PRINCIPLES OF HOME INSPECTION

Second Edition

Systems & Standards

Carson Dunlop & Associates

Dearborn™
Home Inspection
EDUCATION

This publication is designed to provide accurate and authoritative information in regard to the subject matter covered. It is sold with the understanding that the publisher is not engaged in rendering legal, accounting, or other professional service. If legal advice or other expert assistance is required, the services of a competent professional should be sought.

President: Mehul Patel

Executive Director of Product Development: Kate DeVivo

Senior Editorial Project Manager: Laurie McGuire

Director of Production: Daniel Frey

Production Editor: Caitlin Ostrow

Creative Director: Lucy Jenkins

Senior Production Artist: Virginia Byrne

Vice President of Product Management: Dave Dufresne

Senior Product Manager: Brian O'Connor

Published by Dearborn Home Inspection

30 South Wacker Drive, Suite 2500

Chicago, IL 60606-7481

(312) 836-4400

www.dearbornhomeinspection.com

Printed in the United States of America.

08 09 10   10 9 8 7 6 5 4 3 2

ISBN-13: 978-1-4277-7847-5

ISBN-10:   1-4277-7847-7

CONTENTS

INTRODUCTION

This book has two primary goals:

■ To provide you with a sound introduction to the components, materials, and mechanics of building systems that you will encounter and evaluate as a home inspector;

■ To provide you with a solid understanding of inspection processes, strategies, and standards of practice that will help define the scope of your inspections.

SCOPE OF CONTENT

Home inspection requires comprehensive technical knowledge of building systems and practices, which are always evolving. Home inspectors must acquire a significant range of knowledge and skills to be proficient.

This book is intended as a starting point for prospective inspectors. It is a comprehensive *introduction* to home inspection. As such, it focuses on the most common, geographically widespread house systems and components you are likely to encounter. Certain systems that are used in narrow regions of the United States that are becoming obsolete, or that are too new to have become prevalent are omitted in order to better focus on critical components and general strategies.

All major house systems are covered, including:

■ Exterior

■ Roofing

■ Structure

■ Insulation and ventilation

■ Interior

■ Electrical

■ Heating and cooling

■ Plumbing

In addition, the book provides an introduction to report writing, a critical task for home inspectors.

The depth of this book is sufficient to allow the general practitioner home inspector to conduct a performance-based inspection of a house. There is always more material that you can study and other courses that you can take. Where relevant, we reference other volumes in the *Principles of Home Inspection* series that provide further depth on topics in this book.

APPROACHES AND FEATURES

As authors of this text, we are home inspectors, not professional educators. So we went to education design specialists at the university level to help develop the layout, organization, and approach of this book. We hope that the combination of our content and their teaching format creates an efficient, enjoyable learning experience that develops real understanding.

This book takes a consistent approach to presenting house systems and components:

1. *Background information* about the component is provided, including its function, materials, and relationship to surrounding components and systems.

2. Typical *problems* of the component are summarized and then discussed in more detail.

3. Practical *implications* of each problem are presented.

4. The discussion concludes with *strategies* for locating and evaluating the problems.

This consistent presentation is designed to help you easily locate and retain key information as well as develop a methodical approach to your own inspections.

Learning features of the book include:

- Learning objectives: At the beginning of each chapter you will find a list of concepts you should master by the end of the chapter.

- Implications and strategies: These designations help form a consistent presentation of the basic information that home inspectors need to know in order to identify and evaluate problems.

- Margin notes and boldface terms: These tools help you find and review key concepts and terminology.

- Over 340 detailed technical illustrations: Paralleling text, these illustrations show what components and systems *should* look like, as well as what they look like when they are damaged or failing.

- Inspector in the House: Real inspectors provide advice and insight based on some of their most challenging and intriguing inspections.

- Review questions and answers: Over 900 end-of-chapter questions help test your understanding and retention of key concepts and techniques.

STANDARDS

Standards help define a consistent scope of professional practice for home inspectors to use in their day-to-day work. They stipulate the obligations and limits of your job and help clients know exactly what to expect.

When Standards are referenced throughout this book, we specifically mean the ASHI® (American Society of Home Inspectors) Standards of Practice. The ASHI Standards are not the only standards for home inspectors, but we present them in this book because they are thorough, widely used, and a good example of home inspection standards generally. Even if your state or professional organization uses different standards, you are likely to find many similarities between them and the ASHI Standards.

The Standards provide a list of things you must inspect, and a list of things you are not required to inspect. They provide no information on *how* to inspect things.

CODE REFERENCES

Being familiar with codes can be helpful in your work as a home inspector. Therefore, where applicable, this book includes code references. You should remember, however, that a home inspection is not a code compliance inspection. Codes are useful in knowing what is required in new homes, but most existing homes will not comply with all requirements of current codes. Codes are updated regularly, and different codes are used in various jurisdictions over time.

Unless otherwise noted, code references in this book are based on the International Residential Code (IRC), 2006 version. Although a number of building codes exist, the IRC is widely adopted and increasingly recognized as a primary reference. Electrical references are based on the National Electrical Code (NEC) 2008 version.

Part of your responsibility as a home inspector is to learn the rules that apply where you work. They may vary from IRC 2006, especially with respect to numbers. Numbers are not always based on extensive research or demonstrable performance results, but sometimes on experience and tradition. As a result, they can vary from code to code.

We believe it is far more important to understand the rationale for code issues than to know the exact numbers. Therefore, when citing code, this book consistently references the safety and performance issues behind it. You can always look up a number quickly. You can't quickly look up the understanding that allows you to make competent professional judgments in the field.

One of the dangers of using codes is that inspectors rely on a simple number or rule to write up a defect. It takes them off the hook from making a reasoned value judgment. While inspectors might like it, it doesn't provide great value to homebuyers. Some things perform just fine, even though they don't comply with current codes. Remember that your goal as a home inspector is to determine whether a house can perform its intended functions safely and consistently, rather than apply a set of rules without regard for why they exist.

ACKNOWLEDGMENTS

Many students and instructors who used the first edition of this book provided useful feedback to help make the second edition even better. We are grateful to them for their support. In particular, the authors and publisher would like to thank the following:

Contributors
Daniel Friedman
Richard Malin

Reviewers
Don Norman, Kaplan Professional Schools

SUPPLEMENTS

In addition to this core text, Dearborn Home Inspection Education publishes the following volumes, which provide additional breadth and depth of coverage of home inspection topics:

Principles of Home Inspection: Air Conditioning & Heat Pumps

Principles of Home Inspection: Chimneys & Wood Heating

Principles of Home Inspection: Communication & Professional Practice

Principles of Home Inspection: Electrical Systems

Principles of Home Inspection: Exteriors

Principles of Home Inspection: Gas & Oil Furnaces

Principles of Home Inspection: Hot Water boilers

Principles of Home Inspection: Insulation

Principles of Home Inspection: Interiors

Principles of Home Inspection: Plumbing

Principles of Home Inspection: Roofing

Principles of Home Inspection: Steam, Electric & Wall/Floor Heating

Principles of Home Inspection: Structure

STANDARDS
AND REPORTS

LEARNING OBJECTIVES

By the end of this chapter you should be able to:

- explain the purpose of having standards of practice for home inspectors

- define the terms *inspect, readily accessible, installed, normal operating controls,* and *readily openable access panels* as they pertain to the Standards of Practice of the American Society of Home Inspectors (ASHI®)

- give practical examples of things that home inspectors do and do not have to do as defined by the Standards of Practice

- recognize what actions violate the Code of Ethics of ASHI

- list four reasons written reports are needed

- list ten common components of the body of the report, and give an example of each

INTRODUCTION   Standards of practice and report writing may seem like odd topics with which to launch a book on home inspection. You may be eager to get to the meat of this topic—the technical discussions of home systems and structures you'll be inspecting. But understanding the scope of a home inspection is critical to your day-to-day work as an inspector. Standards of practice and a code of ethics help define what you must do, what you could do, and what you should *not* do as a home inspector. And a written report to your client is the tangible product you deliver, as well as required by most standards of practice and states that regulate the practice of home inspection. To succeed in your business, you must be able to write an evaluation of the house that speaks clearly to your clients and satisfies standards of practice.

1.1   STANDARDS OF PRACTICE

We'll start our discussion by looking at the scope of a home inspection as defined by the American Society of Home Inspectors (ASHI®). The ASHI Standards are widely used, but they are not the only standards for home inspectors. Several states have their own standards, as do other organizations. In many cases, there are strong similarities among standards, but others are quite different from the ASHI Standards.

The complete Standards[1] are presented here, but we'll focus on the general portions for now. In later chapters, we'll reference the system-specific, technical portions as appropriate.

1.1.1   The ASHI Standards of Practice

The following are the ASHI Standards of Practice effective October 15, 2006.

1.   INTRODUCTION

The American Society of Home Inspectors®, Inc. (ASHI®) is a not-for-profit professional society established in 1976. Membership in ASHI is voluntary and its members are private home inspectors. ASHI's objectives include promotion of excellence within the profession and continual improvement of its members' inspection services to the public.

2. PURPOSE AND SCOPE

2.1   The purpose of the Standards of Practice is to establish a minimum and uniform standard for home *inspectors* who subscribe to these Standards of Practice. *Home inspections* performed to these Standards of Practice are intended to provide the client with objective information regarding the condition of the *systems* and *components* of the home as *inspected* at the time of the *home inspection*. Redundancy in the description of the requirements, limitations, and exclusions regarding the scope of the *home inspection* is provided for emphasis only.

---

[1]   ASHI Standards of Practice reprinted under license from the American Society of Home Inspectors.
© American Society of Home Inspectors 2002. All rights reserved.

2.2   *Inspectors* **shall:**

A. adhere to the Code of Ethics of the American Society of Home Inspectors.

B. *inspect readily accessible*, visually observable, *installed systems* and *components* listed in these Standards of Practice.

C. *report*:

  1. those *systems* and *components inspected* that, in the professional judgment of the *inspector*, are not functioning properly, significantly deficient, *unsafe*, or are near the end of their service lives.

  2. recommendations to correct, or monitor for future correction, the deficiencies *reported* in 2.2.C.1, or items needing *further evaluation*. (Per Exclusion 13.2.A.5 *inspectors* are NOT required to determine methods, materials, or costs of corrections.)

  3. reasoning or explanation as to the nature of the deficiencies *reported* in 2.2.C.1, that are not self-evident.

  4. *systems* and *components* designated for inspection in these Standards of Practice that were present at the time of the *home inspection* but were not *inspected* and the reason(s) they were not *inspected*.

2.3   **These Standards of Practice are not intended to limit *inspectors* from:**

A. including other inspection services or *systems* and *components* in addition to those required in Section 2.2.B.

B. designing or specifying repairs, provided the *inspector* is appropriately qualified and willing to do so.

C. excluding *systems* and *components* from the inspection if requested by the client.

3.   STRUCTURAL COMPONENTS

3.1   **The *inspector* shall:**

A. *inspect:*

  1. *structural components* including the foundation and framing.

  2. by probing a *representative number* of *structural components* where deterioration is suspected or where clear indications of possible deterioration exist. Probing is NOT required when probing would damage any finished surface or where no deterioration is visible or presumed to exist.

B. *describe:*

  1. the methods used to *inspect under-floor crawl spaces* and attics.

  2. the foundation.

  3. the floor structure.

  4. the wall structure.

  5. the ceiling structure.

  6. the roof structure.

3.2   **The *inspector* is NOT required to:**

A. provide any *engineering* or architectural services or analysis.

B. offer an opinion as to the adequacy of any *structural system* or *component*.

4. EXTERIOR

4.1 **The *inspector* shall:**

A. *inspect:*

1. *siding* flashing, and trim.

2. all exterior doors.

3. attached or adjacent decks, balconies, stoops, steps, porches, and their associated railings.

4. the eaves, soffits, and fascias where accessible from the ground level.

5. vegetation, grading, surface drainage, and retaining walls that are likely to adversely affect the building.

6. adjacent or entryway walkways, patios, and driveways.

B. *describe*:

1. *siding.*

4.2 **The *inspector* is NOT required to inspect:**

A. screening, shutters, awnings, and similar seasonal accessories.

B. fences.

C. geological and/or soil conditions

D. *recreational facilities*.

E. outbuildings other than garages and carports.

F. seawalls, break-walls, and docks.

G. erosion control and earth stabilization measures.

5. ROOFING

5.1 **The *inspector* shall:**

A. *inspect*:

1. roofing materials.

2. *roof drainage systems*.

3. flashing.

4. skylights, chimneys, and roof penetrations.

B. *describe*:

1. roofing materials

2. methods used to *inspect* the roofing.

5.2 **The *inspector* is NOT required to inspect:**

A. antennae.

B. interiors of flues or chimneys that are not *readily accessible*.

C. other *installed* accessories.

6. PLUMBING

6.1 **The *inspector* shall:**

A. *inspect:*

1. interior water supply and distribution *systems* including all fixtures and faucets.

    2. drain, waste, and vent *systems* including all fixtures.

    3. water heating equipment and hot water supply *system*.

    4. vent *systems*, flues, and chimneys.

    5. fuel storage and fuel distribution *systems*.

    6. drainage sumps, sump pumps, and related piping.

  B. *describe*:

    1. water supply, drain, waste, and vent piping materials.

    2. water heating equipment including energy source(s).

    3. location of main water and fuel shut-off valves.

6.2 **The *inspector* is NOT required to:**

  A. *inspect:*

    1. clothes washing machine connections.

    2. interiors of flues or chimneys that are not *readily accessible*.

    3. wells, well pumps, or water storage related equipment.

    4. water conditioning *systems*.

    5. solar water heating *systems*.

    6. fire and lawn sprinkler *systems*.

    7. private waste disposal *systems*.

  B. *determine:*

    1. whether water supply and waste disposal *systems* are public or private.

    2. water supply quantity or quality.

  C. operate *automatic safety controls* or manual stop valves.

7. ELECTRICAL

7.1 **The *inspector* shall:**

  A. *inspect:*

    1. service drop.

    2. service entrance conductors, cables, and raceways.

    3. service equipment and main disconnects.

    4. service grounding.

    5. interior *components* of service panels and sub panels.

    6. conductors.

    7. overcurrent protection devices.

    8. a *representative number* of *installed* lighting fixtures, switches, and receptacles.

    9. ground fault circuit interrupters.

  B. *describe:*

    1. amperage and voltage rating of the service.

    2. location of main disconnect(s) and sub panels.

    3. presence of solid conductor aluminum branch circuit wiring.

    4. presence or absence of smoke detectors.

    5. *wiring methods*.

7.2   The *inspector* is NOT required to:

    A. *inspect:*

        1. remote control devices.

        2. *alarm systems* and *components*.

        3. low voltage wiring *systems* and *components*.

        4. ancillary wiring *systems* and *components* not a part of the primary electrical power distribution *system*.

    B. measure amperage, voltage, or impedance.

8.   HEATING

8.1   The *inspector* shall:

    A. open *readily openable access panels*.

    B. *inspect:*

        1. *installed* heating equipment.

        2. vent *systems*, flues, and chimneys.

    C. *describe:*

        1. energy source(s).

        2. heating *systems*.

8.2   The *inspector* is NOT required to:

    A. *inspect:*

        1. interiors of flues or chimneys that are not *readily accessible*.

        2. heat exchangers.

        3. humidifiers or dehumidifiers.

        4. electronic air filters.

        5. solar space heating systems.

    B. determine heat supply adequacy or distribution balance.

9.   AIR CONDITIONING

9.1   The *inspector* shall:

    A. open *readily openable access panels*.

    B. *inspect:*

        1. central and through-wall equipment.

        2. distribution *systems*.

    C. *describe*:

        1. energy source(s).

        2. cooling *systems*.

9.2   The *inspector* is NOT required to:

    A. *inspect* electronic air filters.

    B. determine cooling supply adequacy or distribution balance.

    C. *inspect* window air conditioning units.

10. INTERIORS

10.1 The *inspector* **shall** *inspect*:

A. walls, ceilings, and floors.

B. steps, stairways, and railings.

C. countertops and a *representative number* of *installed* cabinets.

D. a *representative number* of doors and windows.

E. garage doors and garage door operators.

10.2 The *inspector* **is NOT required to** *inspect*:

A. paint, wallpaper, and other finish treatments.

B. carpeting.

C. window treatments.

D. central vacuum *systems*.

E. *household appliances.*

F. *recreational facilities.*

11. INSULATION AND VENTILATION

11.1 The *inspector* **shall:**

A. *inspect:*

    1. insulation and vapor retarders in unfinished spaces.

    2. ventilation of attics and foundation areas.

    3. mechanical ventilation *systems.*

B. *describe:*

    1. insulation and vapor retarders in unfinished spaces.

    2. absence of insulation in unfinished spaces at conditioned surfaces.

11.2 The *inspector* **is NOT required to disturb insulation.**

See 13.2.A.11 and 13.2.A.12.

12. FIREPLACES AND SOLID FUEL BURNING APPLIANCES

12.1 The *inspector* **shall:**

A. *inspect:*

    1. *system components.*

    2. chimney and vents.

B. *describe:*

    1. fireplaces and *solid fuel burning appliances.*

    2. chimneys.

12.2 The *inspector* **is NOT required to:**

A. *inspect:*

    1. interiors of flues or chimneys.

    2. firescreens and doors.

    3. seals and gaskets.

    4. automatic fuel feed devices.

5. mantles and fireplace surrounds.

6. combustion make-up air devices.

7. heat distribution assists (gravity fed and fan assisted).

B. ignite or extinguish fires.

C. determine draft characteristics.

D. move fireplace inserts or stoves or firebox contents.

13. GENERAL LIMITATIONS AND EXCLUSIONS

13.1 General limitations

A. The *inspector* is NOT required to perform any action or make any determination not specifically stated in these Standards of Practice.

B. Inspections performed in accordance with these Standards of Practice:

1. are not *technically exhaustive*.

2. are not required to identify concealed conditions, latent defects, or consequential damage(s).

C. These Standards of Practice are applicable to buildings with four or fewer dwelling units and their garages or carports.

13.2 General exclusions:

A. *Inspectors* are NOT required to determine:

1. conditions of *systems* or *components* that are not *readily accessible*.

2. remaining life expectancy of any *system* or *component*.

3. strength, adequacy, effectiveness, or efficiency of any *system* or *component*.

4. the causes of any condition or deficiency.

5. methods, materials, or costs of corrections.

6. future conditions including but not limited to failure of *systems* and *components*.

7. the suitability of the property for any specialized use.

8. compliance with regulatory requirements (codes, regulations, laws, ordinances, etc.).

9. market value of the property or its marketability.

10. the advisability of purchase of the property.

11. the presence of potentially hazardous plants or animals including, but not limited to, wood destroying organisms or diseases harmful to humans including molds or mold-like substances.

12. the presence of any environmental hazards including, but not limited to, toxins, carcinogens, noise, and contaminants in soil, water, and air.

13. the effectiveness of any *system installed* or method utilized to control or remove suspected hazardous substances.

14. operating costs of *systems* or *components*.

15. acoustical properties of any *system* or *component*.

16. soil conditions relating to geotechnical or hydrologic specialties.

B. *Inspectors* **are NOT required to offer:**

1. or perform any act or service contrary to law.
2. or perform *engineering* services.
3. or perform any trade or any professional service other than *home inspection*.
4. warranties or guarantees of any kind.

C. *Inspectors* **are NOT required to operate:**

1. any *system* or *component* that is *shut down* or otherwise inoperable.
2. any *system* or *component* that does not respond to *normal operating controls*.
3. shut-off valves or manual stop valves.

D. *Inspectors* **are NOT required to enter:**

1. any area that will, in the opinion of the *inspector*, likely be dangerous to the *inspector* or other persons or damage the property or its *systems* or *components*.
2. *under-floor crawl spaces* or attics that are not *readily accessible*.

E. *Inspectors* **are NOT required to inspect:**

1. underground items including but not limited to underground storage tanks or other underground indications of their presence, whether abandoned or active.
2. items that are not *installed*.
3. *installed decorative* items.
4. items in areas that are not entered in accordance with 13.2.D.
5. detached structures other than garages and carports.
6. common elements or common areas in multi-unit housing, such as condominium properties or cooperative housing.

F. *Inspectors* **are NOT required to:**

1. perform any procedure or operation that will, in the opinion of the *inspector*, likely be dangerous to the *inspector* or other persons or damage the property or its *systems* or *components*.
2. describe or report on any *system* or *component* that is not included in these Standards and was not *inspected*.
3. move personal property, furniture, equipment, plants, soil, snow, ice, or debris.
4. *dismantle* any *system* or *component*, except as explicitly required by these Standards of Practice.

Glossary of Italicized Terms

Alarm Systems
Warning devices *installed* or freestanding including but not limited to smoke detectors, carbon monoxide detectors, flue gas, and other spillage detectors, and security equipment

Automatic Safety Controls
Devices designed and *installed* to protect *systems* and *components* from unsafe conditions

Component
A part of a *system*

Decorative
Ornamental; not required for the proper operation of the essential *systems* and *components* of a home

Describe
To identify (in writing) a *system* or *component* by its type or other distinguishing characteristics

Dismantle
To take apart or remove any *component*, device, or piece of equipment that would not be taken apart or removed by a homeowner in the course of normal maintenance

Engineering
The application of scientific knowledge for the design, control, or use of building structures, equipment, or apparatus

Further Evaluation
Examination and analysis by a qualified professional, tradesman, or service technician beyond that provided by the *home inspection*

Home Inspection
The process by which an *inspector* visually examines the *readily accessible systems* and *components* of a home and which *describes* those *systems* and *components* in accordance with these Standards of Practice

Household Appliances
Kitchen, laundry, and similar appliances, whether *installed* or free-standing

Inspect
To examine any *system* or *component* of a building in accordance with these Standards of Practice, using *normal operating controls* and opening *readily openable access panels*

Inspector
A person hired to examine any *system* or *component* of a building in accordance with these Standards of Practice

Installed
Attached such that removal requires tools

Normal Operating Controls
Devices such as thermostats, switches, or valves intended to be operated by the homeowner

Readily Accessible
Available for visual inspection without requiring moving of personal property, *dismantling*, destructive measures, or any action that will likely involve risk to persons or property

Readily Openable Access Panel
A panel provided for homeowner inspection and maintenance that is *readily accessible*, within normal reach, can be removed by one person, and is not sealed in place

Recreational Facilities
Spas, saunas, steam baths, swimming pools, exercise, entertainment, athletic, playground or other similar equipment, and associated accessories

Report
Communicate in writing

Representative Number

One *component* per room for multiple similar interior *components* such as windows, and electric receptacles; one *component* on each side of the building for multiple similar exterior *components*

Roof Drainage Systems

Components used to carry water off a roof and away from a building

Shut Down

A state in which a *system* or *component* cannot be operated by *normal operating controls*

Siding

Exterior wall covering and cladding; such as aluminum, asphalt, brick, cement/asbestos, EIFS, stone, stucco, veneer, vinyl, wood, etc.

Solid Fuel Burning Appliances

A hearth and fire chamber or similar prepared place in which a fire may be built and that is built in conjunction with a chimney; or a listed assembly of a fire chamber, its chimney, and related factory-made parts designed for unit assembly without requiring field construction

Structural Component

A *component* that supports non-variable forces or weights (dead loads) and variable forces or weights (live loads)

System

A combination of interacting or interdependent *components*, assembled to carry out one or more functions.

Technically Exhaustive

An investigation that involves *dismantling*, the extensive use of advanced techniques, measurements, instruments, testing, calculations, or other means

Under-floor Crawl Space

The area within the confines of the foundation and between the ground and the underside of the floor

Unsafe

A condition in a *readily accessible, installed system* or *component* that is judged to be a significant risk of bodily injury during normal, day-to-day use; the risk may be due to damage, deterioration, improper installation, or a change in accepted residential construction standards

Wiring Methods

Identification of electrical conductors or wires by their general type, such as non-metallic sheathed cable, armored cable, or knob and tube, etc.

1.1.2   Notes on the Standards

Inspect

The Standards are clear on the meaning of **inspect.** When we inspect, we have to look at and test the components listed in the standards. We look at them if they are **readily accessible** or if we can get at them through **readily openable access panels.** These are panels designed for the homeowner to remove. They are within normal reach, can be removed by one person, and are not sealed in place.

Testing

We test components and systems by using their **normal operating controls** but not the safety controls. We turn thermostats up or down, open and close doors and windows, turn light switches and water faucets on and off, flush toilets, etc.

We do not test heating systems on high limit switches, test pressure relief valves on water heaters and boilers, overload electrical circuits to trip breakers, etc.

Systems Shut Down

We do not start up systems that are shut down. If the furnace pilot is off, we don't light it. If the electricity, water or gas is shut off in the home, we don't turn it on. If the disconnect for the air conditioner is off, we don't turn it on.

Accessible

We have to inspect house components that are **readily accessible.** That means we don't have to move furniture, lift carpets or ceiling tiles, **dismantle components,** damage things, or do something dangerous. The exception is covers that would normally be **removed by homeowners during routine maintenance.** The furnace fan cover is a good example because homeowners remove this to change the furnace filter. Many inspectors use tools as the threshold. If tools are required to open or dismantle the component, it is not considered **readily accessible.**

Installed

We only have to inspect things that are **installed** in homes. This means we don't have to inspect window air conditioners or portable heaters, for example.

Deficiencies

We have to report on systems that are **significantly deficient.** This means they are unsafe or not performing their intended function. Although the standards are not explicit, we are not required to identify every minor defect in a home. Failing to report a sticking door latch or cracked pane of glass would not be a meaningful breach of the standards. Some common sense is needed here, determining the effect the issue will have on the safety, usability, and durability of the home.

End of Life

We are required to report on any system or component that in our professional opinion is **near the end of its service life.** This is tricky since we don't know whether inspectors will be held accountable for failed components on the basis that they should have known the component was near the end of its life. With the wisdom of hindsight, it may be hard to argue that the component could not have been expected to fail, when in fact, it did. The situation is also tricky because it includes not only **systems** but individual **components** as well. For many systems there are broadly accepted life expectancy ranges, but these aren't available for some individual components. Reasonable criteria may also be the apparent condition of the component.

Remaining Life

We are not required to determine the remaining life of systems or components. This is related to, but different than, the end of service life issue. If the item is new or in the middle part of its life, we don't have to predict service life, even though the same broadly accepted life expectancy ranges would apply. It's only when the item is near the end, in your opinion, that you have to report it.

Reporting Implications

We have to tell people in writing the **implications** of conditions or problems unless they are self-evident. A cracked heat exchanger on a furnace has a very different implication for a homeowner than a cracked windowpane, for example. It's not enough to tell a client that they have aluminum wiring. We have to tell them of the potential fire risk.

Describe the Implications

It's much better to tell someone to fix a loose railing because someone may fall down the stairs than to quote a specific code requirement. People will only take your recommendations seriously if they understand the implications of making the improvement. *"What will happen if I don't?"* is a fair question from a client about any of your recommendations. You don't need codes or bylaws to advise people on how to make house components perform their intended functions.

Tell Client What to Do

We have to tell the client in the report what to do about any conditions we found. We might recommend they repair, replace, service, or clean the component. We might advise them to have a specialist further investigate the condition. It's all right to tell the client to monitor a situation, but we can't tell them that their roof shingles are curled and leave it at that. We have to tell them what to do about the aluminum wire to reduce the fire risk.

What We Left Out

We have to report anything that we would usually inspect but didn't. We also have to include in our report why we didn't inspect it. The reasons may be that the component was inaccessible, unsafe to inspect, or was shut down. It may also be that the occupant or the client asked us not to inspect it.

Can It Do the Job?

Our approach is to look at each functional component in the home and evaluate whether it is able to perform its intended function. Roofs are supposed to shed water, gutters are supposed to collect water, chimneys are supposed to vent exhaust products, furnaces are supposed to heat homes, plumbing systems are supposed to carry supply and waste water, etc. We use our knowledge and experience to form a professional opinion.

Can Go Further

The Standards allow you to deal with other systems and conditions beyond those covered by the standards. For example, you may want to include inspections of water quality, septic systems, radon, and termites. We can also specify repairs if we are qualified and choose to.

Can Do Less

The Standards also suggest that you do not have to inspect everything that is included in the Standards **if requested by the client.** Clients can hire you to simply look at the roof, for example. However, if a client hires you to do a home inspection, you can't choose to omit the electrical system. Clients sometimes, during the course of a home inspection, ask us not to look at the furnace, for example, because their brother-in-law is going to replace it for them. This is acceptable, but document it in your report.

Not Technically Exhaustive

The Standards indicate that home inspections are not technically exhaustive. This means that we are not taking measurements, using instruments, doing testing, or performing calculations. Another way to think of it is to say that we are doing a visual field performance evaluation.

We are looking at things that are installed in homes and determining whether they are doing their jobs, to the extent we can by looking at them.

- We do not have to measure framing lumber size, spans, or spacing.
- We don't have to measure duct size and runs.
- We don't have to test the quality of the grounding electrodes on electrical systems.
- We don't have to do smoke tests on furnaces to look for cracked heat exchangers.
- We don't have to use manometers to evaluate airflow through duct systems.
- We don't have to use pitot tubes or pressure gauges to analyze water supplies.
- We don't have to trip circuit breakers or measure the current flow through individual branch circuits.
- We don't have to evaluate the design of roof trusses.
- We don't have to perform heat loss calculations.

Four Dwelling Units

The Standards cover buildings that include up to four dwelling units. The Standards also include garages and carports for these buildings. This includes detached garages. We don't have to inspect common elements or areas in condominiums and cooperatives.

The Causes of Problems

We don't have to indicate the cause of a problem. In many cases, it won't matter. If the window is broken, we don't have to speculate what the cause was. In some cases, it's helpful to identify the cause so the problem won't recur. If we find the furnace is badly rusted around the bottom, we might recommend replacement of the furnace. However, it would be helpful to point out to the client that the furnace is rusting because there is a chronic foundation leakage problem. Similarly, you may tell someone to replace the stained and sagging drywall on a part of a ceiling. It's important, however, to let people know that the shower stall above that ceiling leaks every time it is used.

Don't Say How to Fix

Home inspectors should not be writing repair specifications. The Standards say that we don't have to report on the methods, materials, and costs of corrections. Most home inspectors give some general advice on improvements but stay away from specifics. There is usually more than one way to approach a problem, and unless you have specific expertise, you shouldn't be telling contractors how to go about fixing things.

Costs

The Standards don't require you to give ballpark costs for improvements. You don't have to be an estimator. On the other hand, the market reality in many areas is that home inspectors do typically give ballpark costs for improvements. This adds another dimension to a home inspection. There are many cost estimating books available, and some of the premium reporting systems include cost estimate numbers for many house components.

Special Use

Home inspectors don't have to tell clients whether the basement can be set up as a hairdressing salon, for example. There are often special physical issues and usually bylaw and code issues involved in specialized uses of homes. Evaluating whether a home is suitable for this kind of thing is well beyond the scope of a home inspection.

Code Compliance

A home inspection is not a code compliance inspection, nor is it a bylaw inspection. Most existing homes will not meet all current codes. There are several codes that apply to each house. There is typically a building code, electrical code, gas code, plumbing code, and so on. No one person can be comprehensively knowledgeable about all current codes. Further, codes change on a regular basis. It's simply not realistic to expect anyone to know all current code requirements on all aspects of a home.

Performance-Based Inspection

Since we're not doing code inspections, what are we using as a yardstick? All codes are written for specific reasons. A good home inspector has a strong background in codes and knows what constitutes good practice. Every well-written code item boils down to common sense. For example, you may not know exactly how tall railings have to be, but you can get a sense standing beside a railing whether or not you're likely to fall over it if you stumble. With very little experience, you'll also get very good at knowing what average railing heights and stair rises are, for example.

Market Value

Home inspectors should not offer any comment on the price of the home or its value. We are commonly asked at the end of the inspection if the house is good value or if it's priced right. This is a question that you need to defer to a real estate professional. Home inspectors hate it when real estate agents question the inspector's findings or offer technical advice to homeowners during an inspection. In the same sense, real estate agents hate it when inspectors wander into the world of real estate. The world works better all around if everyone stays within their scope of work.

What You Can't See

The Standards tell us in several different ways that if you can't see it, you don't have to inspect it.

Insects, Rodents, or Wood-Destroying Organisms

We don't have to identify termites, rats, or even rot-causing fungi. However, you do have to report on any damage to the structure or other components. You can think of insects, rodents, and wood-damaging organisms as **causes** of the problems that you do have to identify.

Cosmetics

We don't have to comment on anything subjective. Home inspectors should not comment on architectural or decorating issues. Again, you don't want to be outside of your scope. This is a very dangerous place to be.

Breaking the Law

The Standards say you don't have to do anything that's against the law. This is common sense, of course.

Warranties or Guarantees

The Standards say that you don't have to offer warranties or guarantees. Most home inspectors do not. There are warranty programs that people can purchase on homes, but they are, in effect, insurance policies.

Licensed Work

Inspectors shouldn't do anything that requires an occupational license, including engineering or architectural services, unless they have such a license. For example, in some areas, a license is required to comment on wood-destroying organisms. In these areas, home inspectors should not offer comment. In other areas, only licensed technicians can dismantle and evaluate heating systems. Again, stay within your scope. You are performing a visual inspection of the performance of installed house components.

Danger and Damage

You don't have to go anywhere that is dangerous for you. We recommend that you don't walk on steeply sloped roofs, for example. You also don't have to do anything that may damage the property. You don't have to use a crowbar to force open access hatches.

Don't Turn Utilities On

The inspector does not have to inspect components that have been shut off. If the gas, water, or electricity to the house is not on at the time of the inspection, home inspectors are not required to turn them on. As a matter of fact, you should avoid turning them on. Things are usually turned off for a reason. There may be a safety issue. In most cases, you won't know and you risk causing serious damage or injury by activating systems that are shut down.

Disturbing Things

We don't have to move insulation, furniture, suspended ceiling tiles, storage, tree branches, earth, snow, or ice to get a better look. This can be an important point. We recommend that you document limitations caused by any of these things. When someone calls you in six months to complain that you didn't identify a crack in a foundation wall, it's helpful if your report says that part of the foundation wall was not visible because of storage. You may not remember what was there at the time of the inspection, and it's almost certain that your client won't remember. Many complaints about home inspectors' work are the result of things that only become obvious after the inspection.

Hazardous Substance

We don't have to look for poisons, cancer-causing agents, or noise contamination. Indoor air quality and environmental inspections have become a separate profession.

Operating Costs

We are often asked how much it will cost to heat the house or what the electrical bills will be. Home inspectors should not speculate about these. There are so many variables to this question, that your best guess is just going to be a stab in the dark. In some cases, historical information is available that will help people with this issue.

Code of Ethics

The Standards require adherence to the Code of Ethics of the American Society of Home Inspectors. These are described in the next section.

1.2   THE ASHI CODE OF ETHICS

The following are the ASHI Code of Ethics effective June 13, 2004.[2]

---

[2]   ASHI Code of Ethics reprinted under license from the American Society of Home Inspectors. © American Society of Home Inspectors 2002. All rights reserved.

1.2.1   Code of Ethics

Integrity, honesty, and objectivity are fundamental principles embodied by this Code, which sets forth obligations of ethical conduct for the home inspection profession. The Membership of ASHI has adopted this Code to provide high ethical standards to safeguard the public and the profession.

Inspectors shall comply with this Code, shall avoid association with any enterprise whose practices violate this Code, and shall strive to uphold, maintain, and improve the integrity, reputation, and practice of the home inspection profession.

1. **Inspectors shall avoid conflicts of interest or activities that compromise, or appear to compromise, professional independence, objectivity, or inspection integrity.**

   A.   Inspectors shall not inspect properties for compensation in which they have, or expect to have, a financial interest.

   B.   Inspectors shall not inspect properties under contingent arrangements whereby any compensation or future referrals are dependent on reported findings or on the sale of a property.

   C.   Inspectors shall not directly or indirectly compensate realty agents, or other parties having a financial interest in closing or settlement of real estate transactions, for the referral of inspections or for inclusion on a list of recommended inspectors, preferred providers, or similar arrangements.

   D.   Inspectors shall not receive compensation for an inspection from more than one party unless agreed to by the client(s).

   E.   Inspectors shall not accept compensation, directly or indirectly, for recommending contractors, services, or products to inspection clients or other parties having an interest in inspected properties.

   F.   Inspectors shall not repair, replace, or upgrade, for compensation, systems or components covered by ASHI Standards of Practice, for one year after the inspection.

2. **Inspectors shall act in good faith toward each client and other interested parties.**

   A.   Inspectors shall perform services and express opinions based on genuine conviction and only within their areas of education, training, or experience.

   B.   Inspectors shall be objective in their reporting and not knowingly understate or overstate the significance of reported conditions.

   C.   Inspectors shall not disclose inspection results or client information without client approval. Inspectors, at their discretion, may disclose observed immediate safety hazards to occupants exposed to such hazards, when feasible.

3. **Inspectors shall avoid activities that may harm the public, discredit themselves, or reduce public confidence in the profession.**

   A.   Advertising, marketing, and promotion of inspectors' services or qualifications shall not be fraudulent, false, deceptive, or misleading.

   B.   Inspectors shall report substantive and willful violations of this Code to the Society.

1.2.2   Notes on the Code of Ethics

The Code of Ethics is sprinkled with words like **objectivity, reputation, integrity, genuine conviction,** and **good faith.** These are commendable concepts, and this document requires home inspectors to adhere to them. Let's look at some of the specific requirements.

Conflicts of Interest

The first item in the Code of Ethics deals with various conflicts of interest that can confront home inspectors. While there are several, one of the most common is the fact that they have done some work on this house. It's obviously not appropriate for inspectors to inspect houses that they built. How could they possibly be impartial? Similarly, you can't inspect homes in which you have a financial interest.

You cannot make payment of your fee dependent on when or whether the home sells.

Paying for Referrals

You can't pay real estate agents when they send clients to you. You cannot compensate anyone for including you on a list of suppliers. The protection of the client is at the heart of this issue and home inspectors must not only be ethical, but must also be perceived as ethical.

Can't Get Paid Twice

Home inspectors can't accept compensation from more than one party for the same service unless everyone agrees. You can't do an inspection for Client A and then sell the report to Client B. Remember, the report doesn't belong to you; it belongs to Client A.

You also can't be paid for recommending other products or services.

Don't Fix the House

You cannot use the home inspection to get work in another field. As you step off the ladder and tell the client that the roof is worn out, you shouldn't be handing them a business card with a quotation for a new roof. People will wonder whether the house really needs a new roof and whether the purpose of the inspection is to create work for a contracting or remodeling business. Many home inspectors are involved in construction-related businesses, but the two roles must be kept distinct for 12 months after the inspection.

Consulting, Not Contracting

The Standards say we are permitted to provide other inspection services and specify repairs. The distinction seems to be that consulting work is acceptable but contracting work is not. To sum up our interpretation, if you are a mechanical engineer, you can offer to do a design analysis of the heating and ductwork system for an additional fee, but you cannot offer to replace the furnace, at least not within a year after the inspection.

Don't Guess

Item two in the Code of Ethics says that you must act in good faith toward clients. One aspect of this is offering opinions only when they are based on experience and conviction. We shouldn't bluff our way through inspections or guess at things we don't know. We also shouldn't tell people what they want to hear rather than what we know to be true.

Confidentiality

Respecting confidentiality is also part of treating your clients in good faith. The inspection results belong to your clients. They bought them. The inspection results don't belong to you. You are entitled to keep a copy as the producer, but the actual product belongs to your client. As a result, you cannot discuss the inspection results with real estate agents, sellers, or other interested parties without the client's permission. This rule is important and will come back to haunt you if you break it.

Don't Lie or Cheat

Item three of the Code deals with maintaining the good reputation of home inspectors and their profession. Inspectors must not lie about or misrepresent their services or qualifications.

Report Code Violations

Inspectors are asked to report any violations of the Code of Ethics by other members to the Association. While the intent is clear and commendable, this is a difficult issue in practice. For example, will members ever report other members for competitive or personal reasons, rather than professional integrity reasons?

So now you have a sense of the rules of the game. Without getting into the technical specifics of home inspection, you should have a good sense of what constitutes an inspection and what your important obligations are.

1.3   REPORT WRITING

Why Write Reports?

Some home inspectors view reports as a necessary evil, while others see them as an opportunity to promote their business and protect themselves and their clients. Let's look at some of the reasons you should write reports.

Standards Say So

1. The ASHI **Standards require a written report.** Since the large international associations' standards of practice call for written reports, you may have a tough time defending yourself if someone makes a claim against you and you have not provided a written report.

Help the Client

2. The obvious customer service reason to provide a written report is to **help your client.** Clients will only understand about 50 percent of what you say in the field and only remember about 10 percent of that for any length of time. A written report documents your findings for your clients so they can refer to it in the future.

   Reports can be written many different ways. It's helpful to think of your clients' needs before settling on a report-writing format. All home inspection reports are, to a greater or lesser extent, educational documents for the benefit of the client.

Liability Control

3. Reports are written to **protect inspectors from claims** that may be made subsequently by clients. If a claim is made against an inspector, the words spoken during the inspection have very little importance. The written report takes on tremendous significance. The report can help with or ruin a home inspector's defense against a claim.

Marketing Tool

4. Some inspectors use their report as a **public relations document** designed to help increase their credibility, enhance their image, and generate more business. Most home inspectors recognize that clients show their reports to friends, families, and real estate agents. This is especially true if they are impressed with the report. It helps them say to their peers, *"Look at how smart I am. I did the prudent thing in getting an inspection and was clever enough to find a wonderful inspector who gave us this terrific report."*

Report Distribution

The report is the exclusive property of your client. Your client may choose to distribute the report to anyone they choose, including the real estate agents, seller of the property, and so on. You should not distribute the report or discuss it with anyone.

Third-Party Liability

Many home inspectors say in their contract that the report is for the exclusive use of their client and no use by a third party is intended. Inspectors do not want to be responsible to anyone except the client.

1.3.1   How Is the Report Created?

Inspectors may document their notes by writing or using a keyboard or other electronic means to record their information. Some inspectors dictate their field notes.

The Final Copy

The final copy may be on paper, CD-rom, DVD, memory stick, posted on the Internet, or delivered via e-mail.

1.3.2   When Are Reports Delivered?

Generally speaking, there are two options for report delivery.

1. On-site reporting
2. Report delivery at a later date

Some people prepare and deliver their finished report on site. Others go back to their home or office to generate the report and send it out from there via mail, courier, fax, e-mail, etc. There are advantages and disadvantages to both approaches.

Advantages of On-Site Reporting

- On-site reports do not slow down the real estate transaction and real estate agents like this.

- Clients often appreciate being in a position to make their decision with all the facts in front of them immediately after the inspection. Clients sometimes have to make their decisions very quickly. Conditional offers can be quite short, or the inspection may be arranged near the end of the conditional offer period.

- Home inspectors who prepare their reports on site can go back as they fill out the report and check things they have omitted. This is much easier than realizing that you have forgotten to check a fireplace when you are back in the office.

- Home inspectors want to be paid on site to minimize receivables. If the report is delivered on site, it's easier to ask for payment.

- The work is completed when you leave the site. No additional time or money is required for report preparation. Your overhead may include less hardware, software, supplies, and staff if you generate reports on site.

- Inspectors who prepare reports on site can forget the house as soon as they leave it. Inspectors who prepare their reports later may have to store information about one or more houses in their head.

- Inspectors who provide on-site reports often have reduced travel time because they do not have to go back to an office to prepare the report. They also do not have to proofread reports. This again may reduce travel time as well as working time.

Advantages of Reports Delivered after the Inspection

- The presentation of on-site inspection reports can be weak. Relying on handwriting for reports may be a disadvantage. Portable computer systems and printers help resolve this problem.

- Reports delivered after the inspection allow you to think about what you want to say. You may do research and provide better information in the final report, in some cases.

- The advantage of proofreading, of course, is that it allows you to catch mistakes. With on-site report delivery there is often no proofreading. For multi-inspector firms, a senior inspector can review the work of other inspectors at the office before it gets into the hands of clients. This may help with quality control and consistency.

- Reports prepared after the fact can be bound and include customized additions, such as photos of the home, articles, illustrations, and copies of pertinent maintenance tips.

One of the dangers of written reports, whether they are provided on site or after the inspection, is the possibility for discrepancies between what was said and what was included in the report. Your verbal comments should be consistent with your written report. People are quick to pick up inconsistencies and resent having the bad news buried in a written report that was not explained on site. This unprofessional approach is likely to cause problems for the inspector.

1.3.3   Report Format

There are many report writing options. They can generally be categorized as

- checklist
- narrative
- combination

Reports can be filled out by hand or computer-generated. Reports can be a very few pages or can be a few hundred pages. While many home inspectors spend hundreds of hours developing their own inspection report formats, others purchase prepared inspection formats. There are many prepared reporting systems available.

1.3.4   What Should the Report Contain?

Opinions vary about what home inspection reports should contain. We will try to present this discussion in a generic format and try to separate the essential items from the optional ones. In short, the essential items are those required by the standards of practice of an association, such as ASHI.

Common Report Components
Reports may contain some or all of the following:

- contract
- detailed scope of work, including standards of practice
- a report summary or executive summary (before or after the body of the report)
- the body of the report
- limitations to the inspection
- client questionnaire
- maintenance tips and cost estimates

With respect to meeting the standards, only the body of the report is required. Most inspectors provide something in addition. Let's talk about these briefly before we discuss the body of the report.

Contract

The decision to include a contract is a business decision rather than one that affects the practice of the inspection itself. It has become common for inspectors to use pre-inspection agreements or contracts. Most rely to some extent on the advice of their attorneys and other business advisors in the use and wording of contracts.

Getting Your Contract Signed
If you use a contract, you'll want to establish some policy about when the contract is signed. While it is ideally signed before people arrive at the inspection, many inspectors settle for having it signed at the beginning of the inspection. Some inspectors do not get the contracts signed until the end of the inspection. We do not recommend this practice. You may want to discuss it with your legal advisors.

Scope of Work

The contract may contain or may refer to a scope of work such as a standards of practice of an association. Agreeing on a scope of work before the inspection is one of the best ways to align client expectations and control your liability. Unless clients are told what is and what is not included in an inspection, they might reasonably expect inspectors to provide any and all pertinent information about the property. Clients might reasonably call back when anything goes wrong with the house.

Scopes Are Common

Most professions have a scope of work that is agreed upon before the service is provided. You can't play a game without rules, and home inspection is like a game. Without any rules, a home inspection can be anything and is likely to be something different to everyone.

Limitations

Some inspectors include limitations in their contract document. Others include them in the body of the report, and some do both. As long as they are communicated to the client, we don't think it matters where they are presented. The ASHI Standards of Practice have a number of general limitations. Inspectors also have specific limitations that arise during inspections. These might include such things as

- snow on the ground preventing an examination of the grading
- cold weather preventing an inspection of the air conditioning system
- the roof inspection limited by the presence of snow and ice, solar panels, trees overhanging the roof, excessive height, or steep slope of the roof (making it unsafe to climb)
- carpeting over steps, decks, and porches
- no access under decks and porches
- storage that limited visibility
- vehicles in garages restricting access
- attics and crawlspaces that were not accessible or were viewed only from an access hatch
- finishes covering structural components (usually mentioned if these components are typically exposed)
- electrical power turned off
- fuse blocks that could not be pulled to check them without disconnecting the power
- cover on a service panel or main distribution panel that could not be opened
- data plates on equipment missing or not legible
- temperatures too high or too low to test equipment
- water turned off or winterized, preventing testing of the plumbing system
- gas shut off, preventing testing of the heating system
- pilots turned off, preventing testing of gas-fired equipment
- no fuel available in oil tanks for combustion equipment
- some areas that could not be accessed at the request of the occupant
- fireplaces or wood stoves that could not be examined because they were in use

In short, you should include in your report any part of the inspection that you would normally have completed but could not because of these circumstances.

Client Questionnaire

Some home inspectors provide a questionnaire for their clients to complete. This provides a valuable source of feedback and, in some cases, can be used as a marketing tool.

Letter to the Homeowner (Seller's Letter)

Some inspectors provide a letter to the occupant of the home explaining the inspection process. This is a courtesy as well as a marketing piece.

Report Summary or Executive Summary

Many reports include a brief summary. It can be as short as one sentence or it can be a page. The summary provides an overview of the inspection results and recognition of the fact that clients often want the house summed up in a very few words so that they can simplify things and make their buying decision based on this. We encourage you to write the report summary carefully if you use one. You want to make it clear that it does not provide all of the details that your full report does. You do not want to be accused of leaving out critical information in the report summary.

Costs and Priorities

If you provide ballpark costs and priorities for work to be done, these can be included in the summary. Again, this goes beyond the standards.

Maintenance Tips, Filing Systems, and Cost Estimates

Some inspection reports contain general maintenance recommendations and informational articles for homeowners. These may be general or specific and can be cursory or quite detailed.

Filing Systems and Cost Estimates

Some reports go even further, providing a filing system for people to keep track of household bills, including utility costs. Some reports include generic ballpark costs for various home repairs and improvement projects as an aid to their clients. These sorts of things go well beyond the standards, of course, and are marketing tools.

The Body of the Report

As we've already suggested, the body of the report can take several forms. It can also include a number of components. Again, some components are required by the Standards and others are optional. Here are ten common report components and an example statement of each.

Common Report Components

1. Scope/contract—optional

   "The structural inspection includes a visual examination of all exposed structural members, and probing of exposed wood members where damage to finished surfaces will not be caused."

2. Descriptions—required

   "The concrete block foundations support wood-frame, brick-veneer exterior walls."

3. Conditions or evaluations—required

   "The two northern-most floor joists in the basement are rotted and unable to perform their intended function."

4. Causes of conditions—optional

   "The damage to the joists is a result of moisture penetration through the top of the foundation wall."

5. Implications of conditions—required unless self-evident

   "Failure of the flooring system in this area should be anticipated. It is impossible to predict when the floor structure might fail, since it will be determined in part by the loads imposed. The failure may be sudden and catastrophic."

6. Recommended actions—required

   "The floor structure in this area should be strengthened as necessary."

7. Limitations—optional

   "There may be similar damage to other structural members concealed by interior finishes."

8. Life expectancy—optional

   "The air conditioner compressor has an anticipated remaining useful life of one to three years."

9. Priorities—optional

   "It is recommended that the fuse sizes be appropriately matched to the wire sizes in the electrical panel immediately."

10. Ballpark costs—optional

    "The approximate cost for the structural repairs described above is $500 to $1,000."

Some Closing Thoughts

There are a few points to make with respect to report writing.

Consistent Depth

- Report your inspections at a consistent depth from system to system. Don't go into a lot more detail on the heating system just because you have a better understanding of heating systems than other house components.

- Stay within your scope. Resist the temptation to comment on other things. If asked about such items, either defer or recommend the appropriate specialist.

Facts versus Opinions

- Distinguish facts from opinion. Only report as fact what you have seen and know to be true. Where you are offering a professional opinion based on deduction and less than complete information, make that clear. Be wary of using words like these:

  - Satisfactory
  - Good condition
  - Operable
  - Sound
  - Serviceable

  You may instead want to say, *"No problems were identified in the components inspected visually"* or simply, *"No deficiencies noted."*

Bad Situations

- Sometimes you'll see very poor roof flashing details or chimney caps, for example, that may lead to problems. You find no evidence of the resultant problems. Should you report these conditions? We usually describe these as *"vulnerable"* or *"susceptible"* and recommend monitoring. We explain the potential implications to our clients so they can watch for the problems that may result. We also mention "possible concealed damage."

■ While it may be accurate to describe the roof as being *"shot,"* it may be more helpful to say something like, *"the roof covering is near the end of its life—replacement should be planned within the next year."* Many home inspectors don't realize how little home buyers know. When you use the word **roof,** many clients think of the roof structure, sheathing, and covering in its entirety, although you only meant the roof covering.

House Isn't Necessarily Bad

■ Many clients interpret the news that the roof is worn out as an indication that the entire house is inferior. It's helpful to advise clients that roof coverings wear out on a regular basis and this is no reflection on the quality of this home. Similar comments apply with respect to heating systems, water heaters, and cooling equipment, for example.

No Code Comments

■ Don't quote code references. Some inspectors do this to remove subjective issues and provide an authoritative source to justify their recommendations. However, there are significant risks in doing this.

　■ Once you have quoted a code, you have assumed a position as an expert on all codes unless you state otherwise.

　■ Measuring existing homes against current codes is unfair and may be misleading to a client.

　■ It is unlikely that any one person could ever know all the applicable code issues for residential properties.

　■ It's an even larger task to know what the applicable codes were at the time of construction for houses of all ages. Clearly this is not practical.

It is good to learn as much as you can about applicable codes. However, you should also have an understanding of the rationale behind the code issues. It's appropriate to point out problems that may be covered by codes, although you don't need to frame your comments as code compliance issues. If you describe the **condition** and tell the client the **implication,** your authority can be common sense. Clients are much more likely to act on recommendations that they understand, rather than those that are dictated without a rationale statement. It helps clients to understand why something is a problem, and what will happen if they don't address it.

In summary, the goal of your written report is to share with clients your understanding of the physical condition of the home. If your report is well written, the client will develop the same mental picture of the home that you have developed. A well-written report will also make clear the extent and limitations of your scope of work.

The Clients' Perception

When the report is prepared and presented properly, the client will recognize that they have received wonderful value for their investment in the home inspection and know that they have reduced their risk of home buying. They will understand that there is some risk remaining and that the home inspector should not bear responsibility for unforeseen problems.

REVIEW QUESTIONS

1. Decribe in one sentence what home inspection must provide for clients.

2. List three components of written reports.

3. List two general limitations to home inspections.

4. List ten general exclusions to home inspections.

5. List 13 things inspectors are not required to do as part of an inspection.

6. Define **technically exhaustive** within the scope of a home inspection.

7. Define **inspector** within the context of the Standards of Practice.

8. Summarize in one sentence each of the three elements of the Code of Ethics.

9. List four reasons written reports are needed.

10. List two delivery options for providing the report.

11. List three general types of report forms.

12. List ten common components of the body of the report.

13. Give a one-sentence example of each of these components. Use different examples than those provided in the Chapter.

14. Which components are required by the Standards?

15. What elements over and above the ten you have listed might be included in home inspection reports?

CHAPTER

2

EXTERIORS

By the end of this chapter you should be able to:

- identify eight types of exterior siding material

- recognize soffits and fascia

- describe how windows and doors are made weather-tight

- describe the function of trim, flashings, and caulkings

- list the common problems with each of the types of siding, soffits, fascia, windows, doors, trim, flashing, and caulking

- recognize structural and safety components, including steps, railings, columns, beams, joists, floors, roofs, skirting, doors, drains, and walls

- assess the grading of the land around a house and recognize the effects of poor grading

- identify what gutters and downspouts are made of and assess their condition

- understand how window wells are built, what common problems can be found with them, and the implications of the problems

- inspect walks, driveways, and grounds for their condition and usability to the occupant

- understand how retaining walls are built and how they fail

- list the common implications of failure or non-performance for each component

- describe the inspection strategy and tools necessary to identify common problems with each component

INTRODUCTION

The exterior of a house encompasses many components. To help understand them better, we can group exterior components into three broad categories: exterior cladding, exterior structures, and surface water control and landscaping.

The inspection of the exterior is important because problems in this part of a building can be expensive to repair. Exterior problems can lead to damage to the structure and interior of the building. The exterior inspection is challenging because some of the components are not readily seen from grade level.

Functions

The function of the building exterior is to—

1. protect the building structure and interior from damage due to water and snow, wind, pests, and mechanical damage

2. provide reasonable security

3. enhance the appearance of the house

While windows and doors are part of the exterior and we look at them in this chapter, they are dealt with in more detail in the Chapter 6, *Interiors*.

2.1   OVERVIEW OF EXTERIOR CLADDING

The exterior surfaces form the skin of the house, and are referred to as **cladding.**
Cladding components include—

■   wall surfaces

■   soffits and fascia

■   windows and doors

■   trim, flashings, and caulking

There are many different styles and materials in exterior cladding. You will learn how to recognize them, how they tend to fail, and what to advise your client. We will also discuss techniques for inspecting cladding.

2.2   WALL SURFACES

In this section we are going to look at exterior wall surfaces, including several types of cladding. We are going to address siding, soffits and fascia, doors and windows, and trim flashing and caulking. Our discussions here are focused on weather-tightness. We think of the exterior as a weather-tight skin for the building.

Materials

There are many siding materials, including—

■   brick, stone, and concrete

■   traditional and synthetic stucco

■   wood siding

■   metal and vinyl siding

■   asphalt shingles

■   cement-based siding

■   clay and slate shingles

■   plywood, hardboard, and OSB (oriented strandboard)

Ideal Wall Claddings

We will discuss the most commonly used types later in this chapter.

The best wall systems are highly resistant to water, wind, mechanical damage, and vermin entry. They are inexpensive and easy to install, are low maintenance, have great cosmetic appeal, and provide good security. They also provide thermal insulation and have a long life expectancy. Most sidings only do some of these things well. There are no perfect siding materials.

2.2.1   General Inspection Issues

Some of the common problems with any wall system include—

1. Water penetration
2. Too close to grade
3. Too close to roofs
4. Planters and gardens against the wall
5. Vines

Water Penetration

Most serious wall problems are related to water in one way or another. Keep in mind that exterior water may get past flashings by:

How Water Moves

- being driven by wind
- running down the wall (gravity)
- wicking into the wall (capillary action)

IMPLICATIONS

Concealed Damage

You should watch for water damage to wall systems, although in many cases you won't be able to see it. If the siding is deteriorating, there is a good indication that there is some damage behind it. However, in many cases (e.g., metal or vinyl siding and synthetic stucco) the siding looks fine while the sheathing and wall structure behind deteriorate.

Drying Potential

The ability of a wall system to dry often determines the amount of damage done to the cladding and the structure. Wall systems that include sidings with good drying potential, such as aluminum or vinyl, may be less likely to suffer damage than synthetic stucco, for example, which has poor drying potential.

STRATEGY

As you look at exterior wall surfaces, look first at the cladding materials and see if they're in good repair. Second, try to determine how water might get into the wall system and whether there are any areas where you might reasonably suspect concealed damage. Your inspection of the inside of the building should focus on the vulnerable areas that you noticed outside. In some cases, the water getting into the wall system will show up on interior finishes, allowing you to confirm your suspicions. However, damage to wall assemblies doesn't always show up on the building interior, at least not in the early stages.

Pay attention to the drying potential of the wall system. Brick veneer systems with vented rain screens have good drying potential, whereas most stucco systems do not.

Too Close to Grade

Wall cladding materials should be six inches above grade to protect the cladding system and the structure from water damage (see Figure 2.1).

Masonry

Masonry should usually be at least four inches above grade.

F I G U R E 2.1   Clearances from Grade for Siding Stucco and Masonry

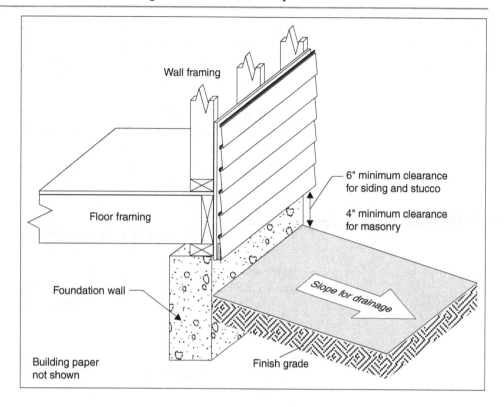

Other Sidings

Most other sidings, including wood and wood-based products, stucco, fiber-cement, metal, and vinyl, should be at least six inches above grade.

IMPLICATIONS

It's easy to recognize the damage to the wall cladding materials. This may include—

- spalling (crumbling or flaking) and cracked brick and missing mortar
- obstructed weep holes in masonry veneer
- rotted wood
- swollen, buckled, or cracking wood-based products
- peeling paint
- staining
- rusted fasteners
- rusted lath and weep screed on stucco

The more serious and concealed implications are the damage to the wall and floor structures behind the siding. This includes rot and insect damage at sheathing, studs, sill plates, headers, and floor joists, for example.

Damage to interior finishes and components is also possible. Sometimes it's not visible until considerable damage has been done. This may be the first indication of a problem.

STRATEGY

Check around the building perimeter for adequate clearance between siding and grade. Can you see part of the foundation? Where the siding is below or too close to grade, look first for damaged siding. If possible, probe to look for damage to the structural members behind.

Note the areas where siding is too close to grade and check inside the building for evidence of water leakage and damage. Try to find the top of the foundation wall. How far above grade is the top of the wall?

Masonry veneer walls typically have weep holes and flashings near the bottom of the wall. Look to see if these have been buried. Buried weep holes can lead to considerable damage to the brick veneer and the structure.

Too Close to Roofs

Siding materials should not be chronically wet. We've talked about this with respect to grade level. It's also true where the bottom of the siding intersects a roof. Best practice is to keep the siding material two inches above the roof. Most people settle for a one-inch clearance. There are step flashings under the siding and roof, so it's okay to keep the siding above the roof surface. The wall won't leak.

IMPLICATIONS

Again, water damage to the siding and possibly to the structure behind are the implications of siding being too close to the roof.

Most sidings discolor if they are chronically wet. Paint may peel. Stucco may soften and crumble. Brick may crack and spall, especially if the moisture in the brick freezes. Efflorescence may develop on the brick.

STRATEGY

Look for a one- to two-inch separation of siding and roofing materials, as shown in Figure 2.2. Where there is little or no clearance, look and probe for deteriorated siding materials.

Planters or Gardens

Gardens should not be built against houses such that earth is held against the siding. A raised planter with three sides and the building acting as the fourth side is a poor arrangement. The situation is worsened when people water their gardens and the soil is perpetually damp.

IMPLICATIONS

The implications of planters and gardens against siding are damage to the siding and wall structure behind and below.

STRATEGY

Look for siding to be six inches above exterior grade. If the siding itself is susceptible to water damage, it should be eight inches above grade.

F I G U R E 2.2 Appropriate Clearance Between Siding and Roof

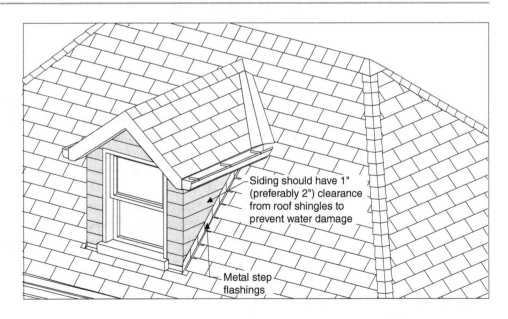

Siding should have 1" (preferably 2") clearance from roof shingles to prevent water damage

Metal step flashings

Where you see raised gardens or planters, look for evidence of damage to the siding on the outside and look for evidence of water penetration and damage on the interior.

Raised planters close to buildings should have four sides and should be set out roughly two inches from the siding.

Vines

Several types of vines and ivies grow on buildings. Many people are prepared to live with the disadvantages of these plants to enjoy the cosmetic effect.

Better on Masonry

Masonry walls are more tolerant of vines than is wood siding. Vines should be kept away from all wood trim, including doors, windows, soffits, fascia, and gutters. Vines should be kept off aluminum and vinyl siding.

Inspection Limitation

A wall covered with vines cannot be fully inspected. This includes the trim, soffit, and fascia. This limitation should be noted in the report.

IMPLICATIONS

Vines on walls may facilitate insect and pest entry and moisture deterioration to the wall, because of slow drying. In severe cases, depending on the type of vines, root systems or attachment nodes can damage siding or enter the building, often through trim areas, providing a direct path for water into the building. Some vines can even damage masonry.

STRATEGY

Most home inspectors evaluate vines on a case-by-case basis and pull them back in several areas to look for damage, particularly at the trim. Evidence of moisture damage to the building skin or mechanical damage caused by the vines themselves should be reported. You may recommend removal of the vines but should point out to clients that it may be difficult to remove all traces of the vines, especially from rough-textured stone, brick, or stucco.

2.2.2   Brick, Stone, and Concrete

Types of Brick

Masonry walls are very common in some areas and are almost never seen in others. A wide variety of materials are used. Brick may be clay, calcium silicate (sand and lime), or concrete. Clay bricks are fired at high temperatures, while concrete bricks are formed by the chemical interaction of Portland cement, sand, stone, and water. Calcium silicate bricks are made using high-pressure steam in an **autoclave.**

Stone and Concrete

Stone may be as hard as granite or as soft as limestone or sandstone. Concrete may be plain or decorative blocks or large precast panels. It may also be poured in place, although this is more common on commercial buildings than on homes. Concrete may also be made into bricks, or it may simulate the look of stone. With few exceptions, these materials are laid up in mortar, and a foundation is needed to support the weight.

Load-Bearing or Veneer

Masonry walls may be a load-bearing part of the structure, or may just be siding (masonry veneer) (Figure 2.3). In Chapter 4, *Structure,* we discuss how to differentiate between the two.

Common problems include—

1. efflorescence
2. spalling
3. cracking
4. mortar deterioration
5. missing weep holes or flashings
6. mechanical damage
7. bowing walls

F I G U R E 2.3   Veneer versus Solid Masonry

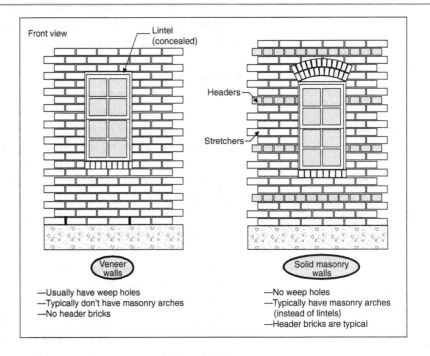

Efflorescence

What Is Efflorescence

Efflorescence is a salt deposit on a masonry or concrete surface that is associated with water moving through walls. The deposits usually are whitish (can be green or brown) and often project one-quarter to one-half inch out from the wall if protected from rain and mechanical abrasion.

There may be a lot of efflorescence immediately after construction, disappearing over the first few years. Seasonal efflorescence is also common, being noticeable only during colder weather.

F I G U R E 2.4   Parapet Walls Prone to Damage

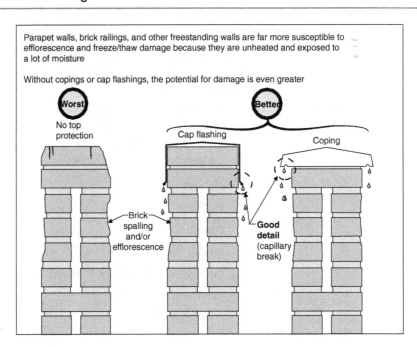

Parapets, etc.

Masonry walls that are exposed to weather on both sides (parapet walls, railings, freestanding walls, etc.) are susceptible to both efflorescence and freeze/thaw damage because the walls can be wetted on two sides and are not heated on either side. The situation is worse if the walls are not protected by effective copings or cap flashings at the top (Figure 2.4).

There may be no damage as a result of the efflorescence, although it may be a sign that the wall is wetted on a recurring basis and may be susceptible to freeze/thaw cycles. In other cases, the pressures exerted by the formation of the salt crystals can spall or flake the wall surface. This is more likely to occur with sealed or glazed bricks that trap water behind the face of the brick.

Pay more attention to efflorescence on old walls than new. Efflorescence is very common on new work and will often dissipate and not reappear. If efflorescence is recurring, there may be a chronic source of moisture that should be eliminated.

Moisture Source

Localized efflorescence usually suggests a localized source of moisture. Try to identify the moisture source and recommend that it be corrected. Look for leaking gutters or downspouts and incorrect grading. On freestanding walls, look for weak joints in coping or cap flashings. On balcony or deck walls, watch for areas where water may be trapped on the floor. Is there an easy path for water to drain off the balcony or deck?

Spalling Masonry and Concrete

Masonry and concrete deterioration is usually in the form of spalling. This is crumbling or flaking of the surface, usually because of efflorescence, freeze/thaw action, or water or mechanical impact, such as sandblasting or high-pressure water washing. Water plays a large role in efflorescence and freeze/thaw damage.

Deteriorating masonry may weaken the structure if the masonry is part of the building skeleton. If the masonry is a veneer, the impact is less severe but can nonetheless be very expensive. Repair or replacement of masonry is costly. Falling masonry units are, of course, dangerous.

A visual examination should reveal deterioration. Pay particular attention to areas near sources of water (near the bottom of the walls, behind downspouts, below gutters, below windows, around chimney breasts, and at any projections out from the wall that might accumulate water).

Look to see whether the masonry extends down to soil level and, if so, pay attention here. Check behind vines and shrubs where water is likely to be held against masonry. Compare the condition of the masonry to similar buildings nearby to see whether mechanical cleaning has changed the surface characteristics.

Cracked Masonry Units or Mortar

As part of the structural evaluation you will be looking for cracks. Cracks are much easier to see in masonry units than in the mortar. Cracks in the mortar are usually at the point of connection to the masonry unit, in a natural shadow line.

Cracked masonry or mortar units may be cosmetic, may be water entry points, or may indicate severe structural problems.

Structure Siding

The cracks allow water into the wall, which may damage the interior skeleton of the building. Moisture entering the cracks can also result in freeze/thaw damage. Cracks may grow with time at a constant (increasing or decreasing) rate and may open and close as seasons change.

Watch for deteriorated mortar and brick movement in the wall, especially at arches. Although the arches have a structural role, the deterioration is usually limited to the area immediately above the window.

FIGURE 2.5   Common Mortar Joints

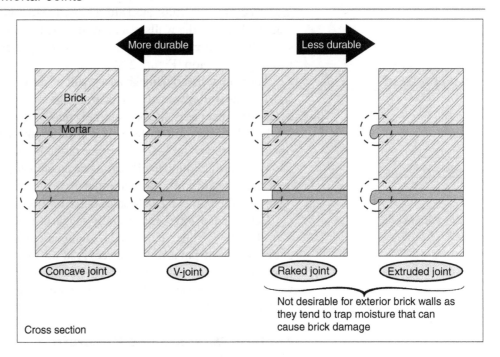

Lintels

Expanding rusting steel lintels over windows and doors often cause horizontal cracks in masonry, radiating out from the top corners of the opening.

Toothed-in Masonry on Additions

Look closely at masonry additions to masonry buildings. Ideally, the masonry at the intersection is toothed in (interlocked), but often this is not the case. There is often some differential movement as the addition settles. This joint can be a source of water penetration.

Seeing Cracks

Small cracks are often best seen by standing back from the wall and looking directly at the wall (rather than on an angle). Several small cracks across the wall surface may indicate considerable movement. One must add up the width of all the cracks. A one-inch crack would be seen by all home inspectors, but sixteen cracks, each one sixteenth of an inch wide and representing the same total amount of movement in the wall, are more likely to be missed. Further discussion of masonry cracks and their structural impact is included in Chapter 4.

Mortar Deterioration

Mortar deterioration is common on masonry, especially areas exposed to considerable wetting. There are several shapes of mortar joints. Figure 2.5 shows some common mortar profiles ranked by durability.

Mortar Strength

Mortar joints should be roughly $3/8$ inch thick with no joint being more than $3/4$ inch thick. Mortar is usually slightly softer than the masonry units themselves, because if the building moves slightly, the mortar joints will fail rather than cracking the masonry units. It is less expensive to repair mortar joints than to replace bricks.

Deteriorating mortar may result in water damage to the building interior and to the masonry. Repointing is relatively expensive, and it is difficult to match the color and texture of old mortar with new.

IMPLICATIONS

STRATEGY

Check the mortar joints for crumbling, failed bonds between the mortar and masonry, and for very soft mortar. Dragging a key or screwdriver across the mortar joints gives a good indication of how soft the mortar is. With a little bit of practice

FIGURE 2.6   Using Weep Holes in the Vented Rain Screen Principle

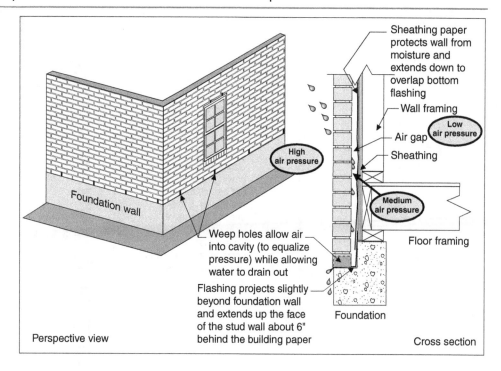

Sheathing paper
protects wall from
moisture and
extends down to
overlap bottom
flashing

Wall framing

Low
air pressure

Air gap

Sheathing

High
air pressure

Medium
air pressure

Foundation wall

Floor framing

Weep holes allow air
into cavity (to equalize
pressure) while allowing
water to drain out

Flashing projects slightly
beyond foundation wall
and extends up the face
of the stud wall about 6"
behind the building paper

Foundation

Perspective view

Cross section

you will be able to evaluate which mortars are acceptably hard and which are soft enough to carve your initials in with your fingernail. Surprisingly, some very soft mortars stand up well.

Missing Weep Holes or Flashings

Function

Modern masonry veneer walls are provided with weep holes to allow water that reaches the back of masonry units to drain out of wall systems. Weep holes are typically created by leaving the mortar out of every fourth or fifth vertical joint in the bottom course of the wall. A flashing at the bottom of the wall directs the water out through the weep holes.

Rain Screen Principle

There is another function of the weep holes that involves the **vented rain screen principle.** This principle uses a two-stage joint to reduce the amount of water that drives through masonry units during wind-driven rains (see Figure 2.6).

The implications of missing weep holes are—

IMPLICATIONS

■ water getting into the structure

■ spalling of the lower masonry units in a wall

In some cases, there will be no problem, or the problems may only appear on the wall exposed to wind-driven rains. In many geographic areas, most of the wind-driven rain comes from one direction, which is not necessarily the direction of the prevailing wind.

STRATEGY

While one should note the absence of weep holes, remedial action should only be recommended where there is evidence of damage. New buildings are the exception. You don't have the test of time on your side in this case, and remedial action should be taken as a precautionary measure.

Check Inside

Weep holes may be present and everything may seem fine, although you may not be able to see the flashing. Look inside the building along the top of the foundation

FIGURE 2.7 Bowing of Masonry Walls

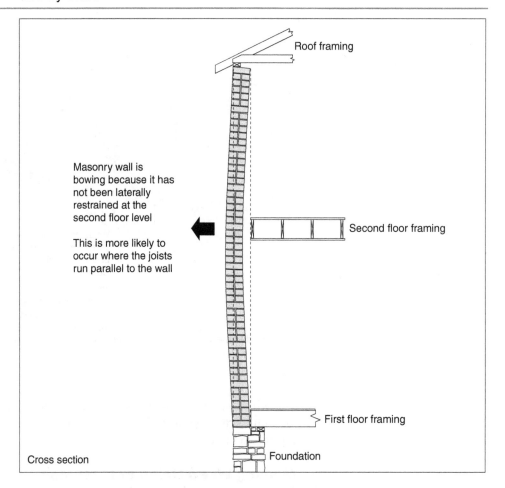

Roof framing

Masonry wall is
bowing because it has
not been laterally
restrained at the
second floor level

Second floor framing

This is more likely to
occur where the joists
run parallel to the wall

First floor framing

Cross section   Foundation

wall. Water streaks running down the foundation wall from the top or efflorescence indicates missing or ineffective flashings.

Mechanical Damage

Mechanical damage is usually clearly evident, often including horizontal displacement of some of the masonry. Partial rebuilding of the wall may be necessary to ensure integrity.

Bowing Walls

Bowing masonry walls (Figure 2.7) are more common on old buildings.

In the early stages of bowing, weather-tightness may be lost. The ultimate implication is failure of the wall itself. Since these may be load-bearing walls, the failure may be catastrophic.

When sighting along exterior walls, don't forget to look up and down the walls. In some cases, a four-foot level or a plumb bob is used to document the amount by which walls are out of plumb. However, if the movement is significant, you can usually see it without aids. Solid masonry walls that lean or bow are generally structural issues rather than cladding issues.

Wall Plates

Look for metal plates or stars on older masonry walls, which suggest the wall has been tied back into the structure to stop bowing. These plates may be on opposite sides of a building, tied together with rods or cables.

You may also see parapet walls bowing or leaning or the tops of masonry walls being pushed out by sagging rafters. These structural issues are dealt with in Chapter 4.

2.2.3 Stucco

Thin Concrete

You can think of stucco as a thin concrete skin applied to a building. Stucco is basically **cement, aggregate,** and **water.** This sounds like concrete, doesn't it? There may be additives used to help hold the mix together, make it more plastic, or speed up or slow down the setting time.

Other Components of Stucco

Stucco is often applied to a **metal lath** or reinforcement that is secured to a wall over **building paper** (felt paper, sheathing paper, or building felt). Edges may be protected with metal trim pieces. Rough masonry surfaces don't use lath or building paper. The stucco is applied directly to the masonry surface.

Purpose of Building Paper

Many installations require building paper behind the reinforcement. The building paper should be vapor permeable.

Lath Options

Older stucco was often applied over horizontal strips of wood lath (like yardsticks) much like plaster was applied on interior walls. Most current applications use metal lath for better performance.

Trim Pieces

Metal trim pieces such as casing beads, control joints, weep screeds, inside corners, and external corners should be corrosion-resistant metals. These pieces provide finished edges and protect vulnerable areas.

Aluminum in Contact with Stucco

Generally speaking, aluminum should not be installed in contact with stucco. The aluminum is prone to oxidation (rusting).

Weep Screed at Bottom

Stucco should terminate about six inches above grade level and there should be a **weep screed,** as shown in Figure 2.8. The weep screed is a metal stop that is exposed below the stucco. This—

■ provides a finished edge

■ allows drainage

■ prevents water from being drawn up into the wall

Home inspectors should watch for missing weep screeds. If there is no weep screed, the stucco may be bonded directly to the concrete foundation. This can lead to water being drawn up into the wall between the stucco and the concrete.

Stucco over Masonry and Stucco over Wood Frame

Stucco over masonry is permanently and securely bonded to the structural masonry or concrete walls. Stucco applied with metal reinforcement over a backing paper is actually a thin concrete slab that is not attached to the supporting structure itself. It is a floating slab, in effect.

Cracking

Compared to stucco applied to masonry or concrete, stucco over wood frame is more vulnerable to cracking as a result of both impact and shrinkage/expansion from changes in temperature and moisture. Control joints help to minimize this problem, but are often missing or not ideally located. Cracks may develop at thin spots in stucco and at corners of door and window openings, because of stress concentrations.

Identifying Stucco over Wood or Masonry

To determine whether stucco is applied over a wood-frame or masonry wall, tap on the stucco. There is a substantial difference between tapping on a masonry wall and on a wood-frame wall. Even with the stucco surfacing, this difference telegraphs clearly.

Is It Really Stucco?

Some hardboard panels imitate stucco. They are 4-foot by 8-foot, 4-foot by 9-foot, or 4-foot by 10-foot sheets. The uniformity of the surface and the trim pieces at the panel intersections are clues that it's hardboard.

Leakage Protection

Traditional stucco may perform well even if there are slight imperfections in the stucco surface. This is because—

■ The building paper provides a second moisture barrier.

■ The lath provides an air space to promote drying and a drainage space for water to run down and escape from the wall.

Let's look at some common stucco problems.

1. Cracks, crumbling, loose, or bulging
2. Incompatible flashings
3. Mechanical damage
4. Rusted lath or trim
5. No weep screed

Cracks, Crumbling, Loose, or Bulging

These defects in stucco may only be siding failures or they may be related to structural movement. From the exterior, you may not be able to tell. If in doubt, wait until you inspect the interior and the rest of the structure before describing cracked, crumbling, loose, or bulging stucco as either a structure or a siding issue. More often than not, it's a siding issue.

IMPLICATIONS

The implications of stucco that is not watertight include water damage to the wood building structure and interior finishes. On any siding problems, appearance may be an issue. Water getting in behind stucco will loosen more stucco around and below. Stucco will eventually fall off in sheets. The emphasis, however, should be on the possible structural damage. Stucco over wood frame is much more susceptible to concealed damage than stucco over masonry.

STRATEGY

Stucco should be inspected visually and by tapping and pressing on the stucco. Pay particular attention to corners and intersections with doors, windows, and other materials. Look for openings where water may enter, and tap those areas carefully. Look along and up and down walls, looking for bulges. Look also for patches and other indications of repairs.

Wind-Driven Rains

Where a building is exposed to prevailing winds or where wind-driven rains come mostly from one direction, inspect those walls more closely.

Tudor Homes

Watch for stucco deterioration and rotted wood on Tudor-style homes with raised wood surfaces. The top edge of these surfaces can catch and hold water against both the wood and stucco. The water often finds its way into the wall system, damaging the stucco, rotting the wood, and rotting sheathing and other structural members.

Crack Patterns

The cracking pattern on stucco may suggest whether the movement is structural or just a siding issue. For example, vertical cracks above and below wall openings suggest building settlement, whereas repetitive vertical cracks across the wall on 16- or 24-inch intervals suggest a siding issue. These cracks may indicate the location of studs.

Cracks may not go through all layers of the stucco. They may only be in the top layer or top two layers. If this is the case, you aren't dealing with building movement and it's most probably an installation related condition.

Nail Popping

Where metal lath is nailed on, nail popping is possible. Nail popping is caused by the shrinkage of framing lumber as it dries. The shrinking lumber retreats from the nail head, leaving the nail head sitting proud. When any force is applied to the wall, the lath and stucco are pushed back against the framing member that has retreated, and the nail head stays put, often popping off some of the stucco around the nail head.

Water Gets Behind

Most stucco finishes will deteriorate quickly if water gets behind the stucco. In this sense, stucco can be a high-maintenance siding, particularly over wood framing. There is also the risk of concealed damage to sheathing and framing, as we keep emphasizing.

F I G U R E 2.8 Weep Screed on Stucco Installation

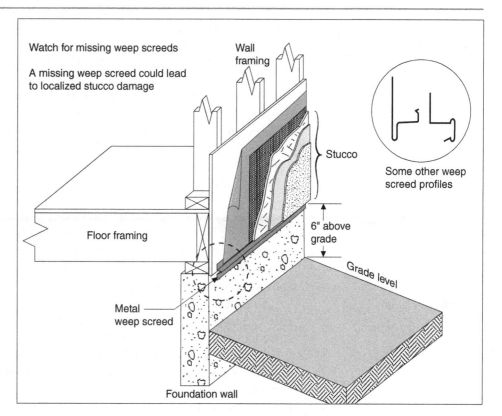

Watch for missing weep screeds

A missing weep screed could lead
to localized stucco damage

Wall framing

Stucco

Some other weep
screed profiles

Floor framing

6" above
grade

Grade level

Metal
weep screed

Foundation wall

Incompatible Flashings

Aluminum flashing will corrode if directly exposed to stucco. Aluminum must be coated or separated by another material to prevent corrosion.

Flashings will fail as they corrode, and the expansion of the corroding metal may cause the stucco to crack and eventually fall off.

When inspecting stucco, look at flashings and watch for evidence of rust, whether the metal is aluminum or steel. Corrosion on aluminum will be white, and corrosion on steel will be reddish-brown.

Mechanical Damage

Stucco applied over wood framing is susceptible to mechanical damage. Stucco over masonry is less susceptible, but it can be damaged.

Mechanical damage may allow water to enter the wall, deteriorating stucco, the building structure, and interior finishes.

Look for evidence of damage. Push on stucco near high-traffic areas, and watch for loose sections, bulges, or cracks.

Rusted Lath or Trim

Metal components in stucco walls are usually protected from weathering by covering them with stucco or providing corrosion protection on the metal.

As metal rusts, it expands. This can cause the stucco surface to pop off the wall. Rusted metal may also allow water to wick into the wall system through or behind the stucco.

Look for rust stains on the surface of stucco. You should not be able to see any lath through the stucco surface. Look at corners, intersections and along lower edges for evidence of rusting on any metal trim.

No Weep Screed

Good detailing of stucco work calls for a metal trim piece along the bottom of the stucco finish (Figure 2.8).

IMPLICATIONS

STRATEGY

The bottom edge of the stucco may deteriorate if a weep screed is missing, and water may be drawn up into the wall system between the foundation and the stucco.

Check for a metal weep screed along the bottom edge of stucco. Where it is missing, recommend further investigation and possible corrective action. In some cases, the bottom of the stucco is caulked as an interim corrective measure. Adding a metal weep screed after original construction is disruptive and expensive.

2.2.4   Synthetic Stucco (EIFS)

The use of **Exterior Insulation and Finish Systems (EIFS)** increased sharply in the 1990s. These lightweight systems, sometimes referred to as **synthetic stucco,** offer a wide variety of colors, ease of architectural detailing, good insulation levels, and a reduction of thermal bridging. These systems are also relatively low cost. Figure 2.9 shows the basic components.

What's in a Name?

Synthetic stucco may be called EIFS, thincoat, softcoat, or PB stucco (polymer-based). Traditional stucco may be called hardcoat, cement stucco, Portland cement stucco, lime-cement stucco, thickcoat, or PM stucco (polymer-modified).

Synthetic stucco can suffer all of the problems of traditional stucco, but, in addition, a unique and possibly widespread problem has been identified: concealed water damage to buildings. A detailed exploration is beyond the scope of this book, but we will briefly look at the problem and its probable causes, because the topic of EIFS has become a hot one. In the early 1990s, problems were found on many rel-

F I G U R E 2.9   Synthetic Stucco (EIFS)

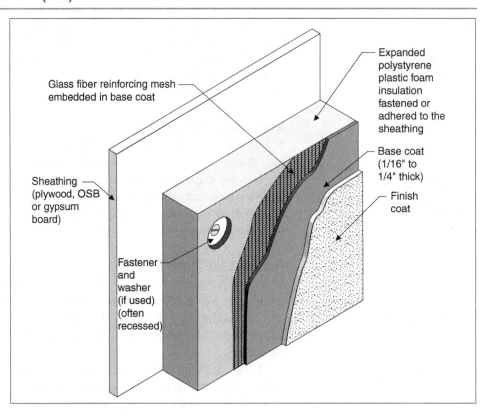

Glass fiber reinforcing mesh
embedded in base coat

Expanded
polystyrene
plastic foam
insulation
fastened or
adhered to the
sheathing

Sheathing
(plywood, OSB
or gypsum
board)

Base coat
(1/16" to
1/4" thick)

Finish
coat

Fastener
and
washer
(if used)
(often
recessed)

F I G U R E 2.10   Kickout Prevents Siding/Wall Damage

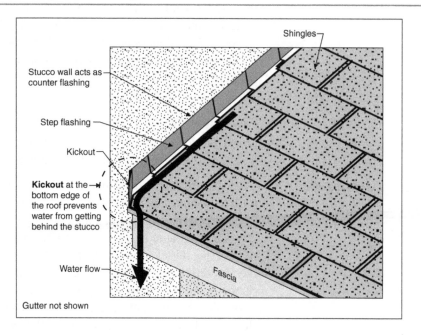

Shingles

Stucco wall acts as counter flashing

Step flashing

Kickout

Kickout at the bottom edge of the roof prevents water from getting behind the stucco

Water flow

Fascia

Gutter not shown

atively new EIFS homes in the southeastern United States. Similar problems have been found in other areas of North America.

Rainwater is getting into walls through imperfections in these face-sealed synthetic stucco systems. This includes joints around windows and doors and penetrations for railings, wiring, plumbing, vents, etc. The water trapped in the wall systems causes mold and rots the sheathing, studs, flooring, and other framing members.

Concealed Damage

EIFS houses often look good until sections of the wall finish are removed, revealing concealed water damage. Damage can take place within the first year of the home's life.

Why is this happening?

Leaky Details

On the surface, we can blame poor design and installation practices that leave many leaky penetrations through the stucco membrane. Poor flashing and caulking work allows water into the walls. Cracks in the stucco surface will also let water through. Window and door assemblies often leak as well, allowing water into walls. The most severe damage is often below and beside windows.

Kickouts

Missing **kickouts** at the bottom of roof/wall intersections are also common problems. A kickout is a flashing that diverts water running down a steep roof away from a vulnerable wall detail (Figure 2.10).

Leaky Windows

Most windows leak slightly, usually through the sills. Even with good flashings and caulking, some water is likely to get into wall systems. (Welded seam vinyl windows are considered by some to be the most leak resistant.)

Leaky Stucco

Thin base coats with cracks or voids and exposed reinforcing mesh are workmanship issues that contribute to the problem.

Condensation

Water condensing out of air as it moves through walls, either from inside the house during cold weather or from outside during warm weather, is a possible contributor. Because the damage seems to be concentrated around penetrations exposed to rain, condensation is not thought to be a major issue. Interior air/vapor barriers, however, do reduce the **drying potential** of wet walls, helping to keep the wall cavities wet longer, promoting rot.

Stucco Surface Not the Problem

Evidence suggests that water passing through the EIFS membrane itself is not the problem unless there are cracks, voids, or exposed reinforcing mesh. Traditional stucco is more prone to field cracking and bulging than EIFS because the EIFS is more flexible. Traditional stuccos are brittle and won't tolerate much substrate movement.

Most stucco installations, traditional or synthetic, are less than perfect. So why is there so much damage with EIFS? Let's look at some key differences between traditional stucco and EIFS.

- Traditional stucco has building paper. EIFS does not.

- Traditional stucco has metal lath, forming an air space to promote drying and a drainage path for water to escape. EIFS does not.

Reduced Drying Potential

EIFS systems do not dry out as quickly as other wall systems. While all stucco walls will let some water past their surface, the EIFS systems are much more likely to trap the water in the walls. Let's look at why this is true.

The synthetic stucco itself is not a vapor barrier. The plywood is not a vapor barrier, but it is close to being one. OSB is more vapor permeable. The expanded polystyrene insulation (sometimes called **beadboard**) is not a vapor barrier either, but it, too, is close. Usually, OSB, plywood or polystyrene exterior sheathings do not pose a problem because, although the materials don't let much vapor through them, air leakage through the joints allows the wall cavity to dry to the outside. **Air-transported moisture** movement into and out of walls is usually much more important than **vapor diffusion** in wetting and drying walls.

Joints Are Sealed

No Air Leakage

With conventional stucco, we have only plywood or OSB sheathing, not both sheathing and insulation. More importantly, the joints are not sealed. They are covered with loose-fitting, overlapped building paper. But with EIFS, the joints in the insulation board are tightly sealed by the base coat. There is no air leakage through the wood sheathing and insulation, and as a result, the drying potential of EIFS walls is poor. Water that gets into the wall system tends to stay there a long time.

Summary of Main Causes

The three main causes of problems with EIFS in our opinion are—

- lack of building paper acting as a backup moisture barrier
- no drainage plane
- poor drying potential

IMPLICATIONS

Lawsuits, Material Banned

Serious damage can be done to homes. Repairs in the thousands of dollars are common, and some homes have been demolished rather than repaired. The problem is doubly serious because it can be very difficult to visually identify.

Class action lawsuits have been filed, and EIFS has been banned in some jurisdictions. Some insurance companies and mortgage lenders are reluctant to get involved in houses with EIFS wall coverings.

STRATEGY

The best way to identify EIFS is to tap it with your knuckle. The foam backer board gives a sharp, hollow ring. It feels like it would be easy to drive a screwdriver through it (because it is!). Tapping on conventional stucco will produce more of a dull thud. EIFS buildings often look sculpted.

After identifying EIFS, remind yourself of the history of the product in your area. Is it used often? Is it known to be problematic? How much precipitation do you get? The recommendation you make has to take this information into account.

Which Homes Are Most Likely to Have Problems?

It's impossible to be certain, but the chances of water damage with an EIFS house (and many others) increase with the following factors:

- The home is in a high rainfall area (U.S. southeast is worse than the southwest).

- Heavy rains are often accompanied by wind.

- The building is exposed to strong winds (a house on a top of a hill standing alone is worse than a house in a low-lying area in a subdivision).

- There is no overhang or only a small roof overhang (wide roof overhangs keep water off the walls).

- There are many penetrations and connections to the wall systems (complicated houses are worse).

- Attention to detail at openings is poor.

- Maintenance of caulking at openings is poor.

- The stucco surface is not vertical. Many manufacturers say that EIFS should not be used on surfaces that are more than 45 degrees off vertical.

The Worst Areas

Damage is frequently worst—

- around and below windows

- at the bottom of roof/wall intersections where kickouts are missing or ineffective

On the exterior, check the following:

Exterior

1. Exposure

   Is the house design vulnerable to wall wetting?

   - exposure to wind-driven rains

   - little or no roof overhang

   - no gutters or soffits

   - near horizontal surfaces

2. Roof/wall connections

   - Is the stucco touching the roof?

   - Where is the flashing draining to?

   - Are there kickouts at the bottom of the flashing?

3. Gutters, especially end caps against walls

4. Chimneys, including chases that surround metal chimneys

5. Door and window openings

   - Are there head (cap) flashings?

   - Are there flashings below windowsills (a rare detail in residential construction, but now called for by some EIFS system manufacturers)?

   - Is there caulking? Is it intact?

6. Openings for electrical conduits, receptacles, lights, telephone wires, cable television, air conditioning refrigerant lines, pipe penetrations including hose bibbs, shutters, house numbers, etc.

7. Vent openings for fans, clothes dryers and furnace, boiler, water heater exhausts and intakes, etc.

8. Railing and deck connections

9. Cracks, bulges, peeling, fungus, exposed reinforcing mesh or metal trim

10. Evidence of repairs—this can include patching or painting

Interior

On the interior, particularly around openings, look for these indications:

1. Stains on walls, floors, and ceilings
2. Rusting carpet tack strip (note: pulling back broadloom goes beyond the Standards)
3. Peeling paint
4. Damaged flooring (e.g., warped hardwood)
5. Elevated moisture levels in drywall and/or subflooring (If you go beyond the Standards in this area, you can use your moisture meter for this.)

In crawlspaces and unfinished basements, look for these:

1. Mold or rot on joists, sills, rim joists, and subflooring
2. Stains on foundations coming from sill area

Moisture Doesn't Always End Up Where It Starts

Water getting through EIFS walls by wind, gravity, or capillary action may follow troweled adhesive marks horizontally some distance before going through joints in sheathing, for example. Water can travel along joints in the insulation as well in the sheathing. Water can be carried directly to the building interior through pipes and ducts that penetrate the wall. Water that finds the end grains of wood, including plywood sheathing and subflooring, can do considerable damage quickly.

Hidden Damage?

It's important to remember that a visual inspection cannot tell the whole story. It is possible that damage within the wall system has no outward indication. If your area has a history of EIFS houses with damage, or if you notice conditions that make you suspect hidden damage, recommend further testing. Even if you see nothing that makes you suspicious, you should let your clients know about the problems some homes have had with this system.

2.2.5   Wood Siding

Life Expectancy Depends on Maintenance

Properly installed and maintained wood siding can last hundreds of years. It seldom does, however, as maintenance is often neglected. Owners should understand the need to look after wood siding. As with most sidings, particular attention should be paid to changes in direction or material and around openings.

Tight but Loose

Siding must be tight enough to prevent water penetration and vermin entry, but must be loose enough to dry quickly front and back, after wetting. Good siding has good drying potential.

Avoid Vines

Vines on wood siding will hold water and reduce drying potential. We recommend removal of vines or ivy from wood siding.

Lumber Grades and Species

Many different grades and species of woods are used in siding. Cedar and redwood are among the best as these species have natural decay-resistant resins. Better grades of lumber with low moisture content and few knots will perform best. You usually won't be able to determine the species and grade during an inspection, but you may be able to diagnose problems associated with wet or knotty lumber.

Narrow, Thick, Rough, Short

The best performance from wood siding is achieved with boards eight inches wide or less (less shrinkage), thicker boards (less likely to cup and split), rough-textured boards (holds finish better) and shorter length lumber (less shrinkage).

Wood Shingles and Shakes

Wood shingles and shakes are usually **western red cedar, white cedar, redwood, or cypress** (Figure 2.11). Other materials such as **pine** may also be used. The first

F I G U R E 2.11   Wood Shingles and Shakes

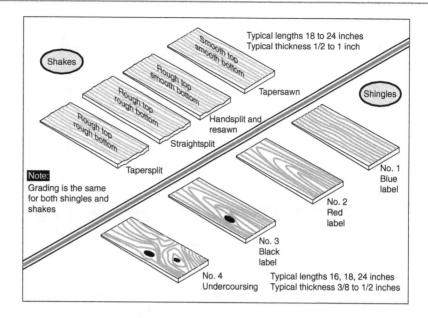

Shingles

materials mentioned have a natural resistance to rot. Pine shingles are usually pressure treated to enhance rot resistance.

Shingles come in 16-, 18-, and 24-inch lengths. A double layer of shingles is usually used on siding.

Shakes

Shakes are typically 18 or 24 inches long. Shakes 32 inches long are sometimes available. Shakes may be **tapersplit, handsplit and resawn, straightsplit,** or **tapersawn.**

Panels

Shingles or shakes can also be mounted on a piece of plywood or fiberboard to make up panels. The panels are typically four or eight feet long. They are installed much like siding boards.

Now we'll look at some common problems with wood board siding and shingles and shakes.

1. Rot
2. Splitting
3. Warping
4. Paint/stain problems
5. Loose

Rot

Rotted wood often requires replacement, and rot can spread if the situation is not corrected.

Rot Is Fungus

Rot is actually a fungus, and the fungus spores are always in the environment ready to attack. When the moisture content of the wood is above 20 percent, and external temperatures are between 40°F and 115°F, rot should be expected.

IMPLICATIONS

Wood loses its structural integrity when rot sets in. Rotted siding is usually replaced unless the rot is very localized. In special cases, such as historical buildings, rotted wood can be injected with epoxy to restore it.

STRATEGY

Inspect by probing and pressing as well as looking at wood. In some cases, rotted wood that has been painted over looks to be in good condition. Probing the wood

F I G U R E 2.12   Vertical Siding—Butt Joint

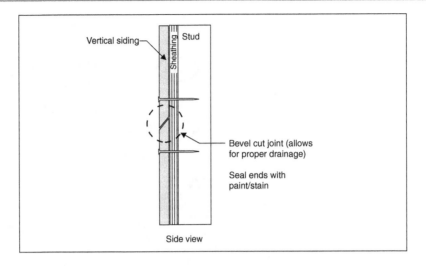

will show whether rot is present. Pay particular attention to areas where rot is most likely to get a foothold. These include areas close to the ground, at joints and end grains, or where siding is within an inch of a roof surface, on dormers or porches, for example.

End Grains
Wood is more susceptible to rot at the end grains than along the length of the board. Since the ends of boards are susceptible, pay attention to these areas during your inspection. Butt joints should always occur over studs or other rigid supports.

Wood siding may have the bottoms of the boards cut back on a 45-degree angle (bevel), which helps water drip off the face of the board rather than be wicked into the end grain. While this detail is not required, it indicates good work.

Mitered Corners
If the outside corners are mitered, pay particular attention to these. Any imperfection in the joint exposes end grains of wood to moisture. Rot can get a foothold here. Corner boards or caps are a better way to finish outside corners.

F I G U R E 2.13   Joints in Siding Boards

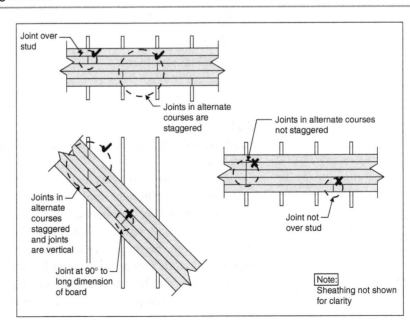

Vertical Siding Butt Joints

Butt joints on vertical siding boards should be cut on a bevel so the upper board overlaps the lower board and drainage will be by gravity to the outside of the joint (Figure 2.12). Cut ends should be sealed with paint or stain to prevent moisture penetration. Inspect butt joints in any board siding carefully.

Joints in Diagonal Siding

When siding is installed on the diagonal, the joints should be cut so that they are both mitered and the joint is vertical (Figure 2.13). Joints at 90 degrees to the long dimension of the board may trap water in the joint.

Staggered Joints

Watch for joints in alternate courses of horizontal or diagonal siding or shingles lining up vertically. It is much better if these joints are staggered.

Splitting

Split boards or siding will allow water penetration into the building. Split wood exposes new unpainted (unstained) surfaces to weathering and may result in rapid deterioration of the wood itself.

STRATEGY

Check for split wood and recommend repair or replacement of any split sections. Check that wood shingles are not butted together side to side. They should be spaced roughly $3/8$ inch apart to allow for swelling when they're wet. Failure to space them will cause buckling and splitting.

Warping

Warping of wood siding usually appears shortly after original installation.

IMPLICATIONS

Warped wood will not be weather-tight and may allow vermin entry.

STRATEGY

Look for warped pieces of wood and recommend that they be resecured or replaced.

Replace Warped Boards

Sometimes warped boards can be flattened with nails or screws, although this will often split the boards. If warping is not isolated to one or two pieces of wood, additional ventilation on the back side of the siding may be necessary. This can sometimes be achieved with shims on lap siding.

Paint and Stain Problems

You will often find exterior wood in need of paint or stain. Some wood is not painted or stained when originally installed. In other cases, paint or stain needs to be redone.

Paint and Stain Protect Wood

Paint or stain gives a desired look and protects against weathering. Most paints or stains prevent decay, although there are some exceptions. Exterior finishes that include color are better than clear finishes because they provide better protection from ultraviolet light.

Types of Finishes

Paints and varnishes are **surface finishes,** while stains and preservatives are **penetrating finishes.** Both are suitable for exterior siding, each with their own advantages.

Drying Potential

Drying potential is important with respect to paint. Siding should be vented so that the wood can dry quickly after it has been wet. Quick drying prevents rot and mold. Good drying potential is also important to stop cupping. Wet wood swells. If the front of the board is dry and the back is wet, the board will tend to cup. Back painting and good ventilation help ensure that the front and back surfaces of siding boards wet and dry at about the same rate.

Cedar, Redwood, and Pressure-Treated Wood

Woods like cedar and redwood have natural resins that resist rot. These woods are more durable and, according to some, do not require paint or stain. Others maintain that even these woods should be protected with paint or stain, as their life expectancy will be extended considerably. The same issues are raised with pressure-treated wood, which is injected with chemicals such as copper chromium arsenate to increase the weather resistance of the wood. Paint or stain will also prolong the life of pressure-treated wood.

FIGURE 2.14   Strapping for Vertical Siding

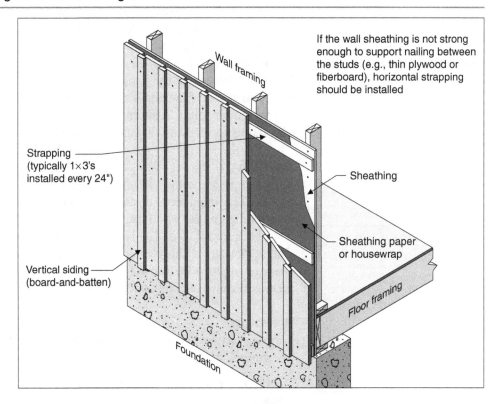

If the wall sheathing is not strong enough to support nailing between the studs (e.g., thin plywood or fiberboard), horizontal strapping should be installed

Wall framing

Strapping (typically 1×3's installed every 24")

Sheathing

Sheathing paper or housewrap

Vertical siding (board-and-batten)

Floor framing

Foundation

Discoloration

Paint and stain also help to maintain a uniform look to wood surfaces. Wood walls with no paint or stain are often darkened near grade level as a result of splashing, snow accumulation, or wood/soil contact. This permanent discoloration is unsightly and may result in premature deterioration in these areas.

IMPLICATIONS

Wood that is unfinished will be more susceptible to rot, splitting, warping, and attack from ultraviolet light. Paint also slows the rate at which wood fibers are worn away by weathering.

STRATEGY

Look for paint or stain that is peeling, cracking, checking, or blistering. This can be a result of moisture in the wall surface, preparation problems, or application problems.

Disintegration

Over time, especially with exposure to sun, paint will break down as a result of ultraviolet radiation. This process is called **chalking.** You can usually confirm this by rubbing a finger on the surface—the chalk will come off. You may also see the ground, shrubs, or wall below the painted area stained by the chalking. This is a normal aging process.

Loose

Loose boards, shakes, or shingles should be resecured.

Strapping

Wood siding boards installed vertically usually require strapping, so the nails go into something more solid than sheathing, as shown in Figure 2.14. Horizontal wood siding should be nailed into studs. This is especially true at end joints. Butt joints should be over a stud, and both boards should be nailed to the stud.

It's common to find siding boards that are not well secured where they meet openings, such as doors and windows, and at roof/wall intersections, for example.

IMPLICATIONS

Loose boards will not be watertight and will not protect against vermin entry. They may also pose a danger if they fall on someone.

Check for loose boards, shakes, or shingles by touching as well as looking. Pay particular attention to areas that are concealed from view (behind shrubs, etc.). Pull on the bottom board to make sure it's well secured. (Don't pull too hard!)

2.2.6   Plywood, Hardboard, and OSB Siding

These manufactured wood products have become popular in the last few decades because of their ease of installation, low cost, and variety of surface finishes. They add rigidity to a building and are effective at reducing air and noise movement through walls. They can be made to look like natural wood or stucco, or they can be profiled like board-and-batten, for example.

Rot and Insect Damage

Manufactured wood products display some of the same properties of wood and have some unique properties. Like wood, they are subject to rot and insect attack. Most require paint and stain to ensure their durability. They are also prone to water absorption along the edges.

Plywood Siding

Plywood is the original structural panel. It comes in boards as well as panels, 4 feet × 8 feet, 4 feet × 9 feet, or 4 feet × 10 feet. It's a relatively low-cost siding because it is easy and quick to apply.

Hardboard Siding

Hardboard is a type of fiberboard. Fiberboard is produced using high temperature and pressure to form wood or other plant fibers into panels. Hardboard is a very dense, compressed wood fiberboard. In hardboard, the wood fibers come from wood chips that have been mechanically or thermally broken down.

Shapes and Sizes

Hardboard sold as siding comes in either panel or board form for lap siding (Figure 2.15). The panels are typically 2 feet × 8 feet, 4 feet × 8 feet, and 4 feet × 9 feet.

F I G U R E 2.15   Hardbord Siding

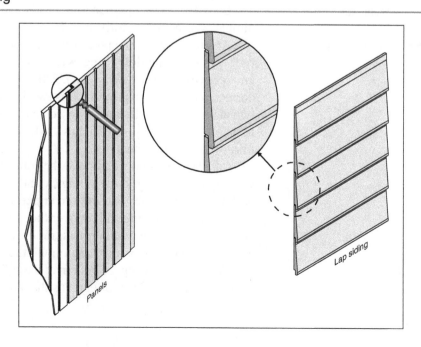

osʙ Siding

osʙ, or **oriented strandboard,** is a version of **waferboard.** Waferboard has been used since the 1970s in structural and non-structural applications. Manufacturers of osʙ siding generally apply a surface coating of some kind to the board. They may also impart a textured or patterned surface or machine grooves into the board.

Inspection issues frequently include the following:

1. Rot, swelling, and delamination

2. Buckling and cracking

3. Loose

4. Mechanical damage

Rot, Swelling, and Delamination

Any wood product will rot if the moisture content is consistently above 20 percent and temperatures are in the 40–115°F range. In this sense, hardboard, osʙ, and plywood react much the same as conventional wood. However, when these materials get wet without rotting, they may behave differently than conventional lumber. Hardboard will swell more than lumber. This reduces strength and can lead to cracking, which, if left unsealed, allows even more water in. In addition, natural wood will shrink back when it dries whereas some hardboard swelling is permanent.

Plywood and osʙ may swell and are also prone to ply delamination. Water may break down the adhesive, allowing the plies to separate. This dramatically reduces the strength.

There have been class action lawsuits involving several siding products. You should become familiar with controversial siding products used in your area.

| IMPLICATIONS |

The appearance and performance of the wood are destroyed once rot, swelling, or delamination is established.

| STRATEGY |

Look for evidence of rot, swelling, or delamination anywhere moisture can enter the system. Mold at edges indicates high moisture levels. This is a red flag. These products are particularly vulnerable at exposed edges, including the bottom edge of lap boards. Squeeze or probe exposed edges to check for deterioration. Joint and flashing details are often poorly made and should be checked closely. Where paint or stain has not been well maintained, the risk of rot is higher.

Check at Nailheads

Look for swelling around nailheads, particularly in hardboard. Look also for dimples caused by overdriven nails.

Siding Touching Roofs

Another area to watch is any wood-based sidings that terminate above a sloped roof. Typically, the siding creates the counter flashing for the step flashings (which are interwoven with the shingles). Although many people do not like the look, it is correct to cut the siding so that it is two inches above the roof surface. This leaves two inches of metal flashing exposed below the bottom of the siding at the roof/wall intersection. Although two inches is ideal, we find even one-inch clearance works fairly well in most situations.

Cutting the wood well above the roof prevents the bottom of the siding from wicking moisture up. If the siding extends down to the asphalt shingles, the wood will be wet more often and for longer periods. This can lead to discoloration in the short term and warping and rot over the long term. Look for deterioration of wood siding along the edges of dormers, for example, or where a two-story building has a one-story addition or a garage joining the wall.

At Grade

Check closely along the bottom of the siding, especially where it is close to grade level. Watch for planters or gardens that have soil touching siding.

FIGURE 2.16   Z Flashings

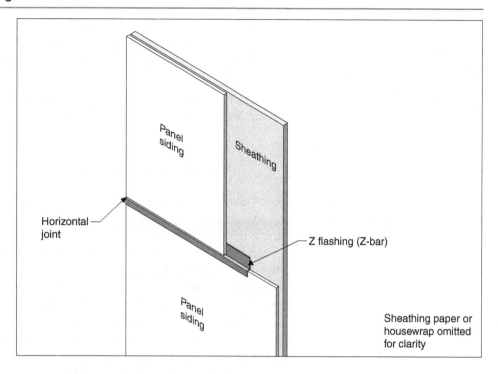

Horizontal joint

Panel siding

Sheathing

Z flashing (Z-bar)

Panel siding

Sheathing paper or housewrap omitted for clarity

Corners and Openings

Check details at corners, penetrations, and door and window openings. These are vulnerable areas, especially if the corner boards aren't big enough to cover the ends of the siding boards.

Buckling and Cracking

This is most commonly found with hardboard. When hardboard is used as a plank siding, the fasteners must allow the planks to expand and contract lengthwise without restriction.

IMPLICATIONS

Buckling and cracking can allow water entry and expose edges to moisture attack.

STRATEGY

Sight along the walls looking for buckled siding. Also, look up the walls to see if overlaying pieces of siding fit properly against the pieces below. Watch for cracking at exposed edges.

Protection at Edges

Look at the vertical panel edges. If they are tongue and groove, neither caulking nor batten strips are required. Otherwise, these should be provided. Look for exposed or deteriorated edges.

Z Flashings

On horizontal joints, a metal **Z** (or Z-bar) flashing extending up behind the upper piece, horizontally across the joint, and down over the front of the lower piece should be provided (see Figure 2.16). Caulking is a less desirable approach. Again, focus on the edges during your inspection.

Loose

Siding that is not well secured will not be watertight.

IMPLICATIONS

Loose siding may allow water or vermin entry.

STRATEGY

Inspect visually and by pushing or pulling on siding to ensure that it is tight and well secured. Look for rusted fasteners. Proper fasteners are corrosion resistant. Dark streaks on the siding suggest rusting nails.

Mechanical Damage

These thin wood products are more susceptible to mechanical damage than conventional wood plank siding. Plywood and OSB can be as thin as $1/4$ inch and hardboard as thin as $5/16$ inch, without continuous sheathing behind supporting the material.

IMPLICATIONS

The implications of mechanical damage include reduced ability to keep water out of the building.

STRATEGY

Inspect carefully for mechanical damage, particularly within the first five feet above grade level, and at patios and decks.

2.2.7   Metal and Vinyl Siding

These siding materials have effectively replaced wood siding in many areas because they are less expensive to install and require less maintenance. Their life expectancy is more than 40 years.

Aluminum

Most modern metal siding is prefinished aluminum. Aluminum siding may be in the form of boards, panels, sheets, or shingles. Expansion and contraction noises are typical of aluminum siding and should not be a concern. Aluminum siding can be repainted, but this then becomes a regular maintenance issue.

Steel

Steel siding is also found but is much less common. It is also usually prepainted. Steel siding will rust if the paint is not well maintained. Older, metal siding may be steel or tin, and it was commonly pressed into patterns to look like brick or stone.

Vinyl Siding

Vinyl siding is extruded polyvinylchloride (PVC). The colors go through the material, so scratching the surface will not reveal a different color below. Also, the color cannot peel or chip off the surface. The material comes in boards. Most vinyl siding can't be repainted. Some of the newer products can be painted successfully.

Drainage Slots

Horizontal siding has drainage holes or slots in the bottom of each piece to allow any water that gets behind the siding to escape.

Good installations of horizontal metal and vinyl siding have the following characteristics:

- They aren't wavy. They are installed over a smooth wall or are furred out from an uneven wall.
- The lap joints are staggered, such that two vertical joints don't line up unless they are separated by three courses.
- The butt end of lap joints face away from main traffic areas so they are less visible.
- The bottom of the siding protects the wall sill area.
- Details at doors, windows and other interruptions are well executed to prevent water entering the wall system.

Common problems include:

1. Buckled or wavy
2. Loose
3. Flashing and caulking defects
4. Mechanical damage
5. Discolored
6. Metal siding not grounded
7. Rust

Buckled or Wavy

Both vinyl and metal siding expand and contract with thermal changes. As a result, the siding must be free to move horizontally. The most common installation mistake with metal and vinyl siding is securing the material too tightly, preventing it from moving.

IMPLICATIONS

Buckled siding doesn't look good, may be blown off or noisy in high winds, and may allow water and vermin into the wall.

STRATEGY

When inspecting metal or vinyl siding, sight along the length to pick up waviness. The buckling is often regular, since all nails are usually driven with similar force.

Check around Lights and Other Penetrations

Local buckling can be caused by installing something through the siding. A light fixture, for example, screwed into the wall through the siding will restrict the siding's movement under expansion and contraction. Surface-mounted fixtures should be installed on mounting blocks—this includes meter bases, shutters, hose bibbs, etc. This rule tends to be broken frequently, sometimes with no resulting problems. Assess each case individually to see how the siding has performed.

Loose

Siding may not be well secured to the building.

IMPLICATIONS

Loose siding can result in water penetration and the siding coming off completely.

STRATEGY

Inspect siding carefully, particularly at corners and intersections with different materials. Don't just look but touch the siding to see if it is loose. Where exterior corners are made with individual caps, these caps are often loose. Pull on them. Moldings at the bottom of siding can be loose and details at door and window openings can also be poorly secured. Pull on the bottom pieces of horizontal siding to ensure it hasn't come loose from its starter stip.

Flashing and Caulking Defects

There are many opportunities for water entry if details are not well finished and sealed. These are discussed in more detail later in this chapter.

IMPLICATIONS

Water and vermin entry are the possible implications of flashing and caulking defects.

STRATEGY

Look carefully at horizontal joints, especially those above windows and doors where water may sit. Where windows project out from the siding, a free-draining cap flashing with a drip edge should be provided, unless the windows are protected by an overhanging eave. If the distance from the top of the window to the soffit is less than one quarter of the width of the overhang, you probably don't need a cap flashing.

Slope of Cap Flashing

Many windows have improperly sloped cap flashings often called **drip caps.** Water may sit on the top of this cap flashing above a window and, if there is any flawed joint, or if the details at either end of the flashing are poorly executed, leakage can occur.

Sills

Windowsills should have a good slope down away from the window and should project at least one inch beyond the siding. A drip groove (capillary break) should be cut in the underside of the sill to prevent capillary action drawing water back along the underside of the sill and into the joint between the siding and the sill.

Flashings below Windows

Good construction practice calls for a flashing below windowsills, as shown in Figure 2.17. This is rarely found on residential construction. There should at least be a trim piece below the sill that secures the siding boards.

Doors, Too

The principles discussed above apply to doors as well as to windows.

FIGURE 2.17 Flashings below Windows

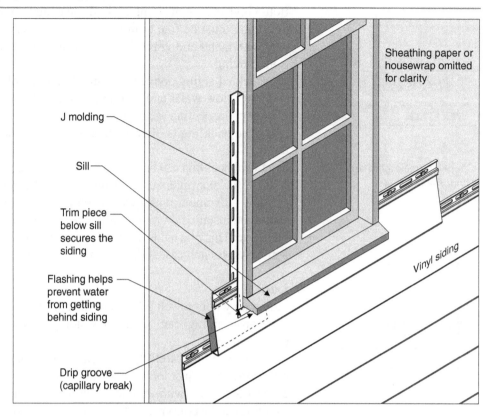

FIGURE 2.18 J Moldings around Windows

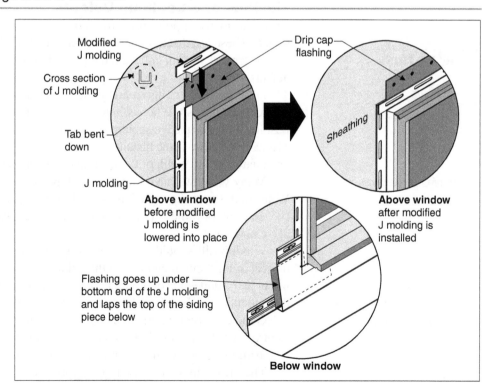

Joint Spacing

When siding is installed horizontally or on the diagonal, there should be at least three feet between joints. Joints in horizontal siding that occur immediately below a window are more susceptible to leakage than others. Pay particular attention to these.

J Moldings above Windows

Metal or vinyl siding should be terminated in a **J molding** around windows and doors, as shown in Figure 2.18. The J molding is not a flashing. A proper drip cap flashing should still be present. The top J molding should be cut at its ends to allow the bottom surface to be bent over the top edge of the side molding. At the bottom of the side J moldings, a piece of flashing is supposed to be installed under the end, lapping the top of the siding board below, for horizontal siding. This detail will not be visible.

Caulking

When using caulking, if the gap is wider than $1/4$ inch, a **backer rod** should be used. This is a foam rope or rod that helps to seal the joint and support the caulking. Look for caulking joints that have failed because they span too large a gap.

Mechanical Damage and Rips

Aluminum siding is susceptible to denting. Vinyl siding is more likely to split, especially when it gets cold. In both cases, replacement of individual damaged pieces is possible, although color or style match may not be perfect.

IMPLICATIONS

Where the surface is not broken, the implications are cosmetic. Where the panels are split or dislodged, water or vermin entry is possible.

STRATEGY

Look for evidence of mechanical damage. It is most often found within five feet of ground level. It is also common on siding around basketball hoops, logically enough. You may also see damaged vinyl siding behind barbeques—the melting is hard to miss.

Rips in vinyl siding can be caused by overnailing in hot weather. The vinyl will shrink when it gets cold, sometimes enough to rip the siding.

Discoloration

Metal or vinyl siding can become discolored by fading in sunlight, by simply being dirty (dust or pollution effects), by having been painted over, or by vandalism.

Green stains on the edges indicate fungus growing beneath the siding. This is due to trapped moisture. The solution may be to drill vent holes in the bottom edges of the siding pieces.

Metal Siding Not Electrically Grounded

Some jurisdictions require that metal siding be grounded to either the house water piping or ground rods.

IMPLICATIONS

Grounding the metal siding is a safety measure. Any live wires that touch the siding could create a dangerous electrical situation, shocking anyone who touched the siding. Grounding provides a safe escape route for electricity.

STRATEGY

Check with your local authorities to see whether siding must be grounded in your area. Also find out how it is most often done and look for the grounding connections during your inspections.

Rust

Modern steel siding is prepainted at the factory, but if paint is scraped off, the exposed steel may rust. Old metal siding may not have been prefinished.

IMPLICATIONS

Rusted siding is unsightly and eventually won't keep the weather out.

STRATEGY

Watch for rusted steel siding, especially where there has been mechanical damage. Rust on aluminum siding is much less common. It appears as whitish surface pits.

FIGURE 2.19   Asbestos Cement Siding

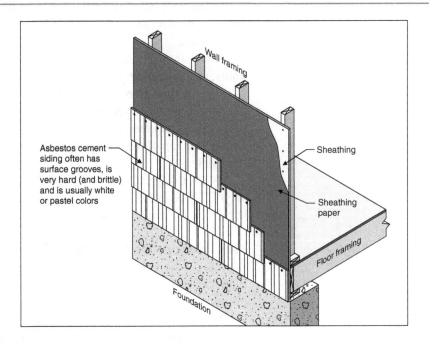

Steel and Aluminum

Small blisters on the surface of aluminum siding, where the enamel is intact, may suggest that the back side is corroding. This indicates inadequate ventilation and perhaps a chronic source of moisture.

2.2.8   Asbestos Cement Siding

Description

Asbestos cement siding (also called mineral fiber siding) is essentially a light concrete panel reinforced with asbestos fibers (Figure 2.19). It was a common siding material in the mid 1900s.

Asbestos cement siding typically comes in large shingles. Sometimes the surface is grooved or mildly corrugated. They are usually painted white or pastel colors. This siding is almost always installed horizontally, with consecutively higher rows overlapping the row below. Be careful when identifying this material. There are other materials very similar in appearance to the asbestos cement shingle.

Asbestos cement is a good siding material that, in many areas, has unfairly developed a bad reputation because of its asbestos content. There is no evidence that there is any health issue associated with this siding while on a building. Asbestos fibers can be a health issue if they are **friable.** This means that fibers are free to float around in the air and may be inhaled by people.

No Friable Asbestos

With asbestos cement siding, the asbestos is not free or friable. People sanding or cutting asbestos cement shingles should consider this, but other than during construction activities, this shouldn't be an issue.

Durable

The siding is extremely durable and its only arguable weakness is that because it is brittle, it is susceptible to mechanical damage. However, most other sidings are also susceptible to mechanical damage, and one has to hit an asbestos cement shingle pretty hard to break it.

Mechanical Damage

Individual pieces of siding may have been damaged. Replacing these is not difficult as long as replacement units can be found.

IMPLICATIONS

Where siding is damaged, moisture and vermin can enter.

STRATEGY

Look for cracked or broken pieces of siding. This is usually impact damage but occasionally is the result of poor fastening or deteriorated fasteners.

2.2.9   Modern Fiber-Cement Siding

Similar to Asbestos Cement

Several fiber-cement siding products currently are sold across North America. These products are similar to the older asbestos cement sidings, but there is no asbestos and the shapes and sizes of planks and panels are different.

Properties

The material is noncombustible. It is termite resistant. It is also rot resistant but should not be installed within six inches of the ground.

Appearance

Panels come in 4-foot × 8-foot, 4-foot × 9-foot, and 4-foot × 10-foot sheets. The surface finishes available are smooth, rough, stucco-like, and many other decorative finishes are also available. Boards come in 12-foot lengths. The widths available are typically 6 to 12 inches. Surface finishes are either smooth or a knotless woodgrain. Fiber-cement siding should be painted.

Potential problems with modern fiber-cement include mechanical damage, missing paint or caulking, and nailing problems.

Mechanical Damage

Fiber-cement siding is brittle and vulnerable to impact damage. As with asbestos cement siding, though, it takes a strong blow to cause damage. Individual pieces are readily replaceable.

IMPLICATIONS

Mechanical damage can facilitate moisture or vermin entry.

STRATEGY

Look for cracked or broken pieces of siding, especially at high traffic areas.

Missing Paint or Caulking

IMPLICATIONS

Missing painting or caulking can result in accelerated siding wear and water penetration into the wall system.

STRATEGY

Check the paint condition on all surfaces. Check caulking for coverage and flexibility at—

- butt joints in panel siding
- windows and doors
- wall penetrations
- inside and outside corner trim

Poor Nailing

Nailing problems include:

- nails that are too short (they should go into framing members at least one inch)
- nails that are not corrosion resistant (electroplate galvanized nails will rust)
- not enough nails (one nail per stud is needed; two nails, if the boards are wide or studs are 24 inches on center)
- nails driven past the board surface (nails should not be sunk into the board)

IMPLICATIONS

STRATEGY

Nailing problems mean that siding is not well secured. Pieces of siding may come off, usually in strong winds.

Look for nails that are rusting, pulling out, missing (face nailing needed on 12-inch planks, for example) or sunk into the planks. You can test the siding by pulling on pieces with moderate force to ensure that they are secure. Watch for boards that have lifted, especially on the windward side of buildings.

2.2.10   Exposed Foundations

You should always be able to see six inches of the foundation wall above grade and below sidings. There are some exceptions to this, however. Masonry veneer walls only require four inches of clearance and, in some cases, brick walls can extend down below-grade. As discussed earlier, the brick must be suitable for below grade use.

Preserved Wood Foundations

Another exception is where preserved-wood foundations are used. While these are not widely used, they are popular in some areas. The pressure treatment used for wood in foundations is much more substantial than for wood used in decks and fences. One may expect to see pressure-treated plywood going right down to grade level. This is the exterior skin of the actual foundation wall. The performance of preserved-wood foundations has not been proven over the long term in many climates in North America. You should watch for evidence of deteriorating wood, particularly where there is soil contact.

Tall Foundations Protect Structure

The main reason that foundation walls extend above grade is to protect the siding and the structure above the foundation from moisture damage. Another benefit to having exposed foundations is resistance to mechanical damage. Damage to siding from lawn mowers, weed trimmers, gardening tools, etc., is much more likely where the siding goes down to grade level.

Assuming that the foundation height is adequate, common exterior foundation issues you may find include:

1. cracks
2. spalling

Cracked Concrete, Masonry, or Mortar

IMPLICATIONS

In mild cases of cracking, moisture entry is possible. In more severe cases, structural stability may be affected. The ability of the foundation to support a masonry veneer wall may also be compromised.

STRATEGY

When inspecting the exposed foundations, look carefully at corners. On poured concrete foundations, it is not unusual for the corners to be weak. Sections of the foundation corners may have cracked or even broken off as a result of poor concrete tamping or careless form removal during construction. Cracks are also common at the corners of doors and windows.

Concealed Areas

Look at concealed areas that are not likely to be noticed by the homeowner. This includes spots behind shrubs, air conditioning units, etc.

Cracked Masonry

Cracked masonry units (bricks, blocks, etc.) are ideally replaced, although if the cracks are small and not highly visible, they are often sealed with a flexible material, such as caulking, as a temporary repair. It is wise to recommend long-term monitoring of foundation cracks to ensure that there is no ongoing structural problem.

F I G U R E 2.20 Parging

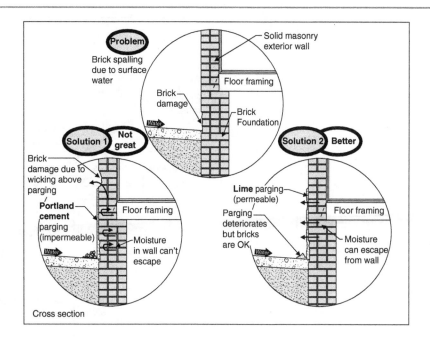

Cross section

Spalling Concrete, Masonry, or Parging

Parging as a Base for Damp-Proofing Materials

Parging (a thin coat of cement plaster) may or may not be present on foundation walls. Below grade, it is typically applied to concrete block walls before a bituminous (asphalt-based) damp-proofing coating is applied.

On the exposed part of foundations, it is common to see the top of the parging and/or the black or dark gray bituminous damp-proofing. The parging is not the damp-proofing; it is the surface that accepts the damp-proofing.

Parging to Prevent Masonry Deterioration

In other cases, parging is used above grade to try to stop the deterioration of concrete or masonry units. This parging is often applied unwisely. If concrete or masonry units are deteriorating near grade level, a Portland cement-based parging does not usually solve the problem. This parging is not vapor permeable, and the problem usually migrates higher up into the wall. Water trapped in the wall cannot escape out through the parging. It is either trapped in the wall or escapes to the outside after wicking up above the parging (Figure 2.20).

Deteriorating masonry may let moisture into the building, and impair the ability of the concrete or masonry units to fulfill their structural roles. This can be very serious.

| IMPLICATIONS |

| STRATEGY |

The first step is to look for and identify any spalling concrete, masonry, or parging. With parging, you can tap on it to determine whether it is tightly bonded to the masonry behind. In many cases, particularly with Portland cement-based parging, the parging has either not bonded properly to the masonry to begin with or is coming away in sheets. A hollow sound heard when tapping indicates a poor bond, and failure may be expected in the short term.

Where parging is in good repair and seems to be intact, watch for spalled masonry just above the parging. Where parging is accompanied by spalling of masonry above, replacement of the parging with a breathable system such as a lime-based parging is usually recommended, but only if the spalling is serious.

F I G U R E 2.21   Soffits and Fascia

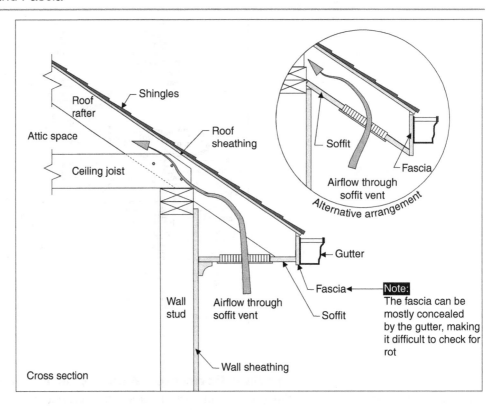

Cross section

2.3 SOFFITS AND FASCIA

Soffits and fascia (Figure 2.21) enclose the rafter ends at the roof overhang and may be made of several materials. You won't always find soffits and fascia. Some architectural styles have open rafters at the eaves and, consequently, no soffits. Across the ends of the rafters, there may or may not be fascia boards behind gutters.

Materials

Soffits and fascia may be wood, aluminum, fiber-cement, hardboard, OSB, plywood, or vinyl, for example.

Venting Roof Spaces

Many soffits have vents to allow air into the unconditioned roof spaces. Vents higher on the roof allow air to escape from the roof spaces.

Inspection Is Difficult

Inspecting soffits and fascia is usually difficult because of a lack of access. Most home inspectors check the soffits and fascia by standing on the ground looking up. Obviously, it's harder on a two-story house than a one-story house, and harder still on a three-story home. You may want to use binoculars to get a better look. Where you get up on the roof, you may be able to get a close look at the soffits and fascia at that point. However, we don't know of any inspectors who move their ladder around the house three feet at a time, getting a close look at the soffits and fascia throughout. Time simply does not permit.

Two Layers

Many older homes have been re-sided with aluminum or vinyl siding. It's common for new aluminum or vinyl soffits and fascia to be added at the same time. These often conceal original wood soffits and fascia. Damage can be covered by the new materials. Home inspectors often cannot identify problems here because it's impossible to see everything.

Let's look at some of the common problems we find in the field.

Common problems include—

1. loose or missing pieces
2. rot
3. damaged
4. paint/stain needed

Loose

Soffits or fascia may have loose or missing pieces.

IMPLICATIONS

The implications of loose or missing pieces of soffits and fascia include wind and water entry into the building as well as the entry of pests such as birds and squirrels.

STRATEGY

As you walk around the building, look for obvious problems with the soffits and fascia. Unless you get a close look at all of it, let your client know the limitations to this part of your inspection. Where you see loose or missing sections, you may also indicate the possibility of concealed damage. Birds' nests, animal droppings, and concealed damage are all issues that should be raised when problems with soffits and fascia are seen.

Rot

Wood and plywood soffits and fascia are susceptible to rot. The fascia is at the lower edge of the roof and, as a result, there may be large volumes of water that run across it. The soffit is typically a horizontal assembly, and any water that leaks or backs up through the lower edge of the roof is likely to collect on the top side of the soffit, which can't be seen. Staining, streaking, and rusting on the soffits walls or metal vent materials are often the only early indication of water in the soffits.

IMPLICATIONS

Rot to soffits and fascia means that these components have to be repaired or replaced. The more serious issue is the possibility of concealed damage to the structure.

STRATEGY

Again, you are confined to looking at soffits and fascia from the ground, perhaps with binoculars. Staining, streaking, peeling paint, rusting vent materials, etc. are indications that there may be concealed rot. Where you are suspicious, you may want to get a closer look, using a ladder. If you don't get a closer look, you should recommend further investigation, and let the client know there may be concealed damage.

Check around Chimneys

Check carefully where exterior chimneys and electrical masts extend up through soffits. Leaking chimney flashings are common and damage to the soffits around chimneys and electrical masts is not unusual.

Damaged

Soffits and fascia can be mechanically damaged.

IMPLICATIONS

The implications of damage are similar to what we've talked about earlier. This includes entry of pests, as well as water and wind entry, possibly resulting in considerable structural damage.

STRATEGY

Use the same techniques we've talked about for loose or rotted soffits to look for damage, again, understanding the restrictions.

Paint/Stain

Aluminum and vinyl products do not need regular maintenance. Most wood products, including plywood, do need regular painting or staining. Paint helps to protect against rotting and deterioration as a result of ultraviolet light. Paint also provides some mechanical protection against water passing over wood.

IMPLICATIONS

The implication of missing or failed paint or stain is deterioration of the wood.

Failures such as bare spots, checking, cracking, peeling, and blistering should be noted. It's risky to specify locations of failure since you are likely to miss some.

2.4 WINDOWS AND DOORS

Windows

Windows provide light, ventilation, and architectural detail to a home. Windows also provide an escape route from the house in the event of a fire, for example. Windows can be made of many materials, including wood, steel, aluminum, and vinyl. Some windows are a combination of more than one of these materials. Each has its advantages and disadvantages.

Evaluation Criteria

You should check windows and doors at several levels. You'll want to look at things like appearance, condition, operability (checked from the inside), security, energy efficiency, comfort (how drafty are they?), and water leakage.

Water leakage is a big performance issue with doors and windows, but it is difficult to evaluate from the exterior. You may see conditions that promote leakage, but you usually won't see the effects of the leakage from the outside.

Common window and door problems that you may see from the exterior include:

1. rot
2. damage
3. paint/stain
4. caulking and flashing problems
5. putty (glazing compound) problems
6. sill slope
7. deteriorated sills
8. frame deformation
9. storm windows and screens missing or damaged
10. cracked or broken glass
11. condensation between panes
12. vines

Poor window performance may result in:

1. water leakage (most windows leak if there is enough water hitting the window hard enough, for a long enough time)
2. air leakage (most windows have some air leakage)
3. difficult operation
4. high heating costs
5. high maintenance and poor appearance

Inside and Out

Let's look at some common problems. Keep in mind that, although some problems can be identified from the exterior, your final judgment shouldn't be offered until you've had a look from the inside.

Rot

Rot is a common problem on wood doors and windows.

STRATEGY

Probe

Inaccessible Windows

Vinyl-clad Wood

It's easy to miss rotted wood, especially if it has been painted recently. While it's not a great long-term approach, many people simply paint over rotted, deteriorated wood. It can look pretty good at first glance.

Some inspectors use a screwdriver or carpenter's awl to probe wood for rot or insect damage. Where you don't want to do damage, you can also use your fingers to push on and squeeze wood. Concentrate on door and windowsills and other horizontal surfaces where water may collect. The longer it takes for the water to leave, the more likely rot is to develop.

Windows that are the hardest to access for inspection, are also the hardest to get to for regular maintenance. Those are the windows that are most likely to be in poor repair. As far as is practical, pay attention to windows that are difficult to access, including those behind overgrown shrubs and high up on the building. The exterior of some windows can be checked from inside the building, if it's easy to open the window and reach out.

Some vinyl-clad wood windows are prone to rot early in their life. Water gets past the vinyl and attacks the wood. This is common with finger-jointed wood windows in particular.

Damage

STRATEGY

Look for obvious signs of mechanical damage, including loose or deteriorated pieces of the window or door itself or the frame.

Check with your hand to see how well various pieces of trim are secured. Many inspectors grab sills and try to rotate them up and down with moderate force. Again, you don't want to create the mechanical damage yourself, so use some common sense.

With vinyl-clad wood windows, try to look at the underside of the sash. Opening casement windows allows for this.

Paint/Stain

We talked about the importance of maintaining paint and stain when we talked about soffits and fascia. The same comments apply to wood doors and windows. Metal and vinyl doors and windows typically do not require regular painting.

Caulking and Flashing Problems

While a detailed discussion of all the possible caulking and flashing configurations is beyond our scope, common sense goes a long way in helping you to know what to look for. If you envision water driving against a wall, door, and window, you can often determine where the weak spots are, if any.

Caulking Problems
Flashing Problems

Caulking may be missing, loose or deteriorated (cracked, shrunk, dried out).

Flashings may be missing, incomplete, ineffective (too small, wrong location, poor slope), rusted, or damaged.

STRATEGY

Check around the top, bottom, and sides of doors and windows for protection against moisture penetration in a driving rain. Use your fingers to check that caulking is pliable and in good repair.

Inspectors do not check every inch of caulking and flashing on a building. A representative sample, usually near grade level, is typically checked on all four walls. Explain to your client that you are only spot checking things like caulking. This way you are less likely to be criticized for overlooking some poor details.

F I G U R E 2.22   Putty (Glazing Compound)

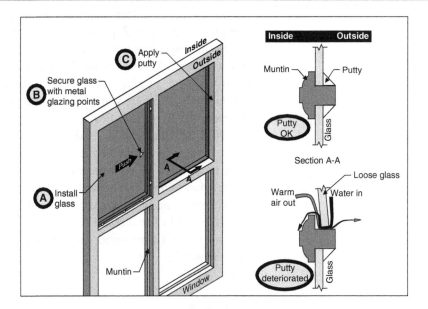

Putty (Glazing Compound) Problems

Putty is used to secure windows in sashes or muntins. This includes windows in doors (Figure 2.22). Not all windows use putty. Caulking or flexible strips have replaced putty on most modern windows.

Failed putty can result in air and water leakage through the window system. Windows may also rattle if putty is dried out and pulled away from the glass.

Check around the perimeter of all glass surfaces to see that putty or some other system is used to maintain a good watertight seal where the glass is supported. Check for putty that has cracked or shrunk, dried out, and pulled away from the glass or the support member. Most putty is painted, and it takes a little practice to determine whether you are looking at deteriorated paint or putty.

Sill Slope

Windowsills

A common window problem is a reverse slope on a windowsill. Windowsills are horizontal surfaces that may collect large amounts of water. Good sills have a pronounced slope, down away from the window. Good sills also include a projection out from the wall so that water running off the sill does not soak the wall below.

Door Sills

The same comments are true of door sills, although reverse slope is less common on door sills.

Capillary Break

Another good detail on windowsills is a groove cut in the underside of the sill, roughly an inch in from the face of the sill, but well away from the wall. This groove runs along the length of the sill, parallel to the wall. This creates a **capillary break** that stops water from running along the underside of the sill back to the wall because of surface tension (Figure 2.23). Some people refer to this as a **drip edge.**

Missing Capillary Breaks

Where this groove is missing, a bead of caulking can be run along the underside of the windowsill where the capillary break would be located. This is not quite as good, but it does create a relatively effective capillary break.

F I G U R E   2.23   Capillary Break

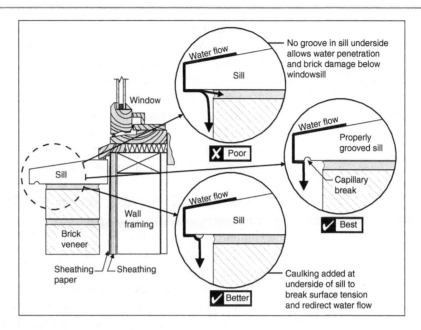

Flashing under Sill

Good detailing on windowsills and door sills includes a flashing below the sill. This has been rare in modern residential construction but is being specified more and more, especially by synthetic stucco manufacturers. Manufactured flashing systems for the bases of doors and windows are available. Whether or not there is a flashing, you should pay close attention to the joint under the sill. It may be made weather-tight with caulking, mortar or flashing, but it's important that it is weather-tight.

STRATEGY

It should become second nature for you to check the sill slopes. This can be done from both the inside and outside. On the outside, you usually only get a good look at the first-floor door sills and windowsills. Remember when you're inside the building to spot-check the sills on the upper floors.

Deteriorated Sills

Windowsills are vulnerable because of their horizontal orientation and the relatively large volume of water they see. Sills are also vulnerable because they typically project from the building face.

Types of Damage

Wooden windowsills are prone to rot, insect attack, and mechanical damage. Metal sills may rust. Masonry sills may crack, spall, or lose mortar. Vinyl sills may crack or be mechanically damaged. Stone or concrete may crack or spall.

STRATEGY

Look at the windowsills from above and below. Probe wood sills for rot, especially at corners. Check metal sills for rust, and check masonry and concrete sills for cracks and spalling.

Look for a good projection beyond the face of the wall and look for a capillary break on the underside of the sill.

Mortar

If the sill is masonry, check for deteriorated mortar joints between the sections. Individual units may come loose if mortar has deteriorated. Deteriorated mortar is also a way for water to get into the walls. If water gets trapped, freezing can damage the masonry units.

Air Conditioners

Check carefully below window air conditioners. Condensate from these units can damage the sills and the wall below.

Door Sills

Door sills may suffer similar deterioration to windowsills.

Frame Deformation

In modern buildings, it is popular to use foam as an insulating and caulking material around door and window openings. The injected foams expand and exert considerable force on the windows. If the foam is a high-expansion type, or too if much foam is used, the window or door frame itself can be deformed.

If their frames are deformed, windows or doors may be stiff or inoperable and the glass may crack.

Make sure windows and doors are level, plumb, and square. Make sure they fit properly in their openings. When inside, check the operation of the doors and windows. From the outside, look for bowing inward near the middle of the tops, sides, or bottoms of door and window openings.

Missing or Damaged Storm Windows and Screens

You'll need to know whether storm windows and screens are typical in your area. Undoubtedly, you'll have an opinion on this already. Modern window systems with double- and triple-glazing systems have made storm windows unnecessary. Screens are removable, and you may find that the screens are not on the windows but stored somewhere in the house or garage.

Storm windows or screens may be missing or damaged.

Are there storm windows and screens in place? Are they in good order? Torn screens, rusted metal frames, storm windows that don't open and close easily (usually only operable from the inside of the building), rotted wood, and deteriorated putty are common problems.

Strangely enough, storm windows and screens do not have to be inspected in an inspection that meets the Standards. However, if your clients expect to find storm windows and screens but don't, you can expect to hear from them.

Cracked or Broken Glass

A common window problem is cracked or broken panes of glass.

It's easy to look for cracked or broken glass. We look from both outside and inside.

Condensation Between Panes

Condensation between panes on sealed multi-glazed windows indicates a failed seal. While the window may be foggy or dirty, and thermal performance is slightly reduced, the window is often not replaced.

Check both outside and inside for condensation (fog) or dirt on the inner surfaces of the glass. Condensation will typically only show up when there is a great temperature difference between indoors and outside.

Vines

We talked about vines earlier. We won't repeat the discussion, but we do recommend that vines be kept away from windows and doors.

2.5   TRIM, FLASHINGS, AND CAULKING

Trim on the exterior of a house may be composed of flashing details or small pieces of siding or other materials such as wood, masonry, or stone.

Trim Functions

Trim may:

■ create architectural detail

F I G U R E 2.24   Flashing over Windows

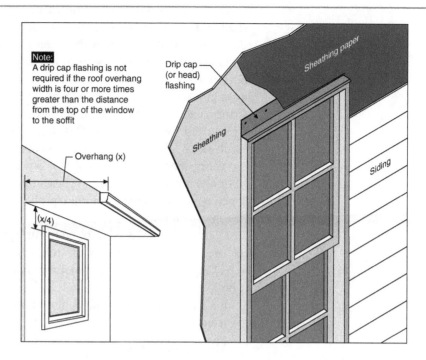

- act as a transition between different materials
- provide tight joints
- provide control joints, weep screeds, or other details on stucco

Flashings protect joints at changes in direction and between different materials. Missing or poor flashing details are often responsible for water damage to walls and floors.

Flashings may be one-part or two-part systems. Two-part flashings include step and counter flashings where walls meet roofs, for example. If the siding is masonry, a metal counter flashing protects the top of the step flashings. The siding material may act as a counter flashing. The only flashing in this case is the step flashing.

Flashings over Windows

Drip cap flashing, sometimes called **head flashing,** is installed over windows and doors on houses with siding (Figure 2.24). These flashings are not typically used on masonry houses where the windows are recessed. Drip cap flashings are sometimes omitted when the windows are close to the top of the wall and the top of the window is protected from wetting by the roof overhang.

Flashings at Bottoms of Walls

Flashings are often provided at bottoms of walls to direct water out of wall cavities (in a vented rain screen, for example) or to protect the bottom edge of siding (stucco, for example).

Some metal and vinyl windows are manufactured with integral drip caps so that a separate flashing is not needed.

Z (or Z-bar) flashing may be used at horizontal joints in panel-type sidings, where one piece of siding is installed above another, or where a siding pattern changes, for example, from horizontal to vertical.

These are just a few examples of the many different types of flashings that you might see on an exterior wall. Flashings are generally designed to be shedding systems. They anticipate water running down a wall surface and are designed to direct the water out away from the wall, protecting openings or joints.

In evaluating exterior trim and flashings, you'll have to use some common sense. Picture water running down the walls and you should be able to predict whether a given detail is likely to be successful or not. Remember that areas that catch water or allow it into wall systems can cause considerable concealed damage.

One of the trickiest aspects of inspecting exterior flashings is that you can't see most of what you'd like to see. In some cases, you can't even tell whether a flashing is in place. Most of the time you have to settle for looking for evidence of non-performance of flashings. In some cases, what seems like an obvious entrance point is protected by a concealed flashing and really isn't a problem. In other cases, details that look good are leakage points.

Your general strategy should be to watch for projecting horizontal surfaces that may collect water or, worse, surfaces that slope down toward the building. Poorly sloped windowsills are a common problem, as are poorly installed cap flashings on the top of windows.

Caulking is designed to bond to surfaces, creating a watertight joint. The joint may be between two pieces of similar material or different materials. Caulking helps keep water out and is sometimes backed up with flashing and building paper or both.

Let's look at some of the common problems we find with flashings, caulking, and trim.

1. Missing flashings
2. Ineffective or incomplete flashings
3. Loose
4. Rust
5. Rot
6. Missing or ineffective caulking

Missing Flashings

Missing flashings are more common than you might think. It's common to find no flashings over doors and windows, for example. In some cases, no damage is done. Protection may be afforded by concealed building paper or a good caulking joint. Neither of these is as reliable as a properly executed flashing detail, but if there is no evidence of leakage, it becomes difficult to justify opening up a wall system to install a flashing. You should, however, make your client know that the installation is not correct, and, although there is no problem now, that the configuration should be monitored.

Well-built homes have two levels of protection against water penetration. Building paper or housewrap behind siding is an example. Strips of building paper around openings behind flashings is another example. Caulking over flashings is a third example.

As with most of the conditions we've been talking about in this section, missing flashings can result in water entry into, and damage to, the wall systems.

On houses with siding, look for flashings over doors and windows. Where it's not visible, look for evidence of water entry points or water damage. Your inspection won't be complete until you check inside the building around this window for damage. Make a note of windows that appear susceptible to leakage from the outside, and check those windows on the inside.

Look at other transitions between materials and changes in direction around the exterior. Are flashing details needed? Are they present? Horizontal seams without flashings are suspect in most applications.

Ineffective or Incomplete Flashings

Flashings can be too short or too small. Horizontal flashings can be ineffective if they have a reverse slope over a window or door. Flashings at roof/wall intersections may be incomplete if there is no counter flashing, for example. Flashings may not extend the full length of the joint. Individual sections of flashings may not be suitably overlapped. Joints in flashings may not be adequately sealed.

IMPLICATIONS
Implications of ineffective or incomplete flashings are similar to those we discussed for missing flashings.

STRATEGY
Make sure that flashings are large enough and arranged so that they can do their job. Make sure trim pieces are complete and are capable of protecting joints. A good example of trim is the batten component of board-and-batten siding. The battens are really trim pieces designed to protect the joints between boards. The battens also provide room to allow the boards to expand and contract.

Loose

While loose flashing is not terribly common, loose trim on siding is very common.

IMPLICATIONS
The implications of loose trim or flashing are the same as we've discussed already.

STRATEGY
You should check flashing and trim for tightness to the building where you can reach it. The best way to do this is to grab it and try to pull it away from the building using moderate force. It's surprising how often things are poorly attached to buildings. Be careful not to do damage with this test. If something starts to pull away from the building, don't keep pulling on it. Simply push it back into position and describe it as "loose."

Rust

On metal flashings and other metal details, rust is a common problem, especially on those components that require regular painting. Prefinished metals often do not require regular maintenance or painting.

IMPLICATION
Rusted flashing and trim pieces will not be able to perform their function as the rust progresses.

STRATEGY
Look at all metal pieces for evidence of rust. Brown to reddish rust is typical of metals containing iron. Whitish coloration is typical of rusting aluminum. Rusting copper is green.

Rot

Rotted wood trim is very common, especially if it is a raised piece of trim, and it's even more vulnerable if it happens to be a horizontal piece. Check these details very carefully.

IMPLICATION
The implication of rotted trim is, of course, non-performance. The trim may be expected to fall off the building and allow water into the wall.

STRATEGY
Check closely for rot. As we've discussed earlier, paint can conceal rotted wood. Both look at and touch wood trim pieces where possible. End grains of wood often rot first. Squeezing near the end grains can reveal rotted wood that's been painted over.

Where there are vertical trim pieces with end grains at the bottom, check here for rot, especially if the trim is close to grade. Any wood that is less than six inches above grade is susceptible to rot because of wetting from splashing and damp soil.

Missing or Ineffective Caulking

Many trim pieces and some flashing pieces are made more weather-tight with caulking. Caulking is also often used as the only defense against water penetration at joints.

We've talked about caulking problems and how caulking fails. We won't deal with the implications again.

Use common sense to determine whether caulking is needed. Caulking should be found, for example, where horizontal boards form a raised surface on wall panels. This is true of Tudor- and Stick-style homes. The horizontal wood members that sit proud of the siding have a horizontal surface that catches water. A bead of caulking that forms a sloped shoulder helps to drain water off and protect the joint between the wood and the siding.

2.6   AN OVERVIEW OF EXTERIOR STRUCTURES

When inspecting the exterior of a house, most inspectors start at one point, often the front door or a front corner, and work their way around. Along the way, exterior structures will be encountered. Usually they are looked at as the inspector comes to them, but sometimes, especially with detached garages, the inspector finds it easier to finish the walk around the house prior to investigating the garage. In this section we'll talk about several exterior structures. We should define some of the things we'll discuss.

- **Porches** are exterior structures at building entrances (Figure 2.25).
- **Decks** are exterior wood structures attached to buildings at an entrance point, usually (Figure 2.26). Decks are commonly supported by posts and the house wall or foundation.
- **Balconies** are exterior structures that project from the building at least one story above grade (Figure 2.27).
- **Garages** are four-walled structures. They can be attached to or detached from the house. A garage has at least one vehicle door and often one or more man doors.
- **Carports** are garages with fewer walls, sometimes none (just posts), and no vehicle door.

Key points to look for with exterior structures include water damage, rot and insect damage, and safety issues.

2.7   PORCHES, DECKS, AND BALCONIES

Most homes will have one or more of these. Although they are accessories to the building in one sense, they are important and can be expensive to repair or replace. They should be included in the inspection.

Let's look at the individual components of these systems. We'll address steps, railings, columns, beams, joists, floors, roofs, and skirting.

2.7.1   Steps and Landings

Function

The floor level of most homes is higher than the exterior grade level. Steps are usually needed to get up to the door. Landings at the top of steps should be large enough to open the door without having to step down off the landing.

FIGURE 2.25 Porches

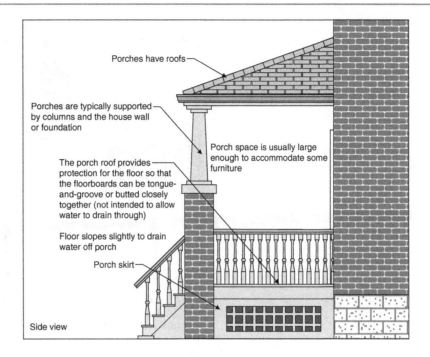

Porches have roofs

Porches are typically supported by columns and the house wall or foundation

Porch space is usually large enough to accommodate some furniture

The porch roof provides protection for the floor so that the floorboards can be tongue-and-groove or butted closely together (not intended to allow water to drain through)

Floor slopes slightly to drain water off porch

Porch skirt

Side view

Concrete Steps

Concrete steps and landings can be built several ways, as shown in Figure 2.28. Settling or heaving problems are common.

Wood Steps

Wood steps and landings should be looked at the same way as interior stairs with respect to dimension and stability and the same as exterior woodwork with respect to wood/soil contact. Wood steps in contact with soil are a frequently found condition that leads to rot and step settlement.

Problems in the following areas are common:

FIGURE 2.26 Decks

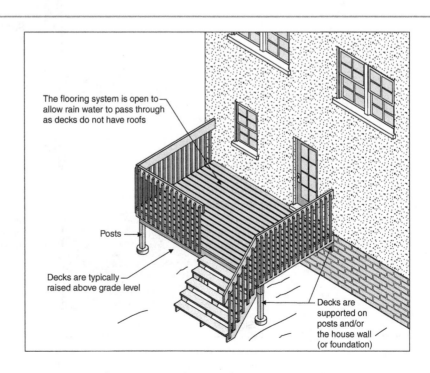

The flooring system is open to allow rain water to pass through as decks do not have roofs

Posts

Decks are typically raised above grade level

Decks are supported on posts and/or the house wall (or foundation)

FIGURE 2.27 Balconies

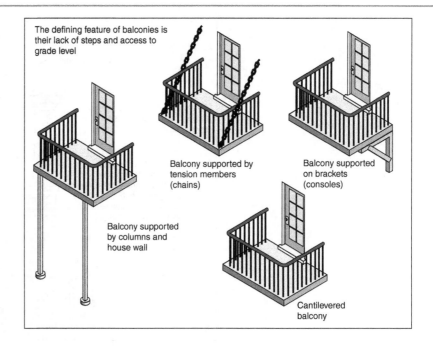

FIGURE 2.28 Support for Concrete Steps

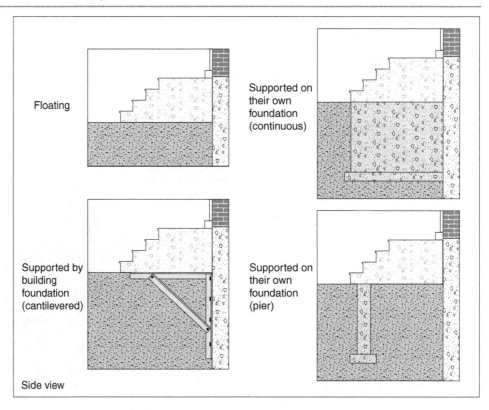

1. Rise, run, tread width (depth), and slope problems
2. Missing or undersized landings
3. Settlement or heaving
4. Spalling masonry or concrete
5. Rot, wood/soil contact, or insect damage
6. Springy, loose, or sagging steps
7. Carpeting over wood

Rise, Run, Tread Width, and Tread Slope Problems

Certain Dimensions Set

A successful staircase is one that is easy to walk up and down. The rise, run, and tread width (depth) have to be within certain guidelines, often dictated by your local jurisdiction. Since this is a safety issue, you don't have much room for latitude or interpretation.

Uniformity

The uniformity of the steps is as important as their rise and run. It is not unusual for the top or bottom step to have a different rise than the rest. This can be a trip hazard and is most serious if it's the top step.

Steps and Landings Should Be Level

Stairs that have settled or heaved may have a slope. Generally speaking, any slope is dangerous.

Rise, Tread Depth, and Nosing

Modern standards for rise and tread depth vary from area to area. You should learn what is acceptable in your area. The maximum rise is typically 7¾ inches. The minimum tread depth (measured horizontally from nosing to nosing) should be ten inches. The nosing is usually ¾ to 1¼ inches deep. Many old staircases will not meet modern standards.

IMPLICATION

A flawed staircase is a safety issue. People may fall on stairs that are improperly arranged.

STRATEGY

Most home inspectors do not measure these dimensions on every set of stairs on every home. With very little practice, one can detect stairs that are outside normal ranges and can pick up irregularities in rise and slope of treads, visually and by walking on them. If it feels awkward, it's probably wrong. Your role is to point out that the steps are not conventional and that people may fall.

Missing or Undersized Landings

Where steps come up to an exterior door, there is often a storm door that opens outward. Good building practice dictates that someone coming up the steps should not be knocked down by someone opening the door from inside. There should be room for the door to swing out over a landing without knocking a person off. Minimum dimensions for landings are often described as 3 feet long and as wide as the steps.

Whether the door to the building opens in or out, there should be a landing. Check your local rules.

IMPLICATION

A missing or undersized landing is a safety issue.

STRATEGY

Advise clients of the benefits of a proper landing, and point out where they are not present.

Landing below Door Sill

Look for a step (minimum six inches high in areas where snow accumulates) going up into the house from the landing or top step. The landing should not be flush with the threshold. Water and snow are likely to get in around the bottom of the door unless there is a step up. The step up into the house should be no more than a typical rise on any step.

Settled or Heaved Steps

Settled steps may be dangerous because of the tread slope and lack of uniformity that result. They may also indicate movement of the entire structure. Repairs to steps that do not have a proper foundation or are not properly supported by the building are expensive. This is especially true of concrete or masonry steps.

The trip hazard that is created is the first implication of settled or heaved steps. An expensive repair is the result. In severe cases, structural problems can develop.

Look carefully at the junction between the steps or landing and the building itself. Where there is settlement, there is often a gap. Where the gap is wider at the top than at the bottom, the steps may be settling down away from the building.

Pay attention to the step uniformity and slope of the treads, both side to side and front to back as you walk up the steps. Pay attention to the slope of the landing (bearing in mind that landings should slope a little to drain water away from the building).

In some cases, frost or expansive soils will cause the steps to heave rather than settle. The resulting problems are similar. It may be safer to describe "movement" rather than mistake heaving for settling or vice versa. Because the movement is often rotational, this is an easy mistake to make.

Spalled Concrete or Masonry

Spalling refers to the crumbling or flaking of the surface of the material.

In some cases, the implications of spalling are only cosmetic. In severe cases, the safety of the stairs may be compromised. Repairs are usually expensive and often involve sandblasting the concrete prior to refinishing.

Check horizontal surfaces and edges, in particular, for spalling, or in some cases, chipping. Look for loose material on the steps or landing. Even in the early stages, this should be documented. Don't mistake a textured non-skid surface for spalling.

Rot, Insect Damage, or Wood/Soil Contact

We discussed earlier in this chapter what makes wood rot and why wood/soil contact is bad.

Wood is weakened with rotting and the steps may shift or collapse when used.

Use an awl or screwdriver to probe wood in vulnerable areas. Pay particular attention to end grains, since wood will rot more quickly here. Where visible, inspect the stair stringers, particularly at the bottoms and at the cutouts for the treads.

Springy, Loose, or Sagging Steps

Steps that display any symptoms of springy, loose, or sagging steps require improvement.

Tread and Stringer Thickness

Exterior wood stair treads are typically $1\frac{1}{2}$ inch thick unless the front of the tread is supported by a continuous riser. In this case, treads are usually one inch thick. Look for stringers to be at least $3\frac{1}{2}$ inches deep at their narrowest point, and at least $9\frac{1}{2}$ inches deep at their widest point. Stringers that span from the ground up to the landing without intermediate support are usually $1\frac{1}{2}$ inches thick.

Again, there are safety implications for springy, loose, or sagging steps.

As you walk up steps, pay attention to the deflection of the treads. Try to walk near the midpoint of the tread between stringers to maximize deflection. Bounce lightly if necessary. Visually check the treads for level, looking for sagging between the stringers. Also look for one end of the individual treads to be lower than the other. This may indicate a failing stringer.

Probe wood near grade level for rot.

FIGURE 2.29 Handrails and Guards

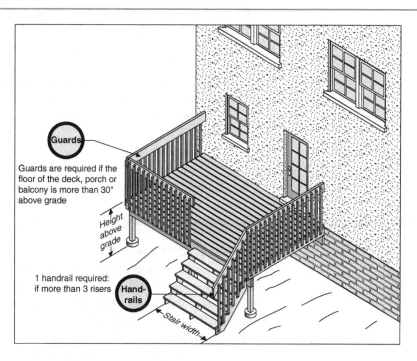

Carpeting on Wood

Carpeting on wood prevents a close inspection and may hold water against the wood. This is a red flag situation.

Carpet on wood steps and decks will hold moisture, inhibit drying, and lead to rot. Premature failure of the wood should be anticipated. Wood covered with carpeting cannot be repainted or stained on a regular basis and cannot be readily inspected for damage.

Explain the disadvantage of the carpeting and recommend its removal for functional reasons. Some people will keep the carpet because of the advantages. Make sure you report your concern about the condition of the wood below the carpeting and your inability to fully inspect it.

2.7.2   Railings (Handrails and Guards)

Handrails provide something to hold when going up or down stairs. **Guards** or **guardrails** keep people from falling off landings, decks, balconies and the open sides of staircases (Figure 2.29).

When Needed

Handrails and guards are safety devices. The implication of non-performance is, of course, falling. Rules vary by jurisdiction. Exterior guardrails are typically required on any porches, decks, or balconies more than 24 or 30 inches above grade. Check your local building standards to see which applies.

Strong and Easy to Grab

Common sense dictates that the handrails must be strong enough to support someone's weight if they stumble. They must also be easy to grab. The handrail section should be at least $1^1/_2$ inches out from any wall so you can get your hand around it, and the part that you grab should be roughly $1^1/_2$ inches across the top surface.

2 × 6 Handrail

A 2 × 6 on edge can meet these criteria and still be a poor handrail. Good handrail design includes a shape at the top that can be easily grabbed in a panic. Grabbing and holding the top of a straight 2 × 6 railing may be difficult. The top of the railing should form a tube or oval, for example, so that you can easily wrap your hand around it.

Guards

Guards should be at least strong enough to support the weight of people leaning against the guard. Many are not.

Problems with handrails and guards include:

1. Missing or loose
2. Rot or insect damage
3. Spindle problems
4. Too low

Missing or Loose

While guards may not be required unless the steps, deck or landing are more than 30 inches above grade, falling backwards off a deck two feet above the ground is dangerous. Irrespective of local building standards, you can offer clients your professional opinion. It's up to your clients whether they provide a guardrail. You do not want to recommend less than what the local building standards are, but you can make recommendations that go beyond the minimum.

IMPLICATION

The implication of missing or loose handrails and guards is a life safety concern.

STRATEGY

The first step is to ensure that handrails and guards are provided.

Railings that are loose are even more dangerous than those that are missing, because they provide a false sense of security. Use every railing and pull on it with progressive and considerable force to ensure that it is secure. Do not lean on a railing or push out on it in such a way that if it lets go, you would fall. Railings that are freestanding at one or both ends are much more difficult to build well. Pay particular attention to these.

Rusted Railings

Metal railings on concrete surfaces usually rust first at their point of penetration into a concrete base. The rusting metal expands and, in some cases, cracks the concrete. The railing may not be very strong. Watch also for damaged concrete where metal railings are attached.

Rot or Insect Damage

While a wood handrail or guard may look secure, closer investigation and probing with a screwdriver, for example, may reveal rot and/or insect damage.

IMPLICATION

A damaged handrail or guard can compromise life safety.

STRATEGY

Look closely at railings, particularly at bottom members, and at horizontal details. Pay particular attention to end grain. These areas tend to rot first.

Missing or Ineffective Spindles

Guards must be constructed so that people cannot fall through. This is particularly important where young children may be expected to test railings. According to many modern standards, spindles (also called balusters) must be designed so that no opening will allow a four-inch ball to pass through. Check with your local authorities to determine what is required in your area. Again, you can recommend something different, but you must know what the minimum standard is for new work.

Spindles should be substantially vertical. Railings with many horizontal details are easily climbed by children and, as such, are a safety hazard. These are not allowed by some authorities.

IMPLICATIONS

Inadequate spindles are a safety issue.

STRATEGY

Use common sense when looking at guards and think about toddlers and small children who love to climb.

Terminology

Some people refer to spindles in railings as **balusters.** The entire railing system may be called a **balustrade.** Freestanding posts at the ends of railings (particularly at steps) are often called **newel** posts.

Too Low

Handrails

Handrails must be at a height that the average person can grab readily as they go up or down steps. In most jurisdictions, they have to be 34 to 38 inches above nosings. Check your area requirements.

Guards

In many areas, the guardrails must be 36 inches high around landings, decks and balconies.

Different Rules

The required height of handrails going up the stairs may not be the same as the required height of the guardrails at the landing around the top of the stairs.

IMPLICATION

Handrails that are too low jeopardize life safety.

STRATEGY

From a safety standpoint, you may want to recommend that the railings be replaced. However, these are often an architectural feature that clients will not want to give up. Raising the issue and ensuring your clients understand the implications is enough for a home inspector. It is not your role to persuade people to make changes to the house, especially on something as subjective as this. Temporary handrails and guards or extenders are possible solutions to maintain architectural appeal over the long term and protect a busy youngster in the short term.

Inspector in the House: Really Making a Point

Everyone likes to feel they are strong. Sometimes it gets us into trouble. Standing on the rear deck about 5 feet above grade, a new inspector and I were explaining to the client the importance of guardrails around a high deck like this. We spoke about how people often lean against railings and there can be a lot of force on them, especially during a party with lots of people and a little alcohol.

My associate grabbed the railing and applied some force—more than the railing could withstand, as a matter of fact. The railing gave way and he would have fallen after it, had the client and I not grabbed him. The point was made, but the damage was done. We were all a little shaken up.

It was very difficult to make the seller understand that the railing was unsafe and not our responsibility to replace. We ended up splitting the cost of replacement.

What was the weak link? In this case there were several, but the most significant was where the railing was (barely) secured to the house wall. We often can't tell by looking where the problem may be.

What did we learn? Test progressively and carefully. Don't put yourself in danger.

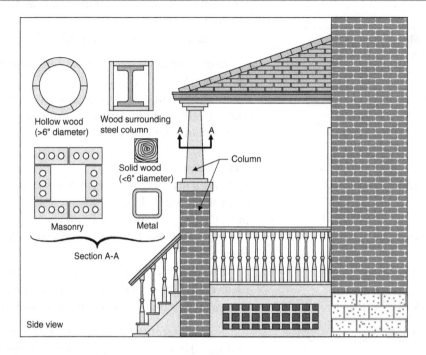

2.7.3 Columns

Functions

Columns typically support the floors and roofs of porches or **porticos** (small roof assemblies over entrances supported by columns). They may also support decks, overhanging living spaces, carports, or balconies. Columns transfer loads from joists or beams to foundations or footings or both.

Materials

Columns can be made of several materials and may be a combination of materials (Figure 2.30). Some columns have a wood upper section and masonry lower section. Most round wooden columns larger than 6-inch diameter are hollow. They are made like barrels. Wooden columns can be solid square lumber.

Common column problems include the following:

1. Leaning, settled or heaved
2. Spalling or cracked
3. Rot, insect damage, wood/soil contact or rust

Leaning, Settled, or Heaved

Most of the time, it is safe to assume that a column was installed straight and plumb. However, columns can shift.

IMPLICATIONS

Columns that have moved may allow the structure they support to fail. These columns may be expensive to stabilize.

STRATEGY

Look carefully at columns, particularly the top and bottom, for evidence of movement. Look at the column from several angles. When standing on the street looking at a house, columns that are out of plumb to the left or right will be visible, but a column that is out of plumb leaning toward the street may not be noticeable.

Impact Damage

If a column is near a laneway or driveway, and has moved or shifted, look for damage that may suggest vehicle impact.

Push on Column

Push on the column near the bottom and near the top, if possible, to ensure that it's well anchored.

Racking Test

Where wooden decks are well off the ground, stand on the deck and shift your weight from side to side to see if the deck moves. If so, diagonal bracing may be necessary. Do the same test on carport roofs.

Rot and Rust

Wood columns sitting in the soil will rot. The bottom of a metal column will rust if it's too close to the soil. Metal and wood columns should have footings that extend above ground more than four inches.

Spalling or Cracked Masonry

IMPLICATIONS

Severe spalling or cracking will weaken the column. This could eventually lead to collapse.

STRATEGY

It's common for brick and block columns to spall and lose mortar at ground level. Often the side of a masonry column most exposed to rain will suffer the most damage.

Masonry will wick water up out of damp soil. This is called **rising damp** in some areas. In cold climates, the moisture will freeze in the masonry, leading to spalling.

Rot, Insect Damage, Wood/Soil Contact, or Rust

STRATEGY

Wood columns are susceptible to rot and insect damage. Watch for wood/soil contact and horizontal surfaces that collect water. Use a screwdriver or awl to probe surfaces, especially at the base of columns.

Metal columns are susceptible to rust.

2.7.4   Beams

Beams may be found on decks, porches, balconies, and carports. They may support a roof or a floor, but in either case, their function and orientation is similar. As discussed in Chapter 4, beams are important load-bearing members, transferring loads from joists to columns or walls (Figure 2.31).

F I G U R E   2.31   Beams

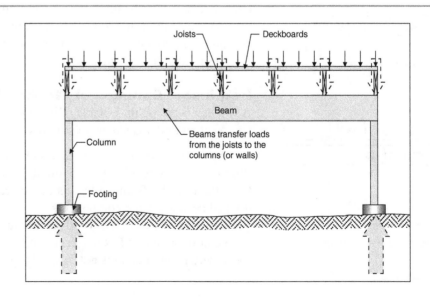

Beam problems to watch for include the following:

1. Sag
2. End support
3. Rotation
4. Rot, insect damage, or wood/soil contact

Sag

Home inspectors should look along beams for evidence of sagging. This suggests non-performance of the beam and may signal expensive repair work or impending sudden structural failure.

IMPLICATION

Structural failure is the ultimate implication. In most cases, sagging beams can be identified and repaired or replaced before things collapse.

STRATEGY

Sight along the beam using other horizontal reference points. Do not line up porch roof beams with gutters. Gutters should never be straight across the face of a structure since they have to slope to work.

Poor End Support

Beams rely on at least 3 inches of end bearing to transfer their loads to concrete or masonry structures below (usually columns or walls). When the supporting elements are wood or metal, at least $1^1/_2$ inches of end bearing are needed.

IMPLICATION

Beams without adequate end support may fall.

STRATEGY

Where visible, look for the correct end bearing for beams. Probe ends of beams with a screwdriver to look for rot.

Examine beams at pockets for signs of the beam having pulled out of its pocket. (The beam end may not have paint on it, or it may be a different color because of less exposure to sun.) At connection points to columns, watch for evidence of movement of the beam relative to the column. Again, a section at the end of the beam may be unpainted, for example.

Check where possible whether beams are mechanically fastened to their supporting members below. Beams should not simply rest on the tops of the columns or pillars. This attachment is often not visible.

Rotation

Beam rotation (twisting) can lead to a lack of support for the joists resting on the beam and can disturb end bearing conditions for joists and the beam.

IMPLICATIONS

Crushing fibers and joist or beam failure may result. In severe cases, building components may fail as a result of beam rotation.

STRATEGY

Ensure that beams have remained relatively square and level.

Rot, Insect Damage, or Wood/Soil Contact

A wooden beam on the outside of a house is susceptible to rot or insect damage.

IMPLICATION

A rotted or damaged beam may result in structure failure.

STRATEGY

Again, look at places where water may be trapped in or against the beam. Probing with a screwdriver is required. Rotted wood can sometimes look just fine from the outside. Built-up beams are susceptible to rot since the water is often trapped between beam components.

Insect Holes

Insect exit holes in the wood surface are clues to possible damage.

Paint and Stain Condition

Paint or stain that has not been well kept up makes wood more vulnerable to rot. Where paint or stain is not in good repair, watch for rot.

Roof Leaks

Beams for structures with roofs (porches, carports, etc.) can be subject to damage if the roof leaks. If you see evidence of roof leakage or damaged trim covering a beam, watch for rot in the beam itself.

2.7.5   Joists

Joists perform similar functions to beams but are smaller and are used to support flooring directly. They transfer loads from flooring or decking to beams or walls. Joists are usually spaced 16 or 24 inches on center in decks, porches, and balconies. Since there are typically several joists in the structure, the failure of any one joist is less important than the failure of a beam. However, the problems we discussed with beams all apply to joists as well.

Wood, Plastic, or Both

Most of the time, you'll see wood joists. There are new products for use in exterior construction. Many of these are recycled plastic, or mixtures of plastic with wood. The same inspection techniques apply, but some problems (e.g., rot) won't be found, and others may develop that are peculiar to these materials. Time will tell.

Joist Support

Joists may be supported on top of beams, ledgerboards, or other framing members (Figure 2.32). Joists may also be supported by metal brackets called **joist hangers.** Joists resting on beams are typically toe-nailed to the beam. While gravity provides a good downward anchoring force, there is less protection against uplift than with a joist hanger. Also, the end of the joist is better restrained from twisting or other lateral movement with a joist hanger.

Sizing of Joist Hangers

These joist hangers and their fasteners may or may not be corrosion resistant. Joist hangers also come in different sizes. A joist hanger intended for a 2 × 4 will not be effective on a 2 × 10.

F I G U R E   2.32   Joist Supports

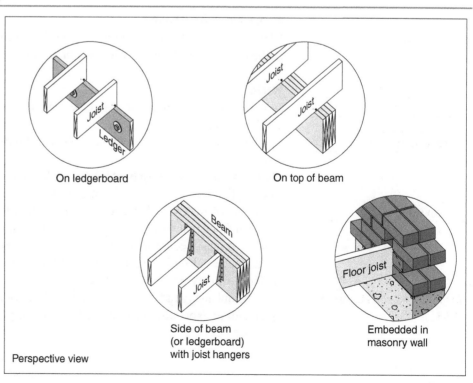

On ledgerboard

On top of beam

Side of beam
(or ledgerboard)
with joist hangers

Embedded in
masonry wall

Perspective view

Nailing of Joist Hangers

With very few exceptions, all of the holes in joist hangers are intended to have nails. Skimpy nailing can lead to failure of the joist hanger and movement of the joist.

End Bearing

The end bearing for joists should be at least $1^1/_2$ inches, even on joist hangers. Joist problems to watch for include the following:

1. Sag
2. Poor end bearing
3. Rotation
4. Rot, insect damage or wood/soil contact
5. Fastener problems
6. Ledgerboard problems
7. Cantilevered joist problems

IMPLICATIONS

The implications for most joist conditions are a weak or bouncy structure. Collapse and personal injury are the most serious implications.

Sag

STRATEGY

One of the best ways to check for joist sagging is to scan the deck or floor surface with your eye at deck level. The other is to bounce while standing on the deck. If you discover a sag, try to determine the reason. You should have a rough idea of what size lumber on what spacing can span what distance. Look for increased loads such as piles of snow drifting or shoveled off the roof onto a deck. If there is access under the structure, look for damage and probe the joists for rot. Watch for missing or ineffective beams.

Porch Floors Are Supposed to Slope

Sagging floors on decks, entrances, porches and balconies are common, but don't mistake a floor sloped to give good drainage for a sag or settlement problem. Porch floors are exposed to driving rain and snow. As a result, the floors are typically built with a slight slope to drain water off the porch away from the house.

Poor End Bearing

STRATEGY

Check for adequate end support at all visible points. Check for rot in the members at the bearing point. Watch for posts or columns that are out of plumb.

Rotation

IMPLICATION

Joist rotation can cause flooring to become uneven. In extreme cases, end bearing can be compromised.

STRATEGY

Sight along joists to check for relative straightness.

Rot, Insect Damage, or Wood/Soil Contact

The implications of rot have been discussed.

STRATEGY

Joists of uncovered structures tend to rot at the top, where water sits. Probe between floor boards to check for rot—more than roughly $1/_8$ inch of penetration indicates weakened lumber. Check also at joist ends, and the undersides, especially if the space below has restricted ventilation. Look for mold and fungus on the surface—it may be black or white.

Header Joists and Pocketed Joists

The outside (header) joist of a porch, deck, or balcony is more susceptible to rot as a result of exposure to moisture. The ends of joists that rest in pocketed masonry can rot quickly.

Fastener Problems

As discussed earlier, joists are usually toe-nailed to the surface they rest on or are hung in joist hangers. Fasteners may be missing, rusted, loose, or the wrong type.

STRATEGY

Look for flush-mounted joists that are nailed without joist hangers or ledgerboards. This is a weak connection—recommend reinforcement. Fasteners should be corrosion-resistant. Hot-dipped galvanized nails are common. Roofing nails, electroplated nails, finishing nails, or drywall screws are not appropriate fasteners, for example.

Check the number of fasteners. Are there enough? Are they rusted or loose?

Poorly Secured Ledgerboards

The ledgerboard is like a joist attached directly to the house wall. Joists are typically supported on the ledgerboard. Joists may sit on top of the ledger or be secured to it with joist hangers.

The ledgerboard may be attached to a wood frame structure by lag bolts into studs or the rim joist every 24 inches. You may also see multiple nails every 16 or 24 inches. For attachment to a concrete or masonry foundation, you may see bolts set into lead plugs, or masonry screws.

IMPLICATIONS

The ledgerboard itself may crack or rot, causing the fasteners to slip. A loose ledgerboard could cause the deck to collapse. This is a life safety issue.

STRATEGY

Check how and where the ledger is attached to the house. Check for signs of the ledger pulling away from the house or of the joists pulling away from the ledger.

Ledger Flashing

Look for rot in the board itself. If possible, probe it with your screwdriver or an awl. The proper ledger construction detail (when installed over a wood frame wall with siding) is to install a flashing that extends up behind the siding and out over the top of the ledger (Figure 2.33). This detail is often omitted.

FIGURE 2.33 Ledgerboard Flashing

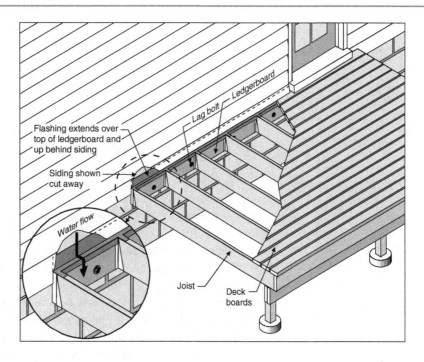

Cantilevered Joist Problems

Many decks and balconies are cantilevered. These are usually a series of joists that have most of their length inside the house, and up to one-third of their length exposed outside. They support a deck or balcony with no vertical support below.

Difficult Details

While cantilevering can be a dramatic architectural detail, it can be very troublesome, functionally.

Problems

Cantilever problems include—

- excess deflection or bounce
- rot and weakness of the deck structure
- rot and water damage to the house wall and interior
- floor unevenness inside the house

Many cantilevers are overextended, and the deck or balcony is springy.

Leaks at Wall

The biggest single problem with cantilevered decks is the difficulty in maintaining a weather-tight joint where the joists pass through the house wall. These joints typically move as a result of expansion and contraction caused by changes in moisture and temperature.

Hard to See

This area is hard to access since it is usually out of sight from above and may be well above eye level when viewed from below. Caulking is usually the only protection of the joint between the cantilevered joists and the house wall. Caulking may be imperfect when installed, or it may deteriorate over time. Rot in the cantilevered joists and water damage to the wall assembly are common problems.

Bumps in Floor inside Home

Where the interior sections of the cantilevered joists are not well secured to other joists and framing members, the inboard ends of the joists can rise, causing bumps in the floor as the outboard ends are depressed.

IMPLICATIONS

Springy decks or balconies are an inconvenience. Weakened framing creates a life safety hazard. Decks or balconies may collapse with people on or below them.

STRATEGY

Cantilevered decks should be viewed with caution. Many inspectors use a ladder if necessary to examine the cantilevered joists at their point of penetration through the wall. Probe the joists with a screwdriver or awl. Look for gaps. Note the location of the cantilever so you can check inside the home for evidence of water damage or a bump in the floor.

2.7.6   Floors

Porches

Porch floors are usually tightly fit tongue-and-groove, one-inch-by-four-inch planks. Porches have roofs that protect the floors. A porch floor system is tight and sheds rain.

Decks

Decks don't have roofs, so the deck boards see more water than porch flooring. Deck boards are usually 2 × 4s or 2 × 6s spaced roughly $3/8$ inch apart. Decking allows the rain to pass through. Decks allow wetting of the joists and beams below, and this helps to explain why decks usually do not last as long as porches.

Canvas Duck

On old porches you may find canvas roofing. These roofs were used where foot traffic was anticipated. Most canvas duck roofs have been replaced. If you see one, it is probably near the end of its life.

Concrete

Some porches or decks have concrete floors. The slab is typically supported by the house wall on one side and by masonry posts or masonry walls on the other sides. Concrete floors should not be supported by wood.

A concrete floor surface should slope away from the house walls.

Look for these flooring problems:

1. Rot, insect damage, or wood/soil contact
2. Sag
3. Paint/stain
4. Poor materials
5. No step up into house
6. Rusted metal
7. Cracked or spalled concrete

Rot, Insect Damage, or Wood/Soil Contact

Wood floors, whether on decks, porches, balconies, or landings, are going to rot eventually.

IMPLICATIONS

Rotting floors can be a safety hazard. People often discover rot by putting a foot through a floor board.

STRATEGY

Walk the entire surface of deck and porch floors. Bounce on the floors near the midspan to check for excessive deflection. Check for rot with a screwdriver or awl, particularly at vulnerable places. By now you know that those are horizontal joints where water might get hung up (at a railing post, for example) or where end joints of wood are exposed.

Sagging

Individual deck or porch boards can sag. This is different from joist sagging. Sagging of floors will show up as a repetitive wavy pattern.

IMPLICATIONS

A sagging floor will be springy and may be weak enough to break under heavy localized loads.

STRATEGY

As you walk on the floors, watch for localized deflection under your foot and sight along the floor looking for a repetitive wavy pattern. It's a good idea to walk heavily on a deck or porch to check for bounce or spring.

Support Spacing

One-inch boards need joists every 16 inches, roughly. One-and-a-half-inch boards (2×6s, for example) need supports at least every 24 inches.

Paint/Stain Needed

Exterior wood lasts longer if it is kept painted or stained.

IMPLICATIONS

Premature rot or ultraviolet damage can occur if paint or stain is not applied.

STRATEGY

Where paint or stain is not present, advise your client that life expectancy will be extended if it is applied. Bear in mind, though, that painting or staining is a high maintenance issue on a traffic surface. With long-lasting wood (cedar, redwood, some pressure-treated wood, for example) it may not be cost effective to paint or stain. We do not consider unpainted or unstained wood on decks as a defect.

Unsuitable Materials

Floors are occasionally made with plywood, waferboard, or other manufactured wood products. These products are generally not successful in outdoor applications, particularly where they are installed horizontally and wetted regularly. Because they are sheet goods, they do not allow water to drain through quickly. Where they are installed with a slope to drain and are well protected with paint or stain, they may work, although when inspecting such systems you should pay very close attention to edges. Edges of plywood tend to delaminate, and edges of waferboard tend to swell with exposure to moisture.

Walking Surfaces

Roof Membrane and Walking Surface

Decks, porches, and balconies should be considered walking surfaces. In some cases, materials such as roll roofing or single-ply roofing membranes are applied. Most roofing materials are not intended to be walking surfaces and will deteriorate as a result of the mechanical and abrasive effect of foot traffic.

There are some single-ply roof membranes that are intended to be walking surfaces. We suggest you visit roofing suppliers and become familiar with the various roofing products. Some inspectors carry samples or brochures of various products so that they can identify unusual systems on site. However, since we are doing a performance-based inspection, your responsibility to the client is to identify deterioration of a roofing membrane as a result of foot traffic, not anticipate it.

IMPLICATION

Use of unsuitable materials may result in a shortened life expectancy for the floor.

STRATEGY

Watch for materials suffering from being used in the wrong application.

IMPLICATION

No Step up into House

Where the deck, porch, or balcony floor is flush with the door threshold, water and snow are likely to get into the house around the bottom of the door. In some cases, the door is also water damaged over time. This problem is common on decks.

STRATEGY

Six-inch Step

Look for a 6-inch step up into the house. A smaller step may be acceptable in areas where snow is not likely to accumulate on the deck or porch floor.

Rusted Metal

Metal floors on balconies and porches are prone to rusting if the metals contain iron or steel. Copper and aluminum oxidize as well, but more slowly. Zinc and lead do not rust like steel does.

IMPLICATIONS

The implications of rust are loss of strength and leakage into areas below.

STRATEGY

Most metal floors are painted. If metal is kept painted, rust is slowed or prevented. Watch for rust, particularly at the edges and penetrations. Check also where paint is missing. Scaling and flaking may mean advanced rust and weakness in the floor structure.

Check from below

Look at the underside of metal flooring for evidence of rusting, including brown or reddish staining.

Tarring Metal Is Bad

Metal roofs covered or patched with roofing cement or other asphalt based products may rust very quickly because water may be trapped between the tar and the metal. This can make things worse instead of better.

Cracked or Spalled Concrete

If it is not severe, cracking or spalling doesn't have serious structural implications. The concrete can be patched and monitored. Severe cracking may be indicating ongoing settlement of the structure, or serious weakening of the slab. Major repairs may be needed.

IMPLICATIONS

Severe spalling usually indicates poor drainage or a poor concrete mix or both. It is unsightly and causes the surface to be uneven, but it rarely poses a serious structural problem.

STRATEGY

Slope

The concrete floor should slope to the outside edges to promote drainage. Any penetrations into the slab should be well caulked. The edge of the concrete should have a drip edge, and ideally a drip edge flashing.

Interior Space Below

If an interior space exists below a concrete porch, balcony, or deck, ensure that the slab is watertight, that the drip edge is adequate, and that the side walls are free of open mortar joints or cracks. Make a note to check the interior space for moisture penetration.

Cracks

Observe the size and location of any cracks in the concrete floor. Cracks the width of a dime or smaller are not immediate concerns, but you should recommend sealing and monitoring. For larger cracks, you may be wise to suggest further investigation. Slab cracking coupled with cracks in support columns or walls suggest movement of the supports. Where the slab shows displacement across a crack, settlement or heaving should be suspected.

2.7.7   Roof Structures

Most of the roof structure will not be visible on a typical porch. Let's look at some of the common problems with roof structures.

Roof structure problems include the following:

1. Movement or settlement
2. Rot, insect damage, or mechanical damage

Movement or Settlement

IMPLICATIONS

Porch roofs that pull away from the house wall may have birds, squirrels, or other pests living in the porch roof. There may or may not be direct connection to the interior of the house. Water penetration into the house walls is a risk if gaps develop. The roof structure can fail catastrophically if early signs of movement are ignored.

STRATEGY

Probe wood for rot, look at connection points to the building and to columns, look for movement of the columns, look for sagging of the beams, and look for evidence of water damage on the underside of the porch roof.

Check Porch Ceiling

Look at the underside of the porch roof, which is often a finished ceiling, for evidence of moisture damage. As porch roof coverings wear out or flashings fail, considerable water damage can be done to the roof structure. Sometimes deterioration of the ceiling indicates problems in the structure. Unfortunately, in some cases, the damage can be quite advanced before it is detectable from below.

Rot, Insect Damage, or Mechanical Damage

Roof structures are similar to other exterior components in that they are vulnerable to rot, insect damage, and mechanical damage.

STRATEGY

Gutters and Downspouts

Pay attention to gutters and downspouts on porch roofs. A gutter that backs up and dumps water into the porch eaves can weaken the main beam running across the front of the porch. If the beam is covered with wood, the trim may show signs of rot. You can often insert a probe through a trim joint to check the beam underneath.

Column Damage

Mechanical damage to columns may be done by cars or trucks when porches are adjacent to driveways. Spalling of concrete or masonry can be an efflorescence or freeze/thaw problem related to rising damp. Rising damp is a capillary action problem where moisture is wicked out of the soil and evaporated off the surface of the column.

2.8   GARAGES AND CARPORTS

The Standards require that garages be inspected whether they are attached or detached. Other outbuildings do not need to be inspected.

Garages

Garages have many of the same features as houses and can be thought of as secondary houses for many aspects of the inspection. Some components and issues are unique to garages. We'll first list some of the components and common problems shared by houses and garages. We'll then look in more detail at the components and issues that are specific to garages.

Carports are simply roof structures supported on columns. They may be attached to the home on one, two, or three sides. Carports don't have walls of their own. There are no vehicle doors, and inspection is relatively simple. There are no inspection issues unique to carports.

It is common for detached wood-frame garages to be in poor condition. Many detached garages are built on mud sills (wood beams directly on the soil supporting the walls). Garage components and systems are often lower quality and less well installed than similar components on houses. Maintenance is often neglected on detached garages.

Unless you adjust their expectations, your clients may expect garages to be just as good as little houses. They rarely are.

Many garage components and problems are similar to house components, so we won't discuss them separately. Just keep in mind that the floors, footings, foundations, walls, roofs, doors, windows, roofs, gutters, and downspouts of garages are subject to the same house conditions discussed throughout this book. If the garage is heated, the heating and chimney system should be inspected as described in Chapters 8 through 11. If there are electrical or plumbing systems in the garage, these should be inspected as described in Chapter 7, *Electrical Systems,* and Chapter 13, *Plumbing.*

Now let's look at some specific garage issues. We'll discuss—

- fireproofing of attached garages
- man doors in attached garages
- garage floors and drainage issues
- vehicle doors and door operators
- combustion appliances in garages

2.8.1   Fireproofing in Attached Garages

Attached garages pose a fire hazard to houses. Building authorities call for fireproofing of garage/house walls and ceilings.

Fireproofing can be achieved several different ways. Find out what the authorities will accept in your area and how most builders accomplish it.

One approach is the use of ½ inch gypsum board on the walls and $^5/_8$ Type X gypsum board on the ceiling, where there is living space above.

Compromised fireproofing is a life safety issue. A fire in the garage may spread to the house.

As you go into the garage, be clear as to exactly what parts of the garage connect to living space. Is it one wall, two walls, three walls? Is it all or part of the ceiling? Look for areas where the tightness of the wall may have been breached or where inappropriate materials have been used.

Be careful if there is ductwork from a forced-air system passing through the garage. There should be no gaps in the ductwork where automobile fumes could enter the house, and there should be no supply or return registers. Additionally, ductwork in garages should be insulated to the level required in your area.

F I G U R E 2.34 Structural Garage Floor

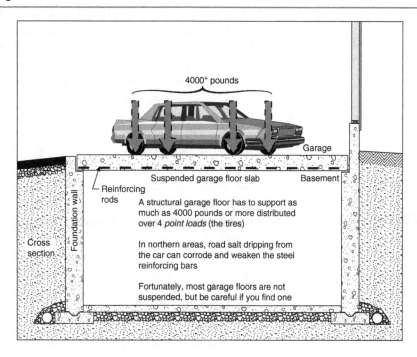

Doors between Garage and House

Doors between the garage and the house should not open into a bedroom and should be 20-minute fire-rated, or a solid exterior-type door at least 1³⁄₈ inches thick. In some areas, a self closer is required.

2.8.2   Garage Floors

Check for the following garage floor conditions:

1. Structural garage floors (needing specialized inspection)
2. Cracked, broken, settled, or heaved floors
3. Drainage problems

Structural Floors

Structural garage floors may need inspection by a specialist (Figure 2.34).

Loads on garage floors are considerable and distress in the floor may be difficult to detect during a visual inspection.

The first thing to determine is whether the garage floor is structural or not. Most slabs simply rest on grade and have no structural function. They are often not supported by the garage foundation.

Garage floors that are suspended require special attention. Because of the weight involved (many cars and vans weigh over 4,000 pounds) and the point loads involved (all of that weight rests on four tires), it is difficult for the home inspector to get a sense of whether the floor is strong enough to support the car over the long term. Again, we are doing a performance-based inspection.

IMPLICATIONS

STRATEGY

Structural Garage Floors

Cracked, Broken, Settled, or Heaved

Garage floor slabs should be at least three inches thick. In some areas, local standards call for them to be four inches thick, and in some cases, they have to be reinforced. Equally important, the substrate should be roughly five inches of well-compacted gravel or clear stone. This provides a stable bearing substrate with good drainage. While all of this is important, you don't get to see how it was built. You only get to see whether it's working or not.

Garage floor slabs should be installed with a slope so that moisture from automobiles will drain out through the overhead door. Slabs that settle or heave may lose this drainage slope and water may pool in the garage, typically against side or front walls.

While special tools are not needed, you should look at the garage floor slab to see that it is relatively uniform and slopes toward the door. Note any areas where the slab has settled and may drain toward a wall. Where you see this condition, look closely at the foundation wall along the wall/floor intersection.

Measuring Settlement

You can often see how much the garage floor slab has dropped by looking for marks on the foundation wall indicating the original position of the slab.

Garage Floor

It is common for a garage floor to settle only around the perimeter in regions where frost footings are used.

Re-sloping

Where a slab has settled and water no longer drains out through the door, additional concrete can be poured to recreate the proper slope on a garage floor.

Hollows below Slabs

Sometimes the garage floor slab does not drop even though the substrate may settle or be eroded below. A hollow sound on the garage floor will indicate settlement of the substrate. Where this is noted, cracking should be anticipated. Since you have no way of knowing how far the substrate has settled, you should recommend further investigation and remedial action.

Check Driveways

Check driveways as well as garage slabs where you suspect subsurface erosion.

Drainage Problems

Modern garage floors in most areas slope to drain water out of the garage through the overhead door and down the driveway. You may find floor drains in garages. These may drain by gravity or by pump.

Garage at Bottom of Driveway

Below grade garages often have a drain just outside the garage door to collect driveway runoff as well as garage floor drainage. These drains often run the full width of the garage door.

Poor Drainage for Below-Grade Garages

Some attached garages are located at the basement level of a house, and the driveway slopes down toward the garage. In these cases, a special drain is provided. Within the garage, the floor slope is the same as that used in conventional modern construction. Water inside the garage flows out through the vehicle door opening. Outside the door, a drain catches the water coming down the driveway and also catches water from the garage. This drain is usually the full width of the garage door.

Undersized, Clogged

Drains may be undersized, clogged, or not at the low point. Covers may be rusted, or exit pipes may be poorly arranged. The walls or floor of the drain may not be sound.

Drainage problems on garage floors can cause water damage to the garage and house.

Authorities in many areas do not permit floor drains in garages because spills of automobile fluids (gas and oil) may find their way into municipal sewer systems. This can be a pollution and life safety problem.

F I G U R E 2.35   Drain Pipes Should Face Down

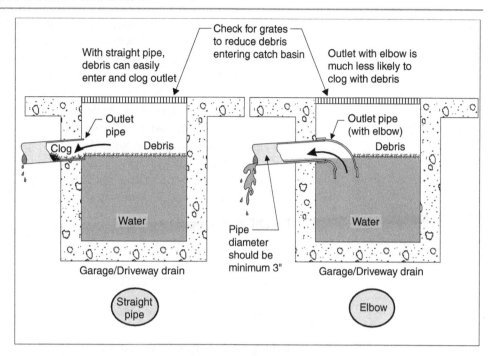

STRATEGY

*Check Garage Door
and Walls*

Look at the bottom of the garage door for evidence of water problems. The garage door, jambs, and operating tracks may show rot or rust, suggesting chronic flooding problems. Look at the inside walls of the garage just above floor level for high watermarks from flooding. Look for stains on the bottom of shelves, or damage to storage in the garage.

Check that the garage floor slopes to a drainage point. In most cases this is out through the vehicle door. If the slope is incorrect, it can usually be corrected by pouring additional concrete on top or by mud jacking, as long as the slab is not still moving. If there is a drain in the garage floor, we do not recommend abandoning it, but we do advise clients of the dangers of automobile fluids entering the drain. You won't normally test this drain. Let your client know this.

*Plumbing Cleanouts
in Garage Floors*

A sump with a grate in the garage floor is not always a floor drain. It may contain a waste plumbing cleanout. Watch for rotted wood walls in such sumps. Watch also for rusted cleanout covers.

Drains Filled with Debris

Look in these drains to make sure that they are not filled with debris. You should be able to see the exit pipe. Exit pipe diameters of less than 3 inches may not be large enough to carry the accumulated rain water away.

Drain Pipe Should Face Down

The end of the pipe in the drain should include an elbow that turns down, as shown in Figure 2.35. Much of the debris that falls into a drain will be floating debris. This includes leaves and twigs. If the drain pipe is simply a hole in the side of the drain, as the water level rises to the drain height, all the floating debris will enter the drain. An elbow only allows water to flow into the drain through a 3-inch-diameter opening that will be below the water surface. Far less debris will enter the drain with this arrangement.

*Check Walls, Floors,
and Cover of Drain*

Make sure the walls, floor, and cover grille are intact. Check to see that the drain is at a low point. It is very common for the paving around the drain to settle, causing low spots to develop. Often water sits in these areas instead of draining into the grate. Recommend correcting the paving.

2.8.3   Vehicle Doors

Types

There are several types of garage doors. Some are hinged at the sides and open like man doors. Some slide sideways on a horizontal track. Most modern doors open overhead. Some of these are solid doors that rotate upward. Many are **sectional** doors with rollers that move in tracks on both sides of the door.

Materials

Garage doors may be of wood, wood-based products, metal or vinyl. They can be insulated. All modern doors have weatherstripping at least on the bottom.

Need to Be Balanced

Overhead garage doors are expensive, heavy, and rarely adjusted perfectly. Springs or counterweights should offset the weight of the door. It should require similarly moderate efforts to open or close the door. A door should stay in position if it is stopped half open. It should not slam shut or spring up.

Problems associated with garage doors include:

1. Difficult to open or close
2. Rot or insect damage
3. Paint/stain
4. Rust or denting
5. Automatic opener problems

Difficult to Open or Close

Doors can be difficult to open or close for a variety of issues.

IMPLICATIONS

Apart from the frustration of getting into and out of the garage, injuries can result from straining on a door that doesn't work properly or from being hit by an overhead door that comes down too quickly or falls off its tracks.

STRATEGY

Open and close the door. It should not take superhuman strength. The same effort should be required to open as to close it. The door should stay where it is if stopped halfway up. If the door goes up or comes crashing down, the springs or counterweights need adjusting.

Sectional Doors

Look at the tracks to see if they are obviously misaligned, twisted, crimped or damaged. Make sure all of the rollers are in place and well secured on sectional doors. Look for evidence of rust, wear from inadequate lubrication, or hardware that has worked loose. This includes the tracks and tension springs as well as the door.

Racking and Sagging

Check the door for racking. When the door is closed, it should fit reasonably tightly along the floor, and there should be no large gaps between the frame and the top or sides of the door. There should be weatherstripping on the bottom of the door. Over time, some sectional doors sag in the middle. Gaps between the floor and the bottom of the door will exist on either end of the door when it's closed.

Rot or Insect Damage

Wood, plywood, and hardboard doors are susceptible to rot and insect damage as we've discussed throughout this chapter. Check carefully at joints, especially with doors that face south or west. Probe through the paint to check the wood beneath. Check any horizontal surfaces carefully. They may trap water and rot first.

Paint/Stain

Wood doors should be painted or stained as necessary. The paint or stain should be applied to the inside and edges of the door and to the outside. Some manufacturers' warranties are voided if this is not done.

FIGURE 2.36 Manual Operation of Automatic Garage Door Openers

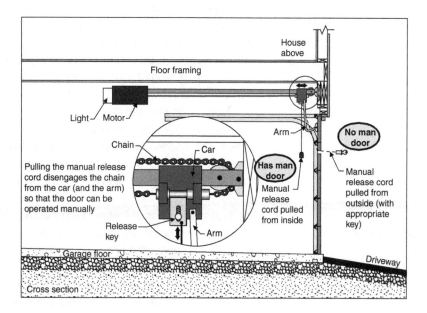

Rust or Denting

Metal or metal-clad doors are susceptible to rust. Pay particular attention to the bottom corners of the door and tracks. Metal doors are often damaged by impact from bicycles, balls, etc. These may or may not affect the door operation.

Automatic Opener Problems

Disengaging the Opener

An automatic opener becomes a problem when it breaks, or if the electricity is off. To open the garage door, it must be disconnected from the opener. Usually the arm is connected to the car via a spring loaded key that fits into the car. A cord and handle is provided so that, when necessary, the cord can be pulled, disengaging the arm from the car.

Vault-Type Garage

This is simple if access to the garage is available through a man door (Figure 2.36). If the garage is only accessible through the vehicle door (similar to a vault), a cable is typically run from the opener disengagement to a keyed lock in the face of the vehicle door. From the outside, a key can be used to unlock the barrel, which allows it to be removed. This pulls on the cable, disengaging the opener.

Auto-Reverse

All automatic door openers **must** have the ability to sense when the door has hit an obstruction on the way down, stop descending, then automatically reverse direction. This is not to prevent damage to car hoods or bumpers. It is to prevent the door from crushing or pinning a child, pet, or fallen adult. It is not enough that the opener stop the door on its way down. It must bring the door back up.

Auto-Stop on Opening

The opener must also sense an obstruction when it is opening the door. This is to prevent crushing people standing on ladders to get to their storage shelving. This isn't as likely as a child running under a closing door, but it still represents a hazard. In this case, the door should stop only—it should not start descending. (This safety feature is not tested during a standard home inspection.)

IMPLICATIONS

Injury may result if the garage door is very stiff to move or comes down quickly, or if the opener or door becomes detached. Missing or defective automatic reversing mechanisms are safety hazards.

STRATEGY

Check Electrical Connection

Test from Inside

Opener May Fall

Where Does It Stop?

Check Chain Drive

Sensitivity Adjustment

Test Auto-Reverse

Don't Damage It!

Auto-Reverse Overridden
in Last Inch

Timed Auto-Reverse

When testing a door with an automatic opener, most inspectors use the hard-wired push button, but not the remote controls.

Look to see how the electrical supply to the openers is arranged. Some jurisdictions are very strict about not allowing extension cords to power garage door operators. This means that an electrical receptacle has to be provided close to the opener. Some jurisdictions require receptacles in garages to be on GFCIS (Ground Fault Circuit Interrupters). Find out what is required in your area.

Look to make sure that the opener is securely installed before operating it. We recommend that you stand inside the garage while testing the opener in case the door closes and cannot be reopened. From inside the garage, you can disconnect the opener and operate the garage door manually. If a problem occurs when you're standing outside the garage, there's nothing you can do about it. Also, if the push button is in the garage, once you close the door you may not be able to get in to activate the button again or disconnect a defective door operator.

Some inspectors will not test an automatic door opener if there is a vehicle parked in the garage under the opener. Poorly adjusted or defective openers may fall, causing damage to vehicles or injury. In some circumstances, openers can cause doors to come off their tracks. Do not stand directly below the door or opener while it is operating.

Operate the door once, paying attention to how smoothly it moves and where it stops. If the door bounces off the garage floor when closing, or stops two inches short of the garage floor, there is an adjustment problem on the closing limit. When the garage door opens, it should not reduce the height of the door opening.

Look for buckling tubes or shafts on chain-driven openers. This may indicate poor adjustment or a defective unit. Many opener kits sold to homeowners have shafts that are thin-walled tubes, packaged in sections. The joints in the sections can be hinge points when under stress, and can buckle. Watch for chains slipping on the sprocket, which may indicate worn sprocket teeth, a loose chain, or an unbalanced door.

Many garage door openers do not automatically reverse properly because the sensitivity adjustment is set too low to overcome a door that does not move freely.

If the door stops for no apparent reason and stays in place or reverses, the auto-reverse sensitivity may be set too high. It is more likely, however, that the door itself requires adjustment.

After the door has been tested once, the automatic reverse features should be tested as described in Figure 2.37. Many people test garage doors by grabbing them at waist height. Depending on the door opener, some will reverse at waist height, but will not reverse when they get down close to the ground level. It is close to ground level where a child may be pinned, and it's here that the reverse mechanism is most important.

Many home inspectors have broken automatic openers while testing the auto-reverse. If the unit doesn't stop, the stress generated while the motor tries to push against the obstruction can break something. Keep your hand on the disconnect cord—pull it if the unit doesn't stop right away.

When testing auto-reversing features, you should note that most doors automatically override their self-reversing feature in the last inch of travel. This is to compensate for uneven garage floors and/or snow or ice on the floor. That's why a two-inch block is used to test the door.

All modern operators have an auto-reverse. Some older units only stop if they meet an obstruction. A door that stops but does not reverse can trap someone under the door. If the door stops but does not reverse, recommend repair or replacement.

Many doors also have an auto-reverse feature that is based on time. If it takes more than 25 seconds, for example, from the start of the closing cycle to the end,

F I G U R E 2.37   Testing Automatic Reverse on a Garage Door Opener

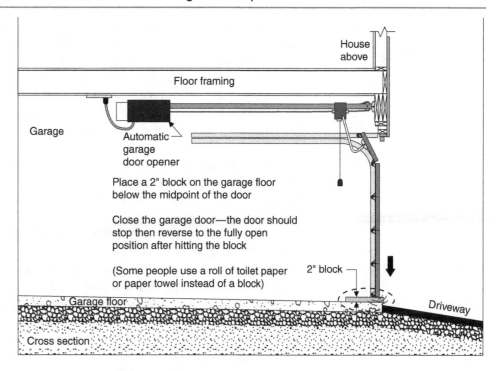

the door may automatically reverse. This is a backup system to the automatic reverse on sensing an obstruction.

Check Photo-Eye

In many jurisdictions, garage door openers have a photoelectric eye that senses obstructions. The eye looks across the full width of the opening. If such a device is in place, you can test the auto-reverse mechanism by breaking the continuity of the beam. This beam is usually located within 6 inches of the floor for the reasons described above.

2.9   SURFACE WATER CONTROL AND LANDSCAPING

Home inspectors look primarily at buildings. We look at the grounds from the perspective of their effect on the home. If the home has 50 acres of land, we do not walk the entire property. Inspectors have different philosophies about how much ground we should cover. This is a business decision you'll have to make. Some turn it into an opportunity by offering to inspect grounds or outbuildings for additional fees.

2.9.1   Lot Grading

It's Really Important!

It is difficult to overemphasize the importance of lot grading. Proper grading facilitates drainage of surface water **away** from the building, resulting in fewer water problems in crawlspaces and basements, and much less risk of deterioration to the foundations due to hydrostatic or frost pressures. Ground sloping toward a building funnels water from rain or melting snow against the building and may cause considerable damage.

Six Inches for the First Ten Feet

While there is disagreement about the exact slope of the grade, and how far it has to be maintained away from houses, a slope of **six inches for the first ten feet** is a common recommendation. Home inspectors usually do not measure these slopes. As a rough guide, you should look for a slope that is visible to the eye.

Impervious Surfaces

Something that is not considered in this simple guideline but warrants consideration is whether or not the ground surface absorbs water or keeps water out. For example, an asphalt or concrete driveway adjacent to a building can have a slope less than six inches over ten feet and still be effective. As long as there is a slope down away from the house of at least one inch over four feet, that should be adequate.

The other side of the coin is that an impervious surface that slopes down toward the house can be a disaster. None of the surface water will soak into an asphalt driveway, so it will all accumulate against the house.

Swales and Catch Basins

Some lot slopes make it difficult to achieve good drainage. **Swales** (shallow ditches) or catch basins can be used on these difficult lots (Figure 2.38), but the potential for problems may remain significant.

Maximum Slopes

There are also structural issues with respect to lot grading on significantly sloped lots. As a rough guideline, lot slopes should not exceed a one-foot rise on average for every two horizontal feet. Where slopes exceed this, the risk of erosion or mud slides may be significant. This will depend on a number of local factors including soil conditions, type and amount of vegetation, amount and intensity of rainfall, etc. You should speak to building authorities, building associations, and builders in your area to determine what is successful in your region with respect to slope stability. Further discussion on building structures and soil conditions can be found in Chapter 4.

F I G U R E 2.38 Swales

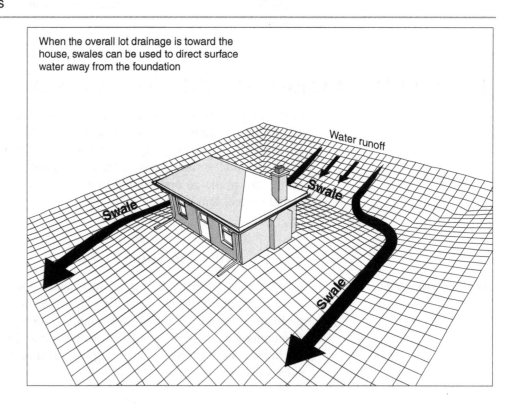

When the overall lot drainage is toward the house, swales can be used to direct surface water away from the foundation

Water runoff

Swale

Swale

Swale

F I G U R E 2.39 Drainage Layer

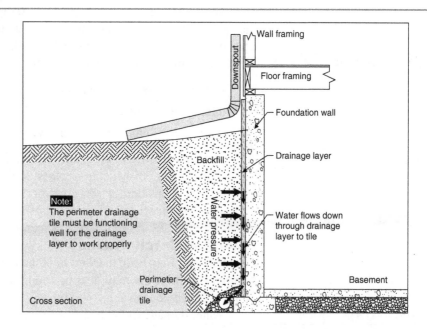

Cross section

Wall framing

Downspout

Floor framing

Foundation wall

Drainage layer

Backfill

Water pressure

Water flows down through drainage layer to tile

Note:
The perimeter drainage tile must be functioning well for the drainage layer to work properly

Perimeter drainage tile

Basement

Is It a Problem or Just a Condition?

One of the challenges of home inspection is to be able to use your professional judgment. You will come across many conditions that are less than ideal but have not resulted in a problem. It is difficult to justify expensive remedial action on a grading situation, for example, where there is no evidence of foundation damage or any moisture problems. Sometimes the grading is horrible, but a sandy soil carries water away so effectively that there are no problems. In this case, let the client know about the condition and the possible result. Tell the client that the situation should be monitored.

Foundation Drainage Material

You may see the top of a drainage material that has been attached to the foundation wall. These drainage materials can take many forms, but many are black plastic in a modified egg-crate, dimpled, or corrugated pattern. They can also be extruded polystyrene. The drainage material holds the soil away from the foundation wall and provides a path for water near the foundation wall to fall straight down to the perimeter drainage tile.

Need Good Drainage Tile

If these systems are well installed, the soil is separated from the foundation wall by this drainage layer (Figure 2.39). If it works correctly, the drainage layer prevents hydrostatic pressure from accumulating against the wall. The water is carried away by the perimeter drainage tile rather than finding its way through imperfections in the foundation wall. This approach relies on good perimeter drainage tile. If the drainage tile is not working properly, or is not present, the solution may not be effective.

Common grading problems include—

1. improper slope
2. clogged catch basins
3. porous material
4. erosion

Improper Slope

Where the grading is flat or slopes toward the building, improvements to the grading are probably necessary. Look for water damage at the exterior wall, where water may be collecting against it, and inside the building, before making a recommendation.

The implications of poor lot grading are—

- wet basements and crawlspaces
- damage to foundations
- damage to siding material, in severe cases

Look at the slope of the grade around the entire building and consider the paths available for runoff. Most inspectors don't use levels. If you can't see any slope, it's suspect. Consider the soil conditions if you have any knowledge of them, and consider whether the surface materials are free-draining.

Clogged Catch Basins

Catch basins may be in the yard or at the bottom of driveways that slope toward the home. Catch basins may also be found at low areas around basement walkouts. Clogged catch basins are common.

Water damage to the house is the serious implication of clogged catch basins.

Look for evidence of backup at the basin. Check the arrangement of the outlet pipe and the condition of the basin walls, floor and cover. Wood walls will eventually rot, and concrete walls can suffer frost damage.

Porous Material at Grade Level

Material that allows water to run through it will not divert water away from the building. This may work if it allows water to percolate down into the soil below the building, but it can also cause a problem if the water gets hung up on an impervious soil just below the surface (Figure 2.40). Good design includes a relatively impervious

F I G U R E 2.40   Water Penetration due to Subgrade Soil Conditions

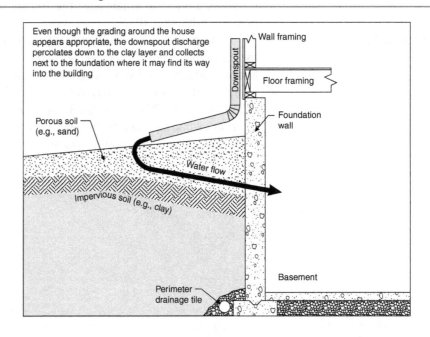

top surface (sod and topsoil qualify) with a more porous soil below. A porous top surface should raise a yellow flag for you.

Porous material at grade level can result in wet basements and crawlspaces and/or foundation damage.

Wherever porous material is on the surface close to the house, there is a possible problem. You won't know whether the porous material extends down past the depth of the footings. You should note this condition as a possible problem, and hold off until you look inside.

Erosion

In some cases, the lot grading is adequate, but there may be soil movement problems. This is particularly true on ravine lots, where a steeply sloped grade may suffer erosion or a land slide.

Erosion may have structural implications for the house.

For the most part, soil issues are best left to specialists, but there are some clues you can watch for.

When looking at ravines or other sloped areas consider these points:

Ravine Lots

- Is there vegetation growing over the whole surface?

Soil Slippage

- Are there bands of freshly exposed topsoil, suggesting recent movement?

Trees Not Vertical

- Are the tree trunks vertical? Virtually all trees grow straight, and tree trunks significantly off vertical may indicate soil movement pushing the tree down the hill.

Cracks in House Walls

- If the slope is at the back of the house, is there cracking visible in the side or back walls of the house? It may be an addition or porch, which is moving relative to the rest of the house.

- Are retaining walls sloped back into the high side at the top? Are they leaning out away from the high side? Retaining walls should be inspected carefully. They will be discussed in more detail later in this chapter.

2.9.2   Gutters and Downspouts

Function

Gutters and downspouts carry water from the roof away from the building, protecting the cladding system and the foundation.

Terminology

Gutters are also called **troughs** or **eavestroughs.** Downspouts are also called **rain water leaders, leaders,** or **conductor pipes.**

When Needed

While not every home requires gutters and downspouts, those that do suffer dramatically if they are not present or are not effective. You will quickly come to know whether gutters and downspouts are typical or not in your area, and, if only on some types of houses, what distinguishes those houses.

Generally speaking, houses with basements or crawlspaces in areas where rainfall is significant should have gutters. Gutters may also be needed to protect siding from damage or discoloration caused by splashing. Where landscaping may be damaged by water running off the edge of a roof, gutters and downspouts should be provided.

Snow and Ice Damming

Gutters and downspouts are not used in some heavy snow areas because **ice damming** problems may be worse with gutters, and because snow and ice can

FIGURE 2.41   Integral Gutter

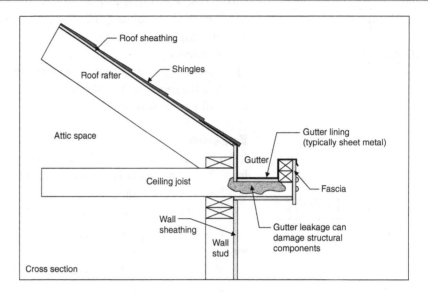

damage gutters or pull them off the building. We discuss ice dams in Chapter 3. In some areas, gutters and downspouts are put up seasonally and are removed for the winter.

Interior Drains

Some houses have interior roof drainage systems instead of gutters and downspouts. This is common on flat roofs, especially those with parapet walls (walls that project above the roof surface) around the perimeter. Interior drains carry water down through the house and out into a sewer system, typically.

Integral Gutters

Sometimes gutters are **integral** with the roof system, and are built into the lower edge of the roof (Figure 2.41). These gutters warrant particularly close inspection, as leakage through the gutters often allows water directly into the building. Gutters hung on the outside of the fascia are less likely to cause damage when they leak. Integral gutters can be rudimentary or elaborate but in all cases, watch for damage from leakage.

Problems

The performance issues with gutters are failure to collect and carry away the water running off the roof.

IMPLICATIONS

The implications of a failed or missing gutter system are potential leakage into the basement or crawlspace, damaged foundations, damage to siding (and with interior drains or integral gutters—damage to soffits, fascia, roof framing, wall systems, and the building interior), and damaged landscaping.

We'll look at problems with gutters first and then at downspout problems.

Gutter Problems

Common gutter problems include the following:

1. Missing
2. Undersized
3. Leaking
4. Loose
5. Damaged
6. Clogged
7. Improper slope

Missing

Home inspectors should report missing gutters where their absence causes dampness in the basement or crawlspace, deterioration to siding, damage to the building interior, or damage to landscaping.

When determining whether the absence of gutters is acceptable, criteria such as existing damage and what is noted on similar nearby houses should be considered.

One of the most difficult things to pick up during an inspection is a missing component. There is no trigger provided, as when something is clearly broken, rusted or worn out. A field checklist will help you look for everything that should be there. We recommend using one, at least for your first few inspections.

Some houses with integral gutters may fool you—they usually can't be seen from the ground. As with any gutter system, try to get a close look from a ladder if necessary. Downspouts may suggest the existence of integral gutters.

Undersized

Gutters must be capable of carrying the runoff from the roof area that the gutters serve. This depends on the local rainfall intensity, the roof area drained, and the slope and size of the gutters. Climatic data from most building codes provides information about local rainfall intensities.

Undersized gutters are more likely to clog with leaves, twigs, and other debris.

With some experience, you will quickly be able to see smaller gutters than what you would expect to find. Do not be misled by steep roofs. They may have a large roof surface but a relatively small **horizontal projection.** (The horizontal area covered by the roof, which is always smaller than the surface area of a sloped roof.) Steep roofs may not need large gutters. On the other hand, the momentum of the water coming off a steep roof may cause it to overshoot narrow or low gutters. Watch for evidence of overshoot. You should also consider how much rain a steep roof will see if the rain is wind driven. Remember that rain doesn't always fall straight down.

One of the other things to watch for is roof shingles that protrude too far out into the gutter, effectively reducing the size of the gutter opening, and promoting overshoot. Generally speaking, shingles should not project more than one inch out over the inner edge of the gutter (Figure 2.42).

Since gutters must slope, the height of the roof above the top of the gutter will vary along the length of the roof. As a general practice, the vertical distance between the roofing material and top of the gutter should be small to minimize water overshooting the gutter.

In some cases, symptoms that look like undersized gutters are the result of undersized or too few downspouts. Gutters and downspouts should be looked at as a system.

Leaking

Gutters may leak along their length, at seams, at end caps, at changes in direction, and at downspout connections. No matter what material is used for the gutters, leaks are most common at seams and changes in direction.

Look carefully at seams and along the bottom of gutters. Look at changes in direction and at downspout connections. Leaks are easy to find during or shortly after a rain, but may be difficult to identify if there has not been any rain recently. Staining or streaking may be helpful, but these may also suggest overflowing gutters.

STRATEGY

Watch for Missing Components

Can't See Some Integral Gutters

IMPLICATIONS

STRATEGY

Excess Shingle Overhang

The Fall from Roof to Gutter

Consider Downspouts, Too

STRATEGY

Check Seams

FIGURE 2.42   Excess Shingle Overhang

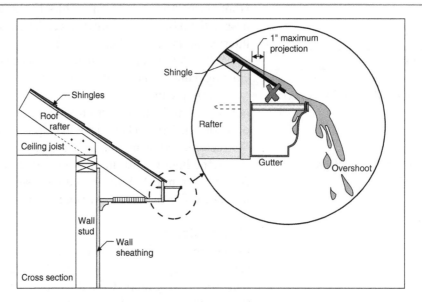

Look for Resultant Damage

Look for damage to fascia, soffits, siding, and landscaping that suggests gutter problems. This includes moss, fungus, peeling paint, and rot. On masonry walls, also look for efflorescence, spalling, and deteriorated mortar.

Patches

If looking at gutters from above, you may notice patching materials in the gutters. This usually indicates attempts to repair leaking gutters. If it is a seam problem, the situation may be localized and minor. If the metal is rusted through, the gutters may be near the end of their life. Sometimes this patching will be on the outside of the gutter and will be obvious from below. Newer sections of gutter may also suggest that part of the gutter system is near the end of its life.

Rust at Bottom

The rusting of galvanized steel gutters can usually be noted on the underside. Often, the rust perforations appear near the centerline of the bottom of the gutter. Steel gutters near the end of their lifespan often look better than they really are because of well-maintained paint. If possible, stand on a ladder and gently push the bottom of the gutter with your hand. Firm resistance means that there's a lot of metal remaining. Very little stiffness means that the gutter should be replaced soon. Be careful, as there's sometimes not much more than the paint between you and the water, and a damaged gutter may mean an irate homeowner. You may also cut yourself if your hand breaks through the metal.

Copper

Copper gutters can develop pinhole leaks, especially with the corrosive action of leaves or needles from trees. You can sometimes see this by looking up from directly below—if you can see the sky, you've got a hole! The more common leak spots in copper gutters are the soldered joints. Thermal expansion and contraction causes the joints to split over time. **Tarring** or caulking copper seams is not a proper repair but is sometimes done instead of more costly resoldering.

Integral Gutters

As we said earlier, consider integral gutters as high-risk areas. If they leak, lots of water gets into the soffit and often in the house wall and ceiling.

Integral gutters are usually found on expensive homes and will often be lined with metal. With time, the joints can open up, and leaks will occur. You may see patching at the seams. Since these are site-built systems, proper repair can be very expensive. A common modern approach (for repairs and new installations) is to line the gutter with a single-ply roofing membrane.

A built-in gutter on a relatively low-slope roof is prone to ice damming. It's not usually possible to determine how high up under the roofing the gutter liner extends. If it is particularly thick and the roofing is somewhat thin, you might see the bump.

Your strategy for integral gutters is to check the exterior eaves and walls and the interior wall and ceiling finishes for evidence of stains, damage, or patching. The gutter framing may be visible from the attic—check for stains or rot. Stains on the sheathing above the gutter could suggest ice damming, especially on a south or west slope.

Can't Check Every Inch

Most inspectors do not inspect every linear foot of gutter around the perimeter of the building. Even if you do this, leaks may not be visible because of their size, because of debris in the gutters, or because the weather has been dry.

Loose

IMPLICATIONS

Gutters that are loose will allow roof water to run behind the gutters. This may cause damage to the soffit, fascia, wall systems, and foundations. Loose gutters may also have an inappropriate slope, which allows the gutters to collect and spill water. The weight of the water will worsen the loosening situation, and eventually the gutters will come off the building.

STRATEGY

When looking up at the gutters from the ground, you can usually see if a gutter has come loose. It will be pulled away from the fascia. Standing back from the house, you may pick up loose gutters because the outside edge of the gutter is lower than the inner edge. This usually means the gutter is pulling down and away from the building. A sag or reverse slope may also mean loose gutters.

Damaged

IMPLICATIONS

The implications of damaged gutters are leaks and water damage as we've discussed.

STRATEGY

Look for evidence of mechanical damage at all locations, but concentrate on spots where ladders would logically be placed and where tree branches or trunks may touch the gutters. Plastic troughing is especially prone to cracking.

Don't Cause Damage

Inspectors should be careful not to damage gutters. Avoid leaning a ladder against a gutter. If the gutter is painted, you are likely to scratch the paint, or even dent or split the gutter. If you have to lean a ladder against a gutter, at least one side of the ladder should rest against a fastener so that it is solidly supported. Consider rigging your ladder ends with cloth or foam to protect gutters. Another alternative is a stand-off for your ladder that puts the load on the roof surface rather than the gutter. Always use best safety practices when working with ladders.

Clogged

IMPLICATIONS

Clogged gutters are common, and while it is just a maintenance recommendation to suggest cleaning on a regular basis, clogged gutters can result in considerable damage.

STRATEGY

Look over the entire length of the system for clogged gutters, if possible. Clogs are often, but not always, at downspouts. You need to be above the gutters either on a ladder or on the roof. It's safer, especially on steep roofs, to look from a ladder, but it takes a lot longer to look at the entire gutter system this way.

People Don't Understand Implications

It's often difficult to impress upon clients the importance of keeping gutters clear. This issue warrants a little time spent with the client, stressing good maintenance and the serious implications of neglect. Flooded basements and foundation damage require more significant repairs than simply replacing the gutters.

Improper Slope

A properly sloped gutter system is usually visible from the ground, standing back from the house. The distance from the top of the gutter to the bottom of the shingles should change noticeably from the high point of the gutter to the downspout. Similarly, you can use the distance between the bottom of the gutter and the bottom of the fascia to check slope.

Typical Slope

Many gutters are nearly horizontal, and while more slope is better, almost any slope will work reasonably well. An ideal slope of approximately 1:25 is never achieved because fascias are too short and gutter runs are too long to allow a gutter to fall roughly one inch every two feet. A slope of 1:200 (one inch drop over a run of 17 feet) is more typical, and is acceptable if there are no low spots.

Some gutters slope from a high end to a downspout at the opposite end. Other gutters slope down from a high point in the middle to downspouts at either end. Either situation is acceptable.

Downspout Problems

Downspout issues may include any of the following:

1. Missing
2. Leaking/damaged
3. Undersized/not enough downspouts
4. Clogged
5. Downspouts discharging onto the ground
6. Downspouts discharging below grade

Missing

Collecting the roof runoff in gutters and having no downspouts is worse than having no gutters. Roof water collected in a gutter and discharged in a concentrated area may cause considerable damage to walls and almost certainly will get into the subgrade area.

Secondary Roofs

It is common for downspouts to be missing on small secondary roofs such as dormers (Figure 2.43). Hip and gable dormers often have gutters but no downspouts. The gutters are often open at the end closest to the roof so water can run onto the main roof surface at the back of the dormer. Water runs down beside the dormer into a gutter below. This arrangement can lead to discoloration and premature roof wear in localized areas.

FIGURE 2.43   No Downspout on Secondary Roof

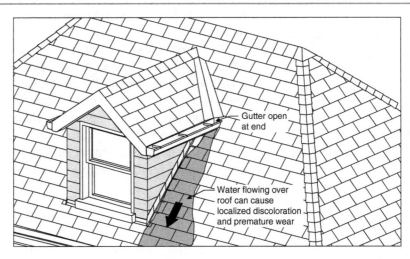

Downspouts Running across Roofs

Some argue that a downspout running across a roof from dormer gutters to the main gutter below is unsightly. It does, however, help the roof last longer. Most inspectors work on a case by case basis to determine whether to recommend downspouts on secondary roofs. It depends on the size and slope of the dormer roof and main roof, the roofing material, and the amount and intensity of rain.

It is usually easy to spot missing downspouts, not only because of the hole in the gutter, but because of the moisture damage below. This includes discoloration, moss, peeling paint, rot, efflorescence, spalling, or cracking on wall surfaces. There is sometimes a hole in the ground below the hole in the gutter, caused by the falling water.

Small Downspouts from Small Roofs

Bay windows, porch roofs, etc., often have gutters but no downspout of their own. In some cases, these gutters are fed through an auxiliary downspout system into a main downspout, typically near the corner of a building. These auxiliary downspouts are usually small diameter, and may run nearly horizontally. Their potential for clogging and leaking is high.

No Downspouts on Small Roofs

Small porch roofs may have gutters but no downspouts, other than a 12 inch elbow that allows water to shoot out into the garden below. Depending on the water volume, this may be effective. Watch for erosion in the landscaping below these areas. In some cases, a downspout is necessary, although a splash block below may prevent erosion. Splash blocks are usually made of concrete or stone.

Leaking/Damaged

The most common downspout leaks are at connections to elbows and at seams.

Downspout Connectors

There are typically two elbows in the connector that joins the gutter to the top of the downspout. Clogging, leaking, and disconnecting are common problems with this connector.

The implications of leaking downspouts are similar to missing downspouts. Depending on the extent and duration of leakage, and whether it occurs near the top or bottom of the wall, damage can be severe.

It may be difficult to spot leaking downspouts except when it is raining. Look carefully for streaking at elbows and connections. The seam on metal downspouts is usually at the back of the downspout against the wall. Where possible, examine this seam. It often splits here because of a clogged downspout and subsequent freeze up.

Damage to Extensions

Mechanical damage can occur anywhere, but is common on downspout extensions which are flattened from being stepped on or driven over by lawn mowers. Ladders and tree branches can also cause mechanical damage.

Undersized/Not Enough Downspouts

A considerable volume of water must be carried during heavy rains. Again, in your local areas, you should become familiar with rainfall intensities and with guidelines for gutter and downspout sizing. You don't need to do a design analysis.

Undersized downspouts cause gutters to overflow, damage walls, and cause basement or crawlspace water problems.

Unless you are doing an inspection in a heavy rain, you can't verify the adequacy of downspouts. Having a rough guideline allows you to raise a yellow flag where the situation is marginal. If a downspout serves more than **35 feet of gutter length,** you should be suspicious.

Clogged

Downspouts are most likely to clog at the elbows on the connector to the gutters. They may also clog along their length or at the bottom, especially if the end is obstructed or crimped.

STRATEGY

Heavily Treed Areas

Look for Water Damage

Clogged downspouts are sometimes visible from the top. Tapping on downspouts will sometimes indicate a clog. A hollow ringing sound means that the downspouts are clear. A dull thud suggests that the downspout is clogged. Watch for clogs at elbows. This usually has to be checked from a ladder.

Where there are tall trees near the house with branches close to or overhanging the roof, clogged gutters and downspouts are more likely.

Again, look for evidence of staining or water damage to walls. Moisture in the basement or crawlspace near the downspout is also a clue.

Downspouts Discharging onto the Ground

Downspouts should discharge at least six feet from the building, and the ground at the discharge point should slope slightly (one inch per foot, for example) away from the building. Common problems include downspouts that discharge too close to the building, or discharge where the ground slope directs water back against the building wall.

Easy to Inspect and Repair

Downspouts discharging above grade are easy to repair or replace if they become damaged or clogged. It is also easy to know whether the gutters and downspouts are working properly during a rain, just by watching the discharge from the downspout extensions. Non-performance can be quickly identified and cured inexpensively.

Splash Blocks

Shorter downspout extensions may require splash blocks to avoid digging holes in lawns and gardens. Splash blocks are often too small. They tend to get moved around and may settle, sloping back toward the house.

Disadvantages

The disadvantages of discharging onto the ground can be traffic problems at building corners (people may trip over downspout extensions) and the necessity to temporarily disconnect or lift downspout extensions when cutting the grass. Some people also feel the downspout extensions are unsightly.

Lots of Water Dumped near House

Another disadvantage of using the above-grade downspout extensions is that they can dump a fair bit of water onto the property near the house. Even if the water does not get into the house, it can pool if drainage is poor. In freezing climates, the ponded water may create ice on sidewalks, patios, and driveways, creating a slip hazard.

Despite these issues, most inspectors believe that this is the best arrangement for downspouts.

IMPLICATIONS

Ineffective downspout discharge can result in damage to the lower section of the building and moisture getting into the basement or crawlspace.

STRATEGY

Where you find above-grade discharge, look for—

- extensions well connected and in good repair
- discharge at least six feet from the house
- ground that slopes down away from the house at the discharge point

Stress Importance to Clients

Downspout extensions are inexpensive, but most home inspectors spend some time explaining their importance to clients. Many are unaware of the important role played by good gutters and downspouts.

Downspouts Discharging into Drains below Grade

Downspouts often disappear into the ground adjacent to the building. On older houses, these extensions may be cast iron, clay tile, or asbestos cement piping. On modern houses, the downspout extensions below grade are often ABS or PVC plastic.

Advantages	The advantages of these systems are—

- there are no unsightly downspout extensions
- water will not be discharged onto the lawn, driveway or grade around the building

Disadvantages	The disadvantages of drains going below grade include the following:
Tough to Inspect	

- It is difficult to see the early indications of non-performance, since water can discharge below grade and collect, saturating the soil for some time before it is noticed.

Repair Is Expensive

- When pipes do get clogged or collapse below grade, repair or replacement is more expensive, often requiring excavation.

Downspouts into Floor Drains

- In many older homes, the downspout extensions extend down below ground beside the foundation, and then run horizontally under the basement floor, terminating in the vertical section of a floor drain pipe, just above the trap. The rain water goes through the floor drain trap out to the street through the **combination sewer** pipe. (In many old houses, there are not separate storm and sanitary sewers. All water is carried in a combination sewer.)

Basement May Flood

Debris can accumulate in the floor drain trap, clogging it. This can cause water to back up into the basement up through the floor drain during heavy rains. Rain water from the roof runs into the gutters, down the downspouts, and to the floor drain. If the floor drain trap is clogged or broken, the water will back up through the floor drain, flooding the basement. Many people confuse this with a sewer backup.

Do Downspouts Drain into Floor Drain Traps?

One of the ways to identify this arrangement is by noting a draft (a cold draft in winter) coming back up through the floor drain (Figure 2.44). Check that the draft is not coming back up through the sewer system. This may happen if the trap has

---

F I G U R E 2.44   Does the Downspout Drain in the Floor Drain Trap?

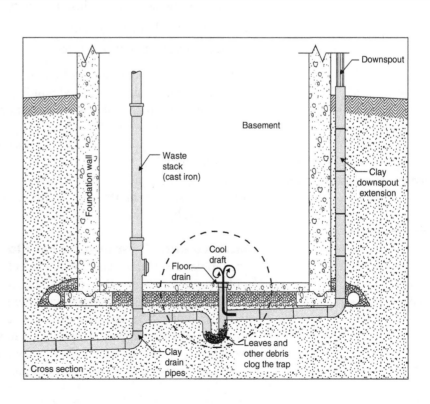

no water. This would cause a sewer odor. If there is a draft of fresh air, it is probably air coming down the downspout, under the basement floor, and into the floor drain above the trap. You may be able to see where the downspout extension discharges into the floor drain.

The implications of downspouts discharging below grade are leaky or flooded basements and sub-grade areas. Foundation damage may also result.

There is not much that can be seen of these downspout extensions during an inspection. The only clues are usually moisture in the building.

In some cases, the top of the downspout extension at grade can be seen to be cracked, broken, or backing up.

In some cases, downspouts drain into below ground pipes that eventually discharge onto the ground at a lower point. Look for this on sloped lots where water can flow by gravity to outlets in the side of hills.

The downspout may drain into a dry well below ground (French drain), or into a storm sewer, which leads to the street. Storm sewers in newer developments often serve downspouts. You probably won't be able to determine where the water is going, but you can learn what's normal for your area. Your job is to look for problems and warn your clients about potential problems.

Downspouts extending below grade do not have to be changed if there are no problems, but clients should be aware that when problems are encountered, they are often expensive. One cost-effective solution is to abandon clogged or collapsed pipes below grade and provide above-grade downspout extensions.

IMPLICATIONS

STRATEGY

Drain out Through Hillsides

Drain to Dry Wells or Storm Sewers

Abandon Below-Grade Downspouts

2.9.3   Flat Roof Drainage

Flat Roofs Aren't Flat!

We should first clear up a misconception. **Flat** roofs should never be perfectly flat. All roofs, even those described as **flat,** should slope toward a drain. Roofers often call these "low" slope roofs.

Three Drain Methods

There are three strategies for controlled draining of flat roofs:

1.   Gutters and downspouts installed along the lower edges of the roof.

2.   An interior drainage system.

3.   Scuppers at the roof perimeter.

Gutters and downspouts are more common on houses. Interior drains and scuppers are more common on commercial buildings, which have larger roof surfaces.

A scupper (Figure 2.45) is a penetration through a **parapet wall** or drip edge that allows water to run off the roof. (A parapet wall is a wall that extends above the roofline.) A scupper is usually connected to a downspout that runs down the outside of the building.

Primary or Secondary Drains

If scuppers are primary drains, they are installed around the perimeter of the roof at low points. If a scupper is an emergency or secondary drain, it is installed about two inches above the roof membrane.

Gutters and Downspouts on Flat Roofs

The problems we talked about with respect to gutters and downspouts apply to flat roofs that are drained with gutters and downspouts.

Scuppers

Roofs that drain through scuppers are similar to gutter and downspout configurations, although several feet of gutter along one side are replaced by a single drainage point (a scupper). Scuppers are more vulnerable to leakage and clogging than gutters. Proper slope is more critical with scuppers than gutters. The downspout issues, as discussed previously, are similar.

FIGURE 2.45   Scupper Drains

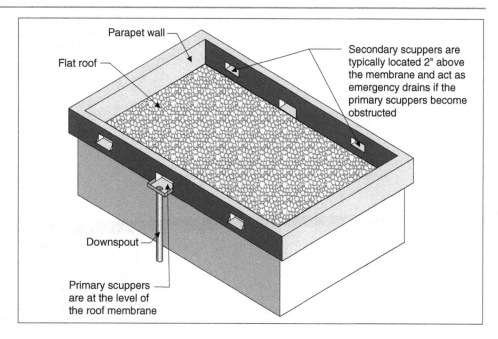

Parapet wall

Flat roof

Secondary scuppers are typically located 2" above the membrane and act as emergency drains if the primary scuppers become obstructed

Downspout

Primary scuppers are at the level of the roof membrane

Interior Drains

As mentioned, these are less common residentially than commercially, so we will not discuss them in detail. Common interior drain problems include the following:

1. Clogged
2. Undersized/not enough drains
3. Drains not at low spots
4. Leaking
5. Absence of scuppers

2.9.4   Window Wells

Where Found

Window wells (Figure 2.46) are typically found where basement windows are completely or partly below the exterior grade level. Wells provide space for light, ventilation, and access to subgrade areas. Window wells have drains to carry away water that collects in them. Alternatively, covers are provided to keep water out of the wells.

Drains

Most window wells have drains that carry water from the well to the storm sewer. These drains can be pipes filled with gravel, or just a gravel column. You won't be able to determine how effective the drain is or, in some cases, whether there is a drain. The drain may be missing or may not be visible because it's below several inches of gravel.

Alternate to Window Well Drains

A common alternate solution is to provide a clear plastic cover that will prevent rain from accumulating in the well. This allows light in through the window, but you can't open the window and get fresh air.

Covers

Another benefit is that covers keep debris out of the window wells. Window wells are great collectors of debris such as blowing papers.

F I G U R E 2.46   Window Well

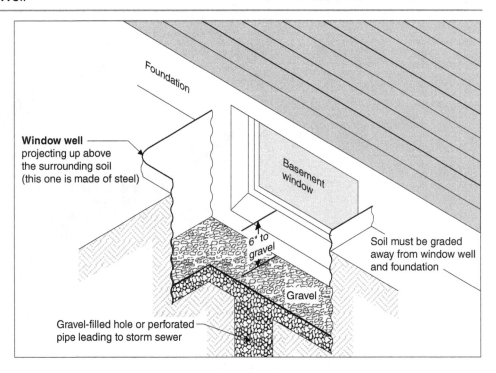

Walls and Floor

Check the walls of the window well to ensure that there has been no movement. The floor of the window well, which is typically gravel, should be approximately six inches below the window frame. Wood/soil contact should be avoided.

Common problems with window wells include the following:

1. Missing

2. Damaged

3. Rot or wood/soil contact or rust

4. Drain problems

Missing

Where basement windows are less than six inches above grade level, wells should be provided.

IMPLICATIONS

Missing wells create wood/soil contact and may create water problems in the foundation or basement. Metal windows and frames may rust. Wood components may rot.

STRATEGY

Check that wells are provided for all windows within six inches of grade.

Damaged

Window well walls are little retaining walls. Where these small retaining walls have moved or suffered damage, improvements will be needed. Concrete walls may be spalled, cracked, or leaning. Wood walls may be rotted, cracked, shifting, or damaged by insect activity. Metal walls may be bowing, broken, or rusted. Masonry walls may be cracked, broken, and shifting. Plastic walls may be bowed or cracked.

IMPLICATIONS

The implications include water damage inside the home and to the structure.

STRATEGY

Poor Grading

Ensure that the walls of window wells are intact and well secured to the building. Probe wood for rot and insect damage. If the walls have deteriorated or pulled away from the building, improvements will be necessary.

Window wells may deteriorate but can also funnel water into the window if the grading around the window well is poor. This is common at the well/wall intersection. Check the grading around window wells carefully.

Wood/Soil Contact

This can occur if window wells are missing or if the floor of the window well is too high.

IMPLICATIONS

Wood/soil contact can lead to rot and insect damage to the well walls (if wood) and to the windows and window frames. It may also allow water into the basement.

STRATEGY

In some cases, the floor of the well can be lowered slightly, although if the walls do not go down deep enough, the walls may have to be modified as well.

Drain Problems

Window wells should have drains (Figure 2.47). These drains can be open pipes that connect to downspout drains or perimeter drainage systems. The pipes may be filled with gravel. In many cases, you won't be able to verify the presence of the drain, but you will see evidence of non-performance if drains are ineffective.

Drains may be—

■ missing

■ not connected

■ broken

■ obstructed

IMPLICATIONS

Water entry into the basement may result from drain problems. Window frames may rust or rot. Well walls may suffer freeze/thaw damage.

F I G U R E 2.47   Drain Problems

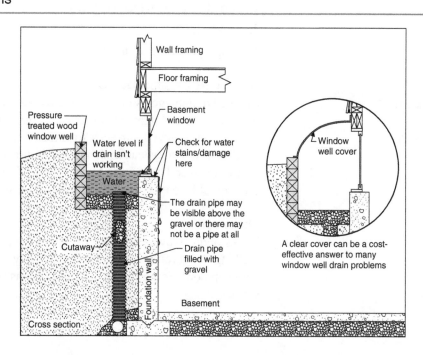

Look for a pipe projecting up through the center of the gravel floor. The top of the pipe may not be visible. The pipe may have been removed, and there may simply be a column of gravel extending down from the gravel in the floor. Look for high watermarks on the glass, sash, frames, or window well walls. Check for rotting wood or rusted metal. When you go inside, look for evidence of water running down the foundation wall below the windows. Look also for stains and damage to the finishes.

Look at the floor of the well. Is it six inches below any wood or metal in the window assembly? Is the well filled with debris?

2.10   WALKS, DRIVEWAYS, AND GROUNDS

Walks, driveways, and grounds are inspected for how they affect the house and its occupants. We don't have to assess the condition of the lawn nor the meandering path leading to the potting shed, for example.

In general, these elements are inspected for trip hazards, maintenance, and drainage.

2.10.1   Walks and Driveways

Walkways can be paths around the house or can be sidewalks at the street. Sidewalks may be the property of the municipality. These do not have to be inspected, although many inspectors do look at them. Some sidewalks are the responsibility of the homeowner. In these cases, the condition of the sidewalk should be reported. You'll have to check with your municipal authorities.

Materials

Walks and driveways can be continuous materials like concrete or asphalt, or can be individual pieces, or units, laid together. These can be stones, brick pavers, concrete slabs, wood pieces, or gravel. Pavers can be mortared in place or laid dry. Walks may be flush with the ground or raised on one or both sides.

We commonly see the following problems with walks and driveways:

1. Cracked or damaged surfaces
2. Uneven
3. Improper slope or drainage

Cracked or Damaged

Cracked or damaged sidewalks or driveways can pose a trip hazard. This is a safety issue. Cracks and damage can also be cosmetic issues.

Checking paved surfaces for cracks or damage is easy. It's harder to notice conditions that may lead to damage in future. Look for missing edging, leaning support walls, wood beginning to rot, soil eroding beside the area, small trees that will grow quickly, pavers beginning to spall, or missing control joints.

Uneven

Walks and driveways should be relatively smooth and even. Unevenness makes walking dangerous, and a severe driveway problem makes it difficult for cars to get in and out. Some of the same conditions that cause cracking can cause uneven surfaces.

Uneven surfaces represent trip hazards. Low areas or pot holes will cause ponding water, leading to moss or ice, both of which are slip hazards.

Check for uneven surfaces by both looking and walking. Again, try to notice conditions that may get worse, even if no problem exists now. Look especially at areas where soil erosion could occur.

Improper Slope or Drainage

Improper Slope

Walkways and driveways should slope away from house walls. If they don't, surface water may get into subgrade areas, and damage the walls. If the driveway slopes down to a garage, a wide drain at the garage door is needed.

Improper Drainage

An improperly draining walk or driveway is one where low spots or unevenness allow water to pond. Ideally, the surface is smooth and sloped to allow water to drain off.

Ponding water can cause moss in summer and ice in winter, both of which are slip hazards. It can also lead to damage to the surfaces themselves, particularly freeze/thaw damage. Ponding against the house can lead to water penetration into the building and damage to the foundation and subgrade areas.

Look for dark stains, moss, or spalling on walk or driveway surfaces. Look for cracks or unevenness that could lead to ponding. On driveways, you may see ruts where cars have compacted the surface.

The most important problem to watch for is driveways that slope toward the house. These can cause considerable water damage to the home.

2.10.2   Grounds

The grounds around a house consist of landscape elements including shrubs, trees, lawns, and patios. Again, we inspect them for their effect on the house.

Common grounds problems include the following:

1. Trees or shrubs too close to house
2. Disturbed ground
3. Patio problems

Trees or Shrubs Too Close to House

Shrubs, trees, or plants too close to the house can cause siding to be scraped or mechanically damaged when the wind blows. They can also prevent air and sunlight from drying wet siding. This can lead to moss, mold, or rot. Trees too close, if tall enough, can overhang the roof and fill the gutters with leaves or needles. Large branches can scrape against the roof. Large, dead branches may fall, damaging the roof, gutters, siding, or windows. Large trees close to the house may have roots that block or collapse sewers, or, in extreme cases, push in the foundation wall.

Planters and Vines

We've talked about problems associated with raised planters in direct contact with the house and with vines growing on wall surfaces.

Look Between House and Vegetation

Look for vegetation that is close enough to the house to have an effect. Often the only way to see if there has been any impact so far is to squeeze behind the plants. Look for scratching or denting, or mold and rot. As usual, check horizontal surfaces carefully, and be aware of which side of the house you are on—east and north sides tend to be more prone to moss and mold.

Disturbed Ground

Patching or Missing Sections

On the lawn, you may notice fresh sod or signs of a recent excavation. On a patio or walkway you may notice patching or sections missing. You should try to determine the reason for it.

IMPLICATIONS

In determining the cause of recent excavation or repair work, you are gathering information that may help you with the rest of your inspection. A patch of sod, or repair to a patio, may simply be due to local damage. A long patch that runs from the house toward the street may be due to recent gas, water, or sewer main work.

These things may suggest recent and possibly current problems.

STRATEGY

Note carefully the location and size of the disturbed or repaired ground or patio areas. Remember that water, sewer, and gas mains usually run from the house to the street. Septic tanks, septic drain pipes, septic beds, and wells are usually in the back or side yards.

Patching along the house wall may be indicating foundation waterproofing work.

Patio Conditions

Patios are typically hard, smooth exterior surfaces used for outdoor living. Outdoor furniture and barbeques are often present. They are most often right at ground level.

Similar to Walks and Driveways

Patio construction varies widely. Common materials include concrete, interlocking brick, wet or dry laid stone, asphalt, granite or manufactured paving units or tree trunk slices.

Problems

Most of the problems that we discussed for walks and driveways apply to patios. Watch for—

1. trip or slip hazards
2. slopes that drain water toward the house

Railings
Patios over Rooms

Look for guardrails if the patio is more than 30 inches off the ground.

There may be living or storage space below the patio, often accessed from the house basement. The patio surface then becomes a roof and should have a membrane built into it. It should also have a well-defined drip edge, ideally with flashing, at its perimeter. You won't be able to observe the roof membrane, as it is covered with the patio surface itself (the concrete, bricks, stones, etc.) or a suitable walking surface. You can, however, check for a drip edge detail, and the watertightness of the sidewalls. Make a note to check the interior space for signs of leakage.

Check the concrete for cracking or spalling. If water penetrates a steel-reinforced slab, the steel may rust. When steel rusts, it expands to six or seven times its normal volume. This can cause even more cracking in the concrete and eventual weakening of the slab.

Drainage

Check for evidence of drainage problems on the surface, including dark stains, moss, or local spalling. Watch for trip or slip hazards and for patio steps that may drain water toward the house.

Railings

Guardrails for patios and decks should be strong and secure and at least 36 inches high. Spindles should be vertical, so the railing is not easy for children to climb. Spindles should be no more than four inches apart, so it's not easy for children to crawl through.

The bottom of a railing that is embedded in a concrete surface should be well sealed, because if water enters, damage will occur. This is especially true of steel railings, which are vulnerable to rust.

STRATEGY

2.11   RETAINING WALLS

Retaining walls hold back earth. They occur on lots with elevation changes. Retaining walls should be inspected, at least to the extent they affect the building. You have a business decision to make as to whether you will inspect all retaining walls, including those that are not likely to affect the building's integrity. Let your client know if there are retaining walls on the property that are not included in your inspection.

Get Permission to Enter Other Properties

Retaining walls are often difficult to see from above. You may have to access other properties to get a look at the retaining wall from below. You should get permission to enter another property to inspect the wall.

Who's Responsible for Wall?

Your client should find out who is responsible for looking after a retaining wall on the property line. Is it your client's or the neighbor's problem? Very often, the property owner on the high side of the wall is responsible for the wall.

Drainage Is Important

The area behind retaining walls should be backfilled with gravel or sand, for good drainage. Ideally, a geotextile fabric is used between the free-draining backfill and the native soil, to prevent clogging. At the base, there should be a weeping tile to direct water away, or drain holes in the face of the wall to let water out. Often the gaps between members of pile or tied-back walls serve as the drain holes.

Water Is the Enemy

While you won't be able to see all the construction details, remember that water and frost are the big enemies of retaining walls.

When inspecting retaining walls, look for the following:

1. Leaning, bowing, or cracking
2. Rot or insect damage
3. Rusting metal or spalling masonry
4. No drainage system

Leaning, Bowing, or Cracking

Retaining walls should lean back slightly into the hill, not away from it. A retaining wall that is vertical or leaning slightly away has probably moved.

Movement may show up as cracks in concrete or masonry walls, for example. Slippage of one wall section relative to another in tied-back retaining walls is another type of movement. Bowing is a common problem with pile retaining walls.

IMPLICATIONS

Retaining walls that have moved or cracked are failing. While sudden collapse is unusual, it is possible, particularly during or after periods of heavy rain. It is impossible, based on a one-time visit, to forecast when rebuilding will be necessary unless the wall has failed already.

STRATEGY

Sight along the wall as well as up and down the wall. Is it vertical or leaning away from the soil it's holding back? Is there bowing of the wall? Has the bottom of the wall slipped? Are there cracks in concrete or masonry units? Is there displacement of individual units? Is there deterioration of the materials that suggests the wall will start to move soon?

Watch for evidence of slumping or other movement of the landscaping on the high side of the wall.

Find the Retaining Walls!

You might have to look behind ivy or other plants to get a good look at a wall. If you notice that the yard is higher than any of its neighbors, go to the edge of the property to look for a retaining wall—sometimes they are hidden. Even if you don't inspect retaining walls that are well away from the house, let your client know they exist.

Insulation to Protect
Against Frost

For cases where the site is small or tight, and free-draining backfill can't be placed all the way to the footing level, extruded-foam insulation board may be placed along the back of the wall to just below grade, and for several feet horizontally away from the wall, again just below grade. If you see this, you will know it was done for frost control. If the wall is cracking badly, moving or leaning, you will know it's not working!

Rot or Insect Damage

All wood retaining walls will eventually fail. Wood in contact with the soil will not last forever. Railway ties that are impregnated with creosote may last 15 to 20 years, but many don't last that long. Conventional pressure-treated wood doesn't have a much longer life expectancy, although the more effective pressure treatment used in preserved wood foundations is more durable. Conventional pressure treating has not always proven effective against termites.

IMPLICATION

Rotted wood loses its strength. The retaining wall won't be able to hold back the soil.

STRATEGY

Assuming movement of the wall is not evident, probe the wood for soft areas. If possible, determine whether there is a free-draining material behind the wood members. This will help keep the wood dry and slow down the rot process.

Pay attention to end grains of wood members. Rot often develops here first. Rot is often accompanied by insect damage. You don't need to identify the type of damage; it's enough to note that the wood has lost strength.

Rusting Metal or Spalling Masonry

IMPLICATIONS

Wall deterioration will lead to localized failures or collapse.

F I G U R E 2.48   Weep Holes in Retaining Wall

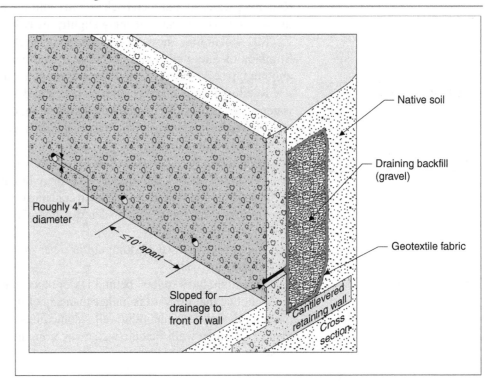

Native soil

Draining backfill (gravel)

Geotextile fabric

Roughly 4" diameter

≤10' apart

Sloped for drainage to front of wall

Cantilevered retaining wall Cross section

Rust can occur in gabion basket frames, piles or shoring, fasteners in wood walls, and reinforcing bars in concrete walls. Rusting fasteners and rebars expand and may damage the surrounding structural members.

Look for spalling in poured concrete, on the faces of hollow-core blocks and on brick walls. You can warn of future damage if you notice dark stains or efflorescence on block or brick walls.

No Drainage System

All retaining walls need a drainage system. Most concrete and masonry retaining walls need weep holes. Gabion, pile, and tied-back retaining walls usually do not as long as there are cracks or gaps in the wall face that will allow water to escape readily. A concealed drainage and tile system may exist behind the wall, but this is unusual in single-family residential construction.

Lack of a drainage system may result in premature failure of the retaining wall. Even if you see no signs of movement or cracking, walls without a drainage system have a shortened life expectancy.

Look for functional weep holes near the bottom of concrete or masonry retaining walls (Figure 2.48). The size and number of the holes is a factor of several things, such as wall height, percolation rate of the soil, slope of the ground surface above the wall, quality and amount of drainage material used, and rainfall frequency and intensity.

Generally speaking, weep holes should be roughly four inches in diameter and not more than 10 feet apart. Check that weep holes are not clogged.

If you can find no evidence of a drainage system, you should note this. If the wall is obviously new, its performance will be unpredictable. If the wall is older and appears intact with a proper slope, your recommendation should be tempered. You may just recommend monitoring.

REVIEW QUESTIONS

1. List three main functions of exterior cladding.

2. List ten exterior wall surface materials that you'll commonly find.

3. List six common problems that are found on all types of wall systems.

4. List seven common problems with masonry walls.

5. Describe efflorescence. What is it?

6. Expanding, rusting steel lintels over windows and doors often cause cracks in what direction in masonry walls?

7. Stucco is made up of _____, _____, and _____.

8. What is the problem with having aluminum in contact with stucco?

9. List three functions of a weep screed.

10. List five common problems with conventional stucco.

11. What is the problem that people are experiencing with EIFS?

12. What is a kickout?

13. List three causes of problems that are unique to EIFS compared to conventional stucco.

14. List six factors that may suggest concealed problems with an EIFS application.

15. List ten areas outside to check for evidence of problems with EIFS installations.

16. List five areas on the interior to check for evidence of problems with EIFS installations.

17. List two areas in basements and crawlspaces to look for with respect to problems on EIFS installations.

18. What is the effect of vines growing on wood siding?

19. For each of the choices below, circle the siding that would perform better.

    a. 12-inch-wide board   - or -   6-inch-wide board

    b. $^3/_4$-inch-wide board   - or - $^3/_8$-inch-thick board

    c. smooth board   - or -   rough-textured board

    d. 6-foot-long board   - or -   12-foot-long board

20. How many layers of wood shingles are typically used in a siding application?

21. List five common problems with conventional wood siding (boards, shingles, or shakes).

22. Hardboard is a type of _____ board.

23. List four common problems with plywood, OSB, and hardboard.

24. What is the life expectancy of vinyl and aluminum siding?

25. List seven common problems with metal and vinyl siding.

26. Why should metal siding be grounded?

27. Asbestos cement shingles should be removed from homes.

    True   False

28. What is the most common problem with asbestos cement shingles?

29. List three common problems with modern fiber-cement shingles.

30. How far should wood siding be kept above grade level?

31. List two common problems to look for on the exterior of exposed foundations.

32. Where are soffits and fascia typically found?

33. What materials are commonly used for soffits and fascia?

34. What are the issues surrounding a double layer of soffit material (e.g., aluminum over wood)?

35. List four common problems with soffits and fascia.

36. List seven different things you would want to evaluate with respect to doors and windows.

37. List twelve common problems with doors and windows.

38. Give three examples of where flashings would typically be found on exterior walls.

39. List six common problems with caulking, trim, and flashings.

40. List three mechanisms by which water may get into wall systems from the building exterior.

41. Why should all the risers in a set of steps be uniform?

42. Rise is usually _____ inches maximum, and tread depth is typically _____ to _____ inches minimum.

43. The nosing is usually _____ inch(es) deep.

44. Minimum dimensions for landings are often stated as _____ feet by _____ feet.

45. Explain why the absence of a landing may be a safety hazard.

46. Describe spalling.

47. What is the best way to check for rot in a wooden stair stringer?

48. Why can carpet on wood porches be bad?

49. Guardrails are typically required on porches, decks, or balconies more than _____ inches above grade.

50. The openings between railing spindles should not be greater than _____ inches.

51. Why should spindles be vertical, not horizontal?

52. Railings on stairways should be between _____ inches and _____ inches above the stair nosing depending on your area.

53. Guardrails should be at least _____ inches high.

54. Why shouldn't you align a beam with a gutter to check for sag?

55. What is the requirement for beam end bearing on masonry?

56. How might paint indicate that a beam has slipped out of its pocket?

57. Beams should be mechanically fastened to their supporting members.

    True   False

58. Joists are usually spaced _____ or _____ inches on center.

59. The metal brackets used to support joists are called _____.

60. What two inspection techniques can you use to check for sagging joists?

61. Two ways to attach a ledgerboard to a wood-frame structure are:

62. Describe the proper way to flash a ledgerboard installed over siding.

63. What is the biggest problem with cantilevered decks?

64. Why are plywood or waferboard sheets poor choices for porch or deck flooring?

65. Why should there be no supply or return registers from heating/cooling ductwork in a garage?

66. Most garage floors are not structural.

    True   False

67. Garage floors that are suspended and have storage or living space below (Circle one)

    a. can be adequately assessed by a home inspector.

    b. should be investigated by a specialist.

68. A good concrete garage floor slab is usually at least _____ inches thick and has _____ inches of gravel beneath it.

69. Which way should garage floors slope?

70. What does a hollow sound on the garage floor indicate?

71. Why do many authorities discourage floor drains in garages?

72. The diameter of a garage drain exit pipe should be at least _____ inches.

73. Why should the end of the drain pipe in a driveway drain turn down?

74. Automatic garage door openers have to be strong because they lift the weight of the door.

    True   False

75. List five problems to look for on a typical sectional garage door.

76. It's best to test a garage door opener from (inside/outside) the garage. (Choose one)

77. If the vehicle door stops two inches short of the garage floor, there is a problem with the _____.

78. What is the recommended way to test the automatic reverse on a garage door opener?

79. What is the commonly recommended slope for ground around a house?

80. Dramatic slope is likely less important if the ground surface is

    Sand   Asphalt

81. Bad grading will always cause wet basements.

True   False

82. Briefly describe a common foundation drainage material.

83. To work well, a foundation drainage layer requires _____.

84. Three possible implications of poor lot grading are _____.

85. What is used to keep soil away from a basement window?

86. Why are porous surface materials near a house a potential problem?

87. List five clues to look for concerning ravine or sloping lots.

88. Briefly state the function of gutters and downspouts.

89. Gutters are also called _____ or _____. Downspouts are also called _____, _____, or _____.

90. Why are gutters and downspouts sometimes left off in northern areas?

91. Steep roofs may have a large surface area but a small _____. This means that their gutters (need to be bigger/can be smaller) than you might expect. (Circle one)

92. Roof shingles should not project more than _____ inches out over the inner edge of the gutter.

93. Gutter leaks are most common at _____.

94. What can cause copper gutters to develop pinhole leaks?

95. A house with integral gutters is more prone to ice damming it if has a steep roof.

True   False

96. A typical gutter slope is _____.

97. What can happen to roof material if a dormer has gutters but no downspouts?

98. List three advantages of downspouts discharging above grade.

99. List three disadvantages of downspouts discharging above grade.

100. List three disadvantages of downspouts discharging into drains below grade.

101. State a simple solution to problems with a below-grade downspout pipe.

102. The top of the gravel in a window well should be _____ inches away from the window frame.

103. What are the risks associated with an improperly draining walkway?

104. List four possible problems that can arise from a large tree growing too close to a house.

105. What might a long stretch of new sod running from the front of the house to the street indicate?

106. What would you tell a client about a retaining wall that is leaning over but not broken, cracked, or damaged?

107. Why might you install insulation on the back of a retaining wall and under the topsoil behind the wall?

108. Ideally, weep holes in a solid retaining wall are at least _____ inches in diameter and not more than _____ feet apart.

C H A P T E R

3

ROOFING

LEARNING OBJECTIVES

By the end of this chapter you should be able to:

■ list three roof functions

■ define roof pitch

■ recognize and distinguish the different types of roofing materials

■ understand the typical conditions for various roofing materials and how to inspect for them

■ know the inspection strategies used to identify roof problems

■ identify the various types of steep roof and flat roof flashings

■ know the materials and locations where flashings are used

■ know the common problems associated with flashings

INTRODUCTION

Functions

The roof inspection is a key and challenging part of the home inspection. Roof functions may include the following—

1. Roofs are designed to protect the building from rain, snow, wind, hail, and, in some cases, fire.
2. Roofs often support some of the mechanical equipment for the house.
3. Some roofs make a strong architectural statement.

Most roofs are not intended to provide insulation for the building. The roof covering itself has no structural role, although most roofs are installed over sheathing, which does have a structural role. The roof covering materials add to the dead load of a building, which must be carried by the rest of the structure.

3.1   GENERAL STRATEGIES FOR STEEP ROOFS

There are two fundamental roofing strategies. Steep roofs shed water, relying on gravity and capillary action. They are not watertight. Steep roofs act more like a series of umbrellas than a weather-tight skin. Flat roofs (called **low-slope roofs** in the roofing profession) use a waterproof membrane or skin to protect the building.

Roof Pitch or Slope

We should review a roofing definition before proceeding. The **pitch** is the slope of the roof, expressed as a ratio of the rise over the run. The run is usually expressed as 12, and a typical slope might be 4 in 12 or 8 in 12. A 45° roof would have a pitch of 12 in 12.

Low Slope versus Flat

In strict roofing terminology, a steep-slope roof is a roof with a pitch greater than 2 in 12, and a low-slope roof has a pitch ranging from 0 in 12 (flat) to 2 in 12. In common usage, people often describe low-slope roofs as flat roofs, and break steep slope roofs into two categories, conventional and low slope. The latter really refers to a low-slope steep roof! Although incorrect according to roofing experts, we will use the more common terms of **conventional**, **low slope**, and **flat** as shown in Figure 3.1.

The Goal

Our goal in the roof inspection is to—

1. Identify the roofing material.
2. Determine whether it is installed properly.
3. Determine whether it is performing properly or is leaking.
4. Determine whether it's near the end of its life.

We will first look at the issues and problems that apply to all steep roofing materials. We will then look at the common roofing materials and problems specific to those.

The roofing inspection is not complete until the interior wall, ceiling and attic surfaces below the roof area are examined. Looking at the underside of the roof sheathing is an important part of the roofing inspection.

To Climb or Not to Climb

You should never walk on a roof when doing so could be dangerous or cause damage. If it is your practice to climb on roofs, at each house you will have to decide whether or not it can be done safely and, if so, how you will gain access to the roof. Safety comes first. You're no help to your client if you injure yourself on the inspection.

Recognize Your Limitations

Because of the nature of roofing, you cannot see everything that you would like to. On a typical roof, at least half the roofing materials are covered. Most of the fas-

F I G U R E 3.1   Roof Slopes

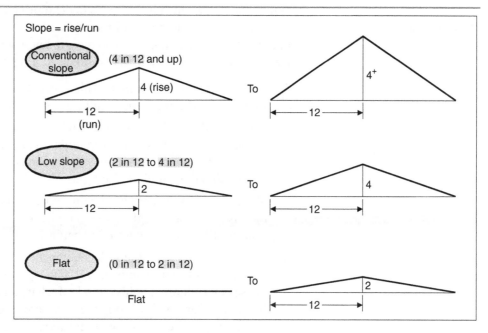

teners and flashing materials are covered. Remember, your roofing inspection isn't complete until you've had a look at the roof from the underside.

Resultant Damage

Considerable damage to the building interior and structure can be done as a result of a roof leak. In some ways, minor roof leaks are worse than major ones. A major roof leak is usually quickly identified and corrected. A minor roof leak may cause considerable damage before it is noticed. If you find evidence of leakage, past or present, tell your client that there might be concealed damage.

Common Problems

Common problems we find on steep roof systems, no matter what the roofing material, include:

1. Old
2. Damaged
3. Patched
4. Missing
5. Exposed fasteners
6. Poor installation
7. Vulnerable areas
8. Ice dam potential
9. Multiple layers

3.1.1   Old

IMPLICATIONS

Worn-out roofs can no longer perform and are prone to leakage.

Age of House

Once you have identified the roofing material, and its normal life expectancy, use any obvious clues to determine the age of the roof covering. On a relatively young house, the roof is often the same age as the house. For example, a 10-year-old house will usually have a 10-year-old roof.

Roof Condition

The next step is to look at the condition of the roofing materials. It is more important to know how much life remains in the roofing material than how old the roof is.

Causes of Aging

When looking at the condition of the roof, you have to know the typical signs of aging for the material. You also have to know what causes it to age and fail. The following are issues with many common roofing materials—

1. Exposure to ultraviolet light. This is usually a function of orientation. Are the roof surfaces facing north, south, east or west?

2. Color. While this is a controversial issue, many believe that darker-colored asphalt shingles wear out before light colored shingles. This may be dependent on climate, including issues such as average summer temperatures and number of hours of direct sunlight.

3. Ventilation. Good ventilation helps to keep the roof cool in summer, and in the case of wood shingles, for example, helps the shingles dry after a rain. Poor ventilation can cause rapid aging.

4. Exposure to winds. A house located in a coastal area or at the top of a hill is exposed to different winds than is a house surrounded by tall trees and other houses in a mature neighborhood. Mechanical action of the wind can cause immediate damage if roofing materials are torn off, or can affect the life expectancy of the roof through the abrasive action of wind-driven rain, hail, snow and debris.

5. Pitch (Slope). Generally, steeper roofs last longer than shallow roofs. Water runs off steep roofs more quickly and the roof dries faster.

6. Complexity. The more complex the roof, the shorter the life expectancy. Complex roofs include those with many changes in direction, many valleys, penetrations and or roof-mounted equipment.

7. Foot traffic. Roofs that are walked on regularly will not last as long as other roofs. Some parts of the roof may see a lot of foot traffic and tend to wear out first. This may be an area where it's easiest to get from one part of the roof to another, or it may be an area below a dormer, where people stand to clean the windows, clear the gutters, paint the trim, etc. If there is equipment on the roof that requires servicing, foot traffic from service people may wear out the roof.

8. Concentrated water on the roof from a drainage system above. It is common for an upper roof to have a gutter or downspout that discharges onto a lower roof. Collecting all the water from the upper roof and allowing it to run across one section of the lower roof will wear out this section prematurely.

9. Tree branches. Branches touching the roof cause abrasion damage and premature failure. Even if the branches don't touch the roof, the overhanging trees drop debris on the roof and shade the roof, slowing the drying process. These factors shorten life expectancy.

How Does the Roof Look?

All these factors should be considered in estimating the remaining roof life. The physical condition of the roof covering, however, is perhaps the strongest indicator. You will have to know what the roof covering looks like when it is new and in good shape. You will also have to know what the roofing material looks like when it is near the end of its life.

Which Sides Wear First?

In many climates, asphalt shingle roofs wear first on the south and west side where the ultraviolet light is the greatest. In wet climates, the wear can be caused by moss and vegetation growing on the roof. This will be more pronounced on the north, or any shaded side of the roof where drying is poor.

Parts of Roof May Be Older

It is not unusual to find that only part of a roof system has been replaced. On the same house, you can have roofing materials of several ages. This is another argument for getting up and walking the roof surface wherever possible. If you can only see three of four sides of a roof from the ground with binoculars, it is possible that the fourth side is older than the three that can be seen.

3.1.2 Damaged

This may include mechanical damage such as broken tiles, holes or tears.

| IMPLICATIONS |

| STRATEGY |

Damage from Snow Removal

A damaged roof covering may not keep the weather out and may allow damage to the building systems below.

When examining the roof, you have to look at the entire surface for flaws. In many cases, the thing that caused the mechanical damage will no longer be visible.

In areas that receive a lot of snow, it is common to find mechanical damage to the lower edge of roofs from shovels and scrapers used to remove snow and ice dams from the roof surface. This damage can also be concentrated on roof areas where there is an adjacent wall. Snow tends to drift on roofs where there is a higher vertical surface adjacent. Snow removal is often necessary here to prevent overloading the roof structure.

3.1.3 Patched

It is common to find previous repairs that have been made on the roof.

| IMPLICATIONS |

| STRATEGY |

Previous repairs present a high risk of future leakage. This is because of the difficulty in making a weather-tight patch, and/or because the substrate (sheathing or building framing) was damaged before the leak was patched, and the roof is spongy in that area.

Patches may be asphalt based products on the roof surface (roofer's mastic, roofing cement, asphalt cement, plastic cement, elastic cement), they may be caulking, or they may show up as roofing materials of a slightly different color, texture, size or style than the original materials. Metal flashings that are unpainted or painted differently from the remainder may indicate patching. If the majority of the metal shows some rusting, but one flashing does not, the flashing has been patched or replaced here.

On some roofing materials, supports for new or patched roofing materials are visible. These may be nail heads, metal hooks or strips of metal, for example.

In some cases, the patches are made with a completely different roofing material. These are easily identified.

Where patches are found, look closely at areas below for evidence of recent moisture. A moisture meter is helpful (although not necessarily conclusive). Patches should be reported as vulnerable areas since it is very common for patches to fail and leak.

3.1.4 Missing

Individual pieces of roofing material may be broken off, or the whole unit may be missing altogether.

| IMPLICATIONS |

Leakage and resultant damage are the obvious implications.

STRATEGY

Again, an inspection of 100 percent of the roof surface area is necessary to identify partially or completely missing units.

3.1.5   Exposed Fasteners

On most roofing systems, nails, screws or other fasteners should not be visible once the work is complete.

IMPLICATIONS

In most cases, exposed fasteners present an increased risk of leakage.

STRATEGY

Some roofing systems have fasteners that are intended to be exposed. Some types of asphalt shingles (Dutch lap and some diamond-shaped shingles, for example), are intended to have exposed fasteners. In addition, some metal roofing has exposed screw heads, by design. Knowledge of proper installation technique is important here.

3.1.6   Installation Problems

Discussion of installation details for the different roofing materials is beyond the scope of this book. We encourage you to become familiar with proper installation practices for the materials commonly used in your area. Where installation does not follow recommended practices, problems are more likely.

IMPLICATIONS

Increased risk of leakage is the implication of installation problems.

STRATEGY

For any given roofing material, you should compare the installation with the recommended practices for—

- minimum slope
- exposure
- fastener type, number and location
- joint alignment
- overhangs at lower edges and rakes
- requirements if any, for underlayment
- the requirement for a waterproof membrane below
- compatible flashing materials
- maximum number of layers recommended

While you won't be able to see everything, installations that clearly deviate from good practice have increased risk of problems, and your inspection should focus on vulnerable areas.

3.1.7   Vulnerable Areas

Anything that restricts the drainage of water off a roof is a vulnerable area. This would include—

- wide chimneys near the lower edge of a roof
- chimneys in valleys

- skylights
- drains from upper roofs that discharge onto lower roofs
- changes in material
- equipment that obstructs drainage
- complicated flashing details
- asymmetric valleys
- patched areas
- roofs that change slope from top to bottom (typically with a lower slope near the bottom edge)

Valleys that are steeper on one side than the other are vulnerable areas because the water coming off the steep side may have enough momentum to drive up under the shingles on the lower sloped side. This is particularly true if the roof surfaces being drained are large.

Areas that show previous repairs are inherently vulnerable. A repair is much more likely to leak than an original roof section, especially a clumsy repair such as roofing cement on a torn valley flashing.

IMPLICATIONS

Increased risk of leakage is the implication of vulnerable areas.

STRATEGY

Look at the roof for places where water may be hung up as it tries to run down the roof. This can often be done effectively while standing at the ridge and looking down the roof surfaces.

In many cases, you won't recommend immediate repairs, but will alert your client to the fact that leakage is more likely here. Pay attention to areas below these vulnerable spots as you go through the rest of your inspection.

3.1.8   Ice Dam Potential

Ice dams only occur in climates where snow accumulates on roofs. Ice dams are most common at the lower edge of roofs, but may also occur near party walls (through which there may be considerable heat loss to the roof area) and around chimneys (again, where heat loss may create localized melting of snow and subsequent re-freezing below).

IMPLICATIONS

Ice dams allow leakage through the roof into the soffit, fascia and wall systems. Leakage may also develop at the interior of the building, although if it does not, the damage can be concealed and go unnoticed for a considerable period.

STRATEGY

Dams are common on low-sloped roofs or roofs that change slope near the eaves. Larger eave overhangs (wide soffits) are more prone to ice dams. Ice dams may also occur where a roof above a heated area extends out over an unheated area such as a porch or balcony.

Where Dams May Occur

As discussed above, ice dams can also occur around party walls in attached homes and around chimneys where localized heat escapes from the building.

North Slopes

Very often, the northern slope of the roof is more vulnerable to ice damming than the southern section. The heat of the sun helps to melt the snow uniformly across the south roof surface and allow water to run off the edge.

In Valleys

Another spot where ice damming frequently occurs is at the bottom of a valley. Melted snow finds its way to the valley and runs down to the bottom. The concentrated water re-freezing in this area can create an ice dam.

Identifying Ice Dams

It is relatively easy to inspect for ice dams in the winter when there is snow on the roof. Icicles hanging off gutters and protruding from soffits or between siding boards, for example, are a dead giveaway that ice damming is taking place. Similarly,

FIGURE 3.2   Ice Dams

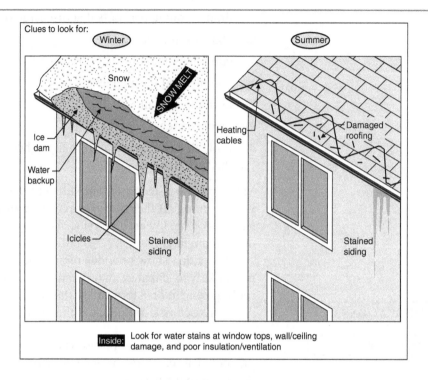

water coming through the wall/ceiling intersection inside along the length of the wall, or near a valley, very often indicates ice damming.

In Summer

It's much more difficult to identify an ice-damming problem during the summer months. Although some of the physical conditions that allow ice dams to form may exist, it is hard to know whether the problem manifests itself or not. Some of the clues that you can look for include (Figure 3.2)—

Wall/Ceiling Damage

1. Evidence of damage along the wall/ceiling intersection on the interior. This looks different from a typical roof leak because it extends along the length of the wall for several feet, typically. A roof leak caused by a puncture or missing shingle rarely leads to leakage that runs horizontally along the wall/ceiling intersection.

Stained Siding

2. Discoloration of siding starting at the soffit and running down the wall. It's unusual for the walls to get wet immediately under the eaves. Where streaking is noticed running down from the wall/soffit intersection, ice damming should be suspected.

Shingle Damage

3. Damage to shingles from axes, hatchets, shovels, or other tools along the lower edge of the roof. This indicates that attempts have been made to break up ice dams.

Heating Cables

4. Electric cables running along the lower part of the roof in a zigzag pattern. These heating cables are often used in an attempt to protect against ice damming. These cables, by the way, provide more opportunity for leakage because they have to be secured through the roof coverings.

Poor Insulation and Ventilation

5. Roofs with poor insulation and ventilation are more likely to suffer from ice damming problems because their attics will be hotter (Figure 3.3).

F I G U R E 3.3   Preventing Ice Dams with Ventilation

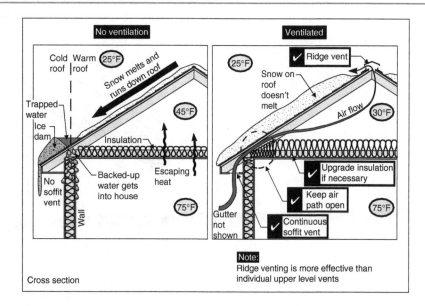

Window Tops

6. The tops of windows may indicate ice damming if evidence can be found of water leakage through the outside or inside of the window top. While it may be leakage, the higher the window and better protected it is by the roof over-hang, the more likely it is to be ice damming.

Check Attic Stained or Rotted Sheathing

7. You might be able to identify an ice-damming problem from the attic space, although this is rare. The water penetration is likely to be near the roof edges and at the bottom of valleys. This area is often obstructed by insulation. Staining, wet areas or rot on the underside of the roof sheathing along the perimeter for any distance may suggest ice damming.

Stains on Insulation

8. In some situations, the insulation may be compressed from the dampness, or there may be stains visible in the insulation, indicating water has been drop-ping onto it. Some old insulation has a Kraft paper barrier on the top. Stains on the paper may be visible.

Sheets or Buckets

9. In some cases, plastic sheeting, buckets or pans may have been placed in the attic to collect water. This suggests either leakage or ice damming.

Configuration

10. Check roof configurations. Roofs with low slopes and wide overhangs are more prone to ice dams.

Monitor

One way to determine whether the problem is ice damming or leakage is to mon-itor the situation seasonally. If the area is wet after a rain, or when there has been no snow on the roof for some time, it is a leak. If the problem only occurs when there is snow on the roof and icicles hanging from the gutters, it is ice damming.

Possible Solutions to Ice Damming

There are several things done to minimize ice damming, including—

1. Upgrading insulation and ventilation

2. Adding eave protection

3. Adding electric heating cables

One of the best is upgrading the attic insulation and ventilation to keep the attic as cold as possible. This will minimize the snow melting on the roof surface. Good soffit venting is essential here. It is also important to seal around penetrations in the attic

FIGURE 3.4   Eave Protection Against Ice Dams

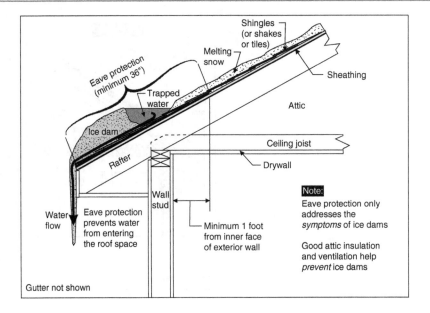

floor to prevent the leakage of warm, moist air from the house into the attic. This warm air contributes to ice dam problems.

Eave protection is recommended in northern climates where ice damming may be an issue (Figure 3.4). Eave protection is a waterproof membrane laid along the lower edge of the roof or anywhere ice dams may cause water to back up under the shingles. This includes chimneys, skylights, valleys, and party walls.

3.1.9   Multiple Layers

New roofs are often added without removing the old roofing material; this reduces the cost of re-roofing.

Multiple layers of roofing may mean faster wear and a shorter life expectancy for the new roofing materials, because of the uneven surface that is created with the second layer lying over the first.

Multiple roof layers often have nails that are too short to penetrate the roof sheathing. Roofing materials are more inclined to be blown off in heavy winds when multiple layers are used.

Adding new roofing over old often means that old flashings are not replaced. These critical components then become the weak link in the "new" roof.

Over-roofing prevents an inspection of the roof sheathing. Roofs are typically only replaced after leakage has occurred. In many cases, the homeowner doesn't know how long the leak has been going on and how much concealed damage may have been done. Putting new shingles over old ones sheds no light on this issue.

Multiple roof layers inhibit the ability of the roof covering materials to dry after a rain. This is particularly important with wood shingles or shakes. This can accelerate deterioration of the roofing.

Count the Layers

Part of your roof inspection should be to determine the number of layers of roofing materials. You have to know how the roofing is applied to verify the number of layers. In most cases, there is a starter of some sort and then the shingles or panels are laid. You can determine the number of layers either from the lower edge of the roof or from the rakes, if there are gables. Understand that, in some cases, roofers will cut off the old roofing material around the edges so that it will look like only one layer when there are really two.

Count the Flashings

In some cases, you can get a look at the number of roofing layers at flashing details, because flashings are often not replaced when new roofing is applied over old. The flashing materials are often durable enough to outlast the roofing covering material. Many flashings, however, are not durable enough to last through two roofing lives, and flashing problems are common when there are multiple layers of roofing.

Check Nails from Below

In some cases, you can determine that there have been two layers of roofing by the nail pattern protruding through the sheathing from below. You have to be careful, however, because as discussed earlier, the shingles may have been removed, but the old nails were driven down into the sheathing. Nails should not be driven through the sheathing where there are open eaves (there are no soffits). This is unsightly from below and makes painting difficult. Sheathing boards often splinter where the nail heads protrude through the underside.

Different Materials?

Asphalt shingles are often installed over wood shingles and, in some cases, over slate. In many cases, this has been done successfully, although you will have to evaluate each case on its own merit.

Inspector in the House: The Sunny Side of the Roof

It was a sunny December morning and the temperature was around freezing. The home was a beautiful two-story Georgian with a cedar shingle roof. I set my ladder up on the south side and got up onto the roof. The slope was modest, about 6 in 12, and I had no trouble moving around—until I stepped over the ridge to the north side of the roof. The sun had not hit that side and a thin layer of frost covered the shingles. In a heartbeat I was sliding down the roof surface, out of control. Instinctively I reached out and grabbed the plumbing stack, and . . . it held!

I crawled very carefully and slowly back up the ridge and over to the south side. I waited until my heart rate slowed a little before going down the ladder and continuing the inspection.

I am now very careful with cold or wet roof surfaces.

3.2 ASPHALT SHINGLES

In this and following sections, we will outline the composition for several common steep roofing materials and then discuss performance issues and inspection techniques.

3.2.1 Composition

Asphalt shingles, also called composition or comp shingles, are made up of (Figure 3.5)—

1. A base material, which may be a fiberglass mat (most common today) or an organic felt

2. An asphalt body or coating

3. Surfacing granules

F I G U R E 3.5   Asphalt Shingle Composition

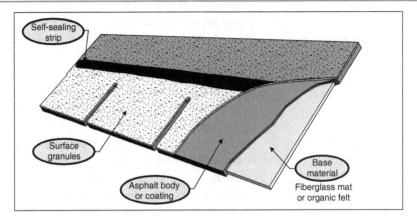

Mats

Glass fiber mats were used in asphalt shingles as early as the 1960s, and are the most common base material in shingles today. The glass mats do not absorb as much moisture as organic felts and are more fire resistant than organic felts. There are, however, performance issues related to glass fiber felt shingles such as cracking and breaking early in their life.

Asphalt

Asphalt is a complex compound available in various types and qualities. Typical asphalt shingles use more than one type of asphalt. The quality of the asphalt has a lot to do with the quality of the shingle.

3.2.2   Conditions Specific to Asphalt

In this section, we'll deal with only the conditions and strategies that specifically apply to asphalt shingles.

Old

STRATEGY

The normal life expectancy of an asphalt-shingled roof is 15 to 25 years. How do you know whether an asphalt-shingle roof is worn out? If you know the life expectancy of asphalt shingles in your area and can estimate the age of the shingles, this is a big help.

Metric Shingles Circa 1978

In areas where metric shingles have become common, you can find out from local suppliers and roofers when the conversion to metric shingles took place. In many areas, this would be in the late 1970s or early 1980s. It's easy to identify metric shingles because the tabs are a little over 13 inches wide, while the imperial tabs are about 12 inches wide. To do this check on every roof, it's very handy to know exactly how long your shoes are. That way, you can quickly tell if you're standing on metric shingles.

Cracks, Cupping, or Clawing

Another way to determine whether the shingles are worn out is to look for evidence of loss of granules, cracking, cupping or clawing. With advanced deterioration, shingles may be torn off. As the asphalt gets older, it becomes more brittle.

Slot Width

On new shingles, the width of the slots between the tabs is typically a quarter of an inch, roughly speaking. As the shingles get old, they shrink, and the slots can be up to one inch wide or more toward the end of the shingle life. Look at the width of the slots as clues to the shingle age.

One other trick is to look in the slots, or cutouts, for evidence of premature wear. There are some shingles that were known to wear prematurely in this area.

FIGURE 3.6   Ridge Shingle Application

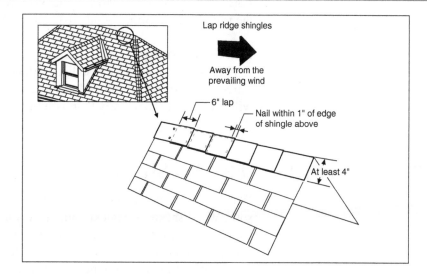

Damaged

Blisters

Sometimes blisters will be noted on relatively young roofs. In some cases, the shingle has a bubble in it. In other cases, the granular material has worn off the bubble and the asphalt material may look like a black dot on the shingle. In advanced cases, this asphalt will be deteriorated. This is often a manufacturing defect.

High Wear Areas

Pay particular attention where foot traffic may be heavy or concentrated water discharges onto the roof from a gutter or downspout above.

Poor Installation

Poorly Installed

Look for proper installation technique. Not all of the installation details will be visible, but where you see some poor installation practices, it's logical to assume there may be others. Look for the leakage that results from poor installation technique. In some cases, poor installation has surprisingly little effect on roofing performance.

Fastener Problems

Nails driven too far in may pull right through the shingle and not hold it in place. Nails that are not driven straight or far enough can sit proud and tear through the overlaying shingle. They may also not hold the shingles securely to the roof. Nails that are too short or not corrosion-resistant will not provide good holding power.

With staples, the same sorts of problems occur. Staples can also be driven crooked, with the result that one side of the staple tears through the shingle it's supposed to secure and the other side of the staple sits high and may tear the overlaying shingle.

Nails may become loose and break through the overlaying shingle. If you see one nail pop, look closely. There may be others.

Hip and Ridge Shingles

These shingles are made up of individual tabs that are bent over the hips and ridges and typically secured in place with two nails (Figure 3.6). They may be more prone to cracking with age because of the bending. Also, hips and ridges may be areas subjected to high foot traffic.

Flaws in the hips and ridges are often forgiving in the sense that very little water runs across these areas. Most of the water runs down the field of the roof, and only the rain that lands directly on hips and ridges has to be carried away.

Multiple Layers

Asphalt shingles are often installed with two layers. Most consider this acceptable. Three layers are not recommended, and some jurisdictions prohibit it, although you will find it more frequently than you might suspect.

3.3   WOOD SHINGLES AND SHAKES

Wood shingles are machine cut, while wood shakes are hand split or mechanically split. Wood shakes are thicker and have a much more uneven surface. Most wood shingles are cedar; however, other materials used include redwood and pine. Wood shingles can be used on roofs with a pitch as low as three in twelve; however, six in twelve or more is recommended. Lower slopes should have higher quality shingles with smaller exposures. Wood shingles vary in length between sixteen inches and twenty-four inches. On a good quality installation, no more than one third of the shingle is exposed to the weather.

Life Expectancy

The life expectancy of wood shingles can be up to thirty to forty years; however, low quality shingles and installation methods deteriorate in fifteen to twenty years. Shakes are thicker and may last longer than shingles. The rate of wear depends largely on material quality, exposure (the amount of shingle that is exposed to the weather), the pitch (the steeper the better), the grade of shingle (there are three), and the amount of sun and shade. Too much sunlight dehydrates the shingles, causing them to become brittle. This results in splitting and cupping of the shingles. Too much shade and moisture causes rot and moss to grow. Wood shingles and shakes can also suffer mechanical damage from tree branches, foot traffic, snow shoveling, etc.

Another factor that affects the life of wood shingles is their ability to dry quickly. It is preferable to install wood shingles over spaced roof sheathing boards rather than plywood sheets. Some experts say the use of plywood will halve the life of the shingles.

As a general rule, when more than ten to fifteen percent of the roof requires repair, it is best to replace the roof covering.

Walk with Care

Be careful walking on wood roofs. They are slippery, especially when wet. Walking on cupped or curled shingles may break them. Incidentally, no golf shoes allowed!

3.3.1   Conditions

We've talked about the basic strategies for the common conditions. Now let's address these as they apply specifically to wood roofs.

Old

It is difficult to pinpoint the age of wood roofs. Determining whether the roof is serviceable is more important. If you go beyond the basics, you may also give the client some idea of the remaining life.

F I G U R E 3.7   Curling, Cupping, and Splitting Wood Shingles

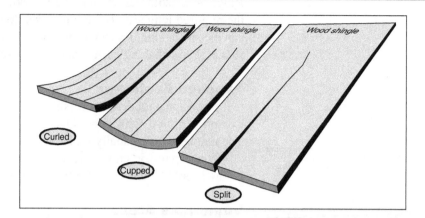

The conditions to watch for include—

1. Rot
2. Cupping (both sides of the shingle or shake lift up)
3. Curling (the bottom of the shingle or shake lifts up)
4. Cracking (splitting)
5. Burn-through or wear-through (where the material becomes so thin that it is no longer water resistant)

Let's look at these individually.

Rot

Look at the bottom edges of shingles or shakes, which tend to rot first. It may be helpful to pinch the bottom edges to see if they are spongy or pulpy. These will rot first because they absorb water more readily than edge grain shingles and because they contain more sapwood. Sapwood does not have the decay-resistant rosins that heartwood does.

Curling, Cupping and Splitting

Shingles that are curling or cupping are usually visible from the ground. A close look is often required to identify split shingles that may simply look like a joint between adjacent shingles, at first glance (Figure 3.7).

Shingles are more prone to curling, cupping and splitting than shakes, because they are thinner.

Flame Pattern

Lower quality shingles that include flat grain and/or grain imperfections are more likely to suffer from curling, cupping and splitting. Watch for the characteristic flame pattern of flat grain shingles.

Wear-Through or Burn-Through

Check the butt thickness of the shingles or shakes. You'll need to know how thick the shingle or shake was when it was new, to be able to evaluate the wear.

Flat grain shingles have much more softwood exposed and are more susceptible to weathering. Watch particularly close for burn-thorough and wear-through on these.

The wear is often near the middle of the exposed part of the shingle or shake.

Missing

Ridge or hip shingles or shakes are most likely to be missing. This is often because the required longer nails were not used to secure these. Incidentally, hip and ridge cap pieces for shingles can be purchased pre-assembled, although this is not so with shakes. Parts of shingles or shakes may also be missing where the material has split.

Exposed Fasteners

On a good installation, there should be no exposed fasteners, with perhaps the exception of two nails at the ridge on the last piece of ridge capping to be installed. The nail heads are usually sealed in this area.

STRATEGY

Where nails or staples are visible, the leakage risk is increased, and the areas below should be checked carefully. Corrective action may be necessary.

Vulnerable Areas

STRATEGY

Vulnerable areas specific to wood roofing are those that cause a roof to stay wet, leading to rot. If the moisture content remains more than 20%, the wood will rot. Watch for condensate from an air conditioner dripping onto a wood roof.

Multiple Layers

STRATEGY

Generally speaking, you should not find multiple layers of wood shingles or shakes. Where you find it, check the performance carefully and advise your client that there is an increased risk of concealed rot and shortened life expectancy.

3.4   SLATE

How Long Does It Last?

Slate is a natural stone roofing product.

Slate can be extremely durable and is expensive. There is a church in England with a 1,200-year-old slate roof. There are also slates that last as few as 15 years (and shouldn't be used for roofing).

Determining Quality of Slate

It is beyond the scope of a home inspector to be able to evaluate the quality of the slate, or to predict with confidence its life expectancy.

Be Careful!

There are many roofing materials that imitate slate, including concrete, rubber and plastic. Make sure it's slate!

3.4.1   Conditions

Let's look at the conditions and strategies specific to slate roofs.

Old/Damaged

Failure Modes

Slate roofs commonly fail because—

1.   The slates wear out.
2.   The fasteners or flashings wear out.
3.   Slates are mechanically damaged.
4.   Installation was poorly done.

Slates Wear Out

The slate itself will eventually break down. As the slate deteriorates, it usually develops a whitish surface, often in the form of a ring around the sides and bottom of the slate. As deterioration progresses, the surface of the slate often turns brown. Delaminations typically occur from the perimeter in toward the center, and the slate eventually disintegrates. Depending on the type of slate and the climate, this is caused by moisture and is accelerated by freeze/thaw cycles.

Evidence of Aging

Slate that is soft or flakes easily when you touch it will be near the end of its life.

Fasteners or Flashings Wear Out

In many cases, the failure of a slate roof is a result of failure of the fasteners or flashings. In many cases, the nails and flashings don't last as long as the slates. Leakage may occur because the flashings have rusted or the fasteners have corroded, allowing the slates to fall off the roof.

Mechanical Damage

Slates are also vulnerable to mechanical damage. Although they are quite strong, they are brittle and if heavy tree branches drop on them, they will break. Nailing too tightly or allowing nails to sit proud will also result in breakage.

Limitations

We recommend you do not walk on slate roofs, so it may be difficult to see any cracked slate(s). Your client should be told of this limitation.

Patched

Many old slate roofs contain patches or repairs. There are several ways of patching roofs, some more successful than others.

Poor Repair Techniques

Poor repair techniques include—

- face-nailing replacement slates in and tarring the nail heads.
- using different roofing materials to replace individual slates.
- worst of all, using asphalt or roofing cement to cover for broken or missing slates.

Tar

Watch for evidence of tar on the roof. This is always a bad thing. Watch for exposed nail heads, usually indicating amateurish repairs.

Exposed Fasteners

On a good roofing installation, you should not see any exposed fasteners.

3.5   CLAY TILE

Clay tiles have been used since the days of the Greek and Roman empires in Europe, China and the Middle East. Clay roofing tiles are expensive and labor intensive to install, but have an indefinite life expectancy. Clay tiles are like slate in that the fasteners and flashings are more likely to fail than the tiles.

3.5.1   Tile Shapes, Colors, and Layout

Tile can be many shapes, but can be roughly categorized as flat or curved.

Curved Tiles

Curved tiles include **Mission** and **Spanish** tile. Mission tile is a two-piece system made up of similarly shaped **pans** and **covers** (Figure 3.8). The pieces may be tapered from top to bottom.

Spanish Tile

The **Spanish** or **S-shaped** tile is a one-piece system that includes a pan and cover all in each piece, with interlocking sides. Variations of this tile shape include the **Roman** and **Greek** tiles, and the **low-profile** S-shaped tiles (Figure 3.9).

This shaped tile is commonly imitated by concrete tile. Be careful when looking at them to be sure it's clay before describing it as such.

F I G U R E   3.8 Clay Tile—Tapered Mission Style

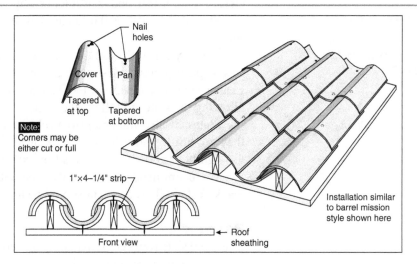

Flat Tile

The second general category is **flat** tiles. These can be either **shingle** or **interlocking** type (Figure 3.10). The shingle tiles are installed like slate with double coverage and a 3-inch head lap, typically. Interlocking tiles are installed as essentially a single layer, with a 3- or 4-inch interlocking overlap. The overlap can be even less, depending on the system. Because of its double coverage, the shingle style, will, of course, be a heavier roof system.

The flat clay tiles may be smooth surfaced, or they may be ribbed to look like wood, or textured to look like slate or other stones.

Colors

A glaze can be any color and can be used on any type of tile. Unglazed tiles are typically terra cotta red. The iron oxides in the clay provide this reddish brown color.

Hip and Ridge Tiles

Hip and ridge tiles are usually secured in place with a single nail with a dab of roofing cement on the nail head, applied to ensure weather-tightness and to help secure the overlaying tile in place.

General

Many manufacturers say that tile roofs should never be walked on. Since fasteners aren't visible, and can be missing or deteriorated, walking on the roof may dislodge a tile. This is, at best, embarrassing and disruptive, and at worst, dangerous to people below and to inspectors who may lose their balance when the tile slips out

STRATEGY

Don't Walk on the Roofs

F I G U R E   3.9 Clay Tile—"S" Style

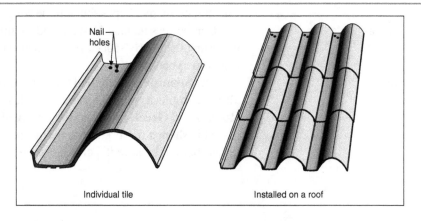

F I G U R E 3.10 Clay Tile—Interlocking Shingle

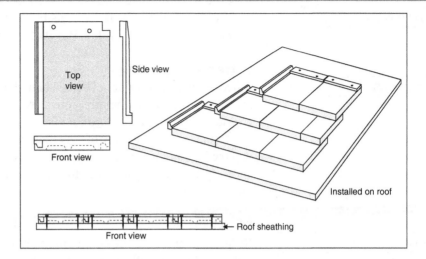

from under foot. Tiles may also break when walked on, especially if people step on the weak points.

The practical recommendation for home inspectors is not to walk on clay tile roofs. As we've discussed, this limits your roof inspection. These limitations should be reported to your client.

Beware of Imitators

Concrete and metal tiles may be manufactured to look like clay. Describing a substitute material as clay can lead to a very expensive request from a client.

3.5.2   Conditions

The problems that you will be looking for include—

1. Installation problems
2. Cracked or broken
3. Pitted or spalling
4. Missing
5. Fastener problems
6. Flashing problems
7. Underlying membrane problems
8. Previous repairs

Installation Problems

Many tile installations are older, and as a result, installation problems will have shown up some time ago. However, on rare new installations, you'll have to look closely.

STRATEGY

If you can identify the tile manufacturer, you may be able to check their installation guidelines. If the roof is new, problems may not have shown up yet. As with any roof, you will be checking for leakage from below.

Cracked or Broken

STRATEGY

Cracked or broken tiles are one of the most common conditions you'll identify.

Hairline cracks are often not visible from the ground, even with binoculars. The client should be aware of this. Pay particular attention to any high traffic areas.

Pitted or Spalling

STRATEGY

Air Pollution

Pitted or spalling tiles are often a manufacturing defect. Some tiles fail after 40 or 50 years. While this would be considered a very good life for most materials, it is considered premature failure for clay.

Pollution is one enemy of clay tiles. The lower edges of individual tiles are usually the last part of the tile to dry, and pollution effects may be visible here first. They show up as discoloration or pitting. Again, these problems may not be visible from the ground.

Missing

STRATEGY

Ridge, hip, and rake tiles are commonly missing. These tiles are subject to wind uplift, and if not well secured, can be blown off.

Watch for tiles that are loose and may soon be missing. Loose tiles are usually identified by a slight misalignment.

Fastener Failures

STRATEGY

Tiles are usually nailed, clipped, tied with wires, supported on slate hooks, hung on wooden battens, held in place with mortar or adhesive, or a combination of these. The caps of Mission tiles are typically nailed to stringers laid vertically on the roof.

The life of most clay tile is indefinite, so the fasteners should be considered the weak link. Fasteners may last 40 to 80 years.

Fastener problems may be difficult to identify unless tiles are missing or loose. Since you can't walk on a tile roof, this will be tough to determine except from the edges. You can put a ladder up against the eaves or gable ends to check a few tiles.

Flashing Problems

STRATEGY

Tile roofs are typical in that their flashing details are among the most vulnerable. Tiles are different, however, in that there are often large voids at hips, ridges, valleys, eaves, and rakes. Tiles are also more difficult to work with than other roofing systems because the tiles themselves are thick, often irregular and difficult to flash to.

Underlying Membranes

STRATEGY

For the most part, you'll only be able to see very small sections of underlying membranes. You will, however, be able to see the result of failed membranes, in the form of leakage.

Asphalt-based roofing membranes laid under tiles are expected to last up to 40 years. Where the slope is low and we are relying on the waterproof membrane below the tiles to keep the water out, it probably makes sense to remove the tiles, establish a new waterproof membrane and re-install the tiles. This is very costly, but the tiles themselves are so expensive and their life expectancy is so long, it's usually worth it.

Previous Repairs

STRATEGY

You can often identify new tiles by a difference in color, or the copper tabs that may have been used to hold them in place. In some cases, there are repair clips used that are not visible.

FIGURE 3.11   Concrete Tiles

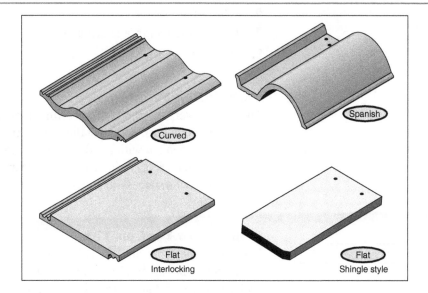

During your inspection, keep an eye out for a supply of replacement tiles. This is a wonderful bonus for someone who owns a tile roof. Matching old tiles is very difficult and expensive. You can sometimes find the name of the manufacturer by looking at the back of the tile.

3.6   CONCRETE TILE

Concrete tiles are available in most of the same configurations as clay tiles and are generally categorized as flat or curved (Figure 3.11).

Flat tiles may be shingle type or interlocking. They may look like slate, wood or clay.

How Long Do They Last?

Since concrete tiles are a relatively young product, it is difficult to know how long they last. One indication can be gained from the fact that many manufacturers provide a 50-year warranty.

Costly

While less expensive than slate and clay tile, concrete tiles are still relatively expensive.

Don't Walk on Concrete Roofs

Concrete roof tiles are brittle, and walking on them can crack or break the tiles. While those who are familiar with the tile layout and pressure points may be able to walk on the tile successfully, we recommend that you do not. Concrete tiles should be treated as clay tiles in this regard.

3.6.1   Conditions

The problems that you should look for include—

1. Installation problems
2. Cracked or broken tiles
3. Pitted or spalling tiles
4. Missing or loose tiles

5. Fastener problems

6. Flashing problems

7. Underlying membrane problems

8. Previous repairs

Installation Problems

There are several methods of installing concrete tiles. Because the tiles are heavy and awkward to work with, installation is expensive. It's common to find that short-cuts have been taken with good installation technique. This may include the installation (or lack thereof) of fasteners, and the execution of flashing details. Much like clay tile, part of a successful concrete tile application is good preparation and layout of the roof.

Cracked or Broken Tiles

STRATEGY

Looking at the roof with binoculars, it may be difficult to see small cracks. Let the client know that this is a limited inspection. Focus on particularly vulnerable areas, such as valleys and areas around roof penetrations. Also, pay particular attention to likely high traffic areas including below dormers and adjacent to television towers used to climb up to the roof.

Pitted, Spalling, or Tiles with Efflorescence

The porosity of concrete tiles is a manufacturing issue. Poor quality concrete will not stand up, especially in freeze/thaw climates. Air entrainment is one method to improve resistance to freezing damage. You won't be able to tell visually whether the tiles have air entrained. You will have to look for evidence of the problems.

Efflorescence

Efflorescence is not serious, but is unattractive. Acrylic sealers help prevent efflorescence on the top surface of the tile. The efflorescence is driven down through the bottom of the tile. When the sealer wears off, after three to five years, the efflorescence has disappeared. This helps explain the weathering that tiles go through in their first few years, where the shiny surface changes to a mat finish.

Missing

STRATEGY

Missing tiles are common along hips, ridges, and rakes. This is a result of wind uplift, in many cases. Ice dams can damage eave tiles or displace rake tiles.

It's easy to look for missing tiles. Also look for tiles that are kicked up at one end or are clearly misaligned. These may well be tiles that will soon be missing.

Fastener Failures

STRATEGY

In most cases, you won't be able to identify the fastener method, except perhaps at eaves, rakes, or valleys. You may be able to push up on the tiles to determine whether they're nailed or screwed. If they push up easily, they're probably just resting on battens. If they push up but are difficult to move, they may be clipped or held in place with wire ties. If they don't move at all, they're probably nailed, mortared or held in place with elastic cement (Figure 3.12). Don't force the tiles up.

Wood Battens

Clay tiles may be hung on horizontal wood battens; so may concrete tiles. Some manufacturers recommend the installation of vertical battens first, to allow water to drain. Others call for gaps or notches in the battens to allow water to escape.

Concrete Tiles Subject to Wind-Driven Rains

Interlocking concrete tiles are not particularly resistant to wind-driven rains, despite their capillary breaks. This is a result of the small overlap of adjacent tiles. In areas prone to strong wind-driven rains, water penetration through tile roofs is

F I G U R E 3.12 How Concrete Tiles Are Secured

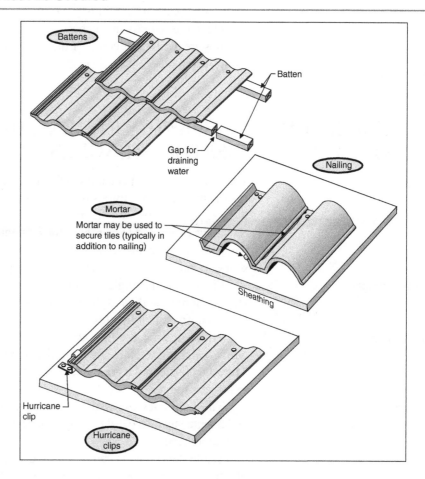

common. Where no waterproof membrane has been provided, watch for water damage as a result. This will generally show up as fairly widespread leakage across the field of the roof, especially on the windward side.

Flashing Problems

As with all roofs, check the intersections with other materials, penetrations and changes in direction carefully.

Underlying Membranes

The membranes are commonly a double layer of roofing felts mopped into hot asphalt. Self-sealing modified bitumen material is becoming popular as a membrane.

You won't be able to see the membrane except at the roofing perimeters, perhaps. Evidence of failure will be viewed mostly from inside and below.

A good membrane laid under a concrete tile roof may last up to 40 years. Removal of the tile, replacement of the membrane, and reinstallment of the tiles is often cost-effective.

Previous Repairs

Previous repairs are obviously the result of previous leaks. The roof is more vulnerable to future leaks in patched areas. You can sometimes pick up patches because the tiles are a different color, or there are visible fasteners used to hold the replacement tiles in place.

3.7 FIBER CEMENT (ASBESTOS CEMENT, MINERAL CEMENT, OR CEMENT ASBESTOS) SHINGLES

These products have been around for most of the 20th century. Portland cement forms the substrate and the fibrous reinforcement adds strength to these products. Up until the 1970s, asbestos was the most common reinforcement. Since then, other materials have been used to reinforce the cement. You won't be able to visually identify what the reinforcement is, and since an environmental inspection is beyond our scope, it may not be an issue for most inspectors.

Brittle and Light

Fiber cement shingles are brittle and are lighter than clay or concrete, but heavier and more rigid than asphalt (composition) shingles. Some are not recommended for use in freezing climates.

Diverse Looks

They are available in many colors and shapes, and are often intended to imitate wood, clay or slate. Rectangular and diamond-shaped shingles are common. They are considered a good quality roofing product with life expectancies in the 30 to 50 year range.

Durable

These shingles are weak with respect to impact, but are otherwise very durable and maintenance-free. Like many roofing products, if properly installed, they require no maintenance.

Many Colors

While the products can be colored with pigments or granules during the manufacturing process, or surface-colored at the factory, they can also be painted in the field. Once painted, ongoing maintenance is needed. It is more common for asbestos cement siding to be painted than roofing.

3.7.1 Conditions

The most common conditions are cracked, broken or missing shingles, because this material is brittle and subject to impact damage.

STRATEGY

Most inspectors walk on asbestos cement shingle roofs unless the slope is too steep. This is the best way to look for cracked, broken or missing shingles. Be careful walking on these. They are very slippery when wet.

Careful Walking on Roofs

On a very old installation, the fasteners may be corroded, allowing the shingles to become loose. You should understand there is a risk in walking on all roofs, because fasteners may become loose. The risk increases with older roofs where fasteners may have rusted.

Efflorescence

Efflorescence may appear on shingles. If it's a new installation, the efflorescence may disappear over time. If the efflorescence persists or is present on an older roof, a mild muriatic acid solution can be used, although it may create lighter patches on the roof.

This Can Look Like Other Materials

Again, be careful to identify the roofing material correctly. There are some very convincing mineral-fiber shingles imitating slate, especially. Some curved fiber-cement roof products manufactured in sheets can be mistaken for concrete or even clay.

Surface Starts Smooth and Roughens
Mineral-fiber shingles usually have a smooth surface when first manufactured unless they were originally ribbed. Over time, the surface becomes rougher and fuzzy, as individual fibers become partially exposed as a result of the cement wearing from the surface. In many cases there is no effect on performance, although over time, if enough of the cement is eroded away, the tile will become extremely brittle and will break under normal loads.

Shingles are also most likely to be broken in areas of high foot traffic.

3.8   METAL ROOFING

There are many types of metal roofs. Copper, galvanized steel, pre-painted or coated steel, terne, and tin are some of the most common. Most metal roofs (particularly copper) are expensive systems. Metal roofs can be installed in sheet form or as shingles. Sheets and shingles can be used on sloped roofs; however, flat roofs are only covered in sheets.

Sheet metal roofs can have many different types of seams. Some are soldered while others are folded and crimped in a variety of ways.

Wear Factors
Like any roofing system there are disadvantages; seams can split, or standing seams can get bent. All metal roofs except copper and pre-painted or pre-coated roofs should be painted on a regular basis. Metal roofs should never be covered with tar, since moisture trapped below the tar causes accelerated rusting.

3.8.1   Metal Shingles

Modern metal shingles are typically steel or aluminum. Steel shingles have corrosion protection, typically in the form of galvanizing (a zinc coating) or galvalume (a zinc/aluminum coating). They may also have baked-on enamel paints, acrylic coatings, and/or stone granules. They usually imitate the look of wood shingles, wood shakes or clay tile. They come with material warranties that range from 25 to 50 years, and are usually nailed, screwed or clipped to plywood sheathing, wood battens, or steel battens.

Conditions—General
The problems you'll be looking for on metal roofing include—

1. Rust
2. Fastener failure
3. Loose or missing shingles or flashing details
4. Installation problems
5. Dented
6. Buckled roofing

IMPLICATIONS

The implication of all these conditions is, of course, leakage.

STRATEGIES

Unless you know that the roof is suitable for walking on, you probably should not get on it. Check the edges and flashings where water may enter the roof and/or become trapped in the roof system. Look for rust, especially where dissimilar metals are in contact. Look for seams that may have been damaged. In areas where ice dams are an issue, pay particular attention to the lower three feet of the roof for damaged interlocks and seams.

Rust is more likely where the materials have to be site cut or bent. This exposes metal that may not have corrosion protection.

3.8.2   Sheet Metal Roofing

Sheet metal roofing has many of the same properties as metal shingle or tile roofing. Sheet metal roofing is commonly seen on old barns. These were usually unpainted galvanized roofs that often were allowed to weather and rust. This is what many people think of when we talk about metal roofing, and as a result, many people don't want anything to do with it. There are, however, some very attractive metal roofs.

Careful with Description

Generally speaking, metal roofing should be considered relatively high quality. Make sure you describe it as a metal roof, rather than guess as to what kind of metal it is. Unless you're absolutely sure, you can get into trouble describing the metal inappropriately.

Conditions

STRATEGY

Your inspection focus should be on—

1.   Rust

2.   Fastener failure

3.   Open or failed seams

Leakage is often through fastener connections. Check for rust around fasteners and watch for fasteners that have pulled through the panel.

Rusting on many metals shows up as small pit holes. These pits are sometimes difficult to see, especially from the ground.

3.9   ROLL ROOFING

Roll roofing material is also known as **selvage roofing.** Roll roofing is an asphalt-based material that is made the same way as asphalt shingles. Roll roofing comes in 36-inch-wide rolls, as its name suggests. **NIS** (Nineteen Inch Selvage) roofing is a type of roll roofing, where roughly half of the 36-inch wide roll is covered with a granular material.

Low Quality

Generally speaking, it is considered a low quality material, especially when installed as a single-ply membrane, as is frequently done. Roll roofing is more common on garages, sheds and other outbuildings than on houses, but you will find it in all applications and it can be used on steep and flat roofs. It is occasionally used as a sacrificial material over built-up roofing in flat applications.

Steep or Flat Roofs

Used as Flashing

Roll roofing is sometimes used as a flashing material. For example, it is commonly the valley flashing material on asphalt shingle roofs. It can also be used as eave protection under shingles.

Roll roofing is usually nailed in place and overlapped. Nail heads are secured with asphalt plastic cement (also known as mastic or elastic cement). The life expectancy of a steep roll roofing application is typically ten years or less.

3.9.1   Conditions

Most of the conditions that apply to asphalt shingle failures apply to roll roofing. Exceptions would be cupping and clawing. Because the material may be installed with different strategies (concealed nails or exposed nails, single layer or double layer) the performance will vary.

The implication of all of these conditions is leakage.

Cracked

Cracks are generally easy to identify. The trick is to look at the entire roof surface.

Blistered

When looking at roll roofing, pay particular attention to seams and overlaps for evidence of blistering. Otherwise it's just a question of looking at the entire roof surface.

Buckling or Wrinkling

Wrinkles or buckles usually wear prematurely and are common failure points.

Check the roof carefully to ensure that the entire roof surface is lying flat.

Open Seams

All seams should be cemented in place. Seams should never face up the slope so that they trap or collect water.

Check that the seams are tight.

Loss of Granular Material

Watch for missing granules, especially in high traffic areas.

Fastener Problems

Fasteners that were not intended to be exposed may be visible if they have popped back through the overlaying surface. These nails should be reseated and sealed.

Where nails are intended to be exposed, ensure that they are properly seated. All nails should be driven through an overlap where asphalt cement has been applied between the two layers of roofing.

Cemented Directly to Sheathing

Roll roofing should never be adhered directly to the roof decking with cement. This may cause the roll roofing to split when the deck moves. You won't be able to tell how the roof was secured unless there has been a failure.

Mechanical Damage

Roll roofing is like asphalt shingle roofing in that it is not able to withstand heavy foot traffic. Pay attention to potential high traffic areas. Mechanical damage, usually in the form of tearing, is easy to see.

Downspout Discharge

Concentrated water running across asphalt roofs, whether shingle or roll roofing, will shorten the life of the roof in this area considerably, because of mechanical wear and tear. Downspouts are much better if continued down to lower gutters rather than discharging onto asphalt roofing.

Multiple Layers
Roll roofing is not a particularly strong or rigid material and will telegraph uneven surfaces below. This can be an aesthetic issue, and if the telegraphing yields ridges, it is possible that premature wear will occur here. In most cases, it's tough to tell how many layers are there unless there has been a failure. Sometimes you can see at the perimeter.

3.10   STEEP ROOF FLASHINGS

Function

Flashings provide weathertight connections for roofs at—

- valleys
- penetrations through the roof
- intersections with other materials
- hips, ridges, eaves, and rakes

Leaks Are Usually at Flashings

Attention to detail on flashings is critical to any successful roof. Even the best roofing materials will leak if the flashings are not installed properly. You'll find that **the majority of roof leaks are flashing related, rather than roofing material related.**

Materials

Common flashing materials include—

- metal (such as steel, aluminum, copper, or lead)
- roll roofing
- felt paper
- rubberized asphalt (modified bitumen)
- and rubber (neoprene)
- there are also a number of composite flashing materials

Locations

Flashings are found at—

- valleys
- chimneys
- pipes or stacks that penetrate roofs
- roof/wall intersections
- sloped roofs which intersect flat roofs
- skylights
- eaves, rakes, hips, and ridges

Different Types

Flashings may be exposed or concealed. Most are at least partly concealed. Some steep roof flashings form a watertight joint, while others are a shedding system. Some are a combination of these.

Although we will touch on some aspects of good installation practices for steep roof flashings, a thorough discussion is beyond the scope of this book. More details can be found in *Principles of Home Inspection: Roofing*.

Careful with Criticism

Ultimately, the performance of the flashings is what matters. In reality, you'll see many liberties taken with good practice. Many times, this doesn't result in leakage. We recommend that you report to your client that there is no evidence of leakage, although the installation technique is not the best trade practice. We

F I G U R E 3.13 Roof Valleys—Open and Closed

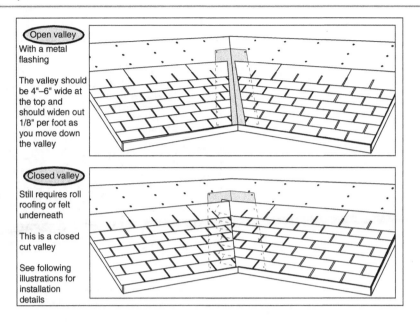

Monitor

typically recommend no action to the client, other than regular monitoring. You should also let the client know if what you've observed is typical for this quality of house in this area.

3.10.1   Valley Flashings

Valley flashings are used where **two different roof slopes come together to form a low trough** or valley. Valleys should be sloped so water runs off one end. Valleys that are flat along their length are likely to be sources of leakage. Valleys obstructed by chimneys or parapet walls, for example, are also likely to leak.

Valley flashings may be visible (open valley) or may be completely covered by the roofing material (a closed valley) (Figure 3.13).

Valley flashings are typically a shedding system rather than a watertight membrane.

Open Valleys

Open valleys have flashing material exposed to the elements along the length of the valley. Valleys should be four to six inches wide at the top and should widen out at a rate of about $^1/_8$ inch per foot as you move down the valley.

Wider at Bottom

There are two reasons the valleys should widen at the bottom.

1. Lower sections of the roof see more water than upper sections. Lower sections of valleys also see more water than upper sections.

2. Valleys that widen as they descend are less likely to hang up snow and ice. Valleys of uniform width are more prone to ice damming.

Open valley flashings for asphalt shingle roofs are typically **roll roofing** (Figure 3.14) or **metal** (Figure 3.15).

F I G U R E 3.14 Valley Flashing (Open)

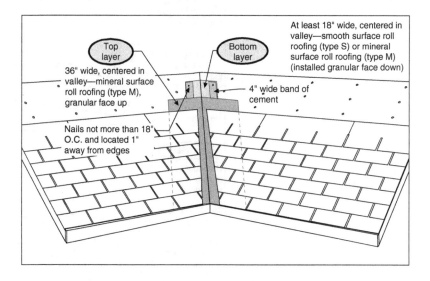

Closed Valleys

Asphalt Only

Closed valleys are commonly used with strip asphalt shingles only. The flashing material is not exposed. The shingles continue through the valley. Individual asphalt shingles (different from the common 3-tab shingles) are not suitable for closed valleys, since they aren't wide enough to carry through the valley without joints. Closed valleys are not recommended for wood. They can be used on clay, concrete, and slate, for example, but are less common. Closed valleys are more difficult to execute and may be more prone to leakage.

Types

With asphalt shingles, there are two types of closed valleys:

1. The closed cut or half-woven (Figure 3.16)
2. Fully woven valley (Figure 3.17)

F I G U R E 3.15 Metal Valley Flashing with Upstand

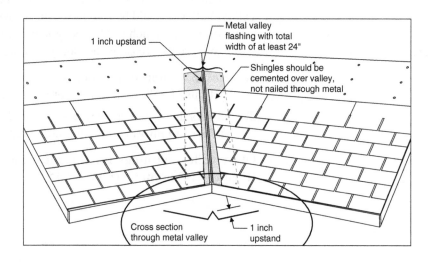

F I G U R E 3.16   Closed Cut (or Half-Woven) Valley

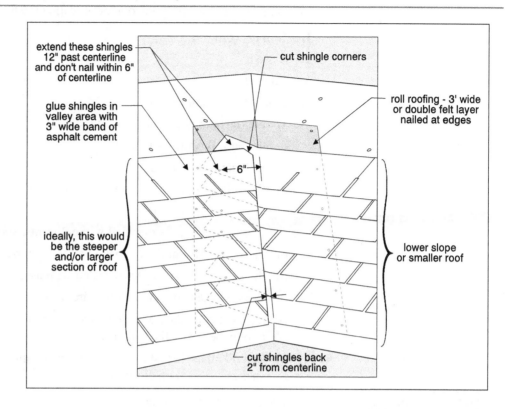

extend these shingles
12" past centerline
and don't nail within 6"
of centerline

cut shingle corners

glue shingles in
valley area with
3" wide band of
asphalt cement

roll roofing - 3' wide
or double felt layer
nailed at edges

6"

ideally, this would
be the steeper
and/or larger
section of roof

lower slope
or smaller roof

cut shingles back
2" from centerline

F I G U R E 3.17   Fully Woven Closed Valley

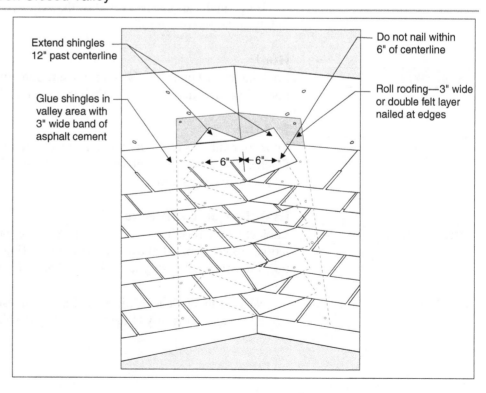

Extend shingles
12" past centerline

Do not nail within
6" of centerline

Glue shingles in
valley area with
3" wide band of
asphalt cement

Roll roofing—3" wide
or double felt layer
nailed at edges

6" 6"

Conditions

Common conditions you'll encounter on valley flashings include—

1. Torn or worn

2. Rusted

3. Patched

4. Installation problems, including

    a) the flashing is cut too short at the eaves

    b) the base flashing is missing

    c) fasteners are exposed

    d) the valley width is uniform over the length of the valley

    e) the points are not cut

    f) there are long runs of metal without joints, subject to buckling

    g) there is no upstand on a metal valley flashing

    h) the shingles have not been sealed with asphalt at the valley

    i) wood shake and shingle joints are broken into the valleys

    j) a closed cut valley does not have the overlaying shingles trimmed back two inches from the centerline

    k) individual asphalt shingles (not strip shingles) or wood shingles or shakes are used on closed valleys

IMPLICATIONS

The implication of all flashing problems (valley or other) is leakage.

Torn or Worn

STRATEGY

Look for tears that may be parallel to or across the length of the valley. Don't mistake a seam for a tear. Look for smooth surfaces indicating worn-off granular surfacing. In this case, the flashing is near the end of its life.

Horizontal tears can be caused by the valley flashing material being wound too tightly at the end of the roll.

Rust

STRATEGY

Looking for rust on metal flashings is easy. Sometimes you can tell that it's surface rust only and sometimes you can see that the metal is rusted all the way through.

Patched

STRATEGY

Look for materials of different color and texture in the valley, suggesting patching. Patches can be shingles, roll roofing, metal, asphalt roofing cement, caulking, and other creative substances.

Installation Problems

STRATEGY

Look at valley flashings from top to bottom for damage resulting from the installation problems listed above. As with all roofing inspection items, your inspection's not finished until you look from below (in the attic and the interior of the home).

Don't Cause Damage

Never walk up valleys. Since the flashing doesn't sit tightly against the sheathing in the valley, it is easy to damage a valley flashing.

Look from Eaves

The best spot from which to inspect the valley flashing is at the eaves. From here, you can sometimes see the following:

- the presence or absence of a base layer
- where the nails occur (preferably just at the outside edges)
- whether the valley flashing runs the full length
- the width of the flashing material
- whether metal valley flashings have returns and cleats at the edges
- whether the shingles were nailed through the valley or cemented in place

Dormer Valleys

Don't forget to check dormer valleys. Flashing dormer valleys is a tricky process. On the main roof side of the valley, the bottom of the valley should have a row of shingles below, so water will shed onto the roof and run down rather than into the roofing system.

Inspector in the House: Never Assume!

As a son who is also a home inspector, I am on call to fix things at my Mom's home. Some time ago, I was called to fix a small roof leak. The bottom of both asphalt roof valleys had been damaged by a raccoon. I shoved a piece of metal under the bottom of the valleys, tarred up the entire valleys, and sprinkled on some brown roof granules—the valleys looked like new. The roof remained leak-free until recently when a heavy snowfall started to melt.

When I got the call about the leak, I thought it must be an ice damming issue, but after clearing away the remaining melting snow, I saw a depression and a 3-inch split in one of the repaired valleys. After much head scratching, my mom mentioned that just before the snowfall, she had hired someone to clean the leaves out of the gutters. It seems he was on the roof with his leaf blower, and had stepped on the repaired valley!

3.10.2   Chimney Flashings

Round metal chimneys are flashed much like pipes. Where the chimney is clad with a siding material, the flashing will be a combination of masonry chimney flashing and roof/wall flashing details. We'll talk about roof/wall flashings in one of the next sections. Let's focus on masonry chimneys since they are the most challenging and are common.

Allowing for Movement

The roof deck may move relative to the masonry chimney, and good flashing details anticipate this. Good chimney flashings are two-part. The base flashings are secured to the deck and the cap flashing is secured to the masonry. The overlap between these two flashings allows movement without disturbing the watertightness.

Typical Materials

Chimney flashings are typically made of galvanized steel, galvalume, lead, copper or lead-coated copper. Aluminum is not generally used since it is not compatible with masonry mortar.

On a chimney, flashing is required at the bottom, sides and top. Each of these would ideally have a base (stepped if it's on the sides) flashing and a cap (counter) flashing; however, bottom (apron) flashings and top (head) flashings (where there is no saddle) are very often one piece.

F I G U R E 3.18 Chimney Flashings—Overview

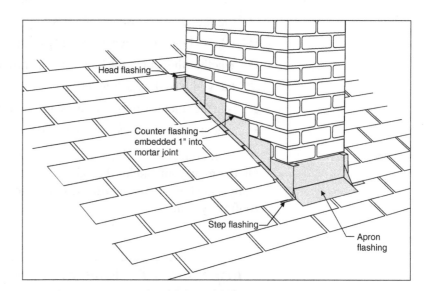

Conditions

When looking at a masonry chimney, look for the following conditions:

1. Rust

2. Damaged (including loose flashings or flashings that are opened at the top)

3. Installation-related problems, such as

    a. missing base or cap flashings

    b. missing bottom, side, or top flashings

    c. tops of flashings not let into mortar joints (asphalt cement and caulking are typical low quality substitutes)

    d. side base flashings not interwoven with shingles

    e. side base flashings too short (length, width or height)

    f. inadequate overlap of base flashings at the side and top

    g. inadequate overlap of cap flashings at the side and top

    h. inadequate height of the cap flashings (bottom, sides or top)

    i. crickets that are missing, loose or damaged

IMPLICATIONS

STRATEGY

Missing

Let into Mortar Joint

The practical implication of all these potential problems is leakage. Not only can interior and structural damage take place, but also the masonry can be damaged over time.

With respect to installation problems, the first thing to check is to make sure that all the required pieces are there (Figure 3.18). The second thing is to check the top of the cap flashing. In many cases, the tops are not let properly into mortar joints.

You should consider any caulked joint at the top of the cap flashing, or a joint that employs asphalt cement, as a temporary situation. Let your client know that this will be an ongoing maintenance issue.

FIGURE 3.19   Chimney Saddle Flashings

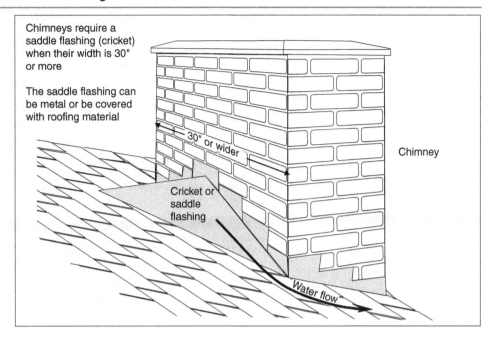

Chimneys require a
saddle flashing (cricket)
when their width is 30"
or more

The saddle flashing can
be metal or be covered
with roofing material

30" or wider

Chimney

Cricket or
saddle
flashing

Water flow

Projection

Lift the shingles carefully to check the horizontal projection of the side base flashings. Make sure that the bottom cap flashing extends down at least four inches onto the shingles.

Cricket

A **cricket** or **saddle** is a peak that deflects water and snow around the chimney, preventing it from accumulating against the topside of the chimney (see Figure 3.19). Make sure there is a cricket if the chimney is 30 inches wide or more. If the chimney is narrow (less than 30 inches wide) and there is no cricket, make sure that the cap flashing on the topside of the chimney extends high enough up the chimney and up the roof.

Check from Below

As with all roofing-related inspections, you aren't finished until you've checked the area below for evidence of leakage.

3.10.3   Pipe or Stack Flashings

In most homes there are round pipes or round metal chimneys, or both, penetrating the roof. Typical examples are plumbing stacks, electrical masts and exhaust vents from fans or combustion appliances.

Materials

These roof penetrations could be plastic, cast iron, steel, aluminum or copper. The flashing materials could be steel, rubber (neoprene), lead, copper or aluminum or a combination of materials.

The flashing details are similar for any of these penetrations.

Installation

■ the roof is shingled from the eaves up to the height of the stack.

■ with asphalt shingles, a shingle is typically cut and slid over the pipe.

■ the flashing flange is then placed over the stack and sealed or nailed in place.

■ once the flange is in place and sealed, the shingling is continued so that at least half, and in some cases almost all of the horizontal section of the flashing flange, is covered with roofing materials.

F I G U R E 3.20   Inspection Issues for Stack Flashings

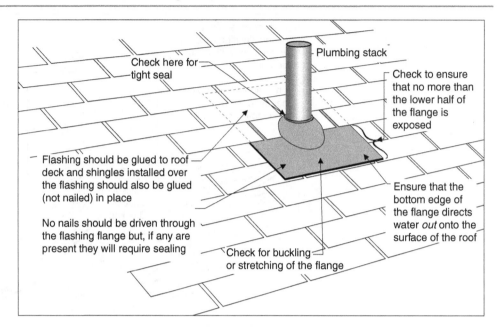

- the shingles (if asphalt) that are on top of the flange are often set in a continuous layer of asphalt cement.
- some roofing authorities recommend that nails not be driven through the flange.

Conditions
Conditions to watch for on these flashings include—

1. Rusted
2. Damaged
3. Vertically misaligned
4. Installation problems

IMPLICATION
In all of these conditions, the implication is the possibility of leakage. Figure 3.20 summarizes the strategy for inspecting stack flashings.

Installation problems include—

1. Missing flashing
2. Improper flashing material (e.g., asphalt cement on asphalt shingles, or rubber flashing flanges on curved concrete tiles)
3. Top half of flange exposed above roofing material, or bottom edge of flange concealed below roofing material
4. Flashing located in a valley
5. Exposed fasteners not sealed
6. Missing fasteners

STRATEGY
Missing components are a very common flashing problem. Most of the installation problems we've listed can be readily seen, if you remember to check for them.

F I G U R E 3.21 Roof/Sidewall Flashings

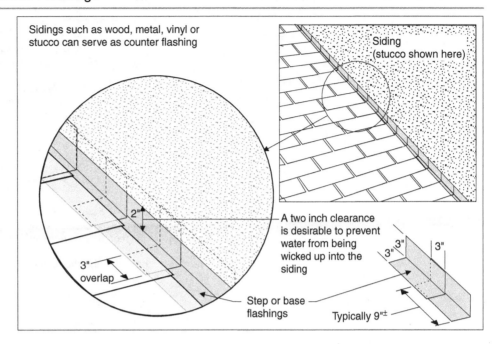

Sidings such as wood, metal, vinyl or stucco can serve as counter flashing

Siding (stucco shown here)

2"

3" overlap

A two inch clearance is desirable to prevent water from being wicked up into the siding

Step or base flashings

3" 3" 3"

Typically 9"±

3.10.4   Roof/Sidewall Flashings

Roof/Sidewall

Many roofs end at a gable or hip. However, the side of a roof can also end up against a wall. This is true with buildings that are part one-story and part two-story, for example, or anywhere the roof height changes from one part of the building to another.

Installation

The flashing approach in this situation is very similar to that used for the sides of chimneys (see Figure 3.21). A step flashing is interwoven with the shingles as they are laid up the roof. The base or step flashing is an L-shaped piece of metal (steel, aluminum or copper, typically). The flashing height and width is typically five inches, although it could be anything from three inches to six inches. Some call for a height of four inches and a width of two inches. The overlap of the metal pieces is typically two to three inches.

Nail to Roof or Wall

The flashings should be nailed to either the roof or the siding but not both. This is to allow for movement. In most cases, the flashing is nailed to the roofing rather than to the siding.

Materials

Materials used commonly include galvanized steel, aluminum, galvalume, lead, copper and lead-coated copper.

Counter Flashing

The siding may serve as the counter flashing if the siding is wood, aluminum, vinyl or stucco, for example. If the adjacent wall is masonry, counter flashings should be provided and let into mortar joints, in exactly the same way they are on chimney side flashings. Aluminum should not be used with masonry, as it is not compatible with mortar.

Terminate Siding above Roof Surface

It is considered good practice to keep the siding acting as a counter flashing away from the roof surface to make it easier to paint the siding, and to keep wood siding materials from soaking up moisture and rotting.

Flashings on Curved Tiles

Spanish, Mission or similarly profiled tiles typically use a different base flashing at sidewalls and the sides of chimneys. These flashings have a vertical lip, anywhere from $1/4$ inch to $1 1/4$ inches tall, along the side of the flashing furthest away

F I G U R E 3.22   Flashing for Roof Intersection with Brick Wall above

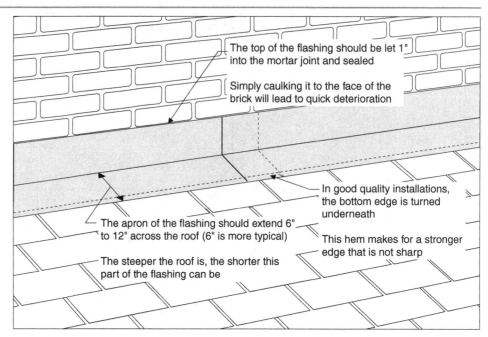

The top of the flashing should be let 1" into the mortar joint and sealed

Simply caulking it to the face of the brick will lead to quick deterioration

In good quality installations, the bottom edge is turned underneath

The apron of the flashing should extend 6" to 12" across the roof (6" is more typical)

This hem makes for a stronger edge that is not sharp

The steeper the roof is, the shorter this part of the flashing can be

from the wall or chimney. This creates a metal trough or pan type flashing. This is usually not a step flashing, but a continuous flashing running up the length of the wall. This flashing is installed before the tiles, and the roof is laid so that the lip in the trough is below the crown or high point of the tile.

The best place to look for this is at the eaves. Water should be able to flow down and discharge out through the bottom of the roof at this point.

Conditions
The conditions to watch for on sidewall/roof flashings include—

1. Loose, damaged or patched

2. Rusted

3. Installation problems, such as

    a. no step and/or no counter flashing

    b. step flashings not tucked under shingles

    c. flashings that are too short or too narrow

    d. siding that is not cut back

    e. inadequate overlap of adjacent pieces of step or counter flashing

    f. inappropriate or missing troughs or pans for curved tiles

    g. counter flashings not let into mortar joints on masonry walls

STRATEGY

There isn't usually much you can see of step flashings at roof/wall intersections. You're probably limited to making sure they're there, well secured, not rusted, and that they appear to be installed properly. You'll want to make sure that wood acting as counter flashing is cut back slightly, to avoid rot. One to two inches is acceptable. As with all roofing issues, it's the resultant leakage you'll be watching for.

Don't Get Fooled

Sometimes when you inspect a roof, you can't see any evidence of step flashing at the roof/wall intersection. If you are looking at two layers of roofing, the step flashing may be concealed.

With asphalt shingles, the following practice is common in some areas when roofing over an old roof at a roof/wall intersection. A strip of roll roofing or Ice and Water Shield (self-sealing modified bitumen membrane) about eight inches wide is nailed onto the roof surface right against the wall. As the new shingles are laid, the shingles are cemented to the strip.

The original step flashing is left in place, but is now concealed by the roll roofing and new shingles. If you look at the eaves, you may be able to see the bottom edge of the step flashing. Otherwise you won't be able to tell whether the step flashing is there or not.

Masonry

Where a steep roof meets a masonry wall at the side, the counter flashings should be let one inch (minimum) into mortar joints, and sealed. In many cases, the counter flashing is just nailed and caulked to the face of the brick wall. This is wrong. The caulking will usually fail within the first two years. This becomes a high maintenance area, vulnerable to leakage. Check these joints carefully.

Snow Drifts

In areas where snow accumulates, this roof/sidewall intersection is a common spot for drifts to develop on roofs. Drifting and subsequent ice damming can pose a challenge to the flashing details here.

3.10.5 Roof Intersections with Walls Above

Similar to Base Flashing for Chimney

A common roof configuration is a roof that runs into a wall at the top. This is ideally treated in much the same way as the base flashing for a chimney. The roofing material is brought up to the wall. A metal base flashing is secured to the wall, typically extending down several inches across the roofing surface (6 inches is typical; 12 inches is very good, but rare). The distance this apron flashing extends is, in part, a function of the steepness of the roof. The higher the pitch, the shorter this flashing can be.

Counter Flashing with Masonry

If the wall above is masonry, a metal counter flashing is added to the wall above the top of the base flashing (Figure 3.22). The top of the counter flashing would ideally be let into a mortar joint, although they are often just nailed into the masonry and caulked at the top.

This is the best approach. Many flashings are one piece rather than the two-piece system we've described here.

Siding Is the Counter Flashing

If the wall is siding, the siding can form the counter flashing. In either case, the counter flashing should not extend right down to the roof. The flashing materials in high quality work have their bottom edge turned under 180° to form a strong edge (hem) without a sharp surface.

Conditions

The common problems are the same ones as we looked for on chimneys, including—

1. Rust
2. Damaged or loose
3. Installation problems, such as—
   a. missing flashings
   b. one-piece flashings on masonry walls
   c. flashings too short
   d. flashings open at the top

    e. wood siding extending down too far

    f. counter flashings on masonry walls not let into mortar joints

    g. flashings nailed through shingles

STRATEGY

The inspection strategies with masonry walls are the same as for chimney flashings (see 3.10.2). It is very common to find only a counter flashing. Where no base flashing is used, the system is weaker but may be satisfactory, depending on several variables including—

1. Roof pitch

2. Exposure to wind driven rains

3. Rainfall

Watch for flashings surface-nailed through shingles to the roof deck. This amateurish technique is likely to cause leakage through the nail holes. Where wood-based wall siding forms the counter flashings, look for the siding to end an inch or two above the roof, to prevent water wicking into the siding.

3.10.6   Hip and Ridge Flashings

In most cases, the hips and ridges are finished with the same roofing tiles or shingles as those in the field of the roof. Some roofs use exposed metal flashings instead. Either approach is acceptable.

Some ridge flashings are also ridge-venting systems (allowing air to escape from the roof space or attic).

Conditions

1. Loose, misaligned or missing hip and ridge pieces

2. Wood hip and ridge pieces coming apart

3. Rust on metal hips and ridges

4. Installation problems, such as

    a. exposed fasteners without plastic cement or caulking

    b. excessive exposure

    c. poor fastening

    d. prefabricated wood, hip and ridge pieces not installed with alternating overlaps

STRATEGY

Look along the hips and ridges for missing, loose or crooked pieces. If you can get up on the roof, lift up on some to ensure they're well secured. Watch for wood sections that may be coming apart.

Look for exposed fasteners. Except for one or two fasteners at each hip and ridge, you shouldn't see any. Where fasteners are exposed, check that plastic cement has been provided to seal the nail heads.

Plastic Cement

Where plastic cement has been used to seal the hip and ridges in place, look for cement that has run out onto the roof, discoloring the roof surface. Plastic cement that is too viscous (flows too easily) will discolor the roof and may not have good holding strength.

Mortar

On concrete or clay tiles, look for missing, cracked, or shrinking mortar. Look also for gaps in curved tile hip and ridges that may allow wind-driven rain or snow to penetrate and that may allow birds and animals into the roof system.

Where the hips and ridges are the same material as the field of the roof, the exposures should be similar.

3.10.7   Skylights

Skylights are a popular architectural detail. They may be found on flat or steep roofs; they may be single, double or triple glazed; they may have flat or curved glazing; the glazing may be glass or acrylic. The units are typically manufactured, but may also be made on site. They may be installed singly or in groups.

Skylights installed in cathedral ceilings or flat roofs don't usually need **light wells** to get to the ceiling level. Skylights installed on steep roofs often have large wells around the skylight extending down through the attic to the ceiling level. These wells often widen as they get closer to the ceiling to allow better light disbursement.

Let's look at some of the problems that you might encounter.

Conditions

Common problems include—

1. Leakage

2. Rot

3. Mechanical damage

4. Patching

5. Cracked or broken glazing

6. Loss of seal on double-glazed units

FIGURE 3.23   Curb-Mounted Skylight in a Sloped Roof

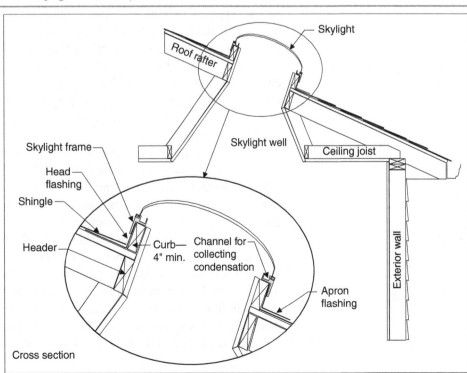

7. Installation problems, including

    a. no curb

    b. low curb

    c. improper or incomplete flashings

    d. wrong application (e.g., a system designed for steep roofing is installed on a flat roof or vice-versa; a system designed for asphalt shingles is installed on a tile roof)

    e. a window is used as a skylight

    f. the skylight is poorly secured to the roof

IMPLICATIONS

There are structural implications to rot around skylights, if the rot is progressive. Most of the other implications of skylight problems are damage to interior finishes as a result of leakage.

Loss of Seal on Double-Glazed Units (Condensation)

STRATEGY

Some double-glazed skylights have sealed glazing where there should be no leakage (in or out) of the air between the two panes. Other skylights are vented, and are intended to have air changes in the space between the glazing units. Most modern skylights are vented, rather than hermetically sealed, and condensation will be only temporary on vented skylights.

If you see condensation or evidence of it (streaks on the glazing surfaces, for example), you should check to see whether the unit is sealed or vented around the perimeter before describing condensation as a problem.

Installation Problems

STRATEGY

Skylights are one of the most troublesome roofing details. Most problems are associated with poor quality installation, although in some cases, it is a problem associated with the quality of the skylight.

Curbs

Look for skylights that are mounted on curbs (Figure 3.23). These are more likely to be successful than curbless skylights or skylights with integral manufactured curbs. Skylights with integral manufactured curbs usually have very small curbs and very small integral flashings. These skylights are more prone to leakage. Some flush-mounted skylights are particularly prone to leakage.

Think of Skylights as Short Chimneys

If you imagine that a skylight mounted on a curb is a very short chimney, it's easy to understand how the flashing details can be done correctly. Base and cap flashing strategies can be used and step flashings along the sides are employed. In some cases, a counter flashing is provided; in other cases the skylight curb itself forms the counter flashing.

On a good quality installation, you're looking for bottom, side and top flashings, each with a base and counter flashing. The side flashings are typically step flashings interwoven with the roofing material. Better skylights have a lip on the frame that extends part way down the side curb, and the skylight frame is fastened to the curb, usually with screws through the lip.

Ice Damming

In areas where snow accumulates on roofs, the heat loss through skylights creates the potential for ice damming around and below the skylight. As heat from the building is lost through the skylight, the snow immediately adjacent to the skylight melts. Since the remainder of the roof is cold, the melted snow running away from the skylight will quickly re-freeze on the roof surface below. This can build up a dam. When subsequent melting snow from around the skylight runs down the roof, it will hit the dam and back up under the roof shingles or skylight flashing.

Self-Sealing Modified Bitumen Material

Many installers extend the flashing around skylights with Ice and Water Shield. This improves the chances for success even in skylights that are otherwise less than ideally installed.

Installation Problems

You should be looking for skylights that are not installed according to manufacturer's recommendations. It is helpful to become familiar with the type of skylights that are commonly used in your area, and obtaining the installation instructions for each of these. Local home shows are a good spot to pick up this information.

Watch for windows that are used as skylights. Generally, anything that has more than a 15° slope off vertical should not be treated as a window. Some people say that windows should be completely vertical. Many authorities require that any glass more than 15° off vertical must be strengthened by **tempering, laminating, wiring, annealing** or equivalent.

Acrylic is more commonly used than glass on skylights because strengthening glass is fairly expensive. The acrylic is strong, although it does scratch easily. Where glass is used on skylights, sometimes special screens are required below the skylight to catch any falling glass in the event the skylight is broken.

Glass or Acrylic

Acrylic skylights usually have curved glazing. Glass skylights are usually flat Tapping on the skylight will help identify the material, with a little practice. Glass skylights sound and feel like windows when you tap. Acrylic skylights sound and feel like plastic.

Safety

You often won't be able to tell if the glass in skylights is appropriately strengthened. If you can get a manufacturer's name and model number, this will allow you to get an answer. Some tempered glass says **tempered** in the corner of the pane. If in doubt, don't guess. Simply tell your client you can't verify that the skylight has the proper safety glazing.

Check the Glazing

Look carefully at all of the glazing for cracks or movement within the frame. Remember that many skylights are double or triple glazed and you have to look at each piece of glazing. Observe whether the edges of the glazing are set in a gasket or terminate in a tray that allows for condensation to drain. Sealed units should never have condensation, while the vented and drained skylights will have condensation from time to time.

Lift up on the Skylight

If you are on the roof and can get to the skylight, you should grab the edge and see if you can lift it off the roof. Be careful here! Don't lift too hard. If the skylight starts to move, you can describe it as being poorly secured without having to lift it all the way off.

Patching

Most skylights leak eventually. If you see evidence of patching on the outside, usually around the flashings, you can assume that the skylight leaked into the building interior.

Structural Issues

Before you go inside to check for evidence of leakage, you should put weight on the framing members around the skylight to ensure that there is no excessive deflection. In some cases, cut structural members are not adequately re-supported. In other cases, slow leaks can cause rot damage to framing members, weakening the structure in the area of the skylight.

Go Inside the Building

From the interior of the building you should always look up at skylights for evidence of leakage, particularly at the bottom corners of the skylight opening. Looking at the skylight from a stepladder gives you a better view, although many inspectors do not take the time to set up a stepladder under each skylight.

If there is evidence of leakage, some inspectors use a moisture meter to try to determine whether the leak is active. If the leak shows wet, you can be relatively certain that the leak is active. If the leak shows dry, the leak may or may not be active, depending on how long it's been since there has been rain or snow. Remember that

F I G U R E 3.24   Flat Roof Drainage Systems

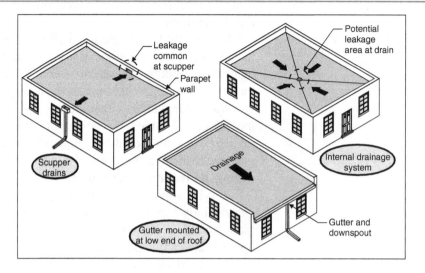

even if a leak shows dry in the summer immediately after a rain, it still may be an active leak during the winter as a result of ice damming.

Identifying the Cause of the Leak

In most cases, it's not possible to find out where the skylight is leaking. Since most of the installation details are concealed from view, you usually can't pinpoint the weak link. In some situations, the "leak" may actually be condensation. Condensate trays and drains may become clogged, preventing the condensate from discharging outside. This can look like a leak, but will typically be only a winter problem, which is when most condensation occurs. Ice damming is also a winter-only problem.

Be Careful

If you see no evidence of leakage, there may be no problem, or the problem may be concealed through recent decorating. We recommend that you be very careful with skylights, and let your clients know that these are susceptible to leakage.

3.11   INTRODUCTION TO FLAT ROOFING

Watertight Skin

Flat roofing is an entirely different strategy than steep roofing. While steep roofing is a shedding system, flat roofing is a watertight skin or membrane that is formed over the top of the building. If you think of a steep roof as an umbrella, houses with flat roofs don't use umbrellas but use wet suits (or to be more accurate, dry suits). Since we have a different approach, there are a whole different set of materials, installation methods and conditions to look for.

Slope

As we stated earlier in this chapter, these roofs are called low-slope roofs by roofing experts. In common usage they are usually referred to as flat roofs and we will use the common terminology in our discussions. Keep in mind that roofs should never be perfectly flat. They should drain water. The drainage system can be gutters and downspouts, centrally located roof drains, and/or scuppers (drainage openings through walls, including parapet walls) (Figure 3.24).

Tough to Seal the Openings

The installation of flat roof is demanding, because not only do we have to make a weather-tight skin over the top of the building, but we have to maintain that weather-tight condition at chimneys, plumbing stacks, skylights, vents, around the edges, etc. It's not as simple as putting a lid on the house and sealing it around the edges.

F I G U R E 3.25   Built-Up Roofing Membrane, 4-Ply

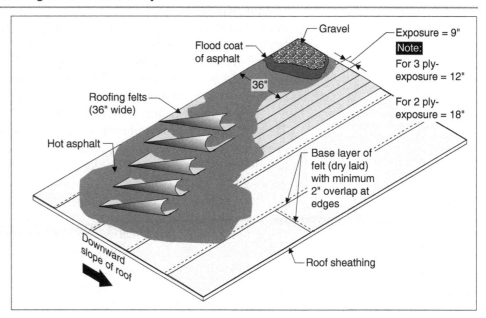

Gravel
Flood coat
of asphalt
Exposure = 9"
Note:
For 3 ply-
exposure = 12"
For 2 ply-
exposure = 18"
36"
Roofing felts
(36" wide)
Hot asphalt
Base layer of
felt (dry laid)
with minimum
2" overlap at
edges
Downward
slope of roof
Roof sheathing

Roof Decks (Sheathing)	Flat roofs on residential buildings usually are wood-framed. On old houses, plank roofing is typical. On newer houses, plywood is more common. The plywood should be exterior grade and should be thick enough to span between roof joists without sagging. Felts should not be mopped directly to wood. These details will be discussed in more detail later in this chapter.
Walking on Flat Roofs	Walking on flat roofs is discouraged except for inspection and maintenance. Wood walkways or concrete paving units should be provided over the roof. Good practice includes the use of a rigid insulation between the roof membrane and walkway.

3.12 BUILT-UP ROOFING

Life Expectancy	The traditional built-up roof is considered to have at least a 20-year life expectancy, and many built-up flat roofs last 30 to 35.
Organic Felts	Figure 3.25 summarizes the components of a built-up roof. The base of an asphalt built-up roof is the felts. These felts are fibrous materials saturated with asphalt. The felts were traditionally made from by-products of the paper, wood and cloth manufacturing industries. These organic (rag or cellulose) felts have been very common.
Asbestos, Fiberglass, and Polyester Felts	Asbestos felts, fiberglass felts and polyester fiber felts are also used. None of these materials is perfect, but all are acceptable. During a home inspection, you won't be able to tell what kinds of felts have been used in a built-up roof system.
Plies	The roofing felts are typically laid anywhere from two to five plies, with each ply being embedded in a full bed of hot asphalt. You normally can't tell how many plies a roof is by looking at it.
Functions of Components	The asphalt is actually the waterproofing material. The felts hold the asphalt in place and provide strength, distribute the forces, and stabilize the layers of asphalt.
Gravel Protection	Asphalt is susceptible to rapid deterioration when exposed to the ultraviolet rays of the sun. The volatiles are boiled out of the asphalt, leaving it brittle and weak.

Flood Coat

Consequently, built-up roof membranes must be protected from ultraviolet light. The traditional protection, called aggregate, may be asbestos, marble, rock slag, gravel or crushed stone. This **gravel** (as it's usually called) is embedded in a **flood coat** of hot asphalt that has been mopped onto the top of the membrane. The flood coat of asphalt holds the gravel and is also a waterproofing layer. It is the primary defense for the felts below. None of the felts should penetrate the flood coat since exposed felts will wick water down into the roofing membrane.

Gravel Alternatives

Some roofs are painted with light colored reflective paints to protect the asphalt. These paints help reflect ultraviolet rays and heat, but can't act as ballast or fire protection. Roofs covered with decks do not require gravel since the decking protects the membrane from ultraviolet (UV) light and helps keep the roof cooler. The decking also acts as ballast.

Difficult to Inspect

Built-up roofs are very difficult to inspect because of the gravel top coating. You can't get a look at the membrane underneath the gravel and in many ways, you're flying blind. While good quality applications last for many years, tracing leaks in built-up roof systems is difficult since the leaks inside buildings are rarely directly below the flaw in the roof above.

3.12.1   Conditions

We're going to look at the membrane problems first, and deal with flashings later. Roof membrane problems include—

1. Old/worn out
2. Mechanically damaged
3. Patched
4. Multiple layers
5. No protective surface (e.g., gravel or paint)
6. Blisters
7. Alligatoring
8. Gravel erosion
9. Ridging and fishmouths
10. Membrane movement/splitting
11. Ponding/vegetation
12. Debris or storage on the roof
13. Exposed felts

Many of the conditions are related to poor installation.

IMPLICATIONS

The implications of any of these conditions are, of course, leakage and damage to the structure.

There are many things that can go wrong. Let's look at some of the individual conditions.

Old/Worn Out

STRATEGY

The key to the inspection of any built-up roof is to walk the roof surface. You'll be looking for all of the conditions we've listed. Depending upon how many of those you find, you may be able to describe the roof as simply "old" and at the end of its life expectancy.

Although we're going to be talking about flashings later, the age and corrosion level of metal flashings also provide clues to the age of the roof membrane.

The age of the roof is less important than the remaining life.

Mechanically Damaged

Built-up roof membranes are relatively susceptible to mechanical damage.

Mechanical damage is usually relatively easy to find. In most cases, mechanical damage that has punctured a membrane will have been corrected. In some cases, you'll find damage that has not penetrated the entire membrane. Repairs should be recommended to prevent deterioration of the roof and eventual leakage in this area.

Patched

It is very common to find that flat roof membranes have been patched.

Look for obvious patches, including areas where gravel has been removed, or additional asphalt-based materials have been poured on the roof. Properly made patches are often invisible because the gravel was removed and replaced after the patching work is done. Sometimes new gravel is used, which may be a different color or texture than the original gravel.

Multiple Layers

It is common for new membranes to be added over old membranes. This is not recommended practice because—

1. It adds weight to the structure below.

2. You are usually replacing a roof because it leaks. Water is trapped in the old membrane. Adding a new watertight membrane may trap water in the roof system. This may lead to rot or cause premature failure of the new membrane.

One of the only ways to determine how many layers there are is to look at the perimeter of the roof. You can sometimes count the drip edge flashings.

Wherever there is more than one, you should describe this as a multiple layer roof and alert the client to the fact that the roof may have a higher maintenance or shorter life than you would otherwise expect.

The absence of multiple drip edge flashings around the perimeter does not necessarily mean there is only one layer of roofing. Sometimes drip edge flashings are removed around the perimeter before adding the second layer of roofing.

No Protective Surface

A protective surface is necessary, as we have discussed earlier, to protect against the rays of the sun and to help keep the roof cool.

The implication is a much reduced life expectancy.

It's easy to identify missing protection. The absence of gravel or paint also lets you have a good look at the membrane. If it's still in good shape, a protective layer can be added to extend the life.

Blisters

When walking roofs in cold weather, be very careful to watch for blisters. Do not step on them or probe them. Blisters should be described as vulnerable spots on the roof. There may be no evidence of leakage below, in which case, repairs are rarely made.

In warmer weather when walking the roof, feel under foot for the sponginess that may be associated with young blisters. You can sometimes see blisters by looking along the roof surface, but you should also walk the entire roof.

Blisters can be cut open, dried, sealed and recovered with gravel.

Alligatoring

Alligatoring is a result of the sun making the top surface of the asphalt brittle. This is because the volatiles, which keep the asphalt flexible, are boiled off. When the membrane is put under tensile stress (e.g., it's cold and the membrane shrinks), the surface cracks in the characteristic alligator skin pattern. Over time, the cracks deepen and eventually allow water through the upper layer of asphalt into the felts.

STRATEGY

Watch for alligatoring in asphalt that has been exposed as a result of either an installation condition or erosion of the gravel surface.

Gravel Erosion (Wind Scouring)

Wind and water running across a roof can scour the gravel away from certain areas. Once the gravel is gone, the sun can attack the asphalt relatively quickly.

STRATEGY

Look for a continuous and uniform gravel cover. Also, make sure the gravel is not sharp so it won't pierce the asphalt. Where gravel is missing, it can usually be replaced, as long as the asphalt and membrane have not already deteriorated dramatically.

In some cases, paint, decking, or other protective covers replace the gravel. As long as these protect the asphalt from the sun and do not interfere with water draining off the roof, they are fine.

Wood Decks on Flat Roofs

Wood decks are ideally installed on sleepers, which are wood stringers (or beams) mopped into the roof surface. The sleepers should run with the slope of the roof, so water can drain.

Posts for deck railings should be flashed into the roof.

The deck should be laid in small sections, and be easy to remove for maintenance or repair.

Look carefully at the doors leading out to wood decks. These are common leakage spots because of—

1. Poor flashing at the door sill
2. Door sills too low

The door sills should be at least six inches above the deck, not the roof surfaces, in areas where snow accumulates. They are rarely high enough.

Ridging and Fishmouths

Ridges in felts may be caused by a number of things, including installation problems related to excessive asphalt moisture, differential thermal expansion of the deck or structure, expansion due to moisture, and slippage of the felts.

Fishmouths are caused where the ridged or wrinkled felts are open at their edge. This may be caused by twisting of the felt roll during application. Figure 3.26 shows ridging and fishmouths.

IMPLICATIONS

One implication of exposed felts is that water is wicked into the membrane through the felt edges. Open fishmouths can also allow water directly into the membrane. Another implication is that the ridging allows the granular material to migrate away from the ridge, and as the membrane is exposed to the sun, it deteriorates more quickly.

F I G U R E 3.26   Ridging and Fishmouths on Flat Roofs

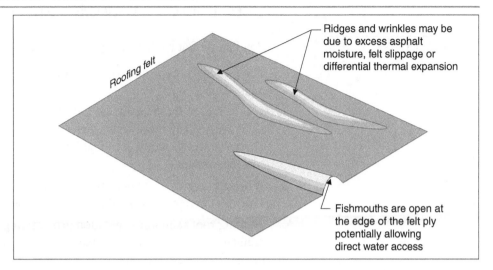

Roofing felt

Ridges and wrinkles may be
due to excess asphalt
moisture, felt slippage or
differential thermal expansion

Fishmouths are open at
the edge of the felt ply
potentially allowing
direct water access

STRATEGY

Protruding Felts

As you walk the roof surface, look for or feel ridges, wrinkles and fishmouths. If they are still covered with gravel, they may not be apparent visually. In cold weather, be careful not to step on any visible ridges for fear of cracking or splitting the membrane.

Open fishmouths are usually easy to identify. Somewhat more subtle are any edges of felts that protrude up through the asphalt and through the gravel. These felts will draw moisture into the membrane, deteriorating it quickly. Prompt repairs should be recommended where this is seen.

Membrane Movement/Splitting

Splitting is a tension failure that differs from cracks that occur as ridges wear. It is also different from the random splitting that occurs with advanced alligatoring. Splitting is a tension failure across the field of the membrane and is usually the result of shrinkage of the membrane relative to the roof deck.

IMPLICATIONS

The implications of membrane movement include flashings being torn loose, membrane splits, seams opening up, and in severe cases, parapet walls or curbs can be pulled over and plumbing stacks can be dislodged.

STRATEGY

Look for splits or open seams around the perimeter and throughout the field. Look at perimeters for flashings, parapets or curbs that have been pulled inward because of membrane shrinkage. Look at roof penetrations for evidence of membrane movement or, in severe cases, misalignment of pipes or stacks that penetrate the roof. Corners are vulnerable to splits, because of different stresses.

Splitting may occur through all plies of the membrane simultaneously, and may extend all or most of the way across the roof width (although not necessarily in a straight line).

Wrinkling

Where there is a perceptible slope, look for wrinkling that indicates part of the membrane has slumped toward the low side of the slope. In some cases, the roof will be displaced outward slightly at the perimeter and may even be overhanging the exterior wall.

Ponding/Vegetation

Any roof that still has water on it forty-eight hours after a rain is defined as a ponding roof.

Ponding on flat roofs has a number of implications:

IMPLICATIONS

1. The prolonged exposure to water is likely to shorten the life of the membrane.

2. The weight of the ponded water deflects the structure and makes the poor slope worse. The more water that accumulates, the more the structure sags. The more the structure sags, the larger the low spot and the more water that can accumulate.

3. When a ponding roof leaks, there is often a large volume of water involved. This can cause significant damage inside the building.

4. Ponding roofs support vegetation growth. Vegetation on the roof impedes drainage, making ponding worse. The roots may also attack and penetrate the membrane, or clog drains.

STRATEGY

Water on the roof is your first clue that there is a ponding problem. Dirt, algae and vegetation are other indications. Look at the roof slope and evaluate the drainage opportunities for water to escape.

It is considered in good practice to have emergency secondary drains, where an interior drainage system is used. This is often in the form of scuppers through parapet walls. The scupper drains may be two inches above the roof membrane so that they do not act as primary drains. They will allow roughly two inches of water to accumulate on the roof before discharging.

Watch for and be critical of vegetation growing on the roof.

Debris or Storage on the Roof

Materials stored on the roof may—

IMPLICATIONS

1. Pierce the membrane

2. Add to the live load on the roof, causing deflection of the structure

3. Impede the drainage off the roof, inhibiting drying

STRATEGY

Part of roof maintenance is to keep the roof clear of debris. When examining a roof, you should be critical of any materials stored on the surface or any debris that has accumulated.

Pay particular attention to drains, because they act as magnets for leaves, twigs, and other debris.

Exposed Felts

IMPLICATIONS

Water will be wicked into the roof via exposed felts, leading to premature failure and leakage.

STRATEGY

Watch for felts sticking up through asphalt

3.13   MODIFIED BITUMEN

Modified bitumen (or mod bit, as it often is called) membranes are an alternative to built-up roofs. Rolls of this rubberized asphalt membrane are typically torched onto the roof, bonded (mopped in) to the roof with hot asphalt, or adhered with a self-adhesive (peel-and-stick) backing. The surface of the membrane may be pro-

F I G U R E 3.27   Single-Ply Modified Bitumen Roof

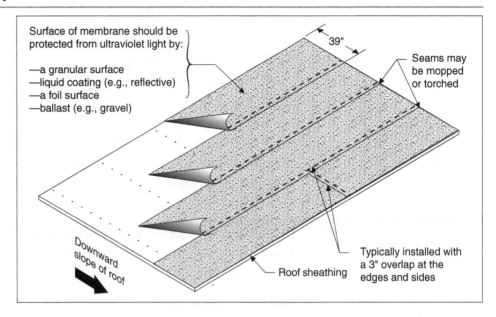

Surface of membrane should be protected from ultraviolet light by:

—a granular surface
—liquid coating (e.g., reflective)
—a foil surface
—ballast (e.g., gravel)

39"

Seams may be mopped or torched

Downward slope of roof

Roof sheathing

Typically installed with a 3" overlap at the edges and sides

tected from ultraviolet rays by a coating of granules, foil, or paint. The sheets are approximately thirty-six to thirty-nine inches wide and usually overlap each other by three inches.

Life Expectancy

Modified bitumen membranes have only been in use since about 1980. A lifespan of fifteen to twenty years is common, but many roofs have failed sooner.

Wear Factors

Many early failures of modified bitumen roofs have been the result of poor installation. Roofs with ultraviolet protection last longer than those without. Two-ply installations are more durable than single-ply. Some types of membranes perform better in a cold or a warm climate. There is no way to determine the type during a home inspection.

Number of Plies

Modified bits are often installed in a single-ply system residentially (Figure 3.27). Higher quality installations are two-ply.

3.13.1   Conditions

Problems on mod bit roofs include—

1. Old/worn out
2. Openings at seams and flashings
3. Surface cracking
4. Loss of granules
5. Slippage of the membrane
6. Blisters
7. Punctures or tears
8. Ponding/vegetation
9. Patched

10. Installation problems, including—

■ seams facing up the slope

■ inadequate overlap of seams at side or ends

■ end seams not staggered

■ inadequate fastening of the membrane to the roof deck

■ poor sealing at seams and flashings (often owing to underheating or overheating the material)

■ inadequate drainage causing ponding

IMPLICATIONS

The implications of all these conditions are leakage and the necessity to repair or replace the roof membrane. We will comment on several of these conditions in the following sections.

Openings at Seams and Flashings

This is a common condition and your inspection should focus on the seams and flashings. Openings in the seams may take the form of fishmouths.

Ponding/Vegetation

While it is unclear whether and to what extent ponding may shorten the life of modified bitumen, it is considered undesirable on any roof. We talked about the implications of ponding and vegetation in 3.12 under Built-up Roofing. The same issues apply.

Patched

It is common to find patches on mod bit roofs. These may indicate previous problems and an increased vulnerability to future leakage.

Installation Problems

STRATEGY

Identification

The inspection of modified bit roofs is similar to the techniques for built-up roofing. The first trick, however, is to identify what kind of roofing membrane you are looking at. If there is an exposed asphalt membrane, or one that has had a coating painted on it, you may be reasonably sure that it's modified bitumen if—

■ the seams are approximately every three feet and,

■ there is some evidence of bleed-out of asphalt at the seams

■ the flashing material is the same as the roofing material

■ there are no nails visible

The above description could also describe "mopped in" roofing felts, but these are usually less than $1/16$ inch thick, whereas mod bit is usually between $1/16$ and $1/8$ inch thick.

If the membrane is covered with a granular surface, then you are sure that it is not a plastic or elastomeric roofing membrane. However, it might be roll roofing (an asphalt-based product that is not modified and is much lower quality). Roll roofing often has nail heads that are exposed and just covered with plastic cement and/or plastic cement along the seams. Roll roofing material is not used for flashings, typically.

Roll roofing is usually 36 inches wide. Mod bit roofing is most often 39 inches (1 meter) wide.

Mod bit is more flexible than roll roofing. If you find a scrap piece on the site, bend it over on itself (180°). The roll roofing will often break along the crease while the mod bit usually won't. The colder it is outside, the more brittle both will be. You can usually pinch a piece off the corner of roll roofing. It's much harder to do this with mod bit.

If you are in doubt as to what the material is, do not go out on a limb. Simply describe it as a "single-ply membrane." Remember, too, that it might be one or two plies. You often won't be able to tell by looking.

Focus on Seams and Flashings   Probably more than half of your inspection time should be devoted to seams and flashings areas. It will not take you long to look at the field of the roof for surface cracks, patching, etc.

High Traffic Areas   Pay particular attention to high traffic areas for wear or mechanical damage. If areas are clearly frequent traffic spots, concrete roof pads should be considered.

Debris   Good roof maintenance includes an absence of debris or foreign materials on the roof. Where these are seen, recommend their removal.

Patches   A small number of small patches is normal and should not be cause for concern. Localized defects are easy to patch in most modified bit systems.

One-Ply or Two-Ply   It's difficult to know whether you are looking at a one-ply or a two-ply system. The side laps on seams should be staggered and sometimes you can see the seams from the base sheet telegraphing through the second sheet. This suggests a two-ply system. However, this could also be an old roof membrane below, so be careful.

Applied over an Old Roof   It is common to use mod bit roofing over old roofs. Good practice requires a new wood sheathing laid over the old roof first. This can be boards, plywood, or OSB (oriented strand board), but should be well secured to the old membrane and should provide a smooth surface for the mod bit. In most cases, you won't be able to verify how many layers are present and whether a re-cover board has been used.

Be careful with exposed membranes. If the membrane has no coating or granular surface, look at the field of the roof closely for premature aging, which often shows up as cracking or blistering.

3.14   SYNTHETIC RUBBER (ELASTOMERIC, EPDM)

EPDM (Ethylene Propylene Diene Monomer) is one of the most common synthetic rubber roofings (Figure 3.28).

Inner Tube   EPDM often looks and feels like the inner tube from a tire. If you stretch it, it rebounds. It is usually black or white, although it can be coated any color.

Reinforcing   The rubber can be plain, or it can be reinforced, typically with a polyester fabric, which may be either embedded in the rubber or laminated to the back.

No UV Protection Needed   In most cases EPDM does not require a protective coating from ultraviolet light or heat. In some cases, coatings are used to enhance appearance or fire resistance. Protective coatings include ballast and Hypalon – a brand name for CPSE (chlorosulphonated polyethylene).

Thickness   The material is typically 0.8 to 1.6 mm (30-60 mils) thick, exclusive of any reinforcement laminated onto the back.

Sheet Size   EPDM is usually laid as a single sheet. The sheets can be up to 50 feet wide and some manufacturers offer single sheets up to 5,000 square feet.

Attaching It to Roof   EPDM can be attached to the roof deck by—

1. Fully or partially adhering to the roof deck with contact cement

2. Mechanically fastened to the roof deck with bars or buttons

3. Laying the EPDM loose and holding it down with ballast

FIGURE 3.28   EPDM Roof Membrane

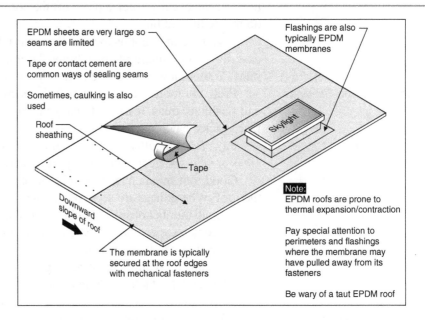

Holding EPDM Down

Ballast is rarely used on single-family residential properties. Ballasted systems provide some protection for the membrane from weathering. Fully adhered systems are commonly used where the slope is significant. Mechanically fastened systems are useful where the roof can't stand the weight of ballast. The mechanically fastened systems are popular in re-roofing applications.

Some of the systems can be fully adhered in hot asphalt. The systems embedded with asphalt typically have a polyester mat laminated onto the bottom, because the asphalt does not bond well to the EPDM.

Compatibility

EPDM is not compatible with some asphalt products, including mastic. Wherever EPDM contacts asphalt products, inspection should be close.

EPDM is attacked by oils. Roof-mounted air conditioners with refrigerant leaks deposit oil onto the roof. Watch for deteriorated EPDM wherever oil may get on it.

Seams

Seams are usually taped or sealed with contact cement. The edges are sometimes sealed with caulking, in addition to the tape or cement. Since the sheets are large, seams may be rare.

Flashings

Flashings for EPDM roofs are typically EPDM membranes.

Life Expectancy

While many manufacturers claim a 20 years' life expectancy, there have been some failures of EPDM roof membranes on much younger installations. Again, because the product is relatively new and continues to evolve with experience, predicting life expectancies is dangerous at this point.

Other Synthetic Products

Other synthetic rubber roofing products include:

Neoprene (a DuPont brand name for polychloroprene). Neoprene has been used for roofing and roofing accessories since the late 1950s.

Hypalon, another DuPont product. It is chlorosulfonated polyethylene (CSPE). This product has been used for roofing since 1966.

Chlorinated polyethylene (CPE), a synthetic rubber that has been around since 1964. This one is compatible with asphalts.

Polyisobutylene (PIB), a synthetic rubber that is compatible with asphalt. It has been around since the mid-1970s.

PUF Roofing

Polyurethane Foam (PUF) roofing is popular in some parts of the country. It is also known as SPF roofing (Sprayed Polyurethane Foam). It has been around since the late 1960s. The system is applied as a liquid spray that foams in place. The foam must be protected from sunlight (ultraviolet rays) with acrylic, acrylic latex, or elastomeric coatings that are often surfaced with ceramic granules, for example.

The advantages are a seamless roof system with no flashings and the insulation value of the foam (an approximate R value of 6.5). The lightweight nature of this roof system does not stress existing structures. In some cases, PUF roofing is applied over old systems without tearing them off.

Possible issues with PUF roofing include a lack of adhesion of the coating to the foam and damage from foot traffic, especially on lower-density foams. Bubbling and blistering may appear as a result of moisture trapped in the roof assembly.

Small repairs can be done with caulking. Larger areas have to be re-foamed and coated, after ensuring that the wet foam has been removed and that the substrate is completely dry.

Unless you are very well versed, or are able to find a brand name somewhere, you will be hard pressed to identify the type of synthetic rubber you are looking at. If you can identify it as a synthetic rubber, you are doing well. If not, be careful just to refer to it as "single-ply."

Thermoplastic

There are other single-ply membranes out there as well, such as polyvinyl chloride (PVC) and Thermoplastic Plefin (TPO). These are plastic-based materials rather than synthetic rubber. They are not commonly found on residential roofs.

3.14.1   Conditions

Watch for the following problems on EPDM roofs:

1. Old
2. Openings at seams or flashings
3. Surface cracking/splitting
4. Patches
5. Punctures/tears
6. Ponding/vegetation
7. Discoloration
8. Installation problems, including
   - not well adhered
   - too taut (tenting)
   - fastener problems
   - inadequate slope, causing ponding
   - wrinkles, ridges or fishmouths
   - poor sealing of seams and/or flashings

IMPLICATIONS

The implications of these problems are leakage and the necessity to repair or replace the roof. Many of these conditions have been discussed already in the context of other roof materials. We will comment on just a couple of them, following.

STRATEGY

Discoloration

Look for damage caused by oil, especially around roof-mounted mechanical equipment (e.g., air conditioner).

No Mastic

Asphalt based roofing mastic should not be used for repairs, since it will attack the EPDM.

Installation Problems

EPDM roofs should be inspected in a similar fashion to other flat roof systems. The most common sources of failure on EPDM roofs are openings at the seams or flashings. Also watch for membranes that are tented (stretched too tightly.) Dislocation of plumbing stacks is caused by membrane movement resulting from shrinkage. In some cases, the membrane pulls away from perimeter flashing details. In severe cases, the membrane can pull a parapet wall inward as the membrane shrinks.

Perimeter Fastenings Can Be Taut

Most detailing on modern EPDM roofs calls for positive securement of the membrane to the roof deck, particularly around the perimeters. Mechanically secured membranes may be most susceptible to damage. The membrane can often be seen to be under stress around the fasteners on mechanically fastened roofs.

Splits

Inspectors should be very careful with taut EPDM roofs. Normal foot traffic, for example, may cause the membrane to split because of the high stresses induced by the tension in the membrane. Watch for battens that have been pulled out of the roof or roofing membranes that are slipping out from under battens.

3.15   METAL ROOFING (AGAIN)

We have talked about metal panel roofing with respect to steep roofing. You may wish to refer back to that to refresh your memory with respect to the various metals and their characteristics.

Flat metal roofing is not a common way to cover an entire house roof. However, flat metal roofs are often used for small roof areas, including balconies and decks, bay window and porch roofs and, in some cases, garage roofs. In some areas, flat roofs on older city row houses were often metal.

Materials

While many metals can be used, the most common materials used today are steel and aluminum. The steel is usually galvanized (protected with a zinc coating), aluminum coated, or coated with a combination of aluminum and zinc.

Flat seams were common on flat roofs traditionally, especially with materials like copper, tin and lead. Modern systems typically use standing seams.

3.15.1   Conditions

The conditions you'll encounter include—

1. Leaks
2. Rust
3. Loose or missing fasteners
4. Bent or damaged metal

Leaks

In some cases, you will identify a leak but won't be able to determine the cause. In this case, you'll just have to report it as such and allow a roofer to locate and correct the leak.

Bent or Damaged Metal

Again, the strategy is to envision water trying to get through the roof system. Look at the field of the roof for loose, bent or rusted field panels. Pay attention to seams for possible openings or weaknesses. Where individual panels are more than ten or twelve feet long, look for evidence of open joints, failed fasteners or bent metal because of thermal expansion and contraction.

When a Leak Isn't a Leak

In colder climates, metal roofs are prone to condensation forming on the underside. Because the metal roof deck will be very cold, any warm moist air leaking from inside the house up to the roof is likely to condense on the underside. Evidence of condensation may show up as a widespread problem rather than a localized one. Where the roof seems to have a large number of leaks for no apparent reason, you may suspect condensation. You may want to check with the homeowner, and if the roof only "leaks" in the winter, this points to condensation as the culprit.

No Asphalt Cement

Asphalt cement should not be used as a patching material on metal roofs. These tend to trap water and accelerate the rusting of the metal. Painting of steel, for example, is a much better approach.

3.16   FLAT ROOF FLASHINGS

Flashings on flat roofs are critical, just as they are on steep roofs. Most roof leaks are at the flashings.

Where Flashings Are Needed

While this is oversimplification, flashings are generally needed—

1. Where the roof ends (the roofing material joins another building material)
2. Where the roof is penetrated, for example, by a pipe or a chimney

General Principles

While there are many flashing issues, a few general principles apply to all situations. These include—

1. Shed the water. There should be no dead flat surfaces in the field of the roof, on top of the chimneys, at the top of parapet walls, at the top of mechanical equipment, etc.

2. Lower materials should be covered by higher materials. Since water flows downhill according to gravity (for the most part), all intersections and details should have the upper material covering or overlapping the lower material.

3. Fasteners should be concealed. If exposed, screws are better than nails.
   - screws should have neoprene washers.
   - screw heads should be caulked as a regular maintenance item.
   - all exposed fasteners should be on vertical rather than horizontal surfaces.

4. All materials must be compatible. Asphalt is not compatible with PVC, and aluminum flashings are not compatible with masonry, for example.

5. Build in redundancy. A "belt and suspenders" approach should be used. Caulking is a temporary material and can be used as the backup watertight joint, but should never be the only watertight joint. This principle is often violated in residential construction.

6. Allow for movement. Metal will expand and contract. Buildings, including their roofs, will deflect with wind loads as well as rain and snow loads.

FIGURE 3.29 Built-Up Flat Roof/Wall Flashing

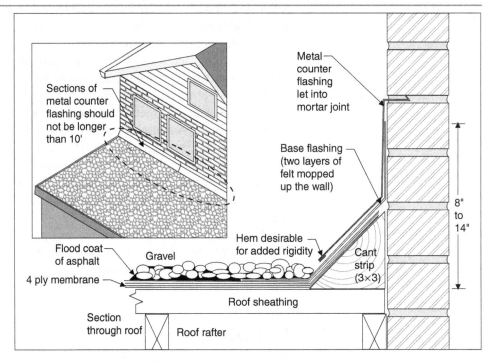

7. Make as few roof penetrations as possible.

- every roof penetration requires a flashing detail and is a possible source of leakage.

- group several roof penetrations together in one box, where possible. This reduces the number of areas susceptible to leakage.

8. Keep roof penetrations away from roof edges. Adequate flashing requires room. Generally speaking, all penetrations should be 18 inches away from roof perimeters, walls or other penetrations.

Residentially, it is rare to find flashings that follow all of these principles or are ideally installed. Our description here of how to do it right won't show up in the field very often. In most cases you are forced to make a judgment call on installations that are not textbook.

Base and Counter Flashings

Wherever a flat roof is penetrated or meets taller building components (a second story wall, parapet walls, chimneys, skylights, etc.) the roof has to be turned up and in effect acts as a large tray. The base and counter flashings make the transition from the membrane to the adjoining material (a masonry or concrete wall, or a metal stack, for example).

Cant Strips

With built-up roofing and modified bitumen, cant strips are used at 90-degree intersections (see Figure 3.29). These are triangular blocks of wood or fiberboard typically, that allow the roofing membrane to make two 45-degree turns rather than one 90-degree turn as the membrane goes up a wall. This makes the membrane less likely to crack at the change in direction.

The roofing membrane typically extends up the cant strip and may go beyond. It may or may not be mopped into the vertical wall.

F I G U R E   3.30   Modified Bitumen Roof/Wall

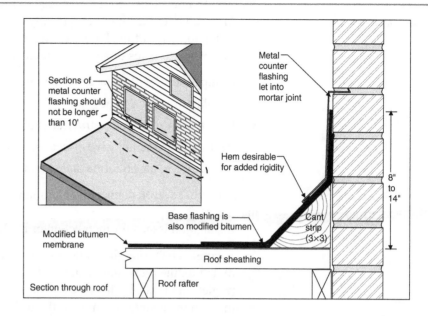

Base Flashing

The base flashing forms a watertight joint to the roof membrane at the bottom and extends up the vertical wall to a point well above the highest expected depth of water (usually eight to 14 inches above the roof deck). The top of base flashing is not sealed to the wall to make a watertight joint. Characteristics of good base flashings include—

1. Resistance to heat and ultraviolet light from the sun

2. Resistance to puncture and to the abrasive effects of wind, rain, and hail

3. Compatibility with the roofing membrane and wall surface

4. The ability to resist slipping or sagging in a vertical or near vertical orientation

5. Flexibility to absorb some movement, especially where differential movement between the roof and wall may occur

6. Resistance to air pollution, chemicals, and roof vegetation

Base flashings are not intended to hold the roof membrane in place. Roof membranes should be secured in place, as necessary, through means independent of the flashings.

Base Flashing Materials

Base flashing materials commonly include—

1. Roofing felts

2. Fabric reinforced asphalt products

3. Modified bitumens

4. Synthetic rubbers (e.g., neoprene)

With modified bitumen, EPDM and PVC, the base flashing materials are very often the same as the roofing material (Figure 3.30). They are installed and bonded to the roofing membrane and the vertical substrates in whatever manner the rest of the membrane is secured (adhesive, hot mopping or torching, for example).

In some cases, the rubber or plastic products will act as both the base and counter flashing. This shortcut can lead to premature failures.

Counter Flashings

Metal counter flashings are typically attached only to the vertical surface. This makes the top edge of the base flashing watertight simply by overlapping it.

The characteristics of a good counter flashing are—

1. Compatibility with adjacent materials
2. Rigidity to remain in position
3. Resistance to heat and ultraviolet light from the sun
4. Resistance to the abrasive effects of water, wind and hail
5. Resistance to air pollution and chemical contamination

Common Counter Flashing Materials

Galvanized steel, copper and aluminum are the most common counter flashing materials.

Installation issues for metal counter flashings include:

1. Securely anchoring the metal into the wall (This is most appropriately done by letting the metal into a one- or two-inch-deep mortar joint or recess (reglet) in the wall. This is less desirably done by screwing a fastening bar through the counter flashing to the wall, and least desirably done by face screwing or nailing the counter flashing to the wall.)
2. Individual pieces of metal should be no longer than ten feet
3. Metal should be fastened at least every 24 inches
4. Joints in metal should be made with a standing seam or locked joints
5. Exposed edges should be turned over 180° to form a rigid hem that leaves no sharp metal exposed
6. Where extending over the top of a wall, flashings should not present a flat surface that may pond water
7. No exposed fasteners in near-horizontal surfaces
8. The bottom of the metal should be above the standing water height

Termination Bar or Clamping Bar

Modified bitumen, EPDM and PVC roofs typically employ the roof membrane material as base flashing, and conventional metal as a counter flashing (see Figure 3.31). With PVC and EPDM, metal counter flashings are sometimes replaced with metal bars called **termination bars** or **clamping bars.** These bars hold the top part of the flashing against the wall. The joint at the top of the flashing is sealed with caulking.

3.16.1   Common Flashing Locations

A discussion of flashing installation details is beyond the scope of this book. Here, we will briefly describe several common situations where flat roof flashing might be required. An in-depth discussion can be found in *Principles of Home Inspection: Roofing.*

Roof Perimeter Flashings

At the edge of a roof, the slope may remain constant, or there may be a curb or parapet wall around the perimeter of the roof. This depends on whether or not the roof is intended to drain water off the edge. If the roof is intended to drain, the slope will not change at the edge. If the roof is tar and gravel or any system with loose rock

FIGURE 3.31   EPDM or PVC Roof/Wall Flashing

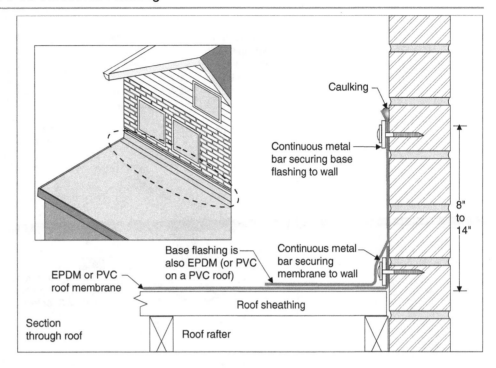

or gravel on top, and there is no curb or parapet wall, there should be a gravel stop to prevent the gravel from being carried off the edge of the roof (see Figure 3.32).

As the roof ends, it has to be terminated somehow. It's typical for the membrane to be turned slightly down over the edge of the roof.

Gravel Stop

Metal **drip edge** flashing is typically used to protect the exposed membrane end. This flashing has a horizontal component that extends onto the roof surface and a vertical component that extends down from the roof, covering the end of the roof membrane, and the top of the wall.

Drip Edge Flashing

Walls

It is common for flat roofs to terminate against walls that are higher than the roof. For example, a one-story garage with a flat roof may be attached to a two-story house. Parapet walls are another example.

A base flashing and counter flashing are typically used (Figure 3.33). If the membrane is asphalt (built-up or mod bit), a cant strip is typically used. This wood or fiberboard triangular piece (typically three inches horizontal and three inches tall) is used to allow the membrane to make two 45° turns rather than one 90° turn. This makes the membrane less susceptible to cracking. The roof membrane typically extends onto the cant strip, but not up onto the vertical wall surface.

Chimneys

Chimney flashings ideally employ a base and counter flashing. For the purposes of flashing, the chimney can be thought of as short walls. One of the shortcuts often taken with chimneys (and walls as well for that matter), is simply to extend the roofing membrane up the vertical wall surface. Sometimes no base flashing is used and sometimes there is no cant strip. Both of these practices make the system weaker and more susceptible to leakage.

F I G U R E 3.32   Built-Up Roofing Membrane-Edge Details

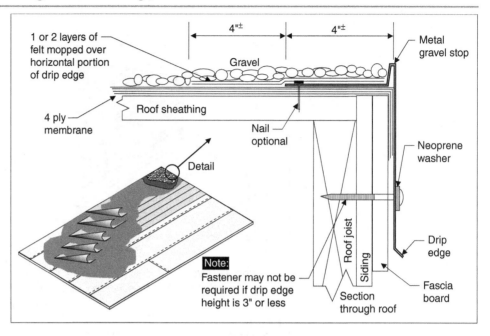

Caps

High-quality chimneys have through-wall flashings at the caps, although this is rare residentially. You should be looking for chimney caps that are sloped to provide drainage (Figure 3.34). Gaps or cracks in caps that allow water into the masonry should be noted. You should tell your client to seal these to prevent water entry.

Caps should project at least one inch beyond the chimney face to reduce wetting of the chimney.

Skylights

On flat roofs, skylights should typically be on 8-inch-high curbs (Figure 3.35). This allows room to provide a cant strip and to provide a base flashing which extends

F I G U R E 3.33   Built-Up Flat Roof/Wall

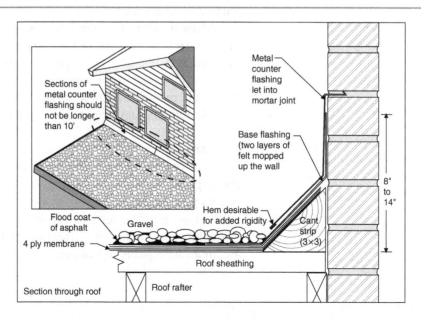

F I G U R E 3.34   Chimney Cap Details

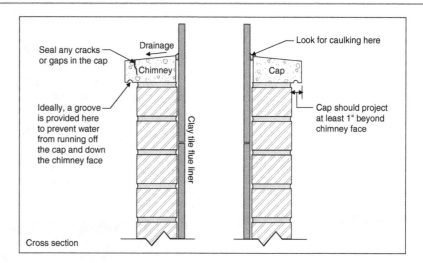

Seal any cracks or gaps in the cap

Drainage

Look for caulking here

Chimney

Cap

Clay tile flue liner

Ideally, a groove is provided here to prevent water from running off the cap and down the chimney face

Cap should project at least 1" beyond chimney face

Cross section

up to the top of the curb. The curb height should always be greater than the highest level that water may accumulate on the roof.

The base flashing often extends up and drapes over the top of the curb. The counter flashing will also often extend up over the top of the curb. The skylight frame is then dropped on, covering the counter flashing and the base flashing below. The skylight is typically mechanically fastened in through the sides of the curb. Screw heads are ideally sealed with caulking. Lift up on the skylight to make sure it's well secured.

Stack Vents or Pipes

Circular penetrations through flat roofs are found on almost every home. These are treated slightly differently than walls. Typically, the roof membrane is laid right up to the base of the pipe or stack. The membrane is not turned up on the stack. A sleeve (stack jack) that is just slightly larger than the outside diameter of the stack is slipped down over the stack. At the bottom of the sleeve is a flat flange that projects out about three inches all the way around. This flange is mopped into the top of the membrane and stripped in with additional layers of roofing felts, or pieces of the roofing membrane if it's a single-ply system (Figure 3.36).

Rectangular or Irregular Shaped Roof Penetrations

Sometimes angle irons or I-beams penetrate roofs. These are very difficult to flash and should be avoided, where possible. In some cases, the only solution to sealing around an irregularly shaped roof penetration is to create a metal box typically about three inches tall with a 3-inch horizontal flange sticking out all the way around the bottom. The box surrounds the penetration and is stripped into the roof with stack flashings.

Pitch Pockets or Pitch Pans

The metal box is then filled with a flexible roofing material. In the old days, pitch was used; today a cold asphalt mastic is used. These pitch pockets are generally not satisfactory and require lots of maintenance to keep them watertight. The flexible material tends to shrink, dry out and crack. The pitch pocket or pitch pan has to be kept full and should be sloped so that water drains away. Otherwise, water will pond in the pan, and leakage is almost inevitable when this happens.

F I G U R E 3.35   Skylight in Flat Roof

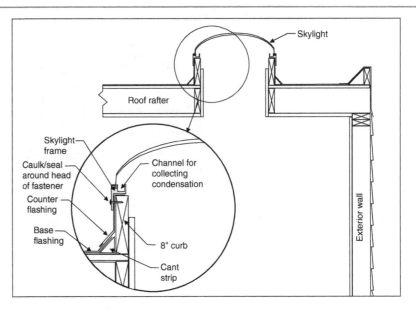

Internal Drains

Internal drains are typically connected to pipes that go down through the house and discharge into a storm sewer. These are often laid into a roof similar to how a stack vent flashing is installed, except that the flange is at the top, and the sleeve extends down below the membrane inside the roof drain in the building.

The roof membrane is laid up to the edge of the drain opening. The drain, which includes a 3-inch flange around the top, is set into the membrane and then stripped in.

Scuppers

Primary and Secondary

Scuppers are simply openings through parapet walls or perimeter curbs that allow water to drain into a downspout running down the exterior of the building. Scuppers are essentially a continuation of the roof membrane. The scupper itself is usually surrounded with a metal box that acts as a flashing and allows water to run through the wall. Good roofing practice includes having primary scuppers at the elevation of the roofing membrane, and secondary scuppers about two inches above, to act as emergency drains in case the primary scuppers are obstructed.

Flat Roofs That Drain onto Steep Roofs Below

Where a flat roof is located above a steep roof, the proper detail is to provide a gravel stop at the top and a counter flashing that extends down over the steep roof for several inches. If the slope of the steep roof is relatively low and wind-driven rain is a risk, a base flashing can be provided that extends from the flat roof membrane down across the sloped roof under the counter flashing. Ice and Water Shield is commonly used for such a transition.

The gravel stop in this case may be used not only to prevent the gravel from escaping off the flat roof, but also to prevent asphalt from flowing off the edge of the flat roof down across the steep roof.

Steep Roofs That Drain onto Flat Roofs Below

Where there is a steep roof discharging onto a flat roof, the flat roof membrane should extend about three feet up under the steep roofing shingles or tiles (Figure 3.37).

F I G U R E 3.36   "Stack Jack" Plumbing Stack Flashing

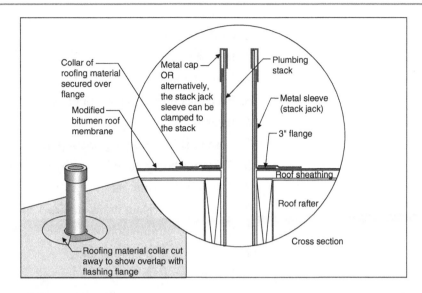

Depending on the material, the shingles may extend down to the flat membrane, but if rigid tiles are used, they should not contact the membrane for fear of piercing it during differential building movement.

Some roofers like to use a metal flashing extending up the steep roof a few inches. This recognizes the possibility that water and/or snow may accumulate at the junction between the flat and steep roof, and many steep roofing materials are not intended to be wet over the long term. Where this detail is used, the top of the metal is overlaid by the shingles or tiles.

3.16.2   Conditions

Now we'll look at what goes wrong with flat roof flashings.

IMPLICATIONS

The implications of the following conditions are roof leakage.

F I G U R E 3.37   Sloped Roof Draining onto Flat Roof

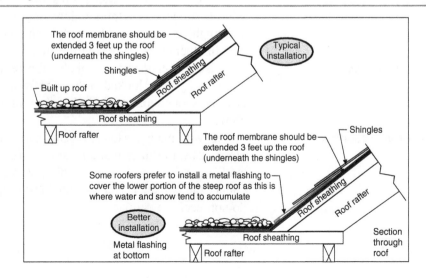

Common flashing problems include—

1. Leaks
2. Old/worn out
3. Rusted metal
4. Loose/bent/sections missing
5. Flashings open at seams or ends
6. Patches
7. Base flashings sagging or slipping
8. Flashings being pulled away by the membrane
9. Fasteners backing out
10. Caulking or sealant dried out/cracked
11. Clamps or termination bars loose
12. Pitch pockets not filled, and
13. Installation problems, including—

- all or part of the flashing assembly may be missing
- incompatible materials (aluminum flashings let into masonry mortar joints or asphalt based products contacting PVC)
- wrong materials for the job (e.g., metal that is too light a gauge)
- flashings too short
- flashings not well secured
- no allowance for expansion and contraction of metal flashings
- exposed fasteners on horizontal surfaces
- horizontal surfaces created that will pond water
- wall counter flashings not let into reglets
- no cant strips for asphalt based products at vertical intersections

Let's take a closer look at installation problems.

Installation Problems

STRATEGY

When inspecting a roof, more time should be spent looking at the flashings than the field of the roof. This discussion should make you sensitive to the many problems with flashings. It is helpful to think of yourself as wind-driven water and see where you might be able to get through flashing details. In some cases, defects are obvious. In other cases, they are invisible.

Look from Inside

Like any other portion of the roof inspection, your flashing inspection is not complete until you've looked at the roof from below. Only from here can you confirm any suspicions about weak flashings, or discover problems that were not visible from above.

Identifying Poor Work

As with many systems, flashings are often poorly installed but do not leak. In other cases, flashings that appear to be first class, do leak. Where you can find no evidence of leakage, but the flashing work is clearly low quality, you should tell the client exactly that. The client should be prepared for flashing problems so that you do not receive a callback.

Leaks—A Final Word   Leaks in flat roofs can be difficult to find because they will often show up on the interior, some distance from the failure point in the roof. Water may travel horizontally along plastic vapor barriers, for example, before coming through ceilings.

Inspector in the House: The Daredevil Client

My clients appeared to be a typical young couple with a toddler in tow. The wife had gone into the house with the real estate agent, leaving Dad and the youngster outside. I said I would get up on the roof to check it out, and be right back. When I got back to the side of the roof where my ladder was, I was horrified to see the husband at the top of my ladder, carrying his toddler in one arm!

I now instruct clients not to follow me up the ladder. Climbing up ladders is much easier than climbing down, and crawling up roofs is much easier than crawling down.

REVIEW QUESTIONS

1. List the three main functions of roofs.

2. The roof covering is typically part of the structure of the home.

    True   False

3. What is the fundamental difference in strategy between a flat roof surface- and a sloped roof surface?

4. Is a sloped roof waterproof? Explain.

5. What is the pitch of the roof and how is it usually expressed?

6. What is the overall goal of the roof inspection? (List four points)

7. Even if you walk on the roof and inspect every inch, there are limitations to your inspection. Explain.

8. Why can a minor leak be more of a problem than a major one?

9. List nine common roof problems you'll find.

10. On a 10-year-old house, how old would you expect the roof surface to be?

11. What are the causes of aging? Try to recall as many as you can.

12. Which side of a roof will wear faster in climates where ultraviolet light is the main aging factor?

13. In general, is there a higher risk of leakage at a patched area of roof?

14. Anything that restricts the drainage of water is a vulnerable area. Give as many examples as you can.

15. What things might you see that suggest patching has been done on a roof?

16. Once a roof is installed, can you see all of the important installation details?

17. What is an ice dam?

18. What causes an ice dam?

19. Which of the following roofs are most prone to ice dams?

    a. A steep sloped roof with a wide soffit

    b. A low-slope roof with a narrow soffit

    c. A low-slope roof with a wide soffit

20. What areas of the roof are most prone to ice dams?

21. List the clues that a house may have had or may be prone to ice damming. These clues may be evident in the summer as well.

22. What are three possible actions to minimize ice damming?

23. Which is the best of the three options above?

24. What are the drawbacks to adding a second layer of roofing over a first?

25. Where can you look on a roof to determine the number of layers?

26. What are the three parts of an asphalt shingle?

27. What is the typical life expectancy of an asphalt shingle roof?

28. List six common failure modes for asphalt shingles.

29. What things do you look for to determine whether the shingles are old?

30. What is the implication of driving nails or staples too deep?

31. What is the implication of not driving nails or staples deep enough?

32. You will never find three layers of asphalt shingles on a roof.

True   False

33. What are the common failure modes for wood shingles and shakes?

34. In what part of the roof are missing shingles or shakes most likely?

35. Slate (choose two answers)

  a.   is a natural product

  b.   is a manufactured product

  c.   lasts longer than asphalt shingles

  d.   doesn't last as long as wood

  e.   is lighter than wood

36. Slate roofs are among the most expensive to install and maintain.

True   False

37. Give four reasons for slate roof failure.

38. Should you walk on slate roofs?

Yes   No

39. Name three poor slate repair methods.

40. What things suggest that the slate is near the end of its life?

41. What general shapes are clay tiles likely to be? (Give two.)

42. What's the difference between a Spanish tile and Mission tile?

43. You should always walk on clay tile roofs.

True   False

44. Give eight conditions to watch for on clay tile roofs.

45. What shapes are concrete tile?

46. What conditions should you watch for? (List eight.)

47. Should inspectors walk on concrete roofs?

48. Fiber-cement shingles contain some of the same components as concrete tiles.

True   False

49. Fiber-cement shingles can be bent without breaking.

True   False

50. Metal roofs are commonly what materials?

51. Six common problems on metal roofs are _____.

52. Another name for roll roofing is _____.

53. Roll roofing is most similar to what other material we've discussed?

54. Roll roofing is commonly used in what flashing detail?

55. What are the common failure modes for roll roofing? (Name four.)

56. Is it more common for a roof to leak at the flashings or at other areas in the roof surface?

57. List as many common flashing materials as you can.

58. List at least five areas where flashings are found.

59. Are valley flashings a watertight or shedding type of flashing?

60. Why should open valleys widen at the bottom? (Two reasons)

61. What are the two common materials that are used for open valley flashing?

62. What are the two types of closed valleys?

63. Give at least three typical valley flashing conditions.

64. What is the best spot from which to inspect the installation of the valley flashing?

65. What are the implications of a valley flashing problem?

66. List as many valley flashing installation problems as you can.

67. A flashing is not required on the bottom edge of the chimney.

True   False

68. Is caulking an acceptable substitute to letting the flashing into the mortar joints?

Yes   No

Why or why not?

69. List as many common masonry chimney flashing conditions as you can.

70. What is the implication of poor chimney flashings?

71. Is your chimney inspection finished when you get off the roof?

Why or why not?

72. Pipe flashings might be found at which roof penetrations?

73. Common stack flashing materials are _____.

74. Common stack flashing conditions include:

75. Roof/sidewall flashings are similar to what flashing we discussed earlier?

76. Step flashings should be nailed to

the wall   the roof   both   either

77. When roof/sidewall flashing is installed, the wood siding can be used as the counter flashing. Why is it considered good practice to keep the siding slightly away from the roof surface? What is the recommended clearance?

78. Roof/sidewall flashings are sometimes improperly installed. Give three examples of typical installation defects:

79. Where a steep roof meets a masonry wall at the side, counter flashing should be used. The counter flashing should be nailed or bolted securely to the face of the brick wall and the joint filled with caulking.

True False

80. Common roof/sidewall flashing materials include:

81. Which metal flashing material is not compatible with masonry mortar, according to some authorities?

82. The primary implication of sidewall flashing problems is _____.

83. Roofs intersecting walls above need flashings similar to _____.

84. Top quality flashings at roofs meeting a masonry wall above are two-piece flashings. Most are _____-piece on homes.

85. Nailing flashings to both the roof and the wall is

    a.   better because it holds the flashing securely.

    b.   worse because it doesn't allow for movement of the wall and roof.

86. Exposed nail heads through the metal flashing into the roof may result in:

87. Some ridge flashing systems have a second function, not related to keeping the roof watertight. What is it?

88. Common hip and ridge conditions include:

89. Fasteners on hips and ridges should be mostly

    a.   exposed

    b.   concealed

90. There are two types of double glazing systems on skylights. Hermetically sealed and _____.

91. Which type of skylight is most likely to be successful, a skylight mounted on a curb or a skylight that is mounted directly on the roof?

On curb   On roof

92. Windows should not be used as skylights. Anything that has more than a _____ degree slope off vertical should not be treated as a window.

93. List as many common skylight conditions as you can.

94. Leaking skylights can lead to structural problems.

True   False

95. Can ice damming be an issue on skylights?

Yes   No

96. During an inspection, you should never lift on the edge of a skylight.

True   False

97. On an interior inspection of a skylight, you might use

    a.   your eyes

    b.   a ladder

    c.   a moisture meter

    d.   both (a) and (b)

    e.   all of the above

98. Is a flat roof system a "shedding" system or a "watertight" system?

Shedding   Watertight

99. Why is it often difficult to identify flaws in the membrane of a built-up roof?

100. What is the purpose of the asphalt, and the felts, in a built-up roof?

101. What is the purpose of the flood coat on a built-up roof?

102. What is the purpose of the gravel on a built-up roof?

103. We have discussed 13 conditions relating to the membrane of a built-up roof. List as many as you can.

104. Is it good practice to apply new built-up roof membranes over old?

Yes   No

105. Any roof that still has water on it _____ hours after a rain is defined as a "ponding" roof.

106. Give two implications of a ponding roof.

107. If it has not rained in a long time, and there is no ponding at the time of the inspection, what are other clues that might lead you to believe that the roof has experienced some ponding?

108. What is the main implication of exposed felts?

109. If you are looking at a single-ply roof surface with a granular surface, what are some clues to differentiate modified bitumen from roll roofing?

110. List nine common problems you'll find on modified bitumen roofs. Don't count installation problems.

111. List six common installation mistakes on modified bitumen roofing.

112. For an EPDM single-ply roof, what is the typical flashing material?

113. EPDM is a kind of:

Plastic   Rubber

114. The most common sources of failure on EPDM roofs are _____ and flashings.

115. Asphalt-based roofing mastic should not be used for repairs on EPDM. Why?

116. A metal surface is a common and inexpensive way to cover large flat roofs.

True   False

117. List at least four different types of metal that have been used for flat roofing.

118. What conditions are commonly found on EPDM, PVC and metal (excluding installation problems)?

a.   EPDM - give 7   **b.**   PVC - give 10

c.   metal - give 6

119. On steep roofs, the most common area for leakage to occur is at the flashings. Where is the most common area for leakage on a flat roof?

120. Why would you not want aluminum flashing on masonry?

121. What is a cant strip and where is it used?

122. The base flashing on a flat roof is a "shedding system."

True   False

123. On a flat roof flashing system, the counter flashing is typically attached to the:

Vertical surface   Horizontal surface

124. When a skylight is installed on a flat roof, an 8-inch-high curb is built for the skylight frame to sit on. Does the skylight frame go over the base flashing or does the base flashing extend up the sides of the skylight frame?

125. What is the purpose of a "pitch pocket"?

126. What is the purpose of a secondary scupper?

127. When a steep roof drains onto a flat roof, the flat roof membrane should extend about _____ feet up under the steep roofing shingles or tiles.

128. List twelve common flashing problems (excluding installation problems).

129. List ten common flashing installation problems.

STRUCTURE

LEARNING OBJECTIVES

By the end of this chapter you should be able to:

- define dead loads and live loads
- list twelve common foundation problems
- list four types of cracks, their characteristics and implications
- describe how crack size can be misleading
- know how to identify pier movement
- understand the function of sills and common sill problems
- list common problems with columns and their implications
- describe the function of beams and common problems associated with them
- list eleven common joist problems
- list nine subflooring problems
- list five concrete floor problems
- list six common problems with masonry walls in addition to cracks
- list seven common wood frame wall problems
- list ten common masonry veneer wall problems
- list eight common header problems
- define rafters, roof joists and ceiling joists and identify the common problems associated with each
- identify different types of trusses, including functions and typical conditions associated with them
- know the function of sheathing, the types available, and common conditions associated with it

INTRODUCTION

Not a Design Review

Not Code Inspection

House Stays Put

Support Live Loads

Home inspectors are often guilty of superficial structural inspections, because structural defects are less common than defects in other areas. However, structural conditions are often the most serious and expensive to correct. In some cases, correction cannot be accomplished cost-effectively and the home may be lost.

Your work as a home inspector is to evaluate the performance of the house structure. On new houses, there isn't much performance over time that you can evaluate, and so you must default to generally accepted building practices, and point out deviations from them. While home inspectors don't do code inspections, a knowledge of code requirements for residential construction is very helpful.

In houses that have been around a few years, you will be looking to see whether the structure is responding satisfactorily. In most cases, this means staying put. While all structures move slightly (they must to carry their loads), the amount of movement should not—

- cause failure of interior finishes
- put undue stress on joints or individual components
- affect the usability and operation of house systems (windows shouldn't jam, pipes shouldn't be broken, electrical wires shouldn't be pulled, etc.)

Perhaps most importantly, the structure should safely support the live loads imposed upon it. Structures that are unsound may allow people to fall, or may crush people.

4.1   FOOTINGS AND FOUNDATIONS

Put simply, the function of a structure is to do nothing. The most successful structures stay still. We will begin our look at structure with footings and foundations.

4.1.1   Fundamentals

We can look at footings and foundations as having two functions:

1. To transfer the live and dead loads of the building to the soil over a large enough area so that neither the soil nor the building will move, and
2. In areas where frost occurs, prevent frost from moving the building.

Dead Loads

Live Loads

Direction of Loads

Dead loads are the weight of the building materials and the soil surrounding the foundations.

Live loads include the weight of people, furniture, snow, rain and wind. Wind may be a vertical force downward, a horizontal force, or an uplift force. A live load may also be exerted by water in the soil around the foundations. Wet soil exerts much more force than dry soil. Frozen soil exerts much more force than wet soil. Expansive soils can exert tremendous force when wet.

The weight of objects is caused by gravity and results in a vertical downward load. Wind can be in any direction, as mentioned earlier. The soil exerts forces in all directions, but foundations usually see the horizontal thrust of the soil on the outside of the foundation wall. The forces of frost are also in all directions. Most frost failures in buildings include horizontal movement (foundation walls cracking, bowing or collapsing inwards) and frost heaving (upward movement of the build-

FIGURE 4.1   Evidence of Frost Heaving

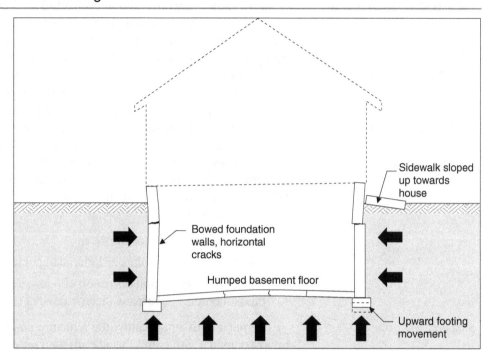

Sidewalk sloped up towards house

Bowed foundation walls, horizontal cracks

Humped basement floor

Upward footing movement

ing as the soil under the building expands due to frost, as shown in Figure 4.1). Expansive soil problems are similar to frost problems.

Soils

Soil Quality Is the Key

Buildings rely on the soil beneath them to stay put. If the soil under the house moves up, down, or sideways, the house is in trouble. Designers or engineers may know quite a bit about the soil conditions at a site and may design the building exactly for those. More commonly, soil conditions are assumed to be a certain type, and footings and foundations are designed with a margin of safety to account for adverse soil conditions, within reasonable limits. Occasionally we guess wrong and the building moves, but for an average site, it costs more to find out how good the soil is over the whole site than to design a system that will work on most soils.

Frost

The Strategy Varies

Have you ever wondered why there are basements in houses in the northern part of North America but not in the southern parts? The answer lies in one word—**frost.** Frost expands soil and exerts tremendous pressure. Frost-induced pressures can lift houses up or push foundation walls in. If you are building in the north, you have to

Basements Where There's Frost

dig down far enough to get below the **frost line**—this is the depth to which frost penetrates into the soil. That's where the footings should be. The foundations have to be tall enough to extend up through the soil above the grade, so we can put the house on top of the foundation. Since we have to dig a trench for the footings and foundations, we may as well create a hole and use the below grade space. That's how basements were invented.

Slab-On-Grade or Crawlspaces Where There's No Frost

If the building is not likely to see frost to any great depth, there's little risk of the building heaving. As a result, the weight of the building can be spread out on footings near the surface. Adding a basement becomes quite expensive. The living space is typically all above grade in areas where frost is not an issue.

FIGURE 4.2 Slab-on-Grade—Floating Slab

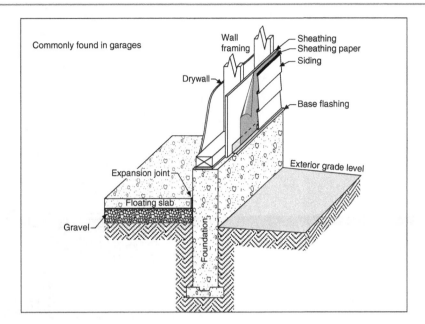

4.1.2   Basements, Crawlspaces, and Slab-On-Grade

There are three common configurations for foundations: Basements, crawlspaces, and slab-on-grade.

Crawlspaces may be built very similarly to basements. They may have continuous perimeter foundations or they may have piers. **Slab-on-grade** refers to a concrete floor slab poured at grade level. These slabs may be supported on continuous foundations, piers or piles and grade beams, or grade beams directly on isolated footings, for example. These foundations often serve as the building floor, as well as the support for the house loads.

Floor slabs may be:

Floating
1. Floating—supported by the ground and independent of perimeter foundations (Figure 4.2).

Supported
2. Supported—the floor slab may be integrated into the foundation system for the building (Figure 4.3). In this case, the foundations support the slab.

Monolithic
3. Monolithic—the slab may be an integral part of the footing (Figure 4.4).

Slabs are typically concrete and may be reinforced, depending on how they're built. Slabs may be thickened, typically on the underside, to support the weight of interior loadbearing members such as columns. Alternatively, the column may go through the slab, and a separate footing may be provided for the column.

4.1.3   Footing and Foundation Types

Spread Footings
This leads us to the configuration of footings. Houses may have spread footings (strip footings) that support the perimeter walls (Figure 4.5). These footings are wide pads that are continuous around the perimeter of the house. In some cases, the pads may be widened and/or thickened to accommodate concentrated loads (a lot of weight in one small area) from fireplaces, pilasters, etc.

FIGURE 4.3   Slab-on-Grade—Supported Slab

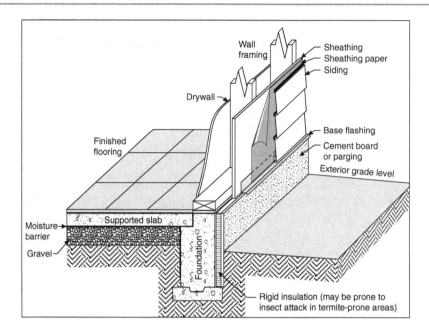

Pilasters

A **pilaster** is a thickening of a foundation wall. It may be thickened to receive the concentrated load of a beam resting on top of the pilaster, or it may be acting as a stiffener to prevent the foundation wall from bowing inward.

Pad Footings

Pad footings are similar to continuous footings except they are usually under a single pier or column. Pad footings spread the load out, usually in a square, with the column or pier sitting in the middle of the square. It's common for houses to have strip footings around the perimeter and pad footings on the building interior under columns.

FIGURE 4.4   Slab-on-Grade—Monolithic Slab

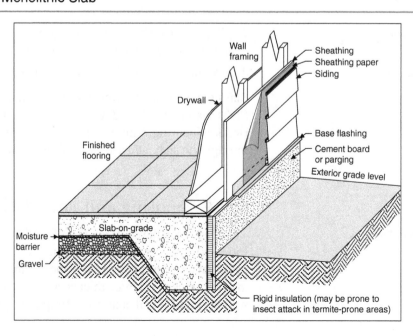

FIGURE 4.5   Strip Footings and Pad Footings

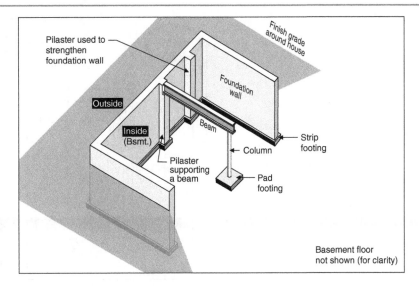

Piles

Piles are used instead of footings, typically where the soil quality is poor (Figure 4.6). They are, generally speaking, more expensive to install and have to be driven into the ground with specialized equipment. They can work one of two ways:

Endbearing

1. Piles can be driven down to a point where they bear on bedrock or other sound substrate.

Friction

2. Piles can be driven into soil far enough that the friction of the soil against the sides of the pile is enough to resist any downward movement.

Incidentally, if a house is supported on piles, they probably won't be visible and you may not know it.

FIGURE 4.6   Pile Foundations

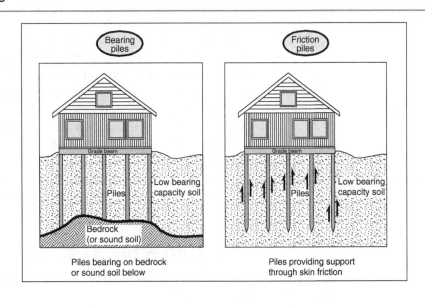

FIGURE 4.7   Pier Foundations

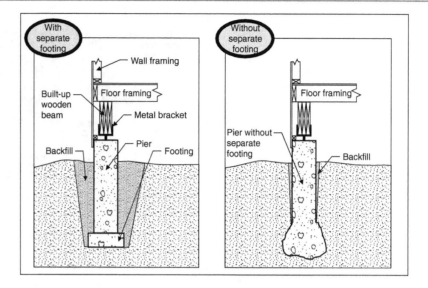

Piers

Piers are columns that may be completely concealed in the soil, or may project above (Figure 4.7). You probably are familiar with the piers that are commonly used to build exterior wood decks and porches. These piers may be poured concrete, often with the concrete poured into a cardboard cylinder in a hole dug in the ground. Piers usually, but not always, have footings. Piers can either be thought of as posts or columns, or can be thought of as short piles that bear on their ends.

Grade Beams

Grade beams are usually concrete beams that are supported on footings, piles or piers and are located at grade. In some cases, they extend below grade, and usually extend only slightly above grade. Grade beams transfer the loads from the building down to the footings or piles.

Caissons

Caissons are foundation systems created by drilling holes and filling them with concrete. A caisson pile is a cast-in-place pile that has a hollow tube driven into the ground. The earth is excavated from the tube, and concrete is poured into the tube. Some caisson piles are flared out at the bottom to create a larger bearing surface. These are sometimes called bell caissons.

Materials

Footings and foundations should be strong so they can transfer loads, and durable with respect to exposure from air, water, soil and insect attack. Most modern footings are concrete (sometimes reinforced) Footings on older buildings may be brick or stone. While we won't talk much about preserved wood foundation systems, these systems sometimes employ a wood footing.

Foundations

Foundations may be concrete, concrete block, cinder block, brick, hollow clay tile (terra cotta), stone (either dry laid or laid in mortar) or wood. Wood was common on very old buildings and has become common where preserved wood foundations are used.

Piles and Piers

Piles are typically concrete, steel or wood. Again, you likely won't see these. Piers might be wood, concrete, concrete block, brick or stone.

4.1.4   Inspection Tips

Before looking at specific conditions of foundations, a couple of general inspection tips are in order.

No Access Into Crawlspaces

Lack of access to a part of a house structure that you ordinarily would see is a red flag. You should document the limitations to your inspection and make your client understand that you couldn't do everything you normally do. This is important because problems that are concealed tend to get ignored. If you can't get into the crawlspace, chances are no one has been in there. Considerable damage or distress may have developed over time. If you fail to make it clear to clients that you couldn't get into a crawlspace, which is important, you'll probably regret it eventually.

Look Inside and Out

As with exteriors and roofing, you have to look at the outside and inside to complete your structure inspection. In many cases, after having looked outside, you'll see something inside. There is nothing wrong with going back outside to have a second look.

4.1.5 Conditions

Common problems found on foundations include:

1. Cracks
2. Bowed, bulging or leaning
3. Mortar deterioration
4. Spalling material
5. Rot
6. Piers moving or deteriorating
7. Pilasters or buttresses pulling away
8. Cold joints
9. Honeycombing
10. Prior repairs
11. Foundation too short
12. Foundation too thin (laterally unsupported)

We'll look more closely at all of the conditions, but let's start with cracking, because it is the most common.

Cracks

Four Types of Cracks

We'll look at four types of foundation wall cracks:

- shrinkage cracks
- settlement cracks
- heaving cracks
- horizontal force cracks

Shrinkage Cracks

Shrinkage cracks are caused by the natural curing of concrete.

IMPLICATIONS

There are usually no structural implications to shrinkage cracks. The foundation wall may leak through shrinkage cracks, which is a nuisance but not a major structural problem.

STRATEGY

Shrinkage cracks are common with poured concrete foundation walls and floors. The cracks usually occur early in the life of the building when the concrete is still curing. While concrete cures for a number of years after it is poured, the majority of the curing takes place early on. Shrinkage cracks usually show up within the first year.

Vertical and Diagonal Cracks Are Common

The most common foundation wall shrinkage cracks are vertical or diagonal. The bottom part of the foundation is restrained by the footing and is less likely to open up due to shrinkage cracking.

Identifying Shrinkage Cracks

Shrinkage cracks typically do not extend into footings or into the structure above. They do not reflect movement of the overall building, simply movement of the foundation component.

Shrinkage cracks do not necessarily have corresponding cracks elsewhere in the building. Cracks due to differential settlement usually do have corresponding cracks in different locations.

Below Windows

Shrinkage cracks, as well as settlement cracks, usually occur at stress concentration points in the wall. Cracks most often radiate down from corners of basement windows.

Crack Size

Shrinkage cracks are usually relatively small, less than $1/8$ inch in width.

Settlement Cracks

Differential Settlement

When one part of the house settles and the rest does not, or two parts settle at different rates, cracking develops. This can be alarming and may or may not be a serious structural problem.

Uniform Settlement

All houses settle when they are built. If the settlement is uniform, there are usually no problems. The house settles slightly as a unit, and since everything moves together, there is no internal stress and no cracking.

Severe Uniform Settlement

Occasionally, uniform settlement can be a problem when the settlement is so dramatic that gas, water and electrical lines are strained and may break. In very severe cases, the foundations may drop to a point where the bottom of wood walls may get their feet in the dirt. Rot can result. This kind of dramatic uniform settlement is rare.

Tipping

There is a type of settlement that is not uniform, but not typically differential either. When a building tips, one part of the building settles more than another; however, the building holds together and no cracks develop. In some cases, no major structural problems develop, although if the building leans to a point where it is no longer stable, or the floors slope to the point where the usability of the house is affected, it can be serious.

Tower of Pisa

The Leaning Tower of Pisa is a good example of a building that tipped, but did not crack much. Eventually, the tipping got to a point where this tall slender building became unstable and had to be resupported.

IMPLICATIONS

The implications of settlement cracking depend on the extent of movement. Possible implications include—

1. None, if the cracks are not noticed
2. Cosmetic issues that make the house appear unstable to the layperson
3. Leakage through the cracks
4. Sloped or uneven floors
5. Utility lines being stressed or broken (plumbing, heating, and gas pipes may break)
6. Flashings for chimneys and pipes may be moved at the roofline, resulting in leakage
7. Chimneys have become unstable or may develop dangerous openings in their flues

8. Floor, roof and ceiling joists and rafters losing their end bearing (which is usually only about an inch and one half) leading to possible floor or roof collapse

9. Collapse of floors, walls and roof if there is enough movement

These implications apply to most of the conditions we'll discuss in this chapter.

As you drive toward the house, look for structural problems in other homes in the neighborhood. Structural problems are often neighborhood specific, especially if they are related to soil conditions.

Check the general topography. Is the land flat or hilly? Is the home you are going to inspect near the top of a hill, on the side of a hill or near the bottom?

How old is the neighborhood? Older neighborhoods that don't show structural problems are more reliable indicators of stability than newer neighborhoods that have not yet stood the test of time.

Talk to municipal building inspectors, homebuilders, septic tank, and sewer people about soil conditions they come across. Is your area known to have weak or expansive soils? Is the problem localized or is it a general problem?

Also ask about high water tables and underground streams. Ask about any areas built on fill or reclaimed land. This will help you identify and understand settlement problems.

Watch for structural problems in hilly areas. If the lots are predominately sloped, problems are more likely to arise. We discussed appropriate lot sloping and the role of the surrounding soil in Chapter 2, *Exteriors*.

When builders work on sloping lots, it is common to create a flat building pad by cutting back into the hill to form the pad for the uphill half of the house. The material that was removed is often deposited on the downhill slope and built up to form an extension of the pad that has been cut in.

You end up with the uphill half of the house built on undisturbed soil, and the downhill half of the house built on fill (Figure 4.8). Differential settlement cracks

FIGURE 4.8 Building Settlement Due to Cut and Fill Excavation

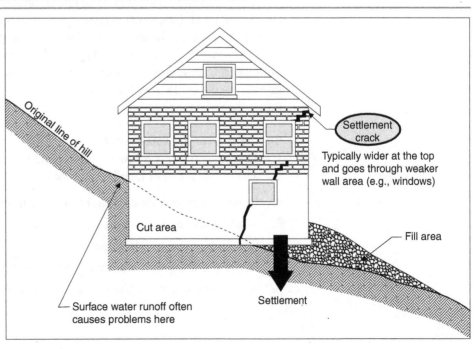

are very common here where the downhill half of the house wants to move and the uphill half wants to stay put.

Usually More Than One Crack

Differential settlement usually results in more than one crack. If, for example, a corner of a building is settling, it will pull away from the walls on either side of the corner. If the downhill half of the house is sliding away from the uphill half, there will usually be cracks in both sidewalls.

Differential settlement cracks usually extend down through the footings and up through the structure. Unlike shrinkage cracks, they will not be restricted to the foundations.

Direction of Cracks

Most cracks due to differential settlement are vertical or diagonal, including stepped cracks.

Crack Size

People often analyze cracks based on size. This is very dangerous, since there are several things that may confuse you. For example, which of these situations is worse?

- a $1/4$ inch wide crack in a wall
- sixteen cracks each $1/16$ of an inch wide

The several smaller cracks indicate more movement than the one large crack, so this is the more serious of the two situations.

Planes of Movement

Don't just focus on crack width. You have to think of movement in all three dimensions. Generally speaking, the more planes of movement, the more serious the problem.

One part of the building may be moving horizontally relative to another. A variation on this is a rotational crack. There will be horizontal movement, but the higher up in the building you go, the more movement there will be, usually. The rotation is usually centered around the footing.

Vertical Shear

One part of the building may drop relative to another. In this case, the crack width may be less than $1/16$ of an inch. However, there can be significant dislocation. One side of the house could drop one inch relative to another and you still wouldn't have a very wide crack. You would have a serious structural problem, though.

Into/out of the Wall Space

You may also end up with movement toward or away from you as you stand looking at a wall surface. One part of the wall may be falling away from you, or part of the wall may be falling toward you.

Pyramids Fall

We've already said that vertical or diagonal cracks are usually related to differential settlement. Cracks often form a pyramid. If two diagonal cracks make a pyramid, most often, the inside of the triangle or the pyramid itself is dropping.

Vees May Be Heaving

If the cracks form an inverted pyramid, this may well be a heaving problem and not related to differential settlement at all. However, this could also be shrinkage or rotation, so be careful. Crushing of material is usually an indicator of heaving rather than shrinkage or rotation.

Cracks Due to Heaving

Heaving refers to upward movement of the building.

The implications of heaving include—

IMPLICATIONS

1. None, if the cracks are so slight they are not noticed
2. Small cracks may only be cosmetic issues
3. Cracks may result in leakage
4. Heaving cracks may cause uneven floors and leaning walls
5. Service lines, interior pipes, wires and ducts may be strained

6. Chimneys may be disconnected

7. Flashing problems may be experienced at plumbing and chimney roof penetrations, for example

8. Floor, roof and ceiling joists and rafters losing their end bearing supports

9. In the most severe cases, structural collapse may occur

STRATEGY

Local Research

You've done some local research into soil conditions, so you should know whether you are in an area of expansive soils. You should also learn the depth of frost in your area and the common building practices with respect to footing depth.

Is the building settling (moving down) or heaving (moving up)? It isn't always easy to tell. If there is a large hump in the center of the house, is it because the interior columns are heaving or because the perimeter is settling? Here are some things you can watch for:

Cracks Opening or Crushing

1. If cracks are open, things are moving apart. If there is crushing around cracks, things are moving together or sliding against each other. Check as many reference points as you can.

Sidewalks and Driveways

2. If driveways, sidewalks and patios around the house have an unnatural slope down toward the house, settlement of the home would be suspected. If these surfaces slope up toward the house, heaving is more likely.

Check Floor Slab

3. If the central part of the house seems to be humped, but there is no cracking or displacement of the floor slab around the columns, it's probably not the columns heaving, but the perimeter settling. On the other hand, if the floor around the central columns shows lots of cracks and the floor slopes up toward the columns all the way around, it's more likely to be heaving.

4. Look at overhead wires coming to the house. Are they at a significantly different angle than neighboring houses?

5. Look at adjacent houses for neighborhood trends.

6. Look at soil lines against buildings. If the front door sill is below grade level, odds are pretty good the house is sinking. If you can see a dirt line six inches above the existing grade line around the perimeter of the house, chances are the house has heaved.

Subtle and Complex

Most situations will not be dramatic or simple. Your investigative and deductive reasoning powers will be tested. As always, if you're not sure, don't guess. Simply report to your client exactly what you saw and advise the client that the information is inconclusive. Recommend further investigation if the movement is dramatic, or monitoring if the movement is less severe.

Don't Guess

Cracks Due to Horizontal Forces (Lateral Thrust)

These cracks are often serious structural problems. As a general rule, horizontal foundation cracks are more serious than vertical or diagonal cracks.

The implication of cracks due to horizontal forces may be—

IMPLICATIONS

- insignificant
- cosmetic
- leakage
- structural distress and ultimately collapse

F I G U R E 4.9   Three Possibilities for Horizontal Cracks and Movement in Foundation Walls

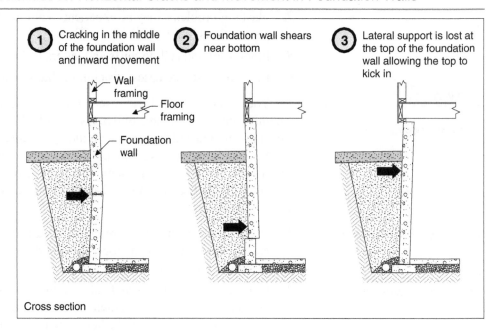

1 Cracking in the middle of the foundation wall and inward movement

2 Foundation wall shears near bottom

3 Lateral support is lost at the top of the foundation wall allowing the top to kick in

Wall framing
Floor framing
Foundation wall

Cross section

STRATEGY

Bowing and Bulging

Common Crack Patterns

Beams Stick out Through the Wall

Brick Overhang

Look from Outside

Some Bowing Not Visible from Outside

Foundation walls that are pushed out of place are not able to carry their vertical or horizontal loads. Any foundation wall that has been pushed out of plumb should be addressed by a specialist.

Horizontal cracks and movement in walls may appear in one of three different ways, as summarized in Figure 4.9.

If the forces are applied slowly and over a long period of time, materials that we normally think of as brittle will flow and bend. Masonry and concrete walls can deform. These **bows** or **bulges** in walls, even if they do not have cracks, indicate movement and often require resupporting.

Walls subjected to horizontal forces often develop horizontal cracks. However, since these walls are usually restrained at the corners (the corner walls act as buttresses) the cracks may die out at the corners. In many cases, the cracks will be diagonal up toward the corner near either end of the wall. Vertical cracks may also appear near the middle of the wall length.

When foundation walls bow inward, beams may punch through the top of the foundation wall. In extreme cases, the beam may actually project outside.

Solid masonry or brick veneer walls above the foundation wall may not move inward with a bowing foundation wall (Figure 4.10) This leads to a significant overhang. If the overhang is more than one inch, there is risk of the masonry wall collapsing.

Look at the base of masonry and veneer walls from outside, If the overhang is most pronounced near the midpoint of the wall and disappears at either end, this suggests that the foundation wall is bowing inward.

The wall may be bowing with no indication from the outside along the top. If the top of the wall is adequately restrained (laterally supported), the foundation wall may not bow at the top and there may be no bow along the length of the wall. The bow or bending of the wall may occur between the top and bottom, with the maximum movement about half-way up the wall. The bowing disappears toward the end of the walls because of the buttressing effect of the foundations at the corners.

F I G U R E 4.10   Excess Brick Overhang Resulting from Bowing Foundation

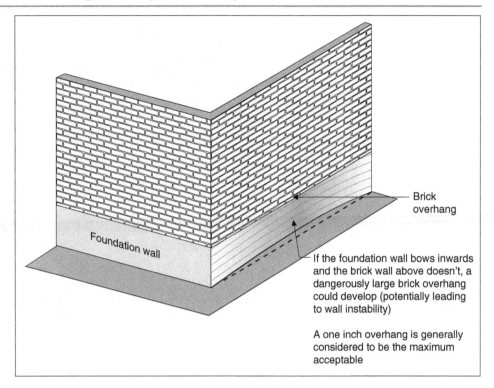

Foundation wall

Brick overhang

If the foundation wall bows inwards and the brick wall above doesn't, a dangerously large brick overhang could develop (potentially leading to wall instability)

A one inch overhang is generally considered to be the maximum acceptable

Loss of Lateral Support

Walls may lean in at the top as joists rot at their ends. If the connection between the top of the foundation wall and the flooring system becomes weak, the lateral support is lost.

Floor joists perpendicular to foundation walls provide good lateral support. Joists parallel to foundation walls need blocking to provide effective lateral support from several joists.

Failure May Be Sudden

Walls may move quickly if there is a heavy rain which saturates the soil, creating substantial pressure against the wall. This may happen not only in particularly heavy rains, but if a downspout becomes disconnected or if gutters are clogged.

Vertical Cracks Occasionally

If the walls are short, soil pressure may cause a vertical crack and the walls will kick in at the midpoint. The horizontal forces are abundantly clear, since the direction of movement is into the basement, despite the fact that the cracks are vertical.

Verifying Inward Movement

If the movement is significant, you'll be able to see it with the naked eye. Cracks will typically be wider on the inside face. A flashlight may be helpful to look into the crack.

A four-foot level (mason's level) is often helpful to verify the direction and amount of movement. Plumb bobs can also be used.

Sight along all house walls, both above and below grade, for leaning, bowing, or bulging.

Check the Height of the Backfill

Building codes have rules for how thick foundation walls of various materials must be, given certain backfill heights. One set of rules applies for foundation walls that are laterally supported, and another set applies for those that are not. Check what is accepted in your area.

Careful with New Houses

Check the height of backfill against the thickness of the wall especially on new construction, where the foundation is too new to display movement (Figure 4.11). Choose a reference point that can be viewed from both inside and out. Basement windows, clothes dryer vents, electrical conduits, etc., are areas that you can use to

F I G U R E 4.11   Determining Height of Backfill

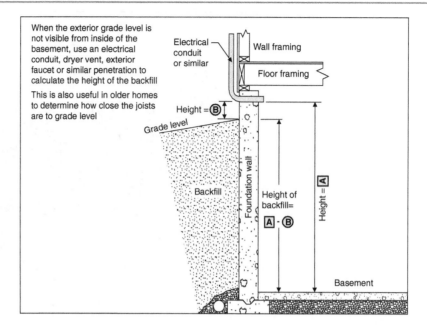

When the exterior grade level is not visible from inside of the basement, use an electrical conduit, dryer vent, exterior faucet or similar penetration to calculate the height of the backfill

This is also useful in older homes to determine how close the joists are to grade level

Electrical conduit or similar

Wall framing

Floor framing

Height = Ⓑ

Grade level

Foundation wall

Backfill

Height of backfill= Ⓐ - Ⓑ

Height = Ⓐ

Basement

compare the height of the foundation wall against the height of the backfill. The foundation wall thickness can be easily checked at basement windows.

Impact Damage

Vehicles can strike and damage the above-grade part of foundation. Watch for this along driveways and parking areas, and inside garages. Landscaping work (including adding a swimming pool) with heavy equipment can also cause impact damage in areas away from normal vehicle traffic.

Different Than Soil Pressure

Impact damage often looks like failure of a foundation wall due to lateral soil pressure but is usually more localized. In some cases, there is evidence on the outside of the impact via scraping or crushing of the exterior foundation face. If there is horizontal displacement such as leaning or bowing, the point of maximum deflection will usually be above grade level.

If all foundation walls are similar and exposed to similar forces, you should question why there would be localized failure at one point. If it is a spot where vehicles can access the foundation, consider this possibility.

Basement Floor Holds the Bottom of Foundations

While good practice dictates that the foundation wall be keyed into the footing, this is often not done and, in some cases, it's not strong enough to stop a foundation from getting pushed inward across the top of a footing. In most cases, the basement floor will stop this.

Basement floors that have been removed to allow for interior drainage systems, or are stopped short and filled with an expansion joint are not necessarily a problem, but lack this built-in protection for the bottom of the foundation wall. Again, we would only comment if we saw evidence of failure.

Bowed, Bulging, and Leaning Foundation Walls

We discussed these conditions when we looked at cracked foundation walls. Bowing, bulging or leaning foundation walls are not always accompanied by cracks. However, the mechanisms and strategies are the same as we discussed earlier.

Mortar Deterioration

Mortar deterioration applies to masonry walls and piers made of stone, concrete block, cinder block, clay tile and brick.

The implications are the same as we've talked about earlier. The ultimate implication is collapse of the structure.

Mortar deterioration may be concentrated on the lower part of the wall or pier. This may be where more moisture leaks through a wall, or where **rising damp** (water drawn up through capillary action) is concentrated.

Testing Mortar Strength

Mortar joints can be probed with an awl or screwdriver to test their integrity. With very little practice, you can get a sense of the mortar strength. Most inspectors do not hack away at mortar. Dragging an awl or screwdriver across the joint with medium force will reveal the strength.

Brick Often Looks Bad

Brick foundations are usually three bricks thick (three wythes). The deterioration visible on the inner face of the brick is often alarming. However, this may be far less serious than a similar-looking mortar deterioration problem on a concrete block wall. Concrete block foundation walls are single thickness (wythe). Deteriorating mortar on a concrete block wall is far more likely to cause the wall to lose its strength than a similar amount of deterioration on a brick wall.

Poured Concrete Is Stronger

Because of the mortar joints, masonry foundation walls are generally not as strong as poured concrete walls.

Spalling Foundation Material

Spalling is splitting, chipping, crumbling or splintering of masonry or concrete.

Deteriorating concrete or masonry can be very serious. Look at the thickness of the foundation wall, and the amount of material that has been lost. What percentage of the wall has been compromised? In some cases, you'll recommend a specialist to determine whether the wall is likely to fail.

How Much Material Is Lost?

Consider where the damage has taken place. If there is lots of spalling near the top of the wall, the wood flooring and wall members may be exposed to moisture and may rot.

Floors and Walls Affected?

Loss of Bearing

Another issue is the loss of bearing surfaces for floors and walls, if the top of the foundation wall is deteriorating.

Rot, Insect or Fire Damage

Rot is the biggest enemy of wood foundations and piers.

When looking for rot, a carpenter's awl is very helpful. Probing wood (other than that used as a decorative interior finish) is required by the Standards where you suspect rot.

Clues

- sometimes rot will show up clearly through cracks or checking in the wood and a crumbling surface.
- there may be fungal growth on the wood.
- the smell of the crawlspace or basement area may tell you that the moisture levels are high and that rot is likely.

Wood/Soil Contact

Pay particular attention where the wood is in direct contact with the soil. Moisture contents in excess of 20% are difficult to avoid where there is wood/soil contact.

Rot

Evaluating the extent of the rot and the amount of weakening of the structure requires considerable experience and expertise. Again, unless you have strong knowledge in this area, or the situation is black and white, call for further investigation.

Insect damage may be found on its own or with rotted wood. You don't have to identify the type or cause of damage, simply that the wood is damaged.

Fire damage to wood members may be superficial or structural. Several factors affect the significance of the damage, including the depth and location of charring and the size, function and location of the components. Where in doubt, recommend further evaluation by a specialist.

Piers Moving or Deteriorating

Piers can be checked for plumb using a mason's level. Look for a gap at the top of the pier. If the pier has settled, it may no longer be carrying the load from the floor or wall system above. Look also for a sag in the floor above the pier. Piers out of plumb by more than ⅓ of the pier thickness should be considered unstable.

Look for bowing or buckling of the pier. Is the beam on top of the pier on the center, or off to one side?

Look for crushing at the top of the pier or the underside of the floor framing member above. Is there adequate end bearing for beams? Is the top of the pier wide enough to carry the full width of the beam? Look also for crushing at the bottom of wood piers.

Hollow concrete block, cinder block, clay tile, and cored brick must be installed with the channels vertical. If the channels are horizontal, the pier will not be as strong.

Look at the pier material itself for rot, mortar deterioration, spalling, cracking or delamination.

In most cases, you won't be able to see whether there is a footing. If there is a concrete floor at the base of the footing, look for cracking and deflection of the concrete around the pier. If the concrete has dropped in this area, settlement is the problem. If the concrete has heaved, there may be a frost or expansive soil issue.

Look for evidence of moisture damage around the bottom of the pier that would indicate rising damp. Probe wooden piers, especially near the bottom and near any wood/soil contact.

Cold Joints

Cold joints are the result of pouring a foundation at two separate times. If part of the foundation is poured and starts to cure, when the second part is poured the visible joint between the two is a **cold joint** or **cold pour.** Cold joints are horizontal or diagonal, although closer to being horizontal than vertical. The joint can be ragged and irregular or it can look like a crack, particularly if it's relatively straight.

Cold joints may be a—

- source of leakage
- weak spot in the wall

The bonding is often less than perfect at the cold joint.

While structural failure of the wall at cold joints is rare, this can be a weak spot. The trick is to be able to identify a cold joint, and differentiate it from a crack. This requires a little bit of experience and a close look.

There are small voids in the concrete at cold joints. This is not true of cracks. Cold joints are not usually as straight as cracks, although cracking may develop along the cold joint. Cold joint patterns are usually different than crack patterns. Cold joints are never vertical and are not necessarily at weak points in the wall.

Watch for leakage through cold joints although this is not a structural problem.

Honeycombing

Honeycombing is large voids or bubbles in poured concrete walls.

Honeycombing shows up as voids in the face of the concrete, often up to one inch in diameter. Very often, the concrete appears to be missing its cement. Large pieces of aggregate are often surrounded by air.

Honeycombing is a weakness in the wall with respect to both moisture penetration and strength. Cracking or bowing of a wall is more likely where there are large sections of honeycombing in the wall. It's also common to find evidence of leakage in a foundation wall where there is honeycombing.

Signs of leakage include—

Identification of Leakage

- moisture on the wall or floor
- streaking or staining running down the wall
- efflorescence (salt deposits on the wall left by evaporating moisture)
- rusting of nails or other metal components in or on the wall
- rusting of metal feet of appliances on the floor, rot on wood trim
- mold, deterioration of cardboard or other paper products against walls or on the floor
- lifted or loose floor tiles
- crumbling drywall
- discolored paneling

Prior Repairs

Prior repairs are the result of past problems.

Try to figure out why the problem occurred in the first place. Is there a natural weak spot in the foundation at this point? Is there a load concentration point outside or above?

Look at whether the repair has been effective. Has the repair itself cracked? This suggests ongoing movement. Is there leakage through the crack? This may only be a nuisance issue, but should be reported. In some cases, walls are stronger where they have been patched than anywhere else. This is true, for example, where epoxy patching is well done.

If the forces that caused the initial problem still exist, a crack will often open nearby. Check around repairs for evidence of new cracks.

Have Walls Been Repaired?

Look for evidence of re-supporting. Have buttresses or pilasters been added? Are there plates on the foundation wall that indicate that reinforcing has been done, perhaps attached to anchors going out into the soil? Have wood or steel channels been installed against the wall to stop further movement? Have new walls been added, inside or out?

Don't Guess

In many cases, it will be tough to look at the cracks in the foundation walls and assure the client that they occurred before the reinforcement was done, and that the cracks have not gotten any larger since reinforcing. Again, without special knowledge, recommend continued monitoring at the least.

Foundation Walls That Are Too Short

The implications of too-short foundation walls include not only the extra soil load imposed by a taller than anticipated backfill height, but also rot to floor and wall assemblies that rest on the foundation.

Look for foundation walls that extend at least six inches above grade, and look for wood members that sit on top of the foundation. If the framing is buried in the

FIGURE 4.12 Lateral Support for Foundation Walls

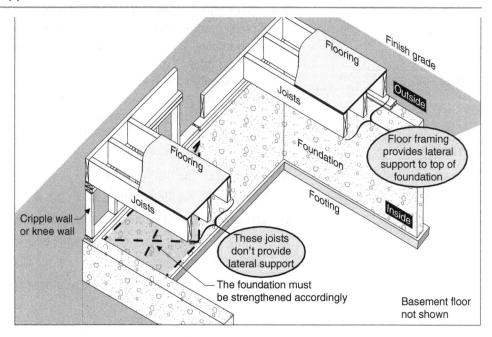

top of the foundation, ensure that the foundation is high enough that the wood members are not below grade.

Concealed Rot at Joist and Beam Ends

While people may get away with this in dry soil environments, it is risky where there is moisture in the soil. Soil moisture will find its way through foundation walls over time. Concealed rot at the end of joists can go unnoticed for some time and lead to structural failure without much warning. Probe these members for evidence of rot.

Foundation Walls That Are Too Thin

Lateral Support

The foundation walls may be too thin for the height of backfill. However, before you make this determination, decide whether the walls are laterally supported (Figure 4.12). The floor system at the top of a foundation wall may or may not provide this support as we've discussed.

Walls May Be Reinforced

You also have to be careful because walls that look too thin may be reinforced with steel. These are stronger than they appear.

STRATEGY

Look at the thickness of the foundation wall, determine whether it's laterally supported, and evaluate the height of soil that it is holding back. Evaluate the age of the building. If there has been no movement and no obvious changes in either the structure of the building or the soil conditions outside, even a marginally undersized foundation wall may be performing adequately.

If It's Not Broken, Don't Fix It

Remember, we're doing a performance-based inspection. If the wall is working, and has been doing so for some time, even though the construction practice is less than ideal, tell your client exactly that. Don't recommend repairs if there is no visible distress on homes that are more than 20 years old.

Unless It's New

If the building or wall is new, however, you will not be able to use the test of time in your determination, and will have to call out the apparently undersized foundation wall for further investigation. Be careful not to be conclusive, remembering that you can't see concealed reinforcement.

F I G U R E 4.13 Basement Floors Provide Lateral Support

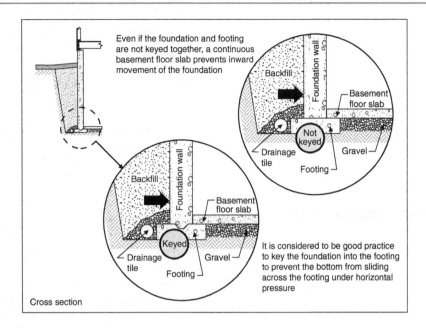

4.2 INTRODUCTION TO FLOORS

Materials

Most suspended floors are wood and most floors resting on the earth are concrete slabs. While there are other systems, we'll restrict our discussion to these.

Function

Floors transfer both live and dead loads to the foundations, footings and ultimately to the soil below the house. Floor systems also provide lateral support for foundation walls (Figure 4.13). In houses with basements, the concrete basement floor provides lateral support for the bottom of the foundation wall and the wood frame first floor typically supports the top of the foundation wall.

Vertical and Horizontal Loads

Floor systems see both vertical and horizontal loads, although most people think of the vertical loads when they think of floors.

To perform their functions, floors must have **strength** and **stiffness.**

Strength and Stiffness

Contrary to common understanding, strength refers to how much load can be applied before something breaks. Stiffness refers to how much bending or **deflection** takes place with a given load.

Strength

Floor systems must be strong enough to carry their loads. If the loads are excessive, the wood or concrete will break and the floors will collapse.

Stiffness
1/360th of Length

Floors also have to be stiff. This means that they have to limit the deflection that takes place when structural members respond to live loads. There will always be some deflection, but if the deflection is too great, damage to the interior finish will result. In some jurisdictions, the maximum allowable deflection is 1/360th of the length of the joist (Figure 4.14). This number is not magic, but comes from the amount of deflection that plaster and drywall will tolerate without cracking. Check what numbers are used in your area.

Avoid Wood/Concrete Contact

In areas at or below grade the best practice is to avoid direct contact of wood with concrete. Polyethylene separators or sill gaskets can be used. Alternatively the wood can be pressure treated. We want to avoid moisture in the concrete being wicked into the wood, causing rot. This applies to beams, columns, joists, and sills.

FIGURE 4.14   Allowable Floor Deflections

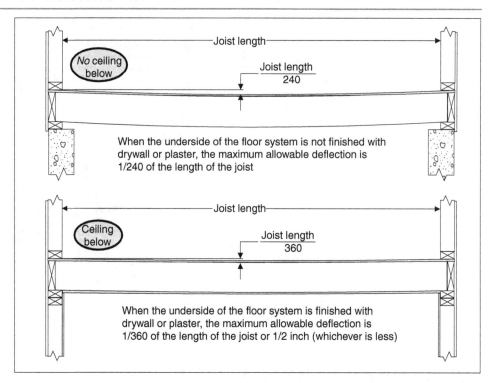

Joist/Beam Pockets

Where beams or joists go into pockets in foundation walls, it's common to keep the sides, top and ends of the wood half an inch away from the concrete to allow air circulation and keep the wood dry. Where the wood has to be embedded, it should be pressure treated and/or field treated with a wood preservative to prevent rot.

Components

We'll look at the five components of wood flooring systems: sills, columns, beams, joists, and subflooring. We'll finish this discussion with a look at concrete floor systems.

4.3   SILLS

Function

A wood sill is typically used to connect the top of the foundation to the wood floor system above. In balloon framing, the sills also connect the wall system to the foundation.

Loads

Sills see primarily compressive loads, but may experience tension (uplift) or shear (lateral) forces due to wind.

Material

Sills might be two by four or two by six or even two by eight lumber, typically the same species and grade as the rest of the lumber. Sills in some areas have to be pressure treated lumber, redwood, cedar or other rot and insect resistant wood.

Sill Gasket

Sills are often separated from the foundation wall by a sill gasket (Figure 4.15). The **sill gasket** is a compressible material designed to—

■   stop air leakage through any gaps between the foundation wall and sill

■   separate the sill from the concrete

The sill should have full bearing on the foundation along its entire length.

F I G U R E 4.15 Sill and Sill Gasket

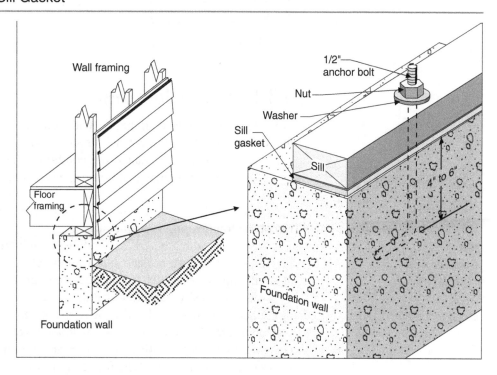

Inside or Outside of Foundation

Sills may be mounted flush with the inside or outside foundation wall face, depending on the wall construction. If the walls are to be wood frame, with masonry veneer, the sills go on the inside part of the foundation, leaving room for the masonry units to rest directly on the foundation. We don't want the masonry resting on the wood. If the walls are to have a siding material, the sills are typically flush with the outside face.

Sills may also be embedded in the concrete foundation as it is poured. There are different approaches, but the function is the same. In some climates, embedding the sills in concrete is an invitation to sill rot.

Should Be above Grade

We have talked about foundation walls and how they should extend at least six inches above finished grade level. Sills should also be well above grade level. Sills are often at or below grade on older homes, as a result of

■ poor construction initially

■ changes to grade level

■ building settlement

Implications of Rot

This is a recipe for problems. Rotted sills are easily crushed by the weight of the house, and will lead to differential settlement of the floors and walls above. Rotted sills also often mean rotted joists and studs. Rotted sills mean the house frame is not well anchored to the foundation.

Common sill problems include—

1. Sills below grade

2. Rot or insect damage

3. Gaps between the sill and foundation

4. Crushed sills

5. Not properly anchored

6. Missing

4.3.1   Sills below Grade

We discussed sills in conjunction with foundation height. When sills are below grade, there is a danger of rot and insect infestation. Even if there is no evidence of dampness or rot, this is a dangerous condition. There could be rot you can't see.

IMPLICATIONS

Sills below grade may result in rot, insect damage or building settlement.

STRATEGY

Siding
Concrete Curb

Basement Stairs

Check the height of a basement window. If the grade level is at or above the top of the foundation, be suspicious.

Watch for siding material extending down to grade level.

If a concrete curb projects out from the plane of the wall, you may be looking at an attempt to prevent water infiltration over the top of the original foundation. This may hide a sill that is below grade.

Where basement walkouts have been converted to finished basement stairs, the wall studs are often close to or below grade level. Watch out for these. If you suspect sills are too low confirm with your tape measure. Measure from the bottom of the floor joists or the top of the foundation to something that can be identified outside (such as a window sill, dryer vent, electrical conduit, etc.).

4.3.2   Rot or Insect Damage

The implications of this and the other problems in this section include—

IMPLICATIONS

- differential settlement
- sloped floors
- sagging floors
- shifting or overturning due to wind or earthquake
- partial collapse
- total collapse of the structure

STRATEGY

More Insulation

Crawlspaces Need Soil Clearance

Crawl Space Ventilation

Look at and probe wood sills with an awl or screwdriver. Pay particular attention to areas that may be close to a water source. If the grade is high in one area, pay particular attention to it.

In some cases, insulation must be temporarily removed to check the sills. This can be done easily with an awl or screwdriver.

Watch for crawlspaces that are shallow. The earth in sub-grade areas should be at 18 inches below floor joists and 12 inches below beams. Where earth is closer, there is a greater risk of rot and insect damage to sills as well as joists and beams.

The risk of rot to sills, joists and beams is also increased where earth-floor crawlspace ventilation is less than 1 sq. ft. of venting for every 150 ft. sq. of floor area. Check your local requirements for venting. These vary with climate and type of floor surface.

Access

There should always be access into under floor spaces. While authorities may specify 16 by 24 inches through a wall, 18 by 24 inches through a floor, or something different, use common sense to determine whether the access is large enough to get through.

4.3.3   Gaps under Sills

IMPLICATIONS

Slight differential settlement and excess heat loss can result from gaps under sills.

STRATEGY

Look for a continuous and level bearing surface under sills. Where foundation walls have an uneven top, a bed of mortar is sometimes used to provide a level surface for the sills. Sill gasket material, which is typically about $1/2$ inch thick, should not be expected to take up significant gaps. This gasket material has no structural strength.

Floor systems built on sills spanning gaps may not deflect until the floor is loaded with furniture and people. Where unusual floor deflection is noted with no apparent cause, it may be a result of sills being pushed down onto the uneven foundation surface by the live loads.

4.3.4   Crushed Sills

STRATEGY

Look for crushing of the sills as you go around the foundation perimeter. Probe for rot and insect damage. Check that there is roughly $1^1/2$ inch end bearing for joists and beams.

4.3.5   Poorly Anchored

Securing Sills to Founations

In modern construction, $1/4$ inch diameter bolts anchored into the foundation wall hold the sill plates down. Many building authorities call for bolts every 6 feet and bolts within 12 inches of every section of sill plate. In seismic (earthquake) prone areas, there are even more requirements. What does your area call for?

STRATEGY

Look for anchor bolts at the appropriate spacings. Check whether the bolts go through the center of the sills. Make sure the sills aren't damaged where the bolts go through. While it is poor practice, sometimes sill plates are set on top of the bolts and hammered until the bolts puncture through the wood. Holes should be drilled in the sills and the sills then slipped over the bolts. In some cases, the sill and bolt are in place, but the bolt misses the sill altogether, or only catches the very edge. Check wheher washers and nuts have been provided and tightened down.

4.3.6   Missing

STRATEGY

All modern construction should have sills. Older houses, particularly solid masonry houses, may not have sills. Joists may bear directly on masonry. This is less desirable, but if time has proven the installation acceptable, you should not criticize. Probe the joists carefully where they enter pockets in the foundation walls. Rot is common here, particularly if the joists are at or near grade level.

4.4 COLUMNS

Materials

Loads

IMPLICATIONS

Columns are designed to transfer loads from beams down through footings to the soil. They are located inside the perimeter of the foundation wall, typically, and may or may not be visible during an inspection. Columns are often concealed within interior wall systems. Columns built into perimeter walls are called **pilasters.**

Columns may be concrete, concrete block, brick, steel or wood, typically. They can be a combination of these.

Columns must be rigid and strong enough to resist crushing and buckling. Columns see mostly compressive loads. They must be durable and well secured to withstand impact loads and mechanical damage.

The implications of column failure may be minor sagging or complete collapse of the structure. Columns are a very important part of the structure.

The common problems that we find with columns include

1. Missing
2. Settled
3. Crushed
4. Leaning
5. Buckling
6. Rust
7. Poorly secured at the top or bottom
8. Mortar deterioration
9. Spalling concrete or brick
10. Mechanical damage
11. Rot or insect damage
12. Heaved
13. Prior repairs

4.4.1 Missing

Missing columns are unusual on original construction. They are most often caused by homeowners trying to make more clear space available in a room. Depending on the house configuration, the results can be catastrophic failure or sagging.

4.4.2 Settled Columns

Columns may settle for the same reason that foundations do (Figure 4.16). Floors around the column may or may not settle with the column.

4.4.3 Crushed

While it is rare for an entire column to be crushed, it is quite common for shims at the top of a column to be crushed, particularly if they are cedar (not a strong wood). Concrete can also be crushed, especially if there is a point load. Wood columns may also be crushed at the top or bottom. If crushed at the bottom, there is often rot involved. The rot weakens the wood, making it susceptible to crushing.

FIGURE 4.16   Reasons for Column Settling

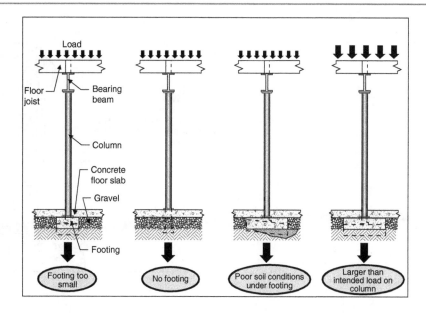

4.4.4   Leaning Columns

STRATEGY

Leaning columns may be catastrophic. Columns cannot lean out of plumb very far without becoming unstable. Generally speaking, if the distance the column is out of plumb exceeds 1/3rd of the column width (in the smallest dimension) the column is unstable (see Figure 4.17). A plumb bob can be used to measure the lean.

FIGURE 4.17   The $^1/_3$ Rule for Column Stability

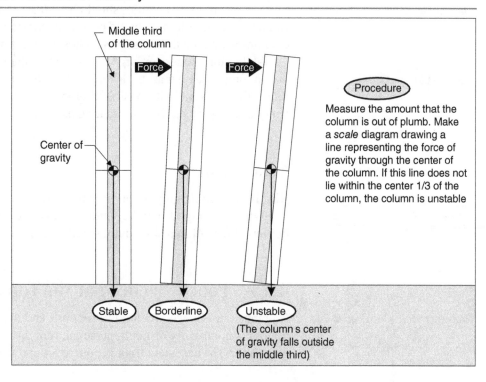

FIGURE 4.18   Column Buckling

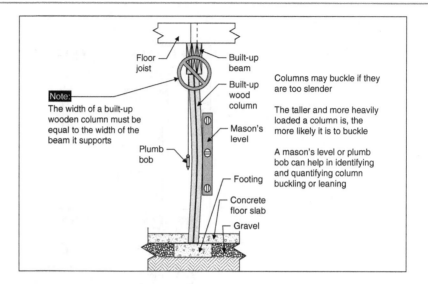

The width of a built-up wooden column must be equal to the width of the beam it supports

Floor joist
Built-up beam
Built-up wood column
Mason's level
Plumb bob
Footing
Concrete floor slab
Gravel

Columns may buckle if they are too slender

The taller and more heavily loaded a column is, the more likely it is to buckle

A mason's level or plumb bob can help in identifying and quantifying column buckling or leaning

4.4.5   Buckling

Columns may buckle if they are too slender. This is a function of their height and loading. Steel columns (lally columns) are typically 3 inches or more in diameter with a wall thickness of about $^3/_{16}$ of an inch. Standard top and bottom bearing plates are four inches by four inches by $^1/_4$ inch thick. Larger top bearing plates may be required to support wood beams.

Rough Rules for Wood Columns

Built-up wood columns should be bolted together with 2 bolts every 16 inches, typically, or nailed together with 2 nails every 12 inches. The bottom of wood columns should not directly contact concrete. Round wood columns should be $7^1/_4$ inch diameter, minimum, typically. Square solid wood columns should be 6 inches by 6 inches minimum.

Masonry and Concrete Columns

Hollow masonry columns should be at least 12 by 12 inches or 10 by 16 inches. Round concrete columns should be 9 inch diameter, minimum, and square concrete columns should be 8 inches by 8 inches, minimum.

Multi-story houses or large concentrated loads require larger columns.

STRATEGY

In some cases, a mason's level is helpful to determine whether a column is buckling, although usually it is visible (Figure 4.18). Reinforcing wood columns to prevent buckling is usually easy, as long as the movement has not been great.

4.4.6   Rust

Rust is most commonly found near the base of columns.

STRATEGY

When looking at metal columns, watch for rust at the bottom. A kick at the bottom of the column should not result in any movement.

4.4.7   Poorly Secured at the Top or Bottom

Problems More Common at Top

Columns must be well secured to footings and to beams above. Securement at the bottom is not usually difficult, since the footing is usually poured below the basement floor. The basement floor is poured around the column, locking it in its proper position on the footing. The exception is when the column is added after original construction. If so, it may be sitting on top of the concrete floor. This raises two questions:

1. Is there a footing?
2. How is the column secured to the floor?

Securing the top of the column to the beam is a much more common problem area.

Is Top Plate Wide Enough?

Is Beam Secured to Column?

Steel to Steel

Look at the beam/column intersection, after checking that the base of the column is surrounded by the concrete floor. Incidentally, it's good practice to use a plastic or building paper slip sheet between the column and the floor slab to prevent floor slab movement of the slab affecting the column.

Make sure the top of the column bearing plate is the full width of the beam. For example, a 4 inch by 4 inch steel plate is not wide enough to support a built-up beam made of four members. A built-up beam made of four two by eights, for example, will be 6 inches wide. The bearing plate needs to be the full width of the beam in order to transfer the loads effectively.

Next, make sure that the beam is not merely resting on the column. If it is a wood beam and the bearing plate is steel, it is common for holes in the bearing plate to be provided, and nails or screws may be used to secure the bearing plate to the beam.

Steel columns may be secured to steel beams by bolting, welding or bendable metal tabs.

Differential movement between the beam and the column can result in catastrophic failure. The loads transferred from beams to columns are significant, and the transfer must be completed effectively. Watch for evidence of movement of the top and bottom of columns.

4.4.8   Mortar Deterioration

Probe suspect mortar with a screwdriver or awl to make sure it is not completely disintegrated. A masonry column has to act as a unit. Repairs are usually not expensive, but are important. Mortar is more important in resisting lateral shear forces than vertical compressive forces. Masonry columns with weak mortar are easily dislodged by impact.

4.4.9   Spalling Concrete or Brick

The implications are similar to what we talked about in concrete and brick foundation spalling. The problem is less likely to arise on interior columns than on perimeter foundation walls, because spalling is often a result of freeze/thaw action. Unless the house has been left unheated, columns are rarely susceptible to freezing temperatures. Spalling is usually concentrated near the column base, and is often a surface problem only. However, if more than about 10% of the column cross sectional area is missing or weakened, further investigation is needed.

4.4.10   Mechanical Damage

This can result from impact as a result of hammers being used to nail things into columns, for example, or careless work nearby. Mechanical damage includes cutting wood with saws, or cutting steel with torches.

Mechanical damage is usually fairly obvious, but concealed columns can't be inspected.

4.4.11   Rot or Insect Damage

Probe the wood close to the basement floor and look for discoloration, checking, mold, and crushing. Watch for wood columns that go through the floor.

4.4.12   Heaved

Occasionally, columns will have heaved and may be hanging from the beam, not touching the floor. (In some cases, this will look like heaving but, in fact, is a result of the bottom of the columns rusting or rotting away.)

The footing and basement floor may heave, pushing the entire house up. When the footing settles back down, the column may not come with it, or may not come down straight. Beam/column or footing/column connections may break. In some cases, part of the basement floor will get stuck between the column and the footing. This is an unstable and dangerous condition.

4.4.13   Prior Repairs

Some repairs are substantial and make columns stronger than they were to begin with. Other repairs are superficial only and do not address the problem. Try to identify the cause of the damage that led to the repair. Where columns have been repaired, try to determine whether the column will be as strong as it was originally.

Inspector in the House: When a Column Is Just a Post

The finished basement was a real feature of this home. It looked great and the workmanship seemed to be very high quality. The basement floor had been lowered—an expensive and tricky bit of structural work. As I looked at all the potentially suspicious areas around the perimeter, I could find no evidence of problems.

I was explaining to the client how well the work was done when there was a crash behind us. We turned around to see the real estate agent lying on the floor beside the post that had been in the center of the room. The agent had leaned against the post and it fell over! It had never been secured at the top or bottom, and when subjected to modest pressure, it simply fell over.

Needless to say I had to retract some of my comments. And we had a discussion about footings under columns—I doubted there was one for this column. Since then, I pay close attention to columns and how they are secured at the top and the bottom.

F I G U R E 4.19   Beams—Shown in Relation to House Structure

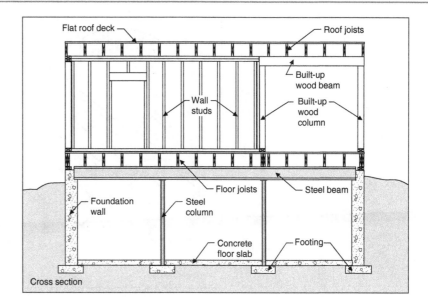

4.5   BEAMS (GIRDERS)

Function

Beams (girders) are large horizontal members that carry the floor loads from the floors, walls and/or roofs to the columns or foundation walls (Figure 4.19). Floor joists rest directly on beams. Walls and columns often sit on floors, so they may rest indirectly on beams.

Materials

Beams are traditionally wood or steel. Wood beams might be solid, built-up, **laminated (glulams), laminated veneer lumber** (LVL—think of it as overgrown plywood), **laminated strand lumber** (LSL) or **parallel strand lumber** (PSL). These last four are known as **engineered wood** products.

Loads on Beams

Beams see primarily vertical loads from the weight of floor systems and the live loads above. Lateral loads or tension (uplift) forces may be induced by wind. Beams might fail in bending or shear. Bending is, of course, a combination of compression (felt by the top part of the beam) and tension (felt by the bottom part of the beam).

Notching Worse in Bottom

Wood is fairly good in both tension and compression, but it is slightly better in compression. A notch cut in the bottom edge of a beam is more likely to result in failure than one cut in the top edge, although as a general rule, notches and holes should not be cut in beams.

Load Transfer

Beams transfer their loads vertically to columns or foundations. Beams may receive their loads on a vertical or horizontal face. Joists may rest on top of beams or be fastened to the sides of beams (Figure 4.20). Joists may also be supported on the bottom flange of a steel beam.

Bearing

Beams require 3 inches of solid bearing at each support point if resting on concrete or masonry, and 1½ inches if resting on wood or metal. The bearing should be the full width of the beam to avoid crushing or rotation. The end bearing should be level and continuous.

Commonly found beam problems include—

1. Rust

2. Rot or insect damage

3. Sag

FIGURE 4.20   Load Transfer

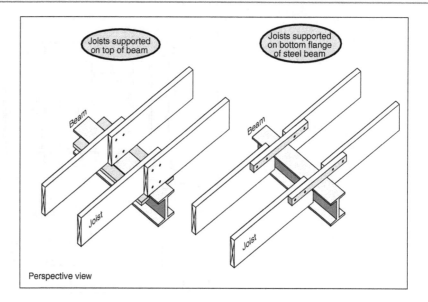

4. Poor bearing
5. Rotated or twisted beams
6. Split or damaged
7. Notches or holes
8. Poor connections of built-up components
9. Weak connections to columns
10. Weak connections to joists
11. Inadequate lateral support
12. Concentrated loads
13. Missing beam sections
14. Prior repairs

4.5.1   Rust

Steel beams can rust, although this is not a common problem.

STRATEGY

If rust is experienced, it is most likely to be where the beam rests in a pocket in an exterior foundation wall. Check this area closely.

4.5.2   Rot or Insect Damage

STRATEGY

We've talked about looking for rot and insect damage in various spots. Again, rot is most likely where the beam rests on the foundation wall near the building exterior. Probe with a screwdriver or awl wherever beams are exposed.

Soil Clearance

We've also discussed the need for beams to be at least 12 inches above the soil in earth-floor crawlspaces.

F I G U R E 4.21   Support for Beam Ends

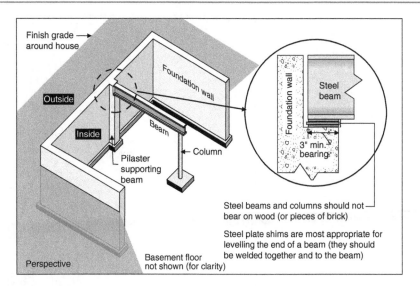

4.5.3   Sag

Beams may sag because they are overspanned for their size. Another way to look at this is to say that they are undersized for their span.

Sight along the underside of beams between supports to look for sag. In some cases, a mason's level is necessary, although if you can't see the sag with your naked eye, it's probably not serious enough to worry about.

4.5.4   Inadequate Bearing

Steel or wood beams should rest on flat, full width bearing surfaces.

Steel beams should only be supported with steel shims (Figure 4.21). Steel shims should be welded to the beam so they will not move. Watch for shims that have slid out from their position. Watch also for wood shims under steel beams. They often crush and creep. Shims will often move because the top surface of the foundation wall is not level.

Wood beams can sit on wood shims, although they should provide continuous bearing on the top and bottom of the shim. The shims should be secured in place with adhesive or mechanical fasteners. The shims should be of a wood at least as hard and dense and the beams.

Beams Rest on Solid Masonry

Beams on masonry walls should rest on a depth of at least 3 inches of solid masonry. Many recommend that the beam ends rest on solid masonry or concrete all the way down to the footing. In any case, beams should not rest on a hollow concrete block.

Space around Beams in Foundation Pockets

Where beams sit in foundation walls, the end, top and sides should have a $1/2$ inch air space to allow the wood to dry out. If a wood beam is buried in a concrete or masonry foundation wall, it is more likely to rot. In some cases, the end of the beam in the foundation is coated with pressure treating chemicals to make the beam more rot resistant.

F I G U R E 4.22   Rotated or Twisted Beams

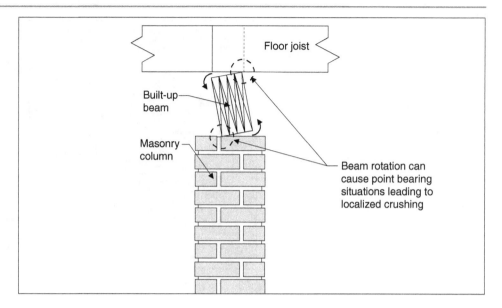

4.5.5   Rotated or Twisted Beams

STRATEGY

Watch for beam rotation creating point bearing situations and crushing at joists, columns and foundations (Figure 4.22).

4.5.6   Split or Damaged Wood Beams

Wood may split as it dries, forming **checks.** Checks generally have a starting and ending point within the beam itself (assuming the beam is solid wood). **Checking** is not considered serious unless the checks go all the way through the beam. Checking in the sides of beams is somewhat more serious than in the tops or bottoms. In most cases, it's not a problem.

Checks

Splits in beams are more serious than checks and are usually the result of notching of the beams or weak end bearing connections. Splitting of beams is a shear failure. Shear failures in beams are unusual without a considerable amount of bending, unless the beam has been weakened by notching or drilling.

Splits

Where you see gaps in a beam, try to identify whether they are the result of checking caused by drying of the wood, or splitting. Splits usually begin at an edge or end of the beam or a notch. Checks are more likely to start and stop within the length of the beam.

STRATEGY

Watch for any places where the beam may be split. Depending on the size and location of the split, the problem may be serious or trivial. You should be able to evaluate the performance of the beam given the damage that it has incurred. Is the beam sagging, twisting or showing evidence of any distress as a result? Has the bearing of the beam been lost or weakened as a result of the split? The older the split is, the more time there has been for problems to manifest themselves.

4.5.7   Notches or Holes

Beams should not be notched and holes should not be drilled. Where this has been done, check for sag, splitting, or rotation of the beam, especially if the notches are in the middle third of the span.

Repairs can be made relatively inexpensively to wood beams, and may make sense as a preventative measure even if you see no signs of distress.

4.5.8   Weak Connections of Built-Up Components

Rather than a single solid beam, a beam may be **built-up** out of two-inch dimensional lumber.

Built-up wood beams are typically made up of three, four or five 2 × 8s or 2 × 10s. These must be nailed or bolted together so that all the individual members act as a single component. Generally speaking, two sets (one for each side) of 2 nails are visible every 18 inches along the length of the beam.

Joints in **individual** beam members are best made over bearing points. Continuous span beams (not simple span beams) may have joints within 6 inches of the end quarter point of the beam span. In this area, the bending forces and the shear forces are relatively low. The joint is permitted near interior supports only, not near the foundation wall. There shouldn't be more than one joint at each quarter point. If there are four 2 × 8s in the beam, three must be continuous through the quarter point. Joints should be at least four feet apart.

STRATEGY

Look for evidence of built-up beam members pulling apart. Where butt joints occur in beam components, ensure that there is no individual sag of these components, nor separation of the joint ends. Sight along the underside of the beam for sagging.

4.5.9   Weak Connections to Columns

STRATEGY

We've talked about the importance of adequate bearing surface for beams on columns. The column bearing plates should be as wide as the beam, and at least $3^1/_2$ inches in length for each beam end supported. Plate modifications are often required on steel columns to achieve this bearing. Where it is not provided, recommend changes.

4.5.10   Weak Connections to Joists

Joists must be properly secured to beams to successfully transfer their load. There are several joist/beam connection methods, some of which are better than others (Figure 4.23).

STRATEGY

Watch for evidence of movement of the joists relative to the beams. The joists and beams should act as a unit. Pay particular attention to notched joists resting on beams or ledger boards, and to mortise and tenon joints.

Joist Hangers

Joist hangers must be the right size for the joists, and must have an adequate number of the proper nails (not roofing nails!) Typically, all nail holes in the hangers should be used. You can't comment on nail type, other than to make sure the head is big enough that it won't pull through. You can check whether there's a nail in each hole.

F I G U R E 4.23   Examples of Weak Joist/Beam Connections

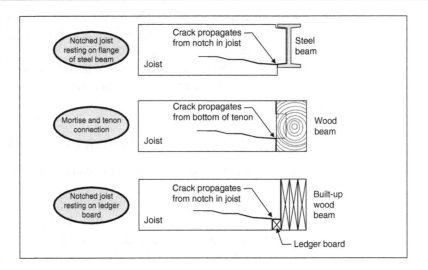

Watch for joists that are sagging or twisted. Either of these may weaken the joist/beam connection. Joists must extend at least $1\frac{1}{2}$ inches onto or into the beam support.

4.5.11   Lateral Support

A vulnerable arrangement with respect to lateral support is wood joists resting on top of a steel beam. Let's look at a few situations.

Look for lateral bracing on either side of steel and wood beams.

1. Floor joists nailed to the tops and sides of wood beams provide adequate lateral bracing.

2. Ribbon boards (1 × 2, for example) run along either side of the top flanges of steel beams and are nailed to the underside of joists to provide lateral bracing. These boards also keep the joists from twisting.

3. Where joists rest inside steel beam flanges against the web, the joists provide adequate lateral support.

4. Where joists are hung off the sides of beams with joist hangers or ledger boards, adequate lateral support is provided.

4.5.12   Concentrated Loads

Where a beam is loaded near its midpoint by a column from above, for example, the beam may be overstressed.

Two Columns Instead of Several Joists

Most beams are **uniformly loaded.** This means that several floor joists and wall studs rest on top of the beam along its length. Where a wall is removed or rooms are rearranged above a beam, loads from the next story may be collected and transferred down through one or two columns instead of a continuous bearing wall. This changes the loading on the beam below from a widely distributed load to a concentrated load (Figure 4.24).

F I G U R E 4.24   Concentrated Loads—Removing or Altering Walls

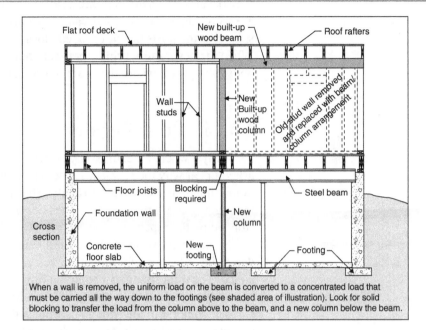

When a wall is removed, the uniform load on the beam is converted to a concentrated load that must be carried all the way down to the footings (see shaded area of illustration). Look for solid blocking to transfer the load from the column above to the beam, and a new column below the beam.

As a general rule, concentrated loads should be carried straight down through the building to a footing. Where a column bears on the mid-span of a beam, the beam is likely to deflect excessively. The solution is to provide a column under the beam, immediately below the column above.

Columns on Subfloors

There is another problem that sometimes occurs when a column rests on a sub-floor. It's common for the subfloor to be supported by joists, and the joists rest on top of a beam. A column may be resting on the subfloor between two joists. The subfloor will deflect once the live loads are applied, by people, furniture, wind and snow.

Think Vertically

The load from the column must be carried continuously. Blocking is required under the subfloor immediately below the column. The blocking can carry the load from the column through the subfloor, down to the beam. The beam, in turn, should have a column immediately below the blocking. At the bottom of the column should be a footing. Any discontinuity in this vertical transferring of loads can lead to structural distress.

As a general rule, when thinking about how structures react, think vertically, try to follow loads down through the building and watch for the weak connections or offsets. We'll talk more about offset vertical loads when we talk about bearing walls.

4.5.13   Missing Beam Sections

Beams Removed

It's rare for beams to be missing entirely. However, it's not unusual for individual sections of beams to have been removed. These areas are usually easy to identify because of the discontinuity in the beams and the lack of support for joists.

Joists Hanging in Mid Air

It is strange how joists, in some cases, can remain seemingly supported in mid air. In reality, the subfloor is holding the joists up and the loads are being transferred to supported joists on either side. If joists are unsupported for long enough, the live loads will usually deflect this area.

Delayed Reactions

The movement may not appear as soon as a section of beam is removed, but may occur with changes in lifestyle and house loading, which always occur when a house changes hands. Just because a beam has been cut out for some time and hasn't sagged or the joists haven't moved, does not mean that we can ignore the situation. When the new family brings their aquarium, bookcase or record collection into the house and puts it where the beam has been cut, the result will be significant.

4.5.14   Prior Repairs

Was Repair Successful?

As always, where a beam or any structural member has been repaired, you should ask yourself why the repair was necessary and whether it is likely to be successful. Some situations are difficult to analyze because a resupported beam has sagged. Has the sagging continued and worsened despite the reinforcing? Has the sagging been stopped by the repair?

Subsequent Movement

Some detective work is required here to evaluate the reinforcement and try to determine whether subsequent movement has occurred since the reinforcing was added. The reinforcing can be in the form of sistering of beams or adding columns below. Sometimes the columns added below are very informal. They are often too slender, do not provide enough bearing at the top, are not well connected at the top, do not rest on a footing, but simply on a thin concrete floor, and are often not connected directly to the floor and/or footing.

Where you see evidence of continued movement, further investigation and repair should be recommended. Where there is no evidence of ongoing movement, you may want to recommend monitoring.

4.6   JOISTS

Function

Joists can be thought of as several small beams. Their function is primarily the same as beams. Joists transfer the dead load of the subfloor and floor finishes as well as the live load of people and furnishings to beams, walls, headers, sills or foundation walls.

Materials

Joists are traditionally solid wood, although there are a large number of engineered wood products, including—

1. Trusses
2. Plywood
3. Wood I beams with flanges (top and bottom pieces) of conventional lumber or laminated veneer lumber and webs (vertical middle piece) of plywood or oriented strand board (OSB)
4. Laminated veneer lumber (LVL)
5. Parallel strand lumber (PSL)
6. Laminated strand lumber (LSL)

Joists can also be made of steel. These may be sheet metal, open web steel joists (trusses) or trusses made of wood and metal.

For the rest of this section, we'll focus on conventional joists.

The Forces That Exist

Joists see vertical loads from above and lateral soil loads from foundation wall thrust and lateral wind loading from above grade walls, for example. Joists provide lateral support for walls.

4.6.1   Rim Joist (Header Joist, Band Joist)

The rim joist, header joist or band joist as it is sometimes called, runs around the perimeter of the house. This joist, which is usually the same dimension as the floor joists, is toe-nailed down into the sill and end-nailed into the joists.

Functions

The rim joist—

1.   Secures the joist ends
2.   Lends support to the walls and floor systems above
3.   Provides a nailing surface for exterior sheathing and siding

Rim joists can be one by tens, rather than two by tens, for example.

Doubling Rim Joists

Where basement windows or crawlspace vents leave the rim joist and sill plate unsupported (because there's no foundation wall under them) the rim joist should be doubled.

4.6.2   Conditions

Common joist problems include—

1. Rot and insect damage
2. Sagging joists (often part of a springy floor)
3. Poor end bearing
4. Rotated or twisted joists
5. Inappropriate notching or holes
6. Split or damaged
7. Weak cantilevers
8. Weaknesses created by openings around stairs, chimneys and windows, etc.
9. Prior repairs
10. Concentrated loads
11. Missing joists

Rot and Insect Damage

We've talked about these on other parts of the floor systems. The causes and strategies are the same. Joists should be at least 12 inches above the soil in earth-floor crawlspaces.

Sagging Joists

STRATEGY

Overspanned joists may sag; they can be identified by measurement. There are span tables in code books and wood design books. Most home inspectors carry some rough rules around in their head. Here are some very broad rules assuming number 1 or 2 grade spruce joists 16 inches on center, and typical 40 psf live and 20 psf dead floor loads:

Rough Span Rules

■   two by sixes can span about nine feet
■   two by eights can span about eleven and a half feet
■   two by tens can span about fourteen feet
■   two by twelves can span about sixteen feet

Spacing joists 12 inches on center results in longer allowable spans:

- two by sixes can span about ten feet
- two by eights can span about thirteen feet
- two by tens can span about sixteen feet
- two by twelves can span about eighteen and three-quarters feet

Use these rough guidelines with caution.

Watch for Additions and Converted Attics

Sagging and overspanned joists are very common on additions and on attics that have been converted to living space. Reinforcing joists during construction work is not expensive or difficult, but stiffening floors once interior finishes are applied is expensive and disruptive.

Sistering Joists or Adding Beam

Overspanned, sagging joists are often **sistered** with additional lumber of the same size. Joists may also be supported by a midpoint beam that cuts the joist span in half.

Stiff Subfloors Help Share Loads

Joists are more likely to sag if there is very little load sharing between joists. The stiffer the subfloor, the more load sharing there is from one joist to the joists on either side. Gluing and screwing the subfloor to the joists, creates a T-shaped beam or truss out of the joists and subfloor that is effective at transferring loads among joists. The goal is to make the floor act as a single strong unit, rather than several individual pieces.

Lots of Strength

Most floor joist systems are strong enough, since they are designed for maximum deflection. Deflection limits are usually far more restrictive than strength limitations. The exceptions are when joists are weakened by rot, insect damage, fire or mechanical damage. Also, look for concentrated loads from walls, columns or heavy furniture above.

Sagging Is Not Sloping

Sagging joists have their low spot in midspan. **Sloping** joists are lower at one end. Sloping joists indicate footing, foundation, beam or column movement, rather than joist failure. Sloping floors are often more serious than sagging floors.

Vibration or Springiness

Test for the vibration potential or springiness of the floor. By bouncing on the floor, and watching the movement of pieces of furniture (especially china cabinets) you can get a sense for the susceptibility of the floor to vibration. Listen to the noise generated as things shake.

Other Causes of Springy Floors

Other causes of bouncy, vibrating floors include long joist spans, smaller depth joists, wide joist spacing, wood species that flex easily, thin subflooring and cantilevered floor joists.

End Bearing

Joists Need Less Bearing than Beams

Joists typically require $1\frac{1}{2}$ inches of end bearing on wood or metal, and 3 inches of end bearing on masonry or concrete.

Joists on Beams

Where joists rest on beams, best practice is to have the joist rest on the full width of the beam, rather than just $1\frac{1}{2}$ inches. Good practice also includes splicing joists that overlap from opposite sides of the beam.

End Support for Joists

Joists can be supported in many ways:

1. They can rest on sill plates on top of foundation walls
2. They can be embedded in masonry or concrete foundation walls
3. They can be supported on the sides of beams with **joist hangers**
4. They can be supported on the sides of beams with **ledger boards**

5. They can be supported in a **mortise and tenon joint** where the end of the joist is trimmed to form a tenon and the beams have a mortise cut-out to receive the tenon

6. Joists can be notched at the end so that only the top part of the joist sits on a beam

7. Joists can be supported on the bottom flange or top flange of steel beams

*Notched Bearing
Is Bad*

One of the weakest configurations is when the joist is notched and only the top inch or so of the joist rests on a beam or foundation wall. This reduces the strength of the joist, and concentrates loads in the top part. Expect to see cracks radiating out horizontally from the top of the notch. This can result in serious structural movement, especially if more than one joist shows this crack. The solution involves supporting the bottom of the joist, often with joist hangers.

*Notching at Bottom Is a
Little Better*

A better, but still less than desirable arrangement, is to notch the bottom one inch or so of the joist and rest the majority of the joist on a ledger board or steel beam flange, for example. The joists are weakened slightly by such an arrangement. Again, watch for horizontal cracks running out from the notch.

Joist Hangers

Steel joist hangers can provide excellent support for joists on the sides of beams. This maximizes the head room in basements and crawlspaces because the beams don't have to sit below the joists. However, joist hangers have to be installed correctly to work properly.

Let's look at joist hanger issues:

1. There are different sized joist hangers for different sized joists. A joist hanger designed for two by fours should not be used on two by tens.

2. Joist hangers have lots of holes in them for nails. Generally speaking, every hole should be filled with a nail. It is very common to find that people have skimped on the number of nails.

3. The right type of nails should be used. Some joist hangers have special nails made for them. Nails used with joist hangers need considerable shear strength and large enough heads that the head won't pull through the joist hanger. Many people mistakenly use roofing nails because of the large heads. Roofing nails do not have good shear strength and may not be able to adequately transfer the loads from the joists to the beam.

4. Joists should rest squarely in the bottom of the joist hangers. When joists don't sit on the bottom, they will settle to the bottom when loaded. This may cause cracking or sagging above, and may pull out some nails in the hangers.

5. Joists should extend fully into the hanger to achieve adequate support.

6. Perpendicular joist hangers should not be used when joists meet beams at a 45° angle, for example.

7. Special joist hangers should be used to support doubled joists.

Ledger Boards

Ledger boards need to be well secured to beams in order to transfer the loads from the joists to the beam (Figure 4.25). Watch for inadequate nailing here. Generally speaking, you're looking for two nails securing the ledger board to the beam below each joist. The joist should also be toe-nailed into the beam.

*Mortise and Tenon
Joints Weak*

The mortise and tenon joints are weak because the joist end is notched both at the top and bottom. Cracking along the bottom of the tenon is common. Extra support below the joist is often required to stop movement.

F I G U R E 4.25   Joists Attached to Beams with Ledger Boards

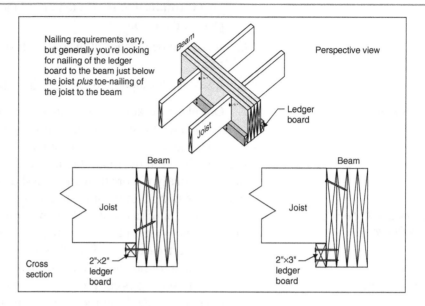

Rotated or Twisted Joists

Ceilings or Strapping

Twisted joists are common only where there is no ceiling provided on the underside of the joists. Drywall or plaster ceilings provide good restraint.

Where the ceiling is unfinished, strapping with one by four boards stops joists twisting. Twisting is a natural tendency for tall thin load bearing members like joists. The strapping should be nailed to the underside of each joist, and should be provided every six or seven feet along the length of the joists.

Blocking or Bridging

Solid blocking or bridging also effectively resists rotating or twisting.

Notching and Holes

Most code books and carpentry books set out rules for notching and holes (Figure 4.26). It's surprising how varied the code requirements are. Some consider the fact that shear stresses are great near ends of joists and bending stresses are great near the midpoint. Bending stresses are more extreme at the top and bottom of joists, and are negligible near the midpoint.

Forces Concentrate

Wood is slightly better in compression than in tension and that's why it's better to notch the top rather than the bottom of joists.

Holes can be anywhere along the length of the joists (although not too close to the ends) and are better near the middle than the top or the bottom.

No Holes Near Top or Bottom

Don't memorize a bunch of rules. You can look at the performance of joists that have been notched or drilled. If the joists have cracked or sagged, you can be reasonably sure that the notching or holes were excessive.

Judge the Performance

Watch for holes drilled near the bottom of joists. It's easier to drill low than get the drill up between the joist spaces and drill through the middle. Also watch for 3 or 4 inch diameter holes cut for waste plumbing from toilets. These weaken joists considerably. Headers and trimmers around 3 inch pipes are a better solution than drilling holes. Watch also for a whole series of holes drilled through joists. Even if they're in the middle, a row of holes 2 feet long will weaken joists considerably.

FIGURE 4.26   Joist Notching and Drilling

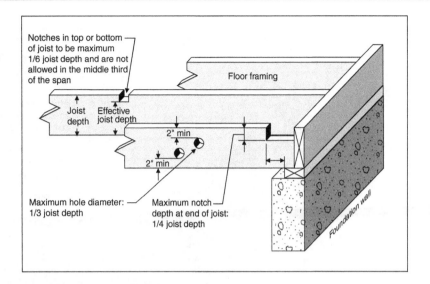

Split or Damaged Joists

Split or damaged joists are common, particularly in unfinished basements where the joists are exposed to the home improvement enthusiast. Follow each joist, end to end. Look at both sides of each joist.

Weak Cantilevers

Amount of Cantilever

Cantilevers are inherently weak structural details and exterior cantilevers are particularly weak. Most modern conventions restrict cantilevers to two feet or so, depending on the size and spacing of the joists, unless there has been special engineering consideration. In some areas, and with some older sets of rules, up to 1/3 of the length of the joist could be cantilevered.

Teeter-Totter Effect

Cantilevering creates a joist that is unsupported at one end and, consequently, subject to deflection and springiness. The other reality of cantilevers is the teeter-totter effect. If joists are cantilevered over an outside wall, for example, bouncing on the cantilevered end puts an upward force on the other end of the joist inside the house.

Hump in Floor Inside

The outside wall is the fulcrum. You'll sometimes find humps in floors at the inner end of the cantilevered joists.

Leakage and Rot Outside

Cantilevered joists are vulnerable to leakage and rot where they pass through an exterior wall. There can be a lot of concealed water damage. Cantilevered joists may rot at the wall penetration point creating an unsafe condition which is difficult to identify.

Look at cantilevers for deflection and springiness, and pay special attention to water damage at the joist/wall joint on outdoor cantilevers.

Weak Openings

Stairwell Openings

Where a floor joist system is interrupted, there will be more connections and concentrated loads. With respect to load transfers around stairwells, we need to double headers and trimmers for modest openings and to engineer the header and trimmer sizes for larger openings.

FIGURE 4.27   Excessive Sagging Around Poorly Framed Stair Openings

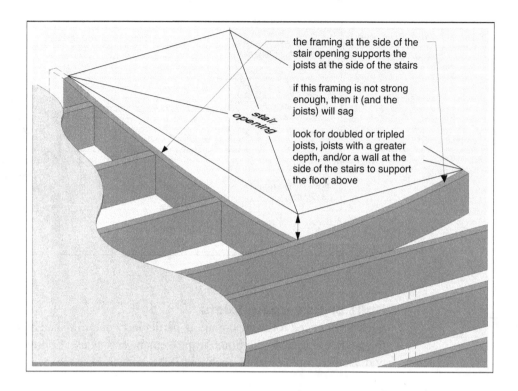

the framing at the side of the stair opening supports the joists at the side of the stairs

if this framing is not strong enough, then it (and the joists) will sag

look for doubled or tripled joists, joists with a greater depth, and/or a wall at the side of the stairs to support the floor above

stair opening

STRATEGY

Where joists cannot rest on walls because of windows, for example, headers are necessary. Headers may be missing or weak, adjacent joists may be overloaded, tail joist-to-header connections may be weak, and header-to-trimmer joist connections may be weak. Watch for deflection around all floor openings.

Fireplaces

Fireplaces and chimneys may also interrupt the floor framing system. Framing members should not touch fireplaces or chimneys. Watch for overheating (charring) of wood framing around fireplaces and chimneys. The weight of a concrete hearth and/or masonry mantle can affect the joists.

Rim Joists

Where rim joists are not supported by foundation walls, because of a basement window, for example, watch for sagging. The rim joists should be doubled over these openings (Figure 4.27).

Prior Repairs

STRATEGY

We've talked about what prior repairs mean and what to watch for. Try to figure out why the joists were repaired and whether or not the repairs are effective. Look for evidence of subsequent movement.

Concentrated Loads

We've talked about some examples of concentrated loads already. Watch for these, including jack posts below headers, columns, water beds, spiral staircases, pianos, fish tanks, book cases, record collections and bath tubs (especially the big ones designed for two or more people).

Partition Walls

Another big enemy of floor joists is the non-load bearing or partition wall. These walls are often not given much structural attention, because they are not carrying the weight of a floor or ceiling joist system above. But partition walls have their own nasty habits.

Considerable Loads

Partition walls have considerable dead weight in the lumber and plaster on both sides. A typical wall weighs 15 pounds per square foot. Every foot along an 8 foot high partition wall weighs 120 pounds. A 10 foot long partition wall weighs 1,200 pounds!

But more than that, people put heavy things against partition walls. Whether it's a dining room with a buffet, sideboard or china cabinet, a kitchen with a refrigerator, stove, dishwasher, base cabinets and upper wall hung cabinets, or a bedroom with a triple dresser and/or water bed, there are considerable loads on joists.

Walls Perpendicular

Where partition walls run perpendicular to joists, their load is spread over several joists. In this case, there is usually very little problem.

Walls Parallel to Joists

The problem crops up where partition walls run parallel to floor joists. A partition wall may end up directly over a floor joist. This can deflect a single joist dramatically. The common recommendation is to double the floor joist under the partition. This makes it awkward to run wires and pipes up through the partition wall (a favorite trick of plumbers and electricians). Joists are often doubled under the partition but set apart three or four inches so services can run up through.

Double the Joist Below

Use Blocking to Span the Bridge Between Joists

Where the partition wall sits mid-span on the subfloor between two joists, the subfloor is likely to deflect considerably. Two by four blocking below the wall spaced every four feet, bridging between the joists, helps transfer the wall load to the two joists.

Doubling Not Enough

There is a common condition found in houses that creates sagging floors despite joist doubling. A stairwell opening typically has double trimmers at either end because these joists are helping to carry the tail joist loads through the header.

A partition wall may be above and parallel to one of the trimmer joists. Doubling or tripling of this trimmer joist may not be enough. It's puzzling because when you go down stairs thinking about the partition wall, you say, *"Great! They've doubled the joist under the partition wall."* If you look downstairs thinking about the stairwell opening, it also looks okay. The problem is that the joist had to be doubled for the partition wall **and** doubled or tripled for the trimmer joist. You need to be thinking about both the partition and the staircase opening.

We need a beam, a load bearing wall or columns under the trimmer joists to carry the concentrated loads. Watch out for this one.

This helps explain why the floor systems sag around stairwell openings in most old houses.

Missing

Strangely, the house will often not move immediately and/or dramatically as a result of one missing joist. Over the long term, however, the effects may show up, particularly if loads are concentrated in this area. Any missing or compromised joist should be written up for immediate repair.

4.7   SUBFLOORING

Materials
Function

Subflooring is typically wood planking, plywood or waferboard.

Think of the subfloor as a series of many small joists or beams. The function is similar to joists and beams. Subfloors carry live loads to the joists, which carry the loads to the beams, which carry the loads to the columns and foundation walls,

FIGURE 4.28   Types of Subflooring

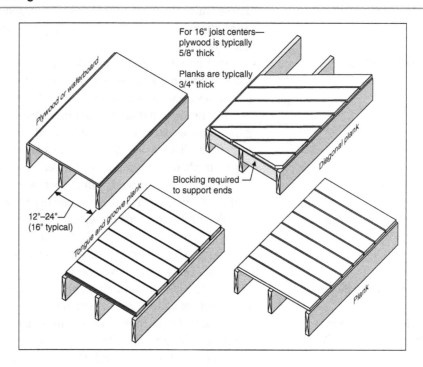

which carry the loads to the footings, which carry the loads to the soil below. We hope the soil stays put.

Span

Subflooring usually spans 12 to 24 inches, with 16 inches being most common. Subflooring is a nominal 1 inch thick plank (about $3/4$ of an inch of actual thickness), or about $5/8$ inch plywood or waferboard, assuming 16 inch centers on the joists.

Plank

If the subflooring is plank, it can be tongue-and-groove although it's usually butt jointed (Figure 4.28). Tongue-and-groove is typically used where resilient flooring is going to be applied above. Butt joints are used where hardwood flooring will overlay the subflooring.

Perpendicular or Diagonal

The plank subflooring is usually perpendicular to the joists although it can also be installed on the diagonal. Diagonal subflooring is considered to have better rigidity with respect to racking of the building, although it can create some problems. All subflooring must be supported at its edges (Figure 4.29). Diagonal subflooring requires additional blocking at the perimeters to support ends of pieces. Spongy floors are often due to unsupported ends of diagonal planking.

Plywood

Plywood subflooring should be installed with its long dimension and face grain perpendicular to the joists. Installing plywood with the subfloor parallel to the joists makes the flooring weaker.

Making Little Trusses

Using glue and screws to fasten the subfloor to the joists makes the whole floor act as a rigid truss.

Stagger the Joints

Joints in plywood or waferboard subflooring should be staggered to increase the rigidity of the floor. Unsupported butt joints and panels should be supported with two by two blocking, or the panels should be tongue-and-groove.

Support the Joints

Small gaps between adjacent panels allow for swelling due to moisture changes without buckling. Gaps of $3/32$ of an inch are typical.

F I G U R E 4.29 Subflooring Edge Support

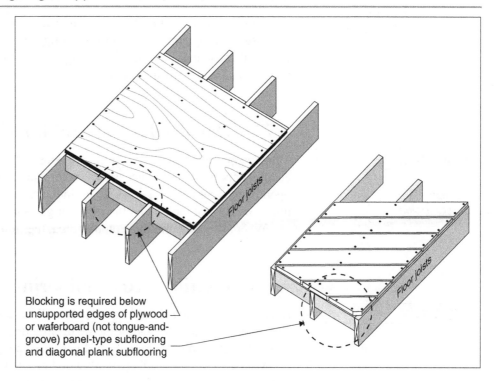

Blocking is required below unsupported edges of plywood or waferboard (not tongue-and-groove) panel-type subflooring and diagonal plank subflooring

Floor joists

Floor joists

Subfloor problems include—

1. Rot and insect damage
2. Sagging or springy subflooring (as a result of being overspanned or undersized)
3. Damaged or cut
4. Cantilevered/unsupported ends
5. Prior repairs
6. Concentrated loads
7. Squeaks
8. Swollen waferboard
9. Cracking ceramic tiles

4.7.1   Rot and Insect Damage

We've talked about this condition with respect to other wood members. Rotted subfloors are common around toilets, bathtubs, shower stalls, etc. Rotted subflooring is also common below radiators on heating systems.

Rotted subflooring may also be found around building perimeters where there is exterior wall or window leakage or condensation which gets hung up on subflooring.

Subfloor damage is common at exterior doorways, particularly at sliding glass doors. Sliding glass doors often suffer condensation. Subflooring may be rotted along the entire length of the door. Watch for this from below, or if you can lift up an edge of the finish flooring, you will sometimes see the damage.

4.7.2   Overspanned or Undersized Subflooring

Subflooring should not deflect more than 1/360th of its span. Weakened or under-sized subflooring can make flooring spongy. This is often localized. A weakened joist will cause subflooring to be springy in that area. Diagonal subflooring with unsupported ends at walls is common.

4.7.3   Damaged or Cut Subflooring

Abandoned Heat Register Holes

Many people cut through subflooring recklessly to accommodate ductwork, piping, etc. Resupporting may be necessary. In carpeted rooms, it's common to find that an opening was cut for a heating register in the wrong place. The heating register was not provided, but the hole in the subfloor gets carpeted over.

Whenever someone steps on that area, the floor is very weak.

4.7.4   Cantilevered Subflooring (Poor End Bearing)

Edges of subflooring should be supported. Where subflooring is cut or terminated and is not over a joist, blocking should be provided. Diagonal plank subflooring that is missing blocking at perimeter walls is very spongy.

Where subflooring edges on plywood or OSB are butted and not tongue-and-groove, you should see blocking. Unsupported edges should have blocking added.

4.7.5   Prior Repairs

As we've discussed, you should try to identify why the repair was necessary and whether it is performing satisfactorily.

4.7.6   Concentrated Loads

Watch for evidence of this and recommend resupporting from below the subfloor.

4.7.7   Squeaks

Squeaks have no structural impact, but may be annoying to inhabitants. Supporting panel edges, leaving gaps between panels, or using tongue-and-groove panels helps reduce squeaks.

4.7.8   Swollen Waferboard

Where you see swollen waferboard, watch also for sagging or breaking. Replacement may be necessary. Fasteners often pull through the swollen subfloor.

4.7.9   Cracked Ceramic Tiles

A common problem in relatively new homes is cracking ceramic tile floors. This is not a structural problem but a failure to recognize that tiles cannot tolerate much deflection without cracking. The subflooring should be more rigid to prevent cracking.

Determining Subfloor Make-Up

The subfloor composition can sometimes be determined by lifting floor heating or cooling registers. Other floor openings may also allow checking the subfloor.

Support Edges of Panel-Type Subflooring

Ceramic tile is less likely to crack if the edges of subflooring are supported by solid blocking, even if the panels are tongue-and-groove type.

4.8   CONCRETE FLOOR SLABS

Structural?

Concrete floor slabs may or may not be an integral part of the structure. You will not usually know whether the floor slab is structural.

Supported or Suspended

Most concrete floor slabs are supported on granular fill or native soil below. Some slabs are suspended with living space, garages, etc., below. Suspended slabs are clearly structural. Suspended slabs may be pre-cast or cast-in-place. They are common commercially, but rare residentially except in high rise construction. Inspection of these can be challenging, and where you suspect any non-performance, a specialist should be consulted.

Slab Thickness

We have seen concrete floor slabs that are $1/2$ inch thick, typically in older homes, and those that are ten inches thick. The most common thickness of supported slabs is three to four inches.

Let's look at some common problems in floor slabs.

4.8.1   Cracked

Cracks in slabs may be

1. Unnoticed
2. Cosmetic
3. Sources of leakage or insect entry (including termites)
4. Safety and comfort issues because floors are uneven
5. Structural issues if the building is unsound

Use the strategies we discussed in the "Footings and Foundations" section (4.1) to quantify the problem. Recommend further investigation where you are unsure.

Identifying Shrinkage Cracks

You can identify shrinkage cracks because they are random and usually show up over the entire floor area. Cracks that follow straight lines or form circles around columns are probably not shrinkage cracks. Shrinkage cracks have no elevation difference from one side of the crack to the other and are rarely $1/8$ inch wide, often much smaller. These cracks may or may not go all the way through the slabs.

Identifying Settling and Heaving Cracks

There are often elevation differences on either side of settling or heaving cracks. The slab surfaces may be tilted on either side of the crack. Walls may not be plumb or floors may not be level.

Cold Joints Aren't Cracks

Watch for cold joints that occur along the edges of slabs. If the concrete foundation and the floor slab are poured at different times, you will get a cold joint around the perimeter of the house between the top of the foundation and the bottom of the floor slab. This is often visible from outside and looks at first glance like a crack. Do not mistake this for a structural crack.

4.8.2   Settled

Slabs may settle with or without cracking.

IMPLICATIONS

The implications may be trivial or significant.

STRATEGY

Sounding (tapping on the floors) for hollowness below will tell you whether there is erosion or missing fill below the slab. This can occur where there are underground streams or expansive soils which have dried out and shrunk. It can also occur where the slab is on organic material that is decomposing, or the subgrade material was disturbed and is recompacting.

Other Movement in Building

Look for other movement in the building. If walls have moved as a result, the slab may be structural and corrective action may be necessary. This can include excavation and repair or replacement of footings, **mud jacking** (injecting a concrete slurry under the slab to fill voids), or monitoring the situation.

4.8.3   Heaved

Slabs may heave with or without cracking.

IMPLICATIONS

Heaved slabs can form a trip hazard and may weaken the structure. Walls may be out of plumb as a result of the heaved slabs.

STRATEGY

Heaved slabs generally require monitoring and investigation by a specialist. It is very dangerous to offer any conclusions about heaved floors based on a one-time visit.

4.8.4   Hollow Below

Loss of support for the slab below can cause settlement.

IMPLICATIONS

STRATEGY

We talked earlier about sounding the floor for hollow areas.

4.8.5   Spalling

Spalling is a breaking away of the concrete surface in chunks or flakes. It may be the result of too much water in the concrete or freeze/thaw action. It is rare in floor slabs, except around the perimeter. Damage is usually localized but should be identified.

4.9   INTRODUCTION TO WALL SYSTEMS

We're going to deal with masonry and wood frame walls only. We will not be dealing with log, post and beam, stacked plank, steel, or concrete walls, either precast panels or poured-in-place.

Functions

Walls have several functions including—

1. Carrying the live and dead loads to the flooring or foundation system.

Resist Racking

2. Resisting racking forces. Houses are generally built as rectangles, and walls help keep them rectangles rather than parallelograms.

Support Finishes

3. Supporting interior and exterior finishes. Exterior siding and interior drywall, for example, are attached to wall systems. In some cases, the wall structure is also the exterior and/or interior finish. For example, in solid masonry construction, the load carrying brick is also the exterior finish.

Hide Mechanicals

4. Providing chases for wires, pipes and ductwork for the house electrical and mechanical systems.

Thermal Insulation

5. Accommodating thermal insulation to minimize heat loss and heat gain.

Sound Insulation

6. Providing sound isolation.

Privacy

7. Providing spatial separation within dwellings, affording privacy.

4.10   SOLID MASONRY WALLS

Materials

Masonry walls may be made of brick, stone, concrete block, cinder block, clay tile or glass block. Solid masonry walls may be single, double or triple **wythe (thickness).** Six inch single wythe masonry walls are common on one-story buildings with walls less than 9 feet high.

What We'll Look at

We'll focus on solid walls in this section and masonry veneer walls in Section 4.12.

Holding the Wythes Together

There are three ways of holding the masonry wythes together, two of which are common.

- header bricks
- metal ties
- diagonal brick bond (rare)

Headers are masonry units that are turned into the wall and straddle both wythes. When the wall is finished, you see only the end of the headers. They look like short bricks. Bricks installed with their long dimension parallel to the wall face are called **stretchers,** if they are horizontal. Sometimes, bricks are installed over windows with their long face parallel to the wall, but the brick is standing on its end. These are commonly called **soldiers.** Figure 4.30 illustrates these different terms and configurations.

There are several types of **metal ties** (brick ties) that can be used to hold the two wythes of a masonry wall together.

Foundations and Footings Are Needed

Masonry walls, including veneer walls, require foundations and footings designed to carry the considerable weight of these wall systems. (Yes, there are a few exceptions!)

Lateral Support

Masonry walls are generally not freestanding. Lateral support can be provided either by vertical or horizontal members. Horizontal support is provided by floor or roof systems. Vertical support is provided by interior or end walls.

Not Strong in Tension
Creep

Masonry walls are a good deal weaker in tension than they are in compression. Tension failures in bowing walls usually occur at mortar joints. Sometimes cracks will appear, but there may be no visible cracks, especially if the movement is very slow. The wall will **creep** as it bows and can move without cracking.

If the masonry wall is load bearing, the wall must rest on concrete, masonry or metal (usually steel, occasionally aluminum). While this is good practice for any

FIGURE 4.30 Brick Wall Terminology

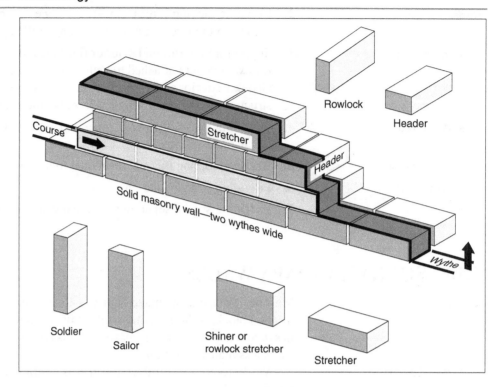

masonry, brick veneer walls which are not load bearing are, in some cases, allowed to rest on wood. Because of the different expansion and contraction properties of these materials, we consider this configuration vulnerable, although some authorities allow it.

Openings in Masonry Walls

Openings for doors and windows use masonry **arches,** or steel, concrete or masonry **lintels** to span the opening. While wood was occasionally used in old construction, wood exposed to the elements may be subject to rot and insect attack. Where you find wood-supporting masonry, look closely.

Arch Outside and Lintel Inside

In some cases, there will be a masonry **arch** for the outer wythe, but a wood **lintel** for the inner wythe of a solid masonry wall (Figure 4.31). This is not normally visible, but can help explain a cracking pattern related to differential movement between the inner and outer wythes of masonry walls.

Let's look at some of the common problems you'll find on masonry walls.

4.10.1   Cracks

Complex

Cracks in masonry walls could be a topic for an entire course. We will discuss the issue in relatively simple terms. These comments will apply to solid masonry, cavity, reinforced and brick veneer walls, for the most part.

When looking at cracks in walls, make sure you don't jump to conclusions. There is a strong temptation to do so. Use a step-by-step approach to analyzing cracks and arrive at a carefully considered opinion. In addition, following are some specific wall issues you can consider.

Cracks at Weak Points

Can you isolate the part that is moving? Walls will crack at their weakest points. These are typically changes in direction or openings, such as doors and windows. These do not always line up exactly with the footing/foundation movement.

F I G U R E 4.31   Arch Outside and Wood Lintel Inside

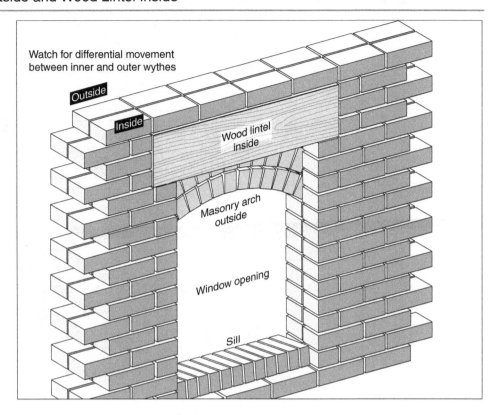

Grouping cracks that are in the same direction and same plane can help simplify your mental picture of what's happening.

Brittle vs. Flexible Materials

Brittle materials such as brick, concrete, plaster, gypsum, stucco, ceramic tile and glass will crack without much movement. In most cases, the cracks go all the way through these materials. However, other materials such as wood can move considerably without visible cracking. Exterior siding made up of several small components may not show any cracking. This includes vinyl and aluminum siding as well as wood clapboard, shingles and shakes. Masonry walls often look worse with less actual movement.

Look in Neglected Areas

One of the ways to discover cracks and get a sense of their age is to look in areas that are not frequently decorated. This includes closets, furnace rooms, etc.

4.10.2   Leaning, Bowing, or Bulging Brick

IMPLICATIONS

Leaning, bowing or bulging walls may collapse. The floors may lose their end bearing as the walls lean, bow or bulge. Masonry walls that have moved need careful analysis.

STRATEGY

You need to look from a distance as well as up close. If you get too close to a wall, you may not see the lean or bow.

Sight along the length and up the height of the wall. Where movement is seen, a plumb line can help to quantify it. Where the movement is horizontal, pulling a tape measure or string tight along the wall can help to measure the amount.

Where movement is noted, follow through the whole house, top to bottom, inside and out to get the entire picture. Is the problem localized or widespread?

FIGURE 4.32 Using Rods and Channels To Stabilize a Settled House

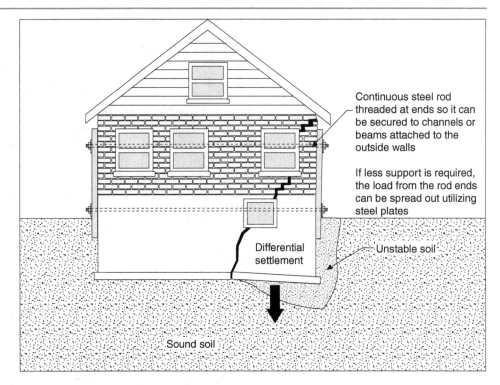

Consider all of the connection points. Will floors, walls and roof systems still be well supported, given this movement?

Corrective Actions

Has anything been done to stop the movement? Look for large metal plates on opposite exterior walls (Figure 4.32). These plates are usually attached to rods or cables that tie opposing walls together and keep them from pulling away from the building. These plates, which may be square, rectangular, circular or star shaped, are often found at the second story floor level.

Metal Plates

Pilasters

Look for external pilasters, sometimes in the form of steel channels bolted to the inside or outside of the building. In some cases, these, too, are interconnected with steel cable.

What to Tell Your Client

When you identify masonry walls that are leaning, bowing or bulging you should recommend further investigation, unless you are sure there are no structural implications. Some destructive investigation is often necessary to closely examine important connections.

Not Okay Just Because It's Old

Do not assume because the bowing, bulging or leaning is old that it is not a problem. This kind of movement can take place slowly over a long period of time. At some point, it becomes serious. You may be close to that point during your inspection.

4.10.3 Mortar Missing or Deteriorated

Mortar is an important structural component in the wall assembly. In most cases, missing or deteriorated mortar is a maintenance issue. However, if walls are severely cracked, or show bowing, bulging or leaning, deteriorated mortar may become important structurally. If the wall is allowed to move as several small units rather than a large single slab, the chances of failure are much greater.

These are the same as we've discussed for other masonry wall problems.

| IMPLICATIONS |
| IMPLICATIONS |

If the mortar is in place, uniform, and looks intact, no further testing is necessary. Mortar joints are typically $^3/_8$ inch wide. If you are suspicious about the mortar quality, dragging a key or screwdriver along it will tell you quickly what kind of shape it's in. If you deeply score the mortar or it falls out as you drag the screwdriver along with moderate force, there may be a serious mortar problem.

As we mentioned, unless the deteriorated mortar is accompanied by severe cracking or wall movement, repair is a maintenance issue rather than a major structural concern.

4.10.4   Deterioration of the Masonry Itself

Brick, stone or concrete walls may suffer deterioration of the masonry units themselves. This often appears as **spalling,** which is deterioration of the surface with chunks or flakes of material coming off the masonry units.

IMPLICATIONS

Widespread

If deterioration is local, this situation may be simply cosmetic. Weather-tightness may be an issue if wind-driven rain, for example, can get into the wall assembly.

If the damage is widespread, there may be structural implications. If more than an inch of a typical masonry unit (about $3^1/_2$ inches thick) is gone, there may be some question about structural integrity.

STRATEGY

Look at masonry units for missing sections, rough surfaces or masonry debris at the base of the walls. Where damaged masonry is accessible, dragging a screwdriver or key, for example, across the surface may reveal how extensively the units are deteriorated.

Where there is doubt about structural integrity, recommend further investigation.

4.10.5   Efflorescence

Efflorescence is usually a cosmetic problem. In most cases it can be washed away and will not reappear.

IMPLICATIONS

STRATEGY

While efflorescence is not likely to be a structural problem, it should be identified and noted. Efflorescence may mask spalling or other deterioration of the masonry. Dragging a screwdriver or key across the surface should remove the efflorescence easily. Check to see whether the masonry units behind have been damaged.

Chemically Cleaning

Masonry walls that have been chemically cleaned may be susceptible to efflorescence for a period of time. Repeated wetting by rain or washing the wall will usually remove the efflorescence in a few weeks. Where efflorescence persists, it can be a cosmetic concern and specialists should be consulted.

4.10.6   Too Close to Grade

While some types of brick can be installed at and below grade, most bricks should be kept at least four to six inches above grade. Brick that is exposed to damp soil may deteriorate unless it is suitable for this application.

IMPLICATIONS

Masonry and mortar may deteriorate as a result of the constant exposure to moisture. Efflorescence may also develop.

STRATEGY

Where masonry is at or near grade, check carefully for deterioration of masonry or mortar. Where you see very old masonry in contact with the ground and there is no deterioration, you need to make a note. On newer buildings, you may note the possibility of deterioration even if none is visible during your inspection. Explain to your client that some types of brick can stand up to this application and others cannot. You can't tell by looking which bricks will be durable.

4.10.7 Prior Repairs

STRATEGY

When you see prior repairs, determine whether they are vulnerable points in the wall. If there are patched cracks, check to see if the patch has re-opened. If so, the movement was not a one-time issue and may or may not still be active.

4.11   WOOD FRAME WALLS

Bearing and Partition Walls

Wood frame walls are very common in single-family residential properties. **Load bearing** wood frame walls carry floor or roof loads from above. **Partition** (non-load bearing) walls do not. However, they are built the same way. Both have bottom plates, studs and double top plates, typically.

How can you tell whether it's a load bearing or partition wall? The answer lies in what's above and below them.

1. Partition walls have no structural elements beneath them to transfer the loads to the foundations and footings.

2. Load bearing walls must have foundations, beams and columns, or another wall system below them to transfer the loads to the soil.

3. Load bearing walls have ends of floor or ceiling joists resting on them. Partition walls don't.

4. If there is another wall directly or almost directly above the wall, it's probably a bearing wall. When removing the wall would remove the support for structural members above, it's a load bearing wall.

5. Door openings in partition walls do not normally require headers. Openings in load bearing walls do need headers.

Deduction versus Observations Results in Opinion versus Fact

Now let's look at some of the problems that we typically find with wood frame walls. Recognize that in most cases you can't see everything. Most of your analysis is going to be by deduction rather than direct observation. Therefore, an element of doubt is built in. Make it clear to your client where you are not reporting a fact, but offering an opinion based on indirect and incomplete evidence.

4.11.1   Rot and Insect Damage

IMPLICATIONS

Since wood frame walls are an integral part of the structure, damage by rot or insects can

1. Weaken the structure,

2. Cause localized deflection, and

3. Lead to ultimate collapse.

STRATEGY

How Condensation Leads to Rot

Worst Damage at Bottom of Wall

Mechanism Reverses in Hot Climates

Roof or Wall Leakage

Roof and Exterior Inspections Help with Wall Inspection

Check Underside of Subfloor

Doors and Windows Wood/Soil Contact

Condensation typically occurs in exterior walls. It is the result of warm moist air from the house leaking into the walls during the winter months. As the warm moist air cools in the wall, the moisture falls out of it. When condensation accumulates in walls, the conditions for rot can easily be met.

The majority of condensation damage is usually at the sole plates and the bottom of the studs because condensation runs down the wall cavities by gravity and accumulates at the sole plate. The end grain of the stud sits on the bottom plate and wicks up moisture that collects on the bottom plate.

This process can take place in reverse in hot humid climates. Hot moist outdoor air (over 100°F with 90% relative humidity) leaking into the walls will be cooled if the house has air conditioning. The inside face of the wall will be much cooler than the outside face. Condensation may form in the walls.

Water leakage into the wall assembly from a faulty roof or gutter system, through siding or through openings in the walls will cause rot damage as well. Gaps around windows are a common water entry point.

Studs, sheathing, siding and interior finishes may be damaged, along with top plates, headers, sole plates, rim joists, joist ends and beam ends.

Your roofing inspection will help to identify areas where the roof may be allowing water into the wall systems. Your exterior inspection will include looking at gutters and downspouts, siding, trim, flashings, etc., where water may get into the wall system. Your interior inspection should also identify damage from leakage or condensation that may affect walls.

The majority of the damage is likely to be done near the bottom of wall cavities where the water gets trapped at the sole plates. You won't usually be able to see these details, although if a basement or crawlspace is unfinished, you can often see evidence of leakage around the perimeter of the house on the underside of the subfloor.

Watch below doors and windows for moisture damage to walls and floors. Leakage and condensation can team up to do considerable damage here. We've talked a couple of times already about the danger of having wood in direct contact with soil.

While the most severe damage occurs at sills and the bottom of studs, wall sheathing can also be damaged by rot and insect attack. Sections of sheathing at the bottom of wall sections are usually most severely damaged. Where there is wood/soil contact, sheathing deterioration is very likely.

4.11.2   Leaning

Wood frame walls should be plumb.

IMPLICATIONS

Walls that lean are inherently unstable and may collapse. Leaning walls may remove the necessary end bearing for joists and beams. Leaning walls usually require further investigation and corrective action.

STRATEGY

Racked structures usually show distress in many areas. Doors and windows often do not operate properly, floors may be sloped, and walls are visibly out of plumb both from the inside and out. Structures that are racked are unlikely to be stable, unless they have been reinforced. You can use a mason's level or plumb bob to verify and quantify the amount of racking. Be wary of "open concept" homes with few interior partitions.

Foundation Movement

As foundations settle, they may lean in or out at the top. In either case, the walls above them may follow the foundations and will no longer be plumb. There is also

F I G U R E 4.33   Wood Frame Bearing Wall with Girts

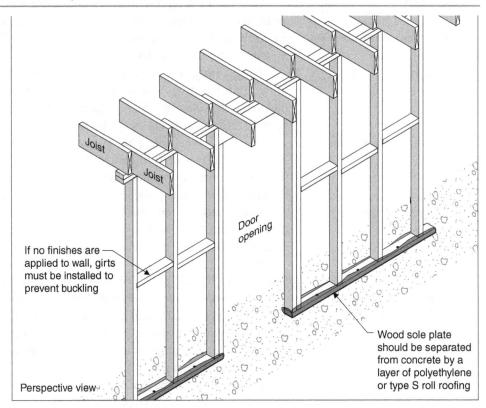

Joist

Joist

Door opening

If no finishes are applied to wall, girts must be installed to prevent buckling

Wood sole plate should be separated from concrete by a layer of polyethylene or type S roll roofing

Perspective view

a risk that the connection between the foundation and wall will be broken, and the wall may no longer be held firmly in place. Foundation movements may be very serious and have serious implications for the floors, walls and roofs above. Where you've identified foundation movement, look for walls that are out of plumb above.

4.11.3 Bowing or Buckling

Buckling and Racking

Load bearing wood frame walls are subject to buckling and racking. They must be braced to prevent this. Most interior finishes including drywall, and most exterior sheathings including waferboard provide this bracing. However, walls may have neither exterior sheathing nor interior finishes. For example, when a house is framed with wood frame bearing walls in the basement or crawlspace these bearing walls are often unfinished. The studs require **girts,** which are horizontal blocks installed near the midpoint of the wall (Figure 4.33).

Girts

Walls that are bowing or buckling may lead to collapse and should be further investigated. Corrective action is often necessary.

IMPLICATIONS

STRATEGY

Look for bearing walls that are bowing inward or outward. Occasionally, the bowing may be localized and may be the result of warped and/or poor quality lumber. This also shows up on partitions. Where the movement is a result of warped studs, there is usually very little pattern to the movement and it's usually localized. Warping can be in opposite directions in adjacent studs, which creates a dramatic visual effect. You may not know whether it's a buckling problem or just warped studs, but before calling for a structural investigation, you should know whether it's a load bearing wall.

FIGURE 4.34   Stud Notching and Drilling

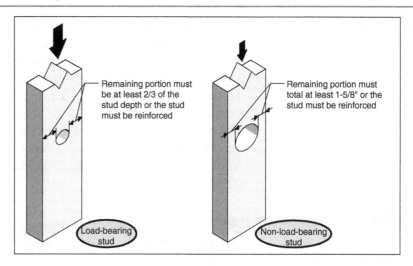

Remaining portion must be at least 2/3 of the stud depth or the stud must be reinforced

Load-bearing stud

Remaining portion must total at least 1-5/8" or the stud must be reinforced

Non-load-bearing stud

Warped or Bowing?

If drywall has no cracks or crushing, you're probably looking at warped studs. If, however, there is cracking plaster or drywall, bowing or buckling could be taking place. Remember, houses are often decorated to help sell them. Repaired plaster or drywall will mislead you.

If you're in a basement with a load bearing wood frame wall, ensure that bracing is provided by interior finishes or girts. You shouldn't be able to step through bearing walls.

Look at Whole Picture

Use all of the evidence at your disposal, not just one or two pieces. If walls have bowed or buckled significantly, you will usually see movement in the areas above as well. Floors may slope down toward the buckled wall, exterior siding may be out of plumb and plaster or drywall in walls above may show unusual cracks. A mason's level or plumb bob will help quantify the problem.

Tall Studs Vulnerable

When walking into rooms with very high ceilings, typical of older Victorian homes, you should be looking for bowing or buckling. The longer studs are more susceptible to bowing and buckling.

4.11.4   Excessive Holes, Notching, or Mechanical Damage

Figure 4.34 summarizes the rules for cutting and notching studs.

IMPLICATIONS

While you won't often see the direct evidence, excessive holes or notching may result in bowing, buckling or leaning walls. The weakened studs may be able to carry their loads most of the time, but when particularly heavy snow or wind loads are experienced, failure may occur quickly. New families with different lifestyles bring new loads to houses and put them in new places. Cracks may develop when people move in, although the damage had been done many years ago.

STRATEGY

We've talked about looking for bowing, buckling and leaning walls already. If the studs are visible, look for evidence of this mechanical damage. However, in most cases, you won't be able to see it.

In some cases, walls are neither drilled nor notched intentionally, but are simply cut accidentally. Damaged wood may have been used in the original framing, or poor quality wood may split, often around knots, under normal loads. Cracks in plaster or drywall may suggest damaged studs behind.

Cutting and Straightening Partition Studs

When warped studs are used to build a partition wall, it's common to straighten the studs before the drywall is installed. This is often done by cutting part way through the stud on a diagonal, near the midpoint. The weakened stud can be pushed back into a vertical position. Very often, the diagonal cut is nailed through to close the slot, which straightens out the stud. If you see this practice, make sure you're looking at a partition wall and not a load bearing wall. In some cases, shims are driven into the cut to help straighten the stud.

Reinforce Load Bearing Studs

If load bearing studs are straightened in this method, the stud must be reinforced. A sistered stud is often nailed across the weakened section. The best practice is to replace the stud, of course.

4.11.5   Sagging Top Plate or Concentrated Loads

Top plates may deflect between studs as a result of concentrated loads.

IMPLICATIONS

This is a localized problem, which can be corrected easily. However, if undetected (which is often the case), this can result in significant settlement of the wall or floor system immediately above. In a worst case, the top plate would collapse altogether, allowing the column or floor system above to fall between the studs. Such catastrophic failure rarely occurs. More typically, you'll get a series of cracks and a sag in the floor or wall above, which prompt people to investigate.

STRATEGY

Be wary of large openings in bearing walls, or bearing walls that have been replaced with a beam and columns. Whenever one load bearing wall sits on another, the loads are uniformly transferred from the upper wall to the lower wall.

Concentrated Loads

When the upper wall is substantially replaced with a header and jack studs, or a beam and two columns, the loads are concentrated. It is a mistake to rest a column which has a considerable load on a top plate of a wood frame bearing wall. A second column should be inserted directly below the upper column to carry loads continuously down. Studs can be sistered to create built-up columns below concentrated loads.

Concentrated Loads on Subfloors

Let's review header and jack studs. A header in an opening in a bearing wall is supported by jack studs under each end. The weight at the bottom of the jack studs may be considerable. In platform construction, walls sit on the subfloor. The subfloor is supported by joists. If the jack stud sits on a piece of subfloor that is spanning between two joists, deflection of the subfloor should be expected. The solution involves adding solid blocking below the subfloor under the jack studs to transmit the loads down to joists, beams, studs or sill plate below.

Concentrated loads are a common cause of localized wall and floor failures.

Offset Bearing Walls

A load bearing wall should rest directly on the load bearing wall or beam below it. As a practical matter, this is often not done because it doesn't fit the room layout. For example, in a side hall home, the living room is wider than the front hall and stairway on the first floor. The basement beam running straight from the front of the house to the back may be directly below the hall/living room wall, or may be offset.

Two Feet of Offset Allowed May Be Too Much

Many authorities allow an offset of up to two feet in bearing walls supporting floors above. In our experience, this often results in floor unevenness. What appears to be a hump often shows up on the floor separating the offset walls. The hump appears to be immediately above the bearing wall or beam below. In reality, it is the offset bearing wall above deflecting the floor beside the lower bearing. The hump may, in part, be caused by the tails of joists kicking up as they are bent down by the wall above, about two feet away from their bearing point.

The offset bearing wall sag and hump configuration is usually not serious and no remedial action is necessary. However, you'll have to evaluate each case.

4.11.6   Lack of Fire Stopping

This problem is more prevalent on balloon frame construction than platform framing. Because balloon frame wall construction is continuous from the foundation up to the roof, a natural chimney can be created in each stud cavity. Good practice dictates that fire stops (e.g., horizontal wood blocks) be provided at each floor level.

Platform framing may require fire stops where pipes or chimneys run up through the building.

IMPLICATIONS

Without fire stops, a house may burn very quickly. Less serious is the fact that more noise may travel through the building vertically than one would expect in exterior wall situations. There can also be considerable heat loss through the convective loops created by these passages.

STRATEGY

With balloon frame construction, try to look up the wall cavities between the studs from the basement or crawlspace. You should not be able to see from one floor level to the next. While wood blocking is the most common fire stopping, thermal insulation also constitutes fire stopping. This will only be found in exterior walls, typically.

4.11.7   Sagging Headers

IMPLICATIONS

This is a localized framing problem and while the ultimate failure may be collapse of the header, most often the result is pyramid shaped cracking of the finishes above the header on both sides of the wall.

Look for distress that is concentrated around the tops of door or window openings. Where the header is the problem, there will be no difficulty with the bottom part of the wall around the opening.

STRATEGY

Sight along the top of the opening for sag. While cracks may accompany sagging header, cracks are often caused by other things. Cracks on the interior that radiate up from the top corners of openings may also result from normal shrinkage of wood framing members or footing/foundation movement.

In any wall system, door and window openings provide many of the clues.

GENERAL STRATEGIES

Although the Standards require you to operate only a representative sample of windows and interior doors (one per room), you may want to operate more for your structural inspection.

Look for doors and windows that are difficult to operate, have clearly been shaved so that they will operate, or have frames out of plumb or out of level. Do not leap to conclusions, since window and door problems alone do not indicate structural difficulties. They are, however, a piece of the puzzle.

Cracking in walls is difficult to analyze definitively. Cracks on interior finishes are doubly difficult because they are often patched to improve cosmetics, or as part of normal decorating. Wallpaper and paneling also mask cracks that would be visible in painted plaster or drywall surfaces.

Cracks Are Clues, Not Answers   The majority of cracks that show only on interior finishes, particularly around doors and windows, are cosmetic only and not important structurally. However, when analyzing structural movement, you should document all these cracks to see whether they fit a pattern of movement throughout the building. A crack by itself doesn't mean much, but a crack may be what tips you off to look for a pattern of movement throughout.

4.12   MASONRY VENEER WALLS

Brick or stone veneer walls are wood frame walls with a masonry siding. The siding is so heavy and thick (typically $2^3/4$ to $3^1/2$ inches thick), it must be supported on the foundation. Veneer walls may suffer a combination of the problems we've talked about for masonry and wood frame walls.

Special Features   There are some issues unique to masonry veneer walls.

1. Brick and wood expand and contract in different directions and at different rates. Clay brick walls get slightly taller after they have been built. Wood frame walls shrink after they have been built, as the wood dries.

2. Brick is brittle and wood is much more flexible.

3. Masonry should not rest on wood (although this is permitted under some circumstances). In veneer walls, we have the two materials side by side with the wood frame providing lateral support for the masonry. The wood frame doesn't carry the vertical load (weight) of the masonry.

4. The masonry does not carry the live or dead loads of the structure. Roof loads, for example, are transferred through the stud walls to the foundation.

5. Brick veneer is not watertight. Wind-driven rains will drive water through most masonry walls. The air gap and sheathing paper behind the brick protect the wall. Other types of wood frame walls rely on their siding materials to keep them dry.

These issues create some interesting conditions in wood frame, brick veneer construction.

Design Considerations   Brick veneer walls should allow for differential movement between the brick and wood frame, and should protect the wood frame walls from moisture, since we can't rely on the brick. Early brick veneer walls did not address these issues.

Brick Ties   Masonry is secured to stud walls with metal ties. In old construction, these metal ties were nails driven part way into studs. As the brick wall was laid up, the heads of the nails were embedded in the mortar joints.

Modern Brick Ties   Modern **brick ties** are typically 1 inch wide "L" shaped galvanized steel straps (Figure 4.35).

In most cases, you aren't going to know where the ties are, how they were installed, how many were used, or whether they are in good condition. You will, however, know that if the masonry veneer is pulling away from the wood wall, that the ties are not working.

F I G U R E 4.35   Masonry Tie Detail on Brick Veneer Wall

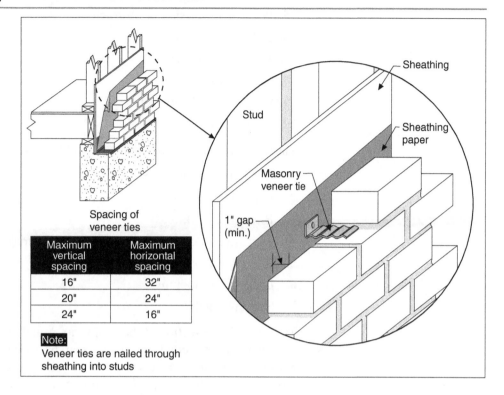

4.12.1   Identifying Masonry Veneer Walls

Some of the characteristics of veneer walls include—

1. The presence of **weep holes** (mostly but not always),

2. The presence of **wood studs** inside (often visible through electrical switch or outlet boxes from the inside, for example,

3. The **absence of header bricks** (bricks turned end ways to lock the two wythes of the masonry wall together),

4. The **absence of masonry arches** (brick veneer construction most often employs steel lintels, although there are some exceptions), and

5. A **single wythe of brick supported on a metal angle** fastened to the exterior of the foundation. This indicates the brick veneer has been added to a building. The foundation wasn't wide enough to carry the brick, so a shelf was attached to the face of the foundation to support the brick. This situation is relatively rare.

4.12.2   Conditions

Common masonry veneer wall problems include—

1. Cracked

2. Bowing or leaning

3. Mortar missing or deteriorating

4. Stone/brick deterioration (including spalling)

5. Weep holes missing or obstructed

6. Efflorescence

7. Too close to grade

8. Wavy brick walls

9. Sagging headers or arches

10. Prior repairs

There may also be wood frame wall problems including—

1. Rot and insect damage

2. Leaning or racking

3. Bowing or buckling

4. Excessive holes, notches or mechanical damage

5. Sagging top plate

6. Lack of fire stopping

7. Sagging lintels

The wood frame section of the wall is not usually visible.

Many of these conditions have been discussed already in the context of solid masonry and wood-frame walls, so we will not reexamine them here, but focus instead on problems unique to masonry veneer walls.

Cracked

The discussion of brickwork cracks in section 4.10.1 applies here. Although the veneer walls are not load bearing, if the foundations move, the veneer walls will move as well. Since this is a rigid, brittle wall system, foundation movement will usually be telegraphed through the veneer.

Missing or Obstructed Weep Holes

IMPLICATIONS

STRATEGY

Missing or obstructed weep holes can result in moisture leakage into the building, deterioration of the masonry wall, and deterioration of the base of the wood frame wall.

Once you have identified the wall as masonry veneer, look for weep holes. Very old wall systems did not have weep holes. Weep holes may be:

1. Open vertical joints (no mortar in every 4th or 5th joint) in the bottom or lower rows of masonry and above openings

2. Plastic screens fitted into open mortar joints (in the same pattern as above)

3. Rope wicks protruding out through the bottom of the wall and over door and window openings.

The rope wicks are useful in drawing moisture out of the wall, but are not a true vented rain screen system, since they do not allow pressurization of the wall cavity.

Young Buildings

Where weep holes are missing and the wall is relatively young, write this up as a deficiency and check for the possible implications. If problems have shown up, corrective action should be recommended. If the problems have not manifested themselves, you may recommend corrective action or monitoring of the situation.

Mature Buildings

If there are no weep holes in a building over 25 years old and there is no deterioration, just recommend monitoring.

FIGURE 4.36   Sagging Interior Header

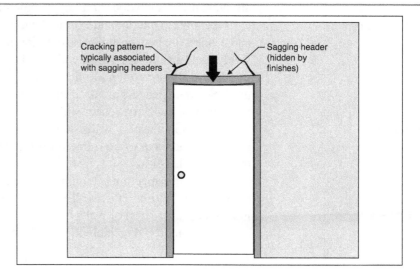

Cracking pattern typically associated with sagging headers

Sagging header (hidden by finishes)

Sagging Lintels

Materials

The lintels for brick veneer walls are typically steel angles. The headers for the wood frame wall inside are most often wood. There is usually no connection between the lintel supporting the brick veneer and the wood headers supporting the wood framing inside.

STRATEGY

Look around lintels for cracking, and sight along the undersides for sag (Figure 4.36). Watch for rust at exposed sections. Mortar joints may be missing mortar at the lintel. There are often weep holes above lintels, especially on wide openings. These help water escape. Where there are no weep holes, it is important that the lintel not be caulked to the brick over the opening. This will trap water in the brick veneer at the lintel, leading to rust.

Prior Repairs

IMPLICATIONS

Prior repairs in brick walls may indicate deterioration or rearrangement of the home. Doors and windows are often moved or blocked off. Where localized deterioration of the masonry has taken place (for example, where a downspout was disconnected and water damaged the brick) localized repairs are common. The masonry veneer is not a load bearing part of the structure, so you're only looking to see that the wall can support its own weight.

GENERAL STRATEGY

As with other masonry walls, you'll want to take a macro look from far away and a micro look from up close at masonry veneer walls.

4.13   ARCHES AND HEADERS (LINTELS)

Function

Arches and headers transfer the loads of walls over openings to the wall systems on either side. They must be strong enough and stiff enough to carry the vertical loads without deflecting and must be durable enough to withstand weathering, since they are exposed to the elements.

Materials

Arches are most often the same masonry as is used in the wall face (e.g., stone, brick, or concrete), although architectural detailing sometimes dictates the use of different materials. For example, stone arches in brick walls are common. Headers are typically steel, wood, or a large single piece of masonry.

Interior and Exterior

Openings in interior and exterior bearing walls require headers or arches. Arches and headers are both common on exterior masonry walls. Headers are almost exclusively used in interior wood walls and exterior wood frame walls with siding. Headers are more common with masonry veneer although arches are sometimes used. Separate headers are used for the exterior masonry and for the interior wood framing on a masonry veneer wall.

End Bearing

Headers in masonry walls should typically have six inches of full and level end bearing. Headers in wood frame walls typically have $1^1/_2$ inches of end bearing (on the jack studs below).

Since our inspection is looking at success or failure, we're not going to analyze arch design. With arches we'll look for vertical movement (sag) and horizontal movement (outwards) of walls beside openings.

Common problems include—

1. Missing
2. Cracks
3. Mortar deteriorating or missing
4. Stone or brick deterioration
5. Sagging, leaning, or rotating
6. End bearing
7. Rust
8. Rot/insect damage

4.13.1 Missing

Missing arches or headers are usually the result of amateurs adding a window or door.

IMPLICATIONS

On a masonry wall, the implications are a cracking pattern that forms a triangle over the opening. Even if all the bricks fell out of this triangle, the brick wall would eventually stabilize as it created its own arch. The window may be damaged, the wall may leak and/or the window may become loose.

In a wood frame wall, the implications may be more severe. Wall, floor and roof systems may drop over the opening.

STRATEGY

Every opening wider than a few inches should have an arch or a lintel. Steel lintels are sometimes difficult to see and wood headers are rarely visible. However, you will see the effect of the arch or header missing.

4.13.2 Cracks

IMPLICATIONS

The implications of cracks around openings can be

1. Cosmetic
2. Water leakage into the wall system
3. Localized masonry failure
4. Wall, floor and roof collapse

STRATEGY

Where cracks occur in or around arches or headers, use the same kind of reasoning that you used in looking at wall cracks in general.

- are the cracks localized or extensive?
- what directions of movement do they indicate?
- how big are they?
- how old are they?
- do they form a triangle over the opening? If so, it is probably a localized arch or header issue.
- are the cracks horizontal and radiating out from the top of the opening? If so, it is probably a rusting steel lintel.
- is there displacement of the wall associated with the cracking? If so, repairs may be urgent.

4.13.3   Sagging, Leaning, or Rotating Headers or Arches

IMPLICATIONS

STRATEGY

These conditions can result in localized or widespread failure above, depending on whether the wall is masonry or wood frame.

As mortar deteriorates in the arches, it is common for masonry units in the arches to slip out of position, or for the whole arch to bow outward. Rotating arches or headers indicate the need for immediate repair.

Rusting steel lintels may pitch forward, causing the wall above to rotate outward. Again, immediate repairs are called for.

Sagging headers may lose their end bearing or fail suddenly. Replacement of the header is called for. In most cases, you won't be able to tell whether the header is sagging because it was undersized, the load increased, or the header weakened.

4.13.4   End Bearing

Four Inches or 1¹/₂ Inches

Headers should be considered small beams and require appropriate end bearing. Steel lintels resting on masonry require 4 inches of continuous end bearing. Check what is accepted in your area. Again, the acid test is, "Is it working?" Wood headers typically require $1^1/_2$ inches of end bearing.

4.13.5   Rust

Rusting is a common problem with steel lintels.

The structural components above the lintel may fail if the steel lintel is rusted.

IMPLICATIONS

STRATEGY

The top edge of the exposed flange of lintels should not be caulked. This will trap water inside the wall. This is a common mistake made by homeowners. When caulking windows, this gap seems to cry out for caulking. The underside of the lintel flange can be caulked to the top of the window or door.

Look for evidence of rusting and the horizontal cracks radiating out from the opening as we've discussed.

4.13.6 Rot and Insect Damage

Wood headers are subject to rot and insect damage as are all other wood components. Be particularly suspicious of wood headers exposed on the face of the wall. These are often found in older masonry buildings.

In some cases, solid masonry walls have a brick arch supporting the outside wythe of brick and a wood header supporting the inner wythe. In most cases, this won't be visible to you. However, failure of this wood header due to rot or insect damage can cause movement of the inner wythe of brick. This is usually accompanied by moisture and deterioration of the interior finishes, but this is not always apparent. Cracking around and above openings on exterior surfaces of masonry walls that are otherwise unexplained may be the result of failure of a wood header supporting the inner wythe of the masonry wall.

4.14 AN OVERVIEW OF ROOF STRUCTURE

We looked at roofing coverings extensively in Chapter 3. We will not repeat observations made there, but focus instead on structural aspects of roofing.

Like many parts of the inspection, a look at the roof framing is required both from outside the building and inside. A **macro** and **micro** approach are necessary.

Macro

From far away, you're looking for things like—

1. A sag in the rafter or ridge system
2. Dishing in the field of the roof
3. Spreading of the roof rafters (often visible at the soffits), or the top of the walls

Micro

The micro look will include identifying things such as—

1. Poor end bearing
2. Weak connections (especially in earthquake or hurricane areas)
3. Rot or insect damage
4. Mechanical damage
5. Fire damage
6. Cracks or sagging of the interior finishes

4.15 RAFTERS, ROOF JOISTS, AND CEILING JOISTS

The functions of rafters, roof joists and ceiling joists include—

1. Carry the live loads of wind, rain, snow and people
2. Carry the dead loads of roof sheathing, roof coverings, and roof-mounted equipment
3. Support the dead loads of insulation and ceiling finishes
4. Laterally support the walls of the building, preventing racking and wall or roof spreading
5. Create an attic space, a ventilation space and support for soffits and fascia

F I G U R E 4.37   Roof Joists versus Roof Rafters

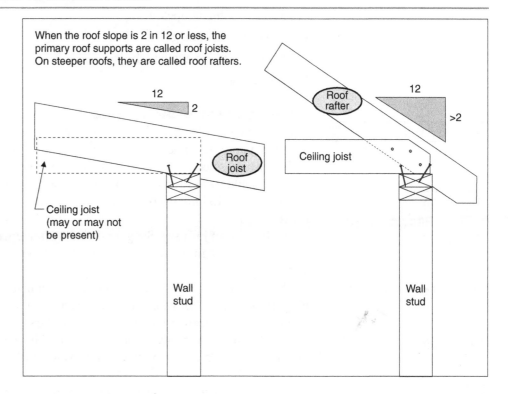

When the roof slope is 2 in 12 or less, the primary roof supports are called roof joists. On steeper roofs, they are called roof rafters.

4.15.1   Definitions

Rafters

Rafters (Figure 4.37) are found on steep roofs. They are typically 2 by 4s, 2 by 6s, 2 by 8s or 2 by 10s. The rafters support the sheathing and typically run from the roof peak down to the eaves. The rafters carry the dead load of the sheathing and roofing material, and the live loads above. Rafters may also carry the ceiling loads below on cathedral ceilings.

Roof Joists

Roof joists are found on low-slope roofs. Their functions are similar to rafters. Roof joists may span continuously from one side of the house to another or may be supported on an interior bearing wall. They may carry ceiling loads.

Ceiling Joists

Ceiling joists are horizontal members used with rafters and roof joists. They carry the dead loads of the interior finishes and insulation. In some cases, they also carry storage, although they are typically not designed to carry the same loads as floors.

Close the Triangle

Ceiling joists often tie the bottoms of opposing rafters together. This closes the triangle formed by the two rafters and prevents rafters from spreading. Ceiling joists may also support knee walls, ridge posts, or struts, for example, helping to transmit live loads down to bearing walls.

4.15.2   Conditions

Problems commonly encountered with rafters, roof joists and ceiling joists include

1. Sagging rafters or ridges
2. Rafter spread
3. Poor end bearing

4. Weak connections
5. Weak framing at openings
6. Rot or insect damage
7. Mechanical damage or splitting
8. Fire damage

Sagging Rafters and/or Ridge

The implications of sagging ridge or rafters may be simply cosmetic, or may lead to roof collapse. In some cases, the roof sags to a given position and is stabilized, perhaps by intermediate supports. Although the roof continues to show a sag, it may be quite stable. Don't jump to conclusions looking from the outside.

IMPLICATIONS

STRATEGY

Not Sagging Sheathing

Remember to look from far away and up close. You're looking for a dishing in the roof surface or a sag at the ridge. Be careful not to confuse sagging sheathing with rafter or roof joist sag. Sagging sheathing is a repetitive pattern between rafters or roof joists. Sagging rafters or roof joists will be on a large scale across the roof surface.

Rafters Pulling Away from Ridge

Look at the ridge for evidence of rafters pulling away from a ridge board or slipping off the ridge. On gable ends, you can often see the tops of the rake boards moving apart, indicating movement of the rafters.

Hip and Valley Rafter

The connections between jack rafters and hip or valley rafters is a weak point on most roofs. Watch for evidence of movement of the jack rafters relative to hip or valley rafters.

Lower Roof Level Sees Snow Drifts

Rafter sag in cold climates on a lower roof in a multi-level roof house is often a result of the weight of the drifting snow which builds up on a low roof against a wall. Check low roofs carefully for sag.

Expect Some Sag

Some ridge sag may be normal, particularly on roofs with rafters. Usually the support at the ends of the ridge is sturdier than the support in the middle. Consider a typical gable roof. The end of the roof is supported by a gable end wall. At all other areas, the ridge is supported by opposing rafters. Once the loads are applied, there will be a natural curve to the ridge that is often noticeable. What is considered normal may depend on age and how wide the house is and takes some experience to discern.

Rafter Spread

Rafter spread is the result of vertical loads (live and dead) on the rafters. Since the rafters are at an angle to these applied loads, the bottom of the rafter wants to slip out (Figure 4.38).

Rafter spread can result in—

■ the rafters, soffits and fascia sliding out away from the walls
■ the walls themselves may be pushed outward if the rafters are well secured to the walls.

IMPLICATIONS

STRATEGY

Leaning Walls/Gap Between Wall and Soffit

Look at the roof surface from the ground outside. A sagging ridge may indicate rafter spread. A dishing roof surface may also mean rafter spread. Make sure the top of exterior walls are plumb and not leaning outward. Look near the middle of walls rather than the ends. Watch for a gap between the soffit and the exterior wall. You can see this from the ground. The gap is usually wider near the midpoint of the wall and closes at the corners. Rafters usually only spread where they are not restrained by gable end walls or hips.

How Are Rafters Restrained?

Check in the attic whether the ceiling joists tie opposing rafter bottoms together. If they do not, rafter spread is more likely. Where ceiling joists are perpendicular

F I G U R E 4.38   Roof Spreading

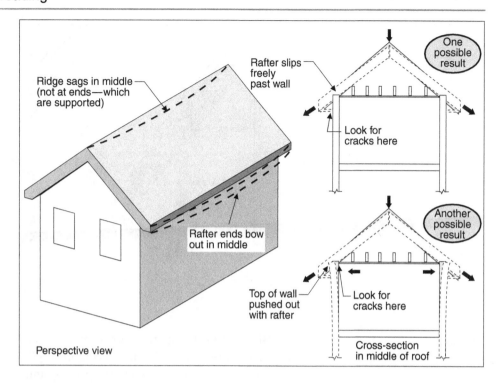

Perspective view

to rafters, 1 by 4s were used to tie the bottoms of rafters to several ceiling joists. While the approach varied dramatically, usually at least three or four ceiling joists were involved, and about every 3rd rafter was secured. Modern codes require rafter ties on every rafter. These 2 by 4 ties should span the width of the attic.

Ceiling Cracks

Cracks in interior ceilings running parallel to the outside wall and within a foot or two of the wall may indicate rafter spread. These cracks may be the result of one or two ceiling joists being pulled outward as the braces joining the rafter bottoms to the ceiling joists move outward.

Cracks at Wall/Ceiling Triangle Broken

Watch also for a crack at the wall/ceiling intersection along exterior walls. This may indicate the exterior walls are being pushed outward by the rafters. Where ceiling joists or rafters are cut to accommodate attic access hatches, dormers, skylights or chimneys, localized rafter spread may occur because of the discontinuity in the ceiling joists or rafters.

Ridge Beam Prevents Spread

If the house has a ridge beam, the rafters will not spread since they are supported at the top. Rafters can only spread if the connection at the peak is allowed to drop. A ridge beam working properly will not allow this to happen.

Poor End Bearing

Generally speaking, $1^1/_2$ inch end bearing is required when rafters are supported by wood or metal and three inches of end bearing is required on concrete or masonry.

IMPLICATIONS

Where bearing is not adequate, the ends of wood members may crush, and rafters and/or joists may fall off their support.

STRATEGY

While it's difficult to get a look at end bearing, it may be worth the trip, especially if you see some misalignment of the house walls.

Heel Bearing Not Toe

If you can get a look at the connections, check that the bottom of sloped framing sloped framing members rest on their heels rather than their toes. While $1^1/_2$ inch end bearing is all that is required, it must be $1^1/_2$ inch on the **bottom edge** of a rafter.

F I G U R E 4.39   Rafter Endbearing

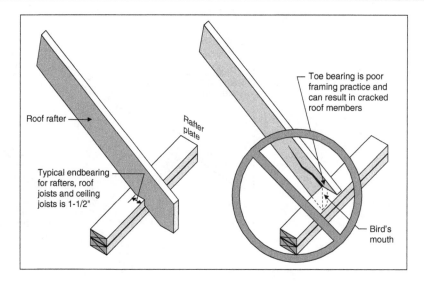

Bird's mouth

Toe bearing is poor framing practice and can result in cracked roof members

Roof rafter

Rafter plate

Typical endbearing for rafters, roof joists and ceiling joists is 1-1/2"

Bearing

Bird's mouths, as they are sometimes called, should always be cut in the bottom of rafters, never in the top (Figure 4.39). Where rafters are bearing on their toes, watch for splits parallel to the grain running up from the bird's mouth.

Angle Bearing Often Weak

Also watch where rafters are cut on an angle to bear against an opposing rafter, a ridge board or a ridge beam. The rafter face must be flush against the opposing member. If the cut is at the wrong angle and there is a point bearing, the wood is likely to crush and the rafter will drop. This applies at valleys and hips as well.

Weak Connections

STRATEGY

Check for evidence of movement at all connections. Watch for nails that have pulled out and wood that has slid against an adjacent piece. Look also at hip and valley rafters for the full length of the cut face of the jack rafter resting flush against the hip or valley rafter. Look for movement around openings for dormers, skylights, access hatches, chimneys and any other interruption in the framing pattern.

Condensation Causes Rust

High humidity levels are often experienced in attics, resulting in condensation problems. This can not only rot wooden members but can rust metal fasteners.

Joist Hangers

Where joist hangers have been used in roof framing, watch for the same conditions as we talked about for joist hangers on floor framing. This includes the wrong size or type of joist hanger, not enough nails, the wrong type of nails, the joists or rafter not sitting in the base of the hanger, etc.

Weak Framing at Openings

STRATEGY

Check around openings and watch for localized sag in roof surfaces or ceilings around dormers, skylights and other openings. This is easiest to see from a distance. You can usually spot this from the ground.

When in the attic area, check for evidence of leakage and rot in the framing members immediately below the openings. Flashing leaks are common roofing problems.

Where trimmers can be seen, make sure they have been at least doubled where more than one rafter has been cut, and make sure connections are secure. Headers should also be doubled if more than one rafter has been cut (Figure 4.40). This rule may vary depending on your area. Some authorities will allow two cut rafters with a

F I G U R E 4.40   Openings in Roofs

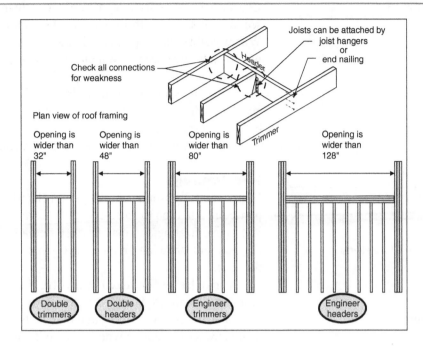

double trimmer and single header. Find out what is allowed in your area. A performance-based inspection (rather than code-based) of these components is suggested.

Cracks in ceilings below openings may indicate movement of framing members.

Rot or Insect Damage
Wood roof framing members are vulnerable to rot and insect damage.

Look for mold that may indicate rot. Look for darkening of both framing members and sheathing. Check around any flashed openings including plumbing stacks, roof vents, chimneys, etc., for evidence of leakage.

Leakage will cause rot and make this area more susceptible to insect attack. Check around the perimeter of the roof. Gutter and downspout backup, ice dam problems, and water collecting from leaks above make these areas susceptible to damage.

STRATEGY

Condensation vs. Leakage

You can sometimes differentiate between condensation and leakage by looking for an overall trend. Condensation is usually much more widespread and results in more uniform damage to the roof area than leakage. Leaks tend to run down sloped roof surfaces, rather than along them horizontally.

Although condensation is usually more uniform, there are a few situations where it can be quite localized. A bathroom exhaust fan discharging into the attic can cause severe condensation.

In cold climates, condensation can form almost immediately after opening the attic hatch. A sudden burst of warm moist air from the house, hitting the roof sheathing, will form a condensation pattern near the hatch. Don't be fooled!

Condensation damage is more likely on lower sloped roofs and flat roofs. Condensation is more likely to develop on well insulated and poorly ventilated roofs. Condensation damage is much more common with plywood or waferboard than on plank sheathing. The gaps in planks seem to allow enough natural ventilation to reduce condensation and rot problems.

Mechanical Damage or Splitting

STRATEGY

Check each visible framing member for integrity. Is the whole piece there, are there sections missing? Are there splits, cracks or checks that obviously weaken the member? Where visible, check particularly closely at bird's mouths for splitting. Check also where nails have been driven close to the edge of boards (a common situation with toe-nailing). This often leads to splitting of the wood at the critical fastener point.

Crushing

Crushing is another form of damage. This is common where end-bearing areas are too small, loads are excessive and concentrated, or the wood has been weakened by rot or insect attack.

Wood failures are often the result of a combination of problems.

Fire Damage

STRATEGY

Check carefully around chimneys and electrical boxes for evidence of charring. Pay particular attention to recessed lights. Early recessed lights, in particular, were subject to overheating and may have started a fire.

Animals Chew Wires

Animals chewing on electrical wires will sometimes start an electrical fire in the attic.

A smoldering fire may not involve the whole house and may self-extinguish. Watch for localized damaged of this sort.

Pyrolysis

Also, watch for charring that may be the result of **pyrolysis.** This phenomenon results from overheating wood repeatedly over time. The auto-ignition temperature of wood (the temperature at which it will burst into flames spontaneously) is typically around 500°F. Prolonged exposure to high temperatures (well below the auto-ignition temperature) can lower the auto-ignition temperature to 200°F to 300°F. This makes the wood far more susceptible to fire and it may eventually burn when exposed to temperatures that wouldn't normally start a fire.

Any charred wood should be examined carefully. Is it from a one time incident? Is it an ongoing process that may worsen, for example, every time a fireplace is used? Treat charred wood with caution. Further investigation may be necessary.

4.16   KNEE WALLS AND PURLINS

Function

Knee walls and **purlins** are designed to reduce the rafter span and prevent rafter sag. They carry the dead loads from the rafters, sheathing and roof covering down to the soil through walls, floors, foundations and footing systems. They also carry the live loads from wind, snow, water, equipment, foot traffic, etc. Knee walls may also support interior finishes and insulation.

Knee Wall Materials

Knee walls are also called **dwarf walls, struts,** or **strongbacks.** They are the same as conventional 2 by 4 stud walls elsewhere in the house. There is a top plate, studs and a bottom plate. Knee walls may be vertical or up to 45° off vertical. If offset, they are often called **struts** or **stongbacks.**

Single Top Plate

There is often a single top plate. This is okay if the studs line up with the rafters they are supporting. Think of knee walls as small bearing walls supporting rafters.

Purlin Materials

Purlins are 2 by 4s or 2 by 6s, typically. The purlin should be the same size as the rafter, at least. Think of purlins as small beams that run under the midpoint of all the rafters.

Purlin Posts

Purlins are supported by 2 by 4 posts or struts. If the purlins are 2 by 4s, the posts are usually every 4 feet. If the purlins are 2 by 6s, the posts are usually every six feet. If the posts are longer than 8 feet, they should be braced to prevent them from buckling. Purlin posts can also be up to 45° off vertical.

What They Rest on

Knee walls and struts ideally rest on bearing walls. Sometimes they bear close to, but not directly on, bearing walls. Where the walls or posts rest on joists, the joists should be the next size larger than they otherwise would be.

The concentrated loads exerted by knee walls or purlins and posts may cause sagging and cracking of ceilings below.

1. Knee walls or struts buckling, bowing or leaning
2. Sagging rafters
3. Sagging top plate
4. Sagging purlins
5. Weak connections
6. Rot and insect attack
7. Mechanical damage and splitting
8. Fire damage

Again, we will not comment on conditions discussed previously.

4.16.1   Buckling, Bowing, or Leaning

STRATEGY

Look at these vertical or near vertical members for bowing. Are they straight? Have they slipped out of position at the top or at the bottom? Were they originally vertical and no longer vertical?

Look for roof sag resulting from this movement.

4.16.2   Sagging Rafters

STRATEGY

From outside, watch for evidence of rafter sag. This can also be picked up inside from within the roof space. Sighting along the rafters can help although if significant, it should be visible from most angles.

Watch for ceiling cracks, especially below the bottom of knee walls or struts for purlins.

Check the connections for evidence of movement. Have the walls, posts or purlins shifted?

4.16.3   Sagging Top Plate on Knee Walls

Single top plates are common on knee walls. This is okay as long as the rafters line up with the studs below.

STRATEGY

Sight along the top plate, looking for deflection. From the exterior of the building, a repeated sagging pattern might be noticed. It is easy to confuse this problem with sagging sheathing which we'll discuss later. Again, don't draw any conclusions until you've had a look inside the roof space.

4.16.4   Sagging Purlins

STRATEGY

A 2 by 6 purlin should be installed so that the rafters rest on the 2 inch surface of the purlin, not the 6 inch surface. Purlins laid flat to the underside of the rafters are less effective.

Again, the sagging purlins will show up as sagging rafters from the outside. Make sure your inspection includes a look both inside and out. When in the attic, look to see whether the rafters are sagging. If the sag is not there, but in the purlins (where the purlin spans from one post or strut to the next), the pattern will be different, although you may not pick it up from the outside.

Sight along the purlins as well as sighting along the rafters. This should tell you which are sagging.

4.16.5   Weak Connections

STRATEGY

Check all visible connections for movement. Metal gusset plates may work loose or may not have been secured well originally. Watch for rotation of framing members. This may suggest weak connections.

4.17   TRUSSES

Materials

The functions of trusses are the same as rafters, roof joists and ceiling joists.

The most common materials (and the only ones we'll be dealing with) are wood with metal or plywood **gusset plates.** Gusset plates are connectors that join chords and webs in trusses (Figure 4.41).

Chords

Trusses have top and bottom **chords** that form the perimeter triangle. There are typically two top chords and one bottom chord, although this can vary, depending on the truss. A parallel chord truss, for example, has one top and one bottom chord.

F I G U R E 4.41   Roof Truss Components

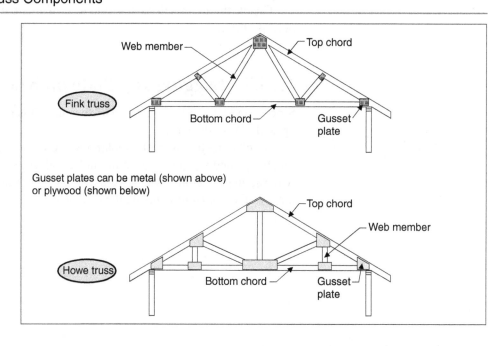

A scissor truss, designed to create a cathedral ceiling, has two bottom chords and two top chords.

Roof sheathing is typically fastened to the top chords and ceiling finishes are typically attached to the bottom chords. These chords are typically made of 2 by 4s, 2 by 5s, or 2 by 6s.

Webs

Webs are the internal components of trusses. Webs typically run from the top chord to the bottom chord. They may be vertical or at an angle to the vertical. Some webs are in compression and others are in tension. It's not easy to visually determine which webs are being squeezed and which are being pulled.

Bracing of Compression Webs

The webs are wood members, often 2 by 3s or 2 by 4s. Tension webs are stretched and are not inclined to buckle. Compression webs, however, are squeezed from either end and are prone to buckling. As a result, compression webs are often braced with 1 by 4s, running along several trusses. The braces are fastened to the midpoints of all the compression webs to prevent them from buckling. Many truss manufacturers staple paper signs to their trusses with the words "brace here" to help with proper assembly. You can see these signs and if there are no braces, you'll know something was left out.

Trusses Need Lateral Support

Trusses require lateral support to prevent rotation or sideways movement. Diagonal bracing is often used during construction to keep the trusses in place until the sheathing and ceiling finishes are installed. The drywall below and plywood, waferboard, strand board or plank sheathing on top, provide adequate stiffening and lateral support for most trusses.

Spacing
Sheathing Sag

It is common to find trusses spaced 24 inches on center. This has some implications for both sheathing and drywall. It's common to find that the sheathing sags between trusses. This is because—

1. The sheathing wasn't thick enough, or

2. The sheathing has been weakened, often by rot resulting from condensation.

Drywall Sag

Drywall ceilings often sag below trusses. This is often in part because the trusses are 24 inches on center. It's good practice to strap the undersides of trusses with 1 by 4s, every 16 inches. This allows the drywall to be fastened every 16 inches rather than every 24 inches.

Condensation

Another cause of drywall sag during winter construction is condensation. Figure 4.42 shows several common truss shapes.

Truss Spans and Sizes

We can't tell in the field whether the spans are acceptable and whether the truss chords and webs are the right size. We have to rely on the designer. However, we can look at the performance of the truss. If there is movement, we can describe that, without knowing whether it's a design problem or some other difficulty. As in most areas, we identify non-performance rather than analyze the design.

Common truss problems include—

1. Sag

2. Buckled webs

3. Weak connectors

4. Rotation or lateral movement

5. Poor end bearing

6. Notches and holes

7. Rot or insect damage

8. Mechanical damage or splitting

9. Fire damage

FIGURE 4.42   Truss Types

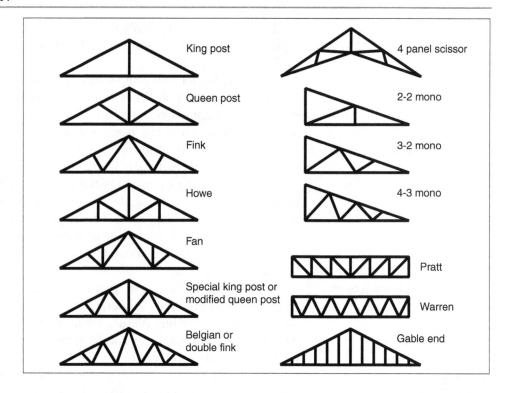

4.17.1   Truss Sag

When looking at roof framing, be careful not to confuse truss sag with sheathing sag. The sagging of sheathing creates a repetitive wave pattern across the roof. A sagging truss will more often show up as a large dish in the roof.

As we've talked about before, you have to look inside and out. One of the common problem areas in truss roofs is where a higher roof is adjacent to a lower level roof.

In snowy areas, snow will drift on the lower roof adjacent to a wall extending above the roof. The concentrated load created by this drifting snow may cause sagging or even break truss members in this area. Your roofing inspection should include a careful look at lower roof areas adjacent to higher parts of the building.

4.17.2   Buckled Webs

When looking at trusses, pay attention to all interior webs. You won't necessarily know which are in compression and which are in tension, but look for buckling, bending, and poor connections.

4.17.3   Weak Connections

Weak truss connections are a fairly common problem. They may be caused by—

1. Gusset plates or connectors missing
2. Connectors not applied in the right location

3. Connectors not fully seated because of
    a. poor original assembly
    b. rough handling
    c. warping wood
    d. rotational or movement of truss components, due to racking
4. Rusted connectors
5. Rotted wood
6. Cut, damaged or split wood at the connectors

While you may not get a look at all the connectors, this should be part of your focus when looking at trusses. Are the connectors in place, are they well secured? Is there evidence of slippage?

Most inspectors do not do a 100% inspection and do not pull a great deal of insulation away.

4.17.4   Rotation or Lateral Movement

This problem is most common during construction. Once ceiling finishes and sheathing are in place, it is unusual for trusses to move.

Look at the spacing of trusses. Is it the same between each pair of trusses? Is the spacing the same from top to bottom?

Rotation or lateral movement can be a problem in multi-level homes after the ceilings and roof sheathing are in place. Where one roof overlaps another, it is common not to sheath the underlying roof trusses. These trusses should be laterally braced. They often are missing this bracing.

STRATEGY

Multi-Level Roofs

4.17.5   Poor End Bearing

At the ends of trusses, the top and bottom chords meet. Trusses should rest on walls so that the top and bottom chord transmit their loads directly to the wall. If the truss is too far outboard, the bottom chord will sit on the wall, but the top chord will rest on the bottom chord out beyond the wall. This is not a desirable situation (Figure 4.43).

FIGURE 4.43   Roof Truss Components

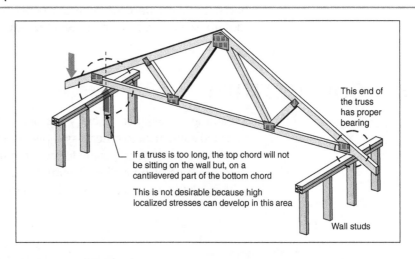

This end of the truss has proper bearing

If a truss is too long, the top chord will not be sitting on the wall but, on a cantilevered part of the bottom chord

This is not desirable because high localized stresses can develop in this area

Wall studs

Parallel Chord Trusses

Since trusses usually extend out beyond the walls, trusses too short to bear on the full wall plate are unusual.

Trusses may be supported by metal hangers, although this is not common. Parallel chord trusses are common on flat and cathedral roofs. Some trusses are designed to bear on their top chord. Some are designed to bear on their bottom chord. It's a mistake to install trusses upside down. You won't be able to tell by looking, other than to see signs of distress near the truss ends. There may be crushing, pulling apart, or bending of truss components.

| STRATEGY |

In most cases, you'll have a difficult time looking at the end bearing of trusses because they'll be surrounded by insulation, and they'll be out at the eaves of the roof where access is difficult. With flat and cathedral roofs, you may not see the trusses at all. Remember to document what you could and could not see.

4.17.6   Notches and Holes

Notches and holes are not permitted in trusses unless the design allowed for them. This would be unusual.

| STRATEGY |

Wherever you see holes or notches in truss members (chords or webs), write this up for further evaluation. Simple sistering or other repairs common with joists and rafters may not work with trusses. It's possible that the truss design allowed for this, but you have no way of knowing.

Where members have been notched or drilled, look for evidence of movement indicating distress. Where you see buckling or sagging, you can be sure that the design did not contemplate these.

Truses that have been cut or damaged should be considered ineffective, and further evaluation by a specialist should be recommended.

Inspector in the House: Beware the Loft

Our client initially was not planning to get a home inspection because he was an accomplished handyman. But the roof had a bit of a sag that worried him.

Lofts had become very popular in our town, and many homeowners were converting attics to living spaces. This home had a very nicely finished loft bedroom, complete with spiral staircase (by the way—this is a means of egress problem in many jurisdictions!) and beautiful railing.

It took some digging to find small access hatches into the knee wall areas on either side of the new room. Once inside, the cause of the roof sag was the owners had cut several webs of the roof trusses to accommodate the new room! Those roof trusses add so much clutter to an attic.

4.18   ROOF SHEATHING

Sheathing is designed to carry the dead load from the roof covering and roof-mounted equipment to rafters, roof joists or trusses. It also carries the live loads from wind, water, snow and people to roof framing members.

Sheathing also provides lateral bracing for roof framing members, including rafters, roof joists and trusses and a nailing surface for roof coverings.

FIGURE 4.44   Installation of Roof Boards

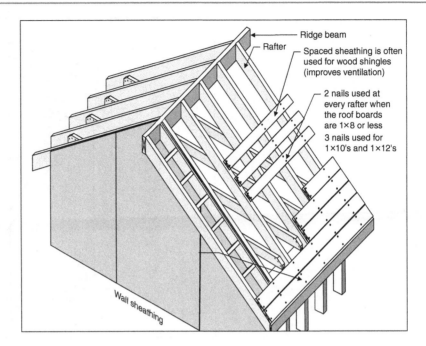

4.18.1   Materials

Wood plank roof sheathing is typically 1 by 4, 1 by 6, or 1 by 8. Joints may be butted or tongue-and-grooved. If tongue-and-grooved, the tongues should face up the roof and the grooves should face down, so water doesn't collect in the grooves.

Plank roofing may be solid or spaced (Figure 4.44). Spaced sheathing is common with wood, slate, tile and concrete roof coverings, for example. Asphalt shingles need solid sheathing.

Plywood roof sheathing, typically in 4 ft. by 8 ft. sheets, is common (Figure 4.45). Thicknesses range from $^3/_8$ to $^3/_4$ inch. Plywood roof sheathing should be installed with the long dimension perpendicular to rafters or trusses (the long dimension is laid across the roof)

Waferboard and OSB are also typically laid in sheets across the roof. Thicknesses are similar to plywood, but vary with load, span, roof covering material, etc.

Like Subflooring on Flat Roofs

Sheathing on flat roofs is usually thicker than sloped roofs because the snow loads and/or water loads may be greater. The thickness and strength of sheathing for flat roofs is often the same as subflooring.

No Sheathing Necessary

In some situations, sheathing is not used. Where the roof covering is concrete tile, some manufacturers recommend a wood batten system without sheathing. Battens are typically 2 inch by 2 inch. There is often a moisture barrier (plastic sheet) laid on top of the rafters to collect and drain any water that may make it through the roof coverings. The tiles are often hung on the battens and may also be nailed, screwed, clipped or wire tied to battens.

Where there is no sheathing, the possibility of lateral movement and rotation of individual wood members is greater. The battens do not provide as much lateral support as planking or plywood sheathing.

Edge Support for Panel Sheathing

Plywood waferboard and OSB requires support at all edges unless they are very thick. Local construction guides and codes spell out when edge support is needed. Most panel sheathing rests on the rafters or trusses at either end and/or intermediate supports. At top and bottom edges, support may be provided by—

F I G U R E 4.45   Installation of Panel Type Roof Sheathing

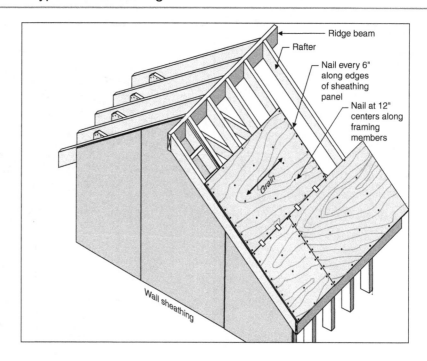

1. "H" clips (see illustration)
2. 2 by 2 blocking
3. Tongue and groove joints in the panels

Gaps Between Panels

Gaps of roughly $1/8$ inch should be provided between each panel to allow sheathing to expand without buckling.

Vertical Joints Staggered

In both plank and panel sheathing, vertical joints should not run continuously up one rafter or one truss. Adjacent vertical joints should be staggered to improve the strength.

Sheathing Spans

Many older buildings had rafters spaced at 16 inches on center. Many modern homes have trusses spaced at 24 inches on center. Although many authorities have allowed $3/8$ inch plywood and $7/16$ inch waferboard on trusses spaced 24 inches on center, sheathing often sagged between trusses. This common problem may be cosmetic only, or it may get to a point where failure is a possibility. In this case, corrective action is taken. The most common corrective action is to replace or overlay the sagging sheathing with a thicker sheathing. A less common solution is to provide intermediate supports under the sheathing, working from inside the attic.

FRT Plywood

Fire Retardant Treated (FRT) plywood has been used since the late 1970s, often on attached homes (row or town homes) rather than detached homes. It was used to replace more expensive parapet walls extending through the roofs at party walls where fire-stopping was needed between dwellings. In many areas, the plywood was required 4 feet out from the party wall on either side of the roof. It was frequently, but not always, installed in this location.

How It Works

Chemicals in the wood are designed to char the wood at relatively low temperatures (typically in the early stages of a fire). This charring raises the auto-ignition temperature of the wood. This will help control the spread of a fire. The charring of the wood weakens it, but in a fire situation, this is a secondary issue.

With some types of FRT plywood, the chemicals were activated at excessively low temperatures, (around 150°F) commonly reached in attics. As a result, the wood was weakened even though there was no fire situation.

The weakened FRT plywood often loses its ability to hold staples. Roof shingles can be blown off in relatively low winds. The sheathing may sag and/or delaminate and can be weak enough that someone walking on the roof could fall through.

4.18.2   Conditions

Common sheathing problems include—

1. Sag
2. Buckled
3. Delaminated
4. Deteriorated FRT plywood
5. Rot and insect damage
6. Mechanical damage and splitting
7. Fire damage

Sagging Sheathing

STRATEGY

Be careful with flat and cathedral roofs. Walk carefully on these and pay attention to how spongy they are, whether or not sag is visible. These roofs have no attic, and are much more prone to rot problems, due to condensation caused by a lack of ventilation.

From the outside, look for a wavy pattern across the surface of the roof. From inside, check the sheathing between rafters or trusses.

Buckled Plywood, Waferboard, or OSB

STRATEGY

Look for panels that are crushed slightly at the edges. They may be buckled up or down. This may be a greater problem where there is more moisture, but can occur in any roof.

Delaminated Plywood

STRATEGY

Again, this is a problem that is often (but not always) associated with flat or cathedral roofs. In conventional attics, it may also be found where there is poor venting, good insulation and lots of moist air leaking into the attic.

Deteriorated FRT Plywood

STRATEGY

Sometimes there are labels (stamps) on the plywood that are visible from the attic that identify it as FRT plywood. However, these may not be visible.

While this plywood is rarely found in detached houses, it is common in town or row houses built in the 1970s and 80s. The FRT plywood may be near the party walls, but you should look at all the sheathing.

Look for evidence of roofing nails or staples that have come loose. Look for delaminating plywood. Look for darkened color on the underside of the plywood. This may look like mold. Look for white dust. These are the salts of the chemicals, creating a type of efflorescence.

REVIEW QUESTIONS

1. What is the function of a footing? A foundation?

2. List the three common foundation configurations and footing types.

3. What is the difference between a strip footing and a pad footing and where would each be used?

4. There are several different materials that a foundation might be made of. List as many as you can.

5. Why is it critical to document how the crawlspace was inspected?

6. Explain the difference between a live load and a dead load. Give examples.

7. What is the difference between a pilaster and a pier?

8. When a foundation is supported on piles, are the piles typically visible for inspection?

9. Name four causes of cracks in foundation walls.

10. Explain the difference between uniform settlement and differential settlement.

11 What is a shrinkage crack and what causes it?

12. Describe a typical shrinkage crack.

13. What is the main implication of a shrinkage crack?

14. If you identify a foundation crack, is it possible to determine the rate of movement at the time of the inspection?

15. It is a good idea to inspect the neighborhood as you are arriving at an inspection. What kinds of things should you look for and how can they help you in your inspection?

16. In general, which crack would be more serious? A crack that has moved in one plane or a crack that has moved in two different planes?

17. It is sometimes difficult to distinguish between a settlement problem and a heaving problem. Give a few examples of how you would distinguish between the two.

18. Cracks due to horizontal forces rarely result in a structural problem.

    True   False

19. Often horizontal forces will cause horizontal cracks in a foundation wall. Why might the crack disappear near the edge of the wall?

20. In your own words, give a definition of lateral support as it applies to foundations.

21. Why might a damaged foundation wall start to move suddenly after a heavy rain?

22. Which is stronger, a poured concrete wall or concrete block wall of the same dimensions?

23. In your own words describe a cold joint as it relates to a concrete foundation.

24. The foundation should extend far enough out of the ground that the wood members are not below grade. Explain why.

25. List five structural components of floors, as defined in this chapter.

26. All of these may be floor functions except:

    a. transferring live and dead loads to the foundation

    b. providing lateral support for foundation walls

    c. carrying the weight of masonry chimneys

27. Floors will bend a little before they break.

    True   False

28. Why is wood contact with concrete near or below grade level discouraged?

29. What is the main function of sills?

30. Why are rotted sills a problem? (three answers)

31. How are sills anchored to foundations?

32. List five common sill problems.

33. Columns transfer live and dead loads:

    a. from joists to footings

    b. from beams to footings

    c. from joists to soil directly

    d. from subfloors to joists

    e. from subfloors to footings

34. List five common column materials.

35. List 12 common column problems.

36. Which column materials are susceptible to crushing?

37. How wide should the top of a column be, relative to the width of the beam above?

38. How may steel columns be fastened to steel beams? (three answers)

39. What tool, in addition to your eyes, is commonly used to inspect columns?

40. Columns are most likely to rot at the

    a. top

    b. middle

    c. bottom

41. Beams carry loads from: (four answers)

    a. floors   **d.** footings

    b. walls   **e.** columns

    c. roofs

42. The two most common beam materials are _____.

43. List four types of engineered wood products used for beams.

44. A beam notched at the top is more likely to cause failure than one notched at the bottom.

    True   False

45. Beams rest on: (two answers)

    a. foundations   **d.** joists

    b. columns   **e.** buttresses

    c. studs

46. The ends of beams should have at least _____ inches of bearing.

47. List 14 common beam problems.

48. Where is rust most likely to be found on a steel beam?

    a. the top

    b. the end

    c. the middle

    d. in the web only

49. Beams sag because they are over_____. Another way of saying the same thing is that the beam is under_____.

50. Steel beams should be shimmed with wood.

    True   False

51. Wood beams should not be supported directly on hollow concrete block.

    True   False

52. Wood beams in pockets in masonry or concrete walls should have $1/2$ inch of air space around the sides, top, and end. Why?

53. Checking of wood beams: (two answers)

    a. indicates failure

    b. requires repair, but not replacement

    c. results from drying

    d. is usually not serious

    e. indicates fire damage

54. Columns that rest on the mid-point of beam spans may (two answers)

    a. indicate very good design

    b. overstress the beam

    c. create a concentrated load

    d. prevent beam sag

    e. create a strong connection

55. The function of joists is to: (three answers)

    a. transfer live loads to beams

    b. transfer dead loads to foundations

    c. transfer live and dead loads directly to columns

    d. transfer live loads to walls

    e. transfer dead loads to subfloors

56. Name five engineered wood products that may replace conventional joists.

57. Joists see vertical loads only.

    True   False

58. List 11 common joist problems you will see on inspections.

59. Roughly how far can these common joists span if spaced 16 inches apart?

    2×8 _____ 2×10 _____ 2×12 _____

60. Joists typically need _____ inches of end bearing when supported by wood.

61. Joists notched at their end are stronger than normal joists.

True   False

62. Joists resting on foundation walls at or near grade level are prone to rot.

True   False

63. List six possible joist hanger problems.

64. How does a ledger board support joists?

65. List four things that can prevent joist twisting.

66. Holes in joists should be near the bottom rather than the middle of the joists.

True   False

67. What is a cantilever?

68. Outdoor cantilevers are particularly vulnerable to moisture damage. Where is the problem most likely to occur and why?

69. Partition walls exert no load on floor joists because they are not load bearing walls.

True   False

70. Name three common subfloor materials.

71. Subfloors act like (two answers)

a. joists

b. foundations

c. columns

d. footings

e. beams

72. What is one possible disadvantage of diagonal plank subflooring?

73. Plywood should be installed with its long dimension parallel to joists.

True   False

74. Common subflooring problems include (give nine) _____.

75. List five common concrete floor problems.

76. Shrinkage crack patterns in concrete floors are usually _____.

a. in circles

b. in straight lines

c. random

d. at 45° to walls

e. at 90° to walls

77. How can you tell if slabs have had their support undermined?

78. List seven functions of walls.

79. List six materials that may be used for masonry walls.

80. Masonry walls are strongest in:

a. compression

b. tension

c. bending

81. List seven common problems with masonry walls.

82. You see large metal plates or stars on the outside of the masonry walls at the top of the first floor level of an older two story building. Why are these here?

83. Patched cracks on brick are a sure sign of serious structural movement.

True   False

84. Bearing walls and partition walls are built in substantially the same way.

True   False

85. Walls see vertical loads only.

True   False

86. Openings in partition walls need headers.

True   False

87. List five differences between a bearing wall and a partition wall.

88. Where is condensation damage likely to be worst?

a. Above windows

b. At the tops of walls

c. At corners of walls

d. At midpoints of walls

e. At bottoms of walls

89. Longer studs are more susceptible than conventional length studs to:

a. settling

b. rotting

c. leaning

d. leaking

e. bowing or buckling

90. Wall framing problems are often tough to identify because wall framing details are usually concealed.

True   False

91. Offset bearing walls: (two answers)

a. are an asset

b. are a serious structural problem

c. are common

d. often result in minor structural problems

e. must always be parallel to joists

92. Missing fire stopping: (three answers)

a. is more common on balloon frame than platform construction

b. is a fire hazard

c. is tough to see on most inspections

d. is only found in masonry houses

e. is never found in masonry houses

93. Interior wall cracks radiating up from the top of windows may mean: (three answers)

    a. sagging lintels

    b. foundation settlement

    c. over-spanned joists

    d. a lack of wall sheathing

    e. shrinkage of framing members

94. In masonry veneer walls:

    a. the masonry is roughly 1 inch thick

    b. the masonry is supported primarily by the wood framing

    c. header courses are found every 7th row

    d. weep holes are often found

    e. metal ties are never used

95. Give five techniques to help differentiate masonry veneer walls from solid masonry walls.

96. List 10 common masonry veneer wall problems. Think of the masonry veneer part only.

97. List seven common veneer wall problems. Think of the wood frame part only.

98. The masonry veneer is a load bearing part of the structure.

True   False

99. Briefly describe the functions of arches and headers. (Hint: use the words "loads," "transfer," and "openings" in your discussion.)

100. What materials are used for arches?

101. End bearing for steel lintels in masonry should be at least _____ inches.

102. End bearing for headers in wood frame walls should be at least _____ inches.

103. List eight common arch and lintel problems.

104. The top of the exposed edge of a steel lintel should be caulked.

True   False

105. Wood lintels on the exterior face of a building are particularly prone to _____ problems.

106. List five functions of roof framing members.

107. Define rafters, roof joists, and ceiling joists.

108. Ceiling joists are often not continuous from one side of the building to the other. In this case they are spliced over a central bearing wall. Why do they have to be securely tied together?

109. How might you tell the difference between roof sheathing sag and rafter sag from the exterior of the house?

110. Explain why a ridge beam helps prevent rafter spread.

111. Proper end bearing is required for rafters and ceiling joists. Generally speaking, what is the minimum recommended end bearing?

112. Give two examples of how you might differentiate between a roof leak and a condensation problem in an attic.

113. What is the main function of a collar tie?

114. What is the difference between a knee wall and a purlin?

115. What can cause sagging of the top plate on a knee wall?

116. On a roof truss, what is the difference between a chord and a web?

117. Why is it common to find sagging of roof sheathing on trusses?

118. Why might a drywall ceiling sag below trusses?

119. There are many different kinds of trusses. List as many as you can.

120. Where are notches and holes commonly permitted in trusses?

Webs   Chords   Neither

121. In both plank and panel roof sheathing, vertical joints should not run continuously up one rafter or one truss. Adjacent vertical joints should be staggered. Explain why.

122. Give three possible causes of sagging sheathing.

123. What is FRT plywood and where was it commonly used?

CHAPTER

5

INSULATION AND VENTILATION

LEARNING OBJECTIVES

By the end of this chapter you should be able to:

- define the terms **insulation, vapor retarder,** and **air barrier,** including their purposes

- describe the implications of inadequate insulation and air/vapor barrier

- name two kinds of house ventilation

- list eight common insulation materials and their forms

- give two reasons it is important to control air movement through building walls and roofs

- indicate whether vapor barriers should be on the warm or cold side of walls

- explain why a moisture barrier should be laid on an earth floor in a crawlspace

- list the functions and types of roof vents

- state at least three precautions you should take when inspecting attics

- list the ventilation-related problems (and their implications) you may find in attics

- list three common problems with wall insulation

- list nine common problems with basement and crawlspace insulation and ventilation

- list seven common areas where insulation may be provided over unheated spaces

INTRODUCTION	In this chapter, you will learn how insulation, air/vapor barriers, and ventilation systems work to keep houses comfortable and structurally sound. While the goal for most homeowners is reduced heating and cooling costs, the home inspector's goal on insulation, air/vapor barriers, and ventilation systems is to identify conditions that may damage the house.
Insulation and Moisture Control	We'll discuss the basics of how insulation works and describe some of the common materials and their characteristics. We'll talk about moisture control, a very important and poorly understood issue. We'll talk about ventilation in two different senses and put the whole package together to look at the house as a group of interrelated systems.
Insulating House Components	We'll discuss how roofs, walls, floors, basements, and crawlspaces are typically insulated and ventilated, and we'll discuss where problems typically crop up.
Ventilation and Air Quality	We'll conclude by discussing some of the ventilation approaches that help maintain good air quality in buildings.
Problem Identification	By the time you have finished this chapter, you'll be able to spot common performance-related problems and understand their implications. You'll be able to make appropriate recommendations. The inspection of insulation and ventilation systems is challenging because so little of these systems can be seen. In many cases, you will have to rely on indirect or incomplete evidence.

5.1   DEFINITIONS AND BASIC CONCEPTS

Before looking at specific components and conditions of insulation inspection, it will be useful to understand some basic terms and concepts.

5.1.1   How Heat Moves

Moving Heat

Heat moves through solids, liquids, gases, and even through a vacuum. Thermal energy or heat always flows from an area of high energy to an area of low energy. Warm materials always transfer their heat to cooler materials. Cool does not flow. Heat flows.

Insulation

Insulation slows the rate of heat loss from a house. In essence, insulation is a material designed specifically to control heat loss.

Know Your Levels

Recommended levels of insulation in roofs, walls, and floors vary depending on your area (Figure 5.1). You should learn what is recommended in new construction in your area. Many older homes have insulation levels far below what is recommended in new construction.

An important basic concept throughout this chapter will be that of **thermal resistance** or R-values. Thermal resistance is the capacity of a material to resist heat transfer.

R-Value per Inch

The thermal resistance of materials is usually measured per inch of thickness. For example, the R-value of a fiberglass insulation might be 3.0 per inch. The value of a 4-inch fiberglass batt is $3.0 \times 4 = 12$. All materials have R-values. Good insulation materials have R-values as high as R-7 or R-8 per inch. Thermal conductors have very low R-values because they are very poor thermal insulators. For example, the R-value of a one-inch-thick concrete slab is 0.08. One inch of stucco has an R-value of 0.2. A one-inch pine board has an R-value of 1.25.

FIGURE 5.1 Recommended Insulation Levels

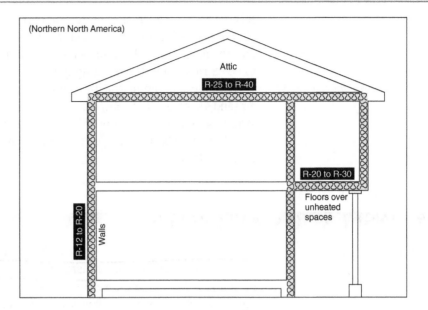

5.1.2   The Role of Air Flow

Still air is a very good insulator. The problem is that air moves around by convection and wind, and the heat travels freely in the air. A good insulation material is one that limits the movement of the trapped air.

Air Barrier

Most insulation materials let some air pass right through them. To mitigate this, an air barrier can be installed. An **air barrier** prevents or restricts air leakage.

5.1.3   The Role of Moisture

Relative Humidity

Relative humity (RH) is the amount of moisture in the air relative to the amount of moisture the air could hold if saturated.

Vapor Barrier

As the temperature of air goes down, its ability to hold moisture is reduced, and the relative humidity goes up. Air which starts out at 70°F at 40% relative humidity will reach 100% relative humidity as it is cooled to 45°F. Therefore, air in the insulation can cool to the point that it deposits moisture in the insulation (whether it be in a wall or attic). This water reduces the effectiveness of the insulation because water is a good conductor of heat. But more importantly, water that gets trapped in the building structure can lead to rot and peeling paint. Therefore, a vapor barrier is required on the warm side of most insulations. A **vapor barrier** (or **vapor retarder**) is designed to restrict the movement of water vapor. An **air/vapor barrier** restricts both vapor diffusion and air leakage.

Drying Potential

Some buildings are able to dry faster than others. Where air can move freely through attics or between siding and sheathing, moisture can be flushed into the outdoor air during periods of low relative humidity. Wall assemblies with wood shingles and shakes, conventional wood siding, and aluminum and vinyl siding have fairly good **drying potential.** Materials like stucco and EIFS (Exterior Insulation and Finishing Systems) do not have good drying potential. This can have an effect on whether (and how much) damage is done to structures due to trapped moisture.

5.1.4   Ventilation, Caulking, and Weather Stripping

Ventilation

It is not possible to create a perfect air barrier. Therefore, wherever possible, the cold side of insulation should be ventilated to remove the moisture-laden air that leaks into the insulation. This allows any moisture that does get through to the cold side to be carried out of the building quickly.

Caulking and Weather Stripping

Insulation, complete with an air/vapor barrier, will not be very effective if the air (and, therefore, the heat) can simply bypass the insulation. Caulking and weather stripping go a long way toward preventing air leakage into and out of a home.

With these basic concepts in mind, we are ready to begin looking at specific insulation materials.

5.2   INSULATION MATERIALS

Function

The purpose of insulation is to slow the rate of heat transfer. This is true in both hot and cold climates. In cold climates, we are trying to stop the flow of heat out of the building. In hot climates, we are trying to slow the movement of heat into the building. Fortunately, insulation works in both directions. For the many climates that need heating and cooling at different times of the year, insulation serves both functions.

All Materials Add to R-Value

The insulation value of walls is more than the value of the insulation itself. All materials have some insulating value, including the plaster or drywall, polyethylene air/vapor barrier, wood sheathing, building paper, siding, and the air films. However, the majority of the R-value of the wall is attributable to the insulation.

5.2.1   Forms of Insulation

Insulation typically takes one of four forms (see Figure 5.2):

1. **Loose fill.** Loose fill, which can be blown or poured, is common in roofs and walls. Materials such as cellulose fiber, glass fiber, mineral wool, vermiculite, and perlite have all been commonly used. Other materials include sawdust, wood shavings, shaved leather, asbestos, and gypsum slag.

2. **Batts or blankets.** Fiberglass and mineral wool commonly come in batts or blankets. Batts are typically 12 to 24 inches wide and fit between ceiling joists, rafters and wall studs. Blankets can be up to six feet wide and are typically laid over ceiling joists.

3. **Rigid boards.** Rigid board insulation can be fit between studs or on the outer face of studs, replacing exterior sheathing. Common board insulations include fiberglass, expanded polystyrene, extruded polystyrene, polyurethane, and polyisocyanurate. These materials are often faced with housewrap-type products, Kraft paper, asphalt-impregnated Kraft paper, or aluminum foil. Some of these materials have very high R-values.

4. **Foamed-in-place insulations.** Foamed-in-place insulations include polyurethane and **polyisocyanate.** Notice it's similar to the word **polyisocyanurate,** but we left out the **"-ur-"** on purpose.

FIGURE 5.2   Forms of Insulation

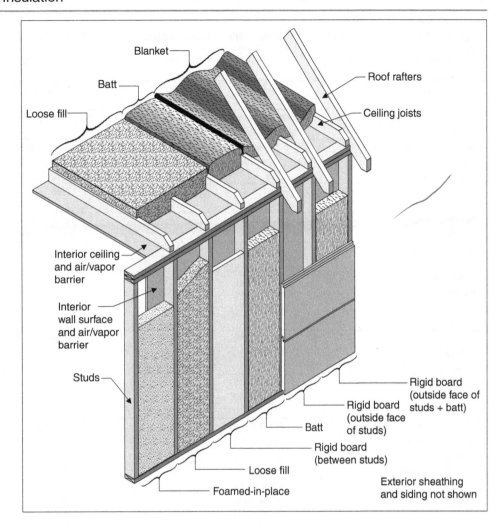

Blanket

Batt

Loose fill

Roof rafters

Ceiling joists

Interior ceiling
and air/vapor
barrier

Interior
wall surface
and air/vapor
barrier

Studs

Rigid board
(outside face of
studs + batt)

Rigid board
(outside face
of studs)

Batt

Rigid board
(between studs)

Loose fill

Foamed-in-place

Exterior sheathing
and siding not shown

5.2.2   Common Insulation Materials and Their Properties

Table 5.1 sets out the properties of various insulating materials. Some of the information in the chart has been approximated, and there are exceptions to these numbers. There are variances with each material, depending on density and other factors, but this is a broad guideline.

Inspection Tip

You'll want to learn to identify the various insulation materials so you can—

■ properly describe them during your inspections, and

■ estimate the total insulation value.

You can find samples of most common insulations at building supply stores. You may want to keep small samples with you, to help identify these materials in the field.

T A B L E 5.1   Properties of Common Insulation Materials

Material (and form)	Approx. R-value per inch	Air Barrier?	Vapor Barrier?	Combustible?	Resistant to Sunlight?	Resistant to Moisture?
Fiberglass (loosefill)	3.0	No	No	No, or slightly	Yes	Somewhat
Fiberglass (batt)	3.2	No	No	No, or slightly	Yes	Somewhat
Fiberglass (board)	4.3	Some have air barrier attached	No	No, or slightly	Yes	Somewhat
Cellulose fiber (loose fill)	3.5	Limited extent	No	Yes, although treated with fire retardants	Yes	No
Mineral wool (loose fill)	3.1	No	No	No	Yes	Yes
Mineral wool (batt)	3.3	No	No	Mostly no	Yes	Yes
Mineral wool (board)	4.3	No	No	No	Yes	Yes
Vermiculite/ perlite (loose fill, poured only)	2.4	No	No	No	Yes	Absorbs moisture if untreated
Expanded polystyrene (board)	4.0	Yes, if joints are sealed	Almost (thicker boards retard more)	Yes	No	Somewhat
Extruded polystyrene (board)	5.0	Yes, if joints are sealed	Almost (thicker boards retard more)	Yes	No	Yes
Closed-cell phenolic plastic (board)	8.0	Yes, if joints are sealed	No	Very slightly	No	Yes
Polyisocyanurate (board)	7.0	Yes, if joints are sealed	Yes	Yes	No	No
Polyurethane (board)	6.3	Yes, if joints are sealed	Yes	Yes	No	No
Polyurethane (foamed-in-place)	6.0	Yes	Sometimes	Yes	No	Somewhat
Isocyanate or polyisocyanate (foamed-in-place)	4.3	Yes	Yes, in typical thicknesses	Yes	Yes	Somewhat

5.3   AIR/VAPOR BARRIER MATERIALS (VAPOR RETARDERS)

The title of this section suggests that air barriers and vapor barriers are the same things. While we often use the same material to do both, the functions are different.

5.3.1   Assume a Heating Situation

In climates like Florida, where cooling is more important, keep in mind that the warm, moist air we're trying to stop is on the outside, rather than the inside. The function of air barriers is the same; the only thing that changes from heating to cooling climates is the direction of movement that causes the problem. In a heating climate, we don't want the warm, moist air to leak into and through the walls to the outside. In a cooling climate, we don't want the warm, moist outdoor air to leak into and through the walls to the inside. For our discussions, we're going to assume climates where heating is a bigger issue than cooling.

Function of Air Barriers

Air barriers are designed to **stop air movement** through the building walls and roof. There are two reasons this is important:

- Air carries heat. We want to minimize the flow of building heat to the outdoors.
- Air carries moisture. This moisture may be deposited in the building structure as it cools and condenses. This can cause damage to the building.

Function of Vapor Barriers

A **vapor barrier, vapor retarder,** or **vapor diffusion retarder** (**VDR**) is designed to protect the building from moisture damage. A VDR minimizes (but does not completely stop) the diffusion of vapor from inside the house to the wall or roof cavity. Air movement is not necessary for vapor diffusion to take place. Air leakage is roughly one hundred times more important than vapor diffusion, with respect to moisture damage to buildings.

As you can see, a vapor diffusion retarder has fewer functions and is less critical than an air barrier. Figure 5.3 summarizes the differences between the two. Let's look at air barriers first.

5.3.2   Air Barriers

What Makes up the Air Barrier?

In a typical home, the air barrier may be thought of as a system, rather than a single component. Many people think only of polyethylene film as an air barrier. People don't usually think of windows as air barriers, but they are. So are drywall, plaster, doors, caulking, weather stripping, and many other building materials.

FIGURE 5.3   Air Barrier versus Vapor Barrier

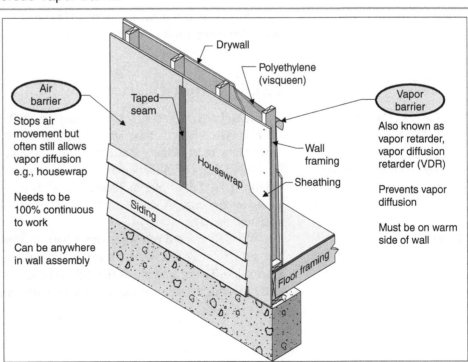

F I G U R E 5.4   Vapor Barrier Location

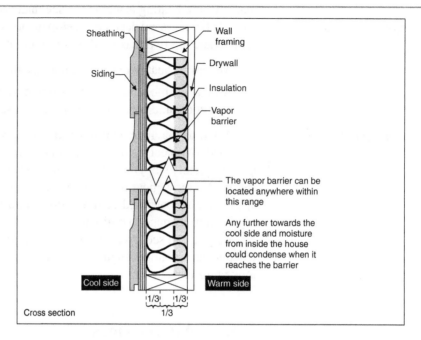

Polyethylene

Polyethylene film is often installed as an air barrier because it is more continuous than other building components. However, polyethylene film is often not continuous, because of a number of factors, including—

- poorly sealed joints;
- discontinuities in the film at partitions, wall/ceiling intersections, wall/floor intersections, door and window openings, etc.; and
- plumbing, electrical, and heating penetrations.

Air barrier systems must be continuous in order to be effective. One hole or unsealed seam can compromise the entire system.

5.3.3   Vapor Barriers

Continuity Not Critical

Unlike air barriers, vapor barriers do not have to be continuous to be effective. Vapor diffusion is a function of the surface area across which the water molecules can move. If we block most of the surface area, we'll stop most of the vapor diffusion.

Must Be on the Warm Side

Vapor barriers must be on the warm side of the wall to perform their function (Figure 5.4). If the water molecules are allowed to move into a cool space, they are likely to condense. A vapor retarder on the cool side will not protect the wall from moisture damage.

Within the Warm Third

A widely quoted rule says vapor barriers don't have to be at the warm face of the insulation. They can be a third of the way through the insulation, closer to the warm side. The research that this rule is based on is a 1950s study of questionable authority, but the rule has been relied on without serious trouble for a long time. It seems to work.

Don't Want Two Vapor Barriers

Consider a wall with a vapor barrier on the inside surface. Can we have a second vapor barrier on the exterior surface? No. Vapor barriers are not likely to be 100 percent effective. We don't want to allow moisture to get into the wall cavity, and then trap it there. We want to allow that moisture to move out through the wall to the outdoors. Any vapor that leaks past the internal vapor barrier should be allowed to flush itself out to the exterior.

Building Paper Vapor Permeable

That's why building paper has traditionally been used on the exterior of buildings. It is very good at stopping external water from getting into the wall. It does, however, stop vapor diffusion moving out through the wall. Housewraps are also vapor permeable.

Cooling Climate

Where air conditioning is an issue, we still want the vapor barrier on the **warm** side of the wall. In this case, it's the **outside.** We don't want the high vapor pressure from the outdoors pushing water vapor into the cooler wall cavities, where it may condense.

In hot climates, the walls store moisture and dry to the inside. Again, in Florida for example, we wouldn't want a vapor barrier on the inside, since that would inhibit drying of the walls.

5.3.4   Summary

We've talked about insulation materials and air/vapor barriers designed to control air and moisture flow in the home. Now let's assume that our efforts to control airflow and moisture have failed. This is a good assumption. What do we do now? Let's look at some ventilation systems.

5.4   VENTING ROOFS

Venting Living Spaces

There are two different kinds of ventilation—one is for living spaces and the other is for unconditioned spaces. Ventilation of living spaces is designed to—

■ Remove excess moisture from sources such as kitchens, bathrooms, and clothes dryers. This helps protect the structure from moisture damage by exhausting the moisture directly rather than allowing it to leak into wall and roof systems.

■ Replace stale, polluted air with fresh air. This helps to maintain good indoor air quality.

A detailed discussion of ventilating living spaces is beyond the scope of this book. For more information, including coverage of heat recovery ventilators and exhaust fans, see *Principles of Home Inspection: Insulation.*

Ventilating Unconditioned Spaces

The second type of ventilation is designed to flush out the warm, moist air that has escaped from the living space (despite our best efforts) before it has a chance to deposit its moisture into the building structure where it can do some damage. This ventilation is most visible on roofs but is also inherent in walls and may be built into sub-grade areas such as crawlspaces. Our discussion here will focus on venting roofs.

Ventilation to Eliminate Heat

There's another good reason to ventilate unconditioned spaces, especially in climates with hot summers. The air in a roof space can become very hot. The sun beating down on a roof surface can drive heat into the roof space. Summer attic temperatures of 130°F are not unusual. If the outdoor temperature is 100°F, it's tough enough to keep a building cool. However, if the air immediately above the building is 130°F, it's even harder to cool. The ventilation system allows the 130°F air to be replaced with 100°F air. Roof ventilation systems flush out the super-heated air and help keep the building cooler.

Prolonged Life of Roof Shingles

Some believe the high temperatures found on poorly ventilated roofs in warm climates contribute to a shortened life expectancy of roofing products such as asphalt shingles.

Purpose

We've touched on three functions of roof venting. Let's review them:

■ Venting allows warm, moist air out of the attic before the moisture condenses on structural members.

■ Venting reduces attic temperatures in the summer by allowing hot air to escape.

■ Venting helps prevent ice dams by keeping the attic cold in winter.

Types and Locations of Vents

The four common types of vents are soffit, ridge, roof, and gable. These are illustrated in Figure 5.5.

FIGURE 5.5   Types and Locations of Roof Vents

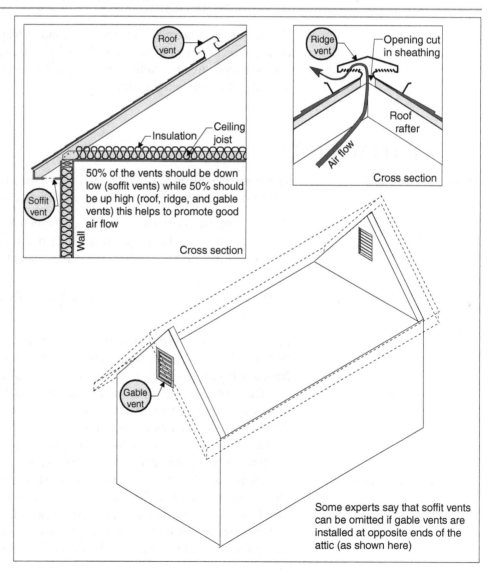

High and Low Vents

Soffit vents typically comprise about 50 percent of the ventilation. Ridge, roof, or gable vents make up the balance. The purpose of low and high vents is to encourage convective air movement through the attic. Air is drawn in through the soffit vents and leaves through the ridge, roof, or gable vents.

Gable Vents at Opposing Ends Vent Both Roof Surfaces

Some experts say that soffit vents can be omitted where there are gable vents at opposing ends of attic areas. While we prefer to see soffit vents, too, we have seen many houses vented this way with no evidence of problems. In many locations, roof vents are required on both sides of a gable roof, for example. This is good practice because wind comes from different directions on different days. If the roof vents are on the downwind side of the roof, air will tend to be drawn out of the roof vents as intended. However, if the roof the vents are on the windward side of a roof, air may be forced into the attic through the roof vents. If there are vents on both sides of the roof, we are assured that air will be drawn out of at least some of the roof vents.

Baffles for Soffit Vents

It's common to find soffit vents blocked by insulation. Good installations include cardboard, plywood, or expanded polystyrene baffles. These baffles prevent insulation from covering the roof vents and allow air to flow up through the soffit vents into the roof space. Baffles also direct the air away from the insulation and help reduce wind washing.

Recommended Amounts of Attic Ventilation

The total vent area is often recommended to be 1/300 of the floor space of the attic. If the attic floor is 600 square feet, we would look for 2 square feet of unobstructed or free vent area (Figure 5.6). At least one square foot of this vent area would be at the soffits, and the other square foot would be at the ridge, roof, or gable vents. The actual vent size has to be larger because the vent area is reduced by louvers or screens to keep out insects, rain, and snow.

Low-Slope, Flat, and Cathedral Roofs

Where the roof slope is below two-in-twelve, or there is a cathedral roof with no attic space, the recommended vent area is often increased to 1/150 of the roof area.

Flat Roofs

Flat roofs typically have ventilation on opposing sides to promote cross ventilation. Since the roof surface is virtually flat, convective airflow does not help much. These roofs are vulnerable to condensation damage.

F I G U R E 5.6   Recommended Amount of Attic Ventilation

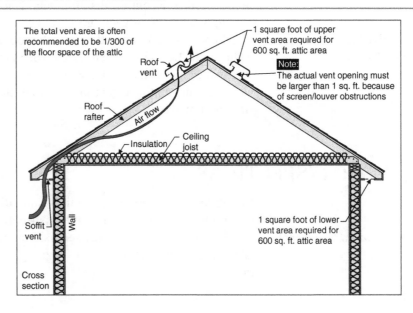

FIGURE 5.7   Venting Mansard and Gambrel Roofs

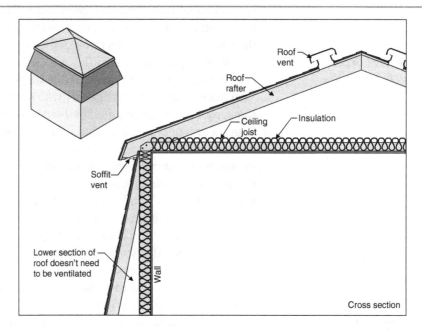

Roofs with a slope of less than two-in-twelve are often ventilated by maintaining $2^1/_2$ inches between the top of the insulation and the underside of the roof sheathing. Cross ventilation may be promoted with 2-inch by 2-inch purlins on top of, and perpendicular to, the roof joists. The insulation level is kept one inch below the top of the joist. The purlin provides another $1^1/_2$ inch of air space. Air can move in any direction with this configuration.

*Vent Spaces on Cathedral
Roofs*

Cathedral roofs with a slope of more than two-in-twelve are often ventilated without purlins. A three-inch air space is often recommended between the top of the insulation and the underside of the sheathing. Vents at the soffits and the ridge allow air to move up the roof space between rafter pairs.

Mansard and Gambrel Roofs

Mansard and gambrel roofs have an upper and lower section with different slopes. Most jurisdictions do not require the steep, lower slope of the roof to be vented (Figure 5.7). Vents are required at the ridge and at the bottom of the upper section. This is a complicated roof detail, and many mansard and gambrel roofs do not enjoy this type of venting.

*Can You Have Too
Much Venting?*

Some people believe there can be too much roof venting, particularly if the ceiling (attic floor) is not well sealed. Too much venting may create negative air pressure in the attic, which will tend to draw warm, moist air out of the living space. As we've discussed, this can promote, rather than prevent, condensation and damage structural members.

5.5   ATTIC INSPECTIONS

Before looking at problem conditions in attics, it will be useful to consider some general issues with respect to attic inspections, including safety issues.

Fall, Shock Hazard, and Irritant

The attic inspection is dangerous. You may fall through a ceiling, damage finishes, get an electric shock, or irritate your lungs, eyes, or skin with insulation materials.

Hot, Cold, and Infested

Attics can be hot in the summer and cold in the winter. They are often very difficult to move through and may be the home for birds and animals you'd rather not meet. Watch for animal droppings, which may pose a health hazard. You may be startled by bats, raccoons, squirrels, mice, and other animals, causing you to lose footing or step carelessly, putting a foot through a ceiling. Bees, hornets, and other stinging insects can also spoil your inspection.

Mask and Goggles

We recommend wearing an appropriate mask with proper filters (HEPA, High Efficiency Particulate Arresting or P100-type) and goggles to keep irritants out of your eyes. We also suggest gloves and long sleeves with tight cuffs when working in an attic.

How Far to Go

When the attic insulation completely covers the ceiling joists, we do not walk through the attic. We simply look at the attic from the access hatch. When you can't see the ceiling joists, it's difficult to know where to step. You may be able to find the ceiling joists with your foot by feeling around through the insulation. However, you may step on a wire or open electrical junction box, or on a joist that has been cut or is cracked. We recommend you do not move through attics where there is risk of damaging the property or injuring yourself. We are also cautious about planks that have been laid as walkways across attic areas. Unless they are clearly well traveled, we move carefully.

Describe Your Inspection

Whether you move through the attic or look at it from the attic access hatch, you should describe in your report how you performed your attic inspection. If you leave clients with the impression your inspection was thorough, you'll have trouble explaining why you didn't identify problems that are discovered later.

Opening Access Hatches

Let's assume you've found the attic access hatch. It's often difficult to get to it and it may be difficult to open. You'll have to use common sense here. We'll remove clothes from a closet and clear stored items from shelves so we can get into an attic. We arrange any materials we move so we are able to replace them in exactly the same order and location.

Hatches Screwed, Nailed, or Painted Shut

Most attic hatches do not require tools to open. Where the hatch has been sealed, you have to decide whether you're prepared to open it. Understand there is some risk of damaging cosmetic finishes.

Use Gloves to Avoid Fingerprints

Bare hands often leave dirty fingerprints on attic hatches. We recommend using gloves to avoid this. You should wipe off any marks you leave on the access hatch and trim. Many inspectors push access hatches open with flashlights to avoid touching them with their fingers.

Drop Cloths and Vacuum Cleaners

Many inspectors use drop cloths below the access hatch and carry battery-powered vacuum cleaners to clean up. It's not unusual for a small amount of insulation to fall through the hatch when removing or replacing it.

Careful with the Hatches

We open all access hatches very carefully. Insulation is often blown into an attic through a roof or gable vent. Twelve inches of loose-fill insulation over an access hatch can create quite a mess in the home when the hatch is opened. Insulation can be an irritant. If you dump insulation on people's clothes, perhaps you should offer to dry-clean them.

Some homes have full staircases leading to attics. Others have pull-down stairs. Be careful when pulling the stairs down. They may come down very quickly if mechanical components are loose or broken.

Stairs

When climbing the stairs, be careful. Treads or stringers may be loose or broken. Bolts may be loose or missing. Some home inspectors have been injured by pull-down stairs.

Access to Secondary Attics

Home inspectors frequently fail to report the fact they could not get into secondary attics. As you look for the attic access hatch, keep in mind what the house looks like from the exterior. Is there only one attic? Many houses have more than one attic or roof space. If some of the roof space is inaccessible, make sure you let your client know, in writing, about this limitation.

Two-story houses with one-story additions should have two attics. Split-level homes typically have two attics and two access hatches. Access to the lower attic is often through a sidewall on the upper floor. This may be in the back of a clothes closet, for example.

Houses with one and a half or two and a half stories often have three attic areas. There are typically at least two knee wall areas and a small attic above an upper floor. There may or may not be access into all of these. If there are dormers, there may be even more attics. A dormer can separate a knee wall attic into two separate areas. Again, there may or may not be access into each. Be sure to let your client know what parts of the house you could not get to.

Common attic problems include the following:

1. Access hatch problems
2. Insulation amount—too little
3. Insulation—wet
4. Insulation—compressed
5. Insulation—gaps or voids
6. Insulation—missing at dropped ceilings
7. Insulation covering recessed lights
8. Insulation inadequate in knee wall areas
9. Insulation inadequate at skylights and light wells
10. Ducts leaking or disconnected, or insulation missing or loose
11. Duct air/vapor barrier missing or damaged
12. Insulation too close to chimneys
13. Air/vapor barrier missing, incomplete, or wrong location
14. Air leakage excessive
15. Venting missing or inadequate
16. Venting obstructed at soffits or roof vents
17. Snow or wet spots below roof vents
18. Turbine vents noisy or seized
19. Power vents operating in winter
20. Power vents inoperative in summer
21. Rafters and sheathing—rot or mold
22. Plywood sheathing delaminating or buckling

5.5.1 Access Hatch Problems

Problems include—

- not insulated or weather-stripped
- missing or inaccessible

The attic access hatch should be insulated, ideally to the same level as the rest of the attic. Rigid or batt insulation can be glued to the top of the hatch. Air leakage around the access hatch can be controlled if the hatch cover is weather-stripped. Sometimes there is no access into the attic.

IMPLICATIONS

Heat loss is an issue where the access hatch is not insulated. Missing hatches should be written up as a limitation to your inspection. Air leaking from the house into the attic is both a heat loss and moisture damage issue. Warm, moist air leaking into the attic can condense on structural members, causing damage.

STRATEGY

As you remove the access hatch, it's easy to see whether it's insulated and weather-stripped. It's a minor recommendation to advise that insulation and weather stripping be added.

Inaccessible

If the hatch is blocked by shelving, for example, or the cover is nailed on, many inspectors will not get into the attic. Report that you didn't gain access to the attic, and why.

5.5.2   Insulation – Too Little

Many older homes will not have as much insulation as is currently recommended. You'll need to know the recommendations for new construction in your area as a benchmark. In some areas, the recommended insulation levels are higher if you have electric heat (because it's more expensive). If this is the case, you should be aware of these requirements and the heating type before you evaluate the insulation.

IMPLICATIONS

The obvious implication of inadequate insulation is heat loss. In areas where snow accumulation and ice dams are an issue, low attic insulation levels promote ice dams.

STRATEGY

To determine the R-value of the attic insulation, you'll need to identify the insulation material and check its R-value per inch. You'll then need to measure the average depth of insulation in the attic. For example, if there are four inches of mineral wool insulation, the R-value will be 13 (3.2×4). If the recommended attic insulation level is R-30, we have only roughly half the insulation level that would be ideal. We would recommend that a client make this improvement, although we would not rank it as a priority measure.

Improvement Rather Than Repair

Clients should understand that adding insulation to an attic is an improvement, rather than a repair. The home has survived with the existing insulation level to this point and would continue to be habitable if no improvements were made. Increased attic insulation will reduce heating costs and may help prevent ice dams. The house may be more comfortable as a result, but this is not necessarily so.

5.5.3   Insulation – Wet

Wet insulation does not insulate very well. Some materials recover their insulating properties as they dry. Others do not.

IMPLICATIONS

Wet insulation won't perform its function. If the amount of moisture is significant, damage to ceiling joists and finishes can result.

STRATEGY

As you look at the attic insulation look for evidence of moisture. In some cases this will appear as a dark patch. In some cases it appears as matted or compressed area of insulation. Cellulose fiber insulation, for example, will be compressed when it's wet and will not rebound. Fiberglass insulation tends to rebound and recover its insulating value as it dries.

Vulnerable Areas of Roof
Below Vents

Check at vulnerable points of the roof, such as chimney flashings and below valleys. We occasionally find piles of snow in the attic under roof vents. This is common where soffit vents have been blocked, and some roof vents act as inlets while others act as outlets for air. Roof vents on windward sides may allow blowing rain or snow in through the vents.

5.5.4   Insulation – Compressed

Insulation works by trapping pockets of air. When insulation is compressed, it can no longer insulate.

IMPLICATIONS

The implication of compressed insulation is reduced insulating values.

STRATEGY

Look for areas where insulation has obviously been compressed. Point out the reduced insulating abilities, and if the area is significant, recommend improvements. Adding insulation over the compressed insulation may be the easiest approach.

5.5.5   Insulation – Gaps or Voids

Attic insulation is not perfectly uniform. It's not unusual to find areas where there is little or no insulation.

IMPLICATIONS

Gaps and voids in insulation can result in increased localized heat loss.

STRATEGY

Check the insulation for uniform depth across the attic.

5.5.6   Insulation – Missing at Dropped Ceilings

Some houses have ceilings that are dropped over bathtub enclosures or kitchen cabinets, for example. Split-level homes have two attic levels. Wherever the attic level changes, it's possible that insulation is omitted on the vertical surfaces separating the upper and lower attic levels (Figure 5.8).

IMPLICATIONS

When insulation is missing at dropped ceilings there may be considerable heat loss through the wall sections between the upper and lower attic levels.

STRATEGY

As you move through the attic, you may see a recess in the insulation. If you can get over to that section, look down for insulation below. Make sure there is insulation on the bottom and sides.

Safety Issue

In some cases, the lowered ceilings for bathtub enclosures are completely filled with insulation. As you look across the attic, you won't notice these recessed ceilings. If you walk through the attic you may discover the recess in a dramatic and unpleasant way. This is another reason to be very careful when walking through attics where you cannot see the ceiling joists.

5.5.7   Insulation Covering Recessed Lights

IMPLICATIONS

Most people who are serious about energy efficiency do not like **recessed lights** (also called **pot lights,** or **high hat lights**) because such fixtures can be the source of considerable air leakage. They are difficult to seal.

F I G U R E 5.8 Missing Insulation at Dropped Ceiling

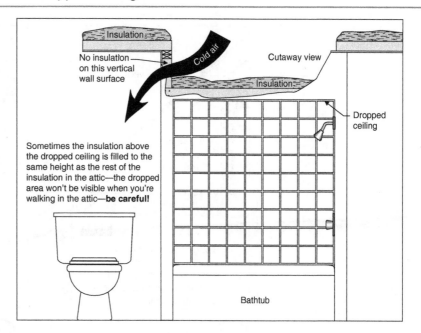

In addition, light fixtures above the ceiling get hot and may be covered with insulation. This poses a fire hazard unless the fixture is designed to be covered with insulation, as some are. Recessed lights that are designed to be covered with insulation typically have a double shell with an air space between to help cool the fixture.

STRATEGY

Where you see recessed light fixtures surrounded by insulation, look for a double shell on the fixture. You may be able to see a designation that includes the letters **IC,** indicating appropriate for use in an **insulated ceiling.**

Boxed-In Fixtures

Some recessed light fixtures have plywood or drywall boxes built around them to keep the insulation away. Insulation was often applied over the box to maintain continuity of the attic insulation while separating the light fixture from the insulation. This arrangement is not common but is acceptable.

5.5.8 Insulation Inadequate in Knee Wall Areas

Knee wall areas form triangles. There are two insulation strategies that can be used (see Figure 5.9.)

Floor and Wall

The most common approach is to insulate the floor and the wall of the attic. If loose-fill or batt insulation is used on the attic floor, solid blocking should be provided at the point where the floor meets the wall. This blocking could be rigid polystyrene insulation or wood, for example. It should be caulked to prevent air leakage from the living space ceiling into the attic. In many cases, this detail is not well done.

The wall should be insulated, and the air/vapor barrier should be on the warm side of the wall, as usual.

Insulating Sloped Roofs and End Walls

The less common approach to insulating knee walls is to add insulation to the underside roof sheathing between the rafters, and to insulate the end walls. This arrangement is less desirable because it does not allow for venting of the roof space and it involves heating a knee wall space that is not living space. In some cases, the knee wall area is used as storage, which may make it desirable to heat and insulate the knee wall areas.

FIGURE 5.9   Insulating Knee Walls

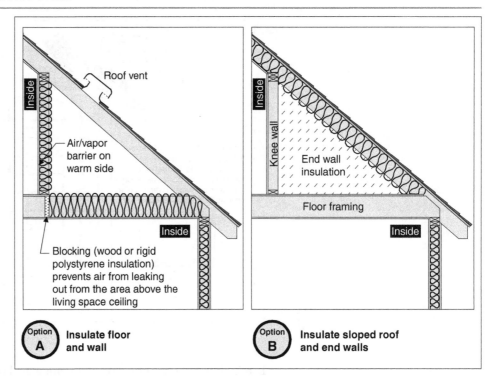

Roof vent

Inside

Air/vapor
barrier on
warm side

Inside

Blocking (wood or rigid
polystyrene insulation)
prevents air from leaking
out from the area above the
living space ceiling

Option A **Insulate floor and wall**

Inside

Knee wall

End wall
insulation

Floor framing

Inside

Inside

Option B **Insulate sloped roof and end walls**

IMPLICATIONS

The implication of inadequate knee wall insulation is increased heating cost.

STRATEGY

Check for insulation on the wall separating the knee wall from the living space, the floor, the rafters, and the end walls. Determine which approach has been followed. If possible, look at the floor/wall intersection for an air barrier between the ceiling joists where the attic joins the living space.

Air/Vapor Barriers and Ventilation

Look for continuous air/vapor barriers on the warm side of the insulation, no matter which approach is taken. Look also for ventilation of knee wall areas. In many cases it will be less than optimum. Look for evidence of mold or rot as a result of restricted air/vapor barrier or venting problems.

5.5.9   Insulation Inadequate at Skylights and Light Wells

Skylights on roofs typically have a light well that extends through the attic. This light well should be insulated to prevent heat loss into the attic. The air/vapor barrier should be on the warm side, which is the side closest to the interior finish. The light wells can be thought of as conventional walls, exposed to the attic. These are similar to knee walls.

IMPLICATIONS

Considerable heat loss can take place through the skylight well. Condensation is another possible implication. Moisture condensing and running down the skylight well surface inside the home is often mistaken for skylight leakage. You can identify the water as condensation by—

■ a lack of insulation;

■ a uniform water accumulation around the perimeter of the skylight (not typical of a leak);

■ the problem occurring only in cold weather; or

■ the problem not appearing during or after rains.

STRATEGY

When you're in the attic, look for insulation and air/vapor barriers on skylight wells. The insulation level would ideally be the same as any wall (R-12 to R-20, for example).

5.5.10 Ducts Leaking or Disconnected, or Insulation Missing or Loose

Heating and air conditioning ductwork in attics should be insulated.

IMPLICATIONS

Implications of missing or loose insulation for ducts include a loss of heat and condensation damage inside the ductwork. Condensation in poorly insulated ducts is often mistaken for roof leakage.

Condensation may also form in the attic itself. Leaking ducts add to heating and cooling costs, and reduce comfort.

In summer, condensation may occur on the outside of ducts. Again, this can look like leakage.

STRATEGY

Look for complete and intact insulation on heating and cooling ductwork in attics or other unconditioned spaces (Figure 5.10). In heating climates, the air/vapor barrier should be on the warm side. The ductwork acts as an air/vapor barrier in most cases. In cooling climates, the air/vapor barrier should be on the warm side. This is the outside of the insulation. The vapor barrier will be covering the insulation as you look at it from the attic in a cooling climate.

Leaky or Disconnected Ducts

Watch for ducts that are disconnected or leaking.

FIGURE 5.10 Ducts in Attics

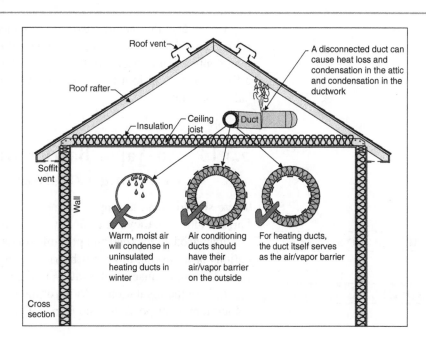

5.5.11 Duct Air/Vapor Barrier Missing or Damaged

The air/vapor barrier on a duct in the heating system is typically the duct itself. The insulation on the outside of the ducts may be exposed. In cooling climates, the air/vapor barrier should be on the outside, or warm side, of the insulation. When inspecting the attic, you should only see the air/vapor barrier covering the insulation. Ductwork is often sold with integral insulation and an external air/vapor barrier.

Air/vapor barriers must be intact to do their job.

IMPLICATIONS

Where the duct air/vapor barrier is missing or damaged, condensation within the insulation or on the outside of the duct can occur. This can rust the duct and damage interior finishes below. Again, this can be mistaken for a roof leak.

STRATEGY

In a heating climate, the duct is the air/vapor barrier. In a cooling climate, look for an air/vapor barrier on the outside of the insulation.

Where an external air/vapor barrier is present, check that it is intact. Recommend that damaged areas be repaired.

5.5.12 Insulation Too Close to Chimneys

Masonry chimneys should have non-combustible insulation surrounding them. Metal chimneys or vents should have no insulation around them for a distance of one to two inches, depending on the type of vent or chimney. Generally speaking, B-vents and L-vents for gas and oil appliances require a one-inch clearance. Metal chimneys for wood stoves and fireplaces typically require a two-inch clearance. There are some exceptions to these guidelines. A boxed-in area is usually constructed to keep insulation away.

IMPLICATIONS

Combustible insulation adjacent to a masonry chimney is a fire hazard. Insulation packed around a metal chimney can lead to overheating and deterioration of the chimney, even if the insulation is non-combustible. This is also a fire hazard.

STRATEGY

Look at masonry and metal chimneys to verify that the insulation is kept away from metal chimneys and that insulation against masonry chimneys is non-combustible.

Check also that an air barrier is provided around the chimney. In many cases, we can look down around metal chimneys through one or even two floor levels. This is not only an air barrier problem but also a fire-stopping problem. There should be a fire stop at each floor level to prevent the quick spread of fire up around the outside of a chimney.

5.5.13 Air/Vapor Barrier Missing, Incomplete, or Wrong Location

There should be an air/vapor barrier on the attic floor. Most attics have air/vapor barriers although they are typically less than perfect (Figure 5.11).

IMPLICATIONS

Increased air leakage and possible rot damage from condensation are the implications of a missing air/vapor barrier. An air/vapor barrier on the cold side of the insulation may cause condensation in the insulation.

STRATEGY

Lift up the insulation to look for an air/vapor barrier. It is usually Kraft paper (older homes) or polyethylene film (1970s and newer homes).

FIGURE 5.11   Air/Vapor Varrier Incomplete or Wrong Location

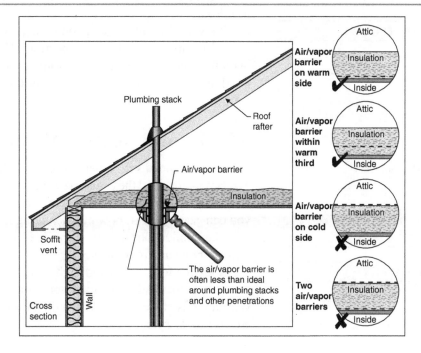

Look for Mold and Rot

Check the air/vapor barrier around roof penetrations such as plumbing stacks. Can air get up into the attic between the air/vapor barrier and the penetration? In most cases the air/vapor barrier is less than perfect. Recognizing this, it's more important to look for evidence of problems (mold and rot) than to criticize a less than perfect installation. Rot and mold are more likely if attic ventilation is poor. Very often, several systems in a house can be slightly less than perfect and we won't have any problems; however, if there are significant deficiencies in a number of systems and house humidity levels are high, rot and mold are likely.

Double vapor barriers or a vapor barrier on the cold side of the insulation are red flags. Look for evidence of condensation damage in and below the insulation. Recommend that the cold-side vapor barrier be removed.

5.5.14   Air Leakage Excessive

In addition to incomplete air/vapor barriers, poor caulking and weather stripping around openings can create air leakage. Common points where air leaks in significant quantities into the attic include—

- access hatches
- plumbing stacks
- light fixtures (especially recessed fixtures)
- chimneys and vents
- ducts
- partitions
- wall/ceiling intersections at the building perimeter
- exhaust fans and their ducts

Again, mold and rot are the risks of excessive air leakage, along with increased heat loss.

STRATEGY

It's very difficult to do a comprehensive air leakage inspection in the attic as part of a conventional home inspection. We recommend you spot-check to get an overall sense of the detail here. More importantly, look for evidence of the rot and mold that indicates damage being caused by the excessive air leakage.

5.5.15   Attic Venting Missing or Inadequate

1:300 Vent Ratio

The recommended venting area is often 1/300 of the floor area of the attic. This is a free-vent area, and the actual size of the vents has to be increased because all vents have louvers, screens, or both. Many vents have a net area stamped into them so you can get an idea of how much venting is present.

IMPLICATIONS

The implications of missing or inadequate venting are condensation and subsequent mold and rot damage.

STRATEGY

Look for soffit vents and high-level vents, or gable vents at opposing ends of the attic. Is there adequate total ventilation? Check that roughly 50 percent of the ventilation is at the soffits. When on the roof you may be able to read the net vent area off roof or ridge vents.

5.5.16   Venting Obstructed at Soffits or Roof Vents

This is one of the most common problems we find in attics.

IMPLICATIONS

The implications of inadequate venting are mold and rot as a result of condensation, and rain and snow being drawn in through high-level roof vents, creating water damage.

Ice Dams

Poor venting may lead to ice damming, since the attic will be warmer than it should be.

STRATEGY

Check that soffit vents are open. Where insulation is deep near the eaves, look for baffles that maintain an air space between the insulation and the underside of the roof sheathing. As you look around the perimeter of the roof, you can often see daylight filtering in through the soffit vents.

You can check roof vents when outside the house and from inside the attic. It's easiest to see mechanical damage and birds' nests from the outside. It's easiest to see missing or undersized sheathing holes for vents from the inside.

5.5.17   Snow or Wet Spots Below Roof Vents

IMPLICATIONS

Water damage is the implication of snow and rain getting into the attic.

STRATEGY

Look for evidence of wet spots, including discoloration and compressed insulation below roof vents.

5.5.18   Turbine Vents Noisy or Seized

Turbine vents are wind-driven roof vents designed to enhance roof ventilation. We do not recommend the use of turbine vents. On calm days they do not help ventilation of the roof to any great extent. On windy days they may lead to excessive ventilation and depressurization of the attic. As we've discussed, excessive depressurization of the attic increases the air leakage from the house into the attic. This increases heating costs and can promote condensation.

Noisy turbine vents are a common problem. Sometimes the turbine vent cannot be made to move. This is not a matter of great concern unless leakage is experienced.

IMPLICATIONS

The noise is a nuisance and usually suggests that the system will seize shortly. There are usually no serious performance implications to a seized turbine vent. In some cases, the vent is vulnerable to rain or snow penetration. We see many turbine vents that are covered with plastic garbage bags because of leakage into the attic through the vents.

STRATEGY

On a calm day, the vents probably won't be turning, although on a hot summer day there may be enough convective airflow out of the attic to move the vents. If you move the vent with your hand, you can sometimes detect a noise problem. In some cases, lubrication can solve the problem, at least temporarily. If the vent is seized or has been bent, damaged, or is corroded, replacement may be necessary. We recommend replacement with conventional roof vents.

5.5.19   Power Vents Operating in Winter

Electric exhaust fans mounted on the roof are useful during the summer to help remove heat from the attic. In the winter, they can depressurize the house and actually increase heat loss. We recommend these not be used during the winter (Figure 5.12).

IMPLICATIONS

Increased heat loss and air leakage into the attic are implications of a power vent operating in the winter.

STRATEGY

Where you see a power vent in the attic, determine whether it's operating. Trace the wiring back to the controls to see how the system is activated (manual switch or thermostat, for example). You may want to explain to the client the reasons for not operating the unit in the winter.

F I G U R E 5.12   Attic Power Vents

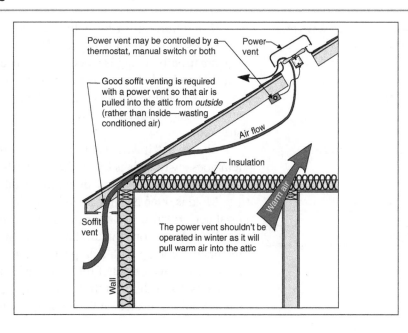

Good Soffit Venting Needed

When the power vent is operating in the summer, good soffit venting is necessary because we want to pull outdoor air into the attic and exhaust the super-heated attic air. We don't want to pull the cool air out of the house into the attic. If soffit vents are missing or obstructed, the negative pressure in the attic will naturally move more air out of the house. If the house is air-conditioned, we are wasting energy by pulling cool air up out of the house and into the attic.

5.5.20   Power Vents Inoperative in Summer

In some cases, the power vent fails to respond to its controls.

IMPLICATIONS

As a result, the attic is likely to be warmer than it would be with the vent operating. This is not a serious problem.

STRATEGY

When you see a power vent in an attic, follow the wiring back to the controls and ensure the vent responds to these. If it does not, recommend the problem be investigated and corrected.

5.5.21   Rafters and Sheathing—Rot or Mold

Mold and rot are common problems inside and outside houses. Mold is usually a surface condition, while rot is caused by fungi capable of decaying wood by breaking down the wood fibers.

Mold may be many colors, including black, green, red, blue, and brown. Although mold can form on almost any surface and will discolor it, mold often does little damage to wood. Small quantities can be readily cleaned off with soap and water or bleach.

Rot

Rot is more serious than surface mold. The rot actually attacks the wood fibers. Brown rot and white rot are the most common. Brown rot is most common on softwoods. White rot is most common in hardwoods. As a result, **brown rot is the enemy of most framing members.**

Identifying Rot

In the early stages, the wood surface becomes dull and discolored. There's often a musty odor. As the rot advances, the wood becomes spongy and crumbly. It can also be stringy. Brown rot can grow to a considerable size on the surface of wood.

Brown Rot Can Look White

White fluffy growths on the surface of wood may indicate brown rot.

Dry Rot—Isn't

Many people refer to dry rot. This is confusing, since dry wood can't rot. What you are usually seeing is wood that has been wet and rotted and subsequently dried out. It's probably best to avoid the term "dry rot."

Other Rots

Brown and white rots are not the only two types. Soft rots, for example, can attack cedar roofing. However, brown rot is the most common enemy of house structures.

Control of Mold and Rot

Simply put, if we keep the moisture content of wood below 20 percent, the problem goes away. This is by far the most effective solution and why it's so important that we control moisture leaking into walls and attics in homes.

IMPLICATIONS

Mold is often accompanied by rot. The implications of rot are weakened structural performance and ultimate failure of the roof structure.

STRATEGY

Rot

Look for rot on structural members throughout. If you can get to the structural members, probing with a carpenter's awl or screwdriver is helpful in determining the presence and extent of rot. A strong light is essential to a proper attic inspection.

Mold

Look for a discoloration on structural members on the attic. Mold forms a slightly raised surface on the wood that can usually be wiped off.

FIGURE 5.13   Delaminating Sheathing

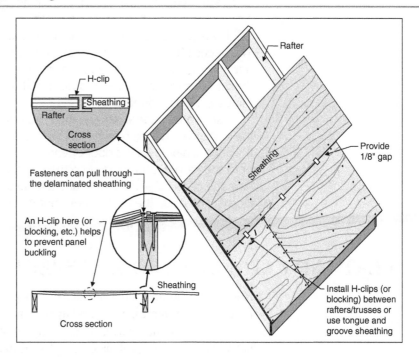

FRT *Plywood Darkening*

Mold is not the cause of the darkening or charring that occurs with some fire-retardant treated (FRT) plywood. Darkened FRT plywood cannot be wiped clean; mold can usually be wiped off.

Inspection Limitations

Unless you can move through the entire attic area, there will be some sections you don't see. This means there may be some rot you will miss. Make sure you document these limitations.

5.5.22   Rafters and Sheathing Delaminating or Buckling

One of the implications of high moisture levels, from either condensation or leakage, is delamination of plywood sheathing (Figure 5.13). This is sometimes accompanied by buckling. Panel-type roof sheathing may lift off the rafters in a regular pattern.

IMPLICATIONS

Delaminated plywood is weakened and may not be able to carry its intended loads. Ultimately the plywood may give way under the weight of foot traffic, for example.

Buckling can weaken the roof by separating the sheathing from the rafters or trusses. If fasteners pull through the sheathing, the entire roof covering and sheathing becomes loose and may be blown off during high winds.

STRATEGY

Check the plywood sheathing, particularly at the panel edges, for evidence of delamination. In many cases, you'll need to make a judgment call as to how severe the delamination is. Where you are unsure, recommend a specialist for further investigation.

Check that the sheathing sits tightly on the top of rafters or trusses over its entire length. Where the sheathing has clearly buckled, make recommendations to reduce moisture levels in the attic and possibly refasten the sheathing.

Inspector in the House: When It Rains . . .

I was just about to finish the inspection and the attic was the only thing left. The access hatch was in the master bedroom closet, and I took all of the clothes out of the closet and placed them on the bed nearby. I always put the clothes on the bed in exactly the same order that I take them out of the closet so I can put things back as I found them.

I set up my ladder and pushed open the hatch. What I didn't know was that the homeowners had blown in extra insulation through the roof vents that covered the access hatch. As the door opened, cellulose insulation rained down all over me, onto the carpet, and even onto the clothes on the bed. I left the house with two garbage bags full of insulation and a large dry cleaning bill. Since then, I carry drop cloths, and open the attic access hatch very slowly!

5.6   FLAT AND CATHEDRAL ROOF INSPECTIONS

Roofs with no attic area are hard to inspect and are difficult to build correctly. Figure 5.14 summarizes several approaches to insulating flat and cathedral roofs.

During a home inspection you may not know which approach, if any, has been taken. You probably will have a tough time identifying the insulation approach, material, total R-value, presence and effectiveness of an air/vapor barrier, and effectiveness of ventilation. As we move through the common problems, we'll discuss some of the inspection strategies, but they are limited, especially when compared to the inspection strategies for attics.

Watch for Water Damage

Rot is the big risk to a home with a flat or cathedral roof. We've discussed the mechanism by which warm, moist air gets carried into roof spaces, cools, condenses and allows mold and rot to get a foothold. Flat and cathedral roofs are vulnerable to this, particularly because visual inspection is usually impossible. Extensive damage can occur before it's apparent in the home. We'll look at some of the conditions that may make a roof susceptible to damage, and some of the clues that suggest damage may have occurred.

It's a Short Inspection

The good news is that it doesn't take nearly as long to inspect flat or cathedral roofs as it does attics. There just isn't very much we can see.

Now let's look at some common problems:

1. Insulation—too little
2. Insulation—wet, compressed or voids
3. Air/vapor barrier—missing or incomplete
4. Venting—missing or inadequate
5. Venting—obstructed

5.6.1   Insulation—Too Little

Since there's no access hatch and usually no way to get a look at the insulation, we won't know whether there is insulation at all, let alone whether the amount is appropriate or not.

F I G U R E 5.14   Insulating Flat and Cathedral Roofs

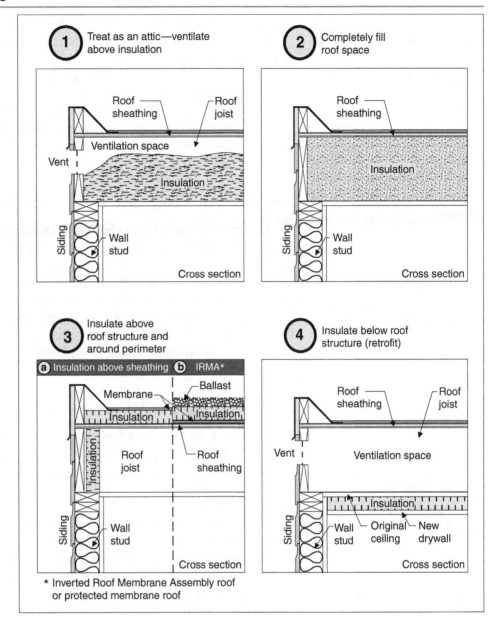

Remove Vents to Check Insulation

Low insulation levels result in higher heating costs but no damage to the structure.

Unless there are holes or gaps in ceilings, there isn't usually an opportunity to look at insulation in flat or cathedral roof cavities. Removing ceiling-mounted light fixtures or exhaust fans can allow a look around electrical junction boxes for insulation. Most home inspectors do not go this far. If you do this kind of investigation, make sure there is no electrical power to the fixtures you are working around.

In some cases, vents applied in fascia boards can be popped out to get a look at the insulation. In some cases, you may be able to determine not only the material but also the amount of insulation.

5.6.2   Insulation—Wet, Compressed, or Voids

IMPLICATIONS

STRATEGY

Again, you won't be able to see much. The evidence is usually indirect.

The implications are reduced insulating values, and if the insulation is chronically wet, mold and rot are risks.

You may see evidence of wet insulation as staining, sponginess, or dampness on the ceiling finishes below. If the evidence is localized, you might suspect a roof leak. If the evidence is widespread, condensation is more likely the culprit. You won't usually see compressed areas or voids, except perhaps as localized areas of melting snow outside when weather conditions allow.

5.6.3   Air/Vapor Barrier—Missing or Incomplete

IMPLICATIONS

STRATEGY

Again, in most cases you won't be able to identify the presence of an air/vapor barrier, let alone problems with it. Remember that many ceiling finishes are effective air/vapor barriers if they are reasonably tight.

The implications of missing or incomplete barriers are increased risk of mold and rot, owing to air leakage into the roof space.

We talked earlier of possibly finding openings to look at the insulation in roof spaces. These same opportunities may allow you to look for an air/vapor barrier. In most cases, however, you simply won't know.

5.6.4   Venting—Missing or Inadequate

IMPLICATION

STRATEGY

Just as we look for vents on attics, we should be looking for vents on flat or cathedral roofs. The venting opportunities on a cathedral roof generally include soffit and ridge vents. On flat roofs, the venting is most often at opposing fascias.

When venting is missing or inadequate, warm, moist air can condense in the roof and cause damage.

On the outside of the building it's relatively easy to look for vents on flat or cathedral roofs. The presence of a good venting system is the exception rather than the rule, especially on older homes. Obvious venting on flat or cathedral older roofs usually indicates upgraded insulation in the roof space.

Channeled Vents versus Cross Ventilation

In many flat or cathedral roofs, vents are at either end of roof joist or rafter runs (Figure 5.15). Ventilation can only move in a straight line through the roof space. Where strapping is added on top of and perpendicular to roof joists and rafters, cross ventilation is possible. Open web trusses also allow cross ventilation. Generally speaking, the more directions ventilation can flow, the better things are.

Lots of Venting

For flat and low-sloped roofs, many recommend ventilation ratios of 1:150. This means there should be one square foot of venting for every 150 square feet of roof space. This ratio refers to net free area of the vents. These are sometimes stamped onto the vents themselves, but in many cases it is difficult to determine.

Two Sides of Roof Minimum

Vents must be on at least two sides of the roof to promote cross ventilation.

5.6.5   Venting—Obstructed

IMPLICATIONS

Vents need to be free and open to operate properly.

Obstructed vents increase the risk of mold and rot damage in the roof space.

FIGURE 5.15   Channeled Vents versus Cross Ventilation

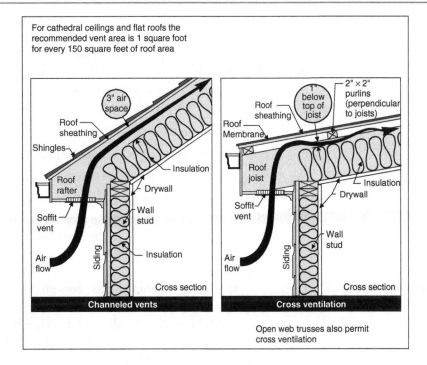

STRATEGY

Look for vents on the outside of the house. If you can get close to them, make sure they are not obstructed. Try to determine the net free area of the vents. On soffit vents, try to look up through the vents with a flashlight. It's not unusual to find that insulation has either been blown right onto the soffit vents or has slipped down onto them. If insulation is touching the soffit vents, the vents are not likely to be effective.

5.6.6   Summary

We recommend you advise clients that flat and cathedral roofs are prone to concealed damage from mold and rot. Without destructive testing, it's almost impossible to know whether there's a serious problem. We've talked about some of the clues, but we've been surprised at the amount of damage found in some roof spaces with no evidence on the interior or exterior of the building.

Moisture Scanners

Moisture scanning devices may provide information about elevated moisture levels in roof spaces. High moisture levels obviously suggest mold and rot problems. The danger is that a low moisture reading does not necessarily indicate that there is no problem. During a dry summer, for example, the framing members may dry out. However, during the heating season, condensation may cause high moisture levels.

Check in Early Winter

Some building experts maintain that early winter is the best time to check roof spaces for high moisture levels. If you are going to perform or recommend these tests, you should be aware of the likely seasonal variations in moisture content in roof spaces.

Describe Limitations

It's important with flat and cathedral roofs to let your clients know that most of your comments are based on indirect evidence because there is very little you can see.

5.7 INSPECTING WALLS ABOVE GRADE

Above-grade walls are not any easier to inspect than flat and cathedral roofs. We don't get much of a look. During your inspection of the structure, you should have determined the makeup of the exterior walls. While there are other possibilities, most are wood frame or masonry. We'll concentrate on these. Log walls and stacked plank walls have no insulation, typically. Stress skin wall panels are mostly insulation.

Wood Frame Walls

Wood frame walls can be insulated three ways:

- The space between studs can be filled.
- Insulation can be added on the interior face of the studs.
- Insulation can be added on the exterior face of the studs.

Traditionally, insulation was either omitted or provided between the studs. Starting in the 1970s, builders in some areas began to provide insulation between the studs and insulating sheathing on the outside of the studs. Other builders moved from two by four to two by six studs to accommodate more insulation without insulating sheathing.

Insulating Sheathing

Insulating sheathing increased wall insulation levels and stopped thermal bridging through studs. On the other hand, it sometimes added a second vapor barrier on the exterior part of the wall—not a good thing. It made siding attachment more difficult, and in replacing conventional sheathing, usually needed diagonal bracing of walls to prevent racking.

Avoid Short Circuits

In some cases, insulation is added to the exterior of a wood frame wall without adding insulation into the wall stud cavity. This approach may be used, for example, where original siding is left in place, insulation is added over the siding, and then a new siding material is provided. The results may not be good, as explained in Figure 5.16.

FIGURE 5.16 Insulation Short Circuit

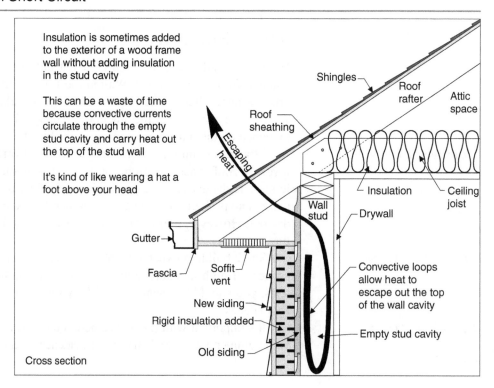

Insulation is sometimes added to the exterior of a wood frame wall without adding insulation in the stud cavity

This can be a waste of time because convective currents circulate through the empty stud cavity and carry heat out the top of the stud wall

It's kind of like wearing a hat a foot above your head

Shingles

Roof rafter

Attic space

Roof sheathing

Escaping heat

Insulation

Ceiling joist

Wall stud

Drywall

Gutter

Fascia

Soffit vent

New siding

Rigid insulation added

Old siding

Convective loops allow heat to escape out the top of the wall cavity

Empty stud cavity

Cross section

Adding insulation to the interior face of a wood stud wall is not common. Even during a renovation, it is disruptive and requires the relocation of window frames and casings as well as electrical outlets and switches. It also makes rooms smaller.

Masonry walls typically do not have enough space within them to add insulation. As a result, most masonry walls have no insulation. Where insulation is provided, it is typically on the interior or exterior face of the wall. Insulation on solid masonry houses is typically only added during renovations. Modern solid masonry walls may have insulation integrated as part of interior or exterior finishes. *Note: we are talking about solid masonry wall construction here, not wood-frame brick veneer or cavity wall construction.*

Let's look at some of the common problems related to wall insulation. Again, there isn't much that we can see, and the big enemy is mold and rot.

1. Insulation—too little

2. Insulation—sagging or voids

3. Air/vapor barrier missing, incomplete or in wrong location

4. Mold or rot suspected

5.7.1   Insulation—Too Little

Recommended levels of wall insulation vary. Typical R-values are R-12 to R-20 in new construction. Older homes will rarely have this much, and many have no wall insulation.

Walls that have no insulation often have R-values in the neighborhood of 4. This is true of wood frame and masonry walls.

Too little insulation results in higher heating costs and, perhaps, lower comfort.

One of the implications of poor wall insulation levels is the **cold wall effect.** This is a phenomenon that makes you feel cool in a room that's at 72°F (perfectly comfortable), if you are sitting close to an uninsulated wall on a winter day. The cold wall effect is a result of heat radiating directly from your body to a cold surface. Heat flows from warm bodies to cold. Sitting beside a cold wall or a window may make you uncomfortable even though the air in the room is perfectly comfortable. The effect is quite dramatic. You can often notice that the side of your body close to the wall is significantly cooler than the other side.

In many cases, you won't be able to find evidence of insulation. We typically remove covers from electrical switches and receptacles on the inside of walls and try to get a look at electrical boxes. You should turn off the electrical power before removing the covers and poking around. You may also find whether or not there is an air/vapor barrier provided as you do this. On masonry walls, electrical boxes are typically shallow and it's unusual to find insulation here. If you don't find any insulation looking from the inside, it is possible that insulation does exist, either within the stud cavities or on the outer surface. You'll have to report that you didn't observe any wall insulation.

You may be able to see evidence of insulation under the siding on the building exterior. This is sometimes visible on the bottom of the siding, near grade level.

If insulation has been blown or poured into wall cavities, there may be evidence in the attic. If the top plates are accessible, check for evidence that these have been drilled or opened up to add insulation.

Foamed-in-Place Insulations

Foamed-in-place insulations such as urea-formaldehyde foam insulation can often be identified around electrical boxes because the foam typically oozes into the box. Evidence is also often visible at the sill plate and top plate.

Check Wall Thickness

You may be able to determine that insulation has been added to the wall by its thickness, if the wall has clearly been built out relative to the other houses in the neighborhood.

Again, if there is no insulation in the wall, we would not describe it as a deficiency, but would indicate that there is room for improvement.

5.7.2   Insulation – Sagging or Voids

In most cases, you won't be able to see what the insulation is doing. However, walls in unfinished spaces, such as knee walls, or insulation on walls in split level homes visible from the attic, can be inspected.

IMPLICATIONS

Sags or voids in insulation can result in increased heating costs.

STRATEGY

Where you can get into unfinished spaces with insulated walls, look for the presence and continuity of insulation.

5.7.3   Air/Vapor Barrier Missing, Incomplete or in Wrong Location

Again, in most cases you're not going to be able to see this condition.

IMPLICATIONS

A missing, incomplete, or cold-side air/vapor barrier may lead to increased air leakage and mold and rot in wall cavities. As we've discussed, good air sealing on a conventional drywall or plaster wall can achieve most of the effectiveness of an air/vapor barrier.

STRATEGY

If you remove covers from electrical switches and outlets (again, shutting off the power first), you may be able to see evidence of a polyethylene air/vapor barrier. (In cooling climates you do not want to see an air/vapor barrier here!) If you are able to look at walls in unfinished areas, such as new walls, you can pull the insulation back slightly and see whether an air/vapor barrier has been provided.

Watch for cold-side vapor barriers. These can cause damage.

Again, in most cases, we would not recommend adding an air/vapor barrier unless we saw evidence of some problems.

5.7.4   Mold or Rot Suspected

IMPLICATIONS

The implications of mold or rot are damage to structural members and possible loss of structural integrity over the long term. Damage to interior finishes and indoor air quality problems are also possible.

STRATEGY

Again, your inspection is going to rely mostly on indirect evidence. Unless there is considerable damage, it's going to be hard to identify this problem without removing interior or exterior finishes.

Damage at Bottom of Walls

Damage is usually concentrated at the bottom of walls. Condensation tends to run down wall studs and get caught on bottom plates. The end grain of the studs sitting on the bottom plates wicks moisture up and, as a result, the bottoms of studs and sill plates show rot first.

In some cases, there's evidence of staining or rusting nail heads on the inner face of the wall near floor level. Damaged subflooring may be visible. In severe cases, there may also be evidence on the inside of the foundation wall below a wood frame wall, for example.

Vented Rain Screen Principle

You should be able to get a sense of the drying potential of the wall. A wall with a vented rain screen is more likely to dry quickly than a face-sealed system. You may be able to see evidence of moisture in walls around electrical boxes. In some cases, you can see staining or rusting if the boxes are metal. You may also see mold in the box or on the surfaces around them. If you have found a missing air/vapor barrier and lots of air leakage paths into the wall, you should suspect concealed damage. This risk is heightened if the exterior siding is stucco or another face sealed system.

Look at Walls and Ceilings

You may also get some clues from the condition of the living spaces. If there is evidence of condensation on walls (especially below windows) or on ceilings, you may be more suspicious of condensation in the wall cavities.

Where to Look

On interior surfaces, look for mold on upper floor levels, particularly in corners or areas behind furniture or clothing in closets. Areas that are cooler have lower airflow, are dark, and are more prone to mold. If you are in an area with prevailing winds, the windward walls will be colder. Look for mold on wall and ceiling surfaces on the windward side. The same is not true of damage inside wall cavities. Air leakage from the house into the walls is more likely on the leeward side than the windward side of the house.

5.8   INSPECTING BASEMENTS AND CRAWLSPACES

Is Insulation Necessary?

Many homeowners ask whether basements and crawlspaces need to be insulated. No part of the house **needs** to be insulated. Insulating the basement and crawlspace will help to reduce heating costs and may improve comfort. Adding basement or crawlspace insulation is an improvement, rather than a repair, like any other insulation upgrade.

The Basement Floor

In some cases, the builder has provided insulation under the concrete floor slab of the basement or crawlspace. In most cases, you won't know whether this is done, and it's not cost-effective to add this insulation, anyway. Home inspectors are usually silent on the issue of sub-slab insulation.

Insulating Basement
Basement Wall Insulation
Is a Bonus

Basement walls can be insulated on the inside or outside. Both are acceptable.

Where no basement wall insulation has been provided, we do not describe the house as having a defect. Basement wall insulation is an improvement, not a necessity.

There are two approaches to insulating crawlspaces, depending on whether the crawlspace is to be part of the heated area of the home or not. We can insulate the walls, creating a heated crawlspace, or insulate the floor above, creating an unheated crawlspace.

Unheated Crawlspaces

If the crawlspace is not to be heated, insulation is usually provided on the underside of the floor above (Figure 5.17). Insulation is typically tucked up between floor joists. The subfloor and flooring material above are usually relied on as the air/vapor barrier. We do not want an air/vapor barrier on the cool underside of the insulation. The insulation can be supported a number of ways, including chicken wire and housewrap. We frequently find insulation sagging or falling out of place.

F I G U R E 5.17   Insulating Crawlspaces

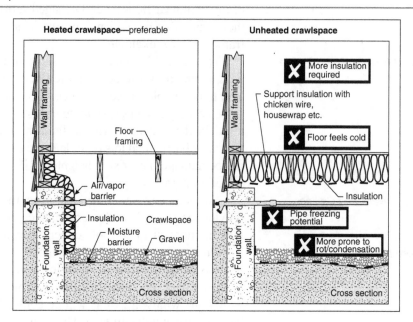

To Vent or Not to Vent?

Most people agree that if the crawlspace is heated, it should not be vented to the outdoors, even in the summer. Unheated crawlspaces are typically vented to the outdoors. A vent ratio of one square foot for every 150 square feet of crawlspace floor area is a common recommendation. Recently, people have challenged the wisdom of venting unheated crawlspaces in hot, humid climates. If the crawlspace is cooler than the outdoor air, leakage of warm, high humidity outdoor air into the crawlspace may result in condensation on building components inside the space. Crawlspaces in drier climates may benefit from ventilation to the outdoors. You should become familiar with local conditions and recommended practices in your area before starting to do home inspections.

Vapor Barriers in Unfinished Crawlspaces

A tremendous amount of moisture can be added to a home through an earth floor. If the crawlspace has an earth floor, a moisture barrier should be provided (Figure 5.18). This is typically polyethylene film sealed at joints and at the perimeter. It's often covered with sand or round gravel to keep the plastic in place. This cuts down tremendously on the amount of moisture in the crawlspace and dramatically reduces the chances of rot in subgrade wooden structural components.

Getting into Crawlspaces

Home inspectors have long discussed whether or not they have to enter crawlspaces. Our philosophy is that if the crawlspace is safe, we should enter it. If there is less than about 18 inches of clearance between the floor and structural members, it may be almost impossible to move through the crawlspace. Different inspectors have different tolerances for how low a crawlspace they will get into. You have to be comfortable that you are not going to be stuck in the space.

Common Access Points

The access into a crawlspace may be a hatch in the floor of the living space, an exterior hatch in the wall near grade level, or an opening in an adjacent basement wall.

Removing Covers

If the access cover to the crawlspace is secured and we are likely to damage the cover or the area around it in opening it, we do not remove the cover. Some inspectors will not remove any covers that require tools. Others are happy to remove four or six screws on an access cover. Still others use a wrecking bar to get into crawlspaces.

FIGURE 5.18   Cover Crawlspace Floor

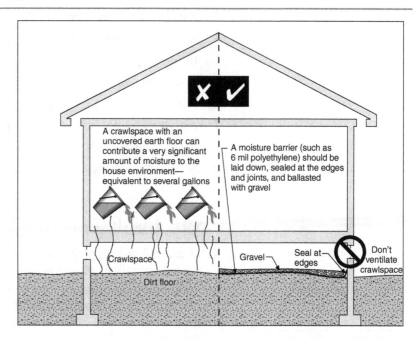

A crawlspace with an uncovered earth floor can contribute a very significant amount of moisture to the house environment— equivalent to several gallons

A moisture barrier (such as 6 mil polyethylene) should be laid down, sealed at the edges and joints, and ballasted with gravel

Crawlspace

Dirt floor

Gravel

Seal at edges

Don't ventilate crawlspace

| Wet Floors | Where the crawlspace has standing water on the floor, we consider that an unsafe condition. The water may be stagnant. In most cases, we don't know the source of the water. It could be raw sewage and a health hazard. Water may also pose an electrical hazard. It's not unusual to find wires on the floor of a crawlspace. If these wires contact wet earth or water, there is a risk of electrical shock. |

Wet Floors

Where the crawlspace has standing water on the floor, we consider that an unsafe condition. The water may be stagnant. In most cases, we don't know the source of the water. It could be raw sewage and a health hazard. Water may also pose an electrical hazard. It's not unusual to find wires on the floor of a crawlspace. If these wires contact wet earth or water, there is a risk of electrical shock.

Animals

We consider a crawlspace unsafe if we can identify animals in the crawlspace or animal waste. Snakes, scorpions, foxes, raccoons, etc. can all be hazardous to your health. Again, different inspectors have different tolerances for the conditions they will endure in a crawlspace.

Dark and Dirty

Most crawlspaces are unpleasant. They are dark, and you will get dirty crawling through them. We don't consider either of these conditions reason to avoid entering a crawlspace. We carry strong lights and disposable coveralls for crawlspace inspections.

Rewards Can Be Great

The information gained from a crawlspace is often significant. Because crawlspaces are unpleasant, most people do not go into them regularly. Problems may develop that in other parts of the home would be found and corrected promptly. Crawlspace problems may go undetected for a long time. We encourage you to access crawlspaces wherever possible.

Access from Basement

In houses with partial basements, the crawlspace is often accessed from the basement, as we mentioned. We encourage homeowners to heat crawlspaces and remove any covers so that the crawlspace communicates directly with the basement. This helps ventilate the crawlspace with warm air and reduces the risk of concealed rot.

Inspection Strategy

If you are inspecting a house with a crawlspace you can't get into, this should raise a yellow flag. Make sure your client understands there may be concealed damage. This is a significant limitation to your inspection.

Let's look at some of the common problems we find related to insulating basements and crawlspaces.

1. Insulation—too little or incomplete
2. Exterior insulation not suitable for use below grade
3. Exterior insulation not protected at top
4. Insulation missing at rim joists
5. Insulation sagging, loose, or voids
6. Exposed combustible insulation
7. Air/vapor barrier missing, incomplete, or wrong location
8. No moisture barrier on basement walls
9. No moisture barrier on earth floor

5.8.1   Insulation—Too Little or Incomplete

Keep in mind that many houses have no basement or crawlspace wall insulation. This is not a problem. Homeowners can add insulation as a home improvement.

Recommended Levels

You should find out what levels of insulation (if any) are recommended in your area for basement and crawlspace walls. You may also want to research whether insulation is recommended all the way down to floor level on basement walls.

STRATEGY

In some cases, it's easy to determine whether insulation has been provided. In other cases, it can be tough to tell.

Inside or Outside?

Insulation can be provided on the inside or outside of foundation walls. It can also be provided on the ceiling, although this is more common in a crawlspace than in a basement.

Look Behind Wall Finishes

Where basement walls are finished, you may be able to determine whether there is insulation by removing covers from electrical receptacles and light switches on perimeter walls. Turn off the electricity first.

Exterior

On the exterior, you may see evidence of the protective coating (e.g., parging, fiber-cement board, or pressure-treated plywood) and a flashing at the top of an insulation material. You'll rarely see the insulation itself on the outside.

Exposed Insulation

Sometimes you can see insulation exposed on basement or crawlspace walls. It may be held in place with tack strips, metal hooks, or a polyethylene vapor barrier and wood strapping. Where the batts are installed between wood studs, the insulation is usually covered by wood paneling or drywall.

Insulation at Rim Joists

You may be able to see whether insulation has been provided around the perimeter of the joist cavity at the top of the basement or crawlspace. It's not unusual to find the basement walls insulated, but no insulation at the rim joists.

5.8.2   Exterior Insulation Not Suitable for Use Below Grade

Some types of rigid fiberglass, mineral wool, and polystyrene boards are suitable for use outside below grade. These are the most common materials used. Conventional fiberglass board or semi-rigid cladding is not suitable for use below grade. Some types of expanded polystyrene are also not suitable for below grade use. Cellulose fiber insulation is not suitable for use below grade, nor is most mineral wool insulation.

IMPLICATIONS

The insulation's performance will be dramatically reduced by moisture if the insulation is not suitable for below grade use.

In most cases, you won't be able to see what type of insulation has been used on the exterior. However, since an inappropriate material suggests an amateurish installation, you may be able to see some of the insulation itself.

5.8.3   Exterior Insulation Not Protected at Top

The top of an exterior installation board should be mechanically protected with a parging, fiber cement board, or pressure-treated plywood, for example. The top of the opening should be covered with a cap or flashing unless the siding extends down over it.

Insulation materials do not stand up well to mechanical damage from lawn mowers, weed eaters, etc.

Many types of insulation are adversely affected by sunlight (polystyrene, for example). Water penetrating the insulation or between the insulation and the foundation can dramatically reduce the insulating value.

You should not be able to see foundation insulation as you look at the building exterior. Where insulation can be seen, improvements are probably necessary.

5.8.4   Insulation Missing at Rim Joists

We've talked about insulating the perimeter of the building above the foundation wall where the joists rest on top of the foundation.

Implications of missing installation are increased heating costs. If air sealing is not well done, moisture damage to structural components is possible. The rim joist area is a vulnerable part of the building. If the exterior grade is too high, the rim joist may be exposed to constant dampness from earth. The exterior grade levels should be at least six inches below the top of the foundation wall. Water accumulating in wall cavities as a result of leakage and condensation will flow by gravity to the bottom of the wall cavity and may end up at the rim joist area.

Where basement walls are not insulated, you would not expect the rim joist area to be insulated. However, where basement walls have been insulated, a consistent approach would include good air sealing of the rim joist area and insulation. The most common approach is to stuff fiberglass batts between the joists.

We touched earlier on the problem of joists embedded in the concrete foundation itself. Where this is done, the perimeter joist bases should not be insulated (Figure 5.19). This promotes rot damage to the ends of the joists. Good air sealing of the joist/concrete joint with caulking is recommended.

5.8.5   Insulation Sagging, Loose, or Voids

Insulation hung on walls is always subject to the forces of gravity. This is particularly true where no wall finish is provided. Wall finishes help to hold the insulation in place.

Increased heat loss is the implication of insulation that is sagging, loose, or has voids. If the insulation is not fit tightly against the wall, convective loops may be formed that dramatically reduce the insulating value.

Where insulation is provided on basement or crawlspace walls, make sure that it is intact. Look for continuity of the insulation and a tight fit against the foundation wall.

F I G U R E 5.19   Don't Insulate Embedded Joints

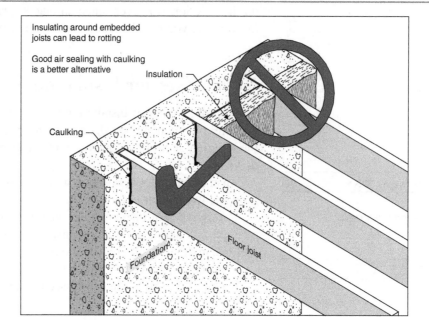

Insulating around embedded joists can lead to rotting

Good air sealing with caulking is a better alternative

Insulation

Caulking

Foundation

Floor joist

Crawlspace or Basement Ceiling Insulation

Where the ceiling of the subgrade area is insulated, it's usually easy to identify sagging or missing pieces of insulation. You'll also want to make sure that an air/vapor barrier has not been provided on the cold side of the insulation.

5.8.6   Exposed Combustible Insulation

Insulation in basements, crawlspace, garages, or any other interior spaces accessible to people, electricity, and heating sources should be covered with drywall or other interior finishes. Combustible wood paneling is acceptable in most areas.

Polystyrene Insulation

When people think of combustible insulations, they usually think of polystyrene. Polystyrene is difficult to ignite but releases a great deal of heat when it burns and produces a toxic black smoke. Cellulose, polyurethane, and polyisocyanurate boards are also combustible.

5.8.7   Air/Vapor Barrier Missing, Incomplete, or Wrong Location

Insulation on basement or crawlspace walls should have an air/vapor barrier. It may be visible polyethylene film. If the insulation is covered with interior finishes, you won't know whether there is an effective air/vapor barrier.

IMPLICATIONS

The implications of a missing air/vapor barrier are condensation on the cold side of the insulation. This won't usually damage the foundation wall, but the moisture can reduce the effectiveness of the insulation and damage a wood strapping or stud wall system used to support the wall insulation.

If the insulation is not covered, you'll be able to identify the presence of an air/vapor barrier. If finishes are provided, you may be able to see the presence of an air/vapor barrier when removing electrical cover plates (after shutting off the power). However, you will not be able to evaluate the effectiveness of the air/vapor barrier.

Watch for double vapor barriers or vapor barriers on the cold side only. Plastic moisture barriers on basement walls should stop at grade level. Insulation on crawlspace ceilings should not be supported by a vapor barrier.

5.8.8   No Moisture Barrier on Foundation Walls

The moisture barrier is applied directly to the foundation wall extending from the floor up to grade level (but not to the top of the foundation wall). If the basement wall has been insulated, you will rarely be able to see this moisture barrier. You may see evidence of it under a stud wall at the floor level.

IMPLICATIONS

Moisture coming through the foundation wall may wet the insulation, reducing its insulating ability. The water may also damage the wood strapping or stud wall assembly that supports the insulation.

STRATEGY

In most cases, you won't be able to see the moisture barrier. If there are gaps in the insulation assembly, you may be able to identify a moisture barrier. You may also be able to see the floor level below the stud wall, as mentioned earlier.

Condensation on Outer Side of Air/Vapor Barrier

A common situation in relatively new homes is condensation of the outer side (closest to the foundation) of a polyethylene air/vapor barrier on an insulated basement or crawlspace wall. It is common to find fiberglass batts held in place with polyethylene film and no moisture barrier on the concrete foundation walls behind.

Concrete Drying

New concrete contains considerable moisture. That moisture may leave the foundation wall on the inner side, often driven by the sun's heat. The moisture is trapped behind the polyethylene air/vapor barrier and condenses. This is very distressing to homeowners and some builders. Water may run down the foundation walls below the insulation.

Normal Condition

There is no real problem here, and in most cases this situation will correct itself within the first several months of occupancy. The amount of moisture in the concrete, in the soil outside, and in the house air all affect this situation. It's one reason that we recommend basements not be finished for at least one year after a new home has been occupied.

5.8.9   No Moisture Barrier on Earth Floor

Controlling moisture migrating out of the soil below a house is important.

IMPLICATIONS

The absence of a moisture barrier on an earth floor can result in elevated moisture levels in the air in crawlspaces and in the living space. These elevated moisture levels can cause damage to the structural members in the crawlspace and other parts of the home.

STRATEGY

Basement and crawlspace floors should be concrete or some other impervious material. Where the floor is earth, recommend that it be covered with at least a polyethylene sheet. The polyethylene sheet should be sealed at the joints and around the perimeter to the foundation walls. A protective gravel or sand coating may be added.

Don't Be Fooled

When looking at a crawlspace or basement floor, make sure you dig down to ensure that there is no moisture barrier, before criticizing the system.

5.9 INSPECTING FLOORS OVER UNHEATED AREAS

Floors over unheated areas are typically cold during the heating season, relative to other floors in the home. This is true even though the room itself is well heated and the air is the same temperature as the other rooms in the house.

Possible Solutions

Several solutions have been tried to make floors more comfortable over unheated spaces. The heated cavity between the floor and insulation below is one approach. The success of this system depends on a number of things, including—

- unobstructed airflow
- good balancing of supply and return air
- good air sealing

The perimeter of this space needs to be well insulated—a detail that was often overlooked.

Sprayed-in-Place Foams

A popular approach in many areas is the use of isocyanate or polyurethane foam insulations. These insulations are foamed in place and covered on the underside. The advantage of these systems is that very good air sealing is achieved by the insulation. This dramatically reduces convective heat loss problems and also reduces air leakage.

Inspection Not Possible

In most cases, you won't be able to determine what insulation, if any, has been provided in floors over unheated spaces. You should point out to your client the potential for cool floors and the limitations to your inspection here.

STRATEGY

Where insulation is exposed, you can identify loose or missing insulation, as well as gaps. If the insulation is exposed, you'll want to make sure there is no air/vapor barrier on the cold side. In most cases, the subfloor and finished flooring usually provide an adequate air/vapor barrier.

Plugs Are Clues

In some cases, you may see clues that insulation has been added in these areas. Plugged holes in the underside of the openings or new finishes both suggest that insulation has been added.

Floors over unheated areas are difficult to inspect and can lead to unhappy clients. Make sure you identify all such areas. They may include spaces—

- above garages
- above porches
- in cantilevered areas
- over breezeways
- below windows that project out from the building
- over unheated crawlspaces or other subgrade areas
- over open areas below houses with pier foundation and no skirting

In most areas, these will be inaccessible areas where you'll simply be raising a question. Insulation improvements in these areas are usually possible at moderate cost. The important thing is to advise your client of the possibility.

Inspector in the House: Dancing in the Attic

Home inspectors are curious and skeptical. We like to see everything and we know that problems are often found in parts of homes where people rarely go. That's why we like to go through attics, even when it may not be safe. Our company policy is, "If the insulation covers the top of the ceiling joists or the bottom truss chord, don't walk the attic."

This is not a story about stepping through a ceiling, but something at least as scary. Failing to follow company policy one day, I stepped into the attic and on the open and live electrical junction box that was buried under the insulation. Luckily I just got a jolt, and did not lose my balance. But that was the last time I wandered through attics, guessing where joists were, and assuming everything was done properly under there. Life is short enough as it is.

REVIEW QUESTIONS

1. The primary function of insulation is to _____.
2. A vapor retarder is designed to _____.
3. What are the implications of an inadequate air/vapor barrier?
4. Name two purposes of house ventilation.
5. Define **relative humidity.**
6. What is meant by **drying potential?**
7. Why are roofs vented in the winter in cold climates?
8. What is the purpose of a heat recovery ventilator?
9. The term *ventilation* might mean two very different things with respect to homes. Explain the two different types of ventilation.
10. Indicate where the air/vapor barrier should be located in the wall assembly in a hot, humid climate.
11. List four common forms that insulation materials may be found in.
12. List 10 common insulation materials. (Hint: vermiculite and perlite only count as one. There are two types of polystyrene.)
13. What forms do these materials come in?
14. What is the function of an air barrier?
15. Indicate two reasons we are interested in controlling air movement through building walls and roofs.
16. Describe the function of a vapor barrier.
17. List two other names for vapor barriers.
18. Is it more important for the air barrier or vapor barrier to be continuous?
19. Should the vapor barrier be on the warm side or cold side of the wall assembly?
20. Should the vapor barrier be on the warm side or cold side of the wall assembly in a hot, humid climate?
21. List three functions of roof vents.
22. List four types of roof vents.
23. What percentage of the total venting should be at the soffits?
24. What percentage of the total venting should be high on the roof?
25. When can soffit venting be omitted safely?
26. What do soffit vent baffles do?
27. How are mansard or gambrel roofs ideally vented?
28. Is it possible to over-ventilate an attic? If so, why is this an issue?
29. What should you wear when inspecting attics? (List three things.)
30. List at least three things that may make attics dangerous.
31. List four common access hatch problems and the implications of each.
32. What are the implications of insulation that is only two inches thick, wet, compressed, interrupted by gaps or voids, or missing?

33. Under what circumstances should insulation cover recessed lights? What is one inspection strategy to help identify recessed lights while in the attic?

34. Will you ever see walls in attics? Where? Should these be insulated?

35. What two things should you be looking for on ducts in attics?

36. How should insulation be handled around masonry chimneys?

37. How should insulation be handled around metal vents?

38. What are the implications of air/vapor barriers that are missing or incomplete?

39. List three common problems with roof vents and their implications.

40. What is suggested by snow on attic insulation below roof vents?

41. List three possible concerns with turbine vents.

42. Should power vents be operating in the winter? Why or why not?

43. What is suggested by mold or rot on rafters and sheathing?

44. Describe in one sentence each, four general approaches to insulating flat and cathedral roofs.

45. List five common problems found with flat roof insulation systems.

46. For each of the problems listed above, describe, in one sentence, the implications.

47. Describe one possible way to get a look at insulation in a flat roof.

48. What things might suggest wet insulation?

49. Describe two strategies used to deal with venting of flat roofs.

50. On a flat roof, where will you most often see the vents?

51. What is an appropriate ratio of vent area to roof area?

52. Basement wall insulation is necessary. True or false?

53. Describe in two sentences each, two strategies for insulating basement walls.

54. Describe in one sentence each, two general approaches to insulating crawlspaces.

55. All crawlspaces should be vented. True or false? Explain.

56. List three safety issues involved in inspecting crawlspaces.

57. List nine common problems with insulation and ventilation in basement and crawlspace areas.

58. List the implications of each of these problems.

59. Describe two possible strategies for keeping floors over unheated spaces warm.

60. List seven areas where floors over unheated spaces may feel cool.

CHAPTER 6

INTERIORS

LEARNING OBJECTIVES

By the end of this chapter you should be able to:

- list the problems and implications related to concrete, wood, carpet, resilient, and ceramic flooring

- list the problems and implications related to plaster, drywall, and wood walls

- describe two inspection strategies that help with ceiling inspections

- list the problems and implications related to plaster, drywall, metal, and wood ceilings

- list five trim problems and their implications

- list ten countertop problems and their implications

- list thirteen cabinet problems and their implications

- list the common problems with stairs and their implications

- list four window functions and eight common window types

- list six frame problems and their implications

- list eight sash problems and their implications

- list six interior trim problems and their implications

- list six glass problems and their implications

- list five hardware problems and their implications

- explain how window size or location can be a problem

- list thirteen door and frame problems and their implications

- list six implications of basement and crawlspace problems

- list twenty signs of moisture in basements and crawlspaces

INTRODUCTION

We look at the building interior for a number of reasons. It provides clues to structural problems and is often the area where water leakage is first detectable. The interior finishes usually reflect the overall building quality, and their condition helps indicate the level of overall maintenance.

The house interior contains the distribution points of the major systems. For example, each room should have an adequate heat supply and sufficient electrical outlets. The concern of the home inspector is function rather than appearance, and emphasis is placed on whether the room will work as it was intended. We do not comment on matters of personal taste.

The major components of the interior inspection are:

- walls, ceilings, and floors
- trim, counters, and cabinets
- stairs
- windows, skylights, and solariums
- doors
- basement and crawlspace leakage

Clients Come with You

While we encourage clients to follow us on all parts of an inspection, we find that they are most interested in being with us as we move through the interior. This is the area where they will have spent most of their time looking at the house, and most of their questions will be related to this area.

6.1   FLOORS

Level, Smooth, and Durable

Floors are designed as walking surfaces and supports for furnishings. Floors can also be part of the architectural appeal of the home.

From a traffic standpoint, floors should be level so they don't trip us, smooth so they're easy to navigate, and durable. Floors typically take more abuse than walls, and walls take more abuse than ceilings. Ceramic tiles designed for walls are not suitable for use on floors, for example.

6.1.1   Materials

Common flooring materials are:

- concrete
- wood
- hardwood or softwood in strip, plank, or parquet styles and engineered wood products
- carpet—wool and synthetic
- resilient—both tile and sheet goods
- ceramic and quarry tile
- stone and marble

FIGURE 6.1   Control Joints in Concrete Floors

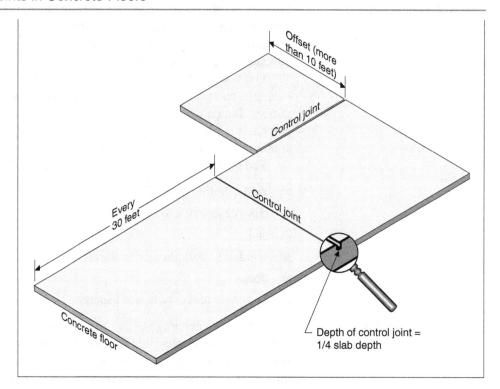

Concrete floor

Offset (more than 10 feet)

Control joint

Control joint

Every 30 feet

Depth of control joint = 1/4 slab depth

Control Joints in Concrete Floors

Concrete floors can be rough, unfinished floors in basements or crawlspaces, or they can be immediately below the finished flooring in slab-on-grade construction. Concrete floors may have control joints to help ensure that any cracks develop where we want them to (see Figure 6.1). If the concrete slabs have steel reinforcement, control joints are often omitted.

6.1.2   General Inspection Strategy

Home inspectors should always know whether they are walking across a wood or concrete floor. You can learn to determine this with experience by both the sound and the feel of the floor as you move across it. In some cases, you may have to bounce on the floor slightly to confirm your suspicions. Try this everywhere you go for the next few days. You'll find that it's relatively easy to do. It's slightly more difficult on ceramic tile floors because they are often wood flooring with a layer of concrete over them.

New Floors over Old

In some cases, new flooring material is laid over old. This is not unusual and may be a matter of mild interest. However, in some cases new flooring has been laid over old because of dramatic settlement or sagging in the old flooring. We have found homes where new flooring systems, including tapered joists, have been installed over old, badly sloping floors. This is not a problem in itself, but it should alert you to considerable movement of the structure. The important question is, "Has the cause of the movement been corrected?"

Rot around Plumbing Fixtures

Rot is one of the biggest enemies of wood flooring. It shouldn't be a surprise that rot is most likely around and below sources of water. While all plumbing fixtures can contribute, toilets are the most common problem area for wood floors. We find more rotted wood subflooring, joists, and beams around toilets than any other plumbing fixture.

Hardwood Below Carpets?   We are very often asked whether there is hardwood flooring beneath wall-to-wall carpeting. You may be able to determine this by lifting heat registers or lifting corners of carpets. (Note: lifting carpets goes beyond the Standards.) If there is hardwood below, you should caution your clients that it may not be in a suitable condition to remove the carpet and expose the hardwood.

6.1.3 Conditions

These are the common flooring problems in houses:

1. Water damage
2. Trip hazard
3. Mechanical damage
4. Loose or missing pieces
5. Absorbent materials in wet areas
6. Concrete
   - cracked
   - settled
   - heaved
   - water penetration
   - efflorescence
   - slopes away from drain
   - hollow below
7. Wood
   - rot
   - warped
   - buckled
   - stained
   - squeaks
   - exposed tongues
8. Carpet
   - rot
   - stained
   - odors
   - buckled
9. Resilient
   - split
   - lifted seams
   - open seams
10. Ceramic, stone, and marble
    - cracked
    - broken
    - loose

- grout missing
- worn
- stained

Water Damage

The implications of water damage may be—

- cosmetic only, if the source of water has been contained
- rot, staining, or other damage to the floor finish
- rot or other damage to structural components

Where you see staining, buckling, warping, rot, efflorescence, or wet spots, you should be looking at several things:

- Is the damage localized or widespread?
- Is there concealed damage? This may be difficult to determine, but you should allow for the possibility.
- What is the source of the water? Again, this may be difficult to tell, especially if the problem is not active (Figure 6.2).
- Is the leak active? If the floor is wet or damp, this is an easy answer. If the floor is dry, the problem may be inactive or intermittent.

Don't Speculate

Your role as a home inspector has been satisfied once you've identified the problem and let the client know the possible implications. You don't have to troubleshoot the problem. You should give the client some direction. Your recommendations may include more than one of these actions:

- Repair the floor;
- Correct the leak;
- Investigate further; or
- Monitor the situation.

Trip Hazard

The implications of trip hazards are personal injury.

Look for unevenness in floor systems. Sometimes you'll discover these accidentally.

Mechanical Damage

Mechanical damage may create unevenness that results in trip hazards. It may result in a loss of continuity in a flooring system. Cuts in resilient flooring in kitchens or bathrooms, for example, can allow water into subflooring.

Look for evidence of mechanical damage in exposed flooring. Remember that in a furnished house, you are not going to see the entire floor. Let your clients know that things may look very different when they take possession of the vacant house. Most houses look considerably worse with no furniture.

Loose or Missing Pieces

Pieces of flooring may have come loose and been lost. This is particularly true of parquet flooring and ceramic tile, for example.

The implications include trip hazards and moisture penetration to subflooring. There are also cosmetic issues.

FIGURE 6.2 Sources of Interior Water Damage

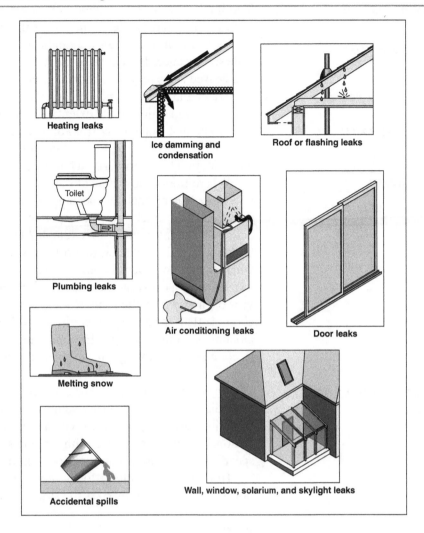

Heating leaks

Ice damming and condensation

Roof or flashing leaks

Toilet

Plumbing leaks

Air conditioning leaks

Door leaks

Melting snow

Accidental spills

Wall, window, solarium, and skylight leaks

STRATEGY

As you walk across floors, look and feel for loose pieces, particularly with wood parquet flooring and ceramic tile, stone, or marble flooring. Many inspectors tap on parquet floors and ceramic tile floors to help identify pieces that are coming loose.

Absorbent Materials in Wet Areas

This is somewhat subjective but is a common sense issue. The classic example is carpeting in bathrooms. Floors in rooms that are likely to get wet should have non-absorbent, moisture-resistant flooring materials.

IMPLICATIONS

Premature deterioration of the flooring is one implication of nonabsorbent materials. Rot damage to subflooring is another. Odors and other indoor air quality issues may create health concerns.

STRATEGY

We look closely for evidence of problems with flooring or subflooring where we find absorbent materials in kitchens and bathrooms. Wood flooring is marginally acceptable, although, again, the potential for moisture damage is considerable.

Alert Your Clients

You may not want to recommend removal of a flooring system, but you should alert your clients to the disadvantage of the situation.

Concrete Floors

The implications of shrinkage cracks are usually not significant. Water and/or efflorescence may appear at the cracks if there is hydrostatic pressure below.

Settled or heaved slabs may indicate structural problems or local problems of little significance. The extent of movement is the best clue as to the severity. Settled and heaved slabs may also be trip hazards.

Water and efflorescence may result in damage to finishes and to the structure. Again, it's a question of the extent and amount of water.

Floors that slope away from drains allow more damage to finishes and structures when floors get wet. Floor drains are typically only found on below grade concrete floors. This is primarily a basement issue.

Where floors show typical random shrinkage cracking, no action is typically necessary. Where cracks are accompanied by settlement or heaving, the location and direction of the cracks may be important. Does the pattern suggest a sinking foundation or heaving column, for example? The extent of movement and the age of the building are valuable clues. In most cases, you won't be able to be conclusive about whether the movement is ongoing based on a one-time visit. However, $1/2$-inch movement in a one-year-old house is far more likely to be significant than in a 100-year-old house. It is often hard to know whether you should be reassuring or alarmist about settled or heaved concrete floors. Common sense tells you to be neither. Document your findings. Explain the limitations and possible implications. Recommend monitoring if the problem is mild and further investigation if the movement is extensive.

Use a similar approach for evidence of water and/or efflorescence at cracks. Remedial actions may include a sump and pump. It helps tremendously to know local conditions. Are you in an area with a high water table or expansive soils? Is this a seasonal problem associated with melting snow and spring runoff? Is the problem specific to the house because of poor control of roof and surface rainwater?

Hollow spaces below floors should be treated much like settled or heaved floors. Figure 6.3 summarizes the strategy to follow.

Wood

Problem conditions for wood include rot, warped, buckled, stained, squeaks, and exposed tongues.

The implications of rot, warped, buckled or stained flooring include—

- cosmetic problems
- trip hazards
- deterioration of the structure below

Squeaks are simply a nuisance; they do not indicate structural problems.

Exposed tongues may result in slivers or splinters for people walking in bare or stocking feet. They may also result in exposed nailheads and resultant injury. There are obvious cosmetic implications and pieces of flooring may become loose and/or lift as a result.

Look for stained, warped, buckled, or rotted flooring. Pay particular attention to areas below sliding glass doors and windows. Leakage and condensation can combine to cause considerable damage in these areas.

Look closely in kitchens and bathrooms for evidence of problems, but focus around toilets. Where possible, go to the floor level below and look up to see if there is evidence of damage to flooring, ceilings, or structural members below the floor-

FIGURE 6.3   Hollow Spaces below Floors

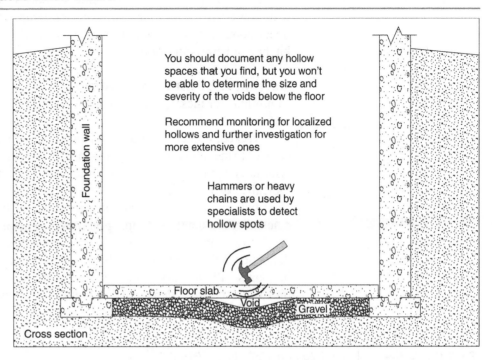

You should document any hollow spaces that you find, but you won't be able to determine the size and severity of the voids below the floor

Recommend monitoring for localized hollows and further investigation for more extensive ones

Hammers or heavy chains are used by specialists to detect hollow spots

Foundation wall

Floor slab

Void

Gravel

Cross section

ing around the toilet. Depending on the extent of the damage and whether or not the problem is active, you may recommend leakage or condensation control measures and flooring replacement. You may also recommend structural repairs.

Squeaks

The first step is to reassure clients that squeaks are common and are not a performance issue. Squeaks can be corrected several ways, but a cost/benefit analysis often convinces people to live with the squeaks.

Carpet

Carpet conditions include rot, stains, odors, and buckling.

IMPLICATIONS

The implications of rot, stains, and odors may be cosmetic. They may also indicate damage to subflooring and framing below. There may be health implications to stains and odors. Buckled carpeting is a trip hazard.

STRATEGY

Look for Moisture

When rot, stains, and/or odors are noted, the first step is to determine whether moisture is still present. Again, if dampness is found you can be conclusive. If the carpet is dry, the problem may be intermittent. You may be able to distinguish between pet odors and general dampness. You may want to recommend further investigation. Carpets that are stained or have odors may have to be replaced. The odors may be in the subflooring as well. There are chemicals that can be used to eliminate these odors. In severe cases, subflooring may have to be replaced. Where rot is noted, structural members below may be damaged.

Buckled

Look for carpeting that has buckled or lifted at the seams and may be a trip hazard. Recommend that this be stretched and resecured.

Resilient Flooring

Resilient flooring may be split or have lifted or open seams.

IMPLICATIONS

Water damage to the subflooring below and trip hazards are the functional implications of these problems.

STRATEGY

Look for splits or tears in resilient flooring. Open or lifted seams are more common on tile floors than sheet goods, simply because there are more seams. Sheet goods typically come in rolls 12 feet wide, and there may be no seams in kitchen or bathroom floors.

Ceramic, Stone, and Marble

Conditions for these floors include loose, grout missing, cracked or broken, worn, and stains.

IMPLICATIONS

Cracked, broken, or loose tiles and tiles with grout missing can lead to water damage to the subfloor and may present trip hazards. Worn tiles may only be cosmetic issues but can be trip hazards if corners are broken or pieces are loose. Stains are typically cosmetic issues only.

STRATEGY

Look for stains and wear and tear. You may be able to see missing grout and cracked or broken tiles. Tapping on tiles also helps to identify loose pieces.

Conventional Flooring

Houses are designed with floor systems that have a considerable amount of deflection. Without proper installation, ceramic tiles over conventional wood floors in houses will often crack. In most cases, this is only a cosmetic problem unless the tiles become loose. Parts A–D of Figure 6.4 show the typical proper installation

FIGURE 6.4 Alternatives for Installing Ceramic Tiles

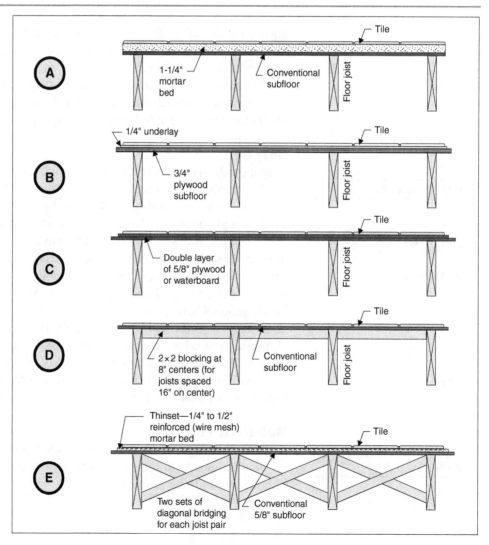

techniques. You also may find cases like part E. Depending on a number of factors, this approach sometimes works. It is more likely to be successful where joist spans are short or there is 12-inch rather than 16-inch joist spacing.

Use Test of Time

Where you see this configuration on a 20-year-old home and there is no cracking on the grout or tile, you can be comfortable that the system has been successful. In a one- or two-year-old house, be more cautious and say that the installation technique is typical, but not ideal. Cracking of tiles or grout may occur. Point out that this is a cosmetic issue.

Checking the Floor

The easiest way to determine how the ceramic tile has been laid is to remove a floor register or grille on a forced air heating or cooling system. Where this can't be done, you may be able to get a look at the floor around edges or at penetrations for plumbing pipes, for example.

Performance-Based Inspection

Where you can't determine exactly how the tile floor has been laid, look at the condition of the floor. Are there cracked, broken or loose tiles or grout? As long as you document the condition of the floor and your limitations in looking at it, you have done your job.

6.2   WALLS

Wall finishes are decorative. They are part of the look of the interior of the home. Most wall finishes also add rigidity to the structure. Drywall prevents wood frame walls from racking, for example. Finishes also conceal and support insulation and air/vapor barriers. Electrical and mechanical systems are also concealed behind wall finishes.

6.2.1   Materials

Common wall finish materials include—

- plaster or drywall, which can have a smooth or textured finish
- wood plank or paneling, which can be solid wood, plywood, or hardboard
- masonry or concrete
- fiber cement paneling

6.2.2   General Inspection Strategy

Flashlight Parallel to Wall

Home inspectors often shine a flashlight beam parallel to wall surfaces when inspecting walls. The light creates a shadow pattern that highlights flaws, irregularities, and patches in the wall.

Push and Tap

Another inspection strategy for walls is to push and tap on the walls. Here we are looking for wall finishes that are loose or pulling away from their substrate. Bulging plaster, for example, is very common in old homes.

Decorating Hides the History

In many cases, fresh paint or wallpaper finishes will conceal considerable movement in walls. This is a limitation that we can't do much about, other than to appreciate that terrific looking interiors do not necessarily mean an absolutely rock-solid structure. The newer the finish, the less history we have to rely on.

Drywall over Plaster

It's very common to replace old plaster covered with multiple layers of paint and/or wallpaper with new drywall right over the old plaster. This sometimes means adjusting baseboard, window and door casings, and other trim and moving electrical boxes, but it is often simpler than trying to repair or replace old plaster walls.

Removing Wallpaper May Remove Plaster

When clients are looking at older homes and are thinking about removing wallpaper, they may ask you if that's a problem. Generally speaking, removing wallpaper is not a big problem. However, removing wallpaper on older plaster walls can often pull a good deal of the plaster off the wall. In some cases, it seems as though it's the wallpaper holding the plaster in place. Disturbing the wallpaper may cause considerable plaster damage.

6.2.3   Conditions

Common wall problems include—

1. Water damage
2. Cracks
3. Mechanical damage
4. Inappropriate finishes in wet areas
5. Plaster and drywall
    - bulging, loose or missing
    - shadow effect
    - crumbling or powdery
    - nail pops
6. Wood
    - rot
    - cracked
    - split or broken
    - buckled
    - loose

Water Damage

IMPLICATIONS

Water damage may be simply cosmetic and a decorating issue. If the wall finish material (plaster, drywall, paneling, etc.) is damaged, there may also be damage to the structure behind.

STRATEGY

We're going to use the same strategy we did when looking at water damage to floors. We'll try to determine—

- the extent
- the source
- whether it's active
- whether there's concealed damage
- what corrective action has to be taken

Common Locations

Water damage to walls is common below windows, bathrooms, roof flashings, and roof penetrations such as chimneys and vents. In many cases, the plaster or drywall interior finish is much less forgiving than the concealed structural components. This is a good thing in that deteriorated interior finishes will alert people to problems and cause them to take corrective action. Although their intent isn't to protect the structure, the happy result is that concealed wood framing members, for example, are protected.

The Exception

Slow or intermittent chronic moisture from small leaks or condensation is much more likely to cause damage to the structure because the interior finishes may not deteriorate. Moisture may be absorbed and held in framing and insulation materials. Very little moisture may get to plaster or drywall finishes. This has become a bigger problem since polyethylene air/vapor barriers have been used. This plastic can protect the interior finish from moisture damage as a result of leakage or condensation within the walls. The plastic barrier traps the moisture where it won't be noticed. There isn't much you can do about this, but you should understand the risk.

Cracks

IMPLICATIONS

STRATEGY

Most cracks are simply decorating issues. Cracks associated with movement to the building are, of course, structural concerns.

Cracks may appear almost independently of the building age. The presence of cracks is more dependent on when the house was last decorated than the age of the building. Most cosmetic cracking is concealed every time walls are painted or wallpapered.

Check inside Closets, under Staircases, etc.

Many inspectors look closely in areas that may not be decorated regularly, such as closets and areas below stairs. There may be more evidence of the history of the home in these spaces. You have to be careful with the information you get here. Considerable cracking, bulging, and loose pieces of plaster may be visible. However, this may indicate neglect rather than any serious problems.

We discussed some clues to consider when determining whether cracks are structural in Chapter 4, "Structure," so we won't repeat them here. If you can't be entirely sure if a crack has structural implications, document your limitations, explain to your client what you have found and why you cannot be conclusive, and recommend further evaluation.

Mechanical Damage

IMPLICATIONS

STRATEGY

Mechanical damage is usually localized and calls for minor repair.

Look at wall surfaces and note holes and other evidence of physical damage. Many walls are damaged by door knobs when there is no effective doorstop.

Inappropriate Finishes in Wet Areas

Areas around bathtubs and showers should have smooth, hard, nonabsorbent finishes to a height of at least six feet above floor level. This can be ceramic tile, glass, marble, plastic laminate, fiberglass, acrylic, and other materials.

Wood Not Appropriate

Wood, drywall, and plaster around bathtubs or showers are not considered appropriate finish materials.

IMPLICATIONS

Absorbent finishes will draw moisture in and are likely to stain or deteriorate. Wood is a good example of this. Plaster or drywall in wet areas will crumble and disintegrate. Textured finishes hold water and foster growth of mold.

STRATEGY

Look carefully at wood and other absorbent or textured finishes in wet areas. If you see evidence of deterioration, you should recommend replacement. Where there is no evidence, you should let clients know of the possible implications. New occupants of a home may have a very different lifestyle. A wood enclosure around a bathtub may not be a problem until people start using the shower, for example.

F I G U R E 6.5   Shadow Effect

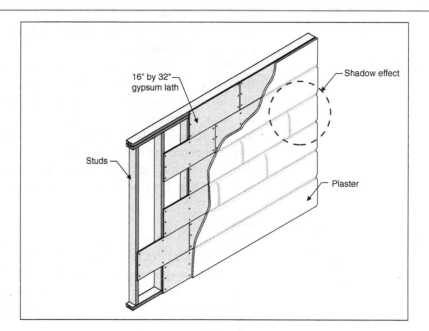

Plaster or Drywall

Conditions for plaster or drywall include:

- bulging, loose, missing
- shadow effect
- crumbling or powdery
- nail pops
- poor joints

Shadow Effect

The meaning of "shadow effect" is perhaps not self-explanatory. It is a cosmetic condition caused on original installation by applying subsequent coats of plaster before previous coats were dry (Figure 6.5).

IMPLICATIONS

Bulging, loose, or missing plaster is certainly a cosmetic issue. It can also be a safety issue. Falling plaster is heavy. Plaster falling from a wall along a stairwell can hurt someone below.

The implications of shadow effect are purely cosmetic.

*Crumbling or Powdery
Plaster or Drywall*

The implications of deterioration depend on the amount of water present and whether the problem is active. Concealed damage to the structure is the big risk. If the problem is ongoing, the source has to be controlled first. The structure behind the damaged wall should be investigated, and only then should the plaster or drywall be repaired. If the problem is not active, removing and replacing the damaged section of plaster and drywall may be all that is required.

*Nail Pops and Poor
Drywall Joints*

Nail pops and poor joints are cosmetic issues and easily corrected.

STRATEGY

We talked about pushing and tapping on walls as a general strategy. We also talked about using a flashlight beam parallel to the wall surface to identify defects. Both of these techniques are valuable in identifying bulging or loose plaster and the shadow effect. Tapping on a wall may also reveal crumbling and powdery plaster or drywall. Poor joints and nail pops may be visible from a distance. The parallel flashlight technique may also be helpful.

Wood

Wood walls can be rotted, cracked, split, broken, buckled, or loose.

IMPLICATIONS

The implications of most interior finish problems are cosmetic. If there is evidence of moisture damage, there may be concealed damage.

STRATEGY

A visual inspection of wood paneling is appropriate. The parallel flashlight technique can be helpful, as can pushing and tapping on the wall to determine its tightness.

6.3   CEILINGS

The function of ceilings is similar to walls. These are primarily decorative. The ceiling finishes typically add some rigidity to the roof structure and help prevent cracking. The ceiling finishes also support the air/vapor barrier and insulation in most cases.

6.3.1   Materials

Ceiling materials are similar to wall materials. They can be plaster or drywall, wood, hardboard, plywood, fiber cement, or concrete. Acoustic tile ceilings are also common. These tiles can be fiberboard or plastic-faced fiberglass. These can be supported on wood strapping or suspended T-bars.

Metal ceilings are common in kitchens of old homes and newer kitchens with traditional design elements. An embossed pattern in the metal is often used to create the look of decorative plaster.

As we discussed with walls, it's not unusual to find that drywall has been applied over old plaster. Acoustic tile ceilings are also often applied below old plaster.

Smooth and Textured

Textured ceilings are very common in some areas because they are quick and inexpensive to install and are more forgiving of imperfections in drywall. Textured finishes should not be used in kitchens or bathrooms because the large surface areas tend to collect dirt and grease and are hard to clean.

6.3.2   Conditions

Let's look at some of the common problems with ceiling finishes.

1. Water damage
2. Cracked, loose, or missing sections
3. Mechanical damage
4. Plaster or drywall
   - bulging, loose, or missing
   - shadow effect
   - crumbling or powdery
   - nail pops
   - poor drywall joints
   - sag
   - textured ceilings in wet areas

5. Wood
   - ▨ rot
   - ▨ cracked, split, or broken
   - ▨ buckled
   - ▨ loose

6. Metal
   - ▨ rust

7. Lighting poor

Water Damage

The issues here are similar to what we talked about on wall systems. The causes, implications, and inspection strategies are similar. Many inspectors lift at least some of the tiles on suspended T-bar ceilings. There is often a good deal of information that can be determined looking above these ceilings.

Check below Fixtures

Operate plumbing fixtures and then check the ceilings below. Revisit the ceiling below bathtubs and showers after operating these fixtures.

Cracked, Loose, or Missing Sections

Truss Uplift

Again, this discussion is the same as for walls. However, there is one additional issue —**truss uplift.**

Truss uplift is a cold weather problem that is not terribly serious from a structural standpoint, but it is very disturbing to homeowners and can cause considerable cosmetic damage.

Winter Only

Truss uplift occurs in the winter only. It occurs because the bottom chord of the truss arches up (Figure 6.6). The ends of the bottom chord rest on the outside wall, but the center portion rises. This usually creates a gap between the top of interior partitions near the center of the house and the ceiling. This gap can be well over an inch. In some cases, the partition wall is rigidly attached to the bottom chord of the

F I G U R E 6.6   Roof Truss Uplift

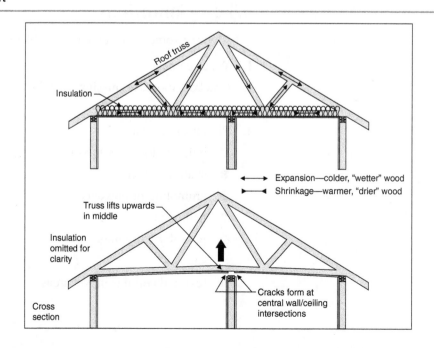

F I G U R E 6.7   Roof Truss Uplift—Remedial Action

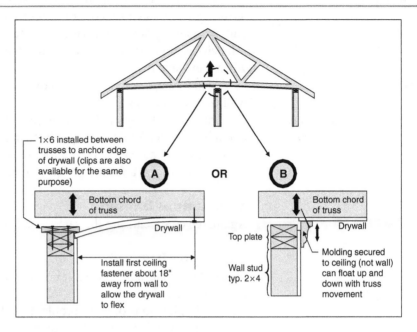

trusses. In this case, the partition wall may be pulled up and a gap may appear between the bottom of the wall and the floor.

Raised Ceiling or Wall

These gaps always look like the wall is dropping (if the gap is at the wall ceiling intersection) or like the floor is dropping (if the gap appears at the wall/floor intersection). This is because we are prisoners of gravity and think that all movement in a vertical plane is down. In this case, however, the movement is up. Either the ceiling is lifting off the wall or the ceiling and wall are lifting off the floor. Close examination and perhaps the help of a mason's level will allow you to verify this.

The cause of truss uplift is not perfectly understood, and the possible explanations are beyond the scope of this book. The bottom line is that it's a cyclical problem: Truss uplift occurs in the winter, but as the warmer months come, the truss will settle back down. The problem repeats itself every winter. The amount of truss uplift may vary depending on weather severity.

Which Trusses Are More Likely to Suffer Uplift?

Trusses with longer spans and lower slopes are more likely to suffer. Trusses in well-insulated attics are more likely to suffer uplift.

Corrective Action

It's not possible to prevent truss uplift.

Moldings

The solutions typically lie in concealing the movement (Figure 6.7). One approach is to use a molding attached to the ceiling but not to the partitions. As the ceiling is lifted up during truss uplift, the molding simply slides up the wall. This is sometimes successful in masking cosmetic deficiencies, although the moldings may scratch the wall surfaces, or the raised moldings will reveal paint of a different color or bare spots on wallpapered sections of the wall.

Float the Drywall

Another solution is to allow the ceiling drywall near the center partitions to float. The drywall is not attached to the trusses within roughly 18 inches of the partition walls. The edge of the ceiling drywall is secured to the wall with a 1 by 6 attached to the top plate or with a drywall clip fastened to the top of the wall. When the truss lifts, the edge of the ceiling drywall stays in place since it's not attached to the bottom chord near the partitions. The drywall bends up over 18 inches to the point where it's attached to the trusses.

When looking at truss roofs, understand that their advantage is their long uninterrupted spans and no need for interior bearing walls, but watch for the uplift problem, particularly at interior partitions near the center of the truss span. Truss uplift is much easier to see in the winter, when the trusses have moved, than in the summer when they have relaxed.

Look for gaps or evidence of movement at the wall/ceiling intersection and the wall/floor intersection.

Trusses most likely to lift are those with long spans, low slopes and lots of insulation in the attic. Again, once you recognize the problem, you can set your client's mind at ease because it is not a serious structural issue. However, if you fail to identify it, you may get a frantic phone call during the winter.

Mechanical Damage
Again, the comments are the same as we offered on walls.

Plaster or Drywall
Many of the conditions for plaster or drywall ceilings are the same as for plaster or drywall walls.

The implications of these problems and strategies for inspecting them are similar to our discussions for walls. You may see sagging or wavy ceilings in relatively new homes, even though the drywall is supported every 16 inches. There are no functional implications. This is purely a cosmetic issue.

Where you see textured ceilings in kitchens and bathrooms, there's no serious functional problem. However, these ceilings may already look quite dirty and may be difficult to keep clean. Resurfacing them with a smooth ceiling finish is a possibility, although rarely a priority for a homeowner.

Wood
Wood ceilings can be rotten, cracked, split, broken, buckled, or loose. These issues are the same as we talked about for walls.

Metal—Rusted

In most cases, the implications of rust on metal ceilings or ceiling components are cosmetic, although, in severe cases, sections of the ceiling may fall.

Look for evidence of rust on exposed metal ceilings. If you can lift suspended tiles, check the wiring and T-bar supports for rust.

Lighting Poor
All living spaces in houses should have adequate electric lighting. We mention lighting here because it is often (though not always) provided from the ceiling.

Rooms or hallways without adequate lighting are a safety hazard.

Look for lighting in each room and in hallways and stairs. Best practice in hallways includes three-way switches so that the lights can be operated from either end. We'll talk about stair lighting shortly, but essentially a stairway is the same as a hall. Three-way switches should be provided to operate the lights from the top or bottom of the stairs. Many make an exception for stairs leading to unfinished basements, for example.

Lighting is often provided at ceiling level, although this is not the case in most living rooms, many family rooms, and some bedrooms. Wall switches may control one or both halves of duplex receptacles. This allows floor or table lamps to be turned on when someone enters the room.

FIGURE 6.8   Kinds of Trim

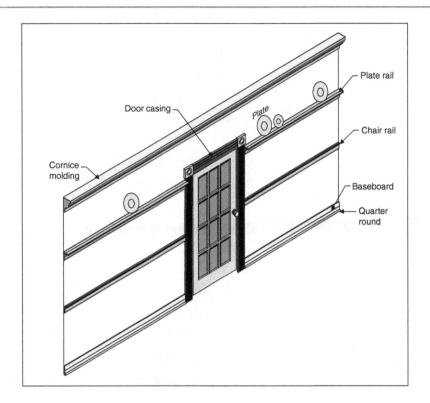

6.4   TRIM, COUNTERS, AND CABINETS

Trim is used to cover joints at changes in material and direction. Trim includes baseboard, quarter round, door and window casings, and floor thresholds (Figure 6.8). Trim is also used to protect walls. Chair rails are an example of this. Trim can be used to add architectural appeal and display ornamentation. Plate rails are an example of this kind of trim. Trim can be used to make wall/ceiling transitions and add architectural detail to walls and ceilings. Cornice moldings and rosettes or medallions are examples of these.

Trim may be made of wood or wood-based products, including fiberboard. Trim may also be marble, ceramics, plaster, or polystyrene (foamed plastic). The more fragile materials such as plaster and polystyrene are commonly used for ceiling trim, which isn't likely to be mechanically abused.

Counters provide working surfaces in kitchens, bathrooms, pantries, and bars. Cabinets provide storage facilities in kitchens, bathrooms, and other rooms.

Most counters are installed over particleboard, although there are some exceptions. Counter materials include—

- plastic laminate
- wood
- marble
- granite or limestone
- synthetic marble or granite
- stainless steel
- ceramic tile

Cabinets may be solid wood, particleboard or metal. Particleboard is often covered with a plastic laminate.

Let's look at some common problems with these systems.

1. Trim problems
   - missing
   - water damage
   - rot
   - loose
   - mechanical damage

2. Counter problems
   - entire top loose
   - loose or missing pieces
   - burned
   - cut
   - worn
   - mechanical damage
   - stained
   - metal rusted
   - ceramic grout missing or loose, ceramic tiles missing or loose
   - substrate rotted

3. Cabinet problems
   - water damage
   - rot
   - stained
   - mechanical damage
   - worn
   - broken glass
   - defective hardware
   - stiff or inoperative
   - not well secured to wall
   - door or drawers missing or loose
   - other pieces missing or loose
   - shelves not well supported
   - rust

Trim Problems

IMPLICATIONS

Missing or damaged trim may be simply a cosmetic problem. Loose trim can allow air leakage into building components, which may result in condensation damage. Rotted or mechanically damaged trim may conceal rot or other damage to building systems behind.

STRATEGY

Look for trim to be continuous, intact, and well secured. Note missing or damaged trim. Where possible, look behind the trim for other damage.

Counter Problems

The implications of a loose countertop may be personal injury if the countertop falls. Poor hygiene is the implication of loose or missing pieces, burned, cut or worn surfaces, mechanical damage, or stained counters and rust. Loose or missing ceramic tiles or grout may also be hygiene issues as well as cosmetic defects.

Rotted substrate may result in the countertop collapsing or sinks, faucets, or basins coming loose.

When looking at countertops, grab the edge and try to lift with moderate force. Don't damage the countertop by applying excessive force. Look for:

- loose or missing pieces, burns, cuts, or worn areas.
- mechanical damage resulting from impact.
- stains on marble, wood and plastic laminates.
- rust on metal countertops.
- loose or missing tiles or grout on ceramics.

When you're looking at cabinetry and plumbing fixtures, check the underside of the countertops, especially around sinks and faucets, for evidence of rot.

Move Cutting Boards

While home inspectors are not required to move household goods, sliding a cutting board or other articles out of the way so you can see the entire countertop can be revealing.

Ask Client to Help?

Many home inspectors get their clients involved when looking at counters and cabinets in kitchens and bathrooms. The evaluation of these systems is somewhat subjective; allowing clients to open and close cupboard drawers and pull out drawers may be helpful to both you and the client.

Cabinet Problems

The implications of water damage may be failure of the cabinets. The implications of damage or wear may be collapse of the cabinet or inoperable doors or drawers, if severe. In many cases, the defects are cosmetic.

Glass

Cracked or broken glass can be a safety issue if glass falls onto people.

Hardware

Defective hardware and stiff or inoperative doors or drawers are functional problems that diminish the usability of the cabinets.

Secured to Wall

Cabinets that are not well secured to a wall are a serious safety issue. Falling cabinets can seriously injure people (Figure 6.9).

Loose or Missing Doors

Doors, drawers, or other pieces that are missing or loose affect the usability of cabinets.

Weak Shelves

Shelves that are not well supported are usually minor problems, unless they are filled with china before giving way. This can cause damage and injury.

Rust

Rusted medicine cabinets are not hygienic, and the cabinet may eventually rust through.

Where water damage is noted, probe for rot and make sure the cabinet structure is intact.

Let the client know about wear or mechanical damage that affects the usability of the cabinetry.

Recommend that broken or cracked glass be replaced. Operate all doors and drawers, looking for hardware or operational deficiencies. In many cases, adjustment or lubrication is all that is required.

Apply moderate upward force on wall-hung cabinets to ensure they aren't loose. Test that shelves are secure by applying moderate downward force to the front edge.

F I G U R E 6.9   Loose Cabinets Can Seriously Injure People

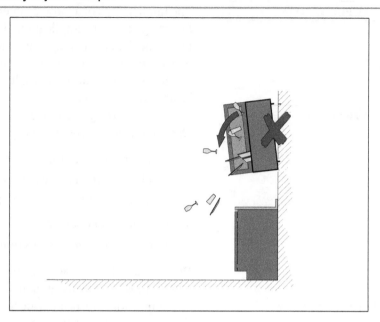

6.5   STAIRS

We looked at several aspects of good stair construction in the "Exterior" chapter. The same guidelines and conditions, such as railing and guard heights and tread sizing, apply to interior stairs, but there are some additional requirements and conditions that you should consider when inspecting indoor stairs. Again, you should consult your local jurisdiction for the rules that apply in your area, but here are some common rules that build on those we've already looked at:

- **Curved Treads**
    - Minimum tread depth, measured 12 inches out from the narrowest part of the tread—10 inches
    - Minimum tread depth, measured at the narrowest part of the tread—6 inches
- **Stairwell Width**—minimum 36 inches
- **Handrail Projections**—maximum 4½ inches into stairwell
- **Headroom**—minimum 6 feet, 8 inches, measured straight up from a diagonal line drawn through the tread nosings

6.5.1   Conditions

As you can imagine, most of the problems with stairs involve disregarding their rules and dimensions. Following are common conditions for stairs (most have been discussed in Chapter 2, "Exterior"):

1. Rot or water damage
2. Mechanical damage

3. Treads
   - too thin
   - excessive rise
   - not uniform
   - excessive nosing
   - inadequate tread depth
   - worn or damaged
   - sloped
   - loose or poorly supported

4. Stringer problems
   - too small
   - too thin
   - excessive span between stringers
   - rot
   - pulling away from wall or treads
   - inadequately secured to header

5. Stairwell width inadequate

6. Headroom inadequate

7. Landings
   - missing
   - too small

8. Handrails
   - missing
   - too high or too low
   - hard to grasp
   - loose or damaged

9. Guardrails
   - missing
   - too low
   - loose or damaged

10. Balusters (spindles) for handrails or guardrails
    - too far apart
    - easy to climb
    - loose or damaged
    - missing

11. Lighting inadequate

IMPLICATIONS

The implications of these problems are:
- personal injury. Stairs that are poorly designed are hazards. People may fall down or off the stairs.
- stairs themselves may collapse.

We won't repeat these implications with each discussion.

FIGURE 6.10 Stringer Movement

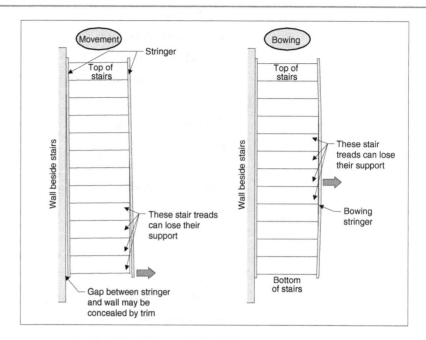

Stringer Problems

Stringers are not always visible. Where they are, check for movement (Figure 6.10). Standing at the top or bottom of a set of stairs, you can look along the staircase and see movement of either stringer in a lateral plane. This may cause stair treads to become loose.

Watch for stringers that run parallel to walls. In some cases, trim is added to the top of the wall as it pulls away from the wall. The trim simply covers what would otherwise be an unsightly gap. The gap may be visible from a closet below, but it is also visible looking along the stringer from the top or bottom of the stairs.

Header Connection

Again in most cases you won't be able to see how the stringer is supported by the header. In most cases, movement can't occur without the bottom of the stringer moving relative to the floor. Watch for movement here as well.

Stairwell Width

You'll get a sense of stairwell width just walking up and down stairs. Basement stairs or stairs to unfinished areas are often narrower. This is acceptable in some juris-dictions and will be common. Similarly, inadequate headroom is often an issue on basement stairs.

Headroom Inadequate

If you have to duck going up or down the stairs, the headroom is inadequate. In many older homes, the headroom is less than ideal. The headroom for basement staircases is very often less than ideal, but it may not be practical to change it.

Landings

You shouldn't be standing on a stair to open a door. Most staircases should have land-ings. Although landings can be omitted at the top of the stairs if the door opens away from the staircase or if there is no door, the best practice includes at least a twelve-

F I G U R E 6.11   Handrail Support

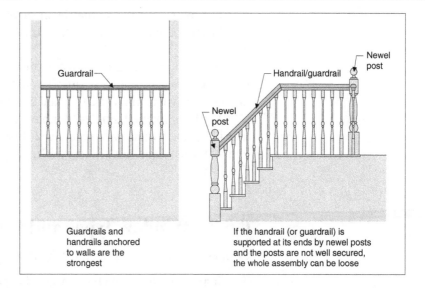

Guardrail

Newel
post

Handrail/guardrail

Newel
post

Guardrails and
handrails anchored
to walls are the
strongest

If the handrail (or guardrail) is
supported at its ends by newel posts
and the posts are not well secured,
the whole assembly can be loose

inch landing at the top of the stairs. Again, rearranging stairs is very expensive and would only be done as a last resort. You should, however, point out the lack of an adequate landing.

Handrails

Handrail problems are obvious and easy to spot with a little practice. Your inspection should include using the handrail as you climb stairs.

Handrails that are not tied into walls, at least at the top and bottom, are most susceptible to problems. Many railings are supported at their ends by **newel posts** (Figure 6.11). If this post is not well anchored to the structure, the handrail can be loose.

The same is true of guardrails. Guardrails anchored to walls at both ends are the strongest, but it is common to find one or both ends of the guardrail secured to a post.

Lighting Inadequate

All stairwells with more than six risers should have lighting controlled by switches at the top and bottom. These are called **three-way switches,** although they only operate the light from two locations. Three-way switches are not usually required at stairs to unfinished areas, such as basements.

Operate the light switches at both the top and bottom of stairs to ensure the light responds to both switches properly. Having the light on as you look at the stairs obviously makes a lot of sense.

6.6   WINDOWS, SKYLIGHTS, AND SOLARIUMS

Functions

Windows allow light and ventilation. Windows can add to the architectural appeal of the home and can provide emergency exits (means of egress).

6.6.1   Materials

Window frames and sashes may be made of wood, vinyl (often polyvinyl chloride), metal (steel or aluminum), or fiberglass. Wood windows may also be vinyl-clad or metal-clad.

Conventional glass is the most common, although laminated, tempered, and wired-glass may be found. Acrylic is common in skylights. Polycarbonates are used in windows where great strength and security are important.

Windows may be single-, double-, or triple-glazed. Single-glazed windows may have storm windows and screens. Double- and triple-glazed windows and skylights may have additional energy efficiency features, such as low-E glass and gas-filled spaces.

6.6.2   Window Types and Components

Common window types include (Figure 6.12)—

- single-hung (only the bottom sash is operable)
- double-hung (both the top and bottom sash is operable)
- casement (the windows may swing in, out, or pivot)
- horizontal sliders
- awning (hinged at top and open outward)
- hopper (hinged at bottom, may open in or out)
- fixed (includes conventional glazing and glass block; glass block may be structural)
- jalousie (typically used only in warm climates, since they do not seal tightly but are good for ventilation)

The main components of windows are frames, sashes, muntins, panes, and mullions (Figure 6.13).

We discussed conditions that contribute to air and water leakage through windows in Chapter 2, section 2.4. We won't repeat that information here, but you should keep it in mind during your inspection of window interiors as well as exteriors. Leakage from outside can affect inside elements of and around windows.

6.6.3   General Inspection Strategy

The interior window inspection is really a follow-up to your exterior window inspection.

Upper Floor Windows

In two- and three-story homes, your inspection of the window exteriors is usually limited by your distance from the windows. You may be able to open upper floor windows when inside the home and get a look at the exterior. You'll want to determine the condition of sills and seals around the perimeter of the window on the exterior. This is where moisture penetration protection is most important.

Don't Fall Out

Sometimes it's not practical to remove screens and glass to get a look outside. You also need to use common sense. Don't risk falling out of the window while straining to get a look.

F I G U R E 6.12   Window Types

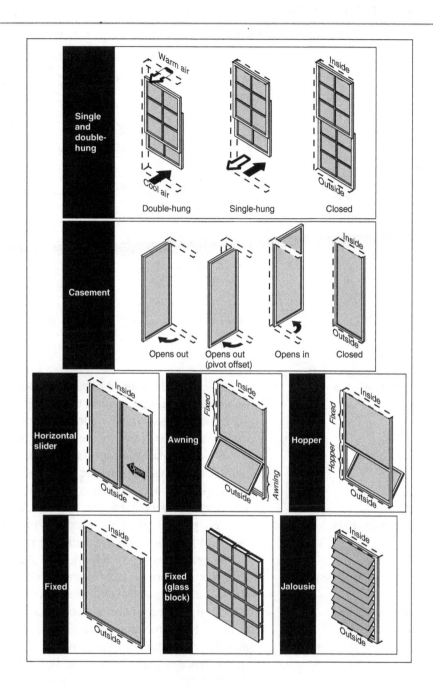

Beware of the Sashless Slider

There is a low-quality window that was used in the 1960s, 1970s, and the 1980s. This horizontal sliding window has a simple pane of glass as the operable component. There is no sash and no weather stripping. An operating knob may be fastened through a hole in the glass or clipped to the edge of the glass. The seal between adjacent panes is simply glass-to-glass. This is not particularly weather-tight.

These windows suffered considerable condensation and leakage problems. Again, many have been replaced, or provided with an external storm window system, even though the original windows were double glass.

Pull Back Curtains

A common home inspector mistake is failure to pull back curtains around windows. Window leakage is common and damage often shows up below the windows at either corner. These corners are typically covered by curtains.

FIGURE 6.13   Window Components

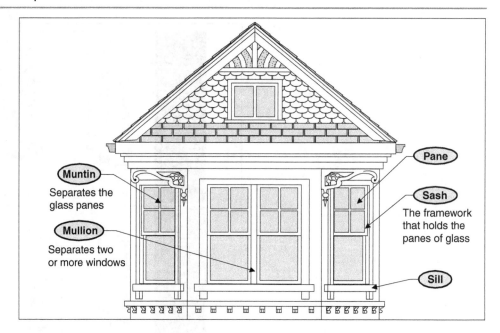

Operate All Windows

Although the standards call for operating one window in each room, we recommend you operate as many as possible. We have found that homeowners are often very disappointed when windows do not operate smoothly. It takes a few more seconds in each room, but we recommend you try each operable window.

Sloped Glazing

Skylights and solariums have glazing units that are not vertical. These are vulnerable to mechanical damage from hail and falling branches, for example. In many areas, glass has to be laminated, tempered, wired, or otherwise strengthened in skylights and solariums. Another common approach is to use acrylic instead of glass.

Strengthened Glass

As a general rule, if the glazing is more than 15 degrees off vertical, some attention has to be paid to strengthening the system to protect against mechanical damage. It's beyond the scope of a home inspection to determine whether glazing has been strengthened since you can't typically determine this by looking. While you may find some clues, there are many cases where you won't be able to be conclusive.

Leakage Is Common

Skylights and solariums are frequently troublesome with respect to water penetration. Problems arise at edges of glass panels that are not vertical. Lips are created that catch and hold water. We encourage you to spend a little extra time looking for evidence of leaks around and below these.

Now let's look at some common window problems.

6.6.4   Conditions

1. Leaks

2. Lintels sagging or missing

3. Frames

■   rot

■   rust

■   racked

- deformed
- installed backward
- drain holes blocked or missing

4. Exterior drip cap missing or ineffective

5. Exterior trim
- missing
- rot
- rust
- damaged, cracked, or loose
- sills with reverse slope
- sill projection inadequate
- drip edge missing
- glazing compound cracked, missing, loose, or deteriorated
- caulking or flashing missing, loose, deteriorated, rusted, or incomplete
- paint or stain needed

6. Sash
- rot
- rust
- inoperable
- stiff
- won't stay open
- sash coming apart
- loose fit
- weather stripping missing or ineffective

7. Interior trim
- rot
- stained
- missing
- cracked
- loose
- poor fit

8. Glass
- cracked
- broken
- loose
- missing
- lost seal on double- or triple-glazed
- excess condensation

9. Hardware
- rust
- broken

■ missing

■ loose

■ inoperable

10. Location

■ sills too low

11. Screens

■ torn

■ rust

■ loose

■ missing

12. Storm windows missing

13. Too small for egress

14. Ice dams at skylights

Leaks

Windows may leak air or water.

Water leakage is an immediate problem with respect to damage to windows and wall assemblies below, as well as to interior finishes.

Air leakage affects heating and cooling costs and may result in concealed rot damage.

Look carefully around and below windows, especially at the corners. Look also for evidence of leakage at the top of the windows. You will sometimes see rust or water stains across the top of a window.

During warm, dry weather it is sometimes difficult to determine whether water damage around the bottom of a window is the result of condensation or leakage. If you can't be certain, allow for both possibilities.

F I G U R E 6.14   Skylight and Solarium Leaks

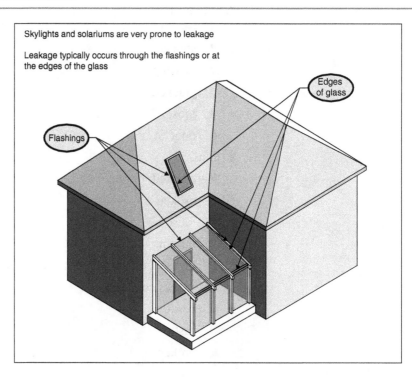

Skylights and solariums are very prone to leakage

Leakage typically occurs through the flashings or at the edges of the glass

Edges of glass

Flashings

Skylights and Solariums

The sloped glazing at skylights and solariums is susceptible to leakage because water gets hung up on the lips and edges supporting the glass (Figure 6.14). Flashings at curbs and solarium/wall intersections are also common leak spots. Look carefully for stains or water marks on the interior below and around the glazing and flashing. Wood sashes, muntins, mullions, and framing members are **very susceptible to rot.** Check carefully, and probe if possible (don't damage finishes).

Lintels Sagging or Missing

This may be more visible from the outside of the building. It's common on large windows or groups of windows. If the lintel or arch is missing or ineffective, you will often see a sag across the top of the window or window group.

IMPLICATIONS

Windows may be difficult to operate and glass may crack. In severe cases, the wall section above may fail.

Frame

Window frame conditions include rot, rust, cracking, deformation, and blocked or missing drain holes.

IMPLICATIONS

The implications of rot, rust, cracking, and deformed frames are poor weathertightness and operability. The window may not open or close. It also may crack, and, if not corrected, windows may have to be replaced.

The implication of blocked or missing drain holes is water leakage into the home.

STRATEGY

If you can get to the exterior sections of the frame, check for rot and rust. Probing wood sections, especially where there are horizontal edges that can collect water, or end grains exposed at corners is a good way to check for this. Don't be too enthusiastic and damage the wood by probing.

Sight along Frames

Check for cracked or deformed frames by sighting along the top, bottom, and sides of windows.

Sill and Drain

Check the sill slope and look for functional drain holes.

Exterior Drip Cap Missing or Ineffective

Water can leak into the window and wall system if the exterior drip cap is missing or ineffective.

IMPLICATIONS

STRATEGY

Look for metal caps that protect the tops of every window in wood-frame walls. You won't see this in masonry or brick veneer construction because the windows are recessed into the wall.

Projection and Slope

Look for a projection of the cap beyond the window. We are looking for water to fall past, not onto, the window. The cap will be nearly horizontal but should slope to drain water away from the wall.

Width

The drip cap should be slightly wider than the window and should not allow water to drain off the side and get behind siding.

Can Sometimes Be Omitted

If the windows are protected by the roof overhang, no drip cap may be needed (see Figure 6.15). As a general rule, if the distance from the top of the window to the soffit is less than one quarter of the soffit width, we don't need a drip cap.

Exterior Trim Problems

Exterior trim includes brick molds, casings, sills, muntins, and mullions. Problems include:

- missing
- rot
- rust
- damaged, cracked, or loose

F I G U R E 6.15   Flashings over Windows

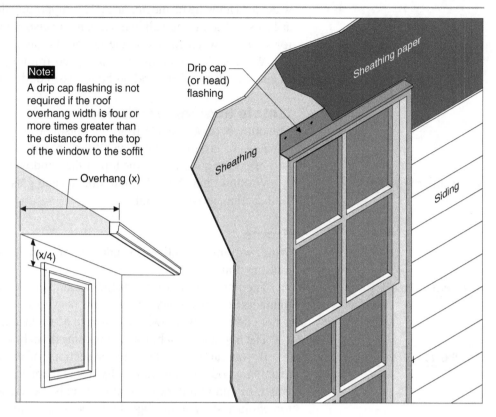

- sills with reversed slope
- sill projection inadequate
- drip edge missing
- putty (glazing compound) cracked, missing, loose, or deteriorated
- caulking or flashing missing, deteriorated, loose, rusted, or incomplete
- paint or stain needed

IMPLICATIONS

STRATEGY

These problems may impact window performance. Leakage of water and air and operation problems are likely results.

You may have identified several of these conditions from your exterior inspection. If you look out through windows, you may pick up these from the interior.

Sashes

Sash conditions include:

- rot
- rust
- inoperable
- stiff
- sashes won't stay open
- sash coming apart
- loose fit
- Weather stripping missing or ineffective

F I G U R E 6.16   Don't Push on Upper Sash

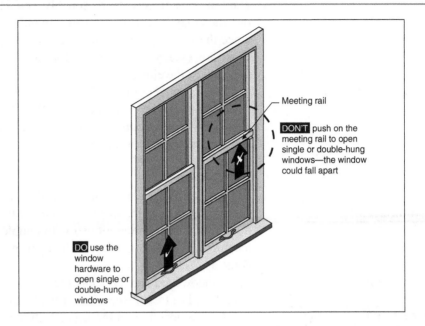

Meeting rail

DON'T push on the meeting rail to open single or double-hung windows—the window could fall apart

DO use the window hardware to open single or double-hung windows

IMPLICATIONS

STRATEGY

Don't Push on Upper Sash

Check Weather Stripping and Fit

IMPLICATIONS

STRATEGY

IMPLICATIONS

Window leakage (air and water) and difficulties in operation are the implications of these problems.

Just as we looked at the frames, we should look at sashes for rot and rust. We recommend testing all operable windows if possible. You may find that windows are painted closed or do not move easily.

There is a strong temptation to push on the upper horizontal part (**meeting rail**) of the sash to open a single- or double-hung window (Figure 6.16). Resist this temptation. Most windows have hardware on the lower rail to open the window. Pushing on the upper rail will eventually lead to separation of the upper rail from the stiles on either side of the sash. The window literally falls apart. Watch for this problem as you operate single- and double-hung windows, and don't contribute to the problem. Use the hardware to pull the window open.

As you operate windows, you'll get a sense of how snugly they fit. When the window is closed, look around the perimeter for obvious gaps or discontinuities in the weather stripping.

Interior Trim

Interior trim can be rotten, stained, missing, cracked, loose, or poorly fit.

These are primarily cosmetic problems, although rot or staining may indicate concealed damage to the structure behind.

Look at casings and the interior stool and apron (fancy names for interior sill and trim) for problems. In some cases, the interior stool is used for storing plants, which are watered regularly. This can cause water damage.

Glass

Window glass can be cracked, broken, loose, or missing. It may have lost its seal or exhibit excess condensation.

Cracked, broken, loose, or missing glass can be both a heat loss and heat gain problem, and it can be a risk of injury. If the glass is loose, it often rattles whenever someone walks through a room. People may be cut on broken glass.

Lost Seals

Lost seals are not particularly serious from an energy efficiency standpoint. The window will still perform reasonably well. However, visibility is often reduced, and the glass may look cloudy, even if there's no condensation present at the moment. Once the seal is gone, condensation will appear and disappear between the panes. This, however, leaves the interior surfaces of the glazing dirty, and the cloudy appearance develops.

Excess Condensation

Excess condensation will usually only occur during cold weather. It is the result of high humidity levels in the house. We talked extensively in Chapter 5, *Insulation*, about how we can control moisture levels inside the house. Eliminating moisture sources and using exhaust fans are obvious steps to control indoor moisture levels.

Hardware
Window hardware can be rusted, broken, missing, loose, or inoperable.

IMPLICATIONS

Windows may not operate at all if hardware is missing or inoperable. Operation may be difficult. As mentioned with double-hung windows, if people push on the meeting rail, rather than using the appropriate hardware, the sash will eventually come apart.

Loss of Security

Window hardware typically includes locking mechanisms. If these are not effective, there is a loss of security for the home.

STRATEGY

As you operate windows, you will recognize hardware problems. If the hardware is working but is obviously rusted or loose, note that in your report.

Location
Window sills may be too low. Windows at stair landings, for example, should have their sills at least 36 inches above floor level.

IMPLICATIONS

If the sills are too low, someone stumbling on the stairs may fall out through the window.

STRATEGY

Check that the windows are at least 36 inches above floor level. When they are lower and there is a risk of falling, you can recommend a guard or rail. Safety glazing may be another option.

Screens
Window screens may have holes or be torn, rusted, loose, or missing. Screens are typically nylon, aluminum, or copper.

IMPLICATIONS

Screens are designed to keep insects and pests out of the home. If they can't do their job, insects will find their way into the house.

STRATEGY

As you're looking at windows, note whether the screens are intact.

Storm Windows Missing
In many climates, storm windows are usually provided. These may have been replaced with double-glazed windows. If single-glazed windows are noted in a heating climate, you may suspect there are storm windows available.

IMPLICATIONS

Heat loss or heat gain are obvious implications of missing storm windows. Excessive condensation levels on the interior surfaces of primary windows is another implication. Adding storm windows will keep the interior glass warmer and reduce condensation. Storm windows also reduce drafts and may improve comfort as a result.

STRATEGY

Look for evidence that storm windows have been installed on the outside in the past. There are often clips used to hold them in place. Check basements, garages, and other outbuildings as you move through these areas. Very often you will come across storm windows.

Most home inspectors don't go so far as to ensure there is a storm for each window, although you can usually get a sense of this. Tell your client that there are no storm windows in place but there are some stored in the house. Some clients will ask sellers to assure them that there are storm windows for all the windows.

Too Small for Egress

In many areas, windows have to be available for use as emergency exits. In some jurisdictions, every bedroom has to have a window that can be used as an emergency exit. Basements also require a window for egress.

Windows to be used for egress must not have a sill more than 44 inches from the floor and must have a clear opening area of 5.7 square feet. When the bedroom is on a grade level floor, the clear opening can be as small as 5 square feet. The minimum width of the opening is 20 inches and the minimum height is 24 inches.

The idea is that someone should be able to crawl out the window if there is a fire that prevents leaving the bedroom through the door.

Code Compliance Inspection?   Home inspectors do not do code compliance inspections. You don't have to refer to the code to let people know the common sense wisdom of providing an emergency escape route. Some inspectors recommend rope ladders and point out bedrooms that do not have a secondary escape route from the house.

6.7   DOORS

Exterior   Exterior doors are a means of entering and leaving a house. They should provide security and privacy. They should be weather-tight and, if they communicate with garages, should be fireproof.

Interior   Interior doors allow passage between rooms. They also afford privacy and some sound protection. They also provide some fire and smoke protection for people in bedrooms.

6.7.1   Materials and Types

Doors   Doors may be made of wood, metal, vinyl, or hardboard. Hardboard doors are usually restricted to indoor use.

Cores   Many doors are hollow-cored. The cores on interior doors may have cardboard reinforcement. Exterior metal doors often have polyurethane insulation as cores. These can provide very good insulation levels.

Sills   Doorsills are typically wood or metal. Sill issues include slope, overhang, support, and weather stripping.

Door Operation   Doors may be **hinged** conventionally (Figure 6.17). They may be **sliding doors** moving in tracks, or suspended from overhead concealed tracks, as is typical of **pocket doors.** Doors may also be **bi-fold,** moving in a track.

Surfaces   Door surfaces may be flush, paneled, louvered, or glazed. Sliding patio doors, for example, are effectively large sliding windows.

French Doors   **French doors** are conventional hinged doors with a difference. These are typically double doors, hinged at either side. Typical French doors are mostly glazing, usually with several muntins breaking the glass up into small panes.

No Mullions   True French doors meet at the center with no middle mullion or frame. Without a mullion or frame to close against, French doors can be leaky, drafty, and less secure than conventional doors. There are several approaches to French door design to maximize the strength, weather-tightness, and security. Your inspection should focus on the meeting point between the two doors, looking for evidence of problems. If they

F I G U R E 6.17 Door Operation

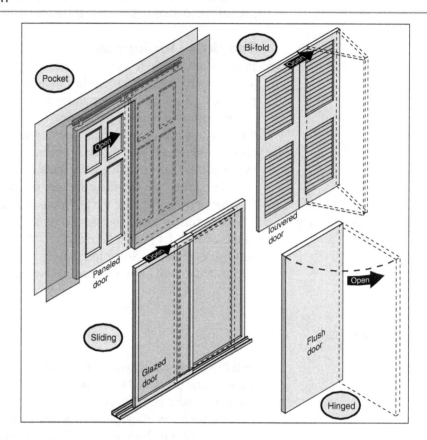

are exterior doors, pay particular attention to the possibility of water damage below the doors in the area of the meeting point.

6.7.2 General Strategy

Doors provide useful clues to the condition of the house structure. Because a door is a rectangular component in a rectangular opening, it's a very good reference spot to look for movement in the building. This is true on both interior and exterior doors. As part of your door inspection, you should be looking for doors that are noticeably out of square. It's common to find doors that have been trimmed as their openings shift, so that the doors will operate freely. Watch for this trimming, which can indicate the direction and amount of movement in the structure.

Not the Whole Story   While the movement of a doorframe can be dramatic, it may be relatively trivial from a structure standpoint. An interior partition wall that is not load-bearing may deflect because of heavy loads along the wall, failure to double the parallel joist below, etc. Movement can be dramatic, but it may not be a huge structural problem. Don't jump to conclusions, but use this information as part of the big picture.

Operate Every Door   The Standards indicate that we have to operate one door per room and operate every exterior door. If possible, try every door. Doors that do not open and close are frustrating to homeowners and, while usually not serious, can be the source of nuisance callbacks. Even if people don't complain, they are often irritated they weren't made aware of the problem.

6.7.3   Conditions

Conditions associated with doors include:

1. Leaks
2. Headers sagging or missing
3. Door and frame
   - rot
   - rust
   - racked
   - deformed
   - damaged
   - delaminated
   - loose or poor fit
   - installed backward
   - drain holes blocked or missing
   - stiff or inoperable
   - swings open or closed by itself
   - dark paint on metal exposed to sun
   - plastic trim on metal door behind storm door
4. Exterior drip cap missing or ineffective
5. Exterior trim
   - missing
   - rot
   - rust
   - damage
   - cracked or loose
   - sills with reverse slope
   - sill projections inadequate
   - sill not well supported
   - sill too low
   - putty (glazing compound) missing, cracked, loose, or deteriorated
   - caulking or flashing missing, deteriorated, loose, rusted, or incomplete
   - paint or stain needed
6. Interior trim
   - rot
   - stained
   - missing
   - cracked
   - loose
   - poorly fit
   - floor stained below

■ doorstops missing or ineffective

■ guides or stops damaged

7. Glass

■ cracked

■ broken

■ loose

■ missing

■ lost seal

■ excess condensation

8. Hardware

■ rusted

■ broken

■ missing

■ inoperable

■ loose

■ doesn't latch

■ hinges on exterior of building

■ self-closer ineffective

9. Storm doors and screens

■ torn or holes

■ rusted

■ loose

■ missing

As we discuss these conditions, many are similar to windows. We won't repeat discussions we've already had.

Leaks

Doors can leak both air and water, just like windows. Because doors are often larger and closer to grade level, leakage can be more of a problem. Watch for leakage both at the top and bottom of the doorframe. Check for water damage in the basement, crawlspace, or floor below exterior doors.

Lintels Sagging or Missing

We talked about this with windows. This is more commonly a problem with sliding glass doors or French doors, because of the wide opening (Figure 6.18). Again, it's often easier to see from outside the home.

Door and Frame Problems

Most of these are similar to the window issues we discussed. Sliding glass doors have tracks at the bottom and should have drain holes. These can be installed backward. Again, the clues are drain holes on the inside and a reverse slope to the sill.

Stiff or Inoperable

Doors may be stiff for several reasons. Rollers and wheels on sliders are often damaged. Tracks can be dirty or damaged.

Pocket Doors

Be sure to operate pocket doors. There are frequently track problems, and repairs can be difficult and expensive because of access problems. Many pocket

FIGURE 6.18 Lintels Sagging or Missing

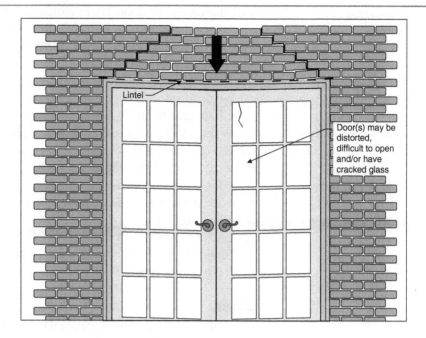

Lintel

Door(s) may be distorted, difficult to open and/or have cracked glass

doors have recessed hardware, and it's very easy for inspectors to walk through an opening and not realize that there is a door into the room.

Doors Swing by Themselves

Doors should stay where they are put. If a door is opened, it should not swing closed. If it's half opened, it should not swing in either direction. Doors that are not hung straight will often move on their own. This is a minor issue but is indicative of the quality of workmanship.

Dark Paint on Metal Doors

Children have been burned touching metal doors that are painted dark colors and exposed to the sun. These doors are often well insulated from behind, and the metal cannot dissipate heat. Dark colors tend to absorb heat, rather than reflect it, and the surface temperature of the metal can be more than 200°F.

Plastic Trim on Metal Doors

Many manufacturers of insulated metal doors recommend against adding a storm door. The heat buildup between the storm and primary doors can be significant. Raised plastic trim on metal doors will sometimes warp and pull away as a result of the heat buildup. Watch for evidence of this. In rare cases, the door itself can warp to the heat.

Exterior Drip Cap Missing or Ineffective
This is the same issue as we discussed on windows.

Exterior Trim
Most of the exterior trim issues for doors are the same as for windows. There are some new issues here we should look at.

Sill Not Well Supported

Doorsills are walking surfaces and in this respect are different from windowsills. Sills are typically cantilevered to a certain extent, and may not be well supported by the structure below. As you walk through doors, make sure you stand on the sill. Watch for any movement of the sill under your weight.

Interior Trim
Again, most of the interior trim issues for doors have been discussed with respect to windows.

Leakage around the base of doors is common. Watch for evidence of staining on the floor below the door. Try to look at the area below the door.

Doorstops prevent doors from swinging into walls. Doorknobs can damage wall finishes. There are several types of doorstops, and virtually any door can be provided with a stop.

Doors typically open either 90 degrees or 180 degrees. Many designers prefer to have doors open 90 degrees against a wall. Doors that open 180 degrees consume more floor area to allow for the door's travel.

When doors are open, they should not block light switches or other systems that require access. This is not something that most home inspectors would mention to clients, but it does suggest poor attention to detail.

Hinged doors typically close against stops at the sides and top. If these stops are loose, damaged, or missing, the door may not close properly or securely. Sliding or rolling doors have end stops. Watch for damage due to excessive force used opening or closing the doors.

Sliding or rolling doors will not operate freely if their tracks or wheels are damaged, dirty, misaligned, or obstructed.

Glass

We've discussed all of these issues with respect to windows. Glass in doors is most often non-operable.

Hardware

Doors should latch positively. Many rely on a tongue and strike plate system. Many doors operate but don't latch because of hardware problems. These can include broken springs, misalignment, missing pieces, etc. You don't need to troubleshoot the problem, but you do need to identify it. Exterior door latching problems are more serious than problems on interior doors.

Exterior doors should have hinges on the inside for security reasons. It's very easy to remove a door by popping hinges. Exterior hinges are an indication of low-quality workmanship and are a security issue. These may mean the door was installed backwards. A majority of hinges are not designed for exposure to the exterior. Look for deterioration.

Many storm doors have self-closers. Again it's common to find problems with these. Open the door and watch to see if it closes and latches properly.

Storms and Screens

Screen doors and storm doors can be torn, rusted, loose, or missing. They may have holes. We talked about these conditions in Section 6.6.4, with respect to windows. The same comments apply.

Inspector in the House: When Seeing Double Is a Good Thing

Most standards call for us to check the operation of all exterior doors. Sometimes that means climbing over sofas and battling with window treatments to check a sliding glass door. The more difficult it is to access, the more likely it is to have issues. This is perhaps because it is rarely used, or possibly because someone does not want you to look at it closely.

During one summer inspection we were almost fooled on this one—when we finally got to the sliding door and operated it, everything seemed fine. When we were re-locking the door, something felt wrong. We saw that one pane of the double glazing was missing! It had apparently broken, and someone had carefully removed all the broken glass. Our client would have been calling us on this one.

6.8   WET BASEMENTS AND CRAWLSPACES

Dampness or water in basements and crawlspaces is the source of more complaints about home inspectors' performance than any other issue. Water in basements or crawlspaces is typically from one of two sources:

- Surface water from rain or snow that lands on the ground around the house or on the roof. This accounts for more than ninety percent of wet basement and crawlspace problems.

- Groundwater—water in the earth below grade level.

Details of the many ways in which water from these two sources can infiltrate the basement is beyond the scope of this book. For a thorough discussion, see *Principles of Home Inspection: Interiors*, which also includes coverage of cures for wet basements. As an inspector, you'll need to know what to look for as evidence of past or current water infiltration, and that is what we'll focus on here.

The implications of wet basements or crawlspaces include—

IMPLICATIONS

- **Nuisance.** Wet basements can damage storage and lead to uncomfortably high interior humidity levels.

- **Damaged carpeting, wall coverings, and furnishings** in finished basement areas.

- **Odors and molds.** If basements are chronically wet, mold may generate unpleasant odors. Some molds are toxic, and there can be a health risk associated with damp, musty basements. Health issues are beyond the scope of an inspection, but you may be asked about the mold issue.

- **Structural deterioration.** Although not common, it is possible for foundation materials to deteriorate as a result of chronic moisture penetrations. We have seen concrete block foundations deteriorate as a result of chronic moisture. Cinder block foundations (made from rock slag rather than concrete) are not usually used below grade because they are susceptible to water damage. We have seen considerable damage to cinder blocks used below grade.

- **Electrical shock or fire hazard.** Wires behind finished walls may corrode or generate short circuits if they become wet. This creates the risk of electrical shock and fire.

- **Damaged insulation.** Where basement or crawlspace walls are insulated on the interior, chronic moisture problems can ruin the insulation.

STRATEGY

Almost all basements get wet at some point. Some new home warranty statistics suggest that 38 percent of homes have water problems in basements within the first five years of their life. The challenge for inspectors is that we are visiting the house at one point in time, and there is often no evidence of a problem. Decorating and finishes may cover the evidence. Concrete can dry up very nicely and not show any evidence of problems.

Can't Predict Frequency   While we know that virtually all basements get wet at some point, it's very difficult to know whether a basement is going to get wet:

- Every time it rains
- Every time it rains with the wind coming from a certain direction
- Every time there is more than one inch of rain in an hour, for example (rainfall intensity)
- Every time it rains more than two inches in total over a week (rainfall volume)
- When there is a 100-year flood (a rain volume that only occurs once every 100 years, according to weather office statistics)
- Only when the ground is frozen (frozen ground can't absorb moisture)
- Only when gutters or downspouts are clogged or leak
- Only when window wells are clogged with debris
- Only when the perimeter drainage tile system fails

Severity   It's difficult to know how often a basement will get wet and under what rainfall conditions. It's also impossible to know how wet it will get. Will the basement:

- Be damp?
- Be wet?
- Have water on the floor? Will it be a trickle, stream, or torrent?
- Flood? Is there likely to be $1/2$ inch or six inches of water in the basement floor?

Report Your Limitations   You get the idea. Predicting basement leakage is a tough game. On one hand, you don't want to be alarmist and point out problems that don't exist. This makes you very unpopular with sellers, for example. On the other hand, you often have suspicions but can't substantiate them. This makes for interesting reporting.

6.8.1   What To Watch for

Let's list some of the clues you can watch for.

- Water or dampness on the walls or floor
- Efflorescence on the walls or floor
- Rot, stains, or water marks on doors, walls, windows, and basement stair stringers
- Rust at baseboard nails, carpet tack strips, columns, or appliances
- Odors and mold
- Rot
- Loose floor tiles (tap on the tiles)
- Damaged basement storage (sagging, stained cardboard boxes, for example)
- Storage kept off floor on pallets or shelves
- Patches in walls
- Patches in floors, especially around the perimeter (possibly indicating perimeter drainage tile inside the foundation)

- A trough at the wall/floor intersection around the perimeter (peripheral drain)
- Sump pumps operating continuously
- A full sump
- One or more spare sump pumps on hand
- An auxiliary electrical supply (battery or generator) for sump pumps
- A high water level alarm on the sump
- Crumbling plaster, drywall, or masonry
- Peeling paint
- Wall cracks with stains
- Recent exterior excavation on the outside
- Evidence of new damp-proofing material on the exterior
- Evidence of a drainage layer or membrane
- A dehumidifier in the basement running constantly

6.8.2   Things That Can Fool You

Should Be Easy

With all these possible indicators, calling out wet basements should be easy. It isn't. Let's look at some of the common situations that can fool you. There are lots of sources of water in basements that may have nothing to do with leakage from the exterior. These include—

- Sweating pipes. Cold water pipes can cool the warm, moist air around them and develop condensation that drips constantly. Over time, this can look like a leak.
- Leaking appliances such as dishwashers and water heaters.
- Leaking plumbing fixtures including toilets, bathtubs, shower stalls, sinks, and basins.
- Leaks from hot water heating systems.
- Leaks from central air conditioning or heat recovery ventilator condensate lines.
- Leaks from above-grade walls, windows, and doors. Water often collects on the tops of foundation walls and runs down the inside, looking like a leak from the exterior. The problems are typically flaws in siding, doors, windows, or flashings. (The clue here is that the foundation wall is stained **above** grade level as well as below.)
- Sewer backup. Basements can flood as a result of water coming back up through floor drains. Backwater valves are used to prevent sewer backup where problems are chronic.
- Condensation and mold in cold rooms—common around the top part of the rooms. Doors to cold rooms should be well weather-stripped. Cold rooms should be vented to the outdoors.

Look at History

There are lots of things that can look like wet basements but are not. In many houses, you will see the history of a number of events. Some of them may include exterior leakage, and others will be caused by the things we've just listed. You're

F I G U R E 6.19   Why Is There a Sump Pump in the Basement?

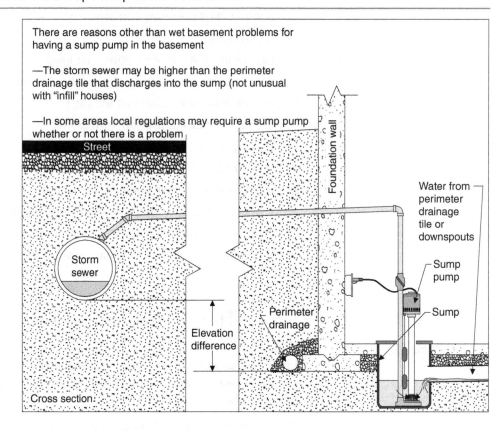

There are reasons other than wet basement problems for having a sump pump in the basement

—The storm sewer may be higher than the perimeter drainage tile that discharges into the sump (not unusual with "infill" houses)

—In some areas local regulations may require a sump pump whether or not there is a problem

going to need some experience to differentiate among the many things that may be going on. The more you see and the more you think while you look, the better you'll get at it.

Analyzing the Sump and Pumps

Many homes have sumps and pumps in the basement. Not all of these are designed to correct or prevent wet basement problems (see Figure 6.19).

6.8.3 Summary

Client Sensitivity

Adjusting client expectations is part of any home inspection. It is as important with respect to wet basements and crawlspaces as with any component of the inspection. Your clients have to understand that almost all basements leak at some point. If we control surface water, we improve matters dramatically. Where ground water is an issue, there are strategies that can be used, but the risks are higher. There are no long-term guarantees, and if nature unleashes a hurricane or torrential rains, there may be no way to keep basements dry.

Determine Client Expectations

Many clients have lived in houses with basements and are aware of the realities. To other clients, the possibility that there may be water in the house comes as a shock and is very unsettling. You are wise to discuss this issue with your client for a minute or so to get a sense of their expectations. If they are unrealistic, you may want to adjust them.

Chapter 6   Interiors   **371**

Inspector in the House: The Longest Crawlspace Inspection

I was alone in the home. The agent, whom I knew well, had let me into the house and then left, with instructions to lock up when I was finished. The crawlspace was accessed through a hatch in the floor of a bedroom closet. I lifted the hatch and got into the crawlspace. I had to hold the hatch open, and once inside the crawlspace, I dropped the hatch back into place.

I made my way through the crawlspace, documented my notes and went back to the access hatch. When I pushed on the hatch, it would not open, although I could wiggle it a little. No matter how hard I tried, the hatch would not open. After a frustrating hour and a half in the crawlspace, I finally heard someone come into the house. I yelled and banged on the hatch with my flashlight until I got their attention. The seller was startled at first and then amused after realizing what had happened. When I dropped the hatch closed, the open closet door had swung over the hatch, effectively locking it down. Since that day, whenever I go into a crawlspace, I find a way to prop the hatch open!

REVIEW QUESTIONS

1. List five common flooring materials.
2. List five general problems with floor systems and their implications.
3. List five concrete flooring problems.
4. List six wood flooring problems and their implications.
5. List four carpet problems and their implications.
6. List three resilient flooring problems and their implications.
7. List five ceramic floor problems and their implications.
8. Where is rot most likely to occur on a wood frame flooring system?
9. List four common wall finish materials.
10. List four general wall problems.
11. List five plaster and drywall problems on walls.
12. List four problems with wood wall and ceiling finishes.
13. List as many of the implications of as many of the problems in Questions 10 to 12 as you can.
14. Name two special inspection strategies you can use on ceilings.
15. List four common ceiling finish materials.
16. List three general ceiling problems.
17. List six plaster and drywall ceiling problems.
18. List one metal ceiling problem.
19. List as many of the implications of the problems in Questions 15 to 18 as you can.
20. List two functions of trim on the interior of homes.
21. List seven trim components commonly found in homes.
22. List seven countertop materials you may find in kitchens or bathrooms.
23. List five common problems with interior trim and their implications.
24. List nine common countertop problems.
25. List twelve common cabinet problems.
26. List as many stair problems as you can.
27. List four window functions.
28. List three common materials used in window frames and sashes.
29. List eight common window types.
30. List two general window problems.
31. List six frame problems.
32. List two exterior drip cap problems and their implications.
33. List ten exterior trim problems.
34. List eight sash problems.
35. List six interior trim problems.
36. List six glass problems.
37. List five window hardware problems.
38. List at least four common problems with storms and screens.

39. Under what circumstances might a window be considered too small?

40. List five functions of exterior doors.

41. List four common door materials.

42. Most wet basement problems come from what two sources?

43. List six implications of wet basements.

44. There are at least 20 common signs that basements have been wet or are vulnerable to wetness problems. See how many you can list.

CHAPTER

7

ELECTRICAL SYSTEMS

LEARNING OBJECTIVES

By the end of this chapter you should be able to:

- recognize the electrical service drop and service entrance and how they should be arranged

- determine the size of the service and how to advise your client about it

- recognize the problems commonly found on the service drop and their implications

- identify common problems found on service entrance conductors and their implications

- understand the function of the service box or service panel

- be familiar with the arrangement and location of the service box

- recognize the common conditions found in service boxes and their implications

- know the functions of grounding and bonding

- understand the common problems found in system grounds and their implications

- identify 15 common problems with branch circuit wiring, and their implications

- recognize conditions found in all panels, as well as those unique to subpanels, fuses, breakers, and panel wires

- understand how wires should be connected and supported

- understand how to identify knob-and-tube wire and the issues associated with it

- know how to identify aluminum wiring and the issues associated with it

- be familiar with common problems at lights and receptacles and their implications

- be familiar with the strategies for inspecting the various components of household electrical systems

INTRODUCTION

The goal of this chapter is to ensure an understanding of the basics of residential electrical systems. You should be able to identify and describe common electrical components, understand the function and importance of each, and recognize adverse conditions that may occur. We will examine the causes and implications of these conditions and appropriate courses of action to be recommended to clients. The systems addressed include—

1. service drop and entrance
2. the grounding system
3. the electrical service box, including the main disconnect and fuses or breakers
4. distribution panels
5. branch circuit wiring
6. lights, outlets, switches, and junction boxes

Electricity has a language all its own. You should know the technical terms but also be able to communicate with clients clearly. For example, clients will understand "wires coming from the street to the house" better than "service drop," and "breakers or fuses" better than "over current protection devices." By the way, most people use the words wire and cable interchangeably, although wire is a single conductor and cable is a group of conductors.

Safety is such a critical issue with respect to inspecting electrical systems that we will mention up front several precautions you should follow:

1. Wear rubber-soled shoes.
2. Do not stand in water or wet areas when touching electrical equipment (sometimes this can't be avoided on the outside of houses).
3. Use insulated tools to remove covers.
4. Do not let your clients stand beside a panel you are working on. They may do something dangerous before you can stop them.
5. Use a voltage detector to ensure that any electrical equipment you are about to touch is not live. Some advocate using lineman's gloves when working on electrical systems.

7.1   SERVICE DROP

Function

The purpose of the service drop and the service entrance is to get electricity safely from the utility into your house.

Overhead Wires to House

The **service drop** is the collection of overhead wires coming from the utility pole (often at the street) to the point of connection to the house (Figure 7.1). People call these the overhead wires or overhead service. Electricians and utilities use the words **service drop.**

Underground Wires

Some utilities use the word **service laterals** to refer to underground services. Here the wires come from the street underground to the house. They may come up out of the ground outside the house to go to an outside meter, or they may go straight into the house.

Drip Loop

Where the service drop or service lateral ends, there is a **splice,** sometimes called the **service point.** This means two wires are joined together. In a service drop this will be at the **drip loop.** The drip loop is a U-shaped bend in the wires that allows water to drip off, so it won't go into the **service entrance.** The drip loop is typically

F I G U R E   7.1   Service Drop

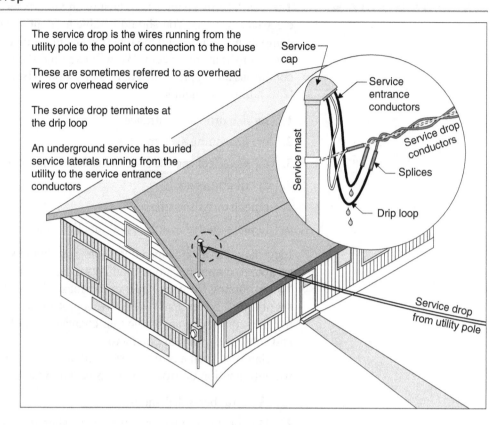

The service drop is the wires running from the utility pole to the point of connection to the house

These are sometimes referred to as overhead wires or overhead service

The service drop terminates at the drip loop

An underground service has buried service laterals running from the utility to the service entrance conductors

Service cap

Service mast

Service entrance conductors

Service drop conductors

Splices

Drip loop

Service drop from utility pole

part of the service entrance. The drip loop also shows that the wires are properly secured to the building and are relaxed.

The drip loop is at the top of the **masthead** (also called **service cap, entrance cap, pothead, weatherhead** or **servicehead**). The wires running from this connection down into the service box are called the **service entrance.** The wires may be in a conduit or may just be a cable. They may be above the roof or below it, attached to the house wall.

Responsibilities

The utility usually provides the service drop and the homeowner is responsible for the service entrance, including the drip loop.

Inspect from Roof? Careful

You have to decide whether you are going to get on the roof. This gives you a better look, although please resist the temptation to touch these wires. Electrical systems can look perfectly safe but be very dangerous.

7.1.1   Service Drop Description

Often Smaller Wires Than Service Entrance Wires

Some home inspectors use the service drop wires to gauge the size of the electrical service. This may be a mistake. These wires are very often smaller than the service entrance wires and in-house wires and may mislead you. These wires are in open air and can carry more electricity than in-house wires because it's so easy for them to dissipate their heat. The wire sizes and ampacities that we normally use are for wires in conduit or cable, not for service drop wires.

Usually Three Wires in Service Drop

The number of wires coming in through the service drop will tell you some things about the house service. There will usually be three wires coming in through the service drop: a black, a red and a white (neutral). Sometimes the neutral is also

F I G U R E 7.2   120/140 Volts

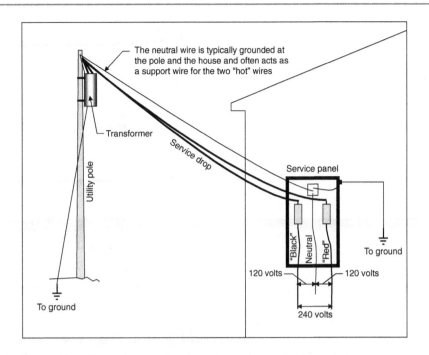

The neutral wire is typically grounded at the pole and the house and often acts as a support wire for the two "hot" wires

Transformer

Service drop

Service panel

Utility pole

"Black"   Neutral   "Red"

To ground

120 volts — 120 volts

To ground

240 volts

the support cable for the red and black. Sometimes there is a separate cable supporting the three conductors. The neutral wire may be bare (no insulation), and in some cases is smaller than the hot wires.

Are there three wires spliced into the service entrance? If so, this will be a typical 240-volt, single-phase residential service (Figure 7.2).

Two wires spliced into the service entrance cable indicate a 120-volt service. This is rare and not adequate for most modern lifestyles.

Four wires coming into the house indicate a three-phase system. This is a commercial electrical system and beyond the scope of a standard home inspection.

Underground service laterals may head straight into the house to the main disconnect. In this case, there are no service entrance conductors as such.

240 Volts

Two Wires for 120-Volt Services

Four Wires Mean 3-Phase Service (Commercial)

No Service Entrance Wires

7.1.2   Conditions

Let's look at some of the service drop problems you'll find:

1. Overhead wires too low
2. Damaged or frayed wires
3. Trees or vines interfering with wires
4. Wires too close to doors or windows
5. Wires not well secured to the house
6. Poor connection between the service drop and service entrance
7. Inadequate clearance from roofs

F I G U R E 7.3   Service Drop Clearances

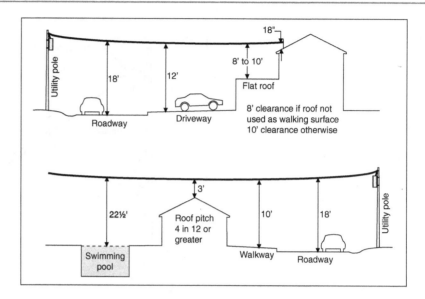

Overhead Wires Too Low

Wires Should Be out of Reach

The wires should be out of reach of people, and safely above places where they may be hit by vehicles, ladders and other equipment (Figure 7.3). The wires need only be 10 feet above a walking surface, 12 feet above a driveway and 18 feet above a roadway. Wires near swimming pools must be 22½ feet away in any direction from the water.

Wires over Roofs

Wires running over a flat roof that is used as a walking surface should be 10 feet above the roof. Otherwise, wires should be 8 feet above the roof. If the roof has a slope greater than 4 in 12, the wires have to be only 3 feet above the roof.

Decks and Balconies

Wires should be out of reach of people on decks, porches and balconies. The wires should be 8 to 10 feet above the floors of these structures.

IMPLICATION

There's an electrical safety issue for people. You don't want to touch service drop wires because of the danger of electrical shock. Wires running just above roofs are dangerous for roofers, and may be damaged by snow or ice in cold climates.

STRATEGY

Check the height of overhead wires coming in, and use common sense as to whether they could be touched by people or vehicles.

Damaged or Frayed Wires

These are usually (but not always) the responsibility of the utility.

IMPLICATIONS

There is the possibility of a short circuit and loss of electrical service to the house. There is also a risk of electrical shock, especially if the wires fall.

STRATEGY

Visually examine these wires from the ground (ideally with binoculars) and look for evidence of mechanical damage or loose insulation. Pieces of insulation hanging off the wires are the most common visible defect.

Trees or Vines Interfering with Wires

Service drop wires should be clear of anything that will cause abrasion.

IMPLICATIONS

The implications are mechanical damage to the wires and reduced ability to dissipate heat.

Check that the wires are clear of any obstructions. Where tree branches or vines interfere with the wires, inform your client. It is possible that the utility will correct this problem.

Wires Too Close to Doors or Windows

Modern electrical codes require that wires be 3 feet away from the sides or bottoms of windows, doors or fire escapes. This is true in some jurisdictions whether the windows open or not, as fixed windows may be replaced with operable windows in the future.

IMPLICATIONS

Again, there is a hazard wherever anyone may be able to touch wires.

STRATEGY

Make a note of situations where wires are too close to windows, doors, or fire escapes. Be careful, since utilities may have accepted this installation. Simply point out the common sense issues and advise your client that the utility is the authority.

Wires Not Well Secured to the House

In most modern installations, the neutral wire supports the red and the black wires. The neutral wire should be attached to the house or to an electrical mast. Rather than looking at all the ways this may be done, you should simply look for a successful connection.

IMPLICATIONS

If the wires come loose, they may fall. This will cut off power to the house, and may result in live electrical wires lying on the ground.

STRATEGY

Look for evidence of movement at the point of connection to the house or mast. Connectors that are starting to pull away, or service drop wires with more sag than is typical, should be noted for further investigation. Watch for the absence of a drip loop (Figure 7.4). This suggests wires under tension.

FIGURE 7.4   Wires Not Well Secured to the House

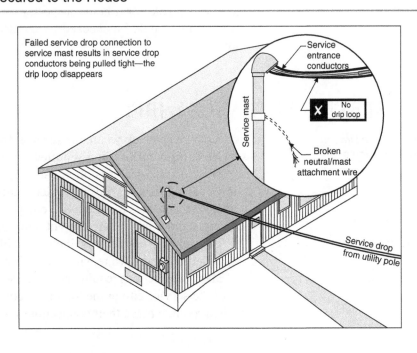

Poor Connection Between the Service Drop and Service Entrance

At the end of the service drop, the wires are joined to the **service entrance wires**. These splices are most often made by the utility, but they can come loose. Connections should be made at a drip loop, which is a relaxed, sagging part of the service entrance cables. The connection should not be at the low point of the loop, since this is where water may collect.

IMPLICATIONS

A poor connection may result in a loss of electrical power to the house and, if the wires fall, there is an electrical hazard.

STRATEGY

Look for evidence of the connection pulling apart. Electrical tape on connections may indicate amateurish work. Many utilities use a heat-shrink seal on this splice.

Inadequate Clearance from Roof

As we discussed earlier, wires can be run over house roofs if they are at least 8 feet above the roof or 10 feet above a walk-out deck. Wires over a roof with a slope of more than 4 in 12 only have to be 3 feet above the roof. If the wires only project 4 feet onto the roof, they only have to be 18 inches above the roof.

IMPLICATIONS

Implications include mechanical damage and possible electrical shock during normal repair and maintenance activities.

STRATEGY

Know what is accepted in your area, and advise your clients of the risks of wires that are too close to the roof.

In some jurisdictions, it was permitted to attach wires virtually to the roof surface. While this is not a desirable situation, the utility may tell your client that this is accepted. The utility is the authority, and you will lose any argument with them.

7.1.3   General Strategy

Use Common Sense

With electrical systems, there are many numbers you can memorize. It's more important to understand the rationale behind things and to use common sense. Overhead service wires should be intact and out of the way. They should be well-supported and the connections should be secure. Rather than citing code, it's perfectly acceptable for a home inspector to say, "These wires are within reach of people. This should be checked by an electrician and the wires may need to be moved."

7.2   SERVICE ENTRANCE WIRES

From Service Drop to Service Equipment

Service wires pick up where the **service drop** wires end. They extend down to the **service equipment (main disconnect, service panel, service box).**

The electrical meter is often part way along the **service entrance wires.** The correct name for these wires is **service conductors.** Where these wires pass through a wall from outdoors to the service equipment, they are properly called (according to some authorities) the **service entrance conductors.**

Three Wires

The service conductors include a black and a red wire, which are hot (ungrounded), and a white wire, which is neutral (grounded).

30 Inches at Top

Many jurisdictions require the service entrance wires to extend at least 30 inches out of the **service cap** at the top of the conduit or masthead. This gives the utility enough room to make their connections and leave a drip loop.

FIGURE 7.5   Using Service Entrance Cable

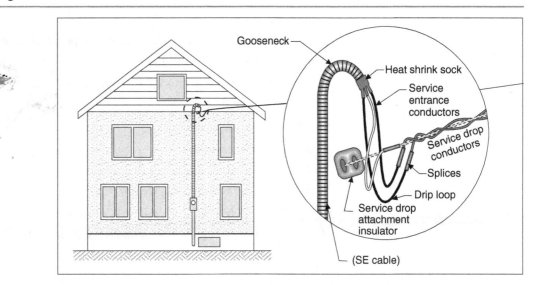

Drip Loop

> A drip loop should be provided whether there is a mast above the roofline or a conduit or cable below the roofline.

Gooseneck on SE Cable

> Where service entrance (SE) cable is used without conduit or masthead, the cable itself is bent downward (like a candy cane or **gooseneck**) before connecting to the service drop wires (Figure 7.5). This discourages water entry into the cable between the wires and the exterior sheathing.

Conduit or Service Entrance Cable

> The service entrance wires may be in a conduit on the outside of the building, or there may be a special **Service Entrance (SE) cable** that does not require a conduit. Either situation is permitted.
>
> Some service drops are attached to the side of a building. Here the conduit will extend up the building and terminate in a service cap.

Mast

> Where the service drop wires are above the roofline, a **service mast** is required. This mast extends up through the roof and terminates in a **service cap.** This mast often forms a conduit that contains the service entrance wires. It is also the mechanical support for the service drop wires. Depending on the height of the mast, guy wires may be necessary to hold the mast straight. The weight of the service drop wires is significant, and poorly supported masts can be bent or even broken.

Flashing

Wires Well above Roof

> Where the mast comes up through the roof, the hole must be properly flashed. Good practice dictates that the service drop wires are attached to the mast within about 12 inches of the top. We don't want the service wires too close to the roof. Many jurisdictions call for them to be 2 feet above the roof surface. This means that the mast usually extends at least 3 feet above the roof.

Service Entrance Wire Type

> If you can see the service conductors at the service cap, you can sometimes check the gauge and find out whether they are copper or aluminum.

Service Size

> The Standards ask you to report the service size (amperage and voltage rating). Based on the gauge of the wire, you can determine whether you have wires suitable for a 60-amp, 100-amp or 200-amp service. The number of service drop wires told you already whether it's a 120 volt or 240 volt service.

Meter Weather-Tight

> You can look to see whether the connections at the meter base are secure and weather-tight.

Let's look at some of the problems that you'll find with service entrance wires:

1. No drip loop
2. No masthead (entrance cap, service cap, pothead, weatherhead)
3. Masthead not weather-tight
4. Service entrance wires too close to the roof
5. Mast or conduit bent
6. Mast or conduit rusted
7. Mast rotted (if wood)
8. Mast, conduit or cable not well secured
9. Mast, conduit or cable not weather-tight
10. Conduit or cable not well sealed at house wall penetration
11. Cable frayed, mechanically damaged or covered by siding

7.2.1 No Drip Loop

We've talked about how the drip loop is designed to prevent water getting into the conduit and to show that the service drop wires are not straining the splices.

IMPLICATIONS

The implications are water entry into the electrical system and possible mechanical stresses on the wires and splices.

STRATEGY

Look for the service entrance wires to have a low spot where they connect to the service drop wires. The wires should be visibly slack.

7.2.2 No Masthead or Service Cap

The implication is water getting into the electrical system.

IMPLICATION

Make sure there is a weather-tight cap on the conduit or mast. This should be arranged so that wires enter the underside of the cap.

STRATEGY

Common sense should tell you whether the connection to the service drop is likely to allow water in.

7.2.3 Masthead Not Weather-Tight

Sometimes there is a service cap (masthead), but it is not tightly installed or not installed at the right angle. It should be weather-tight.

IMPLICATION

The implication is water entering the electrical system.

STRATEGY

Using common sense, make sure the top of the mast, conduit or cable is weather-tight.

7.2.4 Mast or Conduit Bent

The masts or conduits should be straight and, in most cases, vertical.

IMPLICATIONS

The wires may sag reducing overhead clearance or fall, creating a dangerous situation. Weather-tightness may also be lost.

STRATEGY

Make sure the masts and conduits are not bent or pulled out of position. Look at clamps for evidence of movement. Masts taller than 5 feet should have guy wires.

Where there is a mast, look at the roof flashing connection to see if it has been displaced. The drip loop may or may not be intact, depending on how it fails.

7.2.5   Mast or Conduit Rusted

The implications of rusted mast or conduit are—

IMPLICATIONS

1. mechanical failure, allowing wires to fall
2. water entry into the electrical system

STRATEGY

Look for rust at electrical connections. Rust is most likely to occur at horizontal surfaces where water may collect. Pay particular attention to threaded connections where the pipe walls have been made thinner by cutting threads into them.

7.2.6   Mast Rotted

Rot is common on wooden masts, particularly near horizontal surfaces where water may accumulate, and near roof flashings. Wood masts are not allowed on new work in many areas.

IMPLICATIONS

The implications are a loss of strength of the mast and collapse of the wires.

STRATEGY

Look carefully at wooden masts for rot or insect damage. Suggest painting the wood if necessary.

7.2.7   Mast, Conduit, or Cable not Well Secured to the Building

Figure 7.6 summarizes the support requirements for cable, conduit and mast implementations.

IMPLICATIONS

The mast, conduit or cable may pull away from the building, resulting in fallen wires and a dangerous situation. Open joints will allow moisture into the electrical system.

STRATEGY

Rather than memorizing numbers for cable and conduit supports, look for evidence of movement or failure of connectors.

7.2.8   Mast, Conduit, or Cable not Weather-Tight

We've talked about some of the conditions that may cause this already. Common spots where weather-tightness may be compromised include (Figure 7.7)—

1. joints in conduits
2. the service cap (masthead)
3. the flashing at the roof level
4. the meter base

IMPLICATIONS

Water in the electrical system is hazardous. In a best case scenario, the electrical system may shut down. In the worst case, the system may cause an electric shock or start a fire.

FIGURE 7.6   Support Requirements for Service Entrances

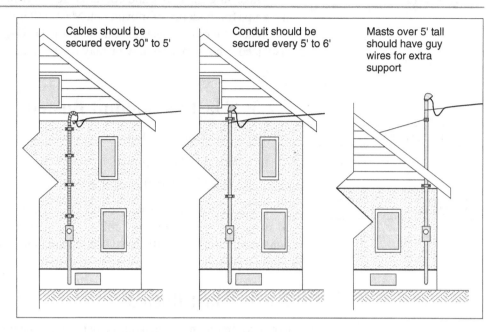

Cables should be secured every 30" to 5'

Conduit should be secured every 5' to 6'

Masts over 5' tall should have guy wires for extra support

STRATEGY

Follow the mast, conduit or cable from top to bottom looking for places where water may enter.

7.2.9   Conduit or Cable Not Well Sealed at House Wall Penetration

IMPLICATIONS

The implications are—

1. water getting into the electrical system causing a shock hazard
2. water getting into the basement causing a nuisance
3. rusting of the service equipment

STRATEGY

Check Inside

Make sure the wall/conduit junction is well sealed, if it's visible.

The conduit or cable may enter the house below grade. In this case, you won't be able to see whether the cable is well sealed where it goes through the wall. You'll have to check this inside when looking at the service equipment.

7.2.10   Service Entrance Cable Frayed, Damaged, or Covered by Siding

IMPLICATIONS

This can create a dangerous electrical condition. Anyone touching the cable could get a shock. If live portions of the cable touch metal siding, the entire skin of the building could become electrically charged. If the cable is covered by wood siding, for example, driving nails through the siding creates a shock hazard.

FIGURE 7.7   Service Entrance—Areas of Potential Water Entry

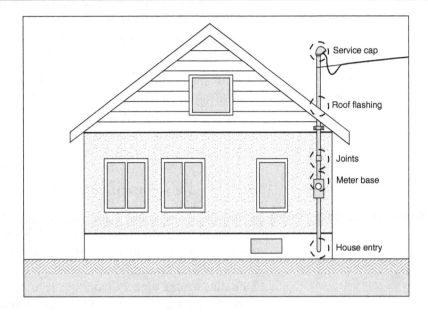

Where cable is used, carefully check its condition. Make sure it is accessible and visible over its entire length. Some authorities allow conduit to be run behind brick siding, for example, since the wires are protected from damage. Cable, however, should never be buried.

7.3   SERVICE SIZE

Anyone buying a house will want to know the service size.

Voltage Is Always 240

The size of the electrical service is a function of both the voltage and amperage. For 999 out of 1,000 houses, the voltage is 240 volts. 120-volt service is becoming very rare.

Ampacity Is the Key

The challenge is to know how much current the system is capable of carrying. People talk about this as the **ampacity** of the service or the **service size.** The common service sizes are 60-amps, 100-amps, and 200-amps, with some others thrown in between. While it's a little too simple to say that small houses are okay with 60-amp services, average houses are okay with 100-amps and big houses need 200-amps, it's not a bad yardstick.

We Don't Do Load Calculations

At the other end of the scale are load calculations, performed to determine exactly what a house needs. Home inspectors don't do these detailed calculations. They use general rules, and good inspectors explain to their clients how lifestyle is a big factor in determining whether the electrical service is adequately sized.

Let's clarify a couple of things:

Not a Safety Hazard

1. An undersized service is not a safety hazard. If you have a 60-amp service in a huge house with many electrical demands, what is likely to happen? If you use enough appliances at the same time, the total current draw through the red and/or black wires will exceed 60 amps and the main fuses or breakers will shut off the power. This is an inconvenience, but it isn't a safety hazard.

Simultaneous Use Is the Problem

2. Undersized services are only a problem when many appliances are used simultaneously. Having an electric stove, an electric water heater, an electric clothes dryer and an electric central air conditioner doesn't mean much, unless you're trying to use them at the same time. Of course, the more large appliances there are, the more likely it is several will be used at one time.

New Construction

60-amp services are considered obsolete and not allowed in new construction.

Adequate electrical capacity is tough to pin down, no matter how much calculation you do, because it's determined by how people use the electricity in the house. Let's look at some general rules.

7.3.1   100-Amp Service

Common

In most modern average-sized houses, 100-amp service is common. It works for most modern lifestyles in a typical three-bedroom, two-story house. It probably won't be enough in a big house. It probably won't be enough if you have electric heat, and it may not be enough if you have a big family and many electrical appliances, including central air conditioning, electric stove, electric clothes dryer, and electric water heater. Large saunas and electric swimming pool heaters may also result in a need for a larger service than 100 amps.

If there is a large workshop, pottery kilns, or some other craft that requires considerable electricity, 100 amps may also be insufficient.

7.3.2   125-Amp and Larger Services

Small Homes with Electric Heat or Bigger Homes

125- and 150-amp services are common in some areas on small houses with electric heat or larger houses without electric heat. They are also found on average-sized houses with more than a typical number of appliances. A 200-amp service would be found on an electrically heated home or a large house.

Very Large Home

In rare cases, you may find a 400-amp electrical service. This is the largest single-phase service available. It's the largest service most utilities will put into a residence. The residence is probably more than 6,000 square feet, or quite large and electrically heated.

7.3.3   Wire Sizes

Wire Gauge—Bigger Is Smaller (AWG)

Logic would suggest that small wires have small numbers and as wires get bigger, the numbers get bigger. Actually, the American Wire Gauge (AWG) system works backwards. A **14-gauge** wire is smaller than a **12-gauge** wire and a **12-gauge** wire is smaller than a **10-gauge** wire.

Don't Use All Numbers

But it's more confusing than that. They don't use every number. For example, they only use 14, 12, 10, 8, 6, 4, 3, 2, 1, and 0.

One of the problems with numbering backwards is once you get down to **0** you don't have any numbers left for bigger wires. So, there is a wire size called **0** and the next bigger wire size is **00**, sometimes shown as **2/0**. The next size after that is **3/0** or **000**. The largest size you'll see in most houses is 4/0 (used in some areas for 200-amp services where the service entrance conductors are aluminum). Figure 7.8 summarizes the wire sizes you'll see most commonly.

Table 7.1 summarizes typical wire sizes for residential wiring in the United States and the amount of current (in amps) that can safely travel through each size. These

FIGURE 7.8   Common Wire Sizes

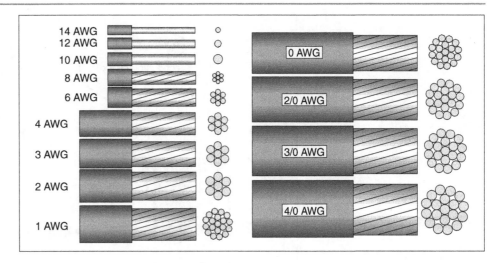

are general rules, and certain variables—such as the temperature rating of the wire and whether it is in free air or enclosed in a raceway or cable—can affect the wire's capacity. Where something doesn't fall into the general rules listed in Table 7.1, there may be a circumstance that makes it okay. Be careful with your criticism.

7.3.4   Determining Service Size

Now that we know how much current each wire can carry, let's see how we identify it in the field.

Check Service Entrance Wires

The best indication of service size is the service entrance wires themselves. Sometimes you can see enough of this wire to read the size on the sheathing at the top of the service entrance conduit. Where the service entrance wires are spliced to the service drop, there should be a drip loop. Not all wire has the size stamped on the outside of it, but if it does, you'll be able to see it here, if you can safely get close enough to look.

TABLE 7.1   Typical U.S. Service Sizes

Minimum Wire Size		Service Size
Copper	Aluminum	(amps)
10*	8*	30
6*	6*	60
6*	4*	70
4	2	100
2	1/0	125
1	2/0	150
2/0	4/0	200

Note: 1. *–not found on new work.
2. All wire gauges are AWG.
3. Several variations are possible depending on the type of wire, the temperature rating, etc.

FIGURE 7.9   Determining Service Size by the Service Entrance Wires

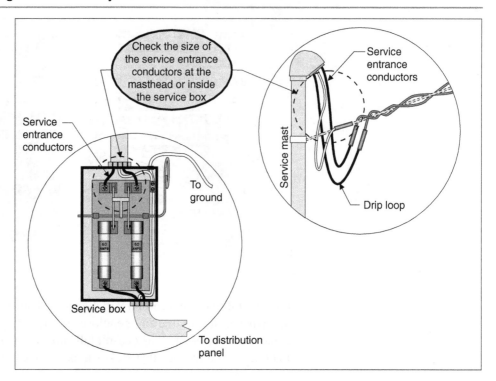

You may also be able to read the wire size at the other end of the service entrance conductors, where they come into the service box or panel (Figure 7.9).

Service Entrance Cable   It may be possible to read the size directly off the sheathing on a service entrance (SE) cable, since there is no conduit.

Copper or Aluminum   You may also be able to tell whether the wire is copper or aluminum. Aluminum wire always has the word ALUMINUM, the letters ALUM, or the letters AL written on the sheathing.

Not Reliable to Measure Bare Wire   It's difficult to identify the wire gauge by looking at the diameter of the bare wire, although some inspectors carry samples of the common wires and compare their samples to what they see in the field. Be careful not to touch any live electrical components.

Don't Measure Cable   Measuring the outside diameter of the cable is risky, since different cable types have different sheathing thicknesses. Measuring the actual conductor size is usually not practical for the home inspector, although there are plastic wire gauges made for this.

Don't Measure Neutral   Sometimes the neutral wire is smaller than the red and the black wires. This is permitted, but can cause you to mistake the service size. You should be sizing the red and the black wires.

Check Main Fuses or Breakers   If you can't size the service entrance conductors, the next best indicator is the size of the main disconnect (assuming there is a single disconnect for the entire home) (Figure 7.10). If the main disconnect is fused, there will be two fuses in the service box. One fuse is for the red service-entrance conductor and the other is for the black. If each of these fuses is rated at 100-amps, you have a 100-amp service. **Be careful: you cannot add the two fuses together.** A 200-amp service would have two fuses, each sized at 200-amps. Where breakers are used, you should see a double-pole 200-amp breaker.

F I G U R E 7.10   Determining Service Size by the Main Disconnect

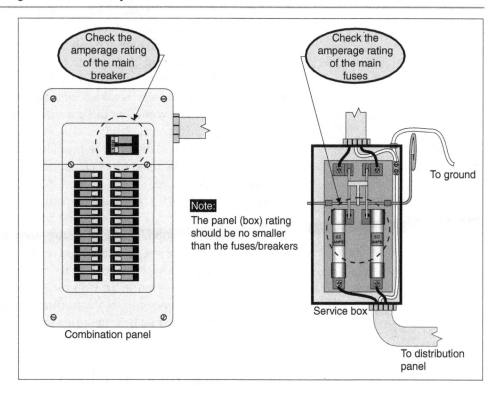

The fuse size may be written on the fuse label, stamped into the body of the fuse, or stamped into one of the metal ferrules at either end of the fuse.

Don't Touch!

In some cases, the fuses will be mounted in the service box with the labels facing the back of the box. You may not be able to read them. Again, do not touch anything in the service box. **This can kill you.** Even if the power to the house is turned off, the service entrance wires coming into the service box will be live, and if any mistake was made hooking it up, the fuses can be live, too.

The fuse or breaker size **usually** indicates the service size, but not always. Some inspectors say, "Apparent 100-amp service," when all they can read is the fuse or breaker size. Some call for an electrician to verify the fuse size.

Limitations

If you can't size the service entrance wires and you can't see the fuse or breaker ratings, report that you could not identify the service size. Home service boxes have a cover that cannot be opened without shutting off the house power. **Do not shut off the house power.** Simply describe the limitation to your client.

Breaker Size Easy to Read

If the main disconnect is a circuit breaker, the breaker size is usually stamped or printed on the handles. You don't have to remove the service box cover to see this.

Sealed Service Box

Some boxes are sealed by the utility for the homeowner's safety and to prevent bypassing the meter or tapping off electricity upstream of the meter, in cases where the meter comes after the service box.

What If Wire Size Doesn't Match Fuse Size?

Determining the size of the breakers or fuses is not as reliable as sizing the service entrance conductors. The fuses or breakers and service entrance conductors **should** be a match in terms of their current rating, but they aren't always. Undersized fuses will cause you to report the service as smaller than it actually is, if you rely solely on the fuse size. This is not a safety concern, since the fuses will cut off the electricity long before the wire overheats.

Overfusing Unsafe

The fuses may be too large for the service entrance conductors. This would lead you to describe the service size as larger than it actually is, if you just read the fuses. This may be an unsafe situation because the fuses may not shut off the electricity quickly enough to keep the service entrance conductors from overheating.

The goal is to identify the service entrance conductor size and make sure it matches the fuses or breakers. We often have to base our determination on the rating of the main fuses or breakers because we can't size the service entrance wires. They are rarely wrong, but there is a slight risk in describing the service based only on fuse or breaker size.

Service Box and Distribution Panel Ratings

The service box and distribution panel have to be big enough to accommodate the service size. The box and panel can be rated for the same or more amps, but not less than the service size.

No Main Fuses or Breakers? Use Wire Size

In some houses, there is no single main disconnect and no service box. There are multiple disconnects to shut off all the house power. Up to six throws (switches or breakers) are permitted to shut off all the electricity in some houses. Your determination of the service size must be based on the service entrance wire size. Adding all of the disconnect ratings will not usually give you an accurate reading of the service size. This total is often more than the service size. It's allowed because not every circuit will be operating at its maximum rating at the same time. In reality, most circuits never operate near their maximum rating.

7.3.5   Advising Your Client

Service Is Adequate

If the service is adequately sized, using normal guidelines, you'll simply report the service size to your client and say that it is adequate for a typical home of this size. You're taking a small risk if you promise that it will be adequate for your client's needs, since you don't know their lifestyle.

Service Too Small

Where the service is undersized you'll report the service size and recommend increasing it. This includes replacing the service drop (or laterals if it's underground), the service entrance conductors, the service box, and usually, the grounding conductor and distribution panel.

Service Marginal

Where the service size is marginal, you'll report the service size and advise your client to live with the electrical service on a trial basis. Since you can't know their lifestyle, you won't be sure.

Tripping Main Breakers

Explain to the client that a marginally-sized service is not a safety issue. If the service box has circuit breakers, the breakers will trip when too much electricity flows. They'll have to turn off some of the electrical appliances and turn the main breakers back on.

Blowing Main Fuses

If the service box has fuses, they may blow. Very few people can change their own main fuses (be careful, because there is still live electricity in the service box even when the house power is shut off). Never recommend that your clients do this. Utilities will come out to replace main fuses in many areas. If the utility won't change the main fuses, ask an electrician.

One Main Fuse Blows

With breakers in the service box, both will always trip. With fuses, one or both may blow. If one blows, roughly half the house will be without power, and none of the 240-volt appliances will work properly.

In the marginal situations, discuss the possibility of having to increase the service size, but explain that this is a convenience improvement rather than a necessity.

FIGURE 7.11 Breaker and Fuse Type Service Boxes

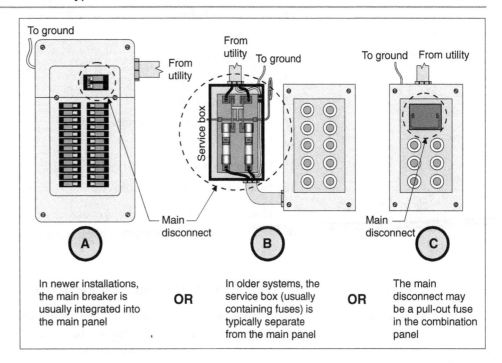

A In newer installations, the main breaker is usually integrated into the main panel

OR

B In older systems, the service box (usually containing fuses) is typically separate from the main panel

OR

C The main disconnect may be a pull-out fuse in the combination panel

7.4 SERVICE BOX

Control Center

The service box (also referred to as the **service equipment** or **service panel**) is the main control center of the house electrical system. It's where all electricity can be shut off with a single switch. It's also where all the electricity can be shut off by the main fuses or breakers if the service is overloaded, or if there is a short circuit or ground fault.

Switch on Outside of Metal Box

Most houses will have a metal service box with a main disconnect switch and main fuses or breakers (Figure 7.11). On breaker systems, the main breakers are also the disconnect switch.

No Single Switch

We've mentioned situations where there may be no service box and there may be up to six throws to disconnect all the electricity in the house. Some inspectors recommend adding a service box with one main disconnect for the whole house. This is a safety improvement. It's easier to throw one switch in an emergency. A single disconnect is currently required for new work in many areas.

Combination Panel

Where there is a service box, it may be a stand-alone box or it may be a combination panel (also called service panel) that incorporates the main disconnect with the distribution panel and all its branch circuit fuses or circuit breakers.

Let's look at some of the problems we'll be watching for on service boxes:

1. Poor access or location
2. Loose
3. Rust or water in box
4. Unprotected openings (cover loose or missing, knockouts missing)
5. Damaged parts
6. Overheating

7. Incorrect fuse or breaker size; box rating too small
8. Service entrance wires exposed in the house
9. Poor connections
10. Improper taps
11. Neutral wire bypasses service box
12. Fused neutral wire
13. Fuses upstream of disconnect switch
14. Obsolete box
15. Exterior box not weather-tight
16. Box not rated for aluminum

IMPLICATIONS

Unless otherwise noted, the implications of these problems are electrical shock or fire.

7.4.1 Poor Access or Location

Service Box Location Locked

Service boxes can be inside or outside and are sometimes in garages. If they're outside, they have to be weather-tight. They can be surface-mounted or recessed into the wall. Service boxes on exterior walls are sometimes locked for security. This may make it impossible to shut off the power quickly in an emergency. If this practice is common in your area, find out what the position of the utility company is. The utility may suggest removal of the lock, or a specific location for the key. Distribution panels should not be locked.

Indoor Locations

Electrical equipment should be at least three feet from indoor gas meters and outdoor gas relief vents. We don't want sparks causing a gas explosion! Boxes should be mounted at eye level and should be easily accessible. As a general rule, the area 30 inches wide and 3 feet in front of the box should not be obstructed. When located inside the house, service boxes should not be in bathrooms, clothes closets, kitchen cupboards or stairwells, for example. Boxes in bathrooms are a shock hazard. Boxes in clothes closets or cupboards are a fire hazard because they may ignite storage or clothing.

IMPLICATION

The box may not be accessible in an emergency to shut off power. Poor locations are fire or safety hazards.

STRATEGY

Make sure the box is accessible. If it's locked, everyone in the house should know where the key is kept.

Watch for boxes too close to gas meters or outdoor gas vents, or in bathrooms, stairwells, clothes closets or cupboards. Use common sense to decide whether the box location presents a hazard. If not, we do not recommend change. Most codes are not retroactive, and authorities also use their discretion in asking people to move service boxes.

7.4.2 Loose or Rusted

STRATEGY

Make sure the box is well secured to its support. Check both the exterior and interior of the box for evidence of rust.

FIGURE 7.12 Panel Openings

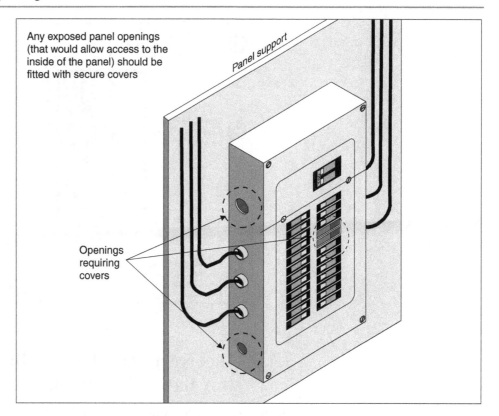

Any exposed panel openings (that would allow access to the inside of the panel) should be fitted with secure covers

Panel support

Openings requiring covers

7.4.3   Unprotected Openings

The panel should not have any openings that people can reach into (Figure 7.12). Covers should be in place and be well secured. Box knockouts that are not used for cables should be intact or replaced with covers.

IMPLICATIONS

A person could be electrocuted putting their finger in the hole while fumbling in the dark to re-set a tripped breaker. A fire in the box is much more likely to be contained if there are no large openings.

STRATEGY

Make sure all openings in the box are protected.

7.4.4   Damaged Parts

Fuse holders, switches and the box itself can be damaged or broken.

STRATEGY

If you can open the service box, look for damaged or broken components. Pay particular attention to fuse holders and switch parts. Check the box and cover as well.

7.4.5   Overheating

STRATEGY

Look for blackened, melted, or charred surfaces. Wire sheathing is often discolored. The smell of burning insulation or sheathing is sometimes a clue. If the box is warm or there are wisps of smoke, there is an immediate and serious problem.

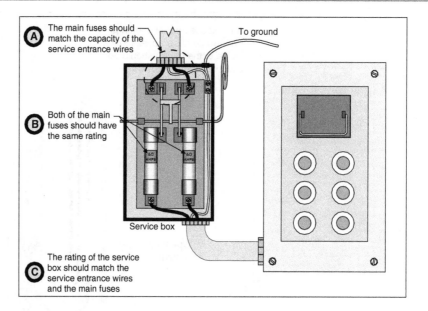

A The main fuses should match the capacity of the service entrance wires

To ground

B Both of the main fuses should have the same rating

60 AMPS   60 AMPS

Service box

C The rating of the service box should match the service entrance wires and the main fuses

7.4.6 Incorrect Main Fuse or Breaker Size; Box Rating Too Small

The fuse or breaker should be (Figure 7.13)—

1. sized to adequately protect the service entrance wires
2. no larger than the rating of the service box

IMPLICATIONS

Fuses or breakers that are too small will shut off the house electricity although the system is still safe. They will unnecessarily restrict the amount of electricity available in the house. Oversized fuses or breakers will not shut off the electricity when the current levels become dangerous. Fire and electrical shock are possible.

STRATEGY

Try to make sure the fuses or breakers are the right size for the wire and for the box. The box rating must be at least as big as the fuses and service entrance wires. Where you can't be sure, let your client know.

Sometimes the fuses or breakers are slightly oversized because there is no breaker available that matches the wire ampacity. It's acceptable, for example, to have 200-amp breakers on wire rated for 180 amps, because you can't buy a 180-amp breaker.

Fuses Same Size

Both fuses should be the same size. If they're different, the client should be advised to have an electrician investigate and correct as necessary. At least one of the fuses is the wrong size.

Breaker Brand

The breaker should be the same brand as the box, in most cases. While there are exceptions, recommend further investigation where the breaker is a different brand than the service box.

7.4.7   Service Entrance Wires Exposed in the House

In most jurisdictions, the service entrance wires, even if in conduit, are not allowed to run through the interior of the house before going into the service box. These wires should come straight into the back of the service box.

STRATEGY

Where service entrance wires run inside the house before going to the service box, recommend further investigation. Again, the utility may have made an exception and permitted this arrangement. You should describe it as unusual and not commit yourself to a position that may make you look foolish.

7.4.8   Poor Connections

Loose connections cause more fires than any other electrical problem. Look at each connection. Sometimes it is clear from a visual inspection that they are physically loose. Sometimes you'll see evidence of overheating or melting as discussed earlier.

Voltage Drop

Loose connections also lead to excessive voltage drop. It's natural to have some loss, or drop, of voltage by the time you get to the end of a long circuit. Most codes allow this to be as much as 3% through a feeder or branch circuit, or 5% total through both. Loose connections lead to too much voltage drop, which you might notice as dim lights, slow motors, etc. It's useful to know this, but the Standards don't require you to test for it.

We do not recommend pulling on connections to make sure they are tight. You may create a loose connection, or worse, electrocute yourself.

7.4.9   Improper Taps

Wires for house services should come off the distribution panel, not off the service box. Where the service box is upstream of the meter (before the meter) any taps off the service box will not be metered and people are stealing the electricity (Figure 7.14).

F I G U R E 7.14   Illegal Taps

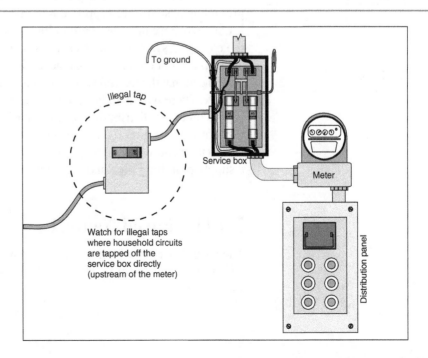

To ground

Illegal tap

Service box

Meter

Distribution panel

Watch for illegal taps
where household circuits
are tapped off the
service box directly
(upstream of the meter)

F I G U R E   7.15   Neutral Wire Shouldn't Bypass the Service Box

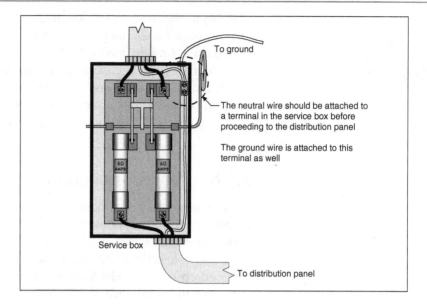

To ground

The neutral wire should be attached to a terminal in the service box before proceeding to the distribution panel

The ground wire is attached to this terminal as well

60 AMPS

60 AMPS

Service box

To distribution panel

IMPLICATIONS

Service boxes are <u>not designed for multiple taps</u> (more than one wire for every fuse, breaker, or wire securement point). There is tremendous potential for loose connections. In addition, the <u>possibility of legal action by the utility exists if people are taking electricity upstream of the meter</u>.

STRATEGY

Look at the service box for wires that are tapped off the box directly.

7.4.10   Neutral Wire Bypasses Service Box

The neutral (white) service entrance conductor should be attached to a terminal in the service box, not in the distribution panel (Figure 7.15).

IMPLICATIONS

The service box is the point in the electrical system where the neutral and grounding systems are supposed to come together. We'll talk more about why this is done when we talk about grounding. If <u>the neutral wire</u> bypasses the <u>service box, the electrical system is not as safe as it should be</u>, because the neutral and ground systems are not connected (balanced), at least not at the proper spot.

STRATEGY

Check that the neutral service conductor is attached to a terminal bar in the service box. There will usually be a white wire, also attached to the terminal bar, which carries on to the distribution panel. There should also be a ground wire attached to the terminal bar directly, connected with a jumper, or bonded by the design of the box to the neutral wire. The ground wire connects to grounding electrodes such as a supply plumbing pipe and a ground rod.

7.4.11   Fused Neutral

The <u>neutral (white) wire in the service box should not run through a fuse</u>. The black wire should have a fuse, and the red wire should have a fuse, but the neutral wire should not.

Dangerous

A fused neutral creates a hazardous situation because the fuse for the neutral may blow before the fuse for the red or the black. People will think that since the fuse is blown and that the appliances don't work, the power to the house is not energized. However, if the white fuse has blown, voltage will be present through the whole house and back through the white wire to where the circuit is interrupted at the fuse.

Modern residential panels are arranged so it's hard to fuse the neutral; however, three-phase panels can be used inappropriately to fuse the neutral on a single-phase service. Some obsolete service boxes were designed with fused neutrals.

STRATEGY

Make sure that only the black and the red wires are fused in the service box. Recommend replacing old boxes with fused neutrals, and rearranging fused neutrals in modern boxes.

7.4.12   Fuses Upstream of Disconnect Switch

The proper arrangement for service box wiring is to have the black and the red service entrance wires attach to the main disconnect switch (Figure 7.16). The main fuses should be after (downstream) the switch. When the switch is thrown, the fuses should be de-energized.

It is possible to wire the service box so the electricity goes through the fuses first and then to the disconnect switch. This makes it more dangerous to change the fuses. This is incorrect and should be reported.

IMPLICATIONS

People may be electrocuted changing fuses, after shutting off power to the house, because they think the fuse holders are de-energized. If the switch is downstream of (after) the fuses, the fuses will always be energized, no matter what position the switch is in.

FIGURE 7.16   The Main Fuses Must Be Downstream of the Disconnect Switch

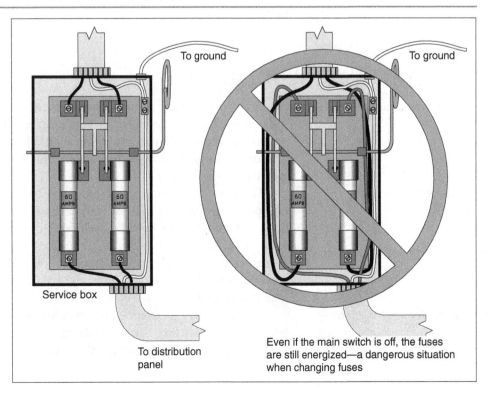

To ground

To ground

Service box

To distribution
panel

Even if the main switch is off, the fuses
are still energized—a dangerous situation
when changing fuses

STRATEGY

Check that the service entrance wires are connected to the "line" side of the switch, rather than the "load" side.

7.4.13   Obsolete Service Box

Any service box with exposed electrical connectors is obsolete. This is typical of some very old ceramic systems. These were often located at ceiling level.

IMPLICATION

The implication is electric shock.

STRATEGY

Any switches not enclosed in a service box should be considered obsolete and replaced. You may be looking at a 30-amp service here.

7.4.14   Exterior Box Not Weather-Tight

Any service boxes mounted on the exterior of buildings should be weather-tight, unless they are mounted inside a weather-tight enclosure.

IMPLICATIONS

Moisture in the box can lead to electrical shock, overheating and fire.

STRATEGY

Where there is the possibility for, or evidence of moisture penetration, improvements should be recommended. Look for water, watermarks and rust in the box. Look for openings, especially on the top, where water could get in.

7.4.15   Box Not Rated for Aluminum

STRATEGY

Where aluminum wire is used in a service box, the box and its components, including breakers, should be rated for use with aluminum (CUAL). The rating may be spelled out on or inside the box.

Where you cannot verify that the box is rated for aluminum, recommend further investigation.

7.5   SYSTEM GROUNDING

Ground Wire Usually Idle

Electricity is confusing enough when we deal with wires that are supposed to carry the current through the house. It gets even more confusing when we talk about wires that normally don't do anything at all. Most people have some difficulty with the concept of **grounding** and its cousin, **bonding.** We'll try to keep it simple and take the mystery out of it.

Equipment Grounding System

There are two types of grounding in homes, with different functions. The **equipment grounding system** is the network of bare wires that runs through the home as part of the branch circuit wiring. This grounding system is connected to the white or neutral service wire coming in from the street. This equipment grounding system protects people from electric shock when electricity gets somewhere it shouldn't and allows fuses to blow and breakers to trip. Think of this as an emergency path for electricity.

Current Flows out to Street

The equipment grounding system connects to the neutral wire coming into the house at the service box. Current in the ground wires in the distribution system flows out the street transformer through the neutral service entrance wire.

F I G U R E 7.17   Electrical Path for Ground and Netural Wires

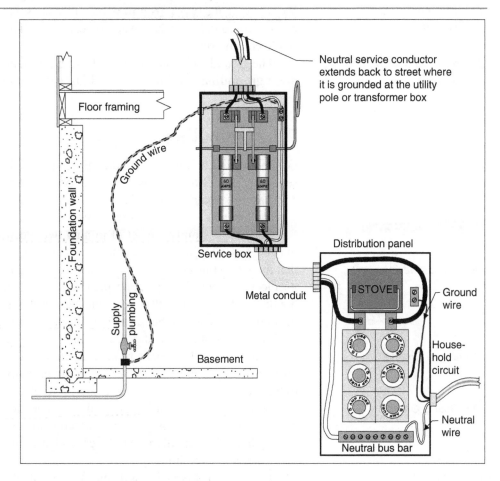

Earth Grounding System

The **earth grounding system** uses a wire to connect the service box to the earth with water pipes, grounding rods, etc. This earth grounding system is a path for lightning or static electricity. It is not intended to carry the emergency current from the equipment grounding system to ground. The only time this earth grounding system would carry electricity from the home would be if there were a fault in the home causing current to flow through the ground wires in the distribution system **and** the neutral service wire out to the street were broken.

7.5.1   Grounding vs. Grounded Neutral Wire

*Grounding (Ground)
versus Grounded*

Let's make sure we understand the difference between the grounding (ground) wire and the grounded neutral wire. The white neutral (grounded) wire carries current on an everyday basis as part of a normal circuit. The electricity flows through the neutral wires and is collected at the neutral bus bar in the distribution panel (Figure 7.17). It then flows to the neutral connection in the service box and is joined to the neutral service entrance wire. This neutral service wire then goes out to the transformer at the street. This is the way electricity is supposed to flow.

Electricity is not supposed to flow through the bare ground wire. The ground wire is normally at rest, available for emergency use only. If something goes wrong, the ground wire will carry electricity safely to the neutral service wire at the service box.

Grounding Electrode Conductors

Let's clarify the terminology we'll use going forward.

We'll refer to the **earth ground wire,** which is the bare wire that connects the service box to the grounding rods or water pipes. It is technically called the **grounding electrode conductor.**

Equipment Grounding Conductors

The ground wires on each branch circuit throughout the house are called **equipment grounding conductors.** We'll just call them **ground wires.**

7.5.2   Bonding

Grounding Defined

Grounding and bonding are frequently confused. Let's start with a simple way to separate them. Grounding is the act of connecting something to the ground (earth), so it has zero electrical potential. Everything that is grounded is connected to ground and can have no electrical energy stored in it.

Bonding Defined

Bonding is simply the act of joining two electrical conductors together. They may be two wires, a wire and a pipe, or they may be two tin cans. Bonding ensures that these two things will be at the same electrical potential. That means you won't get electricity building up in one and not in the other. No current flows between two bonded bodies because they have the same potential. A wire between two electrical outlet boxes bonds them. If a hot (black) wire touches one box, both boxes will have 120 volts of electrical potential and either could give you a shock.

Bonding to Ground

Bonding, itself, doesn't protect anything. However, if one of those boxes is grounded, there can be no electrical energy buildup. If the grounded box is bonded to the other box, the other box is also at zero electrical potential.

The Goal Is Ground

Whether it's a grounding or bonding connection, the goal in house wiring is to have no metal boxes or any other conductive materials near the wires become electrically hot. We want all these to be grounded so they have zero electrical potential and can't give us a shock.

Can't Ground to Gas Piping

The gas piping issue is confusing. You're not allowed to use gas piping to ground the electrical system. It's tempting because the gas piping in houses is usually metal. The gas piping usually goes outside underground and seems like a good way to connect to ground. However, much of the gas underground piping is plastic, which is not a good electrical conductor. This defeats the grounding function.

Bond the Gas Piping

We are not allowed to use the gas piping to ground an electrical system. However, gas piping must be bonded to the electrical grounding systems in most jurisdictions.

That's because we don't want the gas piping to develop an electrical charge. If it does, it could create an arc or spark to something nearby. If gas vapors are present, this could create an explosion.

Most municipalities require that the gas piping be bonded to the house electrical grounding system. Think of the gas piping getting rid of any stray electricity to the grounding system. Remember that we don't want electricity to build up anywhere except within the electrical system. Incidentally, bonding the gas piping usually bonds the furnace and ductwork too, because the piping touches the furnace. Bonding the gas piping is often accomplished with a wire attached to the cold (and sometimes hot) water supply pipe, near the water heater.

Arcing and Sparks

If we build up enough electrical potential in one ungrounded (hot) conductor and bring a second conductor close to it, we can make electricity jump through the air. The potential electrical energy is so great on the hot side that it sees a path to ground that isn't perfect but will bridge the air gap to get to it. This creates a spark. The electricity is said to be arcing between the conductors.

TABLE 7.2 Minimum Sizes for Ground Wires

Service Wire (Copper)	Service Wire (Aluminum)	Grounding Wire (Copper)	Grounding Wire (Aluminum)
2 or smaller	1/0 or smaller	#8	#6
1 or 1/0	2/0 or 3/0	#6	#4
2/0 or 3/0	4/0 or 250 MCM	#4	#2

Note: All wire sizes are AWG except 250 MCM.

7.5.3   Where Does the Grounding System Go?

Ground Wires through the House

We've talked about protecting people in houses by attaching grounding wires to metal boxes, for example, that are close to electrical wires. The fuse panel, metal outlets, flip switches and screw-in light bulbs should all be grounded.

In the first half of the twentieth century, we didn't extend the grounding protection throughout the house distribution system. Since the early to mid-1960s, all new wiring extends the ground protection throughout the distribution network. All branch circuits now include a ground wire.

Grounds Collected at Service Box

The ground wires are collected at the distribution panel and forwarded to the service box. At the service box, the house ground wires are connected to the service box equipment and enclosure. The whole assembly is connected to the service entrance neutral and to a grounding wire that goes to grounding electrodes (e.g., rod or plumbing pipe). In some cases, the system ground may be connected to the grounding electrode conductors at the meter, rather than at the service box.

Two Paths to Ground

This gives the electricity, in theory, two choices to flow to ground. Electricity that comes back to this point can either flow to ground through the neutral service wire, or through the ground wire to the grounding electrode.

Ground Wire from Box to Pipe or Rod

The earth ground wires running from the service box to the grounding electrode are usually copper and are often bare (no insulation). Aluminum grounding wires are permitted if they're kept 18 inches away from the earth and away from moisture or other corrosive environments. Aluminum wires are not as good conductors as copper, so they have to be one size larger than copper wires.

7.5.4   Grounding Wire Size

Table 7.2 summarizes common copper wire sizes for grounding systems. **Note:** 6-gauge copper wire is the largest required if the connection is to a ground rod.

We Don't Check Quality of Ground

A home inspection does not include a check of the quality of the ground system. We're simply looking at the grounding wire, their connections, and the electrodes, where visible, for corrosion, damaged wire and loose connections.

7.5.5   Where Does the Grounding System End?

The goal is to get the electricity to flow to ground. There are several ways to do this, including—

1. through metal water supply pipes
2. through metal rods driven into the ground

3. through wires (often $^1/_2$-inch reinforcing bar) buried in the footings of buildings (UFER ground)

4. buried grounding plates or rings

5. the frames of metal buildings (more common in commercial than residential construction)

6. the metal casings of private water supply wells

A New Issue

In some areas, metal water pipes running to the street water mains are being replaced with plastic. This defeats the grounding system, and is impossible to detect during a home inspection.

Rules Change

Various jurisdictions have different requirements, and like all code issues, the requirements have changed over time. For example, after 1987, grounding to a metal supply water pipe alone is not satisfactory. There must also be a ground rod, because plastic water piping is becoming so popular.

7.5.6 Conditions

IMPLICATIONS

Let's look at what goes wrong with grounding systems. The implications are the same throughout. An ineffective or missing grounding system cannot perform its safety functions. There is greater risk of electrical shock, equipment damage, and fire in houses where the grounding system is not effective.

1. No grounding
2. Ground wire attached to plastic pipe
3. Ground wire after (downstream of) meters and valves, with no jumper
4. Spliced ground wire
5. Poor connections
6. Ground connections not accessible
7. Ground rod cut off
8. Corroded ground wire
9. Undersized ground wire
10. Neutral bonded to ground wire after (downstream of) service box
11. Neutral wires not bonded to ground wire at service box
12. Service box not bonded to ground wire
13. No ground in subpanel feeder wires

No Grounding

STRATEGY

In some cases, you won't find a ground wire from the service box to piping, to a ground rod or to anything else. If it is missing, this is a serious electrical defect and immediate improvement is called for. Clients, real estate agents and existing homeowners may have a tough time understanding how this is important since the house has been operating this way for some time. Explain that this is an emergency safety device and houses can operate for years without it, but the one time they need it (and it will happen) they won't have the protection they should. Is it worth risking someone's life?

FIGURE 7.18   Jumper Wires Needed

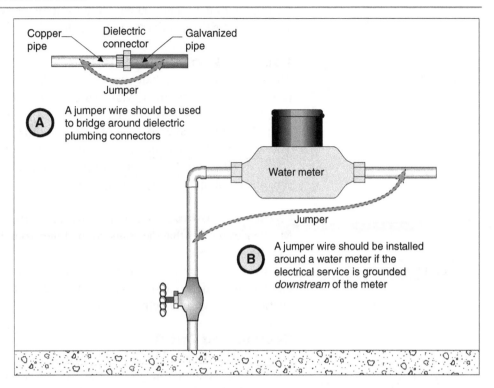

Ground Wire Attached to Plastic Pipe

Plastic piping does not provide a continuous path to ground. Plastic piping is an insulator rather than a conductor. This is the same as having no grounding and immediate improvement should be recommended.

Ground Wire after (Downstream of) Meters and Valves (No Jumper)

Meters, valves and dielectric connectors can interrupt electrical continuity.

Make sure the ground wire is connected as close as possible to the plumbing service entry and upstream of (before) any devices that might interrupt it. Where there are devices such as meters upstream, a jumper should be added around the devices, or the ground wire should be moved upstream of these (Figure 7.18). The jumper should be the same size as the ground wire.

Bonding Gas Piping

In most areas the metallic natural gas piping must be bonded to the grounding system. This applies to new installations, or renovations involving gas piping or electrical service work. It is common to find this bonding wire connected to the plumbing system at the water heater, where the gas and water pipes are close together. In this case, a jumper should be provided around the water meter to maintain continuity of ground for the gas piping (although the electrical system may be properly grounded without this jumper).

Spliced Ground Wire

Ground wires should not be spliced since every splice is a potential poor connection.

Follow the grounding wire where it's visible (where it's not entirely visible, inform your client that you couldn't see it all). Know what is accepted practice in your area. Write up splices if they are not allowed, or if they are poor quality.

Loose or Poor Connections

STRATEGY

The ground wire is typically connected to the service box at one end and to a pipe or ground rod at the other. Make sure the wire is securely fastened at both ends. Where ground wires are attached to pipes, it's not adequate to just wrap the wire around the pipe. The wire must be secured with a clamp approved for that purpose. The wire may be loose in the clamp or the clamp may be loose on the pipe.

Corrosion of the wire, clamp or pipe could result in poor conditions. Where you see this, recommend further investigation.

Ground Connections Not Accessible

Most codes require that the connection of the grounding wire to the piping or ground rods be accessible.

STRATEGY

Where you can't see how the grounding wire is connected, describe that limitation to your client. Advise your client to locate and inspect the quality of these connections, or have an electrician do it.

Ground Rod Cut Off

The ground rod should be a full 8 feet long.

STRATEGY

Look at the top of the ground rod. You should see the data stamped on it. If not, you should describe the ground rod as being suspect. Electricians can check the quality of the ground and it may be okay even if the rod has been cut. Utilities will sometimes allow people to do unconventional things with ground rods. Qualify your criticism, since the installation may be approved by the utility.

Corroded Ground Wire

STRATEGY

Follow the wire through its entire length, if possible. Write up corroded wire or connections.

Undersized Ground Wire

We included a chart earlier describing the minimum sizes for ground wires.

STRATEGY

Check the size of the ground wire against the size of the service wires. Since the wires are often bare, you may not be able to verify the size by reading the sheathing. Compare it to known samples or use a wire measurement device.

Neutral Bonded to Ground Wire after (Downstream of) Service Box

We'll talk about this more in the distribution system, but it's noted here as well, since it's a common defect.

The only place that the neutral wire and the ground wire should be bonded together is at the service box.

The neutral wire carries electricity every day. The equipment ground wires should not. If the neutral and ground are bonded together out in the house distribution system (for example, at an auxiliary panel), the equipment ground wires may carry some everyday electricity. This is not safe.

Note: In combination panels (service box and distribution panel in one cabinet) this bonding is allowed in the distribution panel.

STRATEGY

This will be discovered most often at auxiliary panels. Check that the neutral and ground wires are separated.

FIGURE 7.19   Bond Service Box to Ground

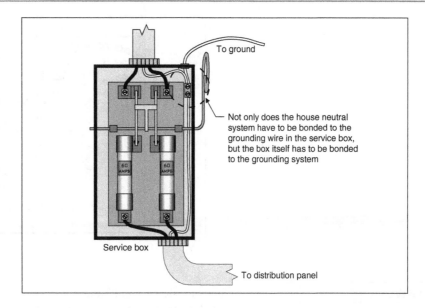

Neutral Wires Not Bonded to Ground Wire at Service Box

The only place that the house neutral should be bonded to the ground is at the service box, but it must be done here. Failure to bond the neutral to the ground at the service box removes some of the emergency safety routes and protection that are available.

Make sure the equipment grounding wires from the house are grouped (usually in the distribution panel) and bonded to the house neutral at the service box. The neutral and ground terminals are often bonded by the design of the box. Some have a removable bonding jumper or screw. Make sure it's in place. If you aren't sure whether one is needed, note the make and model, and call the manufacturer.

Service Box Not Bonded to Grounding Wire

Not only does the house neutral system have to be bonded to the grounding wire in the service box, but also the box itself has to be bonded to the grounding system (Figure 7.19). This is accomplished either with a bonding screw in the neutral terminal block, or with a jumper wire or screw to the box itself.

Combination Panel Includes Service Box and Distribution Panel

Check to make sure the service box itself is bonded to the point where the grounding system and neutral wires come together in the service box.

We have been talking about the service box as though it is separate from the distribution panel. This is true on older systems, but in many modern systems, a combination panel (commonly called a service panel) is used. The service box and distribution panel are in one cabinet, often with two separate covers.

Where there are multiple main disconnects, they should be bonded together, and one should be connected to both the service entrance neutral and grounding electrode wire.

No Ground in Subpanel Feeder Wires

A ground wire in the cable from the service panel to a subpanel is usually needed so the subpanel and all of the branch circuits fed by the subpanel can be adequately grounded (Figure 7.20).

F I G U R E 7.20   Need Ground in Subpanel Feeder Wires

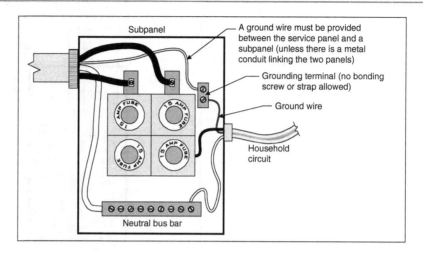

STRATEGY

Check at the subpanel and at the main distribution panel for the presence of a connected ground wire in the subpanel feeder wire.

There may be an exception when the subpanel is adjacent to and bonded to the main distribution panel, most commonly by the metal conduit protecting the feed wires. Where the subpanel is bonded to the main panel by the conduit, a ground wire may not be needed.

7.6 DISTRIBUTION PANELS

It's the Fuse Box

These may also be called **service panels, panelboards, auxiliary panels, subpanels, fuse boxes, fuse panels,** or **breaker panels.** Most people call it the **fuse box,** or the breaker box.

Tree Analogy

So far, we've been talking about bringing electricity into the house. Now we're going to talk about how to spread it around the house. You can think of the service drop and the service entrance conductors as the trunk of a tree. The distribution wires throughout the house are the branches of the tree. The distribution panel is where the branches attach to the trunk.

7.6.1   What Comes in and What Goes out

Wires from Service Box to Panel

Coming into the distribution panel from the service box is a black wire with 120-volt potential, a red wire with 120-volt potential, a neutral wire with no potential, and usually a ground wire (Figure 7.21).

Wires from Panel to Branch Circuits

What goes out of the distribution panel into the house is many black, red, and white wires. Bare ground wires also leave the panel with each circuit (installed after 1960, roughly). The black and the red branch circuit wires carry the electrical energy. The white wires complete the path to ground for each circuit, when the circuit is working. If the distribution system is grounded, the ground wire runs along each circuit ready to pick up any electricity that gets out of hand.

The black and the red wires are connected to fuse or breaker terminals. The white wires are connected to the neutral terminal or bus bar. The ground wires are connected to the panel enclosure (bonded to the panel).

F I G U R E   7.21   Typical Arrangement of Panel Wires

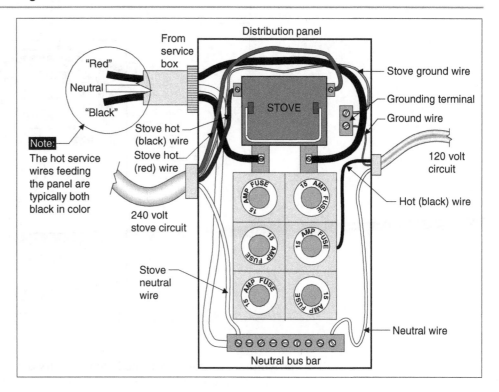

7.6.2   240-Volt Circuits

240-Volt Circuits

Branch circuits can be one of two types. We have heavy-duty 240-volt circuits and we have smaller 120-volt circuits. The 240-volt circuits are used for large appliances, such as electric stoves, electric water heaters, electric clothes dryers, air conditioners and saunas. These large appliances use a red and a black wire from the panel. The potential from the black wire to the red wire is 240 volts.

Big Watts with Small Amps

240-volt circuits allow us to deliver adequate power to the larger appliances and keep the current flow (amps) and wire size relatively small.

Need Two Fuses or Breakers

One of the disadvantages of 240-volt circuits is that you need to have a fuse for the black wire and a fuse for the red wire. These 240-volt circuits have two fuses or breakers. It's important to tie these fuses or breakers together. Otherwise, people would pull out one fuse or shut off one breaker and think the power to the appliance was off. However, when they went to work on it, power would still be delivered through one wire. This can be fatal.

Tie Fuses or Breakers Together

To shut off power to a 240-volt circuit, you have to shut off two circuit breakers or pull out two fuses (Figure 7.22). The fuse pullout blocks on stoves and clothes dryers, for example, force you to do just this. Before you can remove one fuse, you have to pull out the fuse holder, which has both fuses in it.

Linked Breakers

Circuit breakers use either a mechanical tie bar (link) that joins the two breaker handles together, or a fancy breaker that has a single handle but two separate poles.

Balanced 240-Volt Circuits

Most 240-volt circuits have a red wire, black wire and white wire. However, some have only a red wire and a black wire. How can a circuit work with no white wire?

We talked about 240-volt circuits much earlier, and said that when the red wire pulsed, the black wire was at rest, and vice versa. The red and black wires can act

F I G U R E 7.22 Pull-Out Fuse Blocks for 240-Volt Circuits

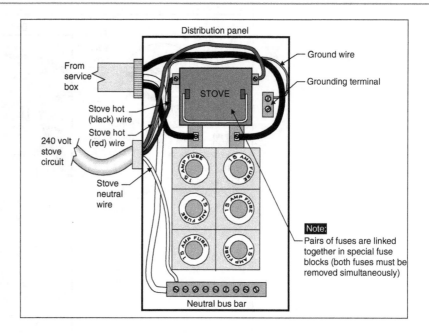

as white wires, but only if the load is exactly the same on the red and black wires, as for a baseboard heater or water heater. Any appliance that has a 120-volt component will need a white wire to carry the unbalanced part of the load. Stoves have 120-volt lights, clocks and timers. Clothes dryers have 120-volt lights, timer and motors. Air conditioners may have 120-volt motors and crank case heaters. All appliances with both 240-volt and 120-volt components need a black, red, **and** white wire.

7.6.3   120-Volt Circuits

As Many As You Want

Some 120-volt circuits use a black wire and a white wire (and a ground wire for safety purposes in newer work). Other 120-volt circuits use a red wire and a white wire. There is no limit to how many circuits you can have in a house. If you wanted to, every outlet could be on its own circuit with its own fuse or circuit breaker, and every light could have its own circuit. This would be expensive and wouldn't give you many advantages. Modern 120-volt circuits accommodate up to about twelve outlets and/or light fixtures on one circuit.

Circuit May Have 12 Outlets

You Won't Know How Many Things Are on Each Circuit

Home inspectors rarely know how many outlets or switches (called electrical **points**) are served by each circuit. It might take two people a couple of hours to figure it out. This obviously isn't practical during a home inspection, although this can be recorded as homeowners label their panels, writing out what each fuse or breaker controls.

Typically 10 to 20 Circuits

We find anywhere from four to 40 general-purpose circuits in the house. These 120-volt circuits serve such things as electrical outlets (receptacles), lights, dishwashers, furnaces, garbage disposals, well pumps, garage door operators, and so on.

7.6.4   Wire Sizes and Fuse Sizes

Match Wire Size to Fuse Size

The wire size is determined by how many amps we need to run through the wire. Recall from Table 7.1 that every wire has a maximum number of amps it can carry safely. Therefore, every wire has a correct fuse (or breaker) size to go along with it. Most people remember some of these, and other ones they have to look up. The common numbers for copper wire are—

14 gauge wire needs **15**-amp fuses or breakers

12 gauge wire needs **20**-amp fuses or breakers

10 gauge wire needs **30**-amp fuses or breakers

8 gauge wire needs **40**-amp fuses or breakers

6 gauge wire needs **60**-amp fuses or breakers

There are exceptions, but most of the time the numbers above apply.

Most circuits for receptacles and lights use 14 gauge wire. Circuits for kitchens, pantries, bathrooms, and utility areas, including receptacles for washing machines and dishwashers, use 12 gauge wire. As a general rule, the 120-volt circuits use 14 or 12 gauge wire.

Wire Size for 240-Volt Circuits

The 240-volt circuits might use 14 or 12 gauge wire but they often use large wire. For example, water heaters, central air conditioners and electric clothes dryers might use 10 gauge wire. Electric stoves and ovens usually use 8 gauge wire. Electric heaters rated at 240 volts may use 12 or even 14 gauge wire. Our job at the distribution panel is to make sure that each fuse or breaker is the right size to protect each wire.

What If the Fuse Is Too Small?

If the fuse or breaker is too small, it will shut down the electrical system before it has to. A fuse that is too small will be a nuisance because it's likely to blow frequently, but it isn't a safety hazard.

What If the Fuse Is Too Big?

If the fuse or breaker is too big, it won't shut off the electricity soon enough. This may allow the wire to overheat and create a dangerous situation. Finding too large a fuse or breaker (often called **overfusing**) is probably the most common electrical problem you will come across.

7.6.5   Panel Descriptions

Combination Panel

Distribution panels are typically steel boxes mounted on a wall, and with a door on the front of the box (Figure 7.23). They are designed to contain an electrical fire inside the panel. The panel can be by itself, or it can be attached to the service box. This **combination panel** or **service panel,** as it's known, has the service entrance wires coming into it. In the service box area, there will be a main disconnect and the main fuses or breakers for the whole house. The wires come out of the service box section into the distribution panel section. Electricity flows out through the various fuses or breakers to all the branch circuits.

Some Panels Have Doors, All Have Covers

Panels may have doors; some do not. All panels have covers that can be removed to inspect or work on the system. As home inspectors, we remove these covers. Homeowners do not need to remove covers to replace fuses or reset breakers.

Remove Panel Covers

The Standards ask us to inspect the interior of panels, so we have to remove the covers so we can match up the size of the wire and the size of the fuses or breakers. Opening the door in the front of the panel is not enough; you have to take the whole cover off. We'll talk about that a little more in Section 7.6.9.

FIGURE 7.23   Inspecting the Service Box and Panels

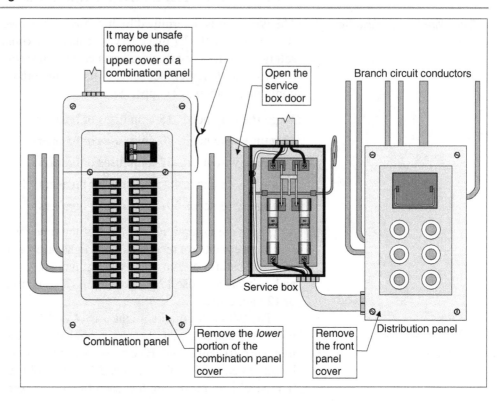

It may be unsafe to remove the upper cover of a combination panel

Open the service box door

Branch circuit conductors

Service box

Combination panel

Remove the *lower* portion of the combination panel cover

Remove the front panel cover

Distribution panel

7.6.6 Location

Panels Can Be Inside or Outside

Distribution panels can be located outside, in garages, or inside the house, often in the basement. Indoor panels are usually located on an exterior wall, adjacent to where the service entrance conductors run down the outside of the house.

At Eye Level, Clear in Front for Access

Distribution panels are supposed to be installed at about eye level so they are convenient. The area 3 feet in front and 30 inches wide should be kept clear.

Bad Locations

There are certain places where you shouldn't find distribution panels, such as close to water, or where access is difficult when the power is out. Some codes prohibit distribution panels in bathrooms, clothes closets, stairwells or kitchen cabinets. These rules vary, depending on what jurisdiction you are in, and when the system was installed. Some areas prohibit panels within 3 feet of indoor gas meters and outdoor gas relief vents.

7.6.7 Subpanels or Auxiliary Panels

Can Be Anywhere

These panels can be located anywhere through the house and can be difficult to find. Sometimes they're beside the main panel, but they can be on the top story of the house, for example, and while they're not supposed to be tucked away in closets, bathrooms, kitchen cabinets, or the like, they often are.

How Do I Know If There Is a Subpanel?

Sometimes you won't know that there's a subpanel, but there are some clues. If the service panel has a 240-volt circuit with no apparent function, it could be going to a subpanel. Sometimes it's even labeled **Subpanel** or **Auxiliary Panel.** If the only major appliances you can find are a stove and electric dryer, and you have three large 240-volt circuits, you should suspect another panel somewhere.

7.6.8   Distribution Panel Size

The panel has to be big enough to handle all the electricity that it might see. For example, if the house has a 100-amp service coming into it, the service panel has to be rated for at least 100 amps. A house with a 200-amp service would need a panel rated for at least 200 amps. That's because the service entrance wires and main fuses or breaker will allow 200 amps, for example, to go through to the distribution panel.

The distribution panel rating can be larger, but not smaller than the service size because it is very likely to see that much current. The panel rating is usually on the inside of the panel cover, although it can be in a number of places.

7.6.9   General Strategy for Inspecting Panels

Be Careful

Although home inspectors are required by the Standards to remove electrical cover plates, we encourage you not to do it unless you have good understanding of electrical systems and are familiar with electrical panels.

Dangerous

Checking the distribution panels is one of the most dangerous parts of home inspection. We'd like to turn off the power in the house before removing the panel cover, but most times that's not practical because the home is occupied. Test the panel with a voltage detector before opening it.

Fuse Pullouts Have to Be Removed to Get Cover Off

A tricky configuration is one where fuse pullouts have to be removed before the panel cover can be pulled off. If you don't notice that until you've got the panel cover loosened, you'll find yourself in an awkward spot, holding onto a cover with no screws in it, but unable to lift it out over the fuse pullouts.

If you're familiar with this kind of panel, you will be tempted to remove the fuse pullouts so you can take the cover off. This has its own set of problems. We normally do not shut off the power in a house for fear of upsetting computers, timers, or life support systems. However, if you don't remove the fuse pullouts, you can't complete the inspection to the Standards. What do you do?

Shutting Off Power

If the panel circuits are labeled, you may know what circuits the pullouts control. For example, if it's a clothes dryer or a water heater, you will probably be fine removing the pullouts. You can check to see whether the clothes dryer is in use. If not, shutting off power to it for a minute or two is seldom a problem. Similarly, disconnecting a water heater for a couple of minutes is not a problem. The catch is, you can't always believe the labels on the panel.

Don't Trust Labeled Panels

You should distrust the panel labeling. Many panels were labeled correctly originally, but subsequent changes are often made without relabeling. Be very careful with this. If the pullout is for a stove, and the timer is set to turn the oven on at 3:00 PM for three hours, you will ruin dinner if you pull the fuses!

Ask the Occupant

One solution is to ask the homeowner (if he or she is present) whether these fuses can be removed so you can perform your inspection.

Report Your Limitations

If you don't get permission, we recommend that you do not pull them out on your own. Write up the limitations to your inspection. Some home inspectors offer to come back and complete the inspection when people know it will be safe to turn off the power. This is a business decision you'll have to make.

Accidentally Tripping Breakers

There are some panels where it's difficult to remove the cover without accidentally tripping breakers. You might trip a breaker pulling the cover off or putting it back on. If you accidentally trip a breaker, you should let the homeowner know, either in person or by leaving them a note.

Swing-Out Panel Covers

Some panel covers are designed with one side that fits behind a couple of lugs, and the other side that rotates into place and is clipped there. Be careful with these covers. Any cover that swings into place can easily pinch a wire. This is more likely to happen, of course, if the box is full or overcrowded with wires. Use considerable care here to avoid problems.

If we've made you hesitant about removing distribution panel covers, that's probably a good thing. It's great to do a good job, but electrocuting yourself is a waste of all those business cards you just had printed.

Inspector in the House: Dinner Will Be Late!

Removing the cover on the electrical panel is usually straightforward, but sometimes it can be a little tricky. With some panels it is easy to trip a breaker inadvertently when removing or replacing the cover. Our most memorable instance was the time we tripped the breaker for the range, and did not realize that dinner was in the oven, with the timer set to start the oven at 4:00 PM. Needless to say, the owners were not happy that we messed up their dinner plans.

7.7 CONDITIONS FOUND IN PANELS

IMPLICATIONS

Let's look at some of the problems we typically find in panels. The implications of most of these are electrical shock and fire, so we won't discuss the implications for each one unless there's something unique.

Because this is confusing enough already, we'll break the problems into six categories so you'll have a better chance of keeping them straight:

- Problems found in all panels
- Problems unique to subpanels
- Problems with fuses or breakers
- Problems with fuses
- Problems with breakers
- Problems with panel wires

7.7.1 Conditions Found in All Panels

Conditions found in all panels include—

1. obsolete and/or fused neutrals
2. damaged panel or components
3. loose or missing door
4. openings in panel
5. panel too small
6. overheating
7. rust or water in panel
8. circuits not labeled
9. panel crowded

FIGURE 7.24   Fused Neutrals in Old Wiring Systems

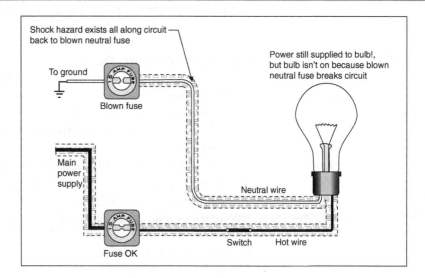

10. poor access

11. installed upside down

12. not suitable for aluminum wiring

13. poor location

14. outdoor panel not weather-tight

Obsolete and/or Fused Neutrals

Exposed Connections

Very old panels do not have covers or doors. Exposed wires can be touched readily. These panels, which are often white ceramic mounted on wooden boards on walls or ceilings, should be replaced.

Fused Neutrals

Another problem with old panels is **fused neutrals** (Figure 7.24). In early electrical work, people thought that if a fuse on the black wire was good, putting a second fuse in the circuit on the white wire would be even better.

Bad Idea

This was later recognized to be a bad idea and is no longer permitted. Why? If there's a 15-amp fuse on the black wire and a 15-amp fuse on the white wire, there are two fuses in the circuit. If the circuit is overloaded, one fuse will usually blow before the other. If the fuse on the white wire blows, the circuit will stop working, and the fuse on the black wire won't blow.

Dangerous

The receptacles won't be operable and the lights will go out. A homeowner would logically think that the power to that circuit was off. However, since the fuse on the black wire hasn't blown, there is actually power all the way through the circuit back to the blown fuse on the white wire in the panel. Someone working on that circuit will get a shock.

STRATEGY

Where you see old panels with exposed connections and/or fused neutrals, recommend replacement of the panels.

Damaged Panel or Components

If there is damage to the walls, door or cover of the panel, the damaged parts should be replaced. Similarly, fuse holders, breaker holders, bus bars, lugs, or terminal screws that are damaged or missing should be repaired or replaced.

Look for damaged cabinet parts or components. Pay particular attention to older Bakelite (brand name for hard, dark brown, plastic-like material) fuse or breaker holders. These are often chipped or broken.

Loose or Missing Door

Some panels are designed with doors. Some are not. This section applies to panels intended to have doors.

Remove the entire front cover (sometimes called the dead-front cover) from the panel. You should also operate the cover door, which homeowners will normally open and close. Make sure the door is present, secure, and operates properly.

Wood Screws Are Wrong

It's common to find that the appropriate machine screws have been lost and wood screws are inappropriately used to secure covers and cover doors. Wood screws have different threads, have pointed ends, are often too long, and can pierce wires. We recommend replacement of wood screws holding panels or doors in place.

Openings in Panel

When the dead-front cover is on, you shouldn't be able to reach into the panel. Knockouts (the metal plates designed to be pried out of the panel sides to allow wires to pass through) should be in place unless there's a wire passing through them. If there is a wire going through a panel, it should be clamped and protected from mechanical damage.

Fuse or breaker slots in the dead-front cover should not be open. Where a knockout or fuse and breaker slot has been removed and the hole is not used, the hole should be covered.

Recommend that openings be covered as a priority improvement.

Panel Too Small

The panel rating must be at least the size of the service entrance so it can handle this current without overheating.

Check the rating on the distribution panel and recommend replacement if it is smaller than the service size. If the panel rating is suitable, but there aren't enough circuits available, a subpanel can be added.

Overheating

Look for evidence of overheating, which includes—

1. warm panel

2. melted insulation, wires or terminals

3. charring or smoke discoloration

4. the smell of burned plastic

Wherever there is evidence of overheating, further investigation should be recommended, even if the panel is not currently warm.

Rust or Water in the Panel

Water in a panel is obviously dangerous since water is a good conductor of electricity. Rust on electrical components not only deteriorates the components but also can lead to poor connections. Where there is rust or water in the panel, repair, replacement or further investigation should be recommended.

Circuits Not Labeled

Many codes call for circuits to be labeled. In many cases, they are not.

Home inspectors should point out that circuit labeling is an important safety issue and recommend circuits be labeled. However, even if circuits are labeled, you won't know whether they are done correctly. Please do not rely on the labeling to be correct.

Crowded

Panels are designed with adequate room for the wires.

If it is hard to get the cover on the panel without pinching wires, it is probably crowded. A panel cleanup should be recommended. With little experience, you should be able to recognize crowded panels.

Poor Access

Panels should be readily accessible. Most codes call for a 30-inch wide, 3-foot deep area at the front to be kept open. The panel should be roughly at eye level and there should be no obstructions to opening the door fully.

Where panel access is restricted, you should recommend that the obstructions be removed or the panel be relocated.

Installed Upside Down

Check to see that the panel is installed in its correct orientation.

Panel Not Suitable for Use with Aluminum Wire

Where aluminum wiring is used in a panel, the panel should be rated for use with aluminum. This is normally on the panel data, often on the inside of the panel door. The panel often says something like, "suitable for use with CU or AL conductors," or "suitable for use with CU/AL rated circuit breakers."

Where you cannot verify that the panel is suitable for use with aluminum, recommend that this be checked. Don't say that the panel is not suitable for use with aluminum, because the labeling may have been removed or concealed. It's safer to write it up as a question.

Poor Location

Watch for panels in bathrooms, clothes closets, stairwells, and kitchen cabinets. Watch also for panels too close to gas meters or gas relief vents.

Use Common Sense

Use common sense to decide whether the panel location presents a hazard. If not, we don't recommend moving it. Codes change, and what used to be common practice is often not acceptable now. Codes will change in the future as well, but codes are not usually retroactive. Authorities use their discretion too, in deciding whether to ask homeowers to move equipment.

Outdoor Panel Not Weather-Tight

Look for outdoor panels to be protected against water entry. Most outdoor panels are flush-mounted, with covers that extend onto the wall surface. Recommend repair or replacement where you see rust or water in the panel.

7.7.2   Conditions Unique to Subpanels

All of the issues that apply to panels also apply to subpanels. The following problems are specific to subpanels:

F I G U R E 7.25   Subpanel Wiring—Disconnect by Subpanel

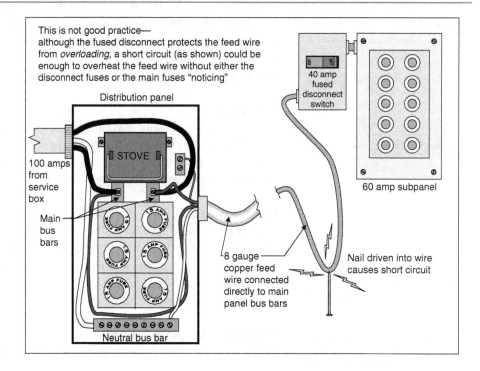

1. subpanel and/or feeder wire not adequately protected
2. neutral and ground wires bonded at subpanel
3. subpanel not grounded

Subpanel and/or Feeder Wire Not Adequately Protected

Subpanels Need Protection

Subpanels are usually smaller ampacity than the service size. For instance, a 100-amp service will have a 100-amp main distribution panel and may have a 40-amp subpanel. The 100-amp main panel is protected by the 100-amp fuses or breakers in the main disconnect. What protects the 40-amp subpanel?

Ideally, there are 40-amp fuses or breakers in the main distribution panel protecting the subpanel and the wire feeding it (which should be 8 gauge if copper, in this case).

When you see a subpanel—

STRATEGY

1. check its rating
2. make sure the feeder wire to the subpanel is sized properly
3. look for fuses or breakers sized properly to protect both the feeder wire and the subpanel

If there are no fuses or breakers to protect the panel and feeder wire in the main distribution panel, the only protection may be the 100-amp main fuses. This is not safe.

Fused Disconnect at Subpanel

Sometimes there is a fused disconnect at the subpanel. In our example, someone might add a 40-amp fused disconnect adjacent to the subpanel (Figure 7.25). This will protect the 8 gauge wire in the event of an **overload.** If the subpanel draws more than 40 amps, these fuses will blow, protecting the 8 gauge wire. However, there is another issue.

FIGURE 7.26 Subpanel Wiring—Disconnect by Main Panel

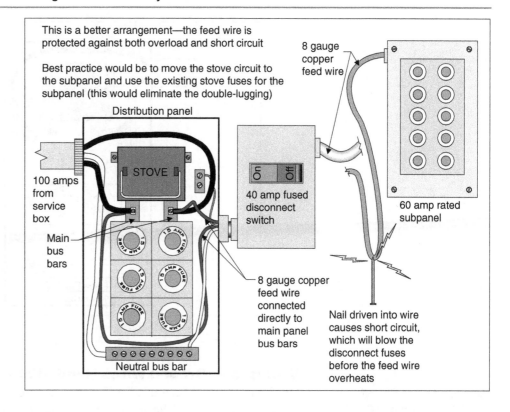

This is a better arrangement—the feed wire is protected against both overload and short circuit

Best practice would be to move the stove circuit to the subpanel and use the existing stove fuses for the subpanel (this would eliminate the double-lugging)

Distribution panel

STOVE

100 amps from service box

Main bus bars

8 gauge copper feed wire connected directly to main panel bus bars

Neutral bus bar

40 amp fused disconnect switch

8 gauge copper feed wire

60 amp rated subpanel

Nail driven into wire causes short circuit, which will blow the disconnect fuses before the feed wire overheats

Fuses Are Best at Beginning of Circuit

Putting the fuses or breakers anywhere in a circuit protects against an **overload** situation, but it does not protect against a **short circuit.** If the main panel is in the basement, and our subpanel with the 40-amp fused disconnect is on the third floor, what happens if someone drives a nail into the 8 gauge wire on the first floor? If the nail bridges the black and the white wires, we get a short circuit.

Short Circuit Doesn't Go Through Fuses

Let's assume 75 amps are flowing where we didn't expect it to be flowing. And it's not flowing through our 40-amp fuses on the third floor! Our 8 gauge wire will overheat and start a fire. The 40-amp fuses on the third floor can't help because they don't see the 75 amps and would never know anything is wrong. The 100-amp fuses in the main disconnect would not blow, because there is only 75 amps flowing.

It's best to put the fused disconnect at the beginning rather than at the end of a circuit (Figure 7.26). That way, the fuses or breakers will see the large current and will shut down the power. The 40-amp fuses should be in or right beside the main panel, not the subpanel.

Complex Rules

Electrical authorities recognize this and prefer to see subpanel feeders fused at the main panel. Different codes make different exceptions, depending on how large the feeder is, how long the feeder is, and whether or not the feeder is mechanically protected (e.g., inside a rigid conduit). These rules become complicated, and are beyond the scope of this program. You may wish to discuss this issue with a utility inspector or electrician.

Call for Help If Unsure

As a home inspector, you are probably justified in recommending further investigation on any system with a subpanel where the fuses or breakers are not at the main panel protecting it. Common sense works well.

F I G U R E 7.27   Don't Bond Neutral and Gound Wires Downstream of Service Box

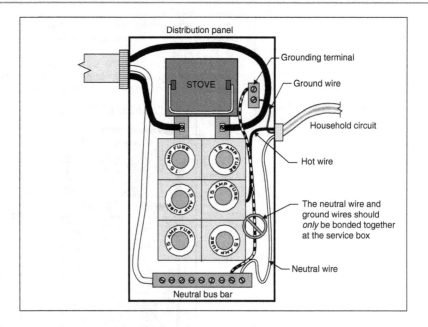

Grounded Wires Should
Not Normally Be Energized

Neutral and Ground Wires Bonded at the Subpanel

This is not allowed (Figure 7.27). The neutral wire should carry the electricity back on an everyday basis. The equipment ground wire should be idle and should only be used in emergencies. If you join the neutral and the ground wires at the subpanel, the ground wire is likely to carry electricity. Its ability to work in an emergency is diminished. More importantly, since it is a bare wire and people don't expect it to be carrying electricity, there's an electrical shock hazard. Ground wires are connected to boxes and equipment cases. If the ground and neutral are joined, the boxes and equipment cases may be energized.

STRATEGY

Check subpanels to make sure the ground and neutral are not bonded together. Some subpanels have bonding screws or jumpers that electrically connect the ground and the neutral bar. Make sure these are not connected. Where they are bonded, or you suspect that they are, recommend that an electrician correct this situation.

No Ground Wire

Sometimes the subpanel does not have an equipment ground wire in the feeder.

STRATEGY

As discussed in Section 7.5 look for a ground wire, unless the main panel and subpanel are connected by metal conduit.

7.7.3   Conditions Found with Fuses or Breakers

Common problems include—

1. Fuses or breakers too big
2. Double taps
3. Multi-wire circuits on one bus

TABLE 7.3   Common Wire Sizes for Larger Appliances

Appliance	Common Copper Wire Size (AWG)
Water Heater	#12, #10
Dryer	#10
Stove	#8
Central A/C	#12, #10, #8
Sauna	#10, #8

Fuses or Breakers Too Big

Overfusing

This is one of the most common electrical problems. You can only verify it by taking the cover off the electrical panel, and comparing the wire size to the size of the fuses or breakers. This is often referred to as **overfusing,** and is an electrical hazard.

STRATEGY

Check the sizes of fuses or breakers against the size of the wires. Where you can't verify they are properly matched, recommend that they be checked. Where fuse pullouts cannot be examined for fear of disconnecting power to an appliance, you should recommend a follow-up inspection of these fuses.

Checking Wire Size

You can usually determine the wire size by reading it off the sheathing. Where you can't, use a comparative technique, checking against known wire samples, either in the panel, or in samples you carry with you.

Color-Coded Fuses

Fuse sizes and breaker sizes can usually be read easily. Color coding on fuses and some breakers also helps. Blue is 15 amps. Orange is 20 amps. Red is 25 amps. Green is 30 amps.

Fuses Only Seem Oversized

Sometimes fuses for electric heaters seem oversized. They are often sized appropriately. For example, 14 gauge wire, which usually requires 15-amp fuses, is all right with 20-amp fuses in many cases with an electric heater. Similarly, 30-amp fuses on 12 gauge wire, which usually needs 20-amp fuses, may also be all right. This assumes that it is copper wire, and that the circuit is dedicated to the permanent electric heater.

Dedicated Circuits

Dedicated circuits for air conditioners often appear overfused, but are acceptable. The data plate on the air conditioner is what determines the fuse or breaker size, and the minimum circuit ampacity.

It's a good idea to know the common wire sizes used for the major appliances. This may allow you to recognize when the wire is inappropriate for the appliance. The table above lists common wire sizes for larger appliances.

Further Evaluation

If you suspect the wire is too small for the load, recommend having it checked by an electrician. If the breaker is correct for the wire, it may trip frequently. In addition, an undersized wire can lead to excessive voltage drop, which will cause the appliance to run incorrectly.

When the Fuse Size Looks Right but Isn't

Sometimes you can be fooled when checking the size of the fuse against the size of the wire at the panel. If you have a 30-amp fuse and a 10 gauge wire, everything will be fine. What you may not know and won't likely discover during a home inspection is that the 10 gauge wire may be spliced with 14 gauge wire at a box somewhere along the circuit. The 14 gauge wire circuit is not adequately protected by the 30-amp fuse.

Watch for Mixed Wire Sizes

Electrical codes don't allow this practice for obvious reasons, but that doesn't mean it's never done. You'd have to be very sharp, and perhaps lucky, to pick this up during

F I G U R E 7.28   Pigtailing to Avoid Double Taps

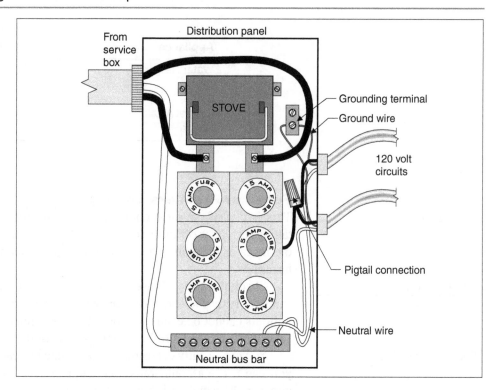

a home inspection. Some inspectors try to follow the entire length of the larger (240V) appliance circuits to check for splices or connection points.

Double Taps

Double tapping (double lugging) is the term for attaching two wires to a single fuse or breaker. Most terminals are not designed to accommodate two wires. The risk of a poor connection is greater with double taps.

Some electrical inspectors will allow double taps if wires are the same size and if the connection looks good. As inspectors, you should always note double taps. Explain that some authorities will accept this situation, but suggest that they have it checked out. Speak to your local utility, inspectors and electricians to see what their position is.

Sometimes double taps are solved by taking the two wires that are attached to a terminal screw and removing them both. The wires are then **pigtailed** together with

Pigtailing

one end of a third short wire (Figure 7.28). The other end of the third wire is attached to the fuse or breaker terminal. This eliminates the double lugging, although it creates one more connection in the box.

Fewer Splices Are Better

Most utilities will accept this solution, although every additional splice is another possible poor connection. Quality work uses the minimum number of connections.

Transformers

Sometimes double taps are accepted where the second wire is a low voltage transformer for a door bell or telephone system, for example. However, double taps are considered more problematic where the two wires are different sizes.

Special Breakers

Some special breakers are designed to hold two wires. In this case, double taps are often permitted. To be on the safe side, you should note all double taps, and let an electrician make the final call.

Multi-Wire Circuits Fed by One Bus

Multi-wire branch circuits including circuits for split receptacles (two 120-volt circuits), and 240-volt circuits, have two hot wires. The two hot wires should be a red and a black. In some cases, circuits will be fed with two blacks or two reds accidentally.

240-Volt Circuits

On a 240-volt circuit, the appliance won't work properly since the appliance is seeing only 120 volts. This situation is usually corrected promptly because the appliance doesn't work properly or doesn't work at all. You won't often see this in the field.

The more subtle situation is the multi-wire 120-volt branch circuit, including split-receptacle circuit. Split duplex receptacles have the top half on one circuit and the bottom half on another. A dishwasher and garbage disposal, for example, can be plugged into the same receptacle without blowing a fuse or tripping the breaker. The top half of the receptacle is on one fuse or breaker and the bottom half is on another.

Split Receptacles

3 Conductor Cable

Normally, electricians run three-conductor cable to these receptacles. This is a cable with a black wire, a red wire and a white wire. The black wire may feed the dishwasher, and the red wire may feed the garbage disposal.

It is important that the black wire and red wire are fed from different bus bars at the panel. That is, the black wire must be fed by the black service entrance conductor and the red wire must be fed by the red service entrance conductor. Why does this matter?

The black wire and the red wire are out of synchronization. This becomes important when we look closely at how the circuit is completed in a split-receptacle multi-wire circuit. We said that the cable had a black, a red and a white wire. The white wire is the return path for both the black and the red wire. Yet it isn't any bigger than the black or the red wire. Won't the white wire be overloaded?

White Wire Serves Red and Black

The answer lies in the black and the red wires being out of synchronization. The current flowing through the neutral wire is much smaller than you would expect.

Breaker Panels Have Staggered Buses

You can usually identify which bus the breakers are attached to. Many modern breakers are finger-jointed so that adjacent breaker positions are on opposite bus bars. You have to be careful, though, because while this applies to most panels, it does not apply to all. Also, there are some panels where **most** of the adjacent breaker positions are on opposite poles, but not all of them. This is something we'll have to leave to the electricians to verify, since we don't touch or dismantle the electrical equipment within the panel.

The same situation applies to fuses. In most situations you'll be able to tell whether the two fuses in a pullout are on different poles. Occasionally you won't be sure.

Twin Breakers

Twin breakers have two breakers that occupy a single slot in a panel. These twins are effectively adjacent breakers on the same pole. Multi-wire branch circuits should not be connected to twin breakers.

One of the clues you can use is to look closely at the neutral wire. The chances are high that if the black and the red both come off the same pole, the neutral wire will have overheated. Look for discoloration or melted insulation, for example, on the white wire. Look closely where it joins the neutral bar in the panel.

7.7.4   Conditions Found with Fuses Only

The items in Section 7.7.3 apply to both fuses and breakers. These problems are specific to fuses:

1. fuses loose
2. fuse holders loose or broken
3. fuses for multi-wire circuits not linked

Fuses Loose

STRATEGY

Where you notice that fuses are loose, they should be written up. We are not supposed to correct deficiencies we find in houses, although you may be unable to resist the temptation to simply tighten the fuse rather than to write up a loose fuse as a defect.

Fuse Holders Loose or Broken

Sometimes the supports for the fuses are worn or broken and will not stay securely in their position in the panel. In other cases, they won't hold the fuses securely. This is particularly true of pullouts, often associated with 240-volt circuits.

STRATEGY

Where fuse holders are loose, or there are pieces obviously broken, replacement of the components or the entire panel should be recommended.

Fuses for Multi-Wire Circuits not Linked

A multi-wire circuit has a red and a black wire. This is typical of all 240-volt circuits. It's also true of 120-volt circuits going to split receptacles, for example. We talked earlier about the danger of these multi-wire circuits. Since there are two conductors that are both hot (black and red) going to the same place, you need two fuses. Removing one fuse and having the circuit not work can be very misleading. People will think there is no electricity in the circuit and start to work on it. Obviously, the other wire will still be hot and people can be electrocuted.

The solution is to make sure that when you disconnect the circuit, you have to pull out two fuses at the same time. Multi-wire circuits should be on fuse pullouts if the two circuits end at the same location (e.g., a duplex receptacle). Where this is not done, recommend rearrangement.

STRATEGY

Look for red wires at the panel. Every one should be on a pullout fuse block. If in doubt, recommend that it be checked. There are some exceptions, so don't take too strong a position.

7.7.5   Conditions Found with Breakers Only

Common problems include—

1. multi-wire circuits not linked
2. too many breakers
3. wrong breaker in panel
4. loose breakers

Multi-Wire Circuits Not Linked

We've talked about requiring fuse pullouts for multi-wire circuits that end at the same location. On circuit breakers, we have to mechanically tie the two breakers together to ensure that both the red and the black are disconnected before we work on the circuit.

F I G U R E 7.29   Special Circuit Breakers for 240 Volts

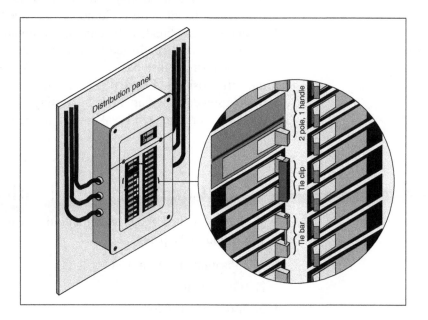

These ties or links may be a metal cap that slips over the breaker handles (Figure 7.29). In some cases, it is a metal bar that slips through the holes in the breaker handles. In other cases, the breaker may have a single handle (throw) but double poles. Any of these is satisfactory.

STRATEGY

Again, watch for red wires in the panel. These will usually be part of a three-conductor cable and part of a multi-wire or 240-volt circuit. When in doubt, get it checked since there are exceptions.

Too Many Breakers

Every panel is designed to accommodate a given number of circuits. Some manufacturers provide half-sized **twin breakers** so you can get two circuits into a spot designed for one breaker in the panel. This is convenient because it allows you to squeeze an extra circuit in, but it can lead to too many circuits in the panel.

STRATEGY

There should not be more circuits used in the panel than the panel is rated for. This information is usually on the panel label. A total of 42 single-pole circuits is the maximum allowed in the largest panel available.

Wrong Breaker in Panel

Every panel manufacturer makes breakers for its panels. Only those breakers designed for that panel should be used in it. Different breakers may not fit properly and may create dangerous, loose connections.

STRATEGY

Question the installation of breakers made by one company in a panel made by a different company. Again, note this as a question rather than a conclusion. The situation should be described as unusual and the possible problem discussed with the client (loose connections, overheating, electrical shock, etc.).

Loose or Damaged Breakers

One breaker that is obviously misaligned from the rest is probably loose. While we do not recommend touching components inside the panel, you should be able to touch the breaker handle safely. Homeowners have to do this to turn the circuit breaker on and off. Any breakers that are loose should be noted for replacement.

Breakers with damaged bodies or handles should be replaced. What do you do when you find a fuse blown or missing? What if you find a breaker tripped or in the "off" position? **Leave it!** There is usually a good reason it is off. You can electrocute someone or start a fire by turning the circuit back on.

Loose or damaged breakers should be reported as a priority item for safety reasons.

7.7.6   Conditions Found with Panel Wires

We haven't talked about branch circuit wiring yet, so we'll only deal with issues you'll find in the panel.

1. Sheathing not removed
2. Overheating
3. Loose connections
4. Damaged
5. Not well secured
6. Wires crossing bus bars
7. Abandoned wires in the panel

Sheathing Not Removed

The sheathing should be stripped off wires inside the panel. The sheathing should remain where the wire is secured by cable clamps as it enters the panel. However, the sheathing should not project more than about an inch into the panel. This makes the wire hard to work with, allows heat to build up and adds fuel to a fire in the panel.

Note any cable sheathing extending more than one inch into the panel. Also make sure that the sheathing does extend into the panel. The sheathing protects the wire where it is clamped in place coming into the panel.

Overheating

We've talked about overheating and how you should look carefully for it on the neutrals of multi-wire circuits. You should also be looking at the termination point of each wire for evidence of overheating: discoloration, melting insulation, smell, and actual heat.

Loose Connections

A loose connection is dangerous. These cause more electrical fires than any other electrical problem. Look for these at the fuse or breaker terminals, the neutral bars, the ground connections, any splices in the panel and at the lugs on the bus bars.

A loose connection may cause excessive voltage drop in the circuit. This may show up as a dim light, for example.

Some inspectors pull gently on the wires to check that they are secured. We consider this dangerous and do not recommend it.

F I G U R E 7.30   Securing Wires

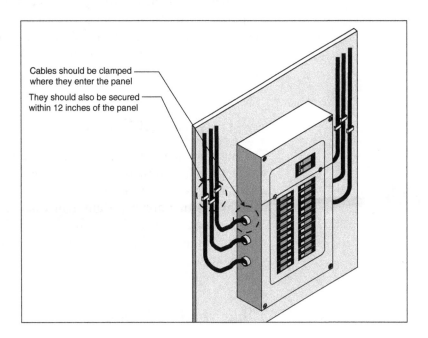

Cables should be clamped
where they enter the panel

They should also be secured
within 12 inches of the panel

Damaged

STRATEGY

Where insulation is missing or split, the wire should be repaired or replaced. Many electricians consider replacement the only respectable repair.

Insulation can also be brittle and broken due to age or overheating. Again, this should probably be replaced.

Not Well Secured

STRATEGY

Cables should be clamped where they come into the panel (Figure 7.30). They should be held securely in place, but not pinched between sharp metal edges.

Look at each cable as it enters the panel and make sure it is well secured. Some inspectors pull lightly on each cable outside the panel to make sure it is well connected to the panel itself.

Wires should also be secured to wall studs or some other firm substrate within 12 inches of leaving the panel.

Wires Crossing Bus Bars

STRATEGY

Wires should not be run across the face of bus bars. Wires should be arranged to run around bus bars down the sides and across the bottoms of panels.

Rerouting wires within the panel is usually not a big problem unless they have been cut too short. In this case, the section of wire will have to be spliced or replaced.

Abandoned Wires in the Panel

STRATEGY

One is never sure whether the wire ends are live. Abandoned wires should be removed from the panel.

7.8 BRANCH CIRCUIT WIRING (DISTRIBUTION WIRING)

Power from Panel to Point of Use

These wires carry the electricity from the main distribution panel or subpanels to the points of use. These include receptacles, lights, switches, and appliances such as stoves, dishwashers, garbage disposals, furnaces, and air conditioners. The job of branch circuit wiring is to get the electricity from the source to the destination safely.

7.8.1 Types of Wires

Copper and Aluminum

The most common household wiring is **copper. Aluminum,** which is silver colored, was a popular alternative from the mid 1960s until the late 1970s. While aluminum wires aren't used much for branch circuits in new work, you'll see them in many existing homes. Aluminum wires are still commonly used for service entrance conductors, and some of the large 240-volt circuits still use aluminum wire (stoves and clothes dryers, for example). We'll talk more about aluminum wire shortly.

7.8.2 Cable Types

NM Cable

There are different types of cable for different uses. The most common distribution wiring in houses is NM (which stands for **Non-Metallic** sheathed cable). This is also called Romex or Loomex, brand names for this type of wire. This cable has a paper, cloth or plastic (most modern) sheathing. This type of wire is widely used, but is not permitted in some areas. Check your rules!

UF BX

UF (undergound feeder) cable is rated for underground use. BX cable (or AC-90 cable) is a flexible metal-jacketed cable. Some people refer to this as **armored cable.** It is typically used where the wire might be subjected to mechanical damage. It was often used to feed furnaces, boilers and water heaters, although most modern codes don't require that.

7.8.3 Wire Insulation and Sheathing

Insulation

The **insulation** refers to the material wrapped around the individual wires. On old wire, it was rubber (knob-and-tube, for example). On more modern wire, it is plastic.

Sheathing

The **sheathing** forms the cable, wrapping around the insulated black, white and/or red wires and the uninsulated ground wire, if there is one. The sheathing is what you can see and touch, typically in the unfinished areas of homes and garages.

Older wires have cloth or paper sheathing. Newer wires have plastic sheathing.

Functions

The function of the insulation is to keep the wires from touching each other within the cable. The function of the sheathing is to provide mechanical protection for the conductors and their insulation.

Certain types of wires are typical of certain time periods. Allowing for regional differences, we can generally say the following wires were used during the periods described in Table 7.4.

TABLE 7.4   Wires and Time Periods of Use

Wire Type	Dates of Use
Knob-and-tube	1920 to 1950
Cloth-sheathed, two- or three-wire cables with no ground wire	1945 to the early 1960s
Cloth-sheathed cable with an integral ground wire	Early 1960s to early 1970s
Cloth-sheathed aluminum cable with integral ground	1964 to 1978
Plastic-sheathed aluminum cable with integral ground	1974 to 1978
Plastic-sheathed copper cable with integral ground	1974 to date

7.8.4   Number of Conductors

Two-Conductor Cables

The knob-and-tube are single-wire cables. Modern wires are typically two or three wires (black, white and sometimes red) and after the mid-1960s, they also included an uninsulated ground wire.

Two-Conductor Plus-Ground Cables

The **two-conductor-plus-ground** cables are used for most normal household circuits (Figure 7.31). (Remember, **conductor** is just a fancy word for **wire.**) The three-conductor-plus-ground cables are typically used for 240-volt appliances and multi-wire branch circuits, including split receptacles.

7.8.5   Wire Sizes

14 and 12 Gauge Wire

Fourteen gauge wire is the most common in residential branch circuits (Figure 7.32). Twelve gauge wire with 20-amp fuses is currently required for at least two circuits.

FIGURE 7.31   Number of Conductors

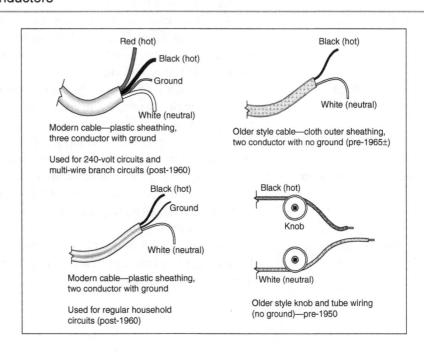

Red (hot)
Black (hot)
Ground
White (neutral)
Modern cable—plastic sheathing, three conductor with ground

Used for 240-volt circuits and multi-wire branch circuits (post-1960)

Black (hot)
Ground
White (neutral)
Modern cable—plastic sheathing, two conductor with ground

Used for regular household circuits (post-1960)

Black (hot)
White (neutral)
Older style cable—cloth outer sheathing, two conductor with no ground (pre-1965±)

Black (hot)
Knob
White (neutral)
Older style knob and tube wiring (no ground)—pre-1950

F I G U R E 7.32   Common Household Wire and Fuse Sizes

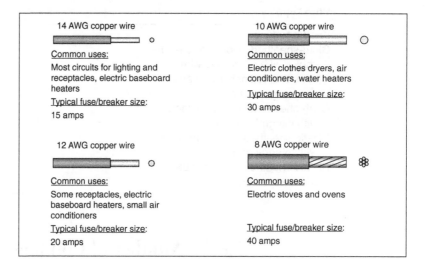

14 AWG copper wire

Common uses:
Most circuits for lighting and receptacles, electric baseboard heaters
Typical fuse/breaker size:
15 amps

12 AWG copper wire

Common uses:
Some receptacles, electric baseboard heaters, small air conditioners
Typical fuse/breaker size:
20 amps

10 AWG copper wire

Common uses:
Electric clothes dryers, air conditioners, water heaters
Typical fuse/breaker size:
30 amps

8 AWG copper wire

Common uses:
Electric stoves and ovens
Typical fuse/breaker size:
40 amps

12 Gauge

Twelve gauge wires are used for some electric baseboard heaters, water heaters, dish washers, garbage disposals, and private well pumps.

10 Gauge

Ten gauge wires are typically used for air conditioners, saunas, electric clothes dryers, some electric water heaters, some cooktops and ovens.

8 Gauge

Eight gauge wire is used for stoves and large air conditioners.

Note: This is all copper wire we're talking about. Aluminum wires are usually one size larger, since aluminum does not conduct electricity as well as copper.

7.8.6   Number of Circuits

12 Points per Circuit

There is no magic number of circuits required in a house. No more than 12 outlets and/or lights should be on a single branch circuit. The acceptable number of circuits is largely a function of lifestyle.

10 to 20 Circuits Typical

The distribution panel and subpanel (if there is one) will tell you the number of circuits in a house. You may have as few as four 120-volt branch circuits or as many as 42. We often see 10 to 20 such circuits. You have to make a judgment call about whether that's adequate.

One Outlet per Room Not Enough

You will get some clues as you move through the house. For example, if there is only one electrical receptacle in each room, that isn't enough. An insufficient number of plugs may encourage people to overuse extension cords, which isn't safe. That usually corresponds with a small number of branch circuits at the panel. People should add more receptacles, and will often have to add more branch circuits.

One Kitchen Counter Outlet Not Enough

If there is only one kitchen counter receptacle, the distribution network may have to be expanded. Remember that this has nothing to do with service size. We're simply talking about adding more branches to the tree. This doesn't change the size of the tree trunk.

More Outlets and Lights May Mean More Circuits

There is a relationship, of course, between the number of branch circuits and the number of outlets and lights. The more outlets and lights you want, the more circuits you should have.

FIGURE 7.33   Types of Connections

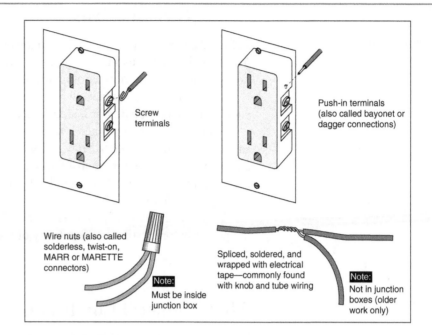

7.8.7   Connectors

No Open Splices

Wires should be connected to each other or to fixtures only inside electrical boxes. Connections can be in the panel box, junction boxes, switch boxes, receptacle boxes, and light boxes, for example. You should not see any open splices in the wire. Knob-and-tube is the only exception to this, and then only on original (pre-1950) work. Knob-and-tube wire should be joined to modern 2-conductor cable in a junction box.

Wires Secured to Terminal Screws

The wires themselves are usually attached to **screw terminals** (Figure 7.33). The wire insulation is stripped off for about three-quarters of an inch. The wire is turned clockwise around the screw head about three-quarters of a turn, and the screw head is tightened to hold the wire in place.

Push-In Connections

There are also **push-in terminals** where about one-half inch of the insulation is stripped off the wire and the wire is pushed straight into a hole, usually in the back of a switch or receptacle. These are also called **bayonet** or **dagger** connections. Many electricians are critical of the quality of push-in terminals, although they do make the work go faster. Some say the wire is easily nicked with this type of connector.

Soldered and Taped Connections Wire Nuts

Wires may also be joined by twisting together, soldering, and wrapping the connection in electrical tape, all inside a junction box. This is rarely done anymore. Most taped connections do not have any soldering and suggest low-quality work. Wires can also be joined with **wire nuts** (also called **solderless connectors, insulated twist-on connectors** or **Marr connectors**). **Marr** and **Marrette** are brand names for a common type of wire nut. Again, these should be inside boxes.

Loose Connections

While there are many ways to secure wires, loose connections are a possibility with any of them. Watch for loose connections and the overheating that results. Be suspicious of taped connections, even inside boxes.

7.8.8   General Strategy for Inspecting Branch Circuit Wiring

Follow the Wiring

Follow the wires where you can, from the panel through to their termination points. You'll typically be testing receptacles, switches and lights as you go through the house. Where wiring runs through unfinished areas, look at the visible wiring.

Look for wiring in places where it shouldn't be (exposed to damage or heat), such as along baseboards or inside closets.

Don't Do Flex Test

Some inspectors recommend flexing wires to make sure they are still pliable. Some say wires should be able to be bent 180° between your fingers. We feel that this is a dangerous test, since if the insulation is brittle and breaks off, you may find yourself holding a hot wire. This can also be a destructive test if the insulation cracks while you're flexing it.

We believe this kind of test is better left to an electrician, who can disconnect the power before testing the flexibility of the wire, and can repair any damage that results.

7.8.9   General Conditions

Let's look at some of the branch circuit wire problems you'll commonly see.

1. Damaged
2. Not well secured
3. Loose connections
4. Open splices
5. Wires too close to ducts, pipes, vents, chimneys and flues
6. Wires too close to the edge of studs or joists
7. Wires run through steel studs without protection
8. Exposed wires on walls or ceilings
9. Exposed wires in attics
10. Indoor cable used outdoors
11. Buried cable not rated for buried use
12. Household wiring used as extension cord or extension cord used as permanent wiring
13. Undersized wire
14. Improper color coding
15. Abandoned wire

Note: We're going to talk about knob-and-tube and aluminum wiring separately. The conditions we'll discuss here apply to knob-and-tube and aluminum wiring as well. Special conditions applying only to those will be discussed separately.

IMPLICATION

The implication for all of these is possible electric shock or fire.

Damaged Wire

Damaged wire includes wire that has been cut or pinched, wire that has been chewed on by pests, burned wire, and wire with cracked (brittle) insulation.

STRATEGY

Follow as much of the wiring as you can to make sure it is intact. Pay particular attention where wire passes through materials, especially if they are sharp. Look closely where wire is held by staples to make sure the staples haven't damaged the wire. Exposed wires are particularly susceptible to damage.

Wires are most likely to be chewed in attics where pests are commonly found.

Wire not Well Secured

Wire should be held in place with **strain relief clamps** wherever it goes into a box. Wire should also be secured within 12 inches of leaving a box, usually with a staple. Wire running through the house should be secured (this includes supporting it by a hole through a joist or stud) every 4$\frac{1}{2}$ feet.

As you follow the wire, make sure it's well supported. It's usually easy to add support. Poorly supported wires are a sign of amateurish work, and should make you look more closely.

Loose Connections

Wherever wires are secured, whether with terminal screws, push-in connectors or solderless connectors, they should be tight. You'll normally just get a look at connections at the panel. The Standards do not require removing cover plates from receptacles or light switches. Many inspectors do this in selected areas to get a look at wall insulation, to determine the type of wire feeding the receptacle, to determine whether the receptacle is suitable for aluminum wire, to look for evidence of overheating, to determine whether a receptacle is a split receptacle, or to determine whether 20-amp rated receptacles are fed by 12 gauge wire.

Wherever you remove cover plates, including at the panel, look at the connections. Be very careful what you touch. We do not recommend that you test connection tightness by touching or pulling on the wires. You should be looking for evidence of loose connections, which is most often overheating.

Open Splices

All connections or splices should be in junction boxes.

Note any connections that are not in boxes. Adding a junction box is usually not a difficult task.

Wires Too Close to Ducts, Pipes, Vents, Chimneys, and Flues

Wires should be at least one inch away from ducts and pipes. Often a piece of insulation is used to separate the wire from the ducts or pipes. This is fine. The distance from vents, chimneys and flues, depends on the fuels. Typically, for a single-wall metal vent connector, the wire should be 6 inches away if the fuel is gas, 9 inches (18 inches in some areas) away if the fuel is oil, and 18 inches away if the fuel is wood. There may be local variations, but this is a good starting point.

As you follow the wire through, make sure the wire won't overheat because it's too close to these heat sources. Pay particular attention to wires run through furnace rooms.

These clearances apply to conduits as well as cables. Plastic conduit is obviously susceptible to high temperatures. Metal conduit may also conduct heat and transfer it into the wires, diminishing their ability to carry electricity.

Wires Too Close to the Edge of Studs or Joists

Wires should be 1$\frac{1}{4}$ inches away from the face of studs or joists.

Where you see wires closer than this to the edge, recommend that protective metal plates be provided over the edge of the joists or studs. There are many places this may happen where you'll never know.

STRATEGY

STRATEGY

STRATEGY

STRATEGY

STRATEGY

Wires Run through Steel Studs without Protection

The raw edges of steel studs can cut non-metallic sheathed wire. In commercial installations, BX (armored) cable or rigid conduit is used. In single family homes, most jurisdictions allow the use of non-metallic sheathed cable with special grommets that protect the wire where it passes through studs.

Wires cannot be fastened directly to metal studs. They must stand off the studs with an insulator at a distance of at least one-quarter of an inch in most areas.

STRATEGY

Where you can look at metal studs, check for damage to the wire. Check for plastic sleeves or grommets where the wires penetrate the studs and make sure wires are not attached directly to the studs.

This is an area that may change since steel frame construction is becoming popular. Other solutions may be developed, and rule changes are expected. Again, you may want to be cautious with your criticism. It may be best to recommend further investigation to confirm your suspicions.

Exposed Wires on Walls or Ceilings

Wires that are not in conduit or are not armored should not be run where they can be damaged by normal day-to-day activities. Wires shouldn't be run along baseboards, around doorframes, in closets, etc. Where these are found, they should be relocated or protected. There are covers available to protect surface-mounted wire.

STRATEGY

Wires should not run on walls where they can be mechanically damaged; for example, anywhere within 5 to 7 feet of the floor. We encourage you to use common sense. No matter where the wire is, if it's likely to be damaged, recommend protection.

Wires run to appliances such as furnaces and water heaters have to be in armored cable in many jurisdictions because they are exposed to damage where they run along beside the appliance. Know what is required in your area and watch for improper work.

Exposed Wires in Attics

Wires should not be run on the tops of ceiling joists in attics. It's easy to step on the wires here, especially if they're concealed below insulation. It's better to run the wires through the ceiling joists. Cables within six feet of the access hatch should be protected from mechanical damage. If there is a stairway or built-in ladder to access the attic, wires should be protected in attic areas with seven feet or more of headroom.

STRATEGY

Check what is accepted in your area. This is a rule you'll find broken all the time, and frankly, most clients won't follow your advice on this one. However, if you don't mention it, an electrical inspector who comes along later will mention it. More importantly, if you don't mention it and someone in the attic electrocutes themselves, chances are good you'll hear about it.

Indoor Cable Used Outdoors

NM cable is suitable for dry environments. It can't be used outdoors.

STRATEGY

Look for indoor-rated cable on exterior wiring.

Buried Cable Not Rated for Buried Use

STRATEGY

Where you can see buried cable coming out of the ground, check to see what type of cable it is. It should be rated for underground use. If you're not sure, jot down the type of wire and phone an electrical supply house or check another reference.

Household Wiring Used as Extension Cord or Extension Cord Used as Permanent Wiring

NM type cable should not be used as portable extension cords. It is not designed to be coiled and flexed the way extension cords are.

STRATEGY

Extension cords should not be fastened in place or concealed in walls, floors or ceilings.

Extension cord arrangements may disappear before your client takes possession of the house. However, if you see this installation, make a note of it and explain the problem to your client.

Undersized Wire

The wire should be a match for the fuse or breaker size and should be continuous throughout the circuit. It is not appropriate to step down the size of the wire after leaving the box.

STRATEGY

Where wiring is visible, check that its size is not reduced in downstream sections. In addition, wiring in the panel should be proper for the fuse size. Where you have a 30-amp fuse, 12 or 14 gauge size is not appropriate. You may have to change the fuse or breaker, or, depending on the appliance served, you may have to change the wire. Another way of saying that the circuit is **overfused** is saying the wire is **undersized.**

Improper Color Coding

Normally, black and red wires signify hot wires and white wires are neutral. But life isn't always simple.

Sometimes white wires can act as black wires. (Don't you just hate it?) Let's look at an example.

When White Wires Are Black or Red

Sometimes electricians want to run 240-volt balanced-load circuits (for example, an electric baseboard heater or water heater). They don't need to use three-conductor cable because the black acts as white when it's at rest, and the red acts as white when it's at rest. We don't need a white wire! However, electricians often don't have two-conductor cable with a black wire and red wire with them. They do, however, almost always have black and white two-conductor cable, so they run a 240-volt circuit with the black wire attached to one breaker and the white wire (acting as a red) attached to another breaker.

Wrap Ends of White Wire with Black Tape

This is acceptable as long as the white wire is color coded at each end to show that it is acting as black or red. Wrapping the last inch or two of wire with black electrical tape is a common way to accomplish this.

STRATEGY

If you look in a panel and see a white wire attached to a fuse or breaker terminal, your first instinct is that it is wrong. This is a good instinct. It might be all right, but if the white wire is acting as a hot (black or red) wire, it should be color coded black at the ends to indicate this. Where this is not done, you should write up the situation as suspect and call for checking by an electrician.

Abandoned Wire

Abandoned wire should always be removed.

STRATEGY

When looking at the ends of an abandoned wire, you can't tell whether it's live. Many people assume it's not. If you're wrong, there's a big price to be paid. The best practice is to remove any abandoned wire so there is no possibility of leaving a live wire exposed.

FIGURE 7.34   Knob and Tube Wiring

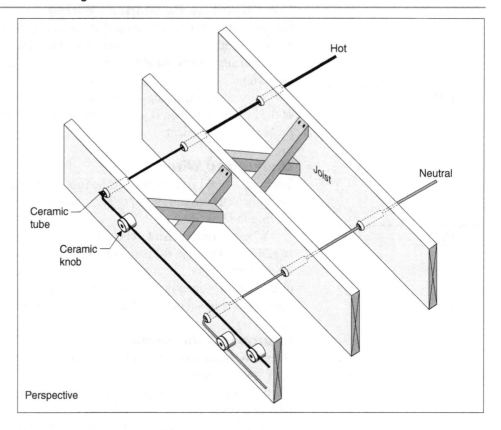

Perspective

7.8.10   Knob-And-Tube Wire Conditions

Most of the problems we have been talking about with respect to panels and wiring also apply to knob-and-tube systems. Some issues are more common with knob-and-tube wiring.

Identifying Knob-and-Tube

Knob-and-tube wiring is easy to identify (Figure 7.34). Two separate cables run to each electrical point, one black, one white. Sometimes the sheathing is black on one and is white on the other, although this isn't always the case. The ceramic knobs and tubes used to support the wire also clearly identify this kind of wiring. Knob-and-tube wiring was common until 1950 and used into the 1960s in some areas. Knob-and-tube wire was made in several gauges. Branch circuit wiring was often 12 gauge.

Remember that there will be no original equipment ground wires anywhere in the distribution system with knob-and-tube wiring. Original connections are often not in junction boxes. Connections are made by splicing, soldering and taping the wires. Knob-and-tube wiring was no longer used by the time multi-wire branch circuits were introduced.

Problems specific to knob-and-tube wiring include the following:

1. Connections not in boxes

2. Brittle wire, insulation or sheathing

3. Wire buried in insulation

4. Fused neutrals

Connections Not in Boxes

The original spliced connections did not have to be in junction boxes. This is acceptable as long as the connections are original, since we have some confidence that the splices are appropriately made by twisting the wires together, then properly soldering, and finally taping with the old, dull black, cloth tape.

Modern plastic electrical tape (the black shiny stuff) on a knob-and-tube connection, or taped connections with knob-and-tube wiring joining modern two-conductor cable, are not acceptable to most authorities. The only knob-and-tube connections that don't have to be in junction boxes are original ones. Knob-and-tube wire should join modern two-conductor cable in a junction box.

Brittle Wire, Insulation, or Sheathing

Older Wire

Another issue with knob-and-tube wiring is the age of the wire. While the copper does not fail under normal work loads, a house wiring system that's been around for a long time may well have been overfused at some time in the past, and the wire may have been overworked. The older it is, the more likely it is to have been abused at some point.

Insulation and Sheathing

The rubber insulation or the cloth sheathing may deteriorate over time, become brittle and start to fall off. This is a function of age and high temperatures. The high temperatures may be high ambient temperatures, or due to overfusing. In either case, watch for insulation problems on knob-and-tube wiring. Resist the temptation to flex the wire to see if it's still supple. You may get a shock or damage the wire.

Problems with the sheathing and insulation are the most common failings of knob-and-tube wiring, other than amateurish modifications and extensions of the circuits.

Wire Buried in Insulation

Hard to Dissipate Heat

This leads us to the discussion of knob-and-tube wiring buried in attic insulation or in wall insulation. This is a controversial issue and different authorities have taken different positions. Some maintain that knob-and-tube wiring shouldn't be buried in insulation because that inhibits its ability to dissipate heat. It's true that all wire can work more comfortably if it's able to dissipate the heat generated as electricity flows through it. But there is a counterpoint.

Separate Wires May Be an Advantage

Since the black wires and white wires are usually separated by several inches in different cables, knob-and-tube might be better able to dissipate heat than modern cable. Modern two-conductor cable has the black wire and white wire less than one-quarter of an inch apart inside a plastic sheathing. It is harder for modern cable to dissipate heat than for knob-and-tube. This is probably only an issue where several cables are bundled together and there is heavy continuous loading on each cable.

Nonetheless, you should find out what is accepted practice in your area. In some jurisdictions, knob-and-tube wiring is only permitted in insulation if the insulation is non-combustible. Find out what your authority thinks is non-combustible. Some consider fiberglass insulation combustible (it really is at certain temperatures). Insulations made of cellulose, wood shavings, shaved leather, most plastics, etc., are combustible. Insulations made from vermiculite, gypsum slag and asbestos are not combustible, although asbestos has other issues.

Fused Neutrals

Because knob-and-tube installations are old, they may connect to old panels. Some of these old panels have **fused neutrals,** which can be dangerous.

T A B L E 7.5 Breaker Sizes for Aluminum Wire

Wire Size	Breaker or Fuse Size
12 gauge	15 amps
10 gauge	25 amps
8 gauge	30 amps
6 gauge	40 amps
4 gauge	55 amps

STRATEGY

When you see knob-and-tube wiring and an old ceramic panel, look for fused neutrals. We discussed these when we talked about problems in panels earlier. If the neutral wire and hot wire are both fused, only one is likely to blow, shutting off the circuit. If the neutral fuse blows, the circuit is live through its entire length. This is dangerous for anyone working on the circuit. Recommend replacement of panels with fused neutrals.

7.8.11 Aluminum Wire Conditions

The common problems specific to aluminum wire are—

1. Connectors not compatible with aluminum

2. No anti-oxidant grease on stranded wires

3. Overheating

Can Be in Old Houses

Aluminum wiring was used from the mid-1960s to the late 1970s. You probably won't find aluminum on branch circuit wiring in houses built after 1980. However, you will often find it in old houses. Electrical work performed in old houses from 1965 to 1978 commonly used aluminum wire.

The appropriate fuse or breaker sizes for common aluminum wire sizes are outlined in Table 7.5.

Connectors Not Compatible with Aluminum

Aluminum Problems

When aluminum wiring was introduced in the 1960s as a less expensive alternative to copper, people had already recognized that it didn't conduct electricity as well as copper. That problem could be handled by using slightly larger wire to carry the same amount of electricity. This was a good decision.

Some problems specific to aluminum weren't recognized for a few years: Aluminum wire—

1. tends to creep out from under terminal screws

2. forms a rust (oxide) that is an electrical insulator

3. is softer than copper and easier to damage when working with the wire

4. was, in some of the early wire, a low quality material, prone to weakness and breaking

Because of these issues, some house fires were attributed to aluminum wiring. By about 1970, the industry had redesigned many connectors specifically for aluminum.

CUAL

These were designated CUAL. They worked well, except on 120-volt branch-circuit receptacles (outlets). Some of the CUAL receptacles did not solve the over-

CO/ALR

heating problems with aluminum wire. A subsequent version known as **CO/ALR** was introduced in the early 1970s, and used tin-plated terminals. This version has worked well.

Switches

In some jurisdictions, CUAL is acceptable for switches. Other jurisdictions prefer a CO/ALR designation on switches. There are also jurisdictions which don't require any special connectors for switches because of the infrequency of problems. Again, learn what's accepted in your area.

Panel and Breakers
Should Be CUAL

Check for aluminum-compatible equipment elsewhere. At the panels, you should verify that the panels and their components are rated for use with aluminum. CUAL is an appropriate designation for service equipment, panels, circuit breakers, dryer receptacles, stove receptacles, etc.

Aluminum Compatible
Wire Nuts

Special wire nuts (also called solderless connectors or twist-on connectors) are designed for use with aluminum. It may be hard to identify them during a home inspection. If you see aluminum wiring in a home, you won't be able to check every connection anyway and you should be recommending an electrician check all connections, including the wire nuts. The best approach to aluminum wiring is to use equipment that is compatible with aluminum. A second choice, allowed in some areas, but discouraged in most, is **pigtailing.** The process involves using a piece of copper wire between the aluminum wire and the receptacle, for example. Pigtailing has the disadvantage of making boxes more crowded and adding more connections.

Pigtailing

Copalum

The aluminum-to-copper wire connection may be made with a proprietary system known as **Copalum.** These are not used at all in some areas. In other areas, they are quite common. Many consider this the best way to work with aluminum wire.

Split-Bolt Connectors

Split bolt connectors can be used to join copper and aluminum wires, although these are more common in industrial applications.

Bad Reputation

In any case, by the time the industry developed these changes to solve the problems with aluminum wiring, aluminum had received such a bad name that most manufacturers stopped making it.

Overheating

Overheating usually is the result of loose connections, slightly corroded connections and/or damaged wires. These problems occur at the ends of the wires where they are connected to fuse or breaker terminals, appliances, wire nuts, or equipment such as receptacles or switches. Receptacles are the most common problem area.

General Strategy for Inspecting Aluminum Wire

STRATEGY

Make sure you identify aluminum wiring if it is visible. Check for appropriate special connectors, or at least pigtailing. Know what approaches are accepted by your local electric company.

Watch for overheating, particularly at receptacles, but at all connections. Consider removing covers from at least some of the kitchen, bathroom and workroom receptacles. Look for anti-oxidant grease on stranded large wire connections (8 gauge and larger).

Remove Covers

Recommend Inspections

Recommend a detailed inspection by an electrician, unless you've evaluated every aluminum wire connection. This may include checking the torque on the breakers.

Recommend annual inspections of the wiring to ensure connections do not become loose.

Replace Small Amount   If there's only a little aluminum wiring in the house, rather than going through a lot of work to investigate, correct and maintain it, it is often simpler to replace it with copper.

Rewiring a whole house with copper is usually not practical or necessary.

Inspector in the House: The Tale of the Underfed Outlets

A few years ago, I was inspecting an older suburban bungalow. The listing bragged about the newly finished basement. The workmanship in the basement showed evidence of a do-it-yourself job—poorly fit trim, doors that did not close properly, and flooring that was not well sealed at the joints. Although there was not much to see, I had my suspicions and dug a little deeper. Removing cover plates from accessible electrical outlets showed an alarming consistency—rather than 12 or 14 gauge wire, the outlets were powered with telephone wire!

The lesson: trust your instincts. If it feels wrong, it probably is. Put another way, if the work that shows is bad, the work that doesn't is often worse.

7.9   LIGHTS, OUTLETS, SWITCHES, AND JUNCTION BOXES

In this section, we'll talk about checking things by taking covers off electrical outlets, light switches and junction boxes.

7.9.1   Conditions at Lights

Let's start by listing some of the common lighting problems we find.

1. Damaged or loose
2. Overheating
3. Inoperative
4. Obsolete
5. Not grounded
6. Missing
7. Poor stairway lighting
8. Conventional lights used in wet areas
9. Improper recessed light installations
10. Improper closet lighting
11. Heat lamps over doors
12. Isolating links needed on pull chains

IMPLICATIONS   The implications will be inadequate lighting and/or shock or fire hazard unless noted otherwise.

We're talking about lights that are permanent fixtures to the house. We do not test floor lamps, table lamps, etc. Testing lights is easy–you simply use the switch to turn them on and off.

STRATEGY

Damaged or Loose

Light fixtures that are damaged or loose may or may not be staying with the house. However, they may be a shock hazard or may be in danger of falling. Recommend they be repaired or replaced, as necessary.

STRATEGY

Overheating

Light fixtures are often out of reach and you may not detect an overheating situation. Where you are close to a light, you may be able to feel the heat, smell the burning insulation, or see evidence of charring or scorching. Many light fixtures get very hot under normal operation, and you have to be careful not to overreact.

Hot

Light bulbs are hot even when working properly. A 100-watt incandescent bulb has a surface temperature of roughly 380°F. A tungsten halogen bulb can be 480° or higher.

STRATEGY

Inoperative

There are many reasons why a light may not work. We should simply describe it as **inoperative** and leave the diagnosis to others.

STRATEGY

Obsolete

Light fixtures with exposed wire connections are obsolete and should be replaced. Any fixture with a bare wire secured to a terminal should be replaced.

STRATEGY

Not Grounded

All modern installations (post 1960) should have grounded light fixtures and light support boxes. However, it is beyond the scope of a home inspection to dismantle light fixtures to determine whether they are grounded.

STRATEGY

Missing

A light fixture should be provided in most rooms. Use common sense here. If part of the house cannot be lit, or cannot be lit from where you enter the room, recommend rearranging the lighting. Wall switches that control receptacles are an acceptable alternative to light fixtures. Lights are not needed in clothes closets, unless it's a walk-in closet.

It is also important that every door into the house has an exterior light. This is a convenience and safety issue.

STRATEGY

Poor Stairway Lighting

If the stairs have more than six treads, you should be able to turn the stairwell lighting on at either the top or the bottom. You may not need switching at both the top and the bottom for an unfinished basement. However, wherever somebody is likely to go up or down the stairs and stay until it gets dark, it makes good sense to provide three-way light switches.

STRATEGY

Conventional Lights Used in Wet Areas

Light fixtures in showers, saunas, or outdoors exposed to the weather, should be suitable for damp environments. These fixtures can usually be identified by a heavy gasket around the diffuser. If it looks like water could get into the light, you should question the installation and have it checked further.

Improper Recessed Light Installations

Two Types

As discussed in Chapter 5, **recessed light fixtures (potlights, can lights, high-hat light fixtures)** can be a fire hazard with respect to insulated ceilings.

Wrong Type of Bulbs

Another problem with recessed lights is the use of conventional light bulbs. Any light bulb that burns with the socket at the top and the bulb facing down is going to have heat collect around the socket. This is not an ideal situation. Light bulbs generally burn cooler and last longer if they burn with the base down. The problem is compounded if we don't use the proper bulbs, which are designed to reflect the light and heat downward.

Oversized Bulbs

Bulbs of the incorrect wattage can also be a problem with recessed lights. Bulbs that are too large build up heat and create a fire hazard. Some fixtures are rated for one size of bulb if they are not in an insulated ceiling, and a smaller bulb if they are in an insulated ceiling.

Many modern recessed lights use small halogen bulbs. These also can get quite hot. The halogen fixtures use small transformers at each light. These transformers should be removable for servicing. The wires on the lights themselves and on the cable coming in should be at least 12 inches long to allow maintenance.

STRATEGY

Be careful with recessed lights and treat all of them as a potential fire hazard. Check the type of fixture, whether it's in an insulated ceiling and for proper recessed light bulbs.

Improper Closet Lighting

STRATEGY

It doesn't make sense to put a light in a closet immediately above a shelf, where things will likely be stored around the light. This can be a fire hazard, and there is a danger of breaking the light and injuring someone with the broken glass.

Closet lights should be mounted on the ceiling away from the shelf, or on the wall above the door.

In some jurisdictions, bare bulbs are not permitted and the lights must be in fixtures. Cages around the bulbs are not acceptable in some areas. Check your local rules.

Heat Lamps over Doors

STRATEGY

Heat lamps have some of the inherent problems we talked about with recessed lights. They can also set fire to things underneath them. Doors should not be able to swing under heat lamps. Heat lamps should not be mounted above shower rods or shower doors. Towels thrown over the top of doors or rods can be ignited by heat lamps. Watch for this, and where you see heat lamps installed inappropriately, recommend they be rearranged.

Isolating Links Needed on Pull Chains

STRATEGY

Lights with metal pull chains to turn them on and off should have isolating links to prevent the pull chains from being alive electrically (Figure 7.35). You can usually see these insulating links. Heavy cardboard or plastic replaces some of the metal links, usually close to the fixture itself. If the pull chain does not have these links, you should question how the chain is electrically isolated from the light. Recommend further investigation.

7.9.2   Conditions at Receptacles (Outlets)

For this part of the inspection you'll need an inexpensive circuit tester, available at hardware or electrical supply stores.

They typically have three lights that indicate wires that are not connected, or are connected improperly. Some testers come with a push button to trip test GFIs. We don't use these models, for reasons discussed later in this section (See "Testing GFIs").

F I G U R E 7.35   Isolating Links Needed on Pull Chains

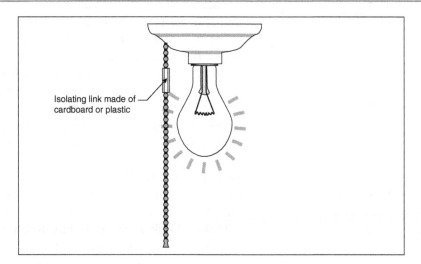

Isolating link made of cardboard or plastic

Now, let's look at branch-circuit outlets and some of their common problems:

1. Damaged
2. Loose
3. Overheating
4. Ungrounded outlets
5. Open neutral or open hot connections
6. Reversed polarity outlets
7. Inoperative
8. Wrong type receptacle
9. No GFIs
10. Overheated neutral on split receptacles
11. Worn receptacles
12. Broken pin or blade in slots
13. Not enough receptacles
14. Too far from basins

The causes will be self-evident for the most part, including mechanical damage, wear and tear or installation error. The implications continue to be shock and fire hazards.

Damaged

Outlets or their cover plates that are visibly damaged should be replaced. This is often mechanical damage caused by furniture.

Loose

Receptacles that are not well secured to their boxes can be dangerous. The hot terminals are often on the sides of outlets. If the outlet is loose in a metal box, it can touch the box, creating a very dangerous situation. When you use a circuit tester (sometimes called a circuit analyzer or plug-in tester), you'll get a sense of whether receptacles are loose.

Overheating

Evidence of overheating on electrical outlets may include discoloration or partial melting of the face. Overheating may also be apparent at the wire connections (melted insulation, charring or scorching, a smell of burned plastic, or warm to the touch) if the cover is removed.

Overheating is more common on aluminum-wired outlets. Overheating may also be more likely on push-in (backwired) receptacles. With aluminum or push-in receptacles, keep overheating in mind as a possibility at all the outlets you look at. In addition, focus on outlets used for heat-generating appliances, such as hair dryers, curling irons, kettles, toasters and microwave ovens.

Ungrounded Outlets

Two Slot Receptacles

Ungrounded receptacles with only two slots can only receive two-prong plugs. It is clear to everyone that the circuit and appliance are not grounded.

Box Not Grounded

There is a safety issue if the box itself is not grounded, as was a common installation practice until the early 1960s. If a hot wire or terminal from the outlet contacts the metal box, the live box becomes a shock and fire hazard.

Three-Slot Receptacles on Ungrounded Circuit

Ungrounded outlets create another safety issue if the old two-slot receptacle is replaced with a modern U-ground receptacle (with a third slot for the ground pin). These are often installed in old houses where there is no ground wire in the branch circuit wiring. A false sense of security is created since the outlet looks grounded, but is not.

It wasn't until the mid 1990s that the addition of a GFI (Ground Fault Interrupter) was considered an acceptable alternative to grounding in an existing installation.

GFI Instead of Grounding

GFI is not as good as grounding, in some respects. Let's look at an ungrounded receptacle with a GFI. If you plug in a power drill (with a grounded three-prong plug) and the hot wire inside the drill touches the metal case, the case will become live. When you pick up the drill, you will get a shock. If the ground pin in the drill plug was connected to a house ground system, you would not have gotten a shock.

However, while you'll get a shock, it will only be for a very brief interval, since the GFI will sense the imbalance in the circuit (as electricity flows through the black wire, through you into ground, but not through the neutral wire) and the breaker will trip.

Ground Only Old Outlets Where Needed

In practice, very few people ground their receptacles in an old house unless there is an appliance that relies on grounding. Any appliance with a three-prong plug relies on grounding. Home computers, for example, dissipate **static charges** through the ground wire. The GFI solution will not be helpful here. We need to ground the outlet.

Partial Update

Most inspectors point out ungrounded outlets but don't recommend complete updating. Clients should be helped to understand the issue and then make their own decisions. Partial updating is common.

When You Think Ungrounded Outlets Are Grounded

Sometimes your tester will tell you that a circuit is grounded even if it's not. For example, if a clothes washing machine is plugged into the outlet and you plug in a tester, there may be an inadvertent path to ground through the washing machine. The flow to ground would be from the ground pin in the tester, through the outlet, through the washing machine plug, back to the washing machine and possibly to the ground below the washing machine or through the water connections to the water piping out to ground.

The path to ground is not through a designed ground connection, but an accidental path through an appliance.

FIGURE 7.36   Reversed Polarity

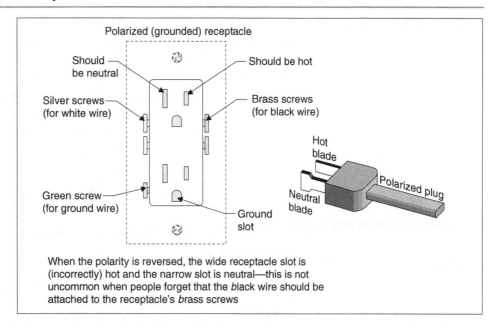

Polarized (grounded) receptacle

Should be neutral

Should be hot

Silver screws (for white wire)

Brass screws (for black wire)

Hot blade

Polarized plug

Neutral blade

Green screw (for ground wire)

Ground slot

When the polarity is reversed, the wide receptacle slot is (incorrectly) hot and the narrow slot is neutral—this is not uncommon when people forget that the *b*lack wire should be attached to the receptacle's *b*rass screws

You can avoid being fooled by unplugging appliances from outlets before testing. However, be careful that you do not disrupt household appliances by unplugging them. Home computers and VCRs, for example, should not be unplugged. Most inspectors don't unplug appliances to test the ground.

Open Neutral or Open Hot Connections

When you use your electrical tester, sometimes it will show **open neutral** or **open hot.** Open means not connected. In either of these cases, the outlet won't work. This is obviously the result of a wiring mistake and the outlet should be rewired. It usually means the wire is not attached to the outlet.

Reversed Polarity Outlets

Your electrical tester will sometimes show **reversed polarity.** What does this mean?

Polarity

Polarity is a confusing issue. Within 120-volt household circuits, if the polarity is correct, the black wire is the hot wire (ungrounded conductor) and the white wire is the neutral wire (grounded conductor). If the polarity is reversed, the white wire is hot and the black is neutral (Figure 7.36).

Switched Appliances

Polarity matters with appliances that have switches. When the appliance is plugged in, power should only go as far as the switch. If polarity is reversed, power will go through the entire appliance back to the switch. If a wire comes loose in the appliance, the entire case of the appliance may be "hot" electrically, even though the appliance is not on. This is a shock hazard.

Home inspectors should check the polarity of receptacles. If the receptacles are not polarized, this is not as issue. Polarized appliance plugs will not fit into non-polarized receptacles because the slots are both narrow. The wide blade for the neutral side will not fit in. We trust none of you will ever admit to filing off the wide flanges on the neutral blade, since this defeats the protection of polarization.

Test Polarity

Where you find polarized receptacles, which include some of the two-slot receptacles and all of the modern U-ground receptacles, we should be checking for polarity with a portable circuit analyzer. You should describe **reversed polarity** receptacles as needing rewiring.

Black Wire to Brass Screw

One of the ways to identify reversed polarity, other than with a tester, is by removing the outlet cover plate. The black wire is typically connected to the brass screw terminal on the outlet, and the white wire is connected to the silver. This color convention is useful but not 100 percent reliable for identifying reversed polarity.

Sometimes the outlet will appear to be wired properly when you take the cover off. The black wire correctly goes to the brass terminal and the white wire correctly goes to the silver terminal. The polarity may have been reversed somewhere upstream, perhaps right at the panel itself. That's why it's not completely reliable to look at the receptacle wiring connections to see if polarity is reversed.

Reversed polarity outlets often go unnoticed for a long time. Many appliances will work just fine. However, the polarity has to be right to provide the protection designed into the system.

Inoperative

STRATEGY

If the outlet is apparently unpowered during your test, it should be written up for improvement. Do not assume there are no hot wires to the outlet. Simply describe it as not working and in need of attention.

*There May Be
Power in Box*

Removing the cover will sometimes show why the outlet is not working. (Occasionally there will be no wires coming into the box!) However, in many cases, it won't be clear and you should not get into a trouble-shooting mode. You can be fooled if the outlet is controlled by a wall switch. Many rooms do not have overhead lights but have a switch on the wall. Make sure you flip the wall light switch before describing the outlet as inoperative. In some cases, both halves of a duplex receptacle are controlled by the wall switch. In other cases, only the top or bottom half of the receptacle is switched.

Switched Outlets

Wrong Type Receptacle

STRATEGY

Some 20-amp receptacles have a neutral slot at right angles to the hot slot. Conventional plugs will not fit into the slots. Others have one T-shaped slot that will accept 15-amp and 20-amp plugs.

In modern construction, 20-amp circuits are required for at least two circuits. These are often in the kitchen and dining room. Receptacles on these circuits should be rated at 20 amps.

*20-Amp Outlets Need
12 Gauge Wire and 20-Amp
Fuses*

Outlets rated at 20 amps should not be used on 15-amp circuits. If they are, recommend that these outlets be replaced. 20-amp outlets can be identified by a slot that is T-shaped rather than straight (Figure 7.37).

No GFIs

GFI and GFCI

A ground fault interrupter (**GFI**) is a special receptacle with ground fault protection. There are also ground fault circuit interrupters (**GFCI**) which are circuit breakers installed at the panel to provide ground fault protection for the whole circuit. Let's make sure we don't get confused between grounding, ground fault circuit interrupters and fuses or breakers.

Grounding

The equipment grounding wire in the branch circuits protects us by providing an emergency path for electricity when the electricity gets where it shouldn't. The ground wire presents a path that's more inviting to the electricity than flowing through us. If grounding systems work properly, we won't get electrical shocks even when things go wrong.

F I G U R E 7.37 Wrong Type Receptacle

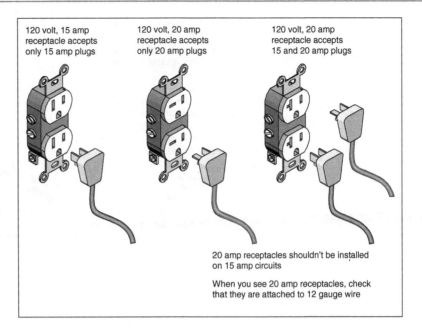

120 volt, 15 amp receptacle accepts only 15 amp plugs

120 volt, 20 amp receptacle accepts only 20 amp plugs

120 volt, 20 amp receptacle accepts 15 and 20 amp plugs

20 amp receptacles shouldn't be installed on 15 amp circuits

When you see 20 amp receptacles, check that they are attached to 12 gauge wire

Fuses and Breakers

Fuses or breakers are safety devices too, but they don't do the same thing as ground wires, nor do they do the same thing as GFCIs. Fuses or breakers shut off power to the circuit if more electricity flows through the circuit than it was designed for. If there is a 25-amp short circuit, for example, in a common household circuit, the 15-amp fuse or breaker will shut off the power. However, if there were an 8-amp electrical current flowing from the black wire through the ground wire (short circuit), the fuse or breaker would be perfectly happy.

GFIs Don't Replace Fuses

Circuits with GFCIs need to have fuses or breakers to shut off the electricity in the case of an overload. So what does a GFI do? A GFI finds electrical **leaks** and shuts off the power if leakage is occurring. It finds leaks by comparing the current flowing out through the black wire to the current flowing back through the neutral (white) wire (Figure 7.38). Where it sees less current coming back through the white than went out in the black, it assumes there is a fault to ground (a leak), and shuts down the circuit.

Find Leaks

You Create a Short Circuit

If you create a short circuit by touching a black and white wire, the GFI may not trip because the current in the black and white wires would be the same. This helps explain why GFIs aren't quite as good as grounding, but are much better than nothing.

Where Are They Used?

GFCI receptacles are currently required for bathrooms and washrooms, outdoors, in garages, above counters for a kitchen sink or wet bar, and in unfinished basements and crawlspaces.

Only Needed Close to Grade Outside

Only the outdoor outlets within $6^1/_2$ feet of grade need GFIs.

Swimming Pools Whirlpool Baths

You also need GFCIs for swimming pool equipment and whirlpool baths, although there are usually no receptacles involved.

Exceptions

There are exceptions to these rules in some cases and so you should be careful how you apply these.

F I G U R E   7.38   Ground Fault Interrupter

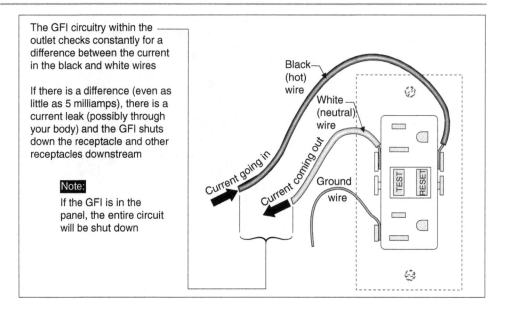

The GFI circuitry within the outlet checks constantly for a difference between the current in the black and white wires

If there is a difference (even as little as 5 milliamps), there is a current leak (possibly through your body) and the GFI shuts down the receptacle and other receptacles downstream

Note:
If the GFI is in the panel, the entire circuit will be shut down

Black (hot) wire
White (neutral) wire
Current going in
Current coming out
Ground wire
TEST RESET

Codes Have Changed

Since we're not doing code compliance inspections and since the requirements for GFIs in different locations came into force in different years, you'll have to make your own decisions as to how far you are going to go. While you could recommend GFIs in all currently required locations in all houses, most inspectors do not. You are wise to get some guidance from the local authorities. What do they recommend on existing homes?

Is It on a GFI or Not?

GFI Outlets Protect Ordinary Outlets Downstream

Sometimes it's difficult to know whether an outlet has **ground fault protection.** Ordinary outlets can be protected by GFIs either at the panel (**a GFCI breaker**), or by a **GFI outlet** upstream. A GFI outlet will protect all outlets wired downstream of it. This is because all electricity flows past the GFI outlet to the other receptacles. The GFI will check all of the electricity flowing through the black wire and measure all of the electricity coming back through the white.

Many electricians put a GFI outlet in a first-floor bathroom in new houses, and put ordinary outlets in other bathrooms in the house on the same circuit. These outlets don't look like they have GFI protection, but they do.

Testing Procedure

There are a couple of ways for you to test this, but all of them involve some walking. If you trip the GFI breaker in one washroom, you can leave it off and check the receptacles in the other washrooms and bathrooms to make sure they are off. Then you can come back, reset the tripped GFI in the first washroom, and check the receptacles in the other bathrooms for proper wiring.

Client Help?

Some people employ their clients as assistants on this kind of test to save some steps. Other inspectors take the extra steps to make sure it's done right.

Testing GFIS

There are two ways to test GFIs within the scope of a home inspection. The first is to use the test button on the GFI receptacle. The second is to use the test button on a plug-in circuit tester. (Not all circuit testers have the ability to test GFIs.)

Test Button on Outlet

If you press a test button and the power to the outlet is not cut off, the GFI is faulty or wired improperly. Your circuit tester should show if there is reversed polar-

STRATEGY

ity, open ground, open hot, etc. The tester also shows whether the power shut off when the test button tripped.

One Test Works, Other Doesn't
Sometimes the test button on the GFI works, but the test button on the circuit analyzer does not. This is usually because the circuit is ungrounded. This should show up on your circuit analyzer. The test button on your circuit analyzer tests the GFI by creating a small fault to the ground wire. If the receptacle is not grounded, this circuit isn't closed and no electricity flows. The tester won't trip, and you will incorrectly report the GFI as defective, if you aren't careful.

Use Outlet Test Button
Most GFIs use an internal test that does not rely on a ground wire. The test button on the GFI outlet is a better test than the one on an external tester. Most electrical authorities will accept GFIs without grounding. In using your circuit analyzer to test GFI receptacles, make sure you test the entire outlet and use the test button on the GFI to help you come to the right conclusion.

Line and Load Sides Reversed (Not Reversed Polarity)
One common problem with GFIs is that they can be wired backwards. The line side of the GFI should be connected to the power supply. The load side of the GFI should be connected to outlets downstream. If it's wired wrong, with the power coming in to the load side, the GFI protection is defeated at this outlet. Outlets downstream will be protected, but not this one. The dangerous part is that the test button will trip but there will still be power to the outlet! That's why it's a good idea to have your circuit tester plugged into the outlet when you trip the GFI test button.

Not on Multi-Wire Branch Circuits
GFIs can't work on multi-wire branch circuits because the current through the black or red wire is usually different from the current through the white. The GFI would trip constantly.

Worn Receptacles
Receptacles that are older and have been heavily used may have loose slots that won't hold plugs tightly. Plugs that tend to move or fall out of receptacles are dangerous because of the poor connection and overheating that can result. They are also dangerous because live parts of the plug blades may be exposed if the plug is not tight in the outlet.

STRATEGY
When you plug in your tester, you can often sense whether the slots are loose. Once the tester is put in, try to move it side to side and up and down. The lights should stay on, and the tester should not move easily.

Where you find worn receptacles, recommend their replacement.

Broken Pin or Blade in Slots
STRATEGY
Where you find an outlet with something broken off in a slot, recommend that it be replaced. This can be dangerous, since whatever is sticking out of the slot may be hot. Furthermore, you can't plug in an appliance.

Not Enough Receptacles
Outlets Every 12 Feet
In older houses, there will usually be fewer receptacles than in newer houses. In modern construction, there should be one outlet about every 12 feet along walls. Any wall 2 feet or longer should have an outlet.

Shouldn't Have to Walk More Than 6 Feet to an Outlet
The actual rules say that any point you walk to on a wall must be within 6 feet of an outlet to one side or the other. Since most appliance cords are about 6 feet long, you shouldn't have to go farther than 6 feet to find a receptacle for your appliance.

Kitchen Counter Outlets
Above kitchen counters, outlets in new construction should be arranged so you don't have to go more than 24 inches in either direction to find an outlet. If the counter space is 12 inches long or more, an outlet is needed above it.

Island Outlets
In new work, outlets are required on work islands in kitchens. Outlets are most often installed on the face of cabinets below the island, or they can be mounted on

STRATEGY

Codes Not Retroactive

Adding Outlets

the island in an upright position on a pedestal (tombstone). They should not be surface-mounted on countertops, because water may get into the outlets.

It is a somewhat subjective call to determine how much electricity is enough for your clients. Most older houses won't have the electrical distribution found in new houses. We recommend that you point this out. We encourage people to see where their electrical needs are focused after they move into a house, rather than make an arbitrary and expensive upgrade of the electrical distribution throughout the house.

Code requirements are usually not retroactive, and you don't have to upgrade electrical distribution on an existing house. Wherever renovations are undertaken, it obviously makes sense to improve electrical distribution at that time since walls are open and running wires is straightforward. It's often required to meet current codes when renovating, anyway.

We'll normally cite a deficiency if there's only one outlet in a bedroom, for example. If there's one outlet on each wall of the bedroom, we usually consider it adequate.

Each branch-wire circuit can have 10 to 12 points. (This is a combination of light fixtures and receptacles. Switches are not included.) In many houses, existing branch circuits are extended to add more outlets.

Too Far from Basins

STRATEGY

*Outlets Beside Basins
Away from Tubs*

Electrical authorities like receptacles in bathrooms to be close to the basin, but they shouldn't be right over the basin since the cord may droop into the water.

Receptacles should be on either side of the basin. The authorities recognize that this is where people use hair dryers, curling irons, electric toothbrushes, electric shavers, and so on.

Inspector in the House: Locked Out of a Garage by a GFI

While inspecting a new town house, I cut the power to the exterior electrical outlet at the back of the building with the GFI (Ground Fault Interrupter) button on my circuit tester. This confirmed that this outlet was protected by a GFI upstream somewhere. So far, so good.

Knowing that these homes typically have one GFI type exterior outlet protecting the other exterior outlets, I went to reset the GFI at the front porch electrical outlet. But there was no outlet there! No problem, I thought; there must be a GFI breaker at the panel.

I was surprised and a little disturbed to find no GFI breaker panel! I did see a label on the panel saying "Exterior/Garage GFI," and I realized the GFI must be in the garage. That makes sense, I thought.

This garage did not have a door into the house—the only access was through the vehicle door. I found the push button for the vehicle door opener but it did not work, because the opener was plugged into the GFI outlet in the garage, and I had tripped the circuit! Naturally, there was no exterior disengagement mechanism for the vehicle door opener.

I could have cut a hole in the garage door and pulled the manual release handle, or cut a hole through the closet beside the garage, and squeezed into the garage. Neither option was appealing, so I finished the inspection and left an apologetic note for the homeowner to call me.

I arranged to go back the next day and, in the basement, found the wire going through the wall to the garage outlet. I punched a small hole through two layers of drywall, and was able to reach through and press the reset button on the GFI. Problem solved!

I patched the small holes in the drywall and have changed my routine for town houses with garages—I never trip an exterior outlet unless I know I can get to the GFI reset.

7.9.3   Conditions at Switches

Common switch problems are listed below. Causes include installation problems, mechanical damage, wear and tear, and mechanical failure. The implications are shock and fire hazards.

1. Damaged
2. Loose
3. Overheating
4. Inoperative

Damaged

STRATEGY

Watch for switches or cover plates that have been mechanically damaged. Recommend replacement. This is a safety issue, since people will be touching the switch handle regularly.

Loose

STRATEGY

Recommend replacement if the switch handle is loose, if the whole switch is loose in the box, or if the box is loose in the wall. These are shock and fire hazards.

Overheating

STRATEGY

Any switch that is warm to the touch, or shows evidence of charring, discoloration or melted plastic, should be considered a serious safety hazard and should be immediately improved. One exception is dimmer switches which are warm to the touch under normal use.

Wattage Rating of Switch

Where a switch controls several bulbs (e.g., a chandelier or several light fixtures), the wattage of the light bulbs may exceed the wattage rating of the switch.

Inoperative

STRATEGY

If the switch does not work, don't try to solve the problem. Just report that the switch does not operate the appliance it is supposed to. The switch could be fine and a light bulb could be burned out, for example.

7.9.4   Conditions at Junction Boxes

All Connections

Junction boxes are used to contain and support switches, outlets and lights. They can be metal or plastic, and come in a large variety of shapes and sizes. Junction boxes may also simply contain wire splices. All modern connections should be made inside a junction box. An electrical panel is considered a junction box.

Accessible

Junction boxes should not be buried in walls, floors or ceilings. They're supposed to be accessible. The presence of many junction boxes acting as splice containers suggests amateur work. Good electrical installations include very few junction boxes.

Covers

Junction boxes should have appropriate cover plates. Often, this is the switch or outlet cover plate. With light fixtures, the light fixture itself forms the cover for the box.

Let's look at the problems with junction boxes. Causes include installation problems and mechanical damage. The implications are, of course, shock and fire hazard.

1. Damaged
2. Missing
3. Loose
4. Not grounded
5. Cover loose or missing
6. Grounded
7. Concealed boxes

Damaged

| STRATEGY |

Damaged boxes should be repaired or replaced.

Missing

| STRATEGY |

Electrical splices made without a junction box are incorrect and a box should be added. Exceptions include original knob-and-tube connections. Modern wire attached to knob-and-tube wiring should have connections in boxes.

Loose

| STRATEGY |

Junction boxes that are not well-secured, or have components such as cover plates that are loose, should be written up for improvement.

Not Grounded

| STRATEGY |

You won't pick up this one often, but if the cover plate is missing, you may be able to see whether the junction box itself is grounded. This is only an issue on metal boxes.

Cover Loose or Missing

| STRATEGY |

Missing or loose cover plates on junction boxes should be replaced or re-secured.

Crowded

| STRATEGY |

This is something you'll only see if the cover plate is missing. A common sense approach is all you need here. While there are several specific rules for various boxes, with little practice you can tell whether a box is crowded. If it's difficult to put the cover on without pinching a wire, it's overcrowded.

Concealed Boxes

| STRATEGY |

Boxes have to be accessible. This is a problem you'll rarely discover, since if the box is concealed, you won't see it.

7.10   SMOKE DETECTORS

Function

Smoke detectors protect people by notifying them of fire in the home, especially when people are sleeping. They usually provide an audible alarm, and some have a visual alarm consisting of a flashing light.

Inspecting Smoke Detectors

The Standards ask us to report the absence of smoke detectors, but do not ask us to test them. We suggest you make it clear to your client whether or not you tested the smoke detectors.

How Many Detectors?

What if there is one detector in the home, but you don't believe that's enough? The Standards only ask you to report the absence of smoke detectors. Our approach is to advise that detectors should be on every floor level of a home, and should be near all sleeping areas. We also advise that interconnecting detectors is a good idea, but expensive to do in an existing home. We stress to clients that maintenance and testing of these safety devices is important.

REVIEW QUESTIONS

1. Service entrance conductors run from the service drop to the service box or service panel.

   True   False

2. The service size is determined by the amperage and voltage ratings of the service.

   True   False

3. Is the service drop overhead or underground?

   Overhead   Underground

4. Are service laterals overhead or underground?

   Overhead   Underground

5. The drip loop is typically part of the service drop.

   True   False

6. The wire size for the service drop must be the same as the wire size for the service entrance conductors.

   True   False

7. How many wires would you typically find in a 240-volt service drop?

8. What would four wires mean?

9. What would two wires usually mean?

10. List seven common problems with service drops.

11. List clearances above ground, swimming pools, and roofs.

12. The service entrance conductors run from the _____ to the _____.

13. All service entrance conductors must be in conduit.

    True   False

14. All service entrance conductors must be attached above roof level.

    True   False

15. The drip loop should be as close to the roof surface as possible.

    True   False

16. List ten common problems with service entrance conductors.

17. List four common areas of water penetration into service entrances.

18. List two functions of the drip loop.

19. Roughly 999 out of 1,000 houses have _____ volts available (insert a number).

20. Roughly 999 out of 1,000 houses have _____ service entrance wires (insert a number).

21. Load calculations are part of a home inspection.

    True   False

22. Implications of an undersized service include—

    a. shock hazard   d. melting insulation

    b. fire hazard   e. nuisance tripping of the main fuses or

    c. shock and fire hazard   breakers

23. What is the largest single-phase service that you are likely to find in a home?

24. What size copper wire would you expect to find on the service entrance for:

    a. A 60-amp service?

    b. A 100-amp service?

    c. A 200-amp service?

25. Which of the following is a reliable way to identify the service size?

    a. the size of the service drop wires

    b. the distribution panel rating

    c. the service box rating

    d. the service entrance conductor size

    e. the service entrance conduit size

26. Aluminum is an acceptable service entrance conductor material.

True   False

27. A fused 200-amp service has two 100-amp fuses in the service box.

True   False

28. If you can't read the size of the fuses in the service box, you should remove them to try to get a better look.

True   False

29. Which of the following is a safety issue?

    a. The main fuses have a lower rating than the service entrance wire.

    b. The main fuses have a higher rating than the service entrance wire.

    c. The service box has a higher rating than the service entrance wires.

    d. The service box has the same rating as the service entrance wires.

    e. The distribution panel has a larger rating than the service entrance wires.

30. The service box can be inside, outside or in a garage.

True   False

31. There can be up to 10 throws to disconnect all of the electricity in the house.

True   False

32. The service box may stand alone or may be combined with the distribution panel.

True   False

33. List 16 common conditions you might find in a service box.

34. The functions of earth grounding systems include _____.

35. The grounding electrode conductor may also be called _____.

36. You are allowed to ground to the gas piping.

True   False

37. The grounding systems are connected to the house neutral at the _____.

38. From the point where the ground and the neutral wires connect, there are two paths to ground. What are they?

39. List five destinations where ground wires can terminate.

40. List 12 common problems found with grounding systems.

41. Distribution panels are also called (list six other names if you can) _____.

42. Wires run directly from the service box to the branch circuits.

    True   False

43. What is the advantage of a 240-volt circuit?

44. What size copper wires are adequately protected by:

    a. 15-amp breakers? _____

    b. 20-amp breakers? _____

    c. 30-amp breakers? _____

    d. 40-amp breakers? _____

45. What size wire is found on most general purpose outlets for lights and receptacles?

46. Which of the following is a safety concern?

    a. a fuse that is too small

    b. a fuse that is too big

47. Subpanels must be immediately adjacent to the main panel.

    True   False

48. Typical distribution panels have 60 circuits.

    True   False

49. Do we normally shut off the power when looking at an electrical system in the house? Why or why not?

50. List 14 conditions that may be found in all panels.

51. Explain why fused neutrals are a bad idea.

52. What is the implication of a panel that is too small for the service?

53. Should the neutral and the ground wires be bonded together at the subpanel?

54. How should the feeder wires to a subpanel from the main panel ideally be protected?

    a. No fusing is necessary.

    b. The main house fuses or breakers will protect the wire.

    c. Fuses should be provided at the subpanel.

    d. Fuses should be provided at the main panel.

    e. None of the above.

55. What are the implications of oversized breakers?

56. What does the term "double tap" mean?

57. The red and black wires of multi-wire circuits should be on separate bus bars.

    True   False

58. List four common problems found only with breakers.

59. List six problems found with wires in panels.

60. What is a split receptacle?

61. What is meant by **linking** in multi-wire branch circuits?

62. List two different branch wire materials you might see.

63. Describe three different cable types you might see.

64. What is the difference between insulation and sheathing?

65. The most common wire size for branch household circuits is _____ gauge.

66. What are the issues on running wire through steel studs?

67. List five common branch circuit wire problems.

68. Give four examples of damaged wire.

69. List three methods for securing wire ends.

70. What is meant by **open splice?**

71. Wire should be _____ inches away from the edge of studs.

72. A grommet is _____.

73. Wires should not be run on wall surfaces without _____.

74. What is the problem with running wire across the top of the attic ceiling joists?

75. Abandoned wire should be _____.

76. Describe how knob-and-tube wiring is visibly different from modern cable.

77. Does knob-and-tube wiring have a ground wire associated with it?

78. List four common problems with knob-and-tube wiring.

79. List three common problems found with aluminum wiring.

80. How would you identify aluminum wiring?

81. When was it used?

82. What caused the problems? (list at least three things)

83. Where is the anti-oxidant grease typically used?

84. List 12 common lighting problems found in houses.

85. How are lights tested?

86. Why should heat lamps not be located over doors?

87. List 14 common receptacle problems.

88. Describe how you would test a GFI receptacle during an inspection.

89. Explain the problem with reversed polarity.

90. Can an outlet be protected by a ground fault interrupter without it being apparent?

91. Outlets should be close to basins.

    True   False

92. List four common problems found with switches.

93. All junction boxes should be concealed.

    True   False

94. List seven common junction box problems.

95. Knob-and-tube wiring was commonly installed without junction boxes.

    True   False

96. One smoke detector is needed in each home, near the kitchen because that's where most house fires start.

    True   False

CHAPTER 8

GAS FURNACES

LEARNING OBJECTIVES

By the end of this chapter you should be able to:

- list and describe the two most common types of gas burners

- describe the function of the gas valve, pilot light and thermocouple, on a residential furnace

- list nine conditions that may be found with gas combustion equipment

- list two problems commonly found with gas furnace heat exchangers

- list six problems found with furnace cabinetry

- describe the setting and function of the three fan/limit controls

- list six problems found with fan controls

- list six conditions found with thermostats

- list twelve conditions that are found with vent connectors

- list eleven problems with duct systems

- outline the four basic components of the inspection and testing procedure for a conventional gas furnace

- list and describe the nine common problems found with high-efficiency furnaces

- describe the life expectancies of different efficiency gas furnaces

INTRODUCTION

We can categorize heating systems by either their fuel or their distribution method. To refer to something as a **gas furnace** does both. The fuel is natural **gas** and the word **furnace** tells us there is a duct system, with supply registers and return grilles.

Components of Gas Furnace

The components of a conventional gas furnace include—

- a **fuel system** (usually steel piping or, less commonly, copper)

- a **combustion air** delivery system (often just the air in the room)

- a **burner** assembly including a gas valve, a pilot and in some cases, a pressure regulator

- a **heat exchanger** to transfer the heat from the flame to the house air

- **controls** to turn the heat on and off, to turn the house air fan on and off and to shut down the system if the temperature gets too high

- a **venting** system **to get rid of the products of combustion,** including a draft hood, vent connector and chimney or vent

- a **distribution system** including ducts and registers to push the warm air through the house and draw cool air back from the house to be reheated

8.1   GAS PIPING

The gas service line may enter the building either through the exterior wall below grade, or through a service riser above grade just outside the house. There is usually a shut-off valve and then the meter. Sometimes there is a regulator upstream of the meter, depending on the gas main pressure.

Pipe Downstream of Meter Is Homeowner's

The piping downstream of the gas meter is usually the responsibility of the home owner. The piping upstream of the gas meter and the meter itself are usually the responsibility of the gas company. We will focus on the portions of gas piping that are the homeowner's responsibility and are visible to home inspectors.

Supply, Branch, and Drop Lines, or Risers

The piping inside the house is called the **gas supply line** or **building line** (Figure 8.1). **Branch lines** run to individual appliances. The branch line terminates in a **drop line,** which is a vertical pipe dropping down to the appliance from an overhead branch line. This drop line is called a **riser** if it carries gas up to an appliance from a branch line below the appliance.

Drip

At the appliance connection point, there is usually a **drip,** sometimes called a **sediment trap**, that includes a nipple and a cap. This pipe extension is usually at least 3 inches long and is intended to catch any water or foreign material that may be in the gas, before the material gets into the appliance itself. This is simply a gravity system, with the solids and liquids falling into the pocket.

Steel, Copper, Brass

The most common gas piping is black steel. Copper, brass, or steel tubing can also be used in some areas but some utilities specifically prohibit the use of copper. In other areas, the use of copper is widespread. You should know what is acceptable in your area.

Steel piping is typically black with malleable iron or steel fittings.

Flex Connectors

Flexible connectors are permitted to connect appliances to the gas piping. There has to be a shut-off valve at the connection to the rigid piping. This valve has to be in the same room as the appliance (Figure 8.2).

Six Feet Long and Accessible

The flexible connectors can't go through walls, floors or ceilings, nor can they be concealed. The flexible connector length is usually limited to 6 feet for stoves and dryers and 3 feet for other appliances.

FIGURE 8.1   Gas Piping Terminology

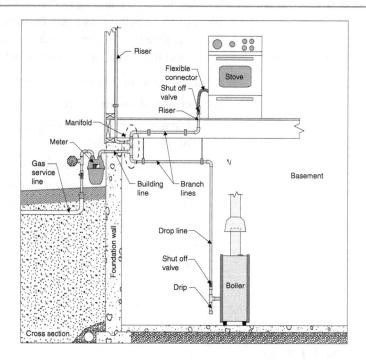

The following problems are typical on gas piping:

1. Leaks
2. Inappropriate materials
3. Inadequate support
4. Rusting
5. No drip leg
6. Missing shut-off valve

FIGURE 8.2   Flexible Gas Appliance Connectors

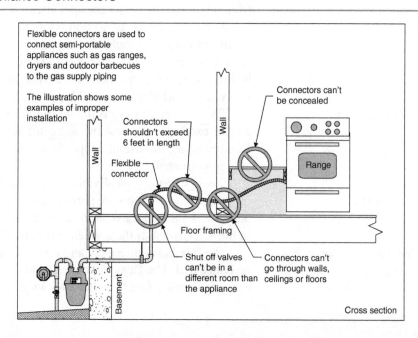

7. Improper connections

8. Plastic pipe exposed above grade

9. Piping in chimneys or duct systems

10. Copper tubing not properly labeled

The implications of all of these problems are possible gas leaks and explosions. We won't mention this repeatedly.

8.1.1   Leaks

Some Leaks Are Too Small to Worry about

Natural gas is perfumed so you can smell it. Some inspectors use combustible gas analyzers to test for leaks. These devices can sense leaks that are so small that the gas company has trouble detecting them. This can cause problems with your relationship with the gas company. You might want to talk to them about what kind of leaks they're looking for.

Any gas leak that is detectable without equipment is a serious one, and the gas company should be notified immediately.

8.1.2   Inappropriate Materials

Inside the house, plastic piping is not allowed, and depending on where you are, copper, brass, or steel tubing may or may not be allowed. Learn what is acceptable in your area.

Looks Like Plumbing Pipe

Black steel is not painted black; it means unfinished or not galvanized. **Galvanized steel** is not used because the zinc coating that makes up the galvanizing may flake off and obstruct gas valves or burners. Gas piping has thick walls, and the connections are threaded.

Gas piping can easily be mistaken for water supply piping or distribution piping on water heating systems. This is especially true if the piping has been painted. You'll have to follow piping from source to destination to know for sure what it's carrying.

Copper tubing for gas can be confused with flexible copper piping for water. To avoid confusion, it should be be marked with a yellow label with "GAS" in black letters every five feet.

8.1.3   Inadequate Support

Horizontal steel piping should be supported as follows:

- ■ $1/2$-inch diameter piping or less should be supported every 6 feet
- ■ $3/4$-inch and one inch piping should be supported every 8 feet
- ■ $1^1/4$- to $2^1/2$-inch piping should be supported every 10 feet

Steel piping should be supported vertically at every floor level.

Tubing

Copper tubing should be supported every 6 feet horizontally and vertically.

Piping cannot be supported on other piping. (Supports designed for piping are required.)

Poorly supported pipe may have weakened connections, resulting in leakage.

STRATEGY

As you examine the pipe, look for missing, too few, broken or ineffective support brackets. Also look for storage of materials on top of or hanging from pipes. Gas piping should not be used to support storage.

8.1.4   Rusting

STRATEGIES

When you find rusted gas piping, recommend further investigation.

8.1.5   No Drip

The drip is intended to catch water or foreign material before it gets into gas valves, burners, etc (Figure 8.3). These are required in areas where the gas contains a lot of water vapor. They are also required on heating appliances.

IMPLICATIONS

Implications include equipment malfunction because of foreign material entering the equipment. There is also a safety issue, as foreign material could block a valve, preventing it from closing completely.

STRATEGY

What Does Gas Company Say

Look for a drip at the bottom of the vertical pipe going into the furnace. There should be a logical place for sediment to be trapped.

Check with your utility. In some cases utilities relaxed the requirement for drips for some time and then reinstituted it. The reintroduction is not necessarily retroactive. Be careful about what you criticize here. A conversation with your local gas company is a good idea.

F I G U R E 8.3   Drip

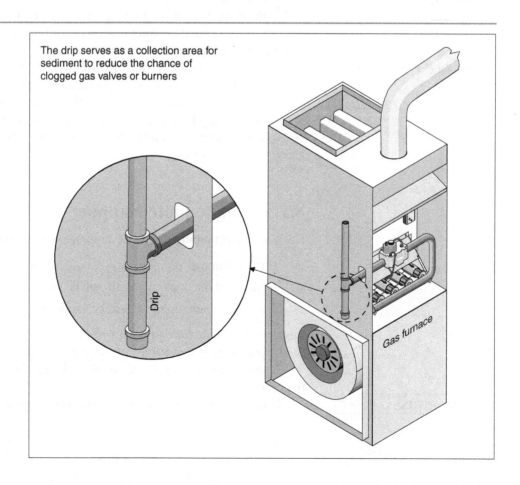

The drip serves as a collection area for sediment to reduce the chance of clogged gas valves or burners

Drip

Gas furnace

8.1.6   Missing Shutoff Valves

A shutoff valve should be as close as possible to the appliance. The only exception would be the shutoff for a gas valve into a gas fireplace or wood-burning fireplace with a gas starter. In these cases, the valve should be outside the fireplace but in the same room (in some areas), within 4 feet of the fireplace.

Inability to shut equipment off in an emergency presents a safety hazard. Maintenance is also more difficult if you have to look for the valve.

Make sure there is a shutoff valve for each appliance. Where one is apparently missing, call for further investigation.

8.1.7   Improper Connections

Teflon tape is sometimes used instead of pipe dope on threaded connections.

Another improper connection is the use of bushings, thread projectors or running threads (close nipples). You want as few connections as possible in a gas piping system. These fittings are normally used where the appropriate length of pipe was not available, and the system is tied together.

Unions (fittings designed to allow pipes to be disconnected relatively easily) are permissible. Do not confuse unions with the other connectors described.

Rigid Connections Where Flex Is Needed

Also improper is the use of a rigid connector when a flexible connector is called for by the local utility. This could be an issue in earthquake areas, or in areas where pulse-type heating systems, for example, require flexible connectors because of the vibration involved in the machine. Again, this is area-specific and you need to know what is acceptable in your jurisdiction.

Teflon tape may not provide a good seal, especially if there is cutting oil left on the pipe threads. Extra connections present extra chances for leaks.

Where you notice tape instead of pipe dope (putty) at the connections, recommend that these connections be checked by the gas company and improved if necessary. A pipe joint tape approved for use with gas is available. It is yellow or orange in color. Teflon tape is typically white.

Look for connections in pipes that have no apparent function. While this should have been inspected during original installation, there are many reasons it may not have been picked up.

8.1.8   Plastic Pipe Exposed above Grade

Plastic pipe should not be exposed above grade. Where it does extend above grade, it should be protected from mechanical damage by metal risers.

Where you see plastic gas piping coming out of the ground, you should criticize it.

8.1.9   Piping in Chimneys or Duct Systems

Gas piping is not allowed in chimneys or in duct systems.

Watch for gas piping disappearing into or coming out of chimneys or duct systems. Where you see it, you should recommend further investigation and possible rearrangement.

Since all of these rules fall within the judgment of the inspector having jurisdiction, allowances may have been made for reasons that are not apparent to us. We should be cautious and describe an installation as unusual in these respects. We should recommend that they be investigated, but let your client know that they may be acceptable.

8.1.10   Copper Tubing Not Properly Labeled

IMPLICATION

Gas tubing may be mistaken for water piping, with disastrous results.

STRATEGY

Look for the word **gas,** or **natural gas,** every 5 feet along the pipe length or a yellow stripe (paint or tape) on the pipe. Where it is not visible, recommend further investigation.

8.2   COMBUSTION AIR

Draft Air per Volume of Gas

For a furnace to work properly, it must have an adequate supply of combustion air. Gas furnaces also require a second source of air to maintain an appropriate draft on the exhaust products. Some people call this **draft air** or **dilution air.** This air is used to help maintain chimney draft and to dilute the products of combustion.

Conventional gas furnaces use roughly 30 cubic feet of air for every cubic foot of gas burned. Many authorities work on 50 cubic feet of air for every cubic foot of gas, building in a safety factor for unforeseen problems.

IMPLICATIONS

The implications of inadequate air are significant. The incomplete combustion process will generate carbon monoxide (a poisonous gas). Further, the lack of dilution air is likely to result in **backdraft** (Figure 8.4). This means that combustion products can't go up the chimney but are dumped back into the room, which is under low pressure (since it's starved for air, because we've pulled all the air into the furnace for the combustion and dilution process). Some people call backdrafting **spillage.** Others consider spillage to be a typical short term condition during start-up of the burner, and not a problem. Backdrafting is ongoing spillage, which is a problem. In this material, we'll use the terms interchangeably.

STRATEGY

When a furnace is operating, it's easy to look for spillage or backdrafting through the draft hood. Some people use a match, cigarette or smoke candle. However, in most cases you can tell simply with your hand. When you put your hand into the base of the draft hood, you should feel cool room air being drawn in. If you feel hot, wet exhaust air coming down onto your hand, spillage is taking place. With a little bit of practice, you can readily identify this. Don't mistake the radiant heat from the hot flue as a downdraft.

Condensation

Another indication of spillage is condensation. Because one of the products of combustion is water vapor, the exhaust products will condense as they come back into the room. The dew point of combustion products is around 125°F. As the gas is cooled, it may cause quite a bit of condensation. Rust around the draft hood may indicate a chronic spillage (backdrafting) problem. Corrosion is a common result of condensation.

Slow Exhaust Movement

Condensation may also occur if the draft is marginally adequate. If the gases don't move quickly enough through the vent connector and up the chimney, they may cool below their dew point and condense although the exhaust products even-

FIGURE 8.4   Backdrafting

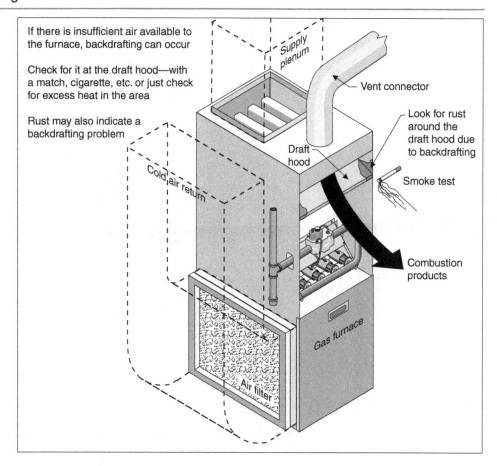

If there is insufficient air available to the furnace, backdrafting can occur

Check for it at the draft hood—with a match, cigarette, etc. or just check for excess heat in the area

Rust may also indicate a backdrafting problem

Supply plenum

Vent connector

Look for rust around the draft hood due to backdrafting

Draft hood

Smoke test

Cold air return

Combustion products

Gas furnace

Air filter

tually get out of the building. This is usually the result of a furnace too small for the chimney or an appliance firing at too low a rate to have the venting system work properly.

Here's a trick to find out what is causing a downdraft condition when the furnace is running:

If you notice that the unit is backdrafting when it's operating, turn the appliance off. With the unit off, use a match or smoke pencil to determine whether there is still a downdraft coming out through the draft hood.

If so, there is a poor draft condition (the chimney is too short or too large or there is a wind condition causing a downdraft, for example). If a match burns without being blown back out of the draft hood or being drawn up into it, you have a neutral condition. This suggests the chimney is blocked.

STRATEGY

When you perform your operating test of the furnace, make sure exhaust products are not spilling out of the draft hood for more than a minute or so on initial start-up. Once the unit has been running for about two minutes, air-flow should be into, not out of, the draft hood.

In a furnace room, test the draft with the door closed to simulate normal operating conditions.

FIGURE 8.5   Monoport Burners

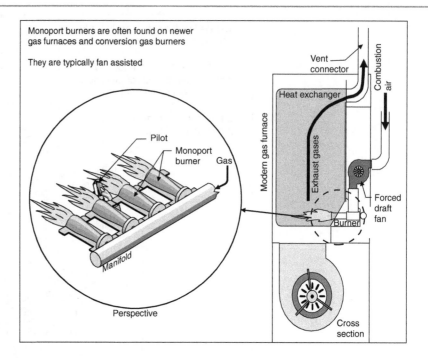

Monoport burners are often found on newer gas furnaces and conversion gas burners

They are typically fan assisted

Pilot
Monoport burner
Gas
Manifold
Perspective

Modern gas furnace
Vent connector
Combustion air
Heat exchanger
Exhaust gases
Forced draft fan
Burner
Cross section

8.3   GAS BURNER

Mono-Port Burner

This section concentrates on the atmospheric or natural draft burner.

There are two basic types of gas burners. One is the **mono-port** (Figure 8.5). This is commonly used on conversion burners, where an oil heating system has been converted into a gas system. These often use a fan assist, and are actually forced draft rather than atmospheric burners. They are common in high efficiency furnaces, and are popular because they work equally well in any orientation. Upflow, downflow and horizontal furnaces can use the same mono-port burners. They can be either **in-shot** burners or **up-shot** burners.

Multi-Port Burner

The second type of gas burner is the one found in most conventional gas furnaces. This is a **multi-port** burner and includes **ribbon, drilled** and **slotted burners** (Figure 8.6). The burners themselves may be made of steel or cast iron.

Crossover Igniter

Most furnaces have more than one burner. One pilot flame usually ignites all the burners. **A crossover igniter** is used to bridge the flame from one burner to the next.

Delayed Ignition

One of the common problems with multi-burner furnaces is delayed ignition of the burners remote from the pilot. This is usually a problem with the cross-over igniter being out of alignment or obstructed in some way.

8.3.1   Flame Patterns

Blue, Stable Flame

The normal flame pattern is substantially blue and the flame is stable. It should not waver or lift off the burner, nor should it float around the edges of the burner or drift out. The normal flame indicates complete combustion. The blue color is not brilliant or intense.

F I G U R E 8.6 Multi-port Burners

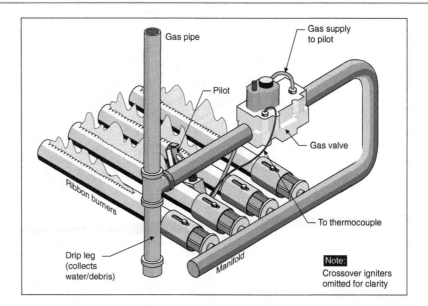

Diagnosing flame patterns is not part of a conventional home inspection. You should, however, be aware that flame irregularities occur and that servicing should be recommended when you see poor flame color or pattern.

8.3.2   Gas Valves, Thermostats, Pilot Lights, and Thermocouples

Gas Valve

The **gas valve** is the main control system for the burner. When the gas valve is closed, gas does not flow into the burner and the furnace isn't on. When the gas valve opens, gas flows into the burner where it is ignited (we hope).

Thermostat

The **thermostat** is the brains of the unit and it decides when the furnace should be on. The thermostat senses the temperature in the living space and as the temperature falls below a set temperature, the thermostat tells the furnace to come on. The thermostat calls for heat, closes the switch and completes the circuit, which energizes the **gas solenoid valve** (electric valve) and allows gas into the burner.

No Pilot

We ignite the gas coming into the burners in a controlled way with a pilot light. What if the pilot isn't on? We don't want to turn on the gas and then try to ignite the mixture once it accumulates. That's a good way to cause an explosion. So how does the furnace make sure this won't happen?

Thermocouple

The automatic safety control is the **thermocouple** (Figure 8.7). The thermocouple has a very specific job. It sits in the pilot flame and senses whether the pilot is on or not. If the pilot is on, the thermocouple allows the electrical current to flow through to the gas valve so that when the thermostat calls for heat and closes its part of the circuit, the gas valve can open.

No Gas Flow

If the thermocouple doesn't sense a pilot flame (because the pilot is out or the thermocouple is defective), the thermocouple will open the circuit and won't let electricity flow through to open the gas valve, even when the thermostat does call for heat. This makes homeowners very unhappy because they don't have any heat. On the other hand, it keeps them from blowing up the house—a pretty good tradeoff.

FIGURE 8.7   Continuous Pilot Light

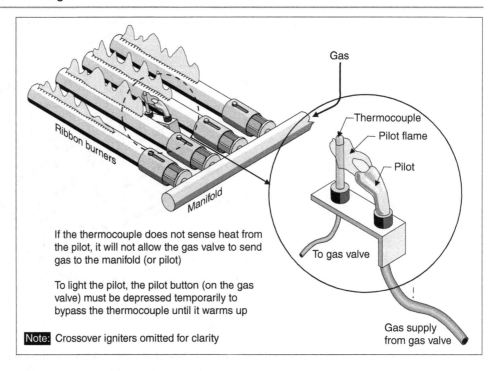

If the thermocouple does not sense heat from the pilot, it will not allow the gas valve to send gas to the manifold (or pilot)

To light the pilot, the pilot button (on the gas valve) must be depressed temporarily to bypass the thermocouple until it warms up

Note: Crossover igniters omitted for clarity

8.3.3 Conditions

Let's look at some of the burner problems that you're likely to encounter:

1. Inoperative
2. Scorching
3. Poor flame color or pattern
4. Flame wavers when house fan comes on
5. Rust
6. Dirt or soot
7. Delayed ignition
8. Gas odor or leak
9. Short cycling

Since it's not your role to be a troubleshooter or a technician for all of these problems, you will recommend servicing of the furnace.

Turn Furnace Off

We recommend that the power to the furnace be shut off during your visual inspection of components inside the furnace. The power to the furnace may be a switch (like a light switch) or a fused disconnect. Trace the 120 volt wiring from the furnace back to find the switch, if necessary. You will have to have the power back on to test the furnace operation.

Inoperative

Your operating test of a gas furnace involves using the normal homeowner controls only. In most cases, this means just turning up the thermostat. If the furnace does not respond, there may be several causes. It is not your role to figure out the cause or fix the furnace.

IMPLICATION

STRATEGY

The implication of an inoperative furnace is no heat.

When the furnace does not respond to its controls, simply report this condition and recommend servicing.

Scorching

This may be visible at the heat rollout shield, at the gas valve, at the wiring, on the faceplate of the heat exchanger or on the cabinetry or cover itself.

IMPLICATIONS

Scorching is a fire hazard. It may also damage the control system for the furnace.

STRATEGY

Where you see evidence of scorching, you should recommend servicing (Figure 8.8). In some cases, you won't be able to tell whether it's an ongoing problem, or is one that has been corrected. Let your client know this. There is usually an efficiency problem as well, if scorching is ongoing, although it is less important than the other hazards involved.

Poor Flame Color or Pattern

STRATEGY

Where the flame is almost completely yellow, is lifting off the burner, is not vertical, is lazy or floating or is wandering around on the burner, you should recommend servicing.

IMPLICATION

The implications are poor efficiency, inadequate heat or no heat.

Flame Wavers When House Fan Comes On

If the flame looks good when the burner comes on, and then is distorted when the house fan comes on, this usually means a crack or hole in the heat exchanger. The air pressure and draft within the burner compartment should not be affected by the house fan coming on. However, where the heat exchanger is cracked, the flame can be distorted away from, or toward, the crack.

F I G U R E 8.8 Scorching

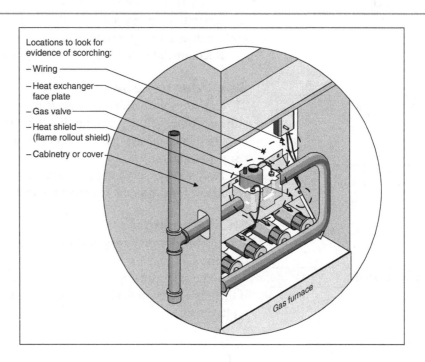

Locations to look for evidence of scorching:

– Wiring
– Heat exchanger face plate
– Gas valve
– Heat shield (flame rollout shield)
– Cabinetry or cover

Gas furnace

IMPLICATIONS

The implications of a cracked heat exchanger are—

- a life safety hazard, since products of combustion may enter the house
- a furnace that probably has to be replaced

STRATEGY

As the burner comes on, watch the flame pattern until the house fan kicks on. Write up any change in the flame pattern as a possibly cracked heat exchanger and recommend further investigation. (This assumes you weren't able to visually identify a crack in the heat exchanger.)

Realize that as the fan turns on, the vibration may cause some flame disturbance, in both color and shape. This is *not* what we are looking for. Also, cracks in the heat exchanger above the flame level will not necessarily affect the flame, but are still problems. These are usually impossible to detect visually.

Rust

IMPLICATIONS

Rust may result in inefficient operation, inadequate heat and a possible gas leak, if the condition is severe enough.

STRATEGY

Use a flashlight and a mirror to look at the burner assembly for rust. You will also be looking at the lower part of the heat exchanger. Fallen rust flakes from the heat exchanger may be obstructing the burners.

Dirt or Soot

IMPLICATIONS

Implications of dirt or soot on the burners are incomplete combustion, inefficient operation and possibly inadequate heat in the house.

STRATEGY

Make a note of any soot or dirt you find on or around the burners and recommend servicing.

Delayed Ignition

IMPLICATIONS

This can lead to flashback or even explosions, as gas can be dumped into the burner chamber without being ignited immediately. If the gas accumulates before ignition, it can cause noisy ignition, result in flame rollout, and possibly blow the pilot out.

STRATEGY

As the thermostat is turned up, watch the burners come on. Look for a smooth start up with no delay and no noise. With a little practice, you can come to recognize an unusual situation quickly.

Recommend servicing where the ignition process is not smooth.

Gas Odor or Leak

IMPLICATION

This, of course, is a life safety issue demanding immediate attention. If the pilot is still on, some people maintain that the chance of an explosion is low because the pilot will burn off any gas that accumulates around the furnace. However, this is a risky assumption.

STRATEGY

Recommend servicing immediately where leaks are detected with your nose. If you need instruments to detect the leaks, they may or may not be significant.

Short Cycling

When a furnace comes on and off every minute or two, it usually indicates a malfunction.

IMPLICATIONS

Sometimes the implications are only inefficiency and perhaps inadequate heat. If there is a crack in the heat exchanger, the implications are life safety and furnace replacement.

Write up short cycling as requiring service. Make sure you have watched for flame wavering when the house fan comes on. This, combined with short cycling, strongly suggests a cracked heat exchanger.

8.4   HEAT EXCHANGERS

Heart of Furnace

The **heat exchanger** is the heart of the furnace. When the heat exchanger fails, you usually have to replace the furnace. If you think of furnaces as having two sides, one is the combustion side and the other is the house-air side (Figure 8.9).

Combustion Side

■   The combustion side includes the burner, the flame side of the heat exchanger, the draft hood, the vent connector and the chimney.

House-air Side

■   The house-air side includes the return-air duct system, the air filter, the blower, the house-air side of the heat exchanger and the supply-air plenum and duct system.

The heat exchanger separates the two sides and moves heat from the combustion side to the house-air side. If everything is working properly, the combustion products never mix with the air in the house.

Steel

The heat exchanger is usually made of steel, often **aluminized** or **galvanized.** Where furnaces are designed for hostile environments, such as indoor pool enclosures, the heat exchangers are sometimes coated with **porcelain,** to protect them against the corrosive chemicals in the environment (chlorine, for example).

F I G U R E 8.9   Heat Exchanger Heat Flow

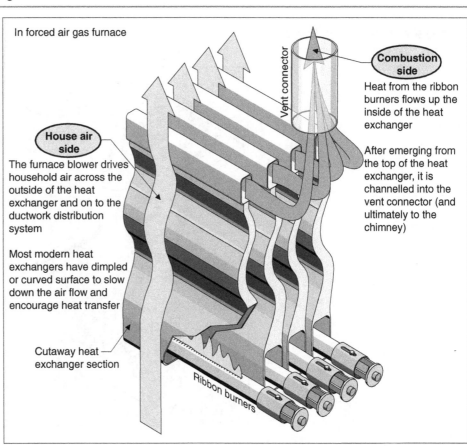

In forced air gas furnace

Combustion side
Heat from the ribbon burners flows up the inside of the heat exchanger

After emerging from the top of the heat exchanger, it is channelled into the vent connector (and ultimately to the chimney)

Vent connector

House air side
The furnace blower drives household air across the outside of the heat exchanger and on to the ductwork distribution system

Most modern heat exchangers have dimpled or curved surface to slow down the air flow and encourage heat transfer

Cutaway heat exchanger section

Ribbon burners

8.4.1   The Flow through a Furnace

Heat exchangers can have more than one cell, depending on how many burners there are. For a simple furnace with a single ribbon burner, the burner runs from the front to the back of the furnace. The heat exchanger will wrap around both sides of the burner and extend upward with walls along either side of the ribbon burner, and walls at the front and back. The heat travels from the burner up through this cavity.

Manifold to Vent Connector
to Chimney
    At the top of this chamber, a **manifold** collects the products of combustion and directs them into the **vent connector** (a metal pipe) attached to the furnace (Figure 8.10). The exhaust products travel through the vent connector, up the chimney and outdoors.

Draft Hood
    The **draft hood** either is built into the furnace cabinetry and forms the outlet of the manifold at the top of the heat exchanger, or is just above the furnace cabinetry at the bottom of the vent connector. The draft hood allows dilution air to be drawn into the vent connector to cool the exhaust and ensure it can move freely up the chimney.

High Temperatures
    Inside the fire side of the heat exchanger, temperatures are high and products of combustion are present. When the burner is operating, the steel walls of the heat exchanger get very hot.

House Air Heats Up
    The house air is moved by the house air fan across the exterior walls of the heat exchanger (usually the two sidewalls and the back wall, although this varies). The house air, which enters at roughly 70°F, picks up heat from the steel heat exchanger walls. The air leaving the top of the heat exchanger may be 140°F.

House Air Flow
    The house air is simply moving in a circle. It goes out through the supply ducts to the registers, to the rooms and comes back through the return grilles, through the return duct system to the furnace.

F I G U R E 8.10   Draft Diverters

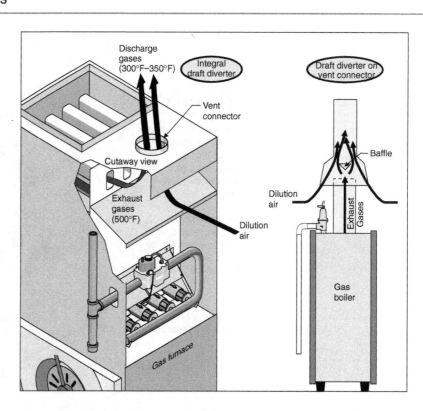

Blower

The **house fan, furnace fan, air handler,** or **furnace blower** (different names for the same thing) pulls the air back through the return system, through the filter, and then pushes the air through the heat exchanger and through the supply duct system out to the supply registers. Every time the air passes the heat exchanger, it gets heated up. This heat is transferred into the living space and the cool air is brought back to be reheated.

8.4.2 Heat Exchanger Issues

Critical

When the heat exchanger fails, combustion products may enter the house. This is at the very least unpleasant and, if there is less than complete combustion, these products may contain poisonous carbon monoxide.

8.4.3 Conditions

We'll leave the strategy discussion for a moment while we look at the common problems: 1) cracks, holes, or rust; 2) soot deposits on the heat exchanger.

Cracks, Holes, or Rust

Cracks

Cracks or holes in heat exchangers can be tricky to find depending on their location. Cracks can be anywhere, but are often close to the burner area. Sometimes they are right at the front of the burner area. Some cracks will be visible without removing the heat shield. Other cracks will be concealed by the heat shield. Rust on the heat exchanger may or may not mean a leak.

Any Direction

Cracks can be horizontal, vertical, or diagonal. Cracks can be at welds or can be in the field of the metal.

Not Visible on Cold Heat Exchanger

Cracks can be very subtle, especially when the sheet metal is cold. The cracks may get wider as the furnace fires and the heat exchanger warms up, expanding the metal.

Holes

Holes can be anywhere, but often develop as a result of rust caused by condensation. Holes may appear at horizontal surfaces where water may collect. These are often accompanied by rust streaks on the heat exchanger walls.

IMPLICATIONS

Unpleasant combustion products, including poisonous carbon monoxide, may enter the house air. This is a life safety issue and the furnace, or at least the heat exchanger, has to be replaced. Failed heat exchangers may cause the furnace to short cycle because hot exhaust products get into the house air and trip the high temperature limit switch.

High humidity levels may be noted in the home as the moist products of combustion enter the house air.

Burner flames may waver when the house air fan comes on because the air pressure changes leak through to the burner side of the heat exchanger.

Heat exchangers can't usually be patched.

We'll talk about inspection strategy for heat exchangers in a minute.

Soot or Deposits on the Heat Exchanger

Black or White

In some cases, you'll find discoloration on the heat exchanger. This can range from black soot to white powdery deposits. These may or may not indicate a weakening of the steel in the heat exchanger. These conditions should be written up for further investigation and servicing as necessary.

IMPLICATIONS

Soot or deposits on the heat exchanger do not necessarily lead to premature failure, but do reduce the efficiency of the heat exchanger and will reduce house comfort, while increasing heating costs.

8.4.4   Inspection Strategy for Furnace Heat Exchangers

Start Simple

Home inspectors have several strategies for looking at heat exchangers. In all of them, we are looking for cracks, holes, rust, soot or deposits on the heat exchanger.

1. Visual Inspection Using a Mirror and Flashlight

Just Looking

This is a minimal inspection. You should make sure the furnace will not come on during this part of your inspection. The front cover of the cabinet has to be removed. Use a flashlight with a telescopic mirror to see as much of the heat exchanger as you can. In a three-burner furnace, for example, you should look into all three chambers in the heat exchanger, from the front to the back along each chamber, if possible.

Only See a Small Part

You'll probably see only a small percentage (5 to 15 percent) of the heat exchanger. If you find a crack, you can be conclusive. There may still be a crack or rust hole, however, even if you can't find one.

2. Watching the Flame Pattern

Visual Inspection

This is a visual inspection within the scope of the Standards. We've talked earlier about turning the burner on and watching the flame. The flame should be steady and should not be disturbed when the house fan comes on. A flame blown or sucked to one side or the other suggests a hole or crack in the heat exchanger.

3. Short Cycling May Be a Clue

Short Cycling

A furnace that cycles on and off frequently and without satisfying the thermostat may have a crack or hole in the heat exchanger. The high-temperature limit switch may be tripping every time the furnace comes on. Watch for this, but remember that there can be other causes of short cycling.

Techniques that go beyond the Standards include use of combustible gas analyzers, carbon monoxide sensors, and light leakage tests. For a discussion of these, see *Principles of Home Inspection: Gas and Oil Furnaces*.

8.5   FURNACE CABINETS

Provides Support and Contains House Air

The cabinet is not an integral part of the furnace; however, it is often used to support components, including the burner, blower and heat exchanger. The cabinet may also be used to contain house air flowing through the furnace. In this sense, part of the cabinetry is acting as a duct system. The cabinetry often supports the flue collar and incorporates the draft hood.

Fan Compartment Cover

There are usually one or two homeowner-removable covers on the cabinet. A fan cover panel provides access to the fan compartment and filter. This panel has no slots or louvered openings in it.

Burner Cover

A second cover panel provides access to the burner. This panel usually has louvered openings to allow combustion air into the burner.

The homeowner can remove this panel to turn the furnace off for the summer and re-light the furnace in the fall or after a pilot outage.

Service people remove these cover panels for normal cleaning, inspection, and adjustment.

Common problems you'll identify on furnace cabinetry include the following:

1. Rust
2. Mechanical damage
3. Missing components/covers
4. Inadequate combustible clearances
5. Obstructed air intakes
6. Scorching

8.5.1   Rust

IMPLICATIONS

STRATEGY

Loss of support for components and air leakage on the house side are implications. Where rust compromises the integrity of the venting system, there can be a life safety issue. Rust may also attack the heat exchanger.

Look for evidence of rust on all four sides of the cabinetry, and on the top and bottom where accessible. Leaking humidifiers and condensate systems from air conditioners are common causes of rust. All rust should be documented and, while it is a bonus to be able to identify the source of the rusting, this is not required. If you're not sure about the source, don't guess.

8.5.2   Mechanical Damage

IMPLICATIONS

STRATEGY

Careful with Covers

Air leakage on the house side may be an issue and if supports for the venting system are compromised, there can be a safety issue.

If the damage obstructs air-flow into either the burner or the draft hood, there are safety issues.

Mechanical damage should be documented for further investigation by a technician unless you're sure there is no performance problem.

You can look foolish if you remove a cover from either the fan compartment or the burner compartment and then can't get it back on. Brute force is generally not the solution. If you have trouble getting a panel cover back in place, take it off and look at the bracket, latch or support mechanism that holds it in place. Ninety-nine times out of a hundred, you just have to line parts up properly and slip them into place by moving the cover in the right direction.

8.5.3   Missing Components

IMPLICATIONS

If the fan cover is missing, in some cases the furnace won't run. In others, the cold air return system will be substantially bypassed as the fan pulls air straight in from the furnace area. This can cause backdrafting and lead to life safety problems, particularly if the furnace is in an enclosed room. People or animals may be hurt by the fan, or get an electrical shock. Since the filter may be bypassed, the heat exchanger, air conditioning coil and supply duct system can get dirty quickly.

The implications of a missing burner cover include the possibility of having high temperature surfaces exposed, allowing people or animals to touch the flame. The cover also protects the burner and controls from mechanical damage and the accumulation of dirt. If the panel is missing, there is also the danger of electrical shock.

You should note any missing cabinet components, including cover panels, and recommend replacement. In some cases, you may find that parts of the sheet metal have literally been cut away. Check all surfaces of the cabinetry.

Don't mistake a draft hood opening for a missing panel cover. Some draft hood openings are an integral part of the cabinetry and form a large rectangular hole. At first glance, it may seem like a cover should be provided here. Some experience with furnaces will help you recognize whether there should be a cover. The absence of any securing mechanism should be a clue, as is the air drawn in through the draft hood and the high temperatures felt if you reach your hand in far enough.

8.5.4   Combustible Clearances

The obvious risk here is fire.

The **data plate** on most furnaces specifies the required clearances from combustibles. Many furnaces are designed for installation on combustible flooring; however, some are not.

Clearances around the front, sides and back should be compared to the data plate. These clearances are usually quite small as the cabinetry provides significant protection and containment of the heat. Usually 30 inches clearance is required in front of any furnace, for service access.

There should also be a clearance indicated for the top or supply plenum (on an upflow furnace). Generally, the supply plenum on an upflow furnace should be at least one inch below a combustible ceiling or framing.

8.5.5   Obstructed Air Intake

The implications are inefficient operation and backdrafting, leading to life safety concerns of carbon monoxide.

Check that air intakes are clear.

8.5.6   Scorching

Scorching on the front of the cabinet is usually the result of flame rollout or flashback. This is a burner malfunction. Very often the controls or burner area behind the panel are scorched as well. It would be unusual to have the panel scorched without the control area also suffering. Scorching on the sides or back of the cabinet may indicate a hole in the heat exchanger. Recommend further evaluation.

Scorching may also be visible around the draft hood. This is usually caused by either a chimney obstruction or a draft problem leading to exhaust spillage and backdrafting.

Scorching may be caused by an over-temperature condition. In furnaces with refractory/fire pots, a failed refractory can lead to scorching and discoloration of the cabinet. The cabinetry may not be properly insulated from high temperatures if the refractory is not doing its job.

IMPLICATIONS

STRATEGY

There is a possibility of fire and electrical shock.

Scorching often suggests inadequate combustion and/or dilution air. There may be a life safety issue associated with combustion products spilling into the house.

Check all exposed surfaces for scorching. Check the inside of the burner cover panel when you remove it. It's common to find evidence of scorching here. Look at the sides and back of the cabinet. A hole in the heat exchanger usually means replacing the furnace. It is also a life safety issue.

8.6   FAN CONTROLS AND HIGH LIMIT SWITCHES

We will discuss these components in the same section since they are prone to the same conditions.

8.6.1   Fan Controls

Fan on and off Cycles

As soon as people thought of putting fans on furnaces, they thought about ways to control them. After some trial and error, people concluded that the furnace fan should not come on at the same time as the burner. When the burner first comes on, the furnace is still cold, and blowing cold air around the house irritates people.

Delay Fan Start up

The solution was to delay the fan until the air in the furnace was warm. A sensor in the house-air side of the heat exchanger measures the air temperature coming off the heat exchanger. When this air is warm enough, it turns on the fan and blows the warm air around the house. The sensor is usually set to turn the house fan on when the furnace air reaches 120°F to 150°F.

The same sensor that turns the fan on is used to turn the fan off, typically when the temperature drops to 80°F to 110°F. This is typically two to four minutes after the burner shuts off.

Manual Override

Summer Switch

Some furnaces have a manual override to allow the fan to be turned on without the furnace. This is sometimes called a **summer switch** because the fan can circulate air through the house during the warm summer weather to provide some cooling.

Switch on Thermostat

Some house thermostats also include a switch, usually labeled **Fan-On-Auto** to override the fan. In the **Auto** position, the fan is controlled by the sensor as we've discussed. In the **On** position, the fan will be on all the time, whether or not the burner is on.

Location of Switch

This switch may be at the thermostat, on the exterior of the furnace cabinet or inside the furnace on the front of the fan/limit control and accessible only by removing the burner cover panel.

Timer

In many modern furnaces, this function is controlled electronically, often based on time, rather than temperature.

8.6.2   Limit Switches

Limit Is Safety Switch

Limit switches are often combined in the same sensor and box as the fan control switch (Figure 8.11). The two are commonly referred to jointly as the **fan/limit**

FIGURE 8.11   Fan/Limit Switch

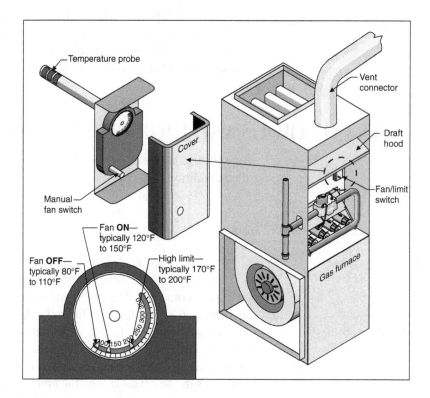

switch. This is not a switch that "limits the fan." It is a switch with two distinct functions. The first is to turn the fan on and off; the second is to control the high-temperature limit. The limit function will shut off the burner if the temperature in the house gets too high (170°F to 200°F, typically). We use the same sensor as we used to control the fan, but the limit is not a normal operating device. It's an emergency safety shutoff or automatic safety control.

The limit switch can be a separate switch and on some furnaces this function is performed separately.

Why It Trips

The furnace may get too hot because the gas valve fails to shut off (defective gas valve or thermostat) or the house-air side may overheat if there is a hole or crack in the heat exchanger. Inadequate air flow through the furnace may also overheat the furnace.

8.6.3   Conditions

Problems with fan controls and limit switches may include the following:

1. Set wrong or defective
2. Scorching
3. Rusting or dirty
4. Mechanical damage

5. Improperly wired

6. Missing cover

We've talked about scorching from flame rollout or flashbacks, so we won't discuss this again.

We've also talked about dirty, rusting and mechanical damage on several furnace components. The same issues apply here.

If the fan control switch is not wired correctly, it can't do its job. The addtion of central air conditioning can result in bypassing the limit switch; however, we usually won't discover this condition on a home inspection.

A missing cover on a fan/limit switch is another condition that a home inspector should identify and recommend correction.

However, the important issue with fan and limit controls is that they be set properly. Let's look at that condition.

Air Conditioning Controls May Accidentally Bypass Fan/Limit

Set Wrong or Defective

The fan should be set to cut in at 120°F to 150°F. The fan should cut out at 80°F to 110°F. The high temperature limit setting should be 170°F to 200°F.

IMPLICATIONS

The implications are poor comfort and high heating bills if the **fan control** is the problem. Burning down the house is the implication of a defective or incorrectly set **limit switch.**

STRATEGY

It goes beyond the Standards to pull the cover off a fan/limit switch to check these settings, although some home inspectors do. On some types, you can see the settings without removing cover plates (other than the burner access panel in the cabinet). Some covers can simply be pulled off. In other cases, they must have screws removed or loosened.

Whether or not you take the covers off fan/limit switches to check the settings, you should do an operational test. You can use a thermometer to check at what temperature the fan turns on and off, although most inspectors don't go this far.

If the device is defective, the settings may be right, but the furnace may not run correctly.

When the thermostat is turned up, normal operation follows this sequence:

1. Thermostat calls for heat.

2. The thermocouple is constantly verifying that the pilot is on.

3. If the pilot is on, the gas valve opens and the burners are ignited.

4. The temperature starts to rise in the house-air side plenum, as heat from the fire side moves through the heat exchanger.

5. When the **fan control** sensor on the house-air side reaches 120°F (for example), the fan will come on.

6. The heat is distributed through the house.

7. When the thermostat reaches its set point, the burner shuts off.

8. The fan keeps running until the **fan control** sensor on the house-air side feels the temperature drop to 80°F, for example.

9. The fan shuts off.

In a runaway burner situation or when there is a hole in a heat exchanger, the sensor may reach 200°F. At this point, it will shut off the burner, even though the thermostat is still calling for more heat. When the temperature drops, the **limit switch** will allow the burner to come back on. If it overheats again, it will shut the burner off again.

Short Cycling

A short-cycling situation may develop where the furnace keeps coming on and off, but the house doesn't get warm. Watch for this situation when testing the furnace.

8.7   THERMOSTATS

Thermostats are designed to turn the heating system on and off at the right times to keep us comfortable. Thermostats aren't mounted on the furnace because people don't live in the furnace room. Thermostats are put in the rooms where we live, and should be in a location that's representative of the average temperature.

The homeowner sets or adjusts the temperature by adjusting a gauge or dial or pushing buttons. Thermostats may use mercury bulbs and bimetallic strips or electronic sensors.

8.7.1   Conditions

Let's look as some of the common problems we'll find with thermostats, keeping in mind that we are not service technicians.

1. Poor location
2. Not level
3. Loose
4. Dirty
5. Damaged
6. Poor adjustment/calibration

Poor Location

Central

Thermostats should be located near the center of the home. They should not see direct sunlight, direct radiated heat from fireplaces, etc.

Not in Kitchens

Thermostats should not be located on exterior walls. They should not be located in kitchens (since kitchens tend to be warmer than the rest of the house).

Not Against Ducts, Pipes, or Chimneys

Thermostats should not be located on walls containing ducts or piping that may be considerably warmer or cooler than the room, nor on walls containing chimneys.

Away from Doors and Windows

Thermostats should not be adjacent to doorways or windows that will be opened frequently during the heating season. These drafts can cause heating systems to come on frequently for short periods.

Five Feet above Floor

Thermostats are usually located about 5 feet above floor level where they are easy to read.

IMPLICATIONS

The house is likely to be less comfortable than it should, since the thermostat will sense the room is either warmer or colder than it actually is. Heating bills may also be higher than they should be.

STRATEGY

If the thermostat is in a poor location, advise that there may be a comfort issue, and that relocating the thermostat is not a big expense.

Not Level

Mercury bulb thermostats must be level to work properly.

IMPLICATION

The set temperature of the thermostat will not be an accurate reflection of the room temperature.

With square or rectangular thermostats, it's easy to check whether the thermostat is within a few degrees of level. With a circular thermostat, it's a little harder to determine. If you pull the cover off (which goes beyond the Standards) most thermostats have either leveling lines or leveling posts that can be checked.

During the heating season, you'll be able to tell whether the room is comfortable. If the thermostat has to be set at 85°F or at 60°F to keep it at roughly 70°F, the thermostat may well be not level. There could also be a calibration problem.

Loose

Mercury bulb thermostats must be well secured to the wall to work properly.

Faulty reading on the thermostat, resulting in large temperature swings or excessive on and off cycles for the furnace, is the implication.

When you are turning the thermostat up to test the heating system, gently grab the thermostat base (not just the cover) and make sure it's well secured.

Dirty

If dirt insulates the bimetallic strip or prevents the contacts from closing the circuit, the thermostat cannot operate the furnace accurately, if at all.

You can get a sense of the cleanliness of the thermostat by looking at the cover. If you remove the cover, you can see the unit itself. Sometimes the cover can be wiped clean, but the thermostat itself is filthy.

Damaged

Implications range from no heat to excessive heat with extreme temperature fluctuations and frequent on/off cycles. Poor comfort and high heating costs are common.

Look for evidence of mechanical damage. If you take the cover off the thermostat, you may be able to identify concealed damage.

Poor Adjustment/Calibration

Don't worry too much about the thermostat being out of calibration by one or two degrees. People will keep the house at whatever is comfortable for them. Whether people feel comfortable with the thermostat set at 71°F or 74°F is not that important. However, if the room feels comfortable and the thermostat is set at 85°F, it may be so far out of calibration that the furnace operation is not predictable.

Excessive temperature fluctuations may result.

Check that the temperature setting of the thermostat is close to the temperature in the house.

8.7.2 Summary

Wherever you see thermostats that do not appear to be operating properly, recommend a technician investigate and correct as necessary. Sometimes you will simply report the furnace as inoperable. You won't know whether the problem is the thermostat, gas valve, pilot, limit switch, or another cause. Don't apologize for not being able to identify the specific problem, but make sure you identify erratic or non-performance of the furnace.

8.8   VENTING SYSTEMS AND VENT CONNECTORS

The function of the venting system on a natural-draft, gas-fired, forced-air furnace is to carry the products of combustion safely and quickly out of the house (before they cool) using the natural buoyancy of the warm gases (convection). The products of combustion get heavier and wetter as they cool. We want to avoid their cooling to the point where they linger in the house or chimney, and we want to get them outside before they condense.

8.8.1   Components

The components of the venting system include—

- the exhaust flue components of the appliance, including the draft hood
- the vent connector
- the chimney or vent

The venting system of the appliance is integral and not much can be seen of it. The **draft hood** may be part of the appliance or may be part of the vent connector at the top of the appliance. The draft hood, incidentally, is also called the **draft diverter.** The vent connector joins the appliance to the chimney.

Materials   Vent connectors are typically single-wall metal pipes on conventional gas furnaces. They are usually made of galvanized steel or aluminum.

Location   They run from the appliance to the chimney, and the shorter the vent connector, the better.

Other Names   Vent connectors are also called **exhaust flues, C vents, vent pipes, stack pipes, flue pipes, chimney connectors,** or **breachings.**

Function   The vent connector allows the exhaust gases to move from the furnace to the chimney.

In Chapter 11, we talk about several chimney and vent problems. Here, we'll focus on vent connector conditions.

8.8.2   Conditions

Let's look first at the general problems that we'll find with vent connectors.

Two fundamental things can go wrong: spillage and condensation.

Spillage (backdrafting) occurs when the exhaust products don't leave the house through the chimney, but enter the house itself. This has safety implications, especially where incomplete combustion is involved and carbon monoxide is produced.

General Strategy   The field test of a venting system is relatively simple. When the furnace is operating, do the exhaust gases leave the house safely through the chimney or vent, or do they spill into the house?

This can be a little misleading, because a chimney that vents properly on the day of the inspection may not vent properly under all weather conditions. When the weather outside is colder or the wind is from a different direction, for example, the operation of the chimney may be quite different. Similarly, a furnace may vent properly with the furnace room door open, but may spill when the door is closed.

High Temperature and Odor   When the appliance is operating, you can identify spillage by the high temperature, high humidity and, in some cases, the odor of the products of combustion entering the house. They may enter any place the venting system is compromised. A common spot for spillage is at the draft hood (diverter hood).

Seeing Condensation

You may be able to see condensation in the venting system. Sometimes it will drip out at seams in the vent connector. You may see it at the draft hood, at the heat exchanger, or dripping into the burner compartment after the burner shuts down. Condensation may only occur during certain seasons. You won't necessarily get condensation on the day of your inspection, even if it is a problem on that furnace.

Evidence of Condensation

Often you only see evidence of condensation, which includes rusting and corrosion. This is sometimes evident along the bottom surfaces of the vent connector, and/or around the draft hood.

Now, let's look at some specific vent connector conditions:

1. Rust
2. Poor slope
3. Too long
4. Poor support
5. Poor connections
6. Inadequate combustible clearances
7. Too small or too big for the furnace
8. Improper material
9. Poor manifolding
10. Vent connector extends too far into the chimney
11. Spillage at the draft hood
12. Obstruction

Rust

IMPLICATIONS

If the vent connector has rusted through, exhaust products will get into the house.

STRATEGY

Look at the entire venting system for evidence of rust. Even small surface rust should be written up for further evaluation by a specialist.

Poor Slope

The vent connector should slope upward going away from the furnace at a minimum of $1/4$ inch per foot.

IMPLICATIONS

Exhaust spillage into the house is the implication.

Another implication of inadequate slope is that condensation may collect in the vent connector system. This can damage the vent connector.

STRATEGY

You don't need any instruments to look at the vent connector and see that it slopes up from the appliance to the chimney connection. The longer the vent connector is, the more difficult it is to achieve this slope.

Vent Connector Too Long

The horizontal run of the vent connector should be as short as possible.

IMPLICATION

Exhaust spillage into the house is the implication. The greater the near-horizontal length of the vent connector, the more difficult it is for exhaust products to travel from the appliance to the outdoors.

STRATEGY

Look for vent connectors to be less than 5 feet long. Where they are 5 to 10 feet long, the situation may be acceptable, but it's marginal. Vent connectors more than 10 feet long should be described as suspect and investigation by a specialist should be recommended.

The vent connector length should be no more than 75% of the chimney height. Most vent connectors are single-wall. When a double-wall B-vent is used as the vent connector, it can be up to 100 percent of the chimney height.

Recommend further investigation where vent connector lengths are suspect. This is a complicated issue and you should not take a firm stand you can't defend authoratively.

Poor Support

Vent connectors should be adequately supported with non-combustible material so they are intact and maintain their slope. Manufacturers set support requirements, often saying supports are needed every 4 feet and at every elbow (Figure 8.12).

IMPLICATIONS

The implications are products of combustion finding their way into the house.

STRATEGY

Common sense is appropriate here. If the slope is appropriate, support is probably adequate.

Poor Connections

Sections of vent connectors should be well secured. Three screws is common. Other connection mechanisms may be acceptable.

IMPLICATION

The implication is leakage of combustion products into the home.

STRATEGY

Visually examine all connections to ensure that they are intact. Sags or changes in direction often indicate a poor connection. Watch for disconnected vent connectors. These are most common where the vent connector joins the chimney or the furnace.

Check the entire circumference of each connection.

Inadequate Clearance from Combustibles

Look for a 6-inch clearance from combustibles on vent connectors unless a B vent is used, in which case a one-inch clearance is all that is required. B vents are double-walled with an air space between the walls.

IMPLICATIONS

If the clearance from combustibles is not adequate, there is a fire hazard.

FIGURE 8.12   Vent Connector Support

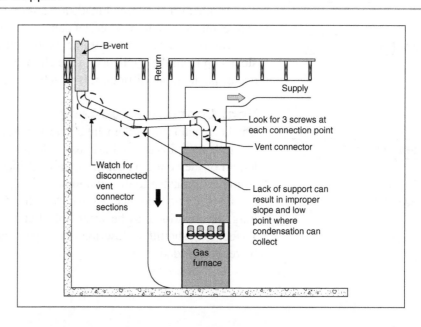

Watch for the clearance from walls and ceilings. Many authorities consider drywall combustible because of the paper surfacing.

Vent connectors should not go through walls or ceilings to connect to remote chimneys. While these arrangements may be allowed in special circumstances, they should be written up as suspect.

Combustible clearances can sometimes be reduced with protective materials.

Vent Connector Too Small or Too Big for the Furnace

The vent connector should usually be the same size as the flue collar on the appliance. Where more than one appliance is manifolded, the vent connector size should increase (Figure 8.13).

The implications are spillage of combustion products and/or condensation.

Check the size of the vent connector and the size of the flue collar on the appliance. If they are different, you should recommend this be checked during regular servicing. Where the vent connector is sized differently, check carefully for spillage during your operating test and look for evidence of condensation along the vent connector, at the bottom of the chimney and at the furnace.

We do not check the design of vent connectors, just as we don't check the design of roof trusses. You are only looking for gross mismatching, checking system performance, and then asking for a specialist's opinion, not offering a conclusion.

Improper Material

The implication is exhaust entering the house.

Unless you are aware of the suitability of the material used, recommend that it be checked.

Look for inspection tags or stickers by authorities having jurisdiction. While it is not a guarantee that the installation is acceptable (we have found many installations where the gas company was subsequently critical of the installation), it is an indication. The absence of an inspection tag may mean there was never an inspection done, or simply that the tag has been misplaced.

Watch for **dryer vent** gauge aluminum used as a vent connector. This is not appropriate. Aluminum must be of a heavier gauge than galvanized steel to be used as a gas appliance vent connector. Dryer vent is very thin.

Watch also for corrugated vent connectors. These are often inappropriate materials.

Poor Manifolding

Multiple vent connectors connected to the same chimney flue should connect to the chimney one above the other. It's good practice to put the smaller appliance vent connector above the larger appliance (Figure 8.14). The exhaust from the larger appliance could choke off the exhaust from the smaller appliance if the smaller one is below.

Exhaust spillage is the implication.

Where the appliance vent connectors are manifolded into a single vent connector before they go into the chimney, make sure the single vent connector is larger than the other two going into it. In addition, the vent connector should be as close to the ceiling level as possible while maintaining combustible clearances.

One has to be careful combining power-vented (forced-draft or induced-draft) appliances with natural appliances. Under some circumstances, the fan from one appliance can push the products of combustion out through the draft hood of the natural-draft appliance, especially if it is idle while the power-vented appliance is working. Again, an analysis of when this is acceptable is beyond the scope of the inspection. Recommend that the situation be checked during regular servicing.

FIGURE 8.13   Size of Vent Connector

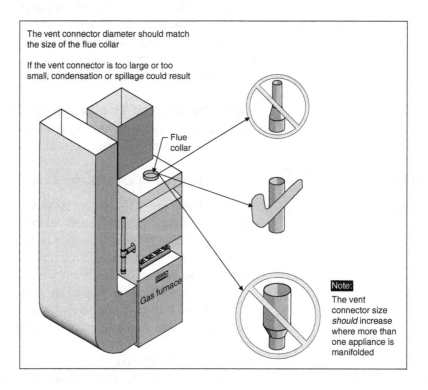

The vent connector diameter should match the size of the flue collar

If the vent connector is too large or too small, condensation or spillage could result

Flue collar

Gas furnace

Note:
The vent connector size *should* increase where more than one appliance is manifolded

Vent Connector Extends Too Far into the Chimney

If the vent connector goes too far into the chimney, it is effectively choked off and can't vent properly.

IMPLICATION

This could allow products of combustion to enter the house.

STRATEGY

If there is a chimney clean-out, use your flashlight and mirror to look up the chimney. You should not be able to see the vent connector projecting into the chimney opening, reducing the chimney diameter.

Check from Above

In some cases, you can get a look down from the top of the chimney, although you can't always see far enough down to determine whether the vent connector projects too far into the flue.

Can't Always Tell

You may not be able to tell whether the vent connector goes into the chimney too far.

Spillage at the Draft Hood

We touched on this a number of times, as a symptom of several problems, but it's important enough to treat it as a condition by itself.

Add Air to Maintain Chimney Draft

Draft hoods break the draft from the burner to maintain a constant airflow through the burner. If the draft hood weren't there, as the draft is established in the chimney, more and more air would move through the burner. This would disturb the burner operation. As the velocity up the chimney changes, more air is drawn in through the draft hood without disturbing the burner.

Deflect Downdrafts

A second function of the draft hood is to deflect downdrafts in the chimney. This prevents them from disturbing or blowing out the flame at the burner.

F I G U R E 8.14 Chimney/Vent Connections

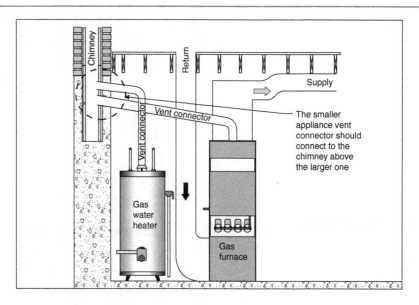

IMPLICATIONS	The implication is the disturbance to the burner operation as discussed.
STRATEGY	While the furnace is operating, check for spillage at the draft hood. A little spillage on start-up for the first minute or two is not a problem, but once the furnace is warmed up there should be no spillage.
Test Not Conclusive	There may be no spillage on the day you test the furnace, but there could be spillage under different weather conditions.

8.9 DISTRIBUTION SYSTEM

Moving Heat through the Home

We've been talking so far about how to get fuel to the furnace, how we burn the fuel and how we get rid of the products of combustion. Now we're going to look at how we move the heat around the house.

Supply Air

The air circulated through the house by the furnace moves in a loop (Figure 8.15). Heat is collected from the heat exchanger by the house air blowing across the heat exchanger. The air is pushed across the heat exchanger by a blower in the duct system located just upstream of the heat exchanger. This blower is an integral part of the furnace.

The air is pushed past the heat exchanger, then into the supply duct system, through the main supply ducts and branch ducts to individual room registers where the warm air is discharged into the room.

Return Air

Another set of grilles (the return grilles) collects the cool air from the rooms and brings it back to the furnace to be heated again. The same fan that **pushed** air past the heat exchanger and through the supply ducts also **pulls** air through the return grilles and return ducts. This air is collected at the furnace and is pulled through a filter. The cool, cleaned return air is then pushed by the fan across the heat exchanger.

F I G U R E 8.15   House Air Flow

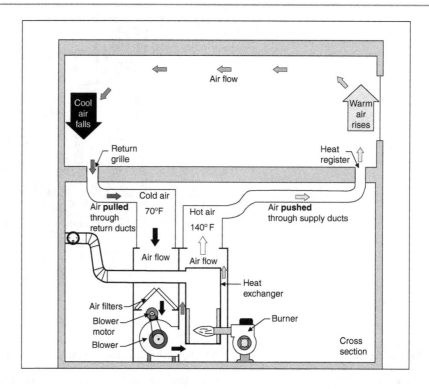

No Air Changes

There is no intentional exhausting of air and no air make-up from the outside. We keep cycling the same air and simply warm it up every time it passes through the furnace.

Distribution Challenges

A good distribution system will deliver approximately the same temperature to all rooms in a house. This is a challenge because—

- not all rooms are the same size
- they don't all face the same direction
- they don't all have the same exposure to cold walls and ceilings (some rooms may have one exterior wall, others may have two or three)
- they don't all have the same number and size of windows
- some rooms tend to generate more heat (kitchens, for example, have refrigerators that warm the room)
- not all rooms are the same distance from the furnace

Complaints Usually Distribution Related

Most complaints are based on the distribution system rather than on the furnace size. Furnaces are usually at least adequately sized for the house, and most are oversized. Duct systems, however, are frequently undersized and/or poorly arranged and balanced.

We'll look at some good practices in distribution design, but before we do, let's touch on the locations of some of the components.

F I G U R E 8.16   Typical Supply and Return Register Locations

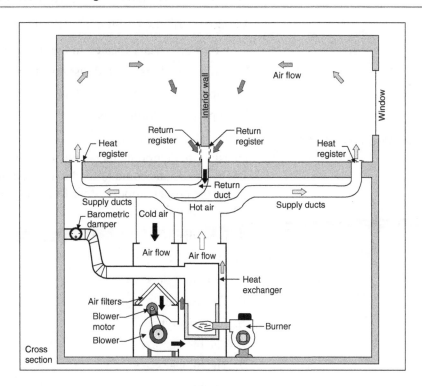

8.9.1   Supply and Return Locations for Heating

Supply

The coldest part of a room is usually on an outside wall, around windows. Consequently, it makes sense to put the warm air into the room near an outside wall below a window (Figure 8.16). The warm air should come into a room at floor level since warm air tends to rise. This gives good mixing of the warm air throughout the room. Rooms with supply registers near ceilings or supply registers on interior walls are likely to be less comfortable.

Return

Cold air returns should be as far away from the supply registers as possible. Cold air returns are usually near floor level on interior walls, often close to the center of a house and frequently near the bottom of stairs, since heavier cool air tends to roll down stairwells.

10 Feet from Fan

Return grilles should be kept at least 10 feet from the furnace, or should be in a separate room. If there is a return grille close to the furnace, the house air fan may create enough suction at the return grille to pull air out of the draft hood or burner compartment causing spillage or flame roll-out at the burner.

No Return in Furnace Room

Return grilles should not be in enclosed furnace rooms for the same reason.

Supply to Each Room

Most residential duct design includes a supply register for each room but does not include a return grille for each room. The best systems do have returns in each room, although this is unusual.

High and Low Returns

Where high and low air returns are provided (typical in houses with central air conditioning), the high level return typically works during the summer and the low-level return works during the winter. Both should not be open at the same time, in most installations.

Balancing

Most residential heating systems are not well balanced. A good balancing exercise is a first step to improving airflow and comfort.

8.9.2 Distribution System Components

A house distribution system is made up of—

1. a blower, usually located in the furnace
2. a filter or filters located just upstream of the blower
3. supply and return duct system
4. supply and return registers

Factors Affecting Air Supply

Duct system calculations are complicated and beyond the Standards, which do not ask us to determine the adequacy or balance of heat supply. Nevertheless, you should understand some of the factors that influence the ability of a duct system to supply the proper amount of air to each room. The following is a list of items that can influence this:

1. Duct size
2. Duct shape
3. Length of duct
4. The number of corners
5. The duct type
6. The blower size
7. The blower speed
8. The blower blade profile
9. The furnace location
10. System extras

8.9.3 Blowers

Very Low Pressure

The blower is contained in the furnace itself and is the source of pressure that moves the air through the ducts. The blower really exerts very little pressure, so it is important for the system that supplies and returns the air through the house be free of obstruction.

Types

Blowers are typically **belt-driven** or **direct-drive** (Figure 8.17). The belt-driven ones are easy to identify because the motor sits beside the fan, and a belt and pulleys drive the fan. The direct-drive units are neater looking, because the motor is mounted inside the body of the fan. There is no belt with direct-drive systems; the shaft at the end of the motor drives the fan.

Common blower problems include the following:

1. Dirty
2. Noisy
3. Inoperative
4. Overheating
5. Rust
6. Poorly secured
7. Running continuously
8. Too small
9. Unbalanced/vibration
10. Fan belt loose, worn or damaged

FIGURE 8.17   Blowers—Belt Drive and Direct Drive

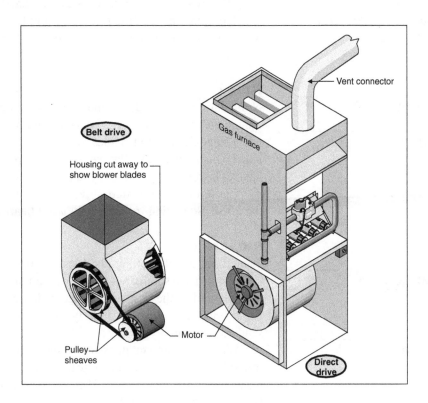

Dirty

IMPLICATIONS	

Dirt on the blower blades dramatically reduces the capacity. This will not only reduce comfort and increase heating costs, but also can overheat and shorten the life of the heat exchanger.

Dirt on the blades can also ruin the balance of the fan. Noise, vibration, and bearing wear can result.

General Inspection Strategies

To inspect the blower, you'll have to remove the blower cover. On some furnaces, a **fan interlock switch** will shut off the furnace when you remove this cover. If a switch is present and is wired correctly, you should be able to inspect the blower without fear of the blower coming on and injuring you.

Turn off Furnace Power

However, if the blower does not have such an interlock switch (and maybe even if it does, since it might be wired incorrectly), the power to the furnace should be shut off while you inspect the blower. There is usually a switch (like a light switch) close to the furnace. It may also be a fused disconnect. If the blower comes on while you are checking it, you can be injured. Your clothing can also be caught by the blower or motor and pulled in.

Summer Switch

Most furnaces have a switch that allows you to run the blower without the furnace running. This is sometimes called the **Summer Switch,** and on other furnaces can be operated by turning a thermostat-mounted switch labeled **Fan-On-Auto** to the **On** position.

You should not run the furnace fan for more than a minute or two with the blower cover missing.

Blower Is the Same as Fan

Incidentally, you'll notice that we use the words **blower** and **fan** interchangeably here; they mean the same thing. **Air handler** means the same thing, too.

Mirror and Flashlight

Ensure that the power to the blower is turned off. Use a mirror and flashlight to look at the fan blades. Sometimes removing the filter allows you to get a better look. If the casing of the blower and motor are dirty, the blades are probably also dirty.

Should Be Checked During Servicing

The cleanliness of the blower should be checked during the furnace servicing. Most inspectors recommend servicing the heating system as soon as a new owner takes possession of a home.

Noisy

IMPLICATIONS

STRATEGY

Noisy fans usually indicate that cleaning or adjustment is needed. There is usually damage being done to belts, bearings and motors if the fan is unusually noisy.

You don't have to troubleshoot the cause of the noise, but you do need to report it and recommend immediate servicing. It is possible that the blower and/or motor will have to be replaced, although you probably won't know this from your inspection.

Get to know the sound of a blower running normally. Listen for variations in the noise. Squealing may indicate worn bearings or a slipping fan belt.

Inoperative

Sometimes the blower simply doesn't work.

IMPLICATIONS

The furnace should not be run with an inoperative fan. Although some heat may be delivered to the house, the heat exchanger is likely to overheat. Operating the furnace in this fashion will likely shorten the life of the heat exchanger, and may void the warranty.

STRATEGY

Where the blower does not respond to normal test procedures, recommend immediate servicing. You can turn on the fan manually with a switch on some furnaces (or on the thermostat). If the fan responds to the switch, it is a control problem rather than a fan problem.

Overheating

The motor or blower may overheat.

IMPLICATIONS

At the least, adjustments are needed and at the worst, replacement of the blower or motor may be required. It is beyond our scope to determine what the appropriate corrective action is.

STRATEGY

When you inspect the blower and motor, if it has been running recently, you may be able to tell by touch that the unit is too hot. If you turn the fan on with the door open (be very careful doing this), you may be able to sense that the unit is overheating.

Overheating is often accompanied with noisy operation and excessive vibration, although this isn't always the case.

Rust

IMPLICATION

Rust on the blower or motor may indicate that premature failure is likely.

STRATEGY

Where you see rust on the blower or motor, recommend further investigation during servicing.

Poorly Secured

The fan and the motor should be securely bolted to the furnace cabinet, preferably with a rubber bushing to minimize vibration.

IMPLICATION

Blowers or motors that are not well secured will be out of alignment and are likely to be noisy and to suffer belt and bearing damage.

STRATEGY

Where the blower or motor is loose, recommend re-securing. You can determine this by putting your hand on the blower or motor and trying to rock it back and forth and side to side. Make sure the power is off and the unit is cool before handling the fan.

Running Continuously

With some exceptions, blowers should not be operating when the furnace is off. People may set the blower to run continuously if they choose. Multi-speed direct drive blowers can also run at low speed to filter and humidify air when the furnace is not on. When the furnace kicks on, they will operate at a higher speed.

IMPLICATIONS

Cool, unpleasant drafts may be experienced. Electrical costs will be higher and the fan and motor life may be shortened.

STRATEGY

If the fan is running continuously, check to see if the **Summer Switch** or fan **On** switch has been set to control this. Sometimes these switches are broken or stuck in the **On** position. In the **Auto** position, the fan should run only when the furnace is on.

Change in Fan Speed

When you operate the furnace, notice whether the fan speed changes. It's possible that the fan is running on low speed by design.

Explain Possibilities

Explain to your clients the choices for fan operation. If there appears to be no intent to have the fan running continuously, it's possible that the fan control switch is defective or has been by-passed. Where the fan is running continuously for no apparent reason, servicing should be recommended to verify that the fan and limit functions have not been compromised.

Too Small

A motor that is too small may result in excessive temperature rise across the heat exchanger. This can shorten the life of the heat exchanger and, in severe cases, can cause the high temperature limit to shut the furnace off.

IMPLICATIONS

An undersized motor will also be unable to deliver adequate air volume through the duct system, especially to the remote registers. The house may be uncomfortable.

The clues that the motor may be too small are—

STRATEGY

1. an excessive temperature rise across the heat exchanger
2. poor air flow at remote registers

There are other possible reasons for these symptoms: a dirty filter or poorly balanced duct system can yield the same result. Don't do any conclusive diagnosis. Report the **symptoms** to the client and explain possible causes, allowing for the possibility that there are other causes.

Unbalanced/Vibration

While excessive vibration and poor balance are often accompanied by noise, this is not always the case.

IMPLICATIONS

The implications include excessive bearing and belt wear and premature failure of the blower and motor.

STRATEGY

Sometimes excessive vibration is apparent throughout the house as the entire duct system may transmit noise and vibration. In other cases, it is only noticeable at the furnace. If you run the furnace fan with the cover off, you can usually see excessive vibration.

Check the alignment of the pulleys on belt driven fans. If they are offset, the belt won't travel easily, and may wear prematurely. This can result in vibration.

Recommend adjustment, cleaning or re-securing as necessary to cure the excessive vibration problem. In some cases, the blower or motor may be damaged and may have to be replaced to solve the problem.

Fan Belt Loose, Worn, or Damaged

If the belt does not transfer energy efficiently from the motor to the blower, the blower won't turn properly. This will result in decreased airflow through the house, causing poor comfort, high heating costs and perhaps a shortened life expectancy for the heat exchanger.

If the belt is too loose, it will slip. This is often accompanied by a squealing noise. If the belt is too tight, the bearings may wear excessively and the motor may have to work too hard. A motor that is overheating may be the result of a fan belt that's too tight.

Look for cracks in the belt. If you are sure you have shut the power off, you can move the belt around so you can see it all. The tension on the belt should be such that you can push the belt in about one inch, at the halfway point between the pulleys. On some units, the movement is designed to be less than this (as little as one-half inch). Again, don't pretend to be a service technician.

Obvious damage or wear to the belt, a slipping belt, or misaligned belt should be reported for improvement.

8.9.4   Filters

Filters either can be conventional mechanical filters or electronic air cleaners. There are other options as well, although these are the two most common.

Filters help clean the house air, making the environment more pleasant. Filters also clean the air before it passes through the blower and heat exchanger. This helps to keep these furnace components working efficiently.

The Standards say we do not have to inspect electronic air cleaners. However, we will touch on them here since they are common, and most inspectors do check them. Let's look at conventional filters first.

Mechanical Filters

Conventional air filters are typically made of fiberglass in a cardboard or plastic frame. There are other types of systems, including pleated fabric-type filters. Some filters are disposable. Other types are washable and can be reused.

Common problems with mechanical filters include—

1. Missing
2. Dirty
3. Installed backwards
4. Wrong size
5. Loose or collapsed

Missing

First, we need to check to see if a filter is present. There are some circumstances where you don't need a conventional filter—

- if there is an electronic air cleaner
- if it's a gravity warm-air furnace rather than a forced-air furnace (i.e., there is no fan)

On the other hand, some furnaces are designed to have two filters. These are often installed at different angles and are required to completely filter the air path.

IMPLICATIONS

STRATEGY

The furnace is likely to get dirty. This reduces efficiency and comfort and increases heating costs. If there is an air conditioning evaporator coil in the supply duct, this coil is likely to become clogged if there is no filter. This will restrict airflow through the system. This not only reduces comfort and increases heating and cooling costs, it can shorten the heat exchanger life.

Make sure there's a filter unless it's a gravity furnace or has an electronic air cleaner. Make sure that the entire air path is protected by a filter. If there is a frame for two filters, make sure there are two in place.

Some Lennox furnaces use a basket type filter. This is a fiberglass filter set in a wire frame. The wire frame is U-shaped and so is the filter. There is a bottom and two sides to the filter, typically. The wire basket alone is not a filter. There has to be a fiberglass filter media attached to it.

Dirty

IMPLICATIONS

Dirty air filters may restrict airflow, reduce comfort, increase costs, ice up air conditioning evaporator coils and overheat the heat exchanger.

STRATEGY

Pull out the filter and check it. If your client is available, you can show them how to change the filter. You can also tell them whether it's a washable or disposable type.

Installed Backwards

Conventional filters have an arrow on the frame that indicates the direction of air flow (Figure 8.18).

IMPLICATION

The filter is more likely to be pulled into the fan and become tangled if it is installed backwards.

STRATEGY

Pull out the filter and make sure that the arrow indicating the airflow is in the right direction. Again, as a courtesy, you can explain to your client how the filter should be installed. Do not correct a filter installed backwards. All the trapped dirt will be released into the furnace if you do. Recommend replacing or cleaning the filter and then installing it properly.

FIGURE 8.18 Air Filter Orientation

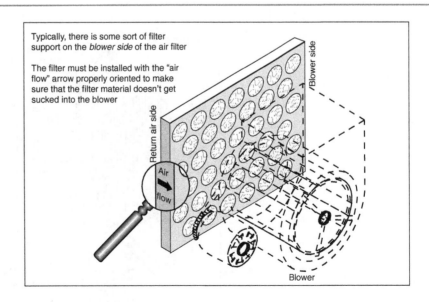

Wrong Size

IMPLICATION

Some of the air will not be filtered.

STRATEGY

Check to see that the filter completely covers the air path. If two filters are needed, make sure both are in place.

Loose or Collapsed Filters

IMPLICATIONS

The implications are a lack of filtering and possible damage to the blower and motor. Since the filters are located immediately upstream of the blower, the blower can pull the filter into the fan and damage the fan.

STRATEGY

Make sure the filter is secure in its frame.

Electronic Air Cleaners

More Efficient

These air cleaners are more efficient than a conventional mechanical filter. They are able to capture small particulate, including pollen and cigarette smoke particles. They are not 100 percent efficient, but are better than mechanical filters if they are well maintained.

Location and Description

The electronic air cleaner is located in roughly the same place as a mechanical filter would be. It includes a metal cabinet and an electrical connection (120-volt). There is a power switch and sometimes a test button on the outside. There is an access door to get at the internal components (Figure 8.19).

Problems we frequently encounter on electronic air cleaners include the following—

1. Dirty
2. Missing components
3. Damaged cells

FIGURE 8.19   Electronic Air Cleaner

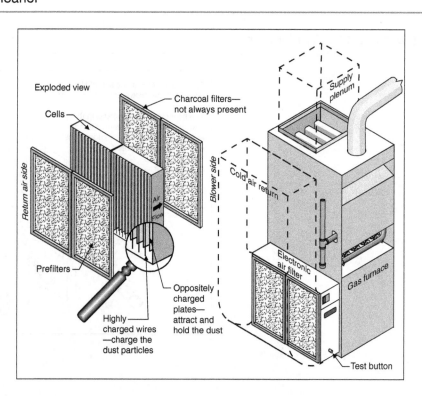

4. Inoperative
5. Improper orientation
6. Mis-wired

Dirty

Reduced airflow and possible overheating of the heat exchanger are implications of a dirty air cleaner.

Explain to your clients the need to clean these regularly. Some units have indicators that show when cleaning is required.

If you are going to inspect electronic air cleaners, understand that there is a danger in opening the unit and putting your hand inside. The power should be shut off and you should wait at least 30 seconds before opening the cover.

Once the cover is removed, you should find a coarse mechanical filter (pre-filter) located upstream of the electronic cells. It should be taken out and inspected. In some cases, there are two filters installed end to end. Check both of them.

The cells should also be taken out and inspected. In some cases, there is only one cell, but often there are two, one behind the other. Be careful handling these; they are delicate, with very fine wires that can easily be broken and dangerously sharp edges.

Don't forget to turn the power back on when you put it back together.

If, after you put the filter and cells back in and put the cover on, the unit crackles and pops continually when you restore the power, turn the power off, wait 30 seconds, take the cells out and reinstall them. It's possible you did not install them snugly enough to make a good electrical connection. If the popping doesn't stop when you turn the power back on the second time, turn the power off and advise the homeowner or his representative, or leave a note that the electronic air cleaner requires cleaning or servicing.

Missing Components

The air cleaner will not work properly with missing cells.

In many air cleaners, there are two cells, installed one behind the other. Make sure when you push the cell in, that it goes all the way to the back of the cabinet. You don't want air to get around the cell.

In addition, make sure there is a prefilter located upstream of the cells.

Damaged Cells

The efficiency of the unit will be reduced where wires or plates are damaged.

When you take the cells out, look for damaged wires or plates. If several wires are broken, repairs may be warranted. Many feel it's not worth the cost of repairing just one broken wire.

Inoperative

Obviously, the unit won't work.

Most of the on/off switches have a power indicator light. If the light is not on, there's probably no electrical power to the unit. Don't try to be a troubleshooter; just report it as inoperative. However, make sure you have checked it with the furnace operating. It's embarrassing to write up a defective electronic air cleaner that's working correctly.

Margin notes:

IMPLICATIONS

STRATEGIES

Danger of Electric Shock

Filter Upstream

Remove Cells

Power Back on
Test after Reassembling

IMPLICATION

STRATEGY

IMPLICATION

STRATEGIES

IMPLICATION

STRATEGY

Installed Backwards or in Wrong Location

The filter should be installed in the return air duct just before (upstream of) the furnace. When you take the cover off, the first thing the air stream should hit is the prefilter. The air should go through this filter first and then go into the electronic cells. The arrows on the cells should point in the direction of the airflow.

The unit will either not work at all or the efficiency will be greatly reduced.

Make sure the filter is in the right location and the cell orientation is proper, with the prefilter before the electronic portion. Electronic air cleaners can usually be installed in a vertical or horizontal orientation.

Mis-wired

The electronic air cleaner should not be energized when the furnace fan is not pulling air across the filter. The unit should be wired into the furnace controls so that the electronic air cleaner will only be energized when the furnace fan is operating.

The unit will produce ozone when operating. High concentrations of ozone can develop around the unit if air is not moving past it. Air should always be flowing past the unit when it is energized.

Look for the indicator light on the air cleaner cabinet. If the furnace is idle (but electrical power to the furnace is on), the power light should not be on. The light should come on when the furnace fan operates.

Tap on Ducts

One of the common tests is tapping on the duct just upstream of the air filter. This usually dislodges a little dust from the duct walls and puts it into the air stream. You'll usually hear a crackling or popping sound, indicating that the system is working properly.

This test may be even more effective than simply using the test button to generate the cracking or popping sound. Many inspectors perform both of these tests to convince themselves that the unit is working as it should.

8.9.5   Duct Systems, Registers, and Grilles

What Makes a Duct

Supply ducts are usually made of sheet metal (galvanized steel) and sometimes of fiberglass. The return duct system, however, carries room temperature air and as such, may not really be ducting material at all. For example, the space created in walls between two studs and two layers of plaster or drywall can form a return air duct.

Return Ducts

Similarly, running across a ceiling, a sheet metal pan nailed to the bottom of two joists can create a return air duct with the sheet metal as the bottom, two adjacent joists as the sides, and the subflooring as the top (Figure 8.20). This may be acceptable on a return duct because of the low temperatures, but is not acceptable as a supply duct.

Materials

Ducts can be made out of galvanized sheet steel, aluminum, copper, fiberglass, paper fiber, clay tile, or asbestos cement. Galvanized steel is the most common. Aluminum ducting is more expensive than steel; copper ducting is more expensive than aluminum. Fiberglass ducts are better at damping sound than metal.

Ducts in Slabs

Galvanized steel is the most common material when the duct system is contained in concrete floor slabs. Paper fiber and clay tile ducts are also used.

Register

We will use the word **register** to describe grilles, registers and diffusers (Figure 8.21). Technically, they are slightly different, but as a practical matter, most homeowners simply call them registers or grilles.

F I G U R E 8.20   Return Ducts in Floor Joists

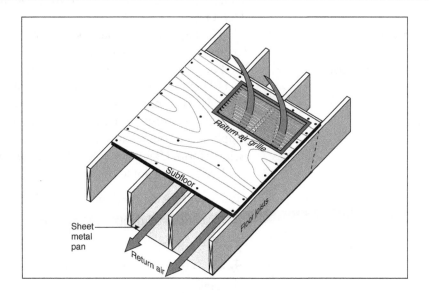

Plenum

Plenums are the large metal connection areas between the furnace and the ducts. The supply plenum is just downstream of the heat exchanger. On an upflow furnace, it should be roughly 3 inches below combustibles. The return plenum is just upstream of the house air fan.

Friction Losses

In moving air through ducts, the goal is to keep the friction losses to a minimum, so we can get the most air into the room. The more changes of direction there are, and the smaller the duct diameter, the greater will be the friction losses. The greater the friction losses, the smaller the volume of air that gets into the room. This is usually measured in cubic feet per minute (cfm) or litres per second (L/s).

F I G U R E 8.21   Supply Air Registers, Diffusers, and Grilles

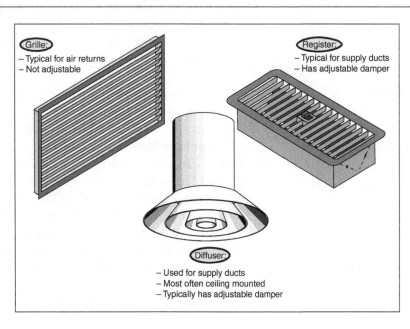

Elbows Bad

Most duct designs turn air gradually through round corners rather than 90 degree angles. Even so, each round elbow is roughly equivalent to about 10 feet of round duct length.

Larger Ducts—Smaller Losses

The larger ducts should be closer to the furnace and get gradually smaller the farther they are from the furnace.

Slow Movement Better

Larger ducts allow sufficient volumes of air to move at lower velocities. Smaller ducts lead to higher velocities, which can create unpleasant drafts and excessive noise. Higher velocities also mean more friction losses.

Leaky Ducts

It is not unusual for a residential duct system to have up to one third of the air supply lost through leaks in the system. The tighter the ducts, the better the system will perform. Cracks or holes in ducts can be filled with caulking or duct tape.

Let's look at some of the problems you're likely to identify.

1. No air or weak airflow
2. Disconnected ducts
3. Dirty ducts
4. Ducts obstructed or collapsed
5. Leaks
6. Rust
7. Uninsulated ducts
8. Registers or grilles in garages
9. Poor location
10. Too few return grilles
11. Registers obstructed, painted shut, or damaged

No Air or Weak Airflow

The room is likely to be cold.

IMPLICATIONS

STRATEGY

Test for Warm Air to All Rooms

The most important test on the furnace is to make sure there is warm air delivered to all the rooms in the house. Many inspectors make a special trip through the the house, just checking the heating distribution. Others incorporate this into their room-by-room inspection. There are advantages to both ways and you can do whatever is most comfortable. Watch for weak airflow or no airflow. This is a very common problem. It's much harder to determine that a house is going to have cold rooms in the summer, than it is in winter. In addition to checking the airflow through the register, you'll probably notice that a room is cool when you walk into it, if it's a problem.

Test Methods

Many inspectors just use their hand to check for airflow. Very few use sophisticated instruments. Some people use paper (anything from tissue paper to note paper) to do a rough comparison of airflow.

Renovations Remove Ducts

Renovated homes will often have areas with no airflow. Many old houses had a gravity warm-air heating system originally. This incorporated supply ducts that ran up through central partition walls of the house. These ducts often terminated in registers in floors or on interior partition walls on the second floor. If first-floor walls have been removed or relocated, there is often no ducting to the second floor registers.

These old systems were less than optimal in that the supply registers were often on interior walls, but that's a different problem.

Testing with Just the Fan

Some inspectors perform this test with just the furnace fan operating, rather than the furnace as well. The advantage to this method is that you do not overheat the house, especially during the summer. This can be unpleasant for the occupant.

Multiple Supply Registers

Many larger rooms require more than one supply register. It's difficult to anticipate whether the number of registers and given air flow will be adequate on the coldest day of the year when you're checking in July.

Use Tissue on Returns

As you're checking the airflow, you have to check the return airflow as well as the supply. Because the grilles are usually larger on the returns, the air velocity is lower and more difficult to sense with your bare hand.

Disconnected

Ducts should be continuous.

IMPLICATION

Inadequate heating is the implication of disconnected ducts.

STRATEGY

Where you can see ducts, picking up disconnected ducts is easy. Where the ducts are concealed, you'll only feel the symptom. No airflow or weak airflow through a register may be caused by disconnected ducts. You often can't be conclusive on this one.

Dirty Ducts

IMPLICATIONS

Fire Hazard

Dirty ducts restrict the airflow slightly and can be a health issue. A bigger issue might be the fire hazard. The dirt that accumulates on the inside of ducts is combustible. A fire in a house can spread quickly through the inside walls of ducts, if there is enough dirt to spread the fire.

STRATEGY

In many cases, it's tough to get a good look at the inside of the ducts other than at the blower and filter area. You should have a look here and any other places that are readily accessible. Looking down supply registers with a flashlight can sometimes give an indication of the cleanliness of the ducts.

Duct Cleaning

Some people clean their ducts on a regular basis. Annual cleaning is not required except under the most unusual circumstances.

Evidence

You can sometimes see evidence of duct cleaning. This is often suggested by round plastic plugs in the ducts about $1\frac{1}{2}$ inches in diameter located at various accessible spots throughout the house. These are often visible in unfinished basements and crawl spaces.

Dirt at Registers

Dirt around supply registers is an indicator that ducts may be dirty. Where you see dirt accumulations, try to get a closer look at the duct interior.

Ducts Obstructed, Crushed, or Collapsed

Obstructed or collapsed ducts retard airflow.

IMPLICATIONS

STRATEGY

Where visible, this can be readily described. In many cases, you won't know whether the duct is disconnected or obstructed or whether there is some other problem. Simply describe the symptom of weak airflow.

Ducts in Concrete Floor Slabs

Where heating ducts are buried in concrete slabs, collapsed ducts are common (Figure 8.22). Water can accumulate in the ducts because of leakage from subgrade soil into the ducts. Standing water in ducts is a health issue, although that's beyond the scope of our inspection. Standing water can also rust metal ducts and eventually the sheet metal will fall and obstruct the airflow. Where the supply ducts are buried in concrete, pay particular attention to the quality of the air. Your nose may tell you of a stagnant water problem in the duct system.

Leakage

Supply ducts will leak their warm air out. Air return ducts can draw air in through gaps in the ducts rather than through the return grilles.

IMPLICATION

The implication is less heat delivered to rooms and/or less return air drawn from rooms.

FIGURE 8.22 Ducts in Concrete Floor Slabs

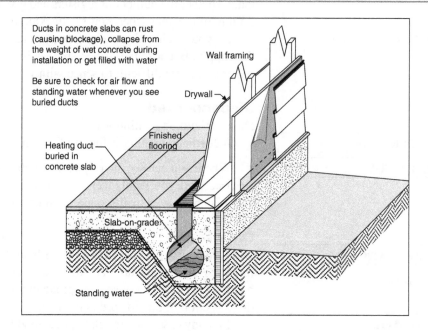

Ducts in concrete slabs can rust (causing blockage), collapse from the weight of wet concrete during installation or get filled with water

Be sure to check for air flow and standing water whenever you see buried ducts

Wall framing

Drywall

Heating duct buried in concrete slab

Finished flooring

Slab-on-grade

Standing water

STRATEGY

Where ducts are exposed, you can check visually and, when the fan is operating, by running your hand over the ducting to feel leakage. Most duct systems would benefit from localized sealing of cracks and holes. Changes in direction are common leakage spots.

Rust

Rusted ducts are not very common. Rust can occur wherever sheet metal is exposed to moisture. Ducts buried in concrete floor slabs are more prone to rusting than other systems.

IMPLICATIONS

If the ducts are compromised, air will leak and heat will be inadequate in the rooms supplied by that duct.

STRATEGY

Where you can see ducts, look for rust. Where you see it, check to see whether it has perforated the duct walls. If there is an active moisture source, recommend that it be corrected. If the duct has been perforated, that section should be replaced.

Pay close attention to ducts near soil or touching basement or crawl space floors. Again, ducts in slabs are the most vulnerable.

IMPLICATIONS

The implications are overheating of electrical components, concealed leakage of gas or water and rusting of dissimilar metals in contact.

STRATEGY

You should question any pipes or wiring you see going into supply ducting.

Pipes or wires are allowed to run through return ductwork in many jurisdictions. Watch for excessive air leakage in this situation.

Uninsulated Ducts

Any ducts going through unheated spaces such as garages, crawl spaces, and attics, should be insulated.

IMPLICATIONS

The implications are heat loss to unheated areas, inadequate heat in the home, and condensation in the ducts.

STRATEGY

Insulated Ducts

Insulation Levels

Insulation Complete?

Unsafe

IMPLICATION

STRATEGY

Good Location

High Returns with Air Conditioning

IMPLICATIONS

STRATEGY

Returns on Outside Walls

Supply and Returns Too Close Together

Basement Registers

Watch for ducts running through unconditioned spaces. Good practice suggests that this be avoided as much as possible. Factory insulated ducts are available. The insulation in this case may be on the inside of the ducting.

Where insulation is field-applied to the outside of a heating supply duct, the vapor barrier should be on the warm side (the side closest to the duct). The outer skin of the insulation is often wrapped to afford mechanical protection. This should not be a vapor barrier.

Insulation levels vary, but generally the insulation should be at least R-4. In cold northern climates, insulation levels well above this are desirable.

If the ducts are insulated, make sure the insulation is continuous along the length and around the diameter. Watch for pieces of insulation that are mechanically damaged or are falling off.

Registers or Grilles in Garages

Forced-air heating systems should not have supply registers or return grilles in garages. Automobile exhaust being drawn into the house is a very real threat.

Some people say you don't have to worry about it in supply registers because the furnace fan will push air into the garage rather than allow air to flow back into the house. This may be true when the furnace is operating, but when the fan is at rest, airflow may very well be from the garage into the house. This is not a safe arrangement!

The implication is a life safety issue with products of combustion from automobiles entering the house.

Where you see ducts running through garages, make sure there are no openings. If there are, recommend that they be closed and sealed.

Poor Location

Supply air registers are ideally located near floor level on outside walls below windows. Return registers are ideally located close to interior walls.

High level return grilles are sometimes used with central air conditioning (because it's the warm air we want to take back to the air conditioner to cool). Most residential installations are a compromise of perfect duct design. You'll have to use your experience and judgment to know whether a system is likely to perform adequately.

The house may be less comfortable than it should.

Watch for supply registers on interior walls. Advise the client that this may produce uneven heat in the room. In many cases, adding auxiliary heat with an electric baseboard heater for occasional use is less expensive then rerouting ducts. Where registers are in less-than-ideal locations, make doubly sure that they are at least delivering good airflow.

Watch for return air grilles on outside walls. While, again, this is not desirable, it may not be worth changing. Let your client know that they may experience some uneven heat distribution. It's almost impossible to quantify the situation, especially since every homeowner has different expectations. You leave yourself open to criticism if you do not mention a less than optimum arrangement.

Similarly, watch for supply and return registers that are too close together. This can lead to short-circuiting with the warm air leaving the supply register and being drawn directly into the return register.

These are often at ceiling level and are less effective because of it. Let your client know that this may be a comfort issue.

F I G U R E 8.23   Return Grille in Furnace Room

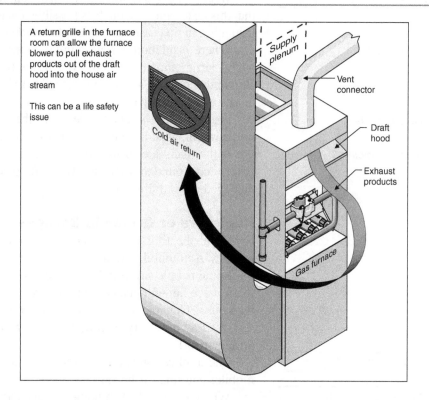

A return grille in the furnace room can allow the furnace blower to pull exhaust products out of the draft hood into the house air stream

This can be a life safety issue

Cold air return

Supply plenum

Vent connector

Draft hood

Exhaust products

Gas furnace

Return Grille in Furnace Room

Return grilles should not be in furnace rooms because the furnace may be starved for combustion air (Figure 8.23). The blower will pull air from the furnace room into the return duct system. This creates low air pressure in the furnace room and can result in starving the burner for air and spillage of exhaust products at the draft hood or burner. Return grilles should be at least 10 feet from the furnace if the furnace is in an open area.

Too Few Return Grilles

Common Defect

This is often a marginal defect in houses. Most older homes have less return air than would be ideal. The cross-sectional area of the return air grilles should be approximately the same as the area of the supply air registers. It's often considerably less.

One Return Serves Several Rooms

Where returns are located in hallways and serve several rooms, the air movement can be obstructed by closing bedroom doors. Where this arrangement exists, bedroom doors should be trimmed at the bottom, to allow air out of the bedroom and into the cold air return system.

Trapped Warm Air Gets Cold

Where the air cannot escape from a bedroom, the bedroom acts like a balloon. The furnace fan pushes air through the ducts, through the register, and into the bedroom. The air pressure builds up in the bedroom because the air can't get out. The bedroom becomes a dead end. The furnace won't push any more air into the bedroom, since there's nowhere for the air to go. This air will cool and the bedroom will feel cold.

Uncomfortable rooms may result.

IMPLICATION

STRATEGY

As you're checking the airflow through supply and return registers, pay attention to how many return registers there are. If there is only one for the entire house, the heating system will probably be uncomfortable. Adding return registers in some cases is relatively straightforward. In other cases, it is quite expensive.

Registers Obstructed, Painted Shut, or Damaged

Common Problem

It's common to find both supply and return registers that are obstructed. Furniture can be backed in tight against walls, obstructing supply registers. Carpets, mats and furniture can cover floor registers. In some cases, you will be unable to find a register in a room because it is obstructed.

IMPLICATION

Inadequate heat distribution will result.

STRATEGY

You should notice these problems as you look for adequate airflow. If you have to lift a carpet to find the return air grille, for example, let your client know that the duct system seems to be working, but that the grille itself should not be obstructed.

Balancing Dampers

Some duct systems provide great opportunity for balancing. There may be balancing dampers adjacent to the main supply plenum, balancing dampers at each branch, balancing dampers below each register and, of course, each register will have a damper to control air flow.

Other systems have very limited opportunity for balancing. These can be retrofit, although it is always more costly to do it after the fact. This is seldom practical if the duct system is inaccessible.

Beyond Scope

Balancing ducts is beyond the scope of a home inspection, but can be suggested as a possible solution to a distribution system that does not seem to be delivering even heat throughout the house.

8.10   INSPECTION AND TESTING PROCEDURE FOR CONVENTIONAL GAS FURNACES

The conventional gas-fired forced-air furnace we've been talking about is a design that has been around since the 1950s. It was by far the most common through the 1960s and 1970s. Let's review the inspection and testing procedure for this system.

1. Look at the furnace after removing the burner cover and fan cover when the furnace is at rest, with the power turned off.
2. Check the heat exchanger.
3. Turn up the thermostat and watch the furnace while it is in operation. This includes looking at the exhaust system including the draft hood, vent connector and chimney.
4. Check the duct system and the airflow through the supply and return registers throughout the home.

Inspector in the House: Canary in a Sauna

It was a Friday afternoon inspection and we turned up the heat to test the furnace. Sadly, we got distracted and forgot to turn it down, so the heat was on full for the entire weekend—the sellers were away. Whether their pet bird died of natural causes or excessive heat we are not sure. We did, however, take a considerable amount of heat ourselves!

Many of our inspectors now leave their keys on the thermostat, so it's hard to leave the house without remembering to turn down the heat.

8.11   MID-EFFICIENCY AND HIGH-EFFICIENCY FURNACES

Mid-efficiency furnaces are the next step beyond the conventional furnaces that we have been discussing. Most of the features and functions are identical; however, mid-efficiency furnaces have two significant additional features, both aimed at reducing energy use.

Electronic Ignition

The first feature is electronic ignition, which permits an intermittent pilot flame instead of a standing (continuous) one. Using this feature, the ignition system comes on to light the burners only when there is a call for heat. This eliminates the consumption of natural gas when the furnace is not heating the home.

Vent Dampers or Induced-Draft Fans

The second feature is some means of closing the venting system when it is not needed. This is accomplished by using either a vent damper (Figure 8.24) or an induced-draft fan. When the venting system is closed off, no house air (which we have paid to heat) will escape up the chimney.

Condensing Furnaces

High-efficiency furnaces include the additional features just described for mid-efficiency furnaces, but go even further. By using various methods, including long, thin heat exchangers (Figure 8.25), these furnaces are able to extract much more heat from the exhaust. As a result, the exhaust gases are cooled to the point that they condense. For this reason, high-efficiency furnaces are also referred to as **condensing furnaces**.

High-efficiency furnaces include a system to collect and dispose of the condensate (Figure 8.26). Because we have a relatively cool exhaust (100°F to 150°F) and a fan to push it, we don't need a chimney anymore; we can vent the exhaust gases directly through the wall. The cool exhaust also permits the use of PVC plastic pipe for venting systems; this is the venting material you'll usually see for high-efficiency furnaces because it is inexpensive and easy to work with.

F I G U R E 8.24   Automatic Vent Dampers

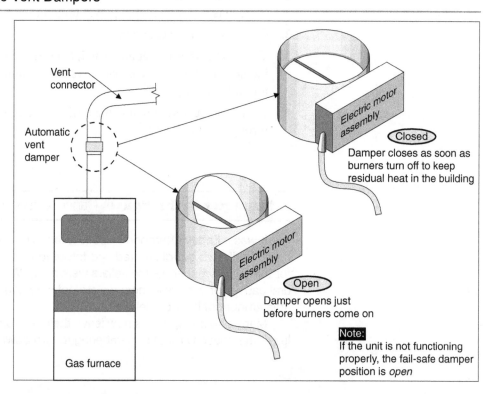

Vent connector

Automatic vent damper

Electric motor assembly

Closed

Damper closes as soon as burners turn off to keep residual heat in the building

Electric motor assembly

Open

Damper opens just before burners come on

Note: If the unit is not functioning properly, the fail-safe damper position is *open*

Gas furnace

F I G U R E 8.25   High-Efficiency Furnaces Have Long Heat Exchangers

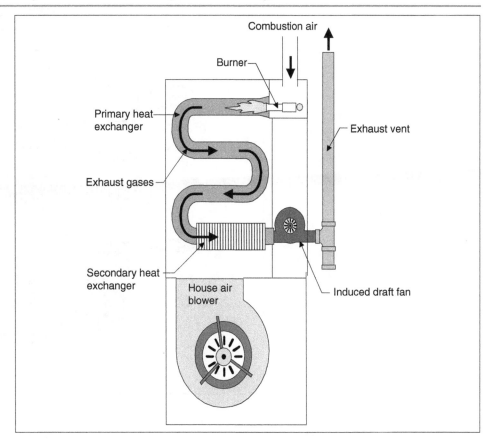

Direct Vent   Many high-efficiency heating systems are **direct-vent** systems; they take their combustion air directly from outside.

Sealed Combustion   These systems are also called **sealed combustion**, because the combustion chamber is not exposed to the house air. It is sealed and only air from outside can get into the combustion chamber. The furnace burner is completely **uncoupled** from the house air.

The outside combustion air intake must be kept clear and must be in a suitable location. Many manufacturers have several rules about where it can be located (for example, not adjacent to a clothes dryer exhaust or a gas regulator not close to a pool, hot tub or spa, above snow level, 4, 8, or 12 inches from the vent termination, depending on manufacturer.)

Both mid-efficiency and high-efficiency furnaces have additional operating and safety controls because they are more complex than conventional furnaces. Many of the controls used in conventional furnaces have been replaced by electronic components in mid-efficiency and high-efficiency furnaces.

Differential Pressure Switch   A **differential pressure switch** usually replaces the air-proving switch. It makes sure the induced-draft fan is running. The differential pressure switch closes when a pressure differential is sensed across the furnace.

For more information on the operation of mid- and high-efficiency furnaces, see *Principles of Home Inspection: Gas and Oil Furnaces.*

FIGURE 8.26   Condensation in High-Efficiency Furnaces

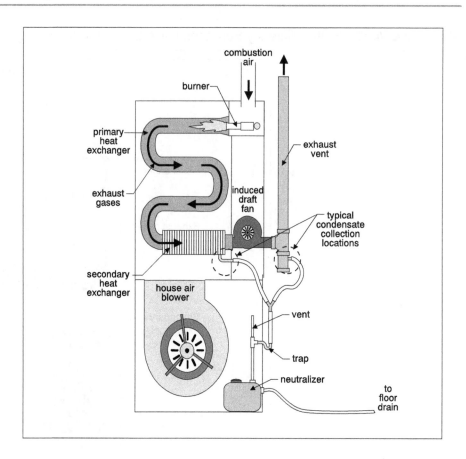

8.11.1   The Cost Savings (?)

Mid- and high-efficiency furnaces are great. They save heat. However, they are much more complicated than conventional furnaces.

High Maintenance

Some service people believe the high maintenance costs involved with high-efficiency furnaces, in particular, offset the annual savings.

Expensive to Buy

When you also consider that mid- and high-efficiency furnaces are more expensive to purchase, and early indications are that their life expectancy may not be as long as conventional furnaces (this is debatable), you may actually spend more money on heating, rather than less.

No Heat!

Then consider the increased number of "no heat" calls because a minor problem has shut down the furnaces.

It's Bound to Get Better

We believe this to be a worst-case scenario, and while there are instances where this may occur, the longer mid- and high-efficiency furnaces are around, the more reliable they are likely to become. This is an emerging technology and things should improve. Indeed, some of the furnaces have already established a good reputation for reliability and some are offering 20-year or even lifetime warranties on heat exchangers.

8.11.2 The Home Inspector's Perspective

From our view, mid- and high-efficiency furnaces can be much tougher to inspect than conventional furnaces, because there are many components and so much we cannot see. With sealed combustion units, you can't get a good look at the burner, let alone the heat exchanger.

With two or three heat exchangers, there is a tremendous amount of heat exchanger you can't see with a mirror and a light.

As in all house systems, a home inspection is a performance test of a field-installed piece of equipment. We are not reviewing the design, doing a code inspection or performing a furnace service check-up. We are there to find out whether the furnace responds to its controls and whether it performs.

8.11.3 Conditions

Let's look at the problems common to mid- and high-efficiency furnaces. These are **in addition to** the problems that apply to conventional furnaces.

1. Vent dampers stuck open or closed
2. Ignition problems
3. Heat exchanger problems
4. Condensate problems
5. Induced draft fan problems
6. Venting problems
7. Differential pressure switch problems
8. Spillage switch problems
9. Poor outdoor combustion air intake location

Vent Dampers Stuck Open or Closed

IMPLICATIONS

The implication of a damper stuck in the open position is heat loss up the chimney during off cycles. The implication of a vent damper stuck in the closed position is no heat if everything works properly or, worse, spillage of combustion products into the house if the burner fires up anyway.

STRATEGY

When the burner starts up and shuts down, you can listen for the vent damper motor. When the thermostat calls for heat, the vent damper motor should open the damper and after the burner shuts off, the motor should close the damper. Operation of this motor can take roughly 15 seconds.

Position Indicator

Some dampers have an external indicator that shows the position of the damper. You should be able to see this indicator move when the system calls for heat, and then move again when it shuts down.

Does Furnace Fire Up?

If the furnace works, that is some assurance the vent damper is working properly, although it's not a guarantee. In addition, if the furnace fails to respond, it may be because of a vent damper problem, although it could be one of several other things, as well.

Look for Spillage

When the furnace is operating, check for spillage of combustion products through the draft hood and burner. This may indicate that the vent damper is stuck closed or partially closed.

Electronic Ignition Problems

We may encounter several problems with electronic ignition. Most of these result in no heat. In many cases, there are problems with ignition systems that you won't be able to diagnose. What you will find is the furnace will not respond to its controls. Don't worry too much about troubleshooting.

To give you an idea of the kinds of things that can go wrong, we'll list some of the conditions:

1. No electrical power
2. Loose electrical connections
3. Poor electrical ground
4. No spark
5. Spark fails to ignite the flame
6. Flame sensor fails to detect the flame
7. Spark won't stop firing after burner is up and running
8. Burner shuts down prematurely
9. Hot surface igniter is cracked

IMPLICATION

The implication is no heat.

STRATEGY

All we can do is verify the burner lights properly. If you can see the spark igniter, make sure that it does go out after the burner ignites. The spark normally shouldn't stay on for longer than about eight seconds.

May Try Several Times

If the burner doesn't respond properly to its controls, you may find that the ignition system tries four or five times to ignite the burner. There can be several problems that will cause the burner not to light, including fuel problems, intake air problems, exhaust problems, condensate accumulation, malfunctioning differential switches, malfunctioning induced-draft fans, etc. It's probably best to stick to the basics. Does the furnace work or not?

Black Line Visible If Igniter Is Cracked

Look for slight black lines in the red-hot igniter during ignition, if you can see it. This is an early sign of failure. This will indicate surface cracking. It resembles the edges of charcoal on a dying wood fire. The flame will still light, but the igniter will probably fail soon.

Heat Exchanger Problems

Common heat exchanger conditions include—

1. rust
2. cracked
3. clogged
4. overheating

IMPLICATIONS

The implications of heat exchanger problems are similar to those in conventional furnaces. A "no heat" condition is possible. More important, there can be life safety issues if the exhaust products leak into the house air.

STRATEGY

If you can get a look at the burner, look for evidence of rust, flakes, or sheets of aluminum coming off aluminized-steel heat exchangers, or sand-like deposits from coated heat exchangers. If possible, use your light and mirror to perform a test similar to the test on conventional furnaces.

Look from Fan Compartment

In some cases, you can look at the second or third heat exchanger from the fan compartment. On some furnaces it's relatively easy to pull the fan out and get a good look. This goes beyond the Standards.

Look for Moisture

If you see evidence of moisture on the outside of heat exchangers, it usually means that condensate is leaking through a hole or a crack. This very likely means a failed heat exchanger.

Sudden Shutdowns

If there is a crack in the heat exchanger, the pressure differential switch may not be satisfied and the furnace may be shut down for safety. While you won't be able to verify this, you should allow for the possibility that unexpected shutdowns can be the result of a heat exchanger failure.

Check Condensate Tubing

It's hard to detect clogged heat exchangers. However, if the clear plastic condensate tubing shows dirt or soot on the tube wall, you may assume that the heat exchanger also has soot on it.

Check Temperature Rise

One operational test we encourage on high-efficiency furnaces is to check the temperature rise across the heat exchanger once the unit is at steady state. Make sure the temperature rise does not exceed that stated on the data plate, a condition which can void the manufacturer's warranty and dramatically shorten the life expectancy of the heat exchangers. Causes of this include dirty filters, blowers or ducts, undersized ducts, blower motor on slow speed, etc.

Heat Switches

Many mid- and high-efficiency furnaces have **heat switches (spillage switches)** to shut off the furnace on high temperature at the front of the burner if there is a flame rollout or spillage condition. When you run the furnace, make sure it runs long enough to reach steady state. If the furnace shuts off because of this high temperature sensor, you should be able to feel heat spilling back out through the front of the burner opening before it shuts off if this is not a direct vent furnace.

Reset Button

Some of these heat switches are automatically reset. Some of them have a push button reset that must be manually operated before the system will work again. Furnaces that shut out on this basis are in distress. It's likely that the heat exchanger is partially clogged.

Condensate Problems

Common condensate conditions include—

1. blocked
2. leaking
3. poor discharge location
4. no neutralizer bath
5. the neutralizer is clogged

IMPLICATIONS

In some cases, blocked or leaking condensate lines will shut down the furnace. In other cases, condensate may accumulate in the heat exchangers, contributing to corrosion. In most furnaces the condensate will accumulate in the secondary or tertiary heat exchanger, not the primary heat exchanger.

Poor discharge locations can be a health issue (if it discharges straight into a plumbing stack for example). They can also cause leakage problem elsewhere in the house. If the condensate runs out onto the floor, damage is likely.

The absence of a neutralizer required in a local jurisdiction is a violation of law. A clogged neutralizer is likely to result in condensate leakage.

STRATEGY

When the furnace is operating, look to see that the condensate is flowing (dripping). Look for the tubing and water to be clean. Dirty condensate or tubing may mean a malfunctioning burner.

Look for evidence of leakage anywhere in the condensate system. Condensate on the house-air side may mean a hole in the heat exchanger.

Induced-Draft Fan Problems

Common conditions with induced-draft fans include damage, worn bearings and being inoperative.

IMPLICATIONS

Induced-draft fans that don't work or don't work properly usually result in a "no heat" condition because the differential-pressure switch or air-vacuum switch is not satisfied.

STRATEGY

When the thermostat is turned up, the first noise you hear should be the induced-draft fan going through a purge cycle. Some inspectors put the blade of their screwdriver against the shaft of the fan and put the handle of the screwdriver against their ear. With a little practice, you can quickly differentiate the sound of good bearings from the grinding noise of bearings in distress. (This goes beyond the Standards.)

Loose Brackets

In some cases, the brackets that support the induced-draft fans can be a problem. Watch the fan in operation for vibration or loose mounting brackets.

Water in Fan Housing

If there are condensate blockages, condensation may pool in the fan housing. Listen for water splashing or spraying, and watch for water dripping out of fan housings when induced-draft fans operate.

Horizontal Fans May Be Better

Many people feel that induced-draft fans installed in a horizontal plane will work better and last longer than those in a vertical plane. Horizontal units usually have the motor mounted above the fan and the fan blades turning through a horizontal plane. This creates fewer low points for condensate to collect.

Failed induced draft fans are probably the most common problem on mid- and high-efficiency furnaces.

Look for metal fan components: these are more likely to fail than plastic.

These motors all have a serial code that often indicates the date of manufacture. Attempt to determine from the code if it has been replaced already, and advise the client they may have to replace fans every three to five years.

Bushings

What typically fails is the inboard bushing in the motor. You can **never** see it. It is the seal between the fan and the atmosphere. Ceramic sleeve bushings have been introduced to combat this problem.

Venting Problems

Common venting problems include—

1. inappropriate material

2. poor location for termination

3. mechanical damage

4. inadequate combustible clearances (mid-efficiency units only)

5. improper slope or support

IMPLICATIONS

Combustion products may enter the house if inappropriate materials are used, if the installation doesn't terminate properly or if there's mechanical damage. If the vent slopes down to the outside, condensate may freeze at the termination, blocking the vent with ice.

The implication of inadequate combustible clearances is, of course, a fire hazard.

Unless stated otherwise in the manufacturer's specification for materials and location, the vent should be—

STRATEGY

- four feet away from windows and building openings, one foot if it's below 100,000 BTU/hour (direct vent appliances only need one foot)

- at least a foot off the ground

Other code requirements may apply in your area as well. For example, there may be a minimum distance from gas meters or air intakes.

Slope

Look for improper slope. A quarter-inch-per-foot slope up moving away from the furnace is required in cold climates. Wrong slopes can lead to frost closure of the discharge.

Damage

Watch for mechanical damage or poor supporting. PVC exhaust piping should be supported about every 3 feet.

Combustible Clearance

On mid-efficiency furnaces, you should be looking for a 6-inch clearance from combustibles. Clearance from combustibles is not an issue on high-efficiency (condensing) furnaces because the exhaust gases are so cool.

Differential Pressure Switch Problems

There are typically two diaphragm switches with tubing running to ports upstream and downstream of the induced-draft fans.

IMPLICATION

If the switches aren't satisfied, the furnace won't come on.

STRATEGY

Check the tubing condition: is it hard or brittle? Check that tubing is well-sealed to the switch and the port.

Spillage Switch Problems

Spillage switch (or heat switch) assembly often includes a copper wire running along the front edge of the heat shield. This high temperature sensor shuts off the furnace if exhaust spillage is detected. (This copper wire makes removal of the heat shield difficult.)

IMPLICATIONS

The implication is no heat if it's a fail-safe type. Another implication is no spillage protection if it's not fail-safe.

STRATEGY

Check that it's not broken.

Poor Outdoor Combustion Air Intake Location

Sealed combustion (direct vent) systems bring outdoor combustion air directly to the furnace, usually through PVC piping. This may be a separate piping system or part of a concentric arrangement with the exhaust piping inside the intake piping. The intake should be able to draw fresh air, with little chance of becoming obstructed. Poor locations include too close to the exhaust vent (varies among manufacturers, 4 to 12 inches), near pools, spas or hot tubs (where corrosive chemicals may be drawn in), too close to the ground or roof (where snow may block the intake), or too close to clothes dryer vents and gas regulators.

IMPLICATION

Lack of combustion air may shut down the furnace. Contaminated combustion air can damage the furnace or cause an explosion.

STRATEGY

Check the location of the air intake. Use common sense and if unsure, recommend that a specialist check further. The manufacturers' recommendations are usually the best source.

F I G U R E 8.27 Gravity Furnace

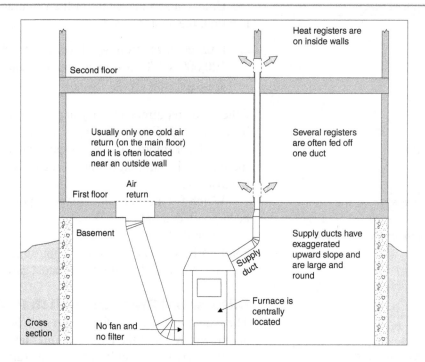

8.12   GRAVITY FURNACES

Gravity warm-air furnaces were popular from the first half of the 20th century until the early 1970s (Figure 8.27). The function of a **gravity warm-air furnace** is to warm the house. Because it is older and less sophisticated than a conventional modern forced-air furnace, it doesn't perform the function quite as well.

The biggest difference between a forced air furnace and a gravity furnace is that gravity furnaces have no fans. Instead, air circulation relies on convection. That is, the warm air rises and the cool air falls naturally.

Fans May Make Air Feel Cool

Fans were sometimes added to gravity furnaces. In some cases these work satisfactorily, although in many cases they do not. The heat exchanger was not designed to see air move quickly past it. In some cases, this air can feel very cool. Adding a fan allows an air filter as well.

No Unique Problems

Gravity furnaces have the same components as conventional forced air furnaces. Consequently, there are no problems that apply only to gravity furnaces. Conditions regarding burners, combustion air supply, venting, gas piping, controls and distribution systems all apply here as well. There obviously won't be fan or filter issues in most cases.

High Failure Probability

Most gravity furnaces are at the end of their useful life, statistically. You should advise clients that furnace replacement may be necessary in the short term.

New Is Better

A modern furnace will provide more even heat, less expensively, while taking up less space in the home. However, the initial replacement may be expensive, because it usually involves relocating the furnace and rearranging ducts.

8.13   LIFE EXPECTANCIES OF FURNACES

Many home inspectors do not speculate on life expectancy. Those who do go beyond the Standards. You may make your decision as to whether or not to give life expectancies for furnaces and other components, based on your market conditions. If most other inspectors in your area do it, you may have a tough time not giving life expectancies. If most don't, you may want to play it safe and not give life expectancies. On the other hand, you may want to differentiate yourself from your competition by giving estimates of life expectancy.

Added Value, Added Risk

The advantage to reporting life expectancies is the benefit to your client. The downside is the added risk you take on by going out on a limb to predict the future.

Remember that the Standards expect you to notify a client if the unit is near the end of its normal life expectancy.

Having said all of that, here are some guidelines we use.

20 to 25 Years

Conventional gas furnaces typically last 20 to 25 years. Furnaces are usually replaced when the heat exchanger fails. Other minor components are typically replaced when they fail.

Problem Furnaces

Some furnaces are known by reputation to fail early on a regular basis. Talk to local installers and service people to get a sense of which furnaces are troublesome in your service area.

Exceptions

Some furnaces last considerably longer than the statistical averages. We have seen conventional forced-air furnaces approaching 40 years of service.

Used Furnaces

Used furnaces are sometimes installed in houses. Home inspectors will often assume the furnace is the same age as the house if the house is less than 20 years old. This is usually, but not always, true.

Mid- and High-Efficiency Furnaces

The life expectancy of mid- and high-efficiency furnaces is more difficult to predict, since these systems have not been around as long as conventional furnaces. Early experience suggests that they are higher maintenance, as might be expected since there are many more components. There is also some question as to the durability of the modern, restrictive heat exchanger.

Different Materials

Several different materials have been used for heat exchangers and inevitably some will perform better than others.

Gravity

Gravity furnaces have not been made for more than 20 years in many areas. Whenever you see one, it is probably safe to say it is close to the end of its life.

Combination Systems

Combination systems are relatively new, and since the furnace side is relatively simple, there is no reason to expect a short life expectancy. If the fan or coil in the furnace fails, it can probably be replaced without replacing the entire furnace.

Age of Furnace

There are several ways of determining the age of a furnace, although the most reliable is the data plate information on the furnace itself. *Preston's Guide* is a useful book that gives an indication of the age of many furnaces and air conditioners based on their model number.

Inspector in the House: "New" Is a Relative Term

We expect new homes to be just that—new. However, when homes are built in cold weather, the heating system often gets quite a workout while the home is being finished. One shiny new furnace in a brand-new home showed us how quickly things can go wrong.

The furnace was obviously new, and looked great from the front. But when we turned it on, the noise caught our attention. When we opened the fan access panel, the filter was not only caked with construction debris, but it had come out of place and was tangled up with the fan.

The inside walls of the cabinet were filthy, and we recommended a specialist check the heat exchanger, air conditioner evaporator coil, and ductwork throughout the home. At the very least, a major cleanup was in order. Not the kind of job you would assume is needed on a new home.

REVIEW QUESTIONS

1. List five of the components of a gas furnace.

2. What is the purpose of the drip on gas piping?

3. One-half-inch diameter black steel piping should be supported every _____ feet, unless it is rising vertically, in which case it must be supported every _____ feet.

4. List six gas piping problems you should watch for.

5. Incomplete combustion of natural gas produces
    a. nitrogen dioxide.   d. carbon monoxide.
    b. carbon dioxide.   e. sulfur dioxide.
    c. ozone.

6. Describe briefly how the pilot light and thermocouple work to ensure safety.

7. The flame wavers over one burner in a gas furnace when the blower comes on. What is the likely cause of this?
    a. The heat exchanger has failed.
    b. The gas valve is faulty.
    c. The blower motor is running too slow.
    d. Airflow across the heat exchanger is insufficient.
    e. The vent is partially blocked.

8. List six problems you'll find on gas combustion equipment.

9. What is meant by **spillage** and **backdrafting** on a gas furnace?

10. Using a mirror and flashlight to view the heat exchanger on a gas furnace allows you to see
    a. less than 20% of the heat exchanger.
    b. 20 to 40% of the heat exchanger.
    c. 40 to 60% of the heat exchanger.
    d. 60 to 80% of the heat exchanger.
    e. all of the heat exchanger.

11. Where possible, why should you watch the flame pattern of a gas furnace?

12. How many panel covers do most conventional gas furnaces have?

13. List six problems commonly found with furnace cabinetry.

14. List and describe the three settings on the fan/limit switch.

15. List six problems commonly found with limit switches.

16. List six problems you may find with a mechanical thermostat.

17. A heating thermostat located in a kitchen will tend to
    a. keep the rest of the house cooler than you want it.
    b. keep the rest of the house warmer than you want it.

18. List the three components of the venting system.

19. List six problems found with vent connectors.

20. Should the smaller appliance vent connect into the chimney above or below the vent from the larger appliance?

   a. Above

   b. Below

21. If there is a chimney clean-out below the vent connection to the chimney, you should look up it to see _____. (List two points)

22. The vent connector should slope

   a. downward going away from the furnace at a minimum of a quarter inch per foot.

   b. upward going away from the furnace at a minimum quarter inch per foot.

   c. downward going away from the furnace at a minimum half inch per foot.

   d. upward going away from the furnace at a minimum half inch per foot.

   e. not at all; it should be horizontal.

23. We like to see vent connectors

   a. less than 3 feet long.

   b. less than 5 feet long.

   c. less than 8 feet long.

   d. less than 10 feet long.

   e. Vent connector length is not a concern.

24. A. What is the typical combustible clearance for a single wall vent?

   B. What is a typical combustible clearance for a B vent?

25. List six common problems with furnace blowers.

26. List two clues that the blower motor may be too small.

27. How much should a belt deflect when it is under proper tension?

   a. about a half an inch   **d.** about two inches

   b. about an inch   **e.** about three inches

   c. about an inch and a half

28. Do our standards require us to look at electronic air cleaners?

   Yes   No

29. List five problems that could be found with mechanical filters in furnaces.

30. Starting at the supply plenum, list the components of the duct system the air travels through to deliver heat to the room, and to re-enter the furnace at the return site.

31. List three things that cause friction loss in duct systems.

32. List six common problems with duct systems.

33. In a heating-only climate, an uninsulated heating duct running through a garage will deliver _____ air to the room at the end of the duct.

   a. warm

   b. cool

34. The vapor barrier on an insulated duct in a heating-only climate should be

    a. on the side of the insulation closest to the duct.

    b. on the side of the insulation furthest away from the duct.

35. Why is it unsafe to have a supply register supplying heat to a garage?

36. List six components that would be found inside the cabinet of a conventional gas-fired forced air furnace.

37. The off-cycle losses of a conventional efficiency furnace total _____ % of the fuel consumed.

38. List eight common problems you may find with mid- or high-efficiency furnaces.

39. It is impossible for a vent damper to fail in the closed position.

    True   False

40. List five reasons why an electronic ignition system may not work.

41. Does condensate leakage out of the induced-draft fan housing cause corrosion problems with the primary heat exchanger?

    Yes   No

42. List five problems commonly found with condensate systems.

43. List three common induced-draft fan problems.

44. List four concerns with mid- or high-efficiency furnace vents.

45. Do the Standards require that we report on the life expectancy of furnaces?

    Yes   No

46. What is the typical life span for a conventional gas furnace?

    a. 5 to 10 years   **d.** 20 to 25 years

    b. 10 to 15 years   **e.** 25 to 30 years

    c. 15 to 20 years

CHAPTER

9

OIL FURNACES

LEARNING OBJECTIVES

By the end of this chapter you should be able to:

- list five problems found with oil storage tanks

- list four problems found with oil fill and vent pipes

- list four problems found with oil supply lines

- list three problems found with the oil filter

- describe in five sentences the basic workings of an oil burner

- list six problems found with oil burners

- describe three different materials commonly used for refractories

- list two problems found with refractories

- describe the function of and problems associated with the primary controller

- describe the operation of a barometric damper

- list five problems commonly associated with the barometric damper

- list twelve problems associated with the vent connector

INTRODUCTION

Different from Gas Furnaces

The second major type of furnaces found in North America is oil-fired. Oil furnaces share many similarities with gas furnaces, such as cabinetry, controls, ducts, registers and grilles, life expectancy and the heat exchanger itself.

Differences from gas furnaces include the storage and delivery of the fuel, the burner itself, the venting of the combustion products and some of the controls. We will highlight the differences in this chapter, rather than repeat whole sections of the gas furnace discussion. We'll start by looking at the fuel system. Then we'll discuss burners, and move to controls and venting.

9.1   OIL STORAGE TANKS

The typical oil-heated house has a fiberglass or steel storage tank. Tanks can be located—

- outside above ground (typically 275 gallons)
- outside underground (often 550 gallons)
- inside the home
- under the home

Regulations for Outdoor Tanks

Most areas now require that outdoor oil storage tanks be cylindrical rather than the older oval shape. This helps protect the tank from tipping over in high winds. In addition, the paint protection specifications are more rigid than they used to be to help protect against rust.

Dikes or Double-Walled Tanks

Many areas also require dikes around the tank to contain any spills or leaks. Alternatively, a double-walled tank may suffice. These regulations are not typically enforced retroactively, so older installations are often oval tanks, with little paint and no dike.

Common oil tank problems include—

1. Poor location
2. Leakage
3. Rusting
4. Underground
5. Empty

9.1.1   Poor Location

5 Feet from Burner
Protect from Damage

The oil tank should not be within 5 feet of any burner.

Oil tanks in garages or outside should be protected from vehicles. Steel posts filled with concrete are often used.

IMPLICATIONS

A fire at the burner could ignite the oil in the tank if the tank is too close. The implication of a tank being hit by a car is an oil spill and possible fire.

STRATEGY

Note the distance between the tank and the burner. In some homes, a concrete block partition may be used to reduce the clearance.

Check that garage tanks are not susceptible to vehicle impact.

9.1.2   Leakage

Because of the odor of oil, homeowners usually detect leaks. A small leak is a nuisance, and a large leak is an environmental problem.

If undetected or unrepaired, the leak could progress, flooding the area around the tank and damaging finishes. If the oil flows towards the burner, a fire could result. Replacement of the tank is usually necessary, depending on the size and location of the leak.

A smell of oil in the basement or near heating equipment does not always indicate a leaking tank. The leak, if one exists, could be at the fill or vent pipes, fuel line, filter or burner.

Spillage and Fill Pipe Leaks

Sometimes the odor is quite noticeable just after the tank is filled. Some spillage may have occured at the filler pipe. There could be a small leak at a joint or connection in the filler pipe. Once the pumping stops and the filler pipe drains, the pipe will stop leaking.

Underside of Tank

Check the underside of the tank for any oil stains or smears. A flashlight and large mirror are helpful. A very slow leak may be very difficult to detect by looking at the underside of the tank. Look closely at seams.

Check Floor below Tank

Inspect the floor under the tank. Dust control products, clay litter or sand are clues, since these materials can be used to absorb the oil from a slow leak. Often a small leak will be tolerated by an owner until a regular service call is arranged. Repair to the filter or fuel line is a straightforward task. A leaking tank may have to be replaced. Figure 9.1 summarizes the areas vulnerable to leakage on an oil storage tank.

F I G U R E 9.1   Oil Storage Tank Leaks

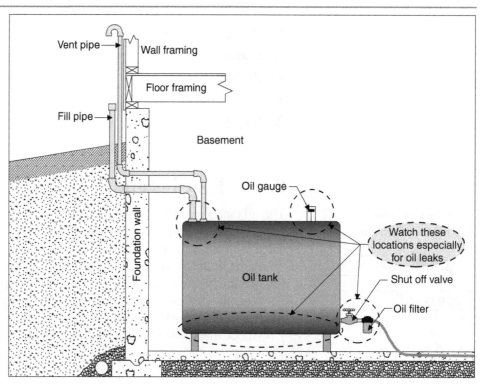

9.1.3   Rusting

Ultimately, fuel leakage is the concern. Severe rusting from a chronically wet basement could weaken legs. There is a risk of the tank toppling over.

Examine the bottom of the tank with a flashlight and mirror. Some minor peeling of paint and surface corrosion is expected, but large amounts of corrosion and scaling should be reported.

Do not poke rusted areas with a screwdriver, as large-scale leakage could result.

Tanks are usually supported at least 4 inches off the floor by four steel legs. Check for signs of rusting and the integrity of the legs. Rusted legs may be resupported by blocks, bricks or wood. Ensure there is no risk of these supports puncturing the tank. Rusted legs suggest basement water leakage.

9.1.4   Underground

The leakage of fuel oil from a buried tank is more than a functional problem. It is also an environmental concern beyond the scope of a home inspection. However, most inspectors at least tell their clients that they don't comment on underground oil tanks. Removal of a tank is a significant expense. Contamination of soil resulting from a leak leads to a much greater expense.

Homeowners converting from oil to another fuel usually have to remove the tank, since most jurisdictions will not allow it to be abandoned and left in place. An existing abandoned tank will require removal in many jurisdictions, even if the conversion was carried out by a previous owner. Any soil contamination has to be cleaned up at the time of tank removal.

An empty tank may eventually rust and collapse, causing soil subsidence problems. Some abandoned tanks are filled with sand or concrete slurry.

Outdoor oil fill and vent pipes that enter the ground outside rather than pass through the walls of the house may suggest the presence of a buried tank. Pipes that pass through the walls of the house likely connect to an indoor tank. Inside tanks may be out in the open, concealed in a closet or partitioned off.

Try to find the oil tank inside the house first, usually near the area where the oil pipes go through the house wall. If the tank cannot be found in the basement, check the crawlspaces.

If necessary, follow the copper fuel-supply line back from the burner. Fuel lines should be buried in or below concrete slab floors (sometimes a patched trench is noted) or embedded in mortar at the joint between the foundation and floor. If the fuel line goes through the wall, there may be a buried tank.

9.1.5   Empty

Oil storage tanks should never be run totally dry. Ideally, the oil supplier refills the tank when it is approximately one-third full, so the home always has heat.

The implications are lack of heat and the potential for freezing plumbing.

The gauge on the top of the tank indicates the oil level in the tank. If the gauge indicates no oil, and the burner runs but does not fire, then an empty tank is likely. Gauges are not always reliable. Some inspectors can tell by tapping on the tank whether there is oil in it. This takes some experience.

F I G U R E 9.2   Fill and Vent Piping

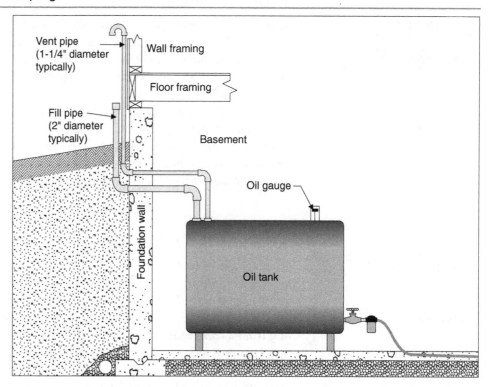

9.2   OIL FILL AND VENT PIPES

The oil fill and vent pipes protrude out of the wall or out of the ground (Figure 9.2). The fill pipe is used to add oil to the tank and the vent pipe allows the air in the tank to escape during filling.

Locations
Oil pipes are usually near the front of the house. Pipes may not be immediately obvious. They may be concealed by shrubs against the house or located in an attached garage or shed.

Size
The fill pipe is typically 2 inches in diameter and the vent pipe is $1^{1}/_{4}$ inch in diameter. They extend from 1 to 4 feet above grade level. They are not always the same length.

Cap and Gooseneck
The cap for the filler pipe is threaded and seals the pipe completely. The vent pipe has a gooseneck on the top, designed to keep rain and water out and allow air to pass.

Pipes Suggest Tank Location
The oil tank is normally inside the house adjacent to the foundation or wall through which the pipes pass. Pipes that enter the ground outside the building suggest the oil tank is underground.

Common fill and vent pipe problems include—

1. Leaks

2. Missing cap

3. Abandoned

4. Damaged/corroded

9.2.1   Leaks

Leaks from oil fill pipes are not common.

IMPLICATIONS

STRATEGY

Stains

Odor

Since oil does not remain in the pipe, the risk of leakage is only during the filling operation.

Look for stains or oil residue along the length of the pipe and at the threaded connections, especially the segment connected to the top of the tank. Oil stains on the inside or outside of the wall below the pipe may also mean leakage.

The odor of oil near the tank and pipes doesn't necessarily mean a leak from the pipe. Leaks at the tank, fuel filters and fuel supply line are more common.

9.2.2   Missing Cap

IMPLICATION

STRATEGY

Rainwater or water from lawn sprinklers may enter the tank if the cap is missing. Water in the oil tank can lead to corrosion and a leak. Children may drop foreign objects into the pipe.

Locate the oil fill and vent pipes and point them out to the client. Ensure that the fill-line cap and vent-line gooseneck are in place.

9.2.3   Abandoned

IMPLICATION

STRATEGY

Abandoned oil pipes are not a problem themselves. There is, however, some risk that a fuel supplier, if not informed of the conversion, may deliver oil through the existing pipes. A messy spill will occur if the oil tank was removed.

Determine if the house has been converted to another fuel. Check whether the tank is in place or removed. Pipes may have also been removed and all that remains is a patch in the foundation. If the tank has been removed, the pipes should ideally be removed or sealed. The pipes are sometimes cut flush with the foundation wall and filled with mortar.

9.2.4   Damaged/Corroded

IMPLICATION

STRATEGY

Leaks or spills can result if the pipe has been damaged.

Pipes should be straight and roughly vertical. Check threaded connections to ensure pieces are tight. Look for rust.

9.3   OIL SUPPLY LINES

The oil supply lines carry oil from the tank to the burner. These lines (there may be one or two) are typically 3/8 inch (minimum) copper although they can also be steel or brass. They are typically visible only at the tank and burner, with most of the length protected from mechanical damage by a mortar bed. A manual shutoff valve is required at the tank outlet or the point where the supply line enters the building.

Two Line Systems

A second (return) line is typically used if the tank is **below** the burner.

Here's what to watch for on the oil supply line(s):

1.   Leaks

2.   Corrosion/mechanical damage

3. Unprotected

4. Undersized

9.3.1   Leaks

IMPLICATIONS

Leaks from the fuel line, if undetected, could drain oil from the tank, since the fuel line is lower than the bottom of the tank. This could result in an expensive cleanup. (One such cleanup in Massachusetts cost $85,000!) A leak in the fuel line would also starve the burner for fuel, affecting the operation of the heating system or shutting it down.

Oil Safety Valve

In some areas, an **oil safety valve** (OSV) is required. This valve senses the suction of the pump, and cuts off the flow of oil if the line is not under suction. Leakage from the line eliminates the vacuum from the pump, shutting down the oil flow.

Firematic Valve

In some jurisdictions a **fire safety valve** (Firematic is a brand name) is required, to cut off the oil flow in event of a high temperature (presumably a fire) at the valve.

STRATEGY

Investigate the source of any oil odor. Inspection can be limited or impossible since the line often is buried below the floor slab or in a bed of mortar. Often, the line is concealed by finishes and storage.

Look for staining or wet spots along the pipe length.

9.3.2   Corrosion/Mechanical Damage

IMPLICATION

The implication is of course, leakage.

STRATEGY

Look along the length of line, wherever it is visible. Check at the tank (it is possible to damage the line during a filter change) and at the burner.

Damage during Service

During the annual burner maintenance, the burner unit must be removed from the furnace/boiler. The line can be disconnected from the burner, or the line may have enough slack that the service technician slides the burner out without disconnecting the line. This increases the risk of damage, such as kinking at the burner.

Rust

Look also for corrosion, typically a green or blue copper oxide (rust) on the line. Badly rusted lines should be replaced.

9.3.3   Unprotected

Lines should be protected. Methods are typically a hard plastic sleeve, or more commonly, burying the line in a mortar bed.

Unprotected lines are easily damaged and may leak or restrict oil flow.

IMPLICATION

STRATEGY

You should not be able to see the majority of the line. If you can, recommend that the line be protected.

9.3.4   Undersized

This condition is common only on lines serving outside, above ground storage tanks. In cold climates, fuel oil thickens and doesn't flow well. Therefore, the oil supply line into the house needs to be much larger than the typical $3/8$-inch-diameter copper line. Usually in these installations, a 2-inch steel line is used, with the line changing to the small copper line about 4 feet inside the house. This distance allows the oil to warm up.

IMPLICATION	If the supply line is undersized, the burner may be fuel-starved and may shut down.
STRATEGY	Where you can trace the outdoor line, check its size. If it's less than 2-inch-diameter, recommend that it be checked by a specialist.

9.4   OIL FILTER

The oil filter is similar to the size and shape of the oil filter on a car. It's usually close to the tank, although it can be close to the burner. Filters can be leaking, dirty or missing.

9.4.1   Leaks

IMPLICATION	This is a minor nuisance unless undetected for a long time. The leak may create an air lock or interrupt the flow of oil to the burner.
STRATEGY	The smell of fuel oil in the vicinity of heating equipment should signal a possible leak from the fuel system. Look at the fuel filter for stray drops of oil. Watch for pie plates or tins on the floor below the filter, or a filter wrapped in plastic bags to collect oil from a slow leak.

9.4.2   Dirty

IMPLICATION	Reduced fuel flow to the burners will affect the output and efficiency of the burner. The fuel pump may work harder, shortening its life. Unreliable operation of the burners can often be corrected by replacing the filter.
STRATEGY	You can't tell if the filter is dirty at an inspection. The client should be informed that the filter is an annual maintenance item.

9.4.3   Missing

IMPLICATION	Impurities in oil or debris from the tank may clog the fuel line, nozzle, etc. Furnace efficiency and heat output could be reduced. Furnace operation could be unreliable if clogs develop frequently.
STRATEGY	The filter is typically installed on the fuel line at the outlet from the tank or near the burners. It is seldom installed anywhere in between because of the increased number of connections required and the inconvenient location.
Not Visible	A filter might be installed but concealed from view if the tank is partitioned or buried behind storage. Look for a canister similar in size and shape to an automotive oil filter.

9.5   OIL BURNER

When we looked at gas burners, we started with **atmospheric burners.** As gas is delivered to the combustion chamber in vapor form, these burners are simple, reliable and inexpensive. With oil, this is not the case. The burners are **forced-draft,** and the exhaust gas temperatures are higher.

FIGURE 9.3   Atomizing Oil Burner

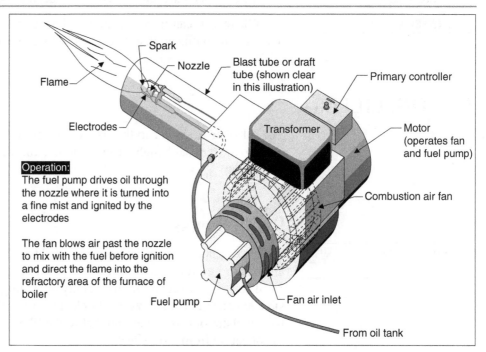

Spark

Nozzle

Blast tube or draft
tube (shown clear
in this illustration)

Primary controller

Flame

Electrodes

Transformer

Motor
(operates fan
and fuel pump)

Combustion air fan

Operation:
The fuel pump drives oil through
the nozzle where it is turned into
a fine mist and ignited by the
electrodes

The fan blows air past the nozzle
to mix with the fuel before ignition
and direct the flame into the
refractory area of the furnace of
boiler

Fuel pump

Fan air inlet

From oil tank

Liquid Fuel

Fuel oil is liquid at the point of delivery to the combustion chamber. This makes the ignition process much more difficult. A few oil burners (**vaporizing** or **pot-type** burners) vaporize the oil before ignition, but they are a special topic. In this section we will deal with the conventional oil burner, the **atomizing burner.** This is also called the **gun type** burner.

Burner Is External

Burners in gas furnaces are usually inside the furnace cabinet. Oil burners are typically outside the furnace cabinet, although the burner is enclosed on some models.

Emergency Shutoffs

Oil burners need 120-volt AC electricity (house power). Oil burners should have a manual oil shutoff valve or an electric switch, or both, located away from the burner as an emergency shutoff.

9.5.1   The Atomizing Burner

Creates an Oil Mist

The **atomizing burner** (Figure 9.3) uses an electric pump and a nozzle to **atomize** the oil (break up the liquid into a spray of fine droplets). This mist is mixed with turbulent air, and is ignited by a high voltage spark. Once the flame is established, the spark stops and the flame continues, until the flow of oil is shut off.

Combustion Air Fan

Air for combustion is drawn into the burner assembly through a fan. This forced-draft fan is powered by the same electric motor that powers the fuel pump. The air enters through an intake port, then is pushed down the **blast tube (draft tube),** through the **head,** to the **electrodes.** The blast tube is the steel cylinder containing the air and fuel delivery line to extend the burner into the fire pot. These are typically 3 inches in diameter, and roughly 1 foot long. The head is contained inside the blast tube, and on a modern **flame-retention head burner** is often at the very end of the blast tube.

Too Much or Too Little Air

Too little combustion air causes—

1. soot (insulating the heat exchanger and reducing efficiency)
2. carbon monoxide
3. inefficient combustion (unburned fuel going up the chimney)
4. cool exhaust gas temperatures (condensation causing corrosion)

Too much air causes—

1. cool exhaust gas temperatures (condensation causing corrosion)
2. reduced efficiency

$^1/_2$-Gallon/Hour Minimum

It is a quirk of oil burners that a steady, stable oil spray cannot be achieved below a flow rate of roughly 0.5 gallons of oil per hour (60,000 BTU/hr output capacity). For this reason, oil furnaces are often oversized for small houses.

9.5.2   Flame Retention Head Burners

Turbulator

Modern atomizing oil burners use a special head, called a **flame retention head** or **turbulator,** to increase the steady state efficiency to about 80% (Figure 9.4). This head swirls the air in the blast tube, to help mix the oil and air. The burn is more efficient and cleaner. The flame pattern is noticeably different compared to the old fashioned burners.

9.5.3   Flame Patterns

The modern flame, at its best, will have a blue core, with a rounded, tight orange flame, and yellow edges. The old style burner looks like a blowtorch, a long, ragged orange/yellow flame with yellow tips. It is quite common with old style burners to

FIGURE 9.4   Oil Burner with Flame Retention Head

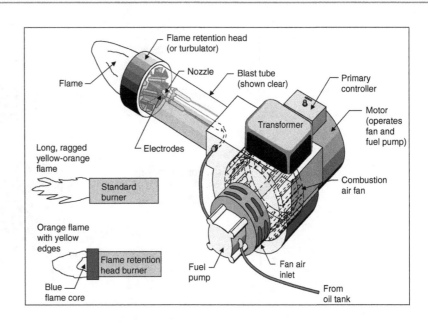

see soot in the combustion chamber. This is a result of the smoky black ends on the flame tips, and visible gray/black smoke above the flame.

9.5.4   Venting System

The combustion air fan pushes air into the burner and through the furnace past the heat exchanger (much like a gas furnace) and out to the vent connector. At the vent connector the exhaust gases are at atmospheric pressure, which is considered negative pressure for venting systems. A **draft regulator** is needed to ensure the exhaust from conventional oil furnaces can flow up the chimney. This draft regulator is usually a **barometric damper** that does the same thing as a draft hood on a gas furnace.

9.5.5   Conditions

Now, let's look at what can go wrong with oil burners (Figure 9.5).

1. Dirty
2. Inoperative
3. Leaking
4. Incomplete combustion
5. Vibrating/noisy
6. Too close to combustibles

Figure 9.5 summarizes how to inspect an oil burner.

FIGURE 9.5   Inspecting an Oil Burner

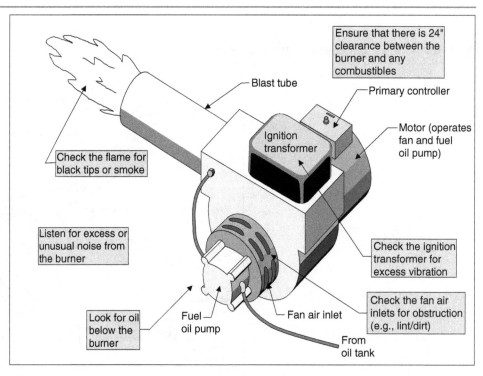

Dirty

An inefficient burner leads to higher heating costs. Severe restriction of the fan inlet can prevent ignition.

You can't check the nozzle or fuel filter during the inspection. They are buried inside the burner.

The color of the flame may give a clue to nozzle condition. A small observation port in the access panel of most modern furnaces and boilers provides a limited view of the combustion chamber. You can often open the door on older cast-iron units to view the flame. The flame should be orange. Different colors may have several causes, not just a dirty nozzle or filter. It is easy during servicing to clean or replace the nozzle and filter.

The fan inlet can usually be checked during a home inspection. The inlet is located on the side of the burner. Typically, a sliding metal plate can be moved to adjust the airflow for the burner. This is where the dust, hair, and so forth, typically build up. Do not change the air intake settings.

Watch for excessive smoke at the combustion chamber. It may mean inadequate air because the fan is dirty.

Inoperative

The implication is no heat. This is obviously a high-priority repair in the winter. Homes with no heat can suffer freezing pipes and frost heaving.

Turn the thermostat up to test the operation of the furnace. The oil burner should ignite almost instantly. In a quiet home, you can usually hear the burner come on.

If the burner does not ignite immediately, check the electric power switch. In most homes with basements, the switch is near the bottom of the basement stairs. The switch should be between the stairs and the appliance. The switch may be a conventional light switch or a fused disconnect.

If the switch is on, check the fuses or breaker panel. Electrical power to the furnace can be proved by operating the furnace air handler (blower) with the manual fan switch. If the power is off, don't turn it on. It may be off for a good reason.

If power is verified and there is still no response from the burner, check the oil level in the tank by looking at the gauge, if there is one. You may be able to tap on the tank and know whether there is fuel in it.

If the tank is not empty, the problem is likely in the fuel line or at one of the burner components. Since the Standards require testing by normal controls only, you do not need to investigate further.

Some inspectors check the refractory for pooling oil. The presence of oil may indicate the pump is working but the fan or igniter is not. **Do not reset the controller** if there is a puddle of oil in the refractory, as an explosion can result. The nozzle may be clogged. Recommend further investigation by a heating contractor. We'll talk about primary controllers shortly.

Leaking

If the leak is on the upstream side of the pump, the burner may not function because of the lack of pump vacuum.

Look for pooling or staining below the burner. Look for pie plates, rags, or paper towels, indicating the owner of the home knows there is a small leak.

Incomplete Combustion

Incomplete combustion causes inefficient performance and soot buildup in the heat exchanger and chimney. This can be a life safety issue if left long enough. Chimney or heat exchanger blockage with soot buildup is a common occurrence on neglected systems. This can spill combustion gases (usually containing carbon monoxide) into the house.

Observe the burner flame for significant black flame tips or smoke. Any time this is seen, you should recommend servicing of the unit, including cleaning the heat exchanger passages and the chimney.

Smoke may mean inadequate air, the wrong nozzle, or a defective refractory.

Delayed ignition is a variation on incomplete combustion. Watch for delayed, sometimes violent ignition. This is usually a spark igniter problem. It can also be related to a nozzle, pump or air supply problem.

A loud bang on start-up may mean there was a pool of oil in the combustion chamber, often a result of delayed shut down of the oil pump at the end of the previous cycle.

Vibrating/Noisy

There is no short-term implication of noisy burners, other than annoyance. However, vibration will accelerate the deterioration of the burner components.

Run the burner and note the noise. Oil burners should produce a steady drone. It is often possible to hear the oil burner noise throughout the entire house. Any uneven or high-pitched noises coming from the burner should be noted. This may mean a bearing problem with the motor, pump, or fan.

Place the back of your right hand on the top of the **ignition transformer.** This is typically a black box roughly 5 inches by 4 inches by 4 inches tall, usually at the top of the burner. It converts house current at 120 volts to very high voltage, so a spark can be generated at the electrode. Using the back of your hand may save your life if there is an electrical problem causing the transformer casing to be energized.

The burner unit should have a slight, steady vibration while running. Dramatic vibration is a cause for concern. A louder rumbling sound may mean the burner is dirty. Recommend inspection and cleaning as necessary.

Too Close to Combustibles

The lack of combustible clearance may result in a fire if something goes wrong at the burner.

Make sure there is no storage piled around or close to the burner. If the furnace has been enclosed in a room, make sure that combustible walls (including drywall) are at least 24 inches from the burner or the front of the furnace.

9.6 REFRACTORY/FIRE POT

The **refractory (fire pot, combustion chamber)** is the chamber in which the oil is burned. The chamber surrounds the flame and radiates heat back to the flame to help with combustion. Gas burners don't typically have a refractory. This is necessary with oil because of the high flame temperature. If the flame touched the metal heat exchanger, the metal would quickly burn through. Since the burner is a gun that throws a horizontal flame like a torch, the refractory is needed to slow down and redirect the heat and combustion gases up toward the heat exchanger.

The refractory is typically stainless steel, cast-iron, or brick and may be lined with soft ceramic felts. Some very old units have a cast-iron refractory. Stainless steel chambers may not be able to withstand the high temperatures associated with flame-retention head burners; a liner is sometimes required to compensate for this.

Retention Head Burners
Need Liner

Modern flame-retention head burners should not have unlined brick refractories, since, to burn efficiently, they need a refractory that heats up quickly and keeps the flame temperature high. Brick refractories heat up slowly, resulting in inefficiencies during start-up. Ceramic felt liners can sometimes be added.

Size

Round combustion chambers are typically 9 to 11 inches in diameter and roughly 13 inches tall. Rectangular chambers might be 9 inches by 9 inches by 13 inches tall. The nozzle is at one side of the chamber, just less than halfway up the wall. An ideal floor area is 80 to 90 square inches, assuming a firing rate of roughly 140,000 BTU/hour.

9.6.1   Crumbling/Cracked/Collapsed

IMPLICATIONS

If the refractory has deteriorated to the point that flame is in direct contact with other components, especially the walls of the heat exchanger or cabinet, premature failure of the furnace will result.

STRATEGY

The view of the refractory is often very limited. The viewing port is usually a small hole, about 1-inch diameter, located about 6 inches above the refractory. It is intended for viewing the flame, and does not provide a good view of the refractory.

Sometimes, large-scale deterioration is visible through the view port. Cracking is an immediate concern.

Ceramic Felt

Ceramic felt refractories are very delicate, and brittle. Large pieces often break off and fall into the bottom of the chamber. This should be noted as an immediate concern, especially if the flame touches the broken area. Ceramic felts are white, woven material, usually about 1/4-inch thick. They can easily be broken by hand.

9.6.2   Saturated

IMPLICATIONS

If the refractory is saturated with oil, it will quickly deteriorate and require rebuilding. Left unrepaired, premature failure of the heat exchanger could result, as the flame burns through the refractory and impinges on the heat exchanger.

STRATEGY

Check the combustion chamber, where accessible, for an accumulation of oil. In addition, look at refractory walls; if they look damp, they are probably saturated.

Limited Access

Access to the refractory is not always possible. Old cast-iron doors are often sealed shut with mortar. Don't break the seal. Newer furnaces have access ports, but the removal of any cover requiring tools is beyond our scope. There is a limited view of the refractory in any case.

Cabinet Clues

In extreme cases, a scorched cabinet, warped frame or glowing hot metal will indicate failed refractories. If you can view the refractory, look for **spalling** (thin sheets of brick falling off), cracking or collapse of the walls.

9.7   PRIMARY CONTROLLER

The **primary controller (primary relay, stack relay, flame sensor, Fire-eye, photo cell, cad cell)** is an automatic safety device to shut off the burner if the flame is out (Figure 9.6). This prevents oil pooling in the combustion chamber, which could be ignited, causing an explosion.

FIGURE 9.6   Primary Controller

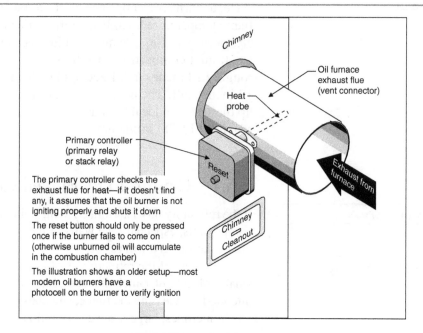

Chimney

Oil furnace
exhaust flue
(vent connector)

Heat
probe

Primary controller
(primary relay
or stack relay)

Reset

The primary controller checks the
exhaust flue for heat—if it doesn't find
any, it assumes that the oil burner is not
igniting properly and shuts it down

The reset button should only be pressed
once if the burner fails to come on
(otherwise unburned oil will accumulate
in the combustion chamber)

The illustration shows an older setup—most
modern oil burners have a
photocell on the burner to verify ignition

*Chimney
Cleanout*

Exhaust from furnace

Two Types

    There are two types of primary controllers. The old style (primary relay, stack relay) is installed in the exhaust flue, and the newer style (flame sensor, Fire-eye, cad cell) is installed on the burner itself. Let's look at the old style first.

Old Style

    The old-style primary controller had a probe that sat in the exhaust flue (vent connector) and used a bimetallic strip, similar to that found in thermostats, to sense combustion of the oil. When the burner is first fired, a signal is sent to the primary controller, starting a timer. Within a minute (more or less), if the bimetallic strip does not sense a temperature rise in the exhaust flue, the burner is shut down. The controller assumes that the burner failed to light, and it stops the pump, so we don't flood the combustion chamber with oil.

Reset Button

    If the primary controller shuts down the burner, a reset button pops, which must be reset to ignite the burner again. **This reset button should be tried only once.** We recommend that home inspectors do not push this button.

New Style

    The new-style primary controller uses a **flame sensor** mounted in the blast tube. This device typically uses a cadmium sulfide eye to sense combustion in the firepot. This device is not visible without dismantling of the burner, and cannot be checked during a home inspection.

    The primary controller is an automatic safety device; we do not test these in a standard home inspection. You should, however, look for primary controllers that are missing, inoperative, or tripped.

9.7.1 Missing

IMPLICATIONS

The combustion chamber may flood with oil if the burner fails to ignite and there is no primary controller to detect this flooding. Unsafe accumulations of oil in the firepot could damage the refractory, since it would become saturated with oil over time. This can also lead to an explosion.

STRATEGIES

Follow the exhaust flue from the furnace or boiler to the chimney. The primary control is a box-like metal device (roughly 6 inches by 5 inches by 3 inches deep) mounted on the flue, upstream of the barometric damper. There is a red reset button on the primary control.

The control box for a modern controller is often on the top of the burner. It is a rectangular box, roughly the same size as the transformer.

9.7.2   Tripped

IMPLICATION

STRATEGIES

If you come across a tripped primary control at an inspection, there will be no heat.

If possible, observe the bottom of the refractory to look for puddles of oil. If there is no pool of oil in the refractory, then the primary control **reset** can be pushed **once** if you are willing to take this responsibility. We are not.

Since it is a safety control that has tripped, indicating a potential problem with the system, the Standards do not require you to reset the primary control and test the unit.

Inspector in the House: Don't Push That Button!

It was early winter and the house was vacant. The agent had arrived early and was opening the house for me. I started on the outside and came inside. I found the agent frantically pushing the reset button on the furnace.

"The furnace keeps stopping!" he complained. I asked him to explain what happened. The house was old so he checked the thermostat. It was set at 72°, but the furnace was not on. He went to the furnace room and found the red **Reset** button on the primary control. He said when he pushed it, the furnace came on for about a minute, then it shut off. Every time he pushed the button, the furnace came on for about a minute.

I asked him how many times he had done this. He indicated between 5 and 10 times. I said, "Don't push it anymore, and we are very lucky the furnace did not start up." I explained that this control shuts the furnace down if no heat is sensed after about a minute. That tells the control the fuel did not ignite. It is important to push the button only once, since every time the furnace tries to start, unburned oil is deposited in the combustion chamber. If you keep pushing the button, you build up a large pool of oil in the chamber. When the furnace does finally start, you have a very dangerous situation, including the risk of an explosion.

I pointed out the words "Push Only Once" on the primary control and the agent agreed to call a service technician.

9.8   BAROMETRIC DAMPER/DRAFT REGULATOR

Venting Oil Furnaces Function

The venting of the combustion products for oil furnaces is similar to, but slightly different from, venting used for gas furnaces. We'll look at the differences here. The **barometric damper** (Figure 9.7) is a metal device mounted on the exhaust flue (vent connector). It ensures an adequate supply of draft air for the chimney. Its job is similar to the draft hood on a gas furnace.

F I G U R E   9.7   Barometric Damper

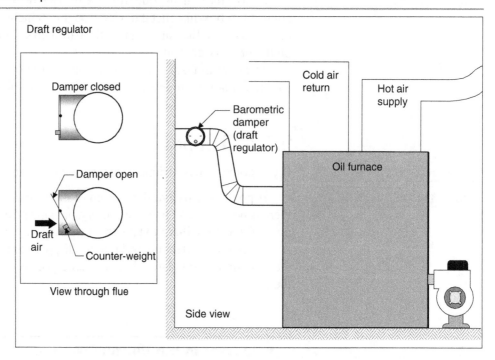

Oil burners, which are forced draft (the fan **pushes** air into the combustion chamber), require a single acting barometric damper. This means that the damper swings only inward to allow draft air into the chimney. The damper won't let the high temperature, sooty exhaust products back into the house.

Description

The damper pivots on its center horizontal axis to allow room air into the flue when the flue pressure is lower than the room air pressure. This air also cools the exhaust and decreases the draft effect on the fire. The damper is weighted, and the adjustment of this weight is critical to the operation of the damper.

Common problems with barometric dampers (draft regulators) include the following:

1. Rusting

2. Inoperative

3. Missing

4. Misadjusted

5. Spillage

9.8.1   Rusting

The exhaust flue and damper are in a hostile environment and can rust. There could be perforations in the damper or the damper housing.

IMPLICATIONS

Rust can obstruct the movement of the damper. A damper that is stuck, whether closed, open or partly open, will affect draft and combustion.

Stuck Closed

If the damper is stuck closed, the chimney can overheat, causing fire. If atmospheric conditions are poor, the lack of draft air could result in poor burner performance.

Stuck Open

If stuck open, heat loss from house air going up the chimney will increase heating costs. A damper stuck open could also allow exhaust products, including carbon monoxide, into the house. This is a potentially lethal condition.

Rust holes may also allow excess heat loss up the chimney or dangerous combustion products into the house.

Look at the condition of the damper inside and outside with a flashlight. Leakage onto the damper should be eliminated.

STRATEGY

Test Damper Movement

Check the movement of the damper with the furnace off by gently pushing the damper open with a screwdriver. The damper should swing back to the closed position. If any stiffness is detected, check inside the flue at the damper for obstructions such as soot or rust.

Check Draft When Furnace Runs

When the furnace starts up, the damper usually swings open and remains slightly open while the burner is on. You can check for room air being drawn into the flue with your hand or a tissue.

9.8.2 Inoperative

IMPLICATIONS

The implications are the same as those of rusting.

STRATEGY

Check the movement of the damper by gently pushing it open with a screwdriver. The damper should swing back to the closed position. If any stiffness is detected, check inside the flue at the damper for obstructions such as foreign debris, soot or rust.

9.8.3 Missing

IMPLICATIONS

The implication of a missing damper is no draft air. Exhaust products will not move properly up the chimney since they are not being supplemented with sufficient volumes of draft air. This affects combustion, possibly producing carbon monoxide and reducing efficiency.

STRATEGIES

Follow the exhaust flue from the furnace to the chimney. The damper is usually installed on the flue itself. Some dampers are installed at the base of the chimney and double as clean-outs. These are more prone to obstruction from debris in the chimney and rusting.

Some Furnaces Don't Use Draft Dampers

Some new, energy-efficient burners do not use a draft damper. These units, sometimes called **high-static burners,** have a powerful fan, capable of overcoming any atmospheric draft conditions. These units are usually labeled as not requiring a barometric damper. Where you cannot see a damper, and are unsure whether one is needed, recommend checking by a specialist.

Calling the Manufacturer

Alternatively, note the make, model and serial numbers, and call the manufacturer. It's great if you can do this while still on site.

9.8.4 Misadjusted

IMPLICATIONS

The damper may remain open when the burner is not in use, increasing heating costs, or the damper may not open sufficiently, reducing the volume of air available for draft purposes. This could lead to incomplete combustion and the production of carbon monoxide.

The damper should be completely closed if the burner is off. Check the damper position when inspecting the flue. Check the position again while the furnace is operating. The damper should swing open. The damper may swing slightly as exhaust products pass through the flue. The damper should swing closed when the burner shuts off.

9.8.5   Spillage

Spillage of combustion gases into the basement is a life safety condition.

With the burner off, look for any obvious holes in the damper itself. Look at the positioning of the damper in the exhaust flue. It should not be installed on an elbow, where combustion gases would bounce off the face of the damper. It should be installed so that the face of the damper is parallel to the flow of gases.

Check for Spillage

Ensure that the damper is closed when the burner is off. With the burner operating, place the palm of your hand at the face of the damper. You should be able to feel the cold draft air moving across your hand into the damper opening. Any hot or wet gases moving across your hand out of the damper, or black soot particles deposited on your hand, mean the damper is spilling.

9.9   VENT CONNECTOR (EXHAUST FLUE)

As with gas furnaces, we need to get the combustion products from the furnace to the chimney. However, as oil combustion products may reach higher flue temperatures of 500°F, the vent connector is typically made of steel (gas furnaces may use aluminum vent connectors).

Many Names

The **vent connector** (also called the **vent,** the **C vent, breeching, exhaust flue** or any of the other names listed in gas furnaces) is the pipe that carries the exhaust gases from the outlet of the heat exchanger to the base of the chimney (vertical flue). The horizontal sections of the vent connector should have a slight uphill slope to allow gravity to move the combustion gases to the chimney.

Look for these vent connector problems:

1. Rusting
2. Poor slope
3. Poor support
4. Too long
5. Inadequate clearance to combustibles
6. Loose connections
7. Too small
8. Unsuitable material
9. Dirty
10. Poor insertion into chimney
11. Poor manifolding
12. Obstruction

9.9.1   Rusting

IMPLICATION

STRATEGIES

Rusting of the exhaust flue can lead to leakage of the combustion gases into the house. This is a life safety issue.

Examine the entire length of the exhaust flue, wherever visible, for rusting. Do not probe the rusted areas with a screwdriver because you may create holes. Check the **bottom** of the flue, and check close to the chimney. This is where the rust is often worst.

If there is more than localized surface rust, especially at seams in the pipe and elbows, recommend replacement of the vent connector.

Patches

Look for mastic patches (a white patch material) at seams and on the outer edges of elbows where prior rust may have perforated and caused leakage of combustion gases. There are often temporary repairs that may fail and sections of the exhaust flue may need to be replaced.

9.9.2   Poorly Sloped Exhaust Flues

Slope is critical to the exhaust flue because the products of combustion must be able to move to the chimney by convection.

IMPLICATIONS

Poor slope can result in backdrafting of combustion gases or inadequate venting of combustion gases. These are life safety issues.

STRATEGIES

Measuring the Slope

The exhaust flue should slope up, away from the furnace at 1/4-inch per foot. Until you get used to estimating the slope of the vent by sight, you may wish to actually measure it with a four-foot spirit level, for example.

9.9.3   Poorly Supported Exhaust Flues

Sections Screwed Together

Exhaust flues are usually made up of individual pieces. These pieces are screwed together. The flue must be supported with wires or straps, typically attached to the framing members above.

IMPLICATIONS

At its worst, the poor support can result in openings in or collapse of the exhaust flue, which will allow combustion gases into the house. This is a life safety issue.

STRATEGIES

You should not be able to push with moderate pressure on the exhaust flue and cause significant deflection in any location. Move along the length of the flue, if it's cool, pushing at each joint to make sure the flue is intact and supported strongly enough so that no movement occurs. Although the numbers differ from jurisdiction to jurisdiction, support every 48 inches is usually required. Make sure the supports are non-combustible and a metal similar to the exhaust flue.

Burn Risk

Hot vent connectors can burn you. Be careful!

9.9.4   Excess Length

Ten feet is a commonly accepted maximum length for vent connectors on oil furnaces (Figure 9.8).

IMPLICATIONS

The implication of excessive vent length is poor drafting, condensation in the venting system and possible spillage of combustion gases into the house.

FIGURE 9.8 Exhaust Flue Length

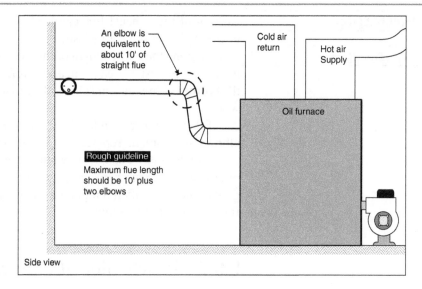

As a general rule, you can use a maximum vent length of 10 feet plus two elbows. Common sense applies here. If evidence of poor draft or backdrafting is visible along the vent, such as corrosion or evidence of poor combustion in the combustion chamber, then the vent length should be checked.

Again, given time, installations can be eyeballed and excess length vents quickly identified. For the first inspections, it is better to actually measure the length of the flue.

Draft inducers (power vents, power venters) are small fans placed in the exhaust flue to improve the draft. These can be used with oil equipment in some areas to reduce the risk of backdrafting on an excessively long flue.

9.9.5   Inadequate clearance to combustibles

Many inspections reveal inadequate clearance to combustibles. Exhaust flues, especially on oil furnaces, are hot enough to ignite many combustibles, yet some people treat exhaust flues as a convenient place to hang storage.

Improper clearance to combustibles can result in fire.

The required clearance to combustibles for a single-wall exhaust flue from an oil furnace is 18 inches in most areas, and 9 inches in others. Some furnace manufacturers specify the appropriate clearance for vent connectors on their furnaces. You should verify this number for your area, and apply it during inspections.

9.9.6   Loose Connections

Loose connections can result in spillage of combustion gases to the house. This is a life safety issue.

Move along the length of the flue, checking each connection as you go. With the burner off, grasp the cool exhaust flue at each joint and attempt to wiggle the connection. There should be minimal play in each of the connections.

3 Screws

Sections of the flue should be screwed together with three self-tapping sheet metal screws at the joints. Old joints that have been repaired with mastic, a temporary patch material, should be reported.

9.9.7   Too Small

IMPLICATION

STRATEGIES

An exhaust flue of insufficient diameter can cause spillage of exhaust gases into the house. This is a life safety issue.

Check in your area to find the proper diameter for exhaust flues. It is common for a 140,000 BTUs input per hour burner to have an exhaust flue of 6 inches diameter. (There are several variables.) Exhaust flues are typically single-wall, so the external flue dimension will be the internal dimension as well. Manufacturers may specify vent connector sizes.

9.9.8   Improper Material

Because of the temperatures and corrosive nature of the exhaust products, very few materials are suitable as exhaust flue material. Typically, we see galvanized steel. Aluminum may be allowed in your area, although it would have to be very thick. Stainless steel is less common than galvanized.

This is a rare problem, usually found only when the homeowner has replaced a failed exhaust flue on his own.

IMPLICATION

The implication is failure of the vent, causing spillage of combustion gases into the home. This is a life safety issue.

STRATEGIES

Look at each section of the vent on its own and determine if it's galvanized steel, typically identified by the zinc spangle on the outside of the pipe.

Stainless steel in an exhaust flue typically has a bluish tinge to it where it has been heated, often identified most easily at the elbows. Stainless steel is also shiny, unlike aluminum, which often has a dull finish.

9.9.9   Dirty

IMPLICATIONS

Dirty flues cause the solid particles in the exhaust gases to collect on the flue material, causing corrosion. In extreme cases, a dirty flue can plug. This would result in combustion gases spilling into the home, which is a life safety issue.

STRATEGIES

You typically cannot observe the inside of vent connectors, and you are not required to do so by the Standards. However, oil burning equipment usually has a barometric damper that lets you see a small portion of the exhaust flue.

9.9.10   Poor Insertion

There is a risk of poor insertion where the vent connector is inserted into a chimney. The vent may not be tightly sealed at the chimney. It should not extend into the flue, but should be flush with the inside face of the chimney wall.

IMPLICATION

Poor insertion can cause spillage of combustion gases to the basement. This is a life safety issue.

STRATEGIES

Open the chimney flue access door, and with a flashlight and mirror, attempt to see if the exhaust flue is flush with the chimney flue. Check the seal of the exhaust flue into the chimney. The exhaust flue should be mortared into a thimble in the chimney so that no gases can leak into the home.

9.9.11   Poor Manifolding

IMPLICATIONS

The implication of poor manifolding can be blockage of the small vent by the combustion products of the large vent. This could cause spillage of combustion gas into the house.

STRATEGIES

If you find multiple vent connectors going into the chimney, make sure that the smaller appliance vent is connected above the larger. Typically, this is an oil furnace and an oil water heater. In this case, the water heater vent has the smaller input, and goes on the top.

9.9.12   Obstruction in Vent Connector

IMPLICATIONS

Obstructions in the vent will cause exhaust gases to be spilled into the house. This is a life safety issue.

STRATEGIES

You cannot see inside the entire length of the vent, so you must rely on the evidence of backdrafting when you run the burner. When the burner is on, you should feel a draft going into the vent connector through the barometric damper. Running your hand along the vent connector, you should not feel exhaust gases leaking out of the connections. Be careful, because when the burner is running, the exhaust flue will be very hot.

REVIEW QUESTIONS

1. List five problems with oil storage tanks.

2. What is the implication of an abandoned buried oil tank?

3. The oil vent pipe allows

    a. oil vapors to vent out of the tank on a hot day.

    b. air to escape from the tank when the tank is filled.

    c. an overflow condition to dump oil back outside.

    d. the oil supplier a second pipe to fill the tank through.

4. List four problems with oil tank fill and vent pipes.

5. List four problems with oil supply lines.

6. Explain why an exterior, above-ground oil storage tank needs a 2-inch oil supply line, rather than the typical 3/8-inch-diameter line.

7. List three problems with oil filters.

8. Natural gas burners on conventional furnaces are natural draft.

    Oil burners in conventional oil furnaces are _____ draft.

9. Since oil is a liquid we have to _____ it before we can ignite it.

10. List six common problems with oil burners.

11. What is the typical required combustible clearance between an oil burner and combustibles?

12. What is the purpose of the refractory in an oil furnace?

13. List three materials that have been used for refractories.

14. What is the purpose of the primary controller in an oil furnace?

    a. it cycles the house air blower

    b. it cycles the burner

    c. it prevents oil accumulation in the combustion chamber

    d. it detects failed heat exchangers

    e. it is a high-temperature limit

15. List three common problems with the primary controller on a conventional oil furnace.

16. What is the purpose of the barometric damper?

17. How do we prevent combustion gases leaking out the barometric damper?

18. List five common barometric damper problems.

19. Every oil furnace must have a barometric damper.

    True   False

20. Since oil combustion gases are hotter than natural gas combustion gases, you will rarely find _____ used as an exhaust vent material.

21. List six problems with oil furnace vent connectors.

22. What is the minimum required clearance to combustibles for a single-wall exhaust flue serving an oil furnace?

a. 1 inch

b. 2 inches

c. 6 inches

d. 18 inches

23. The vent connector from an oil furnace must connect to the chimney above a vent connector from a water heater.

True   False

CHAPTER

10

HOT WATER BOILERS

INTRODUCTION	In this chapter, we will look at hot water boilers and their components. We will not repeat the discussions of fuel supply systems, combustion air, burners, vent connectors, heat exchangers, thermostats, cabinetry, and other components found on both boilers and furnaces. We have discussed all of these in Chapter 8.

10.1   AN OVERVIEW OF BOILERS

The function of the boiler is the same as a furnace: to provide heat so that all parts of the home are comfortable. Boilers fulfill this function in a slightly different way than furnaces.

Boilers Don't Really Boil

Hot water boilers, or what some people call **hydronic heating systems,** don't really boil the water. They typically heat the water to a maximum of 200°F. Normal operating temperatures for many boilers are in the 120°F to 130°F range, depending on a number of factors, including outdoor temperature, design capacity, etc.

10.1.1   Materials

Cast Iron

The oldest boilers, and some modern boilers, have cast-iron heat exchangers. Cast iron is a very high-quality material that works very well for water heating systems.

Steel

Many boilers have steel heat exchangers. On some steel boilers, the exterior jacketing is very heavy plate steel. In other systems, the exterior jacket is light gauge sheet steel forming a cabinet that looks very much like a furnace cabinet. In either case, the exchanger steel is heavy gauge.

Steel heat exchangers are considered lower quality than cast iron, since they are more susceptible to corrosion.

Copper

Many modern boilers use copper tubes. Some have aluminum fins on the tubes, and many have cast-iron headers at either end of the copper tubes. Copper is an excellent heat transfer medium, but copper-tube boilers have a shorter life expectancy than steel and considerably less than cast iron.

Alloys

Some boilers have stainless steel or copper-nickel alloy heat exchangers. These systems are relatively new and their life expectancy and long-term performance are not yet known.

10.1.2   How Boilers Work

Several Fuels

Heat is generated in a boiler by burning oil, natural gas, or propane, for example. There are electric boilers, also.

Water Is the Heat Transfer Medium

Boilers use water to move heat through the house (Figure 10.1). Heat is transferred from the fire side of the heat exchanger, through the heat exchanger, into the water. The heated water is piped to the various rooms of the house where heat is released through radiators, baseboards or convectors. The cooler water returns to the boiler to pick up more heat.

Radiant Heating

In some homes, **radiant heating** is used where the distribution pipes are embedded in floors or ceilings and heat is released along the entire length of these piping grids, buried in the finishes. In radiant systems, there are no radiators or convectors. There is also a lot less for the home inspector to look at!

FIGURE 10.1   How Boilers Work

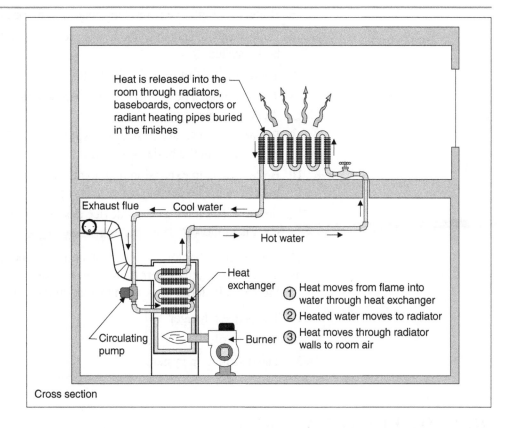

Heat is released into the room through radiators, baseboards, convectors or radiant heating pipes buried in the finishes

Exhaust flue   Cool water

Hot water

Heat exchanger

① Heat moves from flame into water through heat exchanger

② Heated water moves to radiator

③ Heat moves through radiator walls to room air

Circulating pump

Burner

Cross section

10.1.3   Similarities and Differences Between Furnaces and Boilers

Furnaces and boilers both have—

1. burners, fuel supplies, and combustion controls
2. combustion air requirements
3. venting systems
4. heat exchangers
5. cabinets
6. high temperature limit switches
7. thermostats

Because we have talked about all of these systems in Chapter 8, we won't repeat the discussions here, except where there are differences that are important to home inspectors.

The important differences between boilers and furnaces are:

1. Boilers have pipes. Furnaces have ducts.
2. Boilers have radiators, convectors, baseboard heaters, or radiant pipes. Furnaces have registers and grilles.
3. Boilers have pumps instead of fans, with pump controls instead of fan controls. Pumps on boilers are sometimes referred to as **circulators**.

4. Boilers do not have air filters or electronic air cleaners.

5. Boilers cannot have central air conditioning or humidification systems added.

6. Boilers are connected to the house plumbing system (to provide water to the boiler system).

7. There is a control to maintain the boiler water pressure at a desired level.

8. There is often a device to keep the boiler water from getting back into our drinking water.

9. Boilers have a safety device (pressure-relief valve) to prevent water pressure building up in the boiler system.

10. Boilers have an expansion tank to allow the water to expand without creating high pressures when the water heats up.

11. Some boilers have a safety device designed to turn the boiler off if the water level is too low.

Throughout this chapter, we will look at the components that are different from furnaces, occasionally referring back to the furnaces.

We will talk about these components in three groups:

1. The heat exchanger

2. The controls

3. The distribution system

10.2   HEAT EXCHANGERS

Above Burner

The heat exchanger is the heart of the boiler (Figure 10.2). It is usually located above the burner, and sees the products of combustion coming off the burner. At the top of the heat exchanger, the products of combustion are typically directed into the venting system.

The cool water enters the bottom of the heat exchanger and the heated water leaves from the top.

Failures Are Wet

Heat exchangers on boilers are easier on home inspectors than furnace heat exchangers. When a furnace heat exchanger is cracked or has a hole, it's often difficult to tell. When a boiler heat exchanger has a crack or a hole, it's easy to tell. The water leaks out! It may extinguish the burner or result in water spilling onto the floor around the boiler.

Let's look at the specific problems:

1. Leaks

2. Rust

3. Clogged

Leaks

IMPLICATIONS

A leaking heat exchanger typically has to be replaced. Usually you replace the whole boiler when you have to replace the heat exchanger. There are some exceptions, but for the most part, it's safe to say a new boiler is needed when a heat exchanger leaks.

Poor Connections

One exception might be if it is a connection problem. Sometimes sections of heat exchangers are not tightened up securely. Sometimes gaskets fail. In most cases, you won't know, and should decribe the leaking as a potentially serious problem.

F I G U R E 10.2 Heat Exchangers

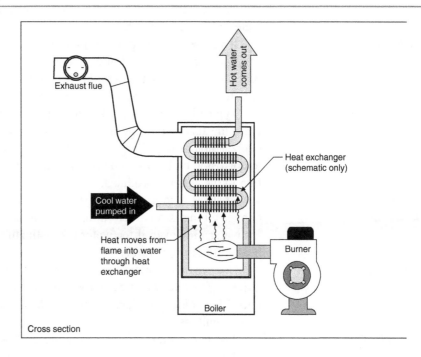

Exhaust flue

Hot water comes out

Heat exchanger (schematic only)

Cool water pumped in

Heat moves from flame into water through heat exchanger

Burner

Boiler

Cross section

Dripping and Hissing

Look for water. Sometimes it's obvious, but sometimes the leak is quite small and is only active when the heating system is firing.

One trick is to look inside the burner compartment at as much of the heat exchanger as you can see, just after the burner shuts off. Look for dripping water and listen for the hissing sound of water hitting the hot combustion chamber components (refractory, for example) and boiling off into steam.

Listen as Burner Is Shut off

Sometimes when you open the burner compartment just after the burner shuts off, you'll see a little puff of steam coming out. This generally means that the heat exchanger has one or more small leaks, allowing water to get through the heat exchanger and into the combustion chamber.

Check Outer Jacket

Don't forget to look at the outside jacket of the boiler. Especially on older cast iron and steam boilers, the jacket is part of the heat exchanger. Look for leaks here too. If it is at a seam, it may only be a gasket problem.

Rust

IMPLICATIONS

Rust on a heat exchanger leads to leaks.

Rust on the fire side of the heat exchanger reduces the boiler's efficiency, increases the heating costs, and may clog the exhaust gas passages, leading to life threatening spillage of exhaust gases into the home.

STRATEGY

Rust is the enemy of boilers. Look for rust on the external parts of the boiler, at the combustion chamber and, using a flashlight and mirror, at whatever parts of the heat exchanger are visible. Look for flaking, scaling rust. Look also for pinhole rusting. Pinholes may be small leaks that scab over with rust scale intermittently; however, they usually mean the heat exchanger is near the end of its life.

Chemicals

Watch for corrosive household chemicals stored near the boiler. These can rust the heat exchanger.

Be Gentle

We don't recommend that you poke aggressively at rust on a heat exchanger with a screwdriver, for example. You may end up with an embarrassing amount of water where it doesn't belong.

Turn Boiler Off

If you're going to poke around inside combustion chambers and heat exchangers, you don't want the boiler to come on. Many home inspectors shut the power off before venturing into a boiler. We think that's a good idea. An equally good idea is to turn it back on when you're done!

Careful with Copper Tube Boilers

Typically, you can't get a good look at a boiler heat exchanger without dismantling the system, going well beyond the Standards. However, one look at a copper-tube heat exchanger can tell you a great deal. These systems are susceptible to corrosion on the fire side of the heat exchanger, typically because of condensation in the exhaust products.

Overheated Heat Exchanger

There is also a potential problem with copper-tube boilers overheating. The copper tubing is relatively thin. It's good at transferring heat from the fire side to the water. However, if the water inside the tubes gets too hot, the copper will overheat and fail prematurely.

Pump Provides Cooling Water

Copper-tube boilers have a pump that pushes water past the heat exchanger quickly. The total water capacity of a copper-tube heat exchanger is only a few gallons. Many of the old, larger, cast-iron heat exchangers have water capacities in the tens of gallons.

Pump Must Be On When Boiler On

The pump must keep introducing cool water to the heat exchanger to avoid overheating the copper tubing. These systems often have a control that won't allow the burner to come on unless the pump is working.

When you are looking at a copper-tube boiler, make sure the pump is working when the burner is on (Figure 10.3).

Clogged

IMPLICATIONS

This can result in reduced efficiency of the heating system. A soot buildup on the heat exchanger, for example, restricts the heat transfer, resulting in more heat going straight up the chimney.

It can overheat the heat exchanger if the exhaust flow across the heat exchanger is restricted.

In severe cases, it can lead to spillage of exhaust products back into the house through the burner.

STRATEGY

With a mirror and flashlight, look for black, sooty deposits on the heat exchanger. These should not be seen at all on gas burners and, although some soot can be expected on an oil burner, watch for measurably thick buildups.

Look for rust on the heat exchanger that can completely obstruct the fins on a copper tube boiler.

Spillage

Check for spillage of combustion gases as you would on any burner. One cause may be a restricted heat exchanger passage.

Cleaning

Where you have identified a partially clogged or heavily sooted heat exchanger, you're probably looking at a maintenance item, rather than a replacement item. This is a far less serious condition in most cases than a leak or severe rusting of a heat exchanger.

FIGURE 10.3   Copper Tube Heat Exchangers

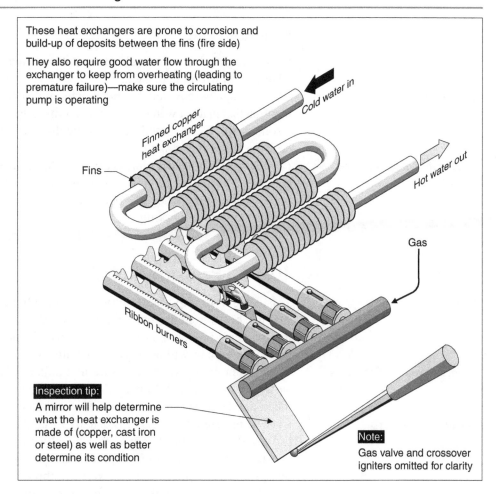

These heat exchangers are prone to corrosion and build-up of deposits between the fins (fire side)

They also require good water flow through the exchanger to keep from overheating (leading to premature failure)—make sure the circulating pump is operating

Finned copper heat exchanger

Fins

Cold water in

Hot water out

Gas

Ribbon burners

Inspection tip:
A mirror will help determine what the heat exchanger is made of (copper, cast iron or steel) as well as better determine its condition

Note:
Gas valve and crossover igniters omitted for clarity

10.3   CONTROLS

As we discuss boiler controls, we will assume we have a closed, forced-water system with a pump. This is the most common system and also has the most complex controls.

Safety Controls and Operating Controls

There are two very different types of controls on a boiler. **Safety controls** do what their name suggests: they help make the system safe. **Operating controls** help the system function efficiently to provide comfortable heat.

Many Variations

There are many ways boilers can be controlled, and we won't include all of them here. We will talk about the most common.

In this section we'll look at four **safety controls:**

1. Pressure relief valve

2. High-temperature limit (aquastat).

3. Low-water cut out

4. Backflow preventer

We will also look at five **operating controls:**

1. Pressure reducing valve

2. Primary control

3. Pump control

4. Zone controls

5. Isolating valve

For each control, we'll talk about what it does and where it's located. We'll look at what can go wrong with each.

Thermostat

Although we covered the **thermostat** more extensively in Chapter 8, we should mention that in a hot water boiler it can turn on the burner, turn on the pump, or open a zone valve. It can sometimes do more than one of these functions, depending on how the boiler is arranged.

Temperature and Pressure Gauge

Most boilers have a **temperature and pressure gauge,** although these are not controls. It is helpful to know the temperature and pressure of the water when the boiler is at rest and when it is operating at steady state. This provides clues to how well the system is working.

10.3.1 Pressure-Relief Valve

Function

This is the most important safety device on a boiler. This valve prevents the pressure in a boiler system from building beyond 30 psi. Excessive pressures can result in superheated water and steam explosions. The pressure relief valve prevents high pressures, with or without high temperatures.

Normal Operating Pressures

The normal operating pressure in a boiler is 12 to 15 psi. The pressure-relief valve, set to relieve at 30 psi, allows pressure to build up with normal heating of the boiler. However, it does not allow the system pressure to get over 30 psi.

Location

The pressure-relief valve is usually located at or near the top of the boiler and is piped down to a discharge point, typically within 18 inches of the floor level.

Don't Test

The Standards do not require us to test safety controls. We do not recommend that you test the pressure-relief valve, although there is a test lever that can be raised. When you raise the lever to test the valve, you actually open the valve and flow water. The valve often will not reseat properly because of some dirt or an internal problem with the valve. Water spilling out onto the floor of the boiler room means an emergency service call, very likely at your expense.

Let's assume we won't be testing safety controls, and look at some of the problems you can identify.

1. Missing

2. Wrong size

3. Wrong pressure setting

4. Poor location

5. No piped extension

6. Pipe too small

7. Pipe threaded, capped, or corroded at the bottom

8. Pipe dripping or leaking

IMPLICATION

The implication of all of these issues is life safety, unless otherwise stated.

Missing

All closed hot water systems should have a pressure-relief valve. We will talk about open systems later, but they are not common. Recommend further investigation wherever you don't see a pressure-relief valve, unless you are sure it is not needed.

F I G U R E 10.4 Pressure Relief Valve

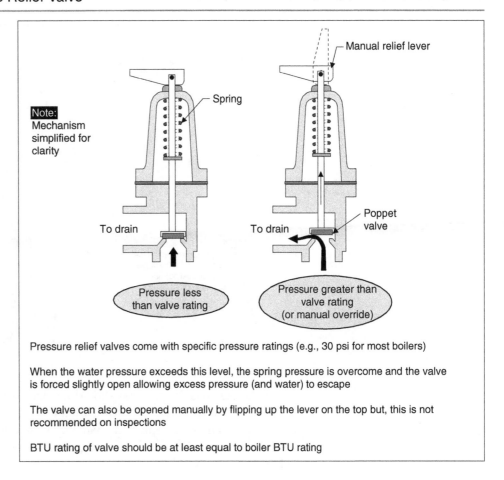

Note:
Mechanism simplified for clarity

Manual relief lever

Spring

Poppet valve

To drain

To drain

Pressure less than valve rating

Pressure greater than valve rating (or manual override)

Pressure relief valves come with specific pressure ratings (e.g., 30 psi for most boilers)

When the water pressure exceeds this level, the spring pressure is overcome and the valve is forced slightly open allowing excess pressure (and water) to escape

The valve can also be opened manually by flipping up the lever on the top but, this is not recommended on inspections

BTU rating of valve should be at least equal to boiler BTU rating

STRATEGY

Look for a valve at or near the top of the boiler. It can be attached to the boiler or to the piping. The valve itself can be brass or steel. It usually has a lever on it to allow for testing. It always has a threaded discharge port at the bottom that should be connected to a discharge pipe extending down to near the floor level.

Wrong Size

The pressure-relief valve should be sized properly for the burner. The valve usually has a tag that indicates its BTU/hr capacity. For example, a burner with 100,000 BTU/hr input should not have a 50,000 BTU/hr-rated relief valve.

STRATEGY

Check the rating on the relief valve against the burner input capacity (Figure 10.4). The relief valve rating should always be equal to or greater than the burner rating.

Set Wrong

The pressure-relief valve is normally set at 30 psi. Many, but not all, of these are preset and cannot be adjusted.

STRATEGY

Very often, you won't be able to tell what the setting is. However, if you can identify the valve as an adjustable type, or if the valve is rated for more than 30 psi and is not adjustable, you should call for further investigation. The tag on the valve usually indicates its setting.

F I G U R E 10.5   Pressure Relief Valve Location

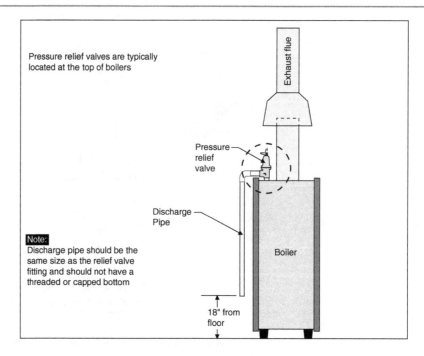

If the tag says **30 psi,** you should be fine. If the tag says 20 to 60 psi, it is adjustable. You won't be able to tell what it is set at. You should call for a specialist to check and either replace the valve or ensure that it is set properly. If the tag on the valve says 60 psi, for example, you should recommend replacement of the valve.

Poor Location

The valve should be located on the top of the boiler or on the piping very close to it (Figure 10.5). The further away from the boiler the valve is placed, the less likely it is to operate quickly and safely.

STRATEGY

Locate the pressure-relief valve. If it's not on or near the top of the boiler, recommend that it be checked during regular servicing. Watch for an isolating valve between the boiler and the relief valve. There should not be one. We don't want to be able to cut off the relief valve from the boiler water pressure.

No Piped Extension

A pressure relief valve should have an extension so that people won't be hit by hot water if the valve discharges.

IMPLICATION

This is a personal safety issue with respect to being scalded, rather than a boiler safety issue with respect to a steam explosion.

STRATEGY

Look for a pipe attached to the pressure relief valve extending down to 6 to 12 inches above floor level.

Pipe Too Small

The pipe diameter should be the same size as the threaded connection on the pressure relief valve.

Check that the pipe diameter is the same as the threaded connection on the pressure relief valve. Three-quarter inch is a common diameter. This information is often included on the tag on the valve. A $1/4$-inch pipe, for example, is too small. A $1/2$-inch pipe is sometimes too small.

Pipe Threaded, Capped, or Corroded at the Bottom
It should not be possible to cap off the piped extension from the pressure relief valve. This would defeat the valve.

Check the bottom of the pipe. It should not be threaded. It should not be capped off. Watch for corrosion that may obstruct the pipe at the bottom.

It's common for the pressure relief valve to operate from time to time over the life of the boiler. In many cases, the operation is intermittent and corrosion may develop at the bottom of the discharge pipe, which is often galvanized steel. This corrosion can reduce the pipe diameter and effectively cap it off. Where you see corrosion, recommend investigation and correction.

Pipe Dripping or Leaking

The implications may be simply replacing the valve or draining a waterlogged expansion tank. However, it is a red flag. Recommend a service technician investigate and correct the cause of the dripping or leaking.

10.3.2   High-Temperature Limit Switch

This switch performs the same function as the **high-temperature limit** on a furnace: it shuts off the boiler if the temperature gets too high (Figure 10.6). This switch is located either in the boiler or in the supply piping just above the boiler. It is typically set at 200°F to 220°F. A common setting is 210°F. On most systems you can look at the limit switch and see its setting.

The limit switch may be missing, set too high, or defective or not wired correctly. As with pressure relief valves, the implication for all of these problems is safety.

Missing

Look for a high temperature limit switch. You may have to remove the front cover panel of the boiler to locate the limit switch. It may be inside the cabinet on the front of the boiler, or it may be on the hot distribution piping just above the boiler, where the heated water leaves the boiler itself.

Set Too High

The high temperature limit switch is usually set around 210°F. If it is set above this, you should recommend that a service person check the setting. If it is set above 250°F, this is a definite safety problem and you should recommend priority correction.

Defective or Not Wired Correctly

Home inspectors will not normally know whether the unit operates properly. Testing safety devices goes beyond the Standards.

FIGURE 10.6 High Temperature Limit Switch

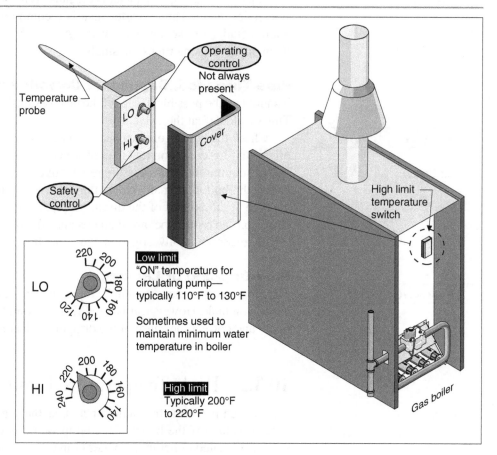

10.3.3 Low-Water Cutout

Function

A **low-water cutout** is a device that shuts off the boiler if the water level is too low (Figure 10.7). This may happen if the boiler leaks, or is drained and then fired. This will overheat and usually crack the heat exchanger, ruining the boiler. Worse, it can generate steam in the piping system if the boiler is partly filled with water. This can be very dangerous.

Low-water cutouts are not found on all residential boilers. Modern installation codes typically will require one, though.

Identifying Them

Low-water cutouts are usually easy to identify. They are usually mounted above the boiler and have a piped connection to the bottom and the top of the boiler or piping. The body of the low-water cutout is often fairly large (larger than a grapefruit) and there is electrical wiring running to the unit. If a nametag is visible, it is usually labeled **low-water cutout.** Some have isolating valves so they can be serviced without draining the boilers.

IMPLICATIONS

Low-water cutouts may be missing, leaking or inoperative. These conditions all have similar safety implications.

Missing

You should know if they are needed in your area. They may only be called for on larger boilers.

FIGURE 10.7   Low Water Cutout

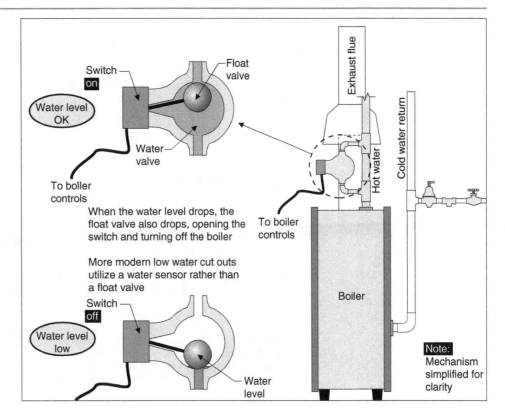

STRATEGY

Look for a low-water cutout mounted on the side of the boiler. If it's not there and is needed, point that out.

Leaking

STRATEGY

Look for evidence of leakage around the low-water cutout and its pipe connections. Obviously, any leakage around a boiler should be noted. Repairs should be recommended.

Inoperative

STRATEGY

Other than being able to identify closed isolating valves, you normally won't be able to tell whether the low-water cutout is working properly. Again, testing safety controls goes beyond our scope.

10.3.4   Backflow Preventer

Function

The **backflow preventer** stops the boiler water from getting back into the drinking water (Figure 10.8). The boiler is connected to the house plumbing system so that we can add water to the boiler. On old systems, this is done manually by opening a valve to allow more water into the boiler system when it was needed.

Modern systems use a **pressure-reducing valve** to add water automatically into the boiler system to maintain its pressure at 12 to 15 psi. Some have a built-in check valve to prevent backflow. Because this pressure-reducing valve (also known as an **automatic water makeup valve**) can fail, like any mechanical device, many jurisdictions require a backflow preventer. This is effectively a double-check valve

F I G U R E 10.8 Backflow Preventer

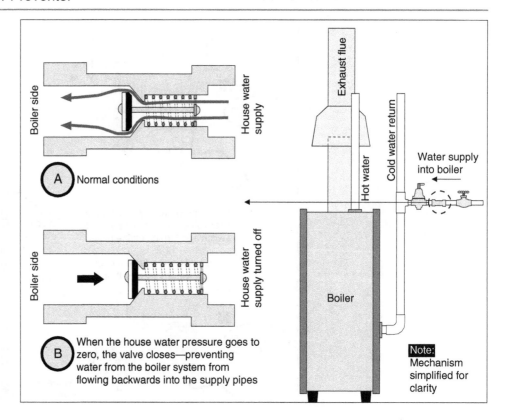

that prevents water from flowing back out of the boiler system into the house plumbing piping. You don't want to drink water that's been in a boiler system for a number of years.

Not all jurisdictions require backflow preventers. You should check to see whether it's necessary in your area.

The backflow preventer is usually next to the **pressure-reducing valve** (which we'll look at shortly) on the short run of connecting piping that joins the cold water supply piping from the plumbing to the boiler itself (Figure 10.9).

The backflow preventer may be missing, leaking or installed backwards.

Missing

The implication is a life safety issue. Putting foul water into our drinking water can obviously make people sick, at the very least.

Know whether backflow preventers are required and under what circumstances. Look for them and make the appropriate recommendations.

Leaking

In most cases, this is a nuisance. In some cases, it can allow backflow.

Look for leaks and recommend that they be corrected.

Installed Backwards

The safety benefit is lost and the boiler can't get any makeup water. Therefore this isn't a common problem.

When looking at a backflow preventer, make sure that the arrow on the valve points toward the boiler.

IMPLICATIONS

STRATEGY

IMPLICATIONS

STRATEGY

IMPLICATIONS

STRATEGY

F I G U R E 10.9 Pressure Reducing Valve Location

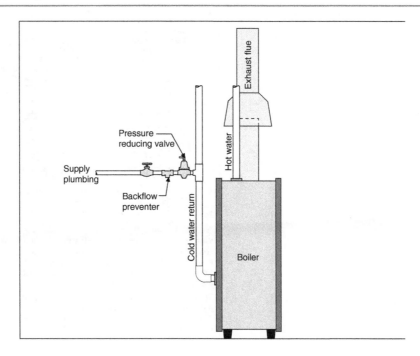

10.3.5   Pressure-Reducing Valve

The **pressure reducing valve** is also called the **automatic make up valve** or the **feed-water pressure regulator.**

Function
     The pressure-reducing valve connects the house plumbing supply system to the boiler water. It is designed to automatically maintain an adequate amount of water in the boiler at the desired pressure (12 to 15 psi) (Figure 10.10).

Location
     The valve is typically on a short connector pipe between the plumbing system and the boiler. It is often close to a **backflow preventer.** The pressure-reducing valve can also be part of an assembly that includes a pressure-reducing valve and a pressure-relief valve.
     When these two units are combined into one component, they should be installed so that the pressure-relief valve is closer to the boiler.

Integral Check Valve
     Some pressure-reducing valves have an integral check valve that prevents water flowing back from the heating system into the plumbing system.

Materials
     These valves are typically made of brass or steel and are very often shaped like a bell. There is no discharge pipe attached to a pressure-reducing valve, because they are not intended to relieve water.
     Common problems include—

1. Set too low
2. Missing
3. Inoperative
4. Leaking
5. Installed backwards

F I G U R E   10.10   Pressure Reducing Valve

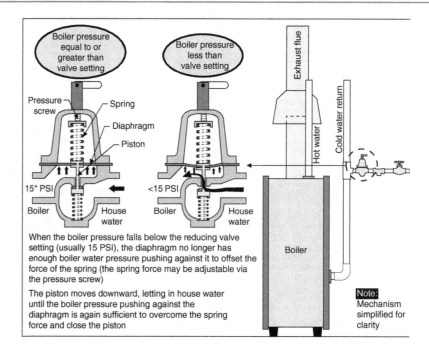

Set Too Low

Pressure-reducing valves are usually factory-set at between 12 and 15 psi. Some are adjustable within this range and beyond (10 to 25 psi range is common).

Tall House Problems

They are rarely faulty, but may be set too low because of the house configuration (Figure 10.11). A tall three-story house with a basement may require a pressure-reducing valve set at more than 12 psi. The pressure at the boiler has to push water up to the top of the heating system. If the radiators on the upper floor are not filled with water, these rooms will be cold.

IMPLICATIONS

The top floor of the house will be cold if the radiators will not fill with water.

STRATEGY

When the system is operating, run your hand along the top floor radiators from bottom to top. If the radiator is not full, you can feel a distinct temperature change on the radiator surface when you get above the water level. The cast iron will feel much cooler.

Don't Operate the Bleed Valves

We'll talk about radiators in a little bit, but you may have already noticed an air bleed valve at one end of the top of the radiator. This allows you to get rid of any air that has accumulated in the system. Some home inspectors go beyond the Standards and operate this bleed valve. This is risky because the valve may not close properly and you may cause a leak. The advantage of doing this is that you can find out whether the water does fill the radiator. When you open the valve, you may get water out immediately. This tells you that the radiator is full and everything is fine.

You may get a rush of air, and eventually water, out of the valve. This is also fine. You have bled some air out of the system and actually improved the efficiency somewhat. The radiator is now filled with water.

You may get air coming out of the bleed valve for a while and then nothing. In this case, you have relieved the little bit of air pressure in the radiator, but since you

FIGURE 10.11   Pressure Set Too Low

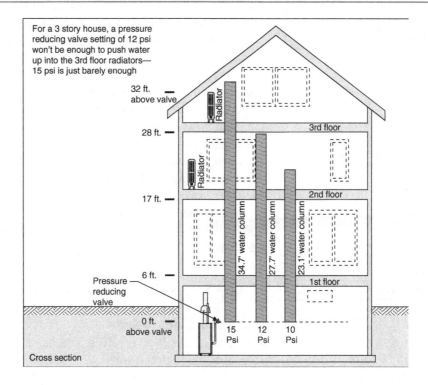

For a 3 story house, a pressure reducing valve setting of 12 psi won't be enough to push water up into the 3rd floor radiators— 15 psi is just barely enough

32 ft. above valve

28 ft.

17 ft.

6 ft.

Pressure reducing valve

0 ft. above valve

3rd floor

2nd floor

1st floor

34.7' water column   27.7' water column   23.1' water column

15 Psi   12 Psi   10 Psi

Cross section

---

got no water, it's possible the radiator isn't full of water. There is one other possibility. The bleed valve may be obstructed so that neither air nor water can get through the valve itself.

Again, we do not recommend operating radiator bleed valves because of the risk of leakage and the possibility of not getting the valve closed properly.

Missing

IMPLICATION

Pressure-reducing valves are not absolutely necessary. They are an operating convenience. You can fill a boiler manually by opening a valve that connects the plumbing system to the heating system.

STRATEGY

A pressure-reducing valve is a plus, but not a necessity. If you advise adding one, make it clear that it's an improvement rather than a repair.

Inoperative

The pressure-reducing valve can be inoperative two different ways.

1. The pressure-reducing valve may be obstructed or defective and no water may get through into the boiler.

2. The pressure-reducing valve may have failed and the water pressure in the boiler system may be too high.

IMPLICATIONS

If the pressure-reducing valve doesn't allow enough water through, the house won't get warm enough, especially on the upper floors. The boiler will eventually run short of water and probably shut down on high-temperature limit or low-water cutout.

If too much pressure is allowed through, the pressure-relief valve will operate constantly. If the pressure-relief valve isn't working or is missing, there is a risk of a pressure build-up and a steam explosion.

The best way to determine whether the pressure-reducing valve is operating properly is to look at the temperature and pressure gauge on the boiler. When the boiler is cold, the pressure should be 12 psi to 15 psi. If the pressure is much lower than this, there may not be enough water in the system. If the pressure range is above this, the pressure-reducing valve may have failed.

High pressure may also result in the pressure-relief valve operating. Watch for a dripping pressure-relief valve pipe.

There are other causes of the boiler pressure being too high and the pressure relief valve dripping. These include an expansion tank that is waterlogged or under-sized, for example.

The temperature gauge may also be defective.

Leaking

Water damage and possible shutdown of the heating system are the implications.

Look for evidence of leakage around the pressure-reducing valve.

Installed Backwards

Most pressure reducing valves have an arrow indicating the proper direction of water flow through the valve.

If the valve is installed backwards, the boiler will not get any makeup water. A more serious implication is in the case of the combination pressure-reducing valve and pressure-relief valve (Figure 10.12). If the assembly is installed backwards, the boiler pressure-relief valve will be upstream of (before) the pressure-reducing valve. This puts it too far away from the boiler, and this important safety device may be compromised.

F I G U R E 10.12   Pressure Reducing/Relief Valve Installed Backwards

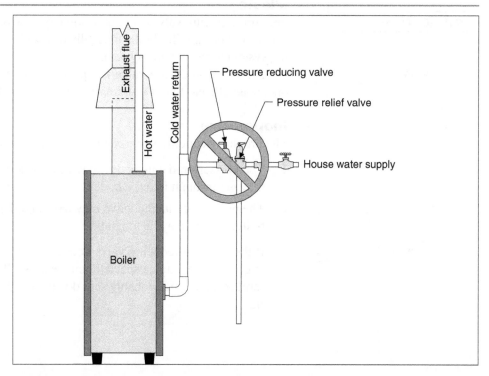

F I G U R E 10.13   Aquastat—Primary Control

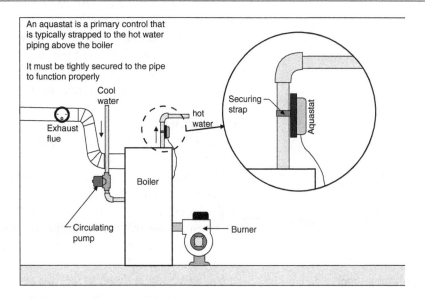

An aquastat is a primary control that is typically strapped to the hot water piping above the boiler

It must be tightly secured to the pipe to function properly

STRATEGY

There is an arrow on the body of the valve. The arrow should point to the boiler.

10.3.6   Primary Control

The **low-temperature limit, operating control aquastat,** or **primary control** as it is sometimes called, is designed to keep the water in the boiler hot so that it can respond quickly to a call for heat (Figure 10.13). Large cast-iron boilers, in particular, take some time to heat up if the water is allowed to cool to room temperature. Many systems are designed to keep the water in the boiler at anywhere from 120° to 200°F, so that the boiler is ready to respond. A typical setting is 140°F. This minimizes thermal lag in the system.

Primary controls can be **strap-on aquastats.** This is a brand name that has become generic for control devices that sense water temperature. These can also be **immersion-type aquastats** with temperature probes in the water itself.

Tankless Water Heaters

Some boilers keep their water hot because domestic hot water is provided by the boiler water as well. Even when the boiler has no demand for heat, the water in the boiler has to be hot so the domestic water can be heated.

Not Always Used

Not all systems have a primary control. Many boilers are allowed to cool to room temperature when there is no demand for heat. The smaller steel and copper tube boilers can heat up more quickly than the old large cast-iron boilers, and so there isn't the same thermal lag built into the system. On these boilers, an operating control is much less important.

Zone Systems

Hot water heating systems with multiple zones often use a primary control to keep the boiler water hot. Various thermostats can activate various zones by turning on a pump or opening a valve. The thermostats on these systems do not activate the burner. The primary control is often the only thing that makes the burner come on and off.

Operating Within a Window

The operating control maintains the boiler water temperature within a range of 10°F, for example. The control can be set to have the boiler come on at 180°F and turn off at 190°F, for example.

If you inspect in an area where hot water heating is common, you will see several control methods. We won't talk about them all, but will include the typical ones. You need to know how systems are normally run in your area.

Primary controls can be inoperative or set incorrectly.

Inoperative

IMPLICATION

If the primary control doesn't work, there will be no heat. This normally results in an emergency service call.

STRATEGY

When you are in a house where the boiler is at rest, you will typically turn up the thermostat to test the heating system. If the boiler water is at room temperature and the burner doesn't come on when the thermostat calls for heat, you may suspect a primary control that's malfunctioning. If the pump comes on when the thermostat is turned up but the boiler fails to fire, this reinforces the possibility of a primary control problem.

Don't Troubleshoot

But let's leave it there, before we get too far into troubleshooting. Have a service technician walk you through, if you want to go further.

Set Incorrectly

The set point on most controls can be adjusted easily. The set point can be either too high or too low. Set points are sometimes changed season to season, or are tied directly to the outdoor temperature.

IMPLICATIONS

There are different implications to different improper settings. If the primary control is set too high, the boiler water may be near the high temperature limit. Keeping water at over 200°F in the boiler is inefficient at best, and may overheat the boiler, shortening its life.

Setting the control too low may mean a long wait for heat when the thermostat calls.

Summer Setting

Some primary controls have at their lower end the setting described as **Summer.** Rather than a temperature setting, this setting allows the homeowner or service person to ensure that the boiler won't come on during the warm summer months.

STRATEGY

If the water temperature on the gauge is over 200°F when the boiler is at rest, you may suspect the primary control is set too high. You can usually look at the setting and determine this. In some cases, the setting indicated is not accurate. When the boiler temperature is over 200°F, you should probably recommend servicing, in any case.

Too High

Too Low

If the primary control is set too low, the burner may not come on, no matter what you do with the thermostat. If the operating control is set to the Summer position, the burner won't fire because it thinks the water is warm enough.

10.3.7   Pump Control

Description and Location

The **pump control** is a thermostatic control and can be an **aquastat.** It looks like the **high-temperature limit** and the **primary control.** It's mounted in the same location (on the hot distribution piping near the boiler) (Figure 10.14).

Function

The pump control is designed to turn the pump on and off. There are a number of ways that boilers may be set up.

FIGURE 10.14 Pump Control

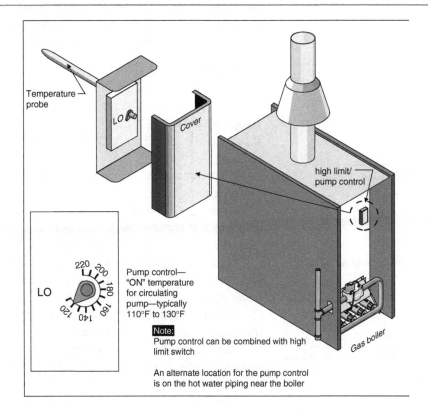

1. Pump runs continuously

Some pumps run continuously and there is no pump control. The pump is always on. The thermostat turns the burner on when there is a call for heat, and the pump continues to work, whether the burner is on or off.

2. Pump on when burner is on

The heating system may be set up so that the pump comes on every time the burner comes on. In this case, there will be no pump control either. When the thermostat calls for heat, the burner is energized and the pump is energized by either the thermostat or burner.

3. Pump control turns pump on

On some systems, the pump is designed to come on when the boiler water temperature gets above a set level (e.g., 110°F to 140°F). The pump control tells the pump to come on and off. When the burner shuts off, the pump will continue to run until the boiler water temperature drops below the set point.

In this arrangement, the house thermostat controls the burner. When there is a call for heat, the burner comes on. The thinking here is that there's no point circulating the water through the boiler and distribution system until the water is warm enough to make that worthwhile. This is similar to the furnace fan arrangement. It may help minimize condensation on start-up.

When you test a hot water heating system, you need to understand all the possible arrangements for the circulator. As you can see, the pump may come on at different times, depending how the system is set up. Don't be too quick to criticize.

There are two pump control problems to look for:

1. Inoperative
2. Set incorrectly

Inoperative

If the pump control is inoperative, the pump will never come on, or will be on all the time.

If the pump does not come on, the heating system will not work comfortably and efficiently.

Some boilers **need** to have the pump working to supply cool water to the heat exchanger. If the heat exchanger isn't constantly fed with cool water, it can overheat. An inoperative pump can ruin a boiler in this case.

Most boilers that rely on the pump have the burner interlocked so that it can only come on once the pump is on. These systems don't use a pump control, so it shouldn't be an issue.

If the pump runs continuously, the heating system will work, although the electrical consumption will be higher.

The first step is to determine whether there is a pump control. It is usually mounted on the hot supply distribution piping from the boiler, just above the boiler itself. It's often very close to the high-temperature limit switch. Don't confuse the two. The high-temperature limit is normally set at 210°F. The pump control is typically set at 110°F to 140°F.

There may also be a primary control designed to keep the water temperature in the boiler at a set level. This is typically between 160°F and 200°F although it can be as low as 110°F or 120°F. It's not unusual to see three controls on the piping just above the boiler. The high temperature limit is the **safety control.** The pump control and primary control for the burner are **normal operating controls.**

About the only way to tell whether the pump control is working is to cycle the boiler through and observe whether the pump comes on when the boiler water temperature reaches the set point of the pump control. You should be able to read the setting on the pump control and watch the boiler water temperature rise at the boiler gauge. If the pump does not come on at the set temperature, you may suspect that either the control or the pump is inoperative. Recommend that this be checked by a service person.

If there is a primary control, but the pump is always on, the control should be serviced.

Set Incorrectly

The pump control can be set too high or too low.

The implications of setting the pump control too low are simply that the pump will run more often than it otherwise would. Since we've already said that some pumps run continuously through the heating season, this isn't a serious problem.

If the setting is too high, the pump won't come on until the boiler water is very hot. It may not come on at all in some cases. This is an efficiency problem and may lead to overheating of the heat exchanger.

Again, when you are operating the boiler, watch the pump. Check the setting of the pump control and make sure the pump comes on at an appropriate boiler water temperature. The pump should always be on by the time the boiler water temperature reaches 150°F. It usually comes on around 110°F, but can be set as high as 140°F.

10.3.8   Zone Control

Large Homes

Large houses with hot water heating often have several zones. Each zone has its own thermostat, which allows the occupants to keep various areas of the house at different temperatures. The zones may be heated by turning pumps on, or by activating electric zone control valves. There are advantages to both approaches.

A full discussion of zoned hot water systems is beyond the scope of this book, but we'll discuss the basics here.

Zone Control with Pumps

Pumps can be used to supply heat to various zones (Figure 10.15). Let's look at a simple two-zone system. There will be a thermostat for each zone. When one thermostat calls for heat, the circulating pump for that zone moves hot water through the distribution piping and radiators for that part of the home. The other thermostat is not calling for heat, and its pump will not be moving water.

Thermostat Starts Pump and Maybe Burner

In some cases, when either one of the thermostats calls for heat, the burner also comes on. This means that the thermostat activates the circulator and the burner. In other cases, the boiler water is kept hot by a primary control. In this arrangement, when the thermostat calls for heat, the appropriate pump comes on and moves the hot water through that zone.

If both thermostats call for heat, both pumps will work, and hot water will be distributed to all parts of the house.

Zone Control with Valves

Let's look at a two-zone system with valves to control the heat (Figure 10.16). If one thermostat calls for heat, the valve to that zone will be opened and the pump will be activated. The **zone valve** may turn the pump on after it opens. We don't want

FIGURE 10.15   Zone Control with Pumps

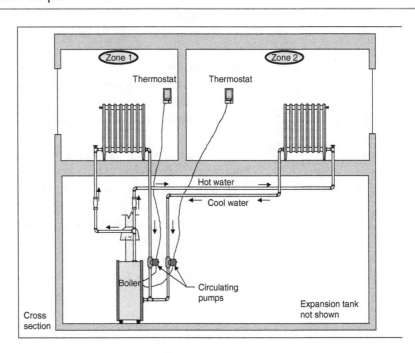

FIGURE 10.16   Zone Control with Valves

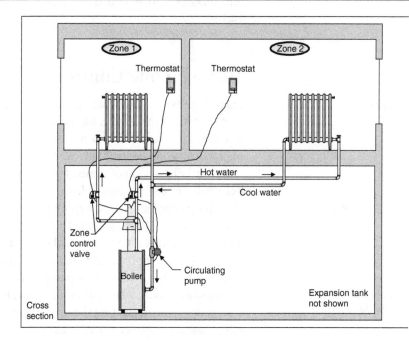

the pump working against closed valves since this will damage the pump. Typically, there is just one pump, although there can be two. The thermostat is usually interlocked with both the valve and the pump.

When both thermostats call for heat, both zone valves are opened and the circulator delivers hot water to all of the piping and radiators in the home.

Again, the boiler may be kept hot with a primary control, or either thermostat could activate the burner.

Multi-zone systems are complex, and it often takes some time to figure out how the system is controlled. In a large home, it can take quite a while just to find all the thermostats.

Zone controls may be inoperative or leaking.

Inoperative

If the zone control system isn't working properly, the pump or valve for that system will not deliver water to that zone, even when the thermostat calls for it.

IMPLICATIONS

The implication of an inoperative zone control is no heat to that zone of the house.

STRATEGY

The best strategy is to turn the thermostats up for all the zones and make sure hot water is delivered to the radiators or convectors in the entire house.

Overheat or No Heat

If the zone control system has failed and the zone valve is stuck open, there is probably no great harm done, although that part of the house may be too warm. However, if a zone control valve is stuck closed, for example, or cannot be opened, the problem is no heat.

It makes sense to have a helper turn the thermostat up and down. This way, you can see and/or hear the valve operate.

Leaking

The implications are water damage and, possibly, no heat.

IMPLICATIONS

STRATEGY

Look at all components of the boiler for leakage. This includes pumps and zone valves.

10.3.9   Isolating Valves

Function

Valves are provided on boilers so that various components can be removed for repair or replacement without draining the whole system.

Location

Valves are commonly found—

- on the supply pipe and return pipe near the boiler
- on either side of the pump (circulator)
- on either side of a low water cut out
- on the pipe connecting the house supplying plumbing to the boiler
- on the supply and return lines of a tankless coil (if used)

More Are Better

Generally speaking, the more valves there are, the better. One valve, strategically placed, can do more than one job. The absence of valves is not a defect, although it is an inconvenience and may result in higher service costs. Don't try to turn any of these valves. Because they aren't used regularly, the packing may be dry and the valve is likely to leak.

Isolating valves may exhibit any of these problems:

1. Leak
2. Inoperative
3. Rust or damage

We've talked about leaks. You know what to look for. You usually won't know if the valve is inoperative, since we recommend you not try them.

Rust or Damage

STRATEGY

Advise your client to ask the service person to operate all valves during regular servicings. Recommend that any obviously damaged valves be repaired or replaced.

Inspector in the House: The Overworked Boiler

It was a very large old home we were inspecting in the fall. The mild weather meant the heating system was not on when we arrived. The client was concerned about adequacy of heat to all parts of the rambling old structure.

We knew that it takes quite a while for cast iron radiators to warm up. We decided to turn the boiler thermostat all the way up at the beginning of the inspection and check the radiators at the end of the process, some four hours after we started. We noticed the house getting quite warm as we did our work, but thought that was a good sign. As we went room to room at the end of the inspection, we were happy to find that all the radiators were indeed hot, except one that needed to be bled.

We were not so happy to get a call of distress from the owner who had just gone to the basement and found water running out of the boiler room door across the carpet of the recreation room. In our enthusiasm, we had failed to consider that running the boiler continuously for so long might cause it to overheat. We raised the water temperature to roughly 200° F, and the water pressure increased from the 15 psi we noted before starting the boiler to 30 psi, at which point the pressure relief valve started to discharge.

The pressure relief valve was doing its job properly, and there might have been no problem except that the basement floor drain was in the middle of the recreation room floor under the carpet. If the high temperature limit switch had been set a little lower, the boiler might have shut off, but it didn't. It was hard to tell the seller he should have added a new floor drain in the boiler room when adding the recreation room, so we paid the cost of cleaning and repairs to the basement.

10.4   DISTRIBUTION SYSTEMS

Move the Heat

The function of the hot water distribution system is the same as the function of the warm air distribution system with furnaces. We are trying to get the heat from the boiler to the rooms we want to heat.

There are four basic components to the distribution system—

1. pump (circulator)
2. pipes
3. radiators, convectors or baseboards
4. expansion tank

Materials

We'll look at each of these components more closely later in this section.

Pumps are traditionally brass, bronze and steel. Piping is traditionally black steel with cast iron fittings. It may also be copper. In modern systems, plastics such as polybutylene and cross-linked polyethylene are used.

Radiators are traditionally cast iron. Convectors can be cast iron, steel or copper. Baseboards may be cast iron, steel, copper, aluminum or a combination of these.

Expansion tanks are typically galvanized steel.

10.4.1   Open and Closed Hot Water Systems

Most modern systems are closed. Some older open systems are still in service. The two systems work very similarly, but you should be able to identify a couple of things.

High Expansion Tank with Overflow

The **open** system is typically a loop using pipes and radiators (Figure 10.17). The system has an **expansion tank** located at the top of the home above the highest radiator. An **overflow pipe,** leading out from this expansion tank, is open to the atmosphere. The pipe may extend out through the roof or wall of the building, discharging outside. Alternatively, it may discharge inside the building into a drainage system.

Function

The expansion tank on an open system allows the water to expand as it heats up. The purpose of putting the expansion tank at the top of the system is to allow the system to be filled, to be able to check the water level, and to create a significant pressure (head) at the boiler, allowing the water to heat up more without getting close to boiling.

FIGURE 10.17   Open Hydronic System

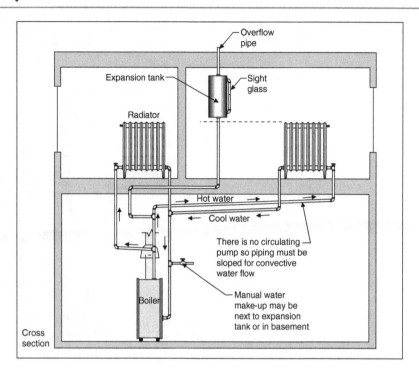

No Pump or Relief Valve	Open systems do not have a pump and they do not have a pressure relief valve in the system. The opening to atmosphere is adequate pressure relief.
	Open systems don't have a pump control or a primary control. Open systems have manual water makeup. There is no pressure-reducing valve and usually no back-flow preventer.
Providing Water Makeup	Open systems have a manual valve that can be used to add water to the system. The expansion tanks typically have **sight glasses** that show how much water is in the tanks. When the water falls below the level of the sight glass, water can be added manually. The valves are sometimes located beside the expansion tank at the top of the home. In other systems, the water make-up valve is located close to
Overfilling	the boiler. Overfilling the system is not a huge problem, since excess water can discharge through the overflow pipe to the outdoors or a safe drain location.
Pump and Pressure Relief	The modern **closed** hot water system has the expansion tank with no sight glass just above the boiler usually at ceiling level (Figure 10.18). It has eliminated the open discharge to atmosphere and has added a **pump.** A pressure-relief valve (set at 30 psi) is needed, since the system now could over-pressurize itself if the burner failed to shut off.
Better Heating	The closed system improves operation and allows for the forced circulating system. The house is more evenly heated. Zone control is possible (and effective) on closed systems.
Don't Need a Pump	A few closed systems do not have a pump. This is not a mistake, but the pumps do add comfort and some efficiency.
Pressure-Reducing Valve	Modern closed systems typically have an automatic water makeup system using a pressure-reducing valve. It automatically adds water to the system as it is needed.
Backflow Preventer	Closed systems often (but not always) have backflow preventers.

FIGURE 10.18 Closed Hydronic System

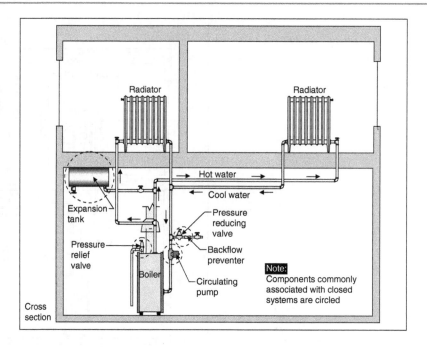

If you see an expansion tank just above the boiler, a pressure-relief valve, a pressure-reducing valve, and a circulating pump, you know for sure you have a closed system. This is what you'll see most of the time.

10.4.2 Balancing

Hot water heating systems can be balanced in a number of ways. In practice, they are usually left alone once they are set up (Figure 10.19).

Pipe Sizing

The original balancing is done in the layout and sizing of the supply and return pipes. The pipe diameters may get smaller as we go further down the system. This is similar to the way supply ducts get smaller as we move further from the furnace.

At the Header

There are often manual valves at main supply headers near the boiler, where the main feeds split to go to various parts of the house.

Radiator Valves

Individual balancing can be done at each radiator. Most radiators have manually operated valves. Some have thermostatically operated valves that are designed to modulate the flow of water through the radiator based on a desired temperature chosen by the occupant. These valves have a dial or gauge allowing you to choose the temperature you want.

Control Flow through Radiators

These valves, whether manual or thermostatic, control the water flow through the radiator. Whenever the pump is working, water will flow through each radiator. Adjusting these valves adjusts the amount of water that flows. If the valve is completely shut off, there will still be water in the radiator and it will still be directly connected to the return side. However, no water will flow through the radiator, and the water in the radiator itself will remain cold, since it isn't circulated past the boiler on a regular basis.

F I G U R E 10.19   Balancing Methods

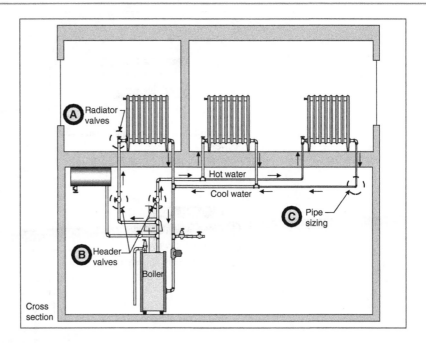

Not on a Series System!

The balancing valves we've been talking about cannot be used on a series loop. If we closed off a valve going into a radiator on a series loop, no water would flow. None of the radiators would get any heat if one radiator valve was closed. This is one clue to identifying a series loop system. There will be no valves on the radiators.

10.4.3   Expansion Tanks

The function of the **expansion tank** is somewhat incidental to the whole distribution system. However, we're going to be referring to them a number of times, so we may as well deal with them now.

Shock Absorber

The expansion tank is an **air cushion** or **shock absorber.** The tank is partially filled with water from the boiler system. The top part of the tank is filled with trapped air.

Water Level Changes in the Tank

If the tank is one-third filled with water when the boiler is cold, the water level will rise when the boiler fires. Air is quite compressible, and can be readily squeezed without increasing pressure dramatically. It acts like an easily compressed spring. When the boiler is operating at steady state, the expansion tank may be two-thirds filled with water.

Material

Expansion tanks are typically galvanized steel. The older tanks were very often unpainted. Modern tanks are usually prepainted at the factory.

Closed System Tanks

On closed systems, there are two types of expansion tanks:

1. Conventional
2. Diaphragm or bladder tank

Tank Differences

The **conventional tank** is just a metal cylinder (Figure 10.20). The **diaphragm tank** has a loose rubber bladder separating the tank into two compartments. One is the air side, and the other is the water side, which is connected to the boiler through a pipe.

F I G U R E   10.20   Conventional Expansion Tank

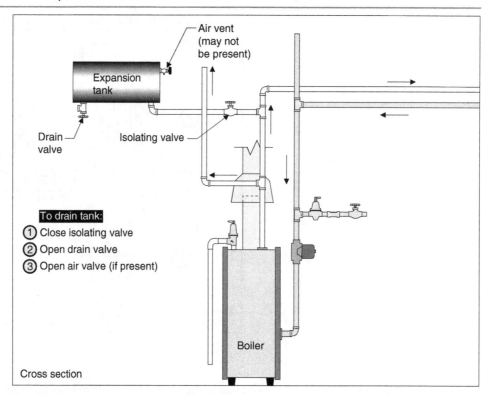

Cross section

Conventional Tank

On closed systems, it's common to find the expansion tank strapped between ceiling joists above the boiler. If the ceiling is plastered, the tank may be barely visible. These tanks are typically cylinders, 8 to 10 inches in diameter and 18 inches to 3 feet long installed horizontally.

Pipe Connections

They typically have one pipe connected to the heating system, usually tapped into the hot water distribution supply pipe coming off the boiler. The expansion tank has a drain valve and may have an air inlet valve that can be opened to allow air into the tank as the water is drained out.

Isolating Valve

The piping between the heating system and the expansion tank usually has an isolating valve that can be manually closed to allow the tank to be drained.

Diaphragm Tanks

Conventional tanks have to be mounted above the boiler. Diaphragm tanks can be anywhere, including above or below the top of the boiler. Tanks can be on the supply or return side of the boiler. Boilers with diaphragm tanks usually have an air vent.

Air Dissolved over Time

The air eventually is lost from the conventional expansion tank. It sometimes leaks out slowly through the air valve, but the majority is dissolved into the water over time.

Waterlogged Tank

When the tank is filled with water, it is said to be **waterlogged.** The system loses its shock absorber. When the boiler comes on, the pressure in the system will rise quickly. If all goes well, the relief valve operates and water leaks out through the discharge pipe from the relief valve. If the relief valve is missing, inoperative or its discharge is obstructed, a dangerous high pressure situation can develop.

A Modern Improvement

Many modern expansion tanks have a rubber (neoprene) diaphragm that separates the air and the water, as discussed. The system works exactly the same, but the flexible rubber diaphragm keeps the air from being dissolved into the water. These systems rarely become waterlogged and are therefore more convenient.

Where Is the Best Spot for the Expansion Tank?

There is some controversy about where the expansion tank is best located. However, for the purposes of a home inspection, as long as it is present and connected to the heating system, we don't have to worry. In most cases, you'll see it on the hot-water supply distribution pipe coming off the top of the boiler. (Conventional tanks on closed systems have to be above the top of the boiler.) If the tank is connected to the return side of the boiler, the system will still work just fine, maybe better.

Expansion tanks are subject to any of the following problems:

1. Leaks
2. Waterlogged
3. Rust
4. Too small
5. Poor discharge location for open tank
6. Poor location for tank

Leaks

IMPLICATIONS

The implications of leakage are water damage and possible overheating of the boiler, if other controls do not work properly.

STRATEGY

Check for leaks at the expansion tank, drain valve, isolating valve, and air inlet.

Waterlogged

IMPLICATIONS

Pressure in the system will rise quickly when the boiler operates. The relief valve should operate. If it does not, the system may become over-pressurized, creating an unsafe condition.

STRATEGY

When the boiler operates, watch the pressure gauge on the boiler. It should move from about 12 to 15 psi when the boiler is cool, up to a maximum of 25 psi. It may not even get above 15 psi. If the gauge gets close to 30 psi and/or the relief valve operates, the expansion tank may be waterlogged. Recommend that this be checked by a service person.

Rust

IMPLICATIONS

A rusted tank is prone to leakage.

STRATEGY

Look at the tank and its fittings for evidence of rust.

Too Small

IMPLICATIONS

The implications of an undersized tank are pressure build-up in the system and discharge of the relief valve.

STRATEGY

We've talked about looking for pressure build-up and discharge of the relief valve. It is usually the result of a waterlogged tank. On new installations, it can be the result of an undersized expansion tank. This is more likely to occur on large homes where the volume of water in the system is considerable.

Poor Discharge Location for Open Tank

IMPLICATION

Water damage to the house is the implication.

STRATEGY

Follow the overflow pipe from the expansion tank on the highest floor, to its end. Where does the water go? It should go outside or into a drain. We find many that end in the attic.

F I G U R E   10.21   Circulating Pump

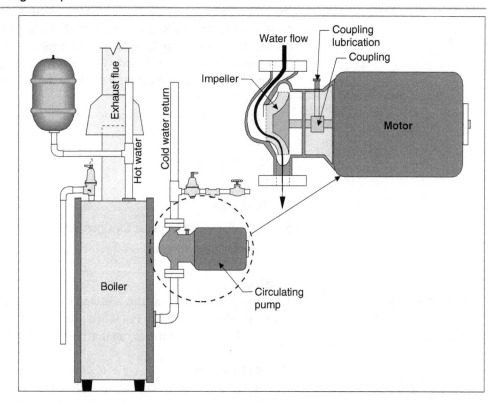

Where you find a poor discharge spot, look for water damage, including rot. Sometimes that intermittent "roof leak" turns out to be an overflow pipe problem!

Poor Location for Tank

The proper location for an expansion tank depends on the system.

The implications of improper location are—

IMPLICATIONS

1. inadequate heat for the upper radiators on open tanks

2. air getting into the boiler from the expansion tank on a closed system

STRATEGY

Watch for these location problems. Remember that diaphragm tanks can be beside the boiler, but conventional tanks can't.

10.4.4   Pumps or Circulators

Function

The **pump** or **circulator** on a hot water heating system has the same function as the fan on a forced air heating system (Figure 10.21). We are pushing the heat transfer medium (water) from the boiler out to the rooms we want to heat.

Works on Return as Well as Supply

Just like the fan on a forced air system, the pump pushes the heated water out to the system and pulls the cool water back. The pump does not create large pressures and is relatively small. It works more like a paddle wheel moving the water slowly through the system, than a fire pump trying to build up pressure.

Location

The pump is typically located on the return piping adjacent to the boiler. Some feel that the pumps work better if they pump away from the boiler. This means putting the pump on the supply piping. Either location is acceptable.

Not Too High or Low

Pumps are usually beside the boiler. They shouldn't be at a low point in the piping because sediment collects here. They shouldn't be at a high point because air bubbles collect here. Air in a pump can damage it.

Electric Motor Driven

The pump is driven by an electric motor and there is often a mechanical coupling between the motor and the pump. The pump is an **impeller-type** and does not shut off the flow of water when the pump is idle. Rather, some flow of water can be expected through the system by convection.

Pump Orientation

The motor should be beside the pump rather than above or below it. The shaft of the motor and pump are designed to be horizontal. If the shaft is vertical, the bearings will fail quickly.

Pumps Need Lubrication

Conventional pumps require lubrication. The electric motor typically has two lubrication ports and the coupler has one. These pumps have been around since the 1930s. Their performance is excellent as long as they are lubricated. If neglected, of course, they will seize.

Another Type of Pump

A more modern and less expensive pump is a **permanently lubricated** pump and motor. The sealed bearings (actually bushings) in the coupler and motor do not require regular maintenance. However, some maintain that their life is shorter than the older type.

A Third Type of Pump

Some pumps are **water lubricated.** The pump and motor are integral in one housing. The water in the heating system lubricates the assembly. The motor is sealed so that it can be immersed in the water. These are common on new systems because they are maintenance-free and are inexpensive. Many modern package boilers are sold with an integral pump, sized correctly for the boiler.

Operating Controls

The pump may be activated by—

1. the thermostat
2. electric power being on to the boiler. (In this case, the pump runs continuously through the heating season.)
3. pump control (aquastat) that senses the water temperature leaving the boiler

Copper Boilers Need Pump On

Copper tube boilers have to have the pump operating before the burner can come on safely. These very thin heat exchangers need a constant supply of cold water to keep them from overheating.

Boiler Condensation a Possibility

Many people feel that the best type of pump control is having the pump come on only when the boiler is up to temperature. (This only applies if the heat exchanger can take the heat without water moving through it.) They feel this will minimize condensation in the boiler.

Another Advantage

When the boiler shuts off, some pumps shut off immediately. This leaves heat in the heat exchanger that finds its way up the chimney. It's more energy-efficient to keep the pump running until the heat exchanger has cooled. We may as well capture as much of the heat as we can.

Continuous Pumping

If the pump runs continuously throughout the heating season, the condensation problem exists, but the efficiency problem on shutdown does not.

Pumps Used for Zone Control

Pumps are sometimes used to control various zones in heating systems. Individual thermostats for various parts of the house can activate their own pumps to move water through that part of the house. Where zone valves are used, one of several zone valves can be opened and the main pump can be activated at the same time, to heat a single zone.

Flow Control Valves

A pump does not provide a positive shutoff to water movement when the pump is at rest. In a zoned system, this can lead to overheating of a zone that's not calling for heat. A flow control valve is often put into the system to prevent water flowing through a zone when the pump is off. When the pump is activated, there is enough force to open the flow control valve. When the pump shuts off, the flow control valve closes, and there will be no gravity or convective flow through that zone.

Reverse Flow Protection

The flow control valve also prevents reverse flow through an idle branch, which is possible on some systems, when another zone is working.

Boiler Kept Hot

The flow control valve is also often used whenever the boiler is kept hot on standby, even if there is only one zone. Without it, the system would operate as a gravity (convective) system when there is no call for heat. The house may overheat.

Look for pumps that are leaky, inoperative, noisy or hot.

Leaks

IMPLICATIONS

The implications are water damage, poor heat circulation and possible overheating of the boiler. There may be an electrical problem as well, if the leak is onto electric controls for the pump or the motor itself.

STRATEGY

Look for evidence of leakage at the pump. Very often there is lubricating oil on and below the pump. Don't mistake this for water leakage. Make sure you look at the pump when it is operating.

Inoperative

When the boiler is running and up to temperature, the pump should be working, unless there is more than one pump. In a zoned system with multiple pumps, only the pump for the zone needing heat will run.

IMPLICATIONS

An inoperative pump will make the house less comfortable, increase the heating costs and may overheat the heat exchanger. Some heat exchangers are very susceptible to damage if the burner fires when the pump is not working. If the pump is interlocked with the burner (copper tube boiler) there will be no heat if the pump doesn't work.

STRATEGY

Make sure the pump operates when the heating system is running. Don't try to troubleshoot pumps that don't come on.

Noisy or Hot

IMPLICATIONS

The implications of a noisy or overheated pump are, at the very least, repairs and possibly replacement of the pump or coupler.

STRATEGY

Squeals, whining, grinding noises and chatter are indications that the pump and/or motor is in distress.

Practice touching pumps and motor casings (be careful!) to get a sense of the normal operating temperature. You should not be burned on contact. The water-lubricated pumps will run cooler. They should be at the return water temperature. The air cooled, conventional electric motor attached to the pump through a coupler should run at the same temperature as any electric motor (hot to the touch).

10.4.5   Pipes

Function

The distribution piping system carries the water from the boiler to the radiator, convector or baseboard. In a radiant system, the piping is also the final distribution mechanism.

Material

The piping on older systems is black steel. It often lasts 70 to 90 years. The fittings may be steel or cast iron. Copper piping is also used. Some modern systems use plastic piping, including polybutylene and cross-linked polyethylene.

Location

Reliable

The piping is run throughout the house and is mostly concealed. Even where it might be exposed in basements or crawl spaces, it is often insulated to keep the heat inside the piping until it gets to the radiators.

For the most part, the piping is not a troublesome part of the hot water heating system.

Look for the following pipe problems:

1. Rust
2. Leaks
3. Crimped
4. Too small
5. Poor support
6. No insulation

Rust

Most piping will rust eventually. However, the black steel piping can last a very long time and copper piping can last almost indefinitely.

Dissimilar Metals

When a steel piping system is extended with copper piping, the possibility of a galvanic reaction is established. The dissimilar metals tend to create an accelerated rusting process and the steel is often sacrificed.

Piping in the Soil

Piping in contact with damp soil can lead to fast rusting. This is true of steel and copper piping. Certain soil types are quite corrosive.

IMPLICATIONS

The implications of rusted pipes are leaking and clogging. Both can lead to inefficiencies, water damage and a no-heat condition.

STRATEGY

Look for evidence of rusting, especially where dissimilar metals join and where pipes are in contact with soil. Also look at connections. Wherever threads have to be cut into pipes, the pipe wall is thinner. Rust may show up first here.

In some cases, rusting can scab over and stop a leak temporarily. If you see evidence of rusting, but no water, there may be an intermittent leak that is going to get worse.

Leaks

IMPLICATIONS

Water damage, a loss of efficiency and a no-heat condition are all possible implications of leaks.

STRATEGY

Look at as much of the visible piping as possible, focusing on connections. One of the most common leakage spots on hot water heating systems is where the piping connects to the radiator. The radiator valves are frequently sources of leaks.

Crimped

This is more of an issue with copper and plastic piping than steel.

IMPLICATIONS

The implications of crimping are reduced flow, reduced comfort and higher heating costs.

STRATEGY

Look for crimping along any exposed pipe lengths.

Too Small

IMPLICATION

The implication of undersized piping is inadequate heating (Figure 10.22).

STRATEGY

Where you see systems extended with pipes that are much smaller than the rest of the distribution system, raise the possibility of a poor comfort condition. You probably won't be able to be conclusive, but you can suggest that people either try it and see for themselves, or have a service person look at the condition.

F I G U R E 10.22   Extending Hot Water Systems

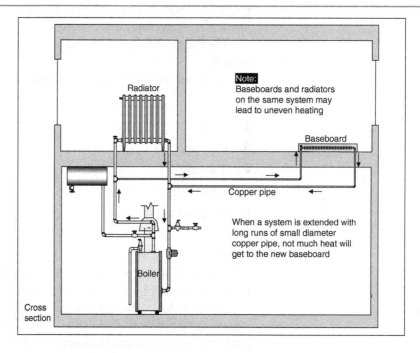

Poor Support

Steel and copper heating pipes are typically supported every 12 feet or less horizontally. Heavy metal straps or hangers are used. Copper or plastic (not steel) hangers should be used on copper pipes.

IMPLICATION

Poor support can result in leaks.

STRATEGY

Look for supports and for sagging pipes.

No Insulation

IMPLICATIONS

There may be no implications. Many pipes are not insulated, but everything works well. However, a lack of insulation can mean overheating, particularly in rooms close to the boiler, or too much heat loss before the water gets to the radiators, which makes rooms cool.

STRATEGY

Look for long runs of uninsulated pipes. In the heating season, you'll be able to identify the hot and cold parts of the house. In the summer, you'll be guessing.

Watch for pipes running through unheated spots, crawlspaces, garages, etc. These pipes should be insulated.

May Contain Asbestos

Some insulation on boilers and pipes contains asbestos. This is an environmental issue in some areas. It's beyond our scope. You can't tell if the insulation contains asbestos by looking.

Do Not Disturb

Our advice is, don't disturb the insulation. We tell our clients that we don't deal with environmental issues such as asbestos, lead, radon, UFFI (urea formaldehyde foam insulation), etc. There are environmental specialists who can help with these issues. Many inspectors do. If you choose to address these issues, we suggest you get some good knowledge first.

10.4.6   Radiators, Convectors, and Baseboards

Function

Radiators, convectors and baseboards have the same function as the registers on supply ducts in forced air systems. This part of the distribution system releases the heat into the room.

Radiators

Radiators are usually cast iron. They can stand on feet, hang on walls or hang from ceilings. Some old radiators were quite decorative; more modern radiators are fairly plain. Radiators are designed to be free-standing, although many people put wooden enclosures around them to make them look better. This does reduce their efficiency to some extent, although it doesn't make them useless.

Convectors

Depending on what part of North America you're from, **convectors** can mean slightly different things. To many, convectors are typically cast iron enclosed in a sheet metal cabinet with openings at the bottom and near the top. They do not radiate heat as directly as radiators, because the hot surface of the cast iron is enclosed by the sheet metal. They do a majority of their heating by convection, drawing cool air at the bottom and expelling the heated air from the top.

Baseboards

Some people think of **convectors** as the low-profile systems that look like baseboard heaters (Figure 10.23). Other people refer to this very low profile system as **baseboard** heating. Baseboards are low profile, often projecting only 3 inches out from a wall surface. They are typically 10 inches tall or less and are encased in a metal cabinet. Again, they have openings at the bottom to introduce cool air, and openings at the top to allow warm air into the room.

The Guts of a Baseboard

Baseboards can be cast iron, steel, copper, aluminum or a combination of these. Copper tubes with aluminum fins are common convector materials. Steel tubes with steel fins are also common (Figure 10.24).

Heats up Slowly, Cools Down Slowly

Cast-iron radiators take a long time to heat up, but once they get hot, they stay hot. Copper-tube baseboards can heat up much more quickly, but also cool down much more quickly when the boiler shuts off.

F I G U R E   10.23   Convector

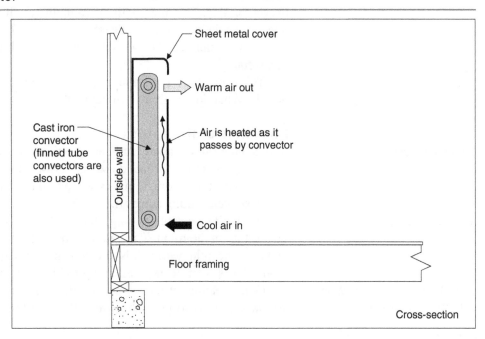

F I G U R E   10.24   Finned Tube Baseboard

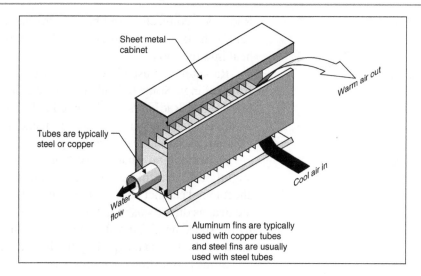

Sheet metal cabinet

Warm air out

Tubes are typically steel or copper

Cool air in

Water flow

Aluminum fins are typically used with copper tubes and steel fins are usually used with steel tubes

Mixing Systems Yields Uncomfortable Heating

Many homes are uncomfortable because they have a combination of radiators and baseboards. If the thermostat is located in a part of the house where there are radiators, the thermostat will respond to the heat given off by the radiators. When the thermostat calls for heat, it will take a while for the thermostat to see the heat from the radiators. However, once the room gets warm, it will tend to stay warm and the thermostat will stay satisfied for a long time. This leads to longer on cycles and longer off-cycles for the boiler.

Overheat

If the same house has baseboards in another part, remote from the thermostat, when the thermostat calls for heat, the baseboards respond quickly and deliver heat to the room fast. This means the room gets comfortable right away. However, since the thermostat is waiting for the cast-iron radiators to warm up, the boiler keeps running. The room with baseboards may actually overheat.

Underheat

When the cast-iron radiators finally get hot and the thermostat is satisfied, the boiler shuts off. The room with the baseboards cools down very quickly and becomes uncomfortable. The room with the radiator is still warm and cozy. The thermostat doesn't see the need for more heat.

As you can see, houses with these combinations can be difficult to heat comfortably.

Think about the same house, but put the thermostat in the room with the baseboards. What do you think will happen?

Location of Radiators

Under Windows

In much the same way as our heating philosophy worked with forced air, it's best to put the radiators on outside walls below windows. Since this tends to be the coolest part of the room, it makes sense to put most of the heat here. That gives us the most even heating across the room.

Convective Loop

We don't have a return air system with hot water, but we do have a convective loop set up in the room. The heavy, cool air is drawn across the floor towards the radiator. The light, warm air is directed up across the cool windows and out into the room. This system works well and provides even heat.

Why Are Radiators Sometimes on Ceilings or High on

Older heating systems were usually convection (gravity) systems. They did not have pumps to push the water through the system. Where the boiler was

the Walls?

located in a basement, people often finished portions of the basement. They wanted to heat these rooms. Since the heat moved only by convection, putting a radiator in the floor in a basement room adjacent to the boiler room was not very effective. This radiator would stay filled with cold water, which was heavy. There would be no incentive for convective flow.

Heat from Boiler Moves Up

People had to put the radiators high up in these rooms so that the water in the radiators would be above the boiler. This allowed for convective flow, with the cold water falling back down toward the boiler, and the lighter, hot water moving to the radiator.

Putting the heat into a room near the ceiling level was a compromise on ideal design, but at least it got some heat into the room.

Auxiliary Heat

One of the downsides of hot water heating is that it's very expensive to upgrade the system. Adding a radiator typically costs several hundred dollars. Where a cool area is identified in a home with hot water heating, it's often more practical to add an electric baseboard heater.

Balancing Valves

Don't Touch!

In most two-pipe systems, most of the radiators have balancing valves. Small radiators in the vestibules and washrooms, for example, may not have balancing valves. The important thing for home inspectors to know about balancing valves is that they should **never** touch them (Figure 10.25)!

They'll Leak!

These valves are not operated on a regular basis. As soon as you turn them, they usually leak. Unless you're prepared to do some emergency repair work, we recommend that you leave them alone.

Look but Don't Touch

We do recommend that you have a close look at the valves and at the piping and flooring below. It's common to find considerable damage here. The leaks at these balancing valves can be particularly troublesome because they're often minor, and can go unnoticed for some time. They can do a fair bit of damage to the woodwork and other components below while this is going on.

F I G U R E   10.25   Radiator Valve Leaks

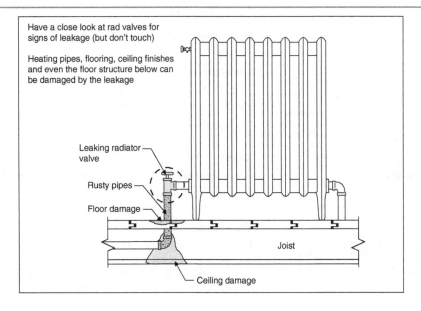

Have a close look at rad valves for signs of leakage (but don't touch)

Heating pipes, flooring, ceiling finishes and even the floor structure below can be damaged by the leakage

Leaking radiator valve

Rusty pipes

Floor damage

Joist

Ceiling damage

Bleed Valves

Air bleed valves should be located near the top of every radiator to let trapped air out, so the water can circulate properly.

Manual-Hand Operated

These valves are usually manual. The valve stem doesn't have to be removed, just loosened. As soon as air starts to rush out, the valve is usually left open until water comes out. As soon as water is delivered, the valve is closed.

Don't Open

Again, we urge you not to operate these valves, although it's pretty tempting sometimes.

Zoned Systems

We talked earlier about how hot water heating systems can be zoned. These systems have multiple thermostats and can use multiple circulating pumps or zone valves to deliver heat to the different parts of the house at different times.

Several Small Houses

The radiators, convectors and baseboards perform the same way on a zoned system, and you can simply think of these as several small house systems.

Mixing Radiators and Baseboards

A zoned system is one application where you might get away with radiators on one thermostat and convectors or baseboards on a different thermostat. In fact, this can be a solution to a problem house with radiators in an old part and baseboards in a new part. Setting up a zoned system can allow both parts of the house to be kept comfortable.

Conditions

Radiators, convectors, and baseboards should be checked for these problems:

1. Leaks
2. Rust
3. Too small
4. Missing
5. Poor location
6. Mixed types
7. Balancing valve problems
8. Bleed valve problems
9. Damaged baseboard fins
10. Obstructed air flow

Leaks

IMPLICATIONS

The implications of a leak are water damage to the home and possibly, a no-heat condition if considerable water is lost.

STRATEGY

Check closely at the balancing valves and bleed valves for evidence of leakage.

Rust

STRATEGY

Look for rust at radiators, convectors, and baseboards. Again, it's most common around the balancing valve.

Too Small

IMPLICATIONS

The room will be uncomfortable.

STRATEGY

You aren't going to do a design analysis of the adequacy of the radiators for each room. What you can use is a little bit of common sense. Pay some attention to the average size and number of the radiators and the average room size as you go through the house. If you see one that is obviously out of step, you should at least raise the question about the comfort of this room.

As we mentioned earlier, it may be more cost effective to add electric baseboard heat than extend a hot water heating system. It's expensive to add more radiators, convectors or baseboards.

Missing

This is an easy one to overlook.

IMPLICATION

The implication is inadequate heat.

STRATEGY

Look for a heating source in each room. In some cases, you can find capped pipes, filled pipe holes in floors or stained flooring where the radiator used to be. Point out to your client the absence of the heat source, and prepare them for the possibility that the heating will be inadequate.

Poor Location

IMPLICATIONS

If the radiators are not located on exterior walls below windows, the room may be uncomfortable. On rooms with many windows, it is sometimes more desirable to use a long, low-profile convector, baseboard or wall-mounted radiator than one or two large radiators. Because there is a great length of the room that's likely to be cool, the heating source should be extended along the same length.

STRATEGY

Where radiators are located on interior walls or are not below walls, point out the possible comfort effects. Again, talk about how auxiliary heat can be added relatively inexpensively, if necessary.

Mixed Types

IMPLICATIONS

We've talked about the comfort implications of mixing various types. Some rooms may get too hot and then get too cold, while other rooms are consistently comfortable.

STRATEGY

Note the type of heating distribution and let your client know of the possible comfort implications.

Balancing Valve Problems

IMPLICATIONS

The implications include water damage. If the valves can't be adjusted, the implication also is poor comfort. If the leakage has damaged the piping or valve body, expensive repairs may be necessary.

STRATEGY

We've already told you to look closely at these valves. We're emphasizing it here because most of us forget, from time to time.

Bleed Valve Problems

IMPLICATIONS

Flooding is one implication of a bleed valve problem. Poor comfort is another, if you can't bleed the air out of the radiator.

STRATEGY

Look for evidence of leakage. This is most often a streak running down the radiator from the bleed valves. Look also for active leakage and mechanical damage to the valve or handle itself.

Damaged Baseboard Fins

IMPLICATIONS

Reduced heating capacity and efficiency are the implications.

Make sure covers are in place on baseboards. Where they are loose or missing, recommend they be resecured and check the fins for damage.

If you can look into baseboards without removing the covers, check the condition of the fins. Fins flattened or bent can be straightened in most cases. There are "fin combs" available to do this.

Obstructed Air Flow

Obstructed baseboards may result in cold rooms.

Look at the bottom of baseboard heaters. Are the intakes open or obstructed? If obstructed, advise your client that simply cutting the carpet back may make the room much more comfortable.

10.4.7   Radiant Heating

Some hot water heating systems don't have any radiators, convectors or baseboards. Instead, pipes are buried in the ceilings, walls and/or floors. Piping embedded in the plaster ceilings is considered one of the most desirable applications.

High Quality Systems

These systems are generally expensive to install but can provide excellent, even heating.

Materials

The piping can be wrought iron, steel, copper or plastic, including polybutylene and polyethylene. The steel and wrought iron are typically only used for floors. They are too heavy for walls and ceilings.

Pipe Size

The piping can be anywhere from $1/4$ inch to 1 inch in diameter. The pipes are laid in grids or coils. The spacing between adjacent pipes should never be more than 12 inches and can be as close as 4 to 6 inches.

Temperature Is an Issue

In a room with 8-foot ceilings, the maximum temperature desired is about 110°F. If the ceilings get warmer than that, they can be uncomfortably warm. When piping is buried in floors, you don't want the temperature above about 85°F.

Water Can't Be Too Hot

This creates a challenge for boiler systems. With radiators, convectors and baseboards, we don't usually worry about the water at the boiler being too hot. However, with radiant systems, we normally run the boiler water around 120°F to 130°F. This is relatively cool.

Water Blender

These low temperatures are often achieved by using a **water blender.** This mixes some cold water with the hot water coming off the boiler to achieve a desired temperature. These are also called **mixing valves** or **tempering valves**.

Balancing Valves

There are often control valves that can be adjusted manually to balance the heating system. They can also be isolating valves, in some cases. Again, these can be located throughout the house and well concealed, or may be adjacent to the boiler.

Hot Spots and Cold Spots

Hot spots on floors can be a problem, especially if the pipes are far apart. If your foot is right on a pipe, it can be quite warm. The area between two pipes can be considerably cooler.

Leaks

Leaks in these systems can cause a lot of damage. Leaks in concrete floor slabs can be tough to find. Considerable erosion of the soil under a slab may take place while the leak is unnoticed.

Since there is nothing much to inspect on radiant systems, we won't go into a lot of detail. Look for the following:

1. Leaks
2. Balancing valves problems
3. Bleed valves problems
4. Cool rooms or parts of rooms

STRATEGY

Checking for Cool Spots

Let System Warm up

Use Your Hand to Feel the Heat

Clean Hands

We've talked about how to look for leaks and balancing and bleed valve problems, with radiators, convectors, and baseboards. The same strategies apply to radiant heating.

While cool rooms are easy to detect in the winter, this can be a challenge in the mild or warm weather. One of the ways to check a radiant system is to feel the surface temperature. First you have to discover where the radiant piping is. Is it in the floors, ceiling, walls or a combination? You may be told, you may find a layout drawing or you may be able to trace the piping and the valves.

If you know where the piping is, you can turn the thermostat(s) up and wait 45 minutes. It takes quite a while for the cold surfaces to warm up. You can do other parts of the inspection while waiting.

Once the system is up to temperature, you can feel the ceiling (for example) surfaces to see if they are warm to the touch. Since rooms may be zoned, some inspectors test the four corners of each room. An inactive area can be felt.

We recommend that your hands be clean while doing this. Use the back of your hand to sense the heat. Because pipes can be several inches apart, you may have to move your hand across the surface to find the heat.

10.5   LIFE EXPECTANCY

Cast Iron

Old cast-iron boilers commonly last 35 to 50 years. We have seen 80-year-old boilers still in service.

Old Steel Boilers

Some older steel boilers typically lasted 20 to 35 years, although most of those are near the end of their life now.

Newer Steel Boilers

The lighter steel and the copper-tube boilers have life expectancies of 15 to 25 years. Some fail as early as 10 years into their life, and there are always those that do better.

Condensation

Condensation causing rust is the big enemy of both the steel and copper-tube boilers.

High Tech Boilers

No one knows for sure how well the newer high-efficiency boilers are going to perform over the long term. Heat exchangers are typically copper, stainless steel or cupro-nickel alloys. Some difficulties have been experienced with the copper heat exchangers on some systems. These are being replaced with stainless steel as they fail.

Inspector in the House: The New Old Boiler

The listing and the feature sheet described the updated heating system, including the new boiler. As we performed the inspection and checked the boiler carefully, we concluded that the boiler was indeed recently installed, but it was 11 years old! A used boiler had been installed. It was not clear whether the seller was aware that they had purchased previously owned equipment, but it did not matter.

The new owner would have been looking to us for a new boiler had we not noted the situation. There are two lessons here: don't assume what you are told or read on a listing is accurate, and check the model and serial numbers to determine the age of heating and cooling systems. There are books that help with determining age and capacity from model and serial numbers. (Carson Dunlop's *Technical Reference Guide* is one such book.)

REVIEW QUESTIONS

1. Copper-tube boilers typically have

   a. better heat transfer characteristics, and longer lifespans than cast-iron boilers.

   b. better heat transfer characteristics, but shorter lifespans than cast-iron boilers.

   c. worse heat transfer characteristics, but longer lifespans than cast-iron boilers.

   d. worse heat transfer characteristics, and shorter lifespan than cast-iron boilers.

   e. have roughly similar characteristics to cast-iron boilers.

2. Which of the following is a similarity between furnaces and boilers?

   a. piping

   b. a low-level safety device

   c. high-temperature limit switches

   d. backflow preventers

   e. a pressure-relief valve

3. Heat exchanger diagnosis on boilers is easier than on furnaces because the heat exchanger will leak when it has failed.

   True   False

4 List the four safety controls found on all hydronic systems.

5. What is the normal operating pressure in a boiler?

   a. 2 to 5 psi

   b. 5 to 9 psi

   c. 9 to 12 psi

   d. 12 to 15 psi

   e. 15 to 18 psi

6. What is the normal setting on the pressure-relief valve?

   a. 10 psi

   b. 20 psi

   c. 30 psi

   d. 40 psi

   e. 50 psi

7. Where is the pressure relief valve typically located? Also, where does it typically discharge?

8. Are we required to test the pressure-relief valve?

   Yes   No

9. Is it possible to have a pressure-relief valve that is too small for the boiler?

   Yes   No

10. What is the common temperature setting for the high temperature limit switch?

    a. 180°

    b. 195°

    c. 210°

    d. 225°

    e. 240°

11. What is the purpose of the low-water cutout on a residential boiler?

12. Why do we need a backflow preventer on a modern hydronic system?

13. What is the safety control that prevents us from getting superheated water in a boiler system?

    a. the circulator

    b. the pressure relief valve

    c. the backflow preventer

    d. the pressure reducing valve

    e. the heat exchanger

14. List four operating controls that we may find on a hydronic system.

15. What is the function of the pressure-reducing valve?

16. In a two-story Victorian home with a boiler in the basement you find a pressure-reducing valve set to 12 psi. Is there a possibility that this valve is set too low?

    Yes   No

17. Is it possible for a boiler to function without a pressure-reducing valve?

    Yes   No

18. You find a boiler with a low temperature limit or primary control. What would be a typical setting for this control?

    a. 50°F

    b. 100°F

    c. 140°F

    d. 180°F

    e. 220°F

19. List three ways that the system can control a circulator (pump).

20. What are the four components in the distribution system for a hot water system?

21. What is the basic difference between an open system and a closed system?

22. Where is the expansion tank typically, in an open system?

23. What is the function of the expansion tank in a closed water system?

24. Where is the expansion tank, typically, in a closed hot water system?

25. List three styles of circulators.

26. List three materials that have been used for distribution piping in hot water systems in the past.

27. When a black steel pipe is extended with copper pipe, what can occur?

    a. The steel pipe may rust at the connection due to galvanic reaction.

    b. The circulator may not be able to overcome the pressure change at the junction.

    c. The copper pipe will wear through with the friction force of the water.

    d. The copper pipe will rust because of the galvanic reaction.

    e. Nothing occurs when steel and copper piping are joined.

28. In a radiant hot water heating system, the pipes serve two purposes.

    What are they?

29. Mixing convectors and radiators in a single hydronic system will often result in uncomfortable heating.

    True   False

30. Where should a radiator be placed in a room?

    a. on an interior wall

    b. on an exterior wall

    c. on an exterior wall below a window

    d. on the ceiling

    e. it doesn't matter; the radiator radiates heat to the room from any location

31. What is the purpose of the bleed valve near the top of the radiator?

32. Why do balancing valves tend to leak when operated?

33. What is the maximum ceiling temperature you would want to have in an 8-foot room with radiant pipe heating?

    a. 70°F

    b. 90°F

    c. 110°F

    d. 130°F

    e. 150°F

34. Do radiant piping systems need bleed valves, since there are no radiators?

    Yes   No

35. What is the average lifespan of a cast iron boiler?

OTHER ASPECTS OF HEATING

LEARNING OBJECTIVES

By the end of this chapter you should be able to—

- list five components of masonry chimneys

- list 24 common masonry chimney problems and their implications

- list 14 common metal chimney or vent problems and their implications

- define creosote

- describe in one sentence two types of wood-burning fireplaces

- list five components of masonry fireplaces and their common problems

- describe the implication of each problem

- identify electric heating systems

- list the common problems encountered with electric heating systems

- describe the implications of each of these problems

We have discussed various heating systems to this point. Most of these heating systems require a chimney or a vent. In this chapter we will concentrate on the chimneys and vents used to get exhaust gases out of the home. We will also look briefly at some less common heating systems, including wood and electric.

11.1   AN OVERVIEW OF CHIMNEYS

Let's start by looking at what chimneys and vents are supposed to do.

1. Chimneys remove the products of combustion from the house.

2. Chimneys should enhance the draft from appliances, assisting in the combustion process and inducing exhaust gases to leave the building.

3. It is a chimney's job to contain a fire in the chimney. We don't want the chimney to spread a fire from a burner or fireplace to other areas of the home. In short, don't burn down the house.

4. Chimneys should prevent poison gases from entering the house—

   ▪ through the appliances

   ▪ through openings in chimney walls

   ▪ through an adjacent idle flue

   ▪ back through upper story windows after leaving the chimney

5. Good chimneys minimize the heat loss from the building, while in use and while idle.

A **chimney** is a vertical device (usually masonry or metal) for **removing** the exhaust products from burning fuels from the house safely (Figure 11.1). Masonry chimneys may have more than one **flue,** which may or may not be **lined.** Metal chimneys are always single flue.

Flues are the interior passages in chimneys through which the gases move upward. **Vents** are metal devices for getting exhaust gases from burning fuels out of the house safely (Figure 11.2). They may be single, double or triple wall vents and may be horizontal, vertical or a combination. Vents are always single flue, although the word **flue** is not normally used in conjunction with vents.

Vent Connectors

Vent connectors are also called **exhaust flues, vent pipes, stack pipes, flue pipes, chimney connectors** or **breechings.** Their function is to transfer the exhaust products from the appliance to the chimney. Most wood stoves, furnaces, boilers and water heaters have vent connectors; fireplaces do not.

Homes with electric heat, high-efficiency furnaces and some mid-efficiency furnaces may have no chimneys. Modern gas fireplaces may not have conventional chimneys. When you're outside a building, don't write up a missing chimney as a defect. One may not be needed.

Chimneys are not intended to hold up other building components. It is not appropriate, for example, to strap a satellite dish, television antenna or tower to a chimney.

Stone, Brick, Concrete Block, Steel, Alloys, Fiber Cement, Concrete

Masonry chimneys are made of stone, brick, or concrete block, typically. Metal chimneys may be made out of galvanized steel, stainless steel or other alloys. Chimneys may be made entirely of asbestos cement (fiber cement) or the asbestos cement may be a chimney liner. Chimneys may also be poured concrete. Chimneys may be covered with wood, stucco, or metal siding, for example.

FIGURE 11.1   Chimneys

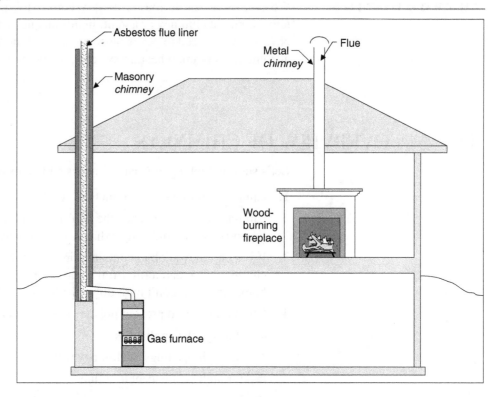

FIGURE 11.2   Vents

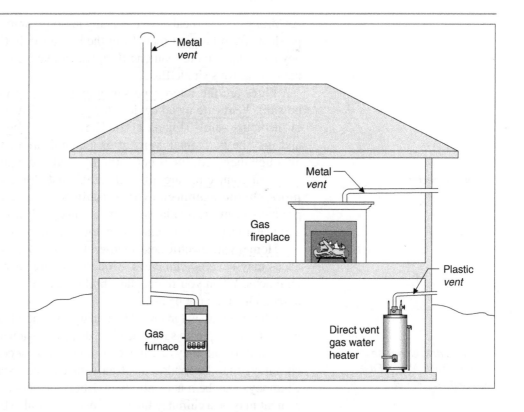

11.1.1 Fuels

Chimneys may see different fuels, including wood, oil, gas, and propane.

Wood

Wood is a fuel that burns hot and may be quite dirty. **Creosote** (the oily or tar-like combustible deposits condensed from the incomplete burning of wood) tends to build up in chimneys serving fireplaces and wood stoves. It's not unusual for temperatures of 800°F to be found in chimneys for wood fireplaces or stoves. Most clay liners used in these chimneys are designed to withstand temperatures of up to 2,000°F. This temperature can be reached in a chimney fire where a buildup of creosote is ignited.

Oil

Oil is a cooler burning fuel than wood and is somewhat cleaner, although it can be sooty. Poorly tuned oil burners can generate lots of incomplete combustion products. Even on properly tuned burners, there is often some soot generated due to incomplete combustion on start-up and/or shut-down.

Temperatures of 500°F

Typical chimney temperatures might be in the 500°F range (with maximums over 700°F) and condensation can be an issue with oil furnaces. The exhaust gases may cool near the top of the chimney. If they reach the dew point, condensation will form on the chimney walls. When the appliances are off, the condensation may freeze in the chimney and can do considerable damage.

Fuel oil contains sulfur. Sulfur can react with condensate to form sulfuric acid which attacks mortar, brick and clay tile.

Gas Temperatures of 350°F

Gas appliances are the coolest of the three. Chimney temperatures are in the 350°F range. Gas is also the cleanest of the three fuels we've looked at. Condensation, however, is a major issue because of the low temperature and large volume of water produced by the combustion of natural gas. A 100,000 BTU/hr gas furnace operating continuously generates 1 gallon of water per hour. We don't want this condensing in the house or in the chimney!

11.1.2 Draft

Draft Quality

Chimneys need house air to maintain their draft. The ability of chimneys to carry exhaust gases away through **natural draft** (or **stack effect**) is a function of several things, including—

1. The chimney height
2. The flue size
3. Any offset from vertical in the chimney
4. The appliance size
5. The number of appliances using the chimney
6. The temperature difference between indoors and out
7. The direction of the prevailing wind
8. Tall structures near the chimney
9. Whether the chimney is interior (running up the center of the building), or exterior (enclosed in, attached to, or adjacent to an exterior wall)
10. The smoothness or roughness of the flue passage

Warm Chimneys Are Best

Generally speaking, the warmer the chimney, the easier it is to maintain good draft. A chimney going up through the center of the house will be warmest. A chimney on the exterior wall, but with three sides interior and only one exterior side (flush with the exterior wall), is the second warmest. The next coldest is a chimney built on an exterior wall, but projecting out from the wall with three exterior sides. The coldest is a freestanding chimney outside the house.

Cold Chimneys

While it's not common with masonry chimneys, metal chimneys are sometimes separate from the house wall but supported by it. The entire outside diameter of these chimneys is exposed to the cold over most of the length of the chimney.

Tall Chimneys Are Better

Taller chimneys usually draw better than short chimneys, at least within the height ranges we usually see on houses.

One-Story Chimney

Watch for homes that are partly one-story and part two-story. A chimney on the one-story section often drafts poorly because of the wind turbulence and downdraft created by the two-story section.

Draft Has to Be Established

It takes a while to establish positive draft when the appliance first comes on. The warm combustion products have to overcome the weight of the column of cold air in the chimney. It's not unusual for appliances to spill or backdraft during start-up.

Flue Size

We mentioned that the size of the flue has a bearing on the quality of the draft. The flue size is determined by a number of factors, including—

1. The fuel that is used
2. The appliance size
3. The number of appliances
4. The chimney height

General rules include—

1. Wood needs a larger flue than oil or gas
2. A larger flue is needed for larger appliances
3. A smaller flue is needed for taller chimneys, all other things being equal

IMPLICATIONS

Flues that are undersized or oversized will tend to backdraft and spill combustion products into the house. Condensation is more likely if the flue size is wrong.

11.1.3 Number of Flues per Chimney

Up to 8 Flues per Chimney

Metal chimneys typically have one flue each. Masonry chimneys may have several flues. Two or three flues is common and there can be six to eight flues, particularly in attached (e.g., row) houses.

Brick Between Flues

Adjacent flues should be separated by a row of brick, typically (Figure 11.3).

11.1.4 Flue Size

We Don't Check Flue Size

A home inspection does not include an evaluation of the suitability of the flue size for the appliance or appliances connected. This requires the consideration of a number of variables, and the expertise of a specialist. Where you have suspicions, call for others to check it out, but you should not normally give opinions on flue sizes.

11.2 MASONRY CHIMNEYS

The basic components of masonry chimneys include (Figure 11.4):

1. Footing and foundation
2. Vent connectors (from appliances)

F I G U R E 11.3 Masonry Chimneys

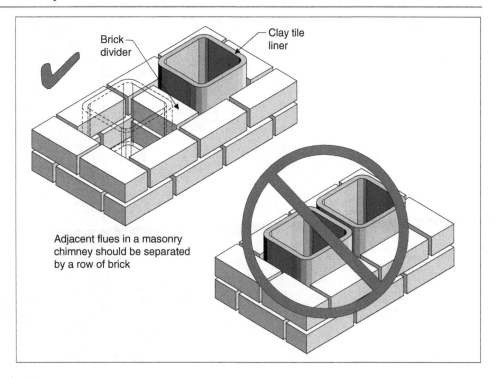

Brick divider

Clay tile liner

Adjacent flues in a masonry chimney should be separated by a row of brick

3. Chimney walls
4. Flue liner (not always present)
5. Cap (or crown as it may be called)

Chimneys with fireplaces will also have all or most of these components:

1. Ash dump and ash pit
2. Hearth (back hearth)
3. Hearth extension (front hearth)
4. Firebox
5. Damper
6. Throat
7. Smoke shelf
8. Smoke chamber
9. Mantel

11.2.1   Footing and Foundation

Concrete, Stone, or Brick

Modern footings are usually concrete, poured with the house footing or poured separately. The footing typically has a projection beyond the chimney foundation that follows the same rules as footings for house foundations. Old footings were often stones or even brick.

Settle Slightly with House

The goal with a fireplace footing is to have it settle the same amount and at the same rate as the rest of the house.

FIGURE 11.4   Basic Masonry Chimney and Fireplace Components

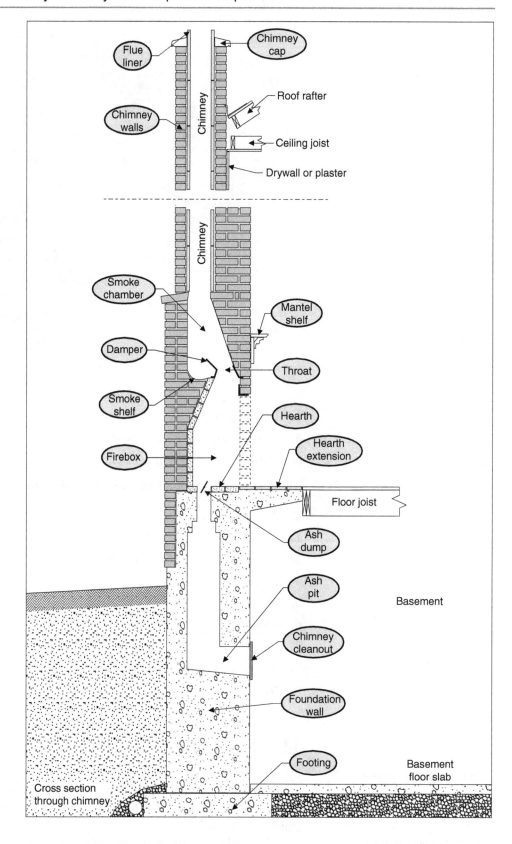

FIGURE 11.5   Chimney Walls

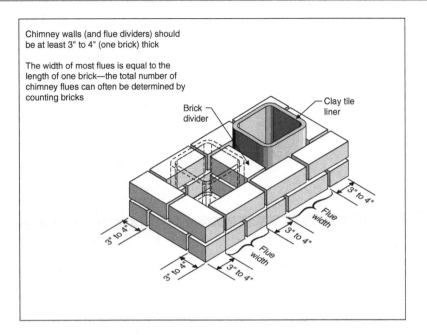

Chimney walls (and flue dividers) should be at least 3" to 4" (one brick) thick

The width of most flues is equal to the length of one brick—the total number of chimney flues can often be determined by counting bricks

Brick divider

Clay tile liner

3" to 4"

Flue width

11.2.2   Vent Connectors

Appliances other than fireplaces are usually connected to masonry chimneys with a metal or asbestos cement **vent connector.** The connection should be made gastight and the vent connector should be flush with the inner edge of the chimney flue. The vent connector should not stop short and should not extend into the chimney flue, restricting the flue.

11.2.3   Chimney Walls

Masonry walls should be at least 3 or 4 inches (one brick) thick, depending on your jurisdiction (Figure 11.5). It is also considered good practice to separate adjacent flues in the chimney by 3 or 4 inches of masonry. In some areas, it is common practice to butt two clay tile liners against each other with no brick between. In many areas, this is considered poor practice, unless there is a single appliance served by both flues. Find out what is acceptable in your region.

Lateral Support

Masonry chimneys extending above their **support** by more than 12 feet require bracing. **Lateral support** is provided if a chimney is part of a masonry or masonry veneer wall. The unsupported height is measured from the point at which the chimney leaves the wall or highest support, usually at the top of the upper floor level. A chimney that passes through an attic is not usually considered laterally supported above the attic floor. The roof sheathing does not normally provide lateral support.

Bracing Not Visible

Chimneys in wood frame houses are laterally unsupported from the top of the foundation wall up, unless metal straps bolted to joists are used. You won't usually be able to see these, so you'll have to look for evidence of movement.

FIGURE 11.6   Clay Tile Flue Liners

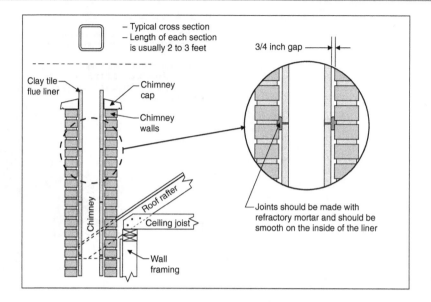

<table>
</table>

Bracing above Roofline

Above the roofline, lateral support is usually metal bracing that ties the chimney back to the roof framing.

Fire Stopping

Non-combustible insulation and/or metal thimbles should provide fire stopping at each floor level.

11.2.4   Flue Liners

Materials

Flue liners may be **clay tile, firebrick, metal,** or **asbestos cement.** Some retrofit liners are made of poured concrete. Metal liners may be rigid or flexible and are made of aluminum or steel.

Functions

Chimney liners offer a smooth inner surface to help facilitate the flow of exhaust gases up through the chimney, and help prevent products of combustion and condensation from getting into the house or chimney masonry. Flue liners make it easier to clean creosote deposits from chimneys. Flue liners also help chimneys resist the high temperatures (1,800 to 2,000°F) that might be involved in a chimney fire.

Clay Tile

Clay tile liners may be round (rare) or rectangular (common) (Figure 11.6). They typically come in 2 or 3 foot long sections. The joints should be made with refractory mortar and should be smooth on the inside. Some have ship lap or other special joints to help stabilize the liners and make a good connection. Many are simply butt jointed.

Gap between Liner and Chimney Wall

Clay tile liners should be set away from the masonry walls of the chimney unless the masonry walls are at least 8 inches thick. A $^3/_4$ inch gap between the liner and the brickwork, for example, is typical. The liners are laterally supported by the mortar joints that extend out to the masonry walls at the top and bottom of each liner section. Again, check the recommended practices in your area.

Bottom Support

The bottom of a clay tile liner should rest on masonry, **not** nails driven into the chimney walls.

Liner Length

The flue liner should extend at least 8 inches below the flue connection at the bottom and roughly 4 inches above the cap.

Liner Projects above Cap

Some authorities say that chimneys should extend 2 to 4 inches or 2 to 6 inches above the cap. A few say **at least** 4 inches above. Again, check the recommended practices in your area.

F I G U R E   11.7   Chimney Offsets

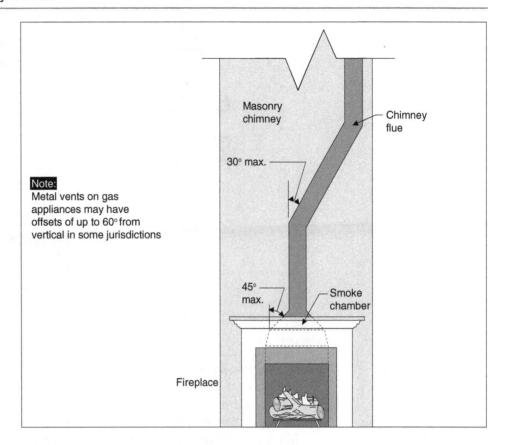

Note:
Metal vents on gas
appliances may have
offsets of up to 60° from
vertical in some jurisdictions

Masonry
chimney

Chimney
flue

30° max.

45°
max.

Smoke
chamber

Fireplace

Aluminum Liners

Aluminum liners should be used only with natural gas or propane. They are usually a flexible, corrugated (accordion type) system. They should not be used with oil or wood fuels. A cap designed for the specific liner should be used. These liners are susceptible to tearing during installation or cleaning. They can also be damaged by acidic condensate from the products of combustion. In most cases, you won't be able to get a good look at either the inside or outside of the liner.

Stainless Steel Liners

Stainless steel liners, which may be rigid or flexible, are suitable for use with gas, propane, oil or wood.

Metal Liners and Insulation

Some jurisdictions don't allow loose fill insulation to be poured around metal liners in masonry chimneys. The danger is that any gap in a liner may allow insulation to fall into the liner and block the flue. Insulation may be required to be a hard-set, high temperature material.

Concrete Liners

Poured-in-place concrete liners are used to line old masonry chimneys. An inflatable bag is inserted into the chimney, held away from the masonry walls with spacers. A concrete slurry is poured around the outside of the bag. The bag is deflated and removed as the concrete cures.

Chimney Offsets

The smoke chamber in a fireplace can have 45° shoulders (offset 45° from the vertical between the damper and the bottom of the flue liner). However, in the chimney itself, offsets of 30° from vertical are usually considered maximum (Figure 11.7). More than this may disturb the draft of the chimney.

Gaps in Joints

Where the chimney is offset, the joints of flue liners should be mitered so that they fit tightly and smoothly. There should be no offset or gap in the liner anywhere along its length. There often is.

FIGURE 11.8   What Makes a Good Chimney Cap?

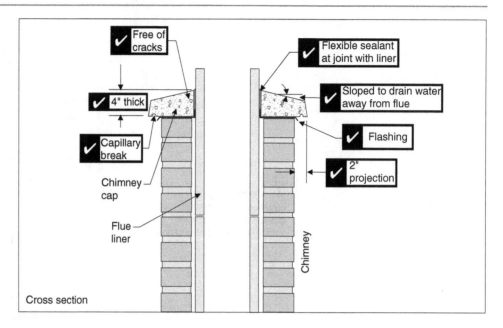

Debris Restricts Flue

Another problem with offsets is the mortar debris that falls from above and accumulates on the shoulder. This can reduce the flue size, restricting flow and creating draft problems.

Sometimes Required on Old Chimneys

Up until roughly 1950 (depending on where you are) flue liners were not required. Many older homes have unlined brick chimneys, used with furnaces, boilers, water heaters and/or fireplaces. In some jurisdictions, these are considered unsafe and must be lined. Other jurisdictions are more lenient and retrofitting liners is only recommended. Eight inch thick masonry chimney walls may not require a liner.

11.2.5   Chimney Caps

Caps, or crowns as they are called in some areas, protect the top of the chimney from weather. They are usually concrete, and may be pre-cast or poured-in-place.

Good Caps

Good caps—

- are 4 inches thick
- are sloped to drain water away from the flue
- are separated from the clay tile liner with a bond break and a flexible sealant
- are free of cracks
- extend 2 inches beyond the face of the chimney on all sides
- have a capillary break (see Figure 11.8) on the underside of the projection
- have a flexible sealant between the cap and liner to allow the cap to move slightly, independent of the chimney masonry

Common Weak Points

Many chimneys don't have good caps. Few have all the characteristics we've listed here. The fewer good points, the greater risk of moisture damage to the inside and outside of the chimney.

Cement Wash

Many chimneys don't have a proper cap. They may have just a thin mortar **wash** on top of the masonry, often with some slope to provide drainage. These are not often durable or functional over the long term.

11.2.6   Condensation

Common

As the products of combustion (exhaust or smoke) cool, they may condense within the chimney. While the goal is to get them out of the chimney before they cool to the point of condensing, it is typical for almost all chimneys to suffer condensation under some conditions. The better the draft of the chimney, the less frequently this will happen.

Unlined Chimneys Vulnerable

Condensation is more likely to damage chimneys without liners. Brick is porous and will draw the condensation into the brick and mortar. When this moisture cools to the freezing point, the condensation freezes, expands and spalls the masonry.

Acidic Exhaust

The products of combustion from wood, oil and gas can be acidic. Damage to the masonry and mortar may be considerable where there is substantial condensation.

Gaps or Cracks in Flue Liners

Where flue liners are not continuous or cracked, localized condensation, efflorescence, and freeze/thaw damage may be noted. This is common near the top of a chimney, which is the coldest part, and where condensation may be worst. The top of the chimney is also the part most exposed to freezing temperatures in cold climates.

Flue Liners Too Tall

In most areas, flue liners are only allowed to extend 4 or 5 inches above the cap. If the liner is too tall, it is more prone to condensation.

11.2.7   Abandoned Chimneys

Remove to Below Roof Level

The best practice for abandoned chimneys is to remove them down to the level of the roof covering and to roof over the opening. This makes it clear that the chimney is not in service. It also avoids deterioration of the above-roof masonry and eliminates the risk of falling masonry units from an abandoned, deteriorating chimney. Removal down to roof level also prevents leakage around chimney flashings at the roof.

11.2.8   Conditions

Common problems with masonry chimneys include—

1. Settling or leaning
2. Cracking
3. Spalling masonry or concrete
4. Loose, missing or deteriorating masonry
5. Loose, missing or deteriorating mortar
6. Efflorescence
7. Excessive offset from vertical
8. Chimney too short
9. Cleanout door too close to combustibles, loose, or missing
10. No liner

11. Cracked or broken liner

12. Incomplete liner

13. Inadequate clearance from combustibles

14. Fire stopping missing or incomplete

15. Cap missing

16. Cap cracked

17. Improper slope on cap

18. No drip edge on cap

19. Creosote buildup in flues

20. Flue obstructed

21. Abandoned openings for flue connections

22. Chimney extender rusted or stuck

23. Too many appliances in flue

24. Undersized screen on spark arrester

We haven't described **poor draft** as a problem because it's easier to evaluate draft as part of the appliance inspection. However, many of the problems listed can affect draft. Draft may be fine during your inspection, but poor on a colder, windier day.

11.2.9   Settling or Leaning

IMPLICATIONS

The implications of settling or leaning chimneys include—

- structural failure (collapse) of the chimney
- fire hazard
- exhaust gas entry into the house
- water leakage into the house
- high maintenance and reduced durability of the chimney and adjacent house components
- damaged or blocked flues

Falling Chimneys

It's not often that chimneys fall, but when they do, property damage, injury, and even death can result. Chimneys with settling footings and foundations often need to be torn down and rebuilt.

Gases Escape

Chimneys that have moved may no longer have tight, continuous flues. Heat and/or poisonous combustion gases may escape from flues and find their way into the house.

Water Leaks

Differential movement between the house and chimney will allow water into the chimney and house systems, typically causing considerable moisture damage over time.

STRATEGY

Look along the entire height of the chimney for gaps or open joints that suggest differential settlement, heaving or leaning.

Check for Plumb

Cracks in masonry may also suggest differential movement. A mason's level or plumb bob is sometimes used to verify and quantify movement. This is a very serious condition, and one that you cannot afford to overlook. Every chimney should be checked to make sure that it is plumb, intact and properly connected to the house.

FIGURE 11.9   3-Sided Chimney

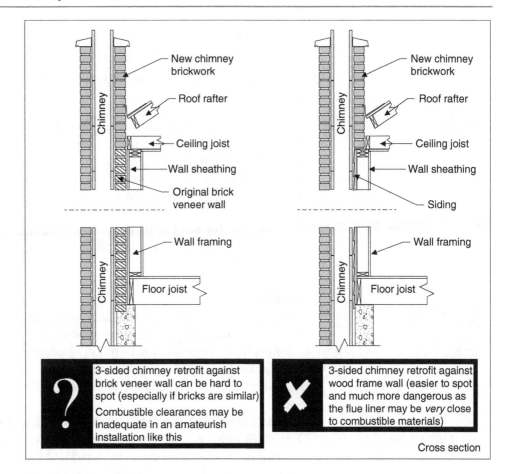

New chimney brickwork

Roof rafter

Ceiling joist

Wall sheathing

Original brick veneer wall

Wall framing

Floor joist

New chimney brickwork

Roof rafter

Ceiling joist

Wall sheathing

Siding

Wall framing

Floor joist

? 3-sided chimney retrofit against brick veneer wall can be hard to spot (especially if bricks are similar)

Combustible clearances may be inadequate in an amateurish installation like this

✕ 3-sided chimney retrofit against wood frame wall (easier to spot and much more dangerous as the flue liner may be *very* close to combustible materials)

Cross section

Tall Chimneys

Watch for chimneys that extend more than 12 feet above the roof or above their last visible support. Are they braced? Are they leaning? Watch for chimneys on two-story houses where the first floor is brick and the second floor is siding. There may be no support for the chimney above the first floor.

Using House Wall as Chimney Wall

Make sure the chimney has four sides! Chimneys added to homes may use the house wall as a fourth side (Figure 11.9). This is not usually acceptable. Call for further investigation where you can't be sure.

Masonry Chimneys Hung on Wood Frame Walls or Metal Brackets

In pre-1920s construction, it is not unusual to find chimneys that start part way up a building wall, supported on the wood frame wall itself. This creates a weak structural condition and a fire hazard, because the framing is tied directly into the masonry. This is a situation that should be reported if you find it. These are common in old houses where each room may have had a wood stove or fireplace, originally.

Cracking

Cracking due to settlement may result in—

IMPLICATIONS

Settling

- structural instability
- a fire hazard
- exhaust gas entry into the house
- increased maintenance and reduced durability
- moisture entry

Overheating

Cracking due to overheating is less likely to be a structural issue but can result in—

- a fire hazard
- exhaust gas entry into the house
- increased maintenance and reduced durability
- moisture entry

STRATEGY

The strategy is similar to what we were looking for on settling and leaning. Again, the inspection should include both inside and out. It's nice to be able to look up and down the flues, although this is almost always restricted, and sometimes not possible at all. Most inspectors do not remove rain caps, spark arresters or animal screens to look down chimneys. Don't lean a ladder against a chimney to look down the flue.

Crack analysis can be tricky. Where you are unsure of the causes and implications of cracks, call for further investigation. Again, chimneys are both structural and life safety issues.

Spalling

IMPLICATIONS

The implications are increased maintenance and reduced durability. In severe cases, replacement of some parts of the chimney may be necessary.

STRATEGY

Spalling is common where moisture accumulates. Watch for horizontal surfaces at shoulders where chimneys change direction or narrow. The corbelled (offset) brick often provides several horizontal ledges for moisture to collect.

Loose, Missing, or Deteriorated Masonry

IMPLICATIONS

The implications may be structural, although in most cases, it is a maintenance and durability issue. In severe cases, there can be a fire hazard and/or exhaust gases may enter the house. Water entry is another possible result.

STRATEGY

In many cases, the loose, missing or deteriorated masonry is visible from the ground. It often occurs at or near the top of the chimney. However, it can occur elsewhere.

Check the Attic

Damage to masonry and mortar may be visible from the attic. We have found a number of cases where loose, missing or deteriorated bricks in the attic allow exhaust gases to enter the attic area.

Inside the Chimney

Loose, missing or deteriorated brickwork may be visible looking down the chimney from the top. Where there is more than one flue, there is usually a single wythe of masonry separating the flues. Particularly on older chimneys with poor or missing caps, this wythe of brick dividing the flues may be deteriorated. It's not unusual to find several courses of brick between the flues are missing. These bricks can often be found by opening the ash pit cleanout at the bottom of the chimney!

Exhaust Gases Get into the House

When these bricks are missing, the possibility of exhaust gases getting back into the house is heightened, because the exhaust gases flow from a working flue into an idle flue.

Blocking the Flue

Another problem is that the masonry and mortar that falls may accumulate at the bottom of the chimney and obstruct the vent connector from an appliance. This is a fire and life safety (carbon monoxide poisoning) hazard.

Loose, Missing, or Deteriorating Mortar

A recent survey showed that more fires in homes were caused by mortar problems in masonry chimneys than any other fireplace or chimney problem. The mortar condition is important! And, there's lots of it we can't see.

While the implications may include structural damage, this is more often a maintenance issue. There is a life safety issue if the deterioration gets to the point where masonry units may fall from the chimney.

Look for the integrity of mortar in all joints. Raking the joints with moderate pressure with a screwdriver, for example, should not result in mortar coming out. Where mortar deterioration is superficial, repointing is possible. Where more than about 1 inch of the mortar has deteriorated, rebuilding may be necessary to ensure structural integrity.

Efflorescence

The implications of efflorescence are usually maintenance. In severe cases, mortar and masonry deterioration are possible.

Efflorescence often indicates a moisture penetration problem. Look for a source of moisture, including cracked liners, cracked or missing caps and loose or missing mortar. Horizontal surfaces that collect water may also lead to efflorescence.

In some cases, chimneys lean not due to structural movement, but due to a combination of weather related factors and condensed exhaust gases from oil burners. This kind of lean usually starts above the roofline. When the sulfur in exhaust products from oil burners condenses on chimneys, the sulfur and water mixture may create sulfuric acid. This acid can damage mortar, masonry and liners.

In some cases, the mortar joints may **swell** as a result of the acid action and/or efflorescence. One side of a chimney typically gets wetter than the other sides because most wind-driven rains come from one direction. Chimneys may lean **away** from the direction of the predominant wind-driven rains because the mortar joints on that side of the chimney swell. This pushes up the masonry units above each mortar joint, causing the chimney to lean. This expansion-of-mortar-joint-induced leaning is typically observed in northern climates on houses with taller chimneys that are, or have been, serving an oil-fired appliance. The top section of the chimney may eventually fall.

Excessive Offset from Vertical

The implications are—

- poor draft, resulting in exhaust gas backdraft into the house
- creosote buildup at the offset
- a chimney that is difficult to clean

If the chimney offset is more than 30°, you should probably point this out to your client and say that it may affect draft under some conditions. This is especially true because it is common for mortar debris falling from above to accumulate at the offset, restricting draft. You usually won't know whether this is an issue or not.

Follow chimney flues and watch for dramatic offsets. In some cases, you'll be able to find evidence of backdraft or spillage as a result, although it's often difficult to be conclusive.

Some inspectors are quick to say that if a fireplace mantel has soot on the front and soot on the ceiling above, the chimney has poor draft. This, however, may only mean that people have started a fire without opening the damper. Be careful about your conclusions.

F I G U R E   11.10   Proper Chimney Height

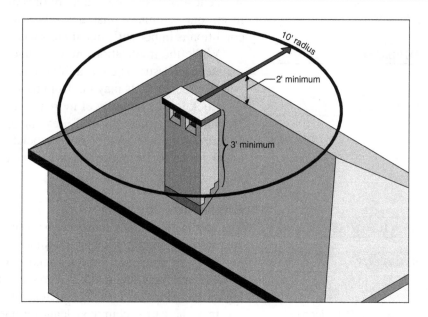

Chimney Too Short

Height Rules

Masonry chimneys should be at least three feet above the roof at the point they go through the roof. They should also be at least two feet higher than anything within ten feet of the chimney, horizontally (Figure 11.10).

IMPLICATIONS

Poor draft is the implication of a chimney that is too short.

STRATEGY

Look for chimneys that extend at least 3 feet above the roofline at their point of penetration and are 2 feet higher than anything within 10 feet of the chimney, horizontally.

Total Chimney Height Too Short

A minimum distance from the top of the appliance or draft hood must also be maintained. This ensures adequate draft to carry the exhaust products away. A chimney or vent should extend:

- at least 11 feet above the unit for an oil-burning appliance.
- at least 5 feet above the draft hood for a gas burner (natural draft).
- at least 15 feet above a wood stove or fireplace.

Where the chimney is shorter, recommend further investigation.

Cleanout Door Too Close to Combustibles, Loose, or Missing

All masonry chimneys need some kind of cleanout at the bottom. Fireplaces may use the firebox or there may be an ash dump, ash pit and cleanout door. Where there is a vent connector, the cleanout should be as far below the vent connector as possible, but not less than 6 inches.

The cleanout door should be tight fitting and non-combustible.

IMPLICATIONS

Cleanout door issues can allow pest entry and heat loss. If hot embers are allowed to fall into the ash pit when the fireplace is operating, a fire hazard results.

STRATEGY

Make sure the cleanout door is in place and well secured. Also make sure there are no combustibles within 6 inches of the door. Some enthusiastic fireplace users clean the fireplace before the ashes and embers have cooled. Allowing hot embers to collect against a cleanout door that touches combustible materials can lead to a fire.

No Chimney Liner

The implications of having no liner are—

- an increased fire hazard
- possible exhaust gas entry into the house
- poor draft
- heavy creosote buildup and difficulty in cleaning

There may be a fire hazard because the chimney walls are hotter if there is no liner. Remember, the liner should be separated from the masonry by $3/8$ to $3/4$ of an inch. This air space provides some insulation and cooling for the masonry.

Check from the top and bottom of the chimney for the presence of a liner. Don't be fooled by the presence of a liner extension sticking out through the top of the chimney. It's common that only one 2-foot piece of liner is provided.

In some jurisdictions, chimneys with 8-inch thick solid walls do not require liners. Most jurisdictions, however, require liners in new construction.

Cracked or Broken Liner

The implications are—

- increased fire hazard
- possible exhaust gas entry into house
- poor draft
- localized heavy creosote buildup

Where possible, look up from the bottom and down from the top with a flashlight. You may be able to see cracks in chimney liners. However, if there is a creosote buildup or the damage is in the middle of the chimney, you may not see it.

Incomplete Liner

The implications include—

1. Fire hazard
2. Possible exhaust gas entry into the house
3. Poor draft
4. Creosote buildup

Look for gaps between adjacent pieces of liner. Gaps with horizontal offsets are the worst. Exhaust products may find their way into the home.

Gap Between Top and Next Section of Liner

It is common to find a gap between the top section of liner and the next-to-top section. Liners are difficult to cut. It is easier for builders to stop the liner a little short at the second-from-the-top section, then fit a full-length section, just supported on nails driven into the closest mortar joint. Condensation gets into the masonry at the gap, and a ring of efflorescence and deteriorated masonry and mortar may develop around the chimney, about 2 feet below the top of the liner extension.

Liner problems must be evaluated individually. Judgment calls as to the safety of various installations can be dangerous. One will find that contractors differ in their recommendations; hence it is easy to find a contractor who will disagree with your analysis of the chimney condition and the necessity for repairs.

Recommend Further
Investigation

Where you see situations that are less than ideal, describe what you see, and let your client know that further investigation is necessary.

Inadequate Clearance from Combustibles

IMPLICATIONS
This is a fire hazard.

STRATEGY
Look at the bottom, middle and top of the chimney wherever it's accessible. At the base of the chimney, if you can look up where it passes through the first floor framing, you should not see any wood/masonry contact. You can often get a look in the attic at the clearance between wood on the attic floor and at the roofline in the masonry.

Watch for Cored Bricks
If you can look down the top of the chimney, you can perhaps see how thick the masonry walls are. Generally speaking, masonry walls should be 3 or 4-inch thick solid masonry. **Cored bricks** (those with holes through the middle) are not appropriate in many areas.

Two Inch Clearance
from Framing
While the rules vary, 2 inches is a common required clearance for framing members from chimneys. Flooring and siding can be closer to chimneys, as long as they are kept 12 inches from the inside surface of the liner. However, framing members are often allowed to come within 1 inch if the chimney is on the exterior of the building. The thinking here is that there will be considerable cooling by the outdoor air. Check your local rules.

Fire Stopping Missing or Incomplete

IMPLICATIONS
This is a fire hazard.

STRATEGY
Look up from the bottom and down from the top where possible. You should not be able to see from one floor to the next around a masonry chimney. The most common fire stopping is sheet metal.

Cap Missing

IMPLICATIONS
The implication is deterioration of the masonry and mortar.

STRATEGY
Any chimney missing a cap should be reported as a potential problem. We usually recommend monitoring this vulnerable condition, unless there is damage visible.

Cap Cracked

IMPLICATIONS
The implications are water leakage into the masonry units and deterioration of the top part of the chimney.

STRATEGY
Chimney cracks are common and are often visible from the sides of the chimney.

Temporary Repairs
However, the best view is looking down from the top. You will often find the cracks have been sealed. As long as these prevent water penetration into the cap, this is acceptable.

Improper Slope on Cap

IMPLICATIONS
Where the cap slopes toward the liners, water and (in freezing climates) ice, will accumulate around the liner and eventually find its way into the chimney.

STRATEGY
The strategy is the same as for missing and cracked caps.

No Drip Edge on Cap

IMPLICATIONS
Moisture accumulation and deterioration to masonry and mortar are the implications.

F I G U R E 11.11   Creosote Deposits

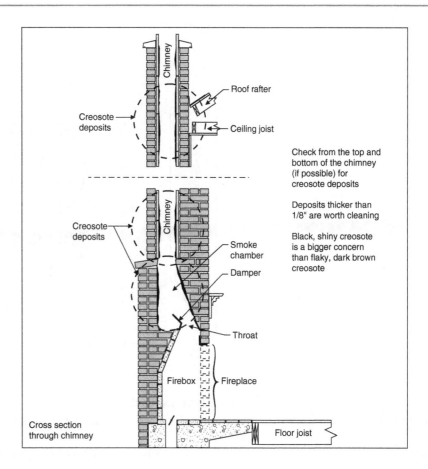

Check from the top and bottom of the chimney (if possible) for creosote deposits

Deposits thicker than 1/8" are worth cleaning

Black, shiny creosote is a bigger concern than flaky, dark brown creosote

Cross section through chimney

Look for a 1 inch (some require 2 inches) overhang on the cap. Highest quality construction also includes a metal flashing that is visible between the top row of masonry and the bottom of the cap. Absence of the flashing shouldn't be called a defect.

If there is no flashing, the overhang should include a **capillary break,** which is usually a groove or slot about $1/4$ inch wide and $1/4$ inch deep in the underside of the overhang. This prevents water from running along the underside of the cap and getting back to the masonry.

Creosote Buildup

This is a fire hazard. Chimney fires often spread from the chimney and involve the rest of the house. Chimney fires also damage chimneys.

Where possible, look down from the top and up from the bottom of the chimney for creosote deposits (Figure 11.11). A depth that exceeds $1/8$ inch should be cleaned. We recommend that every homeowner have their chimney inspected, and swept if necessary, when they move in to a home before using the chimney.

Black shiny creosote that looks like tar is a bigger concern than flaky, dark brown creosote.

FIGURE 11.12   Abandoned Flue Openings

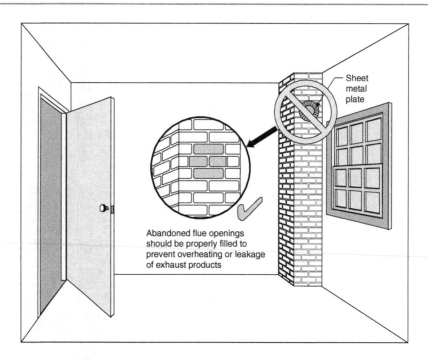

Sheet metal plate

Abandoned flue openings should be properly filled to prevent overheating or leakage of exhaust products

Flue Obstructed

IMPLICATIONS

The implications are poor draft and exhaust gases entering the home. This is a life safety issue.

STRATEGY

Check for obstructions at the cleanout at the bottom of the chimney. This should be at least 6 inches below the lowest vent connector.

Abandoned Openings for Flue Connections

IMPLICATIONS

The implications are fire hazard and exhaust gas entry into the home.

STRATEGY

In old homes, it was not unusual to have heating appliances in each room or at least in several rooms. It was also common to have wood stoves in kitchens. With the advent of central heating systems, most of these appliances have been removed, leaving openings in the chimney.

Seal Opening

The opening must be sealed to prevent exhaust gases getting into the house. The opening should also be as good thermally as the rest of the chimney wall. A single piece of sheet metal, for example, may not be adequate to prevent chimney heat from igniting nearby combustibles (Figure 11.12).

Test for Overheating or Leaks

In many cases, abandoned flue openings have been covered and you won't be able to see them. Where you can, look for evidence of exhaust products leaking past the opening. If possible, have the appliance working and carefully touch the opening to see if temperatures are high. You may also see evidence of overheating such as discoloration or peeling paint, or soot from leaking products of combustion.

Chimney Extender Rusted or Stuck

Swivel Type Extenders

Chimneys sometimes have metal extensions to help with draft problems. These may be straight extensions or extensions that rotate to discharge downwind.

These types of extensions typically have a weather vane on top and are capable of swivelling 360°. The wind pushes the extension into an orientation that allows

F I G U R E   11.13   Wood below Oil on Same Floor Level

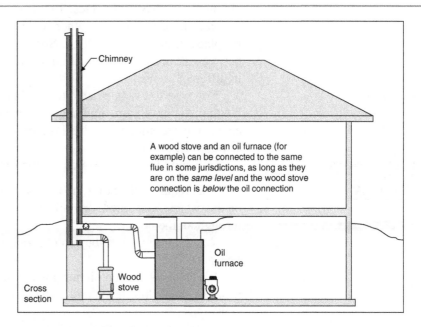

A wood stove and an oil furnace (for example) can be connected to the same flue in some jurisdictions, as long as they are on the *same level* and the wood stove connection is *below* the oil connection

Chimney

Oil furnace

Wood stove

Cross section

the exhaust discharge to face away from the wind. This is supposed to improve the draw and eliminate downdrafts. When they do not swivel, they may **prevent** good draft rather than promote it, especially if they become stuck facing into the wind.

IMPLICATIONS

The implications are poor draft and exhaust gases entering the house.

STRATEGY

Look for rust on the extender, preferably from up close. You may not be able to see it with binoculars from the ground.

If you can get to the chimney, push the extender through 360° to ensure that it rotates freely in both directions. If you can't get to the chimney top you can sometimes see the extender move with wind shifts. If it doesn't move, you can't be conclusive. It may or may not be seized.

Too Many Appliances in One Flue

One Appliance per Flue

Every wood-burning fireplace should have a dedicated flue. Many old houses have two fireplaces on different stories sharing one flue. Back-to-back fireplaces sometimes also share one flue. These are unsafe because the exhaust products from one fireplace can find their way back into the house through the other fireplace.

Seal One Fireplace

Where this condition is found, most inspectors write it up as an immediate safety issue. Many recommend sealing off one of the fireplaces.

Multiple Gas Appliances

Many authorities will permit the connection of two gas appliances to one flue, for example, even if the appliances are on separate floor levels.

Wood Below Oil on Same Floor Level

Wood stoves can sometimes be connected with other appliances to the same flue. Oil fired appliances usually have to be at the same story or floor level. Two oil burning appliances can be on the same flue if they are on the same story. Where a wood stove and an oil-fired furnace, for example, are connected to the same flue, they must be on the same floor and the wood stove connection must be below the oil connection (Figure 11.13). Generally speaking, the heaviest fuel is connected lowest.

Local Rules Vary

These rules vary, depending on location and authority. Sometimes the building code authority and gas utility, for example, are not in agreement. You should know the accepted practices in your working area.

Mutual or Shared Chimneys

In attached row or townhouses, one chimney often serves two dwellings. The chimney may have four flues. Two flues would be for a furnace (or boiler) and a fireplace in one house, the other two flues would be for a furnace (or boiler) and fireplace in the other dwelling. Sometimes these flues are traded back and forth between the houses, sometimes unintentionally. One flue should not serve appliances in different homes.

Tricky Situation

You won't always be able to tell, but be careful with this situation. It's possible that you have more appliances connected to the flue than it seems. Where you are unsure, recommend further investigation. Look up (or down) the chimney as far as possible, for openings.

Fire and life safety hazards are the risks.

IMPLICATIONS

STRATEGY

This requires checking the number and locations of flues (not just chimneys) on the outside, and comparing this with the number, type and location of appliances throughout the house.

Watch for two wood-burning fireplaces on one flue (two gas fireplaces may be all right).

Watch for wood and oil burning appliances sharing a flue (this may be all right if on the same floor level, and if the wood stove enters the chimney below the oil vent).

Watch for a wood-burning fireplace and any other appliance on the same flue (not acceptable).

Call for Help

You may be wise to call for further investigation rather than condemn suspect installations.

Undersized Screen on Spark Arrester

Some chimneys have a screen at the top to prevent sparks or embers escaping and to keep animals and birds out of the chimney. The screen should have openings of at least $^3/_8$ inch.

IMPLICATIONS

STRATEGY

Small screening can easily become clogged with creosote. This can block the chimney, creating a fire and life safety hazard.

Where you see screening at the chimney top, make sure the openings are at least $^3/_8$ inch squares, and check that the screen will not obstruct exhaust gases.

11.3   METAL CHIMNEYS OR VENTS

Metal chimneys and vents are generally characterized by the fuel that they exhaust.

11.3.1   Types of Vents

Gas Burners

Type B vents are designed for natural gas or propane appliances, such as furnaces, boilers and water heaters. They are typically double wall with an air space between. The inner wall may be aluminum or steel and the outer wall is typically galvanized steel (Figure 11.14).

Not Exterior Usually

These units are **not** designed to be exterior chimneys over their entire length unless they are specially approved for such an application. A B vent that runs the entire height of the house outdoors should be checked to ensure that it is approved for this application.

350 °F Normal Temperature

B vents typically see exhaust temperatures of 350°F. They are usually tested for up to roughly 500°F.

FIGURE 11.14   Type "B" Vent

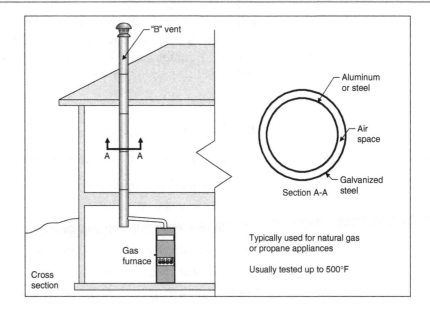

BW Vents

BW vents are oval vents used for wall furnaces. Their construction and function is the same as B vents.

C Vents

C vents are single wall vents, most often used as vent connectors in residential construction. These may be used for gas, oil, or propane. Some areas don't use the term **C vents,** referring to these simply as single wall vents, flues or chimneys.

Gas or Oil Burners

Type L vents are suitable for use with gas, propane, or oil. They can be used instead of a B vent, but a B vent can't be used instead of an L vent. In most cases, L vents are used with oil. Again, this is typically a double wall vent with an air space between. The inner wall is typically stainless steel and the outer wall is galvanized.

Type L vents normally see temperatures of under 750°F. Type L vents are tested for up to 1,000°F.

Indoor Use Only

B vents and L vents can only be used indoors unless they are labeled for exterior use.

Double Wall Insulated

Class A is an obsolete designation for chimneys designed for use with oil and some wood-burning appliances. They can be insulated double-wall chimneys with a stainless steel inner wall and a stainless steel, aluminum or galvanized outer wall. Various insulation materials are used in these chimneys. A 1-inch wall thickness is common.

Triple Wall Uninsulated

These can also be triple wall **uninsulated** chimneys that allow outdoor air to pass between the walls. This **cooling air** prevents overheating of the chimney and nearby combustibles.

Appliance Must Be Approved for Class A Chimney

These chimneys are typically acceptable only for the appliances that they have been tested with. A zero-clearance fireplace, for example, should use only a Class A chimney if it has been tested and approved for use with that specific Class A chimney. Class A chimneys should not be used with wood stoves, furnaces or boilers.

Class A chimneys are rated for 1,000°F continuous use and intermittent temperatures up to 1,400°F.

Factory-Built

650°C Chimneys (Super Chimneys or **629 Chimneys)** are often referred to simply as **factory-built chimneys.** These chimneys are designed for solid fuels and

2-inch Thick Walls

are heavier duty than Class A chimneys. They typically have 2-inch thick insulated walls (sometimes 1-inch), with stainless steel often used as both outer and inner walls. They benefit from a stronger inner liner and more insulation.

These chimneys are tested for up to 2,000°F and are intended to operate at up to 1, 200°F continuously. These are generally required for wood stoves and furnaces, and some factory-built fireplaces.

11.3.2   Conditions

Let's look at some of the common problems with metal chimneys and vents

1. Not labeled for application
2. Sections not well secured
3. Chimney/vent not well supported
4. Inadequate clearance from combustibles
5. Inadequate fire stopping
6. No cap, wrong cap, or obstructed cap
7. Warped, buckled or twisted chimney walls
8. Rusted or pitting
9. Inadequate chimney height
10. Creosote buildup
11. Excessive offset from vertical
12. Not continuous through roof
13. Too many appliances on one flue
14. Adjacent chimneys of different heights

Not Labeled for the Application

With metal vents and chimneys, there are many kinds of equipment on the market. The vent or chimney must be suitable for the fuel and for the appliance that it's used with. For example, a B-vent is not suitable for use with an oil burning appliance, and some wood-burning appliances are not approved for use for Class A chimneys.

IMPLICATIONS

The implication is either fire or life safety, with products of combustion possibly entering the house. Chimneys kill people either by burning the house down or poisoning them with carbon monoxide.

STRATEGY

With metal vents and chimneys, you often find labels that clarify the suitability of the application. Where you can't confirm these, recommend further investigation by a specialist.

Check Data Plate

The appliance data plate may specify what type of vent or chimney is suitable. Look for this plate and follow any clues it provides.

Look for Exterior Use Labels

If a metal chimney runs up the outside of the building, look for labels saying the sections are intended for exterior use. Where you can't be sure, recommend further investigation.

Same Company for All Parts

Look for uniformity of manufacturer on all components. Company X's chimney section should not have Company Y's cap or Company Z's locking bands, for example, in most cases.

Sections Not Well Secured

Because metal vents and chimneys are made of many pieces, each connection is a potential weak spot.

IMPLICATIONS

As we've discussed, the implications are fire and life safety.

STRATEGY

Look at each of the connecting sections. Where they are accessible, you can sometimes test the sections for tightness by pushing, pulling or twisting them. Be careful, they may be hot if they are in use!

Joint Leakage

Look also for evidence of soot or other leakage of combustible products out through joints.

Chimney or Vent Not Well Supported

Chimney sections may fall off the roof and cause damage or injury.

IMPLICATIONS

STRATEGY

Check above Roof Level

It's usually not possible to see how chimneys have been supported as they go up through the house. It is where chimneys project through the roof that support problems usually occur. Any metal chimney taller than 5 feet (or in some cases 6 feet) should be mechanically supported. If you are up on the roof, determine whether a chimney is stable by pushing on it. Be careful not to damage the chimney or push it over, of course. Again, it may be hot!

Supports at Offsets

Supports are required at offsets. These are often not visible, but frequently missing or inadequate. Offsets in chimneys are common problem areas.

Check Bracing

Look for support bars or braces to be well secured at both ends—to the chimney and to the building. Look for loose or corroded supports.

Inadequate Clearance from Combustibles

Combustible clearances for vents and chimneys vary, to some extent, with the manufacturers' recommendations, and the requirements of local authorities. Local authorities can overrule manufacturers' recommendations and call for a greater clearance from combustibles than the manufacturer asks for.

Typical clearances from combustibles are outlined below, although these numbers should be used with caution. Figures should be verified with the individual manufacturers' recommendations and the requirements of local authorities.

B vent	–1 inch
L vent	–1 inch
Class A chimney	–2 to $2^1/_2$ inches
650°C super chimney	–2 inches

STRATEGY

Where the metal vent or chimney is adjacent to the combustible materials, ensure that there are proper stand-offs, thimbles or clearances. There will be many situations where you won't be able to see enough to make a determination in the wall, attic or roof spaces. You can usually get a look where the chimney or vent comes up through the ceiling, into the attic and where it penetrates the roof. Combustible attic insulation (including fiberglass) should be kept 2 inches away from most chimneys.

Clearances Are for Chimney Fires

There are many cases where combustible clearances are not maintained. Although the situation has existed for some years, and people may say that you are overreacting, remember that the clearances are based on emergency situations such as a chimney fire. These are not everyday events, but we don't want to lose the entire house when there is a chimney fire.

Inadequate Fire Stopping

The issues and strategies for this problem are the same as for masonry chimneys.

No Cap, Wrong Cap, or Obstructed Cap

Your clients may ask why masonry chimneys do not always have rain caps, while metal vents and chimneys do. Masonry fireplaces have a smoke shelf that acts as a catch basin for water that comes straight down the chimney. With furnaces and water heaters, the chimney extends down past the vent connector and this, again, acts as a catching area for rainwater that comes straight down.

No Smoke Shelf

Metal chimneys with factory built fireplaces typically have no smoke shelf, so there is no provision to catch rainwater coming down the chimney. The same may be true of boilers and furnaces with metal chimneys. Further, the metal is more prone to rusting and corrosion when wet, especially if there are products of combustion deposited on the inner chimney walls that form acidic compounds when wetted.

Deflects Downdrafts

Another advantage of a rain cap is the deflection of downdrafts. Metal vents and chimneys often draw better than masonry chimneys during adverse wind conditions.

Spark Arrester

For wood-burning appliances, there is usually a spark arrester to prevent burning embers from flying out of the chimney. These are often required by local authorities. The screen size is usually $^3/_8$ to $^1/_2$ inch. (Some consider the $^3/_8$ screening too small because it may be prone to clogging, especially if the chimney is serving a wood-burning appliance.)

Here the implications are—

IMPLICATIONS

- backdraft (spillage)
- moisture entry into the chimney and perhaps the building
- sparks or embers igniting combustibles near the chimney

STRATEGY

If accessible, check that there is a cap in place and that it is secure. Look for birds' nests, creosote or other obvious obstructions at the cap.

Use common sense in judging whether the cap is the right one for the chimney. Does it fit nicely onto the chimney or has it been forced on? Is there a temporary and awkward connection holding it on? Is there a clear passage for products of combustion?

Warped, Buckled, or Twisted Chimney Walls

The implications are fire and life safety.

IMPLICATIONS

STRATEGY

Check the chimney walls anywhere they are exposed, above and below the roofline.

Mirror and Flashlight

You may see interior problems looking up the chimney from the bottom with a flashlight and/or a mirror. Warped or buckled inner walls of metal chimneys or vents are a dangerous situation and, again, immediate action should be recommended.

Rusting or Pitting

Above Roof Section Vulnerable

Rusted or pitted metal chimneys and vents are common, especially on sections above the roofline. B-vents with their galvanized exterior walls have a twenty to thirty year life expectancy, typically. Remember, that unless the B-vent is rated for outdoor use, the entire length of the vent should not be outside running up the exterior of the house. Only the section above the roof surface should be exposed to the elements. This section should be labelled for outdoor use, although the labels are rarely in place.

Early Failures

Some early failures of metal chimneys have been experienced. Corrosion has been found in chimneys serving wood-burning fireplaces less than three years old.

Check Near Roof Level

Insulated Metal Chimneys for Wood

IMPLICATIONS

STRATEGY

Blistering and Discoloring

Check in Attic

This corrosion can occur on the inner or outer walls of the chimney and can occur at any point over the chimney height. In our experience, the most common problem area is just below the point where the chimney penetrates the roof.

This corrosion is common on the insulated metal chimneys used for wood burning appliances. Any corrosion should be identified in your report as a significant safety concern. Recommend further investigation.

The implications are a fire hazard or life safety caused by exhaust gases being trapped in the house.

Check the chimney wherever accessible for corrosion. If you get up on the roof, look at the parts of the chimney above the roof level. Pay particular attention to the cap and to the flashing area where the chimney penetrates the roof.

Blistering paint and discolored metal on the chimney shells are indications of corrosion and possible overheating. Recommend further investigation.

In some cases, metal chimneys are exposed in the attic. If you can access the chimney here, look for rusting just below the roofline, in particular, but check all visible surfaces.

On some appliances, you can look up at the inner wall from below. Remember, this problem can be on relatively new chimneys.

Inadequate Chimney Height

As general rules—

1. B vents should be at least

    ▓ 1 foot above a roof with a slope up to 6-in-12

    ▓ 2 feet above a roof with a slope up to 9-in-12

    ▓ 4 feet above a roof with a slope up to 12-in-12

2. L vents should be at least 2 feet above the roof

3. Metal chimneys for wood-burning appliances should be at least 3 feet above the roof

All of these should also be at least 2 feet higher than anything within 10 feet of the chimney, horizontally.

Poor draft is the major implication here.

IMPLICATIONS

STRATEGY

Check the chimney heights. You'll have to know what fuel is being used and the specific height restrictions in your area. Don't forget to check that the chimney is two feet taller than anything within ten feet horizontally.

Check also that vents or chimneys extend at least 5 feet above draft hoods for gas appliances. Oil burner chimneys should be at least 11 feet tall. Fireplaces and wood stoves need chimneys that are at least 15 feet tall, measured from the top of the appliance.

Creosote Buildup

The issues and strategies for this problem are the same as for masonry chimneys.

Excessive Offset from Vertical

The issues and strategies for this problem are the same as for masonry chimneys.

Not Continuous through Roof

Generally speaking, it is poor practice to have a metal chimney connect to a masonry chimney (Figure 11.15). This presents a problem for inspection and cleaning, in most cases.

F I G U R E 11.15   Metal Chimney Not Continuous through Roof

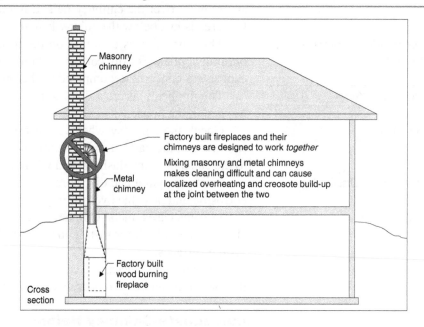

Masonry chimney

Factory built fireplaces and their chimneys are designed to work *together*

Mixing masonry and metal chimneys makes cleaning difficult and can cause localized overheating and creosote build-up at the joint between the two

Metal chimney

Factory built wood burning fireplace

Cross section

IMPLICATIONS

The implications are—

- inspection and cleaning are difficult
- localized creosote build-ups
- poor connections may result in overheating
- leakage may occur at the joint between the metal and the masonry

STRATEGY

Where you find such an arrangement, recommend further investigation by a specialist. Unless you have special knowledge, this is a difficult area to make a decision. At best, this is a marginal situation.

Too Many Appliances on One Flue

The comments we made with respect to masonry chimneys apply to metal chimneys and vents as well.

Adjacent Chimneys of Different Heights

IMPLICATIONS

*Rain Cap Directs
Exhaust Sideways*

STRATEGY

Metal chimneys and vents always have a rain cap. This means that the hot exhaust can contact the adjacent chimney wall. This may overheat and damage the adjacent chimney. It may also lead to condensation on the adjacent chimney, especially when the adjacent one is idle. This can lead to corrosion.

When you see adjacent metal chimneys or vents, check the relative heights. Where one is shorter, check the taller one for damage. Even if none is visible, let your client know of the possible problem. This situation should be monitored.

F I G U R E 11.16   Wood Burning Fireplaces

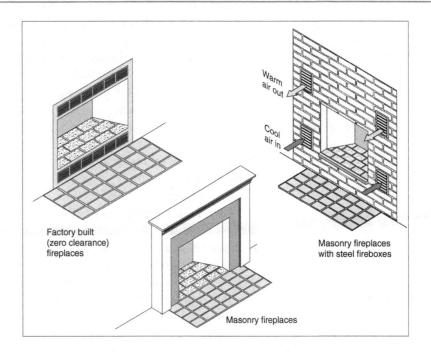

Warm
air out

Cool
air in

Factory built
(zero clearance)
fireplaces

Masonry fireplaces
with steel fireboxes

Masonry fireplaces

11.4   WOOD-BURNING FIREPLACES

Wood Has Been a Fuel for a Long Time

Wood was one of the very early fuels used by humans. In some parts of North America, wood remains a primary source of fuel. In other areas, wood is a secondary or supplemental fuel source.

Wood is also popular for fireplaces. These are **recreational devices** rather than heating appliances in most cases.

A discussion of wood-burning heating methods such as stoves, furnaces, and boilers is beyond the scope of this book. For a thorough discussion, see *Principles of Home Inspection: Chimneys and Wood Heating*. Because fireplaces are very popular in homes, we will focus on them here.

Want Warm Chimneys

Since combustion of wood in fireplaces is rarely 100% complete, we want warm chimneys so that we can minimize the condensation of any unburned gases. If we can keep the gases in a vapor state until they leave the chimney, they won't condense on the chimney walls and cool to form **creosote** deposits.

Cleaning Required

Creosote build-ups have to be removed from chimneys, vent pipes and furnace heat exchangers, on a regular basis.

Life Safety

Experience has shown that wood appliances are more prone to burning homes down than gas or oil appliances. Some of the problems that lead to fires include—

■   poor installation

■   poor quality equipment (not test and listed or certified)

■   overfiring of appliances

■   inappropriate fuels

■   poor maintenance and cleaning

We will look at masonry and factory-built fireplaces (Figure 11.16).

Masonry Fireplaces

Masonry fireplaces are simple. The majority of the components are masonry, including the firebox. The damper is metal and some of the other accessories may be metal. The hearth, foundation and footing are usually concrete or masonry.

Masonry Fireplace, Steel Firebox

Some masonry fireplaces are built with a **steel firebox.** The firebox usually has an integral **damper** and **smoke chamber** as part of the manufactured unit. Steel fireboxes are usually double wall with air circulating between the two walls. Heat circulation (heating room air by passing it through the double walls) is a common feature of steel fireboxes.

Steel Fireboxes Cooler than Masonry

Because of the double wall and air circulation feature, steel fireboxes operate at lower temperatures than masonry fireboxes. This is unfortunate in one sense, because less heat radiates directly into the living space. We may get this back with a good heat circulation system. This may also result in a cooler, slower burning fire because of the cooler firebox walls.

Factory-Built Fireplaces

Factory-built fireplaces, or **zero clearance fireplaces** as they are often called, are less expensive than masonry fireplaces. No footing or foundation is necessary. As their name suggests, the sides and back don't need any clearance from combustibles. The firebox is typically a double wall configuration and air is used to cool the fireplace. Some have insulation to help keep the unit cool.

Listed or Certified

These units must be listed and/or certified as a complete assembly by a recognized testing agency.

Built-In or Free Standing

Factory-built fireplaces can be built into a wall and can look, at first glance, like a masonry fireplace. They can also be freestanding units placed in the center of a room.

Function

Wood-burning fireplaces are basically entertainment devices. They don't add a lot of heat to a home, typically. Many fireplaces actually consume more heat than they provide. If a homeowner is interested in wood as a heating source, a wood stove is a better choice.

Components of Masonry Fireplaces

Masonry fireplaces have the following main components:

1. A footing and foundation
2. A front hearth and back hearth
3. A firebox
4. A damper
5. A throat, smoke shelf and smoke chamber
6. A mantel (face)
7. A chimney (including flue, flue liner and cap).

In addition, you may find the following accessories on fireplaces:

1. Outdoor combustion air
2. Glass doors
3. Heat circulator
4. Gas igniter
5. Ashpit

Components of Factory-Built Fireplaces

Factory-built fireplaces do not need a footing and foundation. They include a hearth but do not have a hearth extension as an integral part of the fireplace. A hearth extension should be provided. They also generally do not have a **smoke shelf** or **smoke chamber.** The throat is an integral part of the firebox sloping up to a damper. The damper connects directly to the metal chimney. Factory-built fireplaces typically do not have an ashpit. The chimney is typically metal.

Combustible Clearances

Combustible clearances around fireplaces are a big issue (Figure 11.17). The rules vary depending on the area that you are working in. As we look at the individual components, we'll talk more about combustible clearances, but let's look at some rough rules for masonry fireplaces.

General Rules

Combustibles should be kept—

- 6 inches from fireplace openings

- 12 inches from fireplace openings if the combustible material sticks out $1^1/_2$ inches from the face

- 4 inches from the firebox (depends on a number of things, including the material used for the firebox. Note: some areas require 8 inch thick walls).

- 2 inches from chimneys (can be as little as $^1/_2$ inch)

- 2 to 9 inches away from outside combustion air inlet ducts (depending on jurisdiction)

Tough to Know

You won't be able to determine whether or not combustible clearances are adequate in many places. You should however, check those that are accessible.

Clearances Different for Factory-Builts

The clearance numbers listed above are typical for masonry fireplaces. Factory-built fireplaces are different and in many cases, zero clearance is acceptable.

Need Clearance at Top of Firebox

Although you won't be able to inspect this in most cases, a common problem with zero clearance fireplaces is inadequate clearance at the **top of the firebox.** The top of the fireplace is almost always enclosed behind room finishes.

Construction Debris

This part of the fireplace needs a clearance from combustibles that varies with each manufacturer. Construction debris that falls onto the top of the fireplace during finishing operations can be a problem. You won't usually be able to see if this is a problem.

Fire Safety

It is good practice to have a smoke detector where there is a wood-burning fireplace. Some jurisdictions also require a carbon monoxide detector.

Fire Extinguisher

A water-based fire extinguisher suitable for use on wood fires should be kept in each room with a fireplace.

Draft Problems

Basement fireplaces, particularly those on exterior walls, are notorious for poor draft. The more complex the fireplace arrangement, the more likely draft problems are to be experienced. Watch for (Figure 11.18)—

- fireplaces with alcoves to store wood

- fireplaces that back onto other fireplaces or barbecues

- fireplaces with dramatic offsets where they connect to the chimney (particularly if the back wall of the smoke chamber has an offset)

Smoke and Soot on the Mantel, Mantel Shelf, and Ceiling

Where there is smoke and soot above the front of a fireplace, you may conclude that there is a draft problem with the fireplace. This may or may not be true. The same condition results from starting a fire with the damper closed, or not establishing a good draft in the chimney before lighting a fire. Based on a one time visit, it is difficult to know whether this condition is chronic or the result of a one-time error.

Failures Are Serious

Obviously a fireplace that does not do its job is a life safety issue. If the fire is not contained, the house can be lost and people can be killed.

Let's look more closely at the individual components and the problems that can occur with them.

F I G U R E   11.17   Combustible Clearance Requirements for Fireplaces

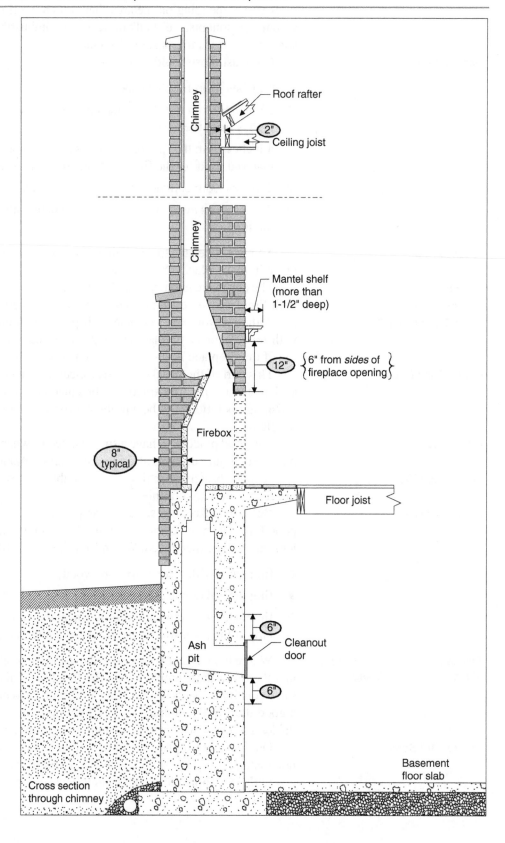

FIGURE 11.18   Problematic Fireplace Designs

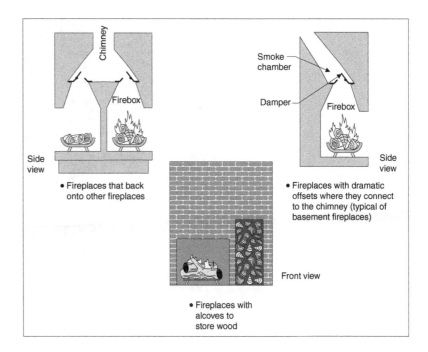

11.4.1   Hearth

Terminology

The fireplace **hearth** is both the floor of the firebox and the floor extension in front of the fireplace. Different terminology is used in different areas. Some people call the **hearth** the floor of the firebox and call the **hearth extension** the part out front. Other people call the part in the firebox the **inner hearth** and the part outside the firebox the **outer hearth.** Still others refer to the part in the firebox as the **back hearth** and the part that extends in front of the firebox as the **front hearth.**

Function

The hearth is designed to contain the fire from below. The part inside the firebox has the fire resting directly on it. There may or may not be a grate inside the firebox. In either case, the hearth has to withstand the direct heat of the fire and embers.

The hearth extension is typically cooler. Its function is to protect combustible flooring from logs that roll out of the fireplace or embers and sparks.

Materials

Inside the firebox, the hearth surface is typically 1 or 2 inch thick **firebrick** (also called **refractory brick**) made to withstand high heat and thermal shock (Figure 11.19). Outside the firebox, the hearth surface may be firebrick, brick, slate, marble, ceramic tile or any other noncombustible material. Both sections of the hearth below the surfacing should be at least 4 inches thick if the hearth is concrete.

Hearth Extension Construction

The front part of the hearth does not sit on the fireplace foundation. It is typically supported on concrete poured on forming boards (e.g., planks, plywood or waferboard). Forming boards should be removed after the concrete has cured. It is considered a fire hazard to leave these in place, although we see this done regularly.

Hearth Extension Dimensions

In many areas, the hearth must extend at least 16 inches out in front of the firebox and 8 inches on either side. In some areas, if the fireplace opening is more than 6 square feet, the hearth must extend 20 inches out in front of the firebox and 12 inches out on either side.

F I G U R E 11.19   Hearth Materials

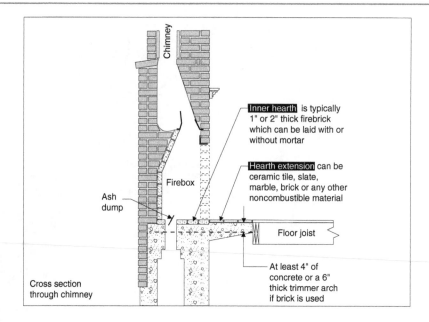

Inner hearth is typically 1" or 2" thick firebrick which can be laid with or without mortar

Hearth extension can be ceramic tile, slate, marble, brick or any other noncombustible material

Chimney

Firebox

Ash dump

Floor joist

At least 4" of concrete or a 6" thick trimmer arch if brick is used

Cross section through chimney

Raised Hearths

Where the fireplace is located above floor level and the hearth extension is at floor level, it is good practice to extend the hearth further. Because the fireplace is raised, embers and sparks that escape from the fireplace can be expected to travel further horizontally before they hit the floor below.

Noncombustible Face Below Firebox

In some cases, the face of the wall below the firebox and above the hearth is combustible. We consider this poor practice and recommend a noncombustible treatment where we see this.

Factory-Built Fireplaces

Factory-built fireplaces do not require a 4 inch thick hearth or hearth extension. A noncombustible hearth extension can typically be installed directly onto a wood floor. Again, a metal strip to stop sparks from getting between the wall and hearth extension is recommended, although not often visible (Figure 11.20).

Common problems with hearths include the following:

1. Too small
2. Gaps or cracks
3. Settled
4. Inappropriate material
5. Wood forms not removed
6. Too thin
7. Evidence of overheating

Too Small

We talked about the minimum dimensions for a hearth extension. Many hearth extensions for coal burning fireplaces were smaller than this. Where the fireplace is being used for wood, the hearth should be extended.

IMPLICATIONS

This is a fire hazard.

STRATEGY

Check that the hearth dimensions are adequate.

F I G U R E 11.20   Hearth Extension for Factory-Built Fireplaces

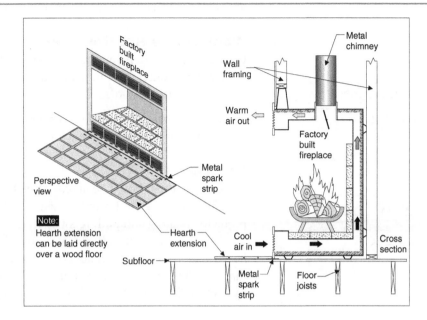

Gaps or Cracks

IMPLICATIONS

Gaps or cracks in the hearth can allow embers to get too close to combustibles. This is a fire hazard.

STRATEGY

Look for gaps or cracks in the hearth or hearth extension and recommend that they be filled. A common crack location is where the hearth joins the hearth extension.

Settled

It is common for the hearth extension to drop relative to the hearth.

IMPLICATION

When the hearth extension settles relative to the hearth, again gaps can develop that may allow embers where they shouldn't be. This is a fire hazard.

STRATEGY

Look for evidence of movement of the hearth extension relative to the hearth. You can check both at the fireplace and below, where there is access from a basement or subgrade area.

Inappropriate Material

The hearth and hearth extension should be noncombustible. The hearth itself should be firebrick. Common brick will deteriorate over time.

IMPLICATIONS

This is a fire hazard.

STRATEGY

Make sure that the floor of the fireplace is firebrick. If it appears to be common brick, recommend inspection by a specialist.

Hearth Extension

Check that the hearth extension is a noncombustible material. If it is combustible, recommend replacement. One of the details that doesn't break this rule but can be dangerous is a noncombustible material surrounded by wood trim. Where the wood trim at the perimeter of noncombustible hearth extension extends above the surface of the extension, embers can be caught by the trim and get into the gap between the trim and hearth extension. This can create a fire hazard. It is better to have the hearth extension flush with or slightly above the flooring. If an ember or spark gets beyond the hearth extension, it's readily apparent. This is a minor point, but may be worth pointing out.

Combustible Wall Face

On raised hearths, watch for combustible wall surfaces below the hearth and above the hearth extension. We recommend that these be noncombustible.

Wood Forms Not Removed

Once the hearth extension has been poured and set, the wood forming boards should be removed from below. In many cases, they are not.

IMPLICATION

This is a fire hazard.

STRATEGY

Check where accessible from below to ensure that wood forms have been removed from the hearth extension.

Too Thin

Concrete hearths should be at least 4 inches thick.

IMPLICATIONS

This can be a fire hazard. A hearth extension that is not thick enough may be prone to cracking and pulling away from the firebox.

STRATEGY

Where visible (usually from below the firebox), check the thickness of the hearth extension. The thickness of the hearth itself is not usually visible. If it is less than 4 inches for concrete (or 6 inches for brick), recommend further investigation by a specialist. Look for evidence of charred wood around the hearth.

Evidence of Overheating

This is a fire hazard.

IMPLICATIONS

STRATEGY

Check below and around the firebox for evidence of charring of combustible materials. Any discoloration of wood close to a fireplace, ashpit, hearth or chimney should be considered a significant indication of a fire hazard.

11.4.2   Firebox

Function

The firebox is the part of the fireplace that contains the fire. It has to be able to withstand the temperatures of the fire. This includes not only the flames, but the bed of hot embers that sits on the fireplace floor for several hours at a time.

Radiate Heat

Good fireboxes help to radiate the heat back into the living space. That is why the side walls of fireboxes are usually sloped inward, and the upper part of the back wall is sloped or curved forward.

Promote Draft

The firebox opening size, shape and depth all have an impact on how well the fireplace draws. Some codes require that the firebox depth be a minimum of 20 inches front to back, other codes require a 12 inch minimum depth. You should know if there is a requirement in your area, and follow it.

Firebrick on Walls

In masonry fireplaces, the walls are typically lined with 2 to 4 inches thick firebrick. Refractory mortar is used for setting the firebrick. This mortar sets very hard, resists high temperatures and is very strong.

Common Brick Not Ideal

Common brick is not recommended for use in fireboxes although you may see it. Watch carefully for deterioration of this kind of brick and recommend further inspection by a specialist.

No Hollow Bricks

Most authorities do not allow the use of hollow bricks in the firebox. Bricks with cores should not be used. You usually won't know.

Wall Thickness

Some codes require 8 inch thickness for the walls of the firebox. In some cases, only the back walls have to be 8 inches thick. Some areas require 10 inch walls if a firebrick liner isn't used. You won't usually know.

F I G U R E 11.21   Metal Firebox Clearance

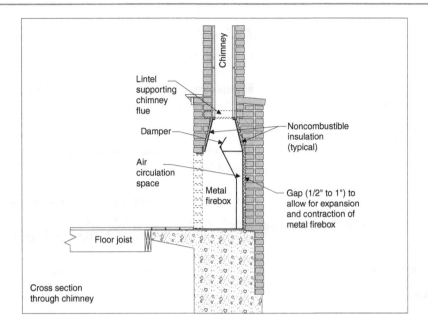

Cross section
through chimney

Metal Firebox Clearance

Metal fireboxes should be **¹/₂ inch to 1 inch away from masonry** (Figure 11.21). This allows the metal to expand and contract without buckling or damaging the masonry. The gap is usually filled with non-combustible insulation. You'll usually see some of this.

Liner Resting on Metal Firebox

One of the common mistakes made with metal fireboxes is that the bottom of the clay tile chimney liner rests directly on the firebox. The liner should rest on masonry or separate steel lintels. The firebox should be clear of the liner so that it won't crack when the firebox expands.

Lintel

The lintel at the front of the fireplace supports the face or breast of the fireplace. It is usually a piece of heavy L-shaped iron or steel. It will expand and contract as the fireplace is in use. It should able to expand without cracking the masonry. Cracks in the face of masonry fireplaces are often the result of lintels that have been installed too tightly. Lintels typically rest on 4 inches of masonry at either end.

Masonry Arch

Lintels aren't the only way to support the fireplace breast. There are also masonry arches, although these are less common.

Factory-Built Fireplace Fireboxes

Fireboxes in factory-built fireplaces often have a thin refractory material in front of the metal. Some of these are made to look like firebrick. These facings often crack and most can be replaced easily (as long as the company is still in business). Some manufacturers say that minor cracking is acceptable and suggest replacement only if serious cracking develops or if pieces are missing. We recommend that you report any cracking refractory in factory-built fireplaces.

Let's look at some of the common firebox problems that we see.

1.   Masonry or mortar loose, missing or deteriorated

2.   Masonry or refractory cracked

3.   Rustout, burnout, buckled or cracked metal fireboxes

4.   Inappropriate materials

5. Designed for coal
6. Too shallow
7. Lintels rusted, sagging or loose
8. Draft suspect

Masonry or Mortar Loose, Missing, or Deteriorated

This can be a fire hazard.

IMPLICATIONS

STRATEGY

Check that all of the masonry and mortar is intact. Tap on the walls of the firebox with the handle of a flashlight or screwdriver. Pay particular attention to the sloped back walls. Listen for a hollow sound and watch for loose brick or mortar.

Masonry or Refractory Cracked

Where individual masonry units or the refractory in a factory-built fireplace is cracked, the integrity of the firebox is in question. Recommend further evaluation by a specialist.

IMPLICATIONS

Again, this may be a fire hazard.

STRATEGY

Check the firebox to ensure that the masonry and/or refractory is tight and intact.

Rustout, Burnout, Buckled, or Cracked Metal Firebox

All of these can be a fire hazard.

IMPLICATIONS

STRATEGY

Use a flashlight to look carefully at the firebox. The rear walls are the most likely to buckle. The welded joints at corners may be vulnerable to cracking. Check carefully along these joints. Where the fireplace is filled with ashes and/or partially burned logs, note this limitation in your report.

Inappropriate Materials

The typical inappropriate material is common brick in a masonry fireplace.

As the brick deteriorates, it may create a fire hazard.

IMPLICATIONS

STRATEGY

Identifying Firebrick

Where common brick is observed, recommend further investigation. Firebrick is often yellow and has a smoother, more dense surface than common brick. The corners of firebrick are often sharper than the rounded corners of common brick. It may take some experience and a few samples, but you should be able to differentiate between firebrick and common brick with practice.

Designed for Coal

Shallow Cast Iron Firebox

Coal burning fireplaces are disappearing from North America. They were typically very shallow fireboxes, often made entirely of cast iron. The width and height of coal fireplaces is less than a typical wood-burning fireplace. Although the temperature of burning coal is higher than wood, the configuration of coal burning fireplaces is often not ideal for wood. Hearth extensions are often undersized as well.

Coal fireplaces may not be safe for burning wood.

IMPLICATIONS

STRATEGY

Where a coal fireplace is identified, recommend that it not be used for burning wood unless a specialist inspects it and makes any necessary modifications.

Firebox Too Shallow

Rumford

Designers such as Count Rumford had intentionally shallow, tall fireboxes to get more heat into the living space. Rumford and other specialty fireplaces often have shallower fireboxes than allowed by current rules.

IMPLICATION

These fireplaces are not allowed in some areas regardless of how well and safely they work.

STRATEGY

There is a school of thought that says that fireplaces should be much more shallow than the conventionally designed fireplace. The problem is that most building authorities do not accept shallow fireboxes. Let your client know that this may be a controversial issue and a specialist should provide further advice.

Lintel Rusted, Sagging, or Loose

IMPLICATIONS

The implications of a weak lintel are collapse of the fireplace face. This is rare, but something you would not be excused for overlooking.

STRATEGY

You'll have to get down on your hands and knees and look up to see the lintel. Look for rust and sagging. Sagging is often accompanied by cracking in the face of the fireplace. Push on the lintel with a screwdriver or other tool to ensure that it is intact. If you grab the lintel with your hand, you will usually have to wash your hand immediately.

Draft Suspect

While an evaluation of the draft is beyond our scope, many of you will feel compelled to advise the client that you don't think the chimney will draw very well.

IMPLICATIONS

The implications of poor fireplace draw can be a life safety issue, especially if the fireplace draws well for a while, then people go to sleep while the fire dies down. A slow burning fire may suffer poor draft allowing products of combustion, including carbon monoxide, back into the home.

STRATEGY

Where you see evidence of poor draft (soot on mantels, faces and ceilings) let your client know about your suspicions. You should also point out that this may be simply the result of accidentally starting a fire with the damper closed. Where you see design configurations that make you suspicious, recommend further investigation. Don't be conclusive with respect to draft.

11.4.3   Damper

Function

The damper is located at the top of the firebox (Figure 11.22). It is designed to allow exhaust products to leave the house when the fireplace is operating and to prevent cold air from entering (or warm air from leaving) the house when the fireplace is idle. Most dampers have to open to 90% of their full area.

Firebox Dampers

Fireplace dampers are usually hinged at the back or the middle. Some are operated with an external handle. Others have a handle inside the firebox.

Damper at Top of Chimney

Some fireplace dampers are located at the top of the chimney rather than at the top of the firebox. This is often done to alleviate draft problems. These systems are usually controlled by chains or cables that hang down in the fireplace. Pivoting-type dampers at the top of the chimney should be located below the top of the flue, even when open. If they project above the flue, they can attract downdrafts. These dampers should be arranged so that they will fail in the open position, so they don't block the chimney accidentally.

Opening Area

Good dampers have the same cross-sectional area as the flue itself. Some jurisdictions require that the damper be as wide as the firebox opening.

F I G U R E 11.22   Firebox Damper

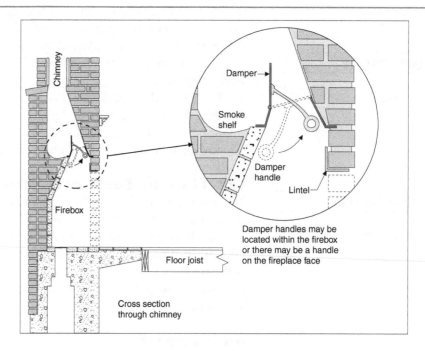

Common damper problems include the following:

1. Missing
2. Inoperative or obstructed
3. Damper or frame rusted
4. Frame loose
5. Too low
6. Undersized

Damper Missing

IMPLICATIONS

The implications are heat loss and downdraft. A missing damper will allow heat to escape up the chimney all the time. Most dampers are also designed to deflect downdrafts coming down the chimney. This isn't true in many factory-built fireplaces, but is true in most masonry fireplaces and masonry fireplaces with a metal firebox. Poor draft may result.

STRATEGY

Make sure there is a damper.

Inoperative or Obstructed

IMPLICATIONS

If the damper cannot be closed, it is a heat loss and possible draft issue. If the damper can't be opened, obviously the fireplace is not operable.

STRATEGY

Operate the damper and make sure that it stays open. Many dampers tend to fall closed. Some fall out of position after you operate them.

Open Carefully

When opening a damper, make sure that debris does not fall into the fireplace. If debris comes down, you should close the damper quickly. Sometimes the debris is dead birds or animals. A more serious problem is a live animal. Opening the damper can allow squirrels, birds, raccoons, et cetera into a home.

Flashlight

Use your flashlight and look up at the damper while you are opening and closing it. Many dampers have to sit in exactly the right position in their frame to function properly. It is easy to accidentally dislodge a damper when testing it.

Damper or Frame Rusted

The damper may be inoperative or may fall out of place.

IMPLICATIONS
STRATEGY

Be Careful Looking Up

When you operate the damper, look at it with a flashlight. Look for evidence of anything more than surface rust.

When you are looking up into a firebox from below, and especially when you are operating the damper, make sure that debris doesn't fall into your eyes. Keep your head slightly out of the firebox or wear protective eyewear. Many inspectors operate the damper slowly without looking up into the firebox at first. Once the damper has moved slightly, they will put their head into the firebox to get a better look, but try not to put their head right under the opening.

Frame Loose

The damper may fall out of place, the damper may be difficult to operate or there may be considerable heat loss up the chimney even when the damper is closed.

IMPLICATIONS
STRATEGY

Check that the frame is tight when you operate the damper. Many people use the damper handle to try to move the frame. You can also use a screwdriver or other tool. If you touch the frame or damper handle with your hand, you are going to want to wash it right away, otherwise you will make a mess of everything else you touch in the house.

Damper Too Low

Many fireplace experts recommend that the damper be at least 8 inches above the bottom of the breast.

IMPLICATION
STRATEGY

This can affect the draw of the fireplace. Smoke may come out through the front of the firebox rather than go up the chimney.

Check the damper height relative to the breast and note if it is too low. In some cases, there may not be a performance implication. As we discussed earlier, some fireplaces that shouldn't draw work perfectly well, and vice versa. Again, avoid conclusions.

Undersized

This may result in poor draft.

IMPLICATIONS
STRATEGY

Where the damper is smaller than the cross-sectional area of the flue (don't measure this, a rough visual estimate is good enough), there may be some draft implications. You don't want to be conclusive, but you can mention that the damper seems small and in some cases there may be draft problems. This can often be overcome by keeping the fire small. Leave it up to a specialist to advise further.

11.4.4   Throat, Smoke Shelf, and Smoke Chamber

Function

Many people believe that this is the most critical part of a fireplace (Figure 11.23). The function is to take the exhaust gases from the large firebox and direct them into the relatively small chimney flue. The goal is to gently compress the exhaust gases without creating backdraft. If it works well, we accelerate the exhaust gases up into the chimney and help to promote good draft. If we don't do it well, we end up with smoke in the house.

F I G U R E   11.23   Throat, Smoke Shelf, and Smoke Chamber

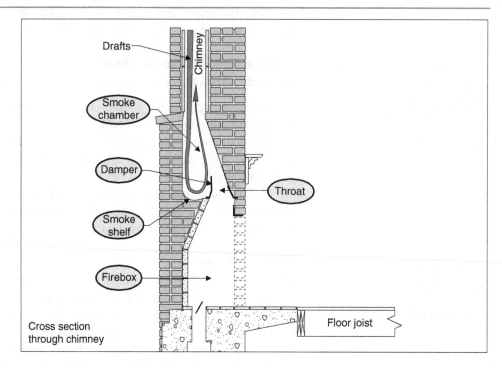

The **throat** is the top of the firebox below and at the damper. The **smoke shelf** is the area behind the damper that is nearly level. It is the bottom of the chimney. The **smoke chamber** is the sloping section of the fireplace above the damper and throat, but below the chimney flue. Typically, the sides and front of the smoke chamber slope. The back of the smoke chamber is usually vertical. This varies.

The throat, smoke shelf and smoke chamber are typically masonry, although the smoke chamber is not usually firebrick.

Factory-built Fireplaces

Factory-built fireplaces do not usually have a smoke shelf or smoke chamber above the damper. Since most of these fireplaces draw quite nicely, the need for a smoke shelf is questionable. It is, however, a standard part of most masonry fireplaces.

Wall Thickness and Slope

The walls of the smoke chamber may have a minimum required thickness of 6 inches. Some jurisdictions do not allow any hollow units. In some cases, the wall thickness has to be 8 inches. A maximum slope for the sides and front is 45° off vertical. Many say that 30° is a much better arrangement and may be required if the smoke chamber is corbelled brick. Good design typically involves the smoke chamber front and both side walls having equal slopes. When the flue is offset to one side of the fireplace or the other, the smoke chamber wall slope has to be asymmetric. This contributes to poor draft, especially if one side of the smoke chamber is vertical and the other has a dramatic slope.

Smooth Walls, Sloped Back

The walls of the smoke chamber should be as smooth as possible. Corbelled brick is not smooth and may contribute to draft problems. Draft problems also can occur when the back wall of the chamber has to be sloped.

Smoke Shelf

The smoke shelf is sometimes flat or almost flat. In other cases it is concave at the bottom, shaped like a cup. Most have a slight slope toward the damper. Part of the thinking is that downdrafts can be stopped and redirected so that they will actually become updrafts and help to improve the overall draft. The absence of a smoke shelf in zero clearance fireplaces may suggest that this theory is flawed.

Let's look at some of the problems we might find with throats, smoke shelves and smoke chambers.

1. Missing
2. Debris
3. Excess slope
4. Uneven slope
5. Wood forms not removed
6. Walls not smooth
7. Rust (metal firebox or factory-built fireplace)

Missing

Masonry fireplaces that do not have a smoke shelf or smooth throat in smoke chamber may suggest amateurish workmanship.

IMPLICATION

Poor draft is the possible implication.

STRATEGY

Look above the damper for evidence of a smoke shelf and look at the walls of the smoke chamber if possible. A mirror may be required with your flashlight here. In many cases, you will find the arrangement less than ideal. However, where there is wide departure from good practice, you should mention the possibility of draft problems, again, without being conclusive.

Debris

A lot of debris may accumulate on the smoke shelf. We talked earlier about being careful opening the damper.

IMPLICATIONS

This can affect draft and can create a mess in the firebox when opening the damper.

STRATEGY

Open the damper carefully and watch that debris does not fall. With a mirror and flashlight you will see any debris behind the damper on the smoke shelf and recommend cleaning.

Recommend Inspection and Sweeping

Any wood-burning fireplace should be inspected (and swept if necessary) before a new homeowner uses it. Because of the life safety issues, we strongly recommend having fireplaces and chimneys checked by specialists.

Excess Slope

Where the sides or front wall of the smoke chamber are more than 45° off vertical, you might be suspicious about the draft.

IMPLICATION

Poor draft is the risk here.

STRATEGY

Check that the front and side slopes have no more of an offset than 45° from the vertical. Where the back wall of the smoke chamber is sloped, again raise a question about draft.

Uneven Slope

Draft problems are the possible result.

IMPLICATIONS

STRATEGY

Check that the two sides of the smoke chamber have similar slopes. Where one is straight and the other has a dramatic slope, the draft may be poor. Again, you cannot be definitive, but it is all contributory.

F I G U R E 11.24   Smoke Chamber Forms Must Be Removed

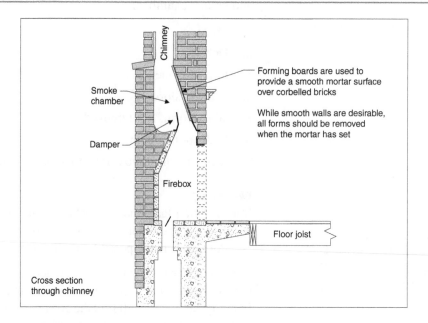

Wood Forms Not Removed

As the smoke chamber is formed, wood may be used above the damper. In new construction, you may be surprised to see wood above. These are usually forming boards (Figure 11.24). They should be taken out when the concrete has cured.

IMPLICATION

This may be a fire hazard, although in most cases, it is not an issue. The wood forms may come loose and jam the damper open or closed.

STRATEGY

When you open the damper and look up at the smoke chamber, look for wood. Where wood is seen, recommend that it be removed.

Walls Not Smooth

Corbelled, rough-surfaced smoke chamber walls are common, but may contribute to draft problems.

IMPLICATION

Poor draft is the implication.

STRATEGY

Where you see rough-surfaced smoke chamber walls, advise your client that this is one other issue that can contribute to draft problems. Don't recommend remedial action based solely on this condition.

Rust

IMPLICATION

The implication is fire hazard.

STRATEGY

As you look at the firebox, use your flashlight and look at the top of the firebox around the damper. When the damper is open, look at the base of the chimney where it joins the firebox for evidence of rust.

11.4.5   Face or Breast

Function

The face (breast) of the fireplace forms the front wall of the chimney and forms the top of the fireplace opening. The face typically extends on either side of the fireplace opening as well. The section above the firebox is supported on the lintel.

F I G U R E   11.25   Settled (Gap at Wall)

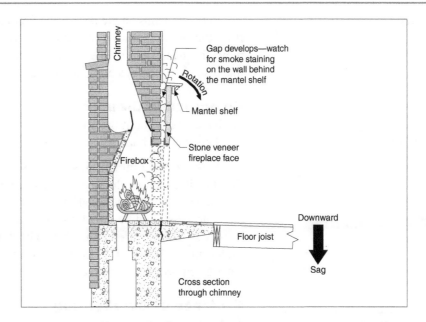

Gap develops—watch
for smoke staining
on the wall behind
the mantel shelf

Rotation

Mantel shelf

Stone veneer
fireplace face

Chimney

Firebox

Downward

Floor joist

Sag

Cross section
through chimney

Too Thick

The breast is typically 4 inches thick. Thicker breasts are sometime criticized as being a source of poor draft.

Let's look at some of the common problems.

1. Cracked

2. Settled (gap at wall)

3. Loose

4. Combustible clearances

5. Evidence of overheating

6. Too thick

Cracked

In most cases, the implications are purely cosmetic. Where the crack goes into the firebox, there is a path for combustion products to get to combustibles. Wood frame walls are often enclosed in the face above the firebox.

Cracked faces may also result from settlement. Other settlement cracks are usually visible in the firebox, chimney or foundation. Where the crack is wider than $1/16$ inch, look for movement of the fireplace relative to surrounding walls and floors.

Settled (Gap at Wall)

It is common for the face to settle and pull away from the house wall (Figure 11.25).

Where there is movement here, exhaust products may be able to escape from the firebox and create a fire hazard.

Look at the joint between the face and the house wall for evidence of movement. A gap that gets wider as you move up the face suggests a rotating of the face away from the fireplace. This may be a result of deflection of the wood floor joists below. This problem is often associated with large, heavy hearth extensions or firewood storage on the floor joists.

IMPLICATIONS

STRATEGY

This may be a fire hazard or the mantel may fall off the face.

Put your hands on the face of the fireplace and try to move it side to side or away from the firebox. Grab it at shoulder level, rather than near the floor level. Try to move the mantel and/or shelf with moderate pressure. Don't use excessive force but make sure that the system is not in danger of falling off the wall.

Combustible Clearances

We have talked about the 6 inch rule.

IMPLICATIONS

STRATEGY

This is a fire hazard.

A Variation

Make sure combustibles are 6 inches away from the fireplace opening. Combustibles above the opening that project more than $1\frac{1}{2}$ inches from the face should be at least 12 inches above the opening. For every $\frac{1}{8}$ inch out from the face, the material should be 1 inch higher than the opening. For example, anything that sticks out 1 inch from the face has to be 8 inches above the opening. Anything that sticks out $1\frac{1}{2}$ inches from the face has to be 12 inches above the opening. Find out what is required in your area.

Evidence of Overheating

This may be a fire hazard.

IMPLICATIONS

STRATEGY

Look for evidence of charring, discoloration or soot and smoke deposits. If the fireplace is operating, use your hand around the face of the opening to get a sense of the temperature.

Too Thick

If the breast of the fireplace is thicker than 6 inches, there may be a draft implication.

IMPLICATION

STRATEGY

Check the breast thickness. Where it is thicker than 6 inches, advise the client that this is one possible contributor to poor draft. It does not necessarily mean that the fireplace will not draw well.

11.4.6   Outdoor Combustion Air

In the 1970s, supplying outdoor combustion air for fireplaces became popular (Figure 11.26). This was done to make fireplaces more efficient, and because modern tighter construction made it harder to supply air to fireplaces. Some jurisdictions require a separate combustion air intake for fireplaces.

Material

A typical configuration includes a screened outdoor air intake and a round metal duct terminating at or near the front of the firebox floor. In the firebox, the inlet may be screened and hooded to prevent embers getting into the duct.

Intakes

The outdoor intakes not only have to be screened, they should be high enough so they won't be blocked by snow. They should be oriented to minimize the effect of wind pressures on the duct. Many intakes face straight down or are hooded.

Operating Damper

The duct should include a damper that can be closed from inside the room near the fireplace. In many cases, the hood can be pushed down flush with the floor to close the air intake.

Let's look at some of the things to watch for with outdoor combustion air intakes:

1. Damper missing
2. Damper stuck

F I G U R E   11.26   Outdoor Combustion Air

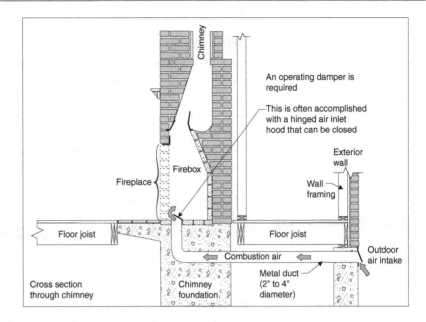

3. Inappropriate material

4. Uninsulated

5. Intake not screened

6. Intake—poor location

7. Intake—not weather-tight

8. Inadequate combustible clearance

9. Disconnected

10. Rusted

11. Hood and screen at firebox missing, damaged or loose

Damper Missing

The implication is heat loss when the fireplace is idle.

Look around the firebox for a way to close the outdoor combustion air intake. Where none is noted, recommend further investigation.

Damper Stuck

You should be able to open or close the damper at or near the firebox.

One implication is considerable heat loss when the fireplace is idle, if the damper is stuck open. If the damper is stuck closed, there will be no outside combustion air.

Operate the damper to ensure that it opens and closes. You may not be able to do this if the fireplace is in use.

Inappropriate Material

The duct supplying outside combustion air should be non-combustible in most jurisdictions.

The implication is a fire hazard.

IMPLICATION

STRATEGY

IMPLICATIONS

STRATEGY

IMPLICATION

If you can see the duct, check the material. If it is combustible, recommend further investigation.

Uninsulated

Condensation and rusting on the duct, and possible overheating of nearby combustibles are the implications.

If you can see the duct, determine whether it is insulated. Where it is not, check with local authorities to determine whether it is required.

Encased in Concrete

If the duct is encased in concrete, it probably won't be insulated. There is no combustible clearance issue, and less of a condensation issue (although it still may cause a problem).

Intake Not Screened

In some areas, $1/4$ inch corrosion resistant screening is required.

Pests may have an easy route into the house. This includes insects and small animals.

Check the outdoor air intake for a screen.

Intake—Poor Location

The intake should be in a spot where it won't be obstructed by snow. It should not be close to the exhaust from other mechanical devices and should not be close to gas regulators, clothes dryer exhausts, etc.

The combustion air intake may not draw any air or may draw air that is not clean.

The fireplace may be starved for air if it cannot draw from the air intake. There is a risk of explosion if the intake draws in natural gas from a regulator vent.

Check with local authorities to see where intakes should be located. Typically, they have to be at least 12 inches above ground level. In heavy snow areas, they may have to be higher. They may have to be located away from other mechanical inlets or exhausts or away from inside corners of buildings, for example.

Where the location is poor, recommend rearrangement.

Intake—Not Weather-Tight

The intake should be sealed to prevent moisture leakage into the building and air leakage out of the building.

Water and air leakage are the implications.

When outside the building, check that the duct is well sealed where it passes through the wall.

Inadequate Combustible Clearances

In many jurisdictions, a 1 inch combustible clearance is required for the first 5 feet away from the firebox. In other areas, clearances may have to be greater.

There is a risk of fire in the home, especially if there is reverse flow and smoke from the fire moves though the duct.

Check what clearances are required in your area if outdoor combustion air intakes are used. Try to get a look at where the combustion air intakes are run. They may be visible from a basement or other sub-grade area. In many cases you won't have access.

Disconnected

The duct should be continuous, of course.

IMPLICATIONS	The outdoor combustion air intake system will not work. Considerable air leakage into another part of the house may result. This may cause high heating bills, for example. The fireplace may not draw properly.
STRATEGY	Where you can see the duct, make sure that it is continuous and intact. When you open the hood or damper at the firebox, look in with a flashlight to make sure there is a duct present.

If you can look into the intake on the exterior, do so to make sure there is a duct connected.

Rust

<table>
<tr><td>IMPLICATION</td><td>Rusted ducts may partially collapse, obstructing the airflow, or may become disconnected.</td></tr>
<tr><td>STRATEGY</td><td>Where the ducts are visible, check them for rust.</td></tr>
</table>

Hood and/or Screen Missing, Damaged, or Loose

At the firebox, there should be a hood to deflect the embers and a screen to prevent embers going into the duct. Check that these are in place, secure, and not mechanically damaged. The air supply should be at the front of the firebox, either inside or just outside.

IMPLICATIONS	The combustion air intake may not allow air into the firebox if the hood and screen are not properly arranged. If the screen or hood are missing, embers may find their way into the duct, creating a fire hazard.
STRATEGY	Check the presence and condition of the hood and screen at the firebox.

Inspector in the House: Life in the Chimney

Inspecting fireplaces is usually straightforward. But sometimes you get surprised. Not too long ago, I was opening a damper to look up the chimney. I was slightly puzzled when the damper was hard to open, because I had done many inspections in that subdivision and was familiar with the type of damper. Some dampers are awkward, some fall out of place easily, but these ones were pretty good. I gave the damper a good shove and was rewarded with success—sort of. The damper opened, which was good, but a very unhappy raccoon came down into the house through the fireplace, which was not so good.

I moved considerably more quickly than I usually do, anxious to get out of the way (raccoons can be vicious and often carry disease), at the same time trying to control the situation. The buyers, seller, and agent were in another room, thankfully. With a fireplace tool, I was able to coax the raccoon out the front door. I'm not sure who was more relieved, me or the raccoon.

I reported the situation and offered to pay for cleaning the living room carpet, which was marked with sooty paw prints. The seller was very gracious and took care of the cleaning herself.

11.5   ELECTRIC HEATING

Electric heat is much simpler than many of the other heating systems we have looked at. So, you can relax. Inspecting electric heating is relatively simple! Let's take a closer look.

Whole House or Supplementary

Electric heat can be the only source of heat in a house or it can be used to supplement other heating systems. The supplementary heat may be **plenum** or **duct heaters,** part of a **combination furnace** or, most commonly, **space heaters** such as electric baseboards.

Types

Electric heating can be broken down into some general categories:

- **Space heaters** including electric baseboard heaters, floor heaters, wall heaters, and ceiling mounted heaters. These may be convection or forced air.

- **Furnaces** (stand-alone or combination systems with wood or oil, for example). A variation on an electric furnace is a **duct heating system** or a **plenum heating system.** These systems are heating elements and controls that are either tucked into the plenum space above the furnace, or tucked into the ductwork of a central air conditioning or heat pump system.

- **Boilers.** Electric boilers are compact and use the same distribution systems as other boilers. Because they are rare, we will not discuss them in this book.

- **Radiant** heating. Electric radiant heating can be in the ceilings, floors or walls (rare).

11.5.1   Efficiency and Load Calculations

Almost 100% Efficient

Because there is no combustion process, there are almost no losses in an electrical heating system. It is very close to 100% efficient.

No Off-Cycle Losses

Because there is no combustion and no chimney, the heat loss from the building is generally less with an electrical heating system than it is with a conventional gas or oil system. As a result, the heating system can be slightly smaller. Some people size electrical heating systems up to 15% smaller than conventional fossil fuel systems because of this.

As a general rule, most houses that are completely heated with electricity would have a 200-amp service. If the electric heating system is to be space heaters, there will probably be several pairs of 15, 20, or 30 amp 240-volt circuits for the space heaters. If the electric system is to be a furnace or boiler, you'll generally see one large set of fuses or breakers at the panel. Radiant heating is usually handled like space heaters, with several smaller circuits. Duct or plenum heaters are treated like furnaces and typically have one large set of fuses or breakers at the panel.

We Don't Check Loads

Determining the total load of electric resistance heaters on each circuit is not within the scope of a home inspection.

Defer to Manufacturers' Recommendations

In some cases, the manufacturer indicates the fuse rating size and wire size. Assuming that the equipment has been listed or certified by a recognized testing agency, these specifications usually take precedence. Table 11.1 provides a sample of a manufacturer's recommendations for wire size and breakers for various electric furnaces. We have added the actual amps that would be drawn assuming the 240-volt circuit, and have identified the wire ampacity. The table assumes copper wire. The first three rows are the manufacturer's specifications. The last two rows are our additions.

TABLE 11.1   Sample Manufacturer's Specifications

Sample Manufacturer's Specifications

1. Heater size (kw)	5	10	15	20	25	30
2. Breaker size	30	60	100	125	150	175
3. Wire size (AWG)	10	8	4	3	2	1
4. Wire ampacity[1]	30	45	85	105	120	140
5. Actual current draw of elements (amps)	21	42	63	84	104	125

[1]This assumes that the wire is rated at 90°C.

11.5.2   General Conditions

The following list of problems associated with all electric resistance heating systems should look familiar if you've already read Chapter 7, *Electrical Systems*. We will not discuss them in detail here.

1. Fuses or breakers missing

2. Fuses or breakers too big

3. Multi-wire circuits on the same bus

4. Fuses or breakers bypassed

5. Fuses or breakers loose

6. No links for 240-volt circuits

7. Wrong breaker for panel

8. Wire overheating

9. Wire damaged

10. Wire not well secured

11. Loose connections

12. Open splices

13. Wires too close to ducts, pipes or chimneys

14. Wires too close to edge of studs or joists

15. Wires exposed on walls or ceilings

16. Wires exposed in attics

17. Wires too small

18. Aluminum wires used without compatible connectors

Now we'll look at specific types of electric heating systems, and the problems unique to each.

11.5.3   Space Heaters

Space heaters do not have distribution ducts or piping systems. They heat only the room or area that they are in. Electric space heaters include—

▪ baseboard heaters

▪ wall mounted heaters

▪ floor mounted heaters

F I G U R E   11.27   Best Location for Electric Heaters

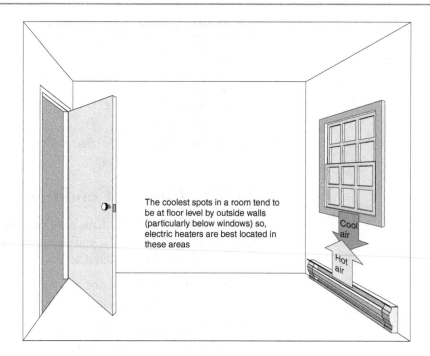

The coolest spots in a room tend to be at floor level by outside walls (particularly below windows) so, electric heaters are best located in these areas

Cool air

Hot air

- ceiling mounted heaters
- toekick heaters which fit under cabinets and deliver heat through the front of the toekick

Convection or Forced Air   These systems may or may not have a fan. In other words, they may be **convection** or **forced air** heating systems. The convection units draw air in at the bottom and discharge heated air out at the top. They need to have free airflow to function properly. The fan units can pull air in from one side and discharge air out though the other, or pull air in from the bottom and discharge it from the top.

Location   Ideal locations of electric heaters are consistent with ideal locations of supply registers on forced air systems or radiators on hot water systems. The heat is typically supplied near floor level on exterior walls, ideally below windows. This tends to be the coolest part of the room and channeling most of the heat to this area results in relatively even temperatures (Figure 11.27).

Dedicated Electrical Service   Electric heaters are usually run on small (12 or 14 gauge) circuits. Permanently installed heaters are almost always on 240-volt circuits. The smaller current draw of a 240-volt circuit allows the wire and fuse or breaker size to be smaller.

Separate Panels   If the house is heated entirely with electric space heaters, there is often a double or second electrical distribution panel with several 20 or 30 amp, 240-volt circuits. These circuits are a balanced load and typically only use two conductor cables. No neutral wire is required to return an unbalanced load. The conductors can be black and red, but are often black and white. The white wire should be designated, with black tape for example, to show that it is acting as a hot wire.

Thermostat Location   Each heater may be controlled by a thermostat on the heater or by a wall thermostat. Alternatively, one wall thermostat can control several heaters in a room. Wall thermostats can be **line voltage** (240 volt) or **low voltage** (12 or 24 volt).

Careful with Wall Thermostats   Wall thermostats have a maximum wattage rating. You can't put an unlimited number of heaters on a single wall thermostat.

Heater Size

Electric space heaters are available in sizes ranging from 75 to 4,800 watts. The most common sizes are 1,000, 1,500 and 2,000 watts. One general rule is to count each linear foot of baseboard as 250 watts. There is no magic to this, and if you are willing to get down on your hands and knees, you can usually read the wattage specifications of the heater.

120 vs. 240

We have talked a little about the advantage of using 240-volt heaters. The portable heaters that are designed to be plugged into convenience receptacles have to be rated at 120 volts. Some permanently installed heaters are also rated at 120 volts. Obviously, we do not want 120-volt heaters wired at 240 volts. This is dangerous. Similarly, we don't want 240-volt heaters wired on a 120-volt circuit. While it's not dangerous, you won't get all the heat you should.

Let's look at some of the things that we will be watching for on electric space heaters. We'll obviously be looking for the general conditions listed earlier. In addition, we'll be looking at—

1. Inoperative heaters
2. Obstructed heaters
3. Dirty or bent fins on heaters
4. 120-volt heaters installed on 240-volt circuits or vice versa
5. Fans—noisy, inoperative, loose or dirty
6. Missing or too few heaters
7. Damaged or rusted heaters
8. Loose or missing covers

Inoperative Heaters

IMPLICATION

No heat is the implication.

STRATEGY

Turn up the thermostat for space heaters. The thermostat may be on the heater or on the wall. Within about 30 seconds, the heating elements or fins should be warm. If it is a convection system, you can usually reach in and touch the fins and feel the heat coming off.

Forced Air

If it is a forced air unit, the fan should start immediately and the air discharged should be warm within approximately one minute.

Obstructed Heaters

Airflow into and out of the heater should not be obstructed. Heaters set directly on the floor should not have their inlets obstructed by carpeting, especially deep pile carpeting.

Drapes can obstruct the heater outlet, as can furniture. Drapes should be at least 8 inches above baseboard heaters or, at least 3 inches out in front and 1 inch above the floor. Manufacturer's recommendations can be checked for specific clearance requirements on different types of heaters.

IMPLICATIONS

This is a fire hazard if furniture or drapes are too close to the heater. At best, heat distribution will be inhibited. The unit may overheat if the inlet or outlet is restricted. The heater may shut off consistently on high temperature. This may also result in no heat or poor comfort as a result of erratic operation.

STRATEGY

Make sure that the airflow surrounding heaters is clear.

Fins Bent or Dirty

IMPLICATIONS

Poor heat transfer from the electric elements into the room air. This may result in uncomfortable room temperature or excessive heating costs.

Use a flashlight and look at the fins on baseboard heaters. Watch for fins that have been bent or jammed together and look for dirt obstructing the airflow between the fins.

120-Volt Heater Installed on a 240-Volt Circuit or Vice Versa

Overheating and heater failure are the implications. This is also a fire hazard.

A 240-volt heater operating at 120 volts will not deliver adequate heat.

Again, this is something that may be difficult to detect during a home inspection. Without doing testing that goes beyond the scope, it will be difficult for you to know which fuse or breaker controls any given heater in the house. Where most of the heaters are clearly on 240-volt circuits (identified by the linked fuses or breakers at the panel), you can check the heaters' dataplate to make sure that they are rated for 240 volts. Many of them are rated for 208/240 volts. These are appropriate for residential 240-volt use.

Fan—Noisy, Inoperative, Loose or Dirty

These fan problems may cause poor comfort, localized overheating of the heater and shut off on thermal cutout.

When the thermostat is turned up, listen to the operation of the fan. Is it working? Is it too noisy? Use a flashlight to ensure that the fan is stable during operation. When the system is idle, use a flashlight to look for dirt on the fan blades or the motor.

Missing or Too Few Heaters

Inadequate heat in some areas is the implication.

Look for a heat source in each room. Use some common sense. If the room has no exterior walls, it may not need heat. But the Standards ask you to note it anyway.

Look for too few or too small heaters in any one area. You'll get a sense of what is commonly used in your area, and will get a sense from the other rooms. Where you see one room that is dramatically different, note it. It's not an expensive undertaking in most cases to add one or two heaters.

Damaged or Rusted Heaters

The heater may become inoperative or unsafe.

Look for and note any damage or rust on heaters.

Loose or Missing Covers

The heater may be susceptible to damage or getting dirty. A missing cover is dangerous if hot elements are exposed to combustibles or accessible to children or pets, for example.

Look for and report any loose or missing heater covers.

11.5.4   Furnaces

Furnaces may be simple electric furnaces or combination furnaces (typically with oil or wood). They may also be duct heaters or plenum heaters introduced into the spaces adjacent to furnaces and/or air conditioners. We'll talk about these all as **furnaces** since they are similar.

FIGURE 11.28   Sequencers

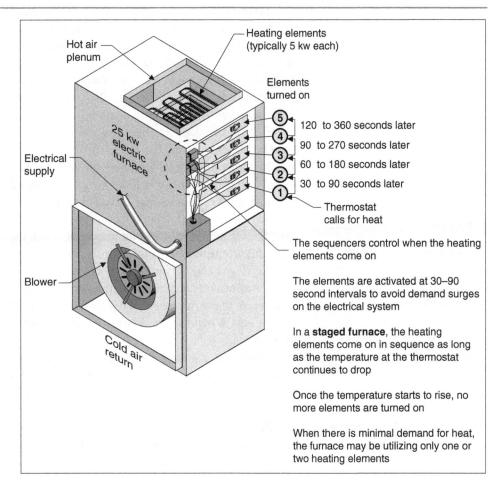

Hot air plenum

Heating elements (typically 5 kw each)

Elements turned on

25 kw electric furnace

Electrical supply

⑤ 120 to 360 seconds later
④ 90 to 270 seconds later
③ 60 to 180 seconds later
② 30 to 90 seconds later
①

Thermostat calls for heat

Blower

The sequencers control when the heating elements come on

The elements are activated at 30–90 second intervals to avoid demand surges on the electrical system

In a **staged furnace**, the heating elements come on in sequence as long as the temperature at the thermostat continues to drop

Once the temperature starts to rise, no more elements are turned on

When there is minimal demand for heat, the furnace may be utilizing only one or two heating elements

Cold air return

Simple

Sizes

The electric furnace is much simpler than gas or oil furnaces.

Electric furnaces typically come in 10 to 30 kilowatt sizes, in increments of 5 kilowatts. A ten-kilowatt heater has a capacity of about 34,000 BTUs. A 30 kilowatt furnace has a capacity of about 102,000 BTUs.

Main Disconnect

There must be a main electrical disconnect for a furnace. In some jurisdictions, it is located at the panel. In other jurisdictions, a disconnect is located at the furnace as well as the panel.

Sequencers

Most electric furnaces have multiple elements. When the thermostat calls for heat, we don't want all of the elements coming on at once. This can cause an electrical surge and a voltage drop, which may cause problems for electronic equipment elsewhere in the house. As a result, electric furnaces have **sequencers** (Figure 11.28). When the thermostat calls for heat, the first element comes on. There is a time delay of 30 to 90 seconds typically, before the next element comes on. Each element comes on in turn, over time. This allows the electrical current flow to gradually build up.

Staged Electric Furnaces

Some furnaces are **variable speed.** These furnaces are **staged** so that if the temperature is mild and the heat demand is not great, only one or two elements may come on. This requires a special thermostat. When the thermostat calls for heat, the first element comes on. If the thermostat senses that the temperature is still dropping, the next element starts. If the thermostat still senses temperature drop, the third element starts and so on. As soon as the thermostat detects a rise in room temperature, no more stages are called to start. When the temperature reaches the set point, the thermostat shuts down all of the elements.

Two Covers but No Access to Elements

Electric furnaces have a fan compartment cover and a cover for the electrical element portion. The elements, however, are not visible after removing the cover designed for homeowner access. You will typically see the wiring to the elements, the sequencers and the relays. The elements, however, are in the air stream and cannot be accessed without partially dismantling the furnace.

Fan/Limit Switch

Electric furnaces are like gas and oil furnaces in that they have a **fan/limit switch.** In some cases, the fan control does not have the fan come on when the plenum temperature gets high enough. The fan may come on as soon as the furnace starts. That is because the heat delivery is very rapid with electricity. It does not have to warm up a heat exchanger before transferring heat to the house air. The fan control may have a small delay both on start-up and shut-down, but it is not unusual to have the fan start and stop simultaneously with the furnace.

High Temperature Shut-Off

A **high temperature limit** is included in the fan/limit switch. A setting of 200°F (similar to gas and oil furnaces) is typical.

Thermal Cutouts or Fusible Links on Elements

Some furnaces have **fusible links** on individual elements that will shut them off in the event of overheating. Others have **thermal cutouts** that will trip if the elements get too hot. When the elements cool, the cutouts will allow the element to come back on.

Sail Switch

Some furnaces have a **sail switch** designed to protect the elements from overheating. This switch will not let the elements heat up unless it senses airflow across them. This switch detects air movement caused by the house air fan. If it doesn't sense that the fan is on, it won't let the furnace come on.

Cool Discharge Temperatures

One of the issues with electric furnaces is a relatively small temperature rise. It is common to have only a 50° to 60°F temperature rise across the furnace. This is smaller than what is common with gas and oil furnaces (it is similar to high-efficiency gas furnaces). Some people feel a "cool breeze" even though adequate heat is being delivered.

Plenum Heaters

Plenum heaters can be used to supplement a furnace or, more commonly, to operate under mild weather conditions instead of the furnace. Where the electrical service in the house is small, the plenum heaters may be arranged to shut down if the electrical demand is high in other parts of the house. You should ask contractors how electric plenum heaters are typically set up in your area.

As with any electric heating system, please refer back to the general conditions described earlier in section 11.5.2. Electric furnaces are smilar to gas and oil furnaces in many ways. You can refer to the earlier chapters for discussions related to similar components, such as cabinets, blowers, thermostats, and ducts.

There are a couple of problems that are specific to electric furnaces:

1. Individual elements, sequencers or relays inoperative
2. Excess temperature rise

Individual Elements, Sequencers, or Relays Inoperative

One of the most difficult things to detect during a visual home inspection is burned out elements on electric furnaces. Because these furnaces may have up to six elements, a normal operating test will not usually reveal whether all of the elements are operative.

IMPLICATIONS

Under cold weather conditions, adequate heat may not be available in the home.

STRATEGY

You won't usually be able to tell just by cycling the furnace and doing a visual examination. You will get heat at the supply registers and the temperature rise (if you measure it) will not be excessive. It might be slightly on the low side, but you'll have a tough time quantifying it.

Using a Clamp-on Ampmeter

Testing the elements with a clamp-on ampmeter goes beyond the scope of a basic home inspection, but it is performed by many inspectors. Clamp-on ampmeters can be used without disturbing electrical connections. As a result, they are relatively safe devices. These measure the current flow through wires by sensing the electrical field around the wire. Clamp-on ampmeters are useful for measuring the current flow through 240-volt circuits. You have to measure the current flow through one leg or the other. You can't do both at the same time.

Testing Strategy

With the furnace at rest, clamp the ampmeter around either the black or the red conductor powering the furnace. This can be done at the furnace or at the electrical panel. Without turning the thermostat up, you may want to turn the furnace fan on using the fan switch or an auxiliary switch on the thermostat. This allows you to isolate the fan current from the electric elements.

Ignore Fan Current

We want to determine the current draw of the fan and then ignore it. The typical current draw from a blower fan is two to five amps. These fans are most often 120 volts. The two to five amps will be drawn through either the red or the black wire. With your ampmeter you can figure out which wire is powering the blower. For this test, you should clamp your meter onto the other wire. This is the wire that does not power the blower.

Turn Up the Thermostat

When you turn up the thermostat, you should watch the ampmeter and look at your watch. What you should see, assuming a 6 element furnace, is the following:

1. When the thermostat comes on, the meter reading will jump from zero to 21 amps as the first element comes on (assuming a 5 kilowatt element, which is the most common).

2. After 30 to 90 seconds, the current draw should jump to 42 amps. This indicates that the second element has come on.

3. After another 30 to 90 seconds, the current draw should jump to 63 amps, indicating that the third element has come on.

4. After yet another 30 to 90 seconds, the meter reading should jump to 84 amps, indicating that the fourth element has come on.

5. And, after another 30 to 90 seconds, the current reading should jump to 104 amps, indicating that the fifth element has come on.

6. After another 30 to 90 seconds, the meter should jump to 125 amps, indicating that the sixth element has come on.

If the time delay between elements is usually 30 seconds, and there is a 60 second delay between any of the steps, you can reasonably assume that one element is not working. If the total current draw is less than the rated current draw, you know that at least one element is not working. You may or may not be able to determine which element isn't working, depending on how well the test is performed, although this part isn't terribly important.

If you don't do this test, tell the client about the inspection limitation of possible inoperative elements.

Excess Temperature Rise

IMPLICATIONS

The implications of excess temperature rise are overheating of the furnace and cutout on thermal overload. This may lead to a "no heat" condition or erratic heating as thermal overloads trip on and off. It can also shorten the life of the heating elements and other components as the furnace overheats.

Duct Heaters

Many duct heaters have an automatic resetting air temperature limit switch set at 200°F and a 250° fusible link or cutout near the elements that must be manually reset.

STRATEGY

While this is a test that goes beyond the Standards, some inspectors use a thermometer with a probe (like a meat thermometer) to test the temperature rise across the furnace. Assuming a 70° temperature coming in, the outlet temperature on an electric furnace might be 120° to 125° typically. Where it is above 130°, recommend further investigation.

Inspector in the House: Follow Your Nose

The nice thing about your sense of smell is that it works even when you are not thinking about it. That's why they put perfume in natural gas, for example—so we can smell it and be warned of a gas leak.

In this case, my sense of smell warned me of my own mistake. The home had electric baseboard heat, and toward the end of the inspection I went through the home and turned up all the heater thermostats. I went through the house again to see if the heaters had gotten warm. As I checked the heater in the living room, my client said he smelled something burning in the front hall. We dashed out there in time to catch the problem before it got out of hand.

I had thrown my coat and scarf on the floor carelessly when I came into the house, not noticing that they came to rest against the hall heater. When I turned up the heat, my scarf started to smolder. I quickly grabbed my coat and scarf and carried them outside before it got serious. I made sure the burning material was extinguished before somewhat sheepishly going back into the home and finishing the inspection.

I reminded the client that drapes and curtains should be kept several inches above electric heaters, which are typically located below windows. I also double checked every heater to make sure there were no electrical outlets above a heater. This can result in burned electrical cords, and in some cases, fires. I'm pretty sure he took the advice seriously and was gracious enough not to dwell on my irresponsible behavior.

REVIEW QUESTIONS

1. List six characteristics of a good chimney.
2. Give a short definition of:
   a. Chimneys
   b. Flues
   c. Vents
3. Chimneys may have multiple flues.
   True   False
4. Masonry chimneys usually help support wood frame structures.
   True   False
5. List four common fuels that need chimneys.
6. List six things that affect chimney draft.
7. List the five basic components of a masonry chimney.
8. Why is condensation an issue in chimneys?
9. List at least 15 common chimney problems.
10. List five implications of chimneys settling or leaning.
11. List four implications of cracked chimneys.
12. What is the maximum that a chimney can be offset from vertical?
13. How far should a masonry chimney extend above the roof?
14. What is the minimum total height for a chimney serving a wood stove?
15. When did masonry chimneys start to get built with clay liners?
16. You can tell whether a chimney is lined by looking for a liner extending above the top.
    True   False
17. Generally speaking, how far should wood framing members be kept away from masonry chimneys?
18. Two wood burning fireplaces can share a single flue, as long as they are on the same floor level.
    True   False
19. B vents are typically used for which fuels?
20. L vents are typically used for which fuels?
21. Class A chimneys are typically used for which fuels?
22. Factory-built chimneys (super chimneys) are typically used for which fuels?
23. Any B-vent can be installed up the outside of a house.
    True   False
24. Metal chimneys often have several flues.
    True   False
25. List 12 common metal chimney vent problems.
26. List at least one implication for each of these conditions.
27. List at least one inspection strategy for each of these problems.

28. Metal chimneys that extend more than _____ feet above the roof should be laterally supported.

29. Metal chimneys for wood fireplaces typically need _____ inches of clearance from combustibles.

30. What part of metal chimneys often rust? (Give the location)

31. It is good practice to connect a metal chimney to a masonry chimney part way up a house so that the exterior part of the chimney is masonry.

    True   False

32. Define creosote.

33. Which chimney is likely to have a heavier creosote deposit—a warm chimney or a cold chimney?

34. List three types of wood-burning fireplaces.

35. Fireplaces can be built in or free standing.

    True   False

36. Fireplaces are designed as a primary heating source in most cases.

    True   False

37. List seven basic components of a masonry fireplace.

38. Factory-built fireplaces do not have a smoke shelf.

    True   False

39. How far should combustibles be from cleanout doors?

40. How far should combustibles be from fireplace openings?

41. How far above fireplace openings should combustibles be if they project out beyond the opening by $1\frac{1}{2}$ inches?

42. How far should combustibles be from the firebox walls?

43. How far should combustibles be from chimneys?

44. How far should combustibles be from an outside combustion air inlet duct?

45. Zero clearance fireplaces do not typically require any clearance from combustibles at the top of the firebox.

    True   False

46. A home inspection includes an analysis of the quality of chimney draw for a fireplace.

    True   False

47. Basement fireplaces typically draw better than first or second floor fireplaces because the chimney is taller.

    True   False

48. Smoke on a mantel always means a poor drafting fireplace.

    True   False

49. Use lines to join the words that belong in pairs.

    Hearth   Front hearth

    Inner hearth   Outer hearth

    Back hearth   Hearth extension

50. Inside the firebox of a masonry fireplace, the surface of the hearth is typically _____.

51. The hearth extension typically sits on _____ inches of _____.

52. Hearths should extend _____ inches out in front and _____ inches to either side of the fireplace opening.

53. If the firebox is raised, the hearth extension can be smaller.

True   False

54. List seven common hearth problems.

55. The function of a firebox is to _____.

56. A common minimum firebox depth requirement is _____ inches.

57. Metal fireboxes should be mortared tightly to the masonry of the fireplace.

True   False

58. Clay tile liners should be supported on metal fireboxes.

True   False

59. Lintels should be mortared tightly into place.

True   False

60. Zero clearance fireplaces require footings and foundations.

True   False

61. List eight common firebox problems.

62. List two functions of a fireplace damper.

63. Can dampers ever be at the top of the chimney?

64. Would you ever find a damper that was permanently open?

65. List six common damper problems.

66. Describe the location and shape of the throat, the smoke shelf and the smoke chamber.

67. Describe the characteristics of a well designed and well built smoke chamber.

68. List seven problems with throats, smoke shelves and smoke chambers.

69. List six fireplace, face or breast problems.

70. List two reasons why outdoor combustion air may be a good idea.

71. List four types of electric heating.

72. List 15 general electrical problems that you might find associated with electric heaters.

73. Which is more dangerous; a 240-volt heater on a 120-volt circuit or a 120-volt heater on a 240-volt circuit?

74. List eight problems specific to electric space heaters.

75. What are common sizes for electric furnaces?

76. Briefly describe the operation of a sequencer.

77. Describe how a staged electric furnace would come on.

78. Can you look at the elements on an electric furnace or boiler?

79. What is the normal setting of a high temperature limit for an electric furnace?

80. What is a sail switch?

81. What is the typical temperature rise on an electric furnace?

82. List two common problem specific to electric furnaces.

AIR CONDITIONING AND HEAT PUMPS

LEARNING OBJECTIVES

By the end of this chapter you should be able to:

- define in one sentence each the function of the compressor, condenser, evaporator and expansion device

- list ten factors that affect how much air conditioning is needed

- explain the implications of an undersized air conditioning system

- explain the implications of an oversized air conditioning system

- describe the location of the air conditioning compressor

- describe in one sentence the function of a crankcase heater

- list eight common compressor problems

- describe the location and function of the condenser fan and the evaporator fan

- list four common condenser fan problems

- list seven common evaporator fan problems

- list eight common duct problems

- list seven thermostat problems

- give the normal life expectancy for conventional air conditioner compressors

- list nine tricks for identifying heat pumps

- list seven common heat pump problems

INTRODUCTION   Central air conditioning is considered a luxury rather than an essential in most parts of the United States Air conditioning systems are more common in the southern areas, and are more common in humid areas than dry areas. There are probably more air conditioners per capita in Florida than in California, for example. You probably know how common central air conditioning systems are in your area.

Scope of Inspection   In this chapter we'll look at split-system air-cooled central air conditioning, since it's the most common system in homes. We inspect permanently **installed** systems with or without ducts. We don't inspect window air conditioners or other systems that can be removed without tools and that plug into 120-volt convenience receptacles. We'll conclude this chapter with a look at heat pumps, a kind of air-conditioner-in-reverse.

12.1   AIR CONDITIONING CAPACITY

Before looking at the specific components of air conditioners and what can go wrong with them, let's consider a general issue which concerns many homeowners: Is the system capacity sufficient to keep the house comfortable during hot weather?

Most home inspectors give their clients some indication as to whether the air conditioning system is sized properly even though it's not required by the Standards. Let's look at the cooling capacity.

Factors Affecting Cooling Load   The amount of cooling required depends on a large number of factors. These include the outdoor temperature; the outdoor humidity; the level of insulation in the house; the amount of air leakage in the house; the amount of southern, east and west facing glass in the house; whether this glass is single-, double- or triple-glazed; whether the glass is a low emissivity glass or gas-filled; and whether window treatments (curtains or blinds) are kept closed or open. Other factors include the amount of shading from trees, roof overhangs, awnings, or buildings and how much heat is generated in the house by the people and equipment inside.

Guidelines   Despite all these variables, most people like to have guidelines. Home inspectors are no exception. In the southern United States, 450 to 700 square feet of floor area per ton of cooling is considered appropriate. In the northern United States, 700 to 1,000 square feet per ton may be adequate. Speak to air conditioning installers and other inspectors in your area to find the appropriate range for your area. (These guidelines assume 8-foot ceilings.)

Duct Capacity Problems   The capacity of the equipment is only one part of the equation. Many air conditioners that under-perform are a result of a duct system incapable of circulating the conditioned air adequately through the system. This is particularly true where air conditioning has been added to a house with ducts that were designed for a heating system only.

Moving Heavy Air with More Obstructions   Adding central air conditioning to an existing furnace system may lead to inadequate air distribution for several reasons. Firstly, the evaporator coil presents an additional obstruction to airflow and reduces the rate of air movement through the system. Secondly, during the cooling season, we are trying to move air that is at 55°F rather than air that is at 140°F (which is what we see in the heating season). The cooler air is more dense (heavier) and more difficult to move through the ducts. We also have to move more air since the difference in temperature between the conditioned air and the room air (about 15°F to 20°F) is less than with a conventional oil or gas furnace (60°F to 70°F).

Air conditioning systems typically move 400 to 450 cubic feet of air per minute per ton through a system. Heating systems only need to move about half this much.

Better to Undersize

Many air conditioning manufacturers and installers recommend slightly undersizing an air conditioning system, rather than oversizing. Either can be a problem.

12.1.1   Undersized

IMPLICATIONS

During moderate weather, the air conditioner may function adequately, but during hot weather, the air conditioner may not be able to achieve a 15°F to 20°F temperature differential between indoors and outdoors.

STRATEGY

The first step is to determine the size of the air conditioning system. This can often be done by reading the model number on the data plate. This is typically located on the outdoor (condenser) unit. The size may be recorded in thousands of BTUs per hour, or in the number of tons.

Preston's Guide

Sometimes it is difficult to translate a model number into a system capacity. **Preston's Guide** is an excellent reference guide with the model, serial numbers and SEER (Seasonal Energy Efficiency Ratings) of many residential air conditioning systems.

Guessing the Size

If the size cannot be determined from the model number on the data plate, the size can be approximated from the Rated Load Amperage (RLA) on the data plate (Figure 12.1). A typical reciprocating compressor will be rated at 6 amps to 8 amps per ton of cooling. The newer high-efficiency units and scroll compressors will draw less electrical current, more like 5 amps per ton. Be clear that this is an approximation only if you report the capacity based on current.

Use House Square Footage

The next step is to roughly calculate the above-grade square footage of the home. Divide the square footage into the number of tons and determine the number of square feet per ton.

If the number of square feet per ton exceeds the ranges we discussed, it is probably best to describe this as marginal or suspect capacity and to recommend further investigation. There may be factors that cause the guidelines not to apply.

Guidelines

It's also possible to find a system that seems to be just fine with respect to capacity using your guideline and yet it isn't really big enough. When considering the square

F I G U R E   12.1   Guessing the Size

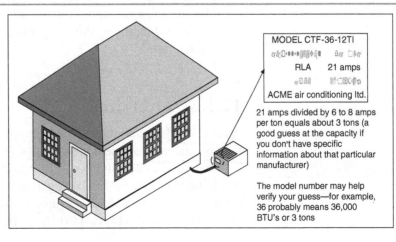

F I G U R E 12.2   Measure Temperature Drop across Inside Cold

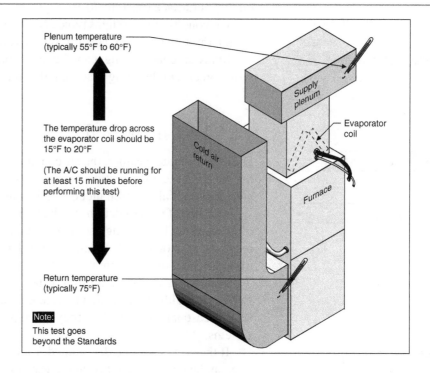

Plenum temperature
(typically 55°F to 60°F)

Supply plenum

Evaporator coil

The temperature drop across
the evaporator coil should be
15°F to 20°F

Cold air return

(The A/C should be running for
at least 15 minutes before
performing this test)

Furnace

Return temperature
(typically 75°F)

Note:
This test goes
beyond the Standards

*Measure Temperature Drop
Across Indoor Coil*

footage of the house, the basement is not usually considered. However, if the basement has a walk-out with a large glass surface facing south, east or west, the air conditioning load may be far greater than contemplated. Lots of skylights change things too.

If the system is adequately sized and is working properly, the air temperature entering the evaporator coil will be whatever the room temperature is (Figure 12.2). Let's say it's 75°F. The air coming off the coil should be 14°F to 22°F cooler (some say 15°F to 20°F). If the inlet temperature is 75°F, the air coming off should be 55°F to 60°F. This can be measured with a thermometer with a sharp probe that is pushed into a joint or hole in the supply plenum immediately downstream of (after) the evaporator coil.

If the temperature drop is different, the problem may be size-related or may indicate a need for servicing. This test should be compared with your approximation of the size of the air conditioner, based on the number of square feet per ton. Make sure the temperature drop is measured after the system has established equilibrium. The unit should run for at least 15 minutes before checking the temperature split. Measuring this temperature split is beyond the Standards but many inspectors do it.

12.1.2   Oversized

An oversized air conditioner is susceptible to short cycling, inadequate dehumidification and large temperature variations in the house.

IMPLICATION

Oversized units will have a shortened life expectancy and will provide a less comfortable environment. The largest comfort issue is the lack of dehumidification. Because the temperature drops rapidly with an oversized unit, there is not enough air movement across the coil to extract the water from the house air. This results in a house that is cool, but with a humid, swamp-like environment. Since compressors experience most damage on start-up, short cycles also mean more start-ups and a shorter life.

Other than the rough guideline test, it is difficult to know whether and how much the unit is oversized. Some utilities indicate that a unit may be as much as 25 percent oversized without adverse effect. The temptation to oversize may become irresistible for installers with respect to heat pumps. Since heat pumps have to deal with a much larger temperature differential from outside to inside, the tendency is to make the heat pump large enough to meet the heating demand. This makes it too large for the cooling load. There are some strategies to address this problem, but within this context, we are watching for oversized cooling units.

One way inspectors identify an oversized air conditioner is by sensing the cold damp environment when walking into a house. Also, an air conditioner that short cycles (turns on and off every five minutes) is a suggestion that the unit may be oversized.

Two surveys have shown that one third to one half of all residential air conditioning systems are oversized.

STRATEGY *(margin label)*

12.2 COMPRESSOR

The compressor is the heart of the air conditioning system. It is the pump that drives the refrigerant through the system.

Location

On conventional split-system systems, the compressor is in the condenser cabinet outdoors or in the attic. It is typically a large, black, hermetically sealed cylinder.

The motor and compressor operate in a refrigerant-filled environment. Opening the condenser cabinet to get at the compressor is going beyond the Standards.

Condensers Hung on Houses

Most condensers sit on the ground but some hang on brackets attached to the building wall. This keeps them out of the dirt and eliminates settling problems. Some claim that this transfers noise and vibration into the house.

Low Temperature Limitations

Compressors shouldn't be tested when the outdoor temperature is below 65°F or when electrical power has been on for less than 12 to 24 hours. Damage can be done to the compressor. The refrigerant in the compressor may condense and mix with the lubricating oil in the base of the compressor. This mix does not provide good lubrication and the compressor may seize.

Sump or Crankcase Heater

There is a sump heater (crankcase heater) on many air conditioning systems that keeps the oil at the base of the compressor warm enough to boil off the refrigerant. The heater usually is on whenever the air conditioning system is powered, but is off when the unit is shut down for the heating season. It's a waste of electricity to keep this heater on year round. The heater may take 12 to 24 hours to warm the oil to the point where all the refrigerant is boiled off. That's why you can't just turn the power on and start up the air conditioner at the beginning of the cooling season.

Delayed Start-Up

Compressors that use capillary tubes as expansion devices are typically low-torque units. This means that on start-up, they expect to see equal pressure on the suction and discharge side of the compressor. The capillary tube allows this equalization of pressure but it takes a little time. When the compressor shuts off, it has a high pressure on the discharge side (as high as 275 psi with some refrigerants) and a low pressure on the suction side (typically 70 psi).

F I G U R E 12.3   Wait Before Restarting a Compressor

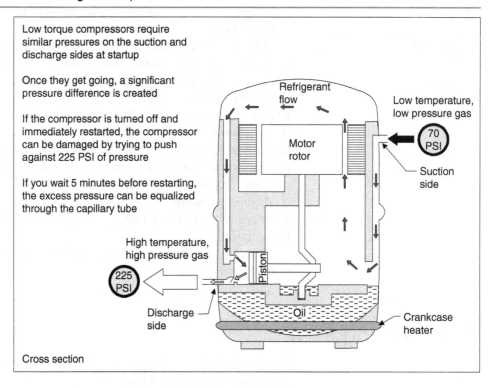

Low torque compressors require similar pressures on the suction and discharge sides at startup

Once they get going, a significant pressure difference is created

If the compressor is turned off and immediately restarted, the compressor can be damaged by trying to push against 225 PSI of pressure

If you wait 5 minutes before restarting, the excess pressure can be equalized through the capillary tube

Cross section

Compressor Damage

If the compressor is asked to start again immediately, it will be trying to push against a high pressure (see Figure 12.3). This can damage the compressor. As a result, most air conditioning systems have a five-minute delay built in that prevents the compressor from coming on just after it has stopped.

Conditions

Common compressor problems include the following:

1. Excess noise/vibration
2. Short cycling or running continuously
3. Out of level
4. Wrong fuse or breaker size
5. Electric wires too small
6. Missing electrical shutoff
7. Inoperative
8. Inadequate cooling

12.2.1   Excess Noise/Vibration

Compressors are not silent when operating. They should run with a monotonous drone. Knocking sounds coming from the compressor are cause for concern. A hum with no background compressor noise may indicate that the compressor is inoperative. No noise at all also indicates that the compressor isn't working.

FIGURE 12.4   Slugging

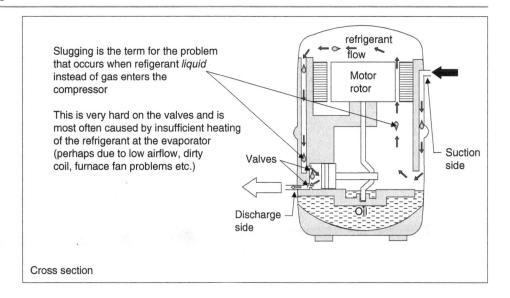

Slugging is the term for the problem that occurs when refigerant *liquid* instead of gas enters the compressor

This is very hard on the valves and is most often caused by insufficient heating of the refrigerant at the evaporator (perhaps due to low airflow, dirty coil, furnace fan problems etc.)

refrigerant flow

Motor rotor

Valves

Suction side

Discharge side

Oil

Cross section

Normal Noises

Scroll-type compressors have a different sound than reciprocating compressors. They have a higher pitched whine. It takes some experience to determine what is typical compressor noise. Some compressors are noisy when new and will break in over time.

Vibration

Some vibration is common with any compressor. Compressors are mounted on rubber feet to isolate this vibration. Excessive vibration, often accompanied by unusual noise, is a sign of severe problems with the system.

IMPLICATIONS

Unusual noises often indicate imminent failure of the compressor. Excess vibration leads to joint failure in the refrigerant line connections. This will allow refrigerant loss, which leads to compressor burnout. Internal damage may also be done to the compressor.

STRATEGY

Compressor noise can be heard best if you are close to the compressor. Make sure you don't confuse the sound of the outdoor coil fan with compressor noise.

Listening with a Screwdriver

Some inspectors remove the outdoor cover and press the tip of a screwdriver against the shell of the compressor and the base of the screwdriver against the ear drum. This will transmit sounds to your ear without background noise from the fan, allowing a more accurate assessment.

Slugging

Compressors that are slugging may be noisy intermittently. Slugging is the introduction of liquid to the intake side of the compressor (see Figure 12.4). Compressors are not intended to work on liquids. They expect to see a gas. The liquid may be oil or liquid refrigerant. In either case, slugging is very hard on a compressor.

When the compressor is running, look for evidence of vibration. This can sometimes be seen through the condenser cover or through the coil. Intermittent vibration or vibration which is readily visible may indicate problems. Look at the rubber mounts to make sure they are secure.

Don't worry about vibration on start-up or shutdown. This is typical. However, a broken mount will show up clearly at start-up and shutdown.

Where noise levels or vibrations are unusual, recommend further investigation.

F I G U R E 12.5   Condensing Unit Out of Level

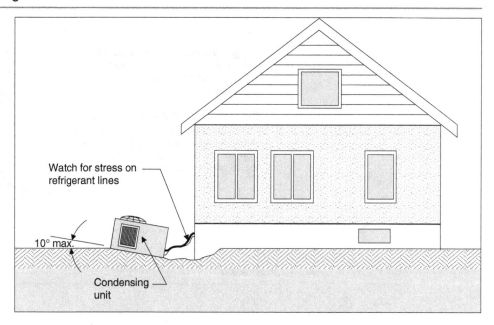

12.2.2   Short Cycling or Running Continuously

IMPLICATIONS

STRATEGY

Compressors that exhibit short cycling or run continuously may result in ineffective cooling and shortened life expectancy of the compressor.

Watch for an air conditioner that never shuts off on a mild day (on a very hot day, it's likely to run continuously) or comes on and off every five minutes. Troubleshooting is beyond our scope, but recommend that the unit be serviced.

12.2.3   Out of Level

The condensing units should be within approximately 10 degrees of level (see Figure 12.5).

IMPLICATIONS

The compressor may not be properly lubricated if the unit is not level.

The other implication of a compressor out of level is slugging. This is very hard on the compressor.

Oil traveling with the refrigerant through the tubing may become trapped if the unit is out of level. This reduces the lubricant available to the compressor and may cause compressor failure.

Another implication of condensing units being out of level is the refrigerant lines breaking as a result of the stresses placed on lines by the unit.

STRATEGY

Look at the condenser unit to see that it is approximately level. No tools are needed. While you are at it, check that the unit is stable and doesn't wobble. Watch for loose or rusted legs.

12.2.4   Wrong Fuse or Breaker Size

The fuse or breaker must be the right size to adequately protect the air conditioner and its wiring. The maximum fuse size is usually on the data plate. Ensure the size is correct.

IMPLICATIONS

Damage to the condenser unit, and possibly a fire, can result from the wrong fuse or breaker size.

STRATEGY

A visual check of the data plate specification against the overcurrent protection device (fuse or breaker) is all that is needed.

If the data plate gives only a fuse size rating, only fuses should be used. Circuit breakers shouldn't be used on this system. If the data plate says "HACR Breaker" this means a **Heating, Air Conditioning, Refrigeration** rated breaker. Most breakers sold today are HACR rated, but look for the rating on the breaker.

No Rating Found

If the data plate is missing or partly illegible, you can approximate the correct fuse or breaker size by using 125 percent of the total of the compressor RLA and the condenser fan FLA (full-load-amperage).

12.2.5   Electric Wires Too Small

The wire carrying electricity to the condenser unit may be too small.
Implications include:

IMPLICATIONS

- overheating of the wire and a possible fire
- excess voltage drop
- an inoperative or poor performing compressor

STRATEGY

Check the data plate to determine the **minimum circuit ampacity.** Make sure the wires serving the condenser unit are large enough to carry this current.

No Data

If the data plate is missing or illegible, you can approximate the minimum wire rating by multiplying the compressor RLA plus the condenser fan FLA (full load amperage) by 125 percent.

12.2.6   Missing Electrical Shutoff

In much of the United States, an outdoor electrical disconnecting means is required within sight of and readily accessible to the condenser unit. Check with your local authorities to determine whether this is needed in your area.

IMPLICATION

A missing electrical shutoff means the unit cannot be serviced conveniently.

STRATEGY

Look for an accessible disconnecting means (switch) for the air conditioner close to the condenser unit. The switch should not be behind or right above the condenser unit because it may not be readily accessible.

12.2.7   Inoperative

IMPLICATION

Obviously, an inoperative compressor means no air conditioning.

STRATEGY

If the compressor doesn't operate when you turn the thermostat down, check first to make sure the fuse or breaker is active. Make sure the thermostat is set to the "Cool" position. If the thermostat is a mercury bulb type, make sure the switch activates by removing the cover and turning the thermostat up and down. You should see the mercury make and break contact as it moves in the bulb.

Delayed Start-Up   Wait for up to seven minutes before determining that the unit is not operative. Many units have a timed start-up delay of up to seven minutes.

It is beyond our scope to troubleshoot compressor failures. This information is intended to give you an appreciation for the complexity of the issue. If the compressor doesn't operate, just record it and recommend further investigation.

12.2.8   Inadequate Cooling

IMPLICATIONS   Poor comfort and high energy costs are the implications of inadequate cooling.

STRATEGY   Measure the temperature drop across the evaporation coil, looking for a 15°F to 20°F drop, roughly. Also, sense how comfortable the house is, if inspecting on a warm day.

12.3   CONDENSER COIL

Function   The outdoor condenser coil transfers heat from the refrigerant into the outdoor air. The refrigerant enters the condenser coil from the compressor as a hot (e.g.,150°F) gas. The gas condenses to a liquid as the 95°F outdoor air (for example) is pushed past the coil by the condenser fan. The air coming off the condenser coil may be 110°F.

Beyond the Standards   The condenser coil is in a cabinet often call the **condenser unit** although it contains the compressor and the condenser fan as well as the condenser coil. This cabinet is not normally opened or serviced by the homeowner. Live 240-volt electrical connections are accessible inside the cabinet. Opening this cabinet is beyond the scope of a home inspection.

Removing the access panel allows you to examine the compressor shell and determine the compressor age from its data plate. You can also look for a failed capacitor (bulging or leaking), oil leaks (which indicate refrigerant leaks) or corroded and obstructed coil fins, for example.

Receivers   Condensers are typically copper tubes with aluminum fins. The bottoms of some condensers are liquid receivers that collect the condensed refrigerant. Some receivers are separate from the condenser. Some modern coils are all aluminum; these may have a shorter life span than copper tube coils.

Noisy   The condenser unit can be noisy. Its location should take this into consideration. A condenser unit that is adjacent to a patio for example, may be a nuisance.

Conditions   Common coil problems include the following:

1. Dirty
2. Damaged or leaking
3. Corrosion
4. Clothes dryer or water heater exhaust too close to condenser

12.3.1   Dirty

The outdoor coil sees unfiltered air pass through it when the system is working. Many modern systems draw air in through the sides and discharge through the top. Other intake and discharge arrangements are used.

Restriction of airflow through the coil leads to poor heat transfer between the coil and the outdoor air. This means the refrigerant leaving the condenser coil will be warmer than it should be. This means that less heat can be removed from the system. Comfort will suffer and energy costs will be high. Over the long term, compressor damage may result.

The condenser coil should be inspected at least from the outside of the condenser cabinet. Many inspectors use a light to ensure that there is free air passage through the coils. Where there is dirt on the coils, cleaning should be recommended as regular maintenance.

12.3.2   Damaged/Leaking

It is common to find the fins on condenser coils damaged. Grilles or louvers are often damaged, and occasionally you'll find mechanical damage to the cabinet itself.

Damaged fins reduce airflow and heat transfer, adversely affecting system performance, comfort and costs.

Look at as much of the fin surface as you can. If the coil is clogged, remove some of the dirt to determine if the fins are bent. Straightening the fins is possible, but leave it to a service person.

Oil Stains

Coils may leak if they are damaged. You won't see refrigerant leaking (it's a colorless gas) but you may see oil stains below the condenser coil. This oil is carried with the refrigerant, and does appear on and below coils or pipes where there are leaks.

12.3.3   Corrosion

Corroded fins are common, particularly on older units.

The implications of a corroded coil are the same as those of a dirty or damaged coil.

The inspection strategy is the same as looking for a dirty coil or damaged fins. Again, some inspectors use a light to look through the coil.

Make sure the condenser is sitting on a pad so that it is above the soil. A cabinet that is partially buried in dirt will be subject to accelerated corrosion.

Look for corrosion on the cabinet and its grilles or louvers.

12.3.4   Clothes Dryer or Water Heater Exhaust Too Close to Condenser

Condensers often are clogged with lint from a clothes dryer discharging nearby.

The lint will clog the fins and the warm air from the dryer or water heater makes it hard to dump the heat outdoors. The fins may be corroded by the acidic water heater exhaust.

STRATEGY

Dryer and water heater vents should be about 6 feet from the condenser. Look for lint on the coil. Recommend moving the vent if it's too close to the condenser.

Inspector in the House: Uncovering the Truth

Many homeowners in our area cover the outdoor condenser coil of their air conditioners in the winter. While some specialists say this may lead to condensation and corrosion, that's another discussion. This simple story is to help you avoid doing what we did.

One of our newest inspectors was on the case in May. The weather was in the high 70s, but it was raining. We usually start our inspections outside and then move into the house. But the hard rain made the inspector start the inspection inside, thinking the rain would probably let up.

Testing the air conditioning is a normal part of the process, and the inspector flipped the thermostat control from Heat to Cool and turned on the air-conditioning unit. He did not know there was a cover on the outdoor unit. Not surprisingly, when the outdoor unit cannot move any air across the condenser coil, the unit does not work very well.

The screeching noise from outside alerted the inspector and everyone within earshot of the problem, as the strap that secured the cover in place was tangled in the fan blades. We were lucky that it only cost us a service call, since there was no major damage done.

What did we learn? The obvious thing is to check the outdoor unit before running the cooling system. The other mistake the inspector made was moving the control from Heat to Cool and starting the unit. We should not be the first to operate a cooling system at the beginning of the season. The refrigerant may have leaked out over the winter and the compressor may be ruined by running the unit. The compressor sump heater may not be on, meaning that there may be liquid refrigerant mixed with the lubricating oil. This, too, may ruin the compressor.

If the system has not yet been operated in cooling mode (a good assumption if the thermostat is set to Heat), recommend servicing before the unit is used.

12.4   EVAPORATOR COIL

Function

The evaporator coil transfers heat from the house air into the refrigerant in the coil. The refrigerant boils inside the coil and the house air temperature drops (e.g., from 75°F to 60°F) as it is pushed past the coil by the house air fan.

Copper Tubes

Evaporator coils are usually copper tubes with up to 14 aluminum fins per inch of tube. This type of coil provides good surface area for heat transfer and allows the coils to be compact. Some modern systems have all aluminum coils, which may have a shorter life than copper tube coils.

A-Coils

The evaporator coil is often an **A-coil** installed with a condensate tray below the bottom of each leg of the "A" (see Figure 12.6). These trays catch the condensate coming off the coil and allow air movement through the coil. The air passes up between the trays through the coil.

Slab Coils

Slab coils (Figure 12.7) are installed on a small angle with a single condensate tray below the lower end of the coil.

Vertical Coils

If the unit is arranged so that airflow across the coil is horizontal, the coil can be vertical with a tray at the bottom.

FIGURE 12.6   A-Coil

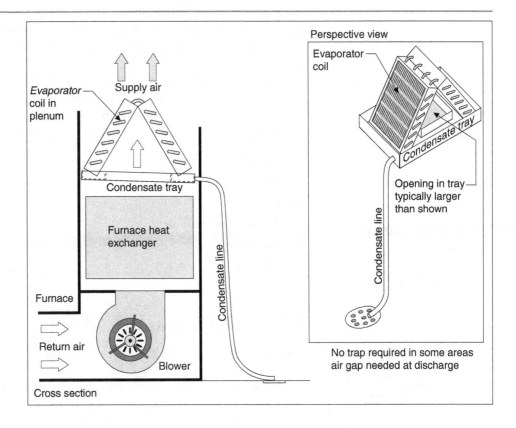

FIGURE 12.7   Slab Coil

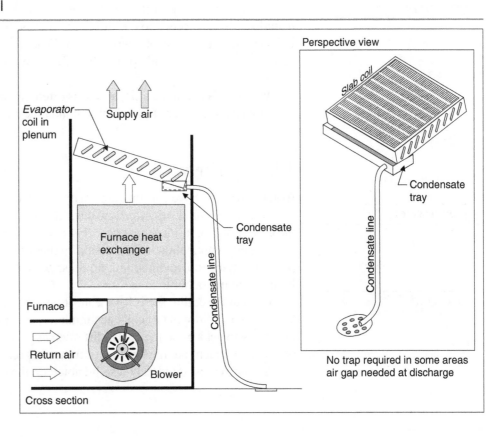

Coil Location

Houses with forced-air heating typically have the evaporator coil just past (downstream of) the furnace heat exchanger. The coil may be in a basement, crawl-space, attic or closet. Houses without a forced-air furnace are often also houses without basements. The evaporator coil, fan and much of the duct system are often in the attic.

Downstream of Furnace Heat Exchangers

Evaporator coils must be downstream of (after) gas, oil or propane furnace heat exchangers. Heat exchangers would rust out quickly if the coils were upstream. The coils can be either before or after electric heating elements.

Conditions

Common evaporator coil problems include the following:

1. No access to coil
2. Dirty
3. Frost
4. Top of evaporator dry
5. Corrosion
6. Damage

12.4.1   No Access to Coil

On many installations, there is no access port in the ductwork to inspect and service the coil.

IMPLICATIONS

If the unit can't be accessed for inspection and cleaning, it will get dirty and suffer from a lack of maintenance. It's also possible that condensate overflow or leakage may occur and go undetected for some time. If the coil is above the furnace heat exchanger (common in an upflow furnace), considerable rusting of the heat exchanger can occur from condensate dripping on to the heat exchanger.

STRATEGY

In some areas, the coils are always accessible. In other areas, coils are rarely installed with an access cover. Find out what is the norm in your area, and if the coils are usually accessible, write up any that are not. Whether the coils are typically accessible or not, it's probably safe to say they need cleaning if there is no access.

When coils are in the attic, access is often awkward and unpleasant, especially on a hot day. However, it is part of a Standards inspection to check these.

12.4.2   Dirty

Evaporator coils have fins that are easily clogged.

IMPLICATION

Dirt on the coil restricts airflow through the coil and inhibits heat transfer across the coil, resulting in inadequate cooling and high operating costs.

Another implication is the possibility that the refrigerant returning to the compressor may be too cold and in a liquid state. The compressor may be damaged if it pumps liquid rather than gas.

STRATEGY

Look at the coil to see if it's clean. If possible, look at the upstream side of the coil where the dirt will typically accumulate. Sometimes a mirror and flashlight are necessary to get a good look. The dirt often accumulates in a mat that can be rolled off the coil, much like the lint that accumulates on a clothes dryer filter.

In some cases, mold may also be noted on the coil.

12.4.3   Frost

If frost is seen on the coil, service is necessary.

IMPLICATION

System performance will deteriorate and compressor damage may result from the suction line containing liquid rather than gas.

STRATEGY

Check the coil for frost. Although no frost should be visible, if there is a small amount of frost on the inlet port of the coil, this may not be a serious problem. Servicing should, however, be recommended.

If frost is visible on other parts of the coil, compressor damage is a distinct possibility and the system should be shut down and recommended for service.

12.4.4   Top of Evaporator Dry

When the evaporator is operating, the entire surface should be covered with condensation.

IMPLICATIONS

If this is not the case, poor comfort and system stress can result.

STRATEGY

If you can look at the coil when the system is or has been operating, check for uniformity of condensation on the coil. This is a secondary indicator to checking the temperature split across the coil. If the split is appropriate, there may not be a problem.

12.4.5   Corrosion

The copper or aluminum fins may corrode.

IMPLICATIONS

All coils will corrode as they age, and as long as there is not a significant reduction of heat transfer or airflow, this is not a major concern.

Corrosion caused by system contaminants is much more serious. These contaminants are usually left over from an improper evacuation of the refrigerant when a component was replaced. The contamination leads to refrigerant line failure, expansion device blockage and corrosion of the soldered joints.

STRATEGY

The coil should be examined through the access port, paying particular attention to the joints at the expansion device and the connection between the refrigerant tubing and the coil. Corrosion of the copper will be green or blue. If the problem is system contamination, the corrosion will be uniform around the joint.

12.4.6   Damage

The fine aluminum fins on the coils can be damaged by aggressive cleaning. If the fins are bent, the airflow will be restricted.

IMPLICATIONS

Such damage can cause reduced airflow and comfort in the house, reduced heat transfer and possible compressor damage.

STRATEGY

When inspecting the coil, look for damage to the fins. In some cases, damaged fins can be straightened.

FIGURE 12.8   Thermostatic Expansion Valve

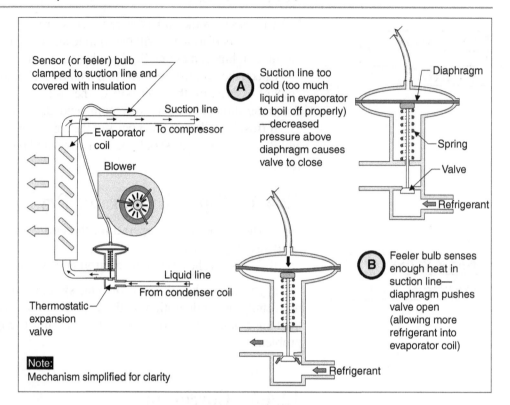

Sensor (or feeler) bulb clamped to suction line and covered with insulation

Suction line
To compressor

Evaporator coil

Blower

Liquid line
From condenser coil

Thermostatic expansion valve

Note:
Mechanism simplified for clarity

A Suction line too cold (too much liquid in evaporator to boil off properly)—decreased pressure above diaphragm causes valve to close

Diaphragm

Spring

Valve

Refrigerant

B Feeler bulb senses enough heat in suction line—diaphragm pushes valve open (allowing more refrigerant into evaporator coil)

Refrigerant

12.5   EXPANSION DEVICE (METERING DEVICE)

Function

This is the device located just upstream of the evaporator coil that changes the refrigerant from a high pressure, high temperature liquid to a low pressure, low temperature liquid.

Capillary Tube

One common expansion device in residential air conditioners is a **capillary tube.** This is a very small-diameter copper tube wrapped into a coil. It simply creates a bottleneck in the liquid line. As the refrigerant comes out of the end of the small-diameter capillary tube, it expands into the larger tube. This lowers the pressure and, consequently, the temperature.

Thermostatic Expansion Valve

Another expansion device is the **thermostatic expansion valve (TXV or TEV),** as shown in Figure 12.8. The TXV is usually found on air conditioning systems larger than three tons, or on combination heat pump and electric furnace packages. The TXV is a more precise metering device than the capillary tube and allows the system to adjust to its environment so that the compressor should never receive liquid refrigerant.

Location

The expansion valve is often visible in the refrigerant lines just outside the duct.

Conditions

Common expansion device problems include the following:

1. Capillary tube defects
2. Thermostatic expansion valve connections loose
3. Clogged orifice
4. Expansion valve sticking

F I G U R E 12.9   Capillary Tube Defects

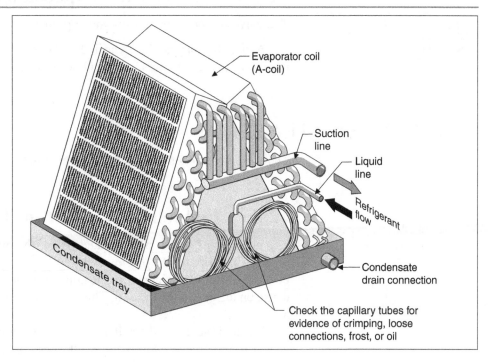

12.5.1   Capillary Tube Defects

The capillary tube may be crimped, disconnected, frosted, or covered with oil (Figure 12.9).

IMPLICATION

Poor cooling performance will result from capillary tube defects.

STRATEGY

If visible through the access port in the duct system, look at the tube for evidence of crimping, loose connections, frost or oil.

12.5.2   Thermostatic Expansion Valve Connections Loose

The TXV may have a loose bulb or loose liquid line connection. The liquid line connection point may also be cracked.

IMPLICATION

These conditions will result in loss of refrigerant and poor system performance.

STRATEGY

Look for evidence of a loose bulb or liquid line connection. Look for evidence of cracking at the liquid line connection.

12.5.3   Clogged Orifice

IMPLICATIONS

If the expansion device is plugged, the refrigerant can't flow and the system will shut down, ideally before the compressor is damaged.

STRATEGY

Troubleshooting air conditioning systems is beyond our scope, but frost near the expansion device may suggest an obstruction.

12.5.4   Thermostatic Expansion Valve Sticking

The valve components may not move properly, resulting in no refrigerant flow.

Again, this may not be identified as the reason for poor system performance or non-performance, but this is beyond our scope.

12.6   CONDENSATE SYSTEM

There are several components to the condensate system.

12.6.1   Condensate Drain Pan (Tray)

Location and Function

The **condensate drain pan,** located below the evaporator coil, catches the condensate that drips off the outside of the coil as the warm moist house air passes over the coil. The cold refrigerant in the coil cools the air, causing the moisture to condense on the outside of the coil. This is how air conditioners dehumidify the house air.

If there is access to the coil, the condensate drain pan can be inspected. If there is no access, you won't be able to see the pan, and as mentioned earlier, you should recommend servicing and the provision of an access panel so that the coil and pan can be inspected and cleaned. The pan should be slightly sloped so water flows to the drain connection. The condensate is piped to a floor drain, sink, outdoors or another suitable discharge point.

Conditions

The common drain pan problem is leaking.

Leaking pans allow water damage to occur to whatever is below. In many areas, the evaporator coil is directly above the furnace heat exchanger. A leaking pan can rust out the furnace heat exchanger, rendering the furnace ineffective and creating an unsafe situation, with a risk of carbon monoxide entering the house.

Look at the pan for evidence of leaking, including cracks, rust, dirt accumulation, a drain line obstruction, improper slope, or poor attachment. Look for staining on the outside of the pan and on whatever components are below.

If there is no access cover, look around and below the cabinetry and furnace components below the coil for evidence of water streaking, staining or rusting.

If the air conditioner is running or has been running recently, look for moisture.

12.6.2   Auxiliary Condensate Drain Pan

Second Line of Defense

Auxiliary pans are typically provided where an evaporator coil is located in an attic or anywhere above finished living space (see Figure 12.10). These are only used when failure of the main drain pan will damage the house. This is a secondary pan, provided because the primary drain will eventually leak.

Causes of Leaks

This pan should be checked for the same conditions as the main condensate drain pan, including rust, dirt accumulation, a blocked drain line, improper slope and poor attachment.

Float Switch

Some drain pans have a float switch that will shut off the system if the water level rises too high, instead of an auxiliary pan. This switch may shut off just the compressor or the compressor and the blower. This switch can be tested by hold-

F I G U R E 12.10   Auxiliary Condensate Line from Attic Evaporator Coil

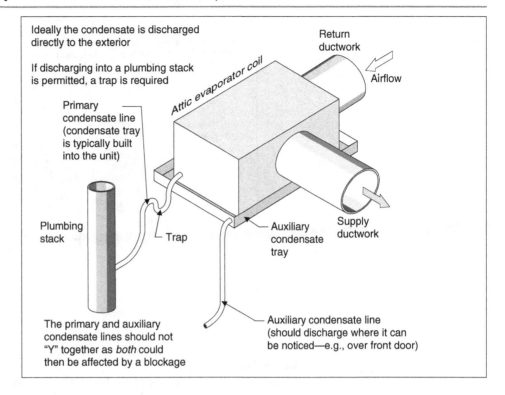

ing it up for roughly five minutes to see whether the unit shuts off. In some cases the whole system shuts down. In some cases only the compressor and condenser fan shut down.

12.6.3   Condensate Drain Line

Function and Material

This drain line carries condensate from the pan to an appropriate discharge point. The line is typically plastic or copper and is usually $^3/_4$-inch diameter. In some areas, the condensate line is insulated to prevent it from sweating as it runs from the evaporator coil to the discharge point.

Separate Drain Pipe Needed for Auxiliary Pan

An auxiliary drain should have a separate drain line from the pan that is not manifolded with the line from the primary pan. A clog in one condensate drain line should not render both pans ineffective. There should be no trap in the auxiliary drain line, which is typically $^3/_4$-inch diameter.

Discharge Point

The discharge point from a primary pan should be out of the way. The discharge point for a secondary pan should be in the way, and hard to ignore; over the front door is good. It should catch your attention, because something is wrong if it's working.

Conditions

Common drain line problems include these:

1. Leaking
2. Blocked
3. No trap
4. Improper discharge point

F I G U R E 12.11 Trap Required in Condensate Line

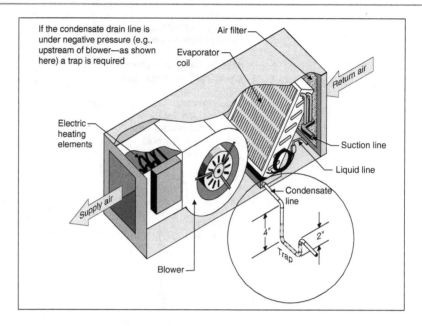

If the condensate drain line is under negative pressure (e.g., upstream of blower—as shown here) a trap is required

Air filter

Evaporator coil

Return air

Electric heating elements

Suction line

Liquid line

Condensate line

4"

2"

Trap

Supply air

Blower

Leaking

A leak will allow condensate to flow where it was not intended. The implications are similar to those we discussed with respect to leakage from the condensate drain pan.

Inspect the length of the condensate drain line looking for active leakage if the unit is running or has been running recently. If the air conditioner is idle, look for evidence of staining, streaking, loose connections or split piping.

Blocked

The implications of blockage are similar to those caused by a leak in the drain pan.

If the unit is operating, make sure water is discharging out of the drain line. If the unit is at rest, pouring water into the drain pan and checking the discharge point will reveal blockages, although this goes beyond the Standards. In some cases, there is a vent (relief opening) downstream of the trap in the condensate drain line. Watch that this is not discharging. If water is coming out of this relief opening, there is probably a blockage in the trap.

Blockages are common at the entry and exit points at the drain line.

No Trap

Traps are often required on condensate drains, especially when the condensate pan is upstream of (before) the house air fan (Figure 12.11). This is typical of air-conditioning-only systems, or air-conditioning-plus-electric-heat. The water in the pan is under negative pressure because it is on the suction side of the pan.

Purpose—Negative Pressure

If the line is under negative pressure, air may be sucked up the drain and the water may not be able to flow down the drain line. In some cases, the drain pan may fill up and overflow. A trap prevents this. Standard traps have a 4-inch drop on the upstream side, and a 2-inch rise on the downstream side. Traps in condensate lines are required in many jurisdictions. In some jurisdictions, if the condensate line is permitted to drain into a waste plumbing pipe, a trap will be required. Check with authorities in your area to determine whether air conditioning condensate lines require traps and, if so, whether there are any specific rules about where and how they are installed. Traps are usually outside the evaporator plenum, as close to the drain pan as possible.

If the condensate line does terminate in a waste plumbing stack, the trap will prevent sewer odor and bacteria from entering the house air supply, at least until the trap water evaporates. However, this discharge point is not allowed in most areas.

Some systems without traps work most of the time. During hot humid weather, the drain pan may overflow. Most would agree that if a condensate line discharges directly into a waste plumbing system, a trap is necessary for health reasons. Incidentally, when the air conditioner hasn't been run for several months (over the winter), the water in the trap will evaporate, and for this reason, direct connection to a waste plumbing stack is not a good idea even if permitted in your jurisdiction.

Trace the condensate line from the drain pan to its discharge point. It should be obvious whether or not a trap has been provided.

Improper Discharge Point

The best place for air conditioning discharge is usually considered to be outside the building onto the ground. The discharge should not run down the exterior of the wall.

Some jurisdictions allow the condensate to drain into a sink or floor drain as long as there is an air gap to prevent siphoning. It may be permitted to discharge the condensate into the tail piece of a basin (upstream of the trap) or into the overflow for a bathtub (again, upstream of the trap). Check with authorities to find what is allowed in your area.

In some areas, the condensate drain line goes down through the floor slab and discharges into the granular material below. This is not considered a good arrangement because you can't see the condensate line working. An obstruction may go undetected until considerable damage is done. Sub-slab gases (such as radon) may also find their way into house when the unit is not running.

We also recommend against discharging the condensate drain line into the waste plumbing stack. There is the issue of a blockage going unnoticed for some time and there is also the possibility of sewer odor backing up into the house air system, as discussed earlier.

Non-performance that goes unnoticed may cause water damage. If discharging into waste plumbing, sewer odor and its associated health issues are other potential implications.

Trace the condensate discharge line to its termination point. Ensure that the end of the line is open, and if the air conditioner is operating, water should be coming out.

12.6.4   Condensate Pump

If the condensate cannot run from the evaporator coil outside by gravity, and if there is no drain or sink nearby that the condensate can be discharged into, a pump is required (Figure 12.12). Condensate pumps are typically low-quality sponge pumps.

Pumps may be inoperative, leaking, or poorly wired.

Inoperative

Since the pump is located outside the evaporator coil housing and duct system, the implication of pump failure is water spilling onto the area around the pump and reservoir.

FIGURE 12.12 Condensate Pump

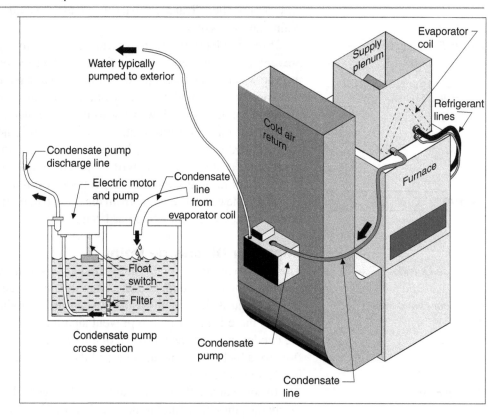

- Water typically pumped to exterior
- Condensate pump discharge line
- Electric motor and pump
- Condensate line from evaporator coil
- Float switch
- Filter
- Condensate pump cross section
- Evaporator coil
- Supply plenum
- Refrigerant lines
- Cold air return
- Furnace
- Condensate pump
- Condensate line

If the system is operating, you can look for water discharging from the condensate line and listen for the pump working.

If the pump does not work, the pump may be inoperative, although you have to be careful. The electrical power to the pump may have been shut off when the air conditioner was shut off for the season. If you're looking at an air conditioning system outside of the cooling season, the condensate pump may not be powered. Be careful not to describe the pump as inoperative under these circumstances.

Leaking

Leakage may result in water damage and a burned-out reservoir pump.

Check the pump and the area around it.

Poor Wiring

Many potential electrical problems can be found at the condensate pump. Because of the proximity of the water and electricity, condensate pumps should be grounded. Many are not. Other common electrical conditions include loose connections, poorly supported wiring, open connection boxes, and overfusing.

Poor wiring can result in fire or electrical shock.

Check the electrical supply to the condensate pump as you check the rest of the electrical system. Ensure that the pump is grounded.

FIGURE 12.13   Refrigerant Lines

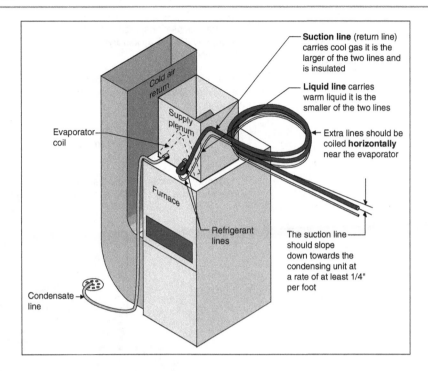

Suction line (return line) carries cool gas it is the larger of the two lines and is insulated

Liquid line carries warm liquid it is the smaller of the two lines

Extra lines should be coiled **horizontally** near the evaporator

The suction line should slope down towards the condensing unit at a rate of at least 1/4" per foot

Evaporator coil

Cold air return

Supply plenum

Furnace

Refrigerant lines

Condensate line

12.7   REFRIGERANT LINES

Function and Material

The lines that carry the refrigerant between the evaporator and condenser coils and through the compressor and expansion device are typically copper.

Suction Line

The larger line typically carries a cool gas and is insulated. This is referred to as the **suction line.** It is also called the **return line.**

Liquid Line

The smaller uninsulated line typically carries a warm liquid. It is most often called the **liquid line.**

Allow Oil to Flow Back to Condenser

Where the evaporator coil is higher than the condensing unit, the suction line should slope down toward the condensing unit with a slope of at least one quarter inch per foot.

Line Coiled Horizontally

Extra lines are usually coiled near the evaporator coil. The line should be coiled horizontally rather than vertically (Figure 12.13). The coils should allow oil to flow down through the coil and back to the condensing unit.

Pressures in the lines may range from 50 psi up to 275 psi. Since the refrigerant is a gas at atmospheric temperature and pressure, if it leaks it will dissipate as a gas. It may leave an oil residue.

Filter/Dryer

In some installations, you will find a **filter/dryer** in the liquid line (Figure 12.14). Filter/dryers clean and dry the refrigerant. They are often added to a system where the compressor has been replaced. They help remove any contaminants. They are roughly the size and shape of a soft drink can. They may be located in the liquid line near the condenser outlet or near the expansion device.

Watch for Frost

Frost accumulation just past the filter/dryer indicates a partially plugged unit and service should be recommended.

Supports and Radius of Bends

Supports for refrigerant lines should be every 5 to 6 feet. Bends in refrigerant lines should have a minimum 12-inch radius.

FIGURE 12.14 Filter/Dryer on the Refrigerant Line

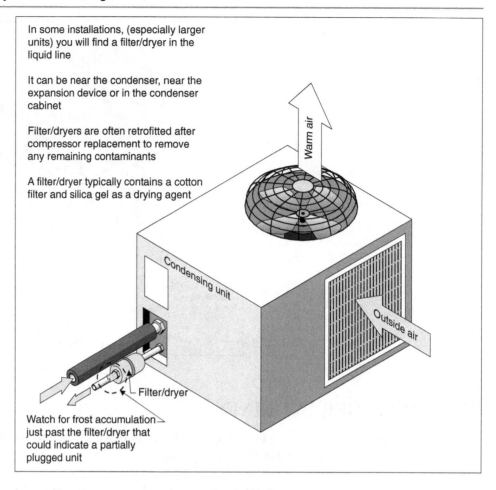

In some installations, (especially larger units) you will find a filter/dryer in the liquid line

It can be near the condenser, near the expansion device or in the condenser cabinet

Filter/dryers are often retrofitted after compressor replacement to remove any remaining contaminants

A filter/dryer typically contains a cotton filter and silica gel as a drying agent

Warm air

Condensing unit

Outside air

Filter/dryer

Watch for frost accumulation just past the filter/dryer that could indicate a partially plugged unit

Conditions

Common refrigerant line problems include the following:

1. Leaking
2. Damage
3. Missing insulation
4. Lines too warm or cold
5. Lines touching each other

12.7.1 Leaking

A leak in a line is usually identified by the oil residue on the line. Because oil travels through the system with the refrigerant, a leak will often show up as an oil stain. Escaping refrigerant boils off and leaves no trace, other than the oil that is left behind.

IMPLICATIONS

If the refrigerant leaks out, the system performance will deteriorate and comfort levels in the house will decrease. Ultimately, the system will shut down or the compressor may fail.

Since refrigerant line joints are usually only at the coils, concentrate on the connections to the coils at either end, where visible. If there is a thermostatic expansion valve, check its connections.

Check along the length of the line for evidence of mechanical damage, particularly in exposed areas and at the interior and exterior penetration points through the house wall. Refrigerant lines need support so that joints aren't stressed under the weight of the lines.

On attic units, pay attention to where the lines disappear into walls or ceilings.

Lines through the Wall

Where refrigerant lines go through walls, the hole in the wall should be considerably larger than the refrigerant lines and the lines should be in conduit where they go through the wall. The ends of the conduit should be sealed with a flexible material at either end to allow movement but to prevent moisture and insect entry into the building and heat loss out of the building.

Oil Stains

Look for evidence of oil stains on the refrigerant lines.

12.7.2   Damage

In some cases, the lines may be crimped or damaged without leakage. Any reduction in the diameter of the lines will act as a pressure restriction, changing the temperature of the refrigerant that passes through the restricted area. This will adversely affect system performance.

IMPLICATIONS

Such damage results in reduced performance of the system.

STRATEGY

Follow the refrigerant lines, looking for evidence of crimping or flattening, particularly at changes in direction or where the lines go through walls or ceilings.

12.7.3   Missing Insulation

The large-diameter line (suction line or gas line) should be insulated along its entire length. The insulation performs two functions.

1. It prevents the suction line from sweating and dripping water inside the house.

2. The insulation also prevents the suction line attracting heat from the outdoors on its way to the condenser coil. We are trying to take heat out of the house and dump it outside. We don't want to gather outside heat and dump it into the suction line before it goes into the compressor.

IMPLICATIONS

System performance will be adversely affected if the outdoor insulation is missing. If the indoor insulation is missing, water damage to the home may result.

STRATEGY

Look for the insulation to be intact along its entire length. Pay particular attention to the outdoor section of the suction line.

12.7.4   Lines Too Warm or Too Cold

Cold Suction Line

When the system is operating, the large insulated suction line should be cold to the touch and sweating at any point where there is no insulation.

Warm Liquid Line

The smaller uninsulated liquid line should be warm to the touch after the system has been operating for 10 or 15 minutes.

Frost

Frost on the suction line may indicate too much refrigerant going through the expansion device, an inoperative house air fan, too much refrigerant or too low an outdoor temperature. Frost on the liquid line may mean the dryer is clogged. Frost on the expansion device may mean the device is clogged with ice.

<table>
<tr><td>IMPLICATIONS</td></tr>
</table>

Lines that are too warm or too cold can indicate a lack of adequate cooling in the house and possible compressor damage.

<table>
<tr><td>STRATEGY</td></tr>
</table>

Touching the lines is a part of any inspection when the air conditioner is operating. Look for the suction line to be at roughly 45°F to 55°F, and the liquid line to be at about 90°F to 110°F. Measurement with instruments is not needed.

If the suction line isn't cold, or the liquid line isn't warm, servicing should be recommended.

12.7.5   Lines Touching Each Other

<table>
<tr><td>IMPLICATIONS</td></tr>
</table>

The liquid and suction lines should not be in contact. If they are, heat transfer between the lines and reduced system efficiency may result.

<table>
<tr><td>STRATEGY</td></tr>
</table>

Make sure these lines don't touch each other.

Inspector in the House: Detective Inspector

I was performing a pre-listing inspection for a seller in the fall. We do a lot of these before the home goes on the market. It was too cold to run the air conditioner but we always do a visual inspection anyway. There was a lot of storage in the furnace room and a pile of firewood outside the house. I had trouble tracing the refrigerant lines from the condenser coil to the evaporator.

Since the client was the seller, I asked if the air conditioner worked. With what may have been the slightest hesitation, she told me the air conditioner had worked fine all summer. As I made my way around the outside, I saw signs of recent excavation along the foundation wall. The homeowner advised they had just had the basement waterproofed to ensure it did not leak. She showed me the listing sheet, which indeed described the recently waterproofed basement.

Moving some firewood allowed me to confirm that the air conditioning lines had been cut for the basement waterproofing to be done! I have not concluded whether or not the homeowner knew about this. Thank goodness we don't have to figure these things out.

By the way, moving the firewood is not required as part of a home inspection, but when you are chasing a clue you sometimes get fanatical about finding the answer.

12.8   CONDENSER FAN

Function

This fan blows outdoor air across the hot condenser coil, cooling the hot refrigerant gas. The gas inside the coil condenses as it cools and the air passing over the coil heats up. This is how we dump the house heat into the outdoor air.

Location and Orientation

The outdoor fan is located in the condenser cabinet. The fan draws air in through the sides of the condenser coil and discharges the warmer air through the top of the cabinet.

Common fan problems include the following:

1. Excess noise/vibration
2. Inoperative
3. Corrosion or mechanical damage
4. Obstructed airflow

12.8.1   Excess Noise/Vibration

IMPLICATIONS

Bearing noise is an indicator of a bearing about to fail, usually from a lack of lubrication.

Unbalanced fan blades will rotate but will eventually cause bearing failure. Unbalanced fan blades are usually a result of mechanical damage or dirt and will not move as much air as they should.

In any case, system failure is the ultimate result of a noisy fan.

STRATEGY

Listen for high pitched intermittent or steady squeals from the fan area. Observe the fan blades for vibration while rotating and listen for a helicopter-type noise. from unbalanced fan blades.

When the fan is not operating, look at the blades to see if they are caked with dirt or are obviously damaged or misaligned.

12.8.2   Inoperative

IMPLICATIONS

When the outdoor fan doesn't work, very little heat will be transferred to the outdoor air, which means that the air conditioning will not perform properly. Over time, compressor failure may result.

STRATEGY

When the unit is running, ensure the fan blades are turning. Most modern fans are axial and turn at approximately 1,800 RPM. Newer quiet low rpm fans may turn at 875 rpm. If the fan is not moving or is moving very slowly, service is required.

12.8.3   Corrosion or Mechanical Damage

IMPLICATIONS

Rusted or damaged fans may not operate. The implications are the same as for an inoperative fan.

In other cases, the fan may turn but with reduced efficiency or speed. This will move less air across the coil and reduce the heat transfer to the exterior air. This, of course, will also reduce the comfort in the house and make the whole system work harder.

STRATEGY

Look closely at the fan and motor for evidence of rusting. A flashlight may be necessary here. Look also for evidence of mechanical damage to the motor casing and fan blades. Check for cracks in the fan blades.

The wisdom of covering condenser units during the winter months is not universally agreed on. Some say they should be covered; others say they shouldn't. People do agree that if a cover is used, it should be breathable, so it won't trap condensation in the unit.

12.8.4   Obstructed Airflow

Intake air should be unobstructed for 1 to 3 feet adjacent to the unit (depending on the manufacturer's recommendations). The clearance on the exit side or top should be 4 to 6 feet.

The airflow through the outdoor fan may be blocked on the intake or exhaust side. A clogged, damaged or corroded condenser coil can block the air supply to the fan.

IMPLICATIONS

Partially or totally restricted fans will lead to non-performance and possible compressor failure.

STRATEGY

Look at the airflow into and out of the fan.

Sunlight or Shade

Some people maintain that air conditioning condensers should be kept out of direct sunlight. Many manufacturers do not consider this a significant issue. Incidentally, manufacturers of heat pumps consider it an asset if the unit is located in the sun.

Discharge Air Is Hot

When checking the operation of the outdoor fan, the air coming off the fan should be warmer than the ambient air temperature, even on a hot summer day. This is one indication that the system is operating properly.

12.9   EVAPORATOR FAN

Function

The indoor fan blows house air across the evaporator coil, cooling and dehumidifying the house air (see Figure 12.15).

Too Much Air

The size of the air handling system has to match the cooling capacity of the air conditioning equipment. If too much air is blown across a coil (the air moves by the coil too quickly), there may not be enough cooling to dehumidify the air. Noise

FIGURE 12.15   Evaporator Fan

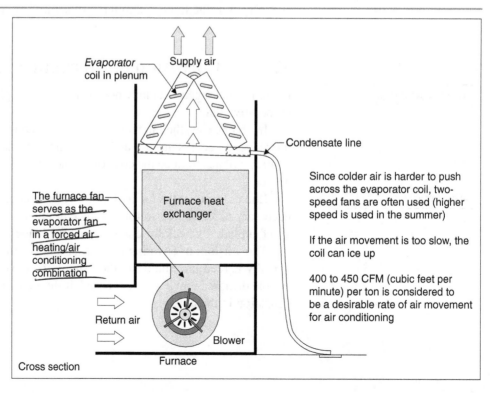

problems will also develop and moisture will be blown off the coil, rusting ducts and damaging finishes downstream. A maximum air velocity of 500 linear feet per minute is typically recommended.

Too Little Air

If the air moves too slowly, the air may be cooled dramatically, but the air may not move quickly enough through the house to achieve good cooling. Another possible impact of inadequate airflow is icing up of the evaporator coil because the coil sees a colder environment than it should.

Need Twice as Much Air for Cooling

Too little air movement is a more common problem than too much air movement is. Roughly twice as much air movement is needed for cooling as heating with a conventional gas furnace, for example.

Fan Coils Hung from Rafters

Fans and coils in attics are often hung from rafters rather than set on ceiling joists to minimize vibration and noise transferred to the living spaces.

Noisy air handlers or air handlers with a great deal of vibration are usually nearing the end of their life. In some cases, lubrication can restore bearing operation and eliminate noise.

Conditions

Common fan problems include the following:

1. Undersized blower or motor
2. Misadjustment of belt or pulley
3. Excess noise/vibration
4. Dirty fan
5. Dirty or missing filter
6. Inoperative
7. Corrosion/damage

Evaporator fans are the same as those found in furnaces. In fact, when an air conditioner is added to a furnace system, the same fan is used for both heating and cooling. Rather than repeat our earlier discussion, please refer to Chapter 8, *Gas Furnaces*, for more information on fans and their associated problems.

12.10   DUCT SYSTEM

Function

The duct system moves cooled dry air through the house and brings warm moist air back to the evaporator coil for cooling and drying (Figures 12.16 and 12.17). A good duct system keeps all parts of the home at roughly the same temperature.

An air conditioning system relies as much on a good duct system as it does on good cooling equipment. Many air-conditioning systems dramatically under-perform as a result of duct problems.

All of Home Served?

Be very careful to ensure that the duct system feeds all parts of the home. Additions and renovations are sometimes not air-conditioned. Watch for electric heat in a room. This may mean no ductwork and, consequently, no cooling. It is very expensive to add air conditioning to spaces that don't have ducts. You don't want to have to provide a client with air conditioning in rooms because you mistakenly told them that the entire house was air-conditioned.

Watch for houses with hot water heat that have had independent air conditioning systems added. These systems often don't cover the whole house.

High Level Return Grilles

Retrofitted air conditioning systems have different needs than heating systems. Heating systems don't usually require a great deal of return air from the upper floors. Air conditioning systems do need good air return from upper levels.

FIGURE 12.16 Flow of Cooled Air–Older-Style Ductwork

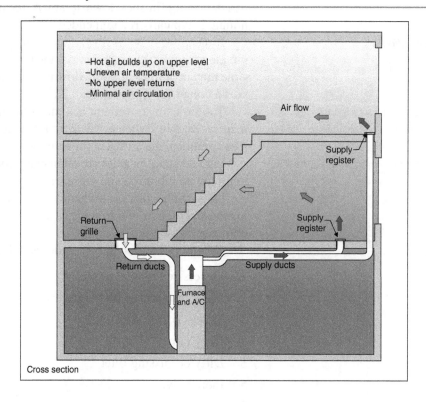

- Hot air builds up on upper level
- Uneven air temperature
- No upper level returns
- Minimal air circulation

Air flow

Supply register

Return grille

Supply register

Return ducts

Supply ducts

Furnace and A/C

Cross section

FIGURE 12.17 Flow of Cooled Air—Modern Ductwork

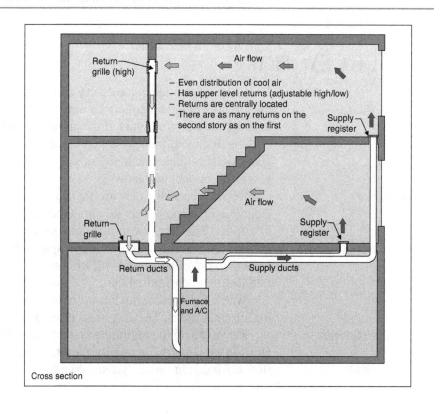

Return grille (high)

Air flow

- Even distribution of cool air
- Has upper level returns (adjustable high/low)
- Returns are centrally located
- There are as many returns on the second story as on the first

Supply register

Return grille

Air flow

Supply register

Return ducts

Supply ducts

Furnace and A/C

Cross section

It is common to find large temperature differences between the first and second floors on air conditioning systems that have been added to ducts designed for heating only.

12.10.1   Duct Insulation

Insulation

Ducts passing through unconditioned spaces, such as attics or crawlspaces, should be insulated and airtight. We don't want to collect heat from these areas, or distribute cool air into these areas. As a general rule, the more ducts that pass through unconditioned spaces, the greater is the challenge for the air conditioning system.

Vapor Barriers

The insulation should have a vapor barrier and, like all vapor barriers, it should be on the warm side of the insulation. In an air conditioning environment, this means the vapor barrier should be on the outside of the insulation. The warm, moist air in the attic or crawlspace may condense if it is cooled. We want to keep the attic and crawlspace air warm, but if we inadvertently cool this air, we don't want condensation to form on the outside of the ducts. The vapor barrier is designed to prevent the warm, moist air from getting close to the ducts where it would inevitably form condensation. It also prevents moisture moving through the insulation by vapor diffusion.

The downside to all of this is that putting the vapor barrier on the outside of ductwork that runs through unfinished spaces creates a vulnerable situation. Vapor barriers are often torn.

12.10.2   Supply and Return Registers

Registers are associated with duct problems, but can be looked at slightly differently. A good-sized air conditioning system and reasonable-sized ducts may still result in poor performance if registers are not of the appropriate size, number and location. Conditioned air is heavier than the room air and may be expected to fall. The warmest air is at the top of the room.

An Ideal Arrangement

Introducing conditioned air near the ceiling on an outside wall allows it to fall through the warm air, creating a relatively even temperature throughout the room. The return registers are ideally located on the opposite (interior) side of the room to enhance circulation through the entire room. The return registers should also be high to carry the warmest air out of the room back to the air conditioner to be cooled.

Many systems are not set up this way and, when the same ducts are used for heating and for cooling, compromises are usually made. Heating systems are best set up with the supply and return registers near floor level, just the opposite of what we talked about for air conditioning registers.

Supply on Outside Walls

During the summer, the warmest part of the room is likely to be the outside wall, especially if there are windows in the wall. It makes sense to introduce the coolest air close to the outside wall. Therefore, the supply register should be located near the outside wall.

Returns on Interior Walls

The return registers should be on an opposite and interior wall. In this regard, heating and air conditioning systems have the same register location goals. For the heating system as well, the supply register should be located near an outside wall (usually below windows) and the return register should be located on an opposite and interior wall.

Heating is the Priority

Real-life compromises often mean that registers are set up with heating as the priority over air conditioning. For example, in a two-story house with the ducts designed primarily for heating needs, the return air grilles typically collect cold air that falls down stairwells to the lower parts of the home. Consequently, the return ducts and grilles are usually located centrally, near the bottom of stairwells, and there is often more air return on the lower level than the upper level.

An ideal return air system for air conditioning would have more return air ducts and grilles on the upper level, and they would be located near the top of the second floor. These grilles would be centrally located and above stairwells.

Cooling Better on First Floor than Second

Since most systems are set up with heating as a priority, it is very common to find houses where the air conditioning system works reasonably well on the first floor, but not nearly as well on the second floor.

Conditions

Common duct problems include the following:

1. Undersized or incomplete
2. Supply and return register problems
3. Dirty
4. Disconnected or leaking
5. Obstructed or collapsed
6. Poor support
7. Poor balance
8. Humidifier damper missing

Further discussion of these problems can be found in section 8.9.5 of Chapter 8, *Gas Furnaces*.

Inspector in the House: Appearances Can Be Deceiving

The house is centrally air conditioned. That's what we assume when we see an air conditioning system connected above the furnace. Sometimes we assume too much.

We assumed too much in the house with the garage that had been converted to a family room. It is difficult to add ductwork to an existing slab-on-grade structure. Adding heating with electric baseboards is relatively easy. Adding air conditioning is tougher. We had to pay for an independent air-conditioning system for this room, because we reported the house as air conditioned and failed to mention there was no air-conditioning for the family room.

We also assumed too much in the 1920s house that was open concept on the first floor. In our area, these homes originally had warm air heating with supply ducts running up the interior walls. When the first floor walls are removed, so are the ducts. The second floor registers often remain and electric heaters are used to keep the second floor comfortable in the winter. But there is no air conditioning, and no easy way to add it.

The worst miss I can remember is the beautifully finished basement apartment with supply registers in the ceramic tile-covered concrete floor. The problem was evident if you lifted the register and looked down. There was no ductwork—only dirt. It's one thing to learn after the inspection that the ducts buried in concrete are rusted, flooded, or collapsed. It's quite another to realize there are no ducts at all. This miss cost us $2,000.

12.11   THERMOSTATS

Conditions

We discussed thermostats in the contxt of furances and won't repeat the information here. You may want to review Section 8.7.

Common thermostat problems include the following:

1. Inoperative
2. Poor location
3. Not level
4. Loose
5. Dirty
6. Damaged
7. Poor adjustment/calibration

Here, we will discuss only inoperative thermostats. The other conditions, and strategies for identifying them, are covered in Chapter 8.

Inoperative

To activate an air conditioning system, the thermostat is turned to a lower temperature than the room temperature. If the air conditioner does not respond after about seven minutes, the system should be described as inoperative.

The thermostat is one component that may cause the system not to operate. There are many other problems that may result in the failure to respond to the thermostat. It's beyond the scope of a home inspection to troubleshoot air conditioning systems, although a bad thermostat can be included as one of the possibilities.

IMPLICATIONS

The air conditioning system won't respond if the thermostat isn't working. It may not start or it may not shut off.

STRATEGY

Turn the thermostat down to see if the system operates. If it does not, you may remove the cover (beyond the Standards) and check that the mercury bulb switch moves properly and that the contacts are working. You may also verify that the low voltage wiring to the thermostat is properly connected. Beyond this, there isn't much you can do.

Calibration

It's possible that the thermostat works, but the calibration is wrong. You may not know this during the inspection, and an analysis of the thermostat calibration is beyond the scope of your inspection.

Indoor Fan Starts Immediately

The air conditioner controls are a little different from the furnace control. When the furnace is activated, the burner typically comes on immediately, but the fan will not come on until the furnace is up to temperature. With air conditioning systems, the indoor fan comes on as soon as the compressor and outdoor fan starts.

12.12   LIFE EXPECTANCY OF COMPRESSORS

Although predicting life expectancies goes beyond the Standards, the Standards require that you identify whether the equipment is near the *end* of its normal life expectancy. Although air conditioners have many components, the compressor is the heart of the unit. It is, by a wide margin, the most expensive component to replace on an air conditioner or heat pump.

Checking the Age

You can determine the age of the unit from the condenser unit data plate. **Preston's Guide** is helpful in this regard. Since compressors are often replaced, the home inspector who goes above and beyond will check on a unit that is more than 5 years old to determine whether the compressor has been replaced. This involves removing the cover from the outdoor condenser unit and checking the compressor itself. There are only a few manufacturers of compressors and the date coding systems can be determined by contacting the manufacturers. Older systems with relatively young compressors are not uncommon. If you aren't going to go this far, when you see old air conditioners, you should allow for the possibility that the compressor has been replaced.

Life expectancies vary. Many people in the southern United States consider 8 to 10 years a typical compressor life expectancy. In more moderate climates, a 10- to 15-year life expectancy is typical, and in northern climates, life expectancies of 15 to 20 years may be appropriate.

Warranty

Many compressors are warranted for five years. This suggests a life expectancy range.

IMPLICATION

The life expectancy may have no implication with respect to existing performance. We may simply be anticipating breakdown. However, older compressors may suffer compression ratio decreases as valves wear. They may also be more expensive to operate because they draw more electricity. Some people recommend replacement of old compressors even if they are still operable, as a way to reduce operating costs through enhanced efficiency.

STRATEGY

The age can be determined from the data plate on the condenser or, as discussed, from the compressor itself. Interpretation of serial numbers is sometimes required to verify age. The compressors typically have a date tag riveted or glued onto the shell of the unit.

Speak with manufacturers and installers in your area to get a sense of the common life expectancies for air conditioning compressors in your climate. If you are going to include life expectancy comments in your reports, make it clear to the client you are dealing with a probability and not a certainty. Many compressors will fail before their normal life is up and others will go well beyond what is expected. You may also ask at what age it makes more sense to replace the whole system, rather than just the compressor.

12.12.1   Ductless Air Conditioning

So far our discussion has focused on air conditioning systems that employ ducts to move cooled air through the house and warm air back to the air conditioner. Let's look briefly at **ductless air conditioning**.

Alternative to Central Systems

Air conditioning is expensive to add to homes that do not have ducts. Ductless air conditioning is becoming a popular option because it is not disruptive to install and can provide several cooling zones. Ductless systems are available as air- or water-cooled units.

Split Systems

There are two common types of ductless systems; **split systems** and **single component systems.** Split systems have a condenser cabinet with a compressor, condenser coil and fan on the ground or on the roof, the same as any central split system. The evaporator coil and house air fan are inside the home, in the area to be cooled. There is a condensate collection and discharge system for the interior component. There are two refrigerant lines, often in a conduit, joining the outdoor condenser unit to the evaporator inside the home.

Compact

Split systems, also called **mini-splits**, are easy to install and require only a 3-inch diameter hole through the house wall. The indoor components can be wall or ceiling mounted and don't take up much space. Some are sold with remote controls so they can be mounted out of the way, high on walls or on ceilings.

Quiet

These have the advantage of an outdoor compressor (the noisiest part of an air conditioner) so the home is quieter. Some interior fans are multi-speed to minimize noise. There are also quieter condenser fans in some systems that operate at very low rpm (less than 900 rpm).

Multi-zone Systems

Split systems can be multi-zone, with one condenser unit serving up to four evaporators in different parts of the home.

Large Capacity

Split systems are available with cooling capacities up to 60,000 BTUs/hr (five tons), large enough for most homes.

Single Component Systems

Single component systems are also called **through-wall** or **package systems.** These are self-contained systems with the condenser, compressor and evaporator all in the same cabinet, installed in the wall of the room or area to be cooled. These units are common in motels and apartments. These single component systems are noisier than split systems because the compressor is in the wall. Some include electric elements for supplementary heating. Single component systems may be wired directly into the panel or may plug into a 240-volt receptacle.

Inspection Issues

The inspection procedures for ductless systems are similar to central systems. There is no distribution system to worry about, and there is often much less you can see, especially on single component systems. There is typically a filter access panel, but that is about all that is accessible. On ceiling and high-wall mounted units, the Standards suggest you don't have to open these panels since they are not within **normal reach.** Dirty air filters are a common problem with ductless systems, especially when the system is out of reach of the average person.

Airflow Issues

Ductless air conditioners can blow air up to 40 feet in an open area, but since there is no distribution system, even cooling in multiple rooms from a single system is unlikely. In small rooms, air can bounce off walls or furnishings and create short cycling and comfort problems. These systems are often located near the top of the stairwell in a two-story home in an effort to cool as much of the home as possible.

Condensate Damage

Condensate discharge systems are often on the building exterior, below the wall-mounted evaporator. Discoloration or damage to the wall is a possibility if the condensate is allowed to run down the wall surface.

12.13   AN OVERVIEW OF HEAT PUMPS

The people who designed, built and sold air conditioning equipment knew that it was fairly expensive. In many parts of North America, the equipment sits idle much of the year. If they could use the same equipment that cools the house in the summer to heat it in the winter, wouldn't that be great! They found with some modifications, they could do just that. The result is the heat pump (Figure 12.18).

Inspecting central air conditioning is hard enough. Inspecting heat pumps is even more challenging. Not only is it an air conditioning system that sometimes acts as a heating system, there is often a back-up heating system to inspect as well. Doesn't seem fair, does it?

A discussion of the mechanics of heat pumps is beyond the scope of this book, but we will get a quick overview and then look at typical conditions of heat pumps.

At first glance, it can be difficult to differentiate heat pumps from air conditioners, especially during the summer months. The following are some of the ways to tell.

1. Look at the data plate. It may say **Heat Pump** on it, or the model number may start with **HP.** If it does not, you can jot down the manufacturer's name and model number and contact the manufacturer.

F I G U R E 12.18 Heat Pump Schematic—Summer Mode

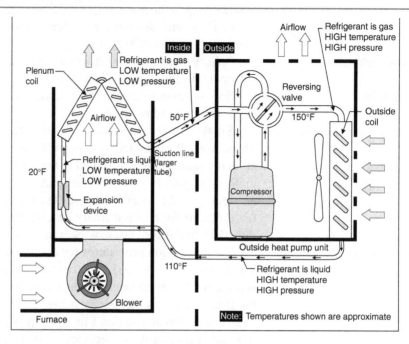

2. If the thermostat has an **Emergency Heat** setting, you can be sure it's a heat pump.

3. If you take the cover off the thermostat (beyond the Standards) and find that it's a two- stage thermostat, this indicates a heat pump. (You must know what you're looking at here.)

4. If both refrigerant lines are insulated, it's a heat pump.

5. If you open the condenser cabinet and find a reversing valve, it's a heat pump.

6. If you find two expansion devices with bypasses, it's a heat pump.

7. If the compressor is indoors and it's an air to air system, it's a heat pump.

8. If there is an outdoor thermostat connected to the control wiring, it's probably a heat pump.

9. If it's winter and the unit is operating, it's a heat pump.

Is It Still Being Used as a Heat Pump?

In many northern climates, heat pumps were often installed with the encouragement of local utilities. For various reasons, they were found to be unsatisfactory. Many have been disconnected as heat pumps and are used only as air conditioners. You won't be able to determine this visually, but your client may want to ask the current owner whether the heat pump is still used for heating. In many cases, it is cheaper to have the back-up heat supply all of the heating, especially if the back-up is a high-efficiency gas furnace. Where the available back-up heat is electricity, heat pumps are more cost effective and more likely to be in service, even in colder climates.

If you're looking at the house in the winter, and the system is operating on the **Emergency Heat** setting, chances are the heat pump is not operative.

12.14   HEAT PUMP CONDITIONS

All of the problems associated with air conditioning components may also be experienced with heat pumps. The following additional problems are common on heat pumps:

1. Oversized for cooling and/or undersized for heating
2. Heat pump inoperative in heating or cooling mode
3. Poor outdoor coil location, including
    a. under the drip line of the roof
    b. where snow drifts accumulate
    c. where air re-circulates and is trapped in an enclosed area, or
    d. where the outdoor coil is exposed to the prevailing wind
4. Outdoor coil is iced up
5. Airflow problems
6. No back-up heat, or back-up heat does not work
7. Old

12.14.1   Oversized for Cooling and Undersized for Heating

Almost all heat pumps in northern climates are undersized for heating. Their sizing should be determined by the cooling load. There is a temptation to oversize for cooling so that the heating load can be satisfied by the heat pump. This is usually poor practice.

IMPLICATIONS

Inappropriate sizing may mean that auxiliary heat is needed in the winter. In the summer, the cooling may produce a damp unpleasant indoor climate and the system may short cycle.

STRATEGY

Since we're not going to do heat loss or heat gain calculations, your estimates of appropriate size will be very rough. Don't go out on a limb and condemn a unit as being undersized or oversized. You're wiser to describe it as suspect, and recommend further investigation. In northern climates, look for auxiliary heat to help the heat pump when it's cold.

12.14.2   Inoperative in Heating or Cooling Mode

IMPLICATIONS

If the system is inoperative in heating mode, there may be no heat, or there may be complete dependence on the auxiliary heat. If the system doesn't work in the cooling mode, there will be no air conditioning and may be no heat.

STRATEGY

Turn the thermostat up to see if the heat pump responds (assuming the outdoor temperature is below 65°F). Check that the heat pump is producing the heat, not the auxiliary heat. If the system is inoperative, a service person should be contacted, since troubleshooting heat pumps is well beyond our scope.

Locked Out

Depending on the outdoor temperature, the type of back-up heat, and the set-up of the system, the heat pump may be operational but locked out.

If the system is set to the cooling mode and the outdoor temperature is above 65°F, the system should respond to lowering the thermostat. If it doesn't respond or doesn't deliver cool air, recommend further investigation. Let your client know that the system may not deliver any heat either, although you can't test that.

12.14.3   Poor Outdoor Coil Location

IMPLICATION

STRATEGY

Inefficient operation, decreased comfort and increased costs will result if the outdoor coil is not well located.

Watch for outdoor units—

- with restricted intake or discharge air flow
- within 6 feet of a clothes dryer, water heater vent or high efficiency furnace vent
- under the drip line of the roof
- below snow drift depth or with no provision for condensate to drain away freely

Some say the best location for a heat pump outside is on the east side of the house, but practical issues are probably more important.

We added furnace discharge vents to the list here. These vents are not an issue for air conditioning systems because the air conditioner and furnace would never operate at the same time. It can be an issue with heat pumps because heat pumps and furnaces may operate at the same time. The moisture in the furnace exhaust may ice up the heat pump coil quickly.

Snow Accumulation Areas

Where snow tends to accumulate, the heat pump should be on a frame or stand several inches above the ground. This helps to prevent snow from blocking the air movement across the coil. There should be 1 to 3 feet of clearance for the intake and 4 to 6 feet for the discharge side.

12.14.4   Coil Iced Up

IMPLICATION

STRATEGY

Poor heating or no heat will result from an iced up coil.

Look for frost or ice on the outdoor coil.

12.14.5   Airflow Problems in House

IMPLICATIONS

STRATEGY

Poor heating and cooling can result from airflow problems.

Perform your tests of the supply registers and return grilles as we have discussed previously.

Poor Register and Grille Location

Watch for supply registers and return grills that favor either heating or cooling. For example, ceiling supply registers are fine for cooling but are not very good for heating.

Low level returns are better for heating than for cooling. Ideal systems have high and low supply registers and return grilles. These are very rare. The best compromise for both heating and cooling is floor registers near outside walls below windows. Return grilles can be high and low with a damper on the low return grille. The damper is open in the heating season for low level return and closed in the cooling season allowing high level return.

Ducts in Unconditioned Spaces

The more of the duct system that passes through unconditioned spaces (attics and crawlspaces), the worse the situation is. Comfort suffers and costs increase. Insulating and sealing ducts helps, but is never 100 percent effective. Warn your clients if there is much ductwork in unconditioned spaces.

12.14.6   Back-Up Heat Problems

IMPLICATION

STRATEGY

The back-up heat may be inactive or ineffective. The result is often inadequate heat in cold weather.

When looking at a heat pump, determine whether back-up heat is needed. You should know this from local installation practices. You can also approximate this by knowing the rough heat loss from the house and determining the heating capacity of the heat pump.

Back-Up Heat

If back-up heat is needed, has it been provided? What type is it? If the back-up heat is electric, it can operate in conjunction with the heat pump. If the back-up heat is gas or oil, the heat pump has to be shut off when the gas or oil burner comes on.

Testing Back-Up Heat

If the back-up heat is electric, it may be several staged elements that come on one at a time as required. You should, as part of your inspection, make sure that auxiliary heat is provided. You should also make sure that it works. Switching to the Emergency Heat setting, and using an ampmeter to measure the current draw through the auxiliary heating circuit is one way to accomplish this. If it is a staged system, you should make sure that each of the auxiliary electric elements comes on appropriately.

Temperature Limitations

You should avoid testing a heat pump in the heating mode above 65°F. Do not run a heat pump in the cooling mode below 65°F.

Back-Up Heat on Constantly

The electric back-up heat should only come on when the heat pump can't deliver enough heat. If the back-up heat is on with the heat pump when the temperature is mild (above 40°F), there may be a wiring or control setting problem. Recommend further investigation.

Five to Seven Minutes Between Cycles

Heat pumps, just like air conditioners, have a built-in time delay to prevent short on/off cycles which create a large pressure for the compressor to try to start up against. This can damage the compressor. Any time the heat pump is shut off, it probably won't recycle for five to seven minutes. A few manufacturers go even longer before allowing the system to re-start.

12.14.7   Old

Heat pump compressors last 8 to 15 years, typically. Use the methods discussed in the Section 12.13 to check the age of the heat pump and compressor.

REVIEW QUESTIONS

1. List ten items that affect the amount of air conditioning needed in a home.

2. How many square feet can one ton of air conditioning cool in Florida?

3. How many square feet can one ton of air conditioning cool in Michigan?

4. Oversized distribution ductwork is a common problem with central air conditioning.

   True   False

5. An undersized air conditioner is better than an oversized one.

   True   False

6. The typical temperature drop from outdoors to indoors with a properly operating air conditioning system would be about 15°F.

   True   False

7. What kind of temperature drop would you expect to find in the house air as it passes over the evaporator coil?

8. A compressor can be thought of as a pump.

   True   False

9. Compressors are typically located indoors on an air-to-air split system air conditioning system.

   True   False

10. What is the function of a sump or crankcase heater?

11. List eight common compressor problems.

12. The condenser coil in a split system is typically located _____.

13. The evaporator coil in a split system is typically located _____.

14. The condenser fan in a split system is located _____.

15. List four condenser problems.

16. List three common configurations of evaporator coils.

17. Evaporator coils should be upstream of furnace heat exchangers.

    True   False

18. List six common evaporator problems.

19. In one sentence, describe the function of a capillary tube.

20. In one sentence, describe the function of a thermostatic valve.

21. List four common expansion device problems.

22. List five possible causes of leaking condensate drain pans.

23. When is an auxiliary condensate drain pan needed?

24. What are condensate drain lines usually made of?

25. Do condensate drain lines ever have a trap?

26. If so, what is its purpose?

27. List two acceptable discharge points for condensate drain lines and one generally unacceptable discharge point.

28. List three common condensate pump problems.

29. Refrigerant lines are usually made of _____.

30. The larger line contains a liquid.

True   False

31. The smaller line is called the suction line.

True   False

32. The larger line is called the return line.

True   False

33. List five common refrigerant line problems.

34. How would you normally identify a leak in a refrigerant line visually?

35. Which line should be cold when the system is operating?

36. Which line should be warm when the system is operating?

37. Which line should be insulated?

38. Where is the condenser fan in a split system located?

39. What is the typical inlet and outlet temperature of air across the condenser fan?

40. List four common condenser fan problems

41. Where is the evaporator fan typically located in a split system?

42. The amount of air that must cross an evaporator coil in a heating climate is less than the amount of air that must cross a conventional furnace heat exchanger coil.

True   False

43. Oversized ducts are a common problem.

True   False

44. High level returns are more appropriate for heating than cooling.

True   False

45. Ducts passing through unconditioned spaces such as attics or crawlspaces should be _____.

46. List seven common problems with thermostats.

47. How long do air conditioning compressors typically last in your area?

48. What is the typical warranty period for a compressor?

49. Heat pumps are generally sized based on the

a. heating load

b. cooling load

c. other

50. The implication of an oversized heat pump during the summer months is:

51. You should not operate the heat pump in the heating mode when the outdoor temperature is above _____.

52. You should not operate the heat pump in the cooling mode when the outdoor temperature is below _____.

53. List at least eight clues that would suggest that you are looking at a heat pump rather than a central air conditioning system.

CHAPTER 13

PLUMBING

LEARNING OBJECTIVES

By the end of this chapter you should be able to:

- describe functional flow

- list three general things that can go wrong with supply plumbing

- list seven different materials used for supply piping

- list two common problems with service piping

- describe 11 problems with supply piping

- identify common types of water heaters

- list the common problems with various types of water heaters

- list eight materials commonly used for drain, waste and vent purposes

- list the common problems with each DWV component

- describe the implication of nonperformance of these components

- describe the inspection strategy for identifying problems

- identify each of the major plumbing fixtures, their function, and how they should be connected to the plumbing system

- list the common problems with each fixture, their implications, and the inspection strategy used to identify them

INTRODUCTION In this chapter, you will learn how plumbing systems work, and how to identify the common components that make up the supply and waste plumbing system. We'll also talk about water heaters, plumbing fixtures and faucets.

13.1   SUPPLY PLUMBING

Supply plumbing is how water gets into the house. Although we can't see much of them during inspections, we'll talk about the **service pipes** or **water entry pipes** that bring the water to the house. We'll also look at the piping inside the house on the supply side. We will talk about the things that cause supply plumbing problems, such as leaks and low water pressure.

13.1.1   How Supply Plumbing Works

Potable Water

We need clean water at several locations throughout the house. We capture the water in piping to keep it where we want it and then push it through the pipes. If we do it right, we'll always have water available when we open a faucet. We call the clean water **potable,** which means we can use it for drinking, cooking and washing.

The Source

Public or Private Water

The source of water for a house is either a municipal supply system, or a private system such as a lake, river, or well. An investigation of the sources is beyond the scope of a professional home inspection, so we will not discuss them here. Either the municipal or private water supply system is assumed to provide us with a continuous supply of clean water at a relatively constant pressure. Since the municipal system is more common, let's use that as our example.

There are three things that can go wrong with supply plumbing:

- **Leaks:** Sometimes we get the water when or where we don't want it. We call these **leaks**. They range from an annoying dripping faucet to a split pipe that floods the house.

- **Not enough water:** People are often confused by this condition. Some say they don't have enough **pressure,** others say they don't have enough **flow** and still others say they don't have enough **volume**. These are different ways of saying the same thing. We'll call these flow/pressure problems.

- **Dirty water:** The water quality may be poor because of a problem with the municipal supply system or a well. The water may also be dirty because it's accidentally mixed with the waste water in the house. All of these situations are dangerous. Some are easy to find and others are just about impossible.

You should determine the flow/pressure performance of the supply plumbing system. Our test of **functional flow** is usually performed at the bathroom that is highest and most remote from the water supply into the house. This is the most rigorous test. Many inspectors get more than two fixtures flowing simultaneously, although you should create a situation that is typical for people living in the home.

A home with eight teenagers is more likely to have a number of fixtures flowing simultaneously than a home with an elderly couple, for example. You can ask your clients some lifestyle questions to get a sense of their needs.

13.1.2 Service Piping (Water Entry Piping)

This is the piping that leads from the city main to the house. In modern construction, the piping is typically $3/4$-inch for a single family home. In some areas, it is common to go to 1-inch pipe if there are more than three bathrooms in the house. The largest pipe size commonly used for single-family homes is $1^1/_2$-inch. Some older houses had $3/_8$-inch diameter piping. Half-inch diameter piping was common in many areas up into the 1960s.

Piping Materials
Water service pipes may be—

- copper
- galvanized steel
- lead
- PVC plastic
- CPVC plastic
- polyethylene plastic
- polybutylene plastic
- cast iron
- asbestos cement
- brass

Piping Identification
Most of the water service piping is not visible. In some cases, it can be seen at its point of entry into the building. In warm climates, it may be seen coming out of the ground and into the building above grade from the outside. In some cases, the service piping is visible at the meter outside the house (warm climates only). In cold climates, the meter is typically inside the house.

Piping in Trenches
Water service piping must be buried at least 12 inches. In cold climates, the piping must be at least 6 inches below the depth of frost.

Protecting Copper Pipe
Where copper piping passes through concrete it is usually wrapped to protect it from corrosion.

Problems with water service pipes include low pressure and leaking.

Low Pressure

Low pressure is often noted inside the building, even though the piping inside the building seems to be a good size and in good condition. The culprit is often old or undersized water service piping, or a combination of both.

IMPLICATIONS

Reduced water pressure and flow are inconvenient for homeowners at best. In severe circumstances, the plumbing system may not be capable of providing showers while any other fixtures are operating.

STRATEGY

Where the water pressure in a large house seems poor for no apparent reason, you may want to check the water meter and recommend possible replacement with a larger commercial type water meter that will not restrict the flow. When you perform your functional flow test, you will get a sense of the strength of the water flow and pressure. It's not always possible to determine where the losses are greatest, and when you can't pinpoint the problem, make sure you include the water service pipe as a possible problem area.

Leaking

A leaking water service pipe may be undetected for some time.

Leaking water service pipes can cause flooding and soil erosion. In milder cases, the leak may be undetected and water pressure and flow may suffer as a result.

Wet spots at the front of the property that are otherwise unexplained suggest a leaking water service pipe. Where a leaking water service pipe is suspected, the water can sometimes be heard flowing through the pipe. Some inspectors will ensure that there is no water being used in the house and then put the tip of a screwdriver against the pipe where it comes into the house. They will then put the handle of the screwdriver against their ear, listening for water flowing through the pipe. In some cases, this can reveal a leaking water service pipe.

Where the water service pipe enters the building below grade, a leaking service pipe may result in a wet spot around the pipe penetration point or at the wall or floor near the point of entry into the house. Where you see dampness in subgrade areas close to a water service entry point, keep in mind the possibility of a leaking pipe outside the house.

13.1.3   Shutoff Valves

Every plumbing system should have a single shutoff valve that allows you to quickly turn off all the water in the house. An important and valuable part of a home inspection is locating this valve and showing the client where it is and what it does. Good shutoff valves are accessible and operable.

Many shutoff valves are **stop and waste** valves (Figure 13.1). This means that there is a bleed or drain valve on the downstream (house) side of the valve. The purpose of this stop and waste valve is to drain all the water out of the supply piping, for example, if the house is to be winterized. On some old valves, the bleed valve operates automatically when the valve is closed. In more modern stop and waste valves, there is a cap on the bleed valve that allows you to decide whether or not water is going to bleed out of the pipe downstream. **Petcock** is another term for the bleed valve on a main shutoff valve.

Let's look at some common problems with shutoff valves.

- missing or cannot be located
- leaking
- inoperable/inaccessible/buried
- damaged handle
- partly closed
- exposed to mechanical damage
- rusted

Missing or Cannot Be Located

Sometimes there is no shutoff valve.

The implication of shutoff valve problems is an inability to shut off all the water quickly in the event of an emergency, such as a flood.

Trace the water supply piping back to its point of entry into the house, looking for a single main shutoff valve. The valve is usually upstream of the meter and

F I G U R E 13.1   Main Shutoff Valve—Stop and Waste

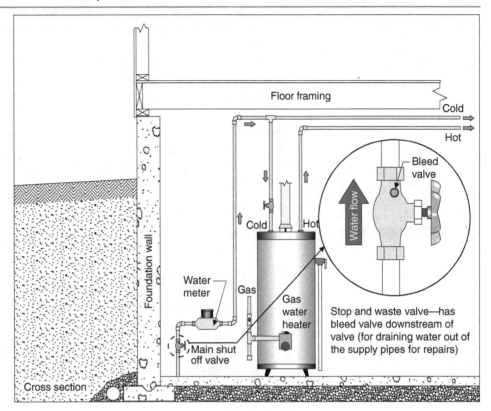

Floor framing

Cold

Hot

Bleed valve

Water flow

Cold   Hot

Water meter

Gas

Gas water heater

Stop and waste valve—has bleed valve downstream of valve (for draining water out of the supply pipes for repairs)

Main shut off valve

Foundation wall

Cross section

upstream of a pressure regulator. If you can't find a shutoff inside the house, check outside for the valve. If you can't find it, write it up as not being located, rather than missing, and recommend further investigation.

Leaking

Sometimes the shutoff valve is leaking.

The implications of a leaking shutoff valve are water damage and perhaps rust forming on the valve, rendering it inoperable over time. If the leak is severe, the water flow and pressure in the house may suffer.

Inoperable/Inaccessible/Buried

Again, people won't be able to shut off the water in an emergency.

Use common sense to determine whether the valve can be turned off easily. Would a homeowner have trouble turning this valve off? If so, recommend improvement.

Damaged Handle

A damaged valve handle is common and can be dangerous.

Not only will it be difficult to close the valve, it is very easy to cut your hand on a valve with a damaged handle.

Make sure the handle is intact.

Exposed to Mechanical Damage

The location of the shutoff valve sometimes makes it prone to mechanical damage.

IMPLICATIONS

If the valve is damaged, there may either be leakage or the valve may become inoperable.

STRATEGY

Watch for valves that are susceptible to mechanical damage. On outdoor, above-grade valves, think about lawnmowers and other landscaping equipment, for example, that may damage the valves.

Rusted

Most of these valves are brass and will not rust. Some, however, have steel handles and other ferric (containing iron) parts.

IMPLICATIONS

The valve may be inoperable.

STRATEGY

Report rust on shutoff valves. If the valve is badly rusted, you should not operate it.

13.1.4   Supply Piping Distribution System in the House

Function

The house supply piping carries water from the service piping to the various points of use, including the water heater, fixtures, appliances such as dishwashers and clothes washers, and hose bibbs.

Materials

Several materials may be used for supply piping. These include:

- Copper
- Galvanized steel
- Brass
- Stainless steel
- Polybutylene (PB)
- Polyethylene (PE)
- Cross-linked polyethylene (PEX)
- CPVC

Not all of these materials are permitted in all areas.

Pipe Sizes

Common supply pipe sizes are $1/2$-inch and $3/4$-inch. On very large homes, 1-inch supply pipes are occasionally found. The longer the run, the larger the pipe diameter should be.

Now let's look at some of the common supply piping problems in houses.

1. Leaking
2. Poor pressure/flow
3. Rust
4. Split/damaged/crimped
5. Poor support
6. Cross connections
7. Excess pressure

8. Excessive noise

9. Combustible piping

10. Suspect connections on polybutylene

11. Non-standard material

Leaking

Leaking supply piping can be very dramatic. Because the piping is pressurized, a leak can do a lot of damage quickly. If there is no functional floor drain, a leaking supply pipe can flood a house.

IMPLICATION

The big risk here is water damage to the home.

STRATEGY

As you look at the visible supply piping in the house you may find leaks. Dramatic leaks are usually found by homeowners and corrected right away. It's the small leaks that you are more likely to find. These may be drips at poor connections or pinholes on galvanized steel pipes that rust over and scab themselves shut temporarily. Some leaks are concealed and you won't see them during an inspection.

Check the Water Meter

If the house has a water meter, you can ensure that all of the plumbing fixtures are off and check the water meter for movement. If you can't tell whether it's moving or not you can come back and check in 10 or 15 minutes and see whether the meter has moved. You can put the tip of a screwdriver on the supply piping and put your ear against the handle of the screwdriver, listening for the sound of water moving through the pipe.

Listen with Screw Driver

Leaks Are Constant

In most cases, supply pipe leaks will be constant. Leaks at fixtures and drain and waste pipes will be intermittent.

Poor Pressure or Flow

This is one of the most common problems, particularly on older homes.

IMPLICATIONS

The implications are less water at each fixture than is desirable. This is most noticeable when more than one fixture is flowing. In severe cases, when fixtures on lower floors are operated, water stops coming out of the fixtures on upper floors.

STRATEGY

Your first and most important job is to point out the low pressure and flow conditions. It's nice to be able to pinpoint the cause, but you won't always be able to do this.

You may be wise to talk to the municipal water departments about any localized supply problems they are having. Undersized mains, old neighborhoods, and neighborhoods that have been substantially expanded can all suffer water supply problems.

Rust

Rust is found on metallic piping only. Galvanized and stainless steel piping are prone to rust. Copper piping does not rust or corrode under normal use, unless the water is acidic.

IMPLICATION

The implication of pipe rusting may be pipe failure.

STRATEGY

If the piping is galvanized steel, rusting is probably a legitimate indication that the pipe is near the end of its life. You have to be careful when looking at rust. Is the pipe rusting from the inside out or is it surface rusting on the exterior only? Galvanized steel piping typically rusts through from the inside, showing first at its threaded connections. Pinhole leaks sometimes scab over and temporarily stop leaking. Surface rust that is the result of condensation or corrosive chemicals in the atmosphere tends to be uniform around the pipe surface and may be more cosmetic than a functional concern.

FIGURE 13.2   Dielectric Union

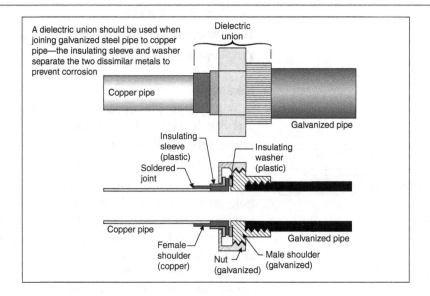

A dielectric union should be used when joining galvanized steel pipe to copper pipe—the insulating sleeve and washer separate the two dissimilar metals to prevent corrosion

Dissimilar Metals

If you come across rusted stainless steel, it will probably be near the end of its life.

Corrosion on copper piping may or may not indicate a serious problem. Where copper piping is directly connected to galvanized steel piping, corrosion usually is the result of **galvanic action.** The steel tends to be the sacrificial metal and it will corrode first and most dramatically. This kind of corrosion also occurs where copper pipes contact sheet metal ductwork, or where copper pipes are supported by iron or steel hangers, for example.

Dielectric Connectors

Special connectors are made to reduce the galvanic action and corrosion of the steel piping by the copper (Figure 13.2). These fittings separate the two materials physically and reduce the flow of electrons between them. In many cases, this is a short-term issue since the galvanized steel piping is probably close to the end of its life anyway.

Split/Damaged/Crimped

Piping that is damaged won't be able to carry water effectively.

IMPLICATIONS

The implications of split, damaged or crimped pipes are leakage and reduced water pressure and flow.

STRATEGY

Wherever piping is visible, make sure it is intact. Watch for crimping and other mechanical damage. If the pipe is split, flooding will usually occur. However, if the pipe is at an outside hose bibb where the water supply has been shut off for the winter, there won't be any leakage. When your client turns on the supply to the hose bibb in the spring, they will find the split pipe and may well ask you to replace it for them.

Plastic pipe can be damaged by sharp hangers. The expansion and contraction of plastic piping can cause wear at hangers and may weaken connections over time.

Vulnerable Locations

Some piping is particularly vulnerable to mechanical damage. You can use common sense to look at supply piping and see whether it is likely to be damaged.

TABLE 13.1   Support Requirements

Piping Material	Maximum Spacing of Supports for Horizontal Piping
copper pipe	6 to 10 feet
copper tubing	6 to 10 feet
galvanized steel	10 to 12 feet
plastic (PE, PEX, PB)	32 inches to 4 feet

Poor Support

Vertical

Horizontal

All piping needs to be adequately supported. Vertical pipes should be supported at every other floor level as a general rule and at least every 24 feet. Copper piping should be supported at each floor level and at least every 10 feet.

Table 13.1 summarizes typical support requirements for horizontal piping runs. Individual codes will vary, so once again, check with your local building authorities. Flexible plastic piping, such as polybutylene, needs very good pipe support, particularly on the hot water piping, because the pipe tends to expand a lot when you heat it up.

Hangers for copper or brass pipe should be copper or brass or should be wrapped so that they are electrically insulated from the copper pipe. This prevents corrosion of the hangers if they are a dissimilar metal.

IMPLICATIONS

The ultimate implication of improper support is leaking pipes. Failures usually occur at joints or connections.

STRATEGY

You won't be able to see the vertical supports for piping in most cases. You will be able to see horizontal piping supports in unfinished basements and subgrade areas (crawlspaces). Where piping is run in attics in warmer climates, you will also be able to see pipe supports there. Rather than applying a bunch of rules for various piping types, it is often more practical simply to look for deflection of the piping. Generally speaking, this is more of an issue with plastic piping than metallic piping.

Watch for plastic piping damage at the hangers, especially if the hangers are metal.

Cross Connections

Cross connections are a possibility wherever the supply plumbing and solid or liquid waste could come together (Figure 13.3). A cross connection is a serious health issue. There is a risk of illness or death if the potable water for drinking, cooking and washing is contaminated with waste. The Standards require us to look for cross connections. Let's look at some of the places we might find them:

1. Fixtures where the faucet spout is below the overflow or flood rim of the fixture. This occurs on older bathtubs and laundry tubs, for example.

2. Fixtures where hand-held showers, extendable faucets or vegetable sprayers can be left in tubs, basins or sinks.

3. Garden hoses left attached to a hose bibb.

4. A toilet tank where the fill water enters at the bottom.

5. A dishwasher where a solenoid valve separates the clean water from the gray water (a term used to describe water that is no longer clean but does not include human waste).

6. A clothes washing machine with a discharge pipe in a laundry tub.

F I G U R E   13.3   Cross Connections

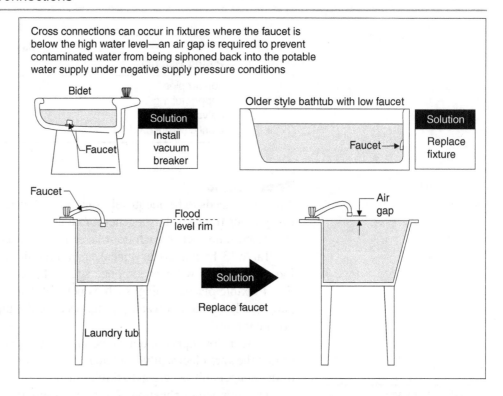

Cross connections can occur in fixtures where the faucet is below the high water level—an air gap is required to prevent contaminated water from being siphoned back into the potable water supply under negative supply pressure conditions

Bidet

Solution
Install vacuum breaker

Faucet

Older style bathtub with low faucet

Solution
Replace fixture

Faucet

Faucet

Flood level rim

Solution
Replace faucet

Air gap

Laundry tub

7. A water softener.

8. A humidifier connected to the supply plumbing system.

9. A lawn or fire sprinkler system.

10. A bidet where water enters the bowl at the bottom.

11. A hot water boiler (boilers are connected to the supply plumbing piping so that make-up water can be provided to the boiler).

12. A swimming pool fill outlet that is located below the flood level of the pool.

13. A trap primer without an air gap.

One of the simplest and most effective ways to prevent cross connections is with a 1-inch vertical air gap. If the supply device (a faucet, for instance) is located above the flood rim of a basin, the water in the basin can't get back into the faucet. Another way to prevent cross connections is with an anti-siphon device, such as a vacuum breaker. This device opens on low pressure, and discharges waste water rather than allowing it to flow backwards through the breaker.

Backflow and Back Siphonage   **Backflow** is a flow occuring in a reverse direction from that intended. A vacuum isn't necessary for backflow. The pressure on the potable water side only has to be very slightly lower than the pressure on the waste water side for backflow to occur.

Back siphonage is also a reverse flow of soiled water into potable water piping, but it doesn't need positive pressure on the downstream (dirty) side. Back siphonage is a specific kind of backflow caused when the potable water piping system is at a lower than atmospheric pressure. A partial vacuum is needed for back siphonage.

Backflow and back siphonage can be prevented by several different arrangements or devices, of which vacuum breakers are the most common (Figures 13.4 and 13.5).

F I G U R E   13.4   Atmospheric Vacuum Breaker

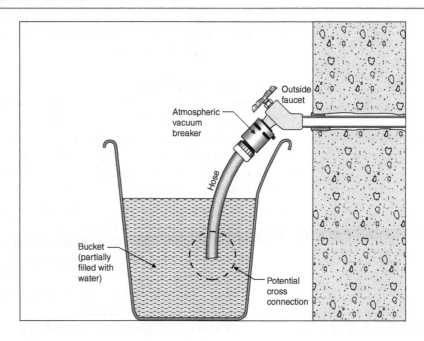

IMPLICATIONS	As we discussed at the outset, the health implications are serious if cross connections exist.

<table>
<tr><td>STRATEGY</td><td>You'll need to be aware of cross connections and what methods your local authorities require to protect against them.</td></tr>
</table>

Excess Pressure

Where the water pressure exceeds 80 or 100 psi (depending on your jurisdiction) pressure regulators may be required to limit the house supply pressure to 80 psi.

IMPLICATIONS	The implications of excess pressure are leaking valves and faucets, as well as solenoid valve failures.

F I G U R E   13.5   Pressure Type Vacuum Breaker

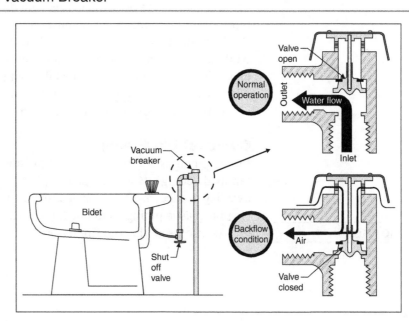

If you use a pressure gauge to check the static pressure on the supply side (beyond the Standards), you can pick up the excess pressure readily. If you don't use a gauge, you may detect the high pressure simply by the force of the water coming out of the faucets.

Excessive Noise

Supply plumbing systems can be noisy. Water hammer is perhaps the most serious of the noise problems.

Water hammer is a loud banging sound in the pipes. It occurs when valves are closed quickly and the water, which is moving with considerable velocity and momentum, has to stop very quickly. The water bounces off the valve and actually creates a vacuum as it bounces away from the valve. The vacuum then violently attracts the water back to the low pressure area and the water again bounces off the closed valve. If the water has enough momentum, it will again bounce off the valve and create a smaller vacuum. The effect of this reverberation sounds a little bit like someone pounding on metal piping with a hammer. Water velocities can be high (up to 3,000 miles per hour) and the forces developed with water hammer can exceed 600 psi.

Noise is always an irritant. In some cases, it may also suggest premature failure of joints and early leakage.

The implications of water hammer can include deterioration of valves, loosening of piping supports and leaking at pipe joints. Metal piping is more susceptible to water hammer than plastic piping. The plastic piping tends to have enough flexibility to absorb some of the energy.

The implications of valve chatter and pipes with rough edges are less serious. Valves often chatter because the washers or seats are worn. The damage caused by pipes rubbing against other materials is not usually an issue over the short term. Over the long term, the abrasive effect can wear through the pipe and cause sudden failure and flooding. In most cases this occurs in concealed wall and floor spaces and is difficult to predict. It is disruptive to interior finishes to locate and correct pipe noises that result from pipes rubbing against framing members, for example.

Where you hear noises from pipes when the system supply piping is tested, you'll need to determine under what circumstances the noise occurs. If the loud banging noise is heard when valves are closed, it's a water hammer problem. If a vibrating noise is heard and it's more noticeable when valves are partly open, it's very likely valve chatter. If the noise increases with the amount of water flowing through the pipe, it may be rough edges on pipe ends.

If the problem is intermittent and occurs after the water has been flowing for a while and again a few minutes after the water has been shut off, it may be the expansion and contraction of metal piping rubbing against framing members or other materials. This typically occurs on the hot water piping.

With the exception of water hammer, these problems are not serious.

Combustible Piping

Plastic piping is combustible. Most jurisdictions allow it to be installed in single-family dwellings. However, plastic piping is not usually allowed to pass from one dwelling to another. The rationale is that a fire might be transmitted through the combustible plastic piping from one home to the next.

As discussed, this is a fire hazard.

F I G U R E 13.6   Polybutylene Pipe—Crimp Fitting

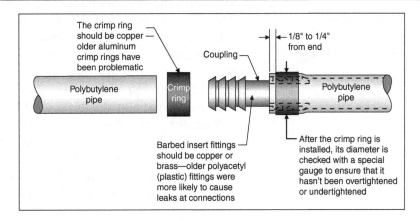

Heat Sources and Plastic Pipe

Where you find plastic piping in homes that are attached to other dwellings, look to see whether the plastic piping passes from one unit to the next. If this appears to be the case, recommend further investigation. At least some sections of the piping may have to be replaced.

Combustible piping should be kept away from heat sources, including exhaust flues for combustion appliances. The required clearances depend on the appliances. Most appliances have rated requirements for clearances from combustibles.

Suspect Connections on Polybutylene Piping

There have been so many problems with polybutylene piping that you should check the exposed connections carefully and let your client know about the potential for leaks at the connections.

The implication is primarily leakage.

Look at exposed connections for evidence of leakage. Polybutylene connections should be at least 18 inches from water heaters. The first 18 inches of piping from the water heater should be metal. Polybutylene piping should not be installed immediately downstream of instantaneous-type water heaters because of the high temperatures.

Insert Fittings on Early Systems were Problems

The barbed insert fittings for polybutylene piping were originally made of polyacetyl (a plastic). Brand names of these fittings included Celcon and Delrin. These systems were used from about 1980 to 1986. Since then, copper and brass fittings have been used.

No Aluminum Crimp Rings

Some of the original crimp rings were aluminum. Some of the aluminum was gold-colored. More modern installations require annealed copper crimp rings. The original crimping tool, which was a combination tool, has also been discarded.

Crimp Rings and Bending the Pipe

Crimp rings should be $^1/_8$-inch to $^1/_4$-inch away from the end of the tube (Figure 13.6). The crimp ring should be perpendicular to the pipe run. The crimp ring should not show evidence of having been crimped more than once. Bends in polybutylene piping should be on a radius that is at least 12 times the tube diameter. For example, the radius of a turn for $^1/_2$-inch piping should be 6 inches minimum.

Protection and Support

Piping that passes through metal wall studs should be protected with sleeves or bushings. Protective sleeves should be used where polybutylene piping runs through floors or concrete slabs.

Metal Hose Bibbs

Polybutylene piping should not be used to make outdoor hose bibb connections. A metal pipe should be used for the hose bibb.

No Circulating Loops

Some authorities say that houses with recirculating loops for hot water piping should not use polybutylene on these loops.

Leak Evidence and Fitting Clues

You should be watching for evidence of leaks, which includes water or a whitish deposit on the pipe surface, usually near fittings. You may also find that there are more fittings than you would expect. This suggests repairs and possible chronic problems. This is especially true if you see different kinds of fittings in the same house.

Heat Sources

Watch for piping close to recessed lights, exhaust flues, or other heat sources.

Summary

Even if you don't see any problems with polybutylene piping, you may want to make your client aware of the issues surrounding polybutylene piping. The bottom line is that crimp rings are questionable, even when well done, and several authorities recommend the use of compression fittings with polybutylene pipe.

Non-Standard Materials

We have listed materials that are approved for water distribution systems. These are the only materials that you should find.

IMPLICATIONS

Leakage, premature failure, poor water pressure and possible health issues, including cross connections, may result from the use of non-standard materials.

STRATEGY

Watch for radiator hose, garden hose, corrugated piping, PVC piping used for hot water supply, and any other piping arrangements that appear unconventional. Where you are unsure as to the suitability of materials, simply raise the question and call for further investigation by a specialist.

13.2   WATER HEATERS

Water heaters are designed to provide hot water at fixtures such as sinks, basins, laundry tubs, bath tubs and showers. We'll concentrate on the most common types, which are gas, oil and electric. These heaters usually have storage tanks with capacities of 30 to 60 gallons.

Most tanks are insulated steel cylinders with an enamel coating on the inner surface. They are referred to as **glass-lined** tanks. The lining helps but does not absolutely prevent corrosion.

Other Materials

Some water heater tanks are copper, some are aluminum and some are an alloy of copper and nickel. Some modern water tanks are plastic coated. The copper-aluminum and copper-nickel alloy tanks all last longer than steel tanks. Some of these can last up to 50 years.

Life Expectancy

Conventional domestic water heaters have life expectancies that vary across North America. In some areas, life estimates are as low as 8 to 12 years. In other areas, life expectancies can be 15 to 25 years.

Temperatures of Hot Water

Water heaters, or **hot water heaters** as they are often (redundantly) called, are designed to raise the water temperature in the house from approximately 50°F to 120° F. Some people call for temperatures of 140° F or even higher but for safety, economy, and conservation reasons there is a trend toward lower temperatures for hot water. Most equipment manufacturers, installers and local authorities now recommend 120°F water.

A water heater is a single pass system that always sees new, not recirculated, water. Because water heaters are constantly exposed to fresh water with lots of oxygen, they are prone to corrosion. As a result, water heaters are usually provided with an anti-corrosion rod or sacrificial anode. Sacrificial anodes sit in the tank water allowing the chemical reaction from the water to attack them rather than the tank.

Water Heater Is Just a Bulge in the Pipe

The water heater is really just a fat part of the piping system where the water passes through. As it passes through, it gets heated. The pressure in the water heater is the same as the pressure throughout the supply plumbing system (typically 60 psi). The pressure on the cold water inlet pipe is virtually the same as the pressure on the hot water outlet pipe.

Vacuum Relief Valves

Some water heaters are provided with a vacuum relief valve on the cold water inlet side. This prevents cross connections by preventing the hot water from backing into the cold water line in the event the cold water pressure is low. The vacuum relief valve also protects against possible collapse of the storage tank by preventing a vacuum inside the tank.

13.2.1   Gas- and Oil-Fired Water Heaters

Burner in Center

On conventional propane-, gas- or oil-fired water heaters, heat is generated by a burner at the bottom of the tank (Figures 13.7 and 13.8). The tank is like a very tall doughnut, with a hole up through the central part of the tank. The exhaust products from the burner go up through this core and heat is transferred through the tank walls from the core into the water. The exhaust products go into a vent connector above the core and into a chimney or vent system.

No Separate Heat Exchanger

Domestic water heaters transfer heat directly from the combustion products through the tank wall and floor into the water. The tank is both the storage compartment and the heat exchanger.

Dip Tube

Cold water is introduced through a **dip tube** near the bottom of the tank (Figure 13.9). The cold water supply pipe usually attaches to the tank at the top. The dip tube carries the cold water down through the tank, discharging it near the bottom of the tank. The hot water is drawn off from the top of the tank.

Thermostat Control

At rest, the tank is filled with water heated to the set temperature (e.g., 120°F). As water begins to be drawn off, the 120°F water leaving the tank is replaced by 50°F water. This cool water activates the thermostat which tells the burner to come on. The burner comes on and heats the water. Depending on how quickly the water is flowing out, the temperature in the tank may rise toward the set temperature, or may continue to drop because cold water comes in faster than the burner can heat it up.

Size Issues

The effective size of a water heater is a function of—

■ the volume of hot water it can keep on hand (capacity)

■ the size of the burner (recovery rate)

The larger the burner, the faster the **recovery rate** of the heater. The recovery rate is the time it takes to heat the tankfull of water from 50°F to 140°F, for example. (Current conventions measure recovery rates over a 90°F temperature rise, even though most of us don't heat water to 140°F anymore.) Generally speaking, the faster the recovery rate, the smaller the tank can be. Oil-fired water heaters typically have larger burners than gas-fired water heaters. Oil water heaters have a faster recovery rate, so their tanks are often smaller than gas water heater tanks.

F I G U R E 13.7   Oil-Fired Water Heater

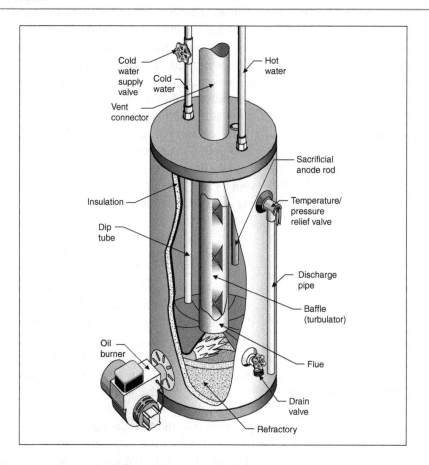

13.2.2   Electric Water Heaters

Electric water heaters work on a different principle (Figure 13.10). There is no core in the center, since there is no burner, and no heat exchanger or venting system is required. Electric water heaters typically employ one or two immersion elements that are similar to the elements in a kettle.

Thermostat Control

The elements are thermostatically controlled. The thermostats are not normally accessible without removing an access panel, and often some insulation. If the electric power to the water heater is on, **there is a risk in removing these access panels and accessing the thermostats.** There are live electrical connections adjacent to the thermostats. Unless you are comfortable and skilled working with electricity, you should leave these access panels closed. The Standards don't ask us to remove these panels during an inspection.

These elements provide the heat and, for the most part, the water configuration is the same as on a gas or oil system. Cold water is introduced near the bottom of the tank and hot water is drawn off near the top. The cold pipe may enter the top of the tank or the side of the tank near the bottom.

FIGURE 13.8 Gas Water Heater

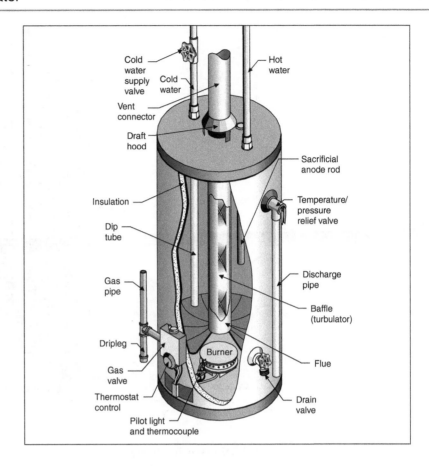

13.2.3 Conventional Tank-Type Water Heaters

Inspection Easy

Inspections of water heaters are very straightforward in that you are looking for hot water and the absence of leaks. Water heaters have many of the same components as and are subject to many of the conditions we discussed with respect to furnaces in Chapters 8–10. We will not repeat that information here, but encourage you to review the components of those systems, their conditions and strategies for inspecting them.

Let's look at some problems we can find with conventional tank-type water heaters.

1. Inoperative (no hot water)
2. Inadequate capacity/recovery rate
3. Leaking
4. Rust
5. Gas burner cover or roll out shield missing/damaged/rusted
6. Damaged tank
7. Inadequate clearance from combustibles
8. Insulation obstructing combustion air or draft hood (gas or oil)
9. Poor location
10. Low water pressure and flow

FIGURE 13.9 Dip Tube in a Water Heater

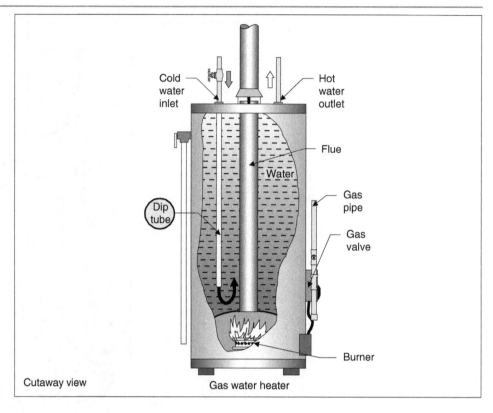

11. Noisy water heater
12. Temperature/pressure relief valve problems
13. Baffle collapsed or missing (gas or oil)
14. Tank not stable/wobbly
15. Hot/cold piping reversed
16. No isolating valve
17. Drain valve problems
18. Propane water heater in low areas

Inoperative (No Hot Water)

IMPLICATIONS

Most people won't do without hot water for any length of time. If there is no hot water in the house, people can't wash comfortably. Dishwashers and clothes washing machines will not work efficiently.

STRATEGY

As you perform your flow tests on the plumbing fixtures, you'll notice if there is no hot water. You may have been able to predict this based on your inspection of the water heater.

Inadequate Capacity or Recovery Rate

How Much Is Enough

The amount of hot water required by a family is very much an issue of lifestyle. There are lots of ways to estimate it, but what is fine for one family of four won't be anywhere near enough for another family of four.

F I G U R E 13.10   Electric Water Heater

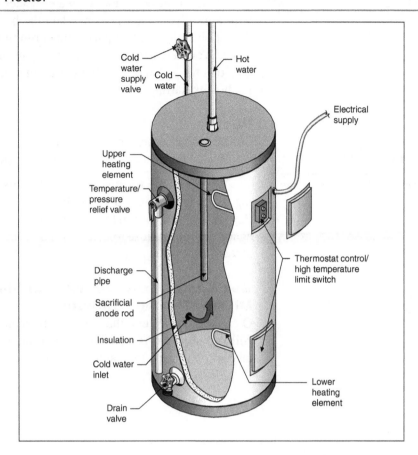

General Rule

IMPLICATIONS

STRATEGY

Here's a very rough guideline. For a family of four, a 40-gallon gas water heater might be considered typical. A 60-gallon electric water heater and a 30-gallon oil water heater might be considered equivalent.

An undersized water heater is frustrating and, although the tank may be filled with hot water during 23 hours of the day, if there isn't enough water to allow everyone to have a shower in the morning, it's going to be considered inadequate.

Most home inspectors don't spend a lot of time interviewing their clients and trying to anticipate their lifestyles. We report on water heater sizes and give people an indication as to whether that's typical. If a family uses more hot water than average, a larger or second water heater will be necessary. Water heaters are not terribly expensive, and an undersized heater should not be a deterrent from buying an otherwise satisfactory house. Further, if the tank size is typical, a high-usage family will probably have to add capacity in whatever home they buy.

Leaking

IMPLICATIONS

A leaking water heater may be simply a nuisance. The water may run over to a floor drain and disappear without any great effect. Serious leaks in water heaters can cause flooding. Obviously hot water leaking out of the plumbing system will reduce the efficiencies of water heaters. Leaks also reduce the pressure and flow available at fixtures throughout the house.

Look for leaks around the water heater and at the top and bottom. Be careful with a gas-fired water heater. When the burner starts up, there will often be condensation in the combustion chamber running down through the center of the water heater. You may hear or see water droplets at the bottom of the heater. Don't mistake this for leakage. The condensation will typically stop within five minutes of the burner starting.

Rust

The tank itself or its feet may be rusted.

Rusted tanks are prone to leakage. Rusted feet may make the tank unstable.

When looking for rust on water heaters, also check the inlet pipes and isolating valves immediately above or beside the tank. Rust in these areas is also common. Pay particular attention to the bottom part of the tank and to the feet. If the tank is against a wall or close to it, a mirror and flashlight may be helpful in getting a look at the inaccessible areas.

Gas Burner Cover or Roll Out Shield Missing/Damaged/Rusted

On gas water heaters, the burner is typically concealed behind a door and a **heat roll out shield** (Figure 13.11). Open the door and move the shield during your inspection to get a look at the burner in operation and at rest.

FIGURE 13.11   Gas Burner Cover and Roll Out Shield

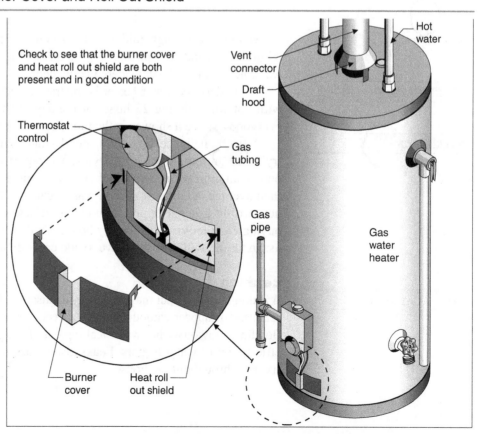

IMPLICATIONS

A missing burner cover or shield will allow the burner to get dirty. It will also allow flames to roll out of the burner in a backdrafting situation. This can be a fire hazard and may damage the controls.

If the burner cover or shield are damaged, they won't be able to do their job. If one of these is rusted, it probably is not easy to operate, and may not be able to perform its function.

STRATEGY

When you remove the cover and move the shield, make sure that both are intact and in good condition. If you see rust on either of these, you might suspect rust on the burner and combustion chamber. You should look more closely.

The rust may also be an indication of leakage. Look carefully for evidence of leakage at the tank or fittings.

Damaged Tank

Mechanical damage of a tank is often in the form of a dent. Sometimes the tank is split along a seam. Surprisingly, the tanks are often watertight, even when they show this kind of damage.

IMPLICATIONS

If the tank leaks, obviously this is a serious implication. If the tank has been dented noticeably, its capacity will be somewhat reduced and a glass lining may be ineffective on the inside. A shorter life expectancy for the tank may result. However, if there is no evidence of leakage and the system is delivering adequate hot water during your inspection, this is not usually something that you'll recommend changing.

STRATEGY

Note any damage to the tank and look for evidence of leakage or premature rusting as a result. Make sure that the tank is still stable on its base and that the draft hood, if it's a combustion type, is intact.

Inadequate Clearance from Combustibles

Most water heaters do not have large requirements for combustible clearances. Clearances of less than 6 inches are common. Some gas units only need 1 inch clearance. There does, however, have to be adequate working space (30 inches wide and deep commonly) around the control side of the heater to service the burner and replace the heater. Doors into closets or rooms with water heaters should be wide enough to allow for removal and replacement.

Combustible Floors

Most gas and oil water heaters are designed for installation on combustible floors, but not carpeting. You're wise to check with the manufacturers of the common systems in your area.

IMPLICATIONS

This is a fire hazard or a service and replacement problem. If someone has built walls around a water heater, the replacement costs are going to be much higher than average.

STRATEGY

Look on the data plate for the required combustible clearances and make sure they are met.

Insulation Obstructing Combustion Air or Draft Hood (Gas or Oil)

IMPLICATIONS

The combustion air inlet for the burner must not be obstructed with insulation. This often happens if the insulation drops down after it's been wrapped around the tank. Similarly, care has to be taken that insulation is not placed around the top of the tank, obstructing the draft hood on a gas water heater. If this happens, combustion may be inefficient at best and the burner may go out. Another possible implication is backdrafting or combustion gas spillage.

Check both the bottom and top of gas fired water heaters for adequate combustion and dilution air. On an oil burner, make sure that the burner itself is not wrapped with insulation and that the combustion air inlet is not obstructed.

Poor Location

Gas or oil-fired water heaters should not be located in sleeping areas, including bedrooms or bedroom closets. We also don't want gas or oil-fired water heaters in clothes closets or bathrooms. We're worried about backdrafting appliances killing people in their sleep and about inadequate combustible clearances. Some areas allow direct vent water heaters in these areas because the chance of backdrafting is very small.

We don't want gas or oil-fired water heaters that are less than 18 inches above the floor in garages. Actually it's the burner and/or pilot that has to be at least 18 inches above the floor. We don't want gasoline vapors to be ignited by a pilot or burner on a water heater. Mechanical protection from vehicles should also be provided for water heaters in garages. Concrete-filled steel pipes set into the floor are one common way to accomplish this.

If the water heater is located outside, it should be on a pad above grade level. We don't want to rust the feet of the water heater.

If a water heater is located above a living space (in warm climates only) a drain pan is usually recommended below the water heater in case of leakage. Pan walls are usually at least 1½ inches high and the pan area is at least larger than the water heater. The pan has to be piped to a suitable location.

There are life safety implications where water heaters are in bedrooms, bathrooms and closets. Fire and explosion are the implications where a water heater is not high enough off a garage floor. Damage to the water heater and possibly fire and explosion are issues if the water heater is not mechanically protected. Water damage to the living space is a possibility if there is no drip pan under a water heater above a living space.

Check for the issues we've talked about and recommend improvements needed.

Low Water Pressure and Flow

Low pressure and flow on just the hot water plumbing is fairly common. Where the piping is galvanized steel, you can expect the rust to be heavier on the hot water piping and the low water pressure on the hot side is not a surprise. The hot water piping arrangement is usually longer than the cold water, so slightly lower pressure may be expected.

The low water pressure and flow reduces the usability of the house plumbing.

If the water pressure is low for no apparent reason, you might recommend flushing of the water heater through the drain valve. Attaching a hose to the drain and directing water to a floor drain or outside the building is fairly straightforward. Most people recommend shutting off the unit and opening the drain valve until the water runs clear.

Some large homes have water service pipes of 1- to 1½-inch diameter. The pressure and flow in these houses can be affected by residential water heaters which typically have ¾-inch connections.

Noisy Water Heater

Water heaters are sometimes noisy because the burner is a problem. Popping sounds at the burner on start up or shut down may be an issue with the gas pressure and/or

F I G U R E 13.12   Temperature/Pressure Relief Valve

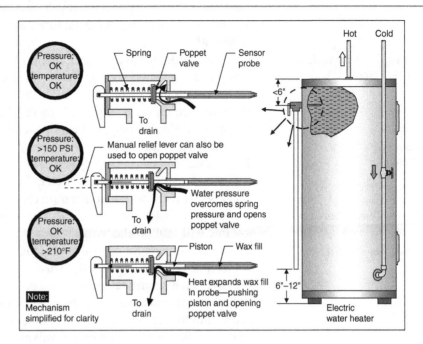

burner adjustment. It may also be condensation dripping onto the burner. This should be checked by a specialist.

Sometimes the water heater rumbles. The rumbling sound appears to come from the tank.

Noisy burners may deliver less hot water than they should and be inefficient. Rumbling sounds indicate sediment in the tank and inefficient operation. Lower recovery rates and sometimes low water pressure and flow result.

If the burner is noisy, recommend servicing. Where a rumbling sound is heard at the water heater, again recommend that the tank be flushed.

Temperature/Pressure Relief Valve Problems

Like hot water boilers, all water heaters must have some way of protecting against high temperatures and high pressures in the tank.

Temperature/pressure relief valves (TPR valves) do two jobs (Figure 13.12). They will open and dump water out of the tank if the temperature exceeds 210°F (just below boiling). They will also open if the pressure in the tank exceeds 150 psi (the maximum normal operating pressure for a water heater). The temperature/pressure relief valve will have a BTU rating stamped on it. Its rating must be the same as or larger than the BTU rating of the water heater.

A temperature/pressure relief valve has to have its probe in the top 6 inches of the tank where it sees the hottest water. Location is more important for temperature than pressure, since the pressure will be uniform throughout the tank.

The temperature/pressure relief valve (TPR valve) has to have a discharge tube attached to it. These tubes used to be metal (typically steel or copper). Now most are plastic, typically CPVC. The discharge tubes cannot have any shutoff valves and have to extend down to a safe location, less than 6 inches above the floor level. This minimizes the chance of spraying anyone with scalding hot water.

IMPLICATIONS

STRATEGY

Temperature/Pressure Relief Valves

Location

Discharge Tubes

Pipe Diameter and Ends

The discharge tubes have to be at least the same diameter as the relief valve. The tube isn't allowed to have any threads or cap on the end because we don't want it to be closed off. The old metal tubes are often rusted on the interior and almost closed off.

Other Ways of Accomplishing the Same Thing

Some systems have an internal high temperature shutoff. Many electric water heaters have an energy cutout (ECO), for example. In an electric water heater, the energy cutout may be inside the tank and not visible, although its presence is usually indicated on the data plate. If there is an ECO, the water heater should have a pressure relief valve only, instead of a temperature/pressure relief valve.

Gas Shut Off on High Temperature

Some gas water heaters use temperature cutouts, such as the Watts 210 valve. This is a valve in the gas supply line to the water heater. There is a temperature probe in the top 6 inches of the water heater. The valve will shut off the gas supply to the water heater if the water temperature exceeds 210°F.

Oil Burner Temperature Control

Oil-fired water heaters may also have an internal high-temperature limit control that will shut off the burner.

Pressure Relief Valve

If the temperature control is provided, we only need a **pressure relief valve**, not a temperature/pressure relief valve. If we have only a pressure relief valve, its location is not so critical because the pressure will build up uniformly in the tank and in the immediate vicinity. The pressure can be sensed anywhere on the tank (not just within the top 6 inches) and in some jurisdictions it can even be on the piping near the tank. There cannot be any valves between the pressure relief valve and the tank itself.

Let's list some of the specific problems you might find on a temperature pressure relief system:

1. Missing relief valve.

2. Undersized relief valve (BTU rating less than water heater).

3. Missing temperature protection (pressure relief valve only, no ECO).

4. Poor location for temperature sensor of temperature/pressure relief valve (must be in top 6 inches of tank).

5. Shut off valve between the pressure relief valve and the tank (not allowed).

6. No discharge tube (dangerous—may scald people).

7. Discharge tube too short or too small diameter.

8. Discharge tube damaged or split.

9. Discharge tube dripping or leaking.

10. Discharge tube capped, threaded or rusted closed.

IMPLICATIONS

Temperature/pressure relief devices are safety items. If any of these conditions exist, safety may be compromised.

STRATEGY

Check temperature/pressure relief valves, high temperature limits and pressure relief valves for all of the problems we've listed above. The life safety issues here are significant.

Baffle Collapsed or Missing (Gas or Oil)

Turbulator

The baffle, or **turbulator** as it is sometimes called, is a stainless steel (typically) helix installed in the flue passage to slow down the gas or oil exhaust products as they move up through the water heater and out toward the vent connector (Figure 13.13). The longer the exhaust products linger in the water heater, the more heat will be transferred into the water.

F I G U R E 13.13   Baffle Collapsed or Missing

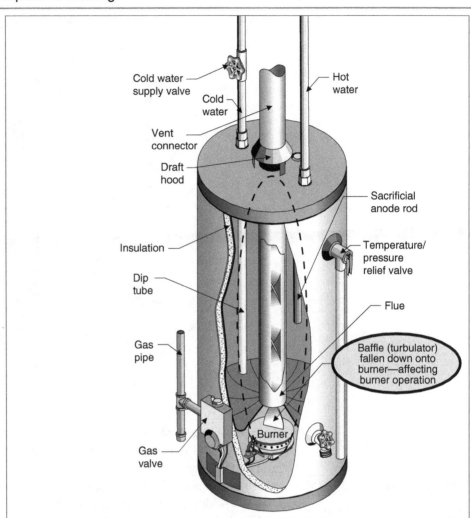

Cold water
supply valve

Cold
water

Hot
water

Vent
connector

Draft
hood

Sacrificial
anode rod

Insulation

Temperature/
pressure
relief valve

Dip
tube

Flue

Baffle (turbulator)
fallen down onto
burner—affecting
burner operation

Gas
pipe

Burner

Gas
valve

<table>
<tr><td>

IMPLICATIONS

</td><td>

The baffle may fall onto the burner, affecting burner operation and reducing the efficiency of the system. A missing or displaced baffle will allow exhaust products to move too quickly through the tanks. This increases fuel consumption.

</td></tr>
<tr><td>

STRATEGY

</td><td>

When looking into the burner compartment on a gas-fired water heater, make sure that the baffle has not fallen down onto the burner. You may be able to look around the draft hood at the top and see the top of the baffle. Where it is not intact, it may have fallen or it may be missing.

In an oil-fired water heater, you may find that the baffle has fallen down into the firepot or refractory. This can sometimes be seen looking in through the viewing port.

</td></tr>
</table>

Tank Not Stable/Wobbly

Tanks need to be well supported and secure on the floor.

IMPLICATIONS

The implications of an unstable tank are leaks, either as water connections are strained or as the tank falls.

STRATEGY

When inspecting a water heater, push and pull with reasonable pressure on the top of the tank to make sure it is not wobbly or loose.

F I G U R E 13.14 Isolating and Drain Valves

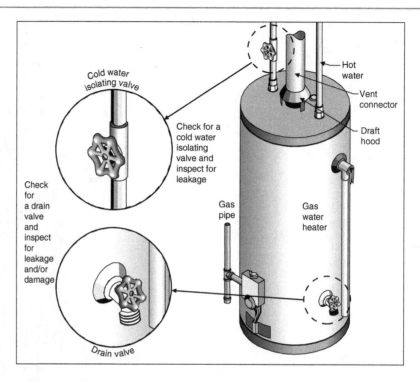

No Isolating Valve

There should be an isolating valve on the cold water inlet in case the tank ruptures and floods (Figure 13.14).

IMPLICATIONS

If there is no isolating valve, the system can't be turned off in an emergency situation. Additional water damage may occur.

STRATEGY

Check that there is an isolating valve on the cold water piping adjacent to the water heater.

Drain Valve Problems

Water heaters should have a drain valve at the bottom. The valve may be missing, damaged or leaking.

IMPLICATIONS

If there is no drain valve, it will be difficult to get the sediment out of the bottom of the tank. This affects the efficiency and amount of hot water available. It can also result in noisy tanks.

If the valve is damaged, it may not be operable. If the valve is leaking, obviously water damage is a possibility.

STRATEGY

Make sure that there is a drain valve and that it appears intact. We do not recommend that you open the drain valve. Hot water will be discharged immediately. The other risk is that the valve will not shut off when you close it. Again, you don't want to create a leak.

FIGURE 13.15 Power-Vented Water Heater

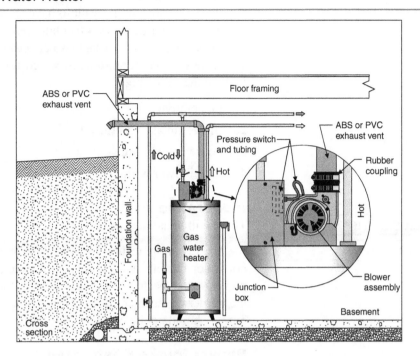

13.2.4 Fan-Assisted Gas Water Heaters

Fan-assisted or power-vented gas water heaters have become popular in some areas. These are typically used with modern heating systems that don't use chimneys. Where the heating system is sidewall-vented or electric, no chimney is needed. It becomes impractical to install or maintain a large chimney for a domestic water heater. If an existing chimney remains in service, it is often too large for the water heater once the furnace or boiler is replaced with a sidewall-venting unit. Oversized chimneys are prone to condensation and deterioration.

Get Rid of the Chimney

A common approach is to replace the water heater with a sidewall-vented unit. **Power-vented** or **fan-assisted** water heaters can be vented through the sidewall using ABS or PVC piping, typically (Figure 13.15).

Added Complexity

Power-vented water heaters have an exhaust fan that requires electricity, controls and a safety device. These water heaters are more complex, more expensive and more prone to failures.

Automatic Ignition Systems

Most power-vented water heaters have either an intermittent pilot or hot surface ignition for the burner. These units do not typically have a standing pilot.

Making Sure the Blower Is On

These water heaters won't operate if the blower is not on. We run the risk of dumping exhaust products into the house and overheating the exhaust piping if the blower is not working. A pressure switch checks to see that the blower is working before the burner is allowed to come on.

Venting Issues

The vents on power-vented water heaters are smaller diameter, typically, than conventional water heater vents. They are plastic vents that do not require any combustible clearances. The vents usually terminate outdoors and have the same rules for termination location as other sidewall-vented appliances.

Slope and Supports for Vents

Since this is not a condensing appliance, the manufacturers may not require any slope on the vent piping. These water heaters do not have a condensate management system, so we don't necessarily want to slope the vent back down to the water heater to collect condensate. Most manufacturers will allow a slope back down toward the appliance, but they don't want to have to handle a lot of condensation. The piping should be supported every 4 feet horizontally, as is typical for plastic piping.

Inspection of power-vented water heaters is similar to conventional water heaters with a few added conditions to watch for. Problems with power-vented systems include the following:

1. Inoperative
2. Blower intake obstructed
3. Poor venting arrangement
4. Poor blower wiring

Inoperative

IMPLICATIONS

There will be no hot water.

STRATEGY

We're simply testing to make sure that hot water is delivered. If you operate hot water faucets and get only cold water, go down to the water heater. If it's a power-vented heater, you should hear the blower operating even before you remove the burner cover to check for burner operation. If the blower is not operating, the burner should not be on.

Blower Intake Obstructed

These systems require considerable amounts of dilution air as discussed.

IMPLICATION

The pressure switch may not be satisfied and the system will not operate. We don't want the water heater to operate if it can't get enough dilution (cooling) air.

STRATEGY

Look to see that the blower intake area is free and open.

Poor Venting Arrangement

Venting issues can be similar to those on high efficiency furnaces. Look for such things as poor termination points, inadequate support, excessive elbows and inappropriate vent size. You may have to refer to an installation manual for details on specific systems. Where the venting system is suspect and you can't verify a problem, recommend further investigation.

Poor Blower Wiring

Any electrically operated device needs to have safe wiring. You should be looking for a grounded system with wiring of an appropriate size. Fuses or breakers for the wiring should be appropriate. The wires should be of a suitable type and adequately secured and protected. Connections should be suitably made inside junction boxes.

Many power-vented water heaters simply use a cord and plug that is put into a 120-volt convenience receptacle. The cord should not be in the path of the exhaust products and should not contact the exhaust piping. In some areas, a dedicated circuit has to be provided for the water heater fan.

IMPLICATION

Electrical problems are safety issues.

STRATEGY

Follow the electrical supply system to the water heater and to the fan itself. Look for the problems we've listed above.

13.3   DRAIN, WASTE, AND VENT PIPING

Waste Includes Solids, Liquids, and Gases

In the discussion of supply plumbing we learned how to get clean water into the house and control it. Now we have to get rid of the waste that includes the solids, liquids and gases. Once again, the concept is very simple; the practice is more complicated.

Flows by Gravity

We get rid of our waste by letting it fall or flow through a series of nearly horizontal and vertical pipes, down through and out of the house. Unlike the supply system, we do not need any pumps or pressure to move the waste, at least not in most cases.

Private or Municipal Sewer System

Once the waste leaves the house, it is no longer the concern of the home inspector. It goes either to a municipal sewage treatment facility (via city sewers), or an on-site facility such as a septic system, for example. There are other options including holding tanks, seepage tanks and cesspools, but we won't address these here, since they are outside the scope of a Standards inspection.

Don't Guess Where Sewage Goes

One word of caution—if you are going to identify the sewage handling system as public or private, we recommend that you do some research. It can cost you several thousand dollars if you are wrong on this one. If you mistakenly tell someone that they are on a public sewage system, you have a serious problem.

The components of the drain, waste and vent plumbing system that we will look at are: drain piping, traps, floor drains, venting systems, sewage ejector pumps, sump pumps, and laundry tub pumps.

Drain, Waste, and Vent Pipes

There are different names for pipes on the waste side of plumbing systems, based on their functions.

- **Soil pipes** carry liquids and solids. The pipe from a toilet is a soil pipe.
- **Waste pipes** carry only liquids according to some authorities and liquids and solids according to others. The terms **drain** and **waste** are often used interchangeably.
- **Drain pipes** are intended to carry liquids and solids (some say liquids only).
- **Vent pipes** carry air only (no liquids or solids).

Most pipe materials are described as DWV (Drain, Waste and Vent), which means they are suitable for solids, liquids, and gases.

13.3.1   Drain Piping

Materials

Drain, waste, and vent piping may include the following materials:

- Copper
- ABS
- PVC
- Cast iron
- Lead (drain and waste only)
- Galvanized steel (typically drain and vent only)
- Brass (typically fittings)
- Clay (underground drain and waste only)

FIGURE 13.16 Connecting Cast Iron Waste Pipe—Hubless

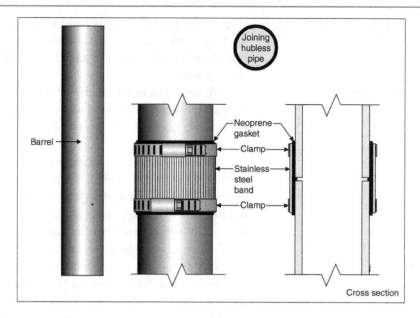

Pipe Supports

Vertical Supports

Generally speaking, vertical supports should be provided at every other floor level. Some areas call for supports at every floor level, particularly with heavy pipe like cast iron. Most areas call for the support of copper piping every 10 feet vertically. Plastic piping needs guides at the mid story height between supports in some jurisdictions. We don't usually see this during a home inspection, so we won't be able to comment.

Sway Bracing

On cast iron waste piping with flexible hangers that are longer than 18 inches, sway bracing is often required to stabilize the pipe in areas where seismic activity is an issue.

Additional Support for Cast Iron Piping

Where cast iron piping has hubless connections (with a sleeve, gasket or shield and clamps) additional supports may be required (Figure 13.16). You should check to see what your area calls for here. Understand, however, that most new work will not include cast iron piping, and that unless supports have been damaged or removed, the age of the system usually proves the success of the installation.

Fittings Cannot Reduce Pipe Diameter

It is critical that the interior of waste pipes be smooth and that size changes always go from smaller to larger. The fittings are not permitted to reduce the interior diameter on waste piping. We don't want to create surfaces or edges that hang up solids.

Bell and Spigot Connections

Bell and spigot connections were common on cast iron pipes, although they have largely been replaced with hubless connectors. The pipes have a male and female end. The pipes are fit together and the base is packed with oakum or jute. This material is sealed in place with molten lead to a depth of at least 1 inch. The oakum or jute is sometimes called **caulking.**

Lead Piping Replacement

Lead piping hasn't been used commonly since the 1950s. It is prone to leakage in most installations after 40 years or so. Galvanized steel supply piping often needs to be replaced after 40 years because of leaks or low pressure. Many home inspectors recommend replacement of lead waste piping whenever galvanized steel supply piping is being replaced. It's common to find both materials at bathrooms, for example. Since changing the supply piping is disruptive, it's a good idea to replace the lead waste piping at the same time.

Galvanized Steel Pipes

Galvanized steel pipes are strong and, when used for vent piping, often have indefinite life expectancies. However, when they are used for drain pipes, they will rust on the inside. The rusting creates an uneven surface which can lead to clogging before the pipes rust through. Galvanized steel pipes very often rust through at the threads first. Galvanized steel drain pipes were commonly used under sinks and laundry tubs.

Copper Piping

Copper drain, waste and vent pipes are considered by many to be the best material. They were popular from the 1950s to the early 1970s.

ABS and PVC

Lightweight plastic ABS and PVC replaced copper drain, waste and vent systems in the 1970s in many areas because they are inexpensive and easy to work with. The chief criticism of these pipes is that they are noisy. In some areas, plastic stacks in walls and ceilings are wrapped with insulation to minimize the noise. This helps, but does not completely eliminate the problem.

Combustibles and Plastic Piping

Plastic piping cannot typically penetrate floors, ceilings or walls that separate two dwellings. Usually, there has to be a fire separation between adjacent dwellings. A plastic pipe would compromise this separation.

Supports for Plastic Piping

Supports for plastic pipes shouldn't rub on the piping. The pipe can wear through as a result of abrasion. The pipe tends to expand and contract as it heats up and cools down and is susceptible to being worn through over time. Insulating the pipe to protect it from hangers is one solution, although this is rarely done. Metal hangers are worse than plastic hangers.

Connecting ABS and PVC

The solvents used to join ABS piping sections together are not the same as the solvents used to connect PVC piping. The solvents are not interchangeable. Where ABS and PVC piping are to be joined together, a special combination solvent can be used.

Sunlight Attacks ABS

In some areas, authorities do not allow plastic piping (especially ABS) outside where it may be exposed to direct sunlight, which will break down the plastic over time. PVC may have UV (ultraviolet) stabilizers that make it more durable outside. Where ABS or PVC stacks extend above roofs, they are supposed to be painted in some jurisdictions, to protect them from the UV rays. Connections are weak spots on drain, waste and vent systems and you should check all connections, paying particular attention to those between dissimilar materials.

We've talked about the general function of drain, waste and vent piping and the common materials used. Let's look at some of the problems we find in the field, starting with drain and waste piping.

Conditions
Common problems with drain, waste and vent piping include the following:

1. Leaks
2. Rust
3. Freezing
4. Split/damaged/crimped
5. Clogged
6. Poor support
7. Cross connections
8. Undersized/overloaded

9. Poor slope
10. Cleanouts missing or inaccessible
11. Exposed to mechanical damage
12. Pipe size reduced downstream
13. Galvanized steel buried in soil
14. Combustible piping
15. Noisy
16. Non-standard materials and patches
17. Missing air gap for dishwashers
18. Clothes washer drainage improper
19. Condensate drain connections improper
20. Poor manifolding

Leaks

Leaks in drain and waste piping systems can be more difficult to find than in supply systems because the pipes are usually idle. Supply pipes are always full of pressurized water. Waste pipes intermittently see water at atmospheric pressure. The implications of a leak can be more serious because of the possible impact of sewage getting into the home. It's one of the reasons that waste pipes cannot run above food preparation areas in some jurisdictions.

IMPLICATIONS

Sewage leaking into the house can make people sick. Leaks can also cause damage to finishes and to the structure.

STRATEGY

You can only verify active leaks in waste plumbing systems by operating the fixtures. In many cases, you will see evidence of leakage but won't know whether it is active until there is water running through the pipes. The more water you run, the more likely you are to find the leaks.

Focus on Connections

We talked earlier about the importance of looking at connections. Wherever the pipe changes direction or materials, we have a potential leak spot.

Freezing Pipes

Where pipes pass through unheated spaces in cold climates, we have the possibility of leakage as a result of freezing. Sometimes the piping is insulated. Touching the insulation, or removing part of it, especially near the bottom of any exposed sections, may reveal a slight leak. Traps in unheated areas are vulnerable to freezing.

Rust

Watch for rusting on metallic piping. Cast iron piping will often leak at small pinholes. The pinhole leaks will often scab over with rust and stop leaking. We strongly recommend that you don't pick or poke at these pinholes. The pipe may be very thin and could collapse if you handle it roughly.

Horizontal Splits in Cast Iron Pipe

Check the top side of horizontal cast iron piping systems. It's not unusual to find a small split running parallel to the length of the pipe.

Rust

Rusted Copper

Rust on copper pipe is typically green. It may be the result of exposure to acids or a corrosive atmosphere. It may also be caused by contact with dissimilar metals.

The implications are ultimately leakage.

IMPLICATIONS

STRATEGY

Most rusting is on cast iron or galvanized steel piping. The majority of it is on the inside of the pipe, and you won't be able to see the rust until it comes through the pipe surface. This can be pinholes, blisters or splits. As we've talked about before, the rust on threaded piping often appears at the threaded connections first.

*Galvanized Steel Piping
Close to Grade*

Surface Rust

Galvanized steel or iron piping should be at least 6 inches above grade. It may have been buried in the soil on original construction or be a result of renovations or earth being moved carelessly in crawlspaces. Where you see earth in contact with galvanized steel piping, look closely for evidence of rusting on the piping exterior.

Rusting on the surface of piping can be caused by condensation or by leaks running along the outer pipe surface. This may be less serious than rust coming through from the inside, but it is often tough to know how extensive the damage is during an inspection.

Freezing

Freezing drain and waste piping is only an issue where the piping is filled with water in cold climates and where the piping is exposed to outdoor temperatures. These conditions may exist in garages and crawlspaces, for example.

IMPLICATIONS

Clogging, splitting, and leaking of the piping are obvious implications.

STRATEGY

In many cases, pipes pass through unheated spaces without insulation. Because the warm water passes through quickly and infrequently, there may be no freeze up problems. However, if there is a faucet that drips, a trickle of water running down the inside of the pipe may be cooled enough to freeze. If uncorrected, the ice can build up to the point of obstructing the drain. This is more common on horizontal pipes but can also happen on vertical pipes.

Insulation and Heat Tracing

Where waste pipes pass through unheated areas, they should be insulated and/or protected from freezing with electric heat tracing wires. Heat tracing is more effective because, although the insulation slows heat loss, it doesn't stop it. If things stay cold enough long enough, insulated pipes may freeze.

Split/Damaged/Crimped Pipe

IMPLICATIONS

The implications of split, damaged or crimped piping are leaks and clogging.

STRATEGY

Follow the lengths of pipes looking for irregularities such as dented or crimped spots, splits or areas of obvious mechanical damage. Watch for abrasion of plastic piping against metal or masonry, for example. Metal hangers on plastic pipes can wear through the piping.

Clogged

You won't always be able to identify clogged piping and where you can find that it is clogged, you will often have difficulty finding the clog.

IMPLICATIONS

This is a health issue since waste will back up in the fixtures.

STRATEGY

We normally find clogged drain pipes by flowing the fixtures. Good plumbing fixtures will drain water out of them as quickly as it can be introduced with both faucets fully open. Many fixtures cannot meet this standard, but that does not mean that they are defective or that the drains are clogged.

15 Seconds to Drain a Basin

You have to use your judgment to determine what is a reasonable amount of time for draining. Many full basins can drain in roughly 15 seconds. If the basin takes more than 30 seconds to drain, there may be an obstruction.

In addition to the drainage piping system, the fixture drain stopper, strainer, outlet pipe or trap may be clogged. Don't be fooled by pop-up drain stoppers that don't pop up high enough to drain freely. Also watch for hair, soap scum, and other junk hung up on strainers. Generally speaking, you would have to observe backup at more than one fixture before describing the waste piping as being clogged.

Poor Support

Generally speaking, you can't see vertical supports except at sub-grade areas and in attics. Supports for horizontal pipes can often be seen in basements or crawlspaces.

Improper slope, clogging and opening at joints are all implications of poor support.

Your first step should be to look at pipes for evidence of movement. If a low spot is visible in a horizontal run, the supports are probably not adequate. Sometimes building settlement or heaving may leave piping unsupported, with the hangers in mid air below the pipe. Watch for pipes that are suspended above their hangers.

Corroded Hangers

Watch for metal piping with metal hangers that are dissimilar. Copper piping, for example, will eventually rust steel hangers.

Sway Bracing

If your area is susceptible to seismic activity, sway bracing may also be necessary for near horizontal pipes.

Cross Connections

Cross connections include the supply and waste piping coming together. Examples are given in the discussion of supply piping earlier in this chapter.

Contamination of a potable water supply is the implication of a cross connection.

Look for the common cross connection areas and recommend rearrangement.

Undersized

Drain and waste pipes have to be large enough to carry away the waste material. The minimum sizes of traps and trap arms for some common fixtures are listed in Table 13.2.

Where drains carry the discharge from multiple fixtures, the drain pipe sizing is determined from **unit loading** tables (unit loading numbers for each fixture are set out in plumbing codes). The drain size depends on several variables including the orientation (vertical or horizontal), the length of the drainage pipe and the length of the vent piping.

Slow drain performance, clogging and possible backup are the implications.

It's beyond the scope of a home inspection to size every drain and vent pipe in the house. For the most part, they're not visible anyway. You should, however, be able to look at individual fixture drains, including their traps, and see if they are suitably sized for the fixture. The chart above is helpful in this regard.

Look under each fixture where visible and ensure that the size of the fixture outlet pipe (tail piece), trap and trap arm (fixture drain) are at least as large as that indicated on the chart.

Poor Slope

Nearly horizontal drain pipes should generally slope at $1/4$ to $1/2$ inch per foot. Large pipes (more than 4-inch) can slope at about $1/8$ inch per foot.

A pipe that has too low a slope will be prone to clogging. A pipe with too steep a slope may be prone to clogging as the liquids flow by quickly and the solids get hung up in the pipe.

Most home inspectors don't measure pipe slope. You should be able to sight along drain pipes and see a positive slope. Where you can't see a slope or you can see an obvious low spot, recommend further investigation.

TABLE 13.2 Minimum Trap and Trap Arm Sizes

Fixture	Minimum Size of Traps and and Trap Arm
single wash basin	1¼ inch
bidets	1¼ inch
dishwashers	1½ inch
kitchen sink with or without dishwasher	1½ inch
laundry tub	1½ inch
bathtubs	1½ inch
floor drains	2 inches
clothes washers	2 inches
showers	1½–2 inches (depending on shower flow rate)

Cleanouts Missing or Inaccessible

There is typically one cleanout for every horizontal drain. The cleanouts can be above grade, in a basement or in a crawlspace. In some cases, the cleanout cap is flush with the basement floor. In some cases, the cleanout is near the base of a stack. It's good practice to have 12 to 18 inches of clear space at the cleanout to gain access depending on the size of the pipe.

IMPLICATIONS

When problems occur, service can be much more expensive if the cleanout is missing or inaccessible.

STRATEGY

Make sure that there is an accessible cleanout provided.

Exposed to Mechanical Damage

In some cases, the pipe is not damaged, but its location makes it vulnerable.

IMPLICATIONS

Mechanical damage causing leakage and/or obstruction of the piping is the implication.

STRATEGY

Watch for piping that may be damaged by opening doors or by vehicles (in garages), or is otherwise susceptible to being bumped. You'll have to use some common sense here.

Pipe Size Reduced Downstream

As waste flows it should never go from a large pipe to a smaller one. The pipe size should always increase downstream and as waste from other fixtures joins in.

IMPLICATION

A poor arrangement is prone to clogging.

STRATEGY

As you follow the waste plumbing system, look for spots where liquid or solid wastes will get hung up. A pipe size reduction is one such area. Watch for traps that are smaller than the fixture tailpiece or trap arms that are smaller than the traps.

Galvanized Steel Pipe Buried In Soil

The implication is premature failure of the pipe as a result of rusting.

IMPLICATIONS

STRATEGY

Check for good clearance (6 inches) of these pipes from the soil. Where the pipe is at or below soil level, recommend rearrangement and further investigation of the pipe.

Combustible Piping

PVC or ABS plastic piping is combustible. It's generally only allowed in single-family homes. There is usually a fire separation between adjacent dwellings or dwellings above each other. A combustible waste pipe that passes from one dwelling to the next compromises the fire separation.

IMPLICATION

This is a fire safety concern.

STRATEGY

If you are in a multi-family building, watch for PVC or ABS piping passing from one dwelling to the next.

Noisy

IMPLICATIONS

This is a nuisance for homeowners. They can insulate the pipe to reduce the noise somewhat, but this is disruptive and expensive.

STRATEGY

Where the waste piping is ABS or PVC plastic, let your client know that some noise should be expected. You can flush a toilet in an upper floor and let your client listen in the room below, so they will have a sense of what to expect.

Non-Standard Materials and Patches

Non-standard materials to watch for include rubber hose (radiator hose), garden hose, corrugated pipe and polyethylene piping. Waste piping materials are not flexible.

Patches are not generally successful on waste piping.

Leaks and related health problems can result from using improper materials.

IMPLICATIONS

STRATEGY

Watch for flexible hoses used as piping and patches on piping material including duct tape. Damaged waste piping should generally be replaced rather than repaired. While repairs are common on cast iron plumbing stacks, they should be considered temporary measures.

Poor Manifolding of Drain Piping

There are several rules for how drain pipes should be interconnected. It's beyond our scope to look at all of these, but you can use some common sense to see whether connections are arranged to encourage the flow of waste in the proper direction.

One example of a poor arrangement is a straight T connection into a waste pipe from fixtures that are back to back or side by side. We don't want the waste from one fixture to flow past the stack and deposit itself in the drain from the other fixture.

Horizontal drain lines joining a vertical stack should connect through:

- 45-degree Y connections
- 60-degree Y connections
- combination Y and one-eighth bends
- sanitary Ts or
- sanitary tapped T branches, for example.

There are other permitted fittings.

Horizontal Drain to Horizontal Drain

When one horizontal drain line connects with another, the connection should be made through a 45-degree Y, combination Y and one-eighth bend, or other similar fitting. Again, the idea is to make the change of direction gradual and to encourage the waste to flow in the desired direction.

Vertical into Horizontal Drains

Vertical into horizontal connections should be made with 45-degree branches or similar fittings (Figure 13.17).

If the vertical pipe is truly vertical, a 60-degree branch may be used.

F I G U R E 13.17   Connecting Vertical Drain Pipes to Horizontal Drain Pipes

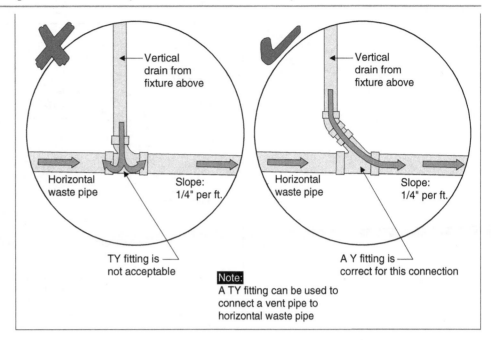

IMPLICATIONS

Poor connections may result in clogging of pipes.

STRATEGY

Look at drain connections from a common sense standpoint.

Watch for connections that will not promote flow of waste in the intended direction. Waste should never be asked to make a sharp 90° turn and should never be asked to flow even slightly uphill.

13.3.2   Traps

Traps are designed to prevent sewer odors from entering the home through the plumbing fixtures. The seal in the trap is provided by the waste water. Every time we use a fixture, we flush out the water that's forming the trap seal and replace it with new water.

Traps are carefully engineered systems. They are designed to be self-scouring so that they don't collect debris, yet retain water to form a seal.

Need to Be Cleaned

Even though traps are designed to flow freely, they sometimes get plugged. Traps should be provided with slip joints (removable threaded connections) that can be removed, or there should be a cleanout plug at the bottom of the trap (Figure 13.18). Slip joints have a disadvantage because they are slightly more vulnerable to leakage than other types of connections. However, the accessibility issue is important.

No Traps for Toilets

The only fixture that doesn't need a trap is the toilet because the water in the toilet bowl acts as a trap. The water in the toilet bowl is replenished every time the toilet is used.

Running Traps

Running traps are traps located in the drainage piping that are not directly connected with a fixture. Many older homes had running traps in the building sewer, typically in the front lawn. These traps were designed to prevent sewer gases from entering the house. Modern homes do not have running traps since they were found to be unnecessary once effective venting systems were designed.

F I G U R E 13.18   Trap Cleanout Required

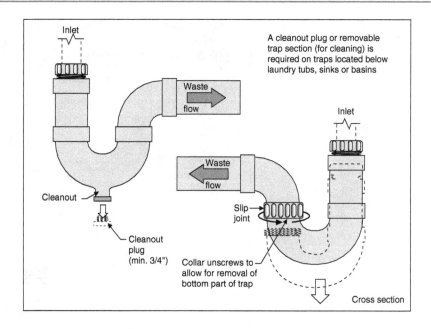

Let's look at some of the problems we find with traps.

1. Missing
2. Wrong type
3. Leak
4. Double trapping
5. Split, rusted or damaged
6. Freezing
7. Tail piece (fixture outlet pipe) too long
8. Trap arm (fixture drain) too short or too long
9. Traps too small or too big
10. Trap primer problems
11. Non-standard shape or material
12. Clogged/no cleanout provision

Missing

Every fixture should be provided with a trap, except for a toilet.

An unhealthy environment in the house will result if sewer gases find their way into the home.

Where you can see below fixtures, look for a trap. If you can't see below the fixture, look down the fixture drain. You should see standing water. You can also use your nose to search for sewer odors.

IMPLICATIONS

STRATEGY

FIGURE 13.19 Illegal Traps

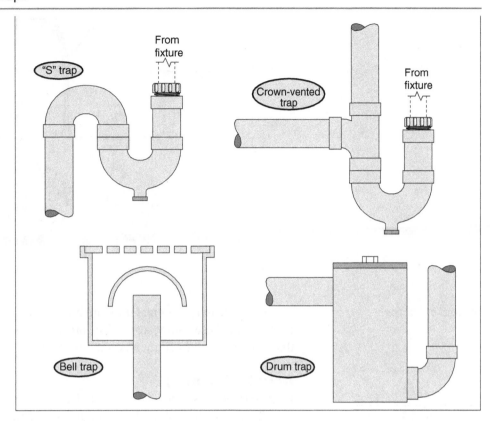

Wrong Type

Residential traps should be **P-type. S-traps, drum traps, bell traps, and crown-vented traps** are usually not permitted (Figure 13.19).

The implication of an S-trap is siphoning. The implication of a crown vented trap is obstruction of the vent and, ultimately, siphoning. Bell traps are unreliable and drum traps are not self-scouring. They tend to accumulate solids.

Look for P-traps. Recommend that other types of traps be replaced or closely monitored for sewer odors or clogging.

Leaks

Leaks are common at traps.

Obviously, waste leaking into the home is a health issue and a water damage issue.

When you are operating each plumbing fixture, look below if possible, and make sure the trap is not leaking. Many inspectors fill the basin and pull the plug, rather than simply run water through. Their thinking is that they will ensure that the tail piece, trap and trap arm are completely flooded. Some leaks only show up when these components are flooded.

You can also watch for evidence of leakage including—

- staining or streaking on the trap
- rusting on cleanout plugs
- buckets or trays below the trap
- water damage on the floor, finishes or structural members below the trap

IMPLICATIONS

STRATEGY

IMPLICATIONS

STRATEGY

Evidence of Leakage

FIGURE 13.20   Double Trapping Doesn't Work

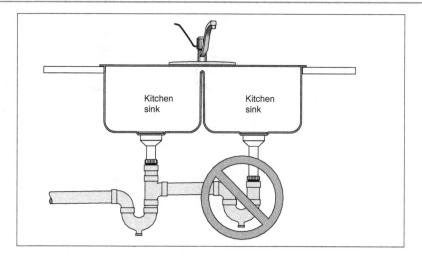

A Word of Caution

Many old tail pieces and traps are brass, often chrome- or nickel-plated. Be careful touching these components. They are sometimes so thin or so badly deteriorated, that simply putting your hand on them can cause them to leak or break.

Double Trapping

Double trapping sounds like a good idea but it's not (Figure 13.20).

IMPLICATIONS

The implication of double trapping is clogging of the trap. If we have double trapping, the velocity coming into the second trap will be reduced and solids are more likely to collect and clog the second trap.

STRATEGY

A common spot for double trapping is under double sinks in kitchens, laundry areas or bathrooms. This can occur elsewhere in the house as well, but may be more difficult to detect.

Split, Rusted, or Damaged

In some cases you won't be able to run the water and find the leaks. In other cases there won't be any apparent leakage but you can see obvious weakness in the trap.

IMPLICATIONS

Trap leakage is the risk here.

STRATEGY

Look at the trap for evidence of splitting, rusting or damage. A mirror and a flashlight are helpful. Looking at just the front of the trap doesn't give you the whole picture, obviously.

Freezing

Traps in cold areas are susceptible to freezing. In most cases, traps will be in heated areas, but traps in bathrooms above unheated garages or crawlspaces, for example, can be vulnerable.

IMPLICATIONS

A freezing trap will split and leakage will result.

STRATEGY

Where plumbing fixtures are close to cold areas, think about the possibility of freezing traps. Pay particular attention to showers and bathtubs, for example, which typically have their drains and traps below the floor level. This can also be an issue on island sinks, where in some jurisdictions it's common to drop the trap below the floor level.

Tail Piece (Fixture Outlet Pipe) Too Long

The vertical or horizontal distance between the fixture and the trap is important. We talked earlier about maintaining adequate waste velocity through the trap.

Most codes call for this distance to be a maximum of 24 inches.

IMPLICATIONS

The implications are siphoning of the trap if the tail piece is vertical, or clogging of the trap if the tail piece is horizontal.

STRATEGY

If you can get a look, check to see how far the trap is from the fixture. Depending on your jurisdiction, it should be no more than 24 or 36 inches.

Trap Arm Too Long or Too Short

The distance from the trap to the vent can't be too long or we may siphon the trap. If the trap arm is too short, waste might splash up into the vent and eventually clog it.

Minimum Trap Arm Length

A trap arm should be at least two pipe diameters long. For example, if the trap is $1\frac{1}{2}$ inch diameter, the trap arm should be at least 3 inches long.

Maximum Trap Arm Length

Many jurisdictions use a 5 foot rule. In some areas, different rules apply based on different pipe diameters. Here is an example of one jurisdiction's rules:

Trap Arm Diameter in Inches	Maximum Trap Arm Length in Feet
$1\frac{1}{4}$	5
$1\frac{1}{2}$	6
2	8
3	12

The object is to have the vent coming off the top of the trap arm higher than the weir of the trap. We don't want the vent pipe flooded because then it won't be able to add air to the trap arm to break the vacuum. Breaking the vacuum is important in preventing direct siphoning of the water in the trap.

IMPLICATIONS

Siphoning the trap or blocking the vent pipe are the implications of trap arms that are too long or too short.

STRATEGY

While it is sometimes difficult to see much, where you can determine the length of the trap arm, check that it falls within the parameters we've outlined above (depending on your jurisdiction). You'll have to find out what rules apply in your area if you are going to call these defects out for improvement. It is more important to look for the functional implications such as siphoning traps, than to memorize rules.

Traps Too Small or Too Big

Most authorities specify minimum trap sizes. Most also make a general comment that the trap size shouldn't be so large that the velocity of the waste slows down to a point where solids will collect in the trap. This is hard to define. As a general rule, the trap should be the same diameter as, or one pipe size larger than, the tail piece (fixture outlet pipe) and the same size as the trap arm. Where the drains from three sinks or basins are manifolded, the trap arm is usually one size larger than the traps and the tail pieces.

IMPLICATIONS

The implications of both an undersized and oversized trap are clogging.

STRATEGY

Traps should be the same size as the trap arm if we are draining a single fixture. Where the trap is a different size, watch for backup and/or siphoning at that fixture.

Nonstandard Shape or Material

Homemade traps, or traps made from different materials than those that are approved, are usually not successful. Their depth of seal may be appropriate, but they won't maintain the proper velocity and self-scouring effect.

IMPLICATION

The trap is not likely to perform well and is more likely to clog or siphon.

STRATEGY

Whenever you see a trap that does not have the characteristic P-shape, you should note it as a questionable performer. Watch also for either a cleanout plug or slip joints that allow the trap to be removed for cleaning.

Clogged

When you are performing your drainage test, you may find that an individual fixture is clogged. Very often, the trap is the problem. While we shouldn't be troubleshooting, you may be able to determine that the trap is clogged. We do not recommend that you remove cleanouts or slip joints to inspect traps. The chances of breaking a fitting or making a mess are significant.

IMPLICATIONS

The fixture will not drain, at least at its normal speed.

STRATEGY

You will be describing drainage problems where fixtures don't get rid of their water in a reasonable amount of time. You may or may not know that it's a clogged trap, but include this as a possibility. This is more likely if only one fixture is slow to drain. If all fixtures in the house are slow to drain, the problem is more likely in a main drain, for example.

13.3.3   Floor Drains

Floor drains are needed to protect the house from water damage. Watch for them during inspections and look for these common problems:

1. Missing
2. Poor location
3. Backup
4. Grate missing, rusted or obstructed
5. No trap
6. Downspout connection upstream of trap
7. No primer or poor primer arrangement

Missing

Every home should be provided with a floor drain. Is it required in your area?

IMPLICATIONS

There is no place for water to go if there is a flood.

STRATEGY

Look for a floor drain. If you can't find one, recommend that it be located or that one be provided.

Poor Location

Floor drains work best if they are at the low point in the floor. Most are not, although they should be relatively close. You'll have to use some common sense to determine whether the location is acceptable or not.

IMPLICATIONS

A considerable amount of water may accumulate and damage the home before it finds it way to the drain if the drain is too high.

F I G U R E 13.21   Backwater Valve

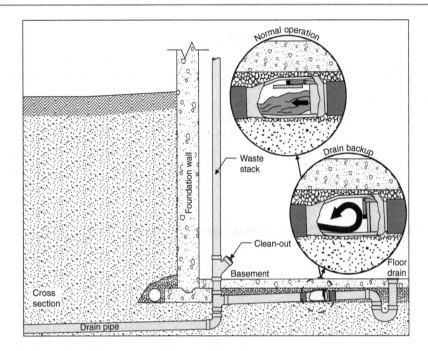

Look to see that the drain is approximately at the low point of the floor. If the house is multi-level, make sure the lowest level has a floor drain.

Backup

Drains may back up for a number of reasons.

If the floor drain backs up, the house may flood.

Look for evidence of the floor drain backing up. Watermarks around the floor close to the drain are one indication. In areas where municipal storm sewers are likely to back up, **backwater valves** are sometimes provided just downstream of the floor drain trap (Figure 13.21). This is a type of check valve designed to protect the home against sewer backup. In most cases you won't know whether one has been provided. In some cases you can see a backflow prevention device just below the floor drain grate. This may be a clue that you should be looking for evidence of prior flooding. Most people do not put these in as a preventative measure. They only get installed after there has been a problem.

Grate Missing, Rusted, or Obstructed

Every floor drain should have a grate with holes in it to allow water to go down.

The drain may become obstructed by materials falling into the 3-inch hole in the floor if the cover is missing. The 3-inch hole for the floor drain is also a safety hazard since someone may step on the hole and twist an ankle, for example. A rusted grate may also be a safety hazard because it may not carry the weight of a person. A rusted or obstructed grate may not let water flow down the drain.

Where the grate is missing, recommend that one be added.

Ensure that there is enough drainage that a large quantity of water can escape through the floor drain. Remember, these are usually 3 inches in diameter, so that the drain can handle large amounts of flooding.

Recommend replacing rusted, damaged or missing grates and cleaning obstructed grates.

No Trap

Every floor drain inside a building should have a trap.

Sewer odors may find their way into the house if there is no trap.

When you look down the floor drain, you should see standing water indicating that there is a trap that is filled. If you see no water, there may either be no trap, or there may be a trap that has had its water evaporate. The trap may also be cracked or broken so that it won't hold water. If you look down and see no water, you should be smelling for sewer odor and recommending further investigation.

13.3.4   Venting Systems

It's hard to see the venting system in a house and, while our discussion will focus on the things that we can check, you should understand that there's a lot that you won't know about the venting system.

Function

The venting system on a house is designed to equalize the air pressure in the waste plumbing system. The venting system should allow air to escape so waste can move through the pipes. Vents should also allow air to be drawn in to prevent a vacuum from forming. We don't want vacuums to form because we don't want the water to be siphoned out of traps. Some people think of venting systems as **trap protectors.** Venting also allows sewer gases to escape outdoors rather than fight their way through the water seal and into the house.

What You Can See

In many houses, the only part of the venting system you can see is the part that extends above the roof. You may be able to see vent piping in the attic, but you can't see the individual vents and branch vents from fixtures. You may be able to see some of the vents in the basement or crawlspace areas. Where there are plumbing fixtures in unfinished areas such as basements, you may see the vents for the fixtures there. For the most part though, the vent system is invisible.

Testing the Venting System

As you flow water at each fixture and watch the functional drainage, you are also testing the venting system. As you watch the water drain out of the fixture, water should go down the drain with about the same noise level right to the end. If the last bit of water gurgles loudly, it's probably because air is being pulled through the water in the trap. This is siphoning the water out of the trap. This characteristic gurgling noise tells us that the venting system is not working.

Toilets Gurgle

The toilet is the exception. It is allowed to gurgle because it is a siphoning fixture. Let's look at some of the common venting problems.

1. Missing
2. Ineffective
3. Poor vent pipe arrangements
4. Too small or too long
5. Island venting problems
6. Vent termination problems
7. Automatic air vents

Missing

Vents should be continuous up through the roof of the building.

IMPLICATIONS

STRATEGY

The drainage system won't work very well and traps might siphon.

When looking at the outside of the building, you should see a vent pipe projecting up through the roof. Where there is none, you can be sure the venting system is missing or incomplete.

Ineffective

Sometimes you can see the vents come up through the roof but when you test the plumbing system, all the fixtures siphon. In this case you should describe the venting system as ineffective.

IMPLICATIONS

STRATEGY

Again, siphoning of traps will allow sewer gases into the house. Drains may be slow because they can't push the water out of the way.

Performing your flow tests on fixtures will tell you whether the venting is working effectively.

When you are on the roof, you can usually hear water flowing through the fixtures by listening at the top of the vent. You can also look for frost closure when on the roof in cold weather.

Poor Vent Pipe Arrangements

Many arrangements for vents are not recommended. You won't be able to see most of them during the inspection, but we'll mention a few. As vents come off trap arms, they should run vertically until they get above the flood rim level of the fixture they are venting (Figure 13.22). This isn't always practical. Sometimes the vents run horizontally. These vents are more likely to become flooded and clogged if there is a backup in the drain system.

The vent has to be on the downstream side of the trap. Occasionally it will be on the upstream side of the trap. This problem is most common on multiple sink or basin arrangements. The only place you should see something on the upstream side of the trap is when it is a cleanout or fresh air intake for a building trap. This will be on the building drain or building sewer and will not be associated with a fixture.

FIGURE 13.22   Horizontal Vent Offset

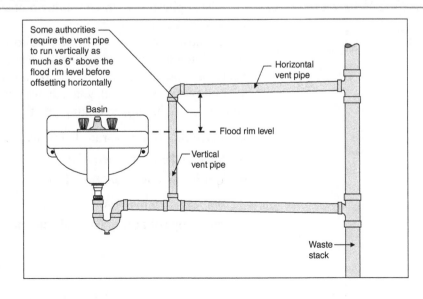

F I G U R E 13.23   Wet Venting

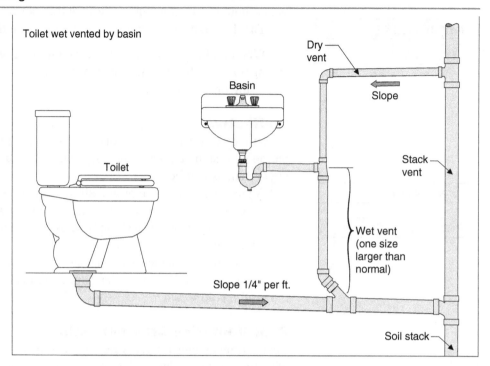

Improper Wet Venting

Wet vents are permitted under some circumstances. (A wet vent is a vent that also acts as a drain for another fixture; Figure 13.23). The fixtures have to be on one floor level and the drain sizes have to be increased to allow for the wet venting. (An exception in some areas allows a basement laundry tub and clothes washing machine standpipe to be wet vented through the drain for a first-floor kitchen sink plus dishwasher.)

It's possible that there is inappropriate wet venting or that the drain pipe serving the wet vent was not increased appropriately in size.

Slope of Vents

The near horizontal vent pipes should slope up slightly away from the trap they are protecting. We want the sewer gases to be able to move up through the venting system by convection. We don't want to create any low spots where condensation may collect. If condensation does develop, it should flow back down through the venting system into the drain and out to the sewer system.

IMPLICATION

The implication of these venting problems is traps losing their seals and allowing sewer gases into the home.

STRATEGY

In most cases you won't be able to inspect the entire venting system. This makes it tough for you to remember what the important issues are on the components that you usually cannot see. If you are doing an inspection where the entire venting system is exposed, you may want to either get some outside help, or refresh yourself as to the proper venting practices in your area. Look for—

- horizontal vent pipe runs below the fixture (less than ideal)
- vent on the wrong side of trap
- wet venting over two floor levels
- non-standard materials
- poor slope of near horizontal vent pipes

Too Small or Too Long

Vent piping can be undersized. Again, for the most part you'll have trouble picking this up. In cold climates, the vent piping extending through the roof may have to be 3-inch diameter to avoid frost closure. In other areas, vent piping can be $1^1/_2$-inch or 2-inch diameter where it passes through the roof.

The minimum vent size for any fixture is $1^1/_4$-inches. This is adequate for a $1^1/_4$- and a $1^1/_2$-inch trap. Anything larger, including a toilet, requires a $1^1/_2$-inch vent.

Just as drain sizes get bigger as you go further downstream, so do vent pipes. The further away from the fixture we get, the larger the vent pipe should be. Vent pipes should never reduce in size.

Maximum Length of Vents

Some jurisdictions limit the length of vent pipes. For example—

Vent Diameter	Maximum Vent Length
$1^1/_4$ inch	45 feet
$1^1/_2$ inch	60 feet
2 inch	120 feet
$2^1/_2$ inch	180 feet
3 inch	212 feet

Again, you are going to have a tough time determining vent sizing and length throughout the house.

IMPLICATION

The implication of undersized or overly long venting is ineffective venting.

STRATEGY

Where you can see vents at fixtures, check their size. Where you can see the vent coming through the roof, make sure it is appropriate.

Island Venting Problems

Kitchen sinks in islands present a special venting problem. Because most home-owners don't want vents running up through the middle of their kitchen, we have to find another way to handle the venting. In some jurisdictions, the trap from the kitchen sink can be below the floor, and a vent can come off the trap arm under the floor and run horizontally to a wall. While this is a less than ideal arrangement, it is not a bad compromise for an otherwise difficult situation. (Why is this less than ideal? Because if the drains back up, the vent will be flooded and may clog.) The alternative (and required) solution in many areas is as illustrated in Figure 13.24.

The Easy Way

The trap comes off the sink in a conventional fashion. The trap arm is connected to a vertical drain that goes down through the floor and also a vent that goes up as high as possible under the counter before turning 180 degrees and coming down to join the horizontal drain below. A nearly horizontal vent comes off this vertical fixture vent. It's called a foot vent and it's $1^1/_2$ inches in diameter. It slopes up slightly until it gets to a wall where it can extend up through the roof or connect to other vents.

The Hard Way

The purpose of the vertical fixture vent making a second connection to the horizontal drain is in anticipation of waste getting up into the loop vent in the event of a backup. If this happens, we want to make sure that the material can drain out and not block the vent.

The drain lines are typically 2-inch and the vent lines are typically $1^1/_2$-inch diameter in this arrangement. In some jurisdictions, island venting may be accom-

FIGURE 13.24   Venting an Island Sink (If Below Floor Trap Is Not Permitted)

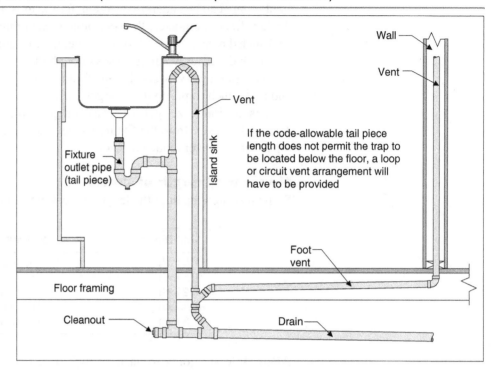

Vent

Wall

Vent

Fixture
outlet pipe
(tail piece)

Vent

Island sink

If the code-allowable tail piece
length does not permit the trap to
be located below the floor, a loop
or circuit vent arrangement will
have to be provided

Foot
vent

Floor framing

Cleanout

Drain

plished by using an air admittance valve. This is a one-way air valve that is installed in place of conventional venting. The AAV should be at least four inches above the drain.

Vent Termination Problems

Flashing

Vents must be tall enough to be appropriately flashed where they extend through the roof.

Not Too Tall

We don't want vents too tall in cold climates because they will be more prone to frost closure. Generally speaking, the maximum height of vent pipes above roofs is 12 inches. Vents that are slightly taller than this are not noteworthy, but where the vents are more than 2 feet tall, for example, and you are in a cold climate, you may worry about frost closure.

Tall Vents

Sometimes vents have to be extended to clear adjacent structures. In this case, there is a risk of frost closure. Vents are sometimes insulated to reduce this risk, although this is rare on houses. If the vent is more than 6 feet tall, consideration should be given to bracing the vent.

*Vent Clearances
from Windows*

Vents have to be at least 2 feet above any operable door or window and 10 or 12 feet away from any door or window at the same elevation or higher. Different areas have different requirements.

Vent Height above Grade

Vent pipes must be at least 10 feet above ground level in most jurisdictions. Again, you may want to check what is appropriate in your area. We mentioned earlier that plastic vents exposed to sunlight have to be painted in some areas to protect against ultraviolet rays attacking the plastic.

IMPLICATION

Vents that are too short may result in flashing leaks at the roof. Vents that are too tall may result in frost closure and possible instability of the vent. Vents that are too close to windows or other building openings may allow sewer gases back into the home. Similarly, vents too close to property lines may allow sewer gases into neighboring homes.

You will need to find out what the standard practices are in your area. Checking the vent terminations is fairly easy. Watch for—

- flashing problems
- too small
- too short (less than 6 inches)
- too tall
- not supported if more than 6 feet tall
- frost closure
- less than 2 feet above doors or windows
- less than 10 feet from door or windows beside or above the vent
- less than 10 feet above grade

Automatic Air Vents

Automatic air vents are similar to air admittance valves; however, automatic air vents are illegal in most areas and you should tell your client that these devices are usually not accepted by authorities (Figure 13.25). However, they may work to some extent. These vents allow air to be drawn in when the waste plumbing system in that area is under negative pressure. This occurs when a vacuum is being formed and the system is about to siphon. These mechanical vents, when working properly, can allow house air to be drawn in and break the vacuum, preventing the siphon problem. The vents do not allow air to be pushed out through the vent, so they don't perform all of the functions of a venting system. Automatic air vents are not recommended for toilets.

The automatic air vents perform only some of the functions of a plumbing venting system. Since they are mechanical devices operating in a hostile environment,

F I G U R E 13.25 Automatic Air Vent

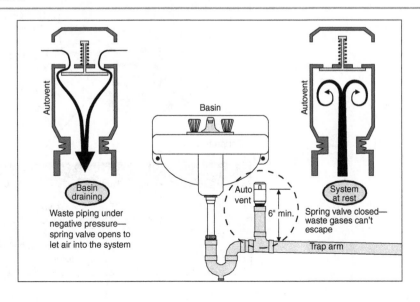

they are prone to failure. Many authorities won't accept their installation and require replacement with a conventional venting arrangement.

When we see an automatic air vent, we advise our client that a full venting system is probably not in place. We perform our plumbing tests and get a sense of whether the device is operating.

If no performance problems are noted, we'll advise the client that this is not an appropriate installation but it may work, at least over the short term. We will let the client know that replacement may be needed.

If there are performance issues, we will recommend replacement with an appropriate venting system right away.

13.3.5   Sewage Ejector Pumps

Sewage ejector pumps are a big deal. They aren't all that common, but if you miss one, neither you nor your client will be happy.

Sewage ejector pumps, also called **sewage pumps, sanitary sewer pumps,** or **solid waste pumps,** are used when there are toilets below the public or private sewer line (Figure 13.26). If waste can't flow to the sewer line by gravity, the waste has to be lifted to be discharged into the sewer.

These pumps are able to pump solids and liquids from the sump or tank up to the sewer. They consist of —

■   a buried tank or sump made of corrosion resistant material (modern ones are often fiberglass or polyethylene) with a sealed, watertight lid. The top of the tank is often flush with the floor of the lowest living space level. A diameter of 18 inches and a 30-inch depth are typical.

FIGURE 13.26   Sewage Ejector Pump

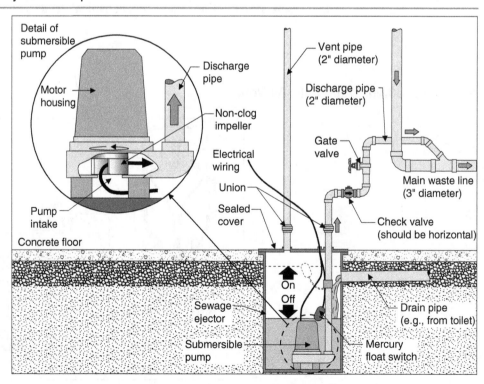

■ a side inlet to receive discharge from toilets and other fixtures. This is typically 3 to 4 inches in diameter.

Electric Pump and Controls

■ an electric pump and motor inside, operated by a float or diaphragm type level sensor to activate the pump. When the liquid level in the tank rises, the pump is activated. Pump motors are typically $1/2$ horsepower.

Pump Arrangements

■ in some cases, a pedestal pump with the motor located above the tank or sump. This makes it easier to see. Most modern sewage pumps have a submersible pump with the pump and motor completely inside the tank.

Electric Supply

These systems can be hard wired or plugged in. Some systems have separate electrics for the automatic controls. These are 120-volt systems.

Union, Check Valve, Gate Valve, in Discharge Line

A discharge pipe, typically 2 inches in diameter, comes off the top of the tank. Some jurisdictions require that the first connection be a union. This makes disassembly and servicing easier. Many installations require a check valve and then a gate valve as we move away from the tank in the discharge line. The check valve is used when the sewage ejector pump is connected to a public sewer system and protects the tank and fixtures that feed the tank from backup of the municipal sewer system. This is necessary since the pump and these fixtures are below the sewer line.

The check valve may have to be in a horizontal section of pipe to work properly. The gate valve is to isolate the tank and check valve from the discharge line for servicing.

Vent Pipe

A vent pipe comes off the top of the tank and vents like any other plumbing fixture. It is typically $1^1/2$ to 3 inches in diameter, with 2-inch diameter piping being the most common.

Check Valves on Sewage Pump Lines

Seasonal properties such as cottages with private sewage disposal systems often have no check valve on the discharge line because any liquids in the line beyond the check valve would freeze during cold weather. With no check valve, the discharge line can run from the pump to a septic tank, for example, without our worrying about burying the line below the frost level. There is less risk of catastrophic sewer backup with a private disposal system than with a municipal sewer connection, so the check valve isn't as critical here.

Let's look at what can go wrong with these sewage pumps.

1. Inoperative
2. Short cycling or running continuously
3. Odor
4. No vent
5. Discharge pipe problems
6. Missing, rusting or inoperative union, gate valve or check valve
7. Alarm sounding
8. Electrical problems

Inoperative

As you do your inspection, you will be testing the plumbing fixtures. Where you find a sewage pump, you should be flowing enough water to make the pump operate.

IMPLICATIONS

There are obvious health implications to an inoperative pump. Waste will back up into the house.

STRATEGY

Flow enough water to ensure that the pump operates. You may have to flow several gallons. Flow all the fixtures that feed into the sump. It's unusual to have an inoperative pump if there are people living in the house. Most people will not live with plumbing fixtures they cannot use.

Short Cycling or Running Continuously

IMPLICATIONS

The life expectancy of the pump and motor is going to be shorter if the pump cycles frequently or if it never shuts off.

STRATEGY

Before you run any water, note whether the pump is running. If so, does it shut off or is it on constantly?

When you run water, watch for the pump cycling on and off several times a minute. If either of these conditions are noted, recommend servicing.

Odor

Sometimes you'll notice an odor in the area of the sewage pump. Sometimes it's the odor that makes you notice that there is a sewage pump.

IMPLICATIONS

Sewer odors are unhealthy and should not be allowed to accumulate in a house.

STRATEGY

Where odors are noted, recommend servicing.

No Vent

Every sewage pump should have a vent coming off the top of the sump and venting to the building exterior.

IMPLICATIONS

If no vent is provided, the pump may not work properly. It may create a vacuum in the sump and may siphon the plumbing fixtures that are connected to it. This will lead to odors getting back into the house. If the vent connection is missing at the top of the sump and the hole is open, sewer gases can enter the house directly.

STRATEGY

Ensure that there are two pipes coming out of the tank lid. One will be the discharge, and the other, the vent. The vent system for sewage pumps should be treated as any other venting system.

Discharge Pipe Problems

Discharge pipes may be leaking, crimped or poorly connected to the sewer piping or the sump.

IMPLICATION

Discharge pipe problems may result in sewage being discharged directly into the home. Obviously this is unsafe.

STRATEGY

When the pump is operating, check the performance of the discharge pipe. Look for leaks or vibration of the piping, which may suggest a blockage. Check that the pipe is well supported and does not sway excessively when in use.

Missing, Rusting, or Inoperative Union, Check Valve, or Gate Valve

All discharge pipes should have a check valve or backwater valve and a gate valve. Many jurisdictions also call for a union before the check valve, to facilitate servicing.

IMPLICATIONS

The implications of problems with these devices are harder work and shorter life for the pump and more difficult servicing. A defective check valve may allow a sewage backup to enter the house.

STRATEGY

Check for a union, check valve and gate valve on the discharge pipe close to the sump. You should determine whether a union is required in your area. If any of the required components are missing, recommend improvements. Check valves usually have to be installed in horizontal piping. Recommend further investigation if the check is on vertical piping (it may be all right).

Alarm Sounding

Sewage will soon back up through the fixtures into the home.

IMPLICATION

Recommend servicing immediately. Don't operate plumbing fixtures feeding the sump. Document this limitation to your inspection.

STRATEGY

Electrical Problems

A number of electrical problems may be found with the supply wiring and controls. Chapter 7 covers these.

This can be a life safety issue.

IMPLICATION

Check that the electrical arrangements to the pump follow good electrical practice. The electrical system should be grounded and well-secured and controls and junction boxes should be intact and well supported. These pumps are typically 120 volts. They can be either plugged in or hard wired.

STRATEGY

We strongly recommend that you use a voltage detector or similar device to ensure that pumps and their controls are safe before touching them.

Inspector in the House: A Work in Progress

The new main floor washroom was very attractive, and a bit of a surprise—there was no other plumbing in this part of the house, and I had seen no vent piping in the attic or above the roof in this part of the house either. But I didn't think too much of it at first. I remembered the locked basement room in the finished basement below and assumed that's why I did not see the plumbing below.

I ran the basin and flushed the toilet. Everything seemed fine, although the waste sounded a little funny. I am a naturally curious type, and wondered why. I asked about access to the locked basement room. The sellers were not home and the agent said she had never seen that room either. She was clever enough to find a key on the top of the door casing and in we went.

We were amazed at what we saw—the hot and cold supply piping were garden hoses, and the waste piping was drained into a 45 gallon drum! That explained the strange noise. We later learned that the owner's son was doing the work and had been out of town for some time. Rather than admit the work was not finished, the sellers created a temporary arrangement. The agent was assured that the work would have been properly completed before the new owners moved in. Our discovery ensured that that happened.

13.4   FIXTURES AND FAUCETS

So far we have looked at the supply piping, water heaters, and the drain, waste and vent system. Now we are going to look at the fixtures where the water is actually used.

13.4.1   Basins, Sinks, and Laundry Tubs

Each of us uses these fixtures every day, so in a sense, inspection is very easy. You're familiar with how to operate these fixtures. There are certainly some things to watch for on inspections.

Let's look at some common problems.

- leaks
- rust
- surface defects
- loose
- overflow missing or inappropriate
- cross connections
- not level
- slow drains

Leaks

Leaks at fixtures are probably the most common problem. The leaks may be at the—

- faucets (especially vegetable sprayers and extendable faucets)
- bowl (especially if the bowl is concrete, synthetic marble or china)
- drain connection or pipe
- trap
- pop-up drain stoppers (where they go through the tailpiece)
- overflow

IMPLICATION

The implication of leaks is primarily water damage.

STRATEGY

As you flow the fixture, look above, around and below for evidence of leakage. Make sure you pull out and operate extendable faucets and vegetable sprayers. Where there are cracks in basins, they may only be surface cracks. It's best to fill the bowl and watch for leaks.

With older enameled steel sinks, it was common to weld a steel overflow onto the front of the sink. It's very common for these to rust out and cause the bowl to leak near the overflow connection, even when no water goes down the overflow (Figure 13.27).

Many of these overflow connections are now siliconed in place, rather than welded.

Rust

Rust is an issue on metal fixtures and on metal faucets, drains and stoppers.

IMPLICATIONS

The implications are mostly leakage related. If the rusting in the bowl is bad, the water may not remain clean as rust flakes come off in the water when the sink is in use.

STRATEGY

Watch for leaks at the faucets, bowls and drain connections. On enameled steel basins, check for rust around the overflow, on both the inside and outside of the bowl.

Surface Defects

Chips, cracks and stains are common in basins and other similar fixtures.

IMPLICATIONS

In many cases these are simply cosmetic defects. Where enamel is chipped away from stainless steel, rusting is the longer term implication.

Where cracks appear in the surface of bowls, leakage through the crack may be the long term implication. Mold growth in the cracks is a common problem.

STRATEGY

Look for surface defects before operating the fixture.

FIGURE 13.27 Rusting Overflow

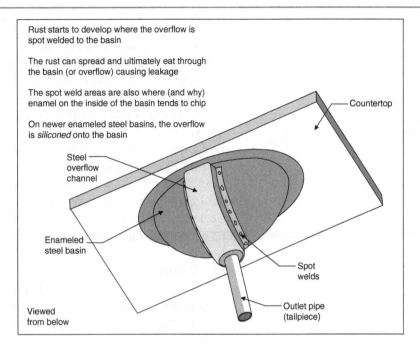

Rust starts to develop where the overflow is spot welded to the basin

The rust can spread and ultimately eat through the basin (or overflow) causing leakage

The spot weld areas are also where (and why) enamel on the inside of the basin tends to chip

On newer enameled steel basins, the overflow is *siliconed* onto the basin

Steel overflow channel

Countertop

Enameled steel basin

Spot welds

Outlet pipe (tailpiece)

Viewed from below

Loose

Basins, sinks and laundry tubs may be supported by countertops, walls, or floors (by pedestals or legs). Wall-hung and pedestal type basins are the most likely to be loose.

IMPLICATIONS

Loose fixtures are likely to strain supply and drain pipes. Leakage is a likely implication. Wall-hung fixtures may fall off the wall and injure someone. Pedestal sinks can also have the tops fall off and injure people. Some pedestal sinks are one piece, although many are two piece with a separate bowl and pedestal. China and cast iron fixtures are extremely heavy and can cause serious injury as well as flooding if they fall.

STRATEGY

With both pedestal and wall-hung fixtures, it's best to test for looseness by lifting on the fixture, rather than pressing down on it. Sinks are not designed to be stepping stools. Putting all your weight on the edge of a pedestal sink or a wall-hung sink, for example, may result in sudden collapse.

Slope on Wall Hung Fixtures

Use some common sense in determining whether the fixture is loose. One of the clues with wall-hung fixtures is that the basin may slope down away from the wall if it's loose. Lifting up gently on the front of the basin will very often allow it to rotate back up into a level position with the back of the basin tight against the wall.

Legs

Many laundry tubs and some basins are supported on legs. The legs may be concrete, metal or plastic. Watch for rusted metal legs and spalling or cracked concrete legs. Again, if you can see deterioration to the legs, there is no need to do any rough physical testing. Your chances of breaking things are significant.

Overflows Missing or Inappropriate

No Overflows on Sinks

Kitchen sinks should not have overflows. Any fixtures that are used for food preparation or dishwashing do not have overflows for fear of trapping food particles and creating an unhealthy situation.

No Overflows on Laundry Tubs
Many laundry tubs also do not have overflows. Double kitchen sinks and double laundry tubs very often have a compromise on overflows. The partition between the two sinks will often be $1/4$ inch lower than the flood rim of the sink. If one of the sinks or tubs overflows, the water will run into the other sink before it spills out onto the floor. This is not completely reliable because the other sink may be in use or its drain stopper may be in place. However, this is certainly better than not having this arrangement.

Basins have overflows, although most home inspectors don't test them.

IMPLICATIONS

We've talked about the implications already. We don't want bits of food being stuck in an overflow in a kitchen. We want to avoid flooding in lavatories where people may be called away to the phone while washing.

STRATEGY

Look for overflows where they should be and where they shouldn't. Where you find an inappropriate installation, recommend rearrangement.

Feel free to test overflows by filling the basin up to the height of the overflow, but be prepared for leakage.

Cross Connections

Cross connections are very common on laundry tubs, and are always a possibility with vegetable sprayers or faucets that can be left lying in a sink full of dirty water.

IMPLICATIONS

The implications of cross connections are obviously health issues. The plumbing system could make people sick.

STRATEGY

Look for cross connections and advise people of the risks inherent in vegetable sprayers and extendable faucets. Most extendable faucets now have integral protection against cross connections, although you typically won't know during an inspection.

Not Level

The laundry tub is the most likely fixture to be out of level. Many laundry tubs have a large, flat base to the tub. If the tub is even slightly out of level, water may pool in the bottom of the tub. This is particularly true of plastic tubs.

IMPLICATIONS

The water pooling in the bottom of the tub is a nuisance and can be a health issue. Stagnant water is not a good thing. A small amount of water will typically evaporate. Rarely is the amount of water enough to raise a serious concern.

STRATEGY

As you test each fixture, you should make sure that when the drain stopper is pulled, the fixture drains completely. Note any areas where water pools in the fixture.

Slow Drains

Slow drains are a common problem on plumbing fixtures. We consider slow drains as:

▪ basins that take more than 30 seconds to empty

▪ sinks or laundry tubs that take more than 60 seconds to empty

IMPLICATIONS

If the drain is slightly slow, most people adjust their lifestyle very slightly and live with it. There are no serious implications. If the drain is so slow that water sits in the drain for extended periods, the fixture may not be usable, and there are health concerns.

STRATEGY

As you perform your operating tests, you'll discover slow drains. Sometimes you can see a strainer or pop-up drain problem and recommend appropriate action. In other cases, you'll advise your client that if they can't live with the slow drain, further investigation is needed to find and correct the problem.

13.4.2   Faucets

Faucets are found on sinks, basins, laundry tubs, bathtubs, showers, bidets and hose bibbs. They are used to deliver hot and/or cold water to fixtures.

The older traditional faucet is known as a **compression faucet.** A threaded stem is turned to open or close the valve. At the end of the stem is a disk with a washer on it. When the valve is closed, the washer is pressed against a seat to prevent water flow (Figure 13.28).

More modern faucets are typically **cartridge** or **ball type.** These faucets align holes in two different materials to allow water to flow and misalign the holes to stop the water flow.

Water Hammer

These modern **washerless faucets,** as they are often called, can be fully opened and closed quickly. This is convenient for the user, but may make a plumbing system prone to water hammer. As part of your test of each plumbing fixture, you will want to close the valves as quickly as an enthusiastic homeowner might. You should then listen for the characteristic banging sound of water hammer.

Single Lever

Another feature of the modern washerless faucet is that many systems now use a single lever or knob to control both the hot and cold water and the volume of water. These faucets are mixing valves that allow you to adjust the ratios of hot and cold water.

Let's look at some of the common faucet problems.

1. Leaks or drips
2. Stiff or inoperative
3. Loose
4. Cross connections
5. Noisy

FIGURE 13.28   Compression Faucet

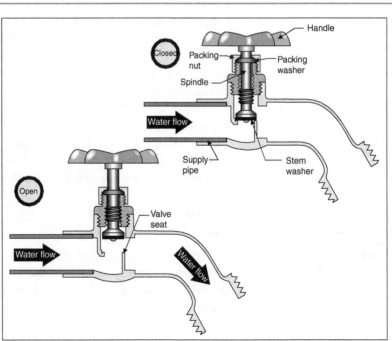

6. Damaged, rusted, loose or missing handles

7. Hot and cold reversed

8. Obstructed aerator

9. Shower diverter inoperative/defective

Leaks or Drips

IMPLICATIONS

The implications of dripping faucets are usually not severe, since the water ends up in the fixture. Over time, you might get some discoloration in the fixture bowl. Leaks through the body of the faucet are usually more dangerous because of the water damage they can do. Damage to countertops caused by leaking faucets is a very common problem at kitchen sinks. If the faucet set or the edge of the sink is not tightly sealed to the countertop, water can get under either the lip of the sink or the faucet base and damage the countertop over time.

STRATEGY

Some leaks are obvious. Others have to be searched out. As you operate the faucets, you should be looking around and below the faucets. This means you have to get down on your hands and knees and look under sinks. Some bathtubs have access panels to the piping on the wall opposite the tub. Look for these panels and check for leakage here.

Vegetable Sprayers

You should operate vegetable sprayers and, if there are extendable faucets, you should pull them out and operate them. It's very common for leaks to develop at the hoses. Some extendable faucets are very subtle. Unless you are thinking about the possibility of an extendable faucet, you may just look at it and operate it as a fixed faucet. It's a good habit to get into the practice of pulling on the spout to see whether it is extendable. If you can get under the fixture, you'll usually see the hose below. This should remind you that you're dealing with an extendable faucet.

Stiff or Inoperative

Faucets should not require superhuman strength to turn the water on and off.

IMPLICATION

It will be difficult to turn the water on and off.

STRATEGY

You will notice stiff or inoperative faucets as you perform your normal test.

Loose

Faucets should be fixed to the wall, to the countertop or to the fixture itself. Many people prefer the faucets fixed to the fixture itself when dealing with kitchen sinks or basins, for example. Many sinks and basins are designed so that if there is leakage around the faucet, the water will run into the sink or basin, rather than onto the countertop or floor.

IMPLICATION

Loose faucets are prone to leakage as a result of strain on fittings. Leaks at the point where the faucets connect to the supply piping system are a concern.

STRATEGY

As you operate faucets, it's very easy to detect loose faucet systems. Understand that a loose faucet is different from a loose handle. Sometimes the handles are not well secured to the faucets. This is a different issue.

Cross Connections

This is a health problem.

IMPLICATION

STRATEGY

Watch for faucet spouts that are below the flood level of fixtures. Advise clients that vegetable sprayers and extendable faucets can form cross connections and should not be left in sinks or other fixtures. These faucets may be protected from backflow, but you usually won't know by looking.

Noisy

Faucets can be noisy in a number of ways. They can bang, chatter or whistle, for example.

The implications of chatter and whistle are valve failure. The implications of water hammer can be flooding if the piping ruptures as a result of the tremendous forces.

As you operate the fixtures, you will notice hammer, chatter and whistle. There's no need to go too far into troubleshooting. You should simply report the problem and recommend correction as necessary.

Damaged, Rusted, Loose, or Missing Handles

There are many problems that you may find with faucet handles.

You may not be able to operate the valves or it may be dangerous to operate the valves. It's very easy to cut your hand on a damaged faucet handle.

This is another problem that's easy to find during your testing of plumbing fixtures.

Hot and Cold Reversed

The hot water should be on the left side and the cold on the right. This is a convention throughout North America, and it applies to single lever as well as dual faucet arrangements.

People can be surprised at best or scalded at worst if they're expecting to get cold water and they get hot.

This is another easy check during your test of plumbing fixtures.

Obstructed Aerator

It's very common for aerators to become obstructed and the water flow and pressure to be poor at a given fixture.

Poor water flow and pressure at that fixture are the implications.

Watch for plumbing fixtures that have considerably lower pressure than other fixtures in the house.

Shower Diverter Inoperative or Defective

We've already talked about having to test the shower. Sometimes you can't get the shower to come on.

Obviously, people can't take showers.

As you test the shower, make sure that the diverter will stay in place. Also ensure that the flow out of the tub spout stops when the shower is operating. In some cases, the diverter doesn't close tightly, and some water will continue to come out of the tub spout while the shower is operating. This is inefficient and makes for low flow and pressure at the showerhead.

13.4.3   Hose Bibbs

Most houses are provided with outdoor hose bibbs (faucets) to connect hoses for watering lawns, washing cars, etc. In some areas these are called **hydrants.** The piping supply to the outside hose bibb is usually metal where it passes through the wall, even if the house has plastic supply piping.

IMPLICATIONS

STRATEGY

IMPLICATIONS

STRATEGY

IMPLICATIONS

STRATEGY

IMPLICATIONS

STRATEGY

IMPLICATIONS

STRATEGY

F I G U R E 13.29 Shut Off Valves for Outside Faucets

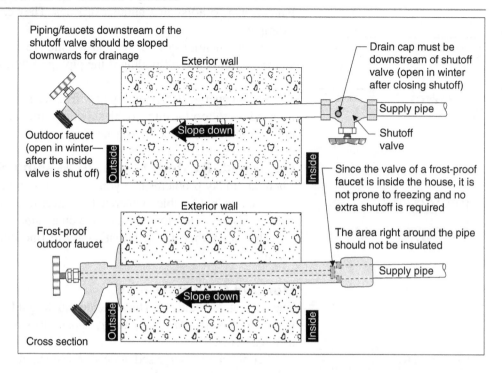

Function

The piping to the hose bibb is connected directly to the cold water supply piping in most cases.

As lengths of hose are added to the faucet, the water supply may be expected to deteriorate because of frictional pressure loss through the hose, so if there is a hose attached, don't criticize the flow based on the amount of water coming out of it.

Conventional Hose Bibbs

Conventional hose bibbs have a compression-type, hand-operated valve outdoors. In freezing climates, there is an indoor shutoff valve as well (Figure 13.29). This is usually a stop and waste valve. This means that the valve shuts off the water to the outdoor faucet and has a drain fitting that allows water to be drained from the pipe between the shutoff and the outdoor faucet. If water is left in the pipe, the pipe may split as the water freezes, even though no more supply water can flow into the pipe. The damage is often not noticed until the following spring when the stop and waste valve is reopened.

Winterizing of Hose Bibbs

Homeowners should be advised that when winterizing a conventional hose bibb, the indoor stop and waste valve should be closed, then the waste should be opened. We also recommend leaving the outdoor faucet open so that any water can drain out of that end. The slope of the pipe going through the wall may prevent the water draining out of the waste valve. An open waste valve inside and an open faucet outdoors assures that there will be no water left in the pipe.

Frost-Proof Faucets

Some outdoor hose bibbs are **frost-proof.** This is just a long stem valve that goes through the wall to the building interior. When the valve is closed, the water flow is shut off inside the house. These systems need to slope down toward outdoors, so that the water in the valve body drains out through the faucet when the valve is shut off. If the pipe slopes down toward the indoor side, water may remain in the valve body as it passes through the wall and freeze during cold weather. This usually ruins the valve, although no leakage may be noted until the valve is opened again.

Don't Operate in Winter

Many inspectors do not operate frost-proof hose bibbs in the winter for fear of creating an ice patch outdoors. They are also sensitive to the possibility that the valve body may be split inside the wall and by operating the valve, they may create an accumulation of water in the valve body where it passes through the wall and cause a freeze-up problem.

Common hose bibb problems include:

1. Leaks or drips
2. Stiff or inoperative
3. No backflow prevention
4. Loose
5. Pipe frozen or split
6. Poor slope on a frost-free hose bibb
7. Mechanical damage

Several of these conditions have been discussed already in the context of faucets; we'll just touch on the unique ones.

No Backflow Prevention

In most areas hose bibbs need to have some kind of backflow prevention device. It can be integral or added to the hose bibb.

IMPLICATIONS

The implication is a cross connection. When a hose is attached to the bibb, the hose may be left in a bucket of dirty water, connected to a pesticide or fertilizer sprayer, or in a roof gutter filled with dirty water, for example. A problem would only arise if the water pressure in the house dropped (because someone shut off the water to work on a plumbing fixture, for example) and the hose bibb was left open. This is not an impossible combination by any stretch of the imagination.

STRATEGY

Look for a backflow prevention device on the end of the hose bibb. If you can't see one, there may be an integral backflow prevention device built into the hose bibb (especially if it's frost-free). You should probably report the absence of a hose bibb backflow prevention device as a question, rather than a conclusion, and recommend that it be checked the first time a plumber is at the house.

Pipe Frozen or Split

Pipe going through the wall can be frozen and split.

IMPLICATIONS

The implications are water damage and the inability to use the hose bibb.

STRATEGY

Since most of this piping isn't visible, you may have trouble determining this condition. Some of the clues to watch for include—

- a closed stop and waste valve during warm weather (you can either tell by looking or opening the hose bibb valve)
- an open valve at a conventional hose bibb during warm weather (this means a closed stop and waste inside)
- leakage to the building interior or exterior when operating a frost-proof hose bibb

Be careful operating frost-proof hose bibbs. If there is leakage, it often shows up only on the inside of the building as you flow the faucet. You risk doing water damage unless someone is watching the inside of the house as you operate these faucets.

You may also be able to see a split pipe, more often on the inside of the wall than the outside. Conventional hose bibbs that are improperly winterized are immediate suspects for frozen or split piping. With frost-proof hose bibbs, an operational test may be possible, but remember the downsides of the test as we discussed earlier.

Poor Slope on Frost-Free Hose Bibbs

We mentioned that the valve body of a frost-free hose bibb has to slope down to the outside to drain water out of the valve body when the valve is shut off.

IMPLICATIONS

A frozen and split valve is the implication. This will result in leakage, of course.

STRATEGY

Sometimes you can see enough of the valve to get a sense of its slope. Sometimes when the valve is shut off, you can put your finger up inside the outlet and feel whether there is water sitting in the valve body. In many cases, it will be hard to know whether or not the slope is correct.

Mechanical Damage

Hose bibbs, like any other faucets, are subject to mechanical damage. Because they are located outside and usually near grade level, their risk of mechanical damage is greater than the average faucet.

IMPLICATIONS

The implications are an inoperative valve or a leak.

STRATEGY

Watch for mechanical damage when operating outdoor hose bibbs.

13.4.4   Toilets

Toilet Types
One- and Two-Piece Toilets

Toilets are classified by their flush mechanism. Figure 13.30 describes two types.

Two-piece toilets are very common. These have a bowl and a tank that may be bolted together on site. There are also one-piece toilets where the bowl and tank are integral.

F I G U R E 13.30   Toilet Flushing Actions

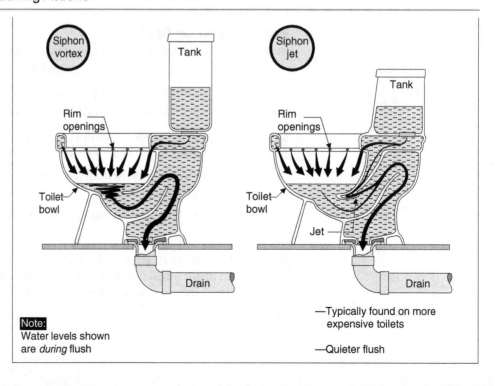

What about Noise?

Toilets are inherently noisy since they are siphoning fixtures. This means they draw some room air with them as they operate. The toilet itself is a trap, and is designed to siphon to some extent.

Sweating Toilets

Since the water supply in the house is often very cold (50°F is common with both a public and private water supply), it's not unusual to find the toilet tank and the toilet fill pipe sweating, particularly in warm, humid weather. If the house is air-conditioned, the toilets will be less inclined to sweat.

Insulated Tanks

Many tanks have an extruded polystyrene foam insulation available as an option that fits against the inside walls of the tank to minimize condensation. These are successful up to a point. Where condensation is a serious problem, the toilet shutoff valve will often be corroded and the escutcheon plate where the fill pipe comes up through the floor or in through the wall will often be rusted. Water damage can also be done to the flooring around the back of the toilet below the bowl and fill pipe.

Mixed Hot and Cold Water to Toilets

One of the unusual but successful solutions to condensation is a mixing valve that mixes some hot water in with the cold water at the toilet supply. If room temperature water is used to fill the toilet tank, there is much less chance of condensation.

Running Toilets Usually Sweat

Toilets that continuously run water through are prone to sweating. We don't want toilets running in any case because of the wasted water. Let's look at some of the common toilet problems.

1. Leaks
2. Loose
3. Flush mechanism inoperative
4. Obstructed
5. Lazy flush
6. Odor around toilet
7. Floor damage suspected
8. Running continuously
9. Shutoff valve missing or inoperative
10. Broken tank lid or seat
11. Surface defects
12. Crowded
13. Cross connection

Leaks

As with most plumbing fixtures, leaks are the big problem. Toilet leaks may occur at a number of locations, including—

- the bowl
- the tank
- supply piping
- the wax ring or gasket that makes the seal where the toilet joins the waste pipe
- the bowl/tank connection
- the bowl refill line (this tube often comes disconnected and may spray water out between the tank and lid when the toilet is refilling)

IMPLICATIONS

STRATEGY

Toilet leaks can waste water and cause water damage.

Before flushing the toilet, look for evidence of leakage around and below the toilet. Make sure you don't confuse sweating (condensation) with leakage. Sweating tends to appear uniformly on the sides and bottom of the tank. It may run down the bowl or supply piping, but initiates around the perimeter of the bowl in a uniform pattern.

Check Under the Lid

Before flushing the toilet, lift the tank lid off carefully (sometimes these are cracked or broken and are sitting precariously in place). Ensure that the bowl refill tube is in place. Ensure that the toilet is not running. Put the tank lid back on and flush the toilet. Watch for evidence of leakage around and below the toilet. Leaks in the supply line and tank will appear whether or not the toilet is flushed. Leaks around and below the bowl may only show up when the toilet is flushed.

Loose
Poorly secured toilets are common.

IMPLICATIONS

STRATEGY

The implications of a loose toilet are leaks, particularly at the wax ring and at the supply piping connection.

Many modern toilets are secured to the toilet flange which is in turn secured to the floor. This is often done with two or sometimes four bolts.

Your inspection should be in two parts here. To check that the bowl is well secured to the floor, some inspectors straddle the bowl and with the insides of their legs, try to move the bowl side to side. They will also push on the front of the bowl to see if the toilet moves front to back. You don't want to use superhuman strength here. You simply want to make sure that it is secure and that the toilet won't move when people sit on it.

We're also interested in knowing whether the tank is well secured to the bowl. To test this, grasp the tank and try to move it side to side and front to back. Watch carefully to see if the connection between the tank and the bowl moves. Again, this is not a test of strength. Use reasonable pressure. If the toilet is a one-piece system, you won't need to check how well the tank is secured to the bowl, since it is integral.

If the toilet is loose, recommend resecuring and watch carefully for leaks below and damaged flooring, subflooring, structural members and finishes below the toilet.

Flush Mechanism Inoperative
Sometimes, nothing happens when you operate the flush lever (or push the button in or lift the operating mechanism).

IMPLICATION

STRATEGY

Obviously, the toilet won't work if you can't initiate a flush.

When you operate the toilet, this failure will become obvious. This is not usually a significant or expensive problem, but it can frustrate the average homeowner.

Obstructed
Nothing strikes more fear into the heart of a home inspector than flushing a toilet and watching the water level in the bowl rise rather than fall. Sometimes the bowl has an adequate capacity to hold the contents of the tank without spilling. In other cases, you won't be so lucky. You will be able to tell your client that the toilet or waste pipe is obstructed. Trying to shut off the toilet isolating valve can elevate the crisis level if it leaks.

Obviously, the toilet won't work and you run the risk of flooding the bathroom if the toilet is obstructed.

When you flush the toilet, watch the flush performance. Obviously, the water in the bowl should be washed down and out of the bowl prior to the water level rising. If the water level rises, rather than drops, the toilet is probably obstructed. It's not unusual to have the toilet and/or waste pipe partially obstructed. The water may not rise to the top of the bowl, but may not flush properly either. This brings us to our next condition.

Lazy Flush

Sometimes the toilet flushes, but not very enthusiastically.

The implication of a lazy flush may be an obstruction, which means that the toilet will be clogged every time solid waste is introduced. If it's a design issue, the toilet will probably have to be replaced. If it's a drain or venting issue, piping revisions in the house may be necessary.

We typically use three or four feet of toilet paper to check the flush function. This isn't a particularly rigorous test, but if the toilet paper won't disappear with a single flush, we have a suspect toilet.

Odor around Toilet

An odor around a toilet usually indicates leakage of the wax ring or gasket where the toilet connects to the waste piping.

There are health implications and damage possibilities to finishes and structural members around and below the toilet.

Your nose will help you complete this part of the inspection.

Floor Damage Suspected

We encourage you to watch for damaged flooring around and below a toilet.

You should step heavily on as much of the flooring immediately adjacent to the toilet that you can. Some inspectors bounce on the flooring. If the floor is spongy, you can usually feel it. Apply your weight gradually, because if the floor is in really bad shape, you might put your foot through it.

Running Continuously

The implications of a running toilet are—

- wasted water.
- sweating (condensation). If a toilet runs continuously, the waste pipe may also sweat over its entire length. This can cause damage to finishes in areas quite remote from the toilet. This can be a difficult problem to diagnose.
- nuisance noise.

You can often see a toilet running by looking into the bowl and/or the tank. You can often hear a toilet running. If you are not sure, you can put a screwdriver to the tank or fill line, if you can get close enough, and put the handle of the screwdriver against your ear. You can also use a flashlight and look down the overflow tube. In some cases, you'll see water flowing at the bottom.

Shutoff Valve Missing or Inoperative

All toilets should have an operable shutoff valve located adjacent to the toilet.

IMPLICATIONS The toilet can't be shut off in an emergency.

STRATEGY Make sure that there is a valve adjacent to the toilet. We don't recommend that you try to operate it. Some inspectors recommend that the first time clients have a plumber in the house, the plumber be asked to make sure that all isolating valves operate. A missing or inoperative shutoff valve is not a problem until it's needed in an emergency.

Broken Tank Lids or Seats

It's not unusual to find the tank lid cracked, broken or even missing. Similarly, seats and seat covers can be cracked, broken or missing.

IMPLICATIONS The toilet may not be usable if the seat is missing or broken. A crack in a seat can pinch skin and be quite painful. Missing or broken tank lids may allow foreign materials into the tank.

STRATEGY Look at the seat, cover and tank lid. Are they present and intact? Most seats and covers have hard plastic stops that are the bearing points. Cracks often develop around these pads.

The seat and cover are usually secured to the bowl with two bolts. Make sure that the seat is well secured to the toilet. It's not usually a big problem to tighten up these bolts, but you should mention a loose seat to the client as a courtesy.

Tank lids simply rest on the tank.

Surface Defects

We talked about surface defects such as cracking and staining on other fixtures. These can be issues on toilets as well. Hairline cracks sometimes do not leak, but should be mentioned as a potential leakage spot. It's very common for toilet tank lids to get dropped and broken.

IMPLICATIONS There may be no performance issues related to the surface defects. They may also be the precursor to a leak as a result of a crack.

STRATEGY We do not make a big deal out of surface defects, but as a courtesy to our client, mention them if we see them, and keep them in perspective.

Crowded

Good practice calls for toilets to have 15 inches on both sides of the center line of the toilet as clear space.

IMPLICATIONS The toilet will still operate, but it is uncomfortable for users. It may also be difficult to install a toilet paper holder.

STRATEGY Where the toilet has less than 30 inches of clear space in total (with the center of the toilet side to side falling at the 15-inch line), note this less than ideal arrangement. You can leave it to your client's discretion to decide whether rearrangement is necessary.

13.4.5   Bathtubs

Common bathtub problems include the following:

1. Leaks
2. Rust
3. Surface defects

F I G U R E 13.31   Inspecting a Tub

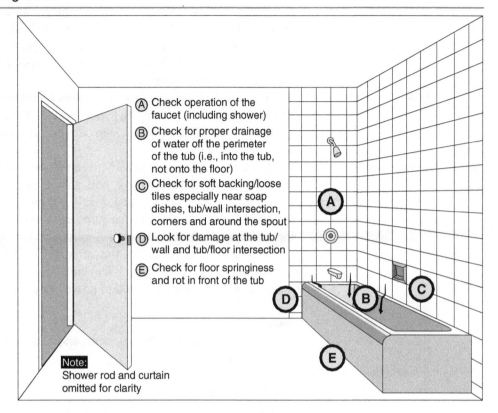

A Check operation of the faucet (including shower)

B Check for proper drainage of water off the perimeter of the tub (i.e., into the tub, not onto the floor)

C Check for soft backing/loose tiles especially near soap dishes, tub/wall intersection, corners and around the spout

D Look for damage at the tub/wall and tub/floor intersection

E Check for floor springiness and rot in front of the tub

Note:
Shower rod and curtain omitted for clarity

4. Cross connections

5. Not level

6. Overflow leaking, disconnected or rusted

7. Loose or unstable

8. Slow drains

Figure 13.31 summarizes the inspection issues for a bathtub; let's look at the conditions more closely.

Leaks

It's unusual for the bathtub itself to leak. It's possible that steel or cast iron will rust through or that acrylic and/or fiberglass may crack, although these are not terribly common problems.

The most common leak issues around bathtubs are those related to—

■ the tub-tile intersection around the perimeter of the tub

■ the drain connection

■ the overflow

Enclosure leakage is covered later in this chapter. Water splashing or running out of the bathtub is not a leak but will cause damage to the tub-floor and tub-wall intersection.

IMPLICATIONS   The leaks may cause water damage. In this sense the implications are the same as for any other leak. Leaks on drain systems are more serious in one sense than supply plumbing leaks. A supply plumbing leak usually results in a flood that will be noticed and corrected immediately. A leak in a drain system may be intermittent, and the amount of water that leaks out may not be great. As a result, the problem may not be diagnosed quickly, leading to concealed damage to the structure from the persistent, intermittent wetting and no opportunity for wood to dry out. When this is coupled with little or no damage to interior finishes below, we can have significant concealed damage.

STRATEGY

We talked earlier about looking below plumbing fixtures before operating them and looking again after they have been tested. If there is access to the piping for the bathtub in a panel on a wall backing onto the tub, you should look at that both before and after testing the fixture.

Tub-tile Gaps and Mold

Look for evidence of gaps between the tub and tile. Deteriorated caulking or caulking heavily discolored by mold should also be pointed out. If you can sense the difference, mold that is under the caulking is more serious than surface mold on the caulking. The mildew that's underneath the caulking indicates that the caulking seal has failed and that water is getting in behind it.

Don't Test Overflows

We recommend not filling the tub up to the overflow level because most overflows leak. You should let your client know that the overflows on bathtubs frequently leak, but we don't feel the need to prove our point.

Rust

We talked about rust on basins, sinks and tubs. This is a similar issue on cast iron and steel bathtubs.

Surface Defects

Again, chips, rust, cracks, and scratches are common various bathtub defects. In most cases, they are just cosmetic, but they can lead to performance problems. Rusting metal will eventually fail, for example. Cracks may be only on the surface of materials but may eventually go all the way through materials.

Again, we talked about this when we looked at basins, sinks, and laundry tubs.

Cross Connections

STRATEGY

Older cast iron bathtubs often have the fill spout below the flood rim of the tub. Watch for this common situation. Also, let your clients know that if there are extendable faucets that can be left below the flood rim of the tub, this is another possible cross connection.

Not Level

This is a fairly common problem with tubs and leads to damage outside the tub at the tub-floor intersection and sometimes at the walls at either end of the tub exterior.

IMPLICATIONS

The apron around the perimeter of bathtubs is usually sloped slightly so that water will drain back into the tub. If the tub is not installed level, the water will tend to drain either out of the front of the tub, or back in along one side or corner of the tub. If the water comes out to the front of the tub, it's going to escape and accumulate, usually at the tub-floor intersection. Sometimes the water gets hung up at the tub-wall intersection at either end of the tub and causes damage here.

If the tub slopes back away from the opening, water will stand on the shelf and be more likely to find its way through the tub enclosure finish (tile, acrylic, marble, etc.) and get into the wall system behind.

STRATEGY

As you test the shower, you'll usually end up with water on the tub perimeter shelf. Watch for evidence of water running in any direction, other than toward the tub. Sometimes you can visually detect a tub that's out of level, although since quarters are usually cramped in a bathroom, you often can't get far enough away to get a good perspective.

Also watch for evidence of damage at the tub-floor intersection and at the tub-wall intersections. Stand on the floor very close to the tub and bounce. The flooring material in a bathroom is usually water resistant (resilient flooring or ceramic tile, for example), but damage to the subfloor below is a concern, especially if it is a wood flooring assembly.

Check the bottom section of the tub enclosure carefully where you see standing water accumulating on the tub shelf.

Overflow Leaking, Disconnected, or Rusting

Problems with overflows are common.

IMPLICATIONS

The overflow isn't used on a regular basis. When the overflow is needed, it will cause water damage below if it's not working properly, even though it is designed to prevent water damage.

STRATEGY

In most cases, you won't be able to get a look at the overflow, so you won't know how well it's connected. Sometimes you can grab the interior fitting in the tub, pull on it and feel that it is not tightly connected. If so, you can criticize the overflow. If you can get a look into an access panel behind the tub, you may be able to see the overflow. In these cases, you may be able to visually identify problems without flowing water. If you choose to test the overflow by filling the tub, be prepared for leakage below!

Loose or Unstable

Bathtubs are typically installed with support from the floor and the perimeter walls. While it's not a common problem, sometimes the tub is not well secured in place.

IMPLICATIONS

The tub is likely to be out of level, and may be more prone to leakage as a result of strained fittings on both the supply and waste plumbing.

STRATEGY

Many home inspectors step into the tub during the course of their inspection. You should be either stepping into the tub or grabbing the edges of the tub and making sure that it won't move. We recommend that you check this out before doing your plumbing tests, otherwise you are stepping into a wet bathtub!

Slow Drains

We consider a slow bathtub drain as one that takes more than 6 minutes to drain water 8 inches deep from a standard 5-foot tub.

13.4.6   Tub and Shower Stall Enclosures

Enclosures around tubs and shower stalls are extremely vulnerable to leakage. This leakage is often concealed for some time and is a difficult issue for home inspectors. Shower stall bases have their own set of problems which we'll talk about shortly.

Enclosures for bathtubs and shower stalls may be ceramic tile, marble or acrylic; any type of durable, water resistant material should work. Ideally, it should also be relatively smooth and easy to clean, as well as being non-porous.

One-piece bathtub or shower enclosures are the easiest to inspect. These are typically acrylic, fiberglass or other laminated plastic-type materials. They have very few seams and, therefore, very few places to leak.

Ceramic Tile

A large percentage of enclosures are ceramic tile. Marble, slate, and limestone are less common, but are treated the same as ceramic tile. We will focus our discussion on ceramic tile shower stall and bathtub enclosures.

Watch Those Exterior Walls

Inspection Tip

In cold climates, it's common to find that shower and bathtub enclosures on an exterior wall are most troublesome. The vapor barrier and insulation details are often poorly executed around tubs and shower stalls on exterior walls. Wall board is not typically installed below the level of a bathtub, for example, and so there is not the traditional support for vapor barriers and insulation in this area. Leakage of warm, moist air into this wall cavity can cause condensation and structural problems resulting in rotted wood. It's often difficult to tell the difference between leakage through the enclosure and condensation problems on exterior cold walls around tub and shower enclosures. Watch for damage here and pay particular attention to these areas and the parts of the house immediately below.

Penetrations and Terminations

How are bathtub and shower enclosures like roofs? With roofs, most of the problems occur at roof penetrations or changes in direction and material. The same is true of bathtub and shower enclosures. Most of the problems occur at penetrations like faucets, soap dishes, grab bars and windows and at changes in direction or material like tub-tile intersections, inside wall corners and outside wall corners where the tile ends. Let's take a look at the problems that we normally find on these very troublesome details. There are two common conditions in bathtub and shower enclosures, and they are usually related. A third problem is less common but is a safety issue.

1. Leaks

2. Loose, broken, or missing tile

3. Electrical problems at the enclosure

Leaks

Leaks in bathtub and shower enclosures are both common and difficult to detect during a home inspection. Leakage can be through grout joints in tile or at any of the penetrations and joints we've talked about.

IMPLICATIONS

The implications of leakage are cosmetic damage to interior finishes below and structural damage to wood members exposed to the moisture. Since this damage is often concealed, the extent of the damage is often not appreciated until the damage is quite advanced.

STRATEGY

With bathtub and shower enclosures, we recommend that you get inside and test these wall systems before flowing any water. Firstly, it's easier on you if you are checking dry surfaces. You don't want to track wet footprints through the house. Secondly, if you see an obvious problem, you may want to avoid running water so you don't cause more water damage.

Look, Tap, and Press

Your testing procedure normally includes a visual inspection of all the surfaces. Focus on the weak areas that we've mentioned. The second part of the inspection is to tap or press on the tiles themselves (or whatever material forms the enclosure). You are looking for sponginess or an unusual amount of give. Sometimes you can see tiles starting to fall off. You may only find a problem when you tap on the surface and hear a hollow ringing sound or push on the tiles and find that they give easily. The tiles around penetrations and just above the tub or just above the shower base are important ones to watch for.

Penetrations

You should also check how well penetrations through the walls are sealed. Some soap dishes and other fixtures are installed through the tile and secured to the wall system behind. Many of the modern soap dishes and other accessories are simply bonded to the tile with a silicone sealant. These are preferable since there is no wall penetration. Obviously, leakage is not nearly so likely here.

Look Behind Escutcheon Plates

Escutcheon plates (the decorative trim rings around pipe penetrations through walls) can sometimes be pulled back easily to determine whether things are well sealed.

Even if there is no leakage, you should note vulnerable areas for water penetration.

Testing the Fixtures

Many home inspectors test bathtubs and showers vigorously. You should make sure that water is not spilling out of the fixture onto the floor during your test. Shower curtains or doors should be in place before operating showers. Some inspectors are also quite diligent about bouncing as much water off the shower walls as they can by moving the shower nozzle. There is a slight risk of creating a leak as you manipulate the shower nozzle, especially if it hasn't been moved recently.

Intermittent Leaks

We have had a number of situations where, despite our best efforts to wet the walls and flow lots of water at a shower head, we have had clients find a leak. Sometimes the leaks will only occur with people standing in the shower. Obviously the water spray is going to bounce and run down the walls in a different pattern if there is someone standing in the shower. Let your clients know that this possibility exists despite your best efforts during the inspection. You should also let them know that shower and tub enclosures are high leakage, high maintenance areas.

Check Adjacent Rooms

After you have flowed water in a tub enclosure or shower stall, you should look closely at adjacent walls in other rooms. Sometimes evidence of leakage will be visible in the walls and/or wall-floor area of adjacent rooms before it shows up either in the bathroom or in the room below, if there is any. Damage to baseboards and quarter round is a common clue that there has been leakage at the bathtub or shower enclosure.

Check the Floor Outside the Tub or Shower

One of the big problems with bathtubs and shower stalls is water spilling out over the front of the tub or through the shower door opening. Damage to the wall below the shower threshold or to the tub facade or tub-floor intersection is common. Make sure you look for this. Many inspectors tap on the wall surface just below a shower threshold and similarly check any area on the face of the tub that is subject to water damage. We've already talked about bouncing on the floor close to the tub to check for sponginess or rotted subflooring. The same kind of test should be done on a shower enclosure, particularly in front of the threshold at either corner of the opening.

Loose, Broken, or Missing Tile

The tiles will not be watertight if they are not secure. If the backer material starts to deteriorate, tiles will eventually fall off the wall. The more immediate concern is that water will get in behind the backer material and attack the wall and floor systems behind and below. Considerable water damage can be done to the structure. If we are lucky, interior finishes that are visible below the tub or shower will give us ample warning of this leakage. Unfortunately, this isn't always the case.

We talked about pushing and tapping on tiles, concentrating on areas around and below penetrations and at the top of the tub or shower base.

In many areas you'll be able to detect differences in grout, color and texture, and in some cases the tiles will be different colors, textures and sizes. This usually indicates a repair. Areas that have been repaired are likely to leak again.

Scanning with a Flashlight

You can hold a flashlight parallel to the wall and scan along the surface looking for irregularities. Sometimes defects can be seen that are not visible looking straight at the wall.

Watch for Windows

Generally speaking, windows in bathtub and shower enclosures are a bad idea. Since virtually all windows contain sills, water can collect here. Also, the presence of a window creates more joints between materials and more changes in direction. An additional problem is the condensation that forms on windows in cold weather when people are showering. Even with double- or triple-glazed windows, you can expect condensation here. This condensation runs down the glass and may get into the window sash or frame or into the sill system and wall below. Look carefully around and below the window for loose tile and soft, spongy backer material. In some cases, people have added a small curtain to cover the window. In effect, the window gets its own shower curtain. While this helps, it may or may not be a positive solution.

Caulk Those Corner Joints

In most new work, the ceramic tiles at interior corners in bathtubs are grouted. We recommend caulking this vertical joint since the grout inevitably cracks as framing members shrink and the building settles very slightly.

Caulking Replacement

The tub-tile or stall enclosure-base connection is particularly vulnerable. Advise your clients that they should plan on replacing the caulking on a regular basis. This means digging out the old caulking and replacing it, rather than adding new caulking over old.

Electrical Problems at the Enclosure

Light Fixtures in Enclosures

Where lighting fixtures are provided inside tub and shower enclosures, they should be a vapor-proof fixture designed for this application. You can usually identify these by the gasket material around the lens.

Receptacles and Switches Near Enclosures

Electric light switches and receptacles should be at least 3 feet away (out of the reach of) shower stalls and bathtub enclosures. We don't want soaking wet people operating electrical equipment.

These are life safety issues.

IMPLICATIONS

STRATEGY

Look for vapor-proof light fixtures and a safe distance from enclosures to switches and receptacles.

13.4.7   Shower Stalls

All shower stalls leak! They don't necessarily leak when you are doing your inspection, but eventually they all leak. Worse than that, shower stalls are very expensive to replace. Worse yet, the leakage can be slow and cause considerable damage without being particularly visible. Be very, very careful with shower stalls. The base or enclosure may be the culprit, but the result is similar.

They leak because they are complicated. The type least likely to leak is a one-piece fiberglass or acrylic shower stall because the floor and walls are made of a single unit (Figure 13.32).

Floors Should Slope

All shower stalls should have a slope of at least $1/4$ inch per foot in toward the drain. The drain obviously should not be at a high point. We don't want water ponding on the floor of the shower stall.

Sills and Thresholds

All shower stalls need to have some way for people to get in to them. They will have a curb or sill at the entrance and it may form a door threshold if there is a shower door rather than a curtain. Typically, the sill or threshold is 1 inch below the top of the liner.

Let's look at some of the common problems with showers themselves. These are in addition to the supply and drain issues and enclosure issues that we've already talked about.

F I G U R E 13.32   One-Piece Shower Stalls

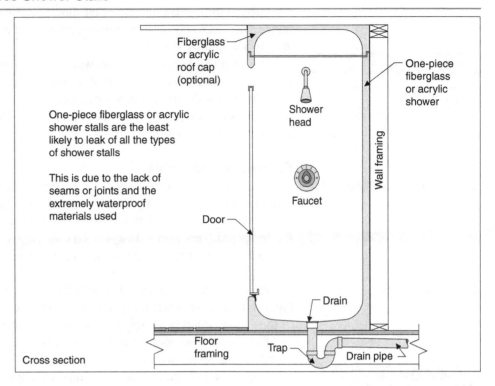

One-piece fiberglass or acrylic shower stalls are the least likely to leak of all the types of shower stalls

This is due to the lack of seams or joints and the extremely waterproof materials used

Fiberglass or acrylic roof cap (optional)

Shower head

Faucet

Door

One-piece fiberglass or acrylic shower

Wall framing

Drain

Cross section

Floor framing

Trap

Drain pipe

1. Leaks
2. Rust
3. Entrance problems
4. Sill and threshold problems
5. Pooling water on the floor
6. Too small
7. Slow drains

Leaks

As always, leaks are the big issue.

One of the tests that many home inspectors perform is a flood test of the shower base itself. Some inspectors plug the drain of the shower stall and flood the base with an inch or two of water. Obviously, we don't want to get the water up over the sill or door threshold. This is a fairly rigorous test. The longer the water stays, the more rigorous the test. Some specialists say the water should stay for 24 hours!

This does not necessarily simulate normal usage and has the added disadvantage of a delayed reaction. In some cases, it will take several hours for the leaks to appear. Obviously a home inspection is not going to last several hours in most cases. We'll leave it to you to decide whether you do this type of test. It does go beyond the Standards and can certainly be revealing.

In one sense, you're not going to see many leaks related to the shower stall by looking inside the stall. You need to be looking around and below for leaks, rather than inside, for the most part. Remember to check the walls and floors in adjacent rooms that back onto the stall.

Rust

It's fairly common to find that metal shower stalls rust. This isn't surprising given their environment. We also mentioned earlier that many metal shower stalls are relatively low quality systems.

IMPLICATIONS

It's tough to keep a rusty shower stall sanitary. Eventually the rust will go through the metal and the shower stall will lose its integrity.

STRATEGY

With metal shower stalls, look carefully in all corners and seams for evidence of rust. In some cases, rust has been painted over. Watch for rough textured surfaces that are usually smooth.

Entrance Problems

Narrow Doors, Non-Tempered Glass

The minimum entrance width is 22 inches for shower stalls. Where they are narrower than this, they should be reported. Also watch for doors that are not tempered glass. In most cases, you'll find an indication in the corner of the door that indicates that it is tempered. This won't always be obvious, however. Where you can't verify that the door is tempered, you may want to raise the question, although this goes beyond the Standards.

Door Opens Inward

Another problem is a shower door that only opens in. There are two disadvantages to this. If the water temperature suddenly gets very hot, people can't get out of the shower quickly. A bigger problem is if someone collapses in a shower stall and falls against the door, it can be very difficult to get the person out. Shower stall doors should open outward.

IMPLICATIONS

Narrow shower entrances, non-tempered glass doors and inward opening doors are all life safety issues.

STRATEGY

Watch for these situations when looking at shower stalls.

Sill and Threshold Problems

Sills and thresholds at shower stalls should be watertight and should be tall enough to control the shower water.

IMPLICATION

In both cases, leakage is the implication.

STRATEGY

Check sills or thresholds carefully. Where these are tile or marble, make sure they are well secured and intact. Ideally, the sills should have a slight slope back into the shower stall so any water that lands on the sill or threshold will drain back into the stall, rather than out onto the floor. With every shower stall, part of your normal routine should be to check outside the sill or threshold carefully for evidence of water damage. It may have been freshly painted, so you may have to be persistent. It is unusual to find no evidence of leakage around and below shower stall sills and thresholds.

Pooling Water on the Floor

Stagnant water sitting in a shower stall is unpleasant and may be unhealthy.

IMPLICATIONS

Before operating the fixture, make sure that there is no water on the floor. Check that the drain is at a low point on the floor.

STRATEGY

When operating the fixture, make sure water does not back up and pool on the floor.

Too Small

We need to watch for shower stalls that are too small. Generally, 30 inches by 30 inches is a minimum size.

Shower stalls that are too small may trap people who collapse in the shower.

While it's not necessary to measure each shower stall with a tape measure, you should have some sense of a 30 inch by 30 inch shower stall and note any that are significantly smaller.

REVIEW QUESTIONS

1. What are three things that go wrong with water supply?

2. Evaluating the quality of the water available at a private source is beyond the scope of a standard home inspection.

   True   False

3. List six materials commonly used for water service piping.

4. What is the typical minimum diameter of water service piping in modern construction?

5. What is the function of a stop and waste valve?

6. List five materials used as water supply piping.

7. When was copper supply piping first used?

   a. 1850s   d. 1960s

   b. 1900   e. 1990

   c. 1930s

8. At what interval is vertical support required for copper piping?

9. What is the recommended horizontal spacing of supports for copper piping?

10. What is the recommended horizontal spacing of supports for galvanized steel piping?

11. Plastic piping needs less support than copper piping because it tends to expand more.

    True   False

12. What is the implication of improper support on piping?

13. Briefly describe a cross connection.

14. List five locations in a house where there may be a cross connection.

15. Is a vacuum necessary to have backflow at a cross connection?

    Yes   No

16. Briefly describe water hammer, and why it occurs.

17. Vertical pipes at ends of runs are one method of preventing water hammer.

    True   False

18. Why can plastic pipe not typically be used between units in shared dwellings?

19. Polybutylene piping failures seem to be concentrated most at

    a. the crimp rings

    b. elbows in the pipes

    c. horizontal splits in the piping

    d. at the connection to fixtures

    e. in vertical pipe runs only

20. Polybutylene supply piping should not be closer than 18 inches to a water heater.

    True   False

21. Can polybutylene piping be used on a hot water recirculating loop?

    Yes   No

22. A house with several different styles of crimp rings should be a cause for concern.

    True   False

23. What is the approximate temperature rise in residential water heaters?

24. A water heater is termed a **single-pass** appliance because _____.

25. What is the biggest impact of the single-pass feature on a water heater?

26. Where is the burner located on gas- and oil-fired water heaters?

27. What is the component that introduces cold water near the bottom of a gas-fired water heater tank?

    a. the drip tube   d. the baffle

    b. the relief valve   e. the vent

    c. the dip tube

28. What are the two methods of rating a water heater?

29. How do these two relate?

30. Which type of water heater has the slowest recovery rate?

31. Which type of water heater has the fastest recovery rate?

32. Water running out of the burner compartment on start-up of a gas water heater suggests _____.

33. Gas and oil-fired water heaters are not allowed in sleeping areas.

    True   False

34. How high above the floor should a gas or oil-fired water heater be in a garage?

    a. 0 inches   d. 18 inches

    b. 6 inches   e. 24 inches

    c. 12 inches

35. Where does the probe for the temperature/pressure relief valve sit in the tank?

36. Where does the discharge tube from the temperature/pressure relief valve have to dump water in a cold climate?

37. Where does the temperature/pressure relief valve have to discharge water in a warm climate?

38. If we only need a pressure relief valve because the water heater has some internal temperature control, where can this pressure relief valve be?

39. What is the purpose of a baffle or turbulator in a gas fired water heater?

40. Why is an explosion with propane more likely than with natural gas?

41. When would a fan-assisted gas water heater typically be used?

42. What is the exhaust pipe material for a fan assisted water heater typically?

43. List the common problems found with fan-assisted gas water heaters.

44. Are fan-assisted water heaters condensing?

45. Describe the function of a trap.

46. Explain briefly why a toilet does not need a trap.

47. A toilet does not need a vent.

True   False

48. A waste pipe is intended to carry solids only.

True   False

49. Why in a cold climate is the trap portion of the drainage system most vulnerable to freezing?

50. Briefly describe the purpose of a trap primer.

51. Explain briefly what is meant by a wet vent.

52. List seven different materials used for piping in drain, waste, and vent systems.

53. Why are leaks more difficult to find in drain, waste and vent systems than in supply systems?

54. Copper pipe does not rust.

True   False

55. List two methods of reducing the freezing risk of pipes in a cold environment.

56. List six locations for possible cross connections in a residence.

57. What is the implication of a cross connection?

58. What is the required slope for nearly horizontal pipes in a drain, waste, and vent system?

59. Pipe size should always increase as you move downstream and more fixtures join in.

True   False

60. Why is PVC or ABS plastic piping usually allowed only in single-family homes?

61. What is the implication of poor manifolding?

62. What is the purpose of a trap?

63. Every trap should be provided with some method of removal or cleaning.

True   False

64. A running trap is a good idea because it provides extra protection.

True   False

65. List four types of traps that are not permitted in residential construction.

66. What is the typical maximum distance between the fixture and the trap?

67. What is the minimum trap arm length?

68. What is the implication of a trap arm that is too long?

69. It's impossible for a trap to be too big.

True   False

70. Where should the floor drain be located?

71. Explain the purpose of a backwater valve.

72. What is the purpose of the venting system?

73. List five common materials used in venting systems.

74. Explain briefly the simple test required to check the venting system when you test functional drainage from a fixture.

75. List seven problems found with vents.

76. The vent is typically located upstream of the trap.

True   False

77. Nearly horizontal vent pipes should slope slightly down away from the trap they are protecting.

True   False

78. The vent diameter must be as large as the trap diameter.

True   False

79. Explain briefly the problems with venting kitchen island sinks.

80. What is the minimum height of vent pipe above the roofline?

81. At least how far should an outdoor vent termination be above an operable door?

    a. 1 foot   **d.** 4 feet

    b. 2 feet   **e.** 5 feet

    c. 3 feet

82. What are the three components required on the discharge line from a sewage ejector pump?

83. What is the typical vent size on a sewage ejector pump?

    a. $1^1/_4$ inches   **d.** $2^1/_2$ inches

    b. $1^1/_2$ inches   **e.** 3 inches

    c. 2 inches

84. What is the purpose of the sewage ejector pump?

85. Why is a check valve necessary when a sewage ejector is connected to municipal sewers?

86. What are the functions of the three pipes connected to a sewage ejector pump?

87. Sewage ejector pumps should not vibrate significantly when running.

True   False

88. What is the purpose of a high level alarm with a sewage ejector?

89. Surface cracking in an acrylic kitchen sink is not usually a concern because there is no leakage.

True   False

90. Testing for loose wall hung basins is best done by putting all your weight on the basin.

True   False

91. List two possible cross connections at basins and sinks.

92. Why is water hammer more common in a house with cartridge faucets than with compression faucets?

93. List eight common faucet problems.

94. List three types of faucet-related noise.

95. How is a cross connection possible with a hose bibb?

96. How is it prevented?

97. List seven common problems with hose bibbs.

98. Describe in two sentences each, two types of hose bibbs.

99. Describe in one sentence a stop and waste valve.

100. What can cause a toilet to sweat?

101. How is a mixing valve used to stop a toilet sweating?

102. Running toilets are less prone to sweating because the water in the tank is constantly replenished.

True   False

103. List three common leak locations in a two-piece toilet.

104. Describe a test used to determine if the toilet connection to the drain piping is loose.

105. Does a toilet need to have a shutoff valve on the supply line?

Yes   No

106. What is the minimum width of space needed for a toilet installation?

   a. 18 inches   **d.** 36 inches

   b. 24 inches   **e.** there is no minimum

   c. 30 inches

107. List seven common bathtub problems.

108. Why does it matter if the tub is slightly out of level?

109. Why are tile enclosures on exterior walls in cold climates more vulnerable than ones on interior walls?

110. List five specific areas where tile enclosures are vulnerable to leakage.

111. Briefly describe a test used to determine if the tiles in an enclosure are bonded well to the backer material.

112. Because there is a watertight liner underneath the tiles in a shower stall base, the floor is not required to slope to drain.

True   False

113. What is the minimum entrance width for shower stalls?

   a. 18 inches   **d.** 30 inches

   b. 22 inches   **e.** there is no minimum requirement

   c. 26 inches

114. Which way should a hinged shower door open in a shower stall?

ANSWERS TO CHAPTER REVIEW QUESTIONS

CHAPTER 1: STANDARDS AND REPORTS

1. Inspections provide the client with information regarding the condition of the systems and components of the home inspected at the time of the home inspection.

2. 1. Things unsafe, inoperative or near the end of their lives
   2. The implications of the deficiencies
   3. The recommendations
   4. What things were not inspected and why

3. 1. Inspections are visual and not technically exhaustive
   2. Inspections applicable to four family units or less and associated garages or carports

4. Inspectors are not required to report on:
   1. Life expectancy
   2. Causes of conditions
   3. Methods, materials or costs of correction
   4. Suitability of property for specialized use
   5. Compliance with regulations
   6. Market value
   7. Advisability of purchase
   8. Components or systems not observed
   9. Presence of pests, including insects
   10. Cosmetic items, underground items or items not permanently installed

5. Inspectors are not required to:
   1. Offer or perform any service contrary to law
   2. Offer warranties or guarantees
   3. Offer engineering, architectural, plumbing or any other job function

4. Calculate the strength, adequacy or efficiency of a system

5. Enter areas or do anything that may damage the property or be dangerous

6. Operate systems that are shut down

7. Operate systems that don't respond to their normal controls

8. Disturb insulation

9. Move personal items, including furniture, equipment, plant life, snow, soil, ice or debris

10. Determine the presence of hazardous substances

11. Evaluate the effectiveness of systems that control hazardous substances

12. Predict future conditions

13. Provide operating costs

14. Evaluate acoustical characteristics of components

6. Technically exhaustive includes dismantling, extensive use of measurements, instruments, testing or calculations.

7. A person hired to examine any system or component of a building, in accordance with these Standards of Practice.

8. 1. Avoid conflicts of interest, real or perceived

2. Act in good faith toward your clients and other interested parties

3. Avoid activities that may harm the public or discredit yourself or the profession

9. 1. The Standards require it   3. To control your liability

2. To help the client   4. Marketing tool

10. 1. On site reports

2. Reports sent after the inspection

11. 1. Checklist

2. Narrative

3. Combination

12. 1. Scope/contract   6. Recommended actions

2. Descriptions   7. Limitations

3. Conditions or evaluations   8. Life expectancy

4. Causes of conditions   9. Priorities

5. Implications of conditions   10. Ballpark costs

13. 1. Scope—the inspection was done according to the ASHI Standards

2. Descriptions—the roofing material is asphalt shingle

3. Conditions or evaluations—the water heater is leaking

4. Causes of conditions—the wet basement is a result of the leaking gutters and downspouts

5. Implications—the uneven stairs are a trip hazard

6. Recommended actions—the 30-amp fuses should be replaced with 15-amp fuses

7. Limitations—No access was gained to the crawlspace

    8. Life expectancy—replacement of the roof covering will probably be necessary within the next three to six years

    9. Priorities—the open electrical box should be provided with a cover immediately and the service should be upgraded to 200 amps within the next year

   10. Ball park—furnace replacement may cost $1,500–$2,500

14. Descriptions, conditions, and implications unless they are self-evident

15.
1. Report summary
2. Client questionnaire
3. Maintenance tips
4. Filing systems
5. Life cycle and cost estimates

Note that none of these elements are required by the Standards.

CHAPTER 2: EXTERIORS

1.
- Protect the structure from water
- Provide reasonable security
- Enhance the appearance of the house

2.
- Brick
- Stone
- Concrete
- Stucco
- EIFS
- Metal and vinyl siding
- Asphalt shingles
- Wood siding
- Cement based siding
- Clay and slate shingles
- Plywood, hardboard and OSB
- Fiber-cement siding

3.
- Water penetration
- Too close to grade
- Too close to roof surface at the bottom of the siding
- Planters and gardens against the wall
- Vines

4.
- Efflorescence
- Spalling
- Cracking
- Mortar deterioration
- Missing weep holes and flashings
- Mechanical damage
- Bowing walls

5. Efflorescence is a whitish powdery salt deposit that is associated with water moving through masonry. Water dissolves the salts from masonry or mortar and deposits them on the surface as crystals when evaporating.

6. Horizontal cracks

7. Cement, aggregate, and water

8. It oxidizes (deteriorates).

9. Provides a finished edge; allows drainage; prevents water from being drawn up into the wall.

10. ▨ Cracks, crumbling, loose or bulging

   ▨ Incompatible flashings

   ▨ Mechanical damage

   ▨ Rusted lath or trim

   ▨ No drip screed

11. Water is getting into the wall system at penetrations and causing structural damage.

12. A flashing used where a wall extends beyond a roof, to shed roof water away from the stucco.

13. Lack of building paper; no drainage plane; poor drying potential

14. ▨ High wind exposure

   ▨ High rainfall area

   ▨ Small or no overhang

   ▨ Lots of penetrations

   ▨ Attention to detail at openings is poor

   ▨ Horizontal stucco surfaces

   ▨ Poor caulking maintenance

15. ▨ Exposure

   ▨ Roof/wall connections

   ▨ Gutters

   ▨ Chimneys

   ▨ Door and window openings

   ▨ Openings for electrical conduits, lights, cable TV lines, refrigeration piping, hose bibbs, etc.

   ▨ Vent openings

   ▨ Railing and deck connections

   ▨ Cracks, bulges, peeling, fungus, exposed reinforcing mesh or trim

   ▨ Evidence of repairs

16. ▨ Stains on walls, floors and ceilings

   ▨ Rusting or rotting carpet tack strip

   ▨ Peeling paint

   ▨ Damaged flooring

   ▨ Elevated moisture levels in drywall or subflooring

17. ▨ Mold, mildew or rot on joists, sills, rim joists and subflooring

   ▨ Stains on foundations coming from sill area

18. Vines hold water, and reduce the drying potential.

19. ▨ 6 inch wide board   ▨ Rough textured board

   ▨ ³/₄ inch thick board   ▨ 6 foot long board

20. Two

21. Rot; splitting; warping; paint/stain problems; loose

22. Fiber

23. ■ Rot, swelling, and delamination   ■ Loose
    ■ Buckling or cracking   ■ Mechanical damage
24. More than 40 years
25. ■ Buckled or wavy   ■ Discolored
    ■ Loose   ■ Metal siding not grounded
    ■ Flashing and caulking defects   ■ Rust
    ■ Mechanical damage
26. So the house shell cannot become electrically charged.
27. False
28. Mechanical damage because the siding is brittle.
29. Mechanical damage; missing paint or caulking; nailing problems.
30. 6 inches
31. Cracks; spalling
32. At the rafter ends.
33. Wood, aluminum, fiber-cement, hardboard, OSB, plywood, or vinyl.
34. ■ Damage on the original layer cannot be detected.
    ■ Soffit vents can be covered up, rendering them ineffective.
35. Loose or missing pieces; rot; damaged; paint or stain needed.
36. Appearance; condition; operability; security; energy efficiency; comfort; water leakage
37. ■ Rot
    ■ Damage
    ■ Paint/stain problems
    ■ Caulking and flashing problems
    ■ Putty (glazing compound) problems
    ■ Sill slope
    ■ Deteriorated sills
    ■ Frame deformation
    ■ Storms and screens missing or damaged
    ■ Cracked or broken glass
    ■ Condensation between panes
    ■ Vines
38. ■ Over windows or doors; at bottoms of walls; at horizontal siding joints in panel type siding.
39. Missing flashings; ineffective or incomplete flashings; loose; rust; rot; caulking missing or ineffective.
40. ■ Rain driven by wind
    ■ Rain running down the wall (gravity)
    ■ Water wicking into the wall (capillary action)
41. Uneven risers are a trip hazard.
42. Rise is 7¾ inches maximum, tread depth is 10 inches minimum.
43. ¾" to 1¼"

44. 3 feet

45. An outward opening door can knock someone off the stairs.

46. Spalling is the crumbling, flaking, chipping, or shaling of the surface of the masonry.

47. Probe the wood with an awl or screwdriver.

48. It prevents close inspection, and holds water against the wood, causing rot.

49. 30 inches

50. 4 inches

51. Horizontal spindles are climbable.

52. 34 to 38 inches

53. 36 inches

54. Gutters slope so they always look off level.

55. 3 inches

56. If the beam has been painted and there are unpainted parts visible at the supports, this may indicate movement of the beam.

57. True

58. 16 or 24 inches

59. Joist hangers.

60. Bounce on the deck; scan the deck with your eye at deck level.

61. Lag bolts every 24 inches or multiple nails every 16 to 24 inches.

62. Flashing extends from under the siding, over the top of the ledgerboard, and down.

63. Rot is found where the joists penetrate the wall.

64. They absorb water readily and rot.

65. To prevent fumes from entering the house.

66. True

67. b

68. 3 inches thick, with 5 inches of well compacted gravel below.

69. To drain (usually towards the door)

70. Settled soil under the slab. The slab is now suspended.

71. Because automotive fluids can find their way into municipal sewers.

72. 3 inches

73. To reduce the amount of debris that gets into the drain pipe.

74. False

75.
- Difficult to open or close
- Rust or denting
- Rot or insect damage
- Automatic opener problems
- Paint or stain problems

76. From inside

77. Adjustment of the closing limit

78. With a two inch block of wood placed in the door's path

79. 6 inch drop over the first 10 feet away from the foundation

80. Asphalt

81. False

82. A black plastic dimpled membrane that acts to relieve hydrostatic pressure in the soil.

83. Perimeter drainage tile.

84. Wet basements and crawlspaces; damage to foundations; damage to siding materials, in severe cases.

85. A window well

86. The earth below them may be impervious, and slope towards the house.

87. ▪ Is there vegetation growing over the whole surface?

   ▪ Are there bands of freshly exposed topsoil?

   ▪ Are the tree trunks vertical?

   ▪ Is there cracking in the walls on the ravine side of the house?

   ▪ Are retaining walls leaning out over the ravine?

88. Gutters and downspouts carry water from the roof away from the building, protecting the cladding system and the foundation.

89. Gutters are called troughs, or eavestroughs. Downspouts are called rain water leaders, leaders, or conductor pipes.

90. Because of ice damming problems.

91. Horizontal projection. Gutters can be smaller.

92. 1 inch maximum projection.

93. Seams and changes in direction.

94. Corrosive action from leaves or needles from trees.

95. False

96. 1 inch drop over 200 inches run

97. Localized discoloration and premature wear occur below the gutter

98. ▪ Easy to repair or replace

   ▪ Easy to know if the downspouts and gutters are working properly

   ▪ With a proper extension, the landscaping is not damaged

99. ▪ Traffic problems at building corners

   ▪ They must be moved or lifted to cut the grass

   ▪ If drainage is poor, the water can pool near the house

100. ▪ Tough to inspect

   ▪ Repair is expensive

   ▪ They may go into the floor drains on old houses which can flood the basement if the floor drain trap is clogged, collapsed, or broken.

101. Redirect the downspout to discharge water above grade with an extension away from the building

102. 6 inches

103. Moss or ice, which are trip hazards. Surface damage of the material itself, and water penetration into the building if the surface is against the house.

104. Trees may—

   ▪ damage the siding

   ▪ prevent air and sunlight from drying the siding

■ heave or push in the foundation

■ damage roofs.

105. A new water or sewer line.

106. It is impossible to tell from a single visit if the wall is in danger of collapse. Leaning walls with no cracks or buckling should be further investigated by a specialist.

107. This is done for frost control.

108. 4 inches in diameter, and not more than 10 feet apart.

CHAPTER 3: ROOFING

1. Protect the building from rain, snow, wind, hail and fire.

Support some of the mechanical equipment for the house.

Make an architectural statement.

2. False

3. Sloped roof surfaces shed water while flat roof surfaces are watertight.

4. Sloped roofs are not waterproof. They are designed to shed water like a series of umbrellas. They are not designed to control standing water.

5. The pitch of the roof is the slope, usually expressed as a ratio of the rise over the run.

6. 1. Identify the roofing material.

2. Determine whether it was properly installed.

3. Determine whether it is performing properly or leaking.

4. Determine whether it is near the end of its life.

7. On a typical roof, the fasteners and most of the flashing materials are concealed. At least half of the roofing materials themselves are also often concealed. Your inspection is also not complete until you look at the underside of the roof.

8. A minor roof leak may cause considerable damage before it is noticed.

9. 1. Old

2. Damaged

3. Patched

4. Missing materials

5. Exposed fasteners

6. Poor installation

7. Vulnerable areas

8. Ice dam potential

9. Multiple layers

10. 10 years old

11.
■ Exposure to ultraviolet light

■ Color

■ Ventilation

■ Wind exposure

■ Pitch

■ Complexity

■ Foot traffic

■ Concentrated water

■ Tree branches

12. South and west

13. Yes

14. ▪ Butterfly roofs
    ▪ Wide chimneys near the lower edge of the roof
    ▪ Chimneys in valleys
    ▪ Skylights
    ▪ Drains from upper roofs discharging onto lower roofs
    ▪ Changes in material
    ▪ Equipment that obstructs drainage
    ▪ Complex flashing details
    ▪ Asymmetric valleys
    ▪ Repaired areas
    ▪ Changes in slope

15. ▪ Asphalt-based products on the roof surface
    ▪ Caulking
    ▪ Differences in color, texture, size or style in the roofing materials used
    ▪ Dissimilar metal flashing, nail heads, metal hooks, strips of metal
    ▪ Different roofing materials

16. No. Many components and details are concealed.

17. An ice dam is a buildup of ice at the bottom of a roof slope.

18. Ice dams are caused by heat escaping from the house and melting the snow on the upper parts of the roof. This melted snow freezes when it gets down to the colder eave area where there is no heat loss from the house.

19. c. A low sloped roof with a wide soffit.

20. ▪ North slopes
    ▪ Bottom of valleys
    ▪ Low sloped roofs
    ▪ Roofs which change slope near the eaves
    ▪ Roofs with wide soffits
    ▪ Roofs over porches or balconies

21. ▪ Evidence of damage at the wall/ceiling intersection
    ▪ Stained sidings starting at the soffits
    ▪ Shingle damage along the lower edge of the roof
    ▪ Zigzag electric heating cables along the lower edge of the roof
    ▪ Poor insulation and ventilation
    ▪ Leakage through the tops of windows
    ▪ Staining in the attic around the perimeter
    ▪ Wet or damaged insulation around the perimeter of the attic
    ▪ Plastic sheets in the attic
    ▪ Roofs with low slopes and wide overhangs

22. Upgrade insulation and ventilation, add eave protection, or add electric heating cables.

23. Upgrading the attic insulation and ventilation

24. ■ The dead load is increased

    ■ Nails may not be long enough to penetrate the roof sheathing

    ■ Old flashings may not be replaced

    ■ The roof sheathing cannot be properly inspected

    ■ Roofing materials may not dry properly

25. Look at the gable ends and lower edges of the roof, at flashings or check the nail pattern protruding through the sheathing from the underside.

26. A base material; an asphalt body or coating; surfacing granules

27. An asphalt shingle roof typically lasts 12 to 25 years.

28. ■ Cupping   ■ Blistering

    ■ Clawing   ■ Loss of granule material

    ■ Cracking   ■ Tearing off

29. Look for loss of granules, cracking, cupping, clawing, missing, or brittle shingles or widening of the slots between the tabs.

30. The fasteners may drive right through the shingles and not hold them in place.

31. These may sit proud and tear through the overlaying shingle. They may not be driven deep enough to hold the shingles in place.

32. False

33. Curling; cupping; splitting; rotting; wear through and burn through.

34. Hips and ridges

35. Both a and c

36. True

37. ■ The slates wear out

    ■ The fasteners or flashings wear out

    ■ Slates are mechanically damaged

    ■ The installation was poorly done

38. No

39. ■ Face nailing new slates

    ■ Replacing slates with metal or other roofing materials

    ■ Covering the damaged area with asphalt

40. The surface of the slates may turn white or brown and may be soft or flake easily

41. Flat or curved

42. Mission tiles come in two pieces—pans and covers. Spanish tiles come in one piece and have interlocking sides.

43. False

44. ■ Installation problems   ■ Fastener problems

    ■ Cracked or broken   ■ Flashing problems

    ■ Pitted or spalling   ■ Underlying membrane problems

    ■ Missing   ■ Previous repairs

45. Flat or curved

46.
- Installation problems
- Cracked or broken tiles
- Pitted or spalling tiles
- Missing or loose tiles
- Fastener problems
- Flashing problems
- Underlying membrane problems
- Previous repairs

47. No

48. True

49. False

50. Copper, stainless steel, galvanized steel, terne, zinc, or aluminum

51.
- Rust
- Fastener failure
- Loose or missing shingles or flashing details
- Installation problems
- Dents
- Buckling

52. Selvage roofing

53. Asphalt shingles

54. Valley flashing

55. Cracking; blistering; buckling; loss of granular material.

56. At the flashings

57. Felt paper; rubberized asphalt; rubber; metal; roll roofing.

58.
- Valleys
- Chimneys
- Pipes or stacks
- Roof/wall intersections
- Sloped roofs which intersect flat roofs
- Skylights
- Eaves
- Rakes
- Hips and ridges

59. Valley flashings are a shedding type of flashing.

60. The lower sections of the valley see more water than the upper sections and valleys that widen as they descend are less likely to collect snow and ice.

61. Roll roofing; metal

62. Closed cut or half woven valley, and fully woven valley

63. Torn or worn; rusted; patched; installation problems.

64. From the eaves

65. Leakage

66.
- The flashing is cut too short at the eaves
- Base flashing is missing
- Exposed fasteners
- Uniform valley width
- Uncut points

- ▣ Excessive lengths of metal without joints
- ▣ Missing upstand (splash diverter)
- ▣ Shingles not sealed with asphalt at the valley
- ▣ Wood shake and shingle joints are broken into the valley
- ▣ Closed cut valleys do not have the shingles trimmed back two inches
- ▣ Individual shingles are used on closed valleys

67. False

68. No, a caulked joint will be an ongoing maintenance item.

69. ▣ Rust

- ▣ Damage
- ▣ Loose
- ▣ Missing base or cap (counter) flashings
- ▣ Missing bottom, side or top flashings
- ▣ Missing reglets
- ▣ Base flashings not interwoven with shingles
- ▣ Side base flashings too short
- ▣ Inadequate overlap of base flashings
- ▣ Inadequate overlap of cap flashings
- ▣ Inadequate height of cap flashings
- ▣ Missing crickets

70. Leakage

71. No, you must also inspect the area below the chimney flashing for evidence of leakage.

72. Plumbing stacks; electrical masts; exhaust vents

73. Steel; rubber; lead; copper; aluminum.

74. Rust; damage; installation problems; vertically misaligned.

75. Flashings at the sides of chimneys

76. Either, but usually to the roof

77. To allow for ease of painting and to keep the end grain of wood siding materials from absorbing water and rotting. The recommended clearance is as much as two inches.

78. ▣ Missing step or counterflashings

- ▣ Step flashings are not tucked under shingles
- ▣ Flashings are too short or too narrow
- ▣ Siding is not cut back
- ▣ Inadequate overlap of adjacent pieces of flashing
- ▣ Inappropriate or missing troughs or pans
- ▣ Counterflashings not let into mortar joints

79. False

80. Galvanized steel; aluminum; Galvalume; lead; copper; lead-coated copper

81. Aluminum

82. Leakage

83. Bottom chimney flashings

84. One

85. b

86. Leakage

87. Ventilation of the roof space

88. Loose, misaligned or missing pieces; separation of wood hips and ridges; rust; installation problems.

89. b

90. Ventilated

91. On curb

92. 15

93. Leakage; rot; mechanical damage; patching; cracked glazing; lost seal; missing or low curb; incomplete flashings; loose; window is used as a skylight.

94. True. Poor installation; low quality skylights; mechanical damage; cracked glazing; condensate drain backup.

95. Yes

96. False

97. e

98. Watertight

99. The gravel coating conceals the membrane.

100. The asphalt is the waterproofing material. The felts hold the asphalt in place, add strength, distribute the forces and stabilize the layers of asphalt.

101. The flood coat holds the gravel in place and provides some waterproofing.

102. The gravel provides ultraviolet protection for the roof.

103.
- Old
- Mechanically damaged
- Patched (temporary repairs)
- Multiple layers
- No protective surface
- Blisters
- Alligatoring
- Gravel erosion
- Ridging
- Fishmouths
- Membrane movements
- Ponding
- Debris or storage
- Exposed felts

104. No

105. 48

106.
- A shortened life expectancy
- Roof structure sag
- A large volume of water available to leak into the building
- Vegetation growth on the roof

107. Look for dirt, algae and vegetation on the roof surface.

108. Water may be wicked into the felts.

109. Roll roofing often has nail heads that are exposed or covered with plastic cement and/or plastic cement along the seams. Roll roofing is typically not used for flashings. Modified bitumen is more flexible than roll roofing and will usually not break if folded. Roll roofing is usually 36 inches wide. Modified bitumen roofing is usually 39 inches (1 meter) wide.

110. Old; openings at seams and flashings; surface cracking; loss of granules; slippage; blisters; punctures; ponding; patching (temporary repairs).

111. ▦ Seams facing up the slope

▦ Inadequate overlap of seams

▦ End seams not staggered

▦ Inadequate fastening of the membrane to the decking

▦ Poor sealing at seams and flashings

▦ Inadequate drainage

112. EPDM

113. Rubber

114. Seams

115. EPDM is not compatible with some asphalt products.

116. False

117. Tin; terne; lead; zinc; copper; aluminum; galvanized steel; stainless steel.

118. 1. EPDM

▦ Old   ▦ Punctures due to tenting

▦ Open seams or flashings   ▦ Ponding

▦ Cracks   ▦ Discoloration

▦ Patches (temporary repairs)

2. PVC

▦ Old

▦ Open seams

▦ Surface cracking or orange peeling

▦ Punctures due to tenting

▦ Ponding

▦ Patching (temporary repairs)

▦ Discoloration

▦ Wrinkling

▦ Ridging or fish-mouthing

▦ Fastener problems

▦ Movement of roof projections

3. **Metal**

▦ Leaking   ▦ Bent or damaged metal

▦ Rust   ▦ Open seams

▦ Loose fasteners   ▦ Failed caulking

119. At the flashings

120. Aluminum is not compatible with masonry

121. Cant strips are triangular blocks used at 90 degree intersections to allow asphalt based roofing materials to make two 45 degree bends.

122. False

123. Vertical surface

124. The skylight frame goes over the base flashing.

125. A pitch pocket is used to flash irregularly shaped roof penetrations.

126. Secondary scuppers act as emergency drains in case the primary drains are obstructed.

127. Three

128.
- Leaks
- Old
- Rusted metal
- Loose seams or ends
- Patches (temporary repairs)
- Sagging or slipping base flashings
- Flashings pulled away by the membrane
- Fasteners backing out
- Dried out caulking or sealant
- Loose clamps or termination bars
- Pitch pockets not filled

129.
- Missing pieces
- Incompatible materials
- Improper materials
- Flashings too short
- Flashings loose
- No allowance for expansion and contraction
- Exposed fasteners on horizontal surfaces
- Horizontal surfaces that collect water
- Missing reglets
- Missing cant strips

CHAPTER 4: STRUCTURE

1. Footings transfer the live and dead loads of the building to the soil over a large enough area so that neither the soil nor the building will move. In areas where frost occurs, footings prevent frost from moving the building. Foundations transfer loads from the building to the footings. Foundations may also act as retaining walls, resisting lateral soil pressure, for example.

2. Common foundation configurations include basements, crawl spaces, and slab-on-grade. Common foundation types include spread footings, pad footings, piles, and piers.

3. A strip footing or spread footing is used under a foundation wall. A pad footing is used under a column. Pad footings distribute concentrated loads. Strip footings handle more evenly distributed loads.

4. Foundation materials include concrete, concrete block, cinder block, brick, clay tile, stone, and wood.

5. Your client has to understand the limitations of your inspection. Crawl spaces can be troublesome. If you couldn't get a good look, your client should understand that there is a greater risk of unforeseen problems.

6. Live loads, such as people, wind, and snow, vary. Dead loads, such as the building materials, are relatively fixed.

7. A pilaster is a thickening of a foundation wall to accommodate the concentrated load of a beam or column. A pier is a stand-alone structural member that can be thought of as a column sunk into the ground.

8. No.

9. Shrinkage, differential settling, heaving, horizontal forces.

10. In uniform settlement, the entire house moves and no cracking develops. With differential settlement, one part of the house moves relative to another. This typically results in cracking.

11. Shrinkage cracks are typically caused by natural curing of concrete.

12. Shrinkage cracks are rarely more than $1/8$ inch wide and typically do not involve displacement of the concrete on either side of the crack. Shrinkage cracks usually show up within the first year of the life of a home. Shrinkage cracks do not extend through the footings or up into the structure above. Shrinkage cracks may occur at stress concentration points such as window openings.

13. The implications of shrinkage cracks may be leakage, but not structural problems.

14. No.

15. Look for structural problems in other homes in the neighborhood. Check the general topography. Houses on side-hill lots may be subject to cut and fill type settlement problems. Houses near the bottom of slopes may experience flooding problems. The general age of the neighborhood is useful information. Older neighborhoods provide a more reliable test of time. You also may know about specific problems such as expansive or weak soils, high water tables, underground streams or reclaimed land.

16. Cracks in more than one plane.

17. ▪ To differentiate between settlement and heaving, check whether cracks are opening, crushing, or sliding type cracks.

   ▪ If sidewalks, driveways and patios slope down toward the house, settlement is more likely. If they slope up towards the house, heaving is more likely.

   ▪ If there is hump in the central part of the house but the columns are not cracked or displaced, the house perimeter is probably settling. If central columns show lots of cracks in the floor area and the floor slopes up toward the column, heaving is more likely.

   ▪ Are overhead electric wires at a different angle than neighboring houses? Is the house higher or lower?

   ▪ Check adjacent houses for similar evidence and neighborhood trends.

   ▪ Look at the soil line against the building. If the front door sill is below grade level, settling is more likely. If you can see a dirt line six inches above the existing grade, heaving is more likely.

18. False.

19. The perpendicular wall reinforces the cracked wall near the end, preventing it from moving.

20. Lateral support is usually a floor system secured to the top of a foundation wall, preventing it from tipping inward.

21. Increase in hydrostatic pressure, or swelling of expansive soils.

22. A poured concrete wall.

23. A cold joint is formed when a foundation is poured at two separate times. The first part of the foundation has started to cure when the second part is poured. At the intersection, a cold joint is created.

24. Wood members are prone to rot if they are at or below grade level.

25. Sills, columns, beams, joists, subfloors

26. c

27. True

28. Avoid moisture and possible rot

29. To connect the top of the foundation to the wood floor system

30. 1. Rotted sills may be crushed and lead to differential settlement

   2. Rotted sills often mean rotted joists and studs

   3. Rotted sills means the house frame is not well anchored to the foundation

31. Sills are typically bolted to the foundation

32. 1) Sills below grade; 2) rot or insect damage; 3) gaps between the sill and foundation; 4) crushed sills; 5) not properly anchored; 6) missing.

33. b

34. 1. Concrete   4. Steel

   2. Concrete block   5. Wood

   3. Brick

35. 1. Missing   7. Poorly secured at the top or bottom

   2. Settled   8. Mortar deterioration

   3. Crushed   9. Spalling concrete or brick

   4. Leaning   10. Mechanical damage

   5. Buckled   11. Rot or insect damage

   6. Rust   12. Heaved

36. 1) Concrete; 2) wood.

37. The same width

38. 1) Bolts; 2) welding; 3) bendable tabs.

39. A level or plumb bob

40. c

41. a, b, c, and e

42. 1) Wood; 2) steel

43. 1. Glulams

   2. LVL—Laminated Veneer Lumber

   3. LSL—Laminated Strand Lumber

   4. PSL—Parallel Strand Lumber

44. False

45. 1) a; 2) b

46. 3 inches

47.
1. Rust
2. Rot or insect damage
3. Sag
4. Poor bearing
5. Rotated or twisted beams
6. Split or damaged
7. Notches or holes
8. Poor connections of built-up components
9. Weak connections to columns
10. Weak connections to joists
11. Inadequate lateral support
12. Concentrated loads
13. Missing sections
14. Prior repairs

48. b

49. Overspanned or undersized

50. False

51. True

52. To avoid rot

53. c and d

54. both b and c

55. a, b, and d

56.

1. Trusses	4. Laminated Veneer Lumber (LVL)
2. Plywood	5. Parallel Strand Lumber (PSL)
3. Wood I-joists	6. Laminated Strand Lumber (LSL)

57. False

58.
1. Rot and insect damage
2. Sagging joists
3. Poor end bearing
4. Rotated or twisted joists
5. Inappropriate notching or holes
6. Split or damaged
7. Weak cantilevers
8. Weaknesses created by openings around stairs, chimneys and windows, etc.
9. Prior repairs
10. Concentrated loads
11. Missing joists

59. 1. Two-by-eights—eleven and a half feet

2. Two-by-tens—fourteen feet

3. Two-by-twelves—sixteen feet

60. $1^1/_2$ inches

61. False

62. True

63. 1. Undersized

2. Inadequate nails

3. Wrong type of nails

4. Joist not bottomed in hanger

5. Joist doesn't penetrate fully into hanger

6. Joists connected to beam at other than 90° with conventional hanger

7. Doubled joists connected to beam with single joist hanger

64. The ledger board is fastened to the beam near the bottom and the joist rests on the top of the ledger board.

65. 1) Bridging; 2) blocking; 3) ceilings; 4) strapping

66. False

67. The member is supported at one end and partway along the length. One end is unsupported.

68. The problem is most likely to occur where the joists pass through the walls because this is the area that is likely to stay wet.

69. False

70. Planking, plywood, waferboard

71. both a and e

72. Unsupported edges may be springy

73. False

74. 1. Rot and insect damage

2. Sagging or springy subflooring

3. Damaged or cut

4. Cantilevered or unsupported ends

5. Prior repairs

6. Concentrated loads

7. Squeaks

8. Swollen waferboard

9. Cracking ceramic tiles

75. 1. Cracked

2. Settled

3. Heaved

4. Hollow below slab

76. c

77. Tap on the slab and listen for a hollow sound

78. 1. Transferring live and dead loads to the flooring or foundation system

2. Resist racking

3. Support interior and exterior finishes

4. Hide electrical and mechanical systems

5. Accommodate thermal insulation

6. Provide sound insulation

7. Provide privacy

79. 1) Brick; 2) stone; 3) concrete block; 4) cinder block; 5) clay tile; 6) glass block

80. a

81. 1. Cracks

2. Leaning, bowing, or bulging

3. Mortar deteriorating or missing

4. Prior repairs

5. Deterioration of the masonry

6. Efflorescence

7. Too close to grade

82. These are typically tying the walls into the building and have been added as result of lack of lateral support.

83. False

84. True

85. False

86. False

87. 1. Partition walls have no structural elements below

2. Load bearing walls rest on foundations, beams or another wall system

3. Ends of floor or ceiling joists rest on load bearing walls but not partition walls

4. Load bearing walls often have a wall directly above. Non-load bearing walls are less likely to have this.

5. Door openings in load bearing walls have lintels. Openings in partition walls do not need lintels.

88. e

89. e

90. True

91. both c and d

92. a, b, and c

93. a, b, and e

94. d

95. Veneer walls have—

1. Weep holes

2. Wood studs behind the masonry

3. No header bricks

4. No masonry arches

5. A single wythe of bricks supported on a metal angle

96. 1. Cracked

2. Bowing or leaning

3. Mortar missing or deteriorating

4. Stone/brick deterioration or spalling

5. Weep holes missing or obstructed

6. Efflorescence

7. Too close to grade

8. Wavy brick walls

9. Sagging lintels or arches

10. Temporary repairs

97. 1. Rot and insect damage

2. Leaning or racking

3. Bowing or buckling

4. Excess notches, holes and mechanical damage

5. Sagging top plate

6. Lack of fire stopping

7. Sagging lintels

98. False

99. Arches and headers transfer dead and live loads above around openings

100. Arches are often the same material as the walls and may be stone, brick or concrete.

101. 4 inches

102. One and one-half inches

103. 1. Missing

2. Cracks

3. Mortar deteriorating or missing

4. Stone or brick deterioration

5. Sagging, leaning or rotating

6. End-bearing

7. Rust

8. Rot or insect damage

104. False

105. Rot

106. 1. Carry live loads of wind, rain, snow and people

2. Carry dead loads of roof sheathing, roof coverings and roof equipment

3. Support dead loads of insulation and ceiling finishes

4. Laterally support building walls

5. Create an attic space, ventilation space and support for soffits and fascia

107. 1. Rafters are sloped structural members on steep roofs that support sheathing and run from the roof peak down to the eaves. They may be 2 by 4 to 2 by 10's and are typically spaced 12 to 24 inches on center.

2. Roof joists are horizontal or nearly horizontal framing members on low sloped roofs that carry the sheathing, roof covering and live loads above to walls or beams. Roof joists can be thought of as low sloped rafters. Some roof joists also carry ceiling finishes.

3. Ceiling joists are horizontal members that support insulation and ceilings. They are used with rafters and may support attic floors. Ceiling joists often tie the bottom ends of opposing rafters together to make a structurally sound triangle of the roof assembly.

108. Ceiling joists help prevent rafters and the tops of walls from being pushed outward by live loads on the roof. Ceiling joists are often in tension, running from the bottom of one rafter to another. They must be continuous to resist these forces.

109. Sagging rafters cause a dishing in the entire roof surface and/or a sag at the ridge. Sheathing sag is a repetitive pattern across the roof between rafters, trusses or roof joists.

110. Rafters are less likely to spread when there is a ridge beam because the rafters hang on this structural member. With a simple ridge board, the rafters are not prevented from dropping at the ridge. A ridge beam, if properly installed, helps prevent the rafters from dropping or spreading.

111. End bearing should be $1^1/_2$ inches on wood and 3 inches on masonry.

112. Condensation tends to be more uniform and widespread than leakage. Condensation is uniform laterally across the roof. Leaks tend to run down sloped roof surfaces following gravity.

113. Collar ties help prevent rafter sag.

114. Knee walls and purlins both provide mid-point support for rafters. Knee walls provide their support by transferring the loads down to ceiling joists and walls or beams below. Purlins act as beams running along the underside of rafters.

115. The top plate of a knee wall may sag if it is a single plate and if the studs are not lined up with the rafters above.

116. A chord is part of the perimeter of a truss. Webs are the internal members.

117. Trusses are further apart than most rafters. Trusses are often 24 inches on center and some common plywood and waferboard sheathings are not thick enough to span 24 inches without sagging under live load.

118. Drywall may sag because $1/_2$ inch drywall cannot span the 24 inches between trusses without sagging, especially if the drywall has been wet as a result of condensation, or during construction and finishing.

119. King post, queen post, fink, howe, fan, belgian or doublefink, scissor, mono, pratt, warren, gable end.

120. Neither.

121. The roof is stronger if vertical joints are staggered. Vertical joints are weaknesses in the roof panel. Lining up all the weakness will tend to make the roof act as several smaller panels rather than one large one.

122. Sheathing may sag due to:

- Overspanning
- Excess loads
- Deteriorated wood
- Panel type sheathing installed in the wrong direction
- Inadequate edge support

123. Fire Resistant Treated (FRT) plywood is typically used in row or town homes close to the party walls to avoid building parapet walls. A chemical treatment in the wood was designed to char the wood at relatively low temperatures raising the auto-ignition temperature of the wood, helping to control the spread of fire.

CHAPTER 5: INSULATION

1. To control heat loss

2. Restrict vapor diffusion

3. Moisture may get into the building structure, causing damage.

4. 1. Flushes moisture from unconditioned spaces in winter and heat from these spaces in summer

2. Provides fresh air for building occupants

5. The amount of moisture in the air relative to the amount it could hold if saturated, expressed as a percent

6. The ability of a material or assembly to dry out after it has gotten wet

7. We were not able to completely stop air leakage into cool roof spaces, so we need to get rid of that warm, moist air.

8. To transfer some of the heat from the air exhausted from the house into the fresh air coming into the house

9. 1. Venting of roof and wall spaces to flush warm moist air out of the building components

2. Exhausting stale air and supplying fresh air to the living space

10. Outer part of the wall, or not at all

11. 1) Loose fill; 2) Batts or blankets; 3) rigid boards; 4) foamed-in-place

12. 1. Fiberglass 6. Extruded polystyrene

2. Cellulose fiber 7. Closed cell phenolic plastic

3. Mineral wool 8. Polyisocyanurate

4. Vermiculite/perlite 9. Polyurethane

5. Expanded polystyrene (EPS) 10. Isocyanate/polyisocyanate

13. 1. Loose, fill, batt, board 6. Board

2. Loose fill 7. Board

3. Loose fill, batt, board 8. Board

4. Loose fill 9. Foamed-in-place

5. Board 10. Foamed-in-place

14. To stop air movement through building walls and roof

15. 1. Minimize heat flow to exterior/interior

2. Minimize moisture flow to building components

16. To protect the building from moisture damage. Designed to protect from moisture due to vapor diffusion, not air movement.

17. Vapor retarder, vapor diffusion retarder (VDR)

18. Air barrier

19. Warm side

20. Warm side

21. 1. Allow warm, moist air out of the attic

    2. Reduce attic temperatures in summer

    3. Helps prevent ice dams in winter by keeping attic cold

22. 1) Soffit; 2) Ridge; 3) Roof; 4) Gable

23. 50%

24. 50%

25. If there are gable vents at opposing ends

26. Prevent insulation from covering the vents

27. 1. Required at the ridge and bottom of upper section

    2. None is required for steep section

28. 1. Yes, if the ceiling is not well sealed

    2. Can cause negative pressure in attic that promotes warm, moist air to enter at a faster rate

29. 1) Mask; 2) goggles; 3) long sleeves with tight cuffs.

30. 1) Fall through the ceiling; 2) electric shock; 3) irritate lungs, eyes, skin.

31.

Problem:	Implications:
1. Not insulated	Results in heat loss
2. Not weather stripped	Results in heat loss and air leakage
3. Missing	Results in heat loss and air leakage
4. Inaccessible	Limits inspection

32.

Problem:	Implications:
1. Two inches thick	Heat loss
2. Wet	Won't work well, damage to finishes
3. Gaps and voids	Localized heat loss, ice damming
4. Compressed	Reduced R-value
5. Missing	Heat loss, ice damming

33. 1. Only if lights are proper type, or installed in drywall boxes

    2. Look for double shell, or "IC" stamp

34. 1) Walls indicate skylights or light wells; 2) yes, should be insulated.

35. 1) Insulation; 2) air/vapor barrier

36. Masonry chimneys should only have noncombustible insulation surrounding them.

37. Vent is contained in a boxed-in area to keep insulation away

38. 1) Air leakage; 2) rot damage; 3) insulation gets wet from condensation.

39. **Problems:** 1) Birds' nests; 2) mechanical damage; 3) undersized openings.

    Implications: 1) Inadequate venting 2) mold/rot from condensation

40. If soffit venting is missing, rain and snow may actually be drawn into the roof vents.

41. 1) No ventilation on calm days; 2) too much ventilation on windy days; 3) noisy or seized

42. No, they can depressurize the attic, increasing heat loss

43. An exhaust fan dumping warm, moist air directly into the attic

44. 1. Treat as an attic—with a little insulation and an air space

   2. Completely fill roof space—in theory it stops airflow

   3. Insulate above sheathing—roof membrane applied over insulation

   4. Insulate below roof structure—lowers ceiling heights, but provides good ventilation

45. Problem:

   1. Too little insulation

   2. Wet, compressed or voids

   3. Missing or incomplete air/vapor barrier

   4. Missing or inadequate venting

   5. Venting obstructed

46. Implications:

   1. Heat loss, no damage to structure

   2. Reduced R-values, mold/mildew/rot

   3. Mold/mildew/rot

   4. Warm, moist air condensing and causing mold, mildew and rot

   5. Mold/mildew/rot

47. 1) Remove ceiling light fixture or exhaust fan covers (with power off); or

   2) pop fascia vents off and look through holes

48. Staining, sponginess or dampness on ceilings

49. 1) Vent the roof space; 2) seal the roof cavity

50. Opposing fascias

51. One square foot of venting for every 150 square feet of roof area

52. False

53. a. Outside—keeps walls warm, no interior space lost, no interior living space lost, etc., but only certain types of insulation are suitable

   b. Inside—inexpensive, can be done at any time, any type of insulation is suitable, etc., but can be difficult to detect leaks

54. 1. Insulate walls, creating a conditioned crawlspace

   2. Insulate floor above, creating an unconditioned crawlspace

55. True if unheated—vent to outdoors to remove warm, moist air in cold climates

56. 1) Wet floors; 2) animals; 3) dark and dirty.

57. 1. Insulation—too little or incomplete

   2. Exterior insulation not suitable for below grade use

   3. Exterior insulation not protected at top

   4. Insulation missing at rim joists

   5. Insulation sagging, loose or voids

   6. Exposed combustible insulation

   7. Air/vapor barrier missing, incomplete or wrong location

8. No moisture barrier on basement walls

9. No moisture barrier on earth floor

58. 1. Higher heating/cooling costs

2. Lower R-value due to moisture

3. Mechanical damage from lawn mowers, weed eaters, etc.

4. Increased heating costs

5. Increased heat loss

6. Risk of fire

7. Condensation on the cold side of insulation and damage

8. Wet insulation, reducing R-value

9. Elevated moisture levels in the crawlspace, possible water damage

59. 1. Heated cavity between floor and insulation below

2. Spray-in-place foams that fill entire cavity

60. 1) Above garages; 2) above porches; 3) in cantilevered areas; 4) over breezeways; 5) below windows projecting out from the building; 6) over unheated crawlspaces; 7) Over open areas below houses with pier foundation and no skirting

CHAPTER 6: INTERIORS

1. 1. Concrete   5. Resilient

2. Wood   6. Ceramic and quarry tile

3. Hardwood or softwood 7. Stone and marble

4. Carpet

2. Problem: **Implications:**

Problem:		Implications:
Water damage	1.	Cosmetic
	2.	Rot, staining or other damage to finish
	3.	Rot or other damage to structural components
Trip hazard	1.	Personal injury
Mechanical damage	1.	Unevenness or loss of continuity in the system
Loose or missing pieces	1.	Trip hazard
	2.	Moisture entry to subflooring
Absorbent materials in wet areas	1.	Premature deterioration
	2.	Rot damage to subflooring
	3.	Odors and air quality issues

3. Problem:

1. Cracked

2. Settled, heaved

3. Water and efflorescence

4. Slope away from drain

5. Hollow below

4. Problem: **Implications:**

Rot	1. Cosmetic problems
	2. Trip hazards
	3. Deterioration of the structure below
Warped	1. Cosmetic problems
	2. Trip hazards
	3. Deterioration of the structure below
Buckled	1. Cosmetic problems
	2. Deterioration of the structure below
Stained	1. Cosmetic problems
	2. Trip hazards
	3. Deterioration of the structure below
Squeaks	1. A nuisance only
Exposed tongues	1. Slivers, splinter or exposed nail heads and possibly injury
	2. Cosmetic

5. Problem: **Implications:**

Rot	1. Cosmetic problems
	2. Possible damage to subflooring below
	3. Health implications
Stains	1. Cosmetic problems
	2. Possible damage to subflooring below
	3. Health implications
Odors	1. Cosmetic problems
	2. Possible damage to subflooring below
	3. Health implications
Buckled	1. Trip hazard
	2. Cosmetic problems

6. Problem: **Implications:**

Split	1. Water damage to subflooring
	2. Trip hazard
Open seams	1. Water damage to subflooring
	2. Trip hazard
Lifted seams	1. Water damage to subflooring
	2. Trip hazard

7. Problem: **Implications:**

Loose	1. Water damage to subflooring
	2. Trip hazard
Grout missing	1. Water damage to subflooring

Cracked or broken	1. Water damage to subflooring
	2. Trip hazard
Worn	1. Cosmetic
	2. Trip hazard if pieces are loose
Stains	1. Cosmetic

8. Around plumbing fixtures, especially toilets

9. 1) Plaster or drywall; 2) wood plank or paneling; 3) masonry or concrete; 4) fiber cement paneling.

10. 1) Water damage; 2) cracks; 3) mechanical damage; 4) inappropriate finishes in wet areas.

11. 1) Bulging, loose or missing; 2) shadow effect; 3) crumbling or powdery; 4) nail pops; 5) poor joints.

12. 1) Rot; 2) cracked, split or broken; 3) buckled; 4) loose.

13. 1. Cosmetic

2. Damage to structure behind

3. Decorating issues

4. Structural movement or settling

5. Minor repair

6. Staining and deterioration

7. Mold growth

8. Life safety from falling plaster

9. Concealed damage

10. Moisture damage

14. 1) Shine flashlight along ceiling; 2) lift tiles on suspended ceilings.

15. 1) Plaster or drywall; 2) wood, hardboard or plywood; 3) fiber cement or concrete; 4) acoustic or suspended tile.

16. 1) Water damage; 2) cracked, loose or missing sections; 3) mechanical damage

17. 1) Shadow effect; 2) crumbling or powdery; 3) nail pops; 4) poor drywall joints; 5) sag; 6) textured ceilings in wet areas

18. Rust

19. 1. Cosmetic

2. Mechanical damage

3. Damage to structure behind

4. Failure of ceiling finishes

5. Safety hazards

6. Staining and deterioration

7. Mold and mildew growth

8. Decorating issues

20. 1) Cover joints at changes of material and direction; 2) protect walls

21. 1. Baseboard

2. Quarter round

3. Door casing

4. Window casing

5. Chair rails

6. Plate rails

7. Cornice moldings

8. Rosettes or medallions

22. 1) Plastic laminate; 2) wood; 3) marble; 4) granite; 5) synthetic marble; 6) stainless steel; 7) ceramic; 8) limestone; 9) synthetic granite

23.

Problem:	Implications:
Missing	Cosmetic
Water damage	Rot; damage to building systems behind
Rot	Damage to building systems
Loose	Damage to building systems behind
Mechanical damage	Cosmetic or air leakage

24. 1) Entire top loose; 2) loose or missing; 3) burned; 4) cut; 5) worn; 6) mechanical damage; 7) stained; 8) metal rusted; 9) substrate rotted.

25. 1) Water damage; 2) rot; 3) stained; 4) mechanical damage; 5) worn; 6) broken glass; 7) defective hardware; 8) stiff/inoperative; 9) not well secured to wall; 10) door or drawers missing/loose; 11) shelves not well supported; 12) rust.

26. GENERAL:

1. Rot/water damage

2. Mechanical damage

TREADS:

3. Excessive rise   7. Worn or damaged

4. Not uniform   8. Sloped

5. Excessive nosing   9. Loose or poorly supported

6. Inadequate tread depth

STRINGERS:

10. Too small   13. Pulling away from wall or treads

11. Too thin   14. Inadequately secured to header

12. Excessive span between stringers 15. Stairwell width inadequate

LANDINGS:

16. Headroom inadequate

17. Landings missing

18. Too small

HANDRAILS:

19. Missing   21. Loose or damaged

20. Hard to grasp   22. Too low or too high

GUARDRAILS:

23. Missing

24. Too low

BALUSTERS:

25. Too far apart   27. Loose or damaged

26. Easy to climb   28. Missing

27. 1) Light; 2) ventilation; 3) architectural appeal; 4) emergency exit.

28. 1) Wood; 2) vinyl; 3) metal.

29. 1) Single hung; 2) double hung; 3) casement; 4) horizontal sliders; 5) awning; 6) hopper; 7) fixed; 8) jalousie.

30. 1) Leaks; 2) headers sagging/missing.

31. 1) Rot; 2) rusted; 3) racked; 4) deformed; 5) installed backwards; 6) drain holes blocked/ missing.

32. 1. Missing—the implication is water leakage

   2. Ineffective—the implication is water leakage

   3. Water leakage

33. 1) Missing; 2) rot; 3) rust; 4) damaged, cracked loose; 5) sills with reversed slope; 6) sill projection inadequate; 7) drip edge missing; 8) putty cracked, missing, loose, deteriorated; 9) caulking/flashing missing, loose, rusted, incomplete; 10) paint or stain needed

34. 1) Rot; 2) rust; 3) inoperable; 4) stiff; 5) sashes won't stay open; 6) sash coming apart; 7) loose fit; 8) weather stripping missing or ineffective.

35. 1) Rot; 2) stained; 3) missing; 4) cracked; 5) loose; 6) poor fit.

36. 1) Cracked; 2) broken; 3) loose; 4) missing; 5) lost seal; 6) excess condensation.

37. 1) Rusted; 2) broken; 3) missing; 4) loose; 5) inoperable.

38. 1) Torn; 2) holes; 3) rust; 4) loose; 5) missing.

39. If the window is required for egress

40. 1) Means of entry and exit; 2) security; 3) privacy; 4) weather-tight; 5) fire resistant if they connect to a garage.

41. 1) Wood; 2) metal; 3) vinyl; 4) hardboard

42. 1) Surface water from rain or snow; 2) groundwater

43. 1) Nuisance; 2) damaged interior finishes and furnishing; 3) odors and mold; 4) structural deterioration; 5) electrical shock or fire hazard; 6) damaged insulation.

44. 1. Water or dampness on walls or floor

   2. Efflorescence on walls or floor

   3. Rot, stains or water marks on walls, doors, windows, basement stairs

   4. Rust at baseboard nails, carpet tack strips, columns, appliances

   5. Odors, mold

   6. Rot

   7. Loose floor tiles

   8. Damaged basement storage

   9. Storage off floor

   10. Wall patches

   11. Floor patches

   12. Trough or trench around floor perimeter

   13. Sump pumps operating continuously

   14. Full sump

   15. Two spare sump pumps

   16. Auxiliary electric supply for pump

   17. High water alarm on sump

   18. Crumbling plaster, drywall or masonry

   19. Peeling paint

20. Wall cracks with stains
21. Recent excavation
22. Evidence of drainage membrane
23. New dampproofing
24. Dehumidifier running constantly

CHAPTER 7: ELECTRICAL SYSTEMS

1. True
2. True
3. Overhead.
4. Underground.
5. False.
6. False.
7. Three.
8. Three phase electricity.
9. 120 volts service
10. 1. Overhead wires too low.
    2. Damaged or frayed wires.
    3. Trees or vines interfering with wires.
    4. Wires too close to doors or windows.
    5. Wires not well secured to the house.
    6. Poor connection between service drop and service entrance.
    7. Inadequate clearance from roofs.
11. ■ above roadway—18 ft
    ■ above driveway—12 ft
    ■ above flat roof—8–10 ft
    ■ above sloped roof—18 inches
    ■ away from water in swimming pool—22½ ft in any direction
    ■ 3 feet above sloped roof with pitch greater than 4 in 12
    ■ above walkway—10 ft
12. From service drop to the service box.
13. False
14. False
15. False
16. 1. No drip loop
    2. No mast head
    3. Mast head not weather-tight
    4. Mast or conduit bent
    5. Mast or conduit rusted
    6. Mast rotted (if wood)

7. Mast conduit or cable not well secured

8. Mast conduit or cable not weather-tight

9. Conduit or cable not well sealed at house/wall penetration

10. Cable frayed, damaged or covered by siding

17. 1) Conduit joints; 2) mast head; 3) roof flashing; 4) meter base; 5) house entry.

18. 1. Prevents water entry into the conduit or service entrance conductors

2. Shows that the service drop wires are not straining the splices

19. 240

20. Three

21. False

22. e

Note: Unless there is overfusing as well, in which case there is a fire hazard.

23. 400 amps

24. a. 6 gauge

b. 4 gauge

c. 2-0 gauge

25. d

26. True

27. False

28. False

29. b

30. True

31. False

32. True

33. 1. Poor access or location

2. Loose

3. Rust or water in box

4. Unprotected opening

5. Damaged parts

6. Overheating

7. Incorrect fuse or breaker size; box rating too small

8. Service entrance wires exposed in the house

9. Poor connections

10. Illegal taps

11. Neutral wire by-passes service box

12. Fused neutral wire

13. Fuses upstream of disconnect switch

14. Obsolete box

15. Exterior box not weather-tight

16. Box not rated for aluminum

34. ■ Grounding systems can help dissipate electricity from lightning.

    ■ Grounding systems can help avoid the buildup of static electricity.

35. The grounding electrode conductor is the ground wire.

36. False

37. Service box

38. Through the neutral service wire or through the grounding electrode conductor to water pipes or ground rods.

39. 1. Metal water supply pipes

    2. Metal rods driven into the ground

    3. Wires buried in the footings of buildings (UFER ground)

    4. Buried grounding plates or rings

    5. The frames of metal buildings (not common in houses)

    6. Metal well casings

40. 1. No grounding

    2. Ground wire attached to plastic pipe

    3. Ground wire after meters and valves with no jumper

    4. Spliced ground wire

    5. Poor connection

    6. Ground connections not accessible

    7. Ground rod cut off

    8. Corroded ground rod

    9. Undersized ground wire

    10. Neutral bonded to ground wire after service box

    11. Neutral wires not bonded to ground wire at service box

    12. Service box not bonded to ground wire

    13. No ground in sub panel feeder wires

41. Service panels, panelboards, auxiliary panels, sub panels, fuse boxes, fuse panels, breaker panels

42. False

43. More electricity can flow at lower amperage ratings.

44. a) 14 gauge; b) 12 gauge; c) 10 gauge; d) 8 gauge

45. 14 gauge

46. b

47. False

48. False

49. We do not shut off the power. This would be a significant inconvenience to the occupant.

50.
1. Obsolete and/or fused neutrals	8. Circuits not labeled
2. Damaged panel or components	9. Panel crowded
3. Loose or missing door	10. Poor access
4. Openings in panel	11. Upside down
5. Panel too small	12. Not suitable for aluminum wiring
6. Overheating	13. Poor location
7. Rust or water in panel	14. Exterior panel not weather-tight

51. These are dangerous because the fuse on the neutral side only blows. The circuit may not work, but there may be voltage throughout the entire circuit.

52. The panel may overheat.

53. No. Because electricity may flow through the ground wire under normal circumstances. The ground wire should be reserved for emergency situations.

54. d

55. Oversized breakers will allow wires to overheat without tripping.

56. Two wires are connected to a single terminal.

57. True

58. 1) Multi-wire circuits not linked; 2) too many breakers; 3) wrong breaker in panel; 4) loose breakers.

59.
1. Sheathing not removed	5. Not well secured
2. Overheating	6. Wires crossing bus bars
3. Loose connections	7. Abandoned wires in the panel
4. Damaged	

60. A split receptacle has the top part of the outlet on one circuit and the bottom part on a different circuit.

61. Linking means that the fuses or breakers for multi-wire branch circuits have to be shut off in pairs.

62. 1) Copper; 2) aluminum

63.
1. NM, Romex, Loomex	3. BX (AC-90), armored cable
2. UF	4. Knob-and-tube

64. Insulation is around the individual wires, and sheathing forms the cables by wrapping around the insulated wires.

65. 14

66. Wire may be damaged by sharp edges of steel studs. Wires passing through holes should be protected with grommets, for example. Wires running parallel to studs should stand off the studs.

67.
1. Damaged
2. Not well secured
3. Loose connections
4. Open splices
5. Wires too close to ducts, pipes, vents, chimneys, and flues
6. Wires too close to the edge of studs or joists
7. Wires run through steel studs without protection

  8. Exposed wires on walls or ceilings

  9. Exposed wires in attics

  10. Cable used outdoors

  11. Buried cable not rated for buried use

  12. Household wire used as extension cords

  13. Undersized wire

  14. Improper color coding

  15. Abandoned wire

68. 1. Cut or pinched

  2. Chewed on by animals

  3. Burned wire

  4. Wire with brittle or cracked insulation

69. 1. Terminal screws

  2. Push-in connectors

  3. Solderless connectors

70. An open splice is a connection that is not made inside a junction box.

71. One and a quarter inches

72. A grommet is a fitting that protects cable from the sharp edges of steel studs.

73. Mechanical protection

74. Because they are not visible and may be stepped on

75. Removed

76. The black and white wires are separate, so the circuit wires usually run in pairs. There are ceramic tubes protecting the wires where they pass through joists or studs. There are ceramic knobs where the wires change direction.

77. No

78. 1) Connections not in boxes; 2) brittle wire, insulation, or sheathing; 3) wire buried in insulation; 4) fused neutrals.

79. 1. Connectors not compatible with aluminum

  2. No anti-oxidant grease on stranded wires

  3. Overheating

80. The conductor itself is silver colored. The sheathing usually has the word ALUMINUM, ALUM or AL.

81. Aluminum wiring was used from the mid 1960s to the late 1970s.

82. Aluminum wire—

  1. Tends to creep out from under terminal screws.

  2. Forms corrosion (oxide) that is an electrical insulator.

  3. Is softer than copper and easier to damage when working with the wire.

  4. Was, in some of the early material, a low quality wire prone to weakness and breaking.

83. Anti-oxidant grease is typically used on stranded aluminum wires.

84. 1. Damaged or loose

  2. Overheating

      3. Inoperative

      4. Obsolete

      5. Not grounded

      6. Missing

      7. Poor stairway lighting

      8. Conventional lights used in wet areas

      9. Improper recessed light used in installations

     10. Improper closet lighting

     11. Heat lamps over doors

     12. Isolating links needed on pull chains

85. Lights are tested by turning them on and off by their switches.

86. A towel thrown over the door may be ignited by a heat lamp.

87. 1. Damaged

      2. Loose

      3. Overheating

      4. Ungrounded outlets

      5. Open neutral or open hot connections

      6. Reversed polarity outlets

      7. Inoperative

      8. Wrong type receptacle

      9. No GFIs

     10. Overheated neutral on split receptacles

     11. Worn receptacles

     12. Broken pin or blade in slots

     13. Not enough receptacles

     14. Too far from basins

88. Use a conventional circuit tester and operate the test button on the receptacle.

89. The collar of a light fixture may be energized, increasing the risk of electrical shock when changing a light bulb.

90. Yes, all outlets downstream of a GFI outlet will be protected.

91. True

92. 1. Damaged

      2. Loose

      3. Overheating

      4. Inoperative

93. False

94. 1. Damaged   5. Cover loose or missing

      2. Missing   6. Crowded

      3. Loose   7. Concealed boxes

      4. Not grounded

95. True

96. False

CHAPTER 8: GAS FURNACES

1. Fuel system, combustion air delivery system, burner assembly, heat exchanger, controls, venting system, distribution system

2. To collect dirt and moisture, separating it from the gas before it gets to the gas valve.

3. 6 feet, and at every floor.

4. Leaks, inadequate support, inappropriate materials, no drip leg, missing shutoff valve, piping in ducts or chimneys, improper connections, plastic pipe exposed above grade, rusting, copper tubing not properly labeled

5. d

6. The pilot flame heats the thermocouple, which senses the flame, allowing the gas valve to open. If the flame goes out, the gas valve is automatically closed.

7. a

8. Rust, scorching, inoperative, delayed ignition, short cycling, poor flame color or pattern, flame wavers when house fan comes on, dirt or soot, gas odor or leak.

9. Spillage (backdrafting) is when the combustion products flow out of the furnace into the room through the burner or draft hood, rather than up the vent. This is a life threatening situation.

10. a

11. Look for changes in the flame pattern when the house air fan turns on. This indicates heat exchanger failure.

12. Two—the blower compartment door, and the burner compartment door.

13. Rust, mechanical damage, missing components, inadequate combustible clearances, obstructed air intakes, scorching

14. Fan off—indicates the temperature at which the house air fan stops (typically 80°F to 110°F)

    Fan on—indicates the temperature at which the house air fan starts (typically 120°F to 150°F)

    High limit—indicates the temperature at which combustion is stopped for safety (typically 170°F to 200°F)

15. Set wrong or defective, scorching, rusting, mechanical damage, improperly wired, missing cover

16. Poor location, not level, loose, dirty, damaged, poor adjustment/calibration.

17. a

18. Draft hood, vent connector, vent.

19. Sections not secured together

    Rusted or pitted

    Poor support

    Poor slope

    Too long

    Inadequate combustible clearances

    Too small or too big for furnace

Improper material

Poor manifolding

Extends too far into chimney

Spillage

Obstruction

20. a

21. Obstructions in the chimney

The connection between the vent connector and the chimney

If the vent connector extends too far into the chimney

22. b

23. b

24. 6 inch clearance for a single wall vent and 1 inch clearance for a B vent.

25. Dirty, noisy, inoperative, overheating, rust, poorly secured, running continuously, too small, unbalanced/vibration, loose, damaged or worn belt.

26. Excessive temperature rise across the heat exchanger; poor airflow at remote registers

27. b

28. No

29. Missing, dirty, installed backwards, wrong size, loose or collapsed

30. The heated air is pushed through the supply plenum, along the supply ducts, out the registers into the room. The air travels across the room from supply register to return grille, through the return ducts to the return plenum, where it re-enters the furnace to be reheated.

31. Duct size, elbows, high velocity, duct shape, length of duct.

32. Disconnected, dirty, removed during renovations, obstructed or crushed, leakage, no air or weak air flow, rust, uninsulated ducts, registers or grilles in garages, poor location, too few return grilles, registers obstructed, painted shut or damaged.

33. cool

34. a

35. Exhaust fumes can enter the house when the furnace is not running.

36. Gas valve, burner(s), heat exchanger, exhaust flue passages, draft hood, fan/limit control, blower, air filter

37. 20%

38. Vent dampers stuck open or closed

Ignition problems

Heat exchanger problems

Condensate problems

Induced draft fan problems

Venting problems

Differential pressure switch problems

Spillage switch problems

Poor outdoor combustion air intake location

39. False

40. No electrical power; loose connections; poor electrical ground; no spark; flame sensor fails to detect flame; hot surface igniter cracked.

41. No

42. Blocked; leaking; poor discharge location; no neutralizer bath; clogged neutralizer

43. Damaged, worn bearings, inoperative

44. Inappropriate materials, poor location for vent termination, mechanical damage, inadequate combustible clearances, and improper slope

45. No, although we have to advise our client if the system is near the end of its normal life expectancy.

46. d

CHAPTER 9: OIL FURNACES

1. Poor location, leakage, rusting, underground, empty

2. The implications include fuel leakage, which is an environmental issue. There may be a significant cost to clean up the soil and remove the tank. There is the issue of removing the tank, because it will eventually collapse. In some areas, the tank is allowed to be filled with sand or a concrete slurry.

3. b

4. Leaks, missing caps, abandoned, corroded

5. Leak, corrosion, mechanical damage, unprotected, undersized

6. The large pipe allows the oil to flow through the line when the temperature is very low. Oil becomes very viscous at low temperatures.

7. Leak, dirty, missing

8. Forced

9. Atomize

10. Dirty, inoperative, leaking, incomplete combustion, vibrating/noisy, too close to combustibles

11. 24 inches

12. Protects the steel of the furnace from the high temperature flame.

13. Fire brick, stainless steel, ceramic felts

14. c

15. Missing, inoperative, tripped

16. The barometric damper ensures adequate draft air supply for the chimney.

17. The damper can only swing one way, so the forced draft burner pressure can close the damper, but not swing it past the vertical position, which would allow flue gases into the house.

18. Rusting, inoperative, missing, misadjusted, inadequate draft air, spillage, improper location.

19. False

20. Aluminum

21. Rusting, poor slope, poor support, too long, inadequate clearance to combustibles, loose connections, undersized
22. d
23. False

CHAPTER 10: HOT WATER BOILERS

1. b
2. c
3. True
4. Pressure relief valve; high temperature limit; low-water cutout; backflow preventer.
5. d
6. c
7. The pressure relief valve is located on top of the boiler, and typically discharges near the floor.
8. No
9. Yes
10. c
11. The low-water cutout prevents boiler damage if the system loses its water for any reason. The cutout prevents the boiler from firing.
12. To prevent contaminated boiler water from flowing backwards into the domestic water piping (drinking water) if the domestic side loses pressure for any reason.
13. b
14. Thermostat; pressure reducing valve; primary control; pump control.
15. The pressure reducing valve drops the domestic water pressure (e.g., 60 psi) down to the pressure required in the hydronic system (e.g., 15 psi).
16. No
17. Yes
18. c
19. The pump can be controlled by water temperature, by the burner control including the thermostat, or be wired to run continuously when there is electrical power to the boiler.
20. Pump, piping, radiators, convectors or baseboards, and expansion tank.
21. The open system operates at atmospheric pressure, the closed system is pressurized. The open system does not have a pump and does not need a pressure relief valve. An open system does not have automatic water make-up (pressure reducing valve).
22. Above the highest level radiator.
23. The expansion tank allows the water to expand as it is heated, so that excess pressure will not build up in the system.
24. Expansion tanks in closed systems are typically located near the boiler, often hung from the ceiling.

25. Pump and motor are mechanically coupled with bearings that have to be oiled.

Pump and motor are close-coupled with permanently lubricated bushings.

Pump and motor are close-coupled with water lubrication.

26. Black steel, copper, cast iron, plastic

27. a

28. Distribute heated water to the rooms, transfer heat to the rooms and return the cooled water to the boiler to be reheated.

29. True

30. c

31. This allows the homeowner to remove trapped air from the radiator, letting the radiator fill with water and heat the room effectively.

32. Because they are turned rarely, the valve packing dries out and shrinks. When the valve is disturbed, a leak occurs here.

33. c

34. Yes

35. 35 to 50 years

CHAPTER 11: OTHER ASPECTS OF HEATING

1.
- Should adequately remove combustion products from the house
- Should prevent poison gases from entering the house
- Minimize the heat loss from the building
- Should keep water, birds, animals, pests out of the house
- Should adequately support their own weight as well as live loads
- Adequately control the fire
- Enhance appliance draft
- Control the fire in the house
- Keep water out of the house

2.
- A structure used to carry exhaust products safely out of the house.
- Interior passages within a chimney which move gases upwards from different fuel burning appliances.
- Metal devices for getting exhaust gases from burning fuels out of the house safely.

3. True

4. False

5. Wood; oil; gas; propane.

6.
- Height
- Flue size
- Any offset from vertical
- Appliance size
- Number of appliances

- Direction of prevailing wind
- The temperature difference between inside and outside
- Tall structures near the chimney
- Whether the chimney is interior or exterior
- The smoothness of the flue passage

7. - Footing and foundation; vent connector; chimney walls; flue liner; chimney cap.

8. Condensation damages the masonry.

9.   1. Settling or leaning
   2. Cracking
   3. Spalling masonry or concrete
   4. Loose, missing or deteriorating masonry
   5. Loose, missing or deteriorating mortar
   6. Efflorescence
   7. Excessive offset from vertical
   8. Chimney too short
   9. Cleanout door too close to combustibles, loose or missing
   10. No liner
   11. Cracked or broken liner
   12. Incomplete liner
   13. Inadequate clearance from combustibles
   14. Fire stopping missing or incomplete
   15. Cap missing
   16. Cap cracked
   17. Improper slope on cap
   18. No drip edge on cap
   19. Creosote buildup in flues
   20. Flue obstructed
   21. Draft inducer fan inoperative
   22. Chimney extender rusted or stuck
   23. Too many appliances on flue
   24. Abandoned opening for flue connections
   25. Undersized screen on spark arrester

10. - Structural failure
- Fire hazard
- Exhaust gas entry into house
- Water leakage into house
- Damaged or blocked flues
- High maintenance and reduced durability of the chimney and adjacent house components

11. Structural instability; fire hazard; exhaust gas entry into house; moisture entry; increased maintenance and reduced durability.

12. 30° maximum

13. Three feet minimum and two feet above anything within 10 feet horizontally.

14. Minimum 15 feet

15. Approximately the 1950s

16. False

17. Minimum two inches

18. False

19. Natural gas and propane

20. Gas and oil

21. Oil and some wood burning appliances

22. Solid fuels

23. False

24. False

25. 1. Not labeled for application

   2. Sections not well secured

   3. Chimney/vent not well supported

   4. Inadequate clearance from combustibles

   5. Inadequate fire stopping

   6. No cap, wrong cap or obstructed cap

   7. Warped, buckled or twisted chimney walls

   8. Rusted or pitting

   9. Inadequate chimney height

   10. Creosote buildup

   11. Excessive offset from vertical

   12. Not continuous through roof

   13. Too many appliances on one flue

   14. Adjacent chimneys of different heights

26. 1. Fire or life safety

   2. Fire and life safety

   3. Chimney sections may fall off and cause damage or injury

   4. Fire hazard

   5. Fire hazard

   6. Corroded flues, backdrafting, sparks or embers igniting combustibles near the chimney

   7. Fire and life safety

   8. Fire or life safety issue of exhaust gases being trapped in the house

   9. Poor draft

   10. Fire hazard

   11. Poor draft

   12. Creosote buildup, poor connections, leakage at joints

13. Backdrafting, life safety issues

14. Corrosion

27. 1. Look for labels that clarify the suitability of the application.

2. Check the connecting sections.

3. Check above roof level. Ensure that it is stable.

4. Check for proper standoffs, thimbles and clearances.

5. Ensure that there are no gaps from top and bottom.

6. Check for a cap and make sure that it is secure.

7. Check the chimney walls anywhere they are exposed, above and below the roof line.

8. Check all accessible sections of chimney for corrosion.

9. Check chimney heights.

10. Check for creosote buildup inside flue.

11. Follow chimney flue and watch for dramatic offsets.

12. Recommend further investigation.

13. Check the number of chimneys against the number of appliances.

14. Check for 16 inch clearance between metal chimneys.

28. Greater than five feet

29. Two inches

30. Above the roof line

31. False

32. Tar-like byproduct of incomplete combustion

33. Cold chimney

34. 1) Masonry fireplaces; 2) factory-built fireplaces

35. True

36. False

37. 1. Footing and foundation

2. Front hearth and back hearth

3. Firebox

4. Damper

5. Throat, smoke shelf and smoke chamber

6. Mantel

7. Chimney

38. True

39. Six inches

40. Six inches

41. Twelve inches

42. Four inches

43. Two inches

44. Two to nine inches

45. False

46. False

47. False

48. False

49. Front hearth—back hearth

Inner hearth—outer hearth

Hearth—hearth extension

50. Firebrick

51. 4 inches of poured concrete

52. 16 inches out and 8 inches to the side, or 20 inches in front and 12 inches to either side

53. False

54. 1) Too small; 2) gaps or cracks; 3) settled; 4) inappropriate material; 5) wood forms not removed; 6) too thin; 7) evidence of overheating.

55. Contain the fire

56. 20

57. False

58. False

59. False

60. False

61. 1. Masonry or mortar loose, missing or deteriorated

2. Masonry or refractory cracked

3. Rust out, burnout, buckled or cracked metal fireboxes

4. Inappropriate materials

5. Designed for coal

6. Too shallow

7. Lintels rusted, sagging or loose

8. Draft suspect

62. 1. Allow exhaust products to leave the house during operation

2. Prevent cold air from entering the house when the fireplace is idle

63. Yes

64. Yes, where gas logs have been inserted.

65. 1) Missing; 2) inoperative or obstructed; 3) damper or frame rusted; 4) frame loose; 5) too low; 6) undersized (too small).

66. 1. Throat—top of firebox below and at the damper

2. Smoke shelf—area behind the damper that is nearly level

3. Chamber—sloping section of the fireplace above the damper and throat, but below the chimney flue

67. The sides and front of the chamber should slope and the back should be vertical.

68. 1. Missing
         2. Debris
         3. Excess slope
         4. Uneven slope
         5. Wood forms not removed
         6. Walls not smooth
         7. Rust

69. 1. Cracked
         2. Settled (gap at wall)
         3. Loose
         4. Combustible clearances inadequate
         5. Evidence of overheating
         6. Too thick

70. 1. Makes fireplaces more efficient
         2. Modern tighter construction made it harder to supply air to fireplaces

71. Space heaters; furnaces; boilers; radiant heating.

72. ▪ Fuses or breakers missing
         ▪ Fuses or breakers too big
         ▪ Multi-wire circuits on the same bus
         ▪ Fuses or breakers bypassed
         ▪ Fuses or breakers loose
         ▪ No links for 240-volt circuits
         ▪ Wrong breaker for panel
         ▪ Wire overheating
         ▪ Wire damaged
         ▪ Wire not well secured
         ▪ Loose connectors
         ▪ Open splices
         ▪ Wires too close to ducts, pipes or chimneys
         ▪ Wires too close to edge of joists or studs
         ▪ Wires exposed on walls or ceilings
         ▪ Wires exposed in attics
         ▪ Wires too small
         ▪ Aluminum wires used without compatible connectors

73. 120-volt heater on a 240-volt circuit

74. ▪ Inoperative heaters
         ▪ Obstructed heaters
         ▪ Dirty or bent fins on heaters
         ▪ 120-volt heaters installed on 240-volt circuits or vice versa
         ▪ Fans—noisy, inoperative, loose or dirty
         ▪ Thermostat overloaded

- Missing or too few heaters
- Damaged or rusted heaters
- Loose or missing covers

75. 10 to 30 kilowatt

76. Sequencers prevent all of the elements from coming on at the same time. A time delay of 30 seconds between elements coming on allows the current flow to gradually build up.

77. When the thermostat calls for heat, only one or two elements will come on. If the thermostat continues to sense that the temperature is still dropping, the next element will start. Once the room temperature begins to rise, no more elements will come on.

78. No

79. 200°F

80. A switch that protects the elements from overheating by making sure there is adequate airflow across them

81. 50 to 60°F

82. 1) Ductwork too small; 2) burned out elements.

CHAPTER 12: AIR CONDITIONING AND HEAT PUMPS

1.
1. Outdoor temperature
2. Outdoor humidity
3. Insulation level in the house
4. Single, double, triple pane windows
5. Whether windows are low e.
6. Whether window coverings are open
7. Amount of shading from trees
8. Roof overhang
9. Awnings or buildings nearby
10. Amount heat generated inside by people and equipment
11. Amount of east and west facing glass.

2. 450 to 700 square feet

3. 700 to 1000 square feet

4. False

5. True

6. True

7. 15-20°F

8. True

9. False

10. It keeps the oil at the base of the compressor warm enough to boil off the refrigerant.

11. 1. Excessive noise/vibration
2. Short cycling or running continuously
3. Out of level
4. Wrong fuse or breaker size
5. Electric wires too small
6. Missing electrical shut off
7. Inoperative
8. Inadequate cooling

12. Outdoors

13. Indoors (above the furnace)

14. Condenser fan is located outdoors

15. 1) Dirty; 2) damaged or leaking; 3) corrosion; 4) dryer or water heater exhaust too close

16. A-coil, slab coil, vertical coil

17. False

18. 1) No access to coil; 2) dirty; 3) frost; 4) top of evaporator dry; 5) corrosion; 6) damage.

19. The capillary tube acts as an obstruction in the line, reducing the pressure and temperature of the liquid refrigerant.

20. A TXV, or TEV acts as a more precise expansion device on larger air conditioners, or heat pumps.

21. 1) Capillary tube defects; 2) thermostatic expansion valve connections loose; 3) clogged orifice; 4) expansion valve sticking.

22. 1. The pan may be cracked, or have an open seam in it.
2. The opening to the drain line may be obstructed.
3. The drain line may be missing or disconnected.
4. The pan may not be sloped properly, allowing water to overflow rather than run to the drain.
5. The pan may be rusted through.
6. The pan may not be properly located below the coil.
7. The pan may be filled with debris, restricting the amount of water it can hold.

23. An auxiliary pan is needed when the evaporator coil is located in an attic, or anywhere over a finished living space.

24. Plastic or copper

25. The condensate line from the primary pan may or may not have a trap. Lines from secondary pans should never be trapped.

26. 1. The trap may be required if the condensate pan is upstream of the house air fan, because the water is under negative pressure.
2. If the condensate is allowed directly into waste plumbing, a trap is required.

27. Acceptable:
1. Outside the building directly into the ground
2. Near the basement floor drain (must be an air gap)

Unacceptable:

1. Into the granular fill beneath the basement floor slab

2. Into the waste plumbing stack

28. 1) Inoperative; 2) leaking; 3) poor wiring.

29. Copper

30. False

31. False

32. True

33. 1) Leaking; 2) damage; 3) missing insulation; 4) lines too warm or cold; 5) lines touching each other.

34. This may be identified by an oil residue below the line set, typically at valves or coil connections.

35. Suction line (large insulated one)

36. Liquid line (small uninsulated one)

37. Suction line

38. The condenser fan is outdoors in the condenser unit.

39. The inlet temperature is outdoor air temperature, and outlet temperature is roughly 15 to 20 degrees F higher than the outdoor temperature

40. 1) Excessive noise/vibration; 2) inoperative; 3) corrosion or mechanical damage; 4) obstructed air flow.

41. Indoors

42. False

43. False

44. False

45. Insulated, with appropriate vapor barriers.

46. 1) Inoperative; 2) poor location; 3) not level; 4) loose; 5) dirty; 6) damaged; 7) poor adjustment/calibration.

47. 1. 8 to 10 years—southern U.S.A.

2. 10 to 15 years—moderate climates

3. 15 to 20 years—northern climates

48. Five years typically

49. b

50. It would cool the house down too fast without dehumidifying the air, resulting in a cool, damp environment.

51. 65°F

52. 65°F

53. 1. Data plate may say "HP" or "Heat Pump"

2. Thermostat has an emergency heat setting

3. Both refrigerant lines are insulated

4. Presence of a reversing valve

5. Compressor is indoors and it's an air-to-air system

6. Presence of an outdoor thermostat connected to control wiring

7. If it is winter and the unit is operating, it's a heat pump.

8. You find a two-stage thermostat.

9. You find two expansion devices.

CHAPTER 13: PLUMBING

1. Pressure or flow is insufficient; leaks; dirty water.

2. True

3.
- Copper
- Galvanized Steel
- Lead
- PVC Plastic
- CPVC Plastic
- Polyethylene Plastic
- Polybutylene Plastic
- Cast Iron
- Asbestos Cement
- Brass

4. $^3/_4$ inch

5. A stop and waste valve shuts off the water supply and allows the system plumbing to be drained.

6. 1. Galvanized steel
   2. Copper
   3. Polybutylene (PB)
   4. Polyethylene (PE)
   5. CPVC (Chlorinated Polyvinylchloride)
   6. Brass (an alloy of tin and zinc)
   7. Stainless steel

7. 1930s

8. At least every ten feet, or every floor level

9. 6 to 10 feet

10. 10 to 12 feet

11. False

12. The implication of improper support is leakage.

13. A cross connection is a piping arrangement in which waste can back up into the supply piping and contaminate it when the pressure drops on the supply side.

14. 1. Fixtures where the faucet spout is below the overflow or flood rim of the fixture
    2. Fixtures where hand held showers, extendable faucets or vegetable sprayers can be left in tubs, basins or sinks
    3. Garden hoses attached to a hose bibb
    4. A toilet tank where the fill water enters at the bottom
    5. A dishwasher where a solenoid valve separates the clean water from the gray water
    6. A clothes washer discharging into a laundry tub
    7. A water softener
    8. A humidifier connected to the supply piping
    9. A lawn or fire sprinkler system

10. A bidet where water enters at the bottom of the bowl

11. A hot water boiler

12. A swimming pool fill outlet located below the flood level of the pool

13. A trap primer without an air gap.

15. No

16. Water hammer is a loud banging sound in the pipes. Water hammer occurs because water moving at several feet per second has to stop abruptly when a valve is turned off. The water bounces off the valve and creates a vacuum as it bounces away from the valve. The vacuum then violently attracts the water back to the low pressure area and the water again bounces off the closed valve. The effect of this is a reverberation, which sounds like someone pounding on metal piping with a hammer.

17. True

18. Because it is combustible

19. The crimp rings

20. True

21. No

22. True

23. 70 degrees Fahrenheit

24. The water heater does not use a recirculating system; it sees the water only once.

25. It is constantly exposed to fresh water and so is more prone to corrosion than a boiler.

26. The burner is at the bottom of the tank.

27. The dip tube

28. 1) The volume of water it can hold; 2) the size of the burner.

29. A large burner means a high recovery rate, which allows a smaller tank to be installed.

30. An electric water heater.

31. An oil-fired water heater.

32. Condensation in the combustion chamber is running down through the center of the water heater and draining out the bottom.

33. True

34. 18 inches

35. In the top 6 inches of the tank

36. 6 to 12 inches above the floor beside the hot water tank

37. 6 to 24 inches above grade level outside of the house

38. Anywhere on the tank, or on piping near the tank in some jurisdictions

39. To slow down the exhaust products as they move up through the water heater

40. Because propane is heavier than air, and can accumulate, especially in a low area.

41. If the house has no chimney or a chimney too large for a water heater

42. ABS or PVC piping

43. 1) Inoperative; 2) blower intake obstructed; 3) poor venting arrangement; 4) poor blower wiring.

44. No

45. A trap prevents sewer gases from entering the house through the fixture drain outlet.

46. The toilet bowl itself is a trap

47. False

48. False

49. It is the only portion of the drainage system which always contains water.

50. The purpose of a trap primer is to ensure there is always water in a floor drain trap to prevent sewer odors entering the home.

51. A wet vent occurs when the drain for one fixture is serving as the vent for another.

52. 1) Copper; 2) ABS plastic; 3) PVC plastic; 4) cast iron; 5) lead; 6) galvanized steel; 7) brass; 8) clay.

53. The pipes are usually idle, and the water is not under pressure

54. False

55. 1) Insulating the pipe; 2) wrapping the pipe with heating cable.

56. 1. Supply faucets below the flood rim of fixtures

    2. Drain connections from dishwashers

    3. Drain connections from clothes washers

    4. Water softeners

    5. Outside house bibbs with hoses attached

    6. Lawn sprinkler systems

    7. Bidets

    8. Vegetable sprayers and extendable faucets at kitchen sinks

    9. Shower wands on bathtubs

   10. Toilets

   11. Supply connections to heating boilers

   12. Trap primers

57. Contamination of a potable water supply.

58. $1/4$ to $1/2$ inch fall per foot run

59. True

60. It is combustible

61. Clogging of pipes

62. To prevent sewer odors from entering the home through the plumbing fixtures.

63. True

64. False

65. 1. S-trap   3. Bell trap

    2. Drum trap   4. Crown vented trap

66. 24 inches

67. At least two pipe diameters

68. Siphoning the trap

69. False

70. At the low point in the floor

71. To protect the home against sewer back up

72. To equalize the air pressure in the waste plumbing system so that the traps won't siphon

73. 1) Copper; 2) galvanized steel; 3) cast iron; 4) ABS plastic; 5) PVC plastic.

74. Listen for gurgling as the last bit of water leaves the drain, and smell for sewer odors.

75. 1. Missing
5. Island venting problems
2. Ineffective/incomplete
6. Vent termination problems
3. Poor vent pipe arrangements
7. Automatic air vents.
4. Too small or too long

76. False

77. False

78. False

79. Kitchen islands are not adjacent to walls; therefore the vent pipe is some distance from the island, often exceeding the maximum allowable distance between trap and vent.

80. 6 inches

81. b

82. 1) A union; 2) a check valve; 3) a gate valve.

83. Two inches

84. To lift the waste from a toilet (and any other fixtures) below the public or private sewer line, up into the sewer. These pumps are needed when waste can't flow by gravity into the sewer system.

85. This protects the ejector tank and house fixtures that feed the tank from back-up of the municipal sewer system.

86. The vent pipe vents sewer gases, the discharge pipe handles the waste, and the drain pipe brings the waste into the pump.

87. True

88. To warn the occupants that the sewage ejector pump has failed.

89. True

90. False

91. 1) Vegetable sprayer left lying in a sink; 2) extendable faucets.

92. Cartridge faucets can be opened and closed more quickly.

93. 1. Leaks or drips
2. Stiff or inoperative
3. Loose
4. Cross connection
5. Noisy
6. Damaged, rusted, loose or missing handles
7. Hot and cold reversed
8. Obstructed aerator
9. Shower diverter inoperative/defective

94. 1) Bang; 2) chatter; 3) whistle.

95. With no backflow prevention device, outside water could be sucked into the plumbing system if the hose is attached, and the supply pressure drops below atmospheric pressure.

96. Install a backflow prevention device

97.
1. Leaks or drips
2. Stiff or inoperative
3. No backflow prevention
4. Loose
5. Pipe frozen or split
6. Poor slope on a frost-free hose bibb
7. Mechanical damage

98.
1. A stop and waste valve prevents water from sitting where the pipe will freeze by isolating the through-wall section of pipe, and draining the trapped water out through the waste valve.
2. A frost-proof valve prevents water from sitting where the pipe will freeze by having the valve body remote from the hose bibb, and a slope to drain to the exterior.

99. Valve shuts off water, drain cock drains water from pipe.

100. Cold supply water on a warm, humid day can cause the toilet tank and toilet fill pipe to sweat, particularly if it is not allowed to warm up because of a running toilet.

101. This valve mixes hot water with the cold water at the toilet supply. There is less incentive for condensation since the warmer water used to fill the toilet won't cool the surrounding air to the dewpoint.

102. False

103. 1) The bowl; 2) the tank; 3) the seal.

104. Grasp the bowl between your legs and try to move the bowl side to side and front to back. Do not use excessive force.

105. Yes

106. c

107. 1) Leaks; 2) rust; 3) surface defects; 4) cross connections; 5) not level; 6) overflow leaking, disconnected or loose; 7) slow drains; 8) loose or unstable.

108. The apron is usually sloped slightly so that water will drain back into the tub. If the tub is not level, water on the apron may drain away from the tub, damaging walls or floors.

109. The vapor barrier and insulation details are often poorly done. Condensation damage is common in this area, as warm house air leaks into the wall and vapor condenses in the cold exterior wall cavity.

110. 1) Faucets; 2) soap dishes; 3) grab bars; 4) windows; 5) changes in direction or material.

111. Tap or press on the tiles, looking for spongy areas or give in the tiles or tiles that sound loose and tinny. Concentrate on areas in Question # 168.

112. False

113. 22 inches

114. Outward

INDEX